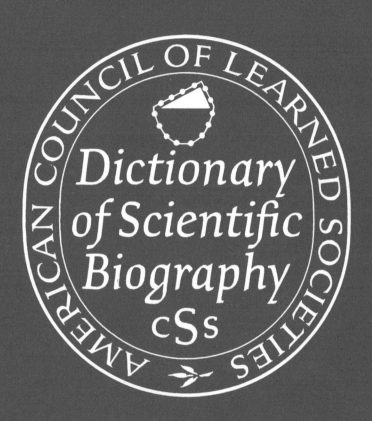

AMERICAN COUNCIL OF LEARNED SOCIETIES

Dictionary
of Scientific
Biography

cSs

DICTIONARY
OF
SCIENTIFIC BIOGRAPHY

PUBLISHED UNDER THE AUSPICES OF
THE AMERICAN COUNCIL OF LEARNED SOCIETIES

The American Council of Learned Societies, organized in 1919 for the purpose of advancing the study of the humanities and of the humanistic aspects of the social sciences, is a nonprofit federation comprising thirty-four national scholarly groups. The Council represents the humanities in the United States in the International Union of Academies, provides fellowships and grants-in-aid, supports research-and-planning conferences and symposia, and sponsors special projects and scholarly publications.

Member Organizations

AMERICAN PHILOSOPHICAL SOCIETY, 1743

AMERICAN ACADEMY OF ARTS AND SCIENCES, 1780

AMERICAN ANTIQUARIAN SOCIETY, 1812

AMERICAN ORIENTAL SOCIETY, 1842

AMERICAN NUMISMATIC SOCIETY, 1858

AMERICAN PHILOLOGICAL ASSOCIATION, 1869

ARCHAEOLOGICAL INSTITUTE OF AMERICA, 1879

SOCIETY OF BIBLICAL LITERATURE, 1880

MODERN LANGUAGE ASSOCIATION OF AMERICA, 1883

AMERICAN HISTORICAL ASSOCIATION, 1884

AMERICAN ECONOMIC ASSOCIATION, 1885

AMERICAN FOLKLORE SOCIETY, 1888

AMERICAN DIALECT SOCIETY, 1889

ASSOCIATION OF AMERICAN LAW SCHOOLS, 1900

AMERICAN PHILOSOPHICAL ASSOCIATION, 1901

AMERICAN ANTHROPOLOGICAL ASSOCIATION, 1902

AMERICAN POLITICAL SCIENCE ASSOCIATION, 1903

BIBLIOGRAPHICAL SOCIETY OF AMERICA, 1904

ASSOCIATION OF AMERICAN GEOGRAPHERS, 1904

AMERICAN SOCIOLOGICAL ASSOCIATION, 1905

ORGANIZATION OF AMERICAN HISTORIANS, 1907

COLLEGE ART ASSOCIATION OF AMERICA, 1912

HISTORY OF SCIENCE SOCIETY, 1924

LINGUISTIC SOCIETY OF AMERICA, 1924

MEDIAEVAL ACADEMY OF AMERICA, 1925

AMERICAN MUSICOLOGICAL SOCIETY, 1934

SOCIETY OF ARCHITECTURAL HISTORIANS, 1940

ECONOMIC HISTORY ASSOCIATION, 1940

ASSOCIATION FOR ASIAN STUDIES, 1941

AMERICAN SOCIETY FOR AESTHETICS, 1942

METAPHYSICAL SOCIETY OF AMERICA, 1950

AMERICAN STUDIES ASSOCIATION, 1950

RENAISSANCE SOCIETY OF AMERICA, 1954

SOCIETY FOR ETHNOMUSICOLOGY, 1955

DICTIONARY
OF
SCIENTIFIC BIOGRAPHY

CHARLES COULSTON GILLISPIE

Princeton University

EDITOR IN CHIEF

Volume IV

RICHARD DEDEKIND—FIRMICUS MATERNUS

CHARLES SCRIBNER'S SONS · NEW YORK

Library of Congress Catalog Card Number 69-18090
SBN684–10115–7

Editorial Staff

MARSHALL DE BRUHL, *MANAGING EDITOR*

SARAH FERRELL, *Assistant Managing Editor*

LOUISE BILEBOF, *Administrative Editor*

LELAND S. LOWTHER, *Associate Editor*

ROSE MOSELLE, *Editorial Assistant*

JANET JACOBS, *Assistant Editor*

ELIZABETH I. WILSON, *Copy Editor*

DORIS ANNE SULLIVAN, *Proofreader*

JOEL HONIG, *Copy Editor*

Panel of Consultants

Contributors to Volume IV

The following are the contributors to Volume IV. Each author's name is followed by the institutional affiliation at the time of publication and the names of articles written for this volume. The symbol † indicates that an author is deceased.

A. F. O'D. ALEXANDER †
DREYER

G. C. AMSTUTZ
University of Heidelberg
ESKOLA

R. CHRISTIAN ANDERSON
Brookhaven National Laboratory
DESSAIGNES

COLETTE AVIGNON
University of Orléans-Tours
EVELYN

NANDOR L. BALAZS
State University of New York at Stony Brook
EINSTEIN

GEORGE B. BARBOUR
University of Cincinnati
FENNEMAN

WILLIAM B. BEAN
University of Iowa
FINLAY

ROBERT P. BECKINSALE
University of Oxford
DELUC

SILVIO A. BEDINI
Smithsonian Institution
DIVINI

WHITFIELD BELL, JR.
American Philosophical Society Library
DIXON, J.

LUIGI BELLONI
University of Milan
DUBINI

ALEX BERMAN
University of Cincinnati
DEROSNE; FÉE

PIERRE BERTHON
Archives, Académie des Sciences, Paris
DUNOYER DE SEGONZAC

KURT-R. BIERMANN
German Academy of Sciences
DEDEKIND; EISENSTEIN

ARTHUR BIREMBAUT
ÉLIE DE BEAUMONT

ASIT K. BISWAS
Department of Energy, Mines and Resources, Canada
DUFOUR; FICHOT

A. BLAAUW
European Southern Observatory
EASTON

L. J. BLACHER
Soviet Academy of Sciences
DOGEL; ESCHSCHOLTZ

H. BOERNER
University of Giessen
ENGEL

UNO BOKLUND
Royal Pharmaceutical Institute, Stockholm
EKEBERG

FRANCK BOURDIER
École Pratique des Hautes Études
DEPÉRET

GERT H. BRIEGER
The Johns Hopkins University
EBERTH

W. H. BROCK
University of Leicester
ERDMANN

THEODORE M. BROWN
Princeton University
DESCARTES

STEPHEN G. BRUSH
University of Maryland
ENSKOG

IVOR BULMER-THOMAS
DINOSTRATUS; DIONYSODORUS; DOMNINUS OF LARISSA; EUCLID; EUDEMUS OF RHODES; EUTOCIUS OF ASCALON

JOHN G. BURKE
University of California at Los Angeles
DUFRÉNOY

HAROLD BURSTYN
Carnegie-Mellon University
FERREL

H. L. L. BUSARD
University of Leiden
DEPARCIEUX; DESPAGNET

RONALD S. CALINGER
Rensselaer Polytechnic Institute
DICKSON

ALBERT V. CAROZZI
University of Illinois
DESOR

BERNARDO J. CAYCEDO
ELHUYAR, F; ELHUYAR, J.

JOHN CHALLINOR
FALCONER; FAUJAS DE SAINT-FOND

SEYMOUR L. CHAPIN
Los Angeles State College
DELISLE, J.-N.

ROBERT CHIPMAN
University of Toledo
DEPREZ

EDWIN CLARKE
University College, London
FERRIER

ARCHIBALD CLOW
British Broadcasting Corporation
DUNDONALD

I. BERNARD COHEN
Harvard University
DELAMBRE

ALBERT B. COSTA
University of Notre Dame
DEWAR; DIXON, H. B.; ERLENMEYER

PIERRE COSTABEL
École Pratique des Hautes Études
DU HAMEL, J. B.

CHARLES COURY
University of Paris
DUVAL

C. F. COWAN
EVANS, W. H.

ALISTAIR C. CROMBIE
University of Oxford
DESCARTES

M. P. CROSLAND
University of Leeds
DULONG

L. W. CURRIER †
EMERSON, B. K.

ŽARKO DADIĆ
Yugoslav Academy of Sciences and Arts
DOMINIS

KARL H. DANNENFELDT
Arizona State University
DIOCLES; DIOCLES OF CARYSTUS

MARGARET DEACON
National Institute of Oceanography
DITTMAR

ALLEN G. DEBUS
University of Chicago
DUCHESNE; FLUDD

ALBERT DELAUNAY
Pasteur Institute
DUCLAUX

BERN DIBNER
Burndy Library
DU MONCEL; FERRARIS

CONTRIBUTORS TO VOLUME IV

D. R. DICKS
University of London
DOSITHEUS; ERATOSTHENES; EUCTEMON

SALLY H. DIEKE
The Johns Hopkins University
DUGAN; DUNCAN; ELKIN

AUBREY DILLER
Indiana University
DICAEARCHUS

CLAUDE E. DOLMAN
University of British Columbia
DOBELL; EHRLICH; ESCHERICH

J. D. H. DONNAY
The Johns Hopkins University
FANKUCHEN

SIGALIA C. DOSTROVSKY
Worcester Polytechnic Institute
DUHAMEL, J.-M.; EUCKEN; EWING,
J. A.; FABRY, C.

A. VIBERT DOUGLAS
Queen's University, Ontario
EDDINGTON

JOHN M. DUBBEY
University College, London
DE MORGAN

K. C. DUNHAM
Institute of Geological Sciences
EVANS, F. J. O.

DAVID R. DYCK
University of Winnipeg
ELLER VON BROCKHAUSEN

JOY P. EASTON
West Virginia University
DEE; DIGGES, L.; DIGGES, T.

SIDNEY M. EDELSTEIN
Dexter Chemical Corporation
DREBBEL

CAROLYN EISELE
*Hunter College, City University of
New York*
ENRIQUES

JON EKLUND
Smithsonian Institution
DUHAMEL DU MONCEAU

VASILY A. ESAKOV
*Institute of the History of Science and
Technology, Moscow*
DOKUCHAEV

JOSEPH EWAN
Tulane University
FERNALD

JOAN M. EYLES
FAREY

V. A. EYLES
DE LA BECHE

EDUARD FARBER †
DÖBEREINER; EDER

W. V. FARRAR
University of Manchester
DONNAN

LUCIENNE FÉLIX
DRACH

E. A. FELLMANN
Institut Platonaeum, Basel
FABRI

EDWIN FELS
DRYGALSKI

BERNARD S. FINN
Smithsonian Institution
EDISON

WALTHER FISCHER
DOELTER

C. S. FISHER
Brandeis University
DEHN; FINE

J. O. FLECKENSTEIN
University of Basel
EMDEN

DONALD FLEMING
Harvard University
DRAPER, J.

MARCEL FLORKIN
University of Liège
DODOENS

PAUL FORMAN
University of Rochester
DUANE

ROBERT FOX
University of Lancaster
DUPRÉ

PIETRO FRANCESCHINI
DELLA TORRE, G.

H. C. FREIESLEBEN
DORNO; ENCKE

DAVID J. FURLEY
Princeton University
EPICURUS

L. K. GABUNA
Soviet Academy of Sciences
DOLLO

GERALD L. GEISON
Princeton University
DUJARDIN

WALTHER GERLACH
University of Munich
ELSTER

CHARLES COULSTON GILLISPIE
Princeton University
DIDEROT

MARIO GLIOZZI
University of Turin
FABBRONI

MARTHA TEACH GNUDI
University of California at Los Angeles
DORN

STANLEY GOLDBERG
Antioch College
DRUDE

J. B. GOUGH
Washington State University
FAHRENHEIT

RAGNAR GRANIT
Nobel Institute for Neurophysiology
FERNEL

NORMAN T. GRIDGEMAN
National Research Council of Canada
DODGSON

M. D. GRMEK
*Archives Internationales d'Histoire des
Sciences*
DODART; ESTIENNE; FERREIN

FRANCISCO GUERRA
DESCOURTILZ; DOMBEY; FEUILLÉE

LAURA GUGGENBUHL
*Hunter College, City University of
New York*
FEUERBACH

HEINRICH GUGGENHEIMER
Polytechnic Institute of Brooklyn
EISENHART

A. RUPERT HALL
*Imperial College of Science and
Technology*
DESAGULIERS

MARIE BOAS HALL
*Imperial College of Science and
Technology*
DIGBY

R. S. HARTENBERG
Northwestern University
EYTELWEIN

JOHN L. HEILBRON
University of California at Berkeley
DUFAY

C. DORIS HELLMAN
*Queens College, City University of
New York*
DÖRFFEL

BROOKE HINDLE
New York University
FARRAR

HEBBEL E. HOFF
Baylor University, College of Medicine
DENIS

J. E. HOFMANN
University of Tübingen
DYCK

S. HOOGERWERF
EINTHOVEN

CONTRIBUTORS TO VOLUME IV

WŁODZIMIERZ HUBICKI
Marie Curie-Skłodowska University
ERCKER

G. L. HUXLEY
Queen's University, Belfast
EUDOXUS OF CNIDUS

AARON J. IHDE
University of Wisconsin
ELVEHJEM; EULER-CHELPIN

ILSE JAHN
University of Berlin
EHRENBERG

S. A. JAYAWARDENE
Science Museum Library, London
FERRARI

JULIAN JAYNES
Princeton University
FECHNER

SATISH KAPOOR
University of Saskatchewan
DUMAS

GEORGE B. KAUFFMAN
Fresno State College
DELÉPINE

G. B. KERFERD
University of Manchester
DEMOCRITUS

PAUL A. KIRCHVOGEL
Landesmuseum, Kassel
FAULHABER

GEORGE KISH
University of Michigan
DELISLE, G.; DUDLEY

MARTIN J. KLEIN
Yale University
EHRENFEST; EINSTEIN

D. M. KNIGHT
University of Durham
DERHAM

J. KOVALEVSKY
Bureau des Longitudes
DELAUNAY; FAYE

CLAUDIA KREN
University of Missouri
DOMINICUS DE CLAVASIO

VLADISLAV KRUTA
Purkinje University, Brno
DUTROCHET; EDWARDS

LOUIS KUSLAN
Southern Connecticut State College
FAVRE

V. I. KUZNETSOV
Soviet Academy of Sciences
FAVORSKY

RODOLPHINE J. CH. V. TER
LAAGE
State University of Utrecht
DONDERS

BENGT-OLOF LANDIN
University of Lund
FABRICIUS

LAURENS LAUDEN
University of Pittsburgh
FERGUSON

P. S. LAURIE
Royal Greenwich Observatory
ELLIS; EVERSHED

GORDON LEFF
University of York
DUNS SCOTUS

HENRY M. LEICESTER
University of the Pacific
DEVILLE

MARTIN LEVEY †
IBN EZRA

JACQUES R. LÉVY
Paris Observatory
ESCLANGON; FABRY, L.

O. LEZHNEVA
Soviet Academy of Sciences
EICHENWALD

G. A. LINDEBOOM
Free University, Amsterdam
EIJKMAN

JAMES LONGRIGG
University of Wisconsin
ERASISTRATUS

SUSAN M. P. McKENNA
University of Michigan
DOWNING

FRANCIS R. MADDISON
Museum of the History of Science, Oxford
DONDI

MUHSIN MAHDI
Harvard University
AL-FĀRĀBĪ

MICHAEL S. MAHONEY
Princeton University
DESCARTES; FERMAT

L. MARTON
National Bureau of Standards
EÖTVÖS

ARNALDO MASOTTI
Politecnico di Milano
FERRO

KIRTLEY F. MATHER
Harvard University
EMMONS, S. F.

ALEXANDER P. D. MAURELATOS
University of Texas
EMPEDOCLES OF ACRAGAS

A. MENIAILOV
Soviet Academy of Sciences
FERSMAN

R. MICHARD
Paris Observatory
DESLANDRES

MIKLÓS MIKOLÁS
Technical University of Budapest
FEJÉR

DONALD G. MILLER
Lawrence Radiation Laboratory
DUHEM

A. M. MONNIER
University of Paris
DEVAUX; ERLANGER; FIESSINGER

JEAN MOTTE
University of Montpellier
DELILE; DRAPARNAUD

JOHN MURDOCH
Harvard University
EUCLID

HENRY NATHAN
OECD, Directorate for Scientific Affairs
FATOU

A. NATUCCI
University of Genoa
FAGNANO DEI TOSCHI, G. C.; FAGNANO
DEI TOSCHI, G. F.

AXEL V. NIELSEN †
DUNÉR

LUBOŠ NOVÝ
Czechoslovak Academy of Sciences
DICKSTEIN; DU BOIS-REYMOND, P. D. G.

ROBERT OLBY
University of Leeds
DILLENIUS; FEULGEN

C. D. O'MALLEY †
DUBOIS; EDWARDES; EUSTACHI;
FALLOPPIO

JANE OPPENHEIMER
Bryn Mawr College
DRIESCH

OYSTEIN ORE †
DIRICHLET

WALTER PAGEL
*Wellcome Institute of the History of
Medicine*
ERASTUS

A. B. PAPLAUSCAS
Soviet Academy of Sciences
EGOROV

LINUS PAULING
Stanford University
DICKINSON

JACQUES PAYEN
*Conservatoire Nationale des Arts et
Métiers*
DESORMES

KURT MØLLER PEDERSEN
University of Aarhus
DOVE

xi

CONTRIBUTORS TO VOLUME IV

MARGARET R. PEITSCH
*Department of Energy, Mines and
Resources, Canada*
FICHOT

P. E. PILET
University of Lausanne
ERRERA

DAVID PINGREE
University of Chicago
DINAKARA; AL-FAZĀRĪ

A. F. PLAKHOTNIK
Soviet Academy of Sciences
DERYUGIN

ERICH POSNER
Birmingham Regional Hospital Board
DOMAGK

WILLIAM B. PROVINE
Cornell University
EAST

EUGENE RABINOWITCH
State University of New York at Albany
EMERSON, R.

SAMUEL X. RADBILL
College of Physicians of Philadelphia
DUNGLISON

NATHAN REINGOLD
Smithsonian Institution
ESPY

SAMUEL REZNECK
Rensselaer Polytechnic Institute
EATON

JOHN M. RIDDLE
North Carolina State University
DIOSCORIDES

GUGLIELMO RIGHINI
Osservatorio Astrofisico di Arcetri
DEMBOWSKI; EMANUELLI

MARIA LUISA RIGHINI-BONELLI
Istituto e Museo di Storia della Scienza
DONATI

GUENTER B. RISSE
University of Minnesota
DÖLLINGER; EHRET; EICHLER

HANS ROHRBACH
University of Mainz
FEIGL

COLIN A. RONAN
DYSON

PAUL LAWRENCE ROSE
St. John's University, New York
DUDITH

K. E. ROTHSCHUH
University of Münster/Westphalia
DU BOIS-REYMOND, E.; ENGELMANN;
FICK

HUNTER ROUSE
University of Iowa
DU BUAT

A. I. SABRA
Warburg Institute
AL-FARGHĀNĪ

MORRIS H. SAFFRON
Rutgers University
DONALDSON; DUGGAR

NORMAN SCHAUMBERGER
*Bronx Community College, City Uni-
versity of New York*
DOUGLAS, JESSE

EBERHARD SCHMAUDERER
DIELS; EMBDEN

CECIL J. SCHNEER
University of New Hampshire
EMMONS, E.

J. F. SCOTT
*St. Mary's College of Education,
Middlesex*
DELAMAIN

EMILIO SEGRÈ
University of California at Berkeley
FERMI

EDITH SELOW
DINGLER

I. P. SHELDON-WILLIAMS
University College, Dublin
ERIUGENA

ELIZABETH NOBLE SHOR
DEGOLYER; EIGENMANN

DIANA SIMPKINS
Northwestern Polytechnic, London
DIXON, H. H.; ELLIOT SMITH; FARMER

JOSEF SMOLKA
Czechoslovak Academy of Sciences
DIVIŠ

PIERRE SPEZIALI
University of Geneva
DINI

NILS SPJELDNAES
University of Aarhus
EBEL; ESCHOLT

WILLIAM H. STAHL †
FIRMICUS MATERNUS

MAX STECK
University of Munich
DÜRER

WALLACE STEGNER
Stanford University
DUTTON

DIRK J. STRUIK
Massachusetts Institute of Technology
DE GROOT; DUPIN; FANO

CHARLES SÜSSKIND
University of California at Berkeley
DE FOREST; FEDDERSEN; FESSENDEN

JUDITH P. SWAZEY
Harvard University
EGAS MONIZ

FERENC SZABADVÁRY
Technical University of Budapest
ESSON; FARKAS

RENÉ TATON
École Pratique des Hautes Études
DESARGUES; DIONIS DU SÉJOUR

KENNETH L. TAYLOR
University of Oklahoma
DES CLOIZEAUX; DESMAREST;
DOLOMIEU; DUPERREY

ANDRÉE TÉTRY
École Pratique des Hautes Études
DELAGE; DUBOSCQ

JEAN THÉODORIDÈS
*Centre National de la Recherche
Scientifique*
FABRE

K. BRYN THOMAS
Reading Pathological Society, Library
DOUGLAS, JAMES

V. V. TIKHOMIROV
Soviet Academy of Sciences
EICHWALD

HEINZ TOBIEN
University of Mainz
DESHAYES; ERMAN; ESCHER VON DER
LINTH

VICTOR A. TRIOLO
Temple University
EWING, J.; FINSEN

HENRY S. TROPP
University of Toronto
FIELDS

G. L'E. TURNER
*Museum of the History of Science,
Oxford*
DOLLOND

H. L. VANDERLINDEN
University of Ghent
DELPORTE

J. J. VERDONK
FINK

KURT VOGEL
University of Munich
DIOPHANTUS; FIBONACCI

WILLIAM A. WALLACE, O. P.
Catholic University of America
DIETRICH VON FREIBERG; DULLAERT OF
GHENT

CHARLES WEBSTER
University of Oxford
ENT

PIERRE WELANDER
Massachusetts Institute of Technology
EKMAN

GEORGE W. WHITE
University of Illinois
EVANS, L.

CONTRIBUTORS TO VOLUME IV

CHARLES A. WHITNEY
Smithsonian Institution, Astrophysical Observatory
DRAPER, H.

L. PEARCE WILLIAMS
Cornell University
DE LA RUE; FARADAY

WESLEY C. WILLIAMS
Case Western Reserve University
DUVERNEY

CURTIS WILSON
University of California at Berkeley
DOPPELMAYR

J. T. WILSON
University of Toronto
DU TOIT

A. E. WOODRUFF
Yeshiva University
DOPPLER

O. WRIGHT
University of London
AL-FĀRĀBĪ

HATTEN S. YODER, JR.
Geophysical Laboratory, Washington
FENNER

A. P. YOUSCHKEVITCH
Soviet Academy of Sciences
EULER

BRUNO ZANOBIO
University of Pavia
FABRICI

DICTIONARY
OF
SCIENTIFIC BIOGRAPHY

DICTIONARY OF
SCIENTIFIC BIOGRAPHY

DEDEKIND—FIRMICUS MATERNUS

DEDEKIND, (JULIUS WILHELM) RICHARD (*b.* Brunswick, Germany, 6 October 1831; *d.* Brunswick, 12 February 1916), *mathematics.*

Dedekind's ancestors (particularly on his mother's side) had distinguished themselves in services to Hannover and Brunswick. His father, Julius Levin Ulrich Dedekind, the son of a physician and chemist, was a graduate jurist, professor, and corporation lawyer at the Collegium Carolinum in Brunswick. His mother, Caroline Marie Henriette Emperius, was the daughter of a professor at the Carolinum and the granddaughter of an imperial postmaster. Richard Dedekind was the youngest of four children. His only brother, Adolf, became a district court president in Brunswick; one sister, Mathilde, died in 1860, and Dedekind lived with his second sister, Julie, until her death in 1914, neither of them having married. She was a respected writer who received a local literary prize in 1893.

Between the ages of seven and sixteen Dedekind attended the Gymnasium Martino-Catharineum in Brunswick. His interest turned first to chemistry and physics; he considered mathematics only an auxiliary science. He soon occupied himself primarily with it, however, feeling that physics lacked order and a strictly logical structure. In 1848 Dedekind became a student at the Collegium Carolinum, an institute between the academic high school and the university level, which Carl Friedrich Gauss had also attended. There Dedekind mastered the elements of analytic geometry, algebraic analysis, differential and integral calculus, and higher mechanics, and studied the nat-

ural sciences. In 1849–1850, he gave private lessons in mathematics to his later colleague at the Carolinum, Hans Zincke (known as Sommer). Thus, when he matriculated at the University of Göttingen at Easter 1850, Dedekind was far better prepared for his studies than were the majority of graduates from the academic high school. At Göttingen, a seminar in mathematics and physics had just been founded, at the initiative of Moritz Abraham Stern, for the education of instructors for teaching in the academic high school. The direction of the mathematics department was the duty of Stern and Georg Ulrich, while Wilhelm Weber and Johann Benedict Listing directed the physics department. Dedekind was a member of the seminar from its inception and was there first introduced to the elements of the theory of numbers. A year later Bernhard Riemann also began to participate in the seminar, and Dedekind soon developed a close friendship with him. In the first semester, Dedekind attended lectures on differential and integral calculus, which offered him very little new material. He attended Ulrich's seminar on hydraulics but rarely took part in the physics laboratories run by Weber and Listing; Weber's lectures on experimental physics, however, made a very strong impression on him throughout two semesters. Weber had an inspiring effect on Dedekind, who responded with respectful admiration. In the summer semester of 1850, Dedekind attended the course in popular astronomy given by Gauss's observer, Carl Wolfgang Benjamin Goldschmidt; in the winter semester of 1850–1851, he attended Gauss's own lecture on the method of least

1

squares. Although he disliked teaching, Gauss carried out the assignment with his usual conscientiousness; fifty years later Dedekind remembered the lecture as one of the most beautiful he had ever heard, writing that he had followed Gauss with constantly increasing interest and that he could not forget the experience. In the following semester, Dedekind heard Gauss's lecture on advanced geodesy. In the winter semester of 1851–1852, he heard the two lectures given by Quintus Icilius on mathematical geography and on the theory of heat and took part in Icilius' meteorological observations. After only four semesters, he did his doctoral work under Gauss in 1852 with a thesis on the elements of the theory of Eulerian integrals. Gauss certified that he knew a great deal and was independent; in addition, he had prophetically "favorable expectations of his future performance."

Dedekind later determined that this knowledge would have been sufficient for teachers in secondary school service but that it did not satisfy the prerequisite for advanced studies at Göttingen. For instance, Dedekind had not heard lectures on more recent developments in geometry, advanced theory of numbers, division of the circle and advanced algebra, elliptic functions, or mathematical physics, which were then being taught at the University of Berlin by Steiner, Jacobi, and Dirichlet. Therefore, Dedekind spent the two years following his graduation assiduously filling the gaps in his education, attending—among others—Stern's lectures on the solution of numerical equations.

In the summer of 1854, he qualified, a few weeks after Riemann, as a university lecturer; in the winter semester of 1854–1855 he began his teaching activities as *Privatdozent,* with a lecture on the mathematics of probability and one on geometry with parallel treatment of analytic and projective methods.

After Dirichlet succeeded Gauss in Göttingen in 1855, Dedekind attended his lectures on the theory of numbers, potential theory, definite integrals, and partial differential equations. He soon entered into a closer personal relationship with Dirichlet and had many fruitful discussions with him; Dedekind later remembered that Dirichlet had made "a new man" of him and had expanded his scholarly and personal horizons. When the Dirichlets were visited by friends from Berlin (Rebecca Dirichlet was the sister of the composer Felix Mendelssohn-Bartholdy and had a large circle of friends), Dedekind was invited too and enjoyed the pleasant sociability of, for example, the well-known writer and former diplomat, Karl August Varnhagen von Ense, and his niece, the writer Ludmilla Assing.

In the winter semester of 1855–1856 and in the one following, Dedekind attended Riemann's lectures on Abelian and elliptic functions. Thus, although an instructor, he remained an intensive student as well. His own lectures at that time are noteworthy in that he probably was the first university teacher to lecture on Galois theory, in the course of which the concept of field was introduced. To be sure, few students attended his lectures: only two were present when Dedekind went beyond Galois and replaced the concept of the permutation group by the abstract group concept.

In 1858, Dedekind was called to the Polytechnikum in Zurich (now the Eidgenössische Technische Hochschule) as the successor to Joseph Ludwig Raabe. Thus Dedekind was the first of a long line of German mathematicians for whom Zurich was the first step on the way to a German professorial chair; to mention only a few, there were E. B. Christoffel, H. A. Schwarz, G. Frobenius, A. Hurwitz, F. E. Prym, H. Weber, F. Schottky, and H. Minkowski. The Swiss school counsellor responsible for appointments came to Göttingen at Easter 1858 and decided immediately upon Dedekind—which speaks for his power of judgment. In September 1859, Dedekind traveled to Berlin with Riemann, after Riemann's election as a corresponding member of the academy there. On this occasion, Dedekind met the initiator of that selection, Karl Weierstrass, as well as other leaders of the Berlin school, including Ernst Eduard Kummer, Karl Wilhelm Borchardt, and Leopold Kronecker.

In 1862, he was appointed successor to August Wilhelm Julius Uhde at the Polytechnikum in Brunswick, which had been created from the Collegium Carolinum. He remained in Brunswick until his death, in close association with his brother and sister, ignoring all possibilities of change or attainment of a larger sphere of activity. The small, familiar world in which he lived completely satisfied his demands: in it his relatives completely replaced a wife and children of his own and there he found sufficient leisure and freedom for scientific work in basic mathematical research. He did not feel pressed to have a more marked effect in the outside world; such confirmation of himself was unnecessary.

Although completely averse to administrative responsibility, Dedekind nevertheless considered it his duty to assume the directorship of the Polytechnikum from 1872 to 1875 (to a certain extent he was the successor of his father, who had been a member of the administration of the Collegium Carolinum for many years) and to assume the chairmanship of the school's building commission in the course of the transformation to a technical university. Along with his recreational trips to Austria (the Tyrol), to Switzerland, and through the Black Forest, his visit to the Paris exposition of 1878 should also be mentioned. On 1 April 1894 he was made professor emeritus but continued to give lectures occasionally. Seriously ill in 1872, following the death of his father, he subsequently enjoyed physical and intellectual health until his peaceful death at the age of eighty-four.

A corresponding member of the Göttingen Academy from 1862, Dedekind also became a corresponding member of the Berlin Academy in 1880 upon the initiative of Kronecker. In 1900, he became a correspondent of the Académie des Sciences in Paris and in 1910 was elected as *associé étranger*. He was also a member of the Leopoldino-Carolina Naturae Curiosorum Academia and of the Academy in Rome. He received honorary doctorates in Kristiania (now Oslo), in Zurich, and in Brunswick. In 1902 he received numerous scientific honors on the occasion of the fiftieth anniversary of his doctorate.

Dedekind belonged to those mathematicians with great musical talent. An accomplished pianist and cellist, he composed a chamber opera to his brother's libretto.

In character and principles, in style of living and views, Dedekind had much in common with Gauss, who also came from Brunswick and attended the Gymnasium Martino-Catharineum, the Collegium Carolinum, and the University of Göttingen. Both men had a conservative sense, a rigid will, an unshakable strength of principles, and a refusal to compromise. Each led a strictly regulated, simple life without luxury. Cool and reserved in judgment, both were warm-hearted, helpful people who formed strong bonds of trust with their friends. Both had a distinct sense of humor but also a strictness toward themselves and a conscientious sense of duty. Averse to any excess, neither was quick to express astonishment or admiration. Both were averse to innovations and turned down brilliant offers for other professorial chairs. In their literary tastes, both numbered Walter Scott among their favorite authors. Both impressed by that quality called modest greatness. Thus, it is not astonishing to find their similarity persisting in mathematics in the same preference for the theory of numbers, the same reservations about the algorithm, and the same partiality for "notions" above "notations." Although considerable, significant differences existed between Gauss and Dedekind, what they had in common predominates by far. Their kinship also received a marked visible expression: Dedekind was one of the select few permitted to carry Gauss's casket to the funeral service on the terrace of the Sternwarte.

Aside from Gauss the most enduring influences on Dedekind's scientific work were Dirichlet and Rie-

mann, with both of whom he shared many inclinations and attitudes. Dedekind, Dirichlet, and Riemann were all fully conscious of their worth, but with a modesty bordering on shyness, they never let their associates feel this. Ambition being foreign to them, they were embarrassed when confronted by the brilliance and elegance of their intellect. They loved thinking more than writing and were hardly ever able to satisfy their own demands. Being of absolute integrity, they had in common the same love for plain, certain truth. Dedekind's own statement to Zincke is more revelatory of his character than any description could be: "For what I have accomplished and what I have become, I have to thank my industry much more, my indefatigable working rather than any outstanding talent."

When Dedekind is mentioned today, one of the first associations is the "Dedekind cut," which he introduced in 1872 to use in treating the problem of irrational numbers in a completely new and exact manner.

In 1858, Dedekind had noted the lack of a truly scientific foundation of arithmetic in the course of his Zurich lectures on the elements of differential calculus. (Weierstrass also was stimulated to far-reaching investigations from such observations in the course of preparing lectures.) On 24 October, Dedekind succeeded in producing a purely arithmetic definition of the essence of continuity and, in connection with it, an exact formulation of the concept of the irrational number. Fourteen years later, he published the result of his considerations, *Stetigkeit und irrationale Zahlen* (Brunswick, 1872, and later editions), and explained the real numbers as "cuts" in the realm of rational numbers. He arrived at concepts of outstanding significance for the analysis of number through the theory of order. The property of the real numbers, conceived by him as an ordered continuum, with the conceptual aid of the cut that goes along with this, permitted tracing back the real numbers to the rational numbers: Any rational number a produces a resolution of the system R of all rational numbers into two classes A_1, A_2 in such a way that each number a_1 of the class A_1 is smaller than each number a_2 of the second class A_2. (Today, the term "set" is used instead of "system.") The number a is either the largest number of the class A_1 or the smallest number of the class A_2. A division of the system R into the two classes A_1, A_2, whereby each number a_1 in A_1 is smaller than each number a_2 in A_2 is called a "cut" (A_1, A_2) by Dedekind. In addition, an infinite number of cuts exist that are not produced by rational numbers. The discontinuity or incompleteness of the region R consists in this property. Dedekind wrote,

"Now, in each case when there is a cut (A_1, A_2) which is not produced by any rational number, then we *create* a new, *irrational* number α, which we regard as completely defined by this cut; we will say that this number α corresponds to this cut, or that it produces this cut" (*Stetigkeit,* § 4).

Occasionally Dedekind has been called a "modern Eudoxus" because an impressive similarity has been pointed out between Dedekind's theory of the irrational number and the definition of proportionality in Eudoxus' theory of proportions (Euclid, *Elements,* bk. V, def. 5). Nevertheless, Oskar Becker correctly showed that the Dedekind cut theory and Eudoxus' theory of proportions do not coincide: Dedekind's postulate of existence for all cuts and the real numbers that produce them cannot be found in Eudoxus or in Euclid. With respect to this, Dedekind said that the Euclidean principles alone—without inclusion of the principle of continuity, which they do not contain—are incapable of establishing a complete theory of real numbers as the proportions of the quantities. On the other hand, however, by means of his theory of irrational numbers, the perfect model of a continuous region would be created, which for just that reason would be capable of characterizing any proportion by a certain individual number contained in it (letter to Rudolph Lipschitz, 6 October 1876).

With his publication of 1872, Dedekind had become one of the leading representatives of a new epoch in basic research, along with Weierstrass and Georg Cantor. This was the continuation of work by Cauchy, Gauss, and Bolzano in systematically eliminating the lack of clarity in basic concepts by methods of demonstration on a higher level of rigor. Dedekind's and Weierstrass' definition of the basic arithmetic concepts, as well as Georg Cantor's theory of sets, introduced the modern development, which stands "completely under the sign of number," as David Hilbert expressed it.

Dedekind's book *Was sind und was sollen die Zahlen?* (Brunswick, 1888, and later editions) is along the same lines; in it he presented a logical theory of number and of complete induction, presented his principal conception of the essence of arithmetic, and dealt with the role of the complete system of real numbers in geometry in the problem of the continuity of space. Among other things, he provides a definition independent of the concept of number for the infiniteness or finiteness of a set by using the concept of mapping and treating the recursive definition, which is so important for the theory of ordinal numbers. (Incidentally, Dedekind regarded the ordinal number and not the cardinal number [*Anzahl*] as the original concept of number; in the cardinal number

he saw only an application of the ordinal number [letter to Heinrich Weber, 24 January 1888].) The demonstration of the existence of infinite systems given by Dedekind—similar to a consideration in Bolzano's *Paradoxien des Unendlichen* (Prague, 1851, §13)—is no longer considered valid. Kronecker was critical because Dedekind, agreeing with Gauss, regarded numbers as free creations of the human intellect and defended this viewpoint militantly and stubbornly. Weierstrass complained that his own definition of a complex quantity had not been understood by Dedekind. Hilbert criticized his effort to establish mathematics solely by means of logic. Gottlob Frege and Bertrand Russell criticized Dedekind's opinion that the cuts were not the irrational numbers but that the latter produced the former. However, even his critics and those who preferred Cantor's less abstract procedure for the construction of real numbers agreed that he had exercised a powerful influence on basic research in mathematics.

Just as Kronecker and Weierstrass had edited the mathematical works of those to whom they felt obligated, so Dedekind worked on the erection of literary monuments to those who had stood close to him. Making accessible the posthumous works of Gauss, Dirichlet, and Riemann occupied an important place in his work. In doing this, he gave proof of his congeniality and the rare combination of his productive and receptive intellectual talents.

Publishing the manuscripts of Gauss on the theory of numbers (*Werke,* vol. II [Göttingen, 1863]) gave him the opportunity of not only making available to wider circles the papers of a man he so greatly respected, but also of commenting on them with deep understanding. Dirichlet's *Vorlesungen über Zahlentheorie* (Brunswick, 1863, and later editions) was edited by him. If, as has been said, Dirichlet was the first not only to have completely understood Gauss's *Disquisitiones arithmeticae* but also to have made them accessible to others, then the same is true, to a great extent, of Dedekind's relationship to Dirichlet's lectures on the theory of numbers. Finally, he collaborated in editing the *Werke Bernhard Riemanns* (Leipzig, 1876; 2nd ed., 1892) with his friend Heinrich Weber and with his accustomed modesty placed his name after Weber's.

The editing of Dirichlet's lectures led Dedekind into a profound examination of the theory of generalized complex numbers or of forms that can be resolved into linear factors. In 1871 he provided these lectures with a supplement, in which he established the theory of algebraic number fields, or domains, by giving a general definition of the concept of the ideal—going far beyond Kummer's theory of "ideal numbers"—

that has become fruitful in various arithmetic and algebraic areas. In several papers Dedekind then, independently of Kronecker and with his approval, established the ideal theory that is held to be his masterpiece. Its principal theorem was that each ideal different from the unit ideal R can be represented unambiguously—with the exception of the order of factors—as the product of prime numbers. In his treatises concerning number fields, Dedekind arrived at a determination of the number of ideal classes of a field, penetrated the analysis of the base of a field, provided special studies on the theory of modules, and stimulated further development of ideal theory in which Emmy Noether, Hilbert, and Philipp Furtwängler participated. Paul Bachmann, Adolf Hurwitz, and Heinrich Weber in their publications also disseminated Dedekind's thoughts and expanded them.

That Dedekind did not stand completely apart from the applications of mathematics is shown by a treatise, written with W. Henneberg, which appeared as early as 1851 and concerns the time relationships in the course of plowing fields of various shapes, and also by the completion and publication of a treatise by Dirichlet concerning a hydrodynamic problem (1861).

Finally, we are indebted to Dedekind for such fundamental concepts as *ring* and *unit*.

It was indicative of the great esteem in which Dedekind was held even in foreign countries that, shortly after his death, in the middle of World War I, Camille Jordan, the president of the Académie des Sciences in Paris, warmly praised his theory of algebraic integers as his main work and expressed his sadness concerning the loss.

Although the association of mathematicians' names with concepts and theorems is not always historically justified or generally accepted, the number of such named concepts can provide an indication, albeit a relative one, of a mathematician's lasting accomplishments in extending the science. By this standard, Dedekind belongs among the greatest mathematicians; approximately a dozen designations bear his name.

BIBLIOGRAPHY

I. ORIGINAL WORKS. For a bibliography of Dedekind's writings, see Poggendorff, I (1863), 534, 1555; III (1898), 340; IV (1904), 305; V (1926), 269; and VI (1936), 538.

His works include *Gesammelte mathematische Werke*, R. Fricke, E. Noether, and O. Ore, eds., 3 vols. (Brunswick, 1930–1932), with a bibliography in III, 505–507; and *Briefwechsel Cantor-Dedekind*, E. Noether and J. Cavaillès, eds. (Paris, 1937). Extracts from his works appear in Oskar Becker, *Die Grundlagen der Mathematik in Geschichtlicher Entwicklung* (Freiburg–Munich, 2nd ed., 1964), pp. 224–245, 316.

II. SECONDARY LITERATURE. On Dedekind and his work, see Kurt-R. Biermann, "Richard Dedekind im Urteil der Berliner Akademie," in *Forschungen und Fortschritte*, **40** (1966), 301–302; Edmund Landau, "Richard Dedekind," in *Nachrichten von der Königlichen Gesellschaft der Wissenschaften zu Göttingen, Geschäftliche Mitteilungen* (1917), pp. 50–70, with a bibliography on pp. 66–70; Wilhelm Lorey, *Das Studium der Mathematik an den deutschen Universitäten seit Anfang des 19.Jahrhunderts* (Leipzig-Berlin, 1916), with personal recollections of Dedekind on pp. 81–83; Karl Mollenhauer, "Julie Dedekind," in *Braunschweigisches Magazin,* **21** (1916), 127–130; Richard Müller, "Aus den Ahnentafeln deutscher Mathematiker: Richard Dedekind," in *Familie und Volk,* **4** (1955), 143–145; Nikolaus Stuloff, "Richard Dedekind," in *Neue Deutsche Biographie,* **3** (1957), 552–553; Hans Zincke ("Sommer"), "Erinnerungen an Richard Dedekind," in *Braunschweigisches Magazin,* **22** (1916), 73–81; "Die Akademien zu Paris und Berlin über Richard Dedekind," *ibid.,* 82–84; and "Julius Wilhelm Richard Dedekind," in *Festschrift zur Feier des 25-jährigen Bestehens des Gesellschaft ehemaliger Studierender des Eidgenössischen polytechnischen Schule in Zürich* (1894), pp. 29–30.

KURT-R. BIERMANN

DEE, JOHN (*b*. London, England, 13 July 1527; *d*. Mortlake, Surrey, England, December 1608), *mathematics*.

Dee was the son of Roland Dee, a London mercer, and his wife, Johanna Wilde. He was educated at St. John's College, Cambridge, receiving the B.A. in 1545 and the M.A. in 1548. He was a fellow of St. John's and a foundation fellow of Trinity College (1546). He traveled to Louvain briefly in 1547 and to Louvain and Paris in 1548–1551, studying with Gemma Frisius and Gerhardus Mercator. Throughout his life Dee made extended trips to the Continent and maintained cordial relations with scholars there.

For more than twenty-five years Dee acted as adviser to various English voyages of discovery. His treatises on navigation and navigational instruments were deliberately kept in manuscript; most have not survived, and are known only from his later autobiographical writings. His "fruitfull Praeface" to the Billingsley translation of Euclid (1570), on the relations and applications of mathematics, established his fame among the mathematical practitioners. Although translated by Billingsley, the Euclid is unmistakably edited by Dee, for the body of the work, especially the later books, contains many annotations and additional theorems by him.

Although Dee was a man of undoubted scientific talents, his interests always tended toward the occult.

His favor in court circles was due largely to his practice of judicial astrology. His interest in alchemy and the search for the philosopher's stone led to the gradual abandonment of other work. His last scientific treatise was a reasoned defense of calendar reform (1583). From that time on, he retreated almost wholly into mysticism and psychic research. Dee was certainly duped by his medium, Edward Kelley, but he himself was sincere. He felt that he had been ill rewarded for his many years of serious study and looked for a shortcut to the secrets of the universe through the assistance of angelic spirits.

BIBLIOGRAPHY

I. ORIGINAL WORKS. A more extensive list is in Thompson Cooper's article in *Dictionary of National Biography*, V, 721–729. *Monas hieroglyphica* (Antwerp, 1564) is presented in annotated translation by C. H. Josten in *Ambix*, **12**, nos. 2 and 3 (1964). "A very fruitfull Praeface . . . specifying the chief mathematical sciences," in H. Billingsley, trans., *Euclid* (London, 1570), was reprinted in *Euclid's Elements*, T. Rudd, ed. (London, 1651) and, with additional material by Dee, in *Euclid's Elements*, J. Leeke and G. Serle, eds. (London, 1661). *Parallaticae commentationis praxosque* (London, 1573) contains trigonometric theorems for determining stellar parallax, occasioned by the nova of 1572. "A plain discourse . . . concerning the needful reformation of the Kalendar" (1583) is in the Bodleian Library, Oxford, MS Ashmole, 1789, i. "The Compendious Rehearsal of John Dee" (1592), BM Cotton Vitellius C vii, 1, is available in "Autobiographical Tracts of Dr. John Dee," James Crossley, ed., *Chetham Miscellanies*, I (Manchester, 1851); it is the main source of biographical information but must be read with caution, since it was written as a request for compensation for injury to Dee's library and reputation. *The Private Diary of John Dee, 1577–1601* was edited by J. O. Halliwell as vol. XIX of Camden Society Publications (London, 1842); a corrected version of the Manchester portions, 1595–1601, was edited by John E. Bailey as *Diary, for the Years 1595–1601* (London, 1880).

II. SECONDARY LITERATURE. There is still no adequate biography of Dee. Both Charlotte Fell-Smith, *John Dee* (London, 1909), and Richard Deacon, *John Dee* (London, 1968), stress Dee's nonscientific activities. The latter has revived the theory, originating with Robert Hooke, that Dee's conversations with the angels were intelligence reports in code. Frances A. Yates, *Theatre of the World* (Chicago, 1969), considers Dee as a Renaissance philosopher in the Hermetic tradition. The book contains interesting discussions of Dee's library and of the mathematical preface to Euclid. It is argued that a revival of interest in Vitruvius was spread among the middle classes of London by Dee's Vitruvian references in the preface.

The best assessment of Dee's scientific work may be found in the books of E. G. R. Taylor, especially *Tudor Geography* (London, 1930) and *Mathematical Practitioners of Tudor and Stuart England* (Cambridge, 1954).

Dee had a remarkable library, and many MSS owned by him are extant. M. R. James, "Lists of MSS Formerly Owned by John Dee," a supplement to *Transactions of the Bibliographical Society* (1921), is the basic work, but many others have been located. See, for example, A. G. Watson, *The Library of Sir Simonds D'Ewes* (London, 1966).

JOY B. EASTON

DE FOREST, LEE (*b.* Council Bluffs, Iowa, 26 August 1873; *d.* Hollywood, California, 30 June 1961), *electronics.*

Lee de Forest grew up in Alabama, where his father, Henry Swift De Forest, a Congregational minister of Huguenot stock, was president (1879–1896) of the Negro Talladega College. His mother was Anna Margaret Robbins, the daughter of a Congregational minister.

After preparation at the Mt. Hermon School in Massachusetts, de Forest entered the three-year mechanical engineering course of the Sheffield Scientific School at Yale University. He graduated in 1896 and returned for graduate work under such luminaries as Josiah Willard Gibbs and Henry Bumstead. De Forest enlisted in the army during the Spanish-American War but saw no action, and he received the Ph.D. on schedule in 1899 with a thesis entitled "Reflection of Hertzian Waves From the Ends of Parallel Wires."

From the first de Forest was interested in radiotelegraphy, and his improvements on the early systems enabled him to obtain financing to compete with Marconi and to interest the U.S. Army and Navy in his equipment. Apparatus constructed by de Forest and his associates was used in an attempt to report the America's Cup yacht races of 1903; and in the early part of the Russo-Japanese War of 1904–1905, his equipment was used by European reporters in sending their news dispatches, until the Japanese put an end to the arrangement.

A search for an improved detector (rectifier) of radio signals led de Forest to an invention that was a substantial improvement over the vacuum diode invented in 1904 by J. A. Fleming: the insertion of a third, control electrode between cathode and anode. De Forest applied for a patent on this "device for amplifying feeble electric currents" in 1906, but this first triode initially served only as a superior detector. A careful reading of the contemporary literature on the subject, exegesis of the subsequent claims made by de Forest (partly for purposes of patent litigation), and additional information unearthed by historical research make it clear that he neither fully understood the operation of the triode nor appreciated its possibilities as an amplifier and high-frequency oscillator until years later. In fact, the triode saw very limited use until after 1912, when Fritz Löwenstein invented the negatively "biased grid" circuit for it and H. D. Arnold and Irving Langmuir set about providing the highest attainable vacuum. But that is not to say that this prototype of all electronic amplifiers was not an invention of the greatest significance, matched in importance only by the invention of the transistor some forty years later. The triode made transcontinental telephony possible for the first time and underlies all technological applications in which weak electrical signals are amplified—including the transistor, which is a type of triode.

Following active participation in the development of the infant radio industry in New York, de Forest went to work for the Federal Telegraph Company in Palo Alto, California. He made California his permanent residence and continued to make inventions at an astonishing rate; he was granted more than 300 patents, many quite speculative, in his lifetime. Besides the triode, de Forest's most important contributions were made in the development of sound motion pictures. He was one of the founder members of the Institute of Radio Engineers in 1912, and in 1915 he received its Medal of Honor. He also received the Elliott Cresson Medal of the Franklin Institute and the Cross of the Legion of Honor from the French government.

De Forest was regarded by many as one of the last of the great individualistic inventors; his companies spent fortunes in fighting over patent rights. Several litigations were carried all the way to the U.S. Supreme Court. He had a deep appreciation of the cultural opportunities of broadcasting and deplored its commercialization. "What have you gentlemen done with my child?" he once asked radio executives. "The radio was conceived as a potent instrumentality for culture, fine music, the uplifting of America's mass intelligence. You have debased this child, you have sent him out in the streets in rags of ragtime, tatters of jive and boogie-woogie, to collect money from all and sundry."

Despite his distaste for the uses of radio, de Forest believed strongly in the future of electronics and participated in its development almost to his death; his last work was on the improvement of magnetic tapes and in thermoelectricity. He received his last patent (on an automatic telephone dialing device) at the age of eighty-four.

De Forest was married four times; his last wife was Marie Mosquini, a motion picture actress, whom he married in 1930 and who survived him. When the Foothill Electronics Museum in Los Altos Hills, Cali-fornia, was established in 1969, she donated his papers and many artifacts to it.

BIBLIOGRAPHY

De Forest's autobiography, somewhat immodestly titled *Father of Radio* (Chicago, 1950), contains his 1920 paper on the history of the triode and a list of most of his U.S. patents. Obituaries are in *New York Times* (2 July 1961), pp. 1 ff.; and in *Proceedings of the Institute of Radio Engineers,* **49** (Oct. 1961), 22A. For a well-documented account of the development of the triode, see B. F. Miessner, *The Early History of Radio Guidance* (San Francisco, 1964).

CHARLES SÜSSKIND

DeGOLYER, EVERETTE LEE (*b.* Greensburg, Kansas, 9 October 1886; *d.* Dallas, Texas, 14 December 1956), *geophysics.*

DeGolyer was the eldest child of John William and Narcissa Kagy Huddle DeGolyer, who had home-steaded in Kansas shortly before the boy's birth. Always interested in mining prospects, the senior DeGolyer moved his family to the lead and zinc center of Joplin, Missouri, and then to Oklahoma during the 1901 land opening. The boy finished high school at the University of Oklahoma preparatory school before entering the University of Oklahoma in the mining engineering course, where he was directed by Charles N. Gould and E. G. Woodruff. During the summer he worked for the U.S. Geological Survey, first as a cook but subsequently as a geologist. In the field in 1907 he impressed C. Willard Hayes, chief geologist of the Survey, who hired DeGolyer two years later to head the exploration staff of the Mexican oil company El Águila. DeGolyer's acquaintance with Sir Weetman Pearson (later Lord Cowdray) from his work in Mexico in 1910 later led to financial backing for DeGolyer's early oil companies, Amerada Petroleum Corporation and Rycade Oil Company.

Already holding a high reputation in oil discovery, DeGolyer resumed his interrupted college career at the University of Oklahoma, receiving the B.A. in 1911, and then returned to Mexico. From 1914 he was an independent oil consultant, and he founded and headed an interlocking series of oil exploration and research companies. His ability and unquestioned integrity led to his frequent employment by his own and other governments as adviser on development of oil fields.

DeGolyer received seven honorary doctorates and the Anthony F. Lucas (1941) and John Fritz (1942) medals of the American Institute of Mining and Metallurgical Engineers. He was a member of the

National Academy of Sciences, Sigma Xi, and Phi Beta Kappa and a charter member of the Society of Economic Geologists and of the American Association of Petroleum Geologists, which awarded him the Sidney Powers Memorial Award in 1950.

DeGolyer made his greatest contributions in the application of physical principles to solution of geological problems. He advocated and developed the theory, earlier suggested by European geologists, that salt domes form by the plastic flow of salt upward from deeply buried beds under the pressure of overlying rocks (1918). He then set out to locate salt domes by geophysical methods. Without question, DeGolyer's development and use of these tools gave the search for petroleum its greatest impetus of the twentieth century. He began with the torsion balance, and in 1924 he found the first salt dome by this method. A subsidiary of Amerada, Geophysical Research Corporation, was set up by DeGolyer to perfect and apply the refraction and reflection seismographs to finding oil fields. In 1927–1928 the company found eleven new salt domes by refraction surveys, but it was the discovery of the Edwards oil field in Oklahoma in 1930 by reflection survey that ushered in the modern era of oil exploration.

A knowledgeable collector of books, DeGolyer assembled one of the world's best libraries for the history of science, especially geology. He presented this library to the University of Oklahoma.

DeGolyer took his own life, after having been ill with aplastic anemia for seven years.

BIBLIOGRAPHY

I. ORIGINAL WORKS. Many of DeGolyer's early papers were on the Mexican petroleum industry. As his field enlarged, later papers summarized world petroleum production and methods. His analysis of salt-dome structure was presented in "The Theory of Volcanic Origin of Salt Domes," in *Bulletin of the American Institute of Mining and Metallurgical Engineers,* **137** (1918), 987–1000. The first two sources cited below list DeGolyer's approximately seventy geological writings, and Denison's memorial contains a complete bibliography that indicates DeGolyer's broad range of interests.

II. SECONDARY LITERATURE. Wallace E. Pratt's "Memorial to Everette Lee DeGolyer," in *Proceedings of the Geological Society of America* for 1957 (1958), 95–103, effectively summarizes the life and career of this energetic man. Further comments and indications of DeGolyer's wide interests are in Carl C. Branson's memorial in *Oklahoma Geology Notes,* **17,** no. 2 (1957), 11–21. A. Rodger Denison, in *Biographical Memoirs. National Academy of Sciences,* **33** (1959), 65–86, describes DeGolyer's personality.

ELIZABETH NOBLE SHOR

DE GROOT, JAN CORNETS, also known as **Johan Hugo De Groot** or **Janus Grotius** (*b.* near Delft, Netherlands, 8 March 1554; *d.* Delft, 3 May 1640), *mechanics.*

The son of Hugo Cornelisz and of Elselinge Van Heemskerck, De Groot (or perhaps a namesake) entered the University of Leiden on 5 February 1575, its opening day. He was a master of liberal arts and philosophy at Douai. Belonging to the Delft patriciate, he was a councillor, and from 1591 to 1595 was one of the mayors. From 1594 to 1617 he was a curator of the University of Leiden, which in 1596 awarded him the doctorate of law. After 1617 he served as adviser to the Count of Hohenlohe.

In 1582 De Groot married Alida Borren, from Overschie. One of their five children was the jurist known as Hugo Grotius.

De Groot was a distinguished amateur scientist, acquainted with the best minds in the Netherlands. Stevin, with whom he collaborated in the construction of windmills, praised him as a man well versed in the whole of philosophy, mentioning Euclid, Alhazen (Ibn al-Haytham), Witelo, music, and poetry. De Groot is best known through the experiment he performed with Stevin, in which they proved that lead bodies of different weights falling on a board traverse the same distance in the same time. This anti-Aristotelian experiment, published by Stevin in his *Waterwicht* (1586, p. 66), anticipated Galileo's famous, but apocryphal, experiment at the Leaning Tower of Pisa. De Groot also befriended Ludolph Van Ceulen, on whose behalf he translated Archimedes' *Measurement of the Circle* from the Greek into Dutch and who submitted to him his approximation of π to 20 decimal places (1586). Van Roomen, in his *Ideae mathematicae* (1593), praises De Groot as one of the better mathematicians of his time.

BIBLIOGRAPHY

Only some Latin and Greek poems, correspondence with his son Hugo—*Hugonis epistolae* (Amsterdam, 1607)—and some MS letters in the library of the University of Leiden are extant.

Secondary literature is C. de Waard, "Groot, J. H. de," in *Nieuw Nederlandsch biographisch Woordenboek,* II (1912), cols. 528, 529, with bibliography; and *The Principal Works of Simon Stevin* (Amsterdam, 1955–1966), esp. vols. I, V.

DIRK J. STRUIK

DE HAAS, WANDER J. See **Haas, Wander J. de.**

DEHN, MAX (*b*. Hamburg, Germany, 13 November 1878; *d*. Black Mountain, North Carolina, 27 June 1952), *mathematics*.

Dehn studied at Göttingen under the direction of David Hilbert and received his doctorate in 1900. He then taught at several schools, served in the army, and was a professor of pure and applied mathematics at Frankfurt University from 1921 to 1935, when the Nazi regime forced him to leave. In 1940 he emigrated to the United States, where he taught at the University of Idaho, Illinois Institute of Technology, St. Johns College (Annapolis), and, from 1945 to 1952, at Black Mountain College, North Carolina. He was a member of the Norwegian Academy of Science, the Strassburger Naturforschung Gesellschaft, and the Indian Mathematical Association.

Dehn was an intuitive geometer. Stimulated by Hilbert's work on the axiomatization of geometry, Dehn showed in his dissertation that without assuming the Archimedean postulate, Legendre's theorem that the sum of the angles of a triangle is not greater than two right angles is unprovable, whereas a generalization of Legendre's theorem on the identity of the sums of angles in different triangles is provable. Following this work, Dehn solved the third of the twenty-three unsolved problems that Hilbert had presented in his famous address to the International Congress of Mathematicians in 1900. This problem concerned the congruence of polyhedra, the geometric properties of which Dehn spent much time studying.

In 1907 Dehn and P. Heegaard contributed a report to the *Encyklopädie der mathematischen Wissenschaften* on the topic of analysis situs (now called topology or algebraic topology), which had become prominent as a result of the works of Poincaré. The article was one of the early systematic expositions of this subject. In 1910 Dehn proved an important theorem concerning topological manifolds that became known as Dehn's lemma. In 1928, however, Kneser showed that the proof contained a serious gap; a correct proof was finally given by C. D. Papakyriakopoulos in 1957.

Following Poincaré, Dehn became interested in the groups that are generated in attempts to characterize topological structures. He formulated the central problems of what was to become an important mathematical field: the word, the transformation, and the isomorphism problems. In the case of fundamental groups these have direct topological significance.

Besides his numerous contributions to the field of fundamental groups, Dehn wrote papers on statics, on the algebraic structures derived from differently axiomatized projective planes, and on the history of mathematics. He supervised the work of eight doctoral candidates in Germany and three in the United States.

BIBLIOGRAPHY

A bibliography of Dehn's works may be found in Wilhelm Magnus and Ruth Moufang, "Max Dehn zum Gedächtnis," in *Mathematische Annalen,* **127** (1954), 215–227. See also C. D. Papakyriakopoulos, "Some Problems on 3 Dimensional Manifolds," in *Bulletin of the American Mathematical Society,* **64** (1958), 317–335.

C. S. FISHER

DEINOSTRATUS. See **Dinostratus.**

DE LA BECHE, HENRY THOMAS (*b*. London [?], England, 10 February 1796; *d*. London, 13 April 1855), *geology*.

De la Beche was the son of an army officer, Lt. Col. Thomas Beach, owner of an estate in Jamaica, who had changed his name to de la Beche. He attended school at Ottery St. Mary, Devonshire, for a short time and then moved with his mother to Dorsetshire, residing first at Charmouth and later at Lyme Regis. In these seaside towns Jurassic rocks were well exposed in sea cliffs, and it is most probable that it was while living at Lyme Regis that de la Beche acquired the interest in geology that led him to make it his career. In 1810 he was sent to the Royal Military College at Marlow. The end of the Napoleonic Wars a few years later, however, made the future for an army officer less promising; and he abandoned the idea of a military career.

De la Beche was then a young man of independent means. In 1817 he was elected a member of the Geological Society of London; and his earliest extant diary, for the year 1818, recording geological observations made between Weymouth and Torquay, confirms that he was already keenly interested in field geology. In 1819 he was elected a fellow of the Royal Society. In the same year de la Beche set out on a long tour through France, Switzerland, and Italy, returning through Germany and the Netherlands. During this lengthy residence abroad he made many geological observations that he later published; he also acquired a command of foreign languages that enabled him, after his return, to keep abreast of advances in geology made outside Great Britain. His first scientific paper—on the depth and temperature of Lake Geneva—was, in fact, published in Geneva (1819).

De la Beche spent the year 1824 in Jamaica, visiting the estate he had inherited. During his stay he studied the geology of the island in some detail, and after his return he gave an account of it to the Geological Society (in *Transactions of the Geological Society of London,* 2nd ser., **2** [1827], 143). The first systematic account of the geology of Jamaica published, it included a colored geological map of the eastern half of the island. In 1829 de la Beche made another extensive Continental tour, the results of which are also apparent in later publications. In 1830 he published *Sections and Views Illustrative of Geological Phenomena,* followed in 1831 by his *Geological Manual,* the popularity of which is indicated by its three editions, as well as translations into French and German. In addition to these books he had already contributed a number of papers on British and foreign geology to the *Transactions of the Geological Society of London* and to other periodicals.

De la Beche's pioneer fieldwork was not confined to rocks of any particular kind or age. In conjunction with his extensive reading of the literature, he had acquired a wide general knowledge of geology, and his publications added considerably to the general stock of geological facts. The value of his published work was greatly enhanced by the clear and simple illustrations, based on sketches made in the field—which, incidentally, demonstrate his skill as an artist. In recording facts he was following the original aim of the Geological Society of London, announced on its foundation in 1807: the collection of geological information rather than the promulgation of geological theories. De la Beche was an accurate observer of those details of rock structure that have a bearing on the origin and mode of formation of particular rocks. Although he has not generally been credited with any outstanding contributions to geological theory, it is evident from his writings, particularly *Researches in Theoretical Geology* (1834), that his interests were not confined simply to recording facts. On the other hand, he made it quite clear that theories must always be regarded as tentative until supported by a sufficient body of factual evidence. In this book he applied his knowledge of mineralogy, chemistry, and physics to a discussion of the broader aspects of theoretical geology; but the views advanced are suggestive rather than dogmatic. For example, he suggested that the original solid crust of the earth, formed by cooling, had floated on a fluid interior of molten rock and that the once continuous crust had been broken up by tidal action to form the earliest separate land masses. This was an idea well ahead of its time.

Until about 1832 de la Beche's career had followed a course parallel to that of a number of his contemporaries, such as Charles Lyell and Roderick Murchison, men of independent means who pursued the study of geology for its own sake and were able to travel extensively in furtherance of that study. Changed circumstances, however, resulted in his spending the rest of his life as a professional geologist. This came about partly because the income from his Jamaica estate had diminished, restricting his freedom to travel, and more directly because he was to become closely involved in the formation and development of an official geological survey of Great Britain. He was the first to suggest that such a survey should be undertaken and was one of the prime movers in establishing it on a permanent basis.

Sometime after 1830 de la Beche had conceived the idea of making a geological survey of Devonshire, possibly because new Ordnance Survey topographic maps, on a scale of an inch to the mile, had recently become available for that area (the lack of accurate topographic maps on which to record geological information had previously constituted a serious difficulty for geologists). In 1832 he submitted a memorandum to the master general of the Ordnance, who was then responsible for the primary topographic survey of Great Britain, offering to make an accurate geological survey of the eight sheets covering Devonshire for the sum of £300, mentioning that originally it had been his intention to carry it out at his own expense but that he was no longer able to do so. Senior government officials had already become aware of the potential economic value to the nation of geological information, and his request was granted with little delay. By 1835 he had completed the task.

De la Beche then proposed that a similar survey should be extended to other parts of the country. This request required more serious consideration, and the government sought the advice of an independent committee of geologists. Their report was favorable; and in the same year the official Geological Survey of Great Britain was established, with de la Beche as director at an annual salary of £500. Work commenced in Cornwall, then an important center of metalliferous mining; and when this area was completed, the survey was extended to the coalfields of South Wales. It was later extended to areas other than those in which mining was active. At its commencement the survey was virtually a one-man affair, but during the next fifteen years de la Beche gradually enlarged the field staff and secured the appointment of such specialists as a paleontologist and a chemist. He also assembled large reference collections of fossils and minerals.

The culmination of de la Beche's official career was reached in 1851, when the Museum of Practical Geology, specially built in Jermyn Street, London, with offices for the survey staff, was opened to the public by Prince Albert. Thereafter he had under his direct charge not only the Geological Survey but also the museum, the School of Mines, and the Mining Records Office. Not long after the opening of these establishments the museum was described by Roderick Murchison as "the first Palace ever raised from the ground in Great Britain, which is entirely devoted to the advancement of Science." The expansion of the Geological Survey and the establishment of its important subsidiary activities on a permanent basis were very largely, if not entirely, due to the imaginative drive and administrative ability of de la Beche. What was perhaps of equal importance, in the long run, was that he succeeded in convincing governmental circles of the desirability of considerable state support for scientific research and the teaching of science.

De la Beche's new responsibilities did not prevent him from carrying out geological work himself. In 1839 he published in London his *Report on the Geology of Cornwall, Devon and West Somerset,* a work that remained valuable for many years because of the mass of mining information it contained that otherwise would probably have been lost. It was the first of the long series of official publications issued by the survey, a series that is still continuing. De la Beche contributed to later memoirs, and he continued to publish papers in scientific periodicals. In 1851 he published (also in London) *The Geological Observer,* an expanded version of an earlier work, *How to Observe* (1835).

While de la Beche, over a period of nearly forty years, contributed much to the general stock of geological knowledge through his publications, his wholehearted and determined efforts to advance the then comparatively new science of geology by every means in his power were no less important. Recognition of the value of his contributions to the science came from the government, in the form of a knighthood conferred on him in 1842, and from his fellow geologists, by election to the presidency of the Geological Society of London in 1847 and the award of this society's highest honor, the Wollaston Medal, in 1855. From about 1850 de la Beche suffered from a form of paralysis, but he continued to attend to his duties until two days before his death.

BIBLIOGRAPHY

I. ORIGINAL WORKS. In addition to the works cited above, de la Beche published *A Selection of the Geological Memoirs Contained in the Annales des Mines* (London, 1824; 2nd ed., 1836), an annotated translation, with a correlation of British with French and German strata.

He also contributed a number of papers, mainly geological, to periodicals. The more important were published in either the *Transactions of the Geological Society of London* or their *Proceedings.* They are listed in the Royal Society's *Catalogue of Scientific Papers 1800–1863,* Vol. II (London, 1868).

De la Beche's official publications (in some instances written in collaboration with other authors) include "Report with Reference to the Selection of Stone for Building the New Houses of Parliament," in *Parliamentary Papers for 1839,* vol. XXX (London, 1839); "On the Formation of the Rocks of South Wales and South-western England," in *Memoirs of the Geological Survey of Great Britain,* **1** (1846), 1–296; and "First and Second Reports on the Coals Suited to the Steam Navy," in *Parliamentary Papers* (London, 1848, 1849) and in *Memoirs of the Geological Survey of Great Britain,* **2,** pt. 2 (1948), 539–630. These reports contain a detailed examination of the physical and chemical characteristics of various British coal seams.

De la Beche's "Inaugural Discourse Delivered at the Opening of the School of Mines and of Science Applied to the Arts," in *Records of the School of Mines,* **1,** pt. 1 (1852), 1–22, is of historical interest as an authoritative contemporary account of the formation and objectives of the Geological Survey and its associated institutions.

II. SECONDARY LITERATURE. No biography of de la Beche has been published, although a number of his diaries and letters are now held by the National Museum of Wales, Cardiff. Accounts of his career are included in J. S. Flett, *The First Hundred Years of the Geological Survey of Great Britain* (London, 1937), pp. 23–56; and E. B. Bailey, *Geological Survey of Great Britain* (London, 1952), pp. 21–51. The former deals especially with his official career, and the latter also assesses his capabilities as a geologist. Some additional matter, based partly on unpublished material, is contained in three short articles by F. J. North: "De la Beche and His Activities, as Revealed by His Diaries and Correspondence," in *Abstracts of the Proceedings of the Geological Society of London,* no. 1314 (June 1936), 104–106; "H. T. de la Beche: Geologist and Business Man," in *Nature,* **143** (1939), 254–255; and "The Ordnance Geological Survey: Its First Memoir," *ibid.,* 1052–1053. L. J. Chubb has described in some detail de la Beche's ancestry, his connection with Jamaica, and the geological work he carried out there in the De la Beche Memorial Number of *Geonotes, the Quarterly Newsletter of the Jamaica Group of the Geologists Association* [of London] (Kingston, Jamaica, 1958).

V. A. EYLES

DELAGE, YVES (*b.* Avignon, France, 13 May 1854; *d.* Sceaux, France, 7 October 1920), *zoology, anatomy, physiology, embryogeny, general biology.*

After passing his *baccalauréat ès-sciences* and *baccalauréat ès-lettres,* Delage went to Paris in 1873 to study medicine. Obliged to interrupt his studies, he accepted a post as *répétiteur* at the *lycée* of La Rochelle. In 1875 he was able to resume his medical studies. At the same time he prepared for the *licence* in natural sciences, which he obtained in 1878. In the same year his teacher, Lacaze Duthiers, chose him to direct the zoological station at Roscoff. He defended his doctoral theses in medicine and in science in 1880 and 1881, respectively. He was *chargé des fonctions de maître de conférences* in zoology at the Sorbonne (1880); *chargé de cours* at Caen (1881); titular professor of zoology at Caen and director of the zoological station at Luc (1884); *chargé de cours* at the Sorbonne (1885); titular professor of zoology at the Sorbonne (1886), a post he occupied until his death; and director of the marine laboratory at Roscoff (1902).

Delage's experimental work was drastically curtailed when he suffered a detached retina, and in 1912 he had to give up teaching. Although he became blind, he continued his work.

A disciple of and assistant to Lacaze Duthiers, Delage at first followed the latter's zoological traditions. His works on crustacean circulation display remarkable skill; and the superb accompanying illustrations are considered classics. The two chief qualities of Delage's work were already manifest: experimental ingenuity and technical ability, both guided by a tenacious will. His penetrating critical mind enabled him to establish new truths that were quite different from what was then generally accepted. His discoveries regarding the *Sacculina* and the embryogeny of the sponges are striking evidence of this ability. The inoculation of the kentrogon larva of the *Sacculina* and the inversion of the laminae in the metamorphosis of sponges are major discoveries that have withstood the test of time. Also worthy of mention are his researches on the nervous systems of the *Peltogaster* and of the *Convoluta,* and on the transformation of a leptocephalus into an eel, which provided the key to the metamorphoses of the Anguillidae; an anatomical study of the *Balaenoptera;* and a monograph on the ascidians.

In experimental physiology Delage investigated the function of the otocysts in various animals and of the semicircular canals in man. He established a new conception in the physiology of the inner ear: the semicircular canals stabilize equilibrium.

A crisis of conscience led Delage to abandon pure zoology for general biology and biomechanics. He now investigated the causes of the manifestations of life in the cell, in the individual, and in the species, considering this area more productive of important results. The book *La structure du protoplasma . . .* (1895) marks the turning point of his scientific career.

The qualities evident in Delage's earlier works are also present in those on merogony, fertilization, and artificial parthenogenesis. He would not consider a question without completely settling it. After Jacques Loeb's discovery of artificial fertilization Delage, through theoretical insights, devised a process of chemical fertilization so perfect that for two years he succeeded in raising to the adult stage sea urchins obtained by this process.

Because of the great importance that he accorded to the action of the environment and to the role of acquired characteristics, Delage was a Lamarckian and, therefore, unwilling to accept the ideas of Weismann and Mendel.

Delage founded the *Année biologique* to publish articles on general biology and was its director for fifteen years. He also planned a great zoological treatise based on his belief that each division of the animal kingdom could be reduced to an ideal type that embodied all the fundamental characteristics of that division.

Among his other activities, Delage constructed and experimented with a bathyrheometer designed to measure the speed of ocean currents. After his blindness had condemned him to meditation, Delage concerned himself with the causes and various states of dreaming.

Delage was not merely an incomparable professor who gave illuminating lectures; he was also a philosopher, a novelist, a short-story writer, a poet, and a polemicist. He belonged to many scientific academies and societies and was elected to the Académie des Sciences in 1901. He worked unceasingly at Roscoff to enlarge the biological station, and there is a monument to him there.

BIBLIOGRAPHY

I. ORIGINAL WORKS. Among Delage's papers are "Sur l'origine des éléments figurés du sang chez les Vertébrés" (1880), his M.D. thesis; "Contributions à l'étude de l'appareil circulatoire des Crustacés Edriophthalmes marins," in *Archives de zoologie expérimentale et générale,* **9** (1881), 1–176, his thesis for the *doctorat ès-sciences;* "Circulation et respiration chez les Crustacés Schizopodes," *ibid.,* 2nd ser., **1** (1883), 105–131; "Évolution de la Sacculine," *ibid.,* **2** (1884), 417–737; "Sur le système nerveux et sur quelques autres points de l'organisation du Peltogaster," *ibid.,* **4** (1886), 17–37; "Études expérimentales sur les illusions statiques et dynamiques de direction pour servir à déterminer les fonctions des canaux semi-circulaires de l'oreille interne," *ibid.,* 535–695; "Sur une fonction nouvelle des otocystes comme organes d'orientation locomotrice," *ibid.,* **5** (1887), 1–26; "Études sur les Ascidies des côtes de France; les Cyntiadées," in *Mémoires de l'Académie des sciences,* 2nd ser., **45** (1892–1899), 323 pp., written with Lacaze Duthiers; "Embryogénie des Éponges. Développement post-larvaire des Éponges siliceuses et fibreuses," in

Archives de zoologie expérimentale et générale, 2nd ser., **10** (1893), 345–499; "Étude sur la mérogonie," *ibid.,* 3rd ser., **7** (1899), 383–418; and "La parthénogenèse expérimentale," in *Rapport du Congrès zoologique. Graz 1910* (1912), pp. 100–162.

Delage's books include *La structure du protoplasma, les théories sur l'hérédité et les grands problèmes de la biologie générale* (Paris, 1895); *Traité de zoologie concrète,* written with E. Hérouard, composed of the following volumes: *La cellule et les Protozoaires* (Paris, 1896), *Les Vermidiens* (Paris, 1897), *Les Procordés* (Paris, 1898), *Mesozoaires et Spongiaires* (Paris, 1899), *Coelentérés* (Paris, 1901), and *Échinodermes* (Paris, 1903); *Les théories de l'évolution,* in the Bibliothèque de Philosophie Scientifique (Paris, 1909), written with M. Goldsmith; *La parthénogenèse naturelle et expérimentale,* in Bibliothèque de Philosophie Scientifique (Paris, 1913), written with M. Goldsmith; and *Le rêve. Étude psychologique, philosophique et littéraire* (Paris, 1920).

II. SECONDARY LITERATURE. A notice on the life and work of Delage is M. Goldsmith, in *Année biologique,* n.s. **1** (1920–1921), v–xix. L. Joubin's speech at the unveiling of the monument to Delage at Roscoff, a biographical notice, and a bibliography constitute *Académie des sciences* (1924), no. 17. The speeches by both Charles Pérez and L. Joubin at the unveiling of the monument are in *Travaux de la Station biologique de Roscoff,* **5** (1926), 1–30.

ANDRÉE TÉTRY

DELAMAIN, RICHARD (*fl.* London, England, first half of the seventeenth century), *mathematics.*

Delamain was a joiner by trade, and after studying mathematics at Gresham College, London, he supported himself by teaching practical mathematics in London. Later he became mathematical tutor to King Charles I, for whom he fashioned a number of mathematical instruments. He was a pupil of William Oughtred, and in the early days of their association the two men became close friends. Unhappily this did not last, and later they quarreled violently over priority in the invention of the circular slide rule, which Delamain described in his *Grammelogia, or the Mathematicall Ring.*

Delamain's fame rests mainly on this essay, a pamphlet of thirty-two pages. The manuscript was sent to the king in 1629, and the work was published the following year. The king retained Delamain's services as tutor at a salary of £40 per annum. A few years later Delamain petitioned for an engineer's post at a salary of £100 per annum. Following an interview with the king at Greenwich in 1637, he was granted a warrant for making a number of mathematical instruments.

The appearance of the *Grammelogia* was the signal for the beginning of the quarrel. Oughtred had in-vented the rectilinear slide rule as early as 1622, but his *Circles of Proportion,* which contained a description of the circular slide rule, was not made public until 1632—by which time the *Grammelogia* had been in circulation for two years. William Forster, a friend and pupil of Oughtred, translated from the Latin and published the *Circles of Proportion,* the preface to which contains some ungenerous references to Delamain, who, it states, purloined the design of the circular slide rule from Oughtred. Delamain retaliated vigorously, attacking both Forster and Oughtred; the latter replied with a pamphlet, *The Apologeticall Epistle,* in which he refers to the "slaunderous insimulations of Richard Delamain in a Pamphlet called *Grammelogia, or the Mathematicall Ring"* and maintains that the latter's horizontal quadrant is no other than the horizontal instrument he had invented thirty years earlier.

Delamain perished in the Civil War sometime before 1645. Oughtred lived until 1660, but his last years were embittered by the dispute with his former friend and pupil.

Delamain was a competent mathematician whose genius lay in the practical realm. He excelled in the construction of a number of mathematical instruments. It is thought that the silver sundial which the king always carried with him and, at his execution, entrusted to Mr. Herbert to be given to the young duke of York, was one of Delamain's creations.

> He likewise commanded Mr. *Herbert* to give his son, the Duke of *York,* his large Ring Sundial of silver, a Jewel his Majesty much valued: it was invented and made by *Rich. Delamaine* a very able Mathematician, who projected it, and in a little printed book did shew its excellent use in resolving many questions in Arithmetick and other rare operations to be wrought by it in the Mathematicks [Wood, *Athenae Oxonienses. History of Oxford Writers,* II, 1692, 525].

BIBLIOGRAPHY

I. ORIGINAL WORKS. Delamain's writings are *Grammelogia, or the Mathematicall Ring* (London, 1630); and *The Making, Description and Use of a Small Portable Instrument for the Pocket . . . Called a Horizontal Quadrant* (London, 1632).

II. SECONDARY LITERATURE. On Delamain or his work, see Florian Cajori, *William Oughtred. A Great Seventeenth Century Teacher of Mathematics* (London–Chicago, 1916), *passim; Dictionary of National Biography;* and E. G. R. Taylor, *The Mathematical Practitioners of Tudor and Stuart England* (Cambridge, 1954), p. 201.

J. F. SCOTT

DELAMBRE, JEAN-BAPTISTE JOSEPH (*b.* Amiens, France, 19 September 1749; *d.* Paris, France, 19 August 1822), *astronomy, geodesy, history of astronomy.*

Delambre's early life resembles those novels of the nineteenth century in which industry overcomes hardship and is rewarded with social distinction and financial gain. He began his education in the local schools of Amiens and eventually won a small scholarship that enabled him to move on to Paris and the Collège du Plessis, where he studied literature (chiefly Latin and Greek) and history. He was especially skilled in languages and began to make translations of works in Latin, Greek, Italian, and English. He was apparently so poor that upon graduation he lived for almost a whole year on a diet of bread and water.[1] He then was engaged as a private tutor in Compiègne and undertook private studies in mathematics, presumably so as to be able to teach this subject along with languages, literature, rhetoric, and history—in which he had received schooling. A local doctor seems to have suggested to Delambre that he might eventually learn astronomy. The opportunity to do so did not occur, however, until 1780, when Delambre had been established in Paris for some nine years. He was thus in his early thirties when he first began to study astronomy, the subject in which he was to establish his reputation.

A most fortunate event that helped Delambre in his career occurred in 1771, when he became tutor to the son of Geoffroy d'Assy (*receveur générale des finances*) in Paris. Eventually d'Assy built a small, private, and apparently well-equipped observatory for Delambre's use—acting on the suggestion made by the astronomer Lalande.[2] Delambre had begun to attend Lalande's lectures at the Collège de France in 1780, and he at once attracted the attention of Lalande when the latter made reference to the Greek poet Aratus, of the third century B.C., author of the astronomical poem *Phaenomena.* Delambre, who was endowed with a prodigious memory, thereupon recited the whole passage in question and went on to discuss various explanations and commentaries that had been made by different scholars. Lalande soon learned that Delambre had written a series of annotations and emendations to his own writings, notably his *Astronomie,* the course textbook. After reading Delambre's notes, Lalande made him an assistant, and eventually Delambre became Lalande's scientific collaborator. Lalande fondly referred to Delambre as his "meilleur oeuvre."[3]

The beginning of Delambre's career as an observer is dated (by himself) on a day in 1786 when only he and Messier, of all the astronomers in Paris, had seen the transit of Mercury across the sun. The event occurred three-quarters of an hour later than the time predicted by Lalande; the other observers, too easily discouraged, had given up. Delambre had more faith in Halley's tables, which predicted the occurrence of the transit an hour and a half later, and so he persevered. This particular episode is cited by Jacquinet[4] as an example of the lack of precision in astronomical tables of that time. Delambre's experience with the transit must have provided a strong incentive for making more accurate tables of various major astronomical phenomena.

Before long there was a public challenge to all astronomers to solve the problems of precise planetary motion. The Académie des Sciences announced a general competition for the prize of 1790 on the subject of the motion of the planet Uranus, which had been discovered by William Herschel in 1781. Some idea of the difficulty of the problem may be gained from the simple fact that these eight years of observation of Uranus represent only about one-tenth of its sidereal period. To determine the orbit and motion of Uranus, Delambre had to consider the perturbations produced by Jupiter and by Saturn: in short, he had to combine a skill in computation with a theoretical understanding of applied celestial mechanics. After winning the prize, he went on to establish himself as a foremost expert in positional astronomy. Eventually there followed tables of the sun, of Jupiter, of Saturn, and of the satellites of Jupiter. The high esteem in which his results were held is shown in the statement by Arago: "In perfecting the methods of astronomical calculation he merits, by reason of the variety and elegance of his methods, a distinguished place among the ablest *géomètres* France can boast."

The above-mentioned tables were published by Lalande in a later edition of his *Astronomie* and earned two further honors for Delambre. In 1792 he was again given the annual prize of the Academy, and he was elected *membre associé* in the section of *sciences mathématiques.* This election was a major factor in his being designated to make the fundamental geodetic measurements on which the metric system was to be based.

In 1788 the Academy decided to establish a "uniform system of measures" founded on some "natural and invariable base." The plan for the new system of measures was formally approved by a decree of the Assembly of 8 May 1790, proposed by Talleyrand; it was approved by Louis XVI on the following 22 August. A commission on the metric system, consisting of Borda, Lagrange, Laplace, Monge, and Condorcet, was thereupon appointed by the Academy. In a report submitted on 19 March 1791,[5] the commissioners rejected two proposed bases for the fundamental unit of measure: the length of a seconds pendulum (at 45° latitude), and one-quarter of the terrestrial equator. Instead they chose one-quarter of a terrestrial meridian, the common practical unit to be a ten-millionth part of this quantity. Accordingly, it was proposed to make a careful and accurate measure along an arc of the meridian through Dunkerque (which had in part been measured by the Cassinis in 1718 and in 1740), extending as far south as Barcelona, giving 9.°5 of arc.

Three fundamental tasks were envisaged. First, to determine the exact difference in longitude between Dunkerque and Barcelona (and to make any needed latitude determinations in between); second, to check by new observations and calculations the triangulations used earlier to find the distance between Dunkerque and Perpignan; third, to make new measurements that could serve for successive triangulations. Clearly a major part of this assignment would be to compute carefully the difference in actual lengths (in *toises*) corresponding to the same difference in latitude at various points along the meridian, so as to be able to determine the actual shape of the earth. While these operations were being performed, other scientists would be engaged in establishing a standard of mass. The instruments, chiefly made by Lenoir according to the plans of Borda, were ready by June 1792, and the work was started shortly afterward.

Originally, the geodetic survey was to be entrusted to Méchain, Cassini, and Legendre. The latter two begged off, and Delambre—just made a member of the Academy—was appointed. It was decided that Delambre would be in charge of the survey from Dunkerque to Rodez, leaving the survey from Rodez to Barcelona in the hands of Méchain. An account of the labors and adventures of Méchain and Delambre is available in their joint publication, *Base du système métrique décimal* (3 vols., Paris, 1806, 1807, 1810). This may be supplemented by Delambre's own *Grandeur et figure de la terre* (Paris, 1912), edited and published from Delambre's manuscript about a century later by G. Bigourdan.

Delambre explains the inequality of the assigned distances (Méchain—170,000 *toises* from Rodez to Barcelona; Delambre—380,000 *toises* from Rodez to Dunkerque) as follows: "The reason for this unequal division was that the Spanish part was entirely new, whereas the remainder had already been measured twice; we were agreed that the former would provide many more difficulties." Then he remarks, "We did not know that the greatest difficulties of all would be found at the very gates of Paris." Méchain, the first

to set out, on 25 June 1792, was arrested at his third observational site, at Essonne, by uneasy citizens who were convinced that his activities had some counter-revolutionary aspects. Only by constant explanation and good fortune was Méchain able to continue, and eventually to carry his survey into Spain. Delambre encountered similar difficulties; and, in addition, when he returned to Paris and had to leave again, he had to seek new passports as the government changed. It seems almost incredible that in time of revolution Delambre was able to continue his work as much as he did. In eight months of 1792, however, he had established only four points of triangulation; but in 1793, despite delays in getting his passport, he made better progress. Then, in January 1794, he received an order from the Committee of Public Safety to stop all observations at once. On his return to Paris he learned that as of 23 December 1793 he had been removed from membership in the commission of weights and measures, along with Borda, Lavoisier, Laplace, Coulomb, and Bresson.

Happily, the enterprise was revivified by the law of 18 Germinal *an* III (7 April 1795), and Delambre and Méchain were able to take up their old assignments, now under the title of *astronomes du Dépôt de la Guerre,* serving under the head of that establishment, General Calon, a member of the Convention. Delambre thereupon set out for Orléans on 28 June 1795 and completed his assignment within four years.

Delambre's task was not merely to make a series of correlated astronomical observations and terrestrial measurements; he had also to carry out extremely laborious calculations. The latter were made especially tedious by the need to convert the observations from the new centesimal units of angle-measure (used in Delambre's instruments) to the older units of degrees, on which all tables of logarithms and of trigonometric functions were then based.

The proponents of the metric system succeeded in establishing a decimal-positional system of mass and length (area and volume), but failed in their attempts to introduce similar systems of time or of angle measure. Delambre's instruments were constructed with the new centesimal divisions, in anticipation of their general adoption. On this score he remarks:

> This subdivision is much more convenient for use with the repeating circle, and would be equally convenient for verniers with any sort of instrument. Some people still prefer the old subdivision out of long habit and because they have never tried the new one, but no one who has ever employed them both wants to return to the former system.
>
> Extending the metric system to the subdivision of the circle, however, required the construction of new trig-

onometric tables. In the year II [1793], M. de Prony was requested to prepare such tables which would leave nothing to be desired in their exactitude and which would constitute the largest and most imposing monument of calculation that had ever been executed or even conceived.[6]

Prony's manuscript, never edited for publication, contained logarithms of sines and tangents to fourteen decimals in tens of centesimal "seconds" and logarithms of numbers from 1 to 100,000 to nineteen decimals. An account was presented to the Institute and was published in 1801 by Lagrange, Laplace, and Delambre, under the title *Notice sur les grandes tables logarithmiques et trigonométriques calculées au bureau du Cadastre sous la direction du citoyen Prony*.

A more usable work was produced by Borda, a set of tables to seven decimals. Completed by Delambre after Borda's death, this work was published in the year IX of the Republic (1801), under the title *Tables trigonométriques décimales, ou tables des logarithmes des sinus, sécantes et tangentes, suivant la division du quart de cercle en 100 degrés, du degré en 100 minutes, et de la minute en 100 secondes; . . . calculées par Ch. Borda, revues, augmentées et publiées par J. B. J. Delambre.*

Méchain died in 1804, and it became Delambre's sole responsibility to complete the computations and to write up the final report. This constituted three volumes containing the history of the enterprise, the observations, and the calculations. The third volume was completed in 1810, some twenty years after the project was begun. When Delambre presented a copy of this work to Napoleon, the emperor responded, "Conquests pass and such works remain."[7]

Delambre's results were put into the hands of a commission of French and foreign scientists, who then determined the unit of length which became the standard meter. Jean Joseph Fourier said that "no other application of science is to be compared with this as regards its character of exactness, utility, and magnitude." The newly constituted Institut de France designated this survey "the most important application of mathematical or physical science which had occurred within ten years" and in 1810 gave Delambre a prize for his share in the great work. The accuracy with which Delambre carried out his task may be seen in a comparison of two base lines: Perpignan and Mélun. Delambre measured both by direct methods. Then, making use of a network of triangulation, he used one to compute the other. According to Fourier, although the distance between the two bases is some 220 leagues, the results of calculation differed from the results of direct measurement by less than three-tenths of a meter, less than one part in 36,000.

By the time of publication of his report on the base of the metric system, Delambre had become a resident member of the newly organized Institut National (*section de mathématiques de la première classe*). He was appointed an inaugural member of the Bureau des Longitudes, founded in 1795. When the Institute was reorganized, he became, on 11 Pluviôse *an* XI (31 January 1803), the first permanent secretary for *les sciences mathématiques*. In 1807, he succeeded Lalande in the chair of astronomy in the Collège de France. In 1813 he published an *Abrégé d'astronomie* and in 1814 a work on *Astronomie théorique et pratique*, based on his lectures. Until 1808, when he moved from the rue de Paradis to the outskirts of the Faubourg Saint-Germain, he continued to make observations from his private observatory, primarily checking stellar positions in the major catalogs from Flamsteed's to Maskelyne's. He also associated himself with Laplace, who was working on the problems of perturbations and other aspects of celestial mechanics, and produced new tables based on these investigations. In the official *éloge*, Fourier wrote:

Before him astronomical calculations were founded on numerical processes, which were at once indirect and irregular. These he has changed throughout, or ingeniously remodeled. Most of those which astronomers use at the present time belong to him, having been deduced from analytic formulas, which, in their application, have been found alike, sure, uniform, and manageable. The new tables which he has given us of the sun, of Jupiter, of Saturn, of Uranus, and of the satellites of Jupiter, at least some of them, may have been considerably improved by recent labors founded on a greater number of exact observations; yet, in the present state of astronomy, and up to this day, the tables of Delambre just mentioned are those employed in the calculations made for the *Connaissance des temps* and for the nautical and astronomical ephemerides of most nations. In addition, the geodetic operation, for which we are chiefly indebted to him, and of which he bore the greatest share, is the most perfect and extensive which has been executed in any country. It has served as the model of all enterprises of the kind which have been since projected.

As scientist, Delambre is remembered primarily for his improvements in astronomical tables and his contributions to the measurement of the earth (and establishment of the base of the metric system). But he had yet another career, begun in the last decades of his life, as historian. Reference has already been made to Delambre's history of the measurement of the earth (and the historical first volume of the *Base du système métrique décimal*). In 1810 Delambre published a major historical work, *Rapport historique sur les progrès des sciences mathématiques depuis 1789.*

Delambre had at one time intended that his treatise on astronomy would be preceded by a *tableau* of the evolution of this science through the ages. But he found the subject so vast that he decided to devote a separate work to it. He began collecting and organizing his materials in 1812, at the age of sixty-three, and he devoted the remainder of his life to compiling a history of astronomy. By the time he was finished, Delambre had completed six volumes, of which the final one (on the astronomy of the eighteenth century) was published posthumously in 1827 by L. Mathieu. The first two volumes (1817) deal with ancient astronomy, a third (1819) with the astronomy of the Middle Ages, and the fourth and fifth with the astronomy of the Renaissance and the seventeenth century. Delambre also helped the Abbé Halma in his translation of Ptolemy's *Almagest* and he wrote an extensive set of notes of such importance that his name appears along with Halma's on the title page.[8]

Delambre's *Histoire de l'astronomie* is a work without parallel in any of the sciences. It is a technical work, written—as he said—"mainly for astronomers, and mathematicians in general." His aim had been to produce a "tableau complet des différens âges de l'Astronomie," that is, "a repository where could be found all the ideas, all the methods, and all the theorems that have served successively for the calculation of phenomena." There is no synthesis, no generalization, no display of insight into the causes for great progress or decline. Delambre rather presents each major chronological period in a series of discrete analyses of one treatise (or other work) after another. Often, in the case of a long book (as Kepler's *Astronomia nova*), the analysis proceeds chapter by chapter. Thus the reader may readily apprehend what a given astronomical work contains, plus a critical estimate of its worth; and he may follow Delambre as he compares and contrasts several works of a given author. But the method is frustrating in the extreme to anyone who may want to trace a particular topic throughout a whole century or more.

As one would expect, Delambre is especially good on astronomical tables and on methods of observation and calculation. A great virtue is the wealth of information on minor figures, for whom no other account may be available. Above all, Delambre spices his presentation with acerb and delightful comments (including critical remarks about style or errors in Greek and Latin) as his statement that Boulliau's

construction is "certainement ingénieuse, mais inutile." Or again, "[We] are writing a history not eulogies." Thus, "The historian owes nothing to the dead save truth. It's not our fault if *in astronomy* Descartes produced nothing but chimeras."[9] Unquestionably the six-volume *Histoire* is the greatest full-scale technical history of any branch of science ever written by a single individual. It sets a standard very few historians of science may ever achieve.

In the course of his geodetic measurements, Delambre gained the service of a young assistant, Leblanc de Pommard. Pommard's mother, then a widow, has been described as "a distinguished Latinist, endowed with solid but not pedantic learning." Delambre married her when he was fifty-five years of age.

Under the Empire, Delambre took on a number of official posts, including *inspecteur général des études* and *trésorier de l'université.* He had the task of establishing a number of *lycées,* including those of Moulins (1802) and Lyons (1803). Despite his "opinions libérales," he became in 1814 a member of the Conseil Royal d'Instruction Publique. He retired from public life in 1815 and was made a *chevalier* of Saint Michel by the royal government. In 1821 he became an *officier* of the Legion of Honor (he had been a *chevalier* since the foundation of the order).

NOTES

1. Mathieu, p. 305*a.*
2. This observatory was situated in the Hotel d'Assy in the rue de Paradis, in the Marais, which is now part of the Archives Nationales. The observatory remained a distinct structure until about 1910 (Jacquinet, p. 195).
3. Lalande listed the date of Delambre's birth in the preface to his *Astronomie,* 3rd ed. (Paris, 1792), p. xxxiii, "parceque, je la regarde comme devant faire époque dans l'histoire de l'astronomie."
4. P. 195.
5. According to the report, "It is apparent here that we are surrendering all claim to the common division of the quarter-meridian into degrees, minutes, and seconds; but this old division could not be kept without harming the unity of the system of measure since decimal division that corresponds to arithmetical gradations is to be preferred for a standard of usage" (Jacquinet, p. 196). See also Delambre's *Grandeur et figure de la terre* (1912).
6. These extracts are taken from Méchain and Delambre, *Base du système métrique.*
7. Delambre wrote this remark in his own copy of this work.
8. In this work, and in his history of ancient astronomy, Delambre adopted a posture which has recently been subject to serious criticism: a "dislike for Ptolemy and the resulting misrepresentation of Hipparchian astronomy as being practically the equivalent of the *Almagest*" (O. Neugebauer, in his preface to the reprint of Delambre's *Histoire de l'astronomie ancienne*).
9. For a critical analysis of Delambre as historian, see I. B. Cohen's introduction to the reprint of Delambre's *Histoire de l'astronomie moderne.*

BIBLIOGRAPHY

I. ORIGINAL WORKS. Delambre published a large number of *mémoires, extraits, notices, éloges,* and other works in the *Connaissance des temps* from 1788 to 1822, and in various publications of scientific societies, including the Académie des Sciences (Paris), and the academies of Berlin and Turin. His major publications, in chronological order, are *Tables de Jupiter et de Saturne* (Paris, 1789); *Tables astronomiques, calculées sur les observations les plus nouvelles, pour servir à la troisième édition de l'Astronomie,* a supp. (with separate pagination) to vol. 1, 3rd ed., of Lalande's *Astronomie* (Paris, 1792)—in the preface Lalande says, "Les tables . . . du Soleil, de Jupiter, de Saturne, et des satellites [de Jupiter], sont de M. de Lambre. . . ."; and *Méthodes analytiques pour la détermination d'un arc de méridien. Précédées d'un mémoire sur le même sujet, par A.M. Legendre* (Paris, an VII [1799]).

The *Tables astronomiques publiées par le Bureau des Longitudes de France,* pt. 1 (Paris, 1806), contains "Tables du Soleil, par M. Delambre"; pt. 2 (Paris, 1808) contains "Nouvelles tables écliptiques des satellites de Jupiter, d'après la théorie de M. Laplace, et la totalité des observations faites depuis 1662, jusqu'à l'an 1802; par M. Delambre"; a separate publication of the latter work, with a slightly different title (*Tables . . . d'après la théorie de M. le Marquis de Laplace . . .*) was issued in Paris, 1817.

Other works are *Base du système métrique décimal, ou Mesure de l'arc du méridien compris entre les parallèles de Dunkerque et Barcelone, exécutée en 1792 et années suivantes, par MM. Méchain et Delambre. Rédigée par M. Delambre. Suite des Mémoires de l'Institut,* 3 vols. (Paris, 1806, 1807, 1810); *Rapport historique sur les progrès des sciences mathématiques depuis 1789, et sur leur état actuel . . .* (Paris, 1810; photo repr., Amsterdam, 1966); *Abrégé d'astronomie, ou leçons élémentaires d'astronomie théorique et pratique* (Paris, 1813); *Astronomie théorique et pratique,* 3 vols. (Paris, 1814); *Histoire de l'astronomie ancienne,* 2 vols. (Paris, 1817); *Histoire de l'astronomie du moyen âge* (Paris, 1819); *Histoire de l'astronomie moderne,* 2 vols. (Paris, 1821); and *Histoire de l'astronomie au dix-huitième siècle.* The six-volume set of histories was repr. in facs., with a preface to vols. I and II by O. Neugebauer, an intro. to vols. IV and V by I. Bernard Cohen, and an intro. to vol. VI by Harry Woolf (New York–London, 1965–1969).

See also *Grandeur et figure de la terre,* with notes and maps (Paris, 1912).

Not included in the above list are certain works edited by Delambre (such as Borda's *Tables trigonométriques décimales . . .*) or reports (such as the one on Prony's tables), even though they are mentioned in the text of the article. But special mention should be made of *Composition mathématique de Claude Ptolémée. Traduite pour la première fois du grec en français, sur les manuscrits originaux de la Bibliothèque Impériale de Paris, par M. [l'Abbé] Halma; et suivie des notes de M. Delambre,* 2 vols. (Paris, 1813–1816; photo repr., Paris 1927).

II. SECONDARY LITERATURE. The major biographical source is Claude Louis Mathieu's article, based on Delambre's manuscript autobiography and other manuscripts, in Michaud's *Biographie universelle* (new ed., Paris, n.d., X, 304–308). Another major source is Pierre Jacquinet, "Commémoration du deux-centième anniversaire de la naissance de J. B. Delambre—son oeuvre astronomique et géodésique," in *Bulletin de la Société Astronomique de France,* 63e annee (1949), 193–207. Jean Joseph Fourier's *Éloge,* prepared for the Académie des Sciences, is available in an English translation by C. A. Alexander in the *Annual report . . . of the Smithsonian Institution . . . for the year 1864* (Washington, 1865), pp. 125–134.

Also available is Joseph Caulle, "Delambre—sa participation à la détermination du mètre," in *Recueil des Publications de la Société Havraise d'Études Diverses,* 103e année (1936), 143–157. Other sources are Charles Dupin, "Notice nécrologique sur M. Delambre," in *Revue encyclopédique,* **16** (1822), 437–460, and the brief account by St. Le Tourneur in the new *Dictionnaire de biographie française,* fasc. 57 (Paris, 1964), p. 675.

As Bigourdan reports, "The Academy of Amiens held a contest for his eulogy; Vulfran Warmé's speech, printed at Amiens in 1824, won for him the *accessit* and a gold medal." A copy of this work, *Éloge historique de M. Delambre, qui a obtenu l'accessit et une medaille d'or au concours de l'Académie d'Amiens* (Amiens, 1824), is in the dossier of Delambre in the library of the Académie des Sciences, Paris, with M. Desboves, *Delambre et Ampère: Discours de réception, suivi de . . . plusieurs lettres inédites de Delambre* (Amiens, 1881). See also David Eugene Smith's *Delambre and Smithson* (New York, 1934).

A summary of the facts of Delambre's life and an evaluation of his work as historian is available in my introduction to the facs. repr. of Delambre's *Histoire de l'astronomie moderne.* In the short biography listed three paragraphs above, Mathieu says of himself: "The author of this article, a student and friend of Delambre and possessor of all his manuscripts, made use of the writings of Delambre, a biographical note written by Delambre himself, and that which he had the opportunity of learning about Delambre during the many years he spent with him. One would have to have heard this modest and sincere man giving an account of his way of life after leaving the Collège du Plessis in order to believe the tiny amount that he spent during one year."

I. BERNARD COHEN

DE LA RUE, WARREN (*b.* Guernsey, 15 January 1815; *d.* London, England, 19 April 1889), *chemistry, invention, astronomy.*

Warren de la Rue was the eldest son of Thomas de la Rue, a printer, and Jane Warren. His early education was at the Collège Sainte-Barbe in Paris. In his teens he entered his father's printing shop and there first came into contact with science and technology. He was one of the first printers to adopt electrotyping and, with a friend, invented the first envelope-making machine. His understanding of machinery and technology was the basis of his contributions to science. De la Rue was not an original thinker but one who perfected instruments and, through these improvements, made accurate observations of theoretical interest.

De la Rue's first scientific contributions were to chemistry, in which he remained interested throughout his life. He made a small improvement of the Daniell constant voltage battery that was announced in his first paper (1836). With August Wilhelm Hofmann, the great German teacher of chemistry in London, he edited an English version of the first two volumes of Liebig and Kopp's *Jahresbericht,* which served to acquaint English chemists with the work of their Continental colleagues. He was an original member of the Chemical Society, serving as its president in the years 1867–1869 and 1879–1880.

De la Rue's major contribution was to astronomy. He was drawn to this science by another inventor-businessman, James Nasmyth, the inventor of the steam pile driver. Nasmyth had been fascinated with the moon for years and had personally drawn some of the best pictures available of our satellite. De la Rue took up astronomy with the purpose of producing more accurate and detailed pictures of the nearby heavenly bodies. He, too, was an excellent draftsman and his drawings of Saturn, the moon, and the sun are superb. His observation of detail was enhanced by improvements he introduced into the polishing and figuring of the thirteen-inch reflecting telescope that he built for his own observatory at Canonbury. His real ability, however, was revealed only when he turned his talents to the application of photography to astronomy. He was able to make stereoscopic plates of the moon's surface, which brought to light details never before noted. He invented a photoheliographic telescope that permitted the sun's surface to be mapped photographically. Applying the stereoscopic methods he had used on the moon, he showed in 1861 that sunspots are depressions in the sun's atmosphere, thus verifying a suggestion made in the eighteenth century by Alexander Wilson of Glasgow.

In later life (1868–1883) De la Rue conducted a series of experiments on electric discharge through gases. They merely multiplied data without leading to any significant theoretical advance.

De la Rue was a fellow of the Royal Society (1850), the Chemical Society, and the Royal Astronomical Society, serving as president of the last-named society from 1864 to 1866. He was also a member and sometime president of the London Institution and member of the Royal Institution and the Royal Microscopical Society.

BIBLIOGRAPHY

De la Rue's published papers are listed in the Royal Society's *Catalogue of Scientific Papers.* The biography that appears in the *Dictionary of National Biography* is generally reliable, although it tends to exaggerate the importance of his contributions to science, particularly chemistry. His correspondence with Michael Faraday, published in *The Selected Correspondence of Michael Faraday,* 2 vols. (London, 1971), reveals his methods and abilities, as well as various aspects of his congenial personality.

L. PEARCE WILLIAMS

DELAUNAY, CHARLES-EUGÈNE (*b.* Lusigny, France, 9 April 1816; *d.* at sea, near Cherbourg, France, 5 August 1872), *celestial mechanics.*

Delaunay's father, Jacques-Hubert, was a surveyor who later bought the office of bailiff. His mother, Catherine, was his confidante all his life, especially after the death of his wife in 1849. A bright pupil in secondary school at Troyes, he showed such a gift for mathematics that he was admitted to the École Polytechnique in 1834 and graduated in 1836, first in his class. He received the newly established Laplace Prize, consisting of the complete works of Laplace, which led to his interest in celestial mechanics.

Although Delaunay was by assignment a mining engineer, he served in various engineering schools and at the University of Paris as professor of mechanics, mathematics, or astronomy. His first researches were on calculus of variations ("De la distinction des maxima et des minima dans les questions qui dépendent de la méthode des variations," 1841, doctor's thesis), on perturbations of Uranus (1842), and on the theory of tides (1844). Delaunay's work in lunar theory started in the 1840's. He published the principle of what is known as the Delaunay method in 1846 and generalized it in 1855.

The Delaunay method, further developed by Anders Lindstedt, Poincaré, and Hugo von Zeipel, was a major contribution to analytical mechanics. It consists of a single procedure permitting elimination from the system of canonical equations, one by one, of all the terms of the disturbing function and hence the building up, term by term, of the solution of the problem. Delaunay applied his method to the moon, computing all the terms up to the seventh order and some additional ones of the eighth and ninth orders. This work was published in 1860 and 1867. It is noteworthy that, in studying the incompatibility between the observed and the computed values of the secular acceleration of the moon, Delaunay suggested that it could be caused by a slowing of the rotation of the earth by tidal friction (1865). This hypothesis is now known to be correct.

There was a long-time rivalry between Delaunay and Le Verrier. Delaunay recognized his colleague's scientific achievements but fought his dictatorial rule over astronomical research. He was appointed director of the Paris observatory in March 1870, after Le Verrier, in a dispute with the staff, was dismissed. But in the two years before his death Delaunay had to devote all his efforts to trying to save the observatory during the Franco-Prussian War and the Commune. He was a member of the Académie des Sciences (1855), the Bureau des Longitudes (1862), and the Royal Society (1869).

BIBLIOGRAPHY

Delaunay's main work is "Théorie du mouvement de la lune," in *Mémoires de l'Académie des sciences,* **28** (1860), entire vol., 883 pages and **29** (1867), entire vol., 931 pages. Most of his findings and scientific discussions were printed in the *Comptes rendus hebdomadaires des séances de l'Académie des sciences* between 1841 and 1872. Among them are "Calcul des inégalités d'Uranus qui sont de l'ordre du carré de la force perturbatrice," *in Comptes rendus hebdomadaires des séances de l'Académie des sciences,* **14** (1842), 371, 406; "Mémoire sur la théorie des marées," *ibid.,* **17** (1843), 344; and "Sur l'existence d'une cause nouvelle ayant une action sensible sur la valeur de l'équation séculaire de la Lune," *ibid.,* **61** (1865), 1023.

The Delaunay method is presented in "Mémoire sur une nouvelle méthode pour la détermination du mouvement de la Lune," *ibid.,* **22** (1846), p. 32; and a modification in "Sur une méthode d'intégration applicable au calcul des perturbations des planètes et de leurs satellites," *ibid.,* **40** (1855), 335.

Further information on Delaunay's life is in Arsène Thévenot, "Biographie de Charles-Eugène Delaunay," in *Mémoires de la Société académique de l'Aube,* **42** (1878), 1–129.

J. KOVALEVSKY

DELÉPINE, STÉPHANE-MARCEL (*b.* St.-Martin-le-Gaillard [Seine Maritime], France, 19 September 1871; *d.* Paris, France, 21 October 1965), *chemistry.*

With his mother's encouragement, Delépine followed in the footsteps of his older brother by studying pharmacy. He received his professional training in Paris, where he studied pharmacy at the École Supérieure de Pharmacie and science at the Sorbonne. From 1892 to 1897 he served as intern in pharmacy

and from 1902 to 1927 as pharmacist of the Hospitaux de la Ville in Paris. In 1898 Delépine became *docteur ès sciences physiques.* From 1895 to 1902, he was *preparateur* to the famous chemist and statesman Marcellin Berthelot at the Collège de France, where he worked on thermochemical determinations and remained until Berthelot's death in 1907.

In 1904 Delépine was appointed *agrégé* at the École de Pharmacie, where he was promoted in 1913 to the rank of professor. He remained there until 1930, when he succeeded Charles Moureu as professor at the Collège de France, thus occupying the chair once held by his mentor Berthelot. Although he inspired a number of students, including Raymond Charonnat and Alain Horeau, his successor, Delépine preferred to do most of his own laboratory work. His retirement in 1941 did not decrease his prolific scientific productivity; during his retirement he added some sixty publications to his 200 articles. He continued to work in his laboratory with the aid of an assistant until six weeks before his death at the age of ninety-four. A scientist of international reputation, Delépine was a member of many societies and was the recipient of numerous honors.

Delépine's work encompassed almost all fields of chemistry. Like Alfred Werner, of whose work he was an ardent proponent, he began his long and fruitful career as an organic chemist. The thesis for his degree in pharmacy dealt with the separation of methylamines by formaldehyde, and his doctoral dissertation involved a primarily thermodynamic study of the amines and amides derived from aldehydes. His name is immortalized in the so-called Delépine reaction for the preparation of primary amines. He determined the structure of aldehyde ammonia and demonstrated the reversibility of the formation of acetals. Delépine's voluminous work on organic sulfur compounds included studies of dithiourethanes, the discovery of the monomeric sulfides of ethylene (whose existence had been considered impossible), and the recommendation of dithiocarbamates as analytical reagents. He discovered that certain compounds containing doubly bound sulfur have the property of spontaneous oxidation accompanied by phosphorescence (oxyluminescence). He also made extensive studies of catalytic hydrogenation in the presence of Raney nickel. His organic work also dealt with terpenes, heterocyclic compounds, pyridine compounds, alkaloids, and aminonitriles.

In the field of inorganic chemistry, Delépine immediately adopted Werner's then controversial views, and his numerous studies of coordination compounds, particularly those of the noble metals, confirmed their geometric and optical isomerism and verified Werner's coordination theory. His classical work on iridium, especially the chloro salts, pyridine derivatives, and oxalates, placed the stereochemistry of this element on a firm basis, just as Werner's work had done for the compounds of cobalt. Delépine also perfected a method for preparing pure tungsten for use in electric light filaments. He was also a master of stereochemistry and crystallography, and he devised the method of active racemates for resolution of coordination compounds and determination of their configurations. In addition, he published several articles on the history of chemistry.

BIBLIOGRAPHY

I. ORIGINAL WORKS. The majority of Delépine's work was published in the *Bulletin de la Société chimique de France,* the *Annales de chimie,* and *Comptes rendus hebdomadaires des séances de l'Académie des sciences.* His masterly summary of the chemistry of iridium is found in P. Pascal, ed., *Nouveau traité de chimie minérale,* xix (Paris, 1958), 465–575.

II. SECONDARY LITERATURE. R. Oesper, in *Journal of Chemical Education,* **27** (1950), 567–568 gives a very brief description of Delépine's work. A 38-page booklet, *Hommage rendu au Professeur Marcel Delépine par ses amis, ses collègues, ses élèves à l'occasion de sa promotion au grade de Commandeur de la Légion d'Honneur, 23 Novembre 1950* (Paris, 1950), consists of eulogies describing his life and work. Two brief obituaries which discuss his life and work are C. Dufraisse, in *Comptes rendus hebdomadaires des séances de l'Académie des sciences,* **261** (1965), 4931–4935; and A. Horeau, in *Annales de chimie,* **1** (1966), 5–6. A detailed description, evaluation, and bibliography of Delépine's work in the field of inorganic chemistry is found in A. Chrétien, *Revue de chimie minérale,* **3** (1966), 187–200.

GEORGE B. KAUFFMAN

DELILE (or **RAFFENEAU-DELILE**), **ALIRE** (*b.* Versailles, France, 23 January 1778; *d.* Montpellier, France, 5 July 1850), *botany.*

The son of Jean-Baptiste Élie Raffeneau-Delile, *porte-malle ordinaire du Roi,* and Marie Catherine Bar, Delile had barely begun his secondary studies at the Collège de Lisieux in Paris when they were interrupted by the Revolution. He completed them in Versailles after having been forced to return there, then became a nonresident medical student in the charitable institutions of the city. At the same time he was introduced to botany at the Trianon gardens.

On 29 Vendémiaire, *an* IV (21 October 1795) Delile was admitted to the École de Santé in Paris as a result of a competitive examination. At the school he met Desfontaines, who was the deciding factor in his joining the Egyptian expeditionary force organized by Bonaparte. He left France on 19 May 1798 as a botanist attached to the expedition.

Delile was in Egypt until the destruction of the French fleet at Aboukir and then returned to France, with an important herbarium, in November 1801. He sailed for America in April 1803 as an assistant commissioner for commercial relations, representing France in Wilmington, North Carolina. In 1806 Delile left that post to work with Benjamin Smith Barton, a physician at the Pennsylvania Hospital in Philadelphia. He resumed his medical studies there and continued them under David Hosack in New York. On 5 May 1807 he defended a thesis entitled "On the Pulmonary Consumption." Three months later Delile was recalled to France in order to resume the editing of a flora of Egypt.

This work was completed in 1809, and Delile was left without employment. His candidacy to succeed Pierre Broussonnet as professor of botany at the Faculty of Medicine of Montpellier had been unsuccessful—Candolle received the appointment—and Delile had to return to the practice of medicine. On 6 July 1809 he defended his doctoral thesis before the Faculty of Medicine in Paris and treated patients without renouncing his other projects. After the collapse of the Empire, Candolle decided to leave France, and in July 1819 Delile was appointed to take his place. From then on, he remained in Montpellier.

Among Delile's published works those relating to Egypt are the most famous, but they represent no more than eight titles out of the sixty that Joly counted in 1859. At first glance the period spent in America seems to have been less fruitful. Only three papers, including his M.D. thesis, were produced. The period in Montpellier, which was the longest, was the one in which Delile published the most; but the works have no definite orientation. There are essays on culture and acclimatization, descriptions of oriental species, and biological observations; none is without importance, yet none is particularly memorable.

However, Delile's published works represent only one part of his research. At his death he left a great many drawings, observations, and unpublished documents. Joly cites four manuscripts that he himself possessed, but they seem to have been lost since then. However, there is an important piece of evidence of Delile's activities in America, a copy of Michaux's *Flora boreali-americana,* annotated in preparation for a revision. This, together with eight cartons of watercolor drawings representing 332 species of fungi—

done during the Montpellier period—may be found in the archives of the Institut Botanique, Montpellier.

BIBLIOGRAPHY

I. ORIGINAL WORKS. Only Delile's most important works are listed here; a more complete list is provided by Joly: "Description de deux espèces de Séné . . .," in *Mémoires sur l'Égypte,* III (Paris, an X [1801]); "Note critique sur le *Ximenia Aegyptiaca,*" *ibid.;* "Observations sur les lotus d'Égypte," in *Annales du Muséum d'histoire naturelle,* **1** (1802); *An Inaugural Dissertation on the Pulmonary Consumption* (New York, 1807), his M.D. thesis; "Description d'opérations rares et nouvelles d'anévrismes, faites avec succès en Angleterre et en Amérique," in *Journal de médecine* (1809); *Dissertation sur les effets d'un poison de Java appelé Upas Tieuté* (Paris, 1809), his M.D. thesis; "Description et dessin d'une tarière spirale, instrument vulgaire aux États-Unis pour abréger les travaux de charpente," in *Mémoires de la Société d'encouragement de Paris* (1812); "Description du Palmier Doum de la Haute-Égypte," in *Descriptions de l'Égypte,* XIX (Paris, 1824); "Florae Aegyptiacae illustratio," *ibid.;* "Flore d'Égypte, explication des plantes gravées," *ibid.;* "Histoire des plantes cultivées en Égypte," *ibid.;* "Mémoire sur les plantes qui croissent spontanément en Égypte," *ibid.; Centurie de plantes d'Afrique du voyage à Méroé, recueillies par M. Cailliaud et décrites par M. Delile* (Paris, 1826); *Fragments d'une flore de l'Arabie Pétrée* (Paris, 1833); "Nouveaux fragments d'une flore de l'Arabie Pétrée," presented to the Academy of Sciences in April 1834; "Première récolte des fruits du ginkgo du Japon en France," in *Bulletin de la Société d'agriculture de l'Hérault* (1835); "Pomone orientale: Designation d'arbres à fruits à importer de Syrie en France," *ibid.* (1840); and "Correspondance d'Orient: De l'horticulture en Égypte," *ibid.* (1841).

II. SECONDARY LITERATURE. On Delile or his work, see N. Joly, "Éloge historique d'Alyre Raffeneau-Delile," in *Mémoires de l'Académie impériale des sciences, inscriptions et belles-lettres de Toulouse,* 5th ser., **3** (1859); Jean Motte, "Delile l'Égyptien, un botaniste à la suite de Bonaparte," in *Science et nature,* no. 18 (1956); and "Matériaux inédits, préparés par Delile pour une flore de l'Amérique du Nord," in *Les botanistes français en Amérique du Nord avant 1850,* Colloques Internationaux du C.N.R.S. no. 63 (Paris, 1957).

JEAN MOTTE

DELISLE, GUILLAUME (*b.* Paris, France, 28 February 1675; *d.* Paris, 25 January 1726), *geography.*

Delisle was the son of Claude Delisle, historian and geographer, and Nicole-Charlotte Millet de la Croyère. Interested in geography and mapmaking from his early childhood, Delisle was taught both by his father and by Gian Domenico Cassini, the director of the Paris observatory. He published his first important work, a set of maps of the continents, a mappemonde,

and a globe, in 1700; these immediately established his fame. He was elected to the French Academy of Sciences in 1702 and ran his own mapmaking establishment in Paris until his death. In 1718 Delisle was given the title *premier géographe du roi,* a distinction no doubt connected with the fact that he tutored the young king, Louis XV, in geography.

Delisle designed and published some ninety maps during his lifetime. These included world maps, maps of continents, and maps of single countries or, in the case of France, provinces. The simple elegance of his work alone would distinguish it from the florid, baroque style affected by his contemporaries and predecessors; but it is the content of his maps that is of importance. Delisle studied under Cassini; and he lived in the era of the great surveys, when a number of places on all continents had their locations accurately determined for the first time, using Cassini's method of observation of the moons of Jupiter. Delisle applied the astronomers' findings to his maps; he omitted guesswork, fantasy, and unnecessary or ornamental detail; he admitted lack of knowledge of unexplored territories; and he insisted on critical use of source materials and dependence on scientifically accurate measurements. He thus acquainted the general public with the results of the work of scientists and became the first modern scientific cartographer.

BIBLIOGRAPHY

Delisle's work can be found in a great many libraries throughout the world, in the form of printed atlases and single maps. Further information can be found in Christian Sandler, *Die Reformation der Kartographie um 1700* (Munich–Berlin, 1905), pp. 14–23.)

GEORGE KISH

DELISLE, JOSEPH-NICOLAS (*b.* Paris, France, 4 April 1688; *d.* Paris, 11 September 1768), *astronomy, geography.*

The ninth child of the historian-geographer Claude Delisle and Nicole-Charlotte Millet de la Croyère, he became known to his contemporaries as Delisle *le cadet* or *le jeune* to distinguish him from his two older brothers. After receiving his early education from his father, he began to develop a taste for mathematics near the end of his formal education in rhetoric at the Collège Mazarin. A solar eclipse in 1706 stimulated this new study and led to instruction in the elements of astronomical calculation under Jacques Lieutaud. He was soon frequenting the Royal Observatory, where he was permitted to copy Jacques Cassini's unfinished lunar and solar tables. When his first attempt to launch his own observational career in the cupola of the Luxembourg Palace was hampered by a lack of instruments, he turned temporarily to the production of various astronomical tables desired by Cassini.

Having equipped his observatory, Delisle began a regular observational program with the lunar eclipse of 23 January 1712. Forced to abandon his observatory in September 1715—when the Duc d'Orleans became regent and installed his eldest daughter, the Duchesse de Berry, in the Luxembourg Palace—he resumed his observations at the end of 1716 in Liouville's former apartment at the Hôtel de Taranne. After almost four years there he moved his instruments to the Royal Observatory and also had some work done in the Luxembourg Palace dome, which he regained in 1722, after the duchess' death in 1719.

This early fulfillment of promise carried Delisle into the Academy of Sciences as a student astronomer attached to Maraldi in 1714, and he quickly began what was to be a long series of contributions—primarily reports of observations of eclipses and occultations—to its *Mémoires*. Since it was also necessary for him to earn a livelihood, he gave mathematics lessons and won a small pension under the regency by drawing up astrological forecasts. An appointment to the chair of mathematics at the Collège Royal in 1718 freed him from such endeavors and also brought him students who aided him in the making and reduction of observations. His best-known students during this period were Godin, Grandjean de Fouchy, and his younger brother, Delisle de la Croyère.

Delisle's growing reputation brought him, in 1721, an offer from Peter the Great to found an observatory and an associated school of astronomy in Russia, an invitation which was transformed into mutually acceptable contractual arrangements in 1725. Planned for four years, Delisle's stay in Russia lasted twenty-two years. There he created an observatory which came to enjoy a good reputation while training many astronomers—with elementary treatises in the preparation of which Delisle participated. Some of these students, as well as his younger brother and the instrument maker who had accompanied him, subsequently engaged in geodetic and cartographic ventures throughout the country, the results of which they communicated to him for a projected, but unrealized, large-scale and accurate map of Russia. To provide corresponding observations for longitude determinations, Delisle published his St. Petersburg observations of eclipses of Jupiter's satellites in each of the first six volumes of the *Commentarii* of Russia's Imperial Academy of Sciences.

Various physical and meteorological data came to

him as well, some of the latter inspired by a "universal thermometer" invented and widely distributed by Delisle. He described this device in a work published in 1738, which also contained his and his brother's numerous observations of aurora borealis in Russia and a record of his own early Paris observations and experiments on light. Furthermore, Delisle returned to an interest in transits of Mercury first manifested in 1723, when he had considered, but failed to demonstrate, that the technique suggested in Halley's famous 1716 paper on the use of transits of Venus to determine the parallax of the sun could be equally utilized in the more frequent transits of Mercury. He now treated this possibility for the 1743 transit of Mercury in a letter to Cassini, which the latter placed in the *Mémoires* of the Paris Academy of Sciences.

That institution took cognizance of the length of Delisle's absence by naming him to veteran status in 1741. This did not change with his return to Paris in 1747, although he resumed attendance at the Academy's meetings. He also returned to his Luxembourg Palace observatory to witness a solar eclipse of July 1748, about which he had prepared an *avertissement* to alert astronomers. In addition he regained his chair at the Collège Royal; most notable among his students in this latter period was Lalande.

One of Delisle's long-standing activities had been the amassing of vast amounts of geographical and astronomical material through an extraordinarily extensive correspondence, through inheritance, and through laborious copying. Because of its great value the French government purchased this collection by giving Delisle the title of *astronome de la marine* and a life annuity of 3,000 livres. Moreover, he obtained a new observatory at the Hôtel de Cluny. It was there, in 1759, that his pupil and assistant, Charles Messier, observed the return of Halley's comet. The place of its reappearance had been the subject of a paper by Delisle in 1757.

In other late works Delisle made some use of his meteorological and cartographic materials from Russia and devoted some attention to longitude determinations. The latter had a significance for transit studies because his perfection of Halley's technique by a simplification of the necessary observations demanded precise longitude information. Having also corrected Halley's planetary tables, Delisle produced an *avertissement* on how to observe the 1753 transit of Mercury and a mappemonde showing the favorable stations. He then determined that the Mercury phenomena were inadequate for parallax determination and concentrated his efforts on the forthcoming transit of Venus in 1761, serving as stimulator and coordinator of its worldwide observation by virtue of another mappemonde and an accompanying memoir distributed through correspondence.

Delisle retired increasingly after this activity. Lalande began to teach in his stead at the Collège Royal in 1761. In 1763 he withdrew to the abbey of Ste.-Geneviève to devote himself to charitable and religious works, although he did publish several maps by his eldest brother, Guillaume. Both the Academy of Sciences and the Collège Royal conferred honors upon him prior to his death from an attack of apoplexy in 1768. His wife, whom he had married before his trip to Russia, died shortly after their return; they had no children.

BIBLIOGRAPHY

I. ORIGINAL WORKS. Delisle's immense collection of observations, maps, and correspondence is scattered among several Paris repositories. He provided a partial description of the collection and some autobiographical materials in a MS preserved in the Bibliothèque Nationale: "Histoire abrégée de ma vie et des mes occupations dans l'astronomie, la géographie et la physique, pour servir d'introduction au catalogue de mes manuscrits et mémoires d'astronomie et de géographie conservés au Dépôt des plans et cartes de la Marine . . .," MS fr. 9678, fols. 24–31. In 1795 the purely astronomical part of the collection was given to the Bureau des Longitudes and became the basis of the archives of the Paris Observatory. That part includes an *abrégé* of his unfinished *Traité complet d'astronomie exposée historiquement et demontrée par les observations,* Archives de l'Observatoire de Paris, A 7 10, and, besides the materials providing the basis for that work, his own early observational journals, which contain a brief autobiographical note on his astronomical beginnings, C 2 14. Only a small part of his correspondence has been printed: E. Doublet, ed., *Correspondance échangée de 1720 à 1739, entre l'astronome J.-N. Delisle et M. de Navarre* (Bordeaux, 1910); and H. Omont, ed., *Lettres de J.-N. Delisle au comte de Maurepas et à l'abbé Bignon sur ses travaux géographiques en Russie (1726–1730)* (Paris, 1919). His contributions to the *Mémoires* of the Paris Academy of Sciences prior to his departure for Russia were as follows: "Sur l'observation des solstices" (1714), pp. 239–246; "Résultat de l'observation de l'éclipse du soleil du 3 mai 1715 au matin, faite au Luxembourg en présence de Madame la Princesse, de M. le Comte de Clermont et de plusieurs autres seigneurs" (1715), pp. 85–86; "Observation de l'éclipse de Vénus par la lune, faite en plein jour au Luxembourg le 28 juin 1715" (1715), pp. 135–137; "Sur l'atmosphère de la lune" (1715), pp. 147–148; "Observation de l'éclipse de Jupiter et de ses satellites par la lune, faite au Luxembourg le 25 juillet 1715 au matin" (1715), pp. 159–160; "Reflexions sur l'expérience que j'ai rapportée à l'Académie d'un anneau lumineux semblable à celui que l'on aperçoit autour de la lune dans les éclipses totales du soleil" (1715), pp. 166–169; "Observation de l'éclipse de lune du 20 septembre 1717 au soir, faite à Montmartre" (1717), pp. 299–301; "Occultation d'Aldebaran par la lune, observée le 9 février 1718 au soir, à l'Hôtel de Taranne" (1718), p. 17; "Sur les projections des éclipses sujettes aux parallaxes; où l'on explique la manière dont les astronomes les considèrent, l'usage qu'ils en font, et où l'on donne l'idée d'une nouvelle projection, qui réduit la détermination géométriques de ces éclipses à une expression plus simple que celle qui se tire des projections ordinaires" (1718), pp. 56–67; "Construction facile et exacte du gnomon pour règler une pendule au soleil par le moyen de son passage au méridien" (1719), pp. 54–58; "Observation de l'éclipse d'Aldebaran par la lune, faite à l'Hôtel de Taranne à Paris le 22 avril 1719, au soir" (1719), p. 318; "Observation de l'éclipse d'Aldebaran par la lune, faite à l'Hôtel de Taranne à Paris, le 30 octobre 1719 au soir" (1719), p. 319; "Détail de l'expérience de la réfraction de l'air dans le vuide" (1719), pp. 330–335; "Sur le dernier passage attendu de Mercure dans le soleil et sur celui de mois de novembre de la présente année 1723" (1723), pp. 105–110; "Observation du passage de Mercure sur le soleil, faite à Paris dans l'Observatoire Royal, le 9 novembre 1723, au soir" (1723), pp. 306–343; "Observations de l'éclipse totale du soleil du 22 mai 1724 au soir, faites à Paris, dans l'Observatoire Royal et au Luxembourg, par MM. Delisle le Cadet et Delisle de la Croyère" (1724), pp. 316–319.

Although some of his observations were reported by himself and others, his only significant contribution to the *Mémoires* during his absence from Paris was the "Extrait d'une lettre de M. Delisle, écrite de Petersbourg le 24 août 1743, et adressée à M. Cassini, servant de supplément au Mémoire de M. Delisle, inséré dans le volume de 1723, p. 105, pour trouver la parallaxe du soleil par le passage de Mercure dans le disque de cet astre" (1743), pp. 419–428.

His contributions to the *Commentarii Academiae imperialis scientiarum petropolitanae* were as follows: "Eclipses satellitum Jovis observatae Petropoli," **1**, 467–474, in collaboration with his brother; "Continuata relatio eclipsium satellitum Jovialium Petropoli," **2**, 491–494; "Observationes altitudinis poli in Observatorio imperiali, quod Petropoli est, habitae," **2**, 495–516; "Tertia series observationum satellitum Jovis in Observatorio imperiali Petropoli factarum," **3**, 425–462; "Continuata relatio eclipsium satellitum Jovis observatarum," **4**, 317–321; "Eclipsium Jovis satellitum in Observatorio petropolitano observatarum continuatio," **5**, 451–457; "Eclipses satellitum Jovis observatae in Imperiali specula astronomica, quae Petropoli est, per integrum annum 1738," **6**, 395–400; "Observationes astronomicae in specula Academiae imperialis scientiarum ab anno 1739–1745, a Josepho Nicolao Delilio cum sociis institutae," **6**, 349–362.

Other publications from this period were a three-part *Abrégé des mathématiques pour l'usage de Sa Majesté impériale de toutes les Russies* (St. Petersburg, 1728), written in collaboration with Jacques Hermann, to which he contributed the second part dealing with astronomy and geography, a *Discours sur cette question: Si l'on peut démontrer, par les seuls faits astronomiques, quel est le vrai système du monde? et si la terre tourne ou non* (St. Petersburg, 1728) which he had read to the Academy, a *Projet de la mesure de la terre en Russie* (St. Petersburg, 1737), and his *Mémoires pour servir à l'histoire et au progrès de l'astronomie, de la géographie et de la physique, recueillis de plusieurs dissertations lues dans les assemblées de l'Académie royale des sciences de Paris et de celle de Saint-Petersbourg, qui n'ont point encore été imprimées, comme aussi de plusieurs pièces nouvelles, observations et réflexions rassemblées pendant plus de 25 années* (St. Petersburg, 1738).

After his return from Russia he placed the following items in the Paris Academy's *Mémoires:* "Observation de l'éclipse du soleil du 25 juillet 1748, faite à Paris au Palais du Luxembourg" (1748), pp. 249–254; "Observations du thermomètre, faites pendant les plus grands froids de la Sibérie" (1749), pp. 1–14; "Observation de l'éclipse de lune du 23 décembre 1749, faite à Paris dans l'Hôtel de Cluny" (1749), pp. 320–321; "Observation de l'éclipse totale de lune du 13 décembre 1750, au matin, faite à Paris dans l'Hôtel de Cluny" (1750), pp. 343–344; "Mémoire sur la longitude de Louisbourg, dans l'Isle Royale" (1751), pp. 36–39; "Observation pour la conjonction de Jupiter avec la lune, du 29 décembre 1751 au soir, faite à Paris dans l'Hôtel de Cluny" (1751), pp. 90–92; "Observation de l'éclipse de lune du 2 décembre 1751 au soir, faite à Paris dans l'Hôtel de Cluny" (1751), pp. 273–274; "Réponse de M. Delisle [à une lettre de M. Bradley]" (1752), pp. 434–439; "Mémoire sur le diamètre apparent de Mercure, et sur le temps qu'il emploie à entrer et à sortir du disque du soleil dans les conjonctions inférieures écliptiques" (1753), pp. 243–249; "Observation de l'occultation de l'étoile ρ du Verseau par la lune, et de la conjonction de l'étoile θ avec la même planète, le 21 novembre 1754 au soir, faites à Paris à l'Hôtel de Cluny" (1754), pp. 382–383; "Détermination de la longitude de l'Isle de Madère, par les éclipses des satellites de Jupiter observées par M. Bory, Lieutenant des Vaisseaux du Roi, comparées avec celles de M. l'abbé de la Caille à l'Isle de France" (1754), pp. 565–571; "Observations des diamètres apparens du soleil, faites à Paris les années 1718 et 1719, avec des lunettes de différentes longueurs; et réflexions sur l'effet de ces lunettes" (1755), pp. 145–171; "Nouvelle théorie des éclipses sujettes aux parallaxes, appliquée à la grande éclipse du soleil qu'on observa le 25 juillet 1748" (1757), pp. 490–515; "Observations du passage de Mercure sur le disque du soleil, le 6 novembre 1756; avec des réflexions qui peuvent servir à perfectionner les calculs de ces passages et les élémens de la théorie de Mercure déduits des observations" (1758), pp. 134–154; "Mémoire sur la comète de 1758" (1759), pp. 154–188; "Mémoire sur la comète de 1759 . . ." (1760), pp. 380–465.

Separately published items of astronomical significance during this later period were his *Avertissement aux astronomes sur l'éclipse de soleil du 25 juillet 1748* (Paris, 1748), the *Lettre de M. Delisle sur les tables astronomiques de M. Halley* (Paris, 1749), the *Avertissement aux astronomes sur le passage de Mercure au devant du soleil, qui doit arriver le 6 mai 1753, avec une mappemonde, où l'on voit les nouvelles découvertes faites au nord de la mer du Sud* (Paris, 1753), and a *Recherche du lieu du ciel où la comète, prédite par M. Halley, doit commencer à paraître* (Paris, 1757).

In the purely geographical realm, he published separately a memoir read to a public assembly of the Academy in 1750 and reported in the *Histoire de l'Académie . . .* of that year (1750), pp. 142–152: *Explication de la carte des nouvelles découvertes au nord de la mer du Sud* (Paris, 1752). His later map publications were noted in *Histoire:* (1763), pp. 112–117; (1764), pp. 158–160; (1766), pp. 114–122.

II. SECONDARY LITERATURE. The laudatory "official" *éloge* for the Academy of Sciences was written by Delisle's student Grandjean de Fouchy and appeared in *Histoire de l'Académie . . .* (1768), 167–183. Equally generous in its praise and somewhat more detailed was Lalande's "Éloge de M. de l'Isle," in *Le nécrologe des hommes célèbres de France, par une société de gens de lettres,* V (Paris, 1770), 1–86. The next treatment of him was quite critical: J. B. J. Delambre, *Histoire de l'astronomie au dix-huitième siècle* (Paris, 1826), pp. 318–327. The rather brief account in J. F. Michaud, ed., *Biographie universelle,* X, 334–335, is inadequate, as is the more recent treatment in Niels Nielsen, *Géomètres français du dix-huitième siècle* (Paris, 1935), pp. 163–166. The first significant attention to his work in Russia was that paid in Petr Pekarski's *Histoire de l'Académie impériale des sciences de Petersbourg* (Paris, 1870), pp. 124–155. The negotiations preceding that trip were treated by J. Marchand in "Le départ en mission de l'astronome J.-N. Delisle pour la Russie (1721–1726)," in *Revue d'histoire diplomatique,* **43** (1929), 1–26; his work there and the maps that he brought back are dealt with in detail in Albert Isnard's "Joseph-Nicolas Delisle, sa biographie et sa collection de cartes géographiques à la Bibliothèque nationale," in *Bulletin de la Section de géographie du Comité des travaux historiques et scientifiques,* **30** (1915), 34–164. On the Delisle materials that went to the Paris observatory, see Guillaume Bigourdan, *Inventaire général et sommaire des manuscrits de la bibliothèque de l'Observatoire de Paris* (Paris, n.d.), taken from *Annales de l'Observatoire de Paris. Mémoires,* **21** (1897), F1–F60. On his Paris observations and observatories, see Bigourdan's *Histoire de l'astronomie d'observation et des observatoires en France,* pt. 2 (Paris, 1930), 20–33, 74–92. On the reputation of the observatory of St. Petersburg under his direction, see Bigourdan's "Lettres de Léonard Euler, en partie inédites," in *Bulletin astronomique,* **34** (1917), 258–319, **35** (1918), 65–96. For brief indications on his teaching at the Collège Royal, see Louis-Amélie Sédillot, *Les professeurs de mathématiques et de physique générale au Collège de France* (Rome, 1869), pp. 128–130. Finally, for an excellent analysis of his contribution to the study of transits and the parallax question, see Harry Woolf, *The Transits of Venus; A Study of Eighteenth-Century Science* (Princeton, 1959), esp. ch. 2.

SEYMOUR L. CHAPIN

DELLA PORTA, GIAMBATTISTA. See **Porta, Giambattista della.**

DELLA TORRE, GIOVANNI MARIA (*b.* Rome, Italy, 12 June 1713; *d.* Naples, Italy, 9 March 1782), *natural sciences.*

Della Torre was born of a noble Genoese family but lived in Naples from his earliest years. He received an ecclesiastical education there and in 1738 was appointed to teach physical sciences in the archiepiscopal lyceum. In 1743 Charles III of Spain, king of the Two Sicilies, named him director of the royal library and royal printing press.

Della Torre was a man of wide culture and of wide scientific curiosity. His studies led him into the history of philosophy, optics, and microscopy (he made several new histological identifications with an excellent compound microscope that he himself had built); in addition, he observed and recorded eruptions of Vesuvius. He was much influenced by the *De rerum natura* of Lucretius.

Della Torre's most important work, however, was as an encyclopedist. His two-volume work, *Scienza della natura* (Naples, 1748–1749; reprinted Venice, 1750—an abridgment, *Institutiones physicae,* was published in Naples in 1753, and a considerably enlarged Neapolitan edition appeared in 1767–1770 as *Elementa physicae*), anticipated the more famous *Encyclopédie,* the publication of which began in 1751.

The *Scienza della natura* is divided into sections, each of which is subdivided into several chapters. The first volume, in five sections, is dedicated to general physics, comprising statics and hydrostatics, dynamics and hydrodynamics (all developed according to the mechanical theories of Galileo and Newton), and includes an entire chapter on thermometry that draws upon the works of Boyle, Perrault, and Fahrenheit. The second volume is also in five sections and deals with the earth (including mineralogy, volcanoes, and earthquakes), the air (including light, sound, and electricity), botany, zoology, and human anatomy. Each volume contains a historical preface and a detailed index. Each is illustrated (there are thirty-one plates in volume I, thirty in volume II); illustrations of particular interest are those of units of measurement, the pendulum, electrostatical machines, the pointing of mortar, the compressed-air gun, the refraction of light rays, and chyliferous vessels in man.

In short, the *Scienza della natura* presents a complete and ordered picture of the state of scientific knowledge in its time. Although Della Torre's work is almost forgotten today, he was strongly influential in establishing the scientific climate of eighteenth-century Italy.

BIBLIOGRAPHY

I. ORIGINAL WORKS. Besides the editions of *Scienza della natura* detailed above, Della Torre published *Storia e fenomeni del Vesuvio col catalogo degli scrittori vesuviani* (Naples, 1755); *Supplemento alla storia del Vesuvio fino all'anno 1759* (Naples, 1759); and *L'incendio del Vesuvio accaduto il 19 Ottobre 1767* (Naples, 1767).

II. SECONDARY LITERATURE. Further material on Della Torre's life and work may be found in *Biographia degli uomini illustri del Regno di Napoli* (Naples, 1834); *Biographie universelle*, X (Brussels, 1847), 242; G. Bruno, "Giovanni Maria Della Torre istologo napoletano," in *Gazzetta sanitaria,* **20** (1949), 156–159; E. D'Afflitto, *Memorie degli scrittori del Regno di Napoli* (Naples, 1782–1788); S. De Renzi, *Storia della medicina in Italia,* V (Naples, 1848), *passim;* G. De Ruggero, *Sommario di storia della filosofia* (Bari, 1930); and M. Schipa, *Storia del Regno di Napoli al tempo di Carlo di Borbone* (Naples, 1904).

PIETRO FRANCESCHINI

DELLA TORRE, MARCANTONIO. See **Torre, Marcantonio Della.**

DELPORTE, EUGÈNE JOSEPH (*b.* Genappe, Belgium, 10 January 1882; *d.* Uccle, Belgium, 19 October 1955), *astronomy.*

Delporte graduated from Brussels University and obtained the doctorate in physics and mathematics with high honors in 1903, at the age of twenty-one. He immediately joined the Royal Observatory of Belgium in Uccle as a volunteer assistant. In 1904 he became assistant, in 1909 associate astronomer, and in 1923 astronomer. He was appointed to the directorship of the observatory in 1936 and retired from official duty in 1947.

From 1903 to 1919 Delporte was attached to the department of meridian astronomy. He made thousands of transit observations of reference stars, among them 3,533 stars for the zones +21° and +22° of the *Carte du ciel,* and conducted careful investigations of the errors of the divisions of the meridian circle. He determined the difference of longitude between the observatories of Paris and Uccle in 1910 and in 1920, and he supervised the installation of the time service at the observatory.

In 1919 Delporte transferred to the department of equatorials and dedicated himself to systematic observations of comets and asteroids. These observations were first performed visually with the thirty-eight-centimeter Cooke refractor; but about 1925, when first the thirty-centimeter-aperture Zeiss astrograph and then the double Zeiss astrograph with forty-centimeter-aperture objectives were installed, a definite investigation of these bodies was organized. The first discovery was the planet Belgica. It was followed by many more discoveries, including Amor and Adonis, which approach nearest to the earth. Delporte's name is also linked with the independent discovery of the comet Dutoit-Neujmin-Delporte. New techniques for accurate determination of position were investigated; and the precise positions were sent regularly to the Astronomisches Rechen-Institut at Heidelberg, where they were used in the determinations of orbits.

In 1930 Delporte edited two volumes for the International Astronomical Union entitled *Scientific Delimitation of Constellations,* with text, maps, and celestial atlas. These volumes fixed the limits of constellations for the entire sky.

Delporte was actively interested in expanding the work of the observatory. The institution was provided with a reflecting telescope one meter in aperture (this was recently enlarged to 1.20 meters and provided with a Schmidt combination), the double astrograph with a forty-centimeter aperture (already mentioned), and an Askania meridian circle with a nineteen-centimeter aperture. He was also responsible for providing the Cooke visual refractor, which had an aperture of thirty-eight centimeters, with a Zeiss objective forty-five centimeters in diameter.

Delporte was an enthusiastic observer, and he inspired many younger astronomers who are continuing his work. After his official retirement he continued to examine plates of asteroids at the observatory, and it was while pursuing this task that he died suddenly.

Delporte received prizes of the Royal Academy of Sciences of Belgium and was a member of the National Committee on Astronomy from its founding in 1919, its vice-chairman in 1930, and its chairman from 1949 until his death. In addition, he was president of the Commission on the Observation of Planets, Comets and Satellites and Ephemerides of the Internation Astronomical Union, corresponding member of the Bureau des Longitudes in Paris, corresponding member of the Academy of Sciences in Paris, and an associate member of the Royal Astronomical Society. He was secretary-editor of the journal *Ciel et terre* of the Belgian Astronomical Society.

BIBLIOGRAPHY

The following major articles appeared in *Annales de l'observatoire de Belgique:* "Observations méridiennes faites au cercle méridien de Repsold," 2nd ser., **10–12** (1907–1910); "Différence de longitude entre Paris et Uccle," *ibid.,* **14** (1913); "Catalogue de 3533 étoiles de repère de la zone +21°. +22°," 2nd ser., **13** (1914); with H. Philippot, "Étude de la division du cercle méridien de Repsold," *ibid.,* **14** (1918); "Forme des tourillons du cercle méridien de Repsold," 3rd ser., **1** (1921); with Philippot, "Positions moyennes pour 1914 d'étoiles de comparaison de la comète 1913 f (Delavan)," *ibid.,* **1** (1922). See also "Observations de la lune et de planètes en 1906 et 1907, et comparaison avec la *Connaissance des temps* et le *Nautical Almanach,*" in *Astronomische Nachrichten,* **178** (1908); "Observations du soleil, de la lune et de planètes en 1908, et comparaison avec la *Connaissance des temps* et le *Nautical Almanach,*" *ibid.,* **181** (1909); "Observations photographiques de petites planètes avec l'astrographe Zeiss de l'Observatoire d'Uccle," in *Journal des observateurs,* **7** (1924); "Petites planetes découvertes à l'Observatoire royale de Belgique," in *Bulletin de la classe des sciences de l'Académie royale de Belgique* (1926).

H. L. VANDERLINDEN

DELUC, JEAN ANDRÉ (*b.* Geneva, Switzerland, 8 February 1727; *d.* Windsor, England, 7 November 1817), *geology, meteorology, physics, natural philosophy, theology.*

Deluc was descended from a family who had emigrated from Lucca, Tuscany, and had settled in Geneva, probably in the fifteenth century. His father, François, refuted the satirical ideas of Bernard Mandeville and others in several treatises that were known to Rousseau, who wrote a diverting description of how much they had bored him.

Deluc received an excellent education, particularly in mathematics and natural science. He then took up commerce, which he combined with political activities. In 1768 he went to Paris on a successful embassy to the duke of Choiseul and in 1770 was nominated to the Council of Two Hundred. His travels widened Deluc's knowledge of landscape, but most of his early writings on natural science were based on numerous excursions to the Alps and the Jura. As was then fashionable, he gradually amassed, with the help of his brother, Guillaume Antoine, a collection of minerals and of flora and fauna. Later his nephew, Jean André Deluc, expanded this collection and took on his uncle's role of voluminous discourser on geological topics, trying, for example, to dissuade Buckland and Murchison from accepting any theory regarding glacial action.

Deluc's commercial affairs failed in 1773 and he left Geneva, returning only once, for a few days. However, his decision to migrate to England afforded him greater opportunity for carrying out scientific research and writing, which he did for another forty-four years. In London, soon after his arrival, he was made a fellow of the Royal Society and appointed reader to Queen Charlotte, a post with an income adequate to allow him ample leisure. During this period of his life Deluc undertook several tours on the Continent and lived for six years (1798–1804) in Germany, where he was a nonparticipant honorary professor of philosophy and geology at Göttingen University. He was also a correspondent of the Paris

Academy of Sciences and a member of several other scientific associations.

Deluc's favorite fields were geology, meteorology, and natural philosophy or theology, as one might expect of a Calvinistic Genevan who made many scientific excursions to the Alps. By nature an inveterate discourser, he would write in a moderate tone on anything, including, for example, the history of the solar system before the birth of the sun. His great aim was to reconcile Genesis and geology; and his orthodoxy, versatility, prolixity, productivity, high social standing, and facility in languages earned him an exalted contemporary position. Georges Cuvier ranked him among the first geologists of his age, whereas Zittel (p. 77) affirms that although Deluc was "held in high respect and favour during his lifetime, his papers have no permanent place in [the] literature."

Deluc believed that the six days of the Creation were six epochs that preceded the present state of the globe, which began when cavities in the interior of the earth collapsed and lowered the sea level, thereby exposing the continents. There was thus a distinction between an older creative, or antediluvian, period and a newer, or diluvian, period. Of the former there survived only a few primordial islands, which accounted for the fossils of large animals and the continuity and antiquity of organic life. In the latter period, which started about 2200 B.C., new geological processes were operative but were so ineffectual or incidental that the landscape remained unchanged. To Deluc mountains were the remnants left upstanding when the adjacent areas had collapsed catastrophically, and the large boulders known today as glacial erratics had been blown out when great interior caverns filled with some expansible fluid had collapsed.

In 1790–1791 and later, in many letters, Deluc opposed Hutton's ideas on present erosion, asserting, for example, that soil is not eroded because if it were there would be none left. In his *Elementary Treatise on Geology* (1809) he claimed rather bombastically that he could now demonstrate "the conformity of geological monuments with the sublime account of that series of the operations which took place during the *Six days,* or periods of time, recorded by the inspired penman." This discursive volume contains, *inter alia,* four of his earlier letters refuting the ideas of Hutton and Playfair. In his later geological writings Deluc occasionally proffers an astute minor observation but rarely, if ever, is the originator of a new idea.

Deluc's meteorological researches were of more lasting value but were also hyperbolized by his contemporaries. He is said to have "discovered many facts of considerable importance" relating to atmospheric heat and moisture, but most of his observations had already been developed further by others. For instance, Deluc noticed the disappearance of some heat during the thawing of ice at a time when Joseph Black had already progressed to a hypothesis of latent heat. Deluc, however, probably can claim to be the originator of the theory, later proved more clearly by John Dalton, that the amount of water vapor contained in any space is independent of the density of the air or any other gaseous substance in which it is diffused.

Deluc's early meteorological interest was mainly in measuring heights by barometer, for which he published improved rules (*Philosophical Transactions* [1771], 158) based on many experiments with hygrometers, thermometers, and barometers, and particularly on the fall in the boiling point of water with diminishing atmospheric pressure and increasing altitude. He devised a hygrometer similar to a mercury thermometer but with an ivory bulb that expanded when moistened and thus caused the mercury to descend (*Philosophical Transactions* [1773], 404). Humboldt compared the merits of this with Saussure's hair hygrometer: the latter proved better for measuring altitude on mountains and the former for use at sea level, but Deluc's hygrometer worked so slowly that its readings could seldom be combined with those of other instruments.

Deluc's influence on popular early nineteenth-century British meteorology texts was considerable. J. F. Daniell, in his *Meteorological Essays and Observations,* based his account of atmospheric evaporation and condensation largely on extracts from "the works of Deluc, who was probably one of the most accurate observers of nature that ever existed, and who seldom, indeed, allowed any hypothetical considerations to warp his description of what he observed" (2nd ed. [1827], p. 506). This hyperbole stemmed from Deluc's visual observations on clouds and ground (radiation) fog, which, he stated, can be seen to change shape and evaporate at the same time that they are forming.

The barometric controversy between H. B. de Saussure, professor of philosophy at Geneva, and Deluc is one of lasting scientific interest. In *Essais sur l'hygromètre* (1783, p. 282) Saussure stated that some of Deluc's findings were based on specious reasoning and inadequate experimentation: "Mr. Deluc supposes that pure air is heavier than air mixed with water vapor. . . . This supposition explains well why a lowering of the barometer is a sign of rain. . . ." Saussure, experimenting with closed containers, had found little difference in weight between dry air and humid air, and considered the differences quite inadequate to explain the large variations in barometric pressure that occurred at ground level in Europe.

Modern meteorology has proved that Deluc was right, whereas Saussure was groping toward the influence of air masses and of the passage of cyclonic depressions and anticyclones.

The significance of Deluc's contributions to physics is greatly exaggerated. In 1809 he sent a long article to the Royal Society discussing the mode of action of the galvanic pile and showing that "in Volta's pile, the chemical effects can be separated from the electrical." This, as a biographer in *Philosophical Magazine* (**50**, 393–394) wrote, ". . . led that ingenious philosopher [Deluc] to construct a new meteorological instrument, very desirable for acquiring a knowledge of atmospherical phaenomena, and which he called the Electric column." The ideas expressed differed so much from those prevalent in London that the council of the Royal Society "deemed it inexpedient to admit them into the *Transactions,*" and the article was also published in *Nicholson's Journal* (**26** [1810]). This "electric column" (or electroscope) consisted of numerous disks of zinc foil and of paper silvered on one side only, piled horizontally in order of zinc, silver, and paper within a glass tube and firmly screwed together. When the uppermost silver was connected by a wire with the lowest zinc disk, an electric current passed along the wire. Today, however, it is hard to see the importance to meteorology and physics of this electric column, which was later improved by Giuseppe Zamboni. It is claimed as a "very valuable discovery" by Deluc's admirers but its principles, at least, had already been stated clearly by Volta on the Continent and probably also during his visit to England.

Deluc's other ventures into physics and chemistry showed all too clearly his inability to assess truly the quality of progress at home and abroad. He strenuously opposed the new chemical theory associated with Lavoisier and attempted to show in two memoirs on that theory, prefixed to his *Introduction à la physique terrestre par les fluides expansibles,* that meteorological phenomena strongly militate against it and in general that the hypothesis of the composition of water (the fundamental point in the theory) has maintained itself only by numerous other hypotheses which are in contradiction with known facts.

BIBLIOGRAPHY

I. ORIGINAL WORKS. Deluc wrote numerous long articles for periodicals, the chief being *Philosophical Transactions of the Royal Society; The Philosophical Magazine and Journal; British Critic,* especially 1793–1795, for letters addressed to J. F. Blumenbach; *Monthly Magazine; Monthly Review,* especially 1790 and 1791, for letters to Hutton; and *Nicholson's Journal.* Many of these letters or articles were republished later in the following books: *Recherches sur les modifications de l'atmosphère,* 2 vols. (Geneva, 1772), 4 vols. (Paris, 1784); *Lettres physiques et morales sur les montagnes et sur l'histoire de la terre et de l'homme.* (*Adressées à la reine de la Grande Bretagne*), 5 vols. (The Hague, 1779); *Idées sur la météorologie,* 2 vols. (Paris, 1786); *Lettres sur l'histoire physique de la terre* (Paris, 1798), abridged trans. by Henry de la Fite (London, 1831); *Lettres sur l'education religieuse de l'enfance* (Berlin, 1799); *Bacon tel qu'il est* (Berlin, 1800); *Lettres sur le christianisme adressées à M. le pasteur Teller* (Berlin-Hannover, 1801; 1803); *Précis de la philosophie de Bacon,* 2 vols. (Paris, 1802); *Introduction à la physique terrestre par les fluides expansibles,* 2 vols. (Paris, 1803); *Traité élémentaire sur le fluide électricogalvanique,* 2 vols. (Paris, 1804); *Traité élémentaire de géologie* (Paris, 1809), trans. by Henry de la Fite (London, 1809); *Geological Travels in the North of Europe and in England,* 3 vols. (London, 1810–1811); *Geological Travels in Some Parts of France, Switzerland and Germany* (London, 1813).

II. SECONDARY LITERATURE. On Deluc or his work, see R. J. Chorley, A. J. Dunn, and R. P. Beckinsale, *History of the Study of Landforms,* I (London, 1964), *passim; Encyclopaedia Britannica,* 11th ed. (1910–1911); a biography in *Gentleman's Magazine* (1817), pt. 2, 629; Charles C. Gillispie, *Genesis and Geology* (Cambridge-New York, 1951; 1959); *passim;* W. J. Harrison, in *Dictionary of National Biography,* XIV (1888), 328–329; C. Lyell, *Principles of Geology,* 12th ed. (London, 1875), I, 80; II, 506, 507; a biography in *The Philosophical Magazine and Journal,* **50,** no. 1 (Nov. 1817), 393–394; and K. A. von Zittel, *History of Geology and Palaeontology,* M. M. Ogilvie-Gordon, trans. (London, 1901), which mentions Deluc's theoretical articles in *Journal de physique*—this otherwise excellent assessment wrongly suggests that Deluc first proposed the term "geology" in its modern sense.

ROBERT P. BECKINSALE

DEMBOWSKI, ERCOLE (*b.* Milan, Italy, 12 December 1812; *d.* Monte di Albizzate [near Gallarate], Italy, 19 January 1881), *astronomy.*

Dembowski was the son of Jan Dembowski, a general of Napoleon, and Matilde Viscontini, an Italian noblewoman. Until he was thirty-one Dembowski was an officer in the Austrian navy; he made several expeditions to the Orient and participated in some minor battles in which he distinguished himself by gallantry.

Having left the navy Dembowski became interested in astronomy. In 1852 he built his own observatory in the village of San Giorgio a Cremano, near Naples, where he made excellent observations of double stars with only a modest telescope of five-inch aperture.

In 1870 he returned to Lombardy and constructed

at Monte di Albizzate, near Gallarate, a new observatory equipped with a telescope of seven-inch aperture by Merz and a meridian circle by Starke. With these new instruments he continued the revision of Struve's *Dorpat Catalogue* that he had begun in Naples. His energy and perseverance in this work produced an internally consistent series of measurements of the distances and positions of double and multiple stars that extends uninterruptedly over a period of twenty-five years.

Dembowski's first publication (1857) contains measurements of 127 double and triple stars selected from Struve's *Dorpat Catalogue;* each measurement represents the mean of ten observations made on the same night. In 1859 he published a reexamination of all the brightest stars in the *Dorpat Catalogue,* and in 1860 he listed—with great accuracy—the positions of fifty-four double stars. These measurements were used by Argelander in his fundamental work on proper motion of 250 stars.

Dembowski was a very active observer. He regularly published (mainly in *Astronomische Nachrichten*) the results of his observations for the benefit of the other astronomers working in the same field.

Following Dembowski's death Otto Struve credited him with having made about 20,000 observations. At the same time, G. V. Schiaparelli urged the Reale Accademia dei Lincei to undertake the collation and publication of Dembowski's scattered observations. The work, edited by Schiaparelli and Struve, appeared two years later.

Dembowski was elected an associate member of the Royal Astronomical Society (London) on 8 November 1878 and was awarded the Gold Medal of that society.

BIBLIOGRAPHY

I. ORIGINAL WORKS. Dembowski's earliest publication is "Misure micrometriche di 127 stelle doppie e triple di catalogo di Struve," in *Memorie della R. Accademia delle scienze di Napoli,* **2** (1855–1857), which was also published in *Astronomische Nachrichten;* his other observations were published in *Astronomische Nachrichten* volumes for 1859, 1864, 1866, 1869, 1870, 1872, 1873, 1874, 1875, and 1876; his collected observations are G. V. Schiaparelli and Otto Struve, eds., "Misure micrometriche di stelle doppie e multiple fatte negli anni 1852–1878," in *Atti della R. Accademia dei Lincei,* **16** and **17** (1883–1884).

II. SECONDARY LITERATURE. The award to Dembowski of the Gold Medal is noted in *Monthly Notices of the Royal Astronomical Society,* **38** (1878), 249; see also obituaries in *Astronomische Nachrichten* (1881) and in *Monthly Notices of the Royal Astronomical Society,* **42** (1882), 148.

GUGLIELMO RIGHINI

DEMOCRITUS (*b.* Abdera, Thrace, *fl.* late fifth century B.C.), *physics, mathematics.*

There were two main chronologies current in antiquity for Democritus. According to the first, which was followed by Epicurus among others, Democritus was the teacher of the Sophist Protagoras of Abdera and was born soon after 500 B.C. and died about 404 B.C. The other chronology puts his birth about 460 B.C., making him a younger contemporary of Socrates and a generation or more younger than Protagoras; in this case, the tradition that he lived to a great age would bring his death well into the fourth century B.C. According to Democritus' own words, he was a young man when Anaxagoras was old, and he may actually have said that he was younger by forty years. Although there was also more than one ancient chronology for Anaxagoras, this statement probably supports the later dates for Democritus, and these have usually been accepted by modern scholars. The question is an important one for our understanding of the history of thought in the fifth century B.C., and it is unfortunate that the occurrence of the name Democritus, presumably as a magistrate, on a fifth-century tetradrachm of Abdera does not help to settle the question, because we cannot be certain that it is the name of the Democritus here discussed nor can the tetradrachm be dated with certainty earlier than 430 B.C. (this would fit with either chronological scheme).

Most of the stories about Democritus are worthless later inventions, but it is probable that he was well-to-do, and stories of extensive travels may have a foundation in fact. He is reported to have said that he visited Athens, but no one knew him there, and from Cicero and Horace we learn that—at least in their time—he was known as the "laughing philosopher" because of his amusement at the follies of mankind. His only certainly attested teacher was Leucippus. The titles of more than sixty writings are preserved from a catalog that probably represented the holdings of the library at Alexandria. Of these we have only some 300 alleged quotations, many of which may not be genuine. More valuable for the understanding of Democritus' theories are the accounts given by Aristotle, Theophrastus, and the later doxographic tradition. Democritus left pupils who continued the tradition of his teachings and one of them, Nausiphanes, was the teacher of Epicurus. Epicureanism represents a further elaboration of the physical theories of Democritus, and surviving writings of Epicurus and others provide further interpretations and sometimes specific information about earlier atomist doctrines.

According to Posidonius in the first century B.C., the theory of atoms was a very old one and went back to a Phoenician named Mōchus, who lived before the Trojan War, in the second millennium B.C. According to others, Democritus was a pupil of Persian magi and Chaldean astrologers, either as a boy in his native Abdera or later in Egypt. Both stories seem to have originated only in the third century B.C. and to be part of the wholesale attempts to derive Greek thought from Oriental sources that followed the "discovery" of the East resulting from the establishment of Alexander's empire. More intriguing is the fact that certain Indian thinkers arrived at an atomic explanation of the universe, which is expounded in the Vaiśeṣika Sūtra and is interpreted by the aphorisms of Kanada. However, the Vaiśeṣika atoms are not quality-free but correspond to the four elements; nor is soul made from these atoms. Moreover, the date of the first appearance of the doctrine in India is probably subsequent to the founding of the Greek kingdom of Bactria, so that coincidences could be due to Greek influences on Indian thought. There is no early evidence of external sources for Democritus' thought; these are not needed, because the doctrines can be shown to have arisen naturally and almost inevitably as a result of the way in which the problems of explaining the physical universe had been formulated by Democritus' immediate predecessors among the pre-Socratics, who were of course Greeks. Consequently, Aristotle is probably right (*De generatione et corruptione,* 325a23 ff.) in explaining his views as developed in reply to the doctrines of the Eleatics. This need not exclude the possibility that the atomists were also influenced by what is sometimes called Pythagorean number-atomism, although whether this preceded or arose only after the time of Leucippus remains uncertain, and it is clear that Democritus did not invent atomism but received the essentials of the doctrine from Leucippus.

By the middle of the fifth century B.C., it seemed to many thinkers that Parmenides, the founder of the Eleatic school, had proved that nothing can come into being out of that which is not, and that anything which is cannot alter, because that would involve its becoming that which is not. Previous attempts to explain the physical universe as derived from one or more primary substances were thus doomed to failure, as they all involved change in the primary substances and so violated Parmenides' conclusions. Anaxagoras, at least in one view of his doctrine, made a heroic attempt to escape from the difficulty by supposing that all substances were always present in all other substances and that apparent change was simply the emergence of the required substance—which had been present unnoticed all the time. The atomism of Democritus was similar in its approach but went

further in depriving the primary constituents of most, but not all, of the qualities apparent in objects derived from them. Moreover, Leucippus had boldly accepted empty space or void—the existence of which the Eleatics regarded as impossible because it would be that which is not—as necessary to make movement possible.

Atoms and void are the bases of Democritus' system for explaining the universe: solid corporeal atoms, infinite in number and shape, differing in size, but otherwise lacking in sensible qualities, were originally scattered throughout infinite void. In general, the atoms were so small as to be invisible. (They were all invisible for Epicurus, but later sources raise the possibility that for Democritus some exceptional atoms may have been large enough to be seen or even that an individual atom might be as big as the cosmos.) The atoms are physically indivisible—this is the meaning of the name *atomos,* which, while not surviving in the fragments of Democritus, must certainly have been used by him. Whether the atoms were conceptually or mathematically indivisible as well as physically is a matter of dispute. But they were certainly extended and indestructible, so that if he thought about it Democritus ought not to have denied mathematical divisibility, especially as the atoms' variety of shape implied the concept of parts within each physically indivisible atom. They are homogeneous in substance, contain no void and no interstices, and are in perpetual motion in the infinitely extended void, probably moving equally in all directions.

When a group of atoms becomes isolated, a whirl is produced which causes like atoms to tend toward like. Within a kind of membrane or garment, as it were, woven out of hook-shaped atoms, there develops a spherical structure which eventually contains earth, sky, and heavenly bodies—in other words a spherical cosmos. The only detailed description of the process ascribes it to Leucippus (Diogenes Laertius, IX, 30 ff.), but there is no reason to doubt that it was repeated by Democritus. There is no limit to the number of atoms nor to the amount of void, and so not one cosmos but many are formed. Some dissolved again before the formation of our cosmos; others coexist with ours, some larger and some smaller, some without sun or moon, and some without living creatures, plants, or moisture. From time to time a cosmos is destroyed by collision with another.

Our earth and everything in it, like everything elsewhere, is compounded of atoms and void, and there are no other constituents of the universe of any kind. Apart from differences in shape, atoms differ in arrangement and position. As Aristotle says, the letter *A* differs from *N* in shape; *AN* from *NA* in arrangement; and Z from N in position, although both have the same shape. We must add, although Aristotle does not say so here, that the spacings between atoms may vary from the zero space of actual contact through increasing distances apart. Soft and yielding bodies and bodies light in weight contain more void than heavier or harder objects of equal extent. Iron is lighter than lead because it has more void, but it is harder because it is denser than lead at particular points, the void not being distributed evenly throughout, as is the case with lead. It is probable that for Democritus the atoms when entangled do not cease to be in motion (their individual movement is naturally less extensive), but they participate in movements of the object of which they are a part. It appears that atoms were not regarded as possessing weight in their own right; this was Epicurus' innovation. But physical objects possess weight, and according to Aristotle, atoms are heavier in proportion to their excess of bulk. Objects as a whole are heavier the greater the proportion of atoms to void. It may be that weight operates only in a developed world and is the result of a tendency of compound objects to move toward the center of a whirl. For Democritus all movement and all change are due to "necessity," but this is an internal cause and not an agency operating from without: it is the necessary result of the natural movement of the atoms. All events are determined, and if Cicero is right at all in saying Democritus attributed events to chance, this can have meant only that they could not be predicted, not that they were not determined.

The perceived qualitative differences between objects depend upon the nature and arrangement of the relevant atoms and void. The importance and novelty of this doctrine were fully appreciated by Theophrastus, who discussed it at some length in his surviving *De sensibus*. It might have seemed sufficient answer to Parmenides' challenging argument to have said that secondary qualities such as colors and tastes were produced by the appropriate arrangement of atoms in the sense that they were present in any object possessing the appropriate atomic configuration and would be altered or disappear when the configuration changed. But Theophrastus complains that Democritus is inconsistent on this point and that, while explaining sensations causally in terms of configurations, he insists that the perceived qualities depend upon the state of the percipient—for example, his health—to such an extent that the qualities exist not in the object but only in the percipient at the time he is perceiving them. According to Sextus Empiricus, Protagoras, in his "Man is the measure" doctrine, had held that there are present in actual objects multiple qualities which are selectively perceived by different percipients. Democritus is said (fr. 156) to have criticized the doctrine of Protagoras at great length, and it could be that he carried the relativism of Protagoras one step further by supposing that secondary qualities did not exist in the configuration of atoms which constitute a thing but only in the consciousness of the percipient. But not all accept Sextus Empiricus' account of Protagoras on this point.

We lack details of many aspects of Democritus' cosmology. The earth is flat and elongated—twice as long as it is broad. Although earlier it strayed about, it is now stationary at the center of the universe. The angle between zenith and celestial pole is explained by the tilting of the earth because the warmer air to the south—under the earth—offered less support than that in the north. Earthquakes are caused by heavy rain or drought changing the amount of water in the cavities of the earth. While some explanations of meteorological phenomena were offered in terms of the theory of atoms (for example, the attraction of like atoms to like as an explanation of magnetism), in general Democritus seems to have followed traditional explanations drawn from earlier pre-Socratics, above all from Anaximander. Unlike Leucippus, who put the sun's orbit outermost in the heavens, Democritus had the normal order of fixed stars, planets, sun, Venus, moon. The moon, like the earth, contained valleys and glens, and its light was derived from the sun.

Two particularly quick-moving constituents of the universe, fire and soul, were for Democritus composed of spherical atoms. Spherical atoms are not themselves either fire or soul but become such by the suitable aggregation of a number of themselves. Such aggregation cannot be by entanglement, which is not possible with spherical atoms, but only by the principle of the attraction of like to like. Whereas air, water, and perhaps earth, and things containing them, were regarded as conglomerations of atoms of all shapes, only the one shape seems to have occurred in fire and soul. Aristotle more than once speaks as if soul and fire were identical, and he adds that the soul can be fed by breathing in suitable atoms from the air around us. In this way, losses of soul atoms from the body can be replaced. When we can no longer breathe, the pressure from the atmosphere outside continues to squeeze out the soul atoms from the body and death results. A slight excess of loss over replacement produces sleep only and not death. Even when death results, the loss of soul atoms takes time, so that some functions, such as growth of hair and nails, continue for a while in the tomb; a certain degree of sensation may also continue for a time, and in exceptional cases, even resuscitation may be possible. We do not know the contents of the work *On Those in Hades,* attributed to Democritus, except that it included reference to such resuscitations.

Within the living body, soul atoms are distributed throughout the whole in such a way that single atoms of the soul and body alternate, and it has sometimes been said that this involves treating isolated atoms as soul atoms and so reintroducing qualities into individual atoms. But such an alternation could be achieved within a lattice pattern of one kind or another for the soul atoms, so that there is no actual inconsistency. These soul atoms are the immediate source of life, warmth, and motion in a living body. In addition to the soul atoms dispersed throughout the body, there is another part of the soul, the mind, located in one part of the body, namely the head.

Sensation for Democritus was based upon touch and was due to images entering the sense organs from outside and producing alterations in the percipient. Sensation is thus the result of the interaction of image and organ. In the case of flavors, there is always a multitude of configurations of atoms present in what is tasted, but the preponderant configuration exerts the greatest influence and determines the flavor tasted, the result being influenced also by the state of the sense organs. In the case of sight, images continually stream off the objects, which are somehow imprinted —by stamping, as it were—on the intervening air. This imprinted air is then carried to the eyes, where its configuration produces the sensation of color. A similar analysis seems to have been offered for hearing and perhaps for smell. Taste, however, entails direct contact between organ and object: large, rough, polygonal shapes produce astringent flavors, and so on.

Thought, like sensation, is the result of a disturbance of the soul atoms by configurations of atoms from outside; it is what occurs when the soul achieves a fresh balance after the movement which is sensation. The details of the process are obscure, and the text of Theophrastus' description is uncertain. But there is no sure evidence to suggest that Democritus held the later theory of Epicurus that it is possible for certain externally originating images to bypass the senses and secure direct access to the mind in thought. For Democritus, thought follows after sensation, and we may believe that Democritus expressed his real view when he said (fr. 125) that the mind takes its evidence from the senses and then seeks to overthrow them, but that the overthrow is a fall for the mind also. Nonetheless, in an important fragment (fr. 11) Democritus did claim that there were two kinds of knowledge, one genuine or legitimate, and the other bastard. To the bastard belong the senses; genuine

knowledge operates on objects too fine for any sense to grasp. This must surely refer to our knowledge of the atomic theory, including the imperceptible atoms and void of which things are composed, but we do not know what mechanical procedure, if any, Democritus envisaged for the acquisition of such knowledge.

It follows from the above view of the soul and the way it leaves the body at death that there is no survival of the individual soul, although the soul atoms themselves survive because, like all atoms, they are indestructible. It might have been expected that this approach would shed doubt on the existence of gods and spirits, especially since we are told that Democritus attributed early man's fear of the gods to his misunderstanding of natural phenomena such as lightning and eclipses. But he accepted that images of beings both beneficent and maleficent, destructible and yet able to foretell the future while being seen and heard, come to men apparently out of the air itself, without any more ultimate source. We do not know what doctrine lies behind this, but it is likely that there was no external source posited for these images other than the soul atoms at large in the air.

The list of Democritus' writings contains the titles of a number of works on mathematics, and it is clear from the few surviving scattered references that his mathematical interests were not inconsiderable. Protagoras had argued that the tangent touches the circle not at one point but over a distance. Democritus treated the sphere as "all angle," and Simplicius explained this as meaning that what is bent is an angle and the sphere is bent all over. It is inferred that he supposed that the sphere is really a polyhedron with imperceptibly small faces, presumably because a physical sphere involves atoms which cannot be further broken down. In such a case he would be in agreement with Protagoras as to the actual relation between tangent and circle while in disagreement as to the apparent relation. But with atoms in an infinite variety of shapes. there is no reason why Democritus could not have posited a perfect physical sphere made up of atoms of indivisible magnitude but with curved faces. In any case Democritus could probably distinguish a physical from a mathematical sphere well enough.

Of very great interest is Democritus' discussion of the question whether the two contiguous surfaces produced by slicing a cone horizontally are equal or unequal. If equal, it might seem that the cone is a cylinder, while if unequal, the cone becomes steplike and uneven (fr. 155). Chrysippus the Stoic, when discussing Democritus' doctrine, declared that Democritus was unaware of the true answer—namely, so he claimed, that the surfaces are neither equal nor unequal. Unfortunately what Democritus' view was remains in doubt. Some suppose that he argued for a stepped physical cone; others that he regarded the dilemma as genuine; and still others that he considered them equal, at least as far as mathematics was concerned. Archimedes records that Democritus was concerned with the ratios of size between cylinders, pyramids, and prisms of the same base and height. While this is evidence of further interest in problems associated with cones of the kind that were so important for the subsequent history of mathematics, we do not actually know the nature of Democritus' discussions concerning them.

Tantalizing references to individual doctrines and the titles of a number of his writings have suggested to some that Democritus' biological work rivaled Aristotle's in both comprehensiveness and attention to detail. The indications that survive do not for the most part suggest that he made any very particular application of atomic theories to biology, and it is probable that his clearly extensive writings were essentially within the general framework of Ionian speculation. More we cannot say through lack of positive information.

Later writers—as well as some from the fifth and fourth centuries B.C.—preserve details which all seem to come from a single account of the origins and development of human civilization. They have in common not only various particular points but also a basic conception—namely, that civilization developed from lower levels to higher, which contrasted strongly with the dominant view that human history represented a continuous decline from an original golden age. The clearest version of this history of culture survives in the *Bibliotheca historica* of Diodorus (bk. I, ch. 8), written in the age of Cicero. It is clear that Democritus held a similar view, and it is possible, although by no means certain, that he originated the whole tradition. Certain features of it, however, are already in Aeschylus' picture of Prometheus and probably in the writings of Protagoras summarized in Plato's dialogue named after the Sophist. Part of Democritus' treatment of the evolution of culture concerned the origin and development of language, taking the view that names were not natural but conventional.

Special problems affect the reconstruction of Democritus' ethical doctrines, to which a very large part of the surviving fragments relate. Many of these are attributed in the manuscript tradition not to Democritus but to an otherwise unknown Democrates, so that their authority for the reconstruction of the views of Democritus is uncertain. Most of the frag-

ments are extremely commonplace, and hardly any are related to atomic theory. The doxographic tradition does, however, suggest that he had a general theory of *euthymia* ("cheerfulness" or "contentment") as the end of ethics. It was based on a physical state, the actual constitution of the body at any one time, of which the external expression is pleasure or enjoyment when the state itself is satisfactory. Even this much is a matter of conjecture, and we do not know how it was all worked out by Democritus.

Most of the fragments dealing with what we would call political questions are as traditional in content as those dealing with ethics. He seems to have had no doubts about the importance of law, although its function was limited to preventing one man from injuring another. It is inferior to encouragement and persuasion, but "it is right to obey the law, the ruler and the man who is wiser" (fr. 47). Democritus had declared that secondary qualities of perception, such as sweetness, existed only by *nomos*, not in reality, and *nomos*, which means "custom" or "convention," is also the word used for "law." It is perhaps not going too far to say that in ethics and politics, just as in physics, Democritus was searching for a truth and a reality behind or beyond the world of appearances; but at the same time, he wished to reaffirm the importance of changing phenomena as the product of an unchanging reality. It is probable that political obedience to the law was regarded as rooted in the well-being of the soul, just as wrongdoing is not to be justified by the thought that one will escape discovery.

BIBLIOGRAPHY

The fragments and testimonia are collected in H. Diels and W. Kranz, *Die Fragmente der Vorsokratiker*, 6th ed., 3 vols. (Berlin, 1951–1952), vol. II. There is a translation of the fragments by K. Freeman, *Ancilla to the Pre-Socratic Philosophers* (Cambridge, Mass., 1966), and the most important are translated and discussed in G. S. Kirk and J. E. Raven, *The Presocratic Philosophers* (Cambridge, 1957). For discussions of Democritus, see V. E. Alfieri, *Gli atomisti* (Bari, 1936) and *Atomos idea, l'origine del concetto dell'atomo nel pensiero greco* (Florence, 1953); C. Bailey, *The Greek Atomists and Epicurus* (Oxford, 1928); T. Cole, *Democritus and the Sources of Greek Anthropology*, American Philological Association Monograph (1967); W. K. C. Guthrie, *History of Greek Philosophy*, vol. II (Cambridge, 1965), ch. 8; A. B. Keith, *Indian Logic and Atomism* (Oxford, 1921); H. Langerbeck, *Doxis Epirhysmie, Studien zu Demokrits Ethik und Erkenntnislehre* (Berlin, 1935); S. Luria, *Zur Frage der materialistischen Begründung der Ethik bei Demokrit* (Berlin, 1964); J. Mau, *Zum Problem der Infinitesimalen bei den antiken Atomisten*, 2nd ed.

(Berlin, 1957); P. Natorp, *Die Ethik des Demokritos, Texte und Untersuchungen* (Marburg, 1893); W. Schmid, *Geschichte der griechischen Literatur,* V (Munich, 1948), 236–350; G. Vlastos, "Ethics and Physics in Democritus," in *Philosophical Review,* **54** (1945), 578–592, and **55** (1946), 53–63.

G. B. KERFERD

DE MOIVRE, ABRAHAM. See **Moivre, Abraham de.**

DE MORGAN, AUGUSTUS (*b.* Madura, Madras presidency, India, June 1806; *d.* London, England, 18 March 1871), *mathematics.*

De Morgan's father was a colonel in the Indian Army; and his mother was the daughter of John Dodson, a pupil and friend of Abraham de Moivre, and granddaughter of James Dodson, author of the *Mathematical Canon.* At the age of seven months De Morgan was brought to England, where his family settled first at Worcester and then at Taunton. He attended a succession of private schools at which he acquired a mastery of Latin, Greek, and Hebrew and a strong interest in mathematics before the age of fourteen. He also acquired an intense dislike for cramming, examinations, and orthodox theology.

De Morgan entered Trinity College, Cambridge, in February 1823 and placed first in the first-class division in his second year; he was disappointed, however, to graduate only as fourth wrangler in 1827. After contemplating a career in either medicine or law, De Morgan successfully applied for the chair of mathematics at the newly formed University College, London, in 1828 on the strong recommendation of his former tutors, who included Airy and Peacock. When, in 1831, the college council dismissed the professor of anatomy without giving reasons, he immediately resigned on principle. He resumed in 1836, on the accidental death of his successor, and remained there until a second resignation in 1866.

De Morgan's life was characterized by powerful religious convictions. While admitting a personal faith in Jesus Christ, he abhorred any suspicion of hypocrisy or sectarianism and on these grounds refused an M.A., a fellowship at Cambridge, and ordination. In 1837 he married Sophia Elizabeth Frend, who wrote his biography in 1882. De Morgan was never wealthy; and his researches into all branches of knowledge, together with his prolific output of writing, left little time for social or family life. However, he was well known for his humor, range of knowledge, and sweetness of disposition.

In May 1828 De Morgan became a fellow of the Astronomical Society; he was elected to the council in 1830, serving as secretary (1831–1838; 1848–1854). He helped to found the London Mathematical Society, becoming its first president and giving the inaugural lecture in 1865. He was also an influential member of the Society for the Diffusion of Useful Knowledge from 1826. De Morgan was a prolific writer, contributing no fewer than 850 articles (one-sixth of the total production) to the *Penny Cyclopaedia* and writing regularly for at least fifteen periodicals.

De Morgan exerted a considerable influence on the development of mathematics in the nineteenth century. As a teacher he sought to demonstrate principles rather than techniques; and his pupils, who included Todhunter, Routh, and Sylvester, acquired from him a great love of the subject. He wrote textbooks on the elements of arithmetic, algebra, trigonometry, calculus, complex numbers, probability, and logic. These books are characterized by meticulous attention to detail, enunciation of fundamental principles, and clear logical presentation.

De Morgan's original contributions to mathematics were mainly in the fields of analysis and logic. In an article written in 1838, he defined and invented the term "mathematical induction" to describe a process that previously had been used —without much clarity—by mathematicians.

In *The Differential and Integral Calculus* (1842) there is a good discussion of fundamental principles with a definition of the limit which is probably the first precise analytical formulation of Cauchy's somewhat intuitive concept. The same work contains a discussion of infinite series with an original rule to determine convergence precisely when simpler tests fail. De Morgan's rule, which is proved rigorously, is that if the series is given by

$$\sum \frac{1}{\phi(n)},$$

then if

$$e = \lim_{n \to \infty} \frac{n\phi'(n)}{\phi(n)},$$

the series converges for $e > 1$ but diverges for $e \leq 1$.

Among his other mathematical work is a system that De Morgan described as "double algebra." This helped to give a complete geometrical interpretation of the properties of complex numbers and, as Sir William Rowan Hamilton acknowledged, suggested the idea of quaternions.

De Morgan's greatest contribution to scientific knowledge undoubtedly lay in his logical researches; and the subsequent development of symbolic logic, with its powerful influences on both philosophy and technology, owes much to his fundamental work. He believed that the traditional method of argument using the Aristotelian syllogism was inadequate in reasoning that involved quantity. As an example De Morgan presented the following argument:

In a particular company of men,
    most men have coats
    most men have waistcoats
∴ some men have both coats and waistcoats.

He asserted that it was not possible to demonstrate this true argument by means of any of the normally accepted Aristotelian syllogisms.

The first attempt to extend classical logic by means of quantifying the predicate and reformulating logical statements in mathematical terms was made by George Bentham in 1827. He rephrased the statement "Every X is a Y" into the equation "X in toto $= Y$ ex parte" with the algebraic notation "$tX = pY$." It was more usual at this time, however, for logicians to make more classical attempts to broaden the Aristotelian syllogistic; and De Morgan's work, which commenced in the 1840's, can be seen as the bridge between this older approach and Boole's analytical formulation. Boole acknowledged his debt to De Morgan and Hamilton in the preface to his first logical work, *The Mathematical Analysis of Logic* (1847).

The Scottish philosopher Sir William Hamilton (not to be confused with Sir William Rowan Hamilton) worked out a system for quantifying the predicate a short time before De Morgan did and unjustly accused him of plagiarism. He had no shred of evidence to support his charge, and De Morgan's work was superior to his in both analytical formulation and subsequent development.

De Morgan invented notations, which he sometimes varied, to describe simple propositions. Objects with certain properties were denoted by capital letters $X, Y, Z, \cdots$ and those without this property by the corresponding small letters $x, y, z, \cdots$. One of his notations was

A	Every X is a Y	as	$X)Y$
E	No X is a Y	as	$X.Y$
I	Some X's are Y's	as	XY
O	Some X's are not Y's	as	$X:Y,$

the symbols A, E, I, O, having their usual Aristotelian meaning. He then worked out rules to establish valid syllogistic inferences. Such results were then written in the form

$$X)Y + Y)Z = X)Z$$
$$Y:X + Y)Z = Z:X$$
$$X)Y + Z)Y = xz,$$

and so on. This notation was superseded by Boole's more algebraic one, but it helped De Morgan to establish valid inferences not always obtainable through the traditional rules. Using the notation of Boolean algebra, the two equations $(A \cap B)' = A' \cup B'$ and $(A \cup B)' = A' \cap B'$ are still referred to as the De Morgan formulas.

De Morgan was also the first logician to present a logic of relations. In a paper written in 1860 he used the notation $X..LY$ to represent the statement that X is one of the objects in the relation L to Y, while $X.LY$ meant that X was not any of the L's of Y. He also presented the idea $X..(LM)Y$ as the composition of two relations L,M, and of the inverse relation L^{-1}. This extension of the idea of subject and predicate was not adopted by any of De Morgan's successors, and the idea lapsed until Benjamin Peirce's work of 1883.

De Morgan was steeped in the history of mathematics. He wrote biographies of Newton and Halley and published an index of the correspondence of scientific men of the seventeenth century. He believed that the work of both minor and major mathematicians was essential for an assessment of mathematical development, a principle shown most clearly in his *Arithmetical Books* (1847). This work describes the many arithmetical books in the author's possession, refers to the work of 1,580 arithmeticians, and contains detailed digressions on such subjects as the length of a foot and the authorship of the popular *Cocker's Arithmetick*. De Morgan's book was written at a time when accurate bibliography was in its infancy and was probably the first significant work of scientific bibliography. Despite a lack of means, he collected a library of over 3,000 scientific books, which is now at the London University library.

De Morgan's peripheral mathematical interests included a powerful advocacy of decimal coinage; an almanac giving the dates of the new moon from 2000 B.C. to A.D. 2000; a curious work entitled *Budget of Paradoxes,* which considers, among other things, the work of would-be circle squarers; and a standard work on the theory of probability applied to life contingencies that is highly regarded in insurance literature.

BIBLIOGRAPHY

I. Original Works. De Morgan's books include *The Elements of Arithmetic* (London, 1830); *Elements of Spherical Trigonometry* (London, 1834); *The Elements of Algebra Preliminary to the Differential Calculus, and Fit for the Higher Classes of Schools etc.* (London, 1835); *The Connexion of Number and Magnitude: An Attempt to Explain the Fifth Book of Euclid* (London, 1836); *Elements of Trig-*

onometry and Trigonometrical Analysis, Preliminary to the Differential Calculus (London, 1837); *An Essay on Probabilities, and on Their Application to Life Contingencies and Insurance Offices* (London, 1838); *First Notions of Logic, Preparatory to the Study of Geometry* (London, 1839); *Arithmetical Books From the Invention of Printing to the Present Time. Being Brief Notices of a Large Number of Works Drawn up From Actual Inspection* (London, 1847), repub. (London, 1967) with a biographical introduction by A. R. Hall; *The Differential and Integral Calculus* (London, 1842); *Formal Logic: or The Calculus of Inference, Necessary and Probable* (London, 1847); *Trigonometry and Double Algebra* (London, 1849); *The Book of Almanacs With an Index of Reference, by Which the Almanac May Be Found for Every Year . . . up to A.D. 2000. With Means of Finding the Day of Any New or Full Moon From B.C. 2000 to A.D. 2000* (London, 1851); *Syllabus of a Proposed System of Logic* (London, 1860); and *A Budget of Paradoxes* (London, 1872).

Articles by De Morgan can be found in *Quarterly Journal of Education* (1831–1833); *Cambridge Philosophical Transactions* (1830–1868); *Philosophical Magazine* (1835–1852); *Cambridge Mathematical Journal* (1841–1845); *Cambridge and Dublin Mathematical Journal* (1846–1853); *Quarterly Journal of Mathematics* (1857–1858); *Central Society of Education* (1837–1839); *The Mathematician* (1850); and *British Almanac and Companion* (1831–1857). He also contributed to *Smith's Classical Dictionary, Dublin Review, Encyclopaedia Metropolitana,* and *Penny Cyclopaedia.*

II. SECONDARY LITERATURE. On De Morgan or his work, see I. M. Bochenski, *Formale Logik* (Freiburg–Munich, 1956), pp. 306–307, 345–347, *passim;* S. De Morgan, *Memoir of Augustus De Morgan . . . With Selections From His Letters* (London, 1882); G. B. Halsted, "De Morgan as Logician," in *Journal of Speculative Philosophy,* **18** (1884), 1–9; and an obituary notice in *Monthly Notices of the Royal Astronomical Society,* **32** (1872), 112–118.

JOHN M. DUBBEY

DENIS, JEAN-BAPTISTE (*b.* Paris, France, 1640 [?]; *d.* Paris, 3 October 1704), *medicine.*

Denis was born in Paris, presumably in the 1640's. He was the son of a hydraulic engineer who was Louis XIV's chief engineer in charge of the works distributing the water of the Seine from the pumps at Marly to the fountains at Versailles.

Denis is said to have studied medicine at Montpellier (1), but no records of his inscription as a medical student or of the conferring upon him of a diploma as doctor in medicine can be found in the very complete archives of the Faculty of Medicine. Niceron says that he obtained "un bonnet de Docteur en cette Faculté" and that "il fut aggrégé à la Chambre Royale" (10). On the other hand, Martin de la Martinière, who was a physician in ordinary to the king, in a letter to Denis accuses him of taking the title of "maître" because of a "lettre de Médecine"

that he obtained in Rheims (2). Nothing has yet been found in Rheims indicating that he obtained such a degree. While in Paris he taught philosophy and mathematics, assuming the title of professor, which he placed at the head of most of his works. No evidence for a degree in mathematics or philosophy has yet been found.

Beginning in 1664, Denis gave public lectures in physics, mathematics, and medicine at his home on the quai des Grands-Augustins in Paris, and published these lectures as conference reports (7). He also joined the group surrounding Habert de Montmort, which met to discuss the new philosophy much like the groups in London that preceded the Royal Society. When the Académie des Sciences was established in 1666, the Montmort group did not participate and continued its own meetings independently of that body.

The discovery of the circulation of blood by William Harvey stimulated experiments on the circulation; intravenous injection was begun by Christopher Wren and Clarke in the 1650's. This was followed by the first trial of transfusion of blood in animals. After discussions at the Royal Society as early as its public meeting of 17 May 1665, an account of successful transfusion in dogs was given by Richard Lower in a letter written to Robert Boyle on 6 July 1665 and submitted by Boyle to the Royal Society. This led to another successful transfusion in November 1666 at the Royal Society (9).

When reports of these experiments reached Paris late in 1666 or early in 1667, the Académie des Sciences immediately set about repeating them, appointing a committee including Louis Gayant, an anatomist; Claude Perrault, the physician noted for the east facade (the Colonnade) of the Louvre; and Adrien Auzout, the astronomer. Gayant performed the first transfusion in Paris on 22 January 1667, using dogs. Transfusion also attracted the interest of the Montmort Academy, which apparently appointed Denis and Paul Emmerez, a surgeon from St.-Quentin, to carry out independent studies. On 3 March 1667 Denis performed a transfusion experiment on two dogs (8). On 2 April 1667 various experiments involving transfusion from three calves to three dogs were made. These were published in the Royal Society's *Philosophical Transactions* (11).

But it was the transfusion of blood in men which was of the greatest interest to Denis, gave him his celebrity, and started the greatest medical controversy of that time. In these experiments he was assisted by Paul Emmerez.

The first transfusion of blood in man was made on 15 June 1667, on a drowsy and feverish young man.

From a lamb he received about twelve ounces of blood, after which he "rapidly recovered from his lethargy, grew fatter and was an object of surprise and astonishment to all who knew him" (4).

The second transfusion was carried out on a forty-five-year-old chair bearer, a robust man who received the blood of a sheep (4). He returned to work the next day as if nothing had happened to him.

The recipient of the third transfusion was Baron Bonde, a young Swedish nobleman who fell ill in Paris while making a grand tour of Europe. He was in such a bad state that he had been abandoned by his physicians; and in despair, having heard of Denis's new cure, his family asked Denis to attempt transfusion of blood as a final recourse. After the first transfusion, which was from a calf, Bonde felt better and began to speak. This improvement lasted only a short time, however, and he died during a second transfusion.

The fourth transfusion patient was a madman, Antoine Mauroy (5), who died during a third transfusion. He may have been poisoned by his wife, who, perhaps to divert suspicion from herself or at the suggestion of the many Paris physicians antagonistic to Denis, accused Denis of having killed her husband. Denis brought the case before the court, and a judgment rendered on 17 April 1668 cleared him of any wrongdoing but forbade the practice of transfusion of blood in man without permission of the Paris Faculty of Medicine. Meanwhile, another transfusion had been made by Denis, on 10 February 1668, on a paralyzed woman. After this, however, the practice of transfusion faded out as suddenly as it had begun.

In 1673 Denis was invited to England by Charles II, who wished to learn about transfusion and other remedies purportedly discovered by Denis. He went to England and successfully treated the French ambassador and several personalities of the court. Despite offers to remain, he became dissatisfied and returned to Paris (10), where he continued his interest in science and mathematics (7) but never practiced medicine or again concerned himself with transfusion. He died suddenly on 3 October 1704.

BIBLIOGRAPHY

1. Jean Astruc, *Mémoires pour servir à l'histoire de la Faculté de Montpellier,* rev. by M. Lorry and P. G. Cavelier, V (Paris, 1767), 378.

2. Martin de la Martinière, *Remonstrances charitables du Sieur de la Martinière à Monsieur Denis* (Paris, 1668).

3. J.-B. Denis, *Lettre à M. L'Abbé Bourdelot . . . pour servir de réponse au Sr. Lamy et confirmer la transfusion du sang par de nouvelles expériences* (Paris, 1667).

4. J.-B. Denis, *Lettre escrite à . . . Montmor . . . touchant une nouvelle manière de guérir plusieurs maladies par la transfusion du sang, confirmée par deux expériences faites sur des hommes* (Paris, 1667).

5. J.-B. Denis, *Lettre escrite à M. . . . touchant une folie invétérée, qui a esté guérie depuis peu par la transfusion du sang* (Paris, 1668).

6. J.-B. Denis, *Lettre écrite à . . . Sorbière . . . touchant l'origine de la transfusion du sang, et la manière de la pratiquer sur les hommes* (Paris, 1668).

7. J.-B. Denis, *Recueil des mémoires et conférences qui ont été présentées à Monseigneur le Dauphin pendant l'année 1672 (1673–1674)* (Paris, 1672–1683).

8. J.-B. Denis, "Extrait d'une lettre de M. Denis, professeur de philosophie et de mathématique, sur la transfusion du sang. De Paris le 9. mars, 1667," in *Journal des sçavans,* **6** (1679).

9. Minutes of the Royal Society (16 Sept. 1663), p. 201.

10. J. P. Niceron, *Mémoires pour servir à l'histoire des hommes illustres de la république des lettres,* XXXVII (Paris, 1727), 77.

11. "An extract of the letter of Mr. Denis . . . touching the transfusion of blood, of April 2. 1667," in *Philosophical Transactions of the Royal Society,* **1,** no. 25 (6 May 1667), 453.

HEBBEL E. HOFF

DEPARCIEUX, ANTOINE (*b.* Clotet-de-Cessous, France, 28 October 1703; *d.* Paris, France, 2 September 1768), *mathematics.*

Deparcieux's father, Jean-Antoine, was a farmer; his mother was Jeanne Donzel. Orphaned in 1715, he was educated by his brother Pierre, who sent him at fifteen to the Jesuit college at Alès. In 1730, after finishing his studies, Deparcieux went to Paris, where he became a maker of sundials. He also investigated problems of hydraulics and conceived a plan for bringing the water of the Yvette River to Paris, which was carried out after his death. In 1746 he was admitted to membership in the Academy of Sciences.

In his *Nouveaux traités de trigonométrie rectiligne et sphérique* (Paris, 1741) Deparcieux gives a table of sines, tangents, and secants calculated to every minute and to seven places, and a table of logarithms of sines and tangents calculated to every ten minutes and to eight places. He also gives the formula for tan $a/2$ in the form of two proportions:

$$\sin s : \sin (s-c) = \sin (s-b) \sin (s-a) : x^2$$

$$\sin (s-a) : r = x : \tan \frac{A}{2},$$

but he did not use the words "cosine" and "cotangent." After long investigations of tontines, individual families, and religious communities, Deparcieux published his results in the famous *Essai sur les probabilités de la durée de la vie humaine* (Paris, 1746; suppl., 1760), one of the first statistical works of its kind. It consists of treatises on annuities, mortality, and life annuities. Deparcieux showed a real progress in his theoretical explanation of the properties of the tables of mortality. However, his tables, which were for a long time the only ones on life expectancies in France, indicated too small a value for the probable life expectancy at every age. He also made further inquiries on the concept of the mean life expectancy.

BIBLIOGRAPHY

On Deparcieux or his work, see J. Bertrand, *L'Académie des sciences et les académiciens de 1666 à 1793* (Paris, 1869), pp. 167, 168, 288, 289; A. von Braunmühl, *Vorlesungen über Geschichte der Trigonometrie,* II (Leipzig, 1903), 90; and G. F. Knapp, *Theorie des Bevölkerungs-Wechsels* (Brunswick, 1874), pp. 68–73.

H. L. L. BUSARD

DEPERET, CHARLES (*b.* Perpignan, France, 25 June 1854; *d.* Lyons, France, 18 May 1929), *paleontology, stratigraphy.*

After submitting a thesis on the Tertiary geology of his native province of Roussillon (1885), Depéret was appointed professor at the Faculté des Sciences of Lyons (1889) and subsequently served as its capable and influential dean, reappointed again and again, for thirty-three years. In 1893 he published, with F. Delafond, a monograph on the Tertiary geology of the Bresse region (between Lyons and Dijon), a work that quickly became a classic. His research on the Tertiary period, especially in the Rhone Valley (where he profited by Fontannes's studies) and in Spain, was accompanied by paleontological studies and often gave rise to detailed geological maps. His *Les transformations du monde animal* (1907), translated into English and German and often reprinted in French, clearly and accurately explains the great problems of paleontology.

Turning to Quaternary geology, until then very obscure, Depéret began in 1906 to present clear and theoretically valid syntheses for the entire world that were based on the theory of eustacy expounded by Eduard Suess and L. de Lamothe. In order to satisfy this theory he conceived of supposed geologic stages called Tyrrhenian and Milazzian and brought about acceptance in France of the notion of alluvial Quaternary terraces of relatively constant altitude (at 20, 30, 60, and 100 meters).

During his lifetime Depéret was considered, both in France and in the Mediterranean countries, to be one of the great masters of science, one whose ideas were adopted without question; extremely powerful

on the administrative level, he had a sense of authority as firm as it was courteous. But after his death it was gradually realized that his paleontological studies were often too hasty; carried away by his theories, which were built upon questionable hypotheses, he had neglected or modified facts inconsistent with those theories. Nevertheless, Depéret did succeed in training loyal disciples and, as a passionate fossil seeker, gathered invaluable paleontological collections for his Lyons laboratory.

BIBLIOGRAPHY

I. ORIGINAL WORKS. Depéret's principal works include *Description géologique du bassin tertiaire du Roussillon* (Paris, 1885); "Recherches sur la succession des faunes de vertébrés miocènes de la vallée du Rhône," in *Archives du Muséum d'histoire naturelle de Lyon,* **4** (1887), 45–313; "Les terrains tertiaires de la Bresse," in *Étude des gîtes minéraux de la France* (Paris, 1893), written with F. Delafond; *Les transformations du monde animal* (Paris, 1907; English trans. New York, 1909; German trans. Stuttgart, 1909); *Notice sur les travaux scientifiques de M. Ch. Depéret* (Lyons, 1913); and "La classification des temps quaternaires et ses rapports avec l'antiquité de l'homme en Europe," in *Revue générale des sciences pures et appliquées* (15 March 1923), 2–8, a résumé of ten notices entitled "Essai de coordination géologique des temps quaternaires" that were published in *Comptes rendus hebdomadaires des séances de l'Académie des sciences* between 1918 and 1922.

II. SECONDARY LITERATURE. On Depéret or his work, see Franck Bourdier, "Origine et succès d'une théorie géologique illusoire: L'eustatisme appliqué aux terrasses alluviales," in *Revue de géomorphologie dynamique,* **10** (1959), 16–29, with 146 references; M. Gignoux, "Charles Depéret," in *Bulletin de la Société géologique de France,* 4th ser., **30** (1930), 1043–1073, with a portrait and a bibliography of 223 titles; and F. Roman, "La vie et l'oeuvre de Charles Depéret," in *Revue de l'Université de Lyon* (July 1929), 304–322.

FRANCK BOURDIER

DEPREZ, MARCEL (*b.* Aillant-sur-Milleron, France, 29 December 1843; *d.* Vincennes, France, 16 October 1918), *engineering.*

Seldom mentioned in English chronologies, Deprez was a major innovator in many fields of technology. After graduating from the National School of Mines, he served as the school's secretary from 1866 to 1872. In this period he invented improved valve and indicator mechanisms for steam engines. During the 1870 siege of Paris he conducted pioneer researches, using instruments of his own creation, on the instantaneous gas pressure, metal strain, projectile velocity, and recoil motion produced in the firing of mortar cannon. For this work and for the invention of a railway dynamometer car he received two prizes from the Académie des Sciences.

Deprez was an early promoter, after 1875, of employing electric power in industry, and he collaborated with d'Arsonval and J. Carpentier in the design and manufacture of a wide variety of direct-current measuring instruments, and adapted small motors to manufacturing and domestic uses. He invented compound winding for voltage and speed stabilization in d.c. machines and showed how the operation of such machines could be fully determined from "open-circuit" and "short-circuit" characteristics.

Convinced of the commercial importance of transmitting power electrically, Deprez presented four dramatic and historic public demonstrations of d.c. electric power transmission, the first at Munich in 1881 and the last in 1886 when he sent seventy-five kilowatts over fifty kilometers of line from Creil to Paris. The 5,800-volt dynamo used was of his own design. He and Carpentier foresaw the advantages of high-voltage a.c. power transmission using transformers and patented the principle in 1881, but they did not develop it commercially.

Deprez was elected to the Académie des Sciences in 1886. In 1890 he was appointed professor of electrotechnology at the Conservatoire des Arts et Métiers. Deprez's work in the areas cited and on other topics, such as the laws of friction, the mechanical equivalent of heat, planimeters, and electric clocks, is described in more than sixty scientific papers, mainly in the *Comptes rendus de l'Académie des sciences*.

BIBLIOGRAPHY

Deprez's works are listed in Poggendorff. *Revue générale de l'électricité* published a special issue (Paris, 1935) commemorating the fiftieth anniversary of Deprez's power-transmission demonstration at Creil. Two obituaries appear in *Comptes rendus de l'Académie des sciences,* **167** (1918), 570–574; and *Electrician* (17 Jan. 1919).

ROBERT A. CHIPMAN

DERHAM, WILLIAM (*b.* Stoughton, Worcestershire, England, 26 November 1657; *d.* Upminster, Essex, England, 5 April 1735), *natural history, natural theology.*

Derham attended Blockley Grammar School and, on 14 May 1675, entered Trinity College, Oxford. He graduated B.A. on 28 January 1679. Ralph Bathurst, the president of the college, recommended him to Bishop Seth Ward, who obtained a chaplaincy for him. He was ordained a deacon of the Church of England in 1681 and priest in 1682, when he was appointed vicar of Wargrave. In 1689 he became vicar of Upminster, not far from London, where he lived for the rest of his life. In 1702 Derham was elected a fellow of the Royal Society, and in 1711–1712 he delivered the course of Boyle Lectures. On the accession of George I in 1714, he was made chaplain to the Prince of Wales, later George II. In 1716 he became a canon of Windsor, and in 1730 was awarded the degree of doctor of divinity by the University of Oxford. Tall, healthy, and strong, he acted as physician as well as parson in Upminster. His eldest son, William, became president of St. John's College, Oxford.

Derham published a number of papers in the *Philosophical Transactions of the Royal Society* on meteorology, on astronomy, and on natural history—his paper of 1724 on the sexes of wasps was admired. But it is for his editing of works by Robert Hooke and John Ray, and for his books on natural theology, that he is remembered. Ray's *Synopsis methodica avium et piscium* had been sent to a bookseller in 1694; but the latter was in no hurry to publish it, and it remained in manuscript on his shelves until the firm went out of business. On its rediscovery, Derham saw it through the press in 1713. Also in 1713 he supervised a new edition of Ray's *Physico-Theological Discourses* and in 1714, a new edition of his *Wisdom of God.* In 1718 Derham edited Ray's *Philosophical Letters* and wrote a short biography of Ray, which did not appear in print until 1760. After Hooke's death Richard Waller edited some of his papers, publishing them in 1705 as *The Posthumous Works of Robert Hooke.* On Waller's death, Hooke's papers passed to Derham, who in 1726 published them as *Philosophical Experiments . . . of . . . Dr. Robert Hooke.* Also in 1726 he prepared a new edition of *Miscellanea curiosa,* a collection of important scientific papers from various sources.

Of Derham's own works, those of greatest interest are *The Artificial Clockmaker, Physico-Theology* (Boyle Lectures), and *Astro-Theology,* all of which were very successful and went through many editions. *Physico-Theology* was translated into French, Swedish, and German, and *Astro-Theology* into German. None of them shows great originality. *The Artificial Clockmaker* is a useful manual containing some of Hooke's ideas on clockwork, notably on the spiral spring balance, which Hooke claimed to have invented before Christiaan Huygens.

Physico-Theology owes much to Ray's *Wisdom of God,* but it became better known in the eighteenth century than Ray's book and was heavily used by

William Paley. Derham's tone was bland; he sought only to show that this is the best of all possible worlds. Venomous reptiles were difficult to account for, but he reflected that they were mostly to be found in heathen countries. Taken seriously, however, the book abounds in arguments from design to God; and anybody who read it would have acquired a respectable amount of natural history—as one would expect from an author who was himself a naturalist and a friend of John Ray.

Astro-Theology was a similar attempt to argue from astronomy to God, and here again Derham was as well qualified as anybody to do it. He made observations with some of Huygens' telescopes and knew Halley and Newton. The main interest of the book is the distinction between the Copernican system and the new system, in which the universe was infinite and every star a sun, presumably surrounded by populated planets. Although works of natural theology such as these seem tedious in style, they do give a useful glimpse of the background of eighteenth-century science in England.

BIBLIOGRAPHY

I. ORIGINAL WORKS. Derham's writings include *The Artificial Clockmaker* (London, 1696); *Physico-Theology* (London, 1713); and *Astro-Theology* (London, 1714). He edited *Philosophical Experiments and Observations of the Late Eminent Dr. Robert Hooke, and Other Eminent Virtuoso's in His Time* (London, 1726).

II. SECONDARY LITERATURE. On Derham or his work, see A. D. Atkinson, "William Derham, F.R.S. (1657–1735)," in *Annals of Science*, **8** (1952), 368–392; the article in *Biographia britannica*, III; and C. E. Raven, *John Ray, Naturalist* (Cambridge, 1950), pp. xiii–xv.

D. M. KNIGHT

DEROSNE, (LOUIS-)CHARLES (*b.* Paris, France, 23 January 1780; *d.* Paris, 21 September 1846), *chemistry, industrial technology, invention.*

Derosne belonged to a family of pharmacists. His father, François Derosne, was associated with the famous Paris apothecary Louis-Claude Cadet (known as Cadet de Gassicourt). After the death of François Derosne in 1796, the Cadet-Derosne pharmacy on the rue St. Honoré was taken over by Charles's older brother, Jean-François, whose chemical analysis of opium (published in the *Annales de chimie* in 1803) foreshadowed the emergence of alkaloid chemistry as an important field of research. For a time Charles was associated with Jean-François in the practice of pharmacy and in several joint scientific and technological

projects. Perhaps the most important result of their collaboration was the investigation in 1807 of the properties of acetone, which they prepared by distilling copper acetate. Both brothers were admitted to the Academy of Medicine in Paris, Jean-François in 1821 and Charles in 1823.

Pharmacy proved too confining, however, for Charles Derosne, who very early in his career demonstrated a remarkable ability for technological innovation. A lifelong interest in improving methods of sugar production led him to introduce new techniques and equipment into sugar technology. In 1808 he refined crude sugar with alcohol, and by 1811 he was able to improve on the methods of beet sugar manufacture described by the contemporary German chemists S. F. Hermbstädt and F. C. Achard. Derosne's innovations and observations were included in his notes to the French translation of Achard's treatise on beet sugar manufacture, published with D. Angar in 1812. Derosne prepared animal charcoal and used it to purify sugar syrup. In 1817 he invented a continuous distillation apparatus and shortly thereafter began to produce other machinery of value in sugar refining at his plant in Chaillot.

Derosne's subsequent partnership with one of his employees, J.-F. Cail, resulted in a rapid expansion and diversification of his business. The Derosne-Cail establishment moved into the manufacture of industrial machinery, locomotives, and railway equipment. By the time of Derosne's death in 1846, an industrial empire had been founded, with factories in Paris, Belgium, Cuba, and Denain, and in 1847 branches were opened in Valenciennes, Douai, and Amsterdam.

BIBLIOGRAPHY

I. ORIGINAL WORKS. Derosne's writings include "Expériences et observations sur la distillation de l'acétate de cuivre et sur ses produits," in *Annales de chimie*, **63** (1807), 267–286, written with J.-F. Derosne; *Traité complet sur le sucre européen de betteraves; culture de cette plante considérée sous le rapport agronomique et manufacturier. Traduction abrégée de M. Achard, par M. D. Angar. Précédé d'une introduction et accompagné de notes . . . par M. Ch. Derosne . . .* (Paris, 1812), the French translation of Achard's work, done with D. Angar; and *De la fabrication du sucre aux colonies et des nouveaux appareils propres à améliorer cette fabrication . . .*, 2 pts. (Paris, 1843–1844), written with J.-F. Cail.

II. SECONDARY LITERATURE. Brief biographies can be found in *Biographie universelle, ancienne et moderne*, L. G. Michaud and J. F. Michaud, eds., new ed., X, 461–462; *Dictionnaire de biographie française*, X (1965), 1144; *Le grand dictionnaire universel*, Pierre Larousse, ed., VI, 513; *La grande encyclopédie*, XIV, 197; and *Nouvelle biographie générale,* J. C. F. Hoefer, ed., XIII, 718. For an account of the growth of Établissements Derosne et Cail, see Bertrand Gille, *Recherches sur la formation de la grande entreprise capitaliste (1815–1848)* (Paris, 1959), p. 69; and Julien Turgan, *Les grandes usines de France, tableau de l'industrie française au XIXe siècle,* II (Paris, 1860–1868), 1–64. See also "Pharmaciens membres de l'Académie de Médecine," in *Figures pharmaceutiques françaises* (Paris, 1953), p. 263. Additional information about Derosne in connection with his work on phosphorus bottles or tubes ("briquets phosphoriques"), the precursors of phosphorus matches, will be found in Maurice Bouvet, "Les pharmaciens et la découverte des allumettes et briquets," in *Revue d'histoire de la pharmacie,* **11** (Mar. 1954), 230–231.

ALEX BERMAN

DERYUGIN, KONSTANTIN MIKHAILOVICH (*b.* St. Petersburg, Russia, 10 February, 1878; *d.* Moscow, U.S.S.R., 27 December 1938), *earth science, oceanography, zoology.*

From 1896 to 1900 Deryugin was a student in the natural sciences section of St. Petersburg University. In 1899 he took part in a scientific expedition to the White Sea; and from that time on, marine organisms and their habitat became his main scientific interest. After graduation Deryugin remained at the university, in the department of zoology and comparative anatomy, to do research and to teach. He also visited the United States and western Europe, where he became acquainted with the organization of foreign research in oceanography. In 1909 he defended his master's thesis and began to lecture in a course entitled "Life of the Sea."

In 1915 Deryugin defended his dissertation for the doctorate in zoology and comparative anatomy. In 1917 he was made a lecturer at St. Petersburg University and, in 1919, professor. From 1920 he combined teaching with substantial research and administrative responsibilities as deputy director and manager of the oceanic section of the State Hydrological Institute in Leningrad.

Deryugin won fame chiefly as taxonomist of a number of groups of marine organisms (fishes, mollusks, and several others). He also studied the distribution of marine fauna in relation to the environment.

In 1915 Deryugin published his chief work, "Fauna Kolskogo zaliva . . ." ("The Fauna of Kola Bay"), in which he gave the first detailed analysis of the system of zones and biological communities (biocenoses) of the Barents Sea. His full description of the pattern of fauna and flora shows their regular distribution in relation to environmental conditions. This broad approach led Deryugin to consider the history of the fauna of the Barents Sea, and then the history of the

sea itself, the structure of the shores and bottom, its geology and petrography, and its hydrology and hydrochemistry.

In 1921 Deryugin reestablished regular hydrological sampling of the Barents Sea (which had been interrupted by the war) along the Kola meridian (33°30′ east longitude) to 75° north latitude and even farther. It soon became clear that the warm currents of the North Cape stream intersected by these samplings frequently change their positions. This discovery had a profound influence on the development of the fishing industry in the Barents Sea, since it showed a connection between the current of warm Atlantic waters and changes of the marine fauna. In particular, as Deryugin demonstrated, these warm currents were responsible for the appearance in the Barents Sea of warm-water forms not previously observed there and for their rapid diffusion to the shores of Novaya Zemlya.

The work of Deryugin and his students, from 1922 on, laid the foundations of present knowledge of the hydrology and biology of the White Sea, a body of water sharply different from other inland seas. Deryugin showed that this comparatively small sea consists of three parts: the basin of the sea itself, the Gorlo Strait, and its funnel. He explained the difference in biological environment between the White Sea and the neighboring Barents Sea by the intensified tidal mingling of waters from the surface to the bottom in the Gorlo Strait, a phenomenon that presented an insurmountable barrier to the dispersion of organisms.

The Pacific Ocean expedition of 1932–1933, which was organized at Deryugin's initiative and worked under his immediate direction, thoroughly investigated the Sea of Okhotsk and the parts of the Sea of Japan, the Bering Sea, and the Chukchi Sea bordering on the Soviet Union. The hydrological samplings were made from six fishing trawlers that collected at depths as great as 3,500 meters. Some work of the expedition was continued in following years. This research, in the course of which the fauna and flora of the Far Eastern seas of the Soviet Union were first seriously studied, brought to light what Deryugin termed a "new world of organisms." In some groups up to 50 percent new forms were found.

Deryugin was responsible for and participated in more than fifty scientific expeditions in twelve bodies of water bordering the Soviet Union. He organized and directed important oceanographic institutions: the Murmansk biological station on the shore of Kola Bay, in Yekaterin Harbor (now Polyarny; 1903–1904) and the Pacific Ocean Scientific Trade Station in Vladivostok (now the Pacific Ocean Scientific Research Institute of Fishing Economy and Oceanography; 1925).

Deryugin gave special attention to the methodological side of oceanographic research. He was responsible for the creation and operation of special methodological stations in the Neva Inlet of the Gulf of Finland (1920), on the White Sea (1931), and on Kamchatka (1932). He organized the design and production of oceanographic instruments in the Soviet Union and spent much of his strength and energy on the planning and building of special ocean research ships.

Deryugin was a member of the Society of Natural Scientists in Leningrad and a life member of the Linnaean Society of Lyons.

BIBLIOGRAPHY

I. ORIGINAL WORKS. The most important of Deryugin's more than 160 published scientific works are "Fauna Kolskogo zaliva i uslovia yeyo sushchestvovania" ("The Fauna of Kola Bay and Its Environment"), in *Zapiski Akademii nauk, fiziko-matematicheskoe otdelenie* ("Notes of the Academy of Sciences, Physics and Mathematics Section"), 8th ser., **34,** no. 1 (1915); "Fauna Belogo morya i uslovia yeyo sushchestvovania" ("The Fauna of the White Sea and Its Environment"), in *Issledovania morey SSSR* ("Investigations of the Seas of the USSR"), no. 7–8 (Leningrad, 1928); "Gidrologia i biologia" ("Hydrology and Biology"), in *Issledovania morey SSSR* ("Investigations of the Seas of the USSR"), no. 11 (Leningrad, 1930), pp. 37–45; "Vlianie prolivov i ikh gidrologicheskogo rezhima na faunu morey i yeyo dalneyshuyu evolyutsiyu" ("The Influence of Straits and Their Hydrological Systems on the Fauna of the Seas and Its Further Evolution"), in *Zapiski Gosudarstvennogo gidrologicheskogo instituta* ("Notes of the State Hydrological Institute"), **10** (1933), 369–374; "Issledovania morey SSSR v biograficheskom otnoshenii" ("Investigations of the Seas of the USSR in Terms of Biogeography"), in *Trudy Pervogo Vsesoyuznogo geograficheskogo sezda (11–18 oktyabrya 1933)* ("Works of the First All-Union Geographical Congress . . ."), pt. 2 (Leningrad, 1934), pp. 36–45; "Uspekhi sovetskoy gidrobiologii v oblasti izuchenia morey" ("The Progress of Soviet Hydrobiology in the Field of Ocean Studies"), in *Uspekhi sovremennoi biologii* ("Progress of Contemporary Biology"), **5,** no. 1 (1936), 9–23; and "Osnovnye cherty sovremennykh faun morey SSSR i veroyatnye puti ikh evolyutsii" ("The Basic Outlines of Contemporary Fauna of the Seas of the USSR and the Probable Course of Their Evolution"), in *Uchenye zapiski Leningradskogo . . . gosudarstvennogo universiteta* ("Scientific Notes of the Leningrad State University"), **3,** no. 17 (1937), 237–248.

II. SECONDARY LITERATURE. Important publications on Deryugin are E. F. Guryanova, "Professor K. M. Deryugin," in *Vestnik Leningradskogo gosudarstvennogo universiteta* ("Leningrad State Herald University"), no. 8 (1949), pp. 81–92; and V. V. Timonov, P. V. Ushakov, and S. Y. Mittelman, "Konstantin Mikhailovich Deryugin kak okeanolog" ("Konstantin Mikhailovich Deryugin as Oceanographer"), in *Trudy Gosudarstvennogo okeanograficheskogo instituta* ("Works of the State Oceanographic Institute"), no. 1, sec. 13 (1947), pp. 9–18.

A. F. PLAKHOTNIK

DESAGULIERS, JOHN THEOPHILUS (*b.* La Rochelle, France, 12 March 1683; *d.* London, England, 10 March 1744), *experimental natural philosophy.*

Desaguliers was taken to Guernsey when he was less than three years old by his Huguenot parents, who in 1694 settled in Islington, where the father taught school and educated his son. After his father's death Desaguliers entered Christ Church, Oxford (28 October 1705), whence he proceeded B.A. in 1709. About this time James Keill abandoned the lectureship in experimental philosophy at Hart Hall that he had held for some ten years; he was succeeded by Desaguliers, who took his M.A. from this college on 3 May 1712. In that year he moved to Channel Row, Westminster, no doubt in the hope of gaining a more remunerative audience. His first book, a translation of *A Treatise on Fortification* from the French of Ozanam, had already appeared (Oxford, 1711).

Continuing in London the style of scientific lecturing he had inherited from Keill, and having taken orders, he was given the living of Whitchurch and Little Stanmore, near Edgeware, to which royal favor later added other benefices. Before long Desaguliers was initiated into No. 4 Lodge of the Freemasons, meeting at the Rummer and Grapes Inn, Channel Row; and by 1719 he had become the third grand master of the recently constituted Grand Lodge of the order. It is said that Desaguliers induced Frederick, prince of Wales, to become a Freemason and also that through him "Freemasonry emerged from its original lowly station and became a fashionable cult" (Stokes). It was at the behest of one such fashionable past grand master, the duke of Wharton (Pope's "scorn and wonder of our days"), that in 1723 Desaguliers (then deputy master) dedicated to the grand master (the duke of Montagu) James Anderson's *Constitutions of the Free-Masons* (in a preface). Others of the Royal Society, to which Desaguliers belonged, joined this distinguished fraternity.

Desaguliers' practical abilities aroused the Royal Society's interest soon after his arrival in London. Late in the winter of 1713/1714, at Newton's suggestion, he was invited to repeat some of Newton's experiments on heat; before long he had become a *de facto* curator of experiments. He was elected a fellow on 29 July 1714, being excused his admission money because of his previous services. Desaguliers continued to furnish the society with experiments until his death. For some time Sir Godfrey Copley's benefaction (1709) of £100 per annum was paid to him; and after the Copley Medal was instituted in 1731, it was awarded to Desaguliers three times as a mark of his experimental ingenuity. Between 1716 and 1742 he contributed no fewer than fifty-two papers to the *Philosophical Transactions,* the earlier ones chiefly on optics and mechanics, the later ones on electricity. In the age of the Bernoullis, Clairaut, Euler, and Maupertuis, Desaguliers' contributions to theoretical mechanics cannot be called outstanding. "Dissertation Concerning the Figure of the Earth" (*Philosophical Transactions,* **33** [1726]) is the most important, yet it follows Keill (correcting his chief error), who followed Huygens (I. Todhunter, *A History of the Mathematical Theories of Attraction . . .* [1873], pp. 103–108). This dissertation was criticized anonymously by Maupertuis in 1741.

In attempting a reconciliation of the measurement of "motion" by the Newtonians (momentum $= mv$) and by the Leibnizians (*vis viva* $= mv^2$), Desaguliers correctly argued that the quantities so expressed were different, and hence the dispute was merely verbal; yet he seems also to have held that the Newtonian concept was better supported by experiment. Desaguliers never employed analytical methods in these papers. In practical mechanics he was highly skilled, being the first English writer to give theoretical analyses of machines on the basis of statics, the ancient treatment of the five simple machines, and elementary dynamics. He was himself a practical improver of various devices, among them Musschenbroek's pyrometer, Stephen Gray's barometric level, Hales's sounding gauge, Joshua Haskins' force pump, and Savery's steam engine. Desaguliers claimed that his improved form of Savery's engine was twice as efficient as the Newcomen pump. He also devised a centrifugal air pump for ventilating rooms, which was employed at the House of Commons. He had the advantage of relying upon Bélidor and his friend Henry Beighton (a Warwickshire engineer) in compiling a very up-to-date account of mechanical practice, including the railroad and steam engine. He clearly understood that a man or a horse could do only a finite amount of work in a given time, no matter what machinery might be used, and understood the fallacy of perpetual motion.

Desaguliers' optical experiments (*Philosophical Transactions,* **29** [1716]) were for the most part repetitions of those described by Newton, made in order to vindicate Newton's accuracy—which had been challenged—and the theoretical conclusions Newton had drawn. Some of them were improved in detail—for example, by the use of a camera obscura. Desaguliers taught that light is a "body" and that reflection, refraction, and diffraction are caused by the varying attractions between light and the media through which it moves. He also hinted at a similarity between the force of electricity and the force of cohesion, which he investigated experimentally. He made little use of the concept of ether (although not wholly avoiding the term), speaking, for instance, of "vacuities" between the particles of matter (the existence of which he thought he could demonstrate experimentally); rather, Desaguliers clung to that part of the Newtonian tradition which emphasized the duality of forces: "There seem to be but two Powers, or general Agents in Nature, which, according to different Circumstances, are concern'd in all the Phaenomena and Changes in Nature; viz. Attraction (meaning the Attraction of Gravity, as well as that of Cohaesion, etc.) and Repulsion" (*Course of Experimental Philosophy,* II, 407). Accordingly, Desaguliers, following Newton's hint, firmly attributed the elasticity of air to a repulsion between its particles. On all such points it might be said that he was "plus Newtonien que Newton," writing of the *Opticks* that it contained a "vast Fund of Philosophy; which (tho' he [Newton] has modestly delivered under the name of *Queries,* as if they were only Conjectures) daily Experiments and Observations confirm," and citing Hales's *Vegetable Staticks* as a book that put several of the "Queries" beyond doubt and showed how well they were founded (*Course of Experimental Philosophy,* preface, pp. vi–vii).

Desaguliers described and demonstrated a great many electrical experiments to the Royal Society (*Philosophical Transactions,* **41, 42;** *Course of Experimental Philosophy,* II, 316–335), although he refrained from so doing until after the death in 1736 of Stephen Gray—who, it is said, lived with Desaguliers and assisted him. This work certainly contributed greatly to the popularization of electrical science. Desaguliers studied charging, conduction, discharge in air, attraction and repulsion, the effects of dryness and moisture, and so forth, using a fragment of thread as detector. He distinguished "electrics per se," which could be charged by friction and so on, from "non-electric bodies," which were incapable of receiving charge directly although they were capable of being electrified indirectly when suitably suspended. Desaguliers did not make a parallel distinction between insulators and conductors, nor did he realize that a "non-electric body" could become an "electric per se" if properly insulated. Nor did he understand the role of leakage to earth in conduction experiments. At a very late stage he commented on the distinction between vitreous and resinous electricity established by Du Fay.

Until the end of his life Desaguliers retained his preeminence as a demonstrative lecturer in the Royal Society, at court, and in his own home (where he took in student boarders). By 1734 he had repeated his course on astronomy, mechanics, hydrostatics, optics, electricity, and machinery more than 120 times. Although he acknowledged that Keill had first "publickly taught Natural Philosophy by Experiments in a mathematical Manner" (the instrument maker Hawksbee had also begun to demonstrate experiments to the public at about the same time), it was Desaguliers who popularized the demonstrative lecture in Britain. (A sample of the scene is provided in two well-known pictures by Joseph Wright of Derby, *ca.* 1760.) "Without Observations and Experiments," he wrote in the preface to the first volume of his *Course of Experimental Philosophy* (1734), "our natural Philosophy would only be a Science of Terms and an unintelligible jargon." By deliberate choice he demonstrated to the eye not only things discovered by experiment but also those "deduc'd by a long Train of mathematical consequences; having contrived Experiments, which Step by Step bring us to the same Conclusions," for he recognized that the Newtonian philosophy was not accessible to all through mathematics. Thus Desaguliers occupies a leading position (along with Keill, Pemberton, and Maclaurin) among those who gave Newtonian science its ascendancy in eighteenth-century England. Not that Desaguliers wholly avoided mathematical reasoning; on the contrary, he employed it continually, but only in simple terms and as an adjunct to empirical evidence. Desaguliers did nothing for serious mathematical physics.

Naturally, Desaguliers was eager to publicize rather than to publish his material. In 1717 he issued as *Physico-Mechanical Lectures* an eighty-page abstract of the twenty-two lectures in the course for the benefit of auditors who did not wish to make their own notes. Two years later one Paul Dawson edited *A System of Experimental Philosophy, Prov'd by Mechanicks . . . As Performed by J. T. Desaguliers.* The lecturer did not produce his own version until 1734 (*A Course of Experimental Philosophy,* Volume I) when he took occasion to denounce this unauthorized version. Meanwhile he was content to print only short syllabi of his lectures: *Mechanical and Experimental Philosophy* (1724) and *Experimental Course of Astronomy* (1725). The former exists in both French and English versions, Desaguliers advertising his willingness to teach in these languages and Latin. At last the long-promised first volume of the *Course* appeared in

1734, containing five long lectures and many additional notes. It is devoted wholly to theoretical and practical mechanics, including both a simple treatment of Newton's system of the world and a description of Mr. Allen's railroad at Bath. Desaguliers attributed the ten-year delay before the appearance of his second tome to his desire to improve the treatment of machines, especially waterwheels; he excused himself for omitting optics altogether, referring the reader to Robert Smith's *Complete System of Opticks.* Continuing with mechanics, in seven lectures he discussed impact and elasticity, *vis viva* and momentum, heat, hydrostatics and hydraulics, pneumatics, meteorology, and more machines. This second volume is even more concerned with applied science and engineering than the first and entitles Desaguliers to be considered a forerunner of the more advanced knowledge of machinery that characterized the Industrial Revolution. Certainly its influence was greater upon practical men and inventors than upon physicists.

Desaguliers was married on 14 October 1712 to Joanna Pudsey, by whom he had several children; the youngest, Thomas, distinguished himself as an artilleryman. About 1739 the construction of the approaches to Westminster Bridge (upon whose design Desaguliers was consulted) necessitated the destruction of Channel Row; he moved his home and classes to the Bedford Coffee House in Covent Garden, where he died. He was buried in the Savoy Chapel, and there is no good reason for supposing him indigent. There are (or were) at least two portraits of Desaguliers: by H. Hysing (1725), engraved by Peter Pelham, and by Thomas Frye (1743), engraved by R. Scaddon.

BIBLIOGRAPHY

I. ORIGINAL WORKS. Desaguliers published translations besides that already mentioned: *Fires Improv'd: Being a New Method of Building Chimneys, so as to Prevent Their Smoaking,* from the French by Nicolas Gauger (London, 1715), mostly about an elaborate form of fire grate; *The Motion of Water and Other Fluids,* from the French by Edmé Mariotte (London, 1718); *The Mathematical Elements of Natural Philosophy,* from the Latin by W. J. 'sGravesande (London, 1720); *The Whole Works of Dr. Archibald Pitcairne,* from the Latin (London, 1727), with G. Sewell; and *An Account of the Mechanism of an Automaton,* from the French by J. de Vaucanson (London, 1742). Most were reprinted.

Desaguliers' own writings, in addition to those already discussed, were *The Newtonian System, an Allegorical Poem* (London, 1728), written on the accession of George II; an Appendix on the reflecting telescope, pp. 211–288 in William Brown's translation *Dr. Gregory's Elements of Catoptrics and Dioptrics* (London, 1735), which contains most of the correspondence between Newton and others relating to the development of Newton's form of that instrument in 1668 and subsequently; and *A Dissertation Concerning Electricity* (London, 1742), the French version of which (Bordeaux, 1742) received a prize awarded by the Académie de Bordeaux (*Course of Experimental Philosophy*, II, 335).

There are MSS by Desaguliers in the Sloane and Birch collections of the British Museum and in the archives of the Royal Society.

II. SECONDARY LITERATURE. Modern studies of Desaguliers include Jean Barlais, in *Les archives de Trans en Provence,* **61**, 281–288, for more on his freemasonry; I. Bernard Cohen, *Franklin and Newton* (Philadelphia, 1956), esp. pp. 243–261, 376–384, mainly on electricity; D. C. Lee, *Desaguliers of No. 4 and His Services to Freemasonry* (London, 1932); Paul R. Major, *The Physical Researches of J. T. Desaguliers,* M. Sc. thesis, London University, 1962, with bibliography; and Jean Torlais, *Un Rochelais grand-maître de la Franc-Maçonnerie et physicien au XVIIIe siècle: Le Reverend J.-T. Desaguliers* (La Rochelle, 1937).

A. RUPERT HALL

DESARGUES, GIRARD (*b.* Lyons, France, 21 February 1591; *d.* France, October 1661), *geometry, perspective.*

One of the nine children of Girard Desargues, collector of the tithes on ecclesiastical revenues in the diocese of Lyons, and of Jeanne Croppet, Desargues seems to have studied at Lyons, where the family lived. The first evidence of his scientific activity places him in Paris on 9 September 1626, when, with another Lyonnais, François Villette, he proposed to the municipality that it construct powerful machines to raise the water of the Seine, in order to be able to distribute it in the city. Adrien Baillet, the biographer of Descartes, declares that Desargues participated as an engineer at the siege of La Rochelle in 1628 and that he there made the acquaintance of Descartes, but there is no evidence to confirm this assertion. According to the engraver Abraham Bosse (1602–1676), a fervent disciple of Desargues, the latter obtained a royal license for the publication of several writings in 1630. It was about this time that Desargues, living in Paris, seems to have become friendly with several of the leading mathematicians there: Mersenne, Gassendi, Mydorge, and perhaps Roberval. Although it is not certain that he attended the meetings at Théophraste Renaudot's Bureau d'Adresses (commencing in 1629), Mersenne cites him, in 1635, as one of those who regularly attended the meetings of his Académie Parisienne, in which, besides Mersenne, the following participated more or less regularly: Étienne Pascal, Mydorge, Claude Hardy, Roberval, and soon Carcavi and the young Blaise Pascal.

In 1636 Desargues published two works: "Une méthode aisée pour apprendre et enseigner à lire et escrire la musique," included in Mersenne's *Harmonie universelle* (I, bk. 6), and a twelve-page booklet with one double plate that was devoted to the presentation of his "universal method" of perspective. The latter publication bore a signature that reappeared on several of Desargues's important works: S.G.D.L. (Sieur Girard Desargues Lyonnais).

Moreover, after presenting his rules of practical perspective, Desargues gave some indication of the vast program he had set for himself, a program dominated by two basic themes: on the one hand, the concern to rationalize, to coordinate, and to unify the diverse graphical techniques by his "universal methods" and, on the other, the desire to integrate the projective methods into the body of mathematics by means of a purely geometric study of perspective, several elements of which are presented in an appendix. This publication appears not to have excited a great deal of immediate interest among artists and draftsmen, who were hardly anxious to change their technique; in contrast, Descartes and Fermat, to whom Mersenne had communicated it, were able to discern Desargues's ability.

The publication in 1636 of Jean de Beaugrand's *Geostatice,* then of Descartes's *Discours de la méthode* in May 1637, gave rise to ardent discussions among the principal French thinkers on the various problems mentioned in the two books: the definition of the center of gravity, the theory of optics, the problem of tangents, the principles of analytic geometry, and so on. Desargues participated very actively in these discussions. Although he made Beaugrand his implacable enemy, his sense of moderation, his concern to eliminate all misunderstandings, and his desire to comprehend problems in their most universal aspect won him the esteem and the respect of Descartes and Mersenne, as well as of Fermat, Roberval, and Étienne Pascal. His letter to Mersenne of 4 April 1638, concerning the discussion of the problem of tangents, illustrates the depth of the insights with which he approached such questions and, at the same time, his inclination to synthesis and the universal. Even though Descartes had prepared for him an introduction to his *Géométrie,* designed to "facilitate his understanding" of it, Desargues did not follow Descartes in his parallel attempts to algebraize geometry and to create a new system of explaining all the phenomena of the universe.

Desargues's goal was at once to breathe new life into geometry, to rationalize the various graphical techniques, and, through mechanics, to extend this renewal to several areas of technique. His profound intuition of spatial geometry led him to prefer a thorough renewal of the methods of geometry rather than the Cartesian algebraization; from this preference there resulted a broad extension of the possibilities of geometry. The *Brouillon project* on conics, of which he published fifty copies in 1639, is a daring projective presentation of the theory of conic sections; although considered at first in three-dimensional space, as plane sections of a cone of revolution, these curves are in fact studied as plane perspective figures by means of involution, a transformation that holds a place of distinction in the series of demonstrations. But the use of an original vocabulary and the refusal to resort to Cartesian symbolism make the reading of this essay rather difficult and partially explain its meager success.

Although he praised the unitary conception that inspired Desargues, Descartes doubted that the use of geometry alone could yield results as good as those that a recourse to algebra would provide. As for Fermat, he reserved his judgment, and the only geometer who really comprehended the originality and breadth of Desargues's views was the young Blaise Pascal, who in 1640 published the brief *Essay pour les coniques,* inspired directly by the *Brouillon project.* But since the great *Traité des coniques* that Pascal later wrote has been lost, Desargues's example survived only in certain of the youthful works of Philippe de La Hire and perhaps in a few essays of the young Newton. The rapid success of the Cartesian method of applying algebra to geometry was certainly one of the basic reasons for the poor diffusion of Desargues's ideas. In any case the principles of projective geometry included in the *Brouillon project* were virtually forgotten until the publication in 1820 of the *Traité des propriétés projectives* of J. V. Poncelet—who, moreover, rendered a stirring homage to his precursor, although he knew his work only from a few brief mentions.

In July 1639 Beaugrand criticized Desargues's work, asserting that certain of his demonstrations can be drawn much more directly from Apollonius. Irritated that Desargues, in an appendix to his study of conic sections, had discussed the principles of mechanics and had criticized Beaugrand's conception of geostatics, Beaugrand wrote in July 1640, a few months before his death, another violent pamphlet against the *Brouillon project.*

In August 1640, Desargues published, again under the general title *Brouillon project,* an essay on techniques of stonecutting and on gnomonics. While refining certain points of his method of perspective presented in 1636, he gives an example of a new graphical method whose use he recommends in stonecutting and furnishes several principles that will simplify construction of sundials. He cites the names of a few artists and artisans who have already adopted the graphical methods he advocates: in particular the painter Laurent de La Hire and the engraver Abraham Bosse. In attempting thus to improve the graphical procedures employed by many technicians, Desargues was in fact attacking an area of activity governed by the laws of the trade guilds; he also drew the open hostility of all those who were attached to the old methods and felt they were being injured by his preference for theory rather than practice.

At the end of 1640 Desargues published a brief commentary on the principles of gnomonics presented in his *Brouillon project;* this text is known only through several references, in particular the opinion of Descartes, who found it a "very beautiful invention and so much the more ingenious in that it is so simple." Since 1637 Descartes had conducted an indirect correspondence with Desargues that had been established through Mersenne, and the two men had exchanged ideas on a number of subjects; in this way Desargues took an active part in the discussions that preceded the definite statement and the publication of Descartes's *Méditations.*

At the beginning of 1641 Desargues had Mersenne propose to his mathematical correspondents that they determine circular sections on cones having a conic for a base and any vertex. He himself had a general solution obtained solely by the methods of pure geometry, a solution that is known to us through Mersenne's comments (in *Universae geometriae mixtaeque mathematicae synopsis* [Paris, 1644], the preface to Mydorge's *Coniques,* pp. 330–331). Roberval, Descartes, and Pascal were interested in the problem, which Desargues generalized in his investigation of the plane sections of cones satisfying the above conditions. References in publications of the period seem to indicate that around 1641 Desargues published a second essay on conic sections, cited sometimes under the title of *Leçons de ténèbres.* But since no copy of this work has been found, one may suppose that there may be some confusion here with another work, either the *Brouillon project* of 1639 or with a preliminary edition of certain manuscripts on perspective that were later included in Bosse's *Manière universelle de Mr Desargues pour pratiquer la perspective . . .* (Paris, 1648). Yet a work that appeared later, Grégoire Huret's *Optique de portraiture et de peinture . . .* (Paris, 1670), specifies (pp. 157–158) that the *Leçons de ténèbres* is based on the principle of perspective that inasmuch as the sections of a cone with a circular base and any vertex are, for all cones, circles for two specific orientations of the cutting plane, therefore in general the projective properties of the circle may be extended to various types of conics, considered as perspectives of circles. This systematic recourse to considerations of spatial geometry obviously does not permit the identification of this work with either the *Brouillon project* of 1639 or the geometric texts of 1648 (mentioned below). But, in the absence of the decisive proof that would be provided by the rediscovery of a copy of the *Leçons de ténèbres,* no definite conclusion can be reached.

Desargues strove to spread the use of his graphical methods among practitioners and succeeded in having them experiment with his stonecutting diagrams without encountering very strong resistance. At the beginning of 1642, however, the anonymous publication of the first volume of *La perspective pratique* (written by the Jesuit Jean Dubreuil) gave rise to bitter polemics. Finding that his own method of perspective was both copied and distorted in this book, Desargues had two placards posted in Paris in which he accused the author and the publishers of this treatise of plagiarism and obtuseness. The publishers asserted that they had drawn his so-called "universal" method from a work by Vaulezard (*Abrégé ou raccourcy de la perspective par l'imitation* . . . [Paris, 1631]) and from a manuscript treatise of Jacques Aleaume (1562–1627) that was to be brought out by E. Migon (*La perspective spéculative et pratique . . . de l'invention de feu Jacques Aleaume . . . mise au jour par Estienne Migon* [Paris, 1643]). Desargues having replied with a new attack, Tavernier and l'Anglois, Dubreuil's publishers, brought out in 1642 a collection of anonymous pamphlets against Desargues's various writings on perspective, stonecutting, and gnomonics, to which they added the *Lettre de M. de Beaugrand . . .* of August 1640, which was directed against his projective study of conics.

Desargues, greatly affected by these attacks, which concerned the body of his work and put his competence and his honesty in question, entrusted to his most fervent disciple, the engraver Abraham Bosse, the task of spreading his methods and of defending his work. In 1643 Bosse devoted two treatises to presenting Desargues's methods in stonecutting and in gnomonics: *La pratique du trait á preuves de Mᵣ Desargues, Lyonnois, pour la coupe des pierres en l'architecture . . .* and *La manière universelle de Mᵣ Desargues, Lyonnois, pour poser l'essieu et placer les heures et autres choses aux cadrans au soleil.* Preceded by an "Acknowledgment" in which Desargues states he has given Bosse the responsibility for the spread of his methods, these works are clearly addressed to a less informed audience than the brief essays that Desargues had published on the same subjects. Their theoretical portion is greatly reduced and more elementary, and numerous examples of applications are handled in a very didactic and often prolix manner. Although only fifty copies of Desargues's essays had been printed, and had been distributed mainly in scientific circles, Bosse's writings were given large printings and were translated into several languages; consequently, they contributed to the diffusion of Desargues's graphical methods among practitioners.

In 1644, however, new attacks were launched against Desargues's work. They originated with a stonecutter, J. Curabelle, who violently criticized his writings on stonecutting, perspective, and gnomonics, as well as the two treatises Bosse published in 1643, claiming to find nothing in them but mediocrity, errors, plagiarism, and information of no practical interest. A very harsh polemic began between the two men, and Desargues published the pamphlet *Récit au vray de ce qui a esté la cause de faire cet escrit,* which contains a number of previously unpublished details on his life and work. He also attempted to sue Curabelle, but the latter seems to have succeeded in evading this action.

Although Desargues apparently gave up publishing, Abraham Bosse wrote an important treatise on his master's method of perspective, commenting in detail on a great many examples of the graphical processes deriving from the "universal method" outlined in 1636. This *Manière universelle de Mᵣ Desargues pour pratiquer la perspective par petit-pied, comme le géométral, ensemble les places et proportions des fortes et foibles touches, teintes ou couleurs* (Paris, 1648) was directly inspired by Desargues and contains, in addition to a reprint of the *Exemple de l'une des manières universelles . . .* of 1636, several elaborations designed "for theoreticians" and others that are purely geometrical. These elaborations, which include the statement and proof of the famous theorem on perspective triangles, should be considered (at least those relating to the theorem should be) as having been written by Desargues. Certain remarks seem to indicate that these theoretical developments may have been the subject of an earlier version published in 1643, under the title of *Livret de perspective,* but no definite proof has yet been established. In 1653 Bosse completed this work with an account of perspective on planes and on irregular surfaces, which included several applications to his favorite technique, copperplate engraving. Desargues's influence is again evident, at least in the first part of this work, but it is less direct than in the *Manière* of 1648.

Meanwhile, relations between the two men had become less close. While continuing his work as an engraver and an artist, Bosse, since 1648, had been teaching perspective according to Desargues's methods at the Académie Royale de Peinture et de Sculpture. He continued to teach there until 1661, when the Academy, following a long and violent polemic in which Desargues intervened personally in 1657, barred him from all his duties, thus implicitly condemning the use and diffusion of the methods of perspective to which it had accorded its patronage for thirteen years. But Bosse continued, through his writings, to conduct a passionate propaganda campaign for his methods.

As for Desargues, after 1644 evidence of his scientific and polemic activity becomes much rarer. Besides the "Acknowledgment" (dated 1 October 1647) and the geometric elaborations inserted in Bosse's 1648 treatise on perspective, Descartes's correspondence (letter to Mersenne of 31 January 1648) alludes to an experiment made by Desargues, toward the end of 1647, in the context of the debates and investigations then being conducted by the Paris physicists on the nature of the barometric space. It seems that while remaining in close contact with the Paris scientists, Desargues had commenced another aspect of his work, that of architect and practitioner. There was no better reply to give to his adversaries, who accused him of wanting to impose arbitrary work rules on disciplines that he understood only superficially and theoretically. Probably, as Baillet states, he had already been technical adviser and engineer in Richelieu's entourage, but he had not yet had any real contact with the graphical techniques he wished to reform. It seems that his new career as an architect, begun in Paris about 1645, was continued in Lyons, to which he returned around 1649–1650, then again in Paris, to which he returned in 1657. He remained there until 1661, the year of his death.

In Paris the authors of the period attribute to Desargues, besides a few houses and mansions, several staircases whose complex structure and spectacular character attest to the exactitude and efficacy of his graphical stonecutting procedures. It also seems that he collaborated, for the realization of certain effects of architectural perspective, with the famous painter Philippe de Champaigne. In the region of Lyons, Desargues's architectural creations were likewise quite numerous; he participated in the planning of several private and public buildings and of rooms whose architecture was particularly delicate. Of Desargues's accomplishments as an engineer, which seem to have been many, only one is well known and is worth mentioning: a system for raising water that he installed near Paris, at the château of Beaulieu. This system, based on the use, until then unknown, of epicycloidal wheels, was described and drawn by Huygens in 1671 (*Oeuvres de Huygens,* VII, 112), by which time the château had become the property of Charles Perrault. Philippe de La Hire, who had to repair this mechanism, wrote about it (see *Traité de méchanique* [Paris, 1695], pp. 10, 368–374).

To complete this description of Desargues's activity, it is necessary to mention the private instruction he gave at Paris in order to reveal his different graphical procedures. Even before 1640 he had several disciples at Paris, as well as at Lyons, where, Moreri states, he was "of great assistance to the workmen . . . to whom he communicated his diagrams and his knowledge, with no motive other than being useful" (*Le grand dictionnaire historique,* new ed., I [Paris, 1759], 297).

In 1660 Desargues was again active in the intellectual life of Paris, attending meetings at Montmor's Academy, such as one on 9 November 1660, at which Huygens heard him present a report on the problem of the existence of the geometric point and sharply discuss the matter with someone who contradicted him. This is the last trace of his activity; the reading of his will at Lyons on 8 October 1661 revealed only that he had died several days before, without stating the date or place of his death, concerning which no document has yet been found.

A geometer of profoundly original ideas, sustained at the same time by a sense of spatial reality, by a much more precise knowledge of the great classic works than he admitted, and by an exceptional familiarity with the whole range of contemporary techniques, Desargues, in his geometrical work, introduced the principal concepts of projective geometry: the consideration of points and straight lines to infinity, studies of poles and polars, the introduction of projective transformations, the general definition of focuses, the unitary study of conics, and so on. Unfortunately, his work, burdened by a too original vocabulary and the absence of symbolism, and known only in a very limited circle, did not receive the audience it deserved. The disappearance of the essential portion of the work of his chief disciple, Blaise Pascal, and the sudden vogue of analytic geometry and infinitesimal calculus prevented the seventeenth century from witnessing the revival of geometry for which Desargues had laid the foundations. His few known forays into other areas of mathematics and mechanics attest to a perfect mastery of all the problems then under discussion and make us regret the absence of any publication by him. In the field of graphical techniques his contribution is of major importance. Between Dürer and Monge he marks an essential stage in the rationalization of the ensemble of these techniques, as much by the improvements he made in the various procedures then in use as by his concern for unity, for theoretical rigor, and for universality. But in this vast area, too, his innovations were bitterly contested and often rejected with contempt, even though the goal of their author was to reduce the burden of the practitioners through a closer and more trusting collaboration with the theorists.

After the reception, often reserved and sometimes malicious, that it received in his time and the oblivion that it experienced subsequently, Desargues's work was rediscovered and fully appreciated by the geometers of the nineteenth century. Thus, like that of all precursors, his work revealed its fruitfulness much more by its remote extensions than by its immediate repercussions.

BIBLIOGRAPHY

I. ORIGINAL WORKS. Desargues's works, most of them published in editions of a small number of copies, are very rare. N. Poudra republished most of them in *Oeuvres de Desargues réunies et analysées . . .,* 2 vols. (Paris, 1864), but they are imperfect. The purely mathematical texts have been republished in an improved form by René Taton, as *L'oeuvre mathématique de Desargues* (Paris, 1951), pp. 75–212, with a bibliography of Desargues's writings and their editions, pp. 67–73. Aside from the polemic writings, prefaces, acknowledgments, and such, listed in the bibliography mentioned above, Desargues's main works and their most recent editions are the following: "Une méthode aisée pour apprendre et enseigner à lire et escrire la musique," in Mersenne's *Harmonie universelle,* I (Paris, 1638), bk. 6, prop. 1, pp. 332–342, repr. in photocopy (Paris, 1963); *Exemple de l'une des manières universelles du S.G.D.L. touchant la pratique de la perspective . . .* (Paris, 1636), also in Abraham Bosse, *Manière universelle de Mr Desargues pour pratiquer la perspective . . .* (Paris, 1648), pp. 321–334 (incorrect title), and in N. Poudra, *Oeuvres de Desargues,* I, 55–84, which follows the Bosse version; *Brouillon project d'une atteinte aux événemens des rencontres du cone avec un plan,* followed by *Atteinte aux événemens des contrarietez d'entre les actions des puissances ou forces* and an *Avertissement* (errata) (Paris, 1639), also in Poudra, I, 103–230, which includes omissions and errors, and in Taton, pp. 87–184, where the original version is reproduced without the figures; *Brouillon project d'exemple d'une manière universelle du S.G.D.L. touchant la practique du trait à preuves pour la coupe des pierres en l'architecture . . .* (Paris, 1640), also in Poudra, I, 305–358, with incorrect plates; original plates repub. by W. M. Ivins, Jr., in *Bulletin of the Metropolitan Museum of Art,* new ser., **1** (1942), 33–45; *Leçons de ténèbres* (Paris, 1640 [?]), which has not been found but may exist; *Manière universelle de poser le style aux rayons du soleil . . .* (Paris, 1640), which has not been found but whose existence is definite, partly reconstructed in Poudra, I, 387–392; and *Livret de perspective adressé aux théoriciens* (Paris, 1643 [?]), which has not been found but is perhaps identical with the last part of Abraham Bosse's *Manière universelle de Mr Desargues pour pratiquer la perspective . . .* (Paris, 1648), pp. 313–343.

II. SECONDARY LITERATURE. Desargues directly inspired three works by Abraham Bosse: *La manière universelle de Mr Desargues, Lyonnois, pour poser l'essieu et placer les heures et autres choses aux cadrans au soleil* (Paris, 1643), also trans. into English (London, 1659); *La pratique du trait à preuves de Mr Desargues, Lyonnois, pour la coupe des pierres en l'architecture* (Paris, 1643), also trans. into German (Nuremberg, 1699); and *Manière universelle de Mr Desargues pour pratiquer la perspective . . .,* 2 vols. (Paris, 1648–1653), also trans. into Dutch, 2 vols. (Amsterdam, 1664; 2nd ed., 1686).

A lengthy bibliography of secondary literature is given in Taton's *L'oeuvre mathématique de Desargues.* The most important works cited are the following (listed chronologically): A. Baillet, *La vie de Monsieur des Cartes,* 2 vols. (Paris, 1691), *passim;* R. P. Colonia, *Histoire littéraire de la ville de Lyon . . .,* II (Paris, 1730), 807 f.; L. Moreri, *Le grand dictionnaire historique,* new ed., I (Paris, 1759), 297; J. V. Poncelet, *Traité des propriétés projectives* (Paris, 1822), pp. xxxviii–xxxxiii; M. Chasles, *Aperçu historique sur l'origine et le développement des méthodes en géométrie . . .* (Brussels, 1837), see index; and *Rapport sur les progrès de la géométrie* (Paris, 1870), pp. 303–306; G. Poudra, "Biographie," in *Oeuvres de Desargues . . .,* I, 11–52; and *Histoire de la perspective* (Paris, 1864), pp. 249–270; G. Eneström, "Notice bibliographique sur un traité de perspective publié par Desargues en 1636," in *Bibliotheca mathematica,* **1** (1885), 89–90; "Die 'Leçons de ténèbres' des Desargues," *ibid.,* 3rd ser., **3** (1902), 411; "Über dem französischen Mathematiker Pujos," *ibid.,* **8** (1907–1908), 97; and "Girard Desargues und D.A.L.G.," *ibid.,* **14** (1914), 253–254; S. Chrzaszczewski, "Desargues Verdienste um die Begründung der projectivischen Geometrie," in *Archiv der Mathematik und Physik,* 2nd ser., **16** (1898), 119–149; E. L. G. Charvet, *Lyon artistique. Architectes . . .* (Lyons, 1899), pp. 120–122; F. Amodeo, "Nuovo analisi del trattato delle coniche di Gerard [sic] Desargues e cenni da J. B. Chauveau," in *Rendiconti dell'Accademia delle scienze fisiche e matematiche* (Naples), ser. 3a, **12** (1906), 232–262; and *Origine e sviluppo della geometria proiettiva* (Naples, 1939), *passim;* J. L. Coolidge, *The History of Geometrical Methods* (Oxford, 1940), pp. 90, 109; and *The History of Conic Sections and Quadric Surfaces* (Oxford, 1949), pp. 28–33; M. Zacharias, "Desargues Bedeutung für die projektive Geometrie," in *Deutsche Mathematik,* **5** (1941), 446–457; W. M. Ivins, Jr., "Two First Editions of Desargues," in *Bulletin of the Metropolitan Museum of Art,* n.s. **1** (1942), 33–45; "A Note of Girard Desargues," in *Scripta mathematica,* **9** (1943), 33–48; *Art and Geometry. A Study in Space Intuition* (Cambridge, Mass., 1946), pp. 103–112; and "A Note on Desargues's Theorem," in *Scripta mathematica,* **13** (1947), 202–210; and F. Lenger, "La notion d'involution dans l'oeuvre de Desargues," in *IIe Congrès national des sciences, Bruxelles . . .,* I (Liège, 1950), 109–112.

Some more recent studies that should be noted are the following (listed chronologically): P. Moisy, "Textes retrouvés de Desargues," in *XVIIe siècle*, no. 11 (1951), 93–95; R. Taton, "Documents nouveaux concernant Desargues," in *Archives internationales d'histoire des sciences*, **4** (1951), 620–630; and "Sur la naissance de Girard Desargues," in *Revue d'histoire des sciences*, **15** (1962), 165–166; A. Machabey, "Gérard [*sic*] Desargues, géomètre et musicien," in *XVIIe siècle*, no. 21–22 (1954), 346–402; P. Costabel, "Note sur l'annexe du Brouillon-Project de Desargues," in *7° Congrès international d'histoire des sciences. Jérusalem, 1953* (Paris, n.d.), pp. 241–245; A. Birembaut, "Quelques documents nouveaux sur Desargues," in *Revue d'histoire des sciences,* **14** (1961), 193–204; and S. Le Tourneur, in *Dictionnaire de biographie française,* X (1964), 1183–1184.

RENÉ TATON

DESCARTES, RENÉ DU PERRON (*b.* La Haye, Touraine, France, 31 March 1596; *d.* Stockholm, Sweden, 11 February 1650), *natural philosophy, scientific method, mathematics, optics, mechanics, physiology.*

Fontenelle, in the eloquent contrast made in his *Éloge de Newton,* described Descartes as the man who "tried in one bold leap to put himself at the source of everything, to make himself master of the first principles by means of certain clear and fundamental ideas, so that he could then simply descend to the phenomena of nature as to necessary consequences of these principles." This famous characterization of Descartes as the theoretician who "set out from what he knew clearly, in order to find the cause of what he saw," as against Newton the experimenter, who "set out from what he saw, in order to find the cause," has tended to dominate interpretations of both these men who "saw the need to carry geometry into physics."[1]

Descartes was born into the *noblesse de robe,* whose members contributed notably to intellectual life in seventeenth-century France. His father was *conseiller* to the Parlement of Brittany; from his mother he received the name du Perron and financial independence from property in Poitou. From the Jesuits of La Flèche he received a modern education in mathematics and physics—including Galileo's telescopic discoveries—as well as in philosophy and the classics, and there began the twin domination of imagination and geometry over his precocious mind. He described in an early work, the *Olympica,* how he found "in the writings of the poets weightier thoughts than in those of the philosophers. The reason is that the poets wrote through enthusiasm and the power of imagination." The seeds of knowledge in us, "as in a flint," were brought to light by philosophers "through reason; struck out through imagination by

poets they shine forth more brightly."[2] Then, after graduating in law from the University of Poitiers, as a gentleman volunteer in the army of Prince Maurice of Nassau in 1618 he met Isaac Beeckman at Breda. Beeckman aroused him to self-discovery as a scientific thinker and mathematician and introduced him to a range of problems, especially in mechanics and acoustics, the subject of his first work, the *Compendium musicae* of 1618; published posthumously in 1650. On 26 March 1619 he reported to Beeckman his first glimpse of "an entirely new science,"[3] which was to become his analytical geometry.

Later in the year, on 10 November, then in the duke of Bavaria's army on the Danube, he had the experience in the famous *poêle* (lit. "stove," "well-heated room"), claimed to have given direction to the rest of his life. He described in the *Discours de la méthode* how, in a day of solitary thought, he reached two radical conclusions: first, that if he were to discover true knowledge he must carry out the whole program himself, just as a perfect work of art or architecture was always the work of one master hand; second, that he must begin by methodically doubting everything taught in current philosophy and look for self-evident, certain principles from which to reconstruct all the sciences. That night, according to his seventeenth-century biographer Adrien Baillet, these resolutions were reinforced by three consecutive dreams. He found himself, first, in a street swept by a fierce wind, unable to stand, as his companions were doing, because of a weakness in his right leg; second, awakened by a clap of thunder in a room full of sparks; and third, with a dictionary, then a book in which he read *Quid vitae sectabor iter?* ("What way of life shall I follow?"), then verses presented by an unknown man beginning *Est et non;* he recognized the Latin as the opening lines of two poems by Ausonius. Before he finally awoke he had interpreted the first dream as a warning against past errors, the second as the descent of the spirit of truth, and the third as the opening to him of the path to true knowledge. However this incident may have been elaborated in the telling, it symbolizes both the strength and the hazards of Descartes's unshakable confidence and resolve to work alone. But he did not make his vision his life's mission for another nine years, during which (either before or after his tour of Italy from 1623 to 1625) he met Mersenne, who was to become his lifelong correspondent, and took part in scientific meetings in Paris. The next decisive incident, according to Baillet, was a public encounter in 1628 in which he demolished the unfortunate Chandoux by using his method to distinguish sharply between true scientific knowledge and mere probability. Among those present was the influential Cardinal de Bérulle, who a few days later charged him to devote his life to working out the application of "his manner of philosophizing . . . to medicine and mechanics. The one would contribute to the restoration and conservation of health, and the other to some diminution and relief in the labours of mankind."[4] To execute this design he withdrew, toward the end of the year, to the solitary life in the Netherlands which he lived until his last journey to Stockholm in 1649, where, as Queen Christina's philosopher, he died in his first winter.

The primarily centrifugal direction of Descartes's thought, moving out into detailed phenomena from a firm central theory (in contrast with the more empirical scientific style of Francis Bacon and Newton), is shown by the sequence of composition of his major writings. He set out his method in the *Rules for the Direction of the Mind,* left unfinished in 1628 and published posthumously, and in the *Discours de la méthode,* written in the Netherlands along with the *Météores, La dioptrique,* and *La géométrie,* which he presented as examples of the method. All were published in one volume in 1637. At the same time his investigation into the true ontology led him to the radical division of created existence into matter as simply extended substance, given motion at the creation, and mind as unextended thinking substance. This conclusion he held to be guaranteed by the perfection of God, who would not deceive true reason. How these two mutually exclusive and collectively exhaustive categories of substance could have any interaction in the embodied soul that was a man was a question discussed between Gassendi, Hobbes, and Descartes in the *Objections and Replies* published with his *Meditations on First Philosophy* in 1641.

It was from these first principles that he had given an account in *Le monde, ou Traité de la lumière* of cosmogony and cosmology as products simply of matter in motion, making the laws of motion the ultimate "laws of nature" and all scientific explanation ultimately mechanistic. This treatise remained unpublished in Descartes's lifetime. So too did the associated treatise *L'homme,* in which he represented animals and the human body as sheer mechanisms, an idea already found in the *Rules.* He withheld these essays, on the brink of publication, at the news of Galileo's condemnation in 1633, and instead published his general system of physics, with its Copernicanism mitigated by the idea that all motion is relative, in the *Principles of Philosophy* in 1644. Finally, he brought physiological psychology within the compass of his system in *Les passions de l'âme* in 1649. This system aimed to be as complete as Aristotle's, which it was designed to replace. It was not by chance that

it dealt in the same order with many of the same phenomena (such as the rainbow), as well as with others more recently investigated (such as magnetism).

A comparison of Descartes's performance with his program of scientific method presents a number of apparent contradictions. He made much of the ideal of a mathematically demonstrated physics, yet his fundamental cosmology was so nearly entirely qualitative that he came to fear that he had produced nothing more than a beautiful "romance of nature."[5] His planetary dynamics was shown by Newton to be quantitatively ridiculous. He wrote in the *Discours,* "I noticed also with respect to experiments [*expériences*] that they become so much the more necessary, the more we advance in knowledge,"[6] yet his fundamental laws of nature, the laws of motion and impact, had to be dismantled by Huygens and Leibniz for their lack of agreement with observation. These apparent contradictions may be resolved in the contrast between Descartes's theoretical ideal of completed scientific knowledge and the actual process and circumstances of acquiring such knowledge. For the modern reader to pay too much attention to his mechanics and to the *Principles,* a premature conception of completed science, can obscure Descartes's firm grasp of the necessity for observation and experiment already expressed in the *Rules* in his criticism "of those philosophers who neglect experiments and expect truth to rise from their own heads like Minerva from Jupiter's."[7]

No other great philosopher, except perhaps Aristotle, can have spent so much time in experimental observation. According to Baillet, over several years he studied anatomy, dissected and vivisected embryos of birds and cattle, and went on to study chemistry. His correspondence from the Netherlands described dissections of dogs, cats, rabbits, cod, and mackerel; eyes, livers, and hearts obtained from an abattoir; experiments on the weight of the air and on vibrating strings; and observations on rainbows, parahelia, and other optical phenomena. Many of his scientific writings reflect these activities and show sound experimental knowledge, although the extreme formalism of his physiological models obscures the question of his actual knowledge of some aspects of anatomy. Attention to the whole range of his scientific thought and practice shows a clear conception not only of completed scientific knowledge but also of the roles of experiment and hypothesis in making discoveries and finding explanations by which the body of scientific knowledge was built up.

Descartes's conception of completed scientific knowledge was essentially that envisaged by Aristotle's true scientific demonstration. It was the geometers' conception of a system deduced from self-evident and certain premises. He wrote,

> In physics I should consider that I knew nothing if I were able to explain only how things might be, without demonstrating that they could not be otherwise. For, having reduced physics to mathematics, this is something possible, and I think that I can do it within the small compass of my knowledge, although I have not done it in my essays.[8]

His optimism about the possibility of achieving such demonstrations seems to have depended on which end of the chain of reasoning he was contemplating. When considering the results of his analysis reducing created existence to extension (with motion) and thought, he seems to have been confident that it would be possible to show that from these "simple natures" the composite observed world must follow. It may be argued that his treatment of motion failed just where his a priori confidence led him to suppose that his analysis (of what was soon seen to be an insufficient range of data) placed his first principles beyond the need for empirical test. But when considering the chain lower down, nearer this complex world, he was more hesitant. He wrote to Mersenne:

> You ask me whether I think what I have written about refraction is a demonstration. I think it is, at least as far as it is possible, without having proved the principles of physics previously by metaphysics, to give any demonstration on this subject . . . as far as any other question of mechanics, optics, or astronomy, or any other question which is not purely geometrical or arithmetical, has ever been demonstrated. But to demand that I should give geometrical demonstrations of matters which depend on physics is to demand that I should do the impossible. If you restrict the use of "demonstration" to geometrical proofs only, you will be obliged to say that Archimedes demonstrated nothing in mechanics, nor Vitellio in optics, nor Ptolemy in astronomy, etc., which is not commonly maintained. For, in such matters, one is satisfied that the writers, having presupposed certain things which are not obviously contradictory to experience, have besides argued consistently and without logical fallacy, even if their assumptions are not exactly true.[9]

The paradox of Descartes as a natural scientist is that his grasp improved the more hopeless he found the immediate possibility of deducing solutions of detailed problems from his general first principles. Standing amidst the broken sections of a chain that he could not cast up to heaven, the experimentalist and constructor of hypothetical models came to life. In Descartes's letter prefaced to the French translation of the *Principles* (1647), he wrote that two, and only two, conditions determined whether the first principles proposed could be accepted as true: "First they must be so clear and evident that the mind of man cannot doubt their truth when it attentively applies itself to consider them"; and secondly, everything else must be deducible from them. But he went on to admit, "It is really only God alone who has perfect wisdom, that is to say, who has a complete knowledge of the truth of all things."[10] To find the truth about complex material phenomena man must experiment, but as the sixth part of the *Discours* shows, the need to experiment was an expression of the failure of the ideal.

As well as being demonstrative, scientific knowledge had to be explanatory; for Descartes the two went together. He wrote, "I have described . . . the whole visible world as if it were only a machine in which there was nothing to consider but the shapes and movements [of its parts]."[11] To such a mechanism it was possible to apply mathematics and calculation, but it was the mechanism that explained. His insistence that even mathematical science without fundamental explanations was insufficient appears in his interestingly similar criticisms of Harvey for starting simply with a beating heart in explaining the circulation of the blood and of Galileo for likewise failing to reduce the mathematical laws of moving bodies to their ultimate mechanisms. He commented on the latter that "without having considered the first causes of nature, he has only looked for the reasons for certain particular effects, and that thus he has built without foundation."[12] By this insistence Descartes here again extracted from the failure of his ideal a fundamental contribution to scientific thinking. He became the first great master to make the hypothetical model, or "conjecture," a systematic tool of research.

Current natural philosophy accepted Aristotle's absolute ontological distinction between naturally generated bodies (inanimate and animate) and artificial things made by man. Hence, in principle no humanly constructed imitation or model could throw real light on the naturally endowed essence and cause of behavior. This distinction had become blurred in the partial mechanization of nature made by some philosophers. Descartes's innovation was to assert the identity of the synthesized artificial construction with the naturally generated product and to make this identification an instrument of scientific research:

> And certainly there are no rules in mechanics that do not hold also in physics, of which mechanics forms a part or species [so that all artificial things are at the same time natural]: for it is not less natural for a clock, made of these or those wheels, to indicate the hours, than for a tree which has sprung from this or that seed to produce a particular fruit. Accordingly, just as those who apply themselves to the consideration of automata, when they

know the use of some machine and see some of its parts, easily infer from these the manner in which others which they have not seen are made, so, from the perceptible effects and parts of natural bodies, I have endeavoured to find out what are their imperceptible causes and parts.[13]

This reduction made the principles of the mechanistic model the only principles operating in nature, thus bringing the objectives of the engineer into the search for the nature of things and throwing the entire world of matter open to the same form of scientific inquiry and explanation. Research, whether into cosmology or physiology, was reduced to the discovery and elucidation of mechanisms. He could construct in distant space the imaginary world of *Le monde* and *L'homme,* and later the world of the *Principles,* as explicitly and unambiguously hypothetical imitations of our actual world, made in accordance with the known laws of mechanics. The heuristic power of the model was that, like any other theory advanced in anticipation of facts, its own properties suggested new questions to put to nature. The main issue in any historical judgment of Descartes here is not whether his own answers were correct but whether his questions were fruitful. In insisting that experiment and observation alone could show whether the model corresponded with actuality, he introduced further precision into his theory of demonstration.

Descartes used the word *demonstrer* to cover both the explanation of the observed facts by the assumed theory and the proof of the truth of the theory. When challenged with the criticism that this might make the argument circular, he replied by contrasting two kinds of hypothesis.[14] In astronomy various geometrical devices, admittedly false in nature, were employed to yield true conclusions only in the sense that they "saved the appearances." But physical theories were proposed as true. He was persuaded of the truth of the assumption that the material world consisted of particles in motion by the number of different effects he could deduce, as diverse as the operation of vision, the properties of salt, the formation of snow, the rainbow, and so on. Thus he made range of application the empirical criterion of truth. He wrote in the *Discours:*

> If some of the matters of which I have spoken in the beginning of the *Dioptrique* and the *Météores* should, at first sight, shock people because I have called them suppositions, and do not seem to bother about their proof, let them have the patience to read them carefully right through, and I hope that they will find themselves satisfied. For it seems to me that the reasonings are so interwoven that as the later ones are demonstrated by the earlier which are their causes, these earlier ones are

reciprocally demonstrated by the later which are their effects. And it must not be thought that in this I commit the fallacy which logicians call arguing in a circle, for, since experience renders the majority of these effects very certain, the causes from which I deduce them do not so much serve to prove them as to explain them; on the other hand, the causes are proved by the effects.[15]

The test implied precisely by the criterion of range of confirmation was the *experimentum crucis.* This is the most obvious feature in common between Descartes's logic of experiment and that of Francis Bacon. Descartes described its function in the *Discours:*

> Reviewing in my mind all the objects that have ever been presented to my senses, I venture truly to say that I have not there observed anything that I could not satisfactorily explain by the principles I had discovered. But I must also confess that the power of nature is so ample and so vast and that these principles are so simple and so general, that I have observed hardly any particular effect that I could not at once recognize to be deducible from them in several different ways, and that my greatest difficulty is usually to discover in which of these ways it depends on them. In such a case, I know no other expedient than to look again for experiments [*expériences*] such that their result is not the same if it has to be explained in one of these ways as it would be if explained in the other.[16]

It was a logician rather than an experimenter who seems to have been uppermost in Descartes's application of this criterion in the same way to very general assumptions, such as the corpuscularian natural philosophy, and to questions as particular as whether the blood left the heart in systole or in diastole. Descartes argued in *La description du corps humain* (1648–1649) that whereas Harvey's theory that the blood was forced out of the heart by a muscular contraction might agree with the facts observed so far, "that does not exclude the possibility that all the same effects might follow from another cause, namely from the dilatation of the blood which I have described. But in order to be able to decide which of these two causes is true, we must consider other observations which cannot agree with both of them."[17] Harvey replied in his *Second Disquisition to Jean Riolan.*

As the great optimist of the scientific movement of the seventeenth century, Descartes habitually wrote as if he had succeeded in discovering the true principles of nature to such an extent that the whole scientific program was within sight of completion. Then, as Seth Ward neatly put it, "when the operations of nature shall be followed up to their staticall (and mechanicall) causes, the use of induction will cease, and syllogisme succeed in place of it." But Descartes would surely have agreed with Ward's qualification that "in the interim we are to desire that men have patience not to lay aside induction before they have reason."[18]

NOTES

1. Fontenelle, *Oeuvres diverses,* new ed., III (The Hague, 1729), 405–406.
2. Part of the *Olympica* incorporated in the *Cogitationes privatae* (1619–1621); see *Oeuvres,* X, 217.
3. *Oeuvres,* X, 156.
4. Baillet, II, 165.
5. *Ibid.,* preface, p. xviii.
6. *Oeuvres,* VI, 63.
7. Rule V; see *Oeuvres,* X, 380.
8. Letter to Mersenne, 11 Mar. 1640; see *Oeuvres,* III, 39. The "Essays" were the volume of 1637.
9. Letter to Mersenne, 27 May 1638; see *Oeuvres,* II, 141–142.
10. *Oeuvres,* IX, pt. 2, 2–3.
11. *Principia philosophiae,* IV, 188; *Oeuvres,* VIII, pt. 1, 315 (Latin); IX, pt. 2, 310 (French, alone with passage in square brackets).
12. Letter to Mersenne, 11 Oct. 1638; see *Oeuvres,* II, 380. For his comments on Harvey, see *Discours V.*
13. *Principia philosophiae,* IV, 203; *Oeuvres,* VIII, pt. 1, 326 (Latin); IX, pt. 2, 321–322 (French, alone with passage in square brackets).
14. Letter to J.-B. Morin, 13 July 1638; see *Oeuvres,* II, 197–202; cf. his letters to Vatier, 22 Feb. 1638, *ibid.,* I, 558–565, and to Mersenne, 1 Mar. 1638, *ibid.,* II, 31–32.
15. *Oeuvres,* VI, 76.
16. *Ibid.,* pp. 64–65; cf. *Principia philosophiae,* III, 46; VIII, pt. 2, 100–101; and IX, pt. 2, 124–125.
17. *Oeuvres,* XI, 241–242; cf. the comments on this controversy by J. B. Duhamel, "Quae sit cordis motus effectrix causa," in *Philosophia vetus et nova.* II, *Physica generalis,* III.ii.2 (Paris, 1684), 628–631.
18. *Vindiciae academiarum* (Oxford, 1654), p. 25.

BIBLIOGRAPHY

Descartes's complete works can be found in *Oeuvres de Descartes,* C. Adam and P. Tannery, eds., 12 vols. (Paris, 1897–1913), together with the revised *Correspondance,* C. Adam and G. Milhaud, eds. (Paris, 1936–   ). Besides these, primary sources for Descartes's life are Adrien Baillet, *La vie de Monsieur Descartes,* 2 vols. (Paris, 1691), which should be read with C. Adam, *Vie et oeuvres de Descartes* (in *Oeuvres,* XII); Isaac Beeckman, *Journal tenu . . . de 1604 à 1634,* C. de Waard, ed., 3 vols. (The Hague, 1939–1953): Marin Mersenne, *Correspondance,* C. de Waard, R. Pintard, B. Rochot, eds. (Paris, 1932–   ).

For Descartes's philosophy and method and their background, see E. Gilson, *Index scolastico-cartésien* (Paris, 1912); *Études sur le rôle de la pensée médiévale dans la formation du système cartésien* (Paris, 1930); *Discours de la méthode: texte et commentaire* (Paris, 1947); Alexandre Koyré, *Entretiens sur Descartes* (Paris–New York, 1944); G. Milhaud, *Descartes savant* (Paris, 1921); L. Roth, *Descartes' Discourse on Method* (Oxford, 1937); H. Scholz, A. Kratzer, and J. E. Hofmann, *Descartes* (Münster, 1951); and Norman Kemp Smith, *New Studies in the Philosophy of Descartes* (London, 1952).

Specific aspects of Descartes's scientific method are discussed in A. Gewirtz, "Experience and the Non-mathematical in the Cartesian Method," in *Journal of the History of Ideas,* **2** (1941), 183–210; and A. C. Crombie, "Some Aspects of Descartes' Attitude to Hypothesis and Experiment," in Académie Internationale d'Histoire des Sciences, *Actes du Symposium International des Sciences Physiques et Mathématiques dans la Première Moitié du XVIIᵉ Siècle: Pise-Vinci, 16–18 Juin 1958* (Paris, 1960), pp. 192–201. An indispensable bibliography is G. Sebba, *Descartes and His Philosophy: A Bibliographical Guide to the Literature, 1800–1958* (Athens, Ga., 1959).

A. C. CROMBIE

DESCARTES: Mathematics and Physics.

In this section, Descartes's mathematics is discussed separately. The physics is discussed in two subsections: Optics and Mechanics.

Mathematics. The mathematics that served as model and touchstone for Descartes's philosophy was in large part Descartes's own creation and reflected in turn many of his philosophical tenets.[1] Its historical foundations lie in the classical analytical texts of Pappus (*Mathematical Collection*) and Diophantus (*Arithmetica*) and in the cossist algebra exemplified by the works of Peter Rothe and Christoph Clavius. Descartes apparently received the stimulus to study these works from Isaac Beeckman; his earliest recorded thoughts on mathematics are found in the correspondence with Beeckman that followed their meeting in 1618. Descartes's command of cossist algebra (evident throughout his papers of the early 1620's) was perhaps strengthened by his acquaintance during the winter of 1619–1620 with Johann Faulhaber, a leading German cossist in Ulm.[2] Descartes's treatise *De solidorum elementis,* which contains a statement of "Euler's Theorem" for polyhedra ($V + F = E + 2$), was quite likely also a result of their discussions. Whatever the early influences on Descartes's mathematics, it nonetheless followed a relatively independent line of development during the decade preceding the publication of his magnum opus, the *Géométrie* of 1637.[3]

During this decade Descartes sought to realize two programmatic goals. The first stemmed from a belief, first expressed by Petrus Ramus,[4] that cossist algebra represented a "vulgar" form of the analytical method employed by the great Greek mathematicians. As Descartes wrote in his *Rules for the Direction of the Mind (ca.* 1628):

. . . some traces of this true mathematics [of the ancient Greeks] seem to me to appear still in Pappus and Diophantus. . . . Finally, there have been some most ingenious men who have tried in this century to revive the same [true mathematics]; for it seems to be nothing other than that art which they call by the barbarous name of "algebra," if only it could be so disentangled from the multiple numbers and inexplicable figures that overwhelm it that it no longer would lack the clarity and simplicity that we suppose should obtain in a true mathematics.[5]

Descartes expressed his second programmatic goal in a letter to Beeckman in 1619; at the time it appeared to him to be unattainable by one man alone. He envisaged "an entirely new science,"

> . . . by which all questions can be resolved that can be proposed for any sort of quantity, either continuous or discrete. Yet each problem will be solved according to its own nature, as, for example, in arithmetic some questions are resolved by rational numbers, others only by irrational numbers, and others finally can be imagined but not solved. So also I hope to show for continuous quantities that some problems can be solved by straight lines and circles alone; others only by other curved lines, which, however, result from a single motion and can therefore be drawn with new forms of compasses, which are no less exact and geometrical, I think, than the common ones used to draw circles; and finally others that can be solved only by curved lines generated by diverse motions not subordinated to one another, which curves are certainly only imaginary (e.g., the rather well-known quadratrix). I cannot imagine anything that could not be solved by such lines at least, though I hope to show which questions can be solved in this or that way and not any other, so that almost nothing will remain to be found in geometry.[6]

Descartes sought, then, from the beginning of his research a symbolic algebra of pure quantity by which problems of any sort could be analyzed and classified in terms of the constructive techniques required for their most efficient solution. He took a large step toward his goal in the *Rules* and achieved it finally in the *Géométrie.*

Descartes began his task of "purifying" algebra by separating its patterns of reasoning from the particular subject matter to which it might be applied. Whereas cossist algebra was basically a technique for solving numerical problems and its symbols therefore denoted numbers, Descartes conceived of his "true mathematics" as the science of magnitude, or quantity, per se. He replaced the old cossist symbols with letters of the alphabet, using at first (in the *Rules*) the capital letters to denote known quantities and the lowercase letters to denote unknowns, and later (in the *Géométrie*) shifting to the *a,b,c; x,y,z* notation still in use today. In a more radical step, he then removed the last vestiges of verbal expression (and the conceptualization that accompanied it) by replacing the words "square," "cube," etc., by numerical

superscripts. These superscripts, he argued (in rule XVI), resolved the serious conceptual difficulty posed by the dimensional connotations of the words they replaced. For the square of a magnitude did not differ from it in kind, as a geometrical square differs from a line; rather, the square, the cube, and all powers differed from the base quantity only in the number of "relations" separating them respectively from a common unit quantity. That is, since

$$1:x = x:x^2 = x^2:x^3 = \cdots$$

(and, by Euclid V, ratios obtain only among homogeneous quantities), x^3 was linked to the unit magnitude by three "relations," while x was linked by only one. The numerical superscript expressed the number of "relations."

While all numbers are homogeneous, the application of algebra to geometry (Descartes's main goal in the *Géométrie*) required the definition of the six basic algebraic operations (addition, subtraction, multiplication, division, raising to a power, and extracting a root) for the realm of geometry in such a way as to preserve the homogeneity of the products. Although the Greek mathematicians had established the correspondence between addition and the geometrical operation of laying line lengths end to end in the same straight line, they had been unable to conceive of multiplication in any way other than that of constructing a rectangle out of multiplier and multiplicand, with the result that the product differed in kind from the elements multiplied. Descartes's concept of "relation" provided his answer to the problem: one chooses a unit length to which all other lengths are referred (if it is not given by the data of the problem, it may be chosen arbitrarily). Then, since $1:a = a:ab,$ the product of two lines a and b is con-

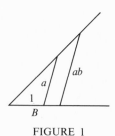

FIGURE 1

structed by drawing a triangle with sides 1 and a; in a similar triangle, of which the side corresponding to 1 is $b,$ the other side will be $ab,$ a line length. Division and the remaining operations are defined analogously. As Descartes emphasized, these operations do not make arithmetic of geometry, but rather make possible an algebra of geometrical line segments.

The above argument opens Descartes's *Géométrie*

and lays the foundation of the new analytic geometry contained therein, to wit, that given a line x and a polynomial $P(x)$ with rational coefficients it is possible to construct another line y such that $y = P(x)$. Algebra thereby becomes for Descartes the symbolic method for realizing the second goal of his "true mathematics," the analysis and classification of problems. The famous "Problem of Pappus," called to Descartes's attention by Jacob Golius in 1631, provides the focus for Descartes's exposition of his new method. The problem states in brief: given n coplanar lines, to find the locus of a point such that, if it is connected to each given line by a line drawn at a fixed angle, the product of $n/2$ of the connecting lines bears a given ratio to the product of the remaining $n/2$ (for even n; for odd n, the product of $(n + 1)/2$ lines bears a given ratio to k times the product of the remaining $(n - 1)/2$, where k is a given line segment). In carrying out the detailed solution for the case $n = 4$, Descartes also achieves the classification of the solutions for other n.

Implicit in Descartes's solution is the analytic geometry that today bears his name. Taking lines *AB, AD, EF, GH* as the four given lines, Descartes assumes that point C lies on the required locus and draws the connecting lines *CB, CD, CF, CH.* To apply algebraic analysis, he then takes the length *AB*, measured from the fixed point *A*, as his first unknown, x, and length *BC* as the second unknown, y. He thus imagines the locus to be traced by the endpoint C of a movable ordinate *BC* maintaining a fixed angle to line *AB* (the axis) and varying in length as a function[7] of the length *AB*. Throughout the *Géométrie*, Descartes chooses his axial system to fit the problem; nowhere does the now standard—and misnamed—"Cartesian coordinate system" appear.

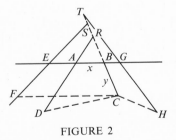

FIGURE 2

The goal of the algebraic derivation that follows this basic construction is to show that every other connecting line may be expressed by a combination of the two basic unknowns in the form $\alpha x + \beta y + \gamma$, where α, β, γ derive from the data. From this last result it follows that for a given number n of fixed lines the power of x in the equation that expresses the ratio of multiplied connecting lines will not exceed

$n/2$ (n even) or $(n - 1)/2$ (n odd); it will often not even be that large. Hence, for successive assumed values of y, the construction of points on the locus requires the solution of a determinate equation in x of degree $n/2$, or $(n - 1)/2$; e.g., for five or fewer lines, one need only be able to solve a quadratic equation, which in turn requires only circle and straightedge for its constructive solution.

Thus Descartes's classification of the various cases of Pappus' problem follows the order of difficulty of solving determinate equations of increasing degree.[8] Solution of such equations carries with it the possibility of constructing any point (and hence all points) of the locus sought. The direct solvability of algebraic equations becomes in book II Descartes's criterion for distinguishing between "geometrical" and "nongeometrical" curves; for the latter (today termed "transcendental curves") by their nature allow the direct construction of only certain of their points. For the construction of the loci that satisfy Pappus' problem for $n \leq 5$, i.e., the conic sections, Descartes relies on the construction theorems of Apollonius' *Conics* and contents himself with showing how the indeterminate equations of the loci contain the necessary parameters.

Descartes goes on to show in book II that the equation of a curve also suffices to determine its geometrical properties, of which the most important is the normal to any point on the curve. His method of normals—from which a method of tangents follows directly—takes as unknown the point of intersection of the desired normal and the axis. Considering a family of circles drawn about that point, Descartes derives an equation $P(x) = 0$, the roots of which are the abscissas of the intersection points of any circle and the curve. The normal is the radius of that circle which has a single intersection point, and Descartes finds that circle on the basis of the theorem that, if $P(x) = 0$ has a repeated root at $x = a$, then $P(x) = (x - a)^2 R(x)$, where $R(a) \neq 0$. Here a is the abscissa of the given point on the curve, and the solution follows from equating the coefficients of like powers of x on either side of the last equation. Descartes's method is formally equivalent to Fermat's method of maxima and minima and, along with the latter, constituted one of the early foundations of the later differential calculus.

The central importance of determinate equations and their solution leads directly to book III of the *Géométrie* with its purely algebraic theory of equations. Entirely novel and original, Descartes's theory begins by writing every equation in the form $P(x) = 0$, where $P(x)$ is an algebraic polynomial with real coefficients.[9] From the assertion, derived inductively, that every such equation may also be expressed in the form

$$(x - a)(x - b) \cdots (x - s) = 0,$$

where $a, b, \cdots, s$ are the roots of the equation, Descartes states and offers an intuitive proof of the fundamental theorem of algebra (first stated by Albert Girard in 1629) that an nth degree equation has exactly n roots. The proof rests simply on the principle that every root must appear in one of the binomial factors of $P(x)$ and that it requires n such factors to achieve x^n as the highest power of x in that polynomial. Descartes is therefore prepared to recognize not only negative roots (he gives as a corollary the law of signs for the number of negative roots) but also "imaginary" solutions to complete the necessary number.[10] In a series of examples, he then shows how to alter the signs of the roots of an equation, to increase them (additively or multiplicatively), or to decrease them. Having derived from the factored form of an equation its elementary symmetric functions,[11] Descartes uses them to eliminate the term containing x^{n-1} in the equation. This step paves the way for the general solution of the cubic and quartic equations (material dating back to Descartes's earliest studies) and leads to a general discussion of the solution of equations, in which the first method outlined is that of testing the various factors of the constant term, and then other means, including approximate solution, are discussed.

The *Géométrie* represented the sum of mathematical knowledge to which Descartes was willing to commit himself in print. The same philosophical concepts that led to the brilliant new method of geometry also prevented him from appreciating the innovative achievements of his contemporaries. His demand for strict a priori deduction caused him to reject Fermat's use of counterfactual assumptions in the latter's method of maxima and minima and rule of tangents.[12] His demand for absolute intuitive clarity in concepts excluded the infinitesimal from his mathematics. His renewed insistence on Aristotle's rigid distinction between "straight" and "curved" led him to reject from the outset any attempt to rectify curved lines.

Despite these hindrances to adventurous speculation, Descartes did discuss in his correspondence some problems that lay outside the realm of his *Géométrie*. In 1638, for example, he discussed with Mersenne, in connection with the law of falling bodies, the curve now expressed by the polar equation $\rho = a\lambda^{\vartheta}$ (logarithmic spiral)[13] and undertook the determination of the normal to, and quadrature of, the cycloid. Also in 1638 he took up a problem posed by Florimond Debeaune: (in modern terms) to construct a curve

satisfying the differential equation $a(dy/dx) = x - y$. Descartes appreciated Debeaune's quadrature of the curve and was himself able to determine the asymptote $y = x - a$ common to the family, but he did not succeed in finding one of the curves itself.[14]

By 1638, however, Descartes had largely completed his career in mathematics. The writing of the *Meditations* (1641), its defense against the critics, and the composition of the magisterial *Principia philosophiae* (1644) left little time to pursue further the mathematical studies begun in 1618.

Optics. In addition to presenting his new method of algebraic geometry, Descartes's *Géométrie* also served in book II to provide rigorous mathematical demonstrations for sections of his *Dioptrique* published at the same time. The mathematical derivations pertain to his theory of lenses and offer, through four "ovals," solutions to a generalized form of the anaclastic problem.[15] The theory of lenses, a topic that had engaged Descartes since reading Kepler's *Dioptrica* in 1619, took its form and direction in turn from Descartes's solution to the more basic problem of a mathematical derivation of the laws of reflection and refraction, with which the *Dioptrique* opens.

Background to these derivations was Descartes's theory of light, an integral part of his overall system of cosmology.[16] For Descartes light was not motion (which takes time) but rather a "tendency to motion," an impulsive force transmitted rectilinearly and instantaneously by the fine particles that fill the interstices between the visible macrobodies of the universe. His model for light itself was the blind man's cane, which instantaneously transmits impulses from the objects it meets and enables the man to "see." To derive the laws of reflection and refraction, however, Descartes required another model more amenable to mathematical description. Arguing that "tendency to motion" could be analyzed in terms of actual motion, he chose the model of a tennis ball striking a flat surface. For the law of reflection the surface was assumed to be perfectly rigid and immobile. He then applied two fundamental principles of his theory of collision: first, that a body in motion will continue to move in the same direction at the same speed unless acted upon by contact with another body; second, that a body can lose some or all of its motion only by transmitting it directly to another. Descartes measured motion by the product of the magnitude of the body and the speed at which it travels. He made a distinction, however, between the speed of a body and its "determination" to move in a certain direction.[17] By this distinction, it might come about that a body impacting with another would lose none of its speed (if the other body remained unmoved) but would

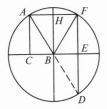

FIGURE 3

receive another determination. Moreover, although Descartes treated speed as a scalar quantity, determination was (operationally at least) always a vector, which could be resolved into components.[18] When one body collided with another, only those components of their determinations that directly opposed one another were subject to alteration.

Imagine, then, says Descartes, a tennis ball leaving the racket at point A and traveling uniformly along line AB to meet the surface CE at B. Resolve its determination into two components, one (AC) perpendicular to the surface and one (AH) parallel to it. Since, when the ball strikes the surface, it imparts none of its motion to the surface (which is immobile), it will continue to move at the same speed and hence after a period of time equal to that required to traverse AB will be somewhere on a circle of radius AB about B. But, since the surface is impenetrable, the ball cannot pass through it (say to D) but must bounce off it, with a resultant change in determination. Only the vertical component of that determination is subject to change, however; the horizontal component remains unaffected. Moreover, since the body has lost none of its motion, the length HF of that component after collision will equal the length AH before. Hence, at the same time the ball reaches the circle it must also be at a distance $HF = AH$ from the normal HB, i.e., somewhere on line FE. Clearly, then, it must be at F, and consideration of similar triangles shows that the angle of incidence ABH is equal to the angle of reflection HBF.

For the law of refraction, Descartes altered the nature of the surface met by the ball; he now imagined it to pass through the surface, but to lose some of its motion (i.e., speed) in doing so. Let the speed before collision be to that after as $p:q$. Since both

speeds are uniform, the time required for the ball to reach the circle again will be to that required to traverse AB as $p:q$. To find the precise point at which it meets the circle, Descartes again considered its determination, or rather the horizontal component unaffected by the collision. Since the ball takes longer to reach the circle, the length of that component after collision will be greater than before, to wit, in the ratio of $p:q$. Hence, if $FH:AH = p:q$, then the ball must lie on both the circle and line FE. Let I be the common point.

The derivation so far rests on the assumption that the ball's motion is decreased in breaking through the surface. Here again Descartes had to alter his model to fit his theory of light, for that theory implies that light passes more easily through the denser medium. For the model of the tennis ball, this means that, if the medium below the surface is denser than that above, the ball receives added speed at impact, as if it were struck again by the racket. As a result, it will by the same argument as given above be deflected toward the normal as classical experiments with air-water interfaces said it should.

In either case, the ratio $p:q$ of the speeds before and after impact depended, according to Descartes, on the relative density of the media and would therefore be constant for any two given media. Hence, since

$$FH:AH = BE:BC = p:q,$$

it follows that

$$\frac{BE}{BI}:\frac{BC}{AB} = \sin \angle AHB : \sin \angle IBG$$

$$= p:q = n \text{ (constant)},$$

which is the law of refraction.

The vagueness surrounding Descartes's concept of "determination" and its relation to speed makes his derivations difficult to follow. In addition, the assumption in the second that all refraction takes place at the surface lends an ad hoc aura to the proof, which makes it difficult to believe that the derivation represented Descartes's path to the law of refraction (the law of reflection was well known). Shortly after Descartes's death, prominent scientists, including Christian Huygens, accused him of having plagiarized the law itself from Willebrord Snell and then having patched together his proof of it. There is, however, clear evidence that Descartes had the law by 1626, long before Golius uncovered Snell's unpublished memoir.[19] In 1626 Descartes had Claude Mydorge grind a hyperbolic lens that represented an anaclastic derived by Descartes from the sine law of refraction. Where Descartes got the law, or how he got it, remains

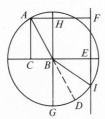

FIGURE 4

a mystery; in the absence of further evidence, one must rest content with the derivations in the *Dioptrique*.

Following those derivations, Descartes devotes the remainder of the *Dioptrique* to an optical analysis of the human eye, moving from the explanation of various distortions of vision to the lenses designed to correct them, or, in the case of the telescope, to increase the power of the normal eye. The laws of reflection and refraction reappear, however, in the third of the *Essais* of 1637, the *Météores*. There Descartes presents a mathematical explanation of both the primary and secondary rainbow in terms of the refraction and internal reflection of the sun's rays in a spherical raindrop.[20] Quantitatively, he succeeded in deriving the angle at which each rainbow is seen with respect to the angle of the sun's elevation. His attempted explanation of the rainbow's colors, however, rested on a general theory of colors that could at the time only be qualitative. Returning to the model of the tennis ball, Descartes explained color in terms of a rotatory motion of the ball, the speed of rotation varying with the color. Upon refraction, as through a prism, those speeds would be altered, leading to a change in colors.

Mechanics. Descartes's contribution to mechanics lay less in solutions to particular problems than in the stimulus that the detailed articulation of his mechanistic cosmology provided for men like Huygens.[21] Concerned with the universe on a grand scale, he had little but criticism for Galileo's efforts at resolving more mundane questions. In particular, Descartes rejected much of Galileo's work, e.g., the laws of free fall and the law of the pendulum, because Galileo considered the phenomena in a vacuum, a vacuum that Descartes's cosmology excluded from the world. For Descartes, the ideal world corresponded to the real one. Mechanical phenomena took place in a plenum and had to be explained in terms of the direct interaction of the bodies that constituted it, whence the central role of his theory of impact.[22]

Two of the basic principles underlying that theory have been mentioned above. The first, the law of inertia, followed from Descartes's concept of motion as a state coequal with rest; change of state required a cause (i.e., the action of another moving body) and in the absence of that cause the state remained constant. That motion continued in a straight line followed from the privileged status of the straight line in Descartes's geometrical universe. The second law, the conservation of the "quantity of motion" in any closed interaction, followed from the immutability of God and his creation. Since bodies acted on each other by transmission of their motion,

the "quantity of motion" (the product of magnitude and speed) served also as Descartes's measure of force or action and led to a third principle that vitiated Descartes's theory of impact. Since as much action was required for motion as for rest, a smaller body moving however fast could never possess sufficient action to move a larger body at rest. As a result of this principle, to which Descartes adhered in the face of both criticism and experience, only the first of the seven laws of impact (of perfectly elastic bodies meeting in the same straight line) is correct. It concerns the impact of two equal bodies approaching each other at equal speeds and is intuitively obvious.

Descartes's concept of force as motive action blocked successful quantitative treatment of the mechanical problems he attacked. His definition of the center of oscillation as the point at which the forces of the particles of the swinging body are balanced out led to quite meager results, and his attempt to explain centrifugal force as the tendency of a body to maintain its determination remained purely qualitative. In all three areas—impact, oscillation, and centrifugal force—it was left to Huygens to push through to a solution, often by discarding Descartes's staunchly defended principles.

Descartes met with more success in the realm of statics. His *Explication des engins par l'aide desquels on peut avec une petite force lever un fardeau fort pesant,* written as a letter to Constantin Huygens in 1637, presents an analysis of the five simple machines on the principle that the force required to lift *a* pounds vertically through *b* feet will also lift *na* pounds *b/n* feet. And a memoir dating from 1618 contains a clear statement of the hydrostatic paradox, later made public by Blaise Pascal.[23]

NOTES

1. Cf. Gaston Milhaud, *Descartes savant* (Paris, 1921), and Jules Vuillemin, *Mathématiques et métaphysique chez Descartes* (Paris, 1960).
2. Cf. Milhaud, pp. 84–87.
3. Defending his originality against critics, Descartes repeatedly denied having read the algebraic works of François Viète or Thomas Harriot prior to the publication of his own *Géométrie*. The pattern of development of his ideas, especially during the late 1620's, lends credence to this denial.
4. In his *Scholarum mathematicarum libri unus et triginta* (Paris, 1569; 3rd. ed., Frankfurt am Main, 1627), bk. I (p. 35 of the 3rd ed.). Descartes quite likely knew of Ramus through Beeckman, who had studied mathematics with Rudolph Snell, a leading Dutch Ramist.
5. *Regulae ad directionem ingenii*, in *Oeuvres de Descartes*, Adam and Tannery, eds., X (Paris, 1908), rule IV, 376–377.
6. Descartes to Beeckman (26 Mar. 1619), *Oeuvres*, X, 156–158. By "imaginary" curve, Descartes seems to mean a curve that can be described verbally but not accurately constructed by geometrical means.

7. Both the term and the concept it denotes are certainly anachronistic. Descartes speaks of the indeterminate equation that links x and y as the "relation [*rapport*] that all the points of a curve have to all those of a straight line" (*Géométrie,* p. 341). Strangely, Descartes makes no special mention of one of the most novel aspects of his method, to wit, the establishment of a correspondence between geometrical loci and indeterminate algebraic equations in two unknowns. He does discuss the correspondence further in bk. II, 334–335, but again in a way that belies its novelty. The correspondence between determinate equations and point constructions (i.e., section problems) had been standard for some time.

8. For problems of lower degree, Descartes maintains the classification of Pappus. Plane problems are those that can be constructed with circle and straightedge, and solid problems those that require the aid of the three conic sections. Where, however, Pappus grouped all remaining curves into a class he termed linear, Descartes divides these into distinct classes of order. To do so, he employs in bk. I a construction device that generates the conic sections from a referent triangle and then a new family of higher order from the conic sections, and so on.

9. Two aspects of the symbolism employed here require comment. First, Descartes deals for the most part with specific examples of polynomials, which he always writes in the form $x^n + a_1x^{n-1} + \cdots + a_n = 0$; the symbolism $P(x)$ was unknown to him. Second, instead of the equal sign, $=$, he used the symbol ∞, most probably the inverted ligature of the first two letters of the verb *aequare* ("to equal").

10. One important by-product of this structural analysis of equations is a new and more refined concept of number. See Jakob Klein, *Greek Mathematical Thought and the Origins of Algebra* (Cambridge, Mass., 1968).

11. Here again a totally anachronistic term is employed in the interest of brevity.

12. Ironically, Descartes's method of determining the normal to a curve (bk. II, 342 ff.) made implicit use of precisely the same reasoning as Fermat's. This may have become clear to Descartes toward the end of a bitter controversy between the two men over their methods in the spring of 1638.

13. Cf. Vuillemin, pp. 35–55.

14. *Ibid.,* pp. 11–25; Joseph E. Hofmann, *Geschichte der Mathematik,* II (Berlin, 1957), 13.

15. The anaclastic is a refracting surface that directs parallel rays to a single focus; Descartes had generalized the problem to include surfaces that refract rays emanating from a single point and direct them to another point. Cf. Milhaud, pp. 117–118.

16. The full title of the work Descartes suppressed in 1636 as a result of the condemnation of Galileo was *Le monde, ou Traité de la lumière.* It contained the basic elements of Descartes's cosmology, later published in the *Principia philosophiae* (1644). For a detailed analysis of Descartes's work in optics, see A. I. Sabra, *Theories of Light From Descartes to Newton* (London, 1967), chs. 1–4.

17. "One must note only that the power, whatever it may be, that causes the motion of this ball to continue is different from that which determines it to move more toward one direction than toward another," *Dioptrique* (Leiden, 1637), p. 94.

18. Cf. Descartes to Mydorge (1 Mar. 1638), "determination cannot be without some speed, although the same speed can have different determinations, and the same determination can be combined with various speeds" (quoted by Sabra, p. 120). A result of this qualification is that Descartes in his proofs treats speed operationally as a vector.

19. See the summary of this issue in Sabra, pp. 100 ff.

20. Cf. Carl B. Boyer, *The Rainbow: From Myth to Mathematics* (New York, 1959).

21. For a survey of Descartes's work on mechanics, which includes the passages pertinent to the subjects discussed below, see René Dugas, *La mécanique au XVIIᵉ siècle* (Neuchâtel, 1954), ch. 7.

22. Presented in full in the *Principia philosophiae,* pt. II, pars. 24–54.

23. Cf. Milhaud, pp. 34–36.

BIBLIOGRAPHY

I. ORIGINAL WORKS. All of Descartes's scientific writings can be found in their original French or Latin in the critical edition of the *Oeuvres de Descartes,* Charles Adam and Paul Tannery, eds., 12 vols. (Paris, 1897-1913). The *Géométrie,* originally written in French, was trans. into Latin and published with appendices by Franz van Schooten (Leiden, 1649); this Latin version underwent a total of four eds. The work also exists in an English trans. by Marcia Latham and David Eugene Smith (Chicago, 1925; repr., New York, 1954), and in other languages. For references to eds. of the philosophical treatises containing scientific material, see the bibliography for sec. I.

II. SECONDARY LITERATURE. In addition to the works cited in the notes, see also J. F. Scott, *The Scientific Work of René Descartes* (London, 1952); Carl B. Boyer, *A History of Analytic Geometry* (New York, 1956); Alexandre Koyré, *Études galiléennes* (Paris, 1939); E. J. Dijksterhuis, *The Mechanization of the World Picture* (Oxford, 1961). See also the various histories of seventeenth-century science or mathematics for additional discussions of Descartes's work.

MICHAEL S. MAHONEY

DESCARTES: Physiology.

Descartes's physiology grew and developed as an integral part of his philosophy. Although grounded at fundamental points in transmitted anatomical knowledge and actually performed dissection procedures, it sprang up largely independently of prior physiological developments and depended instead on the articulation of the Cartesian dualist ontology, was entangled with the vagaries of metaphysical theory, and deliberately put into practice Descartes's precepts on scientific method. Chronologically, too, his physiology grew with his philosophy. Important ideas on animal function occur briefly in the *Regulae* (1628), form a significant part of the argument in the *Discours de le méthode* (1637), and lie behind certain parts of the *Principia philosophiae* (1644) and all of the *Passions de l'âme* (1649). Throughout his active philosophical life, physiology formed one of Descartes's most central and, sometimes, most plaguing concerns.

Descartes hinted at the most fundamental conceptions of his physiology relatively early in his philosophical development. Already in the twelfth *regula,* he suggested (without, however, elaborating either more rigorously or more fully) that all animal and subrational human movements are controlled solely by unconscious mechanisms. Just as the quill of a pen moves in a physically necessary pattern determined by the motion of the tip, so too do "all the motions of the animals come about"; thus one can also explain "how in ourselves all those operations occur which [we] perform without any aid from the reason." Closely associated in the *Regulae* with this notion of animal automatism was Descartes's belief that human sensation is a two-step process consisting, first, of the mechanical conveyance of physical stimuli from the external organs of sense to a common sensorium located somewhere in the body and, second, of the internal perception of these mechanically conveyed stimuli by a higher "spiritual" principle.

Implicit in these two notions and seeming to tie them together is the assumption, evident in broader compass but in as terse a formulation as elsewhere in the *Regulae,* that all phenomena of the animate and inanimate world, with the sole exception of those directly connected with human will and consciousness, are to be explained in terms of mathematics, matter, configuration, and motion.

The fuller working out of his physiological ideas occupied Descartes in the early 1630's, when he was concerned generally with the development of his ontological and methodological views. In 1632 he several times referred to physiological themes and projects in his correspondence, and in June he informed Mersenne that he had already completed his work on inanimate bodies but still had to finish off "certain things touching on the nature of man." The allusion here was to the *Traité de l'homme,* which with the *Traité de lumière* was meant to form *Le monde.* Along with the *Traité de lumière,* however, the *Traité de l'homme* was suppressed by Descartes after the condemnation of Galileo in 1633, and although it thus had to await posthumous publication in the 1660's, his writing of the *Traité de l'homme* proved extremely important in the further maturation of Descartes's physiological conceptions.

The *Traité de l'homme* begins and ends with a proclamation of literary and philosophical license. In the *Traité,* Descartes writes, we deliberately consider not a real man but a "statue" or *machine de terre* expressly fashioned by God to approximate real men as closely as possible. Like a real man, the *machine de terre* will be imagined to possess an immaterial soul and a physical body, and, also like a real man, its physical body will consist of a heart, brain, stomach, vessels, nerves, *et al.* But since we are considering only an artificial man—a contrivance fashioned more perfectly but on the same principles as a clock or water mill—we will not be tempted to attribute the motions and activities of this man to special sensitive or vegetative souls or principles of life. Nothing more than a contained rational and immaterial soul and "the disposition of organs, no more and no less than

in the movements of a clock or any other automaton" will be needed to comprehend the active functioning of this special contrivance formed by God and operated thereafter by the principles of mechanical action. We are to bear in mind, of course, that the man of the *Traité* is remarkably like men we know, but our literary and philosophical license allows us to hypothesize and analogize freely.

Descartes fully exercises his self-proclaimed license in the rest of the *Traité.* He first surveys various physiological processes, giving for each of them not the traditional or neoclassical account of such recent physiological writers as Fernel or Riolan but mechanistic details by which the particular function is performed automatically in the *homme.* Each of Descartes's explanations borrows something from traditionalist physiological theories, but in each case Descartes wields Ockham's razor to strip away excess souls, faculties, forces, and innate heats from the corpuscular or chemical core of explanation.

Digestion, for example, is for Descartes only a fermentative process in which the particles of food are broken apart and set into agitation by fluids contained in the stomach. Chyle and excremental particles are then separated from one another in a filtration performed merely by a sievelike configuration of the pores and vascular openings in the intestines. Chyle particles go through another filtration and fermentation in the liver, where they thereby—and only thereby—acquire the properties of blood. Blood formed in the liver drips from the vena cava into the right ventricle of the heart, where the purely physical heat implanted there quickly vaporizes the sanguinary mass. The expansion of this sanguinary vapor pushes out the walls of the heart and arteries. Expansion with rarefaction is succeeded by cooling; and, as the vapor condenses, the heart and arteries return to their original size. The heart is fitted with a perfect arrangement of valves, and in addition the *homme* is served by a perpetual circulation of blood. (Descartes had read William Harvey's *De motu cordis,* as is also clear from his prior correspondence, but apparently took seriously only the part on circulatory motion rather than on cardiac action.) Cardiac and arterial pulsation is thus continually and automatically repeated throughout the life of the automaton by mechanical means, not under the control of an active diastolic faculty. And while the sanguinary particles are coursing through the vessels, certain of them separate off into special pores, which accounts for both nutrition and the sievelike production of such secretions as bile and urine.

After this mechanistic survey of general physiology, Descartes moves to the nervous system, which he treats in considerable detail. The nerves are said to be a series of essentially hollow tubes with a filamentous marrow and are similar in operation to the water-filled pipes of those hydraulically controlled puppets and mechanical statues found "in the grottoes and fountains in the gardens of our Kings." Filling the spaces in the nerves is a fine, material substance, the animal spirits. These spirits are actually the most quickly moving particles of the blood that have traveled through the arteries in the shortest, straightest path from the heart to the brain. Once conveyed to the brain according to the laws of mechanics and then mechanically separated from the coarser parts of the blood, these most agile particles become "a wind or very subtle flame."

This spiritual wind can flow into the muscles, which are directly connected with the neural tubes. When a particular muscle is inflated by the influx of animal spirits, its belly distends as if by wind billowing a canvas sail, and the ends or insertions of the muscle are necessarily pulled more closely together. The pulling together of the muscular insertions constitutes muscle contraction. Gross movements in the *homme* (including breathing and swallowing) are produced, therefore, as the necessary mechanical effects of animal spirits discharged to one or another muscle group.

The movement of animal spirits is also controlled, however, by the action of the pineal gland in the brain. The rational soul is itself most closely associated with this gland located centrally in the substance of the cerebral marrow, and by directly causing this gland to move, no matter how slightly, the immaterial, willful soul of man can redirect the animal spirits from one set of nervous channels to another. Redirection of animal spirits results, in turn, in the production of different gross muscle movements. The pineal gland can also be, and often is, directly and unconsciously affected by a whole array of supervening influences, among the most important of which are the sensory. In animals, of course, only the supervening influences operate. Since Descartes has already gotten into a discussion of sensation, he now discusses that subject in great detail. He devotes much attention to the external organs of sense, concentrating to a large degree on the visual apparatus. For his discussion here, Descartes was able to draw upon the prior work of sixteenth-century anatomists and natural philosophers that had culminated in Kepler's fine account of the eye as a camera-like optical system. Yet Descartes inserts his optical account of the eye into his already developed physiological system; for once the image is formed on the retina, Descartes explains, the nerves—and with them Descartes's general physiology—take over. Rays of light focused on particular

points of the retina cause specific nerves to jiggle slightly. Since the solid, filamentous part of the nerve is continuous from the sense organ to the brain, the externally caused jiggle is immediately transmitted, like the tug on a bell rope, to the interior of the brain as an internal jiggle. Internal jiggles directly control the streaming of animal spirits in the brain, and the rational soul, operating only at the pineal gland, interprets the patterns of the streams as particular sensations. The soul works "in the dark" this way, too, in all other sensations and in the difficult activity of multilevel perception. The soul "reads" various motions produced in the brain by the nerves and spirits, and interprets particular combinations of motions as taste, odor, color, or even distance.

Descartes moves from this complicated discussion of the five external senses of his *homme* to a consideration of certain internal feelings which it also experiences. The physiology (and psychology) is here, too, based on the manner by which the soul "reads" the messages delivered through the nerves by the spirits, messages which depend, in this instance, upon the internal functioning of the various parts of the body. Thus, when the blood entering the heart is purer and more subtle than usual, it vaporizes very easily in the cardiac chambers, and, as a consequence, it stimulates the nerves placed in the heart in a manner that the soul will associate with joy. All sorts of moods, feelings, and what might be generally labeled chains of somatopsychic effects (Descartes usually calls these "passions") are schematically accounted for in this same manner—by imagining a passive immaterial soul interpreting the varied motions of the spirits as they stream pass the pineal gland.

As a logical extension of his consideration of the "passions," Descartes turns, finally, to a discussion of sleep, dreams, memory, and imagination—other consequences of the interaction of the soul with internal neurophysiology. All these latter psychological phenomena are said to depend on the special motion of animal spirits, sometimes through favored pathways created by habitual or normal daytime activity.

With this discussion (and with his restatement of literary and philosophical license) Descartes terminates the *Traité*. It was obviously written as a full working out of the physiological hints included in the *Regulae* and elaborated in the light of his own philosophical development. A clearly stated dualist ontology runs through the *Traité*, while mechanistic details analogous to those of the *Traité de lumière* are evident at almost every turn.

But the *Traité de l'homme* served not only to clarify and develop Descartes's physiological views; it also quickly became a rich fund of ideas upon which he drew throughout the rest of his intellectual life. In 1637, for example, Descartes published two important works: *Discours de la méthode* and *Dioptrique*. In both he uses physiological ideas from the unpublished *Traité* at important points in his argument. Specifically, in part V of the *Discours*, Descartes employs a summary of his cardiovascular physiology to illustrate how the newly discovered laws by which God orders his universe are sufficient to explicate certain of the most important human functions, and the *Dioptrique* includes a summary of his general theory of sensation as a preliminary to a detailed study of image formation and visual perception. In the 1640's, too, Descartes drew heavily upon the unpublished *Traité*. The complicated arguments of the *Passions de l'âme*, published near the end of that decade, rest firmly on the extensive survey of basic Cartesian physiology incorporated in part I, while Descartes's unruffled assertiveness in his correspondence and later philosophical writings on the "beast-machine" makes full sense only against a background provided by the *Traité*'s automaton.

Descartes, however, had left one major physiological problem untreated in the *Traité:* the reproductive generation of animals and men. He had insisted for reasons of methodological circumspection that the *homme* of the *Traité* was directly contrived by God. The Cartesian program, of course, was to explain all but rational, deliberately willful, or self-conscious behavior in terms of mere mechanism. He had eliminated the souls, principles, faculties, and innate heats of traditional physiology and had systematically replaced them with hypotheses and analogies of purely physical nature. But generation had escaped, and its explanation in mechanistic terms was clearly needed for the logical completion of his system. Recently proposed theories of animal generation had left the subject replete with Galenic faculties and Aristotelian souls, and even William Harvey was soon to show himself content with innate principles and plastic forces as the controlling agents of embryonic development. Descartes, to be consistent, could not accept these explanatory devices and had, therefore, to formulate some alternative.

His correspondence and certain manuscript remains show that Descartes had actually been deeply concerned with the problem of animal generation for a considerable period of time. Earliest references in the former occur in 1629, and snippets of the latter reveal fitful grapplings with the problem, some of them even leading to direct anatomical investigations undertaken, apparently, as a means for providing clues to the processes involved. Descartes's ideas on the subject really seem to have crystallized, however, in the

late 1640's, when he triumphantly announced his "solution" to the long-plaguing problem in a series of enthusiastic letters to Princess Elizabeth. The ideas alluded to in these letters appear to be those published as the *De la formation du foetus,* which Descartes completed not long before his death.

First published by Clerselier in 1664, the *Formation* is a curious essay. Unlike the *Traité de l'homme,* which much preceded it in date of composition, the *Formation* consists mainly of bald assertions and only the vaguest mechanisms. Generation commences when the male and female seeds come together and mutually induce a corpuscular fermentation. The motion of certain of the fermenting particles forms the heart, that of others the lungs. Streaming of particles as the process continues furrows out the blood vessels; later, membranes and fibers are formed which ultimately weave together to construct the solid parts. The formation of the bodily parts is described in these vague terms (no mechanism of organ or vascular development is ever made more precise than this), yet Descartes apparently felt satisfied with his results. For by describing generation in chemical and corpuscular, rather than vital or teleological, terms Descartes had, at least in his own mind, completed the mechanistic program for physiology. Everything in the animal's life, from its first formation to its final decay, now had an automatic, mechanical explanation.

The impact of the Cartesian physiological program, once it was publicly known, was enormous. In two ways—philosophically and physiologically—Descartes transformed long-standing beliefs about animals and men. Philosophically, of course, his notions of mind-body dualism and animal automatism had extremely important implications that were not lost on Henry More, Malebranche, Spinoza, and Leibniz, along with many others in the seventeenth century. The "beast-machine" idea also had continuing ramifications in the eighteenth century, leading, at least according to Aram Vartanian, directly to La Mettrie's *L'homme machine.* Also, according to Vartanian, Descartes's posthumously published views on human function and animal generation exerted important philosophical influence, contributing greatly to the eighteenth-century concern with these biological subjects by many of the *philosophes*. But physiologically, too, Descartes's conceptions had an impact that in many ways was even more impressive than the philosophical influence, because it affected the actual course of contemporary science.

Almost as soon as Descartes published his *Discours de la méthode,* a few professors of medicine began to react to specific Cartesian physiological ideas and to the general Cartesian program. Plempius at Louvain and Regius at Utrecht were among the first. Although Plempius proved relatively hostile to Cartesian ideas (his objections were not unlike those William Harvey was to raise a few years later), Regius became so enthusiastic that for a time he entered into something of a student-teacher relationship with Descartes. As their correspondence for 1641 makes clear, Regius would send his students' theses to Descartes for comment and correction. Descartes would then return them with such specific excisions of classical residues as "In the first line of the Thesis I would get rid of these words: vivifying heat."

The intimate contact between Descartes and Regius marked the beginning of the direct influence of Cartesian ideas and modes of thought on seventeenth-century physiology. That influence was deliberately continued later, even more vigorously after Descartes's death, by such influential figures as Thomas Bartholin and Nicholas Steno. These men, especially Steno, tried to wed the Cartesian method of mechanistic explanation to careful anatomical investigation. Steno was particularly highly regarded by contemporaries for his perfection of the mechanical theory of muscular contraction in his *Elementorum myologiae specimen* (1667) and for his defense of the Cartesian physiological methodology in his anatomically sound *Discours sur l'anatomie du cerveau* (1669).

Many other prominent seventeenth-century physiological writers were influenced by the Cartesian program, either directly by reading Descartes's writings or indirectly through such followers as Steno. Among those deeply influenced by Cartesian physiology were Robert Hooke, Thomas Willis, Jan Swammerdam, and Giovanni Alfonso Borelli. These men saw in Cartesian physiology exactly what Descartes had intended it to be: a method of mechanistic formulation by which traditional categories of physiological explanation could be circumvented. Without Descartes, the seventeenth-century mechanization of physiological conceptions would have been inconceivable.

BIBLIOGRAPHY

The main primary sources—letters, MSS, and published works—are all handsomely printed in the Adam-Tannery *Oeuvres de Descartes*; vol. XI contains the largest sample of relevant works.

Useful secondary studies of Descartes's philosophy which seriously consider his physiological writings range from Étienne Gilson's *Études sur le rôle de la pensée médiévale dans la formation du système Cartésien* (Paris, 1930) to Norman Kemp Smith's *New Studies in the Philosophy of Descartes* (New York, 1966). Two older monographic stud-
ies are also useful: Bertrand de Saint-Germain's *Descartes considéré comme physiologiste* (Paris, 1869) and Auguste-Georges Berthier's "Le mécanisme Cartésien et la physiologie au XVIIe siècle," in *Isis*, **2** (1914), 37–89, and **3** (1920), 21–58. Some of the background to Descartes's treatment of vision is made clear in A. C. Crombie, "The Mechanistic Hypothesis and the Scientific Study of Vision," in *Proceedings of the Royal Microscopical Society*, **2** (1907), 3–112; fundamental aspects of his mechanistic philosophy are discussed in Georges Canguilhem, *La formation du concept de réflexe aux XVIIe et XVIIIe siècles* (Paris, 1955); while the seventeenth-century impact of Cartesian ideas is studied by Berthier (*op. cit.*) and in two helpful general works, Paul Mouy, *Le développement de la physique Cartésienne* (Paris, 1934) and vol. I of Thomas S. Hall, *Ideas of Life and Matter* (Chicago, 1969).

A sense of the influence of Cartesian ideas and methods can also be gleaned from Michael Foster, *Lectures on the History of Physiology* (Cambridge, 1901); and Gustav Scherz's various studies of Nicholas Steno. Finally, see Aram Vartanian, *Diderot and Descartes* (Princeton, 1953) and *La Mettrie's "L'homme machine"* (Princeton, 1960).

THEODORE M. BROWN

DES CLOIZEAUX, ALFRED-LOUIS-OLIVIER LEGRAND (*b.* Beauvais, France, 17 October 1817; *d.* Paris, France, 6 May 1897), *mineralogy, crystallography.*

Born of a family of the old bourgeoisie with a long tradition in the legal profession, Des Cloizeaux studied at the Lycée Charlemagne in Paris, where he came under the tutelage of Armand Lévy, a teacher of mathematics and mineralogy who instilled in him a fascination with minerals and crystals. Lévy encouraged Des Cloizeaux to attend the courses of Alexandre Brongniart at the Muséum d'Histoire Naturelle and those of Armand Dufrénoy at the École des Mines. Also through Lévy, Des Cloizeaux was introduced into Jean-Baptiste Biot's laboratory at the Collège de France. It was through Biot's influence that Des Cloizeaux was commissioned by the government in 1845 to travel to Iceland to study sources of Iceland spar. This voyage also enabled Des Cloizeaux to visit some British mineralogists (Robert Jameson, Thomas Thomson, and George Bellas Greenough, among others) and to inspect mineralogical collections in Scotland and England. In 1846 he returned to Iceland and joined there with members of a German-Danish expedition (including Bunsen and Wolfgang Sartorius von Waltershausen) in studying geysers and minerals. In succeeding years he traveled widely, especially in the Alpine regions, Scandinavia, and Baltic Russia.

In 1843 Des Cloizeaux had become a tutor at the École Centrale. He defended his thesis for the doctorate in 1857 at the Faculté des Sciences of Paris and was appointed professor in the École Normale Supérieure. In 1876 he was made professor of mineralogy at the Muséum in place of Delafosse, whom he had assisted at the Sorbonne since 1873; he taught at the Muséum until 1892. Des Cloizeaux was elected to the Académie des Sciences in 1869, replacing E. J. A. d'Archiac, having failed of election (to his considerable chagrin) in 1862, when Pasteur was chosen instead. In 1889 he served as president of the Academy.

Des Cloizeaux's main achievements fall into two categories: his studies on the form of crystals, and his investigation of the optical properties of crystalline materials. While questions of morphology occupied him early in his career, after 1855 he devoted himself principally to optical problems in crystallography. In both categories his work was characterized by the broad interest of a naturalist attempting to relate the substance under investigation to its mode of origin.

Des Cloizeaux was able, in part through optical methods, to elucidate the interior structure of minerals that had already been subjected to thorough study (for example, quartz).[1] He set out ambitiously to produce a comprehensive work on the structure (but not in the modern sense) of minerals. The result, the *Manuel de minéralogie*, occupied him for thirty-five years but was never completed beyond two volumes. This project began simply as a plan to translate William Phillips' *An Elementary Introduction to Mineralogy* as extended by Henry James Brooke and William Hallowes Miller, but it grew into a text emphasizing Des Cloizeaux's interest in crystallography and serving to establish the crystallographic notation invented by René-Just Haüy and augmented by Lévy.

The most original aspect of Des Cloizeaux's work lies in the field of optical studies of crystals, which he took up in part through the influence of Henri de Sénarmont. He embarked on the gigantic task of determining the optical characters of all known crystals, and although this proved too large an undertaking for one man he did ascertain the optical properties of nearly 500 substances. He was among the first to perceive the great potential utility of the polarizing microscope for investigating minerals, and with improved polarizing microscopes of his own devising he developed techniques for the determination of significant optical characteristics in crystals (e.g., the angle of the optic axis and the dispersions of the optic axes, indicatrix, and bisectrices). His methods and determinations constituted a part of the foundation of petrology. Among his extensions of the knowledge of polarization in crystals was his demonstration of circular polarization in cinnabar and strychnine sulfate.[2]

Inquiring into the effects of heat on crystalline bodies, he found that prolonged heating beyond a certain temperature permanently alters the positions of the optic axes of certain crystals (notably the orthoclase minerals), thereby providing the geologist with a means of determining whether or not certain rocks have been subjected to high temperatures.[3]

Descloizite, a rare mineral consisting of basic lead and zinc vanadate, was named after Des Cloizeaux by his friend and collaborator Augustin-Alexis Damour.[4]

NOTES

1. *Annales de chimie et de physique*, 3rd ser., **45** (1855), 129–316; *Mémoires présentés par divers savants à l'Académie des sciences. Sciences mathématiques et physiques*, **15** (1858), 404–614.
2. *Comptes rendus hebdomadaires des séances de l'Académie des sciences*, **44** (1857), 876–878, 909–912; *Annales de chimie et de physique*, 3rd ser., **51** (1857), 361–367; *Annalen der Physik und Chemie*, **102** (1857), 471–474.
3. *Comptes rendus*, **53** (1861), 64–68; **55** (1862), 651–654; **62** (1866), 987–990; *Annales de chimie et de physique*, 3rd ser., **68** (1863), 191–203; *Annales des mines*, 6th ser., **2** (1862), 327–328; *Annalen der Physik und Chemie*, **119** (1863), 481–492; **129** (1866), 345–350; *Bulletin de la Société géologique de France*, 2nd ser., **20** (1862–1863), 41–47; *Mémoires présentés par divers savants à l'Académie des sciences. Sciences mathématiques et physiques*, **18** (1868), 511–732.
4. *Annales de chimie et de physique*, 3rd ser., **41** (1854), 72–78.

BIBLIOGRAPHY

I. ORIGINAL WORKS. Des Cloizeaux's major work is *Manuel de minéralogie*, 2 vols. in 3 parts (Paris, 1862–1893). Alfred Lacroix's "Liste bibliographique des travaux de A. Des Cloizeaux," in his *Notice historique sur François-Sulpice Beudant et Alfred-Louis-Olivier Legrand Des Cloizeaux* (Paris, 1930), pp. 91–101, is fairly complete. Des Cloizeaux's own *Notice sur les travaux minéralogiques et géologiques de M. Des Cloizeaux* (Paris, 1869) provides annotations, some of them quite extensive, to a list of many of his publications.

II. SECONDARY LITERATURE. On Des Cloizeaux and his work, see Lacroix's *Notice*, referred to above, also in Lacroix's *Figures de savants*, 4 vols. (Paris, 1932–1938), I, 241–272. Contemporary biographical sources include Charles Barrois's funeral speech in *Bulletin de la Société géologique de France*, **25** (1897), 459–460; the eulogy by Adolphe Chatin, in *Comptes rendus hebdomadaires des séances de l'Académie des sciences*, **124** (1897), 983–984; an obituary by Lazarus Fletcher, in *Proceedings of the Royal Society of London*, **63** (1898), xxv–xxviii; and an anonymous sketch in *L'année scientifique* (1897), p. 409. Conrad Burri provides a recent assessment in "Alfred Des Cloizeaux 1817–1897, Ferdinand Fouqué 1828–1904, Auguste Michel-Lévy 1844–1911," in *Geschichte der Mikroskopie*.

Leben und Werk grosser Forscher, III, Hugo Freund and Alexander Berg, eds. (Frankfurt, 1966), 163–176.

KENNETH L. TAYLOR

DESCOTILS, HIPPOLYTE VICTOR. *See* **Collet-Descotils, Hippolyte Victor.**

DESCOURTILZ, MICHEL ÉTIENNE (*b.* Boiste, near Pithiviers, France, 25 November 1775; *d.* Paris, France, 1836), *medicine, natural history.*

Descourtilz was first trained as a surgeon. Following his marriage to the daughter of Rossignol-Desdunes, who had plantations in Artibonite, he went to Saint-Domingue (Haiti) in 1798, on the way visiting Charleston, South Carolina, and Santiago de Cuba. Descourtilz became involved in the Negro revolution and, in spite of the protection of Toussaint L'Ouverture, was nearly executed by Dessalines. He was forced to join the medical service of the Negro army, but in 1803 he escaped and sailed to Cádiz. After reaching Paris, Descourtilz became a doctor of medicine in 1814; he practiced in Orléans; was for a while physician at the Hôtel-Dieu in Beaumont-en-Gâtinais; and retired to Paris, where he was a member of the Société de Médecine Pratique and became president of the Société Linnéenne. Most of his original drawings and manuscripts, as well as his herbarium, were burned in Haiti; and in writing his books he had to rely on the works of Plumier, Joseph Surian, Alexandre Poiteau, and Turpin. His zoological contributions, particularly those on the caiman, were highly praised.

BIBLIOGRAPHY

In *Voyages d'un naturaliste* (Paris, 1809) Descourtilz narrates his adventures during the Haitian revolution and, at the end, deals with the natural history of the isle. Next to be published was *Code du safranier* (Paris, 1810). Pinel presided over his thesis, *Propositions sur l'anaphrodisie . . .* (Paris, 1814), later expanded into a larger volume, *De l'impuissance et de la stérilité . . .* (Paris, 1831). One of his most popular books was *Guide sanitaire des voyageurs aux colonies* (Paris, 1816). *Manuel indicateur des plantes usuelles aux Antilles* (Paris, 1821) appeared as he began, with one of his eight sons, Jean Théodore, to publish his major work, *Flore pittoresque des Antilles,* 8 vols. (Paris, 1821–1829), arranging the material according to medicinal properties. *Anatomie comparée du grand crocodile . . .* (Paris, 1825) was followed by *Des champignons comestibles* (Paris, 1827) and *Cours d'électricité médicale* (Paris, 1832).

Descourtilz is mentioned in Rulx Léon, *Notes bio-bibliographiques. Médecins et naturalistes de l'ancienne colonie française de Saint-Domingue* (Port-au-Prince, 1933).

FRANCISCO GUERRA

DESHAYES, GERARD PAUL (*b.* Nancy, France, 24 May 1797; *d.* Boran-sur-Oise, France, 9 June 1875), *paleontology, malacology.*

Deshayes was the son of a physics professor at the École Centrale in Nancy. He began studying medicine at the University of Strasbourg but left in 1820 and went to Paris, where in 1821 he became *bachelier-ès-lettres.* He then gave up his medical studies and, as an independent scholar, turned to natural history, particularly geology and malacology. Soon after his arrival in Paris he gave private lectures on geology and led field trips. Those who attended included Élie de Beaumont, d'Archiac, Philippe de Verneuil, Constant Prévost, Desnoyers, and Edmond Hébert. His home soon became a center for exchange of scientific ideas as well as social communications. On behalf of the Paris Academy of Sciences, Deshayes was in Algeria from 1840 to 1842 investigating mollusks, especially those of recent origin. Through his own collecting and through items sent by colleagues in many countries, he amassed a great collection of recent and fossil mollusks that was of exceptional importance because of the many original specimens and types it contained. Circumstances forced Deshayes to sell his collection, together with his comprehensive malacological and paleontological library, to the French government in 1868 for 100,000 francs. Both were turned over to the École des Mines in Paris.

In 1869 Deshayes was appointed professor at the Muséum d'Histoire Naturelle in Paris, occupying the chair of conchology once held by Lamarck, whom he highly regarded. This was Deshayes's first and only public post. Despite his advanced age, poor health, and the Franco-Prussian War, he enlarged the museum's malacological collection with tireless zeal and youthful energy. Deshayes was one of the founders of the Société Géologique de France and was several times its president.

An old and worsening heart ailment weakened Deshayes from 1873. He spent some time in Provence and then returned to Boran-sur-Oise, to the region containing the fossils he had described at the beginning of his career. He was survived by his wife and daughter.

In 1824, with his own modest financial means, Deshayes began the publication of *Description des coquilles fossiles des environs de Paris.* This work, interrupted by descriptions of recent and fossil mollusks of the Peloponnesus and India, was completed in 1837. It is among Deshayes's most important works. Along with the painstaking description and illustration of 1,074 species of mollusks, predominantly from the Eocene of the Paris Basin, including 660 species first described by him, there is a division of the Tertiary into three periods. The basis for this division was the proportion of living species among the total number of Tertiary forms: in the first (oldest) period, 3 percent; in the second (middle), 19 percent; in the third (most recent), 52 percent. Deshayes joined this with the premise that since the beginning of the Tertiary there had been a continuous decrease in temperature. This three-part division of the Tertiary (1831) agreed in methodological principles and main features with the subdivision of the Tertiary into Eocene, Miocene, and Pliocene proposed by Lyell. After Deshayes was brought into contact with Lyell, he provided for the latter's use statistical tables of Tertiary mollusk species. They were published in Lyell's *Principles of Geology* and constitute an essential support for Lyell's very important Tertiary subdivisions.

In the following years Deshayes published several large monographs, collections of articles, and compendia. These included a description of fossil mollusks from the Crimea (1838); a work on mollusks from the Algerian expedition, in twenty-five installments interrupted by the February Revolution of 1848 and the actions of envious colleagues (1844–1848); a new edition, in collaboration with Henri Milne-Edwards, of Lamarck's *Histoire des animaux sans vertèbres* (1833–1858); the continuation of a work begun by J.-B. de Férussac, *Histoire naturelle générale et particulière des mollusques* (1839–1851); "Mollusca," in Cuvier's *Règne animal* (1836–1849); an incomplete *Traité élémentaire de conchyliologie* in three volumes (1839–1857); *Conchyliologie de l'île de la Réunion* (*Océan Indien*) (1863); and *Description des animaux sans vertèbres découverts dans le bassin de Paris* (1860–1866).

In this last work, Deshayes returned once more to the subject of his first researches. The publications of 1860–1866 and 1824–1837 present his most important contributions.

Deshayes mastered the entire body of the systematic-taxonomic conchology of his time and presented it brilliantly. Even today, despite later publications by other authors, his descriptions of the mollusks of the Tertiary of the Paris Basin form an indispensable basis for further study. His exposition of the stratigraphy of the Paris Basin in the introduction to his *Description des animaux sans vertèbres* (1860) likewise contains valuable data for an understanding of this sedimentary sequence. Also worth reading are his descriptions in this introduction of the delimitation and definition of species, their life spans, and the reasons for their extinction. Finally, his subdivision of the Tertiary, by means of the proportion of living

species of mollusks established in Lyell's Eocene, Miocene, and Pliocene stages, belongs to the classic methods of biostratigraphy.

BIBLIOGRAPHY

I. ORIGINAL WORKS. Besides many journal articles, Deshayes wrote the following books: *Description des coquilles fossiles des environs de Paris,* 3 vols. (Paris, 1824–1837); *Traité élémentaire de conchyliologie avec l'application de cette science à la géognosie,* 3 vols. (Paris, 1839–1857); *Exploration scientifique de l'Algérie. Histoire naturelle des mollusques,* 25 pts. (Paris, 1844–1848); *Histoire naturelle générale et particulière des mollusques* (Paris, 1820–1851), with J.-B. de Férussac; and *Description des animaux sans vertèbres découverts dans le bassin de Paris,* 3 vols. (Paris, 1860–1866). Lists of Deshayes's papers may be found in Royal Society of London, *Catalogue of Scientific Papers* (*1800–1863*), II (London, 1868), 251–254; and (*1864–1873*), VII (London, 1877), 524.

II. SECONDARY LITERATURE. On Deshayes or his work, see H. Crosse and P. Fischer, "Nécrologie. G. P. Deshayes," in *Journal de conchyliologie,* **24** (1876), 123–127; J. Evans, "Obituary Gérard Paul Deshayes," in *Quarterly Journal of the Geological Society of London, Proceedings,* **32** (1876), 80–82; and K. Lambrecht, W. Quenstedt, and A. Quenstedt, "Palaeontologi. Catalogus bio-bibliographicus," in *Fossilium catalogus,* I, *Animalia,* **72** (The Hague, 1938), 112–113.

HEINZ TOBIEN

DESLANDRES, HENRI (*b.* Paris, France, 24 July 1853; *d.* Paris, 15 January 1948), *astronomy, physics.*

Deslandres was born into a family typical of the mid-nineteenth-century French bourgeoisie. He graduated from the École Polytechnique in 1874 and entered the army, in which he served until 1881, when a strong interest in physical sciences led him to resign his military position. He worked first in the physical laboratories of the École Polytechnique and the Sorbonne, devoting himself to ultraviolet spectroscopy under the guidance of M. A. Cornu.

In 1889 Deslandres joined the staff of the Paris observatory, then headed by Admiral Ernest Mouchez, who sought to develop astrophysics in the institution long dedicated to celestial mechanics under Le Verrier. In 1897 he joined Jules Janssen at his astrophysical observatory in Meudon and became its director in 1908, following Janssen's death. In 1926 the Paris and Meudon observatories were united under his management. Deslandres retired in 1929 but pursued an active scientific life almost until his death at the age of ninety-four.

During his long and successful career Deslandres was elected to essentially all the scientific societies of significance, including the Académie des Sciences (1902; president, 1920), the Royal Society, the Royal Astronomical Society, the Accademia dei Lincei, and the National Academy of Sciences of the United States.

In his bearing, his character, and his style of life Deslandres always remained more akin to the soldier (and the officer) than to the scholar. These consequences of his education also appeared in his scientific work: he was more successful in the experimental and technical aspects of physics and astrophysics than in creating new theories (even though he worked at it with tenacity and ultimately with intuition).

In his thesis Deslandres studied the spectra of molecules such as nitrogen, cyanogen, CH, and water and recognized two simple laws in the disconcerting complexity of the numerous bands, each of which is made up of many tens of lines. These laws bear his name.

First, the frequencies (or wave numbers) v of lines inside a given band can be represented by the parabolic formula

$$v = A + 2Bm + Cm^2,$$

where m is an integer ($m \neq 0$). Then, the constants A associated with various bands of a given system can all be fitted to another parabolic formula involving the integers v' and v''. These laws were at first useful in the empirical study and classification of molecular spectra; later, with the elaboration of quantum mechanics, it became easy to explain them in terms of the structure of molecules. The integers m, v', and v'' were simply the quantum numbers identifying the possible rotational and vibrational energies of the molecule in the initial and final states of a radiative transition; and the various empirical constants in Deslandres's formulas could be related to physical constants that were characteristics of each molecule.

After this splendid success in laboratory spectroscopy, Deslandres turned in 1889 to astrophysics without losing interest in molecules, as is shown by his fine observations of the Zeeman effect on molecular lines. In numerous publications of his late years he sought a unified theoretical interpretation of molecular spectra; he paid little attention to such modernist developments as quantum mechanics.

At the Paris observatory Deslandres attached a spectrograph to the recently built 120-cm. mirror telescope and began observing the spectra of stars and planets, devoting himself to the measurement of line-of-sight velocities through the Doppler-Fizeau effect, the most essential tool of the astronomer in studying the motions and dynamics of celestial bodies. He continued the same type of observations in Meudon with a spectrograph attached to a large re-

fractor with an 83-cm. aperture. Among his most valuable results were the law of rotation of Saturn's ring (1895), which was shown to rotate as a system of independent particles and not as a solid body, and the proof that Uranus (like its known satellites) rotates in the direction opposite to all other planets, a fact of significance to cosmogony.

As an astronomer Deslandres is still better known for his important contributions to the physical study of the sun, particularly for the invention of the spectroheliograph, an instrument that he completed at the Paris observatory in the spring of 1894. It allows one to make photographs of the sun in nearly monochromatic light, the narrow spectral band being selected at will with the help of a dispersing spectrograph. By choosing radiations to which the solar atmosphere is very opaque, one "sees" only its outermost layers, the chromosphere; and a wealth of important phenomena are thus revealed, such as solar plages, prominences, and flares. The spectroheliograph was invented independently by the great American astronomer George Ellery Hale, who actually completed his first instrument more than a year before Deslandres, at Kenwood Observatory in Chicago. However, Deslandres explored with particular tenacity the possibilities of the new method and found useful variants; and for many years he contributed to the description of the structure of the chromosphere and of the complex phenomena of solar activity.

Like Hale, Deslandres believed (and correctly so) that solar activity is dominated by electromagnetic causes; and he attempted imaginative explanations, now of limited interest. However, he showed remarkable intuition in maintaining that the sun produced radio waves, although the crude experiments of Charles Nordmann in 1902 failed to detect them. Solar Hertzian radiation was actually observed only in 1942 by J. S. Hey, and this finding was published shortly after World War II. It is not known whether "the brave soldier" (as Stratton described Deslandres), who then led a rather secluded life, was ever informed that he had been right forty years before.

BIBLIOGRAPHY

I. ORIGINAL WORKS. Deslandres's most important publications are "Spectre du pôle négatif de l'azote. Loi générale de répartition des raies dans les spectres de bandes," in *Comptes rendus hebdomadaires des séances de l'Académie des sciences,* **103** (1886), 375–379; "Loi de répartition des raies et des bandes, communes à plusieurs spectres de bandes . . .," *ibid.,* **104** (1887), 972–976; "Spectres de bandes ultra-violets des métalloïdes avec une faible dispersion," his thesis (Faculté des Sciences de Paris, 1888), no.

619; "Étude des gaz et vapeurs du soleil," in *L'astronomie* (Dec. 1894); and "Recherches sur l'atmosphère solaire. Photographie des couches gazeuses supérieures . . .," in *Annales de l'Observatoire d'astronomie physique de Paris,* **4** (1910).

II. SECONDARY LITERATURE. Short biographies of Deslandres are L. d'Azambuja, in *Bulletin de la Société astronomique de France,* **62** (1948), 179–184; and F. J. M. Stratton, in *Monthly Notices of the Royal Astronomical Society,* **109** (1949), 141–144.

R. MICHARD

DESMAREST, NICOLAS (*b.* Soulaines-Dhuys, France, 16 September 1725; *d.* Paris, France, 28 September 1815), *geology, technology.*

Desmarest was the only child of Jean Desmarest, the local schoolteacher, and Marguerite Clement. Practically nothing is known about his youth until 1740, when his father died. In February 1741 Desmarest's mother remarried, and Nicolas, now in the care of a guardian, was placed in the Oratorian *collège* of Troyes. Here he received a sound education, and when he left Troyes for Paris in late 1746 or early 1747, he embarked upon a scientific career that brought him membership in the Academy of Sciences in 1771. His election to that body followed the scientific work with which his name has remained principally associated: his assertion that the basalt columns found in Auvergne and elsewhere are volcanic in origin. The election to the Academy of Sciences crowned with success what had been an often frustrating campaign for membership, begun as early as 1757.

But Desmarest's profession was not exclusively scientific; much of his energy during his best years was consumed by his duties in the government bureaucracy controlling industry, which culminated in his serving as inspector general of manufactures. After the Revolution suppressed this post, Desmarest found himself working for a time in various minor government agencies and was appointed as a teacher in the *écoles centrales.* He married Françoise Tessier, twenty-five years his junior, on an unknown date. They had a son in 1784, and Desmarest's wife died in 1806.

Despite Desmarest's fame for identifying basalt as volcanic, his general geological orientation was by no means solely volcanological. To the extent that he professed any geological doctrine, it reflected the influence of Guillaume-François Rouelle, whose public courses he had attended in Paris. Rouelle expounded a neptunist outlook regarding the origin of terrestrial formations, and in adopting Rouelle's basic tenets Desmarest rejected forever the notion that volcanoes or an internal heat of the globe had been primarily responsible for producing the earth's essential features. Thus, even though Desmarest greatly expanded the extent to which volcanoes were understood to have produced changes in the earth, he cannot be counted as a genuine volcanist; although he was in a sense the founder of the plutonist side of the basalt controversy, he did not represent the volcanists in the general dispute over modes of geological change that emerged from the confrontation of Wernerian and Huttonian theories of the earth. Indeed, Desmarest's geology did not grow out of, and never became altogether adapted to, a "theory of the earth." Instead, his scientific career developed out of the consideration of more narrowly circumscribed problems. His scientific demeanor always remained rather cautious, and in this regard he reflected a typical Enlightenment aversion to the liabilities of *système.*

After his arrival in Paris, Desmarest lived precariously for a time as a private tutor. His climb toward recognition in the learned world began in 1749, when he assisted Pierre-Nicolas Bonamy in editing the *Suite de la clef,* better known as the *Journal de Verdun.* In subsequent years he may have lived in part on fees for editing books; under his guidance there appeared a collection of the thoughts of the Abbé Louis Du Four de Longuerue (1754) and the seventh edition of *Les élémens de géométrie,* by the renowned Oratorian teacher Bernard Lamy (1758). Of far more significance to Desmarest's line of interest, however, was the French edition of Francis Hauksbee's *Physico-Mechanical Experiments* (1754), which Desmarest edited and to which he added voluminous notes and remarks. In 1751 he won the prize competition of the Académie des Sciences, Belles-Lettres et Arts d'Amiens with an essay arguing that England had once been joined to France by an isthmus whose destruction was recent, natural, and noncatastrophic. The published essay (1753) was accompanied by maps and a cross section of the English Channel prepared by the geographer Philippe Buache; the maps, among the first to employ contour lines to show ocean depths, were used by Desmarest to show that the supposed isthmus still existed not far beneath the waves that had reduced it.

After his success in the Amiens competition, Desmarest continued to direct his attention to scientific questions concerning the earth's surface and internal structure. In the 1754 *Expériences physico-méchaniques,* for example, he supported Hauksbee's attack on a peculiar extension of the terraqueous globe doctrine, according to which the earth's primitive formations had been deposited out of the terraqueous fluid in descending order of the specific gravity of the suspended materials. In 1756, just a few months after the Lisbon earthquake, he published an essay on the propagation of earthquake disturbances, presumed to be caused by the combustion of inflammable matter underground and conveyed by means of the worldwide network of interlocking mountain ranges. The seventh volume of the *Encyclopédie* (1757) brought forth two further contributions by Desmarest to his emerging specialty. "Fontaine" deals for the most part with the ancient problem of the origin of springs, or the manner in which rivers are fed and maintained. Desmarest supported the meteoric theory, claiming that rainfall is sufficient to account for the flow of rivers and that the earth can receive and store water in amounts large enough to account for the continued flow of springs. "Géographie physique" is a more general article outlining the aims and methods of investigating the earth's surface features.

By the late 1750's Desmarest had decided to concentrate on physical geography and the study of rocks, and in the course of several years he traveled extensively in France, observing the Paris region, Champagne, Burgundy, Lorraine, Alsace, Franche-Comté, Guienne, and Gascony. His notes from these travels in the late 1750's and early 1760's indicate a commitment to an organizing scheme like that of Rouelle, which called for a division of the earth's surface features into three categories (*ancienne, intermédiaire, nouvelle*) corresponding respectively to a crystalline inner core, and two different sorts of sedimentary layers, all of them deriving from fluid sources.

In 1757 Desmarest began his most significant and extensive professional occupation outside of science. He was appointed by Daniel-Charles Trudaine, the intendant of finances and director of commerce, to make a study of the woolen cloth industry in France. For over three decades thereafter Desmarest was involved in the analysis and control of French industry as an agent of the royal government. He became expert in the technical aspects of numerous industries and developed special proficiency in papermaking technology. His treatises on the manufacture of paper made him a leader in the rationalization of paper technology in the late eighteenth century. As inspector of manufactures in the *généralité* of Limoges under the intendant Anne-Robert-Jacques Turgot, Desmarest devoted himself especially to agricultural matters. He later held the post of inspector of manufactures of the *généralité* of Châlons and ultimately served as inspector general, director of manufactures, for the entire realm (1788–1791).

It was in his capacity as an agent for Trudaine that Desmarest first traveled to Auvergne in 1763. While on a tour to examine industries south of Clermont-Ferrand, Desmarest noticed prismatic basalt columns in association with hardened lavas, such as had been described by Jean-Étienne Guettard after his 1751 visit to the region. Desmarest's excitement at this discovery appears to have been stimulated initially as much by the mere appearance of the columns as by their possibly volcanic origin. At this time there was considerable interest in the finely sculptured basalts, especially in the articulated columns of County Antrim in Northern Ireland, the celebrated Giant's Causeway. Evidently believing that the articulated columns of Auvergne were the first of that type known outside of Ireland, Desmarest momentarily let chauvinistic pride come to the fore but soon set about investigating the geological significance of the columns' presence among lava flows.

Between 1764 and 1766 Desmarest and François Pasumot drew up a map of the main volcanic district of Auvergne, concentrating especially on the southern, Mont-Dore district. Their geological map was published with Desmarest's first long memoir on the Auvergne basalts, which he delivered before the Academy of Sciences in 1771. This map did not fulfill Desmarest's entire cartographic aim, however, and he continued to work intermittently on the Auvergne geological map for the rest of his life. A much larger and more detailed map than the 1771 version was finally published in 1823 by his son, Anselme-Gaëtan Desmarest.

Desmarest's first public statement on the geological significance of the Auvergne basalts came in a paper he delivered to the Academy of Sciences in the summer of 1765, before departing on a year-long journey in Italy in the company of Duke Louis-Alexandre de La Rochefoucauld. The essential contents of this report are included in the sixth volume of plates for the *Encyclopédie* (1768). Here he argued that the presence of prismatic basalts infallibly indicates the former existence of volcanoes in that area. Hypothesizing that "the regular forms of basalt are a result of the uniform contraction undergone by the fused material as it cooled and congealed, shrinking around several centers of activity," he promised a fuller explanation and substantiation of this supposition in a later work. This he never provided, however, and in his own time other voices were heard saying that a rapid, rather than slow, rate of cooling was responsible for the basalt's columnar shape. But Desmarest's attention had not been confined to basalts of prismatic form. Explaining that the basalts of Auvergne also take the form of ellipsoids composed of concentric layers and of large sheets broken into randomly oriented bundles of regular shape, he found himself leading the way to a study of the relation of these materials to their neighboring or enveloping matter.

71

The notion that prismatic basalts are a volcanic product, rather than rocks of igneous origin, was thus made known to the Academy of Sciences in 1765, and found its way into print in 1768. This opinion became prominent, however, only after 1771, when Desmarest delivered to the Academy of Sciences the lengthy report of his studies on the Auvergne basalts. This was followed by another memoir presented in 1775, and it is in these papers that Desmarest's original contributions to geological science lie. Here he dealt with such problems as the origin of the matter constituting the basalts, the volcanic history of the Auvergne region, and the alterations that the volcanic flows had undergone.

Attempting to reconstruct a mental picture of the former condition of the lava flows whose extremities revealed prismatic basalts, Desmarest was led to a consideration of the destructive effects of flowing water upon the Auvergne terrain. He applied the idea of aqueous degradation, which had become fixed in his mind several years before his first visit in Auvergne, in such a way as virtually to enunciate a principle of uniformity in destructive geological processes. It is noteworthy that he at first took the principle of regularity in cause and rate of degradation as a necessary working hypothesis, but before long began to treat it as a result of his researches. Desmarest utilized his conclusions about Auvergne's physiographical history to hazard a three-stage volcanic history of the region, thus extending historical geology into the field of volcanism.

Desmarest's position on the nature of volcanoes always distinguished between the source of volcanic heat and the molten and solid ejecta. He consistently indicated that volcanoes feed on some combustible or fermenting agent and thus regarded lavas as material heated, as it were, accidentally. Basalt he took to be granite heated moderately—not to an extreme degree. This highly limiting view on the sources of volcanic action, not atypical of his time, naturally placed definite restraints on the possibility of his entertaining truly volcanist ideas, restraints which he always respected. His mature belief, expressed in *Géographie physique,* a large work produced in old age, was that burning beds of underground coal are the most likely cause of volcanic heat, and so he regarded volcanic action as a relatively recent interloper in geological history. Desmarest rejected Hutton's assertion that volcanic heat might be a source of power sufficient to uplift continents. While suggesting that the earth's age must be quite great, he never committed himself to a clear definition of the geological time scale. He retained a faith in the importance of certain catastrophic agencies of terrestrial change and did not regard this as inconsistent with his general adherence to uniformity in degradation.

BIBLIOGRAPHY

I. ORIGINAL WORKS. Desmarest made his scientific debut with *Dissertation sur l'ancienne jonction de l'Angleterre à la France, qui a remporté le prix, au jugement de l'Académie des sciences, belles-lettres & arts d'Amiens, en l'année 1751* (Amiens, 1753), and followed this with *Conjectures physico-méchaniques sur la propagation des secousses dans les tremblemens de terre, et sur la disposition des lieux qui en ont ressenti les effets* (n.p., 1756). Vol. VII of *Encyclopédie, ou dictionnaire raisonné des sciences, des arts et des métiers, par une société de gens de lettres* (Paris, 1757) contains his "Fontaine," pp. 80–101, and "Géographie physique," pp. 613–626. The first published statement of the volcanic origin of prismatic basalt is found in a brief commentary, "Planche VII. Basalte d'Auvergne," in *Recueil de planches, sur les sciences, les arts libéraux, et les arts méchaniques, avec leur explication,* VI (Paris, 1768), pp. 3–4 of section entitled "Histoire naturelle. Règne minéral. Sixième collection. Volcans." Desmarest's detailed studies of the Auvergne basalts were published in three parts, the first two in "Mémoire sur l'origine & la nature du basalte à grandes colonnes polygones, déterminées par l'histoire naturelle de cette pierre, observée en Auvergne," in *Mémoires de l'Académie royale des sciences* for 1771 (1774), 705–775; and the third as "Mémoire sur le basalte. Troisième partie, où l'on traite du basalte des anciens; & où l'on expose l'histoire naturelle des différentes espèces de pierres auxquelles on a donné, en différens temps, le nom de basalte," *ibid.,* for 1773 (1777), 599–670. His general conclusions on the geological history of the Auvergne region were expressed in "Extrait d'un mémoire sur la détermination de quelques époques de la nature par les produits des volcans, & sur l'usage de ces époques dans l'étude des volcans," in *Observations sur la physique, sur l'histoire naturelle et sur les arts,* **13** (1779), 115–126, expanded in "Mémoire sur la détermination de trois époques de la nature par les produits des volcans, et sur l'usage qu'on peut faire de ces époques dans l'étude des volcans," in *Mémoires de l'Institut des sciences, lettres et arts. Sciences mathématiques et physiques,* **6** (1806), 219–289. Desmarest's largest and most comprehensive geological work, which is largely derivative, is a part of the *Encyclopédie méthodique,* entitled *Géographie physique,* 5 vols. (Paris, *an III* [1794–1795]–1828), the last and posthumous volume edited in part by others.

Among the books edited by Desmarest, the most significant is Francis Hauksbee's *Expériences physico-méchaniques sur différens sujets, et principalement sur la lumière et l'électricité, produites par le frottement des corps,* 2 vols. (Paris, 1754).

Foremost among Desmarest's writings in the fields of industry, manufacturing, and agriculture are his essays on papermaking methods: "Premier mémoire sur les principales manipulations qui sont en usage dans les papeteries de Hollande, avec l'explication physique des résultats de ces manipulations," in *Mémoires de l'Académie royale des sciences* for 1771 (1774), 335–364; "Second mémoire sur la papeterie; Dans lequel, en continuant d'exposer la méthode hollandoise, l'on traite de la nature & des qualités des pâtes hollandoises & françoises; De la manière dont elles se comportent dans les procédés de la fabrication & des apprêts: Enfin des différens usages auxquels peuvent être propres les produits de ces pâtes," *ibid.,* for 1774 (1778), 599–687; "Papier. (Art de fabriquer le)," in *Encyclopédie méthodique. Arts et métiers mécaniques,* V (Paris–Liège, 1788), 463–592; and *Art de la papeterie* (Paris, 1789).

The largest and most interesting collections of Desmarest's correspondence are found in the Bibliothèque Nationale, Fonds Français, Nouvelles Acquisitions, MS 803 (letters exchanged by Desmarest and Pierre-Jean Grosley) and MS 10359 (letters from Turgot to Desmarest), and in the Bibliothèque Municipale de Beaune, MS 310 (letters from François Pasumot to Desmarest).

II. SECONDARY LITERATURE. The single most important source of biographical information on Desmarest is a handwritten set of notes by his son, Anselme-Gaëtan Desmarest, "Notes et renseignements sur la vie et les ouvrages de mon père," Bibliothèque de l'Institut de France, Fonds Cuvier, MS 3199. Georges Cuvier depended heavily upon them in preparing his "Éloge historique de Nicolas Desmarets [*sic*], lu le 16 mars 1818," in *Recueil des éloges historiques lus dans les séances publiques de l'Institut royal de France,* II (Strasbourg–Paris, 1819), 339–374. Further references and discussion are found in Sir Archibald Geikie, *The Founders of Geology,* 2nd ed. (London–New York, 1905), pp. 140–175; and Kenneth L. Taylor, "Nicolas Desmarest and Geology in the Eighteenth Century," in Cecil J. Schneer, ed., *Toward a History of Geology* (Cambridge, 1969), pp. 339–356.

KENNETH L. TAYLOR

DESMIER DE SAINT-SIMON, ÉTIENNE J. A. *See* **Archiac, Vicomte d'.**

DESOR, PIERRE JEAN ÉDOUARD (*b.* Friedrichsdorf, near Frankfurt am Main, Germany, 13 February 1811; *d.* Nice, France, 23 February 1882), *glacial geology, paleontology, stratigraphy.*

Desor was of French origin and studied law at the universities of Giessen and Heidelberg. During a short stay in Paris, he was introduced to geology by Élie de Beaumont. His meeting in 1837 in Switzerland with Louis Agassiz marks the turning point of his career; for almost twenty years he was Agassiz's close friend and chief collaborator. Desor's two volumes on the glacial theory were published for the general public, and his reports of Agassiz's expeditions on the Alpine glaciers led to the formation of numerous Alpine clubs.

Desor followed Agassiz to America in 1846, but—for reasons still not understood—their friendship ended suddenly. In the service of federal and state agencies, Desor studied the fauna of the Atlantic shelf aboard the *Bibb;* took part in the Lake Superior land district survey, directed first by C. T. Jackson and then by J. W. Foster and J. D. Whitney; and undertook a study of the coal basin of Pottsville, Pennsylvania, supervised by H. D. Rogers.

Returning to Neuchâtel in 1852 because of his brother's poor health, Desor was appointed professor of geology at the Academy of Neuchâtel. His brother's death in 1858 left him in a financially advantageous situation and enabled him to resign his professorship and return to the study of fossil echinoderms, the geology of the Jura Mountains, and the archaeology of the Bronze Age lake dwellers. From his home at Combe Varin in the Val des Ponts, well-known as a meeting place for natural philosophers, Desor continued his studies and collaborated for twenty years in the preparation of a geological map of Switzerland.

Desor was naturalized in 1859; his subsequent political career led him to the presidency of the Swiss Federal Assembly in 1874. Forced by gout to spend much of his last years on the French Riviera, he devoted his final works to a study of that region's geology and archaeology.

BIBLIOGRAPHY

I. ORIGINAL WORKS. Desor's writings include *Monographies d'échinodermes vivants et fossiles* (Neuchâtel, 1838–1843), 5 pts. in one vol., written with L. Agassiz and G. Valentin; "Aperçu général de la structure géologique des Alpes," in *Bibliothèque universelle,* XXXVIII (Geneva, 1842), 120–149, written with B. Studer; *Excursions et séjours dans les glaciers et les hautes régions des Alpes, de M. Agassiz et de ses compagnons de voyage* (Neuchâtel, 1844); *Nouvelles excursions et séjours dans les glaciers et les hautes régions des Alpes, de M. Agassiz et de ses compagnons de voyage* (Neuchâtel, 1845); "Catalogue raisonné des familles, des genres, et des espèces de la classe des Échinodermes; précédé d'une introduction sur l'organisation, la classification, et le développement progressif des types dans la série des terrains," in *Annales des sciences naturelles (zoologie),* 3rd ser., **6** (1846), 305–374; **7** (1847), 129–168; **8** (1847), 5–35, 355–381, written with L. Agassiz; "On the Drift of Lake Superior," in *American Journal of Science,* 2nd ser., **13** (1852), 93–109; *Synopsis des échinides fossiles,* 2 vols. and atlas (Paris, 1858); *Études géologiques sur le Jura neuchâtelois* (Neuchâtel, 1859), written with A. Gressly; *Les palafittes ou constructions lacustres du Lac de Neuchâtel* (Paris, 1865); *Description des oursins fossiles de la Suisse. Échinides de la période jurassique,* 16 secs. with atlas (Wiesbaden, 1868–1872), written with P. de Loriol; *Le bel âge du bronze* *lacustre en Suisse* (Paris, 1874), written with L. Favre; and *Le paysage morainique, son origine glaciaire, et ses rapports avec les formations pliocènes d'Italie* (Paris, 1875).

The Royal Society's *Catalogue of Scientific Papers* gives a complete list of Desor's publications in II, 266–269; VII, 525–526; and IX, 688–689.

II. SECONDARY LITERATURE. Notices on Desor are L. Favre, "Notice nécrologique d'Édouard Desor (1811–1882)," in *Bulletin de la Société des sciences naturelles* (Neuchâtel), **12** (1882), 551–576; and J. P. Lesley, "Obituary Notice of Édouard Desor," in *Proceedings of the American Philosophical Society,* **20** (1882), 519–528.

ALBERT V. CAROZZI

DESORMES, CHARLES-BERNARD (*b.* Dijon, Côte-d'Or, France, 3 June 1777; *d.* Verberie, Oise, France, 30 August 1862), *chemistry.*

Desormes entered the École Polytechnique at its founding (1794) and he remained there after his studies were completed, becoming *répétiteur* in chemistry under Guyton de Morveau, a position he held until 1804. From this period dates his relationship with Nicolas Clément, his compatriot who later became his scientific collaborator, industrial associate, son-in-law, and friend. (Detailed information on their important joint scientific works can be found in the article on Clément.) Desormes left Guyton de Morveau only in order to devote himself to the alum factory that he established at Verberie in association with Clément and Joseph Montgolfier.

On 5 July 1819 Desormes was elected a corresponding member of the Académie des Sciences; this honor was refused his self-educated son-in-law. From this time, and especially after 1830, Desormes gradually turned away from science in order to devote his time to politics. He was elected *conseiller général* of the department of Oise in 1830, but was defeated as an opposition candidate for parliament in June 1834. He then founded the *Revue de l'Oise,* which became the *Progrès de l'Oise.* Following two further defeats in November 1837 and in July 1842 (shortly after the death of Clément), Desormes was finally elected to the Constituent Assembly on 23 April 1848. He sat with the republicans and participated in the departmental and communal Committee of Administration.

Besides his works in collaboration with Clément, Desormes's scientific *oeuvre* is slight, consisting of three memoirs dating from 1801 to 1804, the period immediately after the appearance of Volta's pile. Historians of science should certainly pay a bit more attention to the dry piles that Desormes then constructed. They were composed of metallic disks separated by a layer of salt paste. The analogous arrangement of Giuseppe Zamboni dates only from 1812.

BIBLIOGRAPHY

For the works that Desormes published in collaboration with his son-in-law Nicolas Clément, see the article on the latter.

The easiest way to gain an overall idea of Desormes's career is to consult *Procès-verbaux des séances de l'Académie tenues depuis la fondation de l'Institut jusqu'au mois d'août 1835,* 10 vols. (Hendaye, 1910–1924). The most relevant of these are II, 312 (6 ventôse *an* IX [25 Feb. 1801]) and II, 316 (11 ventôse [2 Mar.]), reading of a memoir by Desormes on galvanism; IV, 237 (7 Aug. 1809), Desormes admitted to the session upon having presented at least two memoirs; IV, 315 (22 Jan. 1810), Desormes a candidate following the death of Fourcroy; V, 271 (6 Dec. 1813), Desormes proposed as a correspondent; VI, 113 (25 Nov. 1816), same topic; VI, 118 (2 Dec. 1816), Desormes defeated, having received only two votes; VI, 465 (28 June 1819), Desormes a candidate following the death of Clément; VI, 466 (5 July 1819), Desormes elected corresponding member by forty votes; VI, 483 (13 Sept. 1819), Desormes expresses his appreciation; VIII, 216 (23 May 1825), the role of Desormes in the history of the construction of dry cells is recalled; IX, 284 (3 Aug. 1829), same subject, with remarks by Antoine-César Becquerel.

The announcement of Desormes's death is in *Comptes rendus,* **55** (1862), 418.

I. ORIGINAL WORKS. *Considérations sur les routes en général et sur celles du département de l'Oise* (Senlis, 1834); *Des impôts* (Senlis, 1851); "Expériences et observations sur les phénomènes physiques et chimiques que présente l'appareil électrique de Volta," in *Annales de chimie,* **37** (*an* IX [1801]), 284–321; *Proposition relative à la franchise des lettres, adressée au citoyen président de l'Assemblée nationale, présentée le 12 juillet 1848 par le citoyen Desormes . . .* (Paris, 1849).

Desormes also wrote, in collaboration with Guyton de Morveau, "Essai sur l'analyse et la recomposition de deux alcalis fixes et de quelques-unes des terres réputées simples, lu le six floréal an VIII [26 Apr. 1800]," in *Mémoires de l'Académie des sciences,* 1st. ser., III (*an* XI), 321–336; and, in collaboration with Hachette, "Mémoire pour servir à l'histoire de cette partie de l'électricité qu'on nomme galvanisme," in *Annales de chimie,* **44** (*an* XI), 267–284; and "Du doubleur d'électricité," *ibid.,* **49** (*an* XII), 45–54.

II. SECONDARY LITERATURE. See S.-J. Delmont, *Dictionnaire de biographie française,* X (1965), 1501*a*; and *Grande encyclopédie universelle,* XIV (Paris, n.d. [about 1900]), 263.

JACQUES PAYEN

DESPAGNET, JEAN, *alchemy.*

It is unknown where and when Despagnet was born or where and when he died. Very likely he flourished in the first half of the seventeenth century. We know only that he was president of the Parlement of Bordeaux. His son Étienne, who had the same interests as his father, became a councillor of the same parlement in 1617. Very likely it was the latter whom Christian Huygens mentioned in his letters.

Despagnet acquired a great reputation as a hermetic philosopher and alchemist. Only two of his alchemic works, which are considered classics of their kind, are extant: the *Arcanum Hermeticae philosophiae* and the *Enchiridion physicae restitutae,* both published for the first time in Paris in 1623. The *Arcanum* is also attributed to an unknown author called the Imperial Knight; that attribution was denied in 1664 by Étienne, who, when asked about this by Borrichius, affirmed that his father was the author. In the *Enchiridion,* which is an introduction to the *Arcanum,* nature is regarded as a constant expression of divine will, it being understood that the paradisiacal state is the true nature and its attainment is God's will for humanity. The *Arcanum,* a post-Reformation document, illustrates the deepening sense of the spiritual on the part of physical alchemists.

From Fermat's letter of 22 September 1636 to Roberval, it appears that in 1629 Fermat had visited Despagnet at Bordeaux. Fermat also sent Étienne the original of the second book of his *Loca plana restituta,* which he finished in 1629. From Fermat's letter of February 1638 to Mersenne it appears that he had studied the manuscripts of Viète, which were deposited with Étienne Despagnet and were mentioned in the preface of Van Schooten's edition of Viète's *Opera mathematica* (1646). But, according to Fermat, these manuscripts were so antiquated that it was no longer worthwhile to publish them.

BIBLIOGRAPHY

An English translation of the *Arcanum* can be found in W. W. Westcott, *Collectanea Hermeticae,* I (London, 1893).

The best account of Despagnet's works and their several editions can be found in *Nouvelle biographie universelle,* XV (Paris, 1854), 402–403. Some information can also be found in C. Henry, "Recherches sur les manuscrits de Pierre de Fermat," in *Bullettino di bibliografia e di storia delle scienze matematiche e fisiche,* **12** (1879), 535–537; and A. E. Waite, *The Secret Tradition in Alchemy* (London, 1926), pp. 39, 338, 341.

H. L. L. BUSARD

DESSAIGNES, VICTOR (*b.* Vendôme, France, 30 December 1800; *d.* Paris, France, 5 January 1885), *chemistry.*

Dessaignes, the third son of Jean-Philibert Dessaignes, was born at the Collège of Vendôme, a school his father helped establish. In Paris he studied law, receiving his degree when he was twenty-one. Instead of practicing law, however, he immediately enrolled in medical school, where he was diverted still further by a strong interest in chemistry, undoubtedly stimulated by the then preeminent position in research of French chemists. It was not until he was thirty-five that he received a degree in medicine, defending a thesis on the action of various chemical substances on humans. While still a medical student, he exploited his early investigations into metabolic processes. He was able to pursue his interests by having been appointed tax collector in the city of Vendôme, a sinecure in which his law degree was of service.

At thirty-seven Dessaignes married Mlle. Renou, whose brother became the director of the Observatory at Saint Maur. Mme. Dessaignes died soon after the birth of their only son. Dessaignes then devoted well over ten years of his life—as well as most of his savings and income—to the creation of a private laboratory in which he performed the experiments which brought him to the attention of the scientific world.

Dessaignes was awarded the 1860 Jecker prize, consisting of a citation and a cash award of 2,000 francs, for his elucidation of the structure of a number of important, naturally occurring organic acids, such as hippuric, succinic, butyric, and malic acids, as well as quercitol, a desoxyinositol obtained from acorns. He shared the prize with Berthelot, with whom he evidently had formed a warm relationship. The prize brought him attractive offers to teach, but he elected to continue his research. He was named a *chevalier* of the Legion of Honor in 1863 and, at the request of the Académie des Sciences, became the correspondent for chemistry in 1869. Although he had by then ceased all laboratory work, he remained close to the Paris circle of chemists and was honored at a scientific congress at Blois in September 1884, an occasion marked by a laudatory speech by Friedel on behalf of the Academy. That December he developed bronchitis and, although he promptly recovered, was left in a weakened condition. He died after suffering a respiratory collapse; his son, who had become a professor in the school of medicine of Paris, survived him.

Dessaignes was fortunate to have grown up in a place and at a time when French science—especially French chemistry—had reached a peak. The invigorating intellectual climate of Paris, his father's academic influence, and his freedom from financial worries all combined to give Dessaignes the leisure and opportunity to work in the mainstream of science.

Dessaignes studied, determined the structure, and synthesized several important organic substances, principal among these being hippuric acid. This substance was first isolated by J. Liebig in 1829 from horse urine, thus its name. It occurs in the urine of many herbivorous animals, to a lesser extent in that of humans. It was soon found that by administering benzoic acid by mouth the amount of hippuric acid recoverable from human urine could be increased, a laboratory exercise occasionally still used in undergraduate biochemistry courses. Dessaignes found upon hydrolyzing hippuric acid with either acids or bases that he obtained benzoic acid and glycine. The synthesis followed when Dessaignes reacted benzoylchloride and the zinc salt of glycine and obtained a product identical with naturally occurring hippuric acid. The importance of hippuric acid lay in the realization that the body could eliminate unwanted or dangerous foreign materials by reactions with bodily substances to form compounds which could be excreted readily. Such detoxification mechanisms are observed in almost all vertebrates.

Dessaignes also studied the oxidation and reduction of various compounds, converting malic into succinic acid and tartaric into malic acid, all four carbon acids found widely in plant tissues. A knowledge of the transformations between these acids paved the way for the elucidation of metabolic cycles vital to cellular respiration, which, however, awaited the work of Krebs in the twentieth century.

Dessaignes was the sole author of twenty-five articles and coauthor of three others (two with J. Chautard and one with Schmidt). His papers show marked analytical insight and careful, precise experimentation. His life was that of an enlightened but solitary amateur of science in an age which honored perseverance and modesty.

BIBLIOGRAPHY

I. ORIGINAL WORKS. A complete list of Dessaignes's papers may be found in the *Catalogue of Scientific Papers. Royal Society of London* for 1800–1863. J. C. Poggendorff, III, contains a shorter list. Many of the papers were published in substantially the same form in several journals.

II. SECONDARY LITERATURE. An obituary notice of Dessaignes is in *Comptes rendus hebdomadaires des séances de l'Académie des sciences,* **100** (1885), 18, and was reprinted in *Bulletin. Société chimique de France,* **43** (1885), 145.

R. CHRISTIAN ANDERSON

DEVAUX, HENRI (*b.* Etaules, Charente-Maritime, France, 6 July 1862; *d.* Bordeaux, France, 14 March 1956), *plant physiology, molecular physics.*

Devaux was born into a Protestant family of sailors and farmers. After graduation from the University of Bordeaux he worked for five years under the leading botanists of the University of Paris. His doctoral thesis (1889) concerned the gaseous exchanges in plant tissues. He then returned to the University of Bordeaux, where he held the chair of plant physiology from 1906 until his retirement in 1932. Devaux soon displayed his inclination toward physical chemistry, showing as early as 1896 that aquatic plants accumulate polyvalent metallic ions, such as lead, in their cell membranes, even when the surrounding solution contains only traces of the ion. This accumulation is reversed when a large concentration of a monovalent ion, such as sodium or potassium, is added to the external solution. This was exactly the process that, nearly forty years later, was known as ion exchange, a process with wide scientific and industrial applications.

From 1903 on, Devaux was interested in the physics of surfaces. In 1890 Lord Rayleigh, and shortly afterward Agnes Pockels, had demonstrated that the surface tension of water is reduced when a film of oil, presumably one molecule thick, is spread over the surface. Direct evidence of surface films one molecule thick was presented by Devaux in 1903. He applied this demonstration to a wide range of films, particularly to proteins. The apparatus used by Devaux was of the most elegant simplicity: a photographic tray filled with either water or mercury lightly sprinkled with talcum powder. When a minute amount of film-forming substance is deposited on the liquid surface, the talcum particles are repelled and reassemble in the form of a circle. By a simple calculation involving the diameter of this circle, Devaux obtained the molecular weights of film-forming substances, particularly proteins and heavy organic acids. The results were at first ignored in France, but a decade later they were noticed by Irving Langmuir. The famous American physicist, who was to make such important contributions to the study of surfaces, gave full credit in many of his publications to Devaux for having demonstrated that the behavior of monomolecular films depends essentially on the reactivity of specific, or polar groups of the molecules. Devaux's scientific activity continued until his last years. The "wetting" of solid surfaces, the hydration of molecules in surface films, and the evaporation of odorous substances are among the fields to which he made significant contributions.

BIBLIOGRAPHY

I. ORIGINAL WORKS. Devaux's works appeared mainly in local scientific publications of limited circulation, but some of his most important papers appeared in the following accessible journals: "De l'absorption des poisons métalliques très dilués par les cellules végétales," in *Comptes rendus hebdomadaires des séances de l'Académie des sciences,* **132** (1901), 717–719; "Oil Films on Water and on Mercury," in *Annual Report of the Board of Regents of The Smithsonian Institution* (Washington, D.C., 1913), pp. 261–273; "Action rapide des solutions salines sur les plantes vivantes: déplacement réversible d'une partie des substances basiques contenues dans la plante," in *Comptes rendus hebdomadaires des séances de l'Académie des sciences,* **162** (1916), 561–564; "Ce qu'il suffit d'une souillure pour altérer la mouillabilité d'une surface. Étude sur le contact d'un liquide avec un solide," in *Journal de physique,* **4** (1923), 293–309; "La mouillabilité des substances insolubles et les remarquables puissances d'attraction existant à l'interface des liquides non miscibles," in *Comptes rendus hebdomadaires des séances de l'Académie des sciences,* **197** (1933), 105–108; "L'adsorption de l'ovalbumine à la surface libre de ses solutions, lorsque la concentration de celles-ci varie de 10^{-2} à 10^{-8}," *ibid.,* **200** (1935), 1560–1565; "Action de l'acide carbonique sur l'extension de l'ovalbumine à la surface de l'eau, et variations de l'épaisseur de ces lames en couches monomoléculaires," *ibid.,* **199** (1934), 1352–1354; "Détermination de l'épaisseur de la membrane d'albumine formée entre l'eau et la benzine et propriétés de cette membrane," *ibid.,* **202** (1936), 1957–1960; "Sur une représentation macroscopique des lames monomoléculaires et leur comportement à divers états de compression," *ibid.,* **206** (1938), 1693–1696, written with L. Pallu; "Étude expérimentale des lames formées de graines sur le mercure. Possibilité de déterminer sur les lames minces les 3 dimensions principales des molécules," in *Journal de physique,* **9** (1938), 441–446, written with L. Pallu; "Un rapport remarquable entre la constitution cellulaire et la mouillabilité du corps des mousses," in *Comptes rendus hebdomadaires des séances de l'Académie des sciences,* **208** (1939), 1260–1263; "La mouillabilité des surfaces solides," *ibid.,* **210** (1940), 27–29; "Les lames minces hydrophiles," *ibid.,* **211** (1940), 91–94; "L'adsorption d'une couronne de molécules d'eau autour de chaque molécule d'un sel étendu en lame mince," *ibid.,* **212** (1941), 588–590; "L'adsorption hygroscopique d'une couronne de molécules d'eau autour de chaque molécule des substances étendues en lame monomoléculaire sur le mercure," in *Mémoires de l'Académie des sciences de l'Institut de France,* **66** (1942), 1–28; and "L'arrangement des particules flottant sur du mercure, sous l'influence d'un champ électrique," in *Journal de physique,* **4** (1943), 185–196.

II. SECONDARY LITERATURE. Irving Langmuir gives an extensive account of Devaux's early work in surface physics in "The Constitution and Fundamental Properties of Liquids," in *Journal of the American Chemical Society,* **39** (1917), 1848–1906. A complete bibliography up to 1941 can be found in *Actualités scientifiques et industrielles,* no. 932 (Paris, 1942), pp. 23–36. A detailed obituary was published by Gordin Kaplan, "Henri Devaux, Plant Physiologist, Pioneer of Surface Physics," in *Science,* **124** (1956), 1017–1018.

A. M. MONNIER

DEVILLE, HENRI ÉTIENNE SAINTE-CLAIRE (*b.* St. Thomas, Virgin Islands, 11 March 1818; *d.* Boulogne-sur-Seine, France, 1 July 1881), *chemistry.*

Deville was one of the most prolific and versatile chemists of the nineteenth century, making major contributions in most areas of his science. He and his brother Charles, later a well-known physicist, were sons of the French consul in the Virgin Islands, who was a prominent shipowner. The brothers were educated in Paris, where Henri received his medical degree in 1843. Even before graduation he had been attracted to the study of chemistry by the lectures of Thenard. He established a private laboratory in his own quarters and in 1839 published his first paper, a study of turpentine. Soon after receiving his doctorate in medicine, he followed it with one in science.

In 1845, through the influence of Thenard, Deville was appointed professor of chemistry and dean of the newly established faculty of science of the University of Besançon. Here he established such a reputation that in January 1851 he was chosen as professor of chemistry at the École Normale Supérieure in Paris. The facilities for research were at first poor and the instruction elementary. Deville, however, was an excellent teacher and also was active in research. While always interested in teaching beginning students, he greatly improved the research laboratory of the institution. Many outstanding younger chemists were trained by him. From 1853 to 1866 he gave lectures in chemistry at the Sorbonne. Deville was always close to his brother, whose death in 1876 was a heavy blow to him. His health gradually failed, and he retired in 1880. He died the following year.

Deville was essentially an experimentalist and had little interest in chemical theory. He began his laboratory studies at a time when organic chemistry was developing most actively, and his early work was in this field: investigations of turpentine, toluene, and acid anhydrides. However, his analytical skill and his important synthesis of nitrogen pentoxide in 1849 turned his attention to inorganic chemistry. He worked out a process for producing pure aluminum by reducing its salts with sodium. Deville's methods made both metals readily available and drastically reduced their cost, but he himself did not take much part in their later industrial development. He used the sodium obtained by his method for the preparation of such elements as silicon, boron, and titanium. His investigations of the metallurgy of platinum led to honors from the Russian government. In many of his studies, such as those on the artificial production of natural minerals, Deville employed very high temperatures and became a recognized authority on the use of this technique. His measurements of the vapor densities of compounds at various temperatures helped to confirm Avogadro's hypothesis. These studies led Deville to his most notable discovery, the dissociation of heated chemical compounds and their recombination at lower temperatures. He heated such substances as water, carbon dioxide, and hydrogen chloride and then cooled them suddenly to recover the decomposition products. This work led to a better understanding of the mechanism of chemical reactions and to significant developments in physical chemistry.

BIBLIOGRAPHY

I. ORIGINAL WORKS. There is a complete bibliography of Deville's many individual papers in J. Gay, *Henri Sainte-Claire Deville—sa vie et ses travaux* (Paris, 1889). His first paper on dissociation is in *Comptes rendus hebdomadaires des séances de l'Académie des sciences,* **45** (1857), 857–861.

II. SECONDARY LITERATURE. In addition to the book by Gay mentioned above, accounts of Deville are Maurice Daumas, "Henri Sainte-Claire Deville et les débuts de l'industrie d'aluminium," in *Revue d'histoire des sciences,* **2** (1949), 352–357; the obituary by Louis Pasteur, in *Comptes rendus hebdomadaires des séances de l'Académie des sciences,* **93** (1881), 6–9; the paper by R. E. Oesper and P. Lemay, in *Chymia,* **3** (1950), 205–221; and Sijbren Rienks van der Ley, *Iets over de dissociatetheorie van Deville* (Groningen, 1870).

HENRY M. LEICESTER

DEWAR, JAMES (*b.* Kincardine-on-Forth, Scotland, 20 September 1842; *d.* London, England, 27 March 1923), *chemistry, physics.*

Son of Thomas Dewar, a vintner and innkeeper, and Ann Eadie Dewar, young Dewar attended local schools until he was crippled by rheumatic fever at the age of ten. During his two-year period of convalescence he learned the art of violin making and later said that this was the foundation for his manipulative skills in the laboratory. He entered Edinburgh University in 1858. James David Forbes, professor of natural philosophy, and Lyon Playfair, professor of chemistry, directed his interest to physical science. He was assistant to Playfair (1867–1868) and to Playfair's successor, Alexander Crum Brown (1868–1873). Dewar became lecturer on chemistry in the Royal Veterinary College of Edinburgh (1869) and assistant chemist to the Highland and Agricultural Society (1873). He was elected Jacksonian professor of natural experimental philosophy in Cambridge (1875) and Fullerian professor of chemistry at the Royal Institution (1877) and held both chairs until his death. The Royal Institution was the chief center of his experimental activity.

In 1871 Dewar married Helen Rose Banks, daughter of an Edinburgh printer; they had no children. He was president of the Society of Chemical Industry (1887), the Chemical Society of London (1897–1899), and the British Association (1902). Dewar was knighted in 1904. He also served as consultant to government and industry. He was a member of the government committee on explosives (1888–1891) and with Sir Frederick Abel invented the smokeless propellant cordite, a gelatinized mixture of nitrocellulose in nitroglycerin (1889).

Dewar's earliest work (1867–1877) encompassed a wide variety of subjects in physics, chemistry, and physiology. In 1867 he invented a mechanical device to represent Crum Brown's new graphic notation for organic compounds. Playfair sent the device to Kekulé, and Kekulé invited Dewar to spend the summer in his Ghent laboratory. Dewar suggested seven different structural formulas for benzene, including the diagonal formula

and the formula attributed to Kekulé.

In 1870 he proposed the pyridine ring formula, substituting a nitrogen atom for a CH residue in the benzene ring:

He also suggested that quinoline's structure consisted of fused benzene and pyridine rings.

Dewar's early studies included the heats at formation of the oxides of chlorine, the temperature of the sun and of the electric spark, the atomic volume of solids, and the production of high vacua. In 1872 he determined the physical constants of Thomas Graham's hydrogenium (Graham supposed hydrogen to be the vapor of a volatile metal, "hydrogenium") and first used a vacuum-jacketed insulating vessel. Interspersed with these physical researches were physiological investigations on the constitution and function of cystine, the physiological action of quinoline and pyridine bases, and the changes in the electrical condition of the eye under the influence of light.

At Cambridge and the Royal Institution, Dewar continued his varied interests. There were studies on the coal-tar bases; atomic and molecular weight determinations; the chemical reactions at the temperature of the electric arc, in which he noted the formation of hydrogen cyanide in the carbon arc burning in air (1879); and the determination of the monatomicity of sodium and potassium vapor from gas density studies (1883).

The first area to be thoroughly explored was spectroscopy. He joined George Downing Liveing, professor of chemistry at Cambridge, in an attempt to correlate line and band spectra with atomic and molecular states. They published seventy-eight papers between 1877 and 1904. Dewar's interest in spectroscopy stemmed from a fascination with Henri Sainte-Claire Deville's work on dissociation and reversible interactions and Norman Lockyer's controversial speculations on the dissociation of the elements at high temperatures. He contrasted Deville's exact experimental methods with Lockyer's conjectures, which he felt were based on insufficient evidence. Dewar and Liveing accurately determined the absorption spectra of many elements (especially metallic vapors) and compounds. They studied the general conditions affecting the excitation of spectra and, in particular, the ultraviolet emission spectra of many metals. They noted the contrast between single spectral lines, multiplets, and bands, and they attempted to identify the emitting agents for single, multiplet, and band spectra. They classified great, intermediate, and weak intensities with the spectroscopic series as principal, diffuse, and sharp, respectively. Their studies included the differences between the arc, spark, and flame spectra of metals; the emission spectra of gaseous explosions and of the rare gases; and the effect of temperature and concentration on the absorption spectra of rare-earth salts in solution.

Dewar's coming to the Royal Institution in 1877 marked the beginning of his work in cryogenics, his major field of study. In that year Louis Cailletet and Raoul Pictet liquefied small amounts of oxygen and nitrogen. This achievement interested Dewar because hitherto almost all the work on liquefaction of gases had been done at the Royal Institution, especially by

Michael Faraday, who by 1845 had liquefied all the known gases except the six permanent ones (oxygen, nitrogen, hydrogen, nitric oxide, carbon monoxide, and methane). During a Royal Institution lecture in 1878 Dewar gave the first demonstration in Great Britain of the liquefaction of oxygen. His principal interest was not the liquefaction of gases but the investigation of the properties of matter in the hitherto uninvestigated vicinity of the absolute zero of temperature.

In 1884 the Polish physicists Florenty von Wroblewski and Karol Olszewski improved the refrigerating apparatus, prepared moderate amounts of liquid air and oxygen, and measured their physical properties and critical constants. Dewar further improved the apparatus and methods of the Polish scientists and in 1885 prepared large quantities of liquid air and oxygen by compressing the gases at the temperature of liquid ethylene. In 1891 he discovered that both liquid oxygen and ozone were magnetic.

Dewar hoped to liquefy hydrogen; after a decade of work he had not succeeded. The critical temperature of hydrogen is $-241°$C. The lowest temperature attainable with liquid air as a refrigerant is about $-200°$C. His attempts to reach lower temperatures were unsuccessful until 1895, when he took advantage of the Joule-Thomson effect whereby the temperature of a compressed gas decreases with expansion into a vacuum because of the internal work done to overcome molecular attraction. Hydrogen was an exception; its temperature increased slightly. But Dewar showed that hydrogen had a normal Joule-Thomson effect if it was first cooled to $-80°$C. He cooled hydrogen by means of liquid air at $-200°$C. and 200 atmospheres pressure and forced it through a fine nozzle. He obtained a jet of gas mixed with a liquid that he could not collect. The temperature of the hydrogen jet was very low, and by spraying it on liquid air or oxygen he transformed them into solids. Dewar was convinced that he could reach still lower temperatures, and he spent a year making a large liquid-air machine. In 1898 his endeavor ended in success. Cooled, compressed hydrogen liquefied on escaping from a nozzle into a vacuum vessel. With liquid hydrogen he reached the lowest temperature then known. Liquid hydrogen boils at $-252.5°$C. at ordinary pressure. By reducing the pressure he lowered the temperature to $-258°$C. and solidified the hydrogen. He cooled the solid to $-260°$C. With liquid hydrogen, every gas except helium could in turn be both liquefied and solidified.

The lowest temperature attainable with hydrogen was still 13° above absolute zero. Could Dewar close this gap? He turned to the recently discovered helium and predicted that if the critical temperature was not below 8°K., then it should be possible to liquefy helium by methods similar to those for hydrogen. As a source of helium he used the gas bubbling from the springs at Bath, which Lord Rayleigh had found to contain the element. He failed in his liquefaction attempts because the Bath spring gas also contained neon, and in the cooling process the neon solidified, blocking the tubes and valves of the apparatus. In 1908 Heike Kamerlingh Onnes at Leiden, using Dewar's methods, succeeded in liquefying the helium isolated from the mineral monazite. Dewar presented Kamerlingh Onnes's work at a British Association meeting and showed that by boiling helium at reduced pressure he could reach a temperature less than 1° from absolute zero.

Dewar's study of the properties of matter at very low temperatures was made possible by his invention in 1892 of the vacuum-jacketed flask, the most important device for preserving and handling materials at low temperatures. The insulating property of the vacuum was well known, and Dewar had used a vacuum flask in 1872 in making specific heat determinations of Graham's hydrogenium. When he wanted to investigate the properties of liquefied gases, the idea of using a vacuum-jacketed vessel suggested itself to him.

Dewar realized that the insulating capacity of the vacuum flask depended on the state of exhaustion of the space between the inner and outer vessels. In 1905 he discovered that charcoal's adsorptive power for gases was enormously increased at −185°C. By putting a small quantity of charcoal in the evacuated space and filling the flask with liquid air, the cooled charcoal adsorbed the remaining traces of air in the space, producing a vacuum of greater tenuity. Furthermore, the charcoal-containing flasks enabled Dewar to substitute metal vessels for glass ones. Metals gave off small quantities of occluded gas, which would impair the vacuum. Since charcoal would adsorb the gas, metal vacuum vessels became feasible. They could be made both larger and stronger than glass ones. (Such vessels are now called Dewar flasks or vessels.)

Dewar used the different condensability of gases on charcoal to separate or concentrate the constituents of a gas mixture. Charcoal preferentially adsorbed oxygen from air passed over it at −185°C. Collecting the liberated gas in fractions as the temperature rose, he obtained air containing eighty-four percent oxygen. Dewar also separated the rare gases from air by this method. In 1908 he used the carbon-adsorption technique in making the first direct measurement of the rate of production of helium from radium.

Dewar examined a wide range of properties in pioneering explorations on the effect of extreme cold on substances. He determined the properties of all the liquefied gases. He measured the decreased chemical reactivity of substances at low temperatures. He studied the effects of extreme cold on phosphorescence, color, strength of materials, the behavior of metal carbonyl compounds, the emanations of radium (with William Crookes), and the gases occluded by radium (with Pierre Curie).

Dewar established that many vigorous chemical reactions did not take place at all at very low temperatures; oxygen, for example, did not react with sodium or potassium. He wanted to test the effect of cold on fluorine, the most reactive element, and in an 1897 collaboration with Henri Moissan, who had isolated the element in 1886, he liquefied fluorine and examined its properties. After Dewar had liquefied hydrogen, they resumed their investigation and solidified fluorine at −233°C. Even when the temperature was reduced to −252.5°C., solid fluorine and liquid hydrogen violently exploded.

Dewar intended to explore the whole field of cryogenics. Between 1892 and 1895 he joined with John A. Fleming, professor of electrical engineering at University College, London, in an investigation of the electrical and magnetic properties of metals and alloys. Their aim was to determine the electrical resistance from 200°C. to the lowest attainable temperature. They obtained temperature-resistance curves and found that the resistance for all pure metals converged downward in such a manner that electrical resistance would vanish at absolute zero. They gathered accurate information on conduction, thermoelectricity, magnetic permeability, and dielectric constants of metals and alloys from 200°C. to −200°C.

Another area of extensive investigation was low-temperature calorimetry (1904–1913). Dewar devised a calorimeter to measure specific and latent heats at low temperatures. He determined the atomic heats of the elements and the molecular heats of compounds between 80°K. and 20°K. He discovered in 1913 that the atomic heats of the solid elements at a mean temperature of 50°K. were a periodic function of the atomic weights.

World War I prohibited continuation of Dewar's costly cryogenic research. He turned to thin films and bubbles, which had been the subject of the first of his nine courses of Christmas lectures for children at the Royal Institution (1878–1879). He studied both solid films, produced by the evaporation of the solvent from amyl acetate solutions of nitrated cotton, and liquid films from soap. He investigated the conditions for the production of long-lived bubbles and of flat films of great size, the distortions in films produced by sound, and the patterns formed by the impact of an air jet on films.

At the time of his death Dewar was engaged in studies with a delicate charcoal-gas thermoscope that he constructed in order to measure infrared radiation. From a skylight in the Royal Institution he measured the radiation from the sky by day and night and under varying weather conditions. Dewar was a superb experimentalist; he published no theoretical papers.

BIBLIOGRAPHY

I. ORIGINAL WORKS. Dewar's papers were reprinted in *Collected Papers of Sir James Dewar,* 2 vols., Lady Dewar, J. D. Hamilton Dickson, H. Munro Ross, and E. C. Scott Dickson, eds. (Cambridge, 1927); and in George Downing Liveing and James Dewar, *Collected Papers on Spectroscopy* (Cambridge, 1915).

Important papers include "On the Oxidation of Phenyl Alcohol, and a Mechanical Arrangement Adopted to Illustrate Structure in Non-Saturated Hydrocarbons," in *Proceedings of the Royal Society of Edinburgh,* **6** (1866–1869), 82–86; "On the Oxidation Products of Picoline," in *Transactions of the Royal Society of Edinburgh,* **26** (1872), 189–196; "On the Liquefaction of Oxygen and the Critical Volumes of Fluids," in *Philosophical Magazine,* 5th ser., **18** (1884), 210–216; "The Electrical Resistance of Metals and Alloys at Temperatures Approaching the Absolute Zero," *ibid.,* **36** (1893), 271–299; and "Thermoelectric Powers of Metals and Alloys Between the Temperatures of the Boiling-Point of Water and the Boiling-Point of Liquid Air," *ibid.,* **40** (1895), 95–119, written with J. A. Fleming.

See also "The Liquefaction of Air and Research at Low Temperatures," in *Proceedings of the Chemical Society,* **11** (1896), 221–234; "Sur la liquéfaction du fluor," in *Comptes rendus hebdomadaires des séances de l'Académie des sciences,* **124** (1897), 1202–1205; "Nouvelles expériences sur la liquéfaction du fluor," *ibid.,* **125** (1897), 505–511; "Sur la solidification du fluor et sur la combinaison à −252.5° du fluor solide et de l'hydrogène liquide," *ibid.,* **136** (1903), 641–643, written with Henri Moissan; "New Researches on Liquid Air," in *Notices of the Proceedings of the Royal Institution of Great Britain,* **15** (1899), 133–146; "Liquid Hydrogen," *ibid.,* **16** (1902), 1–14, 212–217; "Solid Hydrogen," *ibid.,* **16** (1902), 473–480; "Liquid Hydrogen Calorimetry," *ibid.,* **17** (1904), 581–596; "Studies With the Liquid Hydrogen and Air Calorimeters," in *Proceedings of the Royal Society,* **76** (1905), 325–340; "The Rate of Production of Helium From Radium," *ibid.,* **81** (1908), 280–286; "Atomic Specific Heats Between the Boiling Points of Liquid Nitrogen and Hydrogen," *ibid.,* **89** (1913), 158–169; "Studies on Liquid Films," in *Proceedings of the Royal Institution,* **22** (1918), 359–405; and "Soap Films as Detectors: Stream Lines and Sound," *ibid.,* **24** (1923), 197–259.

II. SECONDARY LITERATURE. A bibliography of Dewar's works was compiled by Henry Young, *A Record of the Scientific Work of Sir James Dewar* (London, 1933). Two detailed studies of his accomplishments are Henry E. Armstrong, *James Dewar* (London, 1924) and Alexander Findlay, in Findlay and William Hobson Mills, eds., *British Chemists* (London, 1947), pp. 30–57. Informative accounts include Henry E. Armstrong, "Sir James Dewar, 1842–1923," in *Journal of the Chemical Society,* **131** (1928), 1066–1706, and *Proceedings of the Royal Society,* **111A** (1926), xiii–xxiii; Ralph Cory, "Fifty Years at the Royal Institution," in *Nature,* **166** (1950), 1049–1053, which has many personal remembrances of Dewar by the librarian of the Royal Institution; Sir James Crichton-Browne, "Sir James Dewar, LL.D., F.R.S.," in *Proceedings of the Royal Society of Edinburgh,* **43** (1922–1923), 255–260; and Hugh Munro Ross, in *Dictionary of National Biography, 1922–1930* (London, 1937), pp. 255–257.

Dewar's cryogenic research was analyzed in "Low-Temperature Research at the Royal Institution" by Agnes M. Clerke, in *Proceedings of the Royal Institution,* **16** (1901), 699–718, and Henry E. Armstrong, *ibid.,* **19** (1909), 354–412, and **21** (1916), 735–785. A more recent study is K. Mendelssohn, "Dewar at the Royal Institution," *ibid.,* **41** (1966), 212–233.

ALBERT B. COSTA

DEZALLIER D'ARGENVILLE, ANTOINE-JOSEPH. *See* **Argenville, Antoine-Joseph d'.**

DICAEARCHUS OF MESSINA (*fl.* 310 B.C.).

Dicaearchus was a distinguished disciple of Aristotle and the author of many books in different fields, none of which is preserved, so that our knowledge of them is fragmentary and often problematical.

On the Soul, six books in dialogue form, espoused the view that the soul is "nothing," immaterial, merely a condition of the body, a "harmony of the four elements"—and consequently perishable and not immortal. The doctrine was not new, but this exposition of it was one of the best. *Descent Into the Cave of Trophonius,* also a dialogue, belittled oracles and recognized only dreams and inspirations as valid sources of prophecy. The same view is attributed to Aristotle. *Tripoliticus,* a dialogue on political theory, advocated a composite constitution, combining the three traditional types of government: monarchy, aristocracy, and democracy. It seems that Dicaearchus saw this exemplified in Sparta, a state to which he was partial. The idea of a mixed constitution was taken up by Polybius. *The Life of Greece,* in three books, dealt with anthropological, moral, and cultural history, including the primitive and the Oriental forerunners of Greek civilization. The work was significant for extending history, on Peripatetic principles, over fields other than the political and military. It was the model for a work by Varro on the Romans.

Dicaearchus' only work on natural science was a

geography, *Tour of the Earth,* following the work of Eudoxus of Cnidus. These two were the first geographers to combine the actual knowledge of lands and seas with the theory of the earth as a sphere, which by then was generally accepted. Measuring a long arc north from Syene (Aswan) and observing the zenith points at the ends, they calculated the circumference to be 400,000 or 300,000 stades (stades varied from 148 to 198 meters). The area of the world then known proved to be only a small part of the surface of the sphere, perhaps 45,000 stades by 30,000 stades. Dicaearchus defended the theory of the earth as a sphere by "measuring" the highest mountains, which he found to be only ten or fifteen stades high, showing that they were insignificant in relation to the curvature of the sphere. Within the known world he sought to schematize the masses of land and sea and mountains—without the aid, of course, of specific latitude, much less of longitude. His successor in this field was Eratosthenes, whose great improvements were practical rather than theoretical.

Among the disciples of Aristotle, Dicaearchus and Aristoxenus of Tarentum, another Dorian from the west, seem to have been particularly congenial, while there was some antipathy between Dicaearchus and Theophrastus, the head of the Peripatetic school. Dicaearchus saw the purpose of knowledge as practical action; Theophrastus, as theoretical contemplation. Among posterity Cicero and Atticus were admirers of Dicaearchus and used his works extensively.

BIBLIOGRAPHY

Additional information may be found in Edgar Martini, "Dikaiarchos 3. Peripatetiker," in Pauly-Wissowa, V, pt. 1 (1903), 546–563; and Fritz Wehrli, *Die Schule des Aristoteles, Texte und Kommentar,* Heft I, *Dikaiarchos* (Basel, 1944; 2nd ed., rev. and enl., 1967).

AUBREY DILLER

DICKINSON, ROSCOE GILKEY (*b.* Brewer, Maine, 10 June 1894; *d.* Pasadena, California, 13 July 1945), *physical chemistry, X rays, crystal structure.*

Dickinson's father, George E. M. Dickinson, was a violin teacher and director of music for the Hyde Park, Massachusetts, city schools; his mother's maiden name was Georgie Simmons. He attended grammar school and high school in Hyde Park and then studied chemical engineering at the Massachusetts Institute of Technology, where he received the B.S. degree in 1915. After two years of graduate work there he was appointed instructor at the California Institute of Technology (called Throop College of Technology until 1918). In 1920 he became the first recipient of the Ph.D. degree from this institute. He remained there all his life; at the time of his death he was professor of physical chemistry and acting dean of graduate studies.

As a graduate student Dickinson became familiar with the technique of determining the atomic structure of crystals by the X-ray diffraction method through his contact with C. Lalor Burdick and James H. Ellis, who carried out, in Pasadena, the first crystal-structure determination made in the western hemisphere. At that time the lack of quantitative information about the interaction of X rays and crystals made the task of the crystal-structure investigator a difficult one. The field was, however, especially well suited to Dickinson, whose outstanding characteristics were great clarity of thought, a mastery of the processes of logical deduction, and meticulous care in his experimental work and in the analysis of data. He carried out many crystal-structure determinations, all of which have been found to be reliable to within the limits of error that he assigned. He determined the structures of a number of crystals containing inorganic complexes, including the hexachlorostannates, the tetrachloropalladites and tetrachloroplatinites, and the tetracyanide complexes of zinc and mercury. His determination (with one of his students, A. L. Raymond) of the structure of hexamethylenetetramine was the first structure determination ever made of a molecule of an organic compound. In a decade he developed the leading American school of X rays and crystal structure.

During the last twenty years of his life Dickinson and his students carried on many researches in other fields, including photochemistry, chemical kinetics, Raman spectroscopy, the properties of neutrons, and the use of radioactive indicators in studying chemical reactions. Through this, as well as through his work on crystal structure, he contributed significantly to the development of the California Institute of Technology.

BIBLIOGRAPHY

For a partial list of Dickinson's chemical and physical publications, see Poggendorff, vol. VI.

LINUS PAULING

DICKSON, LEONARD EUGENE (*b.* Independence, Iowa, 22 January 1874; *d.* Harlingen, Texas, 17 January 1954), *mathematics.*

The son of Campbell and Lucy Tracy Dickson, Leonard Eugene Dickson had a distinguished academic career. After graduating with a B.S. in 1893 as class valedictorian from the University of Texas, he became a teaching fellow there. He received his M.S. in 1894. With the grant of a fellowship he then proceeded to the newly founded University of Chicago, where he received its first doctorate in mathematics in 1896. He spent the following year in postgraduate studies at Leipzig and Paris.

Upon his return to the United States, Dickson began his career in mathematics. After a one-year stay at the University of California as instructor in mathematics, in 1899 he accepted an associate professorship at the University of Texas. One year later he returned to the University of Chicago, where he spent the rest of his career, except for his leaves as visiting professor at the University of California in 1914, 1918, and 1922. He was assistant professor from 1900 to 1907, associate professor from 1907 to 1910, and professor from 1910 to 1939. He married Susan Davis on 30 December 1902; their children were Campbell and Eleanor. At the university his students and colleagues regarded him highly as a scholar and a teacher. He supervised the dissertations of at least fifty-five doctoral candidates and helped them obtain a start in research after graduation. In 1928 he was appointed to the Eliakim Hastings Moore distinguished professorship.

Dickson was a prolific mathematician. His eighteen books and hundreds of articles covered many areas in his field. In his study of finite linear groups, he generalized the results of Galois, Jordan, and Serret for groups over the field of p elements to groups over an arbitrary finite field. He gave the first extensive exposition of the theory of finite fields, wherein he stated and proved for $m = 2, 3$ his modified version of the Chevalley theorem: For a finite field it seems to be true that every form of degree m in $m + 1$ variables vanishes for values not all zero in the field. In linear algebra he applied arithmetical concepts and proved that a real Cayley division algebra is actually a division algebra. He also expanded upon the Cartan and Wedderburn theories of linear associative algebras. He studied the relationships between the theory of invariants and number theory.

While he believed that mathematics was the queen of the sciences, he held further that number theory was the queen of mathematics, a belief that resulted in his monumental three-volume *History of the Theory of Numbers,* in which he investigated diophantine equations, perfect numbers, abundant numbers, and Fermat's theorem. In a long series of papers after 1927 on additive number theory, he proved the ideal Waring theorem, using the analytic results of Vinogradov.

Dickson received recognition for his work. The

American Mathematical Society, for which he was editor of the *Monthly* from 1902 to 1908 and of the *Transactions* from 1911 to 1916, honored him. He was its president from 1916 to 1918 and received its Cole Prize in 1928 for his book *Algebren und ihre Zahlentheorie.* Earlier, in 1924, the American Association for the Advancement of Science awarded him its thousand-dollar prize for his work on the arithmetic of algebras. Harvard in 1936 and Princeton in 1941 awarded him an honorary Sc.D. In addition to his election to the National Academy of Sciences in 1913, he was a member of the American Philosophical Society, the American Academy of Arts and Sciences, and the London Mathematical Society, and he was a foreign member of the Academy of the French Institute.

BIBLIOGRAPHY

Dickson's books are *Linear Groups With an Exposition of the Galois Field Theory* (Leipzig, 1901); *College Algebra* (New York, 1902); *Introduction to the Theory of Algebraic Equations* (New York, 1903); *Elementary Theory of Equations* (New York, 1914); *Algebraic Invariants* (New York, 1914); *Linear Algebras* (Cambridge, Mass., 1914); *Theory and Applications of Finite Groups* (New York, 1916), written with G. A. Miller and H. F. Blichfeldt; *History of the Theory of Numbers* (Washington, 1919–1923), vol. I, *Divisibility and Primality;* vol. II, *Diophantine Analysis;* vol. III, *Quadratic and Higher Forms* (with a ch. on the class number by G. H. Cresse); *A First Course in the Theory of Equations* (New York, 1922); *Plane Trigonometry With Practical Applications* (Chicago, 1922); *Algebras and Their Arithmetics* (Chicago, 1923); *Modern Algebraic Theories* (Chicago, 1926); *Algebren und ihre Zahlentheorie* (Zurich, 1927); *Introduction to the Theory of Numbers* (Chicago, 1929); *Studies in the Theory of Numbers* (Chicago, 1930); *Minimum Decompositions Into Fifth Powers,* vol. III (London, 1933); *New First Course in the Theory of Equations* (New York, 1939); and *Modern Elementary Theory of Numbers* (Chicago, 1939).

Other writings are *On Invariants and the Theory of Numbers,* American Mathematical Society Colloquium Publications, **4** (1914), 1–110; *Researches on Waring's Problem,* Carnegie Institution of Washington, pub. no. 464 (1935).

A. A. Albert, "Leonard Eugene Dickson 1874–1954," in *Bulletin of the American Mathematical Society,* **61** (1955), 331–346, contains a complete bibliography of Dickson's writings.

RONALD S. CALINGER

DICKSTEIN, SAMUEL (*b.* Warsaw, Poland, 12 May 1851; *d.* Warsaw, 29 September 1939), *mathematics, history of mathematics, science education, scientific organization.*

Dickstein devoted his life to building up the organizational structure for Polish science, especially for mathematics. In the eighteenth century Poland's territory had been divided among Prussia, Austria, and Russia; and thus Polish science education and scientific life depended mostly on personal initiative and not on state support. In his youth Dickstein experienced the escalation of national oppression after the unsuccessful uprising of 1863. There was no Polish university in Warsaw at that time, and higher education was provided in part by the Szkola Główna, which was a teachers' college. From 1866 to 1869 Dickstein studied at the Szkola Główna, which was converted into the Russian University in Warsaw in 1869. After 1870 he continued his studies there and in 1876 received a master's degree in pure mathematics.

From 1870 Dickstein taught in Polish secondary schools, concentrating on mathematics; from 1878 to 1888 he directed his own private school in Warsaw. In 1884, with A. Czajewicz, he founded Biblioteka Matematyczno-Fizyczna, which was intended to be a series of scientific textbooks written in Polish. These books greatly influenced the development of Polish scientific literature. In 1888 Dickstein took part in the founding of the first Polish mathematical-physical magazine, *Prace matematyczno-fizyczne*. Later he founded other publications, such as *Wiadomości matematyczne* and the education journal *Ruch pedagogiczny* (1881).

The Poles' efforts after the creation of the Polish university led in 1906 to the founding of Towarzystwo Kursów Naukowych, which organized the university science courses. Dickstein was the first rector of that society. In 1905 he became a founder of the Warsaw Scientific Society, and he was instrumental in the development of the Society of Polish Mathematicians. After the revival of the Polish university in Warsaw he became professor of mathematics there in 1919. His own mathematical work was concerned mainly with algebra. His main sphere of interest besides education was the history of mathematics, and he published a number of articles on Polish mathematicians that contributed to their recognition throughout the world. Of especial note are the monograph *Hoene Wroński, jego życie i prace* (Cracow, 1896) and the edition of the Leibniz-Kochański correspondence, published in *Prace matematyczno-fizyczne,* **7** (1901), and **8** (1902). Appreciation of his historical works was shown in his election as vice-president of the International Academy of Sciences. The list of his scientific works includes more than 200 titles. Dickstein died during the bombardment of Warsaw and his family perished during the German occupation of Poland.

BIBLIOGRAPHY

I. ORIGINAL WORKS. The list of Dickstein's works up to 1917 is contained in a special issue of the magazine *Wiadomości matematyczne;* works from subsequent years are in the memorial volume *III Polski zjazd matematyczny. Jubileusz 65-lecia działalności naukowej, pedagogicznej i społecznej profesora Samuela Dicksteina* (Warsaw, 1937).

II. SECONDARY LITERATURE. Besides the memorial volume, the basic biographical data and an appreciation are contained in A. Mostowski, "La vie et l'oeuvre de Samuel Dickstein," in *Prace matematyczno-fizyczne,* **47** (1949), 5–12.

LUBOŠ NOVÝ

DIDEROT, DENIS (*b*. Langres, France, 5 October 1713; *d*. Paris, France, 31 July 1784), *letters, technology*.

Diderot's importance in the history of science derives from his having edited the *Encyclopédie*—with the partial collaboration of d'Alembert—and from a sensibility that anticipated and epitomized moral, psychological, and social opportunities and stresses attending the assimilation of science into culture.

Early Life and Work. He came from energetic stock. His father, Didier, was a prosperous master-cutler who aspired to higher spheres for his children. His mother, born Angélique Vigneron, was of a family of tanners with a tendency to the priesthood. Diderot was the eldest child of seven. One sister, Angélique, became a nun and died mad. A brother, Didier-Pierre, took orders and became archdeacon of Langres. It may have been fortunate for the Church that nothing beyond the tonsure at the age of thirteen came of the would-be nepotism of a maternal uncle who thought to make a priest of Diderot in order to leave his nephew his own benefice.

Like many of his fellow *philosophes,* Diderot was well-educated by the Jesuits. Having completed their *collège* at Langres, he was sent to Paris in the winter of 1728–1729. There he enrolled in the Collège d'Harcourt and also followed courses in two other famous establishments, the Collège Louis-le-Grand and the Collège de Beauvais. In 1732 he took his degree *maître-ès-lettres* of the University of Paris. Thereafter his father supposed him to be entering upon legal studies. In fact Diderot was enjoying his freedom, intellectual and amorous, in the literary Bohemia of the capital. Abandoning the pretense of law, he drifted into a catchpenny life, ghost-writing sermons for hard-pressed preachers and missionaries, applying himself to mathematics and teaching it a bit, and perfecting his English and undertaking translations—of which the occasional faithlessness expresses wit, not ignorance. For to the ordinary appetites of Grub Street he added that for information, and unlike the hacks around him, he did study. There have been few writers—perhaps only Voltaire—whose lightness of touch has more gracefully dissembled a capacity for work.

The most considerable of these early commissions planted in his mind the idea that burgeoned in the *Encyclopédie.* In 1744 Diderot, together with three other writers, put in hand for the publisher Briasson the translation of *A Medicinal Dictionary: Including Physic, Surgery, Anatomy, Chemistry, and Botany . . .,* a multivolume work that except for Diderot's connection with it would weigh quite forgotten in both languages upon library shelves.[1] Qualifying himself (for he was not the man to remain ignorant of what he was translating), he attended public courses in anatomy and physiology given by one Verdier, and later those of a certain formidable Mlle. Biher. He thus began an adult self-education in science that he long continued and that put him in the way of the medical humanism which forms a still insufficiently appreciated strain in the naturalistic thought of the Enlightenment and which issued in the philosophy of vitalistic materialism. His marriage in 1743 to Anne-Toinette Champion turned out unhappily almost from the start, although their surviving child, later Mme. de Vandeul, was a comfort to him in old age.

In the 1740's Diderot and his fellow writers began to form a recognizable circle of like-minded free spirits on whom he later drew for contributions to the *Encyclopédie.* He met Rousseau in 1742, Condillac in 1744, and came to know d'Alembert, Grimm, Mably, d'Holbach, and others, and to be known to Voltaire, to whose deistic point of view on science he increasingly opposed the naturalistic standpoint he was developing for himself. The publications by which he made himself known for an original writer went far in the direction of overt skepticism. "I write of God," he announced in the opening sentence of *Pensées philosophiques* (1746), embarking upon a celebration of the passions and identifying them with the creative energies of nature, which, it soon appears, is indistinguishable from God. For although the standpoint from which Diderot was attacking absurdities and inequities in the scriptural tradition was ostensibly that of the deism of Shaftesbury, from whom he borrowed many a theological observation, his inspiration in natural philosophy was actually the pantheism of Spinoza, and never Newton.

The *Lettre sur les aveugles* of 1749, his first truly original work, goes further and undermines deism. In it he initiated a device that he employed more regularly in later writings. A prominent contemporary figure is adopted to be spokesman for views that Diderot was just then trying out. Through the person of Nicholas Saunderson, a blind mathematician who was Lucasian professor in Cambridge, Diderot exhibited how unconvincing it is in the eyes of the sightless to base the existence of God upon the evidence for design in nature. The essay combines humanity with skepticism. In handling this favorite psychological puzzle of eighteenth-century sensationalism—how the world appears to a man deprived of one of his senses, or to whom sight or hearing is suddenly restored—Diderot found himself questioning the artificiality with which the associationists, and notably his friend Condillac, abstracted the operation of the five senses one from another in some mechanical and imaginary sensorium.

He ended by disputing as gratuitous the conclusion of the self-styled empiricists that on regaining sight a blind man, once he learned to use his eyes at all, would not recognize the difference between a sphere and a cube without touching them. There was a psychological shrewdness in Diderot that rejected the notion that touch and sight can be independent even for analytic purposes. His sense of what people are really like, related to a highly personal distrust of all abstractions, animates all his writings.

The most widely read of these pre-Encyclopedic writings was almost certainly *Les bijoux indiscrets* (1747). It is a salacious fantasy and, in certain passages in the vein of *Fanny Hill,* a pornographic one, written gaily rather than grossly, and no doubt mainly for gain. Overtones convey the innocence of sensual enjoyment, and the tale is not out of character. It no longer seems so incongruous coming from a champion of humanity as it did prior to the recent recurrence of a cultural symbiosis, at once libertine and libertarian, between open sensuality—aesthetic, gustatory, sexual—disdain for convention, and the belief that freedom is to be asserted against the corruptions and hypocrisies of society and culture and not merely secured within the operations of law and government. The latter would have satisfied Voltaire, but did not interest Diderot. Nor would he with Rousseau reject society and culture. His yearning was for their transfiguration into a congruence with nature.

Such radicalism made itself felt. Inevitably the authorities thought him dangerous and placed him in detention for more than three months in the summer of 1749 in the confines of the château of Vincennes. There he acknowledged authorship of the three works just mentioned—intemperate thoughts that happened to slip out, he called them—and there he continued preparation of what in an executive sense was the great work of his life, the editing of the *Encyclopédie, ou Dictionnaire raisonné des sciences, des arts, et des métiers,* so fully the signet of the French Enlightenment that the word "Encyclopedists" has become almost a synonym for its exponents. Even his imprisonment was one of those enlightened oppressions that did not prevent a subversive character from reading, writing, or receiving friends.

The *Encyclopédie.* Specifying the importance of the *Encyclopédie* in the history of science does not require following in detail the vexed story of its preparation and publication:[2] its commercial origin at the instance of the publisher Le Breton, who intended a straightforward translation from the English of Chambers' *Cyclopaedia* and John Harris' *Lexicon Technicum;* his enlistment of Diderot and d'Alembert in 1747 after a false start with the Abbé de Gua de Malves as editor, d'Alembert to oversee the mathematical subjects; the beating of bushes for contributors and nagging of contributors for copy; the appearance of the first volume in 1751 to applause from the enlightened and muttering from court and clergy; d'Alembert's desertion in 1758 on the eve of the suspension following volume VII and the subsequent prohibition of the enterprise by the authorities; publication, nevertheless, of the remaining ten volumes with the provisional protection of the chief official charged with censorship, the liberal-minded Malesherbes; the triumphant completion of the text of the work in 1766 consisting finally of seventeen volumes of articles and eleven of splendid plates, largely technical in subject matter. This was not merely the work of reference originally imagined by the publisher, who had had to take three other firms into partnership in order to finance the scale to which Diderot in his energy and enthusiasm had expanded it. It was not merely a place to look things up. A proper dictionary, in Diderot's view, should have "the character of changing the general way of thinking."[3]

The ideological impact of the *Encyclopédie* in its social, economic, political, juridical, and theological aspects is naturally more famous than its technical side. Having largely assimilated the ideology of progress, toleration, and government by consent, the general historical consciousness continues to be titillated by the alarm aroused at the time in traditionalist and privileged quarters over articles like "Certitude," by the Abbé de Prades, an emancipated clergyman who preferred the reasonings of Locke to the obscurities of Revelation; "Fornication," which introduces the word as a term in theology; "Salt," which enlarges on the injustice to the poor of excise taxes on items of subsistence; and "Political Authority," which de-

nied the existence in nature of the right of any man to exercise sovereignty over others.

Diderot's purpose, however, was deeper than unsettling the authorities by purveying tongue-in-cheek reflections on superstition and injustice in the guise of information. The technical contents of the *Encyclopédie* were central to that purpose, which was the dignification of common pursuits over and against the artificiality and pretense of the parasitic encrustations in society and reciprocally the rationalization and perfection of those pursuits in the light of modern knowledge. It would be a mistake to seek the scientific importance of the *Encyclopédie* only or even mainly in articles contributed or commissioned by d'Alembert on topics of mathematics, mechanics, or formal science. True, those articles are often (although not always) valuable summaries of the state and resources of a subject, and were so regarded at the time. But technically the central thrust of the *Encyclopédie* was in its descriptions of the arts and trades, and for that the initiative and responsibility were Diderot's, harking back certainly to his provincial background among the thriving artisans of Langres. The account of the cutlery industry is one of the best and clearest in the work, and in the article "Art" is a passage that may be taken as his credo:

> Let us at last give the artisans their due. The liberal arts have adequately sung their own praises; they must now use their remaining voice to celebrate the mechanical arts. It is for the liberal arts to lift the mechanical arts from the contempt in which prejudice has for so long held them, and it is for the patronage of kings to draw them from the poverty in which they still languish. Artisans have believed themselves contemptible because people have looked down on them; let us teach them to have a better opinion of themselves; that is the only way to obtain more nearly perfect results from them. We need a man to rise up in the academies and go down to the workshops and gather material about the arts to be set out in a book which will persuade artisans to read, philosophers to think on useful lines, and the great to make at least some worthwhile use of their authority and their wealth.

Diderot wrote this himself as he did many of the articles describing particular trades and processes. Not in every case was he able to "go down to the workshops" and base his account on actual observation, and a number are composed from printed sources or other secondary information. It was not on the articles alone, however, but on the illustrative plates to which most of them were keyed that Diderot and his publishers relied to fulfill the promise made to subscribers of a systematic description of eighteenth-century industry in its essential processes and principles. Censorship had interrupted publication of articles in 1759, but there could be no objection to going ahead with technical plates containing no sensitive matter. The series began in 1762 and filled the gap until the remaining ten volumes of text could appear all at once four years later. (The supplementary volume of plates and four of text published by Panckoucke were not edited by Diderot.)

Delicate questions arise about the publication of these plates, not concerning Diderot's treatment of the censorship, but rather his originality and treatment of the rights of others. They were preceded in their appearance by angry charges of having been lifted from engravings prepared for the Academy of Sciences. Since its founding in 1666, during the administration of Colbert, that body had been vested with the responsibility of maintaining a scientific surveillance over French industry. Not a line had appeared of its constitutionally prescribed project for a description of arts and trades, although its most recent director, the naturalist and metallurgist Réaumur, had commissioned a large number of plates before his death in 1757. The Academy rushed one volume of these into print in 1761 in order to forestall Diderot, who himself or through agents must indeed have found, bought, or bribed access to Réaumur's plates during the early stages of preparing the *Encyclopédie*. All that can be said in extenuation is that copyright did not exist in the eighteenth century, that title to artistic and literary property was an amorphous matter, and that whoever engraved the various plates it was through Diderot's deeds and misdeeds that they appeared as a collection, a systematic record of industrial life and methods.

At their best the plates of the *Encyclopédie* are executed with the sweep and style of chefs d'oeuvre of technical illustration, notably in the series devoted to the glass industry, in the coverage afforded to Gobelin tapestries, and in depicting the blast furnace and forge. Typically the reader is given something like an anatomy of machines, a physiology of processes. The technique of illustration might be thought to derive from the anatomy of Vesalius two centuries before. Several of his plates are among those that reappear without acknowledgment as do several of Agricola's depicting sixteenth-century mining. Normally the first plate in each series gives an overall picture of an installation and is followed by sectional views, one lengthwise and one crosswise. Thereafter, cutaway representations penetrate to the intermediate assemblies, sometimes shown in place and sometimes in isolation. Finally, there are drawings of the individual parts, pieces, and tools.

The plates exhibit the state of manufacturing processes just before the industrial revolution, then in its earliest, largely unperceived stages in England. Science is often taken to be the fruitful element in technology, the progenitor of industrialization, and so it appears in the *Encyclopédie*, but only if we limit what we understand by the influence of science to its descriptive role. Basic theory had very little to offer the manufacturer in any industry in the eighteenth century, and it was descriptive science addressed to industry that transformed it by rationalizing procedures and publicizing methods. In effect the *Encyclopédie* turned craftsmanship from lore to science and began replacing the age-old instinct that techniques must be guarded in secret with the concept of uniform industrial method to be adopted by all producers.

Not that the changeover was welcomed by practitioners or easily achieved. Many tradesmen, full of suspicion, resisted inquiries or deliberately misinformed Diderot and his associates after accepting their gratuities. Terminology alone created obstacles. Each trade had its own, often barbarous, jargon. A great many artisans had no desire to understand from a scientific point of view what it was they were doing and preferred working by traditional routine. "It is only an artisan knowing how to reason who can properly expound his work,"[4] exclaimed Diderot in a moment of irritation, a remark that might seem to render somewhat circular his fundamental conception of science and reason as the educators of industry, but that brings out the necessity for its rationalization if the truly popular purpose of the *Encyclopédie* was to be achieved in the deepest sense—that is, in the easing of labor, its liberation from routine, and the summons to pride in its enlightenment.

Moral and Philosophic Position. Particular articles in the *Encyclopédie* exhibit the development of Diderot's scientific sensibility into the psychic materialism of his later years, through his reading of chemistry, natural history, comparative anatomy, and physiology, complemented by the experience and observation of humanity, but it is more satisfactory to follow the writings that he found time and inspiration to leave as his literary legacy. The term legacy is deliberate for it was one of the peculiarities of Diderot's intellectual personality that, prolific writer that he was, it seems to have been more important to him to express his mind than to publish and persuade. Of the major books conveying his philosophy of nature, only *De l'interprétation de la nature* was printed during his lifetime, the first edition in 1753 and a revision in 1754, just when he was winding up his researches on the arts and trades. For the rest (to name the important), *Le rêve de d'Alembert, Entretien* *entre Diderot et d'Alembert,* and *Suite de l'entretien* were written in 1769 and published in 1830; the *Supplément au voyage de Bougainville* was begun in 1772 and published in 1796; and the *Éléments de physiologie,* begun in 1774 and taken up again in 1778, was published in 1875. (It was the same with his best literary works: the picaresque novel *Jacques le fataliste* was printed in the completed form in 1796, and the theatrical piece *Est-il bon, Est-il méchant?* in 1834.

Most extraordinary of all, his masterpiece, *Le neveu de Rameau*—a complex dialogue that, in shifting the locus of immorality back and forth between the ostensibly degenerate individual and the actually corrupt society, anticipates the diabolism although not the sexual inversion in the writings of Jean Genet— was first printed in a German translation by Goethe from an inexact manuscript and published in French in a largely faithful version only in 1884. Vicissitudes too complicated to follow here led these manuscripts through various minor German courts and the major court of Catherine the Great in St. Petersburg, which Diderot was persuaded to enliven briefly by his presence in later years.

It is possible to identify sources of much of Diderot's scientific inspiration:[5] the chemistry in the lectures of Rouelle at the Jardin du Roi, the natural history in Buffon, the physiology in Haller, the psychology in La Mettrie, and the medical doctrine in his frequent association with Bordeu. But this record of nonpublication, and the consequent implausibility of supposing that his views could have formed a system exerting a coherent influence upon either contemporary or later writers, make it more reasonable to regard his response to the scientific world picture as an anticipation of the program recognizable later, and rather recurrently than consequentially, as that of biological romanticism—an attempt to construct an account of the operations of nature in categories of organism and consciousness rather than impersonal matter in inanimate motion.

Occasionally it has been supposed in Diderot scholarship that he reached this position in a lifelong progression from some solid Newtonian basis in his youth; and it is true that he published in 1748 (the year of *Les bijoux indiscrets*!) a curious little collection, *Mémoires sur différens sujets de mathématiques;* and further true that in one memoir, the fifth, he mentions that he had studied Newton formerly, "if not with much success, at least with zeal enough," but that to raise questions about Newton today "is to speak to me of a dream of years gone by."[6] Although very interesting in several respects, the memoirs themselves give no reason beyond the title

for thinking that Diderot had in fact ever been seized of Newtonian mathematical physics.

The first and most considerable is a summary of musical acoustics dressed out in elementary mathematical formalism. Its object is to establish that musical pleasure consists in perception of the relations of sounds as they are propagated in nature and is no mere matter of caprice or culture, although such factors certainly affect the judgment. Ever the good encyclopedist, Diderot reported faithfully the work on vibrating strings and pipes of Taylor, d'Alembert, Mersenne, Sauveur, and Euler. Although in no way original physically, the discussion is, nevertheless, a highly individual approach to the physics of beauty in a manner not to be attempted successfully before the work of Helmholtz. The other essays are much slighter. The second and third are geometrical and concern the design of certain devices that Diderot was proposing to mathematical and musical instrument makers. The fourth is a (virtually computerized) program for enlarging the repertory of barrel organs, and rather wickedly suggests that resistance to the improvement of these popular instruments was a function not of musical taste but of the self-interest and restrictiveness of musicians and music teachers. The last reassures those who have failed to master Newton by taking him to task for an allegedly false assumption about air resistance in the pendulum experiments that he reported in the scholium following the sixth corollary to the laws of motion in the *Principia.*

Five years later three volumes of the *Encyclopédie* were in print, and the opening paragraphs of *De l'interprétation de la nature* predict that mathematics is about to go into a decline, and deservedly so. On all grounds it had exaggerated its claim to be the language of science. Metaphysically it falsifies nature by depriving bodies of the qualities of odor, texture, appearance, or taste through which they appeal to our senses. It impoverishes mechanics by requiring it to operate with the superficial measurements of bodies instead of seeking, as the chemist is said to do, for the activity that animates them. Worst of all, it dries up and blights the sensibilities of those who cultivate it and whom it renders inhuman in their judgments. Such will be the effect of any science that ceases to "instruct and please," for the only thing that will make a science appealing and keep it vital is its capacity to improve the character, understanding, and moral fiber of its possessors. Mathematics leads mainly to arrogance, however, pretending to equip a finite intelligence to plumb the infinite where it has no business. Man being insatiable, we need some criterion not found in mathematics by which to establish bounds between what we need to know and the infinite unknown. So let it be our interests, let it be utility, "which, in a few centuries, will establish boundaries for experimental science, as it is about to do for mathematics."[7]

Apparently a formless rumination, *De l'interprétation de la nature* is actually written in an artful stream of consciousness, a reverie on the Experimental Art, the true road to a science of nature. That road lies through craftsmanship, and here we rejoin the editor of the *Encyclopédie*. For Diderot, it is the common touch that opens up the truth, and genius that is to be distrusted, inclining in its pride to draw a mathematical veil of abstraction and obscurity between nature and the people. It is wrong to say that there are some truths too deep or hard for ordinary understandings. Certainly common men will never attach any value to what cannot be proven useful, and they are right. Only a philosophy derived from actually handling objects is innocent in that it involves no a priori ideas. A kind of intuition in the true craftsman has the quality of inspiration for it derives from genuine participation. Such a man will recognize it in himself, in his solidarity with natural objects. In his hands science and nature are one in the actual operation with materials. Not some mathematical abstraction from nature but manual intimacy with nature, living oneness with nature, is the arm of science.

For nature is the combination of its elements and not just an aggregate. It is continuity that science is to seek in nature, not divisibility. The interesting property of molecules is their transience, not their existence. In genetics the notion of *emboîtement* is unacceptable because of its atomistic implications. For there are no fixed limits in nature. Male and female exist in each other (a fascination with hermaphroditism and the merging of the sexes is another motif in his writings that seems curiously up-to-date in the 1970's). Mineral, vegetable, and animal kingdoms blend, species into species, and only the stream of seminal fluid is permanent, flowing down through time. "Tout change; tout passe; il n'y a que le tout qui reste" ("Everything changes; everything passes; nothing remains but the whole");[8] and in *Le rêve de d'Alembert,* Diderot invokes two models to exhibit this unity. The first is the swarm of bees, for the solidarity of the universe is social. It has the oneness of the social insects, among whom laws of community are laws of nature. In the second the universe is a cosmic polyp, time its life unfolding, space its habitation, gradience its structure, and certainly the two ideas that mattered most to Diderot were those of social naturalism and universal sensibility.

In Diderot's philosophic dialogue with a fictitious d'Alembert, that distinguished mathematical colleague admits that the notion of a sensitive matter containing in itself principles of movement and consciousness is more immediately comprehensible than that of a being which is inextended and yet occupies extension, which differs from matter and yet is united to it, which follows its course and moves it without being moved. "Is it by accident," this straw d'Alembert is made to ask,

> that you would recognize an active sensibility and an inert sensibility, in the way that there is a live force and a dead force?—a live force that manifests itself in motion of translation, a dead force that manifests itself by pressure; an active sensibility that is characterized by certain remarkable actions in animals and perhaps in plants, and an inert sensibility the existence of which is assured by the passage to the state of active sensibility?

"Marvelous," Diderot as interlocutor replies, "you said it."[9]

And in the *rêve* that continues the discussion, d'Alembert, apparently ailing, has been put into a trance—it may be a delirium—in which he speaks truths that would not have come to him from the normal detachment of the mathematical analyst quantifying his inert blocks of matter. Now his interlocutors are his mistress, Mlle. de l'Espinasse, and a doctor, Diderot's mentor in medical vitalism, Théophile de Bordeu, who recognizes these verities for what they are and draws them out in a kind of psychic analysis of the realities of a world alive. He it is who sees nature in the perspective of human nature, and who, therefore, knew the answers all the time. "There is no difference," Diderot makes Mlle. de l'Espinasse observe, "between a doctor keeping watch and a philosopher dreaming."[10]

NOTES

1. Scholarship on Diderot occasionally falls into confusion about the identity of this work, published in 3 vols. (London, 1743–1745), attributing it sometimes to the authorship and sometimes to the firm of Ephraim Chambers, publisher of a famous *Cyclopaedia.* In fact the author was Robert James and the publisher T. Osborne. The French translation was published by Briasson in 6 vols. (1746–1748) and entitled *Dictionnaire universel de médecine, de chirurgie, de chymie, de botanique, d'anatomie, de pharmacie, et d'histoire naturelle.* . . .
2. See Jacques Proust, *Diderot et l'Encyclopédie* (Paris, 1963).
3. Quoted in Arthur Wilson, *Diderot: The Testing Years* (New York, 1957), p. 244.
4. Diderot article, "Encyclopédie," in the *Encyclopédie,* vol. V.
5. Jean Mayer, *Diderot, homme de science* (Rennes, 1959).
6. *Op. cit.,* pp. 202–203.
7. *Op. cit.,* par. 6.
8. "Le rêve de d'Alembert," in Paul Vernière, ed., *Oeuvres philosophiques de Diderot* (Paris, 1956), pp. 299–300.
9. "Entretien entre d'Alembert et Diderot," *ibid.,* p. 260.
10. *Ibid.,* p. 293.

BIBLIOGRAPHY

I. ORIGINAL WORKS. There is no modern edition of the works of Diderot, although one is said to be in preparation. The most recent is *Oeuvres complètes,* J. Assezat and M. Tourneux, eds., 20 vols. (Paris, 1875–1877). A useful selection is *Oeuvres philosophiques de Diderot,* Paul Vernière, ed. (Paris, 1956).

There are a number of selections from the *Encyclopédie* in *L'Encyclopédie* (*Extraits*) (Paris, 1934); *The Encyclopédie of Diderot and d'Alembert, Selected Articles,* John Lough, ed. (Cambridge, 1954); *Textes choisis de l'Encyclopédie,* ed., with commentary, by Albert Soboul (Paris, 1962); and *Encyclopedia Selections,* Nelly S. Hoyt and Thomas Cassirer, eds. (New York, 1965).

The undersigned has edited a selection from the technical plates: *A Diderot Pictorial Encyclopedia of Trades and Industry . . . With Introduction and Notes,* 2 vols. (New York, 1959).

II. SECONDARY LITERATURE. The literature on Diderot is immense. Besides works mentioned in the notes, readers will gain entry into it from Abraham Lerel, *Diderots Naturphilosophie* (Vienna, 1950); Jean-Louis Leutrat, *Diderot* (Paris, 1967); J. Lough, *Essays on the Encyclopédie of Diderot and d'Alembert* (London, 1968); René Pomeau, *Diderot, sa vie, son oeuvre, avec un exposé de sa philosophie* (Paris, 1967); and Franco Venturi, *La jeunesse de Diderot* (*1713–1753*) (Paris, 1939).

The exposition of *De l'interprétation de la nature* in this article follows closely the discussion of the significance of Diderot's scientific views for the intellectual history of the Enlightenment in the undersigned's *Edge of Objectivity* (Princeton, 1960), ch. 5.

CHARLES COULSTON GILLISPIE

DIELS, OTTO PAUL HERMANN (*b.* Hamburg, Germany, 23 January 1876; *d.* Kiel, Germany, 7 March 1954), *organic chemistry.*

Diels's father, Hermann, was professor of classical philology at the University of Berlin; his brother Paul, professor of Slavic philology at Breslau; and his brother Ludwig, professor of botany at Berlin. His mother, the former Bertha Dübell, was the daughter of a district judge.

As a student, Diels, with his brother Ludwig, eagerly conducted chemical experiments. He studied chemistry in Berlin from 1895 to 1899 and in 1899 obtained the Ph.D., *magna cum laude,* with a dissertation entitled "Zur Kenntnis der Cyanverbindungen." From 1899 he studied under Emil Fischer and served as his assistant until he became a lecturer in 1904. He became department head in 1913 and in 1914 was appointed associate professor at the Chemical Institute of the Royal Friedrich Wilhelm (now Humboldt) University. In 1916 Diels accepted an invitation from Christian Albrecht University, Kiel, where he served as full professor and director of the Chemical Institute until his final retirement in October 1948.

Diels recorded his personal memories in a manuscript entitled "Werden und Wirken eines Chemieprofessors," as well as in an illustrated diary (Diels was a weekend painter) which has been reviewed in detail by Sigurd Olsen. Diels was considered somewhat reserved, yet possessed of a good sense of humor. He was honest, sensitive, an outstanding educator, and a devoted family man. Diels was married in 1909 and had three sons and two daughters. Toward the end of World War II two of his sons were killed at the eastern front, and air raids completely destroyed the Chemical Institute, the library, and his home. Since there was no possibility of carrying on his work and he was suffering from the general privations, Diels filed for retirement in September 1944, to be effective in March 1945. Nevertheless, in 1946 he agreed to resume the directorship of the Chemical Institute, and at the age of seventy he started anew, under the most primitive conditions in makeshift quarters.

Emil Fischer, Diels's teacher, ended a period of chemistry that Willstätter called the age of simple methods and direct observation. During Diels's time the importance of theoretical chemistry, physicochemical measuring methods, complicated experiments, and teamwork grew to such an extent that in some instances chemical research lost a little of its immediacy.

Diels's work, which was in the field of pure organic chemistry with no significant digressions into biochemistry or into physical chemistry, reveals an outstanding experimenter with original and bold ideas. His *Einführung in die organische Chemie* (1907), which went through nineteen editions by 1962, has a clarity and a precision that have made it one of the most popular textbooks in the field. Diels's lectures, accompanied by experiments, were outstanding and were enthusiastically received by his students.

In 1906 Diels obtained carbon suboxide by dehydrating malonic acid and investigated its properties. In the same year, with E. Abderhalden, he began his research on cholesterol, the structure of which had not yet been determined. He isolated pure cholesterol from gallstones and converted it into "Diels's acid" through cleavage by oxidation. Meanwhile, Windaus had proposed a formula for cholesterol that did not agree with more recent observations. As a result, Diels decided first to establish the aromatic basic structure of cholesterol. Dehydration of cholesterol with sulfur was unsuccessful. Selenium was used next, and in 1927 it yielded a twofold success (Fig. 1): a new, milder, and very effective dehydrating agent had been

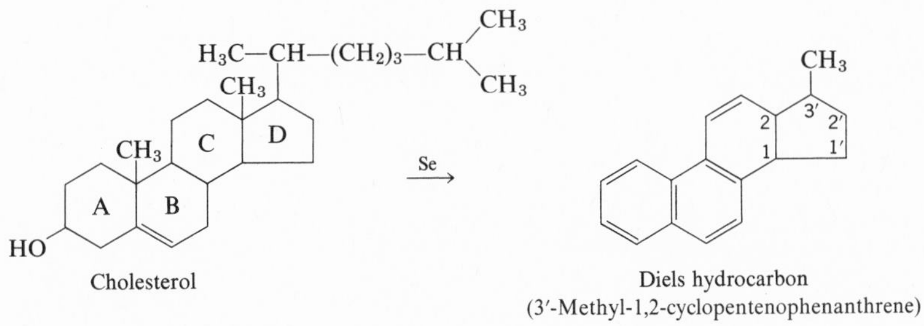

Cholesterol

Diels hydrocarbon
(3'-Methyl-1,2-cyclopentenophenanthrene)

FIGURE 1

discovered; Diels had obtained the aromatic basic structure he had been looking for—3′methyl-1,2 cyclopentenophenanthrene, the structure of which was clarified by Robert Harper, Kon, and Leopold Ruzicka in 1934.

This "Diels hydrocarbon," $C_{18}H_{16}$, the identity of which with the corresponding synthetic product was demonstrated by Diels in 1935, proved to be the basic substance and structure of a number of very important natural products for the chemistry of natural substances. The investigation of these substances corresponded in importance to the discovery of the benzene ring for organic chemistry. The structure and behavior of the sex hormones, the saponins, the cardiac glycosides (digitoxin, strophanthin, etc.), the D vitamins, toad "venom," bile pigments, adrenal-cortex hormones (cortisone), and similar substances could now be clarified.

With Kurt Alder, Diels developed over a period of twenty-two years the diene synthesis, which came to occupy a key position in the theory and practice of organic chemistry. It also yielded new facts concerning the three-dimensional isomerism of the carbon compounds. Starting with Thiele's 1,4-addition theorem and the knowledge of the additive power of azo esters, Diels and Alder attempted in 1928 to combine maleic anhydride with cyclopentadiene (Fig. 2). The dienes (compounds with conjugated carbon double bonds) united with philodienes (compounds with an ethylene radical flanked by carbonyl or carboxyl groups) to form ring-shaped structures. This type of synthesis is not only extraordinarily diverse but also occurs spon-

taneously, even at room temperature, and in general with good yields, without the use of condensing agents and catalysts. The diene system opens at positions 1 and 4, and the terminal carbons are located at the double bonds of the philodienes.

Diels published thirty-three papers on the practical applications of this new method of synthesis. Windaus, in the field of steroids, used it for the separation of ergosterol and its irradiation products. In a series of important terpenes, such as camphor, dl-santene, butadiene, and α-phellandrene, the structure could be confirmed by synthesis, since these substances are composed of isoprene residues, the building blocks of the diene structure. Also, great progress could be made in the synthesis of heterocyclics.

In 1904 Diels participated in the Louisiana Purchase Exposition in St. Louis and received a gold medal for his exhibit. During the academic year 1925–1926 he served as *rector magnificus* of the University of Kiel. His inaugural address was entitled "Über die Bedeutung von Zufall und Instinkt bei grossen chemischen Entdeckungen." In 1931 the Society of German Chemists awarded Diels the Adolf von Baeyer Memorial Medal, and in 1946 the Medical Faculty of Christian Albrecht University awarded him an honorary doctorate. Diels was a member of the academies of sciences of Göttingen and Halle (Leopoldina) as well as the Bavarian Academy of Sciences. In 1950 he and his pupil Kurt Alder shared the Nobel Prize in chemistry for the development of the diene synthesis. In his Nobel address, "Darstellung und Bedeutung des aromatischen Grundskeletts der

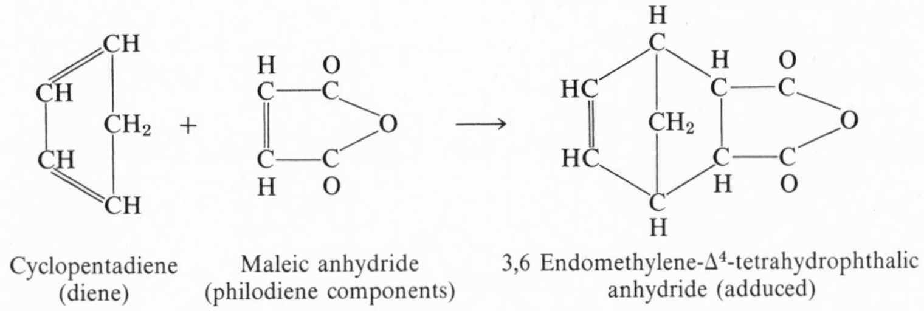

Cyclopentadiene
(diene)

Maleic anhydride
(philodiene components)

3,6 Endomethylene-Δ^4-tetrahydrophthalic anhydride (adduced)

FIGURE 2

91

Steroide," Diels compared his research on cholesterol with his work in diene synthesis.

BIBLIOGRAPHY

Diels's writings include "Über das Kohlensuboxyd I," in *Berichte der Deutschen chemischen Gesellschaft,* **39** (1906), 689, written with B. Wolf; *Einführung in die organische Chemie* (Leipzig, 1907; 19th ed., Weinheim, 1962); "Über die Bildung von Chrysen bei der Dehydrierung des Cholesterins," in *Berichte der Deutschen chemischen Gesellschaft,* **60** (1927), 140, written with W. Gädke; "Über Dehydrierungen mit Selen (II. Mitteil)," *ibid.,* 2323, written with A. Karstens; "Synthesen in der hydroaromatischen Reihe, I. Mitteilung, Anlagerungen von 'Di-en'-kohlenwasserstoffen," in *Justus Liebigs Annalen der Chemie,* no. 460 (1928), 98, written with K. Alder; "Die Dien-Synthesen, ein ideales Aufbauprinzip organischer Stoffe. (Vortrag zum 100. Geburtstag von A. Kekulé)," in *Zeitschrift für angewandte Chemie,* **42** (1929), 911; "'Dien-Synthesen' als Aufbauprinzip und Hilfsmittel organisch-chemischer Forschung," in *Jaarboekie van de Natuur-Philosofische Faculteitsvereniging* (Groningen, 1934); "Über organisch-chemischer Entdeckungen und ihre Bedeutung für Gegenwart und Zukunft," in *Chemikerzeitung,* **61** (1937), 7; "Bedeutung der Diensynthese für Bildung, Aufbau und Erforschung von Naturstoffen," in *Fortschritte der Chemie organischer Naturstoffe,* **3** (1939), 1; "Mein Beitrag zur Aufklärung des Sterinproblems," an address summarized in *Angewandte Chemie,* **60** (1948), 78; and "Darstellung und Bedeutung des aromatischen Grundskeletts der Steroide, Nobelvortrag," in *Les Prix Nobel en 1950* (Stockholm, 1950).

A secondary source is Sigurd Olsen, "Otto Diels," in *Chemische Berichte,* **95,** no. 2 (1962), v-xlvi, with bibliography and photographs.

EBERHARD SCHMAUDERER

DIETRICH VON FREIBERG (*b.* Freiberg, Germany, *ca.* 1250; *d. ca.* 1310), *optics, natural philosophy.*

In Latin his name is written Theodoricus Teutonicus de Vriberg (variants: de Vriburgo, de Vribergh, de Vriberch, de Fridiberg, de Frideberch, Vriburgensis). This has been anglicized as Theodoric of Freiberg and rendered into French as Thierry de Fribourg. Which of the many Freibergs or Freiburgs is the place of his birth is not known for certain; Krebs regards Freiberg in Saxony as the most likely. Dietrich entered the Dominican order (province of Teutonia) and probably taught in Germany before studying at the University of Paris, about 1275–1277. He was named provincial of Teutonia in 1293 and was appointed vicar provincial again in 1310. He earned the title of master of theology at St. Jacques in Paris before 1303. In 1304 he was present at the general chapter of his order held in Toulouse, where he was requested by the master

general, Aymeric de Plaisance, to put his investigations on the rainbow into writing. Dietrich is sometimes cited as a disciple of Albertus Magnus; although he is in Albert's tradition, there is no direct evidence that Albert actually taught him.

Apart from his role as a precursor of modern science, Dietrich wrote extensively in philosophy and theology. He is best characterized as an eclectic, although he generally followed the Aristotelian tradition in philosophy and the Augustinian-Neoplatonic tradition in theology. He opposed Thomas Aquinas on key metaphysical theses, including the real distinction between essence and existence. Crombie argues for an influence of Robert Grosseteste on Dietrich from similarities in their optics, but the evidence is meager; Dietrich certainly rejected the "metaphysics of light" taught by Grosseteste and Roger Bacon, and he did not subscribe to the mathematicist view of nature that was common in the Oxford school. Again, Dietrich's interest in Neoplatonism was more theological and mystical than philosophical. He is credited with having influenced the development of speculative mysticism as it was to be taught by Meister Eckhart and Johannes Tauler, both of whom were German Dominicans.

Dietrich's place in the history of science is assured by his *De iride et radialibus impressionibus* ("On the Rainbow and 'Radiant Impressions,'" i.e., phenomena produced in the upper atmosphere by radiation from the sun or other heavenly body), a treatise composed shortly after 1304 and running to over 170 pages in the printed edition (1914). In an age when scientific experimentation was practically unknown, Dietrich investigated thoroughly the paths of light rays through crystalline spheres and flasks filled with water; and he deduced therefrom the main elements of a theory of the rainbow that was to be perfected only centuries later by Descartes and Newton. He also worked out a novel theory of the elements that was related to his optical researches and wrote on the heavenly bodies, although the latter of these contributions is more the work of a philosopher than of a physical scientist in the modern sense.

The anomalous character of Dietrich's contribution poses a problem for the historian of scientific methodology. One is tempted to see in his use of experiment and mathematical reasoning an adumbration of techniques that were brought to perfection in the seventeenth and later centuries. That there is such a foreshadowing is undeniable, and yet the thought context in which Dietrich worked is so different from the Cartesian and empiricist world views that one must be careful not to force too close an identification in method. The mathematical basis for Dietrich's reasoning stems from the *perspectiva,* or geometrical optics, of the Schoolmen and of Arabs such as Ibn al-Haytham (Alhazen); and his measurements are those of medieval astronomy, based on the primitive trigonometry of Ptolemy's *Almagest.* Dietrich does not propose a "theory" in the technical sense, although there is a hypothetical element in his thinking that can be disengaged on careful reading. Rather, he explicitly locates his own method in the framework of Aristotle's *Posterior Analytics,* which puts him on the search for the causes of the rainbow, through discovery of which he hopes to be able to deduce all of the rainbow's properties. This demonstrative ideal of Aristotelian science, it may be noted, did not exclude the use of dialectical (or conjectural) reasoning by its practitioner, although later Scholastics have tended to overlook the latter element. Dietrich's empiricism also derives from the Aristotelian tradition, even though portions of his theory of knowledge are markedly Augustinian. His optics makes implicit use of a method of resolution and composition that was already known to Grosseteste and that was to be refined considerably by the Averroist Aristotelians at Padua, who educated the young Galileo in its use. The general framework of Dietrich's methodology is, thus, far from revolutionary. What characterizes his contribution is his careful application of a method already known in a general way but never hitherto applied with such skill to the detailed explanation of natural phenomena.

Within this setting Dietrich's methodological contribution may be made more precise, as follows. He was not content merely to observe nature but attempted to duplicate nature's operation by isolating the component factors of that operation in a way that permitted their study at close range. Most of his predecessors had regarded the rain cloud as an effective agent in the production of the rainbow; even when they suspected that the individual drop played a significant role, as did Albertus Magnus, they saw no way of isolating it from the collection that produced the bow. When, for example, they compared the colors of the bow with the spectrum resulting from the sun's rays passing through a spherical flask of water, they tended to equate the flask with a cloud or with a collection of drops. It was Dietrich who apparently was the first to see "that a globe of water can be thought of, not as a diminutive spherical cloud, but as a magnified raindrop" (Boyer, p. 112). This insight, coupled with the recognition that the bow is simply the aggregate of effects produced by many individual drops, ultimately led him to the first essentially correct explanation of the primary and secondary bows. Dietrich, of course, used remarkable

experimental acumen in working out all the implications of his discovery. But his genius consisted basically in immobilizing the raindrop, in magnified form, in what approximated a laboratory situation and then studying at leisure and at length the various components involved in the production of the bows.

Dietrich's work represents a great breakthrough in geometrical optics, and yet a simple error in geometry prevented him from giving a correct quantitative theory of the rainbow. In essence, this came about through his using the "meteorological sphere" of Aristotle as his basic frame of reference. Here the observer was regarded as at the center of such a sphere, and the sun and the raindrop (or cloud) were thought to be located on its periphery. Thus, in Figure 1, the observer is at the center, *B,* while the sun is

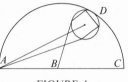

FIGURE 1

behind him at point *A* on the horizon and the much magnified raindrop is elevated at point *D* in front of him. Although this schema permitted Dietrich to use a method of calculation already at hand from medieval astronomy, it automatically committed him to holding that the raindrop and the sun remain always at an equal distance from the observer—an assumption that perforce falsified his calculations.

On the detailed mechanism for the production of the primary, or lower, rainbow (see Figure 2), Dietrich

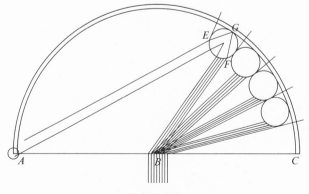

FIGURE 2

was the first to trace correctly the path of the light ray through the raindrop and to see that this involved two refractions at the surface of the drop nearer the observer, i.e., at points *E* and *F,* and one internal reflection at the surface farther from him, i.e., at point *G.* This provided an understanding of why the bow always has a circular form, which was already seen in a rudimentary way by Aristotle; but it also enabled Dietrich to deduce many of the remaining properties of the bow. He was the first to see, for example, that each color in the rainbow is projected to the observer from a different drop or series of drops. He also could deduce, as others before him had merely surmised, that an observer who changes his position sees a different rainbow, in the sense that a completely different series of drops is required for its formation.

This explanation of the primary rainbow alone would have gained for Dietrich a respectable place in the history of optics. He did not stop here, however, but went on to detail the corresponding mechanism for the production of the secondary, or upper, rainbow (see Figure 3). He saw that the light ray, in this case,

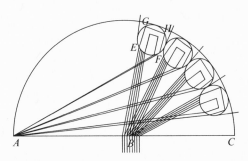

FIGURE 3

follows a path quite different from that in the production of the primary bow, involving as it does two refractions at the surface of the drop nearer the observer, i.e., at points *E* and *F,* and *two* internal reflections at the surface farther from him, i.e., at points *G* and *H.* This insight led immediately to the correct explanation for the inversion of the colors in the secondary bow: the additional internal reflection reverses the ordering of the colors. Thus could Dietrich demolish the competing theories current in his time and go on to deduce other properties of the outer bow: that it is paler in appearance than the inner bow (because of the additional reflection) and that it often fails to appear when the inner bow is clearly seen.

A most interesting part of Dietrich's *De iride*—which led him to compose a companion treatise, *De coloribus* ("On Colors")—is his ingenious but unsuccessful attempt to explain how the colors of the rainbow are generated. It is in these portions of his work, generally passed over rapidly by historians of science, that one can discern in his procedure an interplay between theory and experiment foreshadowing the characteristic methodology of modern science. Dietrich was confident that he had discovered the true "causes" of the bows, and thus he proposed his geometrical explanations of their formation as apo-

dictic demonstrations in the Aristotelian mode. He never was convinced, on the other hand, that he had gotten to the "causes" of radiant color; and thus he had to content himself with the search for the "principles" of such color formation. In this search Dietrich fell back on a Peripatetic argument involving "contraries," the classical paradigm of dialectical reasoning. He used as his analogy the medieval theory of the elements, according to which the four basic contrary qualities of hot-cold and wet-dry, in proper combination, account for the generation of the four elements (fire, air, water, and earth). To employ this, Dietrich had first to establish that there are four colors in the spectrum–and this contrary to Aristotle and almost all of his contemporaries, who held that there are only three. His inductive argument here is superb, and the way in which he employs observation and experiment to overthrow the authority of Aristotle would delight any seventeenth-century thinker. Dietrich was less fortunate in explaining the origin of colors in terms of his two "formal principles" (clear-obscure) and two "material principles" (bounded-unbounded). He did, however, contrive a whole series of experiments, leading to various *ad hoc* assumptions, in his attempt to verify the explanation he proposed. Yet it seems that he was never quite sure of this, and in fact a quite different approach was needed to solve his problem—it was provided by Sir Isaac Newton.

Possibly because of an interest in the elements aroused by his optical studies, Dietrich wrote opuscula entitled *De elementis corporum naturalium* ("On the Elements of Natural Bodies"), *De miscibilibus in mixto* ("On Elements in the Compound"), and *De luce et eius origine* ("On Light and Its Production"). These are neither mathematical nor experimental, but they do shed light on Dietrich's theories of the structure of matter and his analysis of gravitational motion. He also composed treatises relating to astronomy, *De corporibus celestibus quoad naturam eorum corporalem* ("On Heavenly Bodies With Regard to Their Corporeal Nature") and *De intelligenciis et motoribus celorum* ("On Intelligences and the Movers of the Heavens"); the latter has been analyzed by Duhem, who sees it as a retrogression from the astronomical contributions of Albertus Magnus.

For the influence of Dietrich on later optical writers, which was mostly indirect, see the works of Boyer and Crombie cited in the bibliography.

BIBLIOGRAPHY

I. ORIGINAL WORKS. *De iride et radialibus impressionibus,* edited by Joseph Würschmidt in "Dietrich von Freiberg:

Über den Regenbogen und die durch Strahlen erzeugten Eindrücke," in *Beiträge zur Geschichte der Philosophie und Theologie des Mittelalters*, XII, pts. 5–6 (Münster in Westfalen, 1914), contains Latin text, with summaries of chapters in German; an English translation of significant portions of the Latin text with notes, by W. A. Wallace, is to appear in *A Source Book of Medieval Science,* Edward Grant, ed., to be published by the Harvard University Press. The Latin text of *De coloribus, De luce et eius origine, De miscibilibus in mixto,* and portions of *De elementis corporum naturalium* is in W. A. Wallace, *The Scientific Methodology of Theodoric of Freiberg,* Studia Friburgensia, n.s. no. 26 (Fribourg, 1959), pp. 324–376, which contains references to all edited opuscula of Dietrich published before 1959; to these should be added a partial edition of *De visione beatifica* in Richard D. Tétreau, "The Agent Intellect in Meister Dietrich of Freiberg: Study and Text," unpublished Ph.D. thesis for the Pontifical Institute of Mediaeval Studies (Toronto, 1966). A French translation of excerpts from *De intelligenciis et motoribus celorum* is in Pierre Duhem, *Le système du monde,* III (Paris, 1915; repr. 1958), 383–396.

II. SECONDARY LITERATURE. Biographical material can be found in Engelbert Krebs, "Meister Dietrich, sein Leben, seine Werke, seine Wissenschaft," in *Beiträge zur Geschichte der Philosophie und Theologie des Mittelalters,* V, pts. 5–6 (Münster in Westfalen, 1906). Dietrich's work on the rainbow is well detailed in Carl B. Boyer, *The Rainbow: From Myth to Mathematics* (New York, 1959), pp. 110–124 and *passim;* and in A. C. Crombie, *Robert Grosseteste and the Origins of Experimental Science, 1100–1700* (Oxford, 1953), pp. 233–259. Fuller details on Dietrich's methods are in W. A. Wallace, *Scientific Methodology . . .,* cited above. For an account of Dietrich's other scientific accomplishments, see the following articles by W. A. Wallace: "Gravitational Motion According to Theodoric of Freiberg," in *The Thomist,* **24** (1961), 327–352, repr. in *The Dignity of Science,* J. A. Weisheipl, ed. (Washington, D.C., 1961), pp. 191–216; "Theodoric of Freiberg on the Structure of Matter," in *Proceedings of the Tenth International Congress of History of Science, Ithaca, N.Y., 1962,* I (Paris, 1964), 591–597; and "Elementarity and Reality in Particle Physics," in *Boston Studies in the Philosophy of Science,* III, R. S. Cohen and M. W. Wartofsky, eds. (New York, 1968), 236–271, esp. 243–247.

WILLIAM A. WALLACE, O. P.

DIETRICH, BARON DE. *See* **Holbach, Paul-Henri d'.**

DIGBY, KENELM (*b.* Gayhurst, Buckinghamshire, England, 11 July 1603; *d.* London, England, 11 June 1665), *natural philosophy, occult science.*

The son of Sir Everard Digby, executed in 1606 for complicity in the Gunpowder Plot, and of Mary Mulsho of Gayhurst, Digby was brought up a Catholic. In 1617 he accompanied his uncle John Digby (later the first earl of Bristol) on a diplomatic mission to

Spain. He was at Oxford, mainly under Thomas Allen, mathematician and astronomer, from 1618 to 1620, after which he set off on a tour of Europe, to France (where he attracted the attention of Marie de' Medici), Italy, and Spain. On his return in 1623 Digby was knighted, presumably for his share, while in Spain, in entertaining Prince Charles and the duke of Buckingham.

In 1625 Digby secretly married the beautiful Venetia Stanley; five children were born, the marriage being made public after the birth of the second in 1627. In this year Digby set off on a privateering mission to the Mediterranean that involved a dramatic but scandalous attack on Venetian shipping off Scanderoon (Alexandretta; now Iskenderun); this won him considerable fame and financial rewards. Probably in the hope of preferment he was converted to Anglicanism in 1630 but returned to Catholicism on the death of his wife in 1633. His wife's death led Digby to give up his gay public life for study. He had already interested himself in literature, alchemy, and religion; and now he turned to writing seriously upon these subjects. He had settled in France, where he met Hobbes and Mersenne, corresponded with Descartes (whom he visited in Holland), and was in close touch with other English Catholics in semiexile. Digby frequently visited England and, aside from a brief imprisonment in 1642, was free to come and go, in spite of his overt royalism. He became chancellor to the widow of Charles I, Queen Henrietta Maria, and undertook a diplomatic mission to the pope on her behalf; he also twice (1648, 1654–1655) tried to negotiate with Cromwell for toleration of Catholics. In the intervals he wrote on natural philosophy (the *Two Treatises*), religion, and literature; collected books and manuscripts; and collected medical, chemical, and household recipes, which he exchanged with others (such as his young relation by marriage, Robert Boyle).

In 1657 his increasingly poor health led Digby to take the waters at Montpellier, where he gave his famous account of the "powder of sympathy," which cured wounds by being rubbed on the weapon that inflicted them. It was a strong solution of vitriol (copper sulfate) in rainwater, which could be improved by drying in the sun and by mixture with gum tragacanth. It worked by a combination of occult and natural powers, that is, by attraction and by the small material particles given off by all objects.

In the same year Digby corresponded with the mathematicians Fermat, Wallis, and Brouncker, serving as intermediary in a dispute concerning Anglo-French priority rather than mathematical fact. After this Digby undertook a long journey through Germany and Scandinavia and thence, at the Restoration, home to England. He was one of those suggested as a member of the new philosophical society that soon became the Royal Society; his *Discourse Concerning the Vegetation of Plants* was read to them on 23 January 1661; he was named to the council in the charters of 1662 and 1663; and his name appears often in the records of their early meetings. In the *Discourse* Digby discusses germination, nutrition, and growth of plants in chemical and mechanical terms; he finds that saltpeter nourishes plants and concludes that, as "the Cosmopolite" (Alexander Seton, a late sixteenth-century alchemist) had said, there is in air a food of life (saltpeter or niter) and an attractive power for this salt in the plant.

Digby was enormously admired in his own day for the fascination of his personality, the flamboyance of his early life, the romance of his love for Venetia, his position in society, and his undoubted intellectual powers. He was at once a lover of the occult and one who appreciated the new trends in natural philosophy. He never completely emancipated himself from traditional Aristotelianism, influenced, perhaps, by his conscious Catholicism and friendship for the English priest and writer Robert White; yet he read and praised Descartes, Gassendi, and Galileo and could write as scornfully of the "Schoolmen" as they did.

Digby's most important piece of work is the first of the *Two Treatises,* "Of Bodies." Here he displays a clarity and logic of approach that show his appreciation of Descartes. In this work, which deals with both inanimate and animate bodies, he begins with basic definitions. The fundamental properties of bodies are quantity, density, and rarity; and from them motion arises. He discusses motion extensively but qualitatively, although with many admiring references to Galileo's *Two New Sciences* (1638), which not many had read in 1644; he includes Galileo's statement of the law of falling bodies but criticizes Galileo for taking too narrow and strictly functional a view (as Descartes also criticized him). Light is material and in motion; it is in fact fire and can exert pressure, so that when it strikes a body, small particles are carried off with it. Digby's particles, which he sometimes calls atoms, are not fully characterized; they seem neither Epicurean nor Cartesian but certainly are mechanical. The weakness of the work is the lack of precision and definition; this is a general view of natural philosophy, and an interesting one, but Digby had not the ability to explore his subject deeply. Hence, although his book was widely read, it appealed to the virtuoso rather than to the scientist. As a virtuoso himself, Digby may well have intended this, especially in view of the second of *Two Treatises,* "Of Man's Soul."

BIBLIOGRAPHY

I. ORIGINAL WORKS. Digby's writings may be divided into scientific, theological, and personal.

Digby's earliest scientific work is also his most important, *Two Treatises, in One of which, the Nature of Bodies; in the Other, the Nature of Mans Soule, is looked into: in way of discovery, of the Immortality of Reasonable Soules* (Paris, 1644; London, 1645, 1658, 1665, 1669). Best-known is his *Discours fait en une célèbre assemblée, par le Chevalier Digby . . . touchant la guérison des playes par la poudre de sympathie* (Paris, 1658; repr. 1660, 1666, 1669, 1673), English ed., *A late Discourse Made in a Solemne Assembly . . . touching the Cure of Wounds by the Powder of Sympathy* (London, 1658; repr. 1658, 1660, 1664, 1669), and numerous eds. in German, Dutch, and Latin, often appended to other works. His third real scientific work, *A Discourse Concerning the Vegetation of Plants,* read before the nascent Royal Society on 23 January 1661, was first printed at London in 1661 (twice) and, as an appendix to the *Two Treatises,* in 1669; a French trans. was printed at Paris in 1667 and Latin eds. at Amsterdam in 1663, 1669, and 1678. Recipes purporting to come from his MSS were posthumously published in *Choice and Experimented Receipts in Physick and Chirurgery . . . Collected by the Honourable and truly Learned Sir Kenelm Digby* (London, 1668; repr. 1675); these were often selected for inclusion in collections of recipes in other languages. There is also *A Choice Collection of Rare Chymical Secrets and Experiments in Philosophy,* G. Hartman, ed. (London, 1682, 1685). Some of his letters on scientific subjects were printed in John Wallis, *Commercium epistolicum* (Oxford, 1658).

Digby's earliest religious work is *A Conference with a Lady about Choyce of Religion* (Paris, 1638). There followed *Observations upon Religio Medici* (London, 1643; many times repr.); the *Two Treatises* (see above), the theological portion published as *Demonstratio immortalis animae rationalis* (Paris, 1651, 1655; Frankfurt, 1664); *Letters . . . Concerning Religion* (London, 1651); and *A Discourse, Concerning Infallibility in Religion* (Paris, 1652).

The highly miscellaneous personal works include *Articles of Agreement Made Betweene the French King and those of Rochell . . . Also a Relation of a brave and resolute Sea-Fight, made by Sr. Kenelam Digby* (London, 1628); *Sr. Kenelme Digbyes Honour Maintained* (London, 1641); and *Observations on the 22. Stanza in the 9th Canto of the 2d. Book of Spencers Faery Queen* (London, 1643). There are also many posthumously published works, especially *The Closet of the Eminently Learned Sir Kenelme Digbie Kt. Opened* (London, 1669, 1671, 1677, 1910), on food and drink; *Private Memoirs,* Sir N. H. Nicolas, ed. (London, 1827); and *Poems* (London, 1877).

II. SECONDARY LITERATURE. Most important are E. W. Bligh, *Sir Kenelm Digby and His Venetia* (London, 1932), which contains passages not printed in the *Private Memoirs;* and R. T. Petersson, *Sir Kenelm Digby, the Ornament of England 1603–1665* (London, 1956).

MARIE BOAS HALL

DIGGES, LEONARD (*b.* England, *ca.* 1520; *d.* England, 1559 [?]), *mathematics.*

Digges, a member of an ancient family in Kent, was the second son of James Digges of Barham. He was admitted to Lincoln's Inn in 1537 and, if he received the usual education of young gentlemen of the time, may also have attended a university. His works are strongly indebted to contemporary Continental sources, and it is possible that he traveled abroad in 1542.

Digges was interested in elementary practical mathematics, especially surveying, navigation, and gunnery. His almanac and prognostication (1555) contains much material useful to sailors. In 1556 he published an elementary surveying manual, *Tectonicon.* Both of these works went through many editions in the sixteenth century. In 1571 his son Thomas completed and published his more advanced practical geometry *Pantometria,* the first book of which was an up-to-date surveying text. The material in these works is based largely on Peter Apian and Gemma Frisius, but in many cases Digges was the first to describe the instruments and techniques in English.

Digges was a keen experimentalist who gained a reputation, while still quite young, for skill in ballistics. Although his military treatise *Stratioticos* (1579) is largely the work of his son, it is based partly on his notes and the results of his gunnery experiments. The genesis of *Stratioticos* may be found in Digges's association with Sir Thomas Wyatt and others in the preparation of a scheme for an organized militia for Protector Somerset in 1549.

Digges took part in Wyatt's rebellion in 1554. He was attainted and condemned to death but was pardoned for life, probably through the intercession of his kinsman Lord Clinton (later earl of Lincoln), to whom the *Prognostication* was dedicated. He completed payments for the redemption of his property on 7 May 1558 and probably died shortly thereafter.

BIBLIOGRAPHY

I. ORIGINAL WORKS. Digges's writings are *A Prognostication of Right Good Effect* (London, 1555), enl. and retitled *A Prognostication Everlasting* (London, 1556; 11 eds. before 1600); *A Boke Named Tectonicon* (London, 1556; 8 eds. before 1600); *A Geometrical Practise Named Pantometria* (London, 1571, 1591), bk. 1, "Longimetria," repr. by R. T. Gunther as *First Book of Digges Pantometria,* Old Ashmolean Reprints, 4 (Oxford, 1927); and *An Arithmeticall Militare Treatise Named Stratioticos* (London, 1579, 1590).

II. SECONDARY LITERATURE. The *Dictionary of National Biography* article on Leonard Digges is wholly unreliable. Some biographical material can be found in D. M. Loades, *Two Tudor Conspiracies* (London, 1965); and E. G. R. Taylor, *Mathematical Practitioners of Tudor and Stuart England* (Cambridge, 1954). The works on surveying are discussed in E. R. Kiely, *Surveying Instruments* (New York, 1947); and A. W. Richeson, *English Land Measuring to 1800* (Cambridge, Mass., 1967). The *Stratioticos* is discussed in Henry J. Webb, *Elizabethan Military Science* (Madison, Wis., 1965), with reference to Thomas Digges.

JOY B. EASTON

DIGGES, THOMAS (*b.* Kent, England, 1546 [?]; *d.* London, England, August 1595), *mathematics.*

Digges was the son of Leonard Digges of Wotten, Kent, and his wife, Bridget Wilford. He received his mathematical training from his father, who died when Thomas was young, and from John Dee.

Digges was the leader of the English Copernicans. In 1576 he added "A Perfit Description of the Caelestiall Orbes" to his father's *Prognostication.* This contained a translation of parts of book I of Copernicus' *De revolutionibus* and Digges's own addition of a physical, rather than a metaphysical, infinite universe in which the fixed stars were at varying distances in infinite space. He had already published his *Alae seu scalae mathematicae* (1573), containing observations on the new star of 1572 that were second only to those of Tycho Brahe in accuracy. Digges hoped to use these observations to determine whether the Copernican theory was true or needed further modifications, and he called for cooperative observations by astronomers everywhere.

In addition to his astronomical work Digges included a thorough discussion of the Platonic solids and five of the Archimedean solids in his father's *Pantometria* (1571). He also published *Stratioticos* (1579), a treatise on military organization with such arithmetic and algebra as was necessary for a soldier. To this work he appended questions relative to ballistics that were partially answered in the second editions of *Stratioticos* (1590) and *Pantometria* (1591). He was able, on the basis of his own and his father's experiments, to disprove many commonly held erroneous ideas in ballistics but was not able to develop a mathematical theory of his own. These appendixes constitute the first serious ballistic studies in England.

Digges was a member of the parliaments of 1572 (which met off and on for ten years) and 1584 and became increasingly active in public affairs. He was involved with plans for the repair of Dover harbor for several years and served as muster master general of the army in the Low Countries. Apart from his continuing studies in ballistics, his scientific writings cover only a decade; and his promised works on navigation, fortification, and artillery never appeared.

BIBLIOGRAPHY

I. ORIGINAL WORKS. Digges's writings include "A Mathematical Discourse of Geometrical Solids," in Leonard Digges, *A Geometrical Practise Named Pantometria* (London, 1571, 1591), trans. by his grandson Dudley Digges as *Nova corpora regularia* (London, 1634); *Alae seu scalae mathematicae* (London, 1573); "A Perfit Description of the Caelestiall Orbes," in Leonard Digges, *Prognostication Everlastinge* (London, 1576, most later eds.); and *An Arithmeticall Militare Treatise Named Stratioticos* (London, 1579, 1590). For his nonmathematical publications and reports in MS, see the *Dictionary of National Biography*, V, 976–978.

II. SECONDARY LITERATURE. F. R. Johnson, in a letter to the *Times Literary Supplement* (5 Apr. 1934), p. 244, gives information on the dates of Thomas' birth and Leonard's death. The *Dictionary of National Biography* is inaccurate on Thomas' early years, but the account of his later life is useful. For his parliamentary career see J. E. Neale, *Elizabeth I and Her Parliaments* (New York, 1958).

Digges's works are discussed in F. R. Johnson and S. V. Larkey, "Thomas Digges, the Copernican System, and the Idea of the Infinity of the Universe in 1576," in *Huntington Library Bulletin,* no. 5 (Apr. 1934), 69–117; and F. R. Johnson, *Astronomical Thought in Renaissance England* (Baltimore, 1937). For a different interpretation of Digges's infinite universe see A. Koyré, *From the Closed World to the Infinite Universe* (New York, 1957), pp. 34–39. For the ballistics see A. R. Hall, *Ballistics in the Seventeenth Century* (Cambridge, 1952); and for the military treatise H. J. Webb, *Elizabethan Military Science* (Madison, Wis., 1965).

JOY B. EASTON

DILLENIUS, JOHANN JACOB (*b.* Darmstadt, Germany, 1687; *d.* Oxford, England, 2 April 1747), *botany.*

The Dillenius family were civil servants in the state of Hesse who came to Darmstadt at the close of the sixteenth century. Dillenius' grandfather, Justus Dillenius, was a treasury clerk (*Kammerschreiber*), but his father trained as a doctor in the university of Giessen; after several interruptions he completed his studies and was granted a medical licentiate in 1681. Dillenius' mother was the daughter of the clergyman Danile Funk. In 1682 the death of Laurentius Strauss left vacant the chair of medicine in Giessen and Dillenius' father was appointed. In this academic circle the family name, which had already been changed from Dill to Dillen, was altered to Dillenius.

Johann Dillenius followed in his father's footsteps, qualifying in medicine at Giessen in 1713. After a period of practice in Grünberg, Upper Hesse, he was appointed town doctor (*Poliater*) in Giessen. Mean-while his passion for botany developed and led to his election to the Caesare Leopoldina-Carolina Academia Naturae Curiosorum under the name "Glaucias." About this time he contributed several papers on cryptogams to that academy; these show his concern with the study of cryptogamic sexual organs.

Despite the promise of his work Dillenius was not offered a university post in botany in Germany. It was not until the wealthy English consul at Smyrna, William Sherard, learned of his work that he received an invitation to serve as a full-time botanist, working on Sherard's *Pinax.* Dillenius accepted and by August 1721 he was in England. Apparently it was Sherard's intention to endow the existing chair of botany at Oxford and to see that Dillenius was appointed to it. This could not be realized while Gilbert Trowe occupied the unendowed chair. Dillenius had to wait until Trowe's death in 1734, by which time Sherard had died also. In the thirteen years which remained to him Dillenius completed his magnificent *Historia muscorum* (1741) and continued his study of the fungi with the help of his friend George Deering. Neither the projected book on this subject nor Sherard's ill-fated *Pinax* was completed, however, when Dillenius died after a fit of apoplexy.

Dillenius was elected a fellow of the Royal Society in 1724 and served as its foreign secretary from 1727 to 1747. St. John's College, Oxford, admitted him to the degree of M.D. Oxon. in 1734. His labors in Oxford marked a period of activity in botany there which was not equaled until the appointment of John Sibthorp in 1783.

Botany was passing through an exciting phase in its development in Dillenius' student days. The sexual theory of plant reproduction had been established on the basis of experiments with flowering plants conducted by Rudolph Camerarius, but attempts to determine sexual organs in the flowerless plants had met with virtually no success. With regard to classification the state of affairs was likewise more promising for the students of flowering plants than for those who studied the cryptogams. The best work in the latter field had been that by Samuel Doody, incorporated in the second edition of John Ray's *Synopsis plantarum* (1696). William Sherard was particularly concerned about the inadequate state of such knowledge, and in Dillenius he found an enthusiast for the cryptogams.

Dillenius' failure to make headway in Germany, despite the great interest in the subject there, was undoubtedly due to his unwise criticism of the system of classification of A. Q. Bachmann (Rivinus), which was widely accepted in Germany at the time. He attacked Bachmann's system in his *Catalogus plantarum circa Gissam sponte nascentium* (1719), in which the merits and demerits of the various systems of classification are enumerated with impartiality and justice. Dillenius rightly did not approve of Bachmann's use of the regularity and number of petals as the basis for his classification and preferred the system of Ray to those of both Bachmann and Tournefort. Of course Ray's system was not without its faults—and Dillenius did not escape a harsh reply from Bachmann. Needless to say, Dillenius failed in his role of advocate for Ray's system in Germany.

In England, Dillenius worked on the encyclopedia (or *Pinax*) of all the names that had been given to each plant, on the plan originally conceived by Gaspard Bauhin. Fortunately for science, Dillenius interrupted this work frequently to undertake more fruitful tasks, the first of which was the editing of a third and last edition of Ray's *Synopsis plantarum*. This work brought him into close contact with the small but active circle of British botanists who helped him with it, especially Richard Richardson.

When the *Synopsis* appeared in 1724 the number of flowering plant species in it had been increased to 2,200, and many new species of cryptogams had been added, including 150 moss species. This valuable work served British botanists well until the appearance of Linnaeus' *Species plantarum* in 1761.

The years 1724 to 1732 were largely occupied for Dillenius with illustrating, engraving plates, and describing the plants in William Sherard's brother's garden at Eltham, near London. In this work no love was lost between the proud owner of the garden, James Sherard, and the ardent botanist. James Sherard, who wanted a sumptuous tribute to his glory, was greeted instead with a work of great simplicity, the chief merit of which is its very accurate descriptions and botanical illustrations of exotic plants recently introduced to Europe, especially in the genus *Mesembryanthemum*. Sherard never paid Dillenius for the materials needed to print the book, and Dillenius reckoned that he lost some £200 over the work.

Dillenius began putting together in Oxford the oriental plants collected by Dr. Shaw, the Oxford botanist. In 1736 he was Linnaeus' host in Oxford, and in 1741 he published his most important book, *Historia muscorum*, in which he introduced a new classification of the lower plants (some features of which system are still in use to this day). In his desire to be definitive Dillenius put a prodigious amount of work into this book, which meets the high standards demanded by more modern taxonomy. But it is in the tradition of eighteenth-century British taxonomy and fails to break fresh ground in its approach to the subject or to utilize recent European advances in the knowledge of the sexual organs of cryptogams.

BIBLIOGRAPHY

I. ORIGINAL WORKS. Dillenius' works are *Catalogus plantarum circa Gissam sponte nascentium; cum observationibus botanicis, synonymiis necessariis, tempore & locis, in quibus plantae reperiuntur. Praemittitur praefatio et dissertatio brevis de variis plantarum methodis, ad calcem adjicitur fungorum et muscorum methodica recensio . . .* (Frankfurt am Main, 1718); his ed. of John Ray, *Synopsis methodica stirpium britannicarum . . . Editio tertia multis locis emendata, & quadringentis quinquaginta circiter speciebus noviter detectis aucta* (London, 1724), with illustrations; *Hortus Elthamensis, seu plantarium rariorum, quas in horto suo Elthami in Cantio coluit . . . J. Sherard . . . delineationes et descriptiones* (London, 1732; another ed., Leiden, 1774); and *Historia muscorum inqua circiter sexcentae species veteres et novae ad sua genera relatae describuntur et iconobis genuinis illustrantur: cum appendice et indice synonymorum* (Oxford, 1741), of which another issue of the plates with abbreviated indices is *Historia muscorum: A General History of Land and Water, etc. Mosses and Corals, Containing All the Known Species Exhibited by About 1,000 Figures, on 85 Large Royal Quarto Copper Plates . . . Their Names, Places of Growth, and Seasons, in English and Latin, Referring to Each Figure* (London, 1768).

His correspondence with Linnaeus is included in C. Linnaeus, *Epistolae ineditae C. Linnaei; addita parte commercii litterarii inediti, inprimis circa rem botanicam, J. Burmanni, N. L. Burmanni, Dillenii, . . .* (Groningen, 1830); while Bachmann's reply to Dillenius' criticism of his system of classification of Rivinus is A. Q. Rivinus, *Introductio generalis in rem herbarium. Editio tertia. Accedit . . . Responsio ad J. J. Dillenii objectiones* (Leipzig, 1720).

The Dillenian herbarium is preserved at the Botany School, University of Oxford. Dillenius' MSS are in the Sherard Collection in the Bodleian Library, Oxford. There is a portrait of Dillenius holding a drawing of *Amaryllis formosissima* in the Radcliffe Science Library, Oxford, and a copy of it in the Botany School, Oxford.

II. SECONDARY LITERATURE. For details of Dillenius' early life consult A. J. Schilling, "Johann Jacob Dillenius. 1687–1747. Sein Leben und Wirken," in R. Virchow and F. von Holzendorff, eds., *Sammlungen gemeinverständlicher wissenschaftlicher Vorträge*, 2nd ser., **66** (1889), 1–34.

Dillenius' work in England is well-described in G. C. Druce, *The Flora of Oxford. A Topographical and Historical Account . . . With Biographical Notices of the Botanists Who Have Contributed to Oxfordshire Botany During the Last Four Centuries* (Oxford, 1886), pp. 381–385; and *The Dillenian Herbaria. An Account of the Dillenian Collections in the Herbarium of the University of Oxford, Together With a Biographical Sketch of Dillenius, Selections From His Correspondence, Notes etc.* (Oxford, 1907), ed. and with intro. by S. H. Vines.

For biographical information see R. Pulteney, *Historical and Biographical Sketches of the Progress of Botany in England, From its Origins to the Introduction of the Linnaean System,* 2 vols. (London, 1790); and A. Rees, *The Cyclopaedia; or, Universal Dictionary of Arts, Sciences, and Literature* (London, 1819–1820).

On his botanical work see also J. Reynolds Green, *A History of Botany in the United Kingdom From the Earliest Times to the End of the Nineteenth Century* (London, 1914), pp. 162–173; and M. Moebius, *Geschichte der Botanik von den ersten Anfängen bis zur Gegenwart* (Stuttgart, 1968), where his contributions to cryptogamic botany are discussed critically.

ROBERT OLBY

DINAKARA (*b.* Gujarat, India, *ca.* 1550), *astronomy.*

Dinakara, the son of Rāmeśvara and great-grandson of Dunda, was a resident of Bārejya (probably Bariya [or Devgad Baria] in Rewa Kantha, Gujarat). He belonged to the Moḍha *jñāti* (clan) of the Kauśika *gotra* (lineage). He composed two sets of astronomical tables (see essay in supplement); the epoch of both is Śaka 1500 (A.D. 1578). A third set of tables has as epoch Śaka 1505 (A.D. 1583).

The *Kheṭakasiddhi* contains tables for determining the true longitudes of the five star planets that are based on the *Brahmatulya* of Bhāskara II. The *Candrārkī,* which contains tables of solar and lunar motions and of weekdays, *tithis, nakṣatras,* and *yogas,* was largely influenced by the *Mahādevī* of Mahādeva. Dinakara in turn influenced Haridatta II. There exists an anonymous commentary on the *Candrārkī.* The third set of tables, the *Tithisāraṇī,* is also based on the parameters of the *Brāhmapakṣa;* its purpose is to facilitate the computation of the annual *pañcāṅga* (calendar).

BIBLIOGRAPHY

The *Kheṭakasiddhi* is briefly discussed in Ś. B. Dīkṣita, *Bhāratīya Jyotiḥśāstra* (Poona, 1896; repr. Poona, 1931), p. 277. The *Candrārkī* is described and analyzed in D. Pingree, "Sanskrit Astronomical Tables in the United States," in *Transactions of the American Philosophical Society,* n.s. **58** (1968), 51b–53a. Both the *Kheṭakasiddhi* and the *Tithisāraṇī* are analyzed in the forthcoming *Sanskrit Astronomical Tables in England* by D. Pingree.

DAVID PINGREE

DINGLER, HUGO ALBERT EMIL HERMANN (*b.* Munich, Germany, 7 July 1881; *d.* Munich, 29 June 1954), *philosophy.*

Dingler's mother was Maria Erlenmeyer, daughter of the famous chemist Emil Erlenmeyer; his father, Hermann Dingler, was a professor of botany at the University of Würzburg and a noted scholar. His first wife was Maria Stach von Golzheim, by whom he had one daughter; his second wife was Martha Schmitt.

Dingler passed his *Matura* (school-leaving examination) at the Humanistische Gymnasium in Aschaffenburg and then studied mathematics, physics, and philosophy at Erlangen, Göttingen, and Munich. Among his teachers were David Hilbert, Felix Klein, Edmund Husserl, Hermann Minkowski, Wilhelm Roentgen, and Woldemar Voigt. Dingler received his doctor's degree in mathematics and qualified as lecturer in 1912 at the Technische Hochschule in Munich. In 1920 he became an assistant professor at the University of Munich and remained there until 1932, when he accepted a position at the Technische Hochschule in Darmstadt; two years later he was dismissed from the latter on ideological grounds. Dingler could, however, continue his scientific work and have it published; and in 1935 he participated in a scientific conference at Lund in Sweden, where he gave well-attended lectures and seminars. Difficulties during the Third Reich and privations and adversity after its collapse permanently weakened his health, and in 1954 he succumbed to a heart ailment.

While still a student Dingler, stimulated by John Stuart Mill's *Logic,* had encountered the problem of the validity of axioms, which was to concern him throughout his life. Dingler was an independent, self-willed thinker, one who cannot be classified among those who followed any of the contemporary tendencies, although some influences, especially of Husserl and Henri Poincaré, can be ascertained. He designated himself an antiempiricist and considered himself as holding a position much like Kant's. In more than twenty books and numerous articles written from 1907, he treated the Kantian problem: How is pure science possible? In other words, how is exact research as strict, certain, unambiguous knowledge logically and methodologically possible? Dingler's fundamental investigations were concerned exclusively with the logical and methodological aspect of exact research. He called for a reconstruction of the foundations and the elimination of every presupposition in order to be able really to give an ultimate foundation even to the axioms themselves.

The starting point is the "situation" (*Nullpunkt-Situation*), later also called the "untouched" (*Unberührte*):

That, therefore, which is present in the world at the zero point of all conscious knowledge and tradition, that must be the real world, which enters as a partner into the original relationship between the self and the world. It enters there, so to speak, in an "untouched" condition, that is to say, in a condition untouched by all conscious knowledge and tradition [*Grundriss der methodischen Philosophie,* p. 20].

In the untouched state, that which exists (*das Seiende*) is not yet split into subject and object; there are no concepts, no connection of perceptions. The distinction does not appear until the philosopher gives up his passive attitude and decides to will a first principle (*Dezernismus*): "At the beginning of an ordered structuring of knowledge the philosopher must give up his contemplative attitude and decide on the ultimate principles of a meaningful philosophy" (*Der Zusammenbruch,* 2nd ed., ch. 2, sec. 5). This decision progresses from the will to methodical procedure, to unambiguousness, and to system. The will, which is pure and free of strivings, perceives the way to the goal of knowledge. Dingler's voluntarism is a methodical one, as opposed to Schopenhauer's metaphysical voluntarism or to a completely psychological one.

Starting from the presuppositionless zero-situation, Dingler constructed his "system of pure synthesis." We will the existence of concepts and connections; the concepts must be constant and each new thing that is established must have a sufficient basis. In the construction of the system "pragmatic ordering" (the principle of ordered system-thinking) is determinative, since manual and mental steps cannot occur in just any sequence. The construction takes place according to the principle of simplicity. That is, from among the possible logical forms and steps the simplest are chosen, a principle that also has more or less consciously prevailed in the course of history. Dingler gives a historical survey in order to show that what has come about in consequence of a long period of development may also be assimilated with his "system of pure synthesis."

Dingler followed new paths, building on the ideas of Pierre Duhem, in the concept of the experiment. He wished to refute the belief, which had brought about the dominance of experiment, that one could arrive at general laws of nature through induction. For Dingler an experiment is a willed, intentional action. The geometrical forms, which enter into the measuring apparatus and the measurements required in experiment, are produced according to a priori ideas, their properties being determined from within by the definition of the structure. Dingler speaks of "productive or definitional a priori," which relates to the primary, real world; this differs from Kant's a priori, which refers only to appearances. In experi-

ment the appearances of reality are to be reconstructed by means of suitable, invariable "building stones" (elementary forms and modes of action). At the same time it makes these appearances both dependent upon us and subjected to our will, thus creating mental patterns with which the experimental procedure can be planned and made intellectually manageable.

In numerous publications Dingler presented this foundation for the exact sciences, as he had done for geometry and mechanics in *Das Experiment.* He also derived their axioms and completed them. In the posthumous *Aufbau der exakten Fundamentalwissenschaften* (1964) he brought the foundation of arithmetic and geometry from the preaxiomatic, original basis to the fully established science. In addition, he was convinced that his method was applicable in all other fields, including biology (especially evolution), the philosophy of religion, metaphysics, and ethics.

Dingler's attitude toward non-Euclidean geometry, the theory of relativity, and quantum physics has frequently been misunderstood. In his view only a single, completely determined geometry was demonstrable and demonstrated as a fully defined fundamental science: Euclidean geometry. Nevertheless, non-Euclidean geometries were of great importance in terms of method. In one respect Dingler completely opposed the theory of relativity and quantum physics: the theory of relativity operates in the field of number tables, which are furnished by experiment and within the framework of which any intellectual considerations are permissible. The results of experimental measurements (*Zahlenwolke*) are the domain of theoretical physics, which is obliged further to combine formulas, suggest new experiments, and predict new results. Quantum physics (*Feingebiet*) is therefore open to any theoretical train of thought, but cannot yet be made accessible through measurement and experiment. Thus, physicists should renounce ontological explanations of their mathematical results.

In biology Dingler concerned himself especially with problems of evolution and firmly opposed the vitalistic theses that frequently appeared in philosophical circles. In 1943 he wrote an introduction to a collection edited by Gerhard Heberer, *Die Evolution der Organismen,* which was praised as an original accomplishment by Max Hartmann and also appeared in the second edition of the work (1959). In this work Dingler introduced, completely within his system of pure synthesis, a demonstration of the fact of evolution. What he deduced logically, biological research has confirmed experimentally: i.e., the formation of organic substances that have the property of duplicating themselves, reproduction series representing causal chains of evolutionary theory. Dingler saw in the genes, which he named the "restoration apparatus," the chemical basis for the reproduction of inheritable characteristics. In 1932 he outlined a theory of the factors of evolution that later was supported experimentally.

Relative to the extent of his total work, Dingler paid little attention to logic and rejected the claim that classical logic could be demonstrated by mathematical logic.

The political upheavals in Germany hindered the continuous development of Dingler's work and weakened its influence. Dingler, whose thinking was close to the operationalism of P. W. Bridgman, founded no school but nevertheless had a group of followers scattered far beyond Germany. He did not wish to erect a total system, although he occasionally took a position on ethical and religious problems. His concern, as he states in the foreword to his most famous work, *Der Zusammenbruch,* was to help to achieve the "old, great Greek idea of the unity of the mind."

BIBLIOGRAPHY

I. ORIGINAL WORKS. Among Dingler's writings are *Beiträge zur Kenntnis der infinitesimalen Deformation einer Fläche* (Amorbach, 1907), his dissertation; *Über wohlgeordnete Mengen und zerstreute Mengen im allgemeinen* (Munich, 1912), his *Habilitationsschrift; Die Grundlagen der Naturphilosophie* (Leipzig, 1913); *Das Prinzip der logischen Unabhängigkeit in der Mathematik zugleich als Einführung in die Axiomatik* (Munich, 1915); *Die Grundlagen der Physik. Synthetische Prinzipien der mathematischen Naturphilosophie* (Berlin–Leipzig, 1919; 2nd ed., 1923); *Die Kultur der Juden. Eine Versöhnung zwischen Religion und Wissenschaft* (Leipzig, 1919); *Physik und Hypothese. Versuch einer induktiven Wissenschaftslehre nebst einer kritischen Analyse der Fundamente der Relativitätstheorie* (Berlin–Leipzig, 1921); *Der Zusammenbruch der Wissenschaft und der Primat der Philosophie* (Munich, 1926; 2nd ed., 1931); *Das Experiment. Sein Wesen und seine Geschichte* (Munich, 1928); *Philosophie der Logik und Arithmetik* (Munich, 1931); *Geschichte der Naturphilosophie* (Berlin, 1932); *Die Methode der Physik* (Munich, 1938); "Ist die Entwicklung der Lebewesen eine Idee oder eine Tatsache?," in *Biologe,* **9** (1940), 222–232; *Von der Tierseele zur Menschenseele* (Leipzig, 1941–1943); "Die philosophische Begründung der Deszendenztheorie," in Gerhard Heberer, ed., *Die Evolution der Organismen* (Jena, 1943; Stuttgart, 1959); *Grundriss der methodischen Philosophie* (Füssen, 1949); and *Aufbau der exakten Fundamentalwissenschaften,* P. Lorenzen, ed. (Munich, 1964).

II. SECONDARY LITERATURE. On Dingler or his work, see A. Hubscher, *Denker unserer Zeit* (Munich, 1956), 286–290; W. Krampf, ed., *Hugo Dingler. Gedenkbuch zum 75. Geburtstag* (Munich, 1956), with bibliography; "Über die Philosophie H. Dinglers," in *Zeitschrift für philosophische Forschung,* **10** (1956), 287–299; and *Die Philosophie Hugo Dinglers* (Munich, 1955); and H. C. Sanborn, *Dingler's Methodical Philosophy* (Nashville, Tenn., 1950), also in *Methodos,* **4** (1952), 191–220.

E. SELOW

DINI, ULISSE (*b.* Pisa, Italy, 14 November 1845; *d.* Pisa, 28 October 1918), *mathematics.*

Dini, son of Pietro and Teresa Marchionneschi Dini, came from a very modest background. He studied first in his native city, where, at the age of nineteen, he defended a thesis on applicable surfaces. Having won a competitive examination for study abroad, he left the teachers' college founded by his teacher, Enrico Betti, and went to Paris, where he studied for a year under Joseph Bertrand and Charles Hermite. Seven of his publications on the theory of surfaces date from that brief period.

In 1866 Dini taught higher algebra and theoretical geodesy at the University of Pisa; in 1871 he succeeded Betti (who preferred to direct his efforts to mathematical physics) as professor of analysis and higher geometry and, as early as 1877, also taught infinitesimal analysis. He held these two professorships for the rest of his life. Rector of the university between 1888 and 1890 and director of the teachers' college from 1908 to 1918, Dini was also one of the founders of the School of Applied Engineering in Pisa and was its interim director.

From his youth Dini took an active role in public life; he was a member of the city council of Pisa in 1871 and in various other years until 1895. He was elected to the national parliament in 1880 as a deputy from Pisa and was reelected three times. In 1892 he was appointed a senator of the kingdom.

Dini was an upright, honest, kind man who divided his life between teaching and pure research, on the one hand, and the obligations of a public career completely devoted to the well-being of his native city and his country, on the other.

Two periods of equally intense production may be noted in Dini's scientific activity. The first dealt with infinitesimal geometry and centered on studies of the properties of certain surfaces undertaken by Liouville and Meusnier in France and by Beltrami in Italy. These include surfaces of which the product or the ratio of two principal radii of curvature remains constant (helicoid surfaces to which Dini's name has been given); ruled surfaces for which one of the principal radii of curvature is a function of the other; and the problem suggested by Beltrami, and solved in its entirety by Dini, of representing, point by point, one surface on another in such manner that the geodesic curves of one correspond to the geodesic curves of the other. Dini's complete study of the conformable representation of one surface on another resembles the differential parameters introduced by Beltrami and, generally speaking, equations with partial differential coefficients.

Without losing sight of this geometric research, toward which he guided his best students (such as Luigi Bianchi), Dini preferred to devote himself, after 1871, to analytical studies, in which he was inspired by Weierstrass' and Mittag-Leffler's results on uniform functions and by Dirichlet's on series development of functions of a real variable. He discovered the properties of this development through application of an inversion formula more general than Abel's. Dini of course gave preference to the study of functions of a real variable; but his publication on uniform functions, in which he showed that Weierstrass' and Mittag-Leffler's formulas could be obtained through the method used by Betti in his theory of elliptic functions, proves that he was just as content to develop functions of a complex variable.

Dini devoted a volume to Fourier series and a long chapter of his *Lezioni di analisi infinitesimale* to integral equations, in which many original and fruitful ideas appear. Of his last works in mathematical analysis, the greatest number concern the integration of linear differential equations and equations with partial derivatives of the second order. It must also be mentioned that he discovered a method of solving the linear equation

$$a_0 y^{(n)} + a_1 y^{(n-1)} + \cdots + a_n y = X,$$

in which the a's are given functions of x, X being a function of x. Dini also established a theorem for the upper and lower bounds for the moduli of the roots of an algebraic equation.

BIBLIOGRAPHY

I. ORIGINAL WORKS. Dini's main writings are *Fondamenti per la teoria delle funzioni di variabili reali* (Pisa, 1878), trans. into German by J. Lüroth and A. Schepp as *Grundlagen für eine Theorie der Funktionen einer veränderlichen reellen Grösse* (Leipzig, 1892); *Serie di Fourier e altre rappresentazioni analitiche delle funzioni di una variabile reale* (Pisa, 1880); *Lezioni di analisi infinitesimale*, 2 vols. (Pisa, 1907–1915); and *Lezioni sulla teoria delle funzioni sferiche e delle funzioni di Bessel* (Pisa, 1912). There are articles by Dini in *Annali di matematica pura ed applicata, Atti della Reale Accademia dei Lincei, Comptes rendus hebdomadaires des séances de l'Académie des sciences, Giornale di matematiche,* and *Rendiconti del circolo matematico di Palermo.* The work on uniform functions, "Alcuni teoremi sulle funzioni di una variabile complessa," is in *Collectanea mathematica in memoriam Dominici Chelini* (Milan, 1881), pp. 258–276.

II. SECONDARY LITERATURE. Gino Loria examined the life and works of Dini in "Gli scienziati italiani dall'inizio del medio evo ai nostri giorni," in *Repertorio . . . diretto da Aldo Mieli,* I, pt. 1 (Rome, 1921), pp. 137–150. This work includes a complete bibliography of Dini's works (62 titles), a reproduction of an autograph letter, and several details concerning his political activity. Luigi Bianchi, a student of Dini's, wrote "Commemorazione del socio Ulisse Dini," in *Atti della Reale Accademia dei Lincei,* **28** (1919), 154–163; and the article in the *Enciclopedia Treccani,* XII, 909. See also W. B. Ford, "A Brief Account of the Life and Work of the Late Professor Ulisse Dini," in *Bulletin of the American Mathematical Society,* **26** (1920), 173–177.

PIERRE SPEZIALI

DINOSTRATUS (*fl.* Athens, fourth century B.C.), *mathematics.*

According to Proclus (*Commentary on Euclid, Book I;* Friedlein, ed., 67.8–12), "Amyclas of Heraclea, one of the associates of Plato, and Menaechmus, a pupil of Eudoxus who had also studied with Plato, and his brother Dinostratus made the whole of geometry still more perfect." Dinostratus therefore lived in the middle of the fourth century B.C., and although there is no direct evidence his Platonic associations point to Athens as the scene of his activities. He must have ranged over the whole field of geometry, although only one of his achievements is recorded and the record bristles with difficulties. This is the application of the curve known as the quadratrix to the squaring of the circle.

The evidence rests solely on Pappus (*Collection,* IV. 30; Hultsch ed., 250.33–252.3), whose account is probably derived from Sporus (third century). Pappus says: "For the squaring of the circle there was used by Dinostratus, Nicomedes and certain other later persons a certain curve which took its name from this property; for it is called by them square-forming" (τετραγωνίζουσα *sc.* γραμμή, quadratrix). The curve was not discovered by Dinostratus but by Hippias, for Proclus, whose account is derived from Eudemus, says: "Nicomedes trisected any rectilineal angle by means of the conchoidal curves, of which he had handed down the origin, order and properties, being himself the discoverer of their special characteristic. Others have done the same thing by means of the quadratrices of Hippias and Nicomedes" (Friedlein, ed., 272.3–10). It has been usual, following Bretschneider, to deduce that Hippias first discovered the curve and that Dinostratus first applied it to finding a square equal in area to a circle, whence it came to be called quadratrix. It is no objection that Proclus writes of the "quadratrix of Hippias," for we regularly speak of Dinostratus' brother Menaechmus as discovering the parabola and hyperbola, although these terms were not employed until Apollonius; nor is there any significance in the plural "quadratrices." It is a more serious objection that Proclus (Friedlein, ed., 356.11) says that different mathematicians have been accustomed to discourse about curves, showing the special property of each kind, as "Hippias with the quadratrices," for this suggests that Hippias may have written a whole treatise on such curves, and he could hardly have failed to omit the circle-squaring aspect; against this may be set the fact that the angle-dividing property of the curve is more fundamental than its circle-squaring property. It is also odd that Proclus does not mention the name of Dinostratus in connection with the quadratrix; nor does Iamblichus, as quoted by Simplicius (*On the Categories of Aristotle,* 7; Kalbfleisch, ed., 192.15–25), who writes of the quadrature of the circle as having been effected by the spiral of Archimedes, the quadratrix of Nicomedes, the "sister of the cochloid" invented by Apollonius, and a curve arising from double motion found by Carpus. Despite all these difficulties, posterity has firmly associated the name of Dinostratus with the quadrature of the circle by means of the quadratrix.

Pappus, IV.30 (Hultsch, ed., 252.5–25), describes how the curve is formed. Let *ABCD* be a square and *BED* a quadrant of a circle with center *A*. If the radius of the circle moves uniformly from *AB* to *AD* and in the same time the line *BC* moves, parallel to its origi-

nal position, from *BC* to *AD,* then at any given time the intersection of the moving radius and the moving straight line will determine a point *F*. The path traced by *F* is the quadratrix. If *G* is the point where it meets *AD,* it can be shown by *reductio per impossibile* (Pappus, IV.31–32; Hultsch, ed., 256.4–258.11) that

arc $BED:AB = AB:AG.$

This gives the circumference of the circle, the area of which may be deduced by using the proposition, later proved by Archimedes, that the area of a circle is equal to a right triangle in which the base is equal to the circumference and the perpendicular to the radius. If Dinostratus rectified the circle in the manner of Pappus' proof, it is one of the earliest examples in Greek mathematics of the indirect proof *per impossibile* so widely employed by Euclid. (Pythagoras before him is said to have used the method to prove the irrationality of $\sqrt{2}$ and Eudoxus must have used it for his proofs by exhaustion.) It is not out of the question that a mathematician of the Platonic school could have proved Archimedes, *Measurement of a Circle,* proposition 1, which is also proved *per impossibile,* but he may only have suspected its truth without a rigorous proof.

According to Pappus, IV.31 (Hultsch, ed., 252.26–256.3), Sporus was displeased with the quadrature because the very thing that the construction was designed to achieve was assumed in the hypothesis. If *G* is known, the circle can indeed be rectified and thence squared, but Sporus asks two questions: How is it possible to make the two points moving from *B* reach their destinations at the same time unless we first know the ratio of the straight line *AB* to the circumference *BED*? Since in the limit the radius and the moving line do not intersect but coincide, how can *G* be found without knowing the ratio of the circumference to the straight line? Pappus endorsed these criticisms. Most modern mathematicians have agreed that the second is valid, for *G* can be found only by closer and closer approximation, but some, such as Hultsch, have thought that modern instrument makers would have no difficulty in making the moving radius and the moving straight line reach *AD* together. It is difficult, however, as Heath argues, to see how this could be done without, at some point, a conversion of circular into rectilinear motion, which assumes a knowledge of the thing sought. Both objections would therefore seem to be valid.

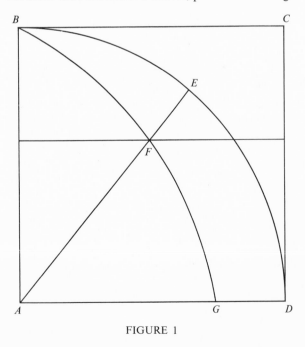

FIGURE 1

BIBLIOGRAPHY

For further reading see the following, listed chronologically: C. A. Bretschneider, *Die Geometrie und die*

Geometer von Euklides (Leipzig, 1870), pp. 95–96, 153–155; Paul Tannery, "Pour l'histoire des lignes et des surfaces courbes dans l'antiquité," in *Bulletin des sciences mathématiques et astronomiques,* 2nd ser., **7,** pt. 1 (1883), 278–284; G. J. Allman, *Greek Geometry From Thales to Euclid* (Dublin, 1889), pp. 180–193; Gino Loria, *Le scienze esatte nell'antica Grecia,* 2nd ed. (Milan, 1914), pp. 160–164; T. L. Heath, *A History of Greek Mathematics,* I (Oxford, 1921), 225–230; Ivor Thomas, *Selections Illustrating the History of Greek Mathematics,* I (London–Cambridge, Mass., 1939), 334–347; B. L. van der Waerden, *Science Awakening* (Groningen, 1954), pp. 191–193; and Robert Böker, in *Der kleine Pauly,* I (Stuttgart, 1964), cols. 1429–1431.

IVOR BULMER-THOMAS

DIOCLES (second century B.C. [?]), *mathematics, physics.*

Nothing is known of the life of this Greek mathematician, but he must have lived after Archimedes (*d.* 212 B.C.) and before Geminus of Rhodes (*fl.* 70 B.C.). Eutocius, a Byzantine mathematician of the fifth and sixth centuries, preserved two fragments of Diocles' work *On Burning Mirrors* in his commentary on Archimedes' *On the Sphere and Cylinder.*

One of these fragments deals with the solution of the problem of the two mean proportionals by means of the cissoid, which Diocles invented. The problem of doubling the cube, the celebrated Delian problem of ancient geometry, had been the subject of mathematical investigation at least as early as the fifth century B.C. Hippocrates of Chios is reported to have discovered that a solution could be found if a way could be devised for finding two mean proportionals in continued proportion between two straight lines, the greater of which line is double the lesser. The question was studied by Plato's Academy and a mechanical solution is even attributed, erroneously, to Plato. Before Diocles, solutions were offered by Archytas, Eudoxus, Menaechmus, Eratosthenes, Nicomedes, Apollonius, Hero, and Philo of Byzantium. All of these, and later solutions, are preserved by Eutocius.

Proposition 4 of Book II of Archimedes' *On the Sphere and Cylinder* presents the problem of how to cut a given sphere by a plane in such a way that the volumes of the segments are in a given ratio to one another. Diocles' solution to the problem, as given in the fragment preserved by Eutocius, was an ingenious geometrical construction that satisfied, by means of the intersection of an ellipse and a hyperbola, the three simultaneous relations which hold in Archimedes' proposition.

Diocles' work *On Burning Mirrors,* judging from the time at which he lived and the work of his predecessors, must have been of considerable scope. It can be assumed that it discussed concave mirrors in the forms of a sphere, a paraboloid, and a surface described by the revolution of an ellipse about its major axis. Apollonius of Perga, a mathematician who was born about 262 B.C., had earlier written a book on burning mirrors, but Arabic tradition associated Diocles with the discovery of the parabolic burning mirror. The Greek *Fragmentum mathematicum Bobiense* contains a fragment of a treatise on the parabolic burning mirror, and some authorities have attributed this work to Diocles. Others consider this attribution very doubtful. William of Moerbeke translated into Latin the fragments of Diocles on mean proportionals and the division of the sphere as a part of his general translation from the Greek of the works of Archimedes and Eutocius' commentaries on them.

BIBLIOGRAPHY

The fragments of Diocles' work can be found in *Archimedis Opera omnia cum commentariis Eutocii iterum,* J. L. Heiberg, ed., III (Leipzig, 1915), 66–70, 160–176.

On Diocles or his work, see Moritz Cantor, *Vorlesungen über Geschichte der Mathematik,* I (Stuttgart, 1907, repr. New York, 1965), 350, 354–355; Thomas Heath, *A History of Greek Mathematics,* 2 vols. (Oxford, 1960), I, 264–266; II, 47–48, 200–203; George Sarton, *Introduction to the History of Science,* I (Baltimore, 1927), 183; Moritz Steinschneider, *Die europäischen Uebersetzungen aus dem arabischen bis Mitte des 17. Jahrhunderts* (Graz, 1965), p. 17; and E. Wiedemann, "Ibn al Haitams Schrift über parabolische Hohlspiegel," in *Bibliotheca mathematica,* 3rd ser., **10** (1909–1910), 202.

KARL H. DANNENFELDT

DIOCLES OF CARYSTUS (*b.* Carystus, Euboea; *fl.* Athens, late fourth century B.C.), *medicine.*

Diocles, the son of Archidamus, also a physician, was still alive shortly after 300 B.C. The Athenians called him a "second Hippocrates" and Pliny the Elder (*Natural History,* XXVI, 10) wrote that Diocles came "next after Hippocrates in time and reputation." Galen and Celsus place him as an equal with Hippocrates, Praxagoras, Herophilus, and Erasistratus. The last three of these physicians were contemporaries of Diocles, and these four raised Greek medicine to a high point in its history. Diocles was a pupil of Aristotle, and he was also a contemporary of such Peripatetics as Theophrastus and Strato. By some, Diocles is considered the leading representative of the dogmatic school, which introduced philosophical speculations into the Hippocratic materials and formalized the medical systems. Diocles saw, however, that philosophical theory could not explain everything, and he is best considered as independent of any school.

Diocles' writings were considerable. The titles of seventeen works are known and more than 190 fragments have been preserved. Unlike the physicians of his time, he wrote in Attic Greek. His writings show a well-polished if simple style, and his language and terminology show the influence of the literary style of Aristotle in scientific writing. The subjects covered in his books range widely.

Diocles' medical writings show the influence of the Aristotelian teleological view of nature. They also indicate that he was the first physician to use a collection of Hippocratic writings, which he may have assembled himself. According to Galen, he was the first to write a book on anatomy and to use that term in the title. While he did not distinguish the nerves from the veins, he did recognize more of the latter than his predecessors. The heart was the source of the blood, which was carried through the aorta and the vena cava. He also described the lungs, ureters, ovaries, fallopian tubes, ileocecal valve, cecum, and the gall bladder with the tube leading to it from the liver. He distinguished between pleurisy and pneumonia and described hepatic and splenic ascites.

In his views on embryology Diocles followed Empedocles. In generation both the man and the woman furnished seed, which contributed to the development of the embryo. The seed, originating in the brain and spinal marrow, was a product of nourishment. Excessive coition was detrimental to the eyes and spinal marrow. In agreement with Empedocles, he felt that the full development of the embryo occurred in forty days, and as the male child grew in the right (i.e., warmer) side of the uterus, it developed quicker than the female. He described human embryos of twenty-seven and forty days. In his studies of sterility, he was especially interested in the mule, and according to Galen, he dissected such animals. Again following Empedocles, he asserted that menstruation occurred during the same period of life for all women, beginning at age fourteen and lasting until sixty. He felt that broad hips, freckles, auburn hair, and manly appearance were certain indicators of fertility. Sterility in the female was attributed to displacement of the uterus.

Diocles' physiology was similar to that of Philistion and was based on the four basic elements of Empedocles—fire, water, air, and earth. The human body also had the four qualities of heat, moisture, cold, and dryness. Health was dependent upon the proper equilibrium of the four elements in the body. Warmth was especially important in the formation of the four humors of blood, phlegm, yellow bile, and black bile. The proper movement of the pneuma, seated in the heart and spreading through the body by means of the veins, had a most important place in health and illness, the latter being independent of outside causes. Fever, disease, or death occurred if the pneuma was hindered by phlegm or bile. Respiration took place through the pores of the skin as well as through the nose and mouth. The Pythagorean number seven was evident in Diocles' view that the seventh, fourteenth, twenty-first, and twenty-eighth days were most critical during illness. Fever was not a disease itself but symptomatic of some morbid condition. He distinguished between continuous and intermittent fevers and also quotidian, tertian, and quartan forms. Like Hippocrates, he stressed practical experience, observation, and the importance of diagnosis and prognosis.

Some indication of Diocles' prominence is seen in the fact that he was known to the rulers of his time. A work on hygiene, written after 300 B.C., was dedicated to the Macedonian prince Pleistarchus, the son of the famous general Antipater. Diocles' letter on hygiene, written between 305 and 301 B.C. and addressed to King Antigone, one of the generals of Alexander the Great, was fortunately preserved by Paul of Aegina, a Greek physician of the late seventh century A.D. Many editions of this work were printed in the sixteenth century in Latin, French, and English.

One of Diocles' works is entitled *Archidamos* in dedication to his dead father. His father had condemned the then current practice of massaging the body with oil, because to do so heated the body too much and made it too dry by rubbing. While refuting his father's arguments, Diocles proposed a compromise: he suggested that in summer a mixture of oil and water be used and in winter pure oil. In the use of oil and water, he is apparently following the idea of a slightly earlier and anonymous work on diet.

Lengthy fragments of Diocles' own work on diet were preserved by Oribasius, physician to Emperor Julian. In this work the Greek physician looked at human life as a whole and by describing the routine of one summer's day prescribed what is suitable and beneficial for men. He made allowances for various ages and changes of seasons. His descriptions are given as ideal standards, dictated by suitable and tasteful behavior—the Aristotelian ethic. He does not describe the various physical exercises, but his whole plan for the day is based on exercise in the morning and the afternoon, revolving around the gymnastics of Greek civilization. His exposition of diet described well the Greek ideals of health, harmony, and balance.

In the history of medical botany or pharmacy, Diocles also deserves recognition. Here, like his colleague Theophrastus, he was probably stimulated to the study of botany by his teacher Aristotle. Diocles was the first scientist to write a herbal on the origin, recognition, nutritional value, and medical use of plants; thus he can be considered the founder of pharmacy. His work was used as a source for all later works until Dioscorides. Two other botanical works, dealing with vegetables and with healing, are practical in nature, but apparently they also advanced the study of plants. Theophrastus, the founder of scientific botany, seems to have made extensive use of the botanical works of Diocles; although he does not name his colleague in his botanical works, in his work *On Stones* he does refer to Diocles as an authority on a certain mineral.

Diocles is credited with two inventions—a bandage for the head and a spoonlike device for the extraction of arrows.

BIBLIOGRAPHY

I. ORIGINAL WORKS. Fragments of Diocles' works are in C. G. Kühn, *Diocles Carystius fragmenta collegit* (Leipzig, 1827); Mauritz Fraenkel, *Dioclis Carystii fragmenta quae supersunt* (Berlin, 1840); Werner Jaeger, "Vergessene Fragmente des Peripatetikers Diokles von Karystos," in *Abhandlungen der Deutschen Akademie der Wissenschaften zu Berlin,* Phil.-hist. Kl., no. 2 (1938); and Max Wellman, "Die Fragmente des sikelischen Aerzte, Akron, Philistion, und des Diokles von Karystos," in *Fragmentsammlung der griechischen Aerzte,* I (Berlin, 1901), 117–207.

II. SECONDARY LITERATURE. On Diocles and his work, see Gustav A. Gerhard, "Ein dogmatischer Arzt des vierten Jahrhunderts vor Christ," in *Sitzungsberichte der Heidelberger Akademie der Wissenschaften,* Phil.-hist. Kl. (1913); W. Haberling, "Die Entdeckung einer kriegschirurgischen Instrumentes des Altertums," in *Deutsche militärärztliche Zeitschrift,* **40** (1912), 658–660; Werner Jaeger, *Paideia, Die Formung des griechischen Menschen,* 3 vols. (Berlin-Leipzig, 1934–1947), trans. into English by G. Highet as *Paideia: The Ideals of Greek Culture,* 3 vols. (New York, 1960), III, 41–44, *passim;* Werner Jaeger, *Diokles von Karystos. Die griechische Medizin und die Schule des Aristoteles* (Berlin, 1938, 1963); George Sarton, *Introduction to the History of Science,* I (Baltimore, 1927), 121; and Max Wellman, *Die pneumatische Schule bis auf Archigenes, in ihrer Entwicklung* (Berlin, 1895); "Das älteste Kräuterbuch der Griechen," in *Festgabe für Franz Susemihl. Zur Geschichte griechischer Wissenschaft und Dichtung* (Leipzig, 1898); and "Diokles von Karystos," in Pauly-Wissowa, *Real-Encyclopädie.*

KARL H. DANNENFELDT

DIONIS DU SÉJOUR, ACHILLE-PIERRE (*b.* Paris, France, 11 January 1734; *d.* Vernou, near Fontainebleau, France, 22 August 1794), *astronomy, mathematics, demography.*

The son of Louis-Achille Dionis du Séjour, counselor at the *cour des aides* in Paris, and of Geneviève-Madeleine Héron, Achille-Pierre studied in Paris at the Collège Louis-le-Grand and then at the Faculté de Droit. A counselor at the Parlement of Paris in 1758, he sat as a member of the Chambre des Enquêtes beginning in 1771 and in 1779 moved to the Grand Chambre, where he was appreciated for his simplicity, his liberalism, and his humanity. He devoted the bulk of his leisure time to mathematical and astronomical research, which brought him election as *associé libre* of the Académie des Sciences on 26 June 1756. (Dionis du Séjour maintained this title at the time of the reorganization of 1785 but resigned it on 14 July 1786 in order to be eligible for election as associate member of the physics section.) His cordiality, his devotion to the cause of scientific research, and his philosophic spirit brought him many friendships; and the quality of his writings earned the respect of Lagrange, Laplace, and Condorcet, among others.

With his friend and future colleague Mathieu-Bernard Goudin, Dionis du Séjour published a treatise on the analytical geometry of plane curves (1756) and a compendium of theoretical astronomy (1761). From 1764 to 1783 he wrote a series of important memoirs on the application of the most recent analytic methods to the study of the principal astronomical phenomena (eclipses, occultations, reductions of observations, determination of planetary orbits, etc.). Revised and coordinated, these memoirs were reprinted in the two-volume *Traité analytique des mouvements apparents des corps célestes* (1786–1789), of which Delambre gives a detailed analysis. The *Traité* is completed by two works, one on comets (1775), in which he demonstrates the near impossibility of a collision of one of these heavenly bodies with the earth, and the other on the varying appearance of the rings of Saturn (1776). All these works are dominated by an obvious concern for rigor and by a great familiarity with analytical methods; if the prolixity of the developments and the complexity of the calculations rendered them of little use at the time, their reexamination in the light of present possibilities of calculation would certainly be fruitful.

In pure mathematics, beyond the study of plane curves, Dionis du Séjour was interested in the theory of the solution of equations, an area where his works have been outclassed by those of his contemporaries Bézout and Lagrange. Finally, in collaboration with Condorcet and Laplace, he undertook a systematic inquiry to determine the population of France. Utilizing the list of communes appearing in the Cassini map of France and the most recent information furnished by the civil registers, this inquiry was based on the empirical hypothesis that the annual number of births in a given population is approximately one twenty-sixth of the total of that population.

The Revolution interrupted Dionis du Séjour's scientific activity. Elected a deputy of the Paris nobility on 10 May 1789, he sat in the National (later Constituent) Assembly until its duties were completed on 30 September 1791. Resigning later from the office of judge of a Paris tribunal, to which post he had been elected on 30 November 1791, he retired to his rich holdings in Argeville, a commune in Vernou, near Fontainebleau, where he died without issue almost a month after 9 Thermidor, having experienced, it seems, a period of difficulties and quite justifiable anxiety.

BIBLIOGRAPHY

I. ORIGINAL WORKS. A list of Dionis du Séjour's papers is in *Table générale des matières contenues dans l'Histoire et dans les Mémoires de l'Académie royale des sciences,* VII-X (Paris, 1768–1809).

His books are *Traité des courbes algébriques* (Paris, 1756), written with Goudin; *Recherches sur la gnomonique, les rétrogradations des planètes et les éclipses du soleil* (Paris, 1761), written with Goudin; *Recueil de problèmes astronomiques résolus analytiquement,* 3 vols. (Paris, 1769–1778), a collection of his papers on astronomy published in the *Histoire de l'Académie royale des sciences; Essai sur les comètes en général; et particulièrement sur celles qui peuvent approcher de l'orbite de la terre* (Paris, 1775); *Essai sur les phénomènes relatifs aux disparitions périodiques de l'anneau de Saturne* (Paris, 1776); *Traité analytique des mouvements apparents des corps célestes,* 2 vols. (Paris, 1786–1789); and *Traité des propriétés communes à toutes les courbes, suivi d'un mémoire sur les éclipses du soleil* (Paris, 1788), written with Goudin.

II. SECONDARY LITERATURE. It should be noted that in any alphabetical listing Dionis du Séjour's name sometimes appears as Dionis, sometimes as Du Séjour, and sometimes as Séjour. On Dionis du Séjour or his work, see the following (listed chronologically): J. S. Bailly, *Histoire de l'astronomie moderne,* III (Paris, 1782), index under Séjour; J. de Lalande, articles in *Magasin encyclopédique ou Journal des sciences, des lettres et des arts,* 1 (1795), 31–34; in *Connaissance des temps . . . pour l'année sextile VIIe de la République* (May 1797), 312–317; and in *Bibliographie astronomique* (Paris, 1803), pp. 750–752 and index; Nicollet, in Michaud, ed., *Biographie universelle,* XI (1814), 401–403, and in new ed., XI (1855), 90–91; J. B. Delambre, *Histoire de l'astronomie au XVIIIe siècle* (Paris, 1827), pp. xxiii–xxiv, 709–735; R. Grant, *History of Physical Astronomy* (London, 1852), pp. 232, 267; J. Hoefer, in *Nouvelle biographie générale,* XV (Paris, 1858), 295–296; Poggendorff, I, 574–575; A. Maury, *L'ancienne Académie des sciences* (Paris, 1864), see index; J. Bertrand, *L'Académie des sciences et les académiciens de 1666 à 1793* (Paris, 1869), pp. 311–312; J. C. Houzeau and A. Lancaster, *Bibliographie générale de l'astronomie,* 3 vols. (Brussels, 1882–1889; repr. London,

1964) I, pt. 2, 1301, 1313, 1341, II, cols. 385, 483, 1078, 1083, 1150, 1207; J. F. Robinet, A. Robert, and J. le Chapelain, *Dictionnaire historique et biographique de la Révolution et de l'Empire,* I (Paris, 1899), 643–644; F. Matagrin, *Vernou et le château d'Argeville* (Melun, 1905), pp. 128–129; A. Douarche, *Les tribunaux civils de Paris pendant la Révolution,* 2 vols. (Paris, 1905–1907), see index; N. Nielsen, *Géomètres français sous la Révolution* (Copenhagen, 1929), pp. 73–79; and Roman d'Amat, in *Dictionnaire de biographie française,* XI (1967), 390–391.

RENÉ TATON

DIONYSODORUS (*fl.* Caunus [?], Asia Minor, third-second centuries B.C.), *mathematics.*

The Dionysodorus who is the subject of this article is recorded by Eutocius as having solved, by means of the intersection of a parabola and a hyperbola, the cubic equation to which (in effect) Archimedes had reduced the problem of so cutting a sphere by a plane that the volumes of the segments are in a given ratio. Of the many bearers of this name in Greek literature, he has usually been identified with the Dionysodorus who is described by Strabo (XII, 3,16) as a mathematician and is included among the men noteworthy for their learning who were born in the region of Amisene in Pontus, on the shore of the Black Sea. But since Wilhelm Cronert published in 1900 hitherto unknown fragments from the Herculaneum roll no. 1044, and especially since Wilhelm Schmidt commented on them in 1901, it has seemed more probable that he should be identified with Dionysodorus of Caunus, son of a father of the same name, who was probably an Epicurean. One fragment (no. 25) indicates that this Dionysodorus succeeded Eudemus as the teacher of Philonides, and another (no. 7) that Philonides published some lectures by Dionysodorus. Eudemus is obviously the Eudemus of Pergamum to whom Apollonius dedicated the first two books of his *Conics,* and Philonides is the mathematician to whom Apollonius asked Eudemus to show the second book. When we recollect that Caunus in Caria is near Apollonius' birthplace, Perga in Pamphylia, it is clear that this Dionysodorus moved in distinguished mathematical company and would have been capable of the elegant construction that Eutocius has recorded. If this identification is correct, he would have lived in the second half of the third century B.C. If he is to be identified with Dionysodorus of Amisene, all that can be said about his date is that he wrote before Diocles, say before 100 B.C. It is clear that he is not the same person as the geometer Dionysodorus of Melos, who is mentioned by Pliny (*Natural History,* II, 112.248) as having arranged for a message to be put in his tomb saying that he had been to the center of the earth and had found the earth's radius to measure 42,000 stades. Strabo, indeed, specifically distinguishes them.

In the passage quoted by Eutocius, *Commentarii in libros II De sphaera et cylindro* (Archimedes, Heiberg ed., III, 152.28–160.2), Dionysodorus says: Let *AB* be a diameter of a given sphere which it is required to cut in the given ratio *CD:DE*. Let *BA* be produced to *F* so that $AF = AB/2$, let *AG* be drawn perpendicular to *AB* so that $FA:AG = CE:ED$, and let *H* be taken on *AG* produced so that $AH^2 = FA \cdot AG$. With axis *FB* let a parabola be drawn having *AG* as its parameter; it will pass through *H*. Let it be *FHK* where *BK* is perpendicular to *AB*. Through *G* let there be drawn a hyperbola having *FB* and *BK* as asymptotes. Let it cut the parabola at *L*—it will, of course, cut at a second point also—and let *LM* be drawn perpendicular to *AB*. Then, proves Dionysodorus, a plane drawn through *M* perpendicular to *AB* will cut the sphere into segments whose volumes have the ratio *CD:DE*.

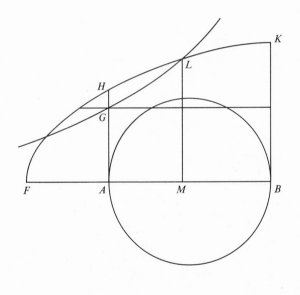

FIGURE 1

It will be more instructive to turn the procedure into modern notation rather than reproduce the prolix geometrical proofs. In his treatise *On the Sphere and Cylinder*, II, 2 and 4, Archimedes proves geometrically that if *r* be the radius of a sphere and *h* the height of one of the segments into which it is divided by a plane, the volume of the segment is equal to a cone with the same base as the segment and height

$$h \cdot \frac{3r - h}{2r - h}.$$

If *h'* is the height of the other segment, and the volumes of the segments stand in the ratio *m:n*, then

$$nh \cdot \frac{3r - h}{2r - h} = mh' \cdot \frac{3r - h'}{2r - h'}.$$

Eliminating *h'* by the relationship $h + h' = 2r$, we obtain the cubic equation in the usual modern form

$$h^3 - 3h^2r + \frac{4m}{m + n}r^3 = 0.$$

If we substitute $x = 2r - h\,(= h')$ we may put the equation in the form solved by Dionysodorus:

$$4r^2:x^2 = (3r - x):\frac{n}{m + n}r.$$

Dionysodorus solves it as the intersection of the parabola

$$y^2 = \frac{n}{m + n}r(3r - x)$$

and the hyperbola

$$xy = \frac{n}{m + n}2r^2.$$

It seems probable (despite Schmidt) that this mathematician is the same Dionysodorus who is mentioned by Hero as the author of the book Περὶ τῆς σπείρας, "On the Tore" (*Heronis opera omnia*, H. Schöne, ed., III, 128.1–130.11), in which he gave a formula for the volume of a torus. If *BC* is a diameter of the circle *BDCE* and if *BA* is perpendicular to the straight line *HAG* in the same plane, when *AB* makes a complete revolution around *HAG*, the circle generates a spire or torus whose volume, says Dionysodorus, bears to the cylinder having *HG* for its axis and *EH* for the radius of its base the same ratio as the circle *BDCE* bears to half the parallelogram *DEHG*.

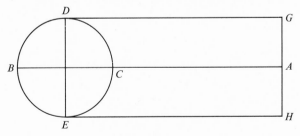

FIGURE 2

That is to say, if *r* is the radius of the circle and $EH = a$,

$$\frac{\text{Volume of torus}}{\pi a^2 \cdot 2r} = \frac{\pi r^2}{a/2 \cdot 2r},$$

whence

$$\text{Volume of torus} = 2\pi a \cdot \pi r^2.$$

109

In an example, apparently taken from Dionysodorus, $r = 6$ and $a = 14$, and Hero notes that if the torus be straightened out and treated as a cylinder, it will have 12 as the diameter of its base and 88 as its length, so that its volume is $9956\frac{4}{7}$. This is equivalent to saying that the volume of the torus is equal to the area of the generating circle multiplied by the length of the path traveled by its center of gravity, and it is the earliest example of what we know as Guldin's theorem (although originally enunciated by Pappus).

Among the inventors of different forms of sundials in antiquity Vitruvius (IX, 8; Krohn, ed., 218.8) mentions a Dionysodorus as having left a conical form of sundial—"Dionysodorus conum (reliquit)." It would no doubt, as Frank W. Cousins asserts, stem from the hemispherical sundial of Berossus, and the cup would be a portion of a right cone, with the nodal point of the style on the axis pointing to the celestial pole. Although there can be no certainty, there seems equally no good reason for not attributing this invention to the same Dionysodorus; it would fit in with his known use of conic sections.

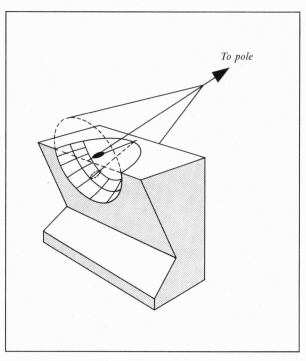

FIGURE 3. Conjectural reconstruction of Dionysodorus' conical sundial.

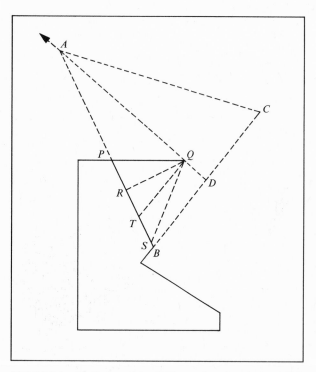

FIGURE 4. Vertical section of Dionysodorus' conical sundial. *PQ* is the style, its nodal point *Q* lying on the axis of the cone, which points to the celestial pole. When the sun is overhead at the equator, the nodal point casts a shadow at *T*, when farthest south at *R*, and when farthest north at *S*.

BIBLIOGRAPHY

On Dionysodorus or his work, see Eutocius, *Commentarii in libros II De sphaera et cylindro,* in Archimedes, Heiberg ed., III, 152.27–160.2; Hero of Alexandria, *Metrica,* II, 13—*Heronis opera omnia,* H. Schöne, ed., III, 128.1–130.11; Wilhelm Cronert, "Der Epikur Philonides," in *Sitzungsberichte der K. Preussischen Akademie der Wissenschaften zu Berlin* (1900), 942–959, esp. frag. 7, p. 945, and frag. 25, p. 952. Wilhelm Schmidt, "Über den griechischen Mathematiker Dionysodorus," in *Bibliotheca mathematica,* 3rd ser., **4** (1904), 321–325; Sir Thomas Heath, *A History of Greek Mathematics,* II (Oxford, 1921), 46, 218–219, 334–335; Ivor Thomas, *Selections Illustrating the History of Greek Mathematics,* II (London–Cambridge, Mass., 1941), pp. 135, 163, 364, 481; René R. J. Rohr, *Les cadrans solaires* (Paris, 1965), pp. 31–32, trans. by G. Godin as *Sundials: History, Theory and Practice* (Toronto–Buffalo, 1970), pp. 12, 13; and Frank W. Cousins, *Sundials* (London, 1969), pp. 13, 30 (correcting Cdynus to Caunus).

IVOR BULMER-THOMAS

DIOPHANTUS OF ALEXANDRIA (*fl.* A.D. 250), *mathematics.*

We know virtually nothing about the life of Diophantus. The dating of his activity to the middle of the third century derives exclusively from a letter of

Michael Psellus (eleventh century). The letter reports that Anatolius, the bishop of Laodicea since A.D. 270, had dedicated a treatise on Egyptian computation to his friend Diophantus. The subject was one to which, as Psellus states, Diophantus himself had given close attention.[1] This dating is in accord with the supposition that the Dionysius to whom Diophantus dedicated his masterpiece, *Arithmetica,* is St. Dionysius, who, before he became bishop of Alexandria in A.D. 247, had led the Christian school there since 231.[2] An arithmetical epigram of the *Greek Anthology* provides the only further information (if the data correspond to facts): Diophantus married at the age of thirty-three and had a son who died at forty-two, four years before his father died at the age of eighty-four.[3] That is all we can learn of his life, and relatively few of his writings survive. Of these four are known: *Moriastica, Porismata, Arithmetica,* and *On Polygonal Numbers.*

Moriastica. The *Moriastica,* which must have treated computation with fractions, is mentioned only once, in a scholium to Iamblichus' commentary on Nicomachus' *Arithmetica.*[4] Perhaps the *Moriastica* does not constitute an original treatise but only repeats what Diophantus wrote about the symbols of fractions and how to calculate with them in his *Arithmetica.*

Porismata. In several places in the *Arithmetica* Diophantus refers to propositions which he had proved "in the *Porismata.*" It is not certain whether it was—as seems more probable—an independent work, as Hultsch and Heath assume, or whether such lemmas were contained in the original text of the *Arithmetica* and became lost with the commentators; the latter position is taken by Tannery, to whom we owe the critical edition of Diophantus.

Arithmetica. The *Arithmetica* is not a work of theoretical arithmetic in the sense understood by the Pythagoreans or Nicomachus. It deals, rather, with logistic, the computational arithmetic used in the solution of practical problems. Although Diophantus knew elementary number theory and contributed new theorems to it, his *Arithmetica* is a collection of problems. In the algebraic treatment of the basic equations, Diophantus, by a sagacious choice of suitable auxiliary unknowns and frequently brilliant artifices, succeeded in reducing the degree of the equation (the unknowns reaching as high as the sixth power) and the number of unknowns (as many as ten) and thus in arriving at a solution. The *Arithmetica* is therefore essentially a logistical work, but with the difference that Diophantus' problems are purely numerical with the single exception of problem V, 30.[5] In his solutions Diophantus showed himself a master in the field of indeterminate analysis, and apart from Pappus he was the only great mathematician during the decline of Hellenism.

Extent of the Work. At the close of the introduction, Diophantus speaks of the thirteen books into which he had divided the work; only six, however, survive. The loss of the remaining seven books must have occurred early, since the oldest manuscript (in Madrid), from the thirteenth century, does not contain them. Evidence for this belief may be found in the fact that Hypatia commented on only the first six books (end of the fourth century). A similarity may be found in the *Conics* of Apollonius, of which Eutocius considered only the first four books. But whereas the latter missing material can be supplied in great part from Arabic sources, there are no such sources for the *Arithmetica,* although it is certain that Arabic versions did exist.

Western Europe learned about a Diophantus manuscript for the first time through a letter to Bianchini from Regiomontanus (15 February 1464), who reported that he had found one in Venice; it contained, however, not the announced thirteen books but only six. In his inaugural address at Padua at about the same time, Regiomontanus spoke of the great importance of this find, since it contained the whole "flower of arithmetic, the *ars rei et census,* called algebra by the Arabs."

Reports concerning the supposed existence of the complete *Arithmetica* are untrustworthy.[6] The question, then, is where one should place the gap: after the sixth book or within the existing books? The quadratic equations with one unknown are missing; Diophantus promised in the introduction to treat them, and many examples show that he was familiar with their solution. A section dealing with them seems to be missing between the first and second books. Here and at other places[7] a great deal has fallen into disorder through the commentators or transcription. For example, the first seven problems of the second book fit much better with the problems of the first, as do problems II, 17, and II, 18. As for what else may have been contained in the missing books, there is no precise information, although one notes the absence, for example, of the quadratic equation system (1) $x^2 \pm y^2 = a$; (2) $xy = b$, which had already appeared in Babylonian mathematics. Diophantus could surely solve this as well as the system he treated in problems I, 27, 30: (1) $x \pm y = a$; (2) $xy = b$, a system likewise known by the Babylonians.

Since in one of the manuscripts the six books are apportioned into seven and the writing on polygonal numbers could be counted as the eighth, it has been supposed that the missing portion was not particularly extensive. This is as difficult to determine as how much—considering the above-mentioned problems, which are not always simple—Diophantus could have increased the difficulty of the problems.[8]

Introduction to the Techniques of Algebra. In the introduction, Diophantus first explains for the beginner the structure of the number series and the names of the powers up to n^6. They are as follows:

n^2 is called square number, $\tau\epsilon\tau\rho\acute{\alpha}\gamma\omega\nu\sigma$ ($\dot{\alpha}\rho\iota\theta\mu\acute{\sigma}$)
n^3 is called cube number, $\kappa\acute{\upsilon}\beta\sigma$
n^4 is called square-square number, $\delta\upsilon\nu\alpha\mu\sigma\delta\acute{\upsilon}\nu\alpha\mu\iota$
n^5 is called square-cube number, $\delta\upsilon\nu\alpha\mu\acute{\sigma}\kappa\upsilon\beta\sigma$
n^6 is called cube-cube number, $\kappa\upsilon\beta\acute{\sigma}\kappa\upsilon\beta\sigma$

The term n^1, however, is expressed as the side of a square number, $\pi\lambda\epsilon\upsilon\rho\grave{\alpha}\ \tau\sigma\hat{\upsilon}\ \tau\epsilon\tau\rho\alpha\gamma\acute{\omega}\nu\sigma\upsilon$.[9]

Diophantus introduced symbols for these powers; they were also used—with the exception of the second power—for the powers of the unknowns. The symbols are: for x^2, $\Delta^{\mathrm{T}}(\delta\acute{\upsilon}\nu\alpha\mu\iota\varsigma)$; for x^3, K^{T}; for x^4, $\Delta^{\mathrm{T}}\Delta$; for x^5, $\Delta\mathrm{K}^{\mathrm{T}}$; and for x^6, $\mathrm{K}^{\mathrm{T}}\mathrm{K}$. The unknown x, "an indeterminate multitude of units," is simply called "number" ($\dot{\alpha}\rho\iota\theta\mu\acute{\sigma}$); it is reproduced as an s-shaped symbol, similar to the way it appears in the manuscripts.[10] No doubt the symbol originally appeared as a final sigma with a cross line, approximately like this: ς; a similar sign is found (before Diophantus) in a papyrus of the early second century.[11] Numbers which are not coefficients of unknowns are termed "units" ($\mu\sigma\nu\alpha\delta\epsilon\varsigma$) and are indicated by $\overset{\circ}{\mathrm{M}}$. The symbols for the powers of the unknowns are also employed for the reciprocal values $1/x$, $1/x^2$, etc., in which case an additional index, ^{x}, marks them as fractions. Their names are patterned on those of the ordinals: for example, $1/x$ is the xth ($\dot{\alpha}\rho\iota\theta\mu\sigma\sigma\tau\acute{\sigma}\nu$), $1/x^2$ the x^2th ($\delta\upsilon\nu\alpha\mu\sigma\sigma\tau\acute{\sigma}\nu$), and so on. All these symbols—among which is one for the "square number," $\square^{os}(\tau\epsilon\tau\rho\acute{\alpha}\gamma\omega\nu$-$os$)—were read as the full words for which they stand, as is indicated by the added grammatical endings, such as ς^{oi} and $\varsigma\varsigma^{oi} = \dot{\alpha}\rho\iota\theta\mu\sigmaί$. Diophantus then sets forth in tabular form for the various species ($\epsilon\hat{\iota}\delta\sigma$) of powers multiplication rules for the operations $x^m \cdot x^n$ and $x^m \cdot x^{1/n}$; thus—as he states—the divisions of the species are also defined. The sign for subtraction, $\wedge$, is also new; it is described in the text as an inverted "psi." The figure is interpreted as the paleographic abbreviation of the verb $\lambda\epsilon\acute{\iota}\pi\epsilon\iota\nu$ ("to want").

Since Diophantus did not wish to write a textbook, he gives only general indications for computation: one should become practiced in all operations with the various species and "should know how to add positive ('forthcoming') and negative ('wanting') terms with different coefficients to other terms, themselves either positive or likewise partly positive and partly negative, and how to subtract from a combination of positive and negative terms other terms either positive or likewise partly positive and partly negative."[12] Only two rules are stated explicitly: a "wanting" multiplied by a "wanting" yields a "forthcoming" and a "forthcoming" multiplied by a "wanting" yields a "wanting." Only in the treatment of the linear equations does Diophantus go into more detail: one should "add the negative terms on both sides, until the terms on both sides are positive, and then again . . . subtract like from like until one term only is left on each side."[13] It is at this juncture that he promised that he would later explain the technique to be used if two species remain on one side. There is no doubt that he had in mind here the three forms of the quadratic equation in one unknown.

Diophantus employs the usual Greek system of numerals, which is grouped into myriads; he merely—as the manuscripts show—separates the units place of the myriads from that of the thousands by means of a point. One designation of the fractions, however, is new; it is used if the denominator is a long number or a polynomial. In this case the word $\mu\sigma\rho\acute{\iota}\sigma\upsilon$ (or $\dot{\epsilon}\nu\ \mu\sigma\rho\acute{\iota}\omega$), in the sense of "divided by" (literally, "of the part"), is inserted between numerator and denominator. Thus, for example, our expression $(2x^3 + 3x^2 + x)/(x^2 + 2x + 1)$ appears (VI, 19) as

$$\mathrm{K}^{\mathrm{T}}\bar{\beta}\ \Delta^{\mathrm{T}}\ \bar{\gamma}\ \varsigma\ \bar{\alpha}\ \dot{\epsilon}\nu\ \mu\sigma\rho\acute{\iota}\omega\ \Delta^{\mathrm{T}}\bar{\alpha}\ \varsigma\ \bar{\beta}\ \overset{\circ}{\mathrm{M}}\ \bar{\alpha}.$$

One sees that the addends are simply juxtaposed without any plus sign between them. Similarly, since brackets had not yet been invented, the negative members had to be brought together behind the minus symbol: thus, $12 - 1/x - 14x = \overset{\circ}{\mathrm{M}}\overline{\iota\beta}\ \wedge\ \varsigma^x\ \bar{\alpha}\varsigma\ \overline{\iota\delta}$ (VI, 22). The symbolism that Diophantus introduced for the first time, and undoubtedly devised himself, provided a short and readily comprehensible means of expressing an equation: for example, $630x^2 + 73x = 6$ appears as $\Delta^{\mathrm{T}}\overline{\chi\lambda}\ \varsigma\ \overline{\sigma\gamma}\ \acute{\iota}\sigma.\ \overset{\circ}{\mathrm{M}}\bar{\varsigma}$ (VI, 8). Since an abbreviation is also employed for the word "equals" ($\acute{\iota}\sigma\sigma\varsigma$),[14] Diophantus took a fundamental step from verbal algebra toward symbolic algebra.

The Problems of the Arithmetica. The six books of the *Arithmetica* present a collection of both determinate and (in particular) indeterminate problems, which are treated by algebraic equations and also by algebraic inequalities. Diophantus generally proceeds from the simple to the more difficult, both in the degree of the equation and in the number of unknowns. However, the books always contain exercises belonging to various groups of problems. Only the sixth book has a unified content. Here all the exercises relate to a right triangle; without regard to dimension, polynomials are formed from the surface, from the sides, and once even from an angle bisector. The first book, with which exercises II, 1–7, ought to be included, contains determinate problems of the first and second degrees. Of the few indeterminate exercises presented there, one (I, 14: $x + y = k \cdot xy$) is transformed into a determinate exercise by choosing numerical values for y and k. The indeterminate exercises I, 22–25, belong to another group; these are the puzzle problems of "giving and taking," such as "one man alone cannot buy"—formulated, to be sure, in numbers without units of measure.[15] The second and all the following books contain only indeterminate problems, beginning with those of the second degree but, from the fourth book on, moving to problems of higher degrees also, which by a clever choice of numerical values can be reduced to a lower degree.[16]

The heterogeneity of the 189 problems treated in the *Arithmetica* makes it impossible to repeat the entire contents here. Many who have worked on it have divided the problems into groups according to the degree of the determinate and indeterminate equations. The compilations of all the problems made by Tannery (II, 287–297), by Loria (pp. 862–874), and especially by Heath (*Diophantus,* pp. 260–266) provide an introductory survey. However, the method of solution that Diophantus adopts often yields new problems that are not immediately evident from the statement of the original problem and that should be placed in a different position by any attempted grouping of the entire contents. Nevertheless, certain groups of exercises clearly stand out, although they do not appear together but are dispersed throughout the work. Among the exercises of indeterminate analysis—Diophantus' own achievements lie in this area—certain groups at least should be cited with individual examples:

I. Polynomials (or other algebraic expressions) to be represented as squares. Among these are:

1. One equation for one unknown:
    (II, 23; IV, 31) $ax^2 + bx + c = u^2$.
    (VI, 18) $ax^3 + bx^2 + cx + d = u^2$.
    (V, 29) $ax^4 + b = u^2$.
    (VI, 10) $ax^4 + bx^3 + cx^2 + dx + e$
                     $= u^2$.
    (IV, 18) $x^6 - ax^3 + x + b^2 = u^2$.

One equation for two unknowns:
    (V, 7, lemma 1) $xy + x^2 + y^2 = u^2$.

One equation for three unknowns:
    (V, 29) $x^4 + y^4 + z^4 = u^2$.

2. Two equations for one unknown ("double equation"):
    (II, 11) $a_1x + b_1 = u^2$,
              $a_2x + b_2 = v^2$.
    (VI, 12) $a_1x^2 + b_1x = u^2$,
              $a_2x^2 + b_2x = v^2$.

Two equations for two unknowns:
    (II, 24) $(x + y)^2 + x = u^2$,
              $(x + y)^2 + y = v^2$.

3. Three equations for three unknowns:
    (IV, 19) $xy + 1 = u^2$,
              $yz + 1 = v^2$,
              $xz + 1 = w^2$.

    (II, 34) $x_i^2 + \sum_{k=1}^{3} x_k = u_i^2 \quad (i = 1 \cdots 3)$.

    (IV, 23) $\prod_{i=1}^{3} x_i - x_k = u_k^2 \quad (k = 1 \cdots 3)$.

    (V, 21) $\prod_{i=1}^{3} x_i^2 + x_k^2 = u_k^2 \quad (k = 1 \cdots 3)$.

4. Four equations for four unknowns:

    (III, 19) $\left(\sum_{i=1}^{4} x_i \right)^2 \pm x_k = u_k^2 \quad (k = 1 \cdots 4)$.

5. Further variations: In V, 5,[17] to construct six squares for six expressions with three unknowns or six squares for six expressions with four unknowns (IV, 20), etc.

II. Polynomials to be represented as cube numbers.

1. One equation for one unknown:
    (VI, 17) $x^2 + 2 = u^3$.
    (VI, 1) $x^2 - 4x + 4 = u^3$.

2. Two equations for two unknowns:
    (IV, 26) $xy + x = u^3$,
              $xy + y = v^3$.

3. Three equations for three unknowns:

    (V, 15) $\left(\sum_{i=1}^{3} x_i \right)^3 + x_k = u_k^3 \quad (k = 1 \cdots 3)$.

III. To form two polynomials such that one is a square and the other a cube.

1. Two equations for two unknowns:
    (IV, 18) $x^3 + y = u^3, \ y^2 + x = v^2$.
    (VI, 21) $x^3 + 2x^2 + x = u^3, \ 2x^2 + 2x = v^2$.

2. Two equations for three unknowns:
    (VI, 17) $xy/2 + z = u^2, \quad x + y + z = v^3$.

IV. Given numbers to be decomposed into parts.

1. From the parts to form squares according to certain conditions:

(V, 9) $1 = x + y$; it is required that $x + 6 = u^2$ and $y + 6 = v^2$.

(II, 14) $20 = x + y$; it is required that $x + u^2 = v^2$ and $y + u^2 = w^2$.

(IV, 31) $1 = x + y$; it is required that $(x + 3) \cdot (y + 5) = u^2$.

(V, 11) $1 = x + y + z$; it is required that $x + 3 = u^2$, $y + 3 = v^2$, and $z + 3 = w^2$.

(V, 13) $10 = x + y + z$; it is required that $x + y = u^2$, $y + z = v^2$, and $z + x = w^2$.

(V, 20) $1/4 = \sum\limits_{i=1}^{3} x_i$; it is required that

$$x_i - \left(\sum\limits_{k=1}^{3} x_k \right)^3 = u_i^2 \ (i = 1 \cdots 3).$$

2. From the parts to form cubic numbers:

(IV, 24) $6 = x + y$; it is required that $xy = u^3 - u$.

(IV, 25) $4 = x + y + z$; it is required that $xyz = u^3$, whereby $u = (x - y) + (y - z) + (x - z)$.

V. A number is to be decomposed into squares.

(II, 8) $16 = x^2 + y^2$.

(II, 10) $60 = x^2 - y^2$.

(IV, 29) $12 = x^2 + y^2 + z^2 + u^2 + x + y + z + u$.

(V, 9) $13 = x^2 + y^2$, whereby $x^2 > 6$ and $y^2 > 6$.

In the calculation of the last problem Diophantus arrives at the further exercise of finding two squares that lie in the neighborhood of $(51/20)^2$. He terms such a case an "approximation" ($\pi\alpha\rho\iota\sigma\acute{o}\tau\eta\varsigma$) or an "inducement of approximation" ($\dot{\alpha}\gamma\omega\gamma\grave{\eta}$ $\tau\hat{\eta}\varsigma$ $\pi\alpha\rho\iota\sigma\acute{o}$-$\tau\eta\tau\sigma\varsigma$). Further examples of solution by approximation are:

(V, 10) $9 = x^2 + y^2$, whereby $2 < x^2 < 3$. This is the only instance in which Diophantus represents (as does Euclid) a number by a line segment.

(V, 12) $10 = x + y + z$, where $x > 2$, $y > 3$, and $z > 4$.

(V, 13) $20 = x + y + z$, whereby each part < 10.

(V, 14) $30 = x^2 + y^2 + z^2 + u^2$, whereby each square < 10.

VI. Of the problems formulated in other ways, the following should be mentioned.

(IV, 36) $xy/(x + y) = a$, $yz/(y + z) = b$, and $xz/(x + z) = c$.

(IV, 38)   The products

$$x_k \cdot \sum\limits_{i=1}^{3} x_i \quad (k = 1 \cdots 3)$$

are to be a triangular number $u(u + 1)/2$, a square v^2, and a cube w^3, in that order.

(IV, 29) $\sum x_i^2 + \sum x_i = 12 \quad (i = 1 \cdots 4)$.

(IV, 30) $\sum x_i^2 - \sum x_i = 4 \quad (i = 1 \cdots 4)$.

(V, 30)   This is the only exercise with units of measure attached to the numbers. It concerns a wine mixture composed of x jugs of one type at five drachmas and y jugs of a better type at eight drachmas. The total price should be $5x + 8y = u^2$, given that $(x + y)^2 = u^2 + 60$.

Methods of Problem-solving. In only a few cases can one recognize generally applicable methods of solution in the computations that Diophantus presents, for he considers each case separately, often obtaining an individual solution by means of brilliant stratagems. He is, however, well aware that there are many solutions. When, as in III, 5 and 15, he obtains two solutions by different means, he is satisfied and does not arrange them in a general solution—which, in any case, it was not possible for him to do.[18] Of course a solution could not be negative, since negative numbers did not yet exist for Diophantus. Thus, in V, 2, he says of the equation $4 = 4x + 20$ that it is absurd ($\ddot{\alpha}\tau\sigma\pi\sigma\nu$). The solution need not be a whole number. Such a solution is therefore not a "Diophantine" solution. The only restriction is that the solution must be rational.[19] In the equation $3x + 18 = 5x^2$ (IV, 31), where such is not the case, Diophantus notes: "The equation is not rational" ($\sigma\dot{\upsilon}\kappa$ $\ddot{\varepsilon}\sigma\tau\iota\nu$ $\dot{\eta}$ $\ddot{\iota}\sigma\omega\sigma\iota\varsigma$ $\dot{\rho}\eta\tau\dot{\eta}$); and he ponders how the number 5 could be changed so that the quadratic equation would have a rational solution.

There are two circumstances that from the very beginning hampered or even prevented the achievement of a general solution. First, Diophantus can symbolically represent only one unknown; if the problem contains several, he can carry them through the text as "first, second, etc." or as "large, medium, small," or even express several unknowns by means of one. Mostly, however, definite numbers immediately take the place of the unknowns and particularize the problem. The process of calculation becomes particularly opaque because newly appearing unknowns are again and again designated by the same symbol for x.

Second, Diophantus lacked, above all else, a symbol for the general number n. It is described, for example, as "units, as many as you wish" (V, 7, lemma 1; M̊ ὅσων θέλεις). For instance, nx is termed "x, however great" (II, 9; ϛ ὅσος δήποτε) or "any x" (IV, 39; ἀριθμός τις). Nevertheless, Diophantus did succeed, at least in simple cases, in expressing a general number—in a rather cumbersome way, to be sure. Thus in IV, 39, the equation $3x^2 + 12x + 9 = (3 - nx)^2$ yields $x = (12 + 6n)/(n^2 - 3)$; the description reads "x is a sixfold number increased by twelve, which is divided by the difference by which the square of the number exceeds 3."

Among the paths taken by Diophantus to arrive at his solutions, one can clearly discern several methods:

1. For the determinate linear and quadratic equations there are the usual methods of balancing and completion (see, for example, the introduction and II, 8); in determinate systems, Diophantus solves for one unknown in terms of the other by the first equation and then substitutes this value in the second. For the quadratic equation in two unknowns, he employs the Babylonian normal forms; for the equation in one unknown, the three forms $ax^2 + bx = c$, $ax^2 = bx + c$, and $ax^2 + c = bx$. Moreover, his multiplication of the equation by a can be seen from the criterion for rationality $(b/2)^2 + ac = \square$ or, as the case may be, $(b/2)^2 - ac = \square$.[20]

2. The number of unknowns is reduced. This often happens through the substitution of definite numbers at the beginning, which in linear equations corresponds to the method of "false position." If a sum is to be decomposed into two numbers, for example $x + y = 10$, then Diophantus takes $x = 5 + X$ and $y = 5 - X$. This is also the case with the special cubic equations in IV, 1 and 2.[21]

3. The degree of the equation is reduced. Either a definite number is substituted for one or more unknowns or else a function of the first unknown is substituted.

(V, 7, lemma 1) $xy + x^2 + y^2 = u^2$; y is taken as 1 and u as $x - 2$; this gives $x^2 + x + 1 = (x - 2)^2$; therefore $x = 3/5$ and $y = 1$, or $x = 3$ and $y = 5$.

(V, 29) $x^4 + y^4 + z^4 = u^2$, with $y^2 = 4$ and $z^2 = 9$; therefore $x^4 + 97 = u^2$. With $u = x^2 - 10$ this yields $20x^2 = 3$. Since $20/3$ is not a square, the method of reckoning backward (see below) is employed.

(IV, 37) $60u^3 = v^2$, with $v = 30u$.

(II, 8) $16 - x^2 = (nx - 4)^2$, with $n = 2$. The "cancellation of a species" (see II, 11, solution 2) is possible with $ax^2 + bx + c = u^2$, for example, by substituting $mx + n$ for u and determining the values

of m and n for which like powers of x on either side have the same coefficient. Expressions of higher degree are similarly simplified.

(VI, 18) $x^3 + 2 = u^2$, with $x = (X - 1)$, yields $(X - 1)^3 + 2 = u^2$; if $u = (3X/2) + 1$, then $X^3 - 3X^2 + 3X + 1 = (9X^2/4) + 3X + 1$, and hence a first-degree equation.

(VI, 10) $x^4 + 8x^3 + 18x^2 + 12x + 1 = u^2$, where $u = 6x + 1 - x^2$.

4. The double equation. (II, 11) (1) $x + 3 = u^2$, (2) $x + 2 = v^2$; the difference yields $u^2 - v^2 = 1$. Diophantus now employs the formula for right triangles, $m \cdot n = [(m + n)/2]^2 - [(m - n)/2]^2$ and sets the difference $1 = 4 \cdot 1/4$; thus the following results: $u = 17/8$, $v = 15/8$, and $x = 97/64$. Similarly, in II, 13, the difference 1 is given as $2 \cdot 1/2$; in III, 15, $5x + 5 = 5(x + 1)$; and in III, 13, $16x + 4 = 4(4x + 1)$.

5. Reckoning backward is employed if the computation has resulted in an impasse, as above in V, 29; here Diophantus considers how in $20x^2 = 3$ the numbers 20 and 3 have originated. He sets $20 = 2n$ and $3 = n^2 - (y^4 + z^4)$. With $n = y^2 + 4$ and $z^2 = 4$, $3 = 8y^2$ and $20/3 = (y^2 + 4)/4y^2$. Now only $y^2 + 4$ remains to be evaluated as a square. Similar cases include IV, 31, and IV, 18.

6. Method of approximation to limits (V, 9–14). In V, 9, the problem is $13 = u^2 + v^2$, with $u^2 > 6$ and $v^2 > 6$. First, a square is sought which satisfies these conditions. Diophantus takes $u^2 = 6\frac{1}{2} + (1/x)^2$. The quadruple $26 + 1/y^2$ (with $y = x/2$) should also become a square. Setting $26 + 1/y^2 = (5 + 1/y)^2$ yields $y = 10$, $x^2 = 400$, and $u = 51/20$. Since $13 = 3^2 + 2^2$, Diophantus compares $51/20$ with 3 and 2. Thus, $51/20 = 3 - 9/20$ and $51/20 = 2 + 11/20$. Since the sum of the squares is not 13 (but 13 1/200), Diophantus sets $(3 - 9x)^2 + (2 + 11x)^2 = 13$ and obtains $x = 5/101$. From this the two squares $(257/101)^2$ and $(258/101)^2$ result.

7. Method of limits. An example is V, 30. The conditions are $(x^2 - 60)/8 < x < (x^2 - 60)/5$. From this follow $x^2 < 8x + 60$ or $x^2 = 8x + n$ ($n < 60$), and $x^2 > 5x + 60$ or $x^2 = 5x + n$ ($n > 60$). The values (in part incorrect) assigned according to these limits were no doubt found by trial and error. In IV, 31, the condition is $5/4 < x^2 < 2$. After multiplication by 8^2, the result is $80 < (8x)^2 < 128$; consequently $(8x)^2 = 100$ is immediately apparent as a square; therefore $x^2 = 25/16$. In a similar manner, x^6 is interpolated between 8 and 16 in VI, 21.

8. Other artifices appear in the choice of designated quantities in the exercises. Well-known relations of number theory are employed. For example (in IV, 38), $8 \cdot$ triangular number $+ 1 = \square$, therefore $8[n(n +$

1)/2] + 1 = $(2n + 1)^2$. In IV, 29, Diophantus applies the identity $(m + n)^2 = m^2 + 2mn + n^2$ to the problem $x^2 + x + y^2 + y + z^2 + z + u^2 + u = 12$. Since $x^2 + x + 1/4$ is a square, $4 \cdot 1/4$ must be added to 12; whence the problem becomes one of decomposing 13 into four squares. Other identities employed include:

(II, 34)　　$[(m - n)/2]^2 + m \cdot n = [(m + n)/2]^2$

(VI, 19)　　$m^2 + [(m^2 - 1)/2]^2 = [(m^2 + 1)/2]^2$

(II, 30)　　$m^2 + n^2 \pm 2mn = \square$

(III, 19)　　$(m^2 - n^2)^2 + (2mn)^2 = (m^2 + n^2)^2$

(V, 15)　　In this exercise the expressions $(x + y + z)^3 + x$, $(x + y + z)^3 + y$, and $(x + y + z)^3 + z$ are to be transformed into perfect cubes. Hence Diophantus takes $x = 7X^3$ and $(x + y + z) = X$, so the first cube is $(2X)^3$. The other two numbers are $y = 26X^3$ and $z = 63X^3$. From this results $96X^2 = 1$. Here again reckoning backward must be introduced. In I, 22, in the indeterminate equation $2x/3 + z/5 = 3y/4 + x/3 = 4z/5 + y/4$, Diophantus sets $x = 3X$ and $y = 4$. In VI, 16, a rational bisector of an acute angle of a right triangle is to be found; the segments into which the bisector divides one of the sides are set at $3x$ and $3 - 3x$, and the other side is set at $4x$. This gives a hypotenuse of $4 - 4x$, since $3x:4x = (3 - 3x)$: hypotenuse.[22]

In VI, 17, one must find a right triangle for which the area plus the hypotenuse = u^2 and the perimeter = v^3. Diophantus takes $u = 4$ and the perpendiculars equal to x and 2; therefore, the area is x, the hypotenuse = $16 - x$, and the perimeter = $18 = v^3$. By reckoning backward (with $u = m$, rather than $u = 4$) the hypotenuse becomes $m^2 - x$ and the perimeter $m^2 + 2 = v^3$. Diophantus then sets $m = X + 1$ and $v = X - 1$, which yields the cubic equation $X^3 - 3X^2 + 3X - 1 = X^2 + 2X + 3$, the solution of which Diophantus immediately presents (obviously after a factorization): $X = 4$.

It is impossible to give even a partial account of Diophantus' many-sided and often surprising inspirations and artifices. It is impossible, as Hankel has remarked, even after studying the hundredth solution, to predict the form of the hundred-and-first.

On Polygonal Numbers. This work, only fragmentarily preserved and containing little that is original, is immediately differentiated from the *Arithmetica* by its use of geometric proofs. The first section treats several lemmas on polygonal numbers, a subject already long known to the Greeks. The definition of these numbers is new; it is equivalent to that given by Hypsicles, which Diophantus cites. According to this definition, the polygonal number

$$p_a^n = \frac{[(a - 2) \cdot (2n - 1) + 2]^2 - (a - 4)^2}{8 \cdot (a - 2)},$$

where a indicates the number of vertices and n the number of "sides" of the polygon.[23] Diophantus then gives the inverse formula, with which one can calculate n from p and a. The work breaks off during the investigation of how many ways a number p can be a polygonal number.

Porisms and Number-theory Lemmas. Diophantus refers explicitly in the *Arithmetica* to three lemmas in a writing entitled "The Porisms," where they were probably proved. They may be reproduced in the following manner:

1. If $x + a = u^2$, $y + a = v^2$, and $xy + a = w^2$, then $v = u + 1$ (V, 3).[24]

2. If $x = u^2$, $y = (u + 1)^2$, and $z = 2 \cdot (x + y) + 2$, then the six expressions $xy + (x + y)$, $xy + z$, $xz + (x + z)$, $xz + y$, $yz + (y + z)$, and $yz + x$ are perfect squares (V, 5).

3. The differences of two cubes are also the sums of two cubes (V, 16). In this case one cannot say whether the proposition was proved.

In solving his problems Diophantus also employs other, likewise generally applicable propositions, such as the identities cited above (see Methods of Problem-solving, §8). Among these are the proposition (III, 15) $a^2 \cdot (a + 1)^2 + a^2 + (a + 1)^2 = \square$ and the formula (III, 19) $(a^2 + b^2) \cdot (c^2 + d^2) = x^2 + y^2$, where $x = (ac \pm bd)$ and $y = (ad \mp bc)$. The formula is used in order to find four triangles with the same hypotenuse. From the numbers chosen in this instance, $a^2 + b^2 = 5$ and $c^2 + d^2 = 13$, it has been concluded that Diophantus knew that a prime number $4n + 1$ is a hypotenuse.[25] In the examples of the decomposition of numbers into sums of squares, Diophantus demonstrates his knowledge of the following propositions, which were no doubt empirically derived: No number of the form $4n + 3$ is the sum of two square numbers (V, 9), and no number of the form $8n + 7$ is the sum of three square numbers (V, 11). Furthermore, every number is the sum of two (V, 9), three (V, 11), or four (IV, 29, and 30; V, 14) square numbers. Many of these propositions were taken up by mathematicians of the seventeenth century, generalized, and proved, thereby creating modern number theory.

In all his multifarious individual problems, in which the idea of a generalization rarely appears, Diophantus shows himself to be an ingenious and tireless calculator who did not shy away from large numbers and in whose work very few mistakes can be found.[26] One wonders what goals Diophantus had in mind in his *Arithmetica*. There was undoubtedly an irresistible drive to investigate the properties of numbers and to explore the mysteries which had grown up around them. Hence Diophantus appears in the period of decline of Greek mathematics on a lonely height as "a brilliant performer in the art of indeterminate analysis invented by him, but the science has nevertheless been indebted, at least directly, to this brilliant genius for few methods, because he was deficient in the speculative thought which sees in the True more than the Correct."[27]

Diophantus' Sources. Procedures for calculating linear and quadratic problems had been developed long before Diophantus. We find them in Babylonian and Chinese texts, as well as among the Greeks since the Pythagoreans. Diophantus' solution of the quadratic equation in two unknowns corresponds completely to the Babylonian, which reappears in the second book of Euclid's *Elements* in a geometric presentation. The treatment of the second-degree equation in one unknown is also Babylonian, as is the multiplication of the equation by the coefficient of x^2. There are a few Greek algebraic texts that we possess which are more ancient than Diophantus: the older arithmetical epigrams (in which there are indeterminate problems of the first degree), the *Epanthema* of Thymaridas of Paros, and the papyrus (Michigan 620) already mentioned. Moreover, knowledge of number theory was available to Diophantus from the Babylonians and Greeks, concerning, for example, series and polygonal numbers,[28] as well as rules for the formation of Pythagorean number triples. A special case of the decomposition of the product of two sums of squares into other sums of squares (see above, Porisms and Lemmas) had already appeared in a text from Susa.[29] One example of indeterminate analysis in an old Babylonian text corresponds to exercise II, 10, in Diophantus.[30] Diophantus studied special cases of the general Pellian equation with the "side and diagonal numbers" $x^2 - 2y^2 = \pm 1$. The indeterminate Archimedean cattle problem would have required a solution of the form $x^2 - ay^2 = 1$. Consequently, Diophantus certainly was not, as he has often been called, the father of algebra. Nevertheless, his remarkable, if unsystematic, collection of indeterminate problems is a singular achievement that was not fully appreciated and further developed until much later.

Influence. In their endeavor to acquire the knowledge of the Greeks, the Arabs—relatively late, it is true—became acquainted with the *Arithmetica*. Al-Nadīm (987/988) reports in his index of the sciences that Qusṭā ibn Lūqā (*ca.* 900) wrote a *Commentary on Three and One Half Books of Diophantus' Work on Arithmetical Problems* and that Abū'l-Wafāʾ (940–988) likewise wrote *A Commentary on Diophantus' Algebra*, as well as a *Book on the Proofs of the Propositions Used by Diophantus and of Those That He Himself* [Abū'l-Wafāʾ] *Has Presented in His Commentary*. These writings, as well as a commentary by

Ibn al-Haytham on the *Arithmetica* (with marginal notations by Ibn Yūnus), have not been preserved. On the other hand, Arab texts do exist that exhibit a concern for indeterminate problems. An anonymous manuscript (written before 972) treats the problem $x^2 + n = u^2$, $x^2 - n = v^2$; a manuscript of the same period contains a treatise by al-Ḥusain (second half of tenth century) that is concerned with the theory of rational right triangles.[31] But most especially, one recognizes the influence of Diophantus on al-Karajī. In his algebra he took over from Diophantus' treatise a third of the exercises of book I; all those in book II beginning with II, 8; and almost all of book III. What portion of the important knowledge of the Indians in the field of indeterminate analysis is original and what portion they owe to the Greeks is the subject of varying opinions. For example, Hankel's view is that Diophantus was influenced by the Indians, while Cantor and especially Tannery claim just the opposite.

Problems of the type found in the *Arithmetica* first appeared in the West in the *Liber abbaci* of Leonardo of Pisa (1202); he undoubtedly became acquainted with them from Arabic sources during his journeys in the Mediterranean area. A Greek text of Diophantus was available only in Byzantium, where Michael Psellus saw what was perhaps the only copy still in existence.[32] Georgius Pachymeres (1240–1310) wrote a paraphrase with extracts from the first book,[33] and later Maximus Planudes (*ca.* 1255–1310) wrote a commentary to the first two books.[34] Among the manuscripts that Cardinal Bessarion rescued before the fall of Byzantium was that of Diophantus, which Regiomontanus discovered in Venice. His intention to produce a Latin translation was not realized. Then for a century nothing was heard about Diophantus. He was rediscovered by Bombelli, who in his *Algebra* of 1572, which contained 271 problems, took no fewer than 147 from Diophantus, including eighty-one with the same numerical values.[35] Three years later the first Latin translation, by Xylander, appeared in Basel; it was the basis for a free French rendering of the first four books by Simon Stevin (1585). Viète also took thirty-four problems from Diophantus (including thirteen with the same numerical values) for his *Zetetica* (1593); he restricted himself to problems that did not contradict the principle of dimension. Finally, in 1621 the Greek text was prepared for printing by Bachet de Méziriac, who added Xylander's Latin translation, which he was able to improve in many respects. Bachet studied the contents carefully, filled in the lacunae, ascertained and corrected the errors, generalized the solutions, and devised new problems. He, and especially Fermat, who took issue with Bachet's statements,[36] thus became the founders of modern number theory, which then—through Euler, Gauss,[37] and many others—experienced an unexpected development.

NOTES

1. Tannery, *Diophanti opera,* II, 38 f. As an example of "Egyptian analysis" Psellus gives the problem of dividing a number into a determined ratio.
2. Tannery, in his *Mémoires scientifiques,* II, 536 ff., mentions as a possibility that the *Arithmetica* was written as a textbook for the Christian school at the request of Dionysius and that perhaps Diophantus himself was a Christian.
3. Tannery, *Diophanti opera,* II, 60 ff.
4. *Ibid.,* p. 72.
5. V, 30, is exercise 30 of the fifth book, according to Tannery's numbering.
6. Tannery, *Diophanti opera,* II, xxxiv.
7. III, 1–4, belongs to II, 34, 35; and III, 20, 21, is the same as II, 14, 15.
8. Problems such as the "cattle problem" do not appear in Diophantus.
9. Or, as in IV, 1, of a cube number.
10. Tannery, *Diophanti opera,* II, xxxiv.
11. Michigan Papyrus 620, in J. G. Winter, *Papyri in the University of Michigan Collection,* vol. III of *Michigan Papyri* (Ann Arbor, 1936), 26–34.
12. Heath, *Diophantus of Alexandria,* pp. 130–131.
13. *Ibid.*
14. Tannery, *Diophanti opera,* II, xli. There are two parallel strokes joined together.
15. Similar problems exist in Byzantine and in Western arithmetic books since the time of Leonardo of Pisa.
16. Heath (in his *Conspectus*) considers the few determinate problems in bk. II to be spurious. Problems 1, 2, 15, and 33–37 of bk. IV become determinate only through arbitrary assumption of values for one of the unknowns.
17. $x^2y^2 + (x^2 + y^2)$, $y^2z^2 + (y^2 + z^2)$, $z^2x^2 + (z^2 + x^2)$, $x^2y^2 + z^2$, $y^2z^2 + x^2$, $z^2x^2 + y^2$.
18. Sometimes Diophantus mentions infinitely many solutions (VI, 12, lemma 2). In VI, 15, lemma, Diophantus presents, besides a well-known solution of the equation $3x^2 - 11 = y^2$ (namely, $x = 5$ and $y = 8$), a second one: $3 \cdot (5 + z)^2 - 11 = (8 - 2z)^2$.
19. Sometimes, for example in IV, 14, the integer solution is added to the rational solution.
20. For example, in VI, 6; IV, 31; and V, 10.
21. In IV, 1, the system $x^3 + y^3 = 370$, $x + y = 10$, corresponds to the quadratic system $xy = 21$, $x + y = 10$, which was a paradigm in al-Khwārizmī. Tannery (*Mémoires scientifiques,* II, 89) shows how close Diophantus was to a solution to the cubic equation $x^3 = 3px + 2q$.
22. Here one sees the application of algebra to the solution of a geometric problem.
23. The *n*th polygonal number has *n* "sides."
24. This is not a general solution; see Tannery, *Diophanti opera,* I, 317.
25. Heath, p. 107.
26. For example, IV, 25, and V, 30; see Heath, pp. 60, 186.
27. Hankel, p. 165; Heath, p. 55.
28. For example, see Hypsicles' formula used in *On Polygonal Numbers.*
29. See E. M. Bruins and M. Rutten, *Textes mathématiques de Suse,* no. 34 in the series Mémoires de la mission archéologique en Iran (Paris, 1961), p. 117.
30. See S. Gandz, in *Osiris,* **8** (1948), 13 ff.
31. See Dickson, p. 459.
32. Tannery, *Diophanti opera,* II, xviii.
33. *Ibid.,* pp. 78–122. Also in "Quadrivium de Georges Pachymère," in *Studi e testi,* CXIV (Vatican City, 1940), 44–76.
34. *Ibid.,* pp. 125–255.
35. Bombelli and Antonio Maria Pazzi prepared a translation of the first five books, but it was not printed.
36. In his copy of Bachet's edition Fermat wrote numerous critical remarks and filled in missing material. These remarks appeared as a supplement, along with selections from Fermat's letters to Jacques de Billy, in Samuel de Fermat's new edition of Diophantus of 1670.
37. The importance of Diophantus is emphasized by Gauss in the introduction to his *Disquisitiones arithmetice:* "Diophanti opus celebre, quod totum problematis indeterminatis dicatum est, multas quaestiones continet, quae propter difficultatem suam artificiorumque subtilitatem de auctoris ingenio et acumine existimationem haud mediocrem suscitant, praesertim si subsidiorum, quibus illi uti licuit, tenuitatem consideres" ("The famous work of Diophantus, which is totally dedicated to indeterminate problems, contains many questions which arouse a high regard for the genius and penetration of the author, especially when one considers the limited means available to him").

BIBLIOGRAPHY

The first Western presentation of the Diophantine problems was by Raffaele Bombelli, in his *Algebra* (Bologna, 1572; 2nd ed., 1579). A Latin translation was produced by W. Xylander, *Diophanti Alexandrini Rerum arithmeticarum libri sex, quorum duo adjecta habent scholia Maximi Planudis. Item liber de numeris polygonis seu multangulis* (Basel, 1575). The text with a Latin translation was prepared by C.-G. Bachet de Méziriac, *Diophanti Alexandrini Arithmeticorum libri sex, et de numeris multangulis liber unus* (Paris, 1621); a new edition was published by Samuel de Fermat with notes by his father, Pierre de Fermat (Toulouse, 1670). There is also the definitive text with Latin translation by P. Tannery, *Diophanti Alexandrini opera omnia cum Graecis commentariis,* 2 vols. (Leipzig, 1893–1895). An English translation, in a modern rendering, is T. L. Heath, *Diophantus of Alexandria, A Study in the History of Greek Algebra* (Cambridge, 1885); the second edition has a supplement containing an account of Fermat's theorems and problems connected with Diophantine analysis and some solutions of Diophantine problems by Euler (Cambridge, 1910; New York, 1964). German translations are O. Schultz, *Diophantus von Alexandria arithmetische Aufgaben nebst dessen Schrift über die Polygon-Zahlen* (Berlin, 1822); G. Wertheim, *Die Arithmetik und die Schrift über die Polygonalzahlen des Diophantus von Alexandria* (Leipzig, 1890); and A. Czwalina, *Arithmetik des Diophantos von Alexandria* (Göttingen, 1952). A French translation is P. Ver Eecke, *Diophante d'Alexandrie* (Paris, 1959). A Greek text (after Tannery's), with translation into modern Greek, is E. S. Stamatis, Διοφαντου αριθμητικα, η αλγεβρα των αρχαιων ελληνων (Athens, 1963).

On Polygonal Numbers appears in a French trans. by G. Massoutié as *Le traité des nombres polygones* (Mâcon, 1911).

Along with the views of the authors in their text editions and translations, the following general criticisms should be consulted: M. Cantor, *Vorlesungen über Geschichte der Mathematik,* 3rd ed., I (Leipzig, 1907), 463–488; P. Cossali,

Origine, trasporto in Italia, primi progressi in essa dell'
algebra (Parma, 1797), I, 56–95; T. L. Heath, *History of*
Greek Mathematics (Oxford, 1921), II, 440–517; B. L. van
der Waerden, *Erwachende Wissenschaft,* 2nd ed. (Basel-
Stuttgart, 1966), pp. 457–470. See also H. Hankel, *Zur*
Geschichte der Mathematik in Alterthum und Mittelalter
(Leipzig, 1874), 2nd ed. with foreword and index by J. E.
Hofmann (Hildesheim, 1965); F. Hultsch, "Diophantus,"
in Pauly-Wissowa, V, pt. 1, 1051–1073; G. Loria, *Le scienze*
esatte nell'antica Grecia (Milan, 1914), pp. 845–919;
E. Lucas, *Recherches sur l'analyse indéterminée et l'arith-*
métique de Diophante, with preface by J. Itard (Paris,
1967); G. H. F. Nesselmann, *Die Algebra der Griechen*
(Berlin, 1842), pp. 244–476; and G. Sarton, *Introduction*
to the History of Science, I (Baltimore, 1927), 336 ff.

Special criticism includes P. Tannery, "La perte de sept
livres de Diophante," in his *Mémoires scientifiques,* II
(Toulouse–Paris, 1912), 73–90; "Étude sur Diophante,"
ibid., 367–399; and "Sur la religion des derniers mathématiciens de l'antiquité," *ibid.,* 527–539.

Historical works include I. G. Bašmakova, "Diofant i
Ferma," in *Istoriko-matematicheskie issledovaniya,* **17**
(1966), 185–204; L. E. Dickson, *History of the Theory of*
Numbers, II, *Diophantine Analysis* (Washington, D.C.,
1920); T. L. Heath, *Diophantus* (see above), ch. 6 and
supplement; K. Reich, "Diophant, Cardano, Bombelli,
Viète. Ein Vergleich ihrer Aufgaben," in *Rechenpfen-*
nige, Aufsätze zur Wissenschaftsgeschichte (Munich, 1968),
pp. 131–150; P. Tannery, *Diophanti opera* (see above), II,
prolegomena; and P. Ver Eecke, *Diophante* (see above),
introduction.

KURT VOGEL

DIOSCORIDES, also known as **Pedanius Dioscorides
of Anazarbus** (*b.* Anazarbus, near Tarsus in Cilicia;
fl. A.D. 50–70), *pharmacy, medicine, chemistry, botany.*

A letter attached to Dioscorides' work as a dedica-
tory preface reveals almost all that is known of his
life. The letter states that Dioscorides lived a soldier's
life; this enabled him to learn at first hand the identity, preparation, and uses of medicines. Galen names
his birthplace,[1] and some manuscript notations add
the name Pedanius. Some authorities believe that
Dioscorides studied at Tarsus and Alexandria and
later attached himself to the Roman army as a military physician. These suppositions are based on his
statement that he led a "soldier-like life" (οἶσδα γὰρ
ἡμῖν στρατιωτικὸν τὸν βίον), his remark that he has
"lived" (συνδιάγοντες) with Areius of Tarsus, and the
likelihood that his travels would have taken him to
Alexandria, where he could have had access to the
library. Dioscorides has been dated both by the mention of his contemporaries and by Galen's use of
Dioscorides' work. Erotian (*fl. ca.* A.D. 60), a commentator of the Hippocratic works who lived during
the Neronian age, mentions Dioscorides (assuming

that the name is not an interpolation).[2] In his letter
to Areius, Dioscorides mentions Laecanius Bassus,
presumed to be C. Laecanius Bassus, consul in A.D.
64, who is spoken of by Pliny and Tacitus.[3] Quintus
Sextius Niger (*fl.* 25 B.C.) is the latest writer whom
Dioscorides cites. Pliny the Elder did not know
Dioscorides' works directly, but certain similarities
between Pliny's and Dioscorides' texts are explained
by their having employed the same written source,
Sextius Niger.[4]

Although numerous treatises in Greek and Latin
are falsely attributed to Dioscorides—both by virtue
of his reputation as a major authority in medicines
for around 1,600 years and because of numerous
editions of his work—only one treatise, Περὶ ὕλης
ἰατρικῆς (*De materia medica*), is now attributed to Dioscorides. The title is taken from book 3 and is the same
title as that of Sextius Niger's lost work. Written
in five books, the treatise discusses over 600 plants,
thirty-five animal products, and ninety minerals in
simple, concise Greek; Dioscorides feared that his
nonliterary style would hinder recognition of the
arduousness of the task he had set himself in collecting information. Of the approximately 827 entries,
only about 130 substances are included in the Hippocratic corpus (since modern subspecies do not always
correspond to Dioscorides' varieties [εἴδη], an exact
count is difficult). Being the author of by far the
largest pharmaceutical guide in antiquity, Dioscorides
added considerably to the knowledge of drugs. More
important, this procedure for relating information on
medicine and his unadorned critical skill determined
the general form of later pharmacopoeias, both Eastern and Western. Galen, always a severe critic, acknowledged Dioscorides' work to be the best of its
kind and showed his respect by numerous citations.[5]

Although an empiricist in method, Dioscorides
apparently belonged to no definite philosophical
school (his friend Areius was a follower of Asclepi-
ades). He cited the need to study each plant in relation
to its habitat, to observe rigorously the plants at all
seasons, to note all parts from the first shoots to the
seeds, to prepare each medicine with precision, and
to judge each medicine by its merits.

Dioscorides claimed that his work surpassed that
of his predecessors in terms of his industry in collecting his information, his unlimited range in finding
medicines, and the arrangement of his material. He
conceded that the older writers transmitted much
accurate information but deplored the fact that recent
writers had introduced the element of controversy to
medicine by speculating vainly on the causes (αἰτίας)
of drugs' powers, while failing to pay proper attention
to their experience in the use of drugs. For each item

generally he gave a Greek synonym, and the names themselves were often of foreign origin, coming from various languages of Africa, Gaul, Persia, Armenia, Egypt, and the like (for which reason linguists are interested in Dioscorides). There follows a deposition on the substance's origin and physical characteristics. He then gives a discourse on the mode of preparation of the medicine and, finally, a list of its medicinal uses with occasional notations of harmful side effects. Often he relates information about how the simple is compounded in a prescription; further, he gives dietetic hints and even tests for detecting a fraudulent preparation.

Even though he faulted earlier writers for their poor classification, Dioscorides' method is not always clear, although he believed his procedure to be superior. His system is as follows (number of items are approximate): book I (129 items), deals with aromatics, oils, salves, trees, and shrubs (liquids, gums, and fruits); book II (186), with animals, animal parts, animal products, cereals, pot herbs, and sharp herbs; book III (158), with roots, juices, herbs, and seeds; book IV (192), with roots and herbs not previously mentioned; and book V (162), with wines and minerals.

Dioscorides says that whenever possible he saw plants with his own eyes but that he also relied on questioning people in the course of his travels and on consulting previously written works. Dioscorides is credited as being the first to recognize the extensive use of medicines from all three of the natural kingdoms—animal, vegetable, and mineral.[6]

Dioscorides cautioned his readers that knowledge of plants was gained by experience: Differences in climates cause wide variations in living patterns—for example, medicines from plants growing in high-altitude windy areas are stronger than those from plants in marshy, shady locations shielded from the wind. Some medicines, such as the white and black hellebore, retain their power for years; others have a shorter effective lifetime. Herbs that are full of branches, such as abrotonum and absinthium, ought to be gathered at seed time. Seeds are best taken when dry; fruits, when ripe; and flowers, before they fall. When the medicine is from sap or juices, the stem should be cut while at full ripeness, but liquids from roots are to be extracted after the plant has lost its leaves.

He notes that storage of medicines is important: Flowers and aromatics should be placed in drug boxes made of limewood. Some herbs are best kept if wrapped in paper (*chartes*) or leaves. Moist medicines may be placed in thick vessels made of such things as silver, glass, or horn. Earthenware is satisfactory if it is not too thin. Brass vessels are suitable for eye medicines and for liquids, especially those compounded with vinegar, liquid pitch, or cedar oil; but tin vessels ought to be used for fats and marrows.

In his preface he names as the older authorities upon whom he relied Iolas the Bithynian, Hexaclides the Tarentine, and Andreas the physician. He also cites various more recent writers whom he called Asclepiadeans (Ἀσκληπιάδειοι)—namely, Julius Bassus, Niceratur, Petronius, Niger, Diodotus, and, most frequently, Crateuas the rhizotomist—and ten other authorities.

Dioscorides was largely responsible for determining modern plant nomenclature, both popular and scientific, because of the reliance of later authorities on his work. Numerous medicines in Dioscorides' work appear in modern pharmacopoeias, among them almond oil, aloes, ammoniacum, belladonna, calamine, calcium hydrate, cherry syrup, cinnamon, copper oxide, coriander, galbanum, galls, ginger, juniper, lavender, lead acetate, marjoram, mastic, mercury, olive oil, opium, pepper, pine bark, storax, sulfur, terebinth, thyme, and wormwood.

The transmission of Dioscorides' text is as important as what it says. Editors and copyists added or subtracted from Dioscorides' writing as a means of contributing their experiences with various drugs in the context of their needs. The numerous and extensive textual modifications make the problem of arriving at a definite understanding of Dioscorides' own Greek text very difficult. Latin, Arabic, and various European vernacular translations reveal greater variations. The study of its transmission is a veritable introduction to the knowledge of Western pharmacy down to the seventeenth century.

Papyri reveal that as early as the second century A.D. recensions had already appeared. The happy survival of a beautifully illustrated manuscript, written entirely in Greek capitals about A.D. 512, demonstrates that by the sixth century Dioscorides' own order of presentation had been completely redone in favor of an alphabetical order. Produced at Constantinople as a wedding gift for Anicia Juliana, daughter of the emperor Flavius Olybrius, the manuscript was offered for the sale price of one hundred ducats to an ambassador of the emperor Ferdinand I by a Jewish physician of Suleiman. The text includes material from other writers. The lavish botanical illustrations in this manuscript and another of the seventh century are the subject of speculation concerning whether the illustrations are from Dioscorides' original work or from Crateuas, the rhizotomist and physician to Mithridates (120–63 B.C.), who was known to paint herbal illustrations with his own hand.[7] A second-century papyrus fragment of Dioscorides' text has illustrations that are different in at least one instance from those in the Juliana manuscript.[8] There is no direct evidence that Dioscorides himself is responsible for the paintings. Plants are drawn in detailed color showing the entire plant, including the root system, flower, and fruit. Certainly the botanical illustrations became standardized, most copyists being content to draw from precedent rather than from nature. One folio (f. 5v) has a portrait purporting to show Dioscorides writing at a desk on the right, while on the left is a painter thought to be Crateuas, drawing a mandrake plant held by Epindia, or Lady Inventiveness, who is standing at the center of the painting.

In the sixth century, Cassiodorus advised some monks: "If you have not sufficient facility in reading Greek then you can turn to the herbal of Dioscorides, which describes and draws the herbs of the field with wonderful faithfulness."[9] Gargilius Martialis (third century) is the first known Latin author to cite Dioscorides. This reference caused some to believe that Martialis was responsible for the first Latin translation; since, however, the other Latin medical writers living before the sixth century failed to cite Dioscorides, it seems more likely that Dioscorides was translated into Latin later than Martialis. Another consideration is Cassiodorus' use of the word *herbarium* to describe Dioscorides' work—but Dioscorides listed all types of substances, not merely plants. Very popular during the early Middle Ages was a pseudo-Dioscoridean text known as *De herbis femininis,* which described and illustrated some seventy-one plants and herbs. Since Cassiodorus referred only to an illustrated herbal, he might possibly have meant *De herbis femininis,* not the complete Dioscorides, especially since Isidore of Seville is known also to have used *De herbis femininis.* Based on Dioscorides, whom the copyists credited with the authorship, the text is severely edited, with additions from other writers. Twenty-seven known manuscripts of *De herbis femininis,* three of which date from the ninth century, testify to its popularity, especially during the early Middle Ages, when the needs of medical science were simpler than those which the full Dioscorides' work was meant to fill.

The Latin West did not have to await the Arabic-Latin translations of the eleventh to thirteenth centuries in order to possess the complete Dioscorides. A Latin translation made in Italy by the sixth century used Dioscorides' original order rather than that of the Juliana manuscript. Although the Latin spelling and grammar are poor, the translation is fairly accurate, with some omissions. The earliest manuscript is written in the eighth-century Beneventan script;

generally manuscripts of this class possess no illustrations.[10] In addition, there was at least one Old English version of Dioscorides.[11]

Stephanus, son of Basilius (Istifan ibn Basīl), translated Dioscorides into Arabic in the second half of the ninth century, but his translation was corrected by Ḥunayn ibn Isḥāq. Another Arabic translation was by Ibn Juljul in the second half of the tenth century in Cordova.[12] Dioscorides greatly influenced Islamic medical botany and therapy, as witnessed by the reliance on his works by such noted writers as Maimonides, Ibn al-Bayṭār, Ibn Sīnā (Avicenna), and Yaḥyā ibn Sarāfyūn (Serapion the Elder).

In the late eleventh or early twelfth century, a popular new edition of Dioscorides was produced in Latin that eclipsed the Old Latin translation. The arrangement was alphabetical. The rubric to a Bamberg manuscript (which contains only the wording of Dioscorides' preface in the Old Latin translation) said that Constantine the African (*d. ca.* 1085) was responsible for the alphabetical order.[13] Whoever the editor was, he meant to bring Dioscorides up-to-date by inserting new drugs—for example, ambergris and zeodary. (The inserted items are related to Constantine's translations of other works and thus support his claim to the editorship.) The main body of the text is close to the Old Latin version and is not a translation from the Arabic. In the section on stones, the editor of this version inserted the text of Damigeron (*ca.* second century B.C.), rather than using Dioscorides'; the editor, however, included only those stones that were in Dioscorides' original. Later thirteenth-century writers—Arnold of Saxony and Bartholomew the Englishman, for example—quote extensively a treatise called *Dioscorides on Stones,* which is actually Damigeron's text and not Dioscorides'. But this is not the only treatise falsely ascribed to Dioscorides: two other notable pseudo-Dioscoridean treatises are *De physicis ligaturis*[14] and *Quid pro quo,*[15] the latter being a guide for drug substitutions.

About 1300, Pietro d'Abano lectured and commented on the alphabetical Dioscorides version and said he knew of another, briefer version. When the text of the Latin alphabetical Dioscorides was first published at Colle di Val d'Elsa, Italy, in 1478 and again at Lyons in 1512, the printer included many of d'Abano's comments.

Judged by the number of editions, printings, and translations, Dioscorides was very popular during the Renaissance. The Greek text was in print in 1499. By this time the list of synonyms following each item had grown extensively to include Arabic and European vernacular words. A translation by Jean Ruelle received twenty-five different editions, and by 1544 approximately thirty-five editions of Dioscorides' translations and commentaries had been produced.[16] The most illustrious edition was Mattioli's, first published in Venice in 1554. So many editions and translations were made from Mattioli's critical Dioscorides that it is said that this printing is the basic work for modern botany.

NOTES

1. *On Simple Medicines,* in *Opera omnia,* C. G. Kühn, ed., XI, 794: ὁ δὲ Ἀναζαρβεὺς Διοσκουρίδης ἐν πέντε βιβλίοις: cf. XIII, 857: ὡς δὲ Διοσκορίδης ὁ Ταρσεὺς ἔδωκεν Ἀρείῳ τῷ Ἀσκληπιαδείῳ.
2. *Das Hippokrates-Glossar des Erotianos,* Johannes Ilberg, ed. (Leipzig, 1893), p. 116; also, *Erotiani,* Ernst Nachmanson, ed. (Uppsala, 1918), p. 51.
3. Pliny, *Natural History,* 26. 4. 5; Tacitus, *Annals,* 15.33.
4. Max Wellmann, "Sextius Niger. Eine Quellenuntersuchung zu Dioscorides," in *Hermes,* **23** (1888), 530–569.
5. XI, 795; see also index, vol. XX, for list of citations.
6. Galen, XI, 794.
7. Vienna MS Med. Gr. 1 and Vienna MS Suppl. Gr. 28; see also L. Choulant, "Ueber die HSS. des Dioscorides mit Abbildungen," in *Archiv für die zeichnenden Künste,* **1** (1855), 56–62.
8. J. de M. Johnson, "A Botanical Papyrus With Illustrations," in *Archiv für die Geschichte der Naturwissenschaften und der Technik,* **4** (1913), 403–408.
9. *Institutiones divinarum et humanarum litterarum,* ch. 31.
10. Munich MS lat. 337.
11. London, BM MS Cotton Vitellius C III, eleventh century, pub. by O. Cockayne, *Leechdoms, Wortcunning and Starcraft of Early England,* 3 vols., I (London, 1864–1866; repr., 1961), 251–325; cf. Oxford Hatton MS 76, early eleventh century, ff. 110–124, an Old English version of *De herbis femininis.*
12. See Madrid BN MS Arab. 125 (Gg 147), twelfth century, cited by Hartwig Derenbourg, *Notes critiques sur les manuscrits arabes de la Bibliothèque Nationale de Madrid* (Paris, 1904), pp. 7–8, 19, 30–31.
13 Bamberg, Staatsbibliothek MS med. 6, thirteenth century, f. 28v.
14. London BM MS Sloane 3848, seventeenth century, ff. 36–40; and Cambridge MS Add. 4087, fourteenth century, ff. 244v–254v.
15. Brno MS MK, fifteenth century, 173–174v; Vatican MS lat. 5373, ff. 36–41; and Vienna MS Pal. 5371, fifteenth century, ff. 121–124v.
16. Jerry Stannard, "P. A. Mattioli and Some Renaissance Editions of Dioscorides," in *Books and Libraries at the University of Kansas,* **4,** no. 1 (1966), 1–5.

BIBLIOGRAPHY

(1) Several modern Greek texts and pseudo-Dioscoridean Greek texts exist. There are two critical Greek texts of the Περὶ ὕλης ἰατρικῆς (*De materia medica*), but both contain other treatises formerly attributed to Dioscorides but now regarded as spurious. Definitely outdated is a two-volume ed. by Curtius Sprengel in *Medicorum Graecorum opera quae exstant,* C. G. Kühn, ed. (Leipzig, 1829–1830), vols. XXV–XXVI, which reprints as authentic three pseudo-Dioscoridean texts: Περὶ δηλητηρίων φαρμάκων (*On Poison Drugs*), Περὶ ἰοβόλων (*On Animal and Deadly Poisons*), and

Περὶ ἁπλῶν φαρμάκων (*On Simple Drugs*), sometimes known as Εὐπόριστα. The best critical ed. is Max Wellmann, *Pedanii Dioscuridis Anazarbei De materia medica libri quinque,* 3 vols. (Berlin, 1906–1914; repr., 1958). In "Dioscorides," in Pauly, *Real-Encyclopädie der klassischen Altertumswissenschaft* (Stuttgart, 1903), Wellmann regarded the treatise *On Simple Drugs* as a third- or fourth-century work falsely assigned to Dioscorides. Subsequently he became convinced that it was a legitimate work of Dioscorides and published it in vol. III of his critical ed. of Dioscorides. His attempt to authenticate this work (not convincing to later authorities) was published as *Die Schrift des Dioscorides* Περὶ ἁπλῶν φαρμάκων (Berlin, 1914). A German trans. of *On Simple Drugs* was prepared by Julius Berendes: "Die Hausmittel der Pedanios Dioskurides," in *Janus,* **12** (1907), 10–33. The oldest MS is Florence, Laur. Gr. 74, 10, fourteenth century; no Latin version has been identified. Berendes has also translated the two other pseudo-Dioscoridean Greek texts that Sprengel mistook as authentic: "I. Des Pedanios Dioskurides Schrift über die Gifte und Gegengifte. II. Des Pedanios Dioskurides Schrift über die giftigen Tiere und den tollen Hund," in *Apotheker-Zeitung,* nos. 92–93 (1905), 933–935, 945–954. A pseudo-Dioscoridean lapidary is printed in F. de Mély, *Les lapidaires de l'antiquité et du moyen âge* (Paris, 1902), I, 179–183.

(2) No accurate trans. of Dioscorides has appeared in a modern European language. Berendes prepared a German trans., *Des Pedanios Dioskurides aus Anazarbos Arzneimittellehre in fünf Büchern* (Stuttgart, 1902), but unfortunately it is based on the inadequate Sprengel ed. Woefully inadequate is an English trans. prepared from the Greek by John Goodyer between 1652 and 1655 but not published until much later in Robert T. Gunther, *The Greek Herbal of Dioscorides* (New York, 1934; repr., 1959).

(3) On the basis of a second-century papyrus, Campbell Bonner observed ("A Papyrus of Dioscorides in the University of Michigan Collection," in *Transactions and Proceedings of the American Philological Association,* **53** [1922], 141–168) that Oribasius' citations to Dioscorides in the fourth century resemble the papyrus text more than they do the alphabetical Greek version found in the Juliana MS (Vienna, Gr.1), sixth century. The papyrus text seems close to Escorial MS Gr. III. R.3, eleventh century, which Wellmann, in his critical text, considered more corrupt. A MS containing a section of Dioscorides in red Greek capitals, dating from around A.D. 600, has parts of four chapters in nonalphabetical order from bk. 3 (in order, chs. 82, 83, 78, and 79 of Wellmann ed.). This MS (Naples MS lat. 2; formerly Vienna MS lat. 16) has a Latin treatise written over the Greek Dioscorides text. It is known to have been at the monastery of Bobbio in the eighth century (erroneously reported by Charles Singer, "The Herbal in Antiquity and Its Transmission to Later Ages," in *Journal of Hellenic Studies,* **47** [1927], 34–35; cf. J. V. Eichenfeld, *Wiener Jahrbücher der Literatur,* **25** [1824], 35–37, and Wellmann, "Dioscorides," in Pauly, *Real-Encyclopädie* [1903], col. 1136).

(4) A facsimile repr. of the Vienna MS Med. Gr. 1, with

beautiful color plates, is published as *De materia medica* (Graz, 1966); cf. Otto Waechter, "The 'Vienna Dioskurides' and Its Restoration," in *Libri,* **13** (1963), 107–111; and G. E. Dann, "Ein Faksimile-Druck des Wiener Dioskurides," in *Zur Geschichte der Pharmazie,* **18** (1966), 9–11.

(5) The Latin text is inadequately treated. The old Latin trans. is found in Munich MS 337, eighth century, and Paris BN, lat. 9332, ninth century, pp. 243–321. K. Hoffmann and T. M. Auracher began editing Munich 337 (*Römanische Forschungen,* **1** [1882], 49–105), and the project was continued by H. Stadler (*ibid.,* **10** [1897], 181–247, 369–446; **11** [1899], 1–121; **13** [1902], 161–243; **14** [1903], 601–637). Stadler had the advantage of the discovery of BN 9332, which he used for editing bks. II–V but he did not reedit bk. I. BN 9332 has missing leaves now in Bern MS A 91.7, ff. 1v–2v. Bk. I, using BN 9332, is reedited by H. Mihuescu, *Dioscoride Latino Materia Medica Libro Primo* (Iaşi, Romania, 1938). The alphabetical Latin Dioscorides is perhaps represented best by Cambridge, Jesus Col., MS Q.D. 2 (44), twelfth century, ff. 17–145; Erfurt MS F 41, fourteenth century, ff. 1–62v; and Vatican MS Urb. lat. 1383, twelfth century, ff. 1–116. Pietro d'Abano's commentary, together with the text of Dioscorides, is found in Paris BN lat. 6819, thirteenth century, ff. 1–70v., and BN 6820, fourteenth or fifteenth century, ff. 1–74. It was apparently the MS BN 6820—probably the exact copy—that the printer Johannes de Medemblich mistook part of d'Abano's commentary for Dioscorides' text. The early printings are covered by Jerry Stannard, "P. A. Mattioli. Sixteenth Century Commentator on Dioscorides," in *Bibliographical Contributions, University of Kansas Libraries,* **1** (1969), 59–81.

(6) A text of *De herbis femininis* is published by Heinrich Kästner, "Pseudo-Dioscoridis 'De herbis femininis,'" in *Hermes,* **31** (1896), 578–636, from only three MS sources. This version is faulty; for instance, London BM Sloane MS 1975, twelfth century, ff. 49v–73, adds some herbs, whereas London BM Harley MS 5294, twelfth century, ff. 43v–58, and Oxford Bodl. Ash. MS 1431, late eleventh century, ff. 31v–43, omit many herbs. Kästner's ed. did not use these MSS. *De herbis femininis* is the only version of the Latin MSS always to be illustrated. No study yet has been made of the drawings.

(7) The best overall treatment by modern scholars remains Max Wellmann's preface to his *Pedanti Dioscuridis,* II, v–xxvi; and his articles "Dioscorides" and "Areios," in Pauly, *Real-Encyclopädie.* Charles Singer (*Journal of Hellenic Studies,* **47** [1927], 1–52) studied the transmission problem and worked with the iconographic aspects; see also his "Greek Biology and Its Relation to the Rise of Modern Biology," in *Studies in the History and Method of Science* (Oxford, 1921), II, 1–101. César E. Dubler has written an extensive examination of the various substances mentioned by Dioscorides as they are transmitted through various medical writers, especially writers in Arabic: *La "Materia Médica" de Dioscórides. Transmisión medieval y renacentista,* 5 vols. (Barcelona, 1953–1959). Vol. I has a valuable concordance which traces the translations of the plants and other substances from Greek to Latin, Arabic, and Castilian. With Elias Terés as coauthor, vol. II prints an Arabic

version of Dioscorides, principally from Madrid BN MS 5006 but with other texts consulted. Vol. III reproduces in facsimile the Salamanca 1570 printing of Don Andrés de Laguna's Castilian trans. first printed in Anvers in 1555. The remainder of the volumes are concerned with commentaries, indexes, etc.

(8) Attempts have been made by modern botanists and other scholars to identify the plants in Dioscorides. The best is Berendes' trans. into German with his own commentary (Stuttgart, 1902). Useful are the following: R. Mock, *Pflanzliche Arzneimittel bei Dioskurides die schon in Corpus Hippocratum vorkommen,* diss. (Tübingen, 1919); R. Schmidt, *Die noch gebräuchlichen Arzneimittel bei Dioskurides,* diss. (Tübingen, 1919); Léon Moulé, "La zoothérapie au temps de Dioscoride et de Pline," in *International Congress for the History of Medicine* (Antwerp, 1920), pp. 451–461; Edmund O. von Lippmann, "Die chemischen Kenntnisse des Dioskorides," in *Abhandlungen und Vorträge zur Geschichte der Naturwissenschaften,* 2 vols. (Leipzig, 1906–1913), I, 47–73; Achille Morricone, "I medicamenti di origine animale recavati dal mare nell'opera di Dioscoride," in *Pagine di storia della medicina,* **7** (1963), 24–28; and Ernst W. Stieb, "Drug Adulteration and Its Detection, in the Writings of Theophrastus, Dioscorides and Pliny," in *Journal mondial de pharmacie,* **2** (1958), 117–134. Attempts to identify some of the plants and animals of the illustrations are made by E. Bonnet, "Étude sur les figures de plantes et d'animaux . . .," in *Janus,* **14** (1909), 294–303, and other of his articles in *Janus,* **8** (1903), 169–177, 225–232, 281–285; and by E. Emmanuel, "Étude comparative sur les plantes dessinées dans le Codex Constantinopolitanus de Dioscoride," in *Schweizerische Apotheker-Zeitung,* **50** (1912), 45–50, 64–72.

JOHN M. RIDDLE

DIRICHLET, GUSTAV PETER LEJEUNE (*b.* Düren, Germany, 13 February 1805; *d.* Göttingen, Germany, 5 May 1859), *mathematics.*

Dirichlet, the son of the town postmaster, first attended public school, then a private school that emphasized Latin. He was precociously interested in mathematics; it is said that before the age of twelve he used his pocket money to buy mathematical books. In 1817 he entered the Gymnasium in Bonn. He is reported to have been an unusually attentive and well-behaved pupil who was particularly interested in modern history as well as in mathematics.

After two years in Bonn, Dirichlet was sent to a Jesuit college in Cologne that his parents preferred. Among his teachers was the physicist Georg Simon Ohm, who gave him a thorough grounding in theoretical physics. Dirichlet completed his *Abitur* examination at the very early age of sixteen. His parents wanted him to study law, but mathematics was already his chosen field. At the time the level of pure mathematics in the German universities was at a low ebb: Except for the formidable Carl Gauss in Göttingen, there were no outstanding mathematicians, while in Paris the firmament was studded by such luminaries as P.-S. Laplace, Adrien Legendre, Joseph Fourier, Siméon Poisson, Sylvestre Lacroix, J.-B. Biot, Jean Hachette, and Francoeur.

Dirichlet arrived in Paris in May 1822. Shortly afterward he suffered an attack of smallpox, but it was not serious enough to interrupt for long his attendance at lectures at the Collège de France and the Faculté des Sciences. In the summer of 1823 he was fortunate in being appointed to a well-paid and pleasant position as tutor to the children of General Maximilien Fay, a national hero of the Napoleonic wars and then the liberal leader of the opposition in the Chamber of Deputies. Dirichlet was treated as a member of the family and met many of the most prominent figures in French intellectual life. Among the mathematicians, he was particularly attracted to Fourier, whose ideas had a strong influence upon his later works on trigonometric series and mathematical physics.

Dirichlet's first interest in mathematics was number theory. This interest had been awakened through an early study of Gauss's famous *Disquisitiones arithmeticae* (1801), until then not completely understood by mathematicians. In June 1825 he presented to the French Academy of Sciences his first mathematical paper, "Mémoire sur l'impossibilité de quelques équations indéterminées du cinquième degré." It dealt with Diophantine equations of the form

$$x^5 + y^5 = A \cdot z^5$$

using algebraic number theory, Dirichlet's favorite field throughout his life. By means of the methods developed in this paper Legendre succeeded, only a few weeks later, in giving a complete proof that Fermat's equation

$$x^n + y^n = z^n$$

has no integral solutions $(x \cdot y \cdot z \neq 0)$ for $n = 5$. Until then only the cases $n = 4$ (Fermat) and $n = 3$ (Euler) had been solved.

General Fay died in November 1825, and the next year Dirichlet decided to return to Germany, a plan strongly supported by Alexander von Humboldt, who worked for the strengthening of the natural sciences in Germany. Dirichlet was permitted to qualify for habilitation as *Privatdozent* at the University of Breslau; since he did not have the required doctorate, this was awarded *honoris causa* by the University of Cologne. His habilitation thesis dealt with polynomials whose prime divisors belong to special arithmetic series. A second paper from this period was inspired by Gauss's announcements on the biquadratic law of reciprocity.

Dirichlet was appointed extraordinary professor in Breslau, but the conditions for scientific work were not inspiring. In 1828 he moved to Berlin, again with the assistance of Humboldt, to become a teacher of mathematics at the military academy. Shortly afterward, at the age of twenty-three, he was appointed extraordinary (later ordinary) professor at the University of Berlin. In 1831 he became a member of the Berlin Academy of Sciences, and in the same year he married Rebecca Mendelssohn-Bartholdy, granddaughter of the philosopher Moses Mendelssohn.

Dirichlet spent twenty-seven years as a professor in Berlin and exerted a strong influence on the development of German mathematics through his lectures, through his many pupils, and through a series of scientific papers of the highest quality that he published during this period. He was an excellent teacher, always expressing himself with great clarity. His manner was modest; in his later years he was shy and at times reserved. He seldom spoke at meetings and was reluctant to make public appearances. In many ways he was a direct contrast to his lifelong friend, the mathematician Karl Gustav Jacobi.

The two exerted some influence upon each other's work, particularly in number theory. When, in 1843, Jacobi was compelled to seek a milder climate for reasons of health, Dirichlet applied for a leave of absence and moved with his family to Rome. A circle of leading German mathematicians gathered around the two. Dirichlet remained in Italy for a year and a half, visited Sicily, and spent the second winter in Florence.

Dirichlet's first paper dealing with Fermat's equation was inspired by Legendre; he returned only once to this problem, showing the impossibility of the case $n = 14$. The subsequent number theory papers dating from the early years in Berlin were evidently influenced by Gauss and the *Disquisitiones*. Some of them were improvements on Gauss's proofs and presentation, but gradually Dirichlet cut much deeper into the theory. There are papers on quadratic forms, the quadratic and biquadratic laws of reciprocity, and the number theory of fields of quadratic irrationalities, with the extensive discussion of the Gaussian integers $a + ib$, where $i = \sqrt{-1}$ and a and b are integers.

At a meeting of the Academy of Sciences on 27 July 1837, Dirichlet presented his first paper on analytic number theory. In this memoir he gives a proof of the fundamental theorem that bears his name: Any arithmetical series of integers

$$an + b, \, n = 0, 1, 2, \cdots,$$

where a and b are relatively prime, must include an infinite number of primes. This result had long been conjectured and Legendre had expended considerable effort upon finding a proof, but it had been established only for a few special cases, such as

$$\{4n + 1\} = 1, 5, 9, 13, 17, 21, \cdots$$
$$\{4n + 3\} = 3, 7, 11, 15, 19, 23, \cdots.$$

The paper on the primes in arithmetic progressions was followed in 1838 and 1839 by a two-part paper on analytic number theory, "Recherches sur diverses applications de l'analyse infinitésimale à la théorie des nombres." Dirichlet begins with a few general observations on the convergence of the series now called Dirichlet series. The main number theory achievement is the determination of the formula for the class number for quadratic forms with various applications. Also from this period are his studies on Gaussian sums.

These studies on quadratic forms with rational coefficients were continued in 1842 in an analogous paper on forms with coefficients that have Gaussian coefficients. It contains an attempt at a systematic theory of algebraic numbers when the prime factorization is unique, although it is restricted to Gaussian integers. It is of interest to note that here one finds the first application of Dirichlet's *Schubfachprinzip* ("box principle"). This deceptively simple argument, which plays an important role in many arguments in modern number theory, may be stated as follows: If one distributes more than n objects in n boxes, then at least one box must contain more than one object.

It is evident from Dirichlet's papers that he searched very intently for a general algebraic number theory valid for fields of arbitrary degree. He was aware of the fact that in such fields there may not be a unique prime factorization, but he did not succeed in creating a substitute for it: the ideal theory later created by Ernst Kummer and Richard Dedekind or the form theory of Leopold Kronecker.

Dirichlet approached the problem through a generalization of the quadratic forms, using the properties of decomposable forms representable as the product of linear forms, a method closely related to the method later used by Kronecker. One part of algebraic number theory, the theory of units, had its beginning in Dirichlet's work. He had earlier written a number of papers on John Pell's equation

$$x^2 - Dy = N,$$

with particular consideration of the cases in which $N = \pm 1$ corresponds to the units in the quadratic field $K(\sqrt{D})$. But in the paper "Zur Theorie der complexen Einheiten," presented to the Berlin Academy on 30 March 1846, he succeeded in establishing the complete result for the Abelian group of units in an algebraic number field: When the field is defined by an irreducible equation with r real roots and s pairs of complex roots, the number of infinite basis elements is $r + s - 1$; the finite basis element is a root of unity.

After these fundamental papers, the importance of Dirichlet's number theory work declined. He published minor papers on the classes of ternary forms, on the representation of integers as the sum of three squares, and on number theory sums, together with simplifications and new proofs for previous results and theories.

In 1863, Dirichlet's *Vorlesungen über Zahlentheorie* was published by his pupil and friend Richard Dedekind. To the later editions of this work Dedekind most appropriately added several supplements containing his own investigations on algebraic number theory. These addenda are considered one of the most important sources for the creation of the theory of ideals, which has now become the core of algebraic number theory.

Parallel with Dirichlet's investigations on number theory was a series of studies on analysis and applied mathematics. His first papers on these topics appeared during his first years in Berlin and were inspired by the works of the French mathematicians whom he had met during his early years in Paris. His first paper on analysis is rather formal, generalizing certain definite integrals introduced by Laplace and Poisson. This paper was followed in the same year (1829) by a celebrated one published in *Crelle's Journal,* as were most of his mathematical papers: "Sur la convergence des séries trigonométriques qui servent à représenter une fonction arbitraire entre deux limites données." The paper was written under the influence of Fourier's theory of heat conduction as presented in his *Théorie analytique de la chaleur.*

Dirichlet and several other mathematicians had been impressed by the properties of the Fourier series on trigonometric series

$$\tfrac{1}{2}a_0 + (a_1 \cos x + b_1 \sin x)$$
$$+ (a_2 \cos 2x + b_2 \sin 2x) + \cdots,$$

particularly by their ability to represent both continuous and discontinuous functions. Such series, although now commonly named for Fourier, had already been used by Daniel Bernoulli and Leonhard Euler to examine the laws of vibrating strings. The convergence of the series had been investigated shortly before Dirichlet in a paper by Cauchy (1823). In the introduction to his own paper Dirichlet is sharply critical of Cauchy on two accounts: first, he considers Cauchy's reasoning invalid on some points;

second, the results do not cover series for which the convergence had previously been established.

Dirichlet proceeds to express the sum of the first n terms in the series corresponding formally to the given function $f(x)$ and examines the case in which the difference between $f(x)$ and the integral tends to zero. In this manner he establishes the convergence to $f(x)$ of the corresponding series, provided $f(x)$ is continuous or has a finite number of discontinuities. Dirichlet's method later became classic; it has served as the basis for many later investigations on the convergence or summation of a trigonometric series to its associated function under much more general conditions.

Dirichlet returned to the same topic a few years later in the article "Über die Darstellung ganz willkürlicher Functionen durch Sinus- und Cosinusreihen," published in the *Repertorium der Physik* (1837), a collection of review articles on mathematical physics on which his friend Jacobi collaborated. An outstanding feature of this article is Dirichlet's abandonment of the until then universally accepted idea of a function as an expression formulated in terms of special mathematical symbols or operations. Instead, he introduces generally the modern concept of a function $y = f(x)$ as a correspondence that associates with each real x in an interval some unique value denoted by $f(x)$. His concept of continuity is, however, still intuitive. For his continuous functions he defines integrals by means of sums of equidistant function values and points out that the ordinary integral properties all remain valid. On this basis the theory of Fourier series is then developed. In a related paper, "Solution d'une question relative à la théorie mathématique de la chaleur" (1830), Dirichlet uses his methods to simplify the treatment of a problem by Fourier: the temperature distribution in a thin bar with given temperatures at the endpoints.

Closely related to these investigations is the paper "Sur les séries dont le terme général dépend de deux angles et qui servent à exprimer des fonctions arbitraires entre des limites données" (1837). The Fourier series can be considered as expansions of functions defined on a circle. In this paper Dirichlet examines analogously the convergence of the expansion in spherical harmonics (*Kugelfunctionen*) of functions defined on a sphere. He later applied these results in several papers on problems in theoretical physics.

Dirichlet's contributions to general mechanics began with three papers published in 1839. All three have nearly the some content; the most elaborate has the title "Über eine neue Methode zur Bestimmung vielfacher Integrale." All deal with methods based upon a so-called discontinuity factor for evaluating multiple integrals, and they are applied particularly to the problem of determining the attraction of an ellipsoid upon an arbitrary mass point outside or inside the ellipsoid.

In the brief article "Über die Stabilität des Gleichgewichts" (1846), Dirichlet considers a general problem inspired by Laplace's analysis of the stability of the solar system. He takes the general point of view that the particles attract or repel each other by forces depending only on the distance and acting along their central line; in addition, the relations connecting the coordinates shall not depend on time. Stability is defined as the property that the deviations of the coordinates and velocities from their initial values remain within fixed, small bounds. Dirichlet criticizes as unsatisfactory the previous analyses of the problem, particularly those by Lagrange and Poisson that depended upon infinite series expansions in which terms above the second order were disregarded without sufficient justification. Dirichlet avoids this pitfall by reasoning directly on the properties of the expression for the energy of the system.

One of Dirichlet's most important papers bears the long title "Über einen neuen Ausdruck zur Bestimmung der Dichtigkeit einer unendlich dünnen Kugelschale, wenn der Werth des Potentials derselben in jedem Punkte ihrer Oberfläche gegeben ist" (1850). Here Dirichlet deals with the boundary value problem, now known as Dirichlet's problem, in which one wishes to determine a potential function $V(x,y,z)$ satisfying Laplace's equation

$$\frac{\delta^2 V}{\delta x^2} + \frac{\delta^2 V}{\delta y^2} + \frac{\delta^2 V}{\delta z^2} = 0$$

and having prescribed values on a given surface, in Dirichlet's case a sphere. This type of problem plays an important role in numerous physical and mathematical theories, such as those of potentials, heat, magnetism, and electricity. Mathematically it can be extended to an arbitrary number of dimensions.

Among the later papers on theoretical mechanics one must mention "Über die Bewegung eines festen Körpers in einem incompressibeln flüssigen Medium" (1852), which deals with the motion of a sphere in an incompressible fluid; it is noteworthy for containing the first exact integration for the hydrodynamic equations. This subject occupied Dirichlet during his last years; in his final paper, "Untersuchungen über ein Problem der Hydrodynamik" (1857), he examines a related topic, but this includes only a minor part of his hydrodynamic theories. After his death, his notes on these subjects were edited and published by Dedekind in an extensive memoir.

In 1855, when Gauss died, the University of Göttingen—which had long enjoyed the reflection of his scientific fame—was anxious to seek a successor of great distinction, and the choice fell upon Dirichlet. His position in Berlin had been relatively modest and onerous, and the teaching schedule at the military academy was very heavy and without scientific appeal. Dirichlet wrote to his pupil Kronecker in 1853 that he had little time for correspondence, for he had thirteen lectures a week and many other duties to attend to. Dirichlet responded to the offer from Göttingen that he would accept unless he was relieved of the military instruction in Berlin. The authorities in Berlin seem not to have taken the threat very seriously, and only after it was too late did the Ministry of Education offer to improve his teaching load and salary.

Dirichlet moved to Göttingen in the fall of 1855, bought a house with a garden, and seemed to enjoy the more quiet life of a prominent university in a small city. He had a number of excellent pupils and relished the increased leisure for research. His work in this period was centered on general problems of mechanics. This new life, however, was not to last long. In the summer of 1858 Dirichlet traveled to a meeting in Montreux, Switzerland, to deliver a memorial speech in honor of Gauss. While there, he suffered a heart attack and was barely able to return to his family in Göttingen. During his illness his wife died of a stroke, and Dirichlet himself died the following spring.

BIBLIOGRAPHY

Many of Dirichlet's works are in L. Kronecker and L. Fuchs, eds., *G. Lejeune Dirichlets Werke, herausgegeben auf Veranlassung der Königlichen Preussischen Akademie der Wissenschaften,* 2 vols. (Berlin, 1889–1897). Included are a portrait; a biography by E. Kummer; correspondence with Gauss, Kronecker, and Alexander von Humboldt; and material from Dirichlet's posthumous papers.

Several of Dirichlet's papers have been reissued in the series Ostwalds Klassiker der exacten Wissenschaften: no. 19, *Über die Anziehung homogener Ellipsoide (Über eine neue Methode zur Bestimmung vielfacher Integrale),* which includes papers by other writers (1890); no. 91, *Untersuchungen über verschiedene Anwendungen der Infinitesimalanalysis auf die Zahlentheorie* (1897); and no. 116, *Die Darstellung ganz willkürlicher Functionen durch Sinus- und Cosinusreihen* (1900).

Dirichlet's lectures have been published in G. Arendt, *Vorlesungen über die Lehre von den einfachen und mehrfachen bestimmten Integrale* (1904); R. Dedekind, *Vorlesungen über Zahlentheorie* (1893); and F. Grube, *Vorle-*

sungen über die im umgekehrten Verhältniss des Quadrats der Entfernung wirkenden Kräfte (1876).

OYSTEIN ORE

DITTMAR, WILLIAM (*b.* Umstadt [near Darmstadt], Germany, 15 April 1833; *d.* Glasgow, Scotland, 9 February 1892), *chemistry.*

Dittmar analyzed samples of seawater collected during the voyage of H.M.S. *Challenger* (1872–1876). He originally qualified in pharmacy, but in 1857 he went to work in Bunsen's laboratory at Heidelberg. There he was befriended by Henry Roscoe, who invited him to England; and when Roscoe became professor of chemistry at Owens College, Manchester, Dittmar accompanied him as his assistant. From 1861 to 1869 he was chief assistant in the chemical laboratory at Edinburgh University.

After spending the next three years in Germany, where he lectured in meteorology at an agricultural college near Bonn, Dittmar returned to Edinburgh in 1872. In 1873 he was appointed assistant lecturer at Owens College but the year after became professor of chemistry at Anderson's College, Glasgow, where he remained until his death.

Dittmar's "Report on Researches Into the Composition of Ocean-Water" (1884) was the result of six years' work on the *Challenger* samples. He improved on existing methods of determining the major constituents of marine salt and confirmed Forchhammer's discovery (1865) that although the salinity of seawater varies from place to place, the ratios of the principal constituents to each other remain almost constant. This showed that calculations of salinity, usually made from measurements of specific gravity, could be done as well, if not better, by determining the weight of chlorine in a sample and multiplying it by a constant factor of 1.8058, the ratio of total salt to chlorine. Dittmar also studied the absorption of gases in seawater and established the proportion of bromine to chlorine.

Dittmar's other work included research on the atomic weight of platinum and on the gravimetric composition of water, for which he was awarded the Graham Medal of the Glasgow Philosophical Society. He was elected a fellow of the Royal Society of Edinburgh in 1863 and of the Royal Society in 1882.

BIBLIOGRAPHY

I. ORIGINAL WORKS. Dittmar's "Report on Researches Into the Composition of Ocean-Water" was published in *Report on the Scientific Results of the Voyage of H.M.S. Challenger: Physics and Chemistry,* I (London, 1884). He also wrote a number of scientific papers and textbooks. See Poggendorff, III, 365–366; IV, 333.

II. SECONDARY LITERATURE. Obituaries of Dittmar are in *Nature,* **45,** no. 1169 (24 Mar. 1892), 493–494; and *Proceedings of the Royal Society of Edinburgh,* **20** (1892–1895), vi–vii. His contribution to oceanography is described in J. P. Riley and G. Skirrow, eds., *Chemical Oceanography,* I (London–New York, 1965), 15, 124–125. His other researches are listed in *Proceedings of the Philosophical Society of Glasgow,* **23** (1891–1892), 310.

MARGARET DEACON

DIVINI, EUSTACHIO (*b.* San Severino delle Marche [near Ancona], Italy, 4 October 1610; *d.* Rome, Italy, 1685), *optical instrumentation.*

Divini was among the first to develop technology for the production of scientifically designed optical instruments. He established himself in Rome about 1646 as a maker of clocks and lenses. In 1648 he constructed an innovative compound microscope with cardboard sliding tubes and convex lenses for the objective and the eyepiece; several years later he developed the doublet lens for microscopes. During the same period he experimented with the construction of telescopes of long focus. It was at this time that Giuseppe Campani of Castel San Felice came to Rome and learned the art of lensmaking. His lenses and instruments were competitive with Divini's, and a bitter rivalry between the two artisans developed into a lasting feud that involved Pope Alexander VII.

Divini constructed long telescopes consisting of wooden tubes with four lenses, of a focal length of seventy-two Roman palms (633 inches). He experimented with the elimination of achromatic aberration in his lenses with some success. He had received some scientific training from Benedetto Castelli, one of Galileo's disciples.

In 1649 Divini published a copper engraving of a map of the moon, based upon his own observations of 1647, 1648, and early 1649, which were made with instruments of his own construction. These instruments incorporated a micrometer of a gridiron design of his own invention.

Divini made a number of astronomical observations, utilizing his instruments. He made observations of the rings of Saturn and the spots and satellites of the planet Jupiter. In his observations he became involved in a controversy with Huygens, in the course of which he published several tracts.

Significant examples of Divini's microscopes and telescopes have survived in such important public collections as those of the Istituto e Museo di Storia della Scienza in Florence, the Osservatorio Astronomico e Museo Copernicano in Rome, the Museo

di Fisica in Padua, and the British Museum in London.

BIBLIOGRAPHY

I. ORIGINAL WORKS. Divini published *Eustachii de Divinis Septempedani brevis adnotatio in systema Saturnium Christiani Hugenii ad Serenissimum Principem Leopoldum Magni Ducis Etruriae fratrem una cum Christiani Hugenii responso ad eumdem Principem* (Rome, 1660); *Eustachius de Divinis Septemedanus pro sua adnotatione in systema Saturnium Christiani Hugenii adversus ejusdem assertionem* (Rome, 1661); *Lettera di Eustachio Divini al conte Carlo Antonio Manzini Si ragguaglia di un nuovo lavoro e compimento di lenti, che servono a occhialoni o simplici o composti* (Rome, 1663); *Lettera di Eustachio Divini con altra del P. Egidio Francesco Gottignes intorno alle macchie nuovamente scoperte nel mese di Luglio 1665, con suoi cannochiali nel pianeta di Giove* (Rome, 1665); and *Lettera sulle ombre delle stelle Medicee nel volto di Giove* (Bologna, 1666).

II. SECONDARY LITERATURE. On Divini and his work see also Silvio A. Bedini, "Seventeenth Century Italian Compound Microscopes," in *Physis,* **5** (1963), 383–397; Giovanni-Carlo Gentili, *Elogio storico di Monsignor Angelo Massarelli di Sanseverino* (Macerata, 1837), pp. 60–86; and Carlo Antonio Manzini, *L'occhiale all'occhio, dioptrica practica* (Bologna, 1660).

SILVIO A. BEDINI

DIVIŠ, PROKOP (also **Procopius Divisch** or **Diwisch**) (*b.* Žamberk, Bohemia, 26 March 1698; *d.* Přímětice, near Znojmo, Moravia, 21 December 1765), *electricity.*

Diviš was one of the most eminent Czech scholars of the mid-eighteenth century. He contributed to the history of science mainly by his studies of atmospheric electricity and by his construction of a lightning conductor. From 1716 he attended secondary school at Znojmo, in southern Moravia. In 1719 he joined the Premonstratensian monastery at Louky, where he completed his study of philosophy and was ordained in 1726. He then taught natural science at the monastery school and introduced practical experiments in the classroom. Diviš also taught theology, becoming doctor of theology at Salzburg in 1733 and doctor of philosophy, probably in 1745 at Olmütz (now Olomouc). In 1736 he was appointed parson in the small village of Přímětice, near Znojmo, where he remained, except for a brief interval, until his death.

Scientific research mattered more to Diviš than his parish duties. Unfortunately, he lived at a great distance from his country's centers of learning (the only universities in Bohemia were those at Prague and Olmütz). He had to keep up with scientific developments through literature, personal contacts, and (chiefly) correspondence. Of the latter, however, only a small portion has been found. Thus circumstance made Diviš more or less self-taught.

During his stay at the monastery of Louky, Diviš concerned himself with practical hydraulics. From his manuscripts it appears that he also worked in chemistry and alchemy. He even constructed a musical instrument called the "denisdor," which resembled a complicated harpsichord and had strings that could be electrified.

Diviš' main interest was electricity. We do not know exactly when he began work in this area, but in 1748 he performed various electrical experiments. He is said to have demonstrated the electric effects of the conductive point in Vienna as early as 1750. By means of unnoticeable pointed wires inserted into his wig, he drew off the electricity from a charged solid body. He had also considered drawing off electricity from clouds, but it is not until early in 1753—only after Dalibard's first experiments—that there is any evidence of Diviš' real interest in and ideas about atmospheric electricity. In that year Diviš also wrote a treatise explaining why the St. Petersburg physicist G. W. Richmann had been killed by a flash of lightning, and sent it to Euler. In a letter dated 24 October 1753, which accompanied the treatise, he hints at his intention of finishing that winter a machine for reducing the severity of thunderstorms and of testing it the following summer. On 15 June 1754, Diviš erected his lightning conductor in the rectory garden of Přímětice.

The basic idea of Diviš' conductor was a consistent application of the point-effect analogy (discovered by Franklin in 1747), that metal points possess the property of allowing electricity to flow away from a charged object. This led Diviš to believe that a thundercloud could be deprived of its charge, thus entirely preventing lightning. Diviš' lightning conductor consisted of a horizontal iron cross with three boxes with twenty-seven points attached to the end of each arm. This complicated *machina meteorologica* was placed on a wooden frame about 108 feet high and connected to the ground by four iron chains. Whether the chains were intended only to increase the stability of so high a structure or whether Diviš was actually aware of the necessity of grounding remains uncertain. At any rate, the grounding made the conductor truly effective, in contrast with the insulated experimental rods of that time. In this respect, Diviš' lightning conductor is considered to be the first to afford actual protection from lightning, although, of course, it did not possess the preventive effects attributed to it by its inventor. The lightning conductor at Přímětice remained standing until 1760,

when the villagers, believing it to be the cause of a great drought, broke the chains and a heavy gale did the rest. Diviš later attached a smaller version to the steeple of his church.

Diviš also was interested in the therapeutic applications of electricity, advocating such treatments and carrying them out. He is said to have cured more than fifty persons. He doubtless was a highly skilled experimenter, but the results he obtained were never beyond the level of the period.

Diviš devoted much attention to the theoretical explanation of electric phenomena. In doing so he referred to Genesis, and in many respects he was influenced by Aristotle and the Scholastics. These influences, together with the general distrust of lightning conductors, seem to have been the main reasons why—despite his continual efforts—Diviš was not more appreciated during the Enlightenment. In 1753 he sought membership in the Berlin Academy of Sciences; in 1755 he took part in a competition at the St. Petersburg Academy; in 1760 he solicited a professorial chair at Vienna University—but all in vain. Likewise, he had great difficulties with his only publication, *Magia naturalis,* which was rejected by the Vienna censors. It was not published until the year of his death, with the help of German Protestants.

BIBLIOGRAPHY

I. ORIGINAL WORKS. Diviš' only published work is *Längst verlangte Theorie von der meteorologischen Electricite, welche er selbst Magiam naturalem benahmet* (Tübingen, 1765; 2nd ed., Frankfurt, 1768). MSS are in National Scientific Library, Olomouc, MSS Dept., sign. III.28. nos. 1–12; National Archives, Brno, Cerroni Collection, no. II.135; and Archives of the Soviet Academy of Sciences, Leningrad: correspondence, fol. 136, op. 2, no. 3; fol. 1, op. 2, no. 39; fol. 1, op. 3, no. 40, 45.

II. SECONDARY LITERATURE. Reports of Diviš' scientific activity are in *Tubingische Berichte von gelehrten Sachen* (1755), pp. 66–73; and *Wochentlicher Intelligenz-Zettel* (Brno, 1758), nos. 3, 4, 7–10.

On Diviš or his work, see E. Albert, "Ein österreichischer Elektrotherapeut aus dem vorigen Jahrhundert," in *Wiener medizinische Presse,* no. 12 (1880), 369–372; I. B. Cohen and R. Schofield, "Did Diviš Erect the First European Protective Lightning Rod, and Was His Invention Independent?," in *Isis,* **43** (1952), 358–364; J. Friess, "Prokop Divisch. Ein Beitrag zur Geschichte der Physik," in *Programm der k. k. Staats-Oberrealschule* (Olomouc, 1884); L. Goovaerts, *Écrivains, artistes et savants de l'Ordre Prémontré,* I (Brussels, 1899), 195–197; K. Hujer, "Father Procopius Diviš—The European Franklin," in *Isis,* **43** (1952), 351–357; F. Pelzel, *Abbildungen böhmischer und mährischer*

Gelehrten und Künstler, III (Prague, 1777), 172–184; and Josef Smolka, "Příspěvky k bádání o Prokopu Divišovi" ("Contribution to the Investigation of Prokop Diviš"), in *Sborník pro dějiny přírodních věd a techniky,* **3** (1957), 122–152; "Divišova korespondence s L. Eulerem a Petrohradskou akademií ved" ("Diviš' Correspondence With L. Euler and the Petersburg Academy of Sciences"), *ibid.,* **8** (1963), 139–162; "B. Franklin, P. Diviš et la découverte du paratonnerre," in *Actes du dixième congrès international d'histoire des sciences* (Paris, 1964), pp. 763–767; and "Prokop Diviš and His Place in the History of Atmospheric Electricity," in *Acta historiae rerum naturalium necnon technicarum* (Prague), spec. iss. **1** (1965), 149–169.

JOSEF SMOLKA

DIXON, HAROLD BAILY (*b.* London, England, 11 August 1852; *d.* Lytham, England, 18 September 1930), *chemistry.*

Dixon was a leading authority on gaseous explosions and created an international interest in combustion research. The son of William Hepworth Dixon, author of popular historical and travel books and editor of *Athenaeum,* Dixon intended to follow a literary career. He did poorly as a classical student at Oxford (1871–1875), however, and transferred to chemistry. He worked with A. V. Harcourt until 1879 and was a lecturer at Trinity and Balliol colleges. In 1886 he assumed the chair of chemistry at Owens College, Manchester, where he founded the Manchester School of Combustion Research. He was elected to the Royal Society in 1886 and was a president of the Chemical Society of London and the Manchester Literary and Philosophical Society.

The only detailed studies of gaseous explosions had been made by Bunsen, and for twenty years his results were accepted as authoritative. Bunsen claimed that his experiments were inconsistent with Berthollet's law of mass action. In his first researches at Oxford, Dixon found Bunsen's conclusions to be erroneous and that the law of mass action applied to gaseous explosions. In 1880 he discovered the incombustibility of purified and dried gases, proving that prolonged drying of gas mixtures rendered them nonexplosive to electric sparks, whereas wet mixtures exploded readily. His publications began the systematic investigation of the effect of moisture on chemical changes.

Dixon's major contribution to combustion research was his detailed study of the rate and propagation of explosions. On the basis of Bunsen's experiments, scientists believed the rates of gaseous explosions were only a few meters per second; but Dixon proved that very great flame speeds were attained and that Bunsen's speeds applied only to the usually short initial phase of explosions. Dixon determined the velocity

and course of explosions, developing his own photographic methods to detect the moving flame. He named the rapid motion of flame "the detonation wave." Another line of combustion research was his measurement of the ignition temperatures of gases and gas mixtures. He was the first to determine these with accuracy.

BIBLIOGRAPHY

Dixon wrote three long papers that serve as detailed monographs on the subjects of flame and explosions: "Conditions of Chemical Change in Gases: Hydrogen, Carbonic Oxide, and Oxygen," in *Philosophical Transactions of the Royal Society,* **175** (1884), 617–684; "The Rate of Explosions in Gases," *ibid.,* **184A** (1893), 97–188; and "On the Movements of the Flame in the Explosion of Gases," *ibid.,* **200A** (1903), 315–352.

Dixon's life and work are chronicled by his students H. B. Baker and W. A. Bone in "Harold Baily Dixon 1852–1930," in *Journal of the Chemical Society* (1931), 3349–3368. The same essay appears in *Proceedings of the Royal Society,* **134A** (1931–1932), i–xvii; and in Alexander Findlay and William Hobson Mills, eds., *British Chemists* (London, 1947), pp. 126–145.

ALBERT B. COSTA

DIXON, HENRY HORATIO (*b.* Dublin, Ireland, 19 May 1869; *d.* Dublin, 20 December 1953), *botany.*

Dixon was the youngest of seven brothers and two sisters; his father, George Dixon, was owner of a soap works; his mother was the former Rebecca Yeates. In 1887 he entered Trinity College, Dublin, with a classical scholarship and prizes in Italian; but in 1891 he graduated with a first-class degree and gold medal in botany, geology, and zoology. He was stimulated by a very active botany department and also by friendship with the physicist John Joly, with whom he collaborated in fruitful research. He then studied in Bonn with Eduard Strasburger until 1893, when he was appointed assistant to E. Perceval Wright, professor of botany in Dublin, and occupied himself reorganizing the botanical gardens and herbarium. Almost all of Dixon's working life was spent in Dublin: he became professor of botany in 1904 and was active in the Royal Dublin Society, receiving the Boyle Medal in 1916 and serving as president from 1944 to 1947. The Royal Society elected him to fellowship in 1908, and he was the Croonian lecturer of 1937. In 1927 he was visiting professor at the University of California. He resigned his chair in 1949 and was elected an honorary fellow of Trinity College, Dublin. He married Dorothea Mary Franks, a medical student, in 1907; they had three sons.

Dixon's early research was suggestive of his potential rather than significant in botany: work on the cytology of chromosomes and first mitosis of spore mother cells of *Lilium* showed that the appearance of bivalents is due to the approach of chromosomes rather than to splitting of some preexisting structure, thus giving the first indication of reduction division.

He started original work soon after graduating and by 1892 had shown how to grow seedlings in sterile culture, foreshadowing later tissue and root culture. He also suggested mutagenic effects to be expected from cosmic radiation. Work on the resistance of seeds to heat, cold, and poisons developed thermoelectric methods of cryoscopy that he was to use again in work on osmotic pressure.

In 1894 Dixon and Joly read their classic paper "On the Ascent of Sap"; they gave an outline of the theory to the Trinity College Experimental Science Association in March and read the full paper to the Royal Society in October. The tension theory of the ascent of sap in trees arose from the combination of Dixon's knowledge of Strasburger's work on transpiration in high trees and Joly's knowledge of work by François Donny and Berthelot on the tensile strength of columns of sulfuric acid and water. This idea was worked out in experiments on transpiration of various trees; and they showed that since leaves can transpire even against high atmospheric pressures, this tension can be maintained. Transmission of internal stress was found to be due to the internal stability of the liquid when mechanically stretched and to the additional stability of minutely subdivided connective tissue; this is unaffected by dissolved gas, and free gas is restricted by the size of the vessel. The tensile stress in the sap is transmitted to the root, where it establishes in the capillaries of the root surface menisci competent to condense water rapidly from the surrounding soil and thus complete the process of transpiration.

Dixon, working alone, continued to perfect the theory in all details. He published a standard account in 1909 and, in 1914, *Transpiration and the Ascent of Sap in Plants,* a comprehensive monograph bringing together theories and experimental work on the subject in a well-argued account. The transpiration stream is raised either by secretory actions in leaf cells, using energy from respiration in the leaves, or by evaporation from the surfaces of leaves, according to the degree of saturation of surrounding cells. The osmotic pressure of turgid mesophyll cells, calculated from cryoscopic measurements of the freezing point of sap, was shown to be enough to raise sap by tension in even the highest tree, through passive vessels, not living cells.

During World War I, Dixon worked on the micro-scopic identification of different kinds of mahogany. Later he returned to problems of transport of organic substances in the phloem, variation in the permeability of leaf cells, and the mechanisms of transpiration. He wrote a textbook on practical plant biology in 1922 and gave three lectures on the transpiration stream at the University of London in 1924. Some of his manuscript notebooks are held at Trinity College, Dublin.

BIBLIOGRAPHY

I. ORIGINAL WORKS. The classic paper "On the Ascent of Sap," written with J. Joly, was recorded in abstract in *Proceedings of the Royal Society,* **57B** (1894), 3–5, and published in full in *Philosophical Transactions of the Royal Society,* **186B** (1895), 563–576. The standard account of the theory was published as "Transpiration and the Ascent of Sap," in *Progressus rei botanicae,* **3** (1909), 1–66, reprinted in abbreviated form in *Report of the Board of Regents of the Smithsonian Institution, 1910* (1911), 407–425. The work on transpiration was brought together in *Transpiration and the Ascent of Sap in Plants* (London, 1914). The other two volumes published by Dixon are *Practical Plant Biology* (London, 1922; 2nd ed., Dublin, 1943); and *The Transpiration Stream* (London, 1924).

II. SECONDARY LITERATURE. Two assessments of Dixon's scientific importance are by W. R. G. Atkins, who worked with him on the cryoscopy of sap, in *Obituary Notices of Fellows of the Royal Society of London,* **9** (1954), 79–93, with portrait and comprehensive bibliography of Dixon's works; and by T. A. Bennet-Clark, in *Nature,* **173** (1954), 239.

DIANA M. SIMPKINS

DIXON, JEREMIAH (*b.* Bishop Auckland, Durham, England, 27 July 1733; *d.* Cockfield, Durham, England, 22 January 1779), *astronomy.*

The fifth child of George Dixon, a well-to-do Quaker, Dixon was educated at John Kipling's school at Barnard Castle, where he displayed interest in mathematics and astronomy. An acquaintance with John Bird, an instrument maker in London and a native of Bishop Auckland, led to Dixon's appointment as assistant to Charles Mason, whom the Royal Society proposed to send to Sumatra to observe the transit of Venus on 6 June 1761. An encounter with a French man-of-war prevented the party from reaching Bencoolen; they observed the transit instead at the Cape of Good Hope, taking so many other measurements that the astronomer royal declared a few years later: "It is probable that the situation of few places is better known."

In 1763 Mason and Dixon were employed to survey the long-disputed boundary between Pennsylvania and Maryland. They were engaged in the delicate and laborious task for nearly five years, hiring local surveyors to assist in observations and calculations and local laborers to cut "vistoes" and set boundary stones. At Dixon's suggestion, and with the approval of the Royal Society, the surveyors calculated the length of a degree of latitude (363,763 feet, or 470 less than the currently accepted figure). The Mason and Dixon survey put a stop at once to quarrels between the two colonies; in political and social significance the line became and remains the most famous boundary in the United States. Dixon was elected a member of the American Society for Promoting Useful Knowledge (later merged with the American Philosophical Society) in 1768.

He was hardly home when the Royal Society sent him—without Mason—to Hammerfest to observe another transit of Venus on 3 June 1769. While there he prepared "A Chart of the Sea Coast and Islands near the North Cape of Europe." Thereafter Dixon lived comfortably at Cockfield, only occasionally resuming his profession. He never married.

BIBLIOGRAPHY

I. ORIGINAL WORKS. Reports from Dixon's three expeditions are in *Philosophical Transactions of the Royal Society,* **52** (1762), 378–394; **58** (1768), 274–323; and **59** (1769), 253–261. The journal of Mason and Dixon in America, 1763–1768, has been edited from the original manuscript in the National Archives, Washington, by A. Hughlett Mason, in *Memoirs of the American Philosophical Society,* **76** (1969).

II. SECONDARY LITERATURE. See H. W. Robinson, "Jeremiah Dixon (1733–1779)—A Biographical Note," in *Proceedings of the American Philosophical Society,* **94** (1950), 272–274; *Report on the Resurvey of the Maryland-Pennsylvania Boundary Part of the Mason and Dixon Line,* Maryland Geological Survey, vol. VII (1908); and Harry Woolf, *The Transits of Venus* (Princeton, 1959), pp. 84–93.

WHITFIELD J. BELL, JR.

DOBELL, CECIL CLIFFORD (*b.* Birkenhead, England, 22 February 1886; *d.* London, England, 23 December 1949), *protozoology.*

Dobell is best-known for his meticulous researches on human intestinal protozoa and for a remarkable monograph on the pioneer microscopist Leeuwenhoek. He was the eldest son and the second of five children of William Blount Dobell, a Birkenhead coal merchant, and his wife, Agnes Thornely. Clifford never used his first Christian name. Owing to his father's unstable business fortunes, his early education was erratic and informal. At thirteen Dobell went to Sandringham School, Southport, as an unhappy boarder. There he headed his class, developed lasting tastes for classical literature and music, and showed talent for art and biological science. Helped by his headmaster, he entered Trinity College, Cambridge, in 1903. He completed one year of medical studies before his tutor, the zoologist Adam Sedgwick, directed his interests toward protozoology. Obtaining his B.A. degree in the natural sciences tripos with first-class honors in 1906, Dobell took the M.A. in 1910 but disdained the Sc.D. until 1942.

He left Cambridge in 1907 to study at Munich under Richard Hertwig and proceeded thence to the zoological station in Naples, where he began investigating the life history and chromosome cycle of the *Aggregata* of cuttlefish and crabs, on which he published an important monograph in 1925. Returning to Cambridge, he was elected a fellow of Trinity College (1908–1914) and won the Rolleston Prize and the Walsingham Medal for original research in biology. He was also awarded the Balfour Studentship, which enabled him to study parasitic protozoa at Colombo, Ceylon. In 1910 Dobell became lecturer in protistology and cytology at the Imperial College of Science and Technology, London. Moving to the Wellcome Bureau of Scientific Research in 1915, he studied amoebic dysentery for the War Office and directed courses in the diagnosis of intestinal protozoal infections. He was elected a fellow of the Royal Society in 1918. The following year Dobell published his classic monograph, *The Amoebae Living in Man,* and was appointed protistologist to the Medical Research Council. He held this position at the National Institute for Medical Research, Hampstead, until death from cerebral hemorrhage in his sixty-fourth year prevented the retirement he dreaded.

Dobell's fastidious tastes and exacting standards limited the scope but not the depth of his interests and accomplishments. Impatient with inaccuracy and scornful of pretentiousness, he was unpopular for his critical tongue, aloof demeanor, and patrician mien; but he was warmhearted within a restricted circle of friends whom he unstintingly admired, such as Adam Sedgwick, D'Arcy Thompson, and David Bruce. In 1937 Dobell married William Bulloch's stepdaughter, Monica Baker. Their happy relationship relieved the lonely, incessant labors of his last twelve years.

Dobell was a self-demanding perfectionist whose tireless industry, stringent observations, and independent conclusions became legendary. He brooked no technical assistants and abhorred teamwork, made personal pets of his experimental *Macaca* monkeys, and carefully infected himself with all manner of intestinal protozoa. These attributes bore special fruit in the sustained researches, begun in 1928 and nearly completed at his death, which elucidated the *in vitro* life histories and the cross-infectivity of practically all known species of human and simian intestinal amoebae. Many of his publications revealed discriminating scholarship in the history of science. His greatest labor of love was the biographical masterpiece *Antony van Leeuwenhoek and His "Little Animals"* (1932). Dobell had to learn seventeenth-century Dutch to decipher and translate his hero's quaint epistles to the Royal Society. This work will probably outlive recollections of his many contributions to experimental biology and medicine.

BIBLIOGRAPHY

I. ORIGINAL WORKS. The most complete bibliography of Dobell's works (121 items, including four posthumous papers) is provided with the obituary by Doris L. Mackinnon and C. A. Hoare (see below). Among his more outstanding publications, many of them lengthy and illustrated with his own beautifully precise drawings, are "The Structure and Life-History of *Copromonas subtilis,* nov. gen. et nov. spec.: A Contribution to Our Knowledge of the Flagellata," in *Quarterly Journal of Microscopical Science,* **52** (1908), 75–120; "Researches on the Intestinal Protozoa of Frogs and Toads," *ibid.,* **53** (1909), 201–277; "On the So-called 'Sexual' Method of Spore Formation in the Disporic Bacteria," *ibid.,* 579–596; "Contributions to the Cytology of the Bacteria," *ibid.,* **56** (1911), 395–506; "A Commentary on the Genetics of the Ciliate Protozoa," in *Journal of Genetics,* **4** (1914), 131–190; "The Chromosome Cycle in Coccidia and Gregarines," in *Proceedings of the Royal Society,* **89B** (1915), 83–94; "On the Three Common Intestinal *Entamoebae* of Man, and Their Differential Diagnosis," in *British Medical Journal* (1917), **1**, 607–612, written with Margaret W. Jepps; "Experiments on the Therapeutics of Amoebic Dysentery," in *Journal of Pharmacology,* **10** (1917), 399–459, written with H. H. Dale; *A Study of 1,300 Convalescent Cases of Dysentery From Home Hospitals: With Special Reference to the Incidence and Treatment of Amoebic Dysentery Carriers,* Special Report Series, Medical Research Committee, no. 15 (London, 1918), 1–28, written with H. S. Gettings, M. W. Jepps, and J. B. Stephens; "A Revision of the Coccidia Parasitic in Man," in *Parasitology,* **11** (1919), 147–197; *The Amoebae Living in Man. A Zoological Monograph* (London, 1919); *The Intestinal Protozoa of Man* (London, 1921), written with F. W. O'Connor; *A Report on the Occurrence of Intestinal Protozoa in the Inhabitants of Britain, With Special Reference to Entamoeba histolytica,* Special Report Series, Medical Research Council, no. 59 (London, 1921), 1–71, with contributions by A. H. Campbell, T. Goodey, R. C. McLean, Muriel M. Nutt, and A. G. Thacker; "The Life History and Chromosome Cycle of *Aggregata eberthi* (Protozoa: Sporozoa: Coccidia)," in *Parasitology,* **17** (1925), 1–136; "On the Cultivation of *Entamoeba histolytica* and Some Other Entozoic Amoebae," *ibid.,* **18** (1926), 283–318,

written with P. P. Laidlaw; and "Researches on the Intestinal Protozoa of Monkeys and Man. I. General Introduction, and II. Description of the Whole Life-History of *Entamoeba histolytica* in Cultures," *ibid.,* **20** (1928), 357–404. This last item was the first in a series of twelve reports on his researches on the intestinal protozoa of monkeys and man that appeared in *Parasitology.* The last to be completed by Dobell himself was "XI. The Cytology and Life-History of *Endolimax nana,*" *ibid.,* **35** (1943), 134–158. R. A. Neal completed and C. A. Hoare edited a final report from Dobell's notes, and they published it posthumously in his name: "XII. Bacterial Factors Influencing the Life History of *Entamoeba histolytica* in Cultures," *ibid.,* **42** (1952), 16–39.

Dobell's historical writings include tributes to Louis Joblot, C. G. Ehrenberg, T. R. Lewis, and Otto Bütschli. Among several obituaries by him the most notable are "Michał Siedlecki (1873–1940). A Founder of Modern Knowledge of the Sporozoa," in *Parasitology,* **33** (1941), 1–7; and "D'Arcy Wentworth Thompson (1860–1948)," in *Obituary Notices of Fellows of the Royal Society,* **6** (1949), 599–617. His biographical magnum opus was *Antony van Leeuwenhoek and His "Little Animals": Being Some Account of the Father of Protozoology & Bacteriology and His Multifarious Discoveries in These Disciplines* (London, 1932; repr., New York, 1958: paperback ed., New York, 1962).

II. SECONDARY LITERATURE. Obituaries include G. H. Ball, "Clifford Dobell, F.R.S.: 1886–1949," in *Science,* **112** (1950), 294; C. A. Hoare, "Clifford Dobell, M.A., Sc.D., F.R.S.," in *British Medical Journal* (1950), **1**, 129–130; C. A. Hoare and D. L. Mackinnon, "Clifford Dobell (1886–1949)," in *Obituary Notices of Fellows of the Royal Society,* **7** (1950), 35–61; Doris L. Mackinnon and Cecil A. Hoare, "Clifford Dobell (1886–1949), In Memoriam," in *Parasitology,* **42** (1952), 1–15; W. H. van Seters, "In Memoriam: Dr. Clifford Dobell, F.R.S. (1886–1949)," in *Nederlandsch Tijdschrift voor Geneeskunde,* **94** (1950), 1274–1276; and H. E. Shortt, "Dr. Clifford Dobell, F.R.S.," in *Nature,* **165** (1950), 219.

Other references to Dobell's work and character are in C. E. Dolman, "Tidbits of Bacteriological History," in *Canadian Journal of Public Health,* **53** (1962), 269–278; and in Paul de Kruif, *A Sweeping Wind* (New York, 1962), pp. 104–106, 111–113.

CLAUDE E. DOLMAN

DÖBEREINER, JOHANN WOLFGANG (*b.* Hof an der Saale, Germany, 13 December 1780; *d.* Jena, Germany, 24 March 1849), *chemistry.*

Döbereiner was the son of Johann Adam Döbereiner, a farm worker who rose to become an estate manager, and Johanna Susanna Göring. He was self-educated, although his mother supervised his early instruction and in 1784 apprenticed him to an apothecary named Lutz. After three years' service with Lutz, Döbereiner made his journeyman's travels through Germany for five years; then he returned to Hof, married Clara Knab, and started a small business manufacturing white lead, sugar of lead, and other pigments and drugs. Almost simultaneously he began publishing articles on these chemicals in the *Neues Berliner Jahrbüch für die Pharmazie,* of which Adolph Ferdinand Gehlen was editor. Döbereiner's business thrived for a few years, but then declined because of personal intrigue and the Napoleonic Wars.

Döbereiner was almost destitute when he was invited to teach at the technical college of the University of Jena, on the recommendation of Gehlen. He became associate professor of chemistry and pharmacy there in August 1810 and in November of that year received the enabling doctorate. Grand Duke Carl August of Saxony-Weimar, the principal patron of the school, may have expected to turn Döbereiner's work to commercial profit, although Goethe, the chief administrator of the Academy and a close friend of Döbereiner, probably had more purely scientific motives in confirming his appointment.

Some of Döbereiner's work at Jena was indeed practical in design. In 1812 he was engaged in the conversion of starch into sugar by Kirchhoff's process, and at a slightly later date he made experiments with illuminating gas (the grand duke had admired gas lighting during a visit to England in 1814). Döbereiner gave up the latter experiments in 1816, however, following an explosion. He also gave a series of lectures on practical chemistry to a group of technicians, and taught special courses for economists and administrators.

Döbereiner made further experiments with spongy platinum, which he prepared by decomposing platinum salts in solution or by exposing them to direct heat. (The grand duke supported him in his work by generous gifts of the precious metal, obtained from his connections in Russia.) He constructed a pneumatic gas lighter (*Platinfeuerzeug*) which consisted of a hydrogenation device that brought hydrogen to impinge on the finely divided platinum; the ensuing oxidation then brought the metal to white heat. In 1828 Döbereiner wrote that about 20,000 of these lighters were in use in Germany and England but, since he had not taken out a patent, they brought him little profit; he added, "I love science more than money."

In addition to his work with the oxides and complex salts of platinum, Döbereiner investigated that form of the metal that Liebig called "platinum black." He studied the role of this material in the process of oxidation of sulfur dioxide and alcohol and proposed its use to manufacture acetic acid from the latter. He decomposed an alloy of raw platinum black and zinc

with dilute acid and found a black powder that contained platinum, palladium, iridium, ruthenium, and osmium; this black powder was even more intensely reactive in air with acids and alcohols than its parent metal—in a dilute acid it easily oxidized its osmium (which could then be sublimated); and it exploded in a shower of sparks when brought into contact with direct heat in air.

Döbereiner was also involved in stoichiometric studies—for which he suggested the use of simple galvanic cells before Faraday—and wrote a book on the subject in 1816. He studied the action of pyrolusite as a catalyst in the production of oxygen from potassium chlorate and developed a method to separate calcium and magnesium by the use of ammonium oxalate or carbonate in the presence of ammonium chloride.

Döbereiner's chief contribution to chemistry, however, was the result of his examination of the weights of the chemical elements—work which aided in the development of Mendeleev's periodic table of all the known elements. Döbereiner's interest in the relationship of elements to each other began as early as 1817; he based his early studies on analogies within certain groups of elements. He found, for example, that the equivalent weight of strontium is almost exactly equal to the mean weight of calcium and barium, and went on to investigate other such triads in alkalies and halogens. (The first members of a group cannot be fitted into such triads; Döbereiner pointed out in 1829 that fluorine and magnesium stand apart.) He further examined such systems of triads in light of other of their qualities—especially specific gravity and affinity—and found, for instance, that the specific gravity (as well as the atomic weight) of selenium is equal to the mean specific gravity (as well as the mean weight) of sulfur and tellurium. He further found that the intensity of chemical affinity decreases in proportion to increased atomic weight of the salt-forming elements in the triads chlorine-bromine-iodine and sulfur-selenium-tellurium but that it increases with atomic weight of the alkali-forming elements in the triads lithium-sodium-potassium and calcium-strontium-barium.

Döbereiner was less successful in formulating rules for the oxides of what he called "heavy metal alumforming substances." He hoped to codify these by "a rigorous experimental revision of the specific gravities and atomic weights," but found the principle of grouping into triads doubtful for iron-manganese-cobalt and nickel-copper-zinc (although lead did seem to represent the proper mean for silver and mercury).

Because of his involvement in practical problems (among others, he was concerned with the fermentation of alcohol and developed methods for improving wine, although he did not publish them in any detail) and because of his heavy and diversified teaching schedule, Döbereiner neglected further development of his work on triads. His merit was civilly rewarded, however, when he was made privy councillor and awarded the Cross of the White Falcon.

BIBLIOGRAPHY

I. ORIGINAL WORKS. Döbereiner's writings include *Lehrbuch der allgemeinen Chemie* (Jena, 1811); *Zur Gährungschemie und Anleitung zur Darstellung verschiedener Arten künstlicher Weine, Biere, usw.* (Jena, 1822, 1844); *Chemie für das praktische Leben* (Jena, 1824–1825); "Vermischte chemische Erfahrungen über Platin, Gährungschemie, usw. Ein Schreiben an die Herren Kastner und Schweigger," in *Journal für Chemie und Physik,* **54** (1828), 412–426; "Gruppierung der Elemente," in *Annalen der Physik,* **15** (1829), 301–307; and *Zur Chemie des Platins in wissenschaftlicher und technischer Beziehung. . .* (Stuttgart, 1836).

II. SECONDARY LITERATURE. Wilhelm Prandtl, *Deutsche Chemiker in der ersten Hälfte des neunzehnten Jahrhunderts* (Weinheim, 1956), pp. 37–78. Döbereiner's publication on the triads was reprinted as no. 66 in Ostwald's Klassiker and was translated in H. M. Leicester and H. S. Klickstein, *Source Book in Chemistry 1400–1900* (New York, 1952).

EDUARD FARBER

DODART, DENIS (*b.* Paris, France, 1634; *d.* Paris, 5 November 1707), *botany, physiology.*

Dodart was the son of Jean Dodart, a notary public who loved belles lettres, and of Marie Dubois, a lawyer's daughter. The family was upper middle class, and through his parents' efforts he received a particularly broad and thorough education. After studying medicine he graduated *docteur régent* from the Faculty of Medicine in Paris on 16 October 1660. Even as a student Dodart so distinguished himself by his learning, his eloquence, and his agreeable nature that Gui Patin, the dean of the Faculty of Medicine and a habitually very severe critic, called him, in a letter to a friend, "one of the wisest and most learned men of this century."

In 1666 Dodart became a professor at the School of Pharmacy in Paris. A well-known practitioner, he was first in the service of the duchess of Longueville and then was physician to the house of Conti. A pious man, Dodart spent much of his time helping the poor, both medically and financially. He was sympathetic to Jansenism and became a close friend of Jean Hamon, a monk-doctor, whom he attended at death and whom he succeeded as doctor at Port-Royal.

Dodart had the title, but did not perform the functions, of physician-adviser to the king. Louis XIV disliked Dodart's connections with Port-Royal, but he yielded to Colbert's appeal that he make Dodart a member of the Academy and to that of Mme. de Maintenon that he give Dodart a place at the court (1698) and named him physician at St. Cyr.

Most of Dodart's scientific activity took place within the framework of the Academy of Sciences, of which he became a member (botanist) in 1673. The Perrault brothers regarded Dodart as a man capable of directing the ambitious *Histoire des plantes,* a project which the Academy had proposed as one of the goals of its research since its founding. In 1676 Dodart published *Mémoires pour servir à l'Histoire des plantes,* a preliminary study and an announcement of a large collective work that never appeared. The *Mémoires* contains a methodological introduction and a model showing how to conduct botanical research. Because of Dodart's recommendation of phytochemical analysis, this work marks a new step in botany.

When the Academy of Sciences was reorganized, Dodart was among the first group of *titulaires* named directly by Louis XIV; on 28 January 1699 he was given the title of pensioner-botanist. He justified this nomination by the publication, in 1700, of studies of the influence of gravitation on development of roots and stems and on the fertilization and reproduction of plants. Dodart was an advocate of the theory of encasement or *emboîtement* of seeds, and he strove tirelessly to apply in botany the embryological ideas of N. Andry and other preformationists. He further described several new species of plants; and Tournefort named the genus *Dodartia* for him.

Botany was not the only field in which Dodart excelled. In 1678 he presented to the Academy an important memoir by La Salle "on certain details of the natural history of North America, particularly of the Iroquois territory." He published a good description of ergotism (1676) and several anatomical-pathological and embryological observations; three memoirs on phonation appeared between 1700 and 1707.

Dodart was the first since Aristotle and Galen to present new ideas on the mechanism of phonation. He nursed the idea of writing a history of medicine; but when Daniel Leclerc published one first, he abandoned this project for a history of music. Studies on the human voice and on the nature of tones were to serve as an introduction to this history. Credit must be given to Dodart for pointing out the fundamental role of the vocal cords in phonation. In opposition to the classic theory, which considered the larynx a type of flute, Dodart stated that "the glottis alone makes the voice and all the tones . . .; no wind instrument can explain its functioning . . .; the entire effect of the glottis on the tones depends on the tension of its lips and its various openings."

Finally, Dodart was, with Perrault, one of the few French physicians of the seventeenth century to understand and properly appreciate the experiments and the theories of the Italian iatromechanics. He performed on himself the "static" (i.e., performed with a balance) experiments of S. Santorio, measuring the changes in weight of his body and in particular the quantity of imperceptible perspiration. He demonstrated that perspiration gradually decreases as one grows older and also noted, for example, how much the strictest Lenten fast may decrease weight and how much time is needed to regain this lost weight. As an advocate of mechanical explanations of vital phenomena, Dodart saw in them a proof of the existence of God. His religious convictions found noble expression in his will (an autograph of which is in the archives of the Academy of Sciences in Paris).

Dodart had one son, Claude-Jean-Baptiste (1664–1730), who was chief physician to Louis XV, and one grandson, Denis le Jeune, who was *maître des requêtes* and *intendant*.

BIBLIOGRAPHY

I. ORIGINAL WORKS. Dodart's main work is *Mémoires pour servir à l'Histoire des plantes* (Paris, 1676), which was divided into "Projet de l'Histoire des plantes" and "Description de quelques plantes nouvelles," the latter illustrated with magnificent plates by Abraham Bosse, Nicolas Robert, and L. de Chatillon. A second edition of the "Projet" appeared in 1679.

Dodart published several articles in the *Mémoires de l'Académie royale des sciences:* "Lettre sur le seigle ergoté" (1676), 562; "Sur l'affectation de la perpendiculaire, remarquable dans toutes les tiges" (1700), 47; "Mémoire sur les causes de la voix de l'homme, et de ses différens tons" (1700), 238–287; "Sur la multiplication des corps vivants considérée dans la fécondité des plantes" (1700), 136–160; "Second mémoire sur la fécondité des plantes" (1701), 241–257; and "Supplément au mémoire sur la voix et sur les tons" (1706), 136–148, 388–410; (1707), 66–81.

His physiological experiments on nutrition and on imperceptible transpiration were published posthumously by P. Noguez as *Medicina statica Gallica* (Paris, 1725).

II. SECONDARY LITERATURE. The basic biographical source remains B. de Fontenelle, "Éloge de M. Dodart," in *Histoire de l'Académie royale des sciences pour l'année 1707* (Paris, 1708), pp. 182–192. The text of his will was published in *Chronique médicale,* **5** (1898), 742–750.

Remarks on his character are in letters by Gui Patin, *Lettres,* J. H. Reveillé-Parise, ed. (Paris, 1846), III, 231, 277, 293; and in the *éloge* of Dodart's son written by Saint-Simon. Biographical notices include the following (listed chronologically): N. F. J. Eloy, "Dodart," in *Dictionnaire historique de la médecine,* II (Mons, 1778), 64–65; J. A. Hazon, *Notice des hommes les plus célèbres de la Faculté de médecine de l'Université de Paris* (Paris, 1778), pp. 135–138; G. Nomdedeu, *Les médecins de Port-Royal* (Bordeaux, 1931); and Roman d'Amat, "Dodart," in *Dictionnaire de biographie française,* XI (Paris, 1967), cols. 417–418. His work in botany is discussed in Y. Laissus and A. M. Monseigny, "Les plantes du roi," in *Revue d'histoire des sciences,* **22** (1969), 193–236.

M. D. GRMEK

DODGSON, CHARLES LUTWIDGE (*b.* Daresbury, Cheshire, England, 27 January 1832; *d.* Guildford, Surrey, England, 14 January 1898), *mathematics, logic.*

Dodgson was the thirdborn of the eleven offspring of Charles Dodgson, a clergyman, and his wife and cousin, the former Frances Jane Lutwidge. All the children stuttered, and Charles Lutwidge himself is said to have spoken without impediment only to the countless nymphets whom, over decades of adulthood, he befriended, wrote wonderful letters to, entertained, and photographed (often nude) with considerable artistry. The obvious inference from this attraction to young girls seems invalid, for he was strongly undersexed. (Even in the Victorian milieu his puritanism was barely credible: for instance, he nursed a project to bowdlerize Bowdler's Shakespeare, and he demanded assurance from one of his illustrators that none of the work would be done on Sundays.) He was never wholly at ease in the company of grown-ups. Friendship with the three small daughters of Dean Liddell resulted in the celebrated *Alice* books, published under a pseudonym that he had first used in 1856 as a writer of light verse—Lewis Carroll. *Alice* brought him fame, money, and the posthumous honor of becoming the most-quoted litterateur in English discursive scientific writing of the twentieth century.

In our concern here with Dodgson's professional achievements, we must bear in mind that his vocational mathematics and his avocational nonsense commingle in a vein of logic that was his salient characteristic as a thinker. For years it was fashionable to point to the gap between mathematics and ingenious nonsense (and the other nineteenth-century master of nonsense, Edward Lear, was most unmathematical); but today we are aware that, at least in some places, the gap is not that wide. The modern view, that Dodgson was all of a piece, is simpler to sustain. His analytical mind is reflected everywhere in his writings, whose quaintness by no means damages clarity. The pity is that his talents were inhibited by ignorance and introversion, for he made no attempt to keep abreast of contemporary advances in mathematics and logic or to discuss his ideas with other academics.

Dodgson's pedestrian career unfolded without hitch. Graduated from Oxford in 1854, he became master of arts there three years later. Meanwhile, in 1855, he had been appointed lecturer in mathematics at his alma mater, Christ Church College, Oxford. In 1861 he was ordained in the Church of England, although he was never to perform any ecclesiastic duties. As a young man he made a trip to Russia, but later journeyings were restricted to London and quiet seaside vacations. Marriage was unthought of, and Dodgson entered into no close friendships. (Perhaps his acquaintanceship with Ellen Terry, the great actress, most nearly qualified for "close friendship.") He took some part in the administration of his college and was proud of his finicky management of its wine cellars. A part-time inventor of trivia, he devised several aids to writing in the dark—to assuage his chronic insomnia and to help dispel the nameless "unholy thoughts" that occasionally pestered him. But generally speaking his placidity was so well rooted that he was able to make the extraordinary statement, "My life is free from all trial and trouble."

As a lecturer Dodgson was drear; and when he gave up the chore, he noted ruefully that his first lecture had been attended by nine students and his last (twenty-five years later) by two. Away from the classroom he wrote assiduously; and his publications, in book form or pamphlet (a favorite medium), are respectably numerous. His scholarly output falls into four main groups; determinants, geometry, the mathematics of tournaments and elections, and recreational logic. He was modest enough to describe his activities as being "chiefly in the lower branches of Mathematics."

Dodgson's work on determinants opened with a paper in the *Proceedings of the Royal Society* for 1866, and this was expanded into a book that appeared the following year. *An Elementary Treatise on Determinants* is good exposition, but favorable reception was prevented by the author's extensive use of ad hoc terms and symbols.

Dodgson's writings on geometry became well known; it was a subject about which he was almost passionate. His initial contribution was *A Syllabus of Plane Algebraic Geometry* (1860), a textbook whose purpose was to develop analytic geometry along rigorous Euclidean lines. He also published pamphlets on this and related themes, in one of which he introduced an original but not particularly meritorious notation for the trigonometric ratios. His most inter-

esting effort in this genre was a five-act comedy entitled *Euclid and His Modern Rivals,* about a mathematics lecturer, Minos, in whose dreams Euclid debates his original *Elements* with such modernizers as Legendre and J. M. Wilson and, naturally, routs the opposition. The book is an attack on the changing method of teaching classical geometry and not, as is sometimes assumed, on non-Euclidean geometry. Indeed, Dodgson showed himself keenly aware of the infirmity of the fifth postulate (on parallels), and he has his oneiric Euclid admit that "some mysterious flaw lies at the root of the subject." The interesting point here is that Riemann's revolutionary geometry was well established during Dodgson's lifetime, and an English translation of the key paper was available. This is yet another instance of Dodgson's being out of touch with the mathematical research of his day. The Euclid drama (which is most engagingly written) apparently was used as ancillary reading in English schools for a number of years.

Least known but quite praiseworthy is Dodgson's work on tournaments and voting theory. His interest stemmed from two sources: the organization of tennis tournaments and the mechanism of arriving at fair decisions by administrative committees. He decided that both matters needed rethinking. As usual, he did not bother to check the literature and so was unaware that the topic had come in for learned discussion in France before and during the Revolution. However, Dodgson unwittingly improved on existing ideas. His initial publication (a pamphlet, in 1873) reviews different methods of arriving at a fair majority opinion, and he sensibly advocates the use of degrees of preference in voting schedules. His whole approach is fresh and thoughtful, and he was the first to use matrix notation in the handling of multiple decisions.

In contrast with his mathematics, Dodgson's work on logic was written entirely under his pseudonym, which clearly testifies to his view that the subject was essentially recreational. Traditional formal logic had long been a barren and overrated discipline; but during his lifetime a renaissance in technique and significance was taking place, and most of the pioneers were his countrymen. Although he was not ignorant of the new trends, their importance either escaped him or was discountenanced. Dodgson was attracted by the contemporary interest in the diagrammatization of the logic of classes, and he had read and appreciated Venn's seminal contributions. In fact, he modified Venn diagrams by making their boundaries linear and by introducing colored counters that could be moved around to signify class contents—a very simple and effective device. On these foundations Dodgson published a game of logic that featured various forms (some very amusing) of the syllogism. His casual realization of the connections between symbolic logic and mathematics might have become vivid and fruitful had he been properly acquainted with what had already been done in the area. But he did not do the necessary reading—there is, for instance, no indication that he had read Boole's *Laws of Thought,* although he owned a copy! Finally, Dodgson was a prolific composer of innocent-looking problems in logic and paradox, some of which were to engage the attention of professional logicians until well into the twentieth century.

BIBLIOGRAPHY

I. ORIGINAL WORKS. The authoritative conspectus of Dodgson's writings, which included sixteen books (six for children) and hundreds of other items, is S. H. Williams and F. Madan, *A Handbook of the Literature of the Rev. C. L. Dodgson* (*Lewis Carroll*) (London, 1931; supp., 1935). Two outstanding books are *An Elementary Treatise on Determinants* (London, 1867) and *Euclid and His Modern Rivals* (London, 1879). His initial publication on election theory, *A Discussion of the Various Procedures in Conducting Elections* (Oxford, 1873), is a rare pamphlet, only one copy being known; it is at Princeton. The Morris L. Parrish Collection of Victorian Novelists, in Princeton University library, contains the biggest mass of Dodgsoniana, much of it MS. Warren Weaver, in *Proceedings of the American Philosophical Society,* **98** (1954), 377–381, tells the history of this collection and gives some examples of its mathematical items. Dodgson's two books on recreational mathematics are now available in a 1-vol. paperback: *Pillow Problems and a Tangled Tale* (New York, 1958). Similarly, his two books on logic are bound together in the paperback *Symbolic Logic, and the Game of Logic* (New York, 1958).

II. SECONDARY LITERATURE. Dodgson's nephew, S. D. Collingwood, published the first biography, in the same year as his subject's death: *The Life and Letters of Lewis Carroll* (London, 1898). It remains a primary source book. Among many subsequent biographies and evaluations, Florence Becker Lennon's *Victoria Through the Looking Glass* (New York, 1945), esp. ch. 15, is notable for its perceptive treatment of Dodgson's serious side. R. L. Green, *The Diaries of Lewis Carroll* (London, 1953), is important, although many of the entries on logic and mathematics have been excised or glossed over. Two papers prepared for the centenary of Dodgson's birth are essential reading: R. B. Braithwaite, "Lewis Carroll as Logician," in *Mathematical Gazette,* **16** (1932), 174–178; and D. B. Eperson, "Lewis Carroll—Mathematician," *ibid.,* **17** (1933), 92–100. His work on tournaments and elections is examined in Duncan Black's *The Theory of Committees and Elections* (Cambridge, 1958). Martin Gardner's *New Mathematical Diversions* (New York, 1966), ch. 4, deals with Dodgson's work on games and puzzles. The same author's earlier books, *The Annotated Alice* (New York, 1960) and *The*

Annotated Snark (New York, 1962), provide remarkable insights into the logico-mathematical undercurrents in Dodgson's fantasia.

NORMAN T. GRIDGEMAN

DODOENS (DODONAEUS), REMBERT (*b.* Mechelen, Netherlands [now Malines, Belgium], 29 June 1516; *d.* Leiden, Netherlands, 10 March 1585), *medicine, botany.*

Dodoens' real name was Rembert van Joenckema. He changed it to Dodoens ("son of Dodo"), Dodo being a form of the first name of his father, Denis Van Joenckema, who came from Friesland to Mechelen at the end of the fifteenth century. (The name was latinized into Dodonaeus, from which the French, who were ignorant of its origins, further transformed it into Dodonée.) The year of Dodoens' birth is generally considered to be 1517, although according to Hunger (1923) 1516 is correct. He was married twice (his wives were Catelyne 'sBruijnen and Marie Saerine) and had five children.

Dodoens studied at the municipal college of Mechelen and went from there to the University of Louvain, where he studied medicine under Arnold Noot, Leonard Willemaer, Jean Heems, and Paul Roels. He graduated as licenciate in medicine in 1535. According to the custom of the time, Dodoens then traveled extensively. Between 1535 and 1546 he was in Italy, Germany, and France, where he visited—among others—Gunther of Andernach in Paris. After these *Wanderjahren* he returned to Mechelen.

In 1548 Dodoens published a book on cosmography. In the same year he became one of the three municipal physicians of Mechelen, the other two being Joachim Roelandts (to whom Vesalius wrote his famous letter on the chinaroot) and Jacob De Moor. During this time Dodoens composed a treatise on physiology (published later) and began his botanical works.

In the beginning of the sixteenth century, it was still believed that no plants existed other than those described by Dioscorides in his *Materia medica* of the first century A.D. The great progress of natural sciences in the sixteenth century was helped by the discovery of printing and by the use of wood-block illustrations. In 1530 the *Herbarum* of Otto Brunfels appeared, followed by those of the men Sprengel called (in addition to Brunfels) the "German fathers of botany," Jerome Bock (1539) and Leonhard Fuchs (1542). Dodoens was their follower.

Dodoens' first botanical work—a short treatise on cereals, vegetables, and fodders, *De frugum historia* (1552)—was followed by an extensive herbarium (1554). In 1553 he published a collection of wood-plates with a vocabulary for the use of medical students. Some of the wood-block illustrations were taken from Fuchs's earlier herbarium. In 1554, Dodoens also published, as *Cruydeboek,* a Dutch version of his *De stirpium historia.* This was a national herbarium devoted to species indigenous to the Flemish provinces. The merit of this book was that rather than proceeding by alphabetical order, as Fuchs had done, Dodoens grouped the plants according to their properties and their reciprocal affinities. These earlier works show a tendency toward medical botany; in a later period Dodoens became more inclined toward a more scientific treatment.

In 1557 negotiations were begun in an effort to persuade Dodoens to accept a chair of medicine in Louvain; they were not successful. In 1574 he left Mechelen for Vienna, where he had been appointed physician to the emperor Maximilian II. He remained there in the same capacity in service of Maximilian's successor, Rudolph II. In Vienna, Dodoens met Charles de l'Écluse (Clusius).

In 1580, wishing to return to his native country, Dodoens left Vienna, but the uncertain conditions prevalent in the Low Countries at that time persuaded him to stop for a year in Cologne. There he published in one volume a dissertation on wine and medical observations (1580; these two texts were later reprinted separately) and synoptic tables on physiology (1581). From Cologne he went to Antwerp, where in 1582 he supervised his friend Plantin's printing of his *Stirpium historiae pemptades sex sive libri XXX* (published in full in 1583 and reprinted posthumously in 1616). In this elaborate treatise, Dodoens' most important scientific work, he divided plants into twenty-six groups and introduced many new families, adding a wealth of illustration either original or borrowed from Dioscorides, de l'Écluse, or De Lobel.

In 1582 Dodoens accepted an offer from Leiden University, to which the curators had invited him for the purpose of enhancing the reputation of the Faculty of Medicine by his appointment. He was offered the high salary of 400 florins, with an additional gift of 100 florins and a travel allowance of 50 florins. The conditions of his appointment required his promise not to take part in religious controversies and to limit his activities to scientific questions.

At Leiden, Dodoens was in charge of the lectures on pathology and general therapeutics; there was then no course on botany at Leiden, and the famous botanical garden was not created until 1587. Dodoens remained in Leiden until his death and was buried there in St. Peter's church. Although he was a renowned physician in his time (first as a Galenist and later as a Hippocratian, as shown by his posthumous *Praxis medica*), his great fame remains based on his botanical work.

BIBLIOGRAPHY

I. ORIGINAL WORKS. Dodoens' writings are *Cosmographica in astronomiam et geographiam Isagoge* (Antwerp, 1548), of which a second edition is *De sphaera sive de astronomiae et geographiae principiis cosmographica isagoge* (Antwerp–Leiden, 1584); *De frugum historia, liber unus. Ejusdem epistolae duae, una de Fare, Chondro, Trago, Ptisana, Crimno et Alica; altera de Zytho et Cerevisia* (Antwerp, 1552); *Trium priorum de stirpium historia commentariorum imagines ad vivum expressae. Una cum indicibus graeca, latina, officinarum, germanica, brabantica, gallicaque nomina complectentibus* (Antwerp, 1553); *Posteriorum trium . . . de stirpium historia commentariorum imagines ad vivum artificiosissime expressa; una cum marginalibus annotationibus. Item ejusdem annotationes in aliquot prioris tomi imagines, qui trium priorum librorum figuras complectitur* (Antwerp, 1554), which was repr. in two vols. as *Commentariorum de stirpium historia imaginum . . . et stirpium herbarumque complures imagines novae . . .* (Antwerp, 1559); *Cruydeboeck in den welcken de gheheele historie, dat es't gheslacht, 't fatsoen, naem, nature, cracht ende werckinghe, van den cruyden, niet alleen hier te lande wassende, maer oock van den anderen vremden in der medecynen oorboorlyck met grooter neersticheyt begrepen ende verclaert es, med derzelver cruyden natuerlick naer datleren conterfeytsel daer by gestelt* (Antwerp, 1554, 1563), French trans. by Charles de l'Écluse as *Histoire des plantes* (Antwerp, 1557), and English trans. by Henry Lyte (1578, 1586, 1595, 1600, 1619); *Historia frumentorum, leguminum, palustrium et aquatilium herbarum, ac eorum quae pertinent. . . . Additae sunt imagines vivae, exactissimae, jam recens non absque haud vulgari diligentia et fide artificiosissime expressae . . .* (Antwerp, 1565, 1566, 1569); *Florum et coronariorum odoratarumque nonnullarum herbarum historia* (Antwerp, 1568, 1569); *Purgantium aliarumque eo facientium, tam et radicum, convolvulorum ac deletariarum herbarum historiae libri IIII. . . . Accessit appendix variarum et quidem rarissimarum nonnullarum stirpium, ac florum quorumdam peregrinorum elegantissimorumque icones omnino novas nec antea editas, singulorumque breves descriptiones continens . . .* (Antwerp, 1574, 1576); *Historia vitis viniqúe et stirpium nonnullarum aliarum: item medicinalium observationum exempla rara* (Cologne, 1580, 1583, 1585, 1621); *Physiologiae medicinae partis tabulae expeditae* (Cologne, 1581; Antwerp, 1581, 1585); *Remberti Dodonoei medici caesarei medicinalium observationum exempla rara. Accessere et alia quaedam quorum elenchum pagina post praefationem exhibet: Antonii Beniveni Florentini medici ac philosophi . . . exempla rara ex libris de curandis hominum morbis Valesci Tharantani et Alexandri Benedicti. Historia gestationis foetus mortui in utero, Mathiae Cornacis, Egidii Hertoghii et Achillis Pirminii Gassari* (Cologne, 1581; Harderwijk, 1584; Antwerp–Leiden, 1585; Antwerp, 1586), and rev. and enlarged ed. of text as second part of *Historia vitis vinique et stirpium* . . . (Harderwijk, 1621); *Stirpium historiae pemptades sex sive libri XXX* (Antwerp, 1583, 1616), Dutch trans. as *Herbarius, seu Cruydeboeck van Rembertus Dodonoeus* . . . by Françoys van Ravelingen (Leiden, 1608, 1618; Antwerp, 1644); *Praxis medica* (Amsterdam, 1616), further ed. and annotated by Nicolai Fontani (Amsterdam, 1640), and Dutch trans. with notes by S. Egbertz and Wassenaar (1624); "Remberti Dodonoei consilium medicinale in melancholia per essentiam," in *Opera Laur. Scholzii* (Basel, 1546); and "Remberti Dodonoei ad Balduinum Ronssaeum Epistola de Zytho, Cormi et Cerevisia," in *Balduini Ronssaei medici celeberrimi opuscula medica* (Leiden, 1590).

II. Secondary Literature. On Dodoens and his work, see F. W. T. Hunger, "Dodonée comme botaniste," in *Janus,* **22** (1917), 151–162; "Over het geboortejaar van Rembertus Dodonaeus," in *Bijdragen tot de geschiedenis der geneeskunde,* **3** (1923), 116–121; "Een tot dusver onuigegeven brief van Rembertus Dodonaeus," *ibid.,* 306–307; P. C. Molhuysen, *Bronnen tot de geschiedenis der Leidische universiteit, 1e part. 1574–1610* (The Hague, 1913); M. A. Van Andel, "Rembertus Dodoens and his Influence on Flemish and Dutch Folk-Medicine," in *Janus,* **22** (1917), 163; E. C. Van Leersum, "Rembert Dodoens (29 juin 1517–10 mars 1585)," *ibid.,* 141–152; P. J. Van Meerbeeck, *Recherches historiques et critiques sur la vie et les ouvrages de Rembert Dodoens (Dodonaeus)* (Mechelen, 1841); and E. Varenbergh, in *Biographie nationale publiée par l'Académie Royale des Sciences, des Lettres et des Beaux-Arts de Belgique,* IV (Brussels, 1878), cols. 85–112.

Marcel Florkin

DOELTER (CISTERICH Y DE LA TORRE), CORNELIO AUGUST SEVERINUS (*b.* Arroyo, Guayama, Puerto Rico, 16 September 1850; *d.* Kolbnitz, Carinthia, Austria, 8 August 1930), *chemical mineralogy.*

Doelter's father, Carl August (*b.* Emmendingen, Baden, 1818), emigrated to Puerto Rico and there married Francisca de Cisterich y de la Torre, whose plantations he managed before becoming a partner of Aldecoa and Company. With his mother, Doelter moved to Karlsruhe, Baden, in 1855 and entered its lyceum in 1860. In 1865 his father brought him to Paris, where he attended the Lycée St. Louis, transferring in 1866 to the Lycée Bonaparte; in 1869 he received the *bachelier* degree and entered the École Centrale des Arts et Manufactures. In the fall of 1870 Doelter enrolled at the University of Freiburg im Breisgau and transferred in the spring of 1871 to Heidelberg. He studied chemistry, physics, mineralogy, and geology, and his most important teachers were Bunsen, J. F. C. Klein, and E. W. Benecke. Following his receipt of the Ph.D. in 1872 he studied

under Suess, F. von Hochstetter, and Carl Hauer in Vienna. In 1873 Doelter became a laboratory assistant at the Imperial Geological Survey, and in 1875 he qualified as a lecturer at the University of Vienna. On 1 May 1876 he was appointed assistant professor of mineralogy and petrography at the University of Graz; he was named full professor in 1883. In 1907 Doelter succeeded Tschermak at the University of Vienna, and in 1911 he became imperial *Hofrat.* He retired in 1921 and continued to live in Vienna, concerning himself chiefly with the preparation of his *Handbuch der Mineralchemie.*

On 24 August 1876 Doelter married Eleonore Fötterle, who bore him one son and one daughter. The marriage was dissolved in 1915, and on 4 October 1919 he married Maria Theresia Schilgerius. His second wife contributed significantly to the maintenance of his ability to work.

Leitmeier described Doelter thus: "Doelter was a fiery spirit. His ability to make rapid connections was astonishing. Much was not matured, and could scarcely have been so considering the extent of the undertakings. He preferred to direct a staff of assistants, giving only suggestions himself."[1] Grengg elaborated:

In lectures or in reports, Doelter stood dispassionately above the material, soberly joining one fact to another, illuminating here and there the possibilities of another view, and frequently even leaving to the audience to select for itself what it found most acceptable. Nevertheless, one always had the impression that a man of considerable understanding and wide views was speaking.[2]

In Graz, Doelter was for a long time editor, and in 1892 also president, of the Naturwissenschaftlicher Verein of Styria; in addition, he was a curator of the Landesmuseum Johanneum. The Akademie der Wissenschaften in Vienna named him a corresponding member on 4 May 1902 and a full member on 2 June 1928. His many students dedicated a *Festschrift* to him in 1920.

The question of the origin of dolomite had brought Doelter to Vienna in 1872. He worked in the eruptive regions of Hungary and South Tyrol for the Imperial Geological Survey. He considered microscopic and chemical investigation of igneous rock and the exact observation of geological occurrence to be the foundation of all petrology. Doelter conducted a thorough survey of the Pontine Islands (1874), of the volcanism of Monte Ferru on Sardinia, and of the volcanic areas of the Cape Verde Islands, which he visited in 1880–1881. On the trip to the Cape Verde Islands he also went to Portuguese Guinea, where he convincingly explained laterite formation and also made ethnographic studies. He repeatedly explored the Monzoni region and Predazzo in South Tyrol and worked in the crystalline areas of Styria.

Doelter insisted on the confirmation of all suppositions through experiment. He first devoted himself to synthesis and prepared nepheline and pyroxenes (1884), a sulfide and a sulfosalt (1886), micas (1888), and a zeolite (1890). In this work he improved Charles Friedel's pressure vessels and used liquid and solid carbon dioxide to obtain higher pressure. Experiments on remelting and recrystallization carried out after 1883 had shown that minerals other than the original ones could be separated out from the fused mass. For example, Doelter obtained an augite andesite from a fused mass of eclogite. He likewise investigated the remelting of rocks and the influence of mineralizers on the occurrence of rock-forming minerals. His *Allgemeine chemische Mineralogie* (Leipzig, 1890) presented the knowledge he had gained of these matters.

In 1890 Doelter studied the absorption of water by dehydrated zeolites and the solubility of silicates in water. At the same time he demonstrated that in electrolysis, fused basalt concentrates iron at the cathode and that, therefore, fused silicates behave like electrolytes and not like alloys. Since the application of the physical-chemical laws developed for aqueous solutions to silicate fusions was hampered by the lack of reliable constants, Doelter began in 1899 to determine the melting points of important minerals and, in 1901, those of mixtures. In 1901 he ascertained the volume increase of liquid and solidified rock fusions relative to the solid parent rock and found that minerals which are difficult to fuse are also difficult to dissolve and very hard (1902). In 1902 Doelter presented a viscosity series from liquid basalt to viscous granite, recognizing the influence of mineralizers on viscosity and on the lowering of the melting point, as well as their catalytic and chemical activity—e.g., in the formation of mica and of tourmaline. Moreover, he found that magmatic differentiation "is nothing else than the final result of mineral segregation."[3] For melting-point determinations he constructed the crystallization microscope built by C. Reichert with the heating oven of W. C. Heraeus (described in 1904; improved in 1909). In 1904 he was able to confirm the suspected influence of the inoculation of solution-melts with seed crystals.

With his *Physikalisch-chemische Mineralogie* (Leipzig, 1905), Doelter showed himself to be, along with J. H. L. Vogt, the most important cofounder of this new discipline, even though he held that the direct transfer of the results of physical chemistry was not always possible, because in silicate fusions a restoration of equilibrium is impeded by the subcooling and by reduced diffusion resulting from viscosity. The chief advantage that he saw in physical chemistry was that it had set the direction that experimental work should follow.

In his *Petrogenesis* (Brunswick, 1906), a masterful work for its time, Doelter experimentally verified, on the whole, Rosenbusch's order of crystallization series and related it to solubility, force and velocity of crystal growth, stability, cooling rates, and percentage of mineralizers. Furthermore, he distinguished (1) density differentiation (liquation), which he demonstrated experimentally; (2) crystallization or cooling differentiation by the freezing of basic facies at the boundary of the surfaces of cooling or by the sinking of the earliest segregation products which later form a rock matrix; and (3) isotectic differentiation, in which a definite association of various minerals separates out. In opposition to the views of Vogt, he was able to verify eutectic differentiation only for quartz-orthoclase and sporadically for fayalite fusions.

Doelter next turned to research on estimation of the number of nuclei in fused masses, on the force of crystallization, and on the measurement of viscosity (1905); in 1911, with H. Sirk, he obtained the first measurement of the absolute viscosity of molten diopside at 1300°C. From 1907 to 1910 Doelter studied the dissociation constants, electrical conductivities, and polarization of solid and fused silicates. He discovered that in the transition from the molten to the crystalline state the conductivity changed irregularly, while in the transition to the vitreous state the change was continuous. He held, in opposition to Groth's conception of lattices of atoms in potassium sulfate, that "one could accept it as more probable that such lattices were made of K' and SO_4'' ions."[4] Even solid, nonconducting sodium chloride could, in his opinion, separate completely or largely into ions, which are fixed in the lattice and which, since they are not mobile, cannot exhibit electrical conductivity.

In addition, Doelter concerned himself with gemmology, particularly with the cause of mineral coloration. In 1896 he began to investigate the influence of Roentgen rays on minerals, and later that of radium rays and of ultraviolet light. He also examined the changes in color resulting from heating minerals in oxidizing, reducing, and inert gases. On the basis of his experience with the coloring agents of synthetic corundums and spinels, Doelter warned against considering analytically or spectroscopically demonstrated trace elements as color pigments, without extensive testing of their behavior when heated in gases and under radiation. Unfortunately these warnings were ignored by many later workers in the field, with the result that contradictory assertions are still published. Doelter even drew upon colloid chemistry in order to clarify these questions—without, however, arriving at any definitive conclusions. Nevertheless his extensive collections of material contain very valuable observations.

Doelter's some 200 works and those of his students have provided the essential experimental basis for modern petrology.

NOTES

1. H. Leitmeier, in *Neue deutsche Biographie,* IV (1959), 25.
2. R. Grengg, in *Montanistische Rundschau,* **22,** no. 19 (1930), 2.
3. *Physikalisch-chemische Mineralogie,* p. 147.
4. *Sitzungsberichte der Akademie der Wissenschaften in Wien,* sec. 1, **117** (1908), 333.

BIBLIOGRAPHY

I. Original Works. Doelter's books include *Bestimmung der petrographisch wichtigen Mineralien durch das Mikroskop* (Vienna, 1876); *Die Vulcane der Capverden und ihre Producte* (Graz, 1882); *Über die Capverden nach dem Rio Grande und Futah-Djallon* (Leipzig, 1884); *Edelsteinkunde* (Leipzig, 1893); *Das Radium und die Farben* (Dresden, 1910); *Die Farben der Mineralien, inbesondere der Edelsteine* (Brunswick, 1915); and *Die Mineralschätze der Balkanländer und Kleinasiens* (Stuttgart, 1916). His *Handbuch der Mineralchemie* was edited by C. Doelter and, from III, pt. 2, with H. Leitmeier; it appeared in 4 vols.: II in three pts., III in two pts., and IV in three pts. (Dresden-Leipzig, 1912–1931). About half of the material is by Doelter.

His papers include "Die Vulcangruppe der Pontinischen Inseln," in *Denkschriften der Akademie der Wissenschaften* (Vienna), Math.-nat. Kl., **36,** pt. 2 (1876), 141–186; "Der Vulcan Monte Ferru auf Sardinien," *ibid.,* **38,** pt. 2 (1878), 113–214; "Die Producte des Vulcans Monte Ferru," *ibid.,* **39,** pt. 2 (1879), 41–95; "Chemische Zusammensetzung und Genesis der Monzonigesteine I–III," in *Tschermaks mineralogische und petrographische Mitteilungen,* **21** (1902), 65–76, 97–106, 191–225; "Der Monzoni und seine Gesteine I–II," in *Sitzungsberichte der Akademie der Wissenschaften* (Vienna), Math.-nat. Kl., sec. 1, **111** (1902), 929–986; **112** (1903), 169–236; "Die Silikatschmelzen I–IV," *ibid.,* **113** (1904), 177–249, 495–511; **114** (1905), 529–588; **115** (1906), 723–755; "Über die Dissoziation der Silikatschmelzen I–II," *ibid.,* **116** (1907), 1243–1309; **117** (1908), 299–336; and "Die Elektrizitätsleitung in Krystallen bei höhen Temperaturen," *ibid.,* **119** (1910), 49–111.

An incomplete list of Doelter's works, without his contributions to *Handbuch der Mineralchemie,* is in Poggendorff, III–VI.

II. Secondary Literature. On Doelter or his work see E. Dittler, in *Zentralblatt für Mineralogie,* pt. A (1930), 476–477; R. Grengg, in *Montanistische Rundschau;* **22,** no. 19 (1930), 1–2; W. Hammer, in *Verhandlungen der Geologischen Bundesanstalt* (Vienna, 1930), 213–214; A. Himmelbauer, in *Almanach der Akademie der Wissenschaften in Wien,* **81** (1931), 314–316; H. Leitmeier, in *Neue deutsche Biographie,* IV (1959), 25–26; and L. J. Spencer, in *Mineralogical Magazine,* **22** (1930), 390–391.

Various biographical information is to be found in the archives at Graz and Vienna.

Walther Fischer

DOGEL, VALENTIN ALEXANDROVICH (*b.* Kazan, Russia, 10 March 1882; *d.* Leningrad, U.S.S.R., 1 June 1955), *zoology.*

His father, A. S. Dogel, was first dissector in the department of histology in Kazan, and then professor in the departments of histology in Tomsk (1888–1894) and in St. Petersburg (1894–1922). V. A. Dogel graduated in 1904 from the natural sciences section of the physics and mathematics faculty of St. Petersburg University and was professor of invertebrate zoology at the university from 1914 to 1955. He occupied the chair of zoology at the (Herzen) Pedagogical Institute for Women from 1908 to 1938, and from 1930 to 1955 was head of the laboratory of fish diseases in the All-Union Institute of Economy for Lake and River Fish and of the laboratory of sea protozoa of the Zoological Institute of the Soviet Academy of Sciences. He was made corresponding member of the Academy in 1939.

Dogel's scientific career was devoted to protozoology and the comparative anatomy of invertebrates. In the area of protozoology he studied the morphology and taxonomy of *Gregarina,* Dinoflagellata, Catenata, Polymastigina, and Hypermastigina (from the intestines of termites) and Infusoria from the stomach of ruminants (Ophryoscolecidae); and he established the evolutionary regularity of the development of protozoa—the phenomenon of polymerization. In ecological parasitology, Dogel studied the relation of the parasitofauna of the animal host to the type of diet and to migrations (among fish and migratory birds), and also to hibernation (among bats). In the area of comparative anatomy and evolutionary morphology, in addition to establishing the taxonomic position of pantopods, Dogel formulated the general evolutionary regularities, in particular the regularity of oligomerization of homologous organs and the means by which it comes about (reduction, fusion of organs, change of function). Dogel was the author of several monographs and textbooks and over 250 specialized works. Among his students were

B. E. Bykhovsky, A. P. Markevich, A. V. Ivanov, E. M. Kheysin, Y. I. Polyansky, A. A. Strelkov, and V. L. Vagin.

BIBLIOGRAPHY

I. ORIGINAL WORKS. Dogel's writings include *Catenata. Organizatsia roda Haplozoon i nekotorykh skhodnykh s nim form* ("Catenata. The Organization of the Genus Haplozoon and Certain Forms Similar to Them"), diss. (St. Petersburg, 1910); *Materialy k istorii razvitia Pantopoda* ("Materials for a History of the Development of the Pantopoda"), diss. (1913); "Monographie der Familie Ophryoscolecidae," in *Archiv für Protistenkunde,* **59** (1927), 1–282; *Uchebnik sravnitelnoy anatomii bespozvonochnykh* ("Textbook of Comparative Anatomy of Invertebrates"), 2 pts. (Leningrad, 1938–1940); *Kurs obshchey parazitologii* ("Course in General Parasitology"), 2nd ed. (Moscow, 1947); *Oligomerizatsia gomologichnykh organov* ("Oligomerization of Homologous Organs," Leningrad, 1954); *Allgemeine Parasitologie,* rev. and enl. by Y. I. Polyansky and E. M. Kheysin (Jena, 1963), trans. as *General Parasitology* (Oxford, 1965); and *Obshchaya protozoologia* ("General Protozoology," Moscow–Leningrad, 1962), written with Y. I. Polyansky and E. M. Kheysin.

II. SECONDARY LITERATURE. On Dogel and his work, see (listed chronologically) Y. I. Polyansky, "Professor Valentin Aleksandrovich Dogel," in *Uchenye zapiski Leningradskogo gosudarstvennogo universiteta. Seria biologicheskikh nauk,* no. 2 (Leningrad, 1939); *Materialy k bibliographii uchenykh SSSR. Seria biologicheskikh nauk. Parazitologia,* no. 2 (Leningrad, 1952); and Y. I. Polyansky, *Valentin Aleksandrovich Dogel* (Leningrad, 1969), which contains additions to the list of Dogel's works.

L. J. BLACHER

DOKUCHAEV, VASILY VASILIEVICH (*b.* Milyukovo, Smolensk province, Russia, 1 March 1846; *d.* St. Petersburg, Russia, 8 November 1903), *natural science, soil science, geography.*

Dokuchaev came from the family of a village priest. He received his elementary education at a church school in Vyazma and then studied at the Smolensk seminary. In 1867 he graduated with distinction from the seminary and was accepted at the St. Petersburg Ecclesiastical Academy. In the same year, having decided not to become a priest, he left the academy and entered the physics and mathematics department of St. Petersburg University to study the natural sciences.

In 1871 Dokuchaev graduated from St. Petersburg University with a master's degree. His dissertation was devoted to the study and description of the alluvial deposits of the Kachna River, on the upper reaches of the Volga, near his birthplace. From that time Dokuchaev's scientific activity was connected with St. Petersburg University, the Society of Natural Scientists, the Free Economic Society, the Mineralogical Society, and the Petersburg Assembly of Agriculturists. With the support of these groups he carried out research on the Russian plains and in the Caucasus. In the fall of 1872 he was made curator of the geological collection of St. Petersburg University, and in 1879 he became *Privatdozent* in geology. Along with his courses in mineralogy and crystallography he began to give a special course, the first anywhere, on Quaternary deposits.

From 1892 to 1895, while remaining a professor at St. Petersburg University, Dokuchaev was occupied with the reorganization and then the direction of the Novo-Aleksandr (now Kharkov) Institute of Agriculture and Forestry (now named for him). There he founded the first department of soil science in Russia and a department of plant physiology that offered courses on microorganisms.

Dokuchaev's first major work, "Sposoby obrazovania rechnykh dolin Evropeyskoy Rossii" ("Methods of Formation of the River Valleys of European Russia"), defended as a doctor's thesis in 1878, was the result of years of profound study of the geological, orographical, and hydrographical peculiarities of the Russian plain, particularly the districts covered by ancient glaciers. He analyzed various earlier hypotheses on the formation of the river plains, particularly those treating valleys as the result of tectonic fissures or receding of the ocean, and he criticized accepted ideas, such as Murchison's "drift theory." Dokuchaev gave a coherent explanation of the genesis of landforms and their relation to specific physical and geographical conditions of the past; on this basis he may be considered one of the founders of geomorphology.

After he began his field studies of Quaternary deposits, Dokuchaev directed his research to the topsoil of European Russia, particularly to chernozem. In 1875 he was invited to write an explanatory note for V. I. Chaslavsky's soil map of European Russia; he then spent several years preparing the map for publication. From 1877 to 1898 he investigated the northern boundary of the chernozem belt: the Ukraine, Moldavia, central Russia, Trans-Volga, the Crimea, and the northern slopes of the Caucasus. His monograph "Russky chernozyom" ("Russian Chernozem," 1883) won numerous honors.

This research attracted the attention of *zemstvos* (village councils) and individual landowners of Saratov and Voronezh provinces; comprehensive research on the natural conditions of these large territories was carried out by a group of young scientists, most of whom were students of Dokuchaev's and worked under his guidance. Their work was important not only for the practice of agriculture but also for the confirmation and development of Dokuchaev's ideas in a new area of natural science—genetic soil science.

Dokuchaev's expeditions to Nizhni Novgorod (1882–1886), Poltava (1888–1896), and other places were conducted according to a special method. In accounts of the expeditions a full description of the natural history of the provinces was given by natural components (geology, soil, water, plant and animal life); and on the basis of an analysis of all the data, an appraisal was made of the agricultural potential. These collections served as the basis for the organization, at Dokuchaev's initiative, of museums of natural history in Nizhni Novgorod and Poltava. Following a plan proposed by Dokuchaev, similar museums were later created in other cities of Russia. Dokuchaev was one of the organizers and leaders of the Eighth Congress of Russian Natural Scientists and Physicians. At his initiative the agronomy and geography sections were separated for the first time. He emphasized the necessity of creating a soil institute and museum and of making a thorough study of the natural history of various areas.

In 1891 there was a severe drought in Russia, and Dokuchaev subordinated his scientific work to the problem of dealing with this disaster. He was commissioned by the Ministry of State Lands to undertake a special expedition that was to devise ways and means of conducting farming, forestry, and water management in the steppe (chernozem) zone. The basis of the work of the expedition was a plan set forth by Dokuchaev in his book *Nashi stepi prezhde i teper* ("Our Steppes Past and Present," 1892), which included preliminary geological, soil, and climatic findings. Three experimental plots in the steppe belt, each about 5,000 hectares, were chosen to survey: Starobelsky, in the watershed between the Don and the Donets; Khrenovsky, between the Volga and the Don; and Veliko-Anadolsky, in the watershed between the Donets and the Dnieper. Of great importance was the network of meteorological stations and rain-gauge points set up on these plots. The careful observations of the climate of the steppe zone made it possible to determine the influence of climatic conditions on agriculture, particularly the role of forests and protective forest belts. Much work was done on artificial forest cultivation, the regulation and use of water resources, and the building of reservoirs.

As head of the Bureau of Soil Science of the Scientific Committee of the Ministry of Agriculture, Dokuchaev also carried out the compilation of a new soil map of European Russia. In 1897, after twenty years of service at St. Petersburg University, he retired for reasons of health. His health having improved slightly, in 1898 Dokuchaev led an expedition to study the soil of Bessarabia; in 1898–1899 and 1900 he studied the Caucasus and the Transcaucasus; and in 1898–1899 he also went to the Trans-Caspian region. Of the results of his research in the Caucasus he wrote that he "not only *predicted* but even *factually proved* the indisputable unusually sharply expressed existence in the whole Caucasus and Trans-Caucasus of *vertical* soil (and, in general, natural history) zones . . . " (*Sobranii sochineny* ["Collected Works"], VIII, 331).

Dokuchaev's last public activity was a series of lectures on soil science and on the results of his three-year study of the soils of the Caucasus, given in Tbilisi in 1900.

Dokuchaev continually sought to popularize the accomplishments of science. He stressed the centralization of all soil work and research and the necessity of creating a soil institute and departments of soil science in universities. He and A. V. Sovetov were responsible for the series *Materialy po izucheniyu russkikh pochv* ("Material for the Study of Russian Soils," from 1885) and *Trudy* ("Works") of the Soil Commission of the Free Economic Society (1889–1899). In 1899, at his initiative, the journal *Pochvovedenie* ("Soil Science") began publication.

A prerequisite for the creation of soil science was Dokuchaev's discovery of soil as a special body that has developed as a result of climate, bedrock, plant and animal life, age of the land, and topography.

Dokuchaev's approach to the evolution of soils allowed him to discover all the complex connections between the soil-forming factors, including the factors of time and human activity. He defined soil as follows:

> It consists essentially of the mineral-organic formations lying on the surface, which are always more or less noticeably colored with humus. These bodies always have their own particular origin; they always and everywhere are the result of the totality of activity of the bedrock, the living and inanimate organisms (plant as well as animal), climate, the age of the country, and the topography of the surroundings. Soils, like every other organism, always have a certain normal structure, normal depth, and normal position and are always related to these in warmth, moisture, and plant growth differently from their bedrock [*ibid.*, II, 260].

Thus, according to Dokuchaev, soils are geobiological formations, the properties of which are closely related to their position on the earth's surface and change regularly as a result of environmental conditions. Starting with the definition of soil and the position that soil depends on soil formers, Dokuchaev created a new classification of soils according to natural history. His methods of classifying soils are now basic for cartographic representation and qualitative appraisal of soils. He distinguished three basic classes of soils: normal, transitional, and abnormal. A more detailed division into sections and types was made after considering the differences in soil formers and their interrelationships. Normal, or zonal, soils are the most typical and most widespread. In the course of time the classification of soils has become more precise and detailed. In Dokuchaev's classifications of 1896 (*ibid.,* VII, 449, inset) and 1898 (*ibid.,* VI, 330, inset) the genetic soil types and soil belts were related to vegetation and climatic belts, which was of great importance "for the accurate and complete *understanding* and *appraisal* of nature and its varied and extremely complex forms" (*ibid.,* VI, 306).

Dokuchaev established the zonality of soil and its coincidence with the zonality of climate, vegetation, and animal life. On this subject he wrote:

> . . . thanks to the known position of our planet relative to the sun, thanks to the rotation of the earth, its spherical shape—climate, vegetation, and animal life are distributed on the earth's surface from north to south, in a strictly determined order . . . which allows the division of the earth's sphere into belts: *polar, temperate, subtropical, equatorial,* and so forth. And since the agents—soil formers, which are subject to known laws in their distribution—are distributed by belts, their results also—the soil—must be distributed on the earth's sphere in the form of definite *zones,* going *more* or *less* (only with certain deviations) parallel to the circles of latitude [*ibid.,* 407].

A view of nature as an entity shaped by a profound mutual interdependence and mutual determination of all its components led Dokuchaev to create the theory of zones of nature. He distinguished five basic geographical zones: boreal, taiga, chernozem (steppe), arid desert, and lateritite (tropical). Tracing the main zones, he noted transitions between them and pointed to the differentiation of natural zones into separate physical-geographical regions.

Dokuchaev stressed that agriculture should be carried out on a zonal basis and defined the main problems of agricultural technology for each zone. The most complete synthesis of his scientific work can be found in his statements on theory of the relationship between "inanimate" and "living" nature. In *Mesto i rol sovremennogo pochvovedenia v nauke i zhizni* ("The Place and Role of Contemporary Soil Science in Science and in Life," 1899) Dokuchaev wrote:

> As is well known, in recent times one of the most interesting *disciplines* in the field of contemporary natural science has developed and become more and more

defined, namely, the theory of the multiple and various *relationships* and *interactions,* and equally *laws* which govern their age-old *changes,* which exist between so-called *inanimate* and *living nature,* between (*a*) the surface rocks, (*b*) the plastic layer of the earth, (*c*) soils, (*d*) surface and underground water, (*e*) the climate of the country, (*f*) plant, and (*g*) animal organisms (including, and even chiefly, the lowest) and man, the proud crown of creation [*ibid.,* 416].

Dokuchaev sought to create a unified science that would embrace "the one, whole, and indivisible nature." The core of this new science would be genetic soil science. His death cut off this work; but it has been continued by, among others, Dokuchaev's student Vernadsky, the creator of the theory of the biosphere.

Dokuchaev's work greatly influenced the development of physical geography and geobotany, and made a great contribution to the study of swamps. His "polygenetic" theory of the genesis of loess significantly anticipated contemporary views. His ideas received wide recognition, and his genetic soil classification was applied in making soil maps of England, the United States, Rumania, and other countries.

BIBLIOGRAPHY

Dokuchaev's works have been gathered in *Sobranii sochineny* ("Collected Works"), 9 vols. (Moscow-Leningrad, 1949–1961). Vol. I contains his most important geological and geomorphological works, including *Sposoby obrazovania rechnykh dolin Evropeyskoy Rossii* ("Methods of Formation of the River Valleys of European Russia," St. Petersburg, 1878). Vol. II contains articles and reports on the study of the chernozem (1876–1885) and *Kartografia russkikh pochv* ("Cartography of Russian Soils," St. Petersburg, 1879). Vol. III consists of *Russky chernozyom* ("Russian Chernozem," St. Petersburg, 1883). Vols. IV and V are devoted to *Nizhegorodskie raboty* ("Nizhni Novgorod Works," 1882–1887). Vol. VI contains works on the transformation of the nature of the steppes, on soil research and soil appraisal, and the theory of zonality and classification of soils (1888–1900), including *Nashi stepi prezhde i teper* ("Our Steppes, Past and Present," St. Petersburg, 1892); *K voprosu o pereotsenke zemel Evropeyskoy i Aziatskoy Rossii. S klassifikatsiey pochv* ("Toward the Question of a Reappraisal of the Soils of European and Asiatic Russia. With a Classification of Soils," Moscow, 1898); *K ucheniyu o zonakh prirody* ("Toward a Theory of Zones of Nature," St. Petersburg, 1899); and *Prirodnye pochvennye zony. Selskokhozyaystvennye zony. Pochvy Kavkasa* ("Natural Soil Zones. Agricultural Zones. The Soils of the Caucasus," St. Petersburg, 1900). Vol. VII consists of various articles and reports, material on the organization of soil institutes, and popular lectures (1880–1900). Vol. VIII contains speeches and correspondence. Vol. IX contains S. S.

Sobolev's article on the development of Dokuchaev's basic ideas, a biographical sketch by L. A. Chebotareva, and archival documents for his biography. A substantial part of the volume is devoted to a bibliography of all his works (pp. 165–247) and of literature on him (pp. 248–322), including 49 items in foreign languages (pp. 315–320).

Recent works on Dokuchaev not listed in the bibliography mentioned above are V. A. Esakov and A. I. Soloviev, *Russkie geograficheskie issledovania Evropeyskoy Rossii i Urala v XIX-nachale XX v.* ("Russian Geographical Research on European Russia and the Urals in the Nineteenth and the Beginning of the Twentieth Centuries," Moscow, 1964), pp. 76–90; *Istoria estestvoznania v Rossii* ("History of Natural Sciences in Russia"), III, S. R. Mikulinsky, ed. (Moscow, 1962), 217–238; and G. F. Kiryanov, *Vasily Vasilievich Dokuchaev, 1846–1903* (Moscow, 1966).

VASILY A. ESAKOV

DÖLLINGER, IGNAZ (*b.* Bamberg, Germany, 27 May 1770; *d.* Munich, Germany, 14 January 1841), *physiology, embryology.*

Döllinger should be considered one of the most able and influential German biologists of the early nineteenth century. Although his initial scientific career was associated with the application of Friedrich W. Schelling's philosophical ideas to physiology and embryology, Döllinger simultaneously conducted microscopical observations related to embryonic and vascular structures. His major achievement was to provide enthusiasm, method, and assistance to the new generation of scientists, such as Karl von Baer, Heinrich Christian von Pander, Johann L. Schönlein, Georg Kaltenbrunner, and Eduard d'Alton. Thus Döllinger symbolizes the successful attempt in Germany to proceed beyond the narrow schemes embodied by *Naturphilosophie* and to instruct students in the virtues of observation and experiment.

As the son of the personal physician to Franz Ludwig von Erthal, ruler of the bishopric of Würzburg and Bamberg, Döllinger received an elaborate education. After completing his studies in philosophy and natural sciences at the University of Bamberg, he began his medical career there, transferring later to Würzburg. Under the sponsorship of Erthal, Döllinger next went to Vienna, where he received the clinical training lacking at the time in Germany. In addition he improved his anatomical knowledge and acquired great skill in vascular injection techniques under the direction of Prochaska. The Vienna sojourn was followed by a journey to the University of Pavia, where Döllinger studied under Johann Peter Frank and Antonio Scarpa.

In 1793 Döllinger returned home after the revolutionary wars had forced Pavia to close its doors. In 1794 he received the M.D. from the University of Bamberg, where he was then named professor of physiology and general pathology; he remained until 1801, when the university was closed as a result of the annexation of the bishopric by Bavaria. In 1803, under the new administration, Döllinger was elected professor of anatomy and physiology at the reorganized University of Würzburg. He remained there for twenty years and was the most important figure at the medical school, attracting a great number of students, especially from Germany and the Russian Empire.

In 1816 Döllinger was accepted as member of the Leopoldinisch-Karolinische Deutsche Akademie der Naturforscher. After being a corresponding member since 1819, he was elected in 1823 to a regular chair at the Bavarian Academy of Sciences. He therefore moved to Munich in order to fill the vacancy left by the anatomist Samuel T. Sömmering. Döllinger's early years in Munich were occupied with the creation and construction of an anatomical amphitheater, which was opened in 1827. Also, after the University of Bavaria had been moved from Landshut to Munich in 1826, he became its professor of human and comparative anatomy. He was elected secretary of the mathematical-physical section of the Bavarian Academy for the years 1827–1830 and 1833–1836, and became a member of the Bavarian Medical Advisory Board in 1836. His health was seriously and permanently affected by the cholera epidemic that ravaged Germany in 1836. Döllinger's last years were spent in virtual seclusion, and he died of a perforated gastric ulcer.

Döllinger's early treatise *Grundriss der Naturlehre des menschlichen Organismus* is an attempt to place the physiological knowledge available at the turn of the nineteenth century within Schelling's philosophical postulates. But in the preface he makes it clear that this formulation will not stifle his spirit of inquiry or hamper further search for knowledge. For him *Naturphilosophie* was pure and absolute philosophical knowledge, which could not determine the finite biological phenomena with which he was dealing.

As a Bavarian academician, Döllinger sought to improve his major research tool, the microscope. With the opticians of the Utzschneider-Fraunhofer Institute at Munich he was instrumental in achieving needed corrections on the aplanatic microscope. He made microscopical observations of the blood circulation, and in his short monograph "Vom Kreislaufe des Blutes" paid special attention to the red and white blood cells and their intravascular and extravascular fates in the different tissues. Döllinger felt that these cells were elementary organic units floating in the serum, and that their chemical transformation was needed for the nutrition and secretion of the different organic structures.

In embryology Döllinger stimulated research on the morphology of the developing chick. He was a believer in the existence of a plastic, organic principle that unfolded its own design within the embryo. He set out to follow this process microscopically and recognized the early stages of embryonic differentiation.

BIBLIOGRAPHY

I. ORIGINAL WORKS. Döllinger's writings include *Grundriss der Naturlehre des menschlichen Organismus, zum Gebrauch bei seinen Vorlesungen* (Bamberg–Würzburg, 1805); *Beyträge zur Entwicklungsgeschichte des menschlichen Gehirns* (Frankfurt, 1814); "Vom Pulse," in *Deutsches Archiv für die Physiologie,* **2** (1816), 356–358; "Versuch einer Geschichte der menschlichen Zeugung," *ibid.,* 388–402; *Was ist Absonderung und wie geschieht sie? Eine akademische Abhandlung* (Würzburg, 1819); "Bemerkungen über die Vertheilung der feinsten Blutgefässe in den beweglichen Teilen des thierischen Körpers," in *Deutsches Archiv für die Physiologie,* **6** (1820), 186–199; and *Vom Kreislaufe des Blutes,* vol. VII in the series Denkschriften der K. Akademie der Wissenschaften (Munich, 1821), pp. 169–228.

II. SECONDARY LITERATURE. On Döllinger or his work, see Burkard Eble, *Curt Sprengel's Versuch einer pragmatischen Geschichte der Arzneikunde* (Vienna, 1837), VI, pt. 1, many refs. between pp. 303 and 618; Albert von Kölliker, *Zur Geschichte der medicinischen Facultät an der Universität Würzburg. Rede zur Feier des Stiftungstages der Julius-Maximilians Universität* (Würzburg, 1871), pp. 31–37; Arthur William Meyer, *Human Generation: Conclusions of Burdach, Doellinger and von Baer* (Stanford, Calif., 1956), pp. 26–32; and Phillip F. von Walther, *Rede zum Andenken an Ignaz Doellinger Dr.* (Munich, 1841).

GUENTER B. RISSE

DOLLO, LOUIS ANTOINE MARIE JOSEPH (*b.* Lille, France, 7 December 1857; *d.* Brussels, Belgium, 19 April 1931), *paleontology.*

Dollo belonged to an old Breton family, several generations of which were sailors and lived in Roscoff. He studied at the University of Lille, where the geologist Jules Gosselet and the zoologist Alfred Giard played major roles in his scientific education. In 1877 he graduated with a degree in civil and mining engineering. In 1879 Dollo moved to Brussels, where he worked first as an engineer in a gas factory. At this time he became acquainted with the works of Kovalevski. Having decided to devote himself to paleontology, in 1882 he became junior naturalist at the Royal Museum of Natural History in Brussels. From 1891 almost to the end of his life he was curator of the vertebrate section there. He began teaching in 1909 as extraordinary professor at Brussels University, where he delivered lectures on paleontology and animal geography.

Dollo never limited himself to paleontology, and through his enthusiastic lectures in natural science he popularized scientific knowledge. He was seriously interested in linguistics—he attempted to compose a grammar of the Bantu languages of the Congo Basin—and biochemistry, and his love of music was well known to all around him. An active member of the Royal Academy of Belgium and a corresponding member of many foreign academies, Dollo won the Kuhlmann Prize in 1884, the Lyell Medal in 1889, and the Murchison Medal in 1912.

Fossil reptiles occupied the central place in Dollo's scientific work. A long series of brief articles contained careful analyses of the phenomena of adaptation among fossil reptiles, especially iguanodonts of the Lower Cretaceous, to certain conditions of existence. These investigations, which laid the foundations for the ethological study of fossil forms, sought to clarify not only their way of life but also the history of their adaptation. The study of the ethological peculiarities of such dinosaurs as *Triceratops* and *Stegosaurus* enabled Dollo to make a rather unexpected discovery: these four-legged forms must have had functionally biped ancestors. His works on fossil turtles and mosasaurians had great methodological importance. Explaining the ethological type of fossil sea turtles, Dollo showed what a complex and tortuous path their historical development had followed. The evolution of land forms that shifted to sea life did not involve simply the movement from the shores to the open sea; adaptation frequently took place in the opposite direction. Studying the hearing apparatus of the mosasaurian, Dollo found several indications of an ability to dive, which were confirmed by other signs in the structure of its skull. Investigation of the teeth of various representatives of this group led to the identification of several types of adaptation to its food. The precision of observation and the depth of analysis are also striking in the works devoted to rhynchocephalians, crocodiles, and ichthyosaurs.

Among Dollo's most significant works is the monograph on lungfishes, which explains the essential characteristics of the evolution of this very interesting group. The basic conclusions of this and other works on fossil and contemporary fish are still valid.

Dollo successfully applied his ethological method of research not only to fossil vertebrates but also to such invertebrates as the cephalopod mollusks and arthropods. However, probably the greatest achievement of this method was its application to the study of certain animals now living. In particular, the ethological analysis of the properties of the extremities of contemporary marsupials allowed Dollo to establish beyond a doubt their origin from ancient forms.

Like Kovalevski, whom he called his teacher and to whom he dedicated a cycle of remarkable lectures published under the title "La paléontologie éthologique" (1909), Dollo was not satisfied with explaining the functional significance of an organ of an animal being studied. He always tried to explain the historical development of, and the reasons for, its adaptation. Guided in his theoretical research by the ideas of Darwin and Kovalevski, Dollo enriched Darwinism by his famous laws on the irreversibility of evolution.

Limitations can sometimes be noted in Dollo's views in connection with his tendency to delimit mechanically the boundaries between paleontology and geology. Some of his conclusions concerning the mode of life of fossil forms also can be shown—and in fact are being shown—to be imprecise. On the whole, however, his works are of indisputably great methodological and theoretical significance. The most important of them remain unsurpassed models of paleobiological research.

BIBLIOGRAPHY

I. ORIGINAL WORKS. Dollo's writings are "Les lois de l'évolution," in *Bulletin de la Société belge de géologie, de paléontologie et d'hydrologie,* **7** (1893), 164–166; "Sur la phylogénie des dipneustes," in *Bulletin de la Société belge de géologie, de paléontologie et d'hydrologie,* **9** (1895), 79–128; "Les ancêtres des marsupiaux étaient-ils arboricoles?," in *Miscellanées biologiques dédiées au Prof. A. Giard à l'occasion du XXVᵉ anniversaire de la fondation de la station zoologique de Wimereux, 1874–1899* (Paris, 1899), pp. 188–203; "Sur l'évolution des chéloniens marins (considérations bionomiques et phylogéniques)," in *Bulletin de l'Académie royale de Belgique. Classe des sciences,* no. 8 (1903), 801–830; and "La paléontologie éthologique," in *Bulletin de la Société belge de géologie, de paléontologie et d'hydrologie,* **23** (1909), 377–421.

II. SECONDARY LITERATURE. On Dollo or his work, see O. Abel, "Louis Dollo. 7 Dezember 1857–19 April 1931. Ein Rückblick und Abschied," in *Palaeobiologica,* **4** (1931), 321–344; P. Brien, "Notice sur Louis Dollo," in *Annuaire de l'Académie royale de Belgique. Notices biographiques* (1951), pp. 69–138; L. S. Davitashvili, "Lui Dollo," in *Voprosy istorii estestvoznania i tekhniki* ("Problems in the History of Natural Sciences and Technology"), **3** (1937), 108–120; and V. Van Straelen, "Louis Dollo (1857–1931)," in *Bulletin de la Musée d'histoire naturelle de Belgique,* **9,** no. 1 (1933), 1–6.

L. K. GABUNIA

DOLLOND, JOHN (*b.* London, England, 10 June 1706; *d.* London, 30 November 1761), *optics.*

Dollond was born in Spitalfields, London, of French Protestant parents who had originally lived in Normandy. Although he became a silk weaver, his inclination led him to the study of mathematics, astronomy, and the classical languages in whatever spare time he could find. His eldest son, Peter, joined him as a weaver but, stimulated by the knowledge of mathematics and optics learned from his father, subsequently took up the trade of optical instrument maker. This venture was successful, and John Dollond was consequently persuaded to leave the weaving trade. He joined Peter in business in 1752, and the partnership soon became fruitful.

Some ideas for the improvement of the optical arrangement of lenses in the refracting telescope were incorporated in a letter addressed to James Short, a fellow of the Royal Society, who communicated the letter to the society, where it was read on 1 March 1753. Soon after this, on 10 May 1753, another paper was read to the Royal Society, this time on an improved micrometer (heliometer) for the telescope. Dollond had modified the Savery micrometer by using one object glass cut into two equal segments instead of two whole lenses. The micrometer could now be applied to the reflecting telescope, which was immediately done by James Short.

Dollond is popularly known as the inventor of the achromatic telescope; but although he was anticipated in the discovery by about twenty years, it seems that he independently worked out the necessary lens combinations—and he certainly was the first to publish the invention and develop it commercially. Dollond's early successes in optics brought him to the attention of astronomers and mathematicians. He corresponded with many, including Euler, against whom he defended Newton's opinion that no combination of lenses could produce an image free of color, and that in this respect no improvement could be expected in the refracting telescope.

Eventually Dollond conducted (1757–1758) a series of experiments with different kinds of glass to check Newton's findings. The paper incorporating the results, with the conclusion that the objectives of refracting telescopes could be made "without the images formed by them being affected by the different refrangibility of the rays of light," was read to the Royal Society in June 1758. Dollond's composite objective was patented, but the patent was challenged by a group of London optical instrument makers after his death. In 1766 the court upheld Peter Dollond's right to the patent on the grounds that Chester More Hall, the inventor of an achromatic lens combination in the period 1729–1733, did not exploit the invention commercially or publicize his findings.

It seems unlikely that Hall's invention could have been known to anyone capable of realizing its significance, because the Royal Society not only published Dollond's papers but conferred both the Copley Medal (1758) and membership (1761) upon him. The certificate proposing Dollond for membership was signed in February 1761 by ten men, including scientists of the standing of Gowin Knight, John Smeaton, James Short, William Watson, and John Ellicott. The proposal specifically refers to Dollond's invention of "an Object-Glass, consisting of two Spherical Lenses of different densities, so contrived as to correct the Errors arising from the different refrangibility of the Rays of Light."

Early in 1761 Dollond was appointed optician to King George III. Regrettably, he did not enjoy this honor for long; he died of apoplexy later that year. He left three daughters and two sons, Peter and John. The latter joined his elder brother as a partner in the family firm.

BIBLIOGRAPHY

I. ORIGINAL WORKS. The following were first published in *Philosophical Transactions of the Royal Society* and were reprinted in Kelly's *Life* (see below): "A letter from Mr. John Dollond to Mr. James Short, F.R.S. concerning an Improvement of refracting Telescopes," **48**, pt. 1 (1753), 103–107; "A Description of a Contrivance for measuring small Angles," *ibid.*, 178–181; "Letters relating to a Theorem of Mr. Euler, of the Royal Academy of Sciences at Berlin, and F.R.S. for correcting the Aberrations in the Object-Glasses of refracting Telescopes," *ibid.*, 287–296; "An Explanation of an Instrument for measuring Small Angles," **48**, pt. 2 (1754), 551–564; and "An Account of some Experiments concerning the different Refrangibility of Light," **50**, pt. 2 (1758), 733–743.

II. SECONDARY LITERATURE. Reprinted letters and papers by John and Peter Dollond, Short, Euler, and Maskelyne will be found in John Kelly, *The Life of John Dollond, F.R.S. Inventor of the Achromatic Telescope. With a copious Appendix of all the Papers referred to,* 3rd ed. (London, 1808). For an account of the priority of Chester More Hall and the patent litigation, with references, see Thomas H. Court and Moritz von Rohr, "A History of the Development of the Telescope from about 1675 to 1830 based on Documents in the Court Collection," in *Transactions of the Optical Society,* **30** (1928–1929), 207–260 (sec. IV, 228–235).

G. L'E. TURNER

DOLOMIEU, DIEUDONNÉ (called **DÉODAT**) **DE GRATET DE** (*b.* Dolomieu, Dauphiné, France, 23 June 1750; *d.* Châteauneuf, Saône-et-Loire, France, 28 [16? 29?] November 1801), *geology.*

One of eleven children of François de Gratet, marquis de Dolomieu, and of Marie-Françoise de Béranger, Dolomieu was placed in the Sovereign and Military Order of the Knights of Malta at the age of two. Because of his precocious interest in natural objects, he is supposed to have been sent to Paris for a part of his education before the beginning of his military career. He was a member of the carabiniers in 1764, then served his apprenticeship aboard one of the order's galleys in 1766, achieving the rank of second lieutenant in the same year. He rose to lieutenant in 1774, became a knight in 1778, was promoted to captain in 1779, and commander in 1780.

His career in the Knights of Malta was marked by a long series of difficulties. In 1768, after a duel in which he killed a fellow member of the order, he was sentenced to life imprisonment but was released through the intervention of Pope Clement XIII. In the early 1780's he resigned as *lieutenant du maréchal* of his Langue (Auvergne), following a dispute with the grand master concerning an alleged transgression of the rights of the Langues; he carried on a legal battle for several years thereafter, acquiring some bitter enemies within the order. He finally left Malta in 1791, and his expression of pro-Revolutionary opinion soon began to elicit accusations of his involvement in a plot to destroy the order—which did indeed suffer grave setbacks during the Revolution. Dolomieu eventually played an unwilling role in Napoleon's seizure of Malta in 1798.

Garrisoned in Metz between 1771 and 1774, Dolomieu began to cultivate science under the tutelage of Jean-Baptiste Thyrion, an apothecary who taught chemistry and physics (and who was the mentor of Jean-François Pilâtre de Rozier as well). Dolomieu became the friend of Duke Louis-Alexandre de La Rochefoucauld, who helped secure Dolomieu's election as correspondent of the Royal Academy of Sciences in 1778, and whose mother, the duchess d'Enville, was hostess of a salon where Dolomieu met members of the fashionably learned world. La Rochefoucauld, who had made the grand tour in 1765–1766 in the company of Nicolas Desmarest, helped direct Dolomieu's interests toward mineralogy. In 1775 Dolomieu toured Anjou and Brittany, investigating mines and ironworks and studying the origin of saltpeter. He traveled in the Alps and in Italy in 1776, seeing the region of Vesuvius. His eulogizer Lacépède to the contrary, he probably did not visit Sicily and climb to the summit of Etna.

Dolomieu's determination to pursue geological science became firm in 1778, when he acted as secretary to Prince Camille de Rohan during an embassy of the order to Portugal, where he studied basaltic rocks.

Soon afterward (in 1779 or 1780) he retired from active service with the Knights of Malta and devoted himself to his scientific investigations, although much of his time was taken up in litigation over affairs in the order. He maintained a home in Malta but made frequent journeys for geological and other purposes, traveling in Sicily in 1781, in the Pyrenees (with Philippe-Isidore Picot de Lapeyrouse) in 1782, in Italy and Elba in 1784, Italy and Corsica in 1786, and in the Alps in 1789 and frequently thereafter.

Dolomieu gathered a substantial mineralogical collection, the great bulk of which served him as a pretext for remaining in Malta, despite his ostensible wish to depart because of his political difficulties with the grand master. This collection ultimately became the property of Dolomieu's brother-in-law, Étienne de Drée, part of it later coming to the Muséum d'Histoire Naturelle.

In 1791 Dolomieu made his way to Paris as a strong partisan of the Revolution, to the consternation of his family and many of his noble associates. In that year he wrote to Picot de Lapeyrouse that he refrained from running for public office only on account of the standing it would cost him with relatives. He joined the Club de 1789 and the Club des Feuillants, and styled himself a constitutional monarchist, a liberal position which the march of events soon made conservative. The excesses of the Revolution—most notably the assassination of his friend La Rochefoucauld in August 1792—repelled him, and he turned against these excesses in public rebuke.

During the hard days that followed, from 1792 through part of 1794, Dolomieu lived at La Roche-Guyon, the La Rochefoucauld château. His relatives were incarcerated or executed and his financial resources wiped out. Dolomieu therefore went to work, entering into a contract with the publisher Panckoucke to write the mineralogical portion of the *Encyclopédie méthodique,* a project that Dolomieu never completed. In 1794 he was appointed to teach natural history in the Écoles Centrales of Paris, and he was named *ingénieur* of the Corps des Mines in 1795, which led in 1796 to his assumption of teaching duties in physical geography at the École des Mines. During summer seasons he inspected mines and continued his geological travels in the Alps. When the Academy of Sciences was reconstituted as part of the Institute in 1795, Dolomieu was made a member.

In 1798 Dolomieu joined Napoleon's expedition to Egypt, during which he was maneuvered into taking part in negotiations for the capitulation of Malta. His stay in Egypt was cut short by illness (and perhaps also by his chagrin at having been used by Napoleon); and on the return voyage to France, when a storm forced his ship to put in at Taranto, he and his companions were imprisoned during the Calabrian counterrevolution. Taken to Messina, Dolomieu fell victim to vindictive influences exercised against him at the court of Naples by some of the Knights of Malta. He suffered a trying solitary imprisonment of twenty-one months until his release in March 1801. His return to Paris marked the end of what had become a cause célèbre among French intellectuals, the unconscionable detention of a scientist on the pretext of reasons of war. Having been elected while in prison to Daubenton's former chair, Dolomieu began to teach at the Muséum d'Histoire Naturelle; but his health, seriously affected by his ordeal in prison, failed shortly after his last tour in the Alps. He died a bachelor, in accord with his vow as a Knight of Malta, although he had been known to fancy women.

During his relatively brief career Dolomieu acquired a reputation as one of the most astute geologists. This reputation was not attributable to any remarkable theoretical innovation, although Dolomieu was interested in theory and, indeed, possessed greater theoretical commitments than he readily acknowledged. Instead, he was esteemed as a judicious inquirer within the framework of existing styles of geological research, and it is fitting that he is the eponym of a substance—dolomite—and of the Alpine regions largely composed of it, rather than of a geological principle. He was known primarily for his studies of volcanic substances and regions; among his related interests were earthquakes, the structure of mountain ranges, the classification of rocks, and the fashion in which chemical and mineralogical studies could be applied to historical interpretation of the earth.

Dolomieu ascribed his own interest in volcanoes to the influence of Barthélemy Faujas de Saint-Fond, to whom he wrote from Portugal in 1778 concerning his investigation of the origin of basalt. During the 1770's the new idea that basalt might be of volcanic origin attracted many scientists, especially the French, and Dolomieu rapidly joined the ranks of the adherents of this theory. He accounted for the prismatic form of certain basalts by arguing that they had suffered sudden contraction from the cooling effect of water. His commitment to the proposition that volcanic products are more than casual and accidental creations of the earth, but rather constitute a significant proportion of the earth's features, is reflected in such descriptive writings as *Voyage aux îles de Lipari* (1783) and *Mémoire sur les îles Ponces* (1788), as well as his more analytical papers, most of which were published in *Observations sur la physique.*

Despite his belief in the historical significance of

volcanoes, however, Dolomieu was convinced that aqueous agents were the outstanding causes of geological change. His volcanism was always tempered by this belief. In 1790, at the beginning of the basalt controversy, he declared that "far from extending the empire of subterranean fire, I believe that more than any other [mineralogist] I have circumscribed its true limits and excluded from its domain an infinitude of regions, a multitude of substances that have been attributed to it."[1] He would not join with those who would make volcanoes responsible for the majority of geological events; to his mind, volcanic effects were limited both spatially and temporally. To be sure, volcanic activity was not an ephemeral event and had occurred repeatedly during various stages of the earth's history, but by comparison with aqueous agents it was historically an occasional event of inferior significance. He wrote that "the humid way is the most universal means, the oldest, that which acts quietly in all times and all places, to which almost all of our globe belongs, which everywhere reasserts itself and regains possession of that part of its empire . . . that it yielded momentarily to the dry way." He estimated that no more than one-twentieth of the entire surface of the earth had ever been affected by volcanic action.[2]

In expounding his doctrine of aqueous geological activity, Dolomieu set forth a historical scheme for the earth that contained many of the components of neptunism. He believed that the oldest rocks had been precipitated out of a universal fluid in the earliest epochs from which there remains any evidence. It was perfectly plausible, he acknowledged, that prior to this coagulation the earth may have experienced a history of undeterminable length, but the absence of remnants from this era prevents our knowing anything about it. The history of the earth begins, for our purposes, with a terraqueous globe and the precipitation of matter from the universal fluid.

Dolomieu reasoned that this fluid cannot have been water alone, since so much matter could not have been dissolved without the aid of some other agent, perhaps a principle of fire or light, such as phlogiston (in 1791 Dolomieu had already noted that this principle was being rejected by chemists, but this did not deter him from positing some like essence). Precipitation out of the primordial solvent must have taken place in reverse order of solubility, in a slow and orderly fashion, and upon its completion the solvent material had largely disappeared. The means of its removal posed a problem; perhaps the atmosphere absorbed it.

The next stage in the geological history proposed by Dolomieu was a series of violent upheavals result-

ing in the rearrangement of the originally crystallized rocks. These catastrophes occurred before the creation of mechanical deposits and determined once and for all the major irregularities of the earth's surface. Whatever consideration Dolomieu gave to geological agents of a regular nature, he did not envision them as capable of accomplishing large alterations in the mountains and basins created by these catastrophes. The source of the violent uplifting force causing this sudden rearrangement was uncertain, but might probably be chosen from among three possibilities—interior force, the loss of interior support (as in the creation of underground caverns), or exterior shock. Dolomieu inclined toward the last possibility. On consulting Laplace, Dolomieu was assured that normal gravitational forces could not account for such upheavals, but that either a passing comet or the "accidental" causes of volcanic eruptions might bring about catastrophic uplift.[3]

Following the process of upheaval, alterations in the rearranged depositions were brought about by "transport," or mechanical deposits deriving from degradation of the mountainous uplands. These beds, however, were also disturbed from time to time by catastrophic currents, probably in the form of immense tides. Dolomieu steadfastly held to a belief in recurrent catastrophic alteration of the fundamentally established order of things, and in the greatly variable intensity of geological forces. His fascination with earthquakes was consistent with this catastrophism. Violent means were the principal causes of change in the earth's surface, he thought, and his geological time scale was accordingly short. He thought 10,000 years to be a generous—even excessive—estimate of the extent of the era following the great catastrophic upheavals. Dolomieu therefore opposed the idea of the action of slow and cumulative forces bringing about geological change over a great period of time. Calling upon force rather than time as the cause of such changes, he wrote that "in fashioning the earth such as we inhabit it, nature has not spent time with as much prodigality as some celebrated writers have supposed."[4] Remarks of this nature and his denial that significant consolidation of rocks occurs in the ocean depths, at least along coasts, suggest that Dolomieu may have intended to make known his opposition to the main tenets of Huttonian theory, although no explicit references to Hutton are known among Dolomieu's writings.

Dolomieu's overall geological scheme, then, was not volcanist, but rather shared much in common with the opponents of doctrinaire volcanism. All the same, he was an authority on volcanoes and volcanic action, and spoke with an influential voice on the subject.

One of his major concerns in studying volcanoes was the nature and source of volcanic ejecta. Dolomieu's view of the mineralogical nature of lava depended on the conception of lavas as being warm and viscous, but never especially hot. An intrinsic source of heat within the lava, he believed, maintains the lava's heat at a relatively even and moderate level. The exact identity of this intrinsic heat source was uncertain; it might be (or contain) sulfur, and it might be the same principle responsible for the binding action within certain rocks (such as granite), which always seem hard when unearthed but often crumble upon exposure to air, presumably because of the release of some substance that had joined the parts.

In any case, Dolomieu rejected any possibility of finding the source of volcanic heat in such fuels as coal or oil. On the other hand, there appears to be little ground for attributing to him a belief in an intense central heat within the globe. His investigations in Auvergne did convince him by 1797 that granites lie above the sources of volcanic eruptions and that the interior of the globe may therefore be fluid, but he did not cast aside the opinion that the modest heat of this viscous core comes from an intrinsic chemical source, such as caloric.[5]

The components of lavas are always traceable to a nonvolcanic origin, according to Dolomieu. In lava these components do not decompose, for the most part, but retain their mineralogical character. Volcanic heat does not destroy the older mineral composition, but merely "dilates" or "disunites" the integrant molecules, allowing them to slip past one another without being disaggregated. Lavas are therefore not vitrifications. The sources (*foyers*) of volcanoes are quite deep below the surface of the earth and are not limited to one particular type of rock, which explains the variability in composition of lavas. Many of Dolomieu's writings reflect his serious concern to determine which mineral substances have been subject to volcanic action, as well as the effects of volcanic heat on the resulting rock. His deep knowledge of the precise nature of various volcanic ejecta was perhaps the main foundation of the respect accorded him by other scientists.

There is discernible in the development of Dolomieu's thought a drift toward increasing interest in a theory of mineral classification and lithology, accompanied by a growing interest in what German mineralogists were doing. In the early 1780's Dolomieu secured a shipment of Saxon mineral samples through the assistance of Johann Friedrich Charpentier, professor at the Freiberg Bergakademie, and shortly before his death Dolomieu was planning a trip to Freiberg to visit Werner and perhaps take steps toward a reconciliation of German and French mineralogies.

Dolomieu clearly felt a certain affinity with Werner, but his greatest expressions of mineralogical debt and admiration were reserved for Haüy, whom he regarded as the founder of a new and highly fruitful approach to knowledge of mineral substances. Dolomieu came to believe in the importance of the form and constitution of the constituent structural unit, as opposed to the relative quantity of constituent substances, in determining a mineral substance's characteristics. His commitment to the integrant molecule as the basis of a new mineralogy is recorded in *Sur la philosophie minéralogique, et sur l'espèce minéralogique* (1801), which he had begun to compose during his imprisonment and in which he pursued the hope of raising mineralogy to the degree of precision that had recently been achieved, he thought, by chemistry.

Dolomieu was excited by the prospect of reducing the variety of mineral appearances to the chemical and spatial properties of the unique integrant molecule—which by definition established mineral species. Part of his excitement derived from his recognition that by assuming the integrant molecule to exist, one avoided having to deal with mineral species as only a matter of convention.

In light of Dolomieu's avowed empiricism, it is interesting that he saw this promising new development in mineralogy as the outgrowth of conceptual, not observational, investigation; species cannot be definitively distinguished by any mechanical operation, but only in the mind. On the whole, however, Dolomieu regarded himself as a scientist firmly rooted in observational technique. His many trips in the volcanic regions of Italy, in the Alps, and in other areas of geological interest were part of his program for geological investigation, and his mineral collection appears to have been a major focus of his empirical energies, especially early in his career.

Dolomieu was, however, given to making occasional tributes to experience as the fount of scientific knowledge. The scientists he praised most highly were often observationalists like Horace Bénédict de Saussure. He was inclined to see disputes over geological issues as resolvable by recourse to simple observation, if not by reasonable determination to eliminate unnecessary semantic disagreement. In the turmoil of doctrinaire controversy in geology at the end of the eighteenth century, he saw himself as a practical-minded and moderate scientist with excellent credentials as a mediator between rival extremes.

Dolomite was named after Dolomieu by Nicolas Théodore de Saussure, to whom Dolomieu had given samples of the substance after describing it as a calcareous rock from Tirol that was attacked by acid without effervescence.[6]

NOTES

1. "Sur la question de l'origine du basalte," in *Observations sur la physique*, **37** (1790), 193.
2. *Ibid.*, p. 194.
3. Lacroix, *Déodat Dolomieu*, II, 132.
4. "Mémoire sur les pierres composées," in *Observations sur la physique*, **39** (1791), 394.
5. "Rapport," in *Journal de physique*, **3** (1798), 406–411.
6. *Observations sur la physique*, **39** (1791), 3–10; **40** (1792), 161–173.

BIBLIOGRAPHY

I. ORIGINAL WORKS. Dolomieu's books are *Voyage aux îles de Lipari fait en 1781* (Paris, 1783; German trans., Leipzig, 1783); *Mémoire sur les tremblemens de terre de la Calabre pendant l'année 1783* (Rome, 1784; Italian trans., Rome, 1784; German trans., Leipzig, 1789; English trans., as part of John Pinkerton, *General Collection of the Best and Most Interesting Voyages and Travels in All Parts of the World*, V [London, 1809], 273–297); *Mémoire sur les îles Ponces, et catalogue raisonné des produits de l'Etna* (Paris, 1788); and *Sur la philosophie minéralogique, et sur l'espèce minéralogique* (Paris, 1801; German trans., Hamburg-Mainz, 1802).

Among Dolomieu's principal articles are "Mémoire sur les volcans éteints du Val di Noto en Sicile," in *Observations sur la physique, sur l'histoire naturelle et sur les arts*, **25** (1784), 191–205; "Lettre de M. le commandeur Déodat de Dolomieux, à M. le baron de Salis-Masklin, à Coire dans les Grisons: Sur la question de l'origine du basalte," *ibid.*, **37** (1790), 193–202; "Mémoire sur les pierres composées et sur les roches," *ibid.*, **39** (1791), 374–407; **40** (1792), 41–62, 203–218, 372–403; "Mémoire sur la constitution physique de l'Égypte," *ibid.*, **42** (1793), 41–61, 108–126, 194–215; "Distribution méthodique de toutes les matières dont l'accumulation forme les montagnes volcaniques, ou tableau systématique dans lequel peuvent se placer toutes les substances qui ont des relations avec les feux souterrains," in *Journal de physique, de chimie et d'histoire naturelle*, **1** (1794), 102–125; "Mémoire sur les roches en général, & particulièrement sur les pétro-silex, les trapps & les roches de corne, pour servir à la distribution méthodique des produits volcaniques," *ibid.*, **1** (1794), 175–200, 241–263, 406–428; **2** (1794), 81–105; "Discours sur l'étude de la géologie," *ibid.*, **2** (1794), 256–272; "Lettre à M. Pictet, professeur de physique à Genève, et membre de la Société royale de Londres, sur la chaleur des laves, et sur des concrétions quartzeuses," in *Journal des mines*, **4**, no. 22 (1796), 53–72; "Lettre sur la nécessité d'unir les connaissances chimiques à celles du minéralogiste; Avec des observations sur la différente acception que les auteurs allemands et français donnent au mot chrysolithe," *ibid.*, **5**, no. 29 (1797), 365–376; "Rapport fait à l'Institut National, par Dolomieu, sur ses voyages de l'an cinquième & sixième," in *Journal de physique, de chimie, d'histoire naturelle et des arts*, **3** (1798), 401–427, and *Journal des mines*, **7** (1798), 385–402, 405–432.

Dolomieu's "Osservazioni ed annotazioni relative a spiegare ed illustrare la classazione metodica di tutte le produzioni volcaniche" was published with Torbern Bergman's *De' prodotti volcanici considerati chimicamente dissertazione*, Giuseppe Tofani, trans. (Florence, 1789[?]).

Dolomieu's letters to Barthélemy Faujas de Saint-Fond (1778) were published in the latter's *Recherches sur les volcans éteints du Vivarais et du Velay* (Grenoble-Paris, 1778), pp. 440–446. Alfred Lacroix edited several of Dolomieu's previously unpublished papers and notes, including "Une note de Dolomieu sur les basaltes de Lisbonne, adressée en 1779 à l'Académie Royale des Sciences," in *Comptes rendus hebdomadaires des séances de l'Académie des sciences*, **167** (1918), 437–444; "Un voyage géologique en Sicile en 1781," in *Bulletin de la Section de géographie du Comité des travaux historiques et scientifiques* (1918), 29–213; "L'exploration géologique des Pyrénées par Dolomieu en 1782," in *Bulletin de la Société Ramond* (1917–1918), 120–178; and "Vues générales sur le Dauphiné," in *Bulletin de la Société de statistique, des sciences naturelles et des arts industriels du département de l'Isère*, **40** (1919), 237–282. Dolomieu's Egyptian notes, G. Daressy, ed., appeared as "Dolomieu en Égypte (30 juin 1798–10 mars 1799)," in *Mémoires présentés à l'Institut d'Égypte*, **3** (1922).

II. SECONDARY LITERATURE. The fullest biographical treatment is Alfred Lacroix, *Déodat Dolomieu*, 2 vols. (Paris, 1921), consisting largely of selections from Dolomieu's correspondence and other previously unedited material, preceded by a "Notice historique." A contemporary eulogy is Lacépède's "Notice historique sur la vie et les ouvrages de Dolomieu," in *Histoire de la classe des sciences mathématiques et physiques* (Institut National de France), **7** (1806), 117–138, and in *Journal des mines*, **12** (1802), 221–242.

Information on Dolomieu's mineralogical ideas is in Karl Wilhelm Nose, *Beschreibung einer Sammlung von meist vulkanisirten Fossilien die Deodat-Dolomieu im Jahre 1791 von Maltha aus nach Augsburg und Berlin versandte* (Frankfurt-am-Main, 1797). T. C. Bruun-Neergaard's account of Dolomieu's last summer tour is in *Journal du dernier voyage du C^{en}. Dolomieu dans les Alpes* (Paris, 1802).

See also Kenneth L. Taylor, "The Geology of Déodat de Dolomieu," in *Actes*, XIIth International Congress of the History of Science (1968).

KENNETH L. TAYLOR

DOMAGK, GERHARD (*b.* Lagow, Brandenburg, Germany, 30 October 1895; *d.* Burgberg, Germany, 24 April 1964), *medicine, chemistry, pharmacology.*

Domagk, the son of a teacher, decided to study medicine while still at a scientifically oriented grammar school in Liegnitz (now Legnica). During his first term at the University of Kiel, World War I broke out and Domagk volunteered for active service with a German grenadier regiment. After being wounded he transferred to the German army medical corps and received his M.D. at Kiel in 1921. For a short while he worked as an assistant to the chemist Ernest Hoppe-Seyler and in 1924 became reader (*Privatdozent*) in pathology at the University of Greifswald. In 1925 he accepted a similar post at the University of Münster and married Gertrud Strube. They had four children, and his only daughter was one of the first patients to be treated successfully with prontosil rubrum for a severe streptococcal infection.

Domagk became extraordinary professor of general pathology and pathological anatomy at Münster in 1928 and ordinary professor in 1958.

In 1924 Domagk published a paper on the defensive function of the reticuloendothelial system against infections. As a result of that paper and of his well-known interest in chemotherapy the directors of the I. G. Farbenindustrie appointed him—at the age of thirty-two—director of research at their laboratory for experimental pathology and bacteriology at Wuppertal-Elberfeld. It was the turning point of his career.

Since Paul Ehrlich's discovery of arsphenamine in 1909, chemotherapy had advanced in the field of protozoan and tropical diseases, but hardly any progress had been made in regard to bacterial infections of man; and the I. G. Farbenindustrie had decided on further testing of potential antibacterial agents, along the lines laid down by Ehrlich. Domagk's interest centered on the so-called azo dyes, in which one hydrogen atom had been replaced by a sulfonamide group. These dyes, which had been developed as early as 1909 by H. Hörlein and his collaborators, conferred on textiles a high resistance to washing and light, because of their intimate combination with wool proteins.

In 1932 Domagk's colleagues, the chemists Fritz Mietzsch and Josef Klarer, synthesized a new azo dye, hoping that it would prove to be a fast dye for treating leather. It was -4' sulfonamide-2-4-diaminoazobenzol, which they named prontosil rubrum. Domagk early recognized its protective power against streptococcal infections in mice and its low toxicity, but he withheld publication of his findings until 1935. His paper "Ein Beitrag zur Chemotherapie der bakteriellen Infektionen" has become not only a classic but—measured by strict experimental and statistical yardsticks—a masterpiece of careful and critical evaluation of a new therapeutic agent.

As early as 1933 A. Förster had reported the dramatic recovery of an infant with staphylococcal septicemia after treatment with prontosil rubrum, but Domagk's discovery—after so many years of fruitless searching for specific antibacterial agents—was received with a great deal of skepticism. In 1936

L. Colebrook and M. Kenny of the British Medical Research Council confirmed Domagk's findings and concluded that "the clinical results together with the mouse experiments support the view that . . . there is more hope of controlling these early streptococcal infections by the administration of this or some related chemotherapeutical agent than by any other means at present available." In the first paper on prontosil published in the United States, P. H. Long and E. A. Bliss mentioned Domagk only as one of the investigators of prontosil, but in the same issue of the *Journal of the American Medical Association*, its editor gave Domagk full credit for his significant paper and hoped that "further investigations will disclose a definite group of disorders characterised by high virulence and mortality which can be materially helped by appropriate chemotherapy." Their hopes were indeed fulfilled, but only after workers at the Pasteur Institute in Paris—the Tréfuëls, F. Nitti, D. Bovet, and E. Fourneau—had established that the azo component of prontosil dissociated *in vivo* and that the liberated sulfonamide radical was responsible for the antibacterial effect. This was a very important discovery, because sulfonamide could be produced far more cheaply than prontosil.

Ironically enough, at that very time an agar plate containing an even more powerful antibacterial agent—penicillin—lay forgotten in St. Mary's Hospital in London. Its owner, Alexander Fleming, had become highly interested in prontosil and the sulfonamide derivatives that followed, but in his many papers on antibacterial and antiseptic treatment published between 1938 and 1940 he never mentioned penicillin, the antistaphylococcal action of which he had first observed in 1928.

In 1938 L. E. H. Whitby synthesized sulfapyridine, which soon became the drug of choice in the treatment of the pneumococcal pneumonias. Many other sulfa drugs followed in quick succession. The structural formulas of the most important ones are shown in Figure 1.

Domagk's discovery profoundly changed the prognosis of many dangerous and potentially fatal diseases such as puerperal fever, erysipelas, cerebrospinal meningitis, and pneumonia.

In October 1939, sponsored by American, French, and British scientists, Domagk was awarded the Nobel Prize in physiology or medicine. He duly acknowledged the great honor to the rector of the Caroline Institute; but some weeks later, after having been arrested by the Gestapo, he declined the prize in a letter drafted for him by the German authorities. (After the peace prize had been awarded in 1936 to the German radical and pacifist writer Carl von

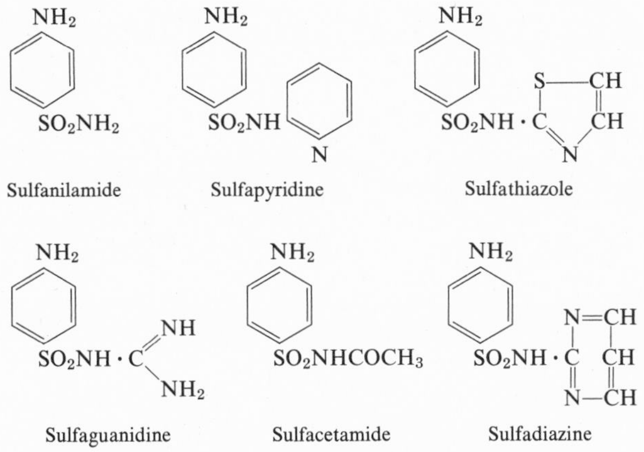

FIGURE 1. Structural formulas of some major sulfonamides.

Ossietzky, who was a prisoner in a concentration camp, Hitler had forbidden any German to accept a Nobel Prize.) Domagk eventually received the Nobel Prize medal (1947), but by then the prize money had been redistributed. He received many other high honors and an honorary professorship of the University of Valencia, and he became doctor *honoris causa* of many European and American universities. He was especially pleased by the award of the Paul Ehrlich Gold Medal and the Cameron Medal of Edinburgh and by his election as a foreign correspondent of the Royal Society of London.

The discovery of the sulfonamides reawakened interest in the sulfones, the derivatives of 4, 4′-diaminodiphenyl-sulfone (DDS) (Fig. 2). Because of their high toxicity the sulfones had never been favored in the treatment of acute bacterial infections, but in 1941, E. V. Cowdry and C. Ruangsiri reported encouraging effects in treating rat leprosy with a DDS derivative, sodium glucosulfone. After G. H. Faget and his co-workers confirmed this in a clinical trial in 1943, the sulfones largely replaced the venerable chaulmoogra oil in the treatment of human leprosy and revolutionized the prognosis of this biblical scourge.

After World War II, with the antibiotics having

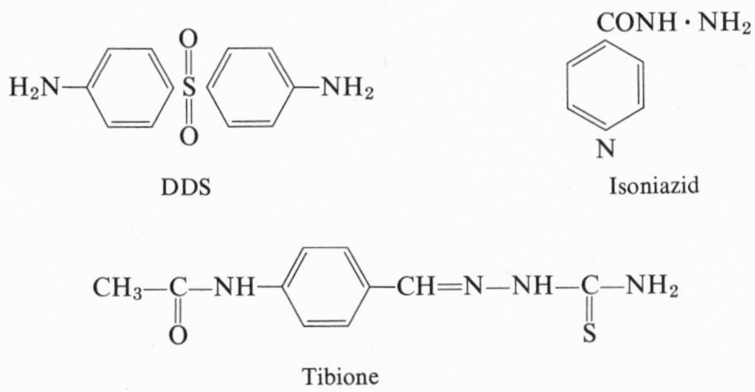

joined the therapeutic armamentarium against acute bacterial diseases, Domagk's interests shifted to the chemotherapy of tuberculosis. The euphoria induced by the discovery of streptomycin had by that time given way to considerable disillusionment because of the rapidly increasing numbers of streptomycin-resistant strains of the tuberculosis mycobacterium.

Together with R. Behnisch, F. Mietzsch, and H. Schmidt, Domagk reported in 1946 on the tuberculostatic action *in vitro* of the thiosemicarbazones of which the 4′-acetyl-aminobenzaldehyde (Conteben, Tibione) seemed to be the most promising compounds. Because of their many and dangerous toxic side effects the thiosemicarbazones never became popular in clinical medicine, but for many years they were used as "second-line drugs" against mycobacteria that were resistant to one or more of the standard antituberculous drugs.

The work of Domagk and his colleagues with the thiosemicarbazones resulted, however, in a supremely important accidental discovery. In 1945 V. Chorine had reported on the tuberculostatic action of the nicotinamides, and his findings were rediscovered by D. McKenzie, L. Malone, S. Kushner, J. J. Oleson, and Y. Subba Row in 1948. This produced no practical results until it became known that the active agents of the nicotinamides were derivatives of isonicotinic acids. In 1951 H. H. Fox tried to prepare isonicotinaldehyde-thiosemicarbazone. An intermediate product, isonicotinoylhydrazine (isoniazid), was tested in New York's Sea View Hospital in 1952 and has since become one of the most potent and reliable drugs in the treatment of tuberculosis.

Finally Domagk turned to the greatest challenge of all, the chemotherapy of cancer. He experimented mostly with ethylene-iminoquinones, but success evaded him as it did so many other workers in that field. In a letter quoted by Colebrook he wrote: "One should not have too great expectations of the future of cytostatic agents."

It is characteristic of Domagk's intensive scientific curiosity and humane outlook that he wrote at the end of his life: "If I could start again, I would perhaps become a psychiatrist and search for a causal therapy of Mental Disease which is the most terrifying problem of our times."

The dawn of the new chemotherapeutic era in Germany was no accident, if only for the traditional close association between the chemical industry and medical research in that country. Nevertheless, twenty-seven years passed between P. Gelmo's first preparation of a sulfonamide in 1908, during Ehrlich's lifetime, and its recognition by Domagk as an *elixirium magnum sterilisans*. Gelmo's original paper,

FIGURE 2. Structural formulas of DDS, isoniazid, and tibione.

"Sulphamides of P-aminobenzene Sulphonic Acid," is in *Journal für praktische Chemie,* **77** (1908), 369–382.

Domagk was fortunate in having adequate chemical help, the lack of which prevented Fleming from advancing with penicillin for eleven years. But here, as in so many similar situations, Pasteur's famous dictum applies: "The lucky chance favors only the prepared mind."

BIBLIOGRAPHY

I. ORIGINAL WORKS. Domagk's writings are "Untersuchungen über die Bedeutung des retikuloendothelialen Systems für die Vernichtung von Infektionserregern und für die Enstehung des Amyloids," in *Virchows Archiv für pathologische Anatomie und Physiologie und für klinische Medizin,* **253** (1924), 594–638; "Ein Beitrag zur Chemotherapie der bakteriellen Infektionen," in *Deutsche medizinische Wochenschrift,* **61** (1935), 250–253; "Über eine neue, gegen Tuberkelbazillen in vitro wirksame Verbindungsklasse," in *Naturwissenschaften,* **33** (1946), 315, written with R. Behnisch, F. Mietzsch, and H. Schmidt; *Pathologische Anatomie und Chemotherapie der Infektions-Krankheiten* (Stuttgart, 1947); "Investigations on the Anti-tuberculous Activity of the Thiosemicarbazones *in vitro & in vivo,*" in *American Review of Tuberculosis and Pulmonary Diseases,* **61** (1950), 8–19; "Chemotherapy of Cancer by Ethylenimino-quinones," in *Annals of the New York Academy of Sciences,* **68** (1957–1958), 1197–1204; and "Über 30 Jahre Arzt," in *Therapie der Gegenwart,* **102** (1963), 913–917.

II. SECONDARY LITERATURE. Writings on Domagk or his work are V. Chorine, "Action de l'amide nicotinique sur les bacilles du genre mycobacterium," in *Comptes rendus hebdomadaires des séances de l'Académie des sciences,* **220** (1945), 150–151; L. Colebrook, "Gerhard Domagk," in *Biographical Memoirs of the Royal Society,* **10** (1964), 39–50; L. Colebrook and M. Kenny, "Treatment of Human Puerperal Infections and Experimental Infections in Mice with Prontosil," in *Lancet* (1936), **1**, 1279–1286; E. V. Cowdry and C. Ruangsuri, "Influence of Promin, Starch and Heptaldehyde on Experimental Leprosy in Rats," in *Archives of Pathology,* **32** (1941), 632–640; G. H. Faget *et al.,* "The Promin Treatment of Leprosy, a Progress Report," in *Public Health Reports,* **58** (1943), 1729–1741; E. Fourneau *et al.,* "Chimiothérapie des infections streptococciques par les dérivés du p-aminophénylsulfamide," in *Comptes rendus des séances de la Société de biologie,* **122** (1936), 652–654; H. H. Fox, "The Chemical Attack on Tuberculosis," in *Transactions of the New York Academy of Sciences,* **15** (1952), 234–242; L. S. Goodman and A. Gilman, *The Pharmacological Basis of Therapeutics* (New York, 1960), pp. 1250–1300.

See also H. Hörlein, "Chemotherapy of Infectious Diseases Caused by Protozoa and Bacteria," in *Proceedings of the Royal Society of Medicine,* **29** (1936), 313–324; editorial in *Journal of the American Medical Association,* **108** (1937), 48–49; P. H. Long and E. A. Bliss, "Para-Amino-Benzene-Sulfonamide and Its Derivatives," *ibid.,* pp. 32–37; D. McKenzie *et al.,* "The Effect of Nicotinic Acid-amide on Experimental Tuberculosis of White Mice," in *Journal of Laboratory and Clinical Medicine,* **33** (1948), 1249–1253; I. J. Selikoff *et al.,* "Chemotherapy of Tuberculosis With Hydrazine Derivatives of Isonicotinic Acid," in *Quarterly Bulletin of Sea View Hospital* (New York), **13** (1952), 27; T. L. Sourkes, *Nobel Prize Winners* (New York, 1967), pp. 214–219; O. Warburg, "Gerhard Domagk," in *Deutsche medizinische Wochenschrift,* **90** (1965), 34, 1484–1486; L. E. H. Whitby, "Chemotherapy of Pneumococcal and Other Infections With 2- (p-aminobenzenesulfonamide) pyridine," in *Lancet* (1938), **1**, 1210–1212.

ERICH POSNER

DOMBEY, JOSEPH (*b.* Mâcon, France, 22 February 1742; *d.* Montserrat, West Indies, 18 February 1794), *medicine, botany.*

The tenth of the fourteen children of Jean-Philibert Dombey, a baker, and Marie Carra, Dombey was orphaned at the age of fourteen. After studying with the Jesuits, he studied medicine at Montpellier and graduated in 1767. Antoine Gouan and Pierre Cusson stimulated Dombey to pursue natural history, and he carried out fieldwork in the Pyrenees, the Alps, and the Vosges. He went to Paris in 1772 and took courses under Antoine-Laurent Jussieu and Lemonnier, and in 1776 he was appointed royal botanist for the study of South American plants that could acclimatize to France.

Dombey left Cádiz in 1777 with the Spanish botanists Hipólito Ruiz and José Pavón, reaching Callao, Peru, in 1778. Dombey studied the Peruvian vegetation, particularly the so-called American cinnamon, searched for platinum and saltpeter, analyzed the Chauchín spa, and made archaeological explorations in Chan Chan, Pachacamac, and Tarma; at Huánuco he found cinchona. In 1781 he went to Chile, exploring the mines of Coquimbo and Copiapó, and returned to France in 1785.

Dombey had promised not to publish his observations prior to those of the Spaniards, and his ill health and disappointments caused him to sell his books and to burn all his notes and observations when he retired to Lyons. In 1793, during the Revolution, he became surgeon at the military hospital of Lyons and afterward was commissioned to take the standards of the decimal system to the United States and to arrange the purchase of grain. His ship was captured by the British and he died in prison, but news of his death did not reach France until October 1794.

Dombey introduced the Araucanian pine, named after him, into naval construction and presented to the Jardin des Plantes, Paris, a great number of specimens and his herbarium, containing more than 1,500 new species. He was made a member of the Academia de Medicina, Madrid, and the Académie des Sciences, Paris.

BIBLIOGRAPHY

I. ORIGINAL WORKS. Since he burned his notes and manuscripts, Dombey's only printed works are "Lettre sur la salpêtre du Pérou et la phosphorescence de la mer," published by Lalande in the *Journal de physique,* **15** (1780), 212–214; and certain observations included by Ruiz and Pavón in the *Flora peruviana et chilensis* (4 vols., Madrid, 1798–1802). Dombey's correspondence has been published as E. T. Hamy, *Joseph Dombey, médecin, naturaliste, archéologue, explorateur du Pérou, du Chili et du Brésil* (*1778–1785*), *sa vie, son oeuvre, sa correspondance* (Paris, 1905). J. Riquelme Salar, "El Doctor Dombey, médico francés; su labor científica en los reinos del Perú y Chile, año 1777–85," in *Proceedings of the International Congress of the History of Medicine,* **1** (1959), 160–162, also contains the correspondence.

II. SECONDARY LITERATURE. On Dombey or his work, see E. Dubois, *Le naturaliste Joseph Dombey* (Bourg-en-Bresse, 1934); and A. R. Steele, *Flowers for the King. The Expedition of Ruiz and Pavón and the Flora of Perou* (Durham, N.C., 1964).

FRANCISCO GUERRA

DOMINGO DE SOTO. *See* **Soto, Domingo de.**

DOMINIC GUNDISSALINUS. *See* **Gundissalinus, Dominicus.**

DOMINICUS DE CLAVASIO, also known as **Dominicus de Clavagio, Dominicus Parisiensis,** or **Dominic de Chivasso** (*fl.* mid-fourteenth century), *mathematics, medicine, astrology.*

Dominicus de Clavasio's birthdate is unknown, but he was born near Turin and was active in Paris from about the mid-1340's. He taught arts at Paris during 1349–1350, was head of the Collège de Constantinople at Paris in 1349, and was an M.A. by 1350. Dominicus received the M.D. by 1356 and was on the medical faculty at Paris during 1356–1357. He was astrologer at the court of John II and may have died between 1357 and 1362.

Dominicus is the author of a *Practica geometriae* written in 1346; a *questio* on the *Sphere* of Sacrobosco; a *Questiones super perspectivam;* a set of *questiones* on the first two books of the *De caelo* of Aristotle, written before 1357; and possibly a commentary on Aristotle's *Meteorology.* He mentions in the *Practica* his intention to write a *Tractatus de umbris et radiis.*

The *questiones* on the *De caelo* have not been edited, although a few that are concerned with physical problems have been examined. They reveal that Dominicus is part of the tradition established at Paris during the fourteenth century by Jean Buridan, Nicole Oresme, and Albert of Saxony. Like these Parisian contemporaries, he adopted the impetus theory as an explanation of projectile motion as well as of acceleration in free fall. Also like his colleagues at Paris, Dominicus considered impetus as a quality. As is true of the *Questiones de caelo* of Albert of Saxony, Dominicus' discussions of impetus reveal the influence of both Oresme and Buridan. If Dominicus were directly familiar with Oresme's conceptions of impetus, he most likely drew them from the latter's early Latin *questiones* on the *De caelo* and obviously not from his much later French *Du ciel.* According to Dominicus, a body in violent motion possessed both impetus and an "actual force" (*virtus actualis*), although the relationship between these factors is unclear. Also, as Nicole Oresme may have done, he may have connected impetus with acceleration rather than velocity.

The *Practica* was a popular work during the Middle Ages and has survived in numerous manuscript versions. It served, for example, as a model for a *Geometria culmensis,* written in both Latin and German near the end of the fourteenth century. The *Practica* is divided into an introduction and three books. The introduction contains arithmetical rules and the description of an instrument, the *quadratum geometricum* of Gerbert. Book I deals with problems of measurement, book II contains geometrical constructions of two-dimensional figures, and book III is concerned with three-dimensional figures. In the course of the *Practica,* Dominicus mentions Ptolemy and the thirteenth-century mathematician and astronomer Campanus of Novara.

The *Questiones super perspectivam* reveal Dominicus' familiarity with the standard authors of the medieval optical tradition, such as Witelo, al-Rāzī (Rhazes), Roger Bacon, Peckham, and Ibn al-Haytham (Alhazen). His work is not based, however, on the influential *Perspectiva communis* of Peckham but is a commentary on the *De aspectibus* of Ibn al-Haytham and the latter's Latin successor, Witelo.

Insofar as his thought has been examined, Dominicus de Clavasio appears not as an innovator but as a fairly conventional continuator of well-established medieval traditions.

BIBLIOGRAPHY

I. ORIGINAL WORKS. H. L. L. Busard, ed., "The *Practica geometriae* of Dominicus de Clavasio," in *Archives for*

History of Exact Sciences, **2** (1962–1966), 520–575, contains the entire text; Graziella Federici Vescovini, "Les questions de 'perspective' de Dominicus de Clivaxo," in *Centaurus,* **10** (1964–1965), 14–28, contains an edition of questions 1 and 6.

II. SECONDARY LITERATURE. On Dominicus or his work, see A. von Braunmühl, *Vorlesungen über Geschichte der Trigonometrie,* I (Leipzig, 1900), 107–110; M. Cantor, *Vorlesungen über Geschichte der Mathematik,* II (Leipzig, 1899), 127, 150–154, 450–452; M. Clagett, *The Science of Mechanics in the Middle Ages* (Madison, Wis., 1959), pp. 635, 636, note; M. Curtze, "Über den Dominicus parisiensis der *Geometria culmensis,*" in *Bibliotheca mathematica,* 2nd ser., **9** (1895), 107–110; and "Über die im Mittelalter zur Feldmessung benutzten Instrumente," *ibid.,* **10** (1896), 69–72; G. Eneström, "Über zwei angebliche mathematische Schulen im christlicher Mittelalter," in *Bibliotheca mathematica,* 3rd ser., **7** (1907), 252–262; Anneliese Maier, *Zwei Grundprobleme der scholastischen Naturphilosophie* (Rome, 1951), pp. 241–243; *An der Grenze von Scholastik und Naturwissenschaft* (Rome, 1952), pp. 121, 209; *Metaphysische Hintergrunde der spätscholastischen Naturphilosophie* (Rome, 1955), p. 365, note; and *Zwischen Philosophie und Mechanik* (Rome, 1958), p. 218; H. Mendthal, ed., *Geometria culmensis. Ein agronomischer Tractat aus der Zeit des Hochmeisters Conrad von Jungingen, 1393–1407* (Leipzig, 1886), which contains the Latin and German texts of the *Geometria culmensis;* K. Michalski, "La physique nouvelle et les différents courants philosophiques au xive siècle," in *Bulletin international de l'Académie polonaise des sciences et des lettres. Classe d'histoire et de philosophie, et de philologie* (Cracow), *année 1927* (1928), 150; P. Tannery, *Mémoires scientifiques,* V, J. L. Heiberg, ed. (Paris, 1922), 329–330, 357–358; Lynn Thorndike, *A History of Magic and Experimental Science,* III (New York, 1934), 587–588; *The Sphere of Sacrobosco and Its Commentators* (Chicago, 1949), p. 37; and E. Wickersheimer, *Dictionnaire biographique des médecins en France au moyen âge* (Paris, 1936), p. 121.

CLAUDIA KREN

DOMINIS, MARKO ANTONIJE (*b.* Rab, Yugoslavia, 1560; *d.* Rome, Italy, 8 September 1626), *physics.*

After finishing his studies in Padua, Dominis lectured on mathematics, logic, and philosophy at Verona, Padua, and Brescia until 1596. Later he was appointed bishop of Senj and then archbishop of Split. The last years of his life were devoted chiefly to theological questions. In his main theological work, *De republica ecclesiastica,* which he wrote during this period and which contributed most to his fame, he urged unity of all Christian churches, their commitment to exclusively spiritual ends, and peace among nations. These beliefs made it necessary for Dominis to flee to England. Soon after his return to Rome he was imprisoned by the Inquisition. He died in a dungeon, and after his death he was found guilty of heresy and his body was burned.

Dominis had written two works on physics by the time he lectured on mathematics in Padua. The first one, *De radiis visus et lucis,* deals with lenses, telescopes, and the rainbow. Dominis knew how light was refracted in its passage from one medium to another, but he was not always consistent in his assertions. He held that it was possible that in some cases light could pass through the border of a medium without being refracted—for instance, into a thin layer of water. In general, his observations on refraction in lenses were correct.

After the invention of the telescope Dominis added its theoretical explanation to his work. His explanation was not entirely satisfactory, however, because his knowledge of the law of refraction was incomplete. He concluded that the image of an object was enlarged by increasing the angle of sight, which he had previously defined correctly. Thus Dominis describes in particular detail the effect on the angle of sight of a lens of greater curvature or of a greater distance between the lens and the object being viewed. With the same thoroughness he examined lens combinations, in particular the combination of a convex object glass and a concave eyepiece. This work led to his discovery of the conditions under which the magnification of an image is possible.

A greater part of *De radiis visus et lucis* is concerned with the rainbow. Dominis held that a rainbow is caused by refraction and reflection in raindrops: upon entering the drop, the light is refracted, then is reflected on the inner side of the drop, and then leaves the drop. This process had already been asserted by Dietrich von Freiberg, but the dependence of Dominis' theory on Dietrich's cannot be proved. Unlike Dietrich, Dominis failed to see that upon leaving the raindrop, the light was refracted again. As for the secondary rainbow, Dominis thought that the light struck on the drops' surfaces more obliquely than in the primary rainbow. His theory does not assert that the secondary rainbow is caused after two reflections on the inner side of the drop. Dominis could not explain the order of the colors in a rainbow because he used the Aristotelian theory of the mixture of darkness and light.

In *Euripus seu de fluxu et refluxu* Dominis is concerned with the tides. The greater part of the book deals with the figure of the earth, advocating sphericity and refuting the opinion of Patricius, who thought that the configuration of the earth was irregular.

Dominis believed the tide was caused by the influence of the moon and the sun on the sea in a manner analogous to the working of a magnet. He adopted Grisogono's theory of a second daily tide caused by the influence of the celestial point opposite the moon or the celestial point opposite the sun. Yielding to objections of his contemporaries, Dominis corrected this theory and introduced the influence of a transpolar circle through the moon and the sun. Dominis summed up the influences of both bodies in any position and thus accounted for all the different elevations of the sea. He was correct in believing that the tide wave was not the result of the lateral transportation of a mass of water, but rather to its rising and falling in depth and place; the wave moves horizontally, but each particle of water vertically. He wrongly ascribed the cause of tide differences in closed seas to characteristics of these seas, such as salinity and warmth.

BIBLIOGRAPHY

I. ORIGINAL WORKS. Dominis' scientific works are *De radiis visus et lucis in vitris perspectivis et iride* (Venice, 1611) and *Euripus seu de fluxu et refluxu maris sententia* (Rome, 1624). His main theological work is *De republica ecclesiastica libri X* (London, 1617).

II. SECONDARY LITERATURE. On Dominis or his work, see R. E. Ockenden, "Marco Antonio de Dominis and His Explanation of the Rainbow," in *Isis*, **26** (1936), 40–49; Carl B. Boyer, *The Rainbow, From Myth to Mathematics* (New York, 1959), pp. 187–192; Josip Torbar, "Ob optici Markantuna de Dominisa" ("On the Optics of Marko Antonije de Dominis"), in *Rad Jugoslavenske akademije znanosti i umjetnosti* (Zagreb), **43** (1878), 196–219; Stanko Hondl, "Marko Antonij de Dominis kao fizičar" ("Marko Antonij de Dominis as Physicist"), in *Vienac*, **36,** no. 2 (1944), 36–48; Žarko Dadić, "Tumačenja pojave plime i oseke mora u djelima autora s područja Hrvatske" ("Explanations of the Tides in the Works of Croatian Authors"), in *Rasprave i gradja za povijest nauka* ("Treatises and Materials for the History of Science"), II (Zagreb, 1965), 87–143. A complete bibliography and discussions of Dominis' life and work (in Croatian) are in *Encyclopaedia moderna,* V–VI (1967), 84–140.

ŽARKO DADIĆ

DOMNINUS OF LARISSA (*b.* Larissa, *fl.* fifth century A.D.), *mathematics, philosophy.*

Domninus was a Syrian Jew of Larissa on the Orontes. (In his entry in the *Suda Lexicon* Larissa is regarded as identical with Laodicea, but they appear to have been separate towns.) He became a pupil of Syrianus, head of the Neoplatonic school at Athens, and a fellow student of Proclus. He therefore lived in the fifth century of the Christian era.

Syrianus thought equally highly of Domninus and Proclus, and Marinus relates how he offered to discourse to them on either the Orphic theories or the oracles; but Domninus wanted Orphism, Proclus the oracles, and they had not agreed when Syrianus died. Marinus implies that Domninus succeeded to Syrianus' chair, but if so, he can only have shared it for a short time with Proclus. Their disagreement widened into a controversy over the true interpretation of Platonic doctrine from which Proclus emerged as the victor in the eyes of the Academy. Domninus withdrew to Larissa, and Damascius, the last head of the Neoplatonic school, while admitting Domninus' mathematical competence, accused him of being old-fashioned in philosophical matters. This may have been a partisan judgment. Nor need we pay much attention to an anecdote related by him and intended to show that Domninus lacked the true philosophic mind: When Domninus was troubled by spitting blood and the Aesculapian oracle at Athens prescribed that he should eat swine's flesh, he had no scruples about so doing despite the precept of his Jewish religion. Equally suspect are Damascius' allegations that when advanced in years Domninus loved only the conversation of those who praised his superiority and that he would not admit to his company a young man who argued with him about a point in arithmetic.

Nothing has survived of his philosophical teachings. A reference by Proclus (*In Timaeum,* I.34B; Diehl, ed., I. 109. 30–110.12) indicates that Domninus took some interest in natural science. He held that comets were composed of a dry, vapor-like substance, and he explained the myth of Phaëthon by the assumption that the earth once passed through such a comet, the substance of which was ignited by the sun's rays and which in turn set the earth on fire.

It is on his mathematical work that his claim to remembrance rests. Nothing was known of this work until 1832, when J. F. Boissonade edited from two Paris manuscripts his Ἐγχειρίδιον ἀριθμητικῆς εἰσαγωγῆς ("Manual of Introductory Arithmetic"), and it was not until 1884 that its importance was recognized. Paul Tannery, who in the following year made a critical revision of Boissonade's text, then perceived that this brief work marked a reaction from the arithmetical notions of Nicomachus and a return to the sounder principles of Euclid. It may not be without significance that, according to Marinus, Proclus had become convinced by a dream that he possessed the soul of Nicomachus of Gerasa. Whereas numbers had been represented by Euclid as straight lines, Nicomachus had departed from this convention and, when dealing with unknown quantities, was forced into clumsy circumlocutions; he also introduced highly elaborate classifications of numbers, serving no useful purpose and difficult to justify. Proclus, according to the *Suda Lexicon,* wrote a commentary on Nicomachus' work, but without openly controverting him, Domninus, in the concise and well-ordered text edited by Boissonade, quietly undermines it. As Hultsch recognized, the book is arranged in five parts: an examination of numbers in themselves, an examination of numbers in relation to other numbers, the theory of numbers both in themselves and in relation to others, the theory of means and proportions, and the theory of numbers as figures. In general Domninus follows Euclid in his classification of numbers and departs from Nicomachus. He is content with the arithmetic, geometric, and harmonic means and finds no use for Nicomachus' seven other means. Like Euclid, he admits only plane and solid numbers. In writing this manual Domninus drew not only upon Euclid and Nicomachus but upon Theon of Smyrna and upon a source used by Iamblichus that has since disappeared.

At the end of the manual Domninus avows his intention of setting forth certain subjects more fully in an ᾿Αριθμητικὴ στοιχείωσις ("Elements of Arithmetic"). Whether he did so is not known, but a tract with the title Πῶς ἔστι λόγον ἐκ λόγου ἀφελεῖν ("How to Take a Ratio out of a Ratio"), edited by C. E. Ruelle in 1883, is almost certainly by Domninus and may have been written as part of the projected *Elements.* "Taking a ratio out of a ratio" does not mean subtraction but manipulation of the ratio so as to get it into other forms.

BIBLIOGRAPHY

Most of what is known about the life of Domninus comes from a long entry in the *Suda Lexicon* (Eva Adler, ed.) that seems to be derived from a lost work by Damascius. There is a short entry in Eudocia, *Violarium* 331, Flach, ed., 239. 7–10. Eudocia's source appears to be the lost *Onomatologos* of Hesychius of Miletus; see Hans Flach, *Untersuchungen ueber Eudoxia und Suidas,* p. 60. A brief notice is given by Marinus, *Vita Procli,* ch. 26, in J. F. Boissonade ed.

Domninus' *Manual of Introductory Arithmetic* may be found in J. F. Boissonade, *Anecdota graeca,* IV (Paris, 1832), 413–429. Paul Tannery commented on it in "Domninos de Larissa," in *Bulletin des sciences mathématiques et astronomiques,* 2nd ser., **8** (1884), 288–298, repr. in his *Mémoires scientifiques,* II (Paris–Toulouse, 1912), 105–117; he revised Boissonade's text at points in "Notes critiques sur Domninos," in *Revue de philologie,* 9 (1885), 129–137, repr. in *Mémoires scientifiques,* II, 211–222; he translated the work into French, with prolegomena, as "Le manuel d'introduction arithmétique du philosophe Domninos de Larissa," in *Revue des études grecques,* **19** (1906), 360–382, repr. in *Mémoires scientifiques,* III (1915), 255–281.

"How to Take a Ratio out of a Ratio" is printed with a French translation, a commentary, and additional notes by O. Riemann, in C. E. Ruelle, "Texte inédit de Domninus de Larissa sur l'arithmétique avec traduction et commentaire," in *Revue de philologie,* **7** (1883), 82–92, with an addendum by J. Dumontier explaining the mathematical import, pp. 92–94.

There is a useful summary by F. Hultsch, "Domninos," in Pauly-Wissowa, *Real-Encyclopädie,* V (1903), cols. 1521–1525.

IVOR BULMER-THOMAS

DONALDSON, HENRY HERBERT (*b.* Yonkers, New York, 12 May 1857; *d.* Philadelphia, Pennsylvania, 23 January 1938), *neurology.*

Donaldson, scion of a banking family, showed an early interest in science, and after studies at Phillips Andover and Yale stayed on an additional year in New Haven to do research in arsenic detection at Sheffield Scientific School (1879–1880) under Russell H. Chittenden. He then received somewhat reluctant parental approval to study medicine at the College of Physicians and Surgeons of New York (1880–1881), but after one year became convinced that his true bent lay in research rather than practice. Donaldson was offered, and accepted, a fellowship at Johns Hopkins, where he spent two years (1881–1883) studying the effects of digitalin on the heart and of cocaine on the nerves controlling temperature. The latter work, done under the supervision of G. Stanley Hall, became the theme of his Ph.D. dissertation (1895). Donaldson next spent almost two years (1886–1887) in Europe at the great neurological centers, studying under such masters as Forel, Gudden, Theodor Meynert, and Golgi. Returning briefly to Johns Hopkins as associate in psychology, he soon followed Hall, who had become president of Clark University, to Worcester, Massachusetts. Here, while assistant professor of neurology (1889–1892), he carried out his classic study on the brain of Laura Bridgman, a blind deaf-mute. This study, characterized as "probably the most thorough study of a single human brain that has ever been carried out," determined the theme that was to dominate all of Donaldson's subsequent research: the growth and development of the human brain from birth to maturity. His early papers were incorporated in a monograph, *The Growth of the Brain: A Study of the Nervous System in Relation to Education* (1895).

In 1892 Donaldson moved to Chicago to join the faculty of the recently opened university. Here he served as professor of neurology and dean of the

Ogden School of Science until 1898, when his teaching career was interrupted by a crippling tubercular infection of the knee which necessitated a prolonged recuperative period in Colorado. From 1891 to 1910 there was a continuous flow of papers concerned with the rate of growth of the brain and spinal cord, and the relationship of their weight and length to that of the entire body.

In 1905, after serious consideration, Donaldson finally decided to accept the distinguished appointment as head of the Wistar Institute of Anatomy and Biology in Philadelphia, a position he was to retain until his death. In 1906 there appeared the first of a long series of papers in which the white or albino rat (rather than the frog) was used as a research tool. Donaldson had already used this animal in his work with Adolf Meyer in Baltimore as early as 1893, but the superiority of the rat over the frog had long been advocated by Shinkishi Hatai, who had joined Donaldson in Philadelphia. He then proceeded to work out the equivalence in age between man and rodent, and as a result of lengthy genetic studies was able to produce the famous Wistar Institute stock of white rats, which have since then figured in innumerable research projects. The fundamental studies on growth, although primarily directed toward the brain and central nervous system, were later expanded to include the muscles, bones, teeth, and viscera.

Among the many distinguished workers associated with Donaldson in Chicago and Philadelphia were Alice Hamilton, John B. Watson, S. W. Ranson, and Frederick S. Hammett. His numerous foreign students included at least twenty Japanese. A member of the American Philosophical Society from 1906, Donaldson served that organization in various important positions until his death. He was also honored with the presidency of the Association of American Anatomists (1916–1918), the American Society of Naturalists (1927), and the American Neurological Society (1937). Both Yale and Clark granted him the honorary D.Sc.

Donaldson was a man of great culture and a true humanist. He loved music, the arts, and literature, but did not neglect to concern himself actively with social problems of the day. From 1888, when he helped to found the Marine Biological Laboratory at Woods Hole, he kept open house each summer for a host of friends and admirers. On his seventy-fifth birthday he was presented with a special volume of the *Journal of Comparative Neurology* (1932), dedicated to him and containing twenty contributions as well as an affectionate eulogy. His first marriage, to Julia Desboro Vaux of New York, produced two sons, one of whom, John C. Donaldson, served as professor of

anatomy at the medical school of the University of Pittsburgh.

BIBLIOGRAPHY

See "The Physiology of the Central Nervous System," in *An American Textbook of Physiology* (1898); and *The Rat* (1924). His diaries (1890–1936), in 49 vols. in manuscript, are at the American Philosophical Society Library, Philadelphia.

A biography is Edward G. Conklin, "Henry Herbert Donaldson (1857–1938)," in *Biographical Memoirs. National Academy of Sciences* (1939), 229–243, with a bibliography and portrait.

MORRIS H. SAFFRON

DONATI, GIOVAN BATTISTA (*b.* Pisa, Italy, 16 December 1826; *d.* Florence, Italy, 20 September 1873), *astronomy.*

Donati studied at the University of Pisa, where he was a pupil of Mossotti. In 1852 he went to Florence, where he worked in the observatory, then called "La Specola." It was directed at that time by Amici, whom Donati succeeded in April 1864. In the years 1854–1873 Donati published about 100 works, many of which were devoted to comets (on 2 June 1858 he discovered the comet that is named after him), astrophysics, and atmospheric physics.

His greatest achievement was the development of a new branch of astronomy based on Fraunhofer's famous discovery and leading to the spectroscopic study of the stars. Indeed, after having been in Spain for the eclipse of the sun of June 1860, he devoted himself completely to the application of spectroscopy to the stars and published the results of his studies in *Annali del Regio museo di fisica e storia naturale.* He pointed out the differences between the spectra of fifteen principal stars and that of the sun. He was also the first to obtain the spectrum of a comet and to interpret the observed features. The sun also was an object of his studies, both as an isolated body and in relation to other celestial bodies.

In 1868 he published two papers on the sun, one (in *Nuova antologia,* **8,** 334–353) on determining its distance from the earth and the other (*ibid.,* **9,** 60–93) on its physical structure. In 1869 he noted that certain phenomena heretofore thought to have had an atmospheric source actually originated in higher regions. He thus formulated the basis of a cosmic meteorology.

His experimental work brought forth first of all a spectroscope with five prisms, which was used in Sicily to observe an eclipse in 1870. He also devised a spectroscope of twenty-five prisms; it was exhibited in Vienna and Donati used it to make a series of remarkable observations in 1872. He noted the results that he obtained through the use of these spectroscopes and described them in *Rapporti sulle osservazioni dell'eclisse totale di sole del 22 dicembre 1870* and in *Memorie della Società degli spettroscopisti italiani.*

During the years 1864–1872 Donati was further occupied with the construction of a new observatory at Arcetri, near the house where Galileo died. The observatory was dedicated on 27 October 1872.

Donati's important work "Sul modo con cui si propagarono i fenomeni luminosi della grande aurora boreale osservata nella notte dal 4 al 5 febbraio 1872" was the first number of the intended periodical *Memorie del Regio osservatorio di Firenze ad Arcetri.* (Publication of the *Memorie* ceased with Donati's death; twenty years later A. Abetti started a new series with the title *Osservazioni e memorie dell'osservatorio astrofisico di Arcetri.*)

Donati died of cholera returning from Vienna, where he had taken part in the International Congress of Meteorology.

BIBLIOGRAPHY

Donati's works include "Intorno alle strie degli spettri stellari," in *Annali del Regio museo di fisica e storia naturale di Firenze per il 1865,* n.s. **1** (1866), 1–21; "Intorno alle osservazioni fatte a Torreblanca in Spagna dell'eclisse totale di sole del 18 luglio 1860," *ibid.,* 21–37; "Osservazioni di comete fatte all'Osservatorio del Regio museo di Firenze dall'anno 1854 fino al 1860," *ibid.,* 37–63; "Osservazioni spettroscopiche di macchie solari fatte a Firenze," in *Memorie della Società dei spettroscopisti italiani raccolte e pubblicate per cura del Prof. P. Tacchini,* I (Palermo, 1871), 52–55; *Rapporti sulle osservazioni dell'eclisse totale di sole del 22 Dicembre 1870 eseguite in Sicilia dalla Commissione Italiana* (Palermo, 1872), pp. 31–39; and "Sul modo cui si propagarono i fenomeni luminosi della grande aurora boreale osservata nella notte dal 4 al 5 febbraio 1872," in *Memorie del Regio osservatorio di Firenze ad Arcetri* (Florence, 1873), pp. 5–31.

MARIA LUISA RIGHINI BONELLI

DONDERS, FRANCISCUS CORNELIS (*b.* Tilburg, Netherlands, 27 May 1818; *d.* Utrecht, Netherlands, 24 March 1889), *physiology, ophthalmology.*

Donders was the youngest of nine children and the only son of Jan Frans Donders and Agnes Elisabeth (Clara?) Hegh. His father (who died when Donders was an infant) was not without means and occupied himself with chemistry, music, and literature, while his wife supervised his business.

Donders therefore passed the earliest years of his life in a family consisting only of women; in 1825 he was sent to a boarding school at Duizel, a village near Eindhoven. He remained there until 1831, working for his tuition as an assistant teacher during the final two years. After a short stay at the French School in Tilburg he attended the Latin School in Boxmeer, from which he graduated *cum laude* on 27 January 1835.

From July 1835 to December 1839 Donders was a student at the military medical school in Utrecht. Since this training conferred the right to treat only military men and their families, he enrolled in the medical faculty of Utrecht University. In February 1840 he was appointed health officer with the garrison in Vlissingen. The same month he passed the doctoral examination in medicine at Leiden and on 13 October 1840 received the M.D. from Leiden University.

Although he was educated as a Roman Catholic, he seems not to have practiced his religion after his time in Utrecht. He pleaded for the separation of religion and science and, according to his statements, was probably a theist or deist.

After he finished his studies Donders remained for some time with the garrison in Vlissingen. In August 1841 he was transferred to The Hague as medical officer. His sojourn there seems to have been important to the development of his career; he read, became familiar with the official and cultural life of that city, and was consulted by the inspector general about the reorganization of the Utrecht military medical school, where he was appointed docent in physiology and anatomy.

In September 1842 he returned to the University of Utrecht, where Gerrit Jan Mulder was intensively occupied with the renovation and expansion of chemistry as a discipline. Mulder requested Donders' cooperation in histological and histochemical research. Important discoveries in embryology and physiology were made in Mulder's laboratory, and Donders was present at the birth of physiological chemistry.

To augment his small income from teaching, Donders translated—among other things—Christian Georg Theodor Ruete's *Lehrbuch der Augenheilkunde.* Indeed, as well as translating the work, he edited it and, where necessary, performed additional experiments. Soon, in addition to his physiological and clinical publications, he began to write articles on ophthalmology. He wrote frequently for the *Holländische Beiträge zu den anatomischen und physiologischen Wissenschaften,* which he published with the physiologists Isaac van Deen and Jacob Moleschott, and for the *Nederlandsch Lancet,* of which he was editor.

His lecture "Blik op de stofwisseling als bron der eigen warmte van planten en dieren" ("Consideration of Metabolism as the Source of Heat in Plants and Animals") was published in 1845. In this work he attributed the regulation of heat mainly to the skin and also mentioned the principle of the law of the conservation of energy.

Donders was appointed extraordinary professor at the University of Utrecht—although there was no vacancy—to retain his services there. He chose to give courses that had not been taught before, including forensic medicine, ophthalmology, and (under the title of general biology) the science of metabolism and histology. He selected the latter term to avoid the word "physiology," in order not to embarrass his beloved teacher, the physiologist J. L. C. Schroeder van der Kolk, with even the appearance of competition.

Because of his courses in the physiology of the eye and its adaptation to pathological problems, Donders was soon consulted as an ophthalmological expert. Although he was urged to establish himself as an ophthalmologist, he hesitated to do so. In 1851 he was invited by Sir James Young Simpson and others to visit the important English eye clinics. This trip was of great significance to him: in England and on his return by way of France he met outstanding English, German, and French physiologists and eye doctors, including Sir William Bowman, Albrecht von Graefe, and Claude Bernard. (In London he also heard about the ophthalmoscope, invented by Helmholtz.) Strengthened by the events of his travels, Donders decided to establish himself as a specialist in diseases of the eye.

In 1852 Donders was appointed ordinary professor at Utrecht and concerned himself especially with ophthalmology. With his own money he opened a polyclinic and managed to obtain the use of the cholera hospital, which, however, soon became too small. A committee of private individuals then raised 40,000 florins to buy a large mansion, which was remodeled as a charity hospital for indigent patients; it opened in 1858. The hospital also functioned as an independent educational institution, primarily at the service of the university, as the university itself provided little opportunity for ophthalmological education. Here Donders established a center for both research and teaching and soon, in addition to university students, many foreign physicians took part in studies on refraction and accommodation anomalies and other ophthalmological problems.

In his autobiography Donders mentions that these years demanded a great deal of his strength. The hospital and the physiological laboratory, his courses in many subjects, research in the laboratory, and work for the press and the university all required his attention. When in 1862 Schroeder van der Kolk died, Donders was offered the professorship in physiology and promised a new laboratory. Donders accepted this offer because, as he said, physiology was his first love. Donders resigned from his ophthalmological practice; he remained, however, as director of the hospital until 1883. The new laboratory, equipped according to his directions, was opened in 1866. Donders' work was not limited to purely scientific studies, and he was often consulted by the university administrators. As dean of the medical faculty he was a capable leader. He was concerned in making science serve the needs of humanity; his publications give an impression of the essential and varied nature of his work.

In 1845 Donders married Ernestine J. A. Zimmerman, the daughter of a Lutheran minister in Utrecht. She died in 1887, after a long illness marked by mental depression. Shortly after he retired in 1888, Donders married the painter Abrahamine Arnolda Louisa Hubrecht, a daughter of his friend, the state councilor P. F. Hubrecht. Although Donders complained about his health in the diaries and correspondence of his last years, he appeared healthy and youthful until the time of his retirement. He died less than a year later, of a progressive brain disease, possibly a tumor.

BIBLIOGRAPHY

I. ORIGINAL WORKS. Donders published more than 340 works, mainly on ophthalmology and physiology, of which about a hundred are of a clinical, pathological, or physiochemical nature. Much of his work was published in French, English, or German. *On the Anomalies of Accommodation and Refraction of the Eye with a Preliminary Essay on Physiological Dioptrics* (London, 1864) has been translated into various languages, but has never appeared in Dutch. Also of importance are his *Handleiding tot de natuurkunde van den gezonden mensch*, written with A. F. Bauduin, 2 vols. (Utrecht–Amsterdam, 1851, 1853); *De voedingsbeginselen. Grondslagen eener algemeene voedingsleer* (Tiel, 1852); and P. B. Bergrath, trans., *Die Nahrungsstoffe, Grundlinien einer allgemeine Nahrungslehre* (Crefeld, 1853), a semipopular work taken from articles in the *Geneeskundige Courant* that was intended to give both the physician and the educated layman an outline of the elements of nutrition as a basis for a rational diet.

II. SECONDARY LITERATURE. On Donders and his work see Sir William Bowman, "In Memoriam F. C. Donders," in *Proceedings of the Royal Society,* **49** (1891), vii–xxiv; F. P. Fischer and G. ten Doesschate, *Franciscus Cornelis Donders* (Assen, 1958), a very extensive monograph in

Dutch, which includes a reprint of the above; M. A. van Herwerden, "Eine Freundschaft von drei Physiologen," in *Janus,* **20** (1915), 174–201, 409–436; "Die Freundschaft zwischen Donders und von Gräfe," *ibid.,* **23** (1918); J. Moleschott, *Franciscus Cornelis Donders, Festgruss zum 27 Mai 1888* (Giessen, 1888); P. J. Nuel, "F. C. Donders et son oeuvre," in *Annales d'oculistique,* 14th ser. (année 52), 5–107, of which pp. 5–45 are biographical and pp. 45–107 contain a systematic bibliography of works by Donders and his students; C. A. Pekelharing *et al.,* Paula Krais, trans., *F. C. Donders Reden gehalten bei der Enthüllung seines Denkmals in Utrecht am 22 Juni 1921* (Leipzig, 1922), which contains a German bibliography of Donders' work based on the one by Nuel; R. A. Pfeiffer, "F. C. Donders," in *Bulletin of the New York Academy of Medicine* (October 1936); H. J. M. Weve and G. ten Doesschate, *Die Briefe Albrecht von Gräfes an F. C. Donders* (Stuttgart, 1936); and *Het Jubileum van Professor F. C. Donders gevierd te Utrecht op 24 en 28 Mei 1888. Gedenkboek uitgegeven door de commissie* (Utrecht, 1889), of which pp. 115–132 contain an autobiographical essay.

RODOLPHINE J. CH. V. TER LAAGE

DONDI, GIOVANNI (*b.* Chioggia, Italy, 1318; *d.* Milan, Italy, 22 June 1389), *horology, astronomy, medicine.*

Dondi was the son of Jacopo (Giacomo) de'Dondi dall'Orologio, municipal physician at Chioggia; his work parallels closely that of his father, with whom he has often been confused. When the family moved to Padua in 1349, Giovanni Dondi became physician to Emperor Charles IV. In 1350 or 1352 he was appointed professor of astronomy at the University of Padua and later was a member of each of the four faculties of medicine, astrology, philosophy, and logic. He lectured on medicine at Florence around 1367–1370. He was ambassador to Venice in 1371; the following year he was a member of a committee of five citizens appointed to establish boundaries between Carrara and the Venetian Republic. Later he was befriended by Gian Galeazzo Visconti of Pavia and from 1379 to 1388 was connected with the University of Pavia; in 1382 he was living in the Visconti palace.

Dondi wrote, probably before 1371, a brief treatise, *De modo vivendi tempore pestilentiali,* mostly concerning diet during times of plague. After 1372 he followed his father's interest in balneology with a treatise describing the hot springs near Padua and methods of salt extraction, *De fontibus calidus agri Patavini consideratio ad magistrum Vicentium.* He also wrote *Quaestiones aliquae in physica et medica.* A friend of Petrarch and Cola di Rienzo, Dondi shared their interest in the ruins and inscriptions of ancient Rome.

Dondi's father, Jacopo, had designed a clock (hence the "dall'Orologio" added to the family name) which was installed in 1344 in the Torre dei Signori of the Palazzo del Capitanio at Padua. Giovanni Dondi's fame rests on an elaborate astronomical clock which he designed and spent sixteen years constructing, completing it in 1364. Petrarch, praising Dondi's astronomical attainments in his will, referred to this "planetarium," and there are early descriptions of it by Dondi's friends Phillippe de Mézières (in his *Songe du vieil pèlerin,* written between 1383 and 1388) and Giovanni Manzini, *podestà* of Pisa (letter to Dondi 11 July 1388). Dondi himself wrote a detailed description of his planetary clock, a treatise known as the *Tractatus astrarii* or *Tractatus planetarii,* copiously illustrated with diagrams of the dials, wheels, and other components. In this treatise, Dondi says, "I derived the first notion of this project and invention from the subtle and ingenious idea propounded by Campanus [of Novara] in his construction of equatoria, which he taught in his *Theorica planetarum*"; the astrarium is one of the earliest geared equatoria, driven by clockwork. A heptagonal frame bears dials for the sun, moon, Mercury, Venus, Mars, Jupiter, and Saturn; below, there are dials or displays showing the twenty-four hours, the times of sunrise and sunset, fixed feasts, movable feasts, and the nodes of the moon's orbit. The astrarium was acquired by Gian Galeazzo Visconti and installed in 1381 in the ducal library in the Castello Visconteo in Pavia. Regiomontanus, who saw the astrarium in 1463 and mentioned it in his introductory lecture on the mathematical sciences at the University of Pavia, said in 1474 that he had such a mechanism under construction in his workshop at Nuremberg. The existence of the astrarium is last recorded when it was offered in 1529 or 1530 to that lover of clocks, Emperor Charles V; it was then so dilapidated that Gianello Torriano (later the emperor's clockmaker) considered it beyond repair and undertook to make a similar device. Two modern replicas of the astrarium have been completed; that now in the Museum of History and Technology, Washington, D.C., is 4′4″ in overall height, 1′6″ in maximum diameter, and contains 297 parts, of which 107 are wheels and pinions.

Dondi's treatise is of great importance in the history of medieval horology and technology; the only known earlier detailed description of any sort of clock is that by Richard of Wallingford of his astronomical clock installed in St. Albans Abbey (about 1330). Both treatises, written within a century of the invention of the mechanical clock escapement, demonstrate the rapid development of clockwork and the constant concern to mechanize astronomical demonstrational instruments that is so evident in the long tradition of European public astronomical clocks.

BIBLIOGRAPHY

I. ORIGINAL WORKS. Dondi's works include *De modo vivendi tempore pestilentiali*, Karl Sudhoff, ed., in *Archiv für Geschichte der Medizin*, **5** (1911), 351–354; and *De fontibus calidus agri Patavini consideratio ad magistrum Vicentium*, printed in *De Balneis* (Venice, 1553), with Jacopo de'Dondi's brief treatise on the extraction of salt from the hot springs near Padua. Eleven manuscripts have survived of the treatise on the astrarium; these are Padua, Bibl. Capitolare Vescovile, D. 39; Venice, Bibl. Naz. Marciana, 85. Cl. Lat. VIII. 17; Milan, Bibl. Ambrosiana, C. 221 inf. and C. 139 inf.; Padua, Bibl. Civica, CM 631; Oxford, Bodleian, Laud Misc. 620; London, Wellcome Historical Medical Library, 248; Cracow, Bibl. Universytetu Jagiellońskiego, 577 and 589; Eton College, 172. Bi a. l; Salamanca, Universidad, 2621, item 12, 25r–72v (? fragments). A twelfth MS, Turin, Bibl. Naz. XLV, was destroyed by fire in 1904. The MS Padua, Bibl. Capitolare Vescovile, D. 39, has been reproduced in facsimile with transcription and commentary in Dondi's *Tractatus Astrarii*, trans., with introduction and glossary, by Antonio Barzon, Enrico Morpurgo, Armando Petrucci, and Giuseppe Francescato (Vatican City, 1960). Illustrations reproduced from other manuscripts, especially Bodleian, Laud Misc. 620, may be found in works cited below.

II. SECONDARY LITERATURE. On Jacopo and Giovanni de'Dondi and their works, see George Sarton, *Introduction to the History of Science*, III (Baltimore, 1948), 1669–1671, 1672–1677; Lynn Thorndike, *A History of Magic and Experimental Science*, III (New York, 1934), 386–397; and *Giovanni Dondi dall'Orologio, medico, scienziato e letterato* (Padua, 1969). Silvio A. Bedini and Francis Maddison discuss the history of the astrarium and its antecedents, list the MSS, and give a full bibliography in "Mechanical Universe. The Astrarium of Giovanni de'Dondi," in *Transactions of the American Philosophical Society*, n.s. **56,** pt. 5 (1966). Also see G. H. Baillie, "Giovanni de'Dondi and his Planetarium Clock in 1364," in *Horological Journal* (April–May 1934); H. Alan Lloyd, "Giovanni de'Dondi's Horological Masterpiece 1364," in *La Suisse horlogère*, international ed., no. 2 (July 1955), 49–71; and H. A. Lloyd, *Some Outstanding Clocks Over Seven Hundred Years, 1250–1950* (London, 1958), pp. 9–24, which describe the construction and appearance of the astrarium.

FRANCIS MADDISON

DONNAN, FREDERICK GEORGE (*b.* Colombo, Ceylon, 5 September 1870; *d.* Canterbury, England, 16 December 1956), *physical chemistry.*

Donnan, the son of a Belfast merchant, was born while his parents were temporarily abroad. He was educated at Belfast Royal Academy and at Queen's College, Belfast; after graduation he spent three years at Leipzig with Wislicenus and Ostwald, then a year at Berlin under van't Hoff. This unusually long apprenticeship to chemistry was completed with a period spent working with Ramsay at University College, London, to the teaching staff of which he was appointed in 1901. Three years later he became professor of physical chemistry at the University of Liverpool; he was made a fellow of the Royal Society in 1911 and succeeded Ramsay at University College in 1913. Donnan was drawn into industry during World War I, and for several years he worked on problems connected with the manufacture of "synthetic" ammonia and nitric acid, both in London and with the firm of Brunner, Mond in Cheshire. These industrial connections and interests were retained for the rest of his life, and even after his retirement in 1937 he continued to act as a consultant. His London house was destroyed in 1940, and he retired to Kent with his sisters; he was unmarried.

Donnan, having worked with both Ostwald and van't Hoff, was one of the main agents by whom the "new" physical chemistry was introduced into Britain. Van't Hoff had interested him in the problems of colloids, soap solutions, and osmotic pressures, and this interest led to his major paper, "The Theory of Membrane Equilibrium in the Presence of a Nondialyzable Electrolyte" (1911). This examined the effect of confining, by means of a membrane, a mixture of ions, one of which cannot pass through the membrane because of its large size. (In the absence of a membrane, the equilibrium of a protein with a salt solution is a similar case.) The theory of the Donnan membrane equilibrium has important applications in colloid chemistry and in the technologies of leather and gelatin, but above all in the understanding of the living cell, where it can give a quantitative account of ionic equilibria both within the cell and between the cell and its environment.

None of Donnan's subsequent work approaches this in importance. In later years he guided his department in London on a very loose rein, welcoming promising young men and leaving them free to follow their own interests. A wealthy, cultured, and highly articulate man, fond of travel and much given to hospitality, he became interested in the speculative and cosmological aspects of biology, and many of his later publications concern these topics. He wrote no book but was the author of more than 100 papers.

BIBLIOGRAPHY

The most informative obituary notices are those of F. A. Freeth, in *Biographical Memoirs of Fellows of the Royal Society*, **3** (1957), 23–29, which includes a portrait and a complete bibliography; W. E. Garner, in *Proceedings of the Chemical Society* (1957), 362–366, with portrait; and C. F. Goodeve, in *Nature*, **179** (1957), 235–236.

W. V. FARRAR

DOPPELMAYR, JOHANN GABRIEL (*b.* Nuremberg, Germany, 1671 [?]; *d.* Nuremberg, 1 December 1750), *astronomy, mathematics, physics, history of mathematics.*

Doppelmayr's father, Johann Siegmund Doppelmayr, was a merchant who made a hobby of experiments in physics and, according to his son, was the first to introduce into Nuremberg an air pump equipped with a lever and standing upright "like a flower vase."

After graduating from the Aegidien Gymnasium, Doppelmayr entered the University of Altdorf in 1696 with the intention of studying law; but there he heard the lectures on mathematics and physics of Johann Cristoph Sturm, founder of the Collegium Curiosum sive Experimentale and reputedly the most skilled experimenter in Germany. For a brief while in 1700 Doppelmayr attended the University of Halle, but he then decided to give up law for physics and mathematics, and spent two years traveling and studying in Germany, Holland, and England.

After Doppelmayr's return to Nuremberg, he was appointed in 1704 to the professorship of mathematics at the Aegidien Gymnasium, a post he held until his death. His life was devoted to lecturing, writing, astronomical and meteorological observation, and physical experimentation; his reputation was such as to gain him memberships in the Academia Caesarea Leopoldina, the academies of Berlin and St. Petersburg, and the Royal Society of London.

Doppelmayr's writings are not marked by originality; they do, however, provide an index of the scientific interests and information current in Germany, and particularly of the transmission of science from England, Holland, and France into Germany during the first half of the eighteenth century.

Among the astronomical works are *Kurze Erklärung der Copernicanischen Systems* (1707), *Kurze Einleitung zur Astronomie* (1708), and translations of Thomas Streete's astronomy (1705) and of John Wilkins' defense of the Copernican system (1713). His major work, however, is the *Atlas novus coelestis* (1742), a collection of diagrams with explanations intended as an introduction to the fundamentals of astronomy. Besides star charts and a selenographic map, the *Atlas* includes diagrams illustrating the planetary systems of Copernicus, Tycho, and Riccioli; the elliptic theories of Kepler, Boulliau, Seth Ward, and Mercator; the lunar theories of Tycho, Horrocks, and Newton; and Halley's cometary theory.

Doppelmayr's writings on mathematics include *Summa geometricae practicae;* a memoir on spherical trigonometry; an essay on the construction of the sundial; and a translation (with appendices by Doppelmayr) of Nicolas Bion's treatise on mathematical instruments.

Of lasting value for historians is Doppelmayr's *Historische Nachricht* (1730), a 314-page folio volume giving biographical accounts of over 360 mathematicians, artists, and instrument makers of Nuremberg. The biographies are arranged chronologically from the fifteenth to the eighteenth century.

In physics Doppelmayr continued the experimental tradition of Sturm. His *Physica experimentis illustrata* (1731) is a list, in German, of 700 experiments and demonstrations given before the Collegium Curiosum. The procedures are not described in any detail; they are designed to illustrate such topics as the "subtlety" or fineness of subdivision of various materials, electric and magnetic "effluvia," simple machines, the principles of hydrostatics, the optics of the eye, and so on.

More important is the *Neu-entdeckte Phaenomena* (1744), a well-organized and accurate summary of the electrical experiments and theories of Hawksbee, Gray, and Dufay. This work no doubt helped to create and inform the popular interest in electrical phenomena that spread through Germany in the mid-1740's. In the last two chapters Doppelmayr proposes a hypothesis to explain away electrical attraction and repulsion as caused by air movements; Dufay's discovery of the opposite characters of vitreous and resinous electricity is reduced to a difference in electric strength of different materials; and in general Doppelmayr returns to the earlier and less promising theoretical outlook of Hawksbee.

Doppelmayr's electrical investigations continued until his death, which followed a severe shock suffered while experimenting with one of the newly invented condensers.

BIBLIOGRAPHY

I. ORIGINAL WORKS. Doppelmayr's writings include *Eclipsis solis totalis cum mora* (Nuremberg, 1706); *Kurze Erklärung der Copernicanischen Systems* (Nuremberg, 1707); *Kurze Einleitung zur Astronomie* (Nuremberg, 1708); *Neue vermehrte Welperische Gnomonica* (Nuremberg, 1708); *Neu-eroffnete mathematische Werck-Schule* (Nuremberg, 1st ed., 1712, 2nd ed., 1720, 3rd ed., 1741), a trans. of Nicolas Bion's *Traité de la construction et des principaux usages des instruments de mathématique; Johannis Wilkins Vertheidigter Copernicus* (Leipzig, 1713), a trans. of Wilkins' essay of 1640 on the probability of earth's being a planet; *Summa geometricae practicae* (Nuremberg, 1718, 1750); *Grundliche Anweisung zur Verfertigung grossen Sonnenuhren und Beschreibung derselben* (Nuremberg, 1719), also in Latin as *Nova methodus parandi sciaterica solaria;* "Animadversiones nonnullae circa eclipsium observationes," in *Academiae Caesareo-Leopoldinae Carolinae naturae curiosum ephem-*

erides, **2** (1715), Centuriae III et IV, app., 133–136; "Animadversiones circa usum vitrorum planorum in observationibus astronomicis," *ibid.,* **4** (1719), Centuriae VII et VIII, 457–459; "Circa trigonometriam sphaericum," in *Academiae Caesareae Leopoldina-Caroliniae naturae curiosum acta physico-medica . . . exhibentia ephemerides . . .,* **2** (1730), 177–178; *Historische Nachricht von den Nürnbergischen Mathematicis und Künstlern* (Nuremberg, 1730); *Physica experimentis illustrata* (Nuremberg, 1731); *Atlas novus coelestis* (Nuremberg, 1742); and *Neu-entdeckte Phaenomena von bewundernswürdigen Würckungen der Natur, welche bei fast allen Körper zukommenden elektrischen Krafft . . . hervorgebracht werden* (Nuremberg, 1744). J. H. von Mädler mentions as Doppelmayr's first work a Latin trans. (1705) of Streete's *Astronomia Carolina* (1661). George Hadley, in *Philosophical Transactions of the Royal Society,* **42** (1742), 245, refers to published barometrical observations by Doppelmayr for the years 1731–1735.

II. SECONDARY LITERATURE. On Doppelmayr or his work, see *Allgemeine deutsche Biographie,* V, 344–345; J. H. von Mädler, *Geschichte der Himmelskunde,* I (Brunswick, 1873), 129; J. G. Meusel, *Lexikon der vom Jahr 1750 bis 1800 verstorbenen teutschen Schriftsteller* (Leipzig, 1802–1816), II; *Neue deutsche Biographie,* IV, 76; and G. A. Will, *Nürnbergisches Gelehrter-Lexicon,* I (Nuremberg, 1755), 287–290.

CURTIS WILSON

DOPPLER, JOHANN CHRISTIAN (*b.* Salzburg, Austria, 29 November 1803; *d.* Venice, Italy, 17 March 1853), *mathematics, physics, astronomy.*

Christian Doppler was the son of a noted master stonemason. Although he showed talent in this craft, his poor health led his father to plan a career in business for him. Doppler's mathematical abilities were recognized by the astronomer and geodesist Simon Stampfer, at whose advice Doppler attended the Polytechnic Institute in Vienna from 1822 to 1825. Finding the curriculum too one-sided, Doppler returned to Salzburg and pursued his studies privately. He completed the Gymnasium and subsequent philosophical courses in an unusually short time, while tutoring in mathematics and physics. From 1829 to 1833 he was employed as a mathematical assistant in Vienna, and wrote his first papers on mathematics and electricity. In 1835 Doppler was on the point of emigrating to America; he had sold his possessions and had reached Munich when he obtained a position as professor of mathematics and accounting at the State Secondary School in Prague. In 1841 he became professor of elementary mathematics and practical geometry at the State Technical Academy there, during the tenure of which he enunciated his famous principle. He had become an associate member of the Königliche Böhmische Gesellschaft der Wissen-

schaften in Prague in 1840 and was made a full member in 1843. Doppler moved to the Mining Academy at Schemnitz (Banská Štiavnica) in 1847 as *Bergrat* and professor of mathematics, physics, and mechanics. As a result of the turbulence of 1848–1849 he returned to Vienna; there, in 1850, he became director of the new Physical Institute, which was founded for the training of teachers, and full professor of experimental physics at the Royal Imperial University of Vienna, the first such position to exist in Austria. Doppler had suffered from lung disease since his years at Prague. A trip to Venice in 1852 was of no avail, and he died there the following year, survived by his wife and five children.

Doppler's scientific fame rests on his enunciation of the Doppler principle, which relates the observed frequency of a wave to the motion of the source or the observer relative to the medium in which the wave is propagated. This appears in his article "Ueber das farbige Licht der Doppelsterne und einiger anderer Gestirne des Himmels" (read 25 May 1842). The correct elementary formula is derived for motion of source or of observer along the line between them; the extension to the motion of both at the same time appears in an article of 1846. Doppler mentions the application of this result both to acoustics and to optics, particularly to the colored appearance of double stars and to the fluctuations of variable stars and novae. The reasoning in the latter arguments was not always very cogent; for example, he believed that all stars were intrinsically white and emitted only or mainly in the visible spectrum. The colors which he believed to be characteristic of double stars, then, were to have their origin in the Doppler effect. It should be noted that Doppler worked under rather isolated circumstances, being the earliest important physicist in Austria in the nineteenth century. He was unable to justify in his own mind the application of his principle to transverse vibrations of light, an extension performed by B. Bolzano shortly afterwards.

The first experimental verification of the acoustical Doppler effect was performed by Buys Ballot at Utrecht in 1845, using a locomotive drawing an open car with several trumpeters. Buys Ballot also criticized the unsound assumptions upon which Doppler had based his astronomical applications. Doppler replied to these and similar criticisms in a rather stubborn and unconvincing fashion. The acoustical effect was also noted and commented on at the British Association meeting in 1848 by John Scott Russell and by H. Fizeau in the same year, perhaps without knowledge of Doppler's work. Fizeau pointed to the usefulness of observing spectral line shifts in the application to astronomy, a point of such importance that the principle is sometimes called the Doppler-Fizeau principle. Although in 1850 the Italian astronomer Benedict Sestini had published data on star colors apparently supporting Doppler's application of his principle to double stars, its valid astronomical use had to wait until proper spectroscopic instrumentation was available, beginning with the work of the English astronomer William Huggins in 1868. The optical effect was first confirmed terrestrially by Belopolsky in 1901. Modified by relativity theory, the Doppler principle has become a major astronomical tool.

Doppler's principle itself was criticized by the Austrian mathematician Joseph Petzval in 1852, on the basis of an incorrect mathematical argument. Doppler defended himself to good effect in this situation. Doppler also published works of less importance on related optical effects (Bradley's aberration of light; dependence of intensity on the motion of the source; the deviation of waves by a rotating medium, as, for example, an ethereal atmosphere rotating with a star), optical instruments, and topics in mathematics and physics, especially in geometry, optics, and electricity.

BIBLIOGRAPHY

I. ORIGINAL WORKS. Doppler's papers on his principle and related topics are found in *Abhandlungen von Christian Doppler,* ed. with notes by H. A. Lorentz (Leipzig, 1907), Ostwald's Klassiker der exakten Wissenschaften, no. 161. A list of most of his publications appears in Poggendorff, I, 594–595. The statement of his principle, "Ueber das farbige Licht der Doppelsterne und einiger anderer Gestirne des Himmels," in *Abhandlungen der Konigl. Böhmischen Gesellschaft der Wissenschaften,* 5th ser., **2** (1842), 465, was also published separately (Prague, 1842). The extension of motion to both source and observer appeared in *Annalen der Physik und Chemie,* **68** (1846), 1–35.

II. SECONDARY LITERATURE. See the obituary by Anton Schrötter in *Almanach der Kaiserlichen Akademie der Wissenschaften,* **4** (1854), 112–120; further information appears in Julius Scheiner, "Johann Christian Doppler und das nach ihm benannte Prinzip," in *Himmel und Erde,* **8** (1896), 260–271. Some of his ideas and accomplishments are described in B. Bolzano, "Christ. Doppler's neueste Leistungen auf dem Gebiete der physikalischen Apparatenlehre, Akustik, Optik und optischen Astronomie," in *Annalen der Physik und Chemie,* **72** (1847), 530–555.

A. E. WOODRUFF

DÖRFFEL, GEORG SAMUEL (*b.* Plauen, Vogtland, Germany, 21 October 1643; *d.* Weida, Germany, 16 August 1688), *astronomy, theology.*

Son of Friedrich Dörffel, pastor in Plauen, Georg Dörffel was best known for his representation of the orbit of a comet as a parabola with the sun at the focus. He was married three times and had nine children.

Dörffel studied philosophy, theology, Oriental languages, and mathematics, receiving the degrees of bachelor (Leipzig, 1662), master (Jena, 1663), and bachelor of theology (Leipzig, 1668; dissertation, 1665). He became his father's substitute in Plauen in 1667 and his successor in 1672. In 1684 he became ecclesiastical superintendent in Weida. He had an excellent astronomical library and good eyesight but observed mostly with an old-fashioned astronomical radius. It consisted of a long arm and a short arm at right angles to each other, with a fixed sight at the end of the long arm and two movable sights at the ends of the transversal. His comet observations with it were accurate to one or two minutes. His home was not favorable for observing because of neighboring buildings.

Dörffel found no observable parallax for the comet of 1672 and measured its angular distance from fixed stars. From measurements made with a quadrant on 27 March, he calculated its latitude and longitude and length and breadth. He depicted its apparent path as circular and noted that it moved in the same direction as the planets. Dörffel published his report while the comet was still visible but growing fainter. He realized that it was soon to be lost in the light of the moon. He considered God responsible for comets. In the last half of the seventeenth century, skepticism existed about astrological predictions. Dörffel, although he accepted the ancient belief that comets were evil omens, said of the comet of 1672 that it signified something new that was not good, but that he would not predict specific events which might follow. His next recorded astronomical activity concerns the comet of 1677.

In 1680 Dörffel shifted his attention from the apparent path to the actual path of comets. He noted Apian's statement that comets' tails are directed away from the sun and appreciated Tycho Brahe's observations of the nova of 1572 and the comet of 1577 as forcing abandonment of the concept of the incorruptibility of the heavens. Although not the first to suggest a parabolic path for a comet, Dörffel was the first to describe the path of the comet of 1680, and possibly other comets, as a parabola with the sun at the focus (*Astronomische Betrachtung*). Although he had the comet move around the sun while that body moved around the stationary earth, he was not a confirmed anti-Copernican. Using the radius of the earth's circular orbit around the sun and his observations of the comet's elongation from the sun, he projected the comet's path on the ecliptic. Probably the first (25

August) observer of Halley's comet in 1682, he described it briefly in print and at greater length in correspondence with Gottfried Kirch.

Dörffel's interests extended to the computation of lunar eclipses, to occultations, to meteors, including computation of their paths, and to mock moons. In 1685 he published his discovery, mentioned in 1682, of a new method to determine the distance of a body from the earth, with observations from only one site, utilizing the earth's diurnal rotation and expressing the distance in semidiameters of the earth.

Dörffel's writings, which were in German and anonymous or signed only with initials, were soon superseded by Newton's *Principia*. They received little attention until the mid-eighteenth century, when they began to be of historical interest and appealed to German national pride. In 1791 J. H. Schröter named a lunar mountain range after him.

BIBLIOGRAPHY

I. ORIGINAL WORKS. *De definitione et natura demonstrationis* (Dörffel, resp.; Bernhard v. Sanden, praes.) (Leipzig, June 1662); *Exercitatio philosophica de quantitate motus gravium* (Erhard Weidel, praes.) (Jena, 14 February 1663); *. . . Disputatio philologo-theologica de gloria templi ultimi, ex Hagg. cap. II vers. 6–9, adversus Judaeos asserta . . . sub praesidio Johannis Adami Scherzeri, . . . 1666 . . . eruditorum examini publice subjecit . . .* (Leipzig, n.d.), 2nd ed. in appendix to J. A. Scherzer's *Collegii antisociniani . . . .* 2nd ed. (Leipzig, 1684); *Tirocinium accentuationis ad lectionem Biblicam practice accommodatum* (Plauen, 1670); *Warhafftiger Bericht Von dem Cometen/Welcher im Mertzen dieses 1672. Jahrs erschienen: Dessen Lauff/ Art und Beschaffenheit/ sampt der Bedeutung/ hiermit fürgestellet wird/ und in Plauen observire worden. Von M.G.S.D.* (1672); *Bericht Von dem neulichsten im Mertzen dieses 1672 Jahres erschienenem Cometen/ Auss einem zu Plauen gedrucktem Bedencken wiederholet und vermehret* (1672); *Extract eines Schreibens aus Plauen im Voigtland an einen guten Freund, von dem neuen Cometen. Welcher im April dieses 1677. Jahrs am Himmel erschienen* [Plauen, 1677]; *Neuer Comet-Stern welcher im November des 1680sten Jahres erschienen, und zu Plauen im Voigtlande dergestalt observiret worden, sampt dessen kurtzer Beschreibung, und darüber habenden Gedanken* [Plauen, 1680?]; *Astronomische Betrachtung des Grossen Cometen/ Welcher im ausgehenden 1680. und angehenden 1681. Jahre höchstverwunderlich und entsetzlich erschienen: Dessen zu Plauen im Voigtlande angestellte tägliche Observationes, Nebenst etlichen sonderbahren Fragen und neuen Denckwürdigkeiten/ sonderlich von Verbesserung der Hevelischen Theoriae Cometarum, . . .* (Plauen, 1681); *De incertitudine salutis aeternae contra Aloysium Richardum,* German title, *Der ärgste Seelen-Gifft Des Trostlosen Pabstthums* (Jena [?], 1682); *Eilfertige Nachricht, von dem*

itzund am Himmel stehenden neuen Cometen, welcher am 15. Augusti dieses 1682sten Jahres zum erstenmahl, zu Plauen im Voigtlande ist gesehen worden (Plauen, 1682); "Observatio eclipseos lunae totalis, d. XI. Febr. A. 1682 . . . Symmista Plav. in Variscia, instituta, et cum novissimis tabb. Horroccio-Flamstedianis, vix sensibiliter discrepantibus, collata," in Gottfried Kirch, *Annus III. Ephemeridum motuum coelestium ad . . . M. D. C. LXXXIII* (Leipzig, 1683), recto G_1; *Neues Mond-Wunder/ Wie solches den 24. Jenner dieses angehenden 1684. Jahres/ zu Plauen im Voigtlande/ gesehen worden: Neben einem kurtzen Bedencken/ was hiervon zu halten sey* (Plauen, n.d.); "Calculus Eclipseos Lunaris penumbratilis Anno 1684 d. 17/ 27 Jun. ex Tabbulis Flamstedianis" in Gottfried Kirch, *Ephemeridum motuum coelestium Annus IV* (Leipzig, 1684), recto D_4; "Methodus nova, phaenomenorum coelestium intervalla a terris facillime determinandi, non variata statione seu loco observationis, neque captis eorundem altitudine vel azimutho," in *Acta eruditorum* (1685), pp. 571–580; and *Gedächtnisspredigt Herrn Hanns George v. Carlowitz gehalten den 19. des Christmonds 1686.*

MS letters from Dörffel to Gottfried Kirch are preserved in the University Library, Leipzig.

II. SECONDARY LITERATURE. See Angus Armitage, "Master Georg Dörffel and the Rise of Cometary Astronomy," in *Annals of Science,* **7** (1951), 303–315; Rudolf Gerlach, in *Neue deutsche Biographie,* IV (1959), 30–31; Norbert Herz, *Geschichte der Bahnbestimmung von Planeten und Kometen,* II (Leipzig, 1894), pp. 252–260; Abraham Gotthelf Kästner, "Nachrichten von Georg Samuel Dörfeln . . . ," in Leipzig Gesellschaft der freyen Künste, *Sammlung einiger ausgesuchten Stücke der Gesellschaft,* III (Leipzig, 1756), 252–263; Curt Reinhardt, *Mag. Georg Samuel Dörffel. Ein Beitrag zur Geschichte der Astronomie im 17. Jahrhundert* (Plauen, 1882), a doctoral dissertation presented at Leipzig; and Baron de Zach, *Correspondance astronomique,* VII (1822), 136–138; VIII (1823), 397–399.

C. DORIS HELLMAN

DORN, GERARD (*b.* Belgium [?]; *fl.* Basel, Switzerland, and Frankfurt, Germany, 1566–1584), *medicine, alchemy, chemistry.*

As an early follower of Paracelsus, Dorn contributed significantly, through his translations and commentaries and through his own writings, to the rapid dissemination of Paracelsian doctrines in the late sixteenth century, and his influence has been revived in the twentieth century through its importance to C. G. Jung's studies of alchemy. Yet little appears to be known of his life. His contemporary Michael Toxites referred to him as Belgian (*Belga*).[1] He was a student of the Paracelsist Adam of Bodenstein, to whom he dedicated his first book,[2] but where he received his doctorate remains unclear. For several years he appears to have worked, perhaps on commission, as a translator for the Basel publisher Peter Perna. The dedications of his books indicate that he was still living in Basel in 1577–1578, but by 1581–1584 he apparently had taken up residence in Frankfurt.

Dorn's translations of Paracelsus include works on chemistry, astronomy, astrology, and surgery as well as on therapeutics and pharmacology. His dictionary of Paracelsian terms was influential not only in its Latin editions but also in later Dutch (1614), German (1618), and English translations (1650, 1674). Like Paracelsus he directed attention to the utility of chemistry in medicine, and he defended Paracelsus' new medicine against the attacks of the traditionalist Thomas Erastus. But it was Paracelsus' attempt to build a cosmic philosophy from an amalgamation of hermetic Neoplatonism and chemistry that attracted Dorn most strongly. His objective was not to transmute baser metals into gold, but to change manifest into occult forms, the impure into the pure. Believing that the education of his time was too pagan and scholastic, he presented the operations of alchemy not only as a material procedure but also as a spiritual process of striving toward "sublimity of mind."[3] "Transform yourselves into living philosophical stones," he exhorted.[4]

Dorn was also indebted to John of Rupescissa on the quintessence and to Nicholas of Cusa in his application of numerical symbols[5] to Paracelsian principles. He felt an affinity for the English mathematician and astrologer John Dee, whose symbol of unity (*monas*) he incorporated into the title-page vignette of his *Chymisticum artificium*.[6] His elaborations of Paracelsian concepts and his own meditations, as reprinted in the *Theatrum chemicum*,[7] came to have a special meaning for C. G. Jung, whose later works are based on profound and lengthy researches into philosophical alchemy. Jung's summation of the significance of alchemical symbolism for psychology and religion was notably influenced by Dorn's concept of a unitary world (*unus mundus*) and, like Dorn, he drew a parallel between the alchemical act and the moral-intellectual transformation of man. With this interpretation he placed alchemy in a new perspective in the history of science, medicine, and theology.

NOTES

1. Paracelsus, *Onomastica II,* Michael Toxites, ed. (Strasbourg, 1574), p. 430.
2. *Clavis totius philosophiae chymisticae* (Lyons, 1567), dedication dated Basel, 1566.
3. *Ibid.,* p. 126.
4. Cited by C. G. Jung, in *Psychology and Alchemy,* 2nd ed. (Princeton, 1968), p. 148.
5. *Clavis,* chs. 7–9; *Monarchia triadis in unitate soli deo sacra,* appended to *Aurora thesaurusque philosophorum Paracelsi* (Basel,

1577), pp. 65–127; and his "De spagirico artificio Io. Trithemi sententia," in *Theatrum chemicum,* I (Strasbourg, 1659), 390–391.
6. *Chymisticum artificium naturae theoricum et practicum* (n.p., 1568).
7. *Theatrum chemicum,* I, 192–591.

BIBLIOGRAPHY

I. Original Works. Bibliographies (listed chronologically) of Dorn's writings are given by K. Sudhoff, "Ein Beitrag zur Bibliographie der Paracelsisten im 16. Jahrhundert," in *Centralblatt für Bibliothekswesen,* **10** (1893), 385–391; J. Ferguson, *Bibliotheca chemica* (Glasgow, 1906), I, 220–222; D. Duveen, *Bibliotheca alchemica et chemica* (London, 1949; repr. London, 1965), 177–179; and J. R. Partington, *A History of Chemistry* (London, 1961), II, 159–160. The *De summis naturae mysteriis* and the *Aurora thesaurusque philosophorum,* presented by Dorn as translations of Paracelsian writings, are considered by Sudhoff to be Dorn's own works: *Versuch einer Kritik der Echtheit der Paracelsischen Schriften* (Berlin, 1894), nos. 125, 177. A. E. Waite's translation of the *Aurora* in *The Hermetic and Alchemical Writings of Paracelsus* (London, 1894; repr. New Hyde Park, N.Y., 1967) does not include, as might be inferred from Partington, either the tract *Monarchia triadis in unitate soli deo sacra* (alternate title of the *Monarchia physica*), which was issued with the *Aurora* (Basel, 1577), pp. 65–127, or the *Anatomia viva,* also issued with *Aurora,* 129–191, on the chemical examination of urine by distillation, which also was probably Dorn's own work and was ascribed to him by Huser in his German translations of the *Aurora* of 1605 and 1618—see Sudhoff, *op. cit.,* nos. 267, 302; see also no. 469. W. Pagel has suggested that, under the name Dominicus Gnosicus Belga, Dorn was the author of a commentary, first printed in 1566, to the *Seven Hermetic Treatises:* "Paracelsus: Traditionalism and Medieval Sources," in L. G. Stevenson, ed., *Medicine, Science and Culture; Historical Essays in Honor of Owsei Temkin* (Baltimore, 1968), pp. 58–60; and "The Eightness of Adam and Related 'Gnostic' Ideas in the Paracelsan Corpus," in *Ambix,* **16** (1969), 131–132.

II. Secondary Literature. The fullest accounts of Dorn are given by J. R. Partington, *A History of Chemistry* (London, 1961), II, 159–160; L. Thorndike, *A History of Magic and Experimental Science,* V (New York, 1941; repr. New York, 1954), 630–635; and R. P. Multhauf, *The Origins of Chemistry* (London, 1966), 241–243, 288–289. Other references are in W. Pagel, *Paracelsus; An Introduction to Philosophical Medicine in the Era of the Renaissance* (Basel, 1958), pp. 189–194; and *Das medizinische Weltbild des Paracelsus* (Wiesbaden, 1962), p. 111. The works of C. G. Jung in which Dorn is most frequently cited are vols. XII, XIII, and XIV of his *Collected Works: Psychology and Alchemy,* 2nd ed. (Princeton, 1968); *Alchemical Studies* (Princeton, 1967); and *Mysterium coniunctionis* (New York, 1963). Further references relevant to Dorn's alchemical philosophy and to his influence on Jung are M.-L. von Franz, "The Idea of the Macro- and Microcosmos in the Light of Jungian Psychology," in *Ambix,* **13** (1965), 22–34;

G. H., review of T. Burckhardt's *Alchimie: Sinn und Weltbilt, ibid.,* **8** (1960), 177–180; A. Jaffé, "The Influence of Alchemy on the Work of C. G. Jung," in *Alchemy and the Occult. A Catalogue of Books and Manuscripts From the Collection of Paul and Mary Mellon Given to Yale University Library,* compiled by Ian MacPhail (New Haven, 1968), I, xxi, xxii, xxix; II, 394; W. Pagel, "Jung's Views on Alchemy," in *Isis,* **39** (1948), 44–48; and his review of I. B. Cohen's *Ethan Allen Hitchcock, Discoverer of the True Subject of the Hermetic Art, ibid.,* **43** (1952), 374–375; H. J. Sheppard, "A Survey of Alchemical and Hermetic Symbolism," in *Ambix,* **8** (1960), 35–41; and R. S. Wilkinson, "The Alchemical Library of John Winthrop, Jr. (1606–1676)," *ibid.,* **9** (1963), 33–51; **10** (1966), 139–186.

Five of Dorn's works were in Winthrop's library; the copy that belonged to John Dee bears his initials and the comment in his hand that Dorn used his *monas* without permission. The existence of one of the world's most substantial alchemical libraries in seventeenth-century New England adds another dimension to the Puritan mind.

Martha Teach Gnudi

DORNO, CARL W. M. (*b.* Königsberg, Prussia [now Kaliningrad, U.S.S.R.], 3 August 1865; *d.* Davos, Switzerland, 22 April 1942), *biometeorology.*

The son of Carl Dorno and the former Emma Lehnhard, Dorno came from an old Königsberg merchant family. In 1891 he took over his father's business; and the following year he married Erna Hundt, from Hamburg, who bore him one daughter. When Dorno was thirty-three years old, he began to study chemistry, physics, political economy, and law at Königsberg University, capping his studies with a doctorate in chemistry in 1904. After his daughter contracted tuberculosis, he moved the family to Davos, an alpine town frequented by consumptives; here he became concerned with determining the factors that made the climate beneficial. In order to conduct research he established a private physical-meteorological observatory, financing it with his personal fortune.

From the beginning Dorno sought the exact measurement and recording of solar and celestial radiation, separately and combined, to determine the total energy and the energies of single spectral regions. For this purpose it was necessary to construct better instruments. Aided by R. Thilenius, Dorno constructed a pyrheliograph, based on older pyrheliometer principles, with a continuous intensity scale that permitted its use in atmospheric investigations, and the Davos frigorimeter. With the information recorded by his new instruments Dorno investigated the annual and diurnal variation of radiation, not only for Davos but also for other places at various latitudes and altitudes.

At high altitudes the intensity of solar radiation is nearly constant; this is the most important factor in the beneficial effects of high-altitude air. On the highest peaks radiation is higher in winter than in summer because of the ellipticity of the earth's orbit. For the most part water vapor diminishes radiation, especially ultraviolet radiation. Dorno's investigations on the ultraviolet were so pioneering that the radiation between 2,900 and 3,200 angstrom units is called Dorno's radiation. He also deduced the concept of biological cooling and was thus the founder of bioclimatology.

Dorno's daughter died in 1912; but rather than return to Germany, he decided to devote his life to the work he had begun. The loss of his fortune after World War I brought him many difficulties, but the Swiss government took over his observatory and its financial maintenance, permitting him to observe and publish freely as before. In 1926 Dorno retired as director but remained very active in meteorological-physiological studies. Since the mid-1930's he had suffered from difficulties with his vision, which gradually worsened, so that at last he could no longer continue his scientific work.

Among Dorno's honors were an honorary M.D. from the University of Basel (1922) and the title of "professor" from the Prussian government.

BIBLIOGRAPHY

Dorno's writings are *Studien über Licht und Luft des Hochgebirges* (Brunswick, 1911); *Dämmerungs- und Ringerschein. 1911–1917* (Brunswick, 1917); *Physik der Sonnen- und Himmelsstrahlung* (Brunswick, 1919); *Himmelshelligkeit, Himmelspolarisation und Sonnenintensität, 1911–1918* (Brunswick, 1919); *Klimatologie im Dienste der Medizin* (Brunswick, 1920); "Fortschritte in Strahlungsmessung (Pyrheliograph)," in *Meteorologische Zeitschrift,* **39** (1922), 303–323; *Meteorologische - physikalische - physiologische Studie Muottas-Muraigl* (Davos, 1924); "Über die Verwendbarkeit von Eder's Graukeilphotometer im meteorologische Dienst," in *Meteorologische Zeitschrift,* **42** (1925), 87–97; "Davoser Frigorimeter," *ibid.,* **45** (1928), 401–421; *Assuan, eine meteorologische-physikalische-physiologische Studie* (Davos, 1932); and *Das Klima von Agra, eine dritte und letzte meteorologische-physiologische Studie* (Davos, 1934).

On Dorno, see R. Süring, "Carl Dorno," in *Meteorologische Zeitschrift,* **59** (1942), 202–205.

H. C. Freiesleben

DOSITHEUS (*fl.* Alexandria, second half of the third century B.C.), *mathematics, astronomy.*

He was a friend or pupil of Conon, and on the latter's death, Archimedes, who had been in the habit of sending his mathematical works from Syracuse to

Conon for discussion in the scientific circles of Alexandria, chose Dositheus as the recipient of several treatises, including *On the Quadrature of the Parabola, On Spirals, On the Sphere and the Cylinder* (two books), and *On Conoids and Spheroids.* At the beginning of the first of these Archimedes says, "Having heard that Conon has died, who was a very dear friend of mine, and that you have been an acquaintance of his and are a student of geometry . . . I determined to write and send you some geometrical theorems, as I have been accustomed to write to Conon" (Heiberg, ed., II, 262). The preambles to the other works make it clear that Dositheus on his side often wrote to Archimedes requesting the proofs of particular theorems. Nothing is known about Dositheus' own mathematical work.

His astronomical work seems to have been concerned mainly with the calendar. He is cited four times in the calendar attached to Geminus' *Isagoge* (Manitius, ed., p. 210 ff.) and some forty times in Ptolemy's *Phaseis* for weather prognostications (ἐπισημασίαι) such as formed part of a *parapegma,* a type of almanac, originally engraved on stone or wood and later transmitted in manuscript form—like the two mentioned above—giving astronomical and meteorological phenomena for the days of each month (cf. A. Rehm, "Parapegmastudien," in *Abhandlungen der Bayerischen Akademie der Wissenschaften,* phil.-hist. Abt., n.s., vol. **19** [1941]). Dositheus may have made observations in the island of Cos (*Phaseis,* p. 67. 4, Heiberg, ed.—but the text here is insecure; cf. *proleg.* cliii note 1) as well as in Alexandria.

According to Censorinus (*De die natali,* 18, 5), Dositheus wrote on the *octaëteris* (an eight-year intercalation cycle) of Eudoxus, and he may be the Dositheus Pelusiotes (Pelusium, at the northeastern extremity of the Egyptian delta) mentioned as providing information about the life of Aratus (*Theonis Alexandrini vita Arati,* §2, Maas, ed.—but spelled here Δωσίθεος).

BIBLIOGRAPHY

In addition to the works cited in the text, see F. Hultsch, "Dositheos 9," in Pauly-Wissowa, *Real-Encyclopädie,* X (1905), cols. 1607–1608.

                                                  D. R. DICKS

DOUGLAS, JAMES (*b.* Baads, Scotland, 21 March 1675; *d.* London, England, 2 April 1742), *medicine, natural history, letters.*

Douglas was the second son of William Douglas of Baads, near Edinburgh, and his wife, the former Joan Mason. They were an obscure but industrious family of small landowners, a minor branch of the widespread Douglas clan. Of their twelve children, four became fellows of the Royal Society—Walter, James, John, and George—although only James and John, both physicians, produced work of lasting importance. Nothing is known of the early schooling of James Douglas; but on 23 July 1699 he was granted the degree of *docteur* by the Faculty of Medicine of the University of Rheims, and it is likely that he had obtained the M.A. at Edinburgh in 1694. He was working in London by 1700 and early decided on a career in obstetrics and anatomy. In 1705 he read his first paper to the Royal Society and was granted fellowship in 1706. He became fellow of the Royal College of Physicians in 1721. To his contemporaries he was sufficiently outstanding to receive mention in Pope's *Dunciad,* and he was a friend of Sir Hans Sloane, founder of the British Museum; the physician Richard Mead; and William Cheselden, whose lateral operation for removal of bladder stones he described.

Douglas married Martha Wilkes, aunt of John Wilkes, the political reformer and rake. They had two children, but neither married and both died young. Following her husband's death, Martha Douglas gave lodging to William Hunter and to his brother John during their early days in London.

By 1707, when he published his handbook of comparative myology, Douglas had realized the importance of anatomical teaching to the advancement of medicine; and he was among the first to advertise classes, which were well attended. His major publication in this field was that on the peritoneum (1730), an excellent monograph that drew attention to the duplicature of the peritoneal membrane, at that time a controversial subject. In this book there is a short description of the structure later known as the pouch of Douglas and still recognized by that name. There are also the ligament, the line, and the semilunar fold of Douglas. In the Hunterian Library of the University of Glasgow, donated by will of its founder, William Hunter, are no fewer than sixty-four unpublished manuscripts by Douglas, on many aspects of anatomy, natural history, grammar, and orthoepy, and the Blackburn Collection in that library contains an enormous number of documents, drawings, and notes, nearly all in Douglas' hand.

Douglas was also a collector of editions of the works of Horace; and he published a magnificent catalog of his library of Horatiana, containing 557 volumes.

In the Hunterian Library may also be seen an interesting series of case notes, written at the bedside of his patients, dating from 1704 and illustrating the problems of diagnosis and treatment at that time.

They show, too, that he acted as consultant to the London midwives, being called for medical treatment during pregnancy as well as for the complications of labor.

In obstetrical science Douglas carefully studied the anatomy of the female pelvis and of the fetus; in 1735 he attended Anne, princess of Orange, daughter of George II, in Holland. He was also concerned, in 1726, in the exposure of Mary Toft, the "rabbit woman" of Godalming.

In 1719 James assisted his younger brother John, a brilliant but irascible physician, in the promulgation of John's ideas in introducing suprapubic lithotomy, one of the earliest attempts at routine abdominal surgery in England.

Douglas' publications on natural history include a well-produced monograph on the "Guernsay-lilly" (*Nerine sarniensis*) and a paper to the Royal Society on the flamingo (1714). Both demonstrate the care and method of his presentation.

His greatest contribution to the future, however, lay in his encouragement of William Hunter, who came to him as a resident pupil in 1741. The brilliant young student and his shrewd master established an intimate relationship, and on Douglas' death in 1742 Hunter wrote a touching letter to his mother. (The letter is now in the Royal College of Surgeons of England.) During the single year of their contact, Hunter became interested in the anatomical subjects on which Douglas had worked. Thus the anatomy of aneurysms, of the bones, of the "cellular membrane," and above all of the gravid uterus were topics upon which William Hunter elaborated at various later dates. It is not too much to say that the encouragement and training received by Hunter during this formative period was an important factor in those developments in British medical education for which he and his brother John were so largely responsible.

BIBLIOGRAPHY

I. ORIGINAL WORKS. Douglas' writings are *Myographia comparatae specimen, or a Comparative Description of All the Muscles in a Man and a Quadruped*... (London, 1707); *Bibliographiae anatomicae specimen sive catalogus omnium pene auctorum qui ab Hippocrate ad Harveium rem anatomicum* ... (London, 1715); *Index materiae medicae* ... (London, 1724); *Lilium Sarniense: or a Description of the Guernsay-Lilly* ... (London, 1725); *The History of the Lateral Operation* (London, 1726); *An Advertisement Occasion'd by Some Passages in Sir R. Manningham's Diary* ... (London, 1727); *Arbor Yemensis fructum café ferens: or a Description and History of the Coffee Tree* (London, 1727); *A Description of the Peritoneum and of ... the Membrana Cellularis* (London, 1730); and *Catalogus editorum Quinti Horatii Flacci ab an. 1476 ad an. 1739 quae in bibliotheca Jacob. Douglas . . . adservantur* (London, 1739).

Eleven articles that appeared in the *Philosophical Transactions of the Royal Society* between 1706 and 1731 are listed in K. Bryn Thomas, *James Douglas of the Pouch* ... (London, 1964), p. 198. Unpublished MSS in the Blackburn Collection at the Hunterian Library of the University of Glasgow are catalogued and annotated in the book by Thomas (above) pp. 85–193; a: 1 in J. Young and P. H. Aitken, *A Catalogue of the Manuscripts in the Library of the Hunterian Museum* ... (Glasgow, 1908), p. 425 ff.

II. SECONDARY LITERATURE. Besides Thomas' book (see above) one may also consult J. C. Carpue, *A Description of the Muscles... With the Synonyma of Douglas* (London, 1801); Börje Holmberg, *James Douglas on Pronunciation, c. 1740* (Copenhagen, 1956); and D. Watson, *The Odes, Epodes, and Carmen seculare of Horace ... With a Catalogue of the Editions of Horace From 1476 to 1739 in the Library of James Douglas* (London, 1747).

K. BRYN THOMAS

DOUGLAS, JESSE (*b.* New York, N.Y., 3 July 1897; *d.* New York, 7 October 1965), *mathematics.*

Douglas became interested in mathematics while he was still a high school student; in his freshman year at the City College of New York he became the youngest person ever to win the college's Belden Medal for excellence in mathematics. He graduated with honors in 1916 and began graduate studies with Edward Kasner at Columbia University. From 1917 to 1920 (in which year he was awarded the doctorate) he also participated in Kasner's seminar in differential geometry; here he developed his love for geometry and first encountered the problem of Plateau.

From 1920 to 1926 Douglas remained at Columbia College, teaching and doing research, primarily in differential geometry. Between 1926 and 1930 he was a National Research fellow at Princeton, Harvard, Chicago, Paris, and Göttingen; during this period he also devised a complete solution to the problem of Plateau, of which the essential features were published in a series of abstracts in the *Bulletin of the American Mathematical Society,* between 1927 and 1930, while a detailed presentation appeared in the *Transactions of the American Mathematical Society* for January 1931. This solution won Douglas the Fields Medal at the International Congress of Mathematicians in Oslo in 1936.

Douglas was appointed to a position at the Massachusetts Institute of Technology in 1930 and taught there until 1936; he was a research fellow at the Institute for Advanced Study at Princeton in the academic year 1938–1939 and received Guggenheim Foundation fellowships for research in analysis and geometry in 1940 and 1941. From 1942 until 1954 he taught at Brooklyn College and at Columbia University, then in 1955 returned to City College, where he spent the rest of his life.

Douglas' work with the problem of Plateau was again rewarded in 1943 when he received the Bôcher Memorial Prize of the American Mathematical Society for his memoirs "Green's Function and the Problem of Plateau" (in *American Journal of Mathematics,* **61** [1939], 545 ff.), "The Most General Form of the Problem of Plateau" (*ibid.,* **61** [1939], 590 ff.), and "Solution of the Inverse Problem of the Calculus of Variations" (in *Transactions of the American Mathematical Society,* **50** [1941], 71–128). The problem of Plateau was apparently first posed by Lagrange about 1760, and had occupied many mathematicians—most notably Riemann, Weierstrass, and Schwarz—in the period from 1860 to 1870. The problem is concerned with proving the existence of a surface of least area bounded by a given contour. Prior to Douglas' solution, mathematicians had succeeded in solving a number of special cases, as when, in the nineteenth century, a solution was obtained for a contour that is a skew quadrilateral having a plane of symmetry. Douglas' solution of 1931 is highly generalized; indeed, it is valid when the contour is any continuous, closed, nonintersecting curve whatever (Jordan curve)—it may even be in space of any number of dimensions. (R. Garnier in 1927 and T. Radó in 1930 had succeeded in solving the problem with less generality by using alternative methods.)

Having disposed of the most fundamental instance of the problem of Plateau—a single given contour and a simply connected minimal surface—Douglas went on to consider surfaces bounded by any finite number of contours and to consider surfaces of higher topological structure—as, for example, one-sided surfaces or spherical surfaces with any number of attached handles or any number of perforations. Between 1931 and 1939 he gave solutions to such problems as these and formulated and solved other general forms of the problem.

The problem of Plateau did not represent Douglas' sole mathematical interest, however. In 1941 he published a complete solution of the inverse problem of the calculus of variations for three-dimensional space—a problem unsolved until then, although in 1894 Darboux had stated and solved the problem for the two-dimensional case. In addition to publishing some fifty papers on geometry and analysis, Douglas' work in group theory is notable; in 1951, he made significant contributions to the problem of determining all finite groups on two generators, A and B, which have the property that every group element can be expressed in the form $A^r B^s$, where r and s are integers.

BIBLIOGRAPHY

I. ORIGINAL WORKS. *Scripta mathematica,* **4** (1936), 89–90, contains a bibliography of Douglas' publications prior to 1936. A complete bibliography of his works is on file in the mathematics department of the City College of New York.

II. SECONDARY LITERATURE. Some information on Douglas' life prior to 1936 may be found in *Scripta mathematica,* **4** (1936), 89–90. In the near future the National Academy of Science will publish a biography of Douglas, including a complete bibliography of his publications. An obituary of Douglas can be found in the *New York Herald Tribune* (8 Oct. 1965).

NORMAN SCHAUMBERGER

DOVE, HEINRICH WILHELM (*b.* Liegnitz, Prussia [now Legnica, Poland], 6 October 1803; *d.* Berlin, Germany, 4 April 1879), *meteorology, physics.*

The son of Wilhelm Benjamin Dove and the former Maria Susanne Sophie Brückner, Dove belonged to a prosperous family of apothecaries and merchants in Liegnitz. His delicate health led him to choose an academic career instead of following the family profession. Dove was an open-minded, communicative person who was interested not only in science but also in politics, history, and philosophy, all of which he studied at the University of Breslau, which he entered in 1821. His doctoral thesis, on climatology, was presented in 1826 to the University of Königsberg, where he lectured until 1829, when he went to Berlin. He became a professor there in 1844. On 26 October 1830 he married Franziska Adelaide Luise Etzel.

Dove devoted much of his time to lecturing, becoming a great popular success. Mainly an experimental physicist, he improved and devised many scientific instruments and illustrated his lectures with elegant experiments. His great interest in education was shown when, in 1837–1849, he edited the *Repertorium der Physik,* for which he wrote many of the articles himself: on the progress of physics, meteorology, theory of heat, optics, magnetism, and electricity. His contribution to physics centered on observations of the earth's magnetism; polarization phenomena, especially the optical properties of rock crystals; and induced electricity.

Dove's principal interest was meteorology. A great step forward in that field had been the extension, in 1780, of a network of thirty-nine observation stations to cover many European countries. This had been organized by the Societas Meteorologica Palatina in Mannheim, Germany, which had demanded uniformity in the mounting and operation of the standard instruments. At the beginning of the nineteenth century, stations were established in Russia and North

America, and Humboldt used their observations to draw maps indicating the distribution of temperature throughout the areas covered. This new field, climatology, also interested Dove, who used the many observations to draw maps showing the monthly mean distribution of heat at the earth's surface. These maps demonstrated how the winds, land masses, and seas influenced heat distribution.

H. W. Brandes emphasized that not only climate but other variables were important in meteorology. In Breslau, Dove studied meteorology with Brandes, and after thorough study of Brandes' meteorological data he formulated his "Drehungsgesetz" ("law of rotation") (1827), which states that the order of meteorological phenomena at a single place on the earth's surface corresponds to what would happen if there were great whirligigs rotating clockwise in the atmosphere. With a southwest wind the temperature rises, and it rains. The wind then moves to the west, the temperature falls, and the barometer rises. When the wind is northeast, the barometric pressure is at a maximum and the temperature at a minimum. Then the pressure begins to fall until the wind again blows from the southwest. It was Dove's great contribution to meteorology to be the first to find a system in weather changes.

Further progress occurred in 1857, when Buys Ballot, one of Dove's students, found that winds arise because of differences in atmospheric pressure. Throughout his life Dove defended his own law, which, in contrast with Buys Ballot's, was founded on the assumption that wind is the primary factor by which weather phenomena should be explained.

Dove was interested in expanding the international collaboration between meteorological institutions that had started with the establishment of the Societas Meteorologica Palatina. He assembled meteorologists from several European countries in Geneva in 1863, but it was not until 1873, with the first international meteorology meeting in Leipzig—in which Dove took no part—that the collaboration was expanded to any great extent.

Dove was director of the Prussian Institute of Meteorology from its founding in 1849, and he was three times elected vice-chancellor of the University of Berlin. In 1853 he received the Copley Medal of the Royal Society, and he was a member of several scientific societies.

BIBLIOGRAPHY

I. ORIGINAL WORKS. Dove's scientific writings are listed in the Royal Society's *Catalogue of Scientific Papers*, **2**, 329–335; **7**, 553–554; and in Neumann's biography (see below), p. 72 ff. Most of them were published in *Abhandlungen* and *Monatsberichte der Preussischen Akademie der Wissenschaft* and J. C. Poggendorff's *Annalen der Physik und Chemie*. The most important meteorological writings are *Meteorologische Untersuchungen* (Berlin, 1837); "Das Gesetz der Stürme," in *Monatsberichte der Preussischen Akademie der Wissenschaft*, **52** (1840), 232–239; and *Die Verbreitung der Wärme auf der Oberfläche der Erde* (Berlin, 1852).

II. SECONDARY LITERATURE. Further information may be found in "Heinrich Wilhelm Dove," in *Nature*, **19** (10 Apr. 1879), 529–530; Hans Neumann, *Heinrich Wilhelm Dove. Eine Naturforscher-Biographie* (Liegnitz, 1925); and *Neue deutsche Biographie*, IV (1959), 92 f.

KURT MØLLER PEDERSEN

DOWNING, ARTHUR MATTHEW WELD (*b.* Carlow, Ireland, 13 April 1850; *d.* London, England, 8 December 1917), *astronomy*.

Downing's chief contribution was the computation of precise positions and movements of astronomical bodies; he was also one of the founders of the British Astronomical Association. The younger son of Arthur Matthew Downing, Esq., of County Carlow, he received his early education under Philip Jones at the Nutgrove School, near Rathfarnham, County Dublin. He thence proceeded in 1866 to Trinity College, Dublin, where he obtained the scholarship in science and graduated B.A. in 1871, gaining the gold medal of his year in mathematics. He took his M.A. degree in 1881, and in 1893 Dublin University granted him the honorary degree of D.Sc.

In 1872 Downing was appointed assistant at the Royal Observatory, Greenwich, to commence 17 January 1873. There he was placed in charge successively of the library and manuscripts, the time department, and the circle computations. Reduction of the circle, altazimuth, and equatorial observations came to constitute his major responsibility, but he also served as one of four regular observers with the transit circle and altazimuth. Following his election as fellow of the Royal Astronomical Society in 1875, he communicated seventy-five papers to the society, dealing principally with the correction of systematic errors in different star catalogs and with the computation of fundamental motions of the heavenly bodies. Among the papers is a calculation done in collaboration with G. Johnstone Stoney of perturbations suffered by the Leonid meteors, which predicted and explained the relative sparseness of the 1899 shower.

Downing's next appointment, as superintendent of the Nautical Almanac Office, extended from 1 January 1892 to his statutory retirement on 13 April 1910. During this period he brought out the *Nautical Almanac* for the years 1896 to 1912, gradually instituting various improvements therein, including increasing the number of ephemeris stars, introducing Besselian coordinates into the eclipse and occultation lists, and expanding the sections on planetary satellites. He also replaced the solar and planetary tables of Le Verrier with those of Simon Newcomb and George Hill, dropped the obsolete Lunar Distance Tables, and introduced into the *Almanac* the physical ephemerides of the sun, moon, and planets.

As one of the founders in 1890 of the British Astronomical Association and subsequent nurturer of its early development, Downing contributed significantly to amateur astronomy. His consistent advance publication of particulars of astronomical occurrences, such as eclipses and occultations, constituted a valuable service to observers in many countries.

In 1896 Downing was elected fellow of the Royal Society and officiated in Paris at the important International Conference of Directors of Ephemerides, which sought to attain uniformity in the adoption of astronomical constants. In 1899 he revised Ernst Becker's *Tafeln zur Berechnung der Precession*, adapting them to a new value of the precessional constant first derived by Simon Newcomb in response to a formal request presented to him at the Paris meeting. The epoch adopted for the tables was 1910, but they were constructed to be useful for at least ten years before and after that year. In 1901 Downing compiled a revised version of Taylor's *Madras Catalogue* of 11,000 stars, reduced without proper motion to the equinox of 1835. His sudden death in 1917, following several years of illness, was from a recurrent heart complaint.

Downing was secretary (1889–1892) and vice-president (1893–1895) of the Royal Astronomical Society, as well as vice-president (1890–1891) and second president (1892–1894) of the British Astronomical Association.

BIBLIOGRAPHY

I. ORIGINAL WORKS. Seventy-five papers communicated to the Royal Astronomical Society are listed in the *General Index to the Monthly Notices of the Royal Astronomical Society* covering vols. **1–52** (1870) and vols. **53–70** (1911). See especially the Downing-Stoney paper "Ephemerides of Two Situations in the Leonid Stream," in *Monthly Notices of the Royal Astronomical Society,* **59** (1898), 539–541. Other joint communications with Stoney on this subject include "Perturbations of the Leonids," in *Proceedings of the Royal Society,* **64A** (1899), 403–409; and two letters to the editor of *Nature:* "Next Week's Leonid Shower," **61** (1899), 28–29, and "The Leonids—a Forecast," **63** (1900), 6. Another paper, by Downing alone, concerning meteors is "The Perturbations of the Bielid Meteors," in *Proceedings*

of the Royal Society, **76A** (1905), 266–270. A report by Downing to the British Astronomical Association on 28 June 1905, concerning his researches on the Bielids, is described in *Journal of the British Astronomical Association,* **15,** no. 9 (1905), 361–363.

Nineteen contributions to *Observatory* (of which Downing was editor of vols. **8–10** [1885–1887]) are in vols. **2–4, 6, 8, 12, 27, 30, 33, 36** and **39**. A determination of the sun's mean equatorial horizontal parallax is in **3**, no. 31 (1879), 189–190. See also *Astronomische Nachrichten,* **96**, no. 2288 (1880), 119–128.

Twenty-one contributions to the *Journal of the British Astronomical Association* are in vols. **1, 3, 8, 10, 15–19,** and **21–22**. Besides accounts of observational phenomena these include "How to Find Easter," **3**, no. 6 (1893), 264–268; and "When the Day Changes," **10**, no. 4 (1900), 176–178, the latter trans. as "Où le jour change-t-il," in *Ciel et terre,* **21** (1900), 84–86. Downing edited the first of the eclipse volumes of the British Astronomical Association dealing with the eclipse of 1896 (he also organized an Association expedition that failed to observe the eclipse because of cloud). He issued in addition several Association circulars giving advance particulars of other current notable eclipses. He was private adviser over many years to the editor of the *Journal of the British Astronomical Association* (see acknowledgment by A. S. D. Maunder, **28**, no. 2 [1917], 67–69).

Ten letters to the editor of *Nature,* two in conjunction with Stoney, see above, are in vols. **17, 59, 61, 63, 65, 71–72, 76, 78,** and **90**. The receipt of advance particulars of various astronomical phenomena from Downing is frequently noted and quoted in the editorial columns of this journal. While superintendent of the Nautical Almanac Office, Downing compiled for the years 1896–1912 the *Nautical Almanac and Astronomical Ephemeris for the Meridian of the Royal Observatory at Greenwich* (for 1896–1901, published London, 1892–1897; for 1902–1912, published Edinburgh, 1898–1909). See seven-page appendix to the *Nautical Almanac* for 1900, which contains a continuation of tables I and III of Damoiseau's *Tables of Jupiter's Satellites for the Years 1900–1910.*

Other contributions are his revision of Becker's *Tafeln . . . Precession: Precession Tables Adopted to Newcomb's Value of the Precessional Constant and Reduced to the Epoch 1910* (Edinburgh, 1899); and his revision of *Taylor's General Catalogue of Stars for the Equinox 1835.0 From Observations Made at the Madras Observatory During the Years 1831 to 1842* (Edinburgh, 1901).

II. SECONDARY LITERATURE. Obituaries are A. C. D. Crommelin, in *Nature,* **100** (1917), 308–309; and A. S. D. Maunder, in *Journal of the British Astronomical Association,* **28**, no. 2 (1917), 67–69. Unsigned obituaries are in *Observatory,* **41**, no. 522 (1918), 70; and *Monthly Notices of the Royal Astronomical Society,* **78**, no. 4 (1918), 241–244. References to his role in founding the British Astronomical Association are made by Howard L. Kelly in *Memoirs of the British Astronomical Association,* **36**, pt. 2 (1948), a Historical Section memoir. Summaries of some of Downing's original papers in *Journal of the British Astronomical*

Association, Monthly Notices of the Royal Astronomical Society, and *Proceedings of the Royal Society* appear in the editor's column of contemporary issues of *Nature.*

SUSAN M. P. MCKENNA

DRACH, JULES JOSEPH (*b.* Sainte-Marie-aux-Mines, near Colmar, France, 13 March 1871; *d.* Cavalaire, Var, France, 8 March 1941), *mathematics.*

Drach was born a few months before the Treaty of Frankfurt, by which Alsace ceased to be French. His father, Joseph Louis Drach, and mother, the former Marie-Josèphe Balthazard, modest farmers from the Vosges, took refuge with their three sons at Saint-Dié. From his youth Drach had to work for an architect in order to help his family. He was, however, able to attend elementary school and, at the urging of his teachers, who obtained a scholarship for him, went on to the *collège* in Saint-Dié and then to the lycée in Nancy. Drach was admitted at the age of eighteen to the École Normale Supérieure. Without attempting to make up his failure of the *agrégation,* and encouraged by Jules Tannery, he devoted himself to research and obtained the *doctorat-ès-sciences* in 1898. He taught at the universities of Clermont-Ferrand, Lille, Poitiers (where he married Mathilde Guitton), Toulouse, and Paris (1913), where his courses in analytical mechanics and higher analysis were well received. Drach was elected to the Académie des Sciences in 1929 and was a member of many scientific commissions. His poor health obliged him to reside in Provence for most of the year. His son Pierre entered the École Normale Supérieure in 1926 and had a brilliant career as a biologist.

After retiring to his estate at Cavalaire, Drach pursued his mathematical researches and indulged his love of reading, being interested in the plastic arts as well as in the sciences. Marked by the ordeals of his youth, he always remained close to the poor and was actively involved in the improvement of land held by the peasants.

Drach's mathematical researches display great unity. Galois's algebraic theory, with its extension to linear differential equations just made by Émile Picard (1887), seemed to him to be a model of perfection. He proposed to elucidate the fundamental reason for such a success in order to be able to extend it to the study of differential equations in the most general cases, asserting that the theory of groups is inseparable from the study of the transcendental quantities of integral calculus.

To what he termed the "geometric" point of view, in which one introduces supposedly given functions whose nature is not specified, Drach opposed the "logical" problem of integration, which consists of classifying the transcendental quantities satisfying the rational system verified by the solutions. For this process he introduced the notion of the "rationality group," whose reducibility and primitiveness he investigated. This bold conception, of an absolute character, foreshadowed the axiomatic constructions that were subsequently developed. In discovering regular methods permitting one to foresee the reductions in the difficulties of integration, Drach gave an account of the results obtained before him by Sophus Lie, Émile Picard, and Ernest Vessiot. He completed these and thus extended the special studies concerning, for example, the ballistic equations and those determining families of curves in the geometry of surfaces, such as the "wave surface."

Besides numerous articles in various journals and notes published in the *Comptes rendus . . . de l'Académie des sciences* over some forty years, Drach, with his colleague and friend Émile Borel, prepared for publication a course given at the Faculté des Sciences in Paris by Henri Poincaré—*Leçons sur la théorie de l'élasticité* (Paris, 1892)—and one given by Jules Tannery at the École Normale Supérieure, *Introduction à l'étude de la théorie des nombres et de l'algèbre supérieure* (Paris, 1895). Moreover, he played a large role in preparing for publication, under the auspices of the Académie des Sciences, the works of Henri Poincaré (11 vols., 1916–1956).

BIBLIOGRAPHY

Drach's papers include "Essai sur une théorie générale de l'intégration et sur la classification des transcendantes," in *Annales de l'École normale supérieure,* 3rd ser., **15** (1898), 243–384; "Sur le problème logique de l'intégration des équations différentielles," in *Annales de la Faculté des sciences de Toulouse,* 2nd ser., **10** (1908), 393–472; "Recherches sur certaines déformations remarquables à réseau conjugué persistant," *ibid.,* pp. 125–164; "Le système complètement orthogonal de l'espace euclidien à *n* dimensions," in *Bulletin de la Société mathématique de France,* **36** (1908), 85–126; "Sur l'intégration logique des équations différentielles ordinaires," in *Cambridge International Congress of Mathematicians. 1912,* I (Cambridge, 1913), 438–497; and "Equations différentielles de la balistique extérieure," in *Annales de l'École normale supérieure,* 3rd ser., **37** (1920), 1–94.

LUCIENNE FÉLIX

DRAPARNAUD, JACQUES-PHILIPPE-RAYMOND (*b.* Montpellier, France, 3 June 1772; *d.* Montpellier, 2 February 1804), *zoology, botany.*

The son of Jacques Draparnaud, a merchant, and Marie-Hélène Toulouse, Draparnaud received his master of arts at the age of fifteen from the École de Droit; his thesis was entitled *De universa philosophia.* After graduating in 1790, he turned to the study of medicine. The Revolution, in which he took an active part, interrupted his studies, sent him to jail, and ruined him financially. He also narrowly escaped the scaffold. Freed in 1794, he withdrew to the École de Sorèze, where he taught physics and chemistry. In 1796 he was assigned the chair of *grammaire générale* at the Écoles Centrales, but he remained there only a short time. In 1802 Chaptal appointed him curator of collections at the Faculté de Médecine of the University of Montpellier and associate to Antoine Gouan, who was then director of the Jardin des Plantes. However, the intrigues of some of his colleagues led Draparnaud to resign in November 1803. He died shortly thereafter of pulmonary tuberculosis, from which he had suffered for many years.

During a scientific career of only fifteen years and despite the obstacles imposed by the Revolution and his illness, Draparnaud published at least forty-five works on politics, philosophy, grammar, physics, mineralogy, zoology (principally malacology), and botany. Besides his observations, he reached certain conclusions in biology and physiology that were remarkably ahead of his time. He introduced in a few words the idea of vital phenomena common to animal and plant life, and attempted to reduce these phenomena to physical and chemical laws.

At his death Draparnaud left numerous manuscripts in various stages of completion. Only one was published: *Histoire naturelle des mollusques terrestres et fluviatiles de la France* (1805); the others have been lost. Among them was one on the history of confervae, to which he attached great importance and on which he had worked for ten years. This work marks him as one of the first algologists. All that is left of it is the herbal of algae, now kept in the Muséum d'Histoire Naturelle in Paris.

BIBLIOGRAPHY

I. ORIGINAL WORKS. A complete list of Draparnaud's works is in Dulieu (1956) and Motte (1964) (see below). The most important include *Discours sur les avantages de l'histoire naturelle* (Montpellier, an IX); *Tableau des mollusques terrestres et fluviatiles de France* (Montpellier, an IX); *Discours sur les moeurs et la manière de vivre des plantes* (Montpellier, an IX); *Discours sur la vie et les fonctions vitales, ou précis de physiologie comparée* (Montpellier–Paris, an X); *Discours sur la philosophie des sciences* (Montpellier–Paris, an X); *Dissertation sur l'utilité de l'histoire naturelle dans la médecine présentée à l'École de Médecine de Montpellier pour obtenir le titre de médecin* (Montpellier, an XI); and *Histoire naturelle des mollusques terrestres et fluviatiles de la France* (Paris–Montpellier, 1805).

II. SECONDARY LITERATURE. On Draparnaud and his work, see J. B. Baumes, *Éloge de Draparnaud* (Montpellier, an XII); L. Dulieu, "Jacques-Philippe-Raymond Draparnaud," in *Revue d'histoire des sciences et de leurs applications,* 9, no. 3 (1956), 236–358; G. Laissac, "Notes sur la vie et les écrits de Draparnaud," in *Revue du midi,* 2 (1843), 81–112, 239–256; J. Motte, "Vie de Draparnaud," in *Opuscula botanica necnon alia,* 7 (1964), 1–79; and J. Poitevin, *Notice sur la vie et les ouvrages de M. Draparnaud, lue à l'assemblée publique de la Société libre des sciences et belles-lettres de Montpellier, le 13 floréal an XII* (Montpellier, an XIII).

JEAN MOTTE

DRAPER, HENRY (*b.* Prince Edward County, Virginia, 7 March 1837; *d.* New York, N.Y., 20 November 1882), *astronomy.*

Draper's family moved to New York City when he was two years old, and there he maintained his principal residence for the rest of his life. His father, John William Draper, was a distinguished physician and chemist. His mother, the former Antonia Coetana de Paiva Pereira Gardner, was the daughter of the attending physician of the emperor of Brazil.

Draper was stimulated to precocity by his parents and by the intellectual milieu of New York City. He swiftly rose to prominence as a gifted inventor and a deft technician who made most of his own equipment. He pursued excellence and innovation; and his principal fame rests not on his medical profession but on his astronomical avocation, pursued at his own expense. Draper maintained intellectual freedom without slipping into isolation, and he is one of America's outstanding "amateur" scientists.

Educated at the University of the City of New York, where his father was professor of chemistry, Draper entered the medical school at the age of seventeen, after two years in college. In 1857 he had completed all his medical studies; he had written a medical thesis on the spleen, illustrated with daguerreotype microphotographs; and he had passed all of his examinations. He was only twenty, however, and since he had not yet reached the age required for graduation, he went abroad for a year with his older brother, Daniel, to relax and study.

During a visit to the observatory of William Parsons, the third earl of Rosse, in Parsonstown (now Birr), Ireland, Draper conceived the possibility of combining photography and astronomy. Returning to America in the spring of 1858, he received his medical diploma, joined the staff of Bellevue Hospital, and began preparations for grinding and polishing a speculum mirror. This tedious task occupied his spare time until the following summer, and it later ended in frustration when the mirror was split by freezing moisture. Draper's father revealed this tale to Sir John Herschel in June 1860 and was advised that glass was preferable to speculum in ease of figuring, lightness, and brightness when silvered. By November 1861 Draper had completed the first of about 100 glass mirrors, and he installed it in his new observatory on his father's estate at Hastings-on-Hudson, New York. His astronomical career began with daguerreotypes of the sun and the moon.

Early in 1860 Draper was appointed professor of natural sciences at the University of the City of New York, and for the next four years his teaching duties had to compete with experiments in photography and the polishing of glass mirrors. Many of these experiments were discussed at the monthly meetings of the American Photographic Society, of which he was a founding member. His monograph "On the Construction of a Silvered Glass Telescope 15-1/2 Inches in Aperture, and Its Use in Celestial Photography," published in 1864 at the request of Joseph Henry, provided a detailed description of his techniques and became the standard reference on telescope making.

Draper's work was interrupted during the Civil War by service as surgeon of the Twelfth Regiment of the New York State Militia. Because of poor health he was discharged in October 1862, after serving for nine months. During 1863 Draper made 1,500 negatives of the lunar face, and a small number of them bore enlargement to a fifty-inch diameter. His work was severely limited by atmospheric tremor and smoky haze, and he commented that "if the telescope could be transported to the Peruvian plateaus, 15,000 feet above the sea, or somewhere near the equator on the rainless west coast of South America, it would accomplish more." He never reached either of these sites, but both have subsequently been utilized.

The interests of the period 1865–1867 (when he was aged twenty-eight to thirty) were interwoven through his life until his sudden death at forty-five. In this interval he published an article on spectrum analysis, completed a textbook on chemistry, and was appointed professor of physiology and dean of the faculty in the medical department. The department had just lost its building and collections in a fire; and Draper led, and partly financed, its rehabilitation until 1873, when he resigned.

In 1867 Draper married Anna Mary Palmer, the daughter of Courtlandt Palmer. Wealthy and charming, Mrs. Draper proved to be a talented assistant in her husband's laboratory as well as a renowned hostess. The Draper dining table was frequently surrounded by celebrated scientists, politicians, and soldiers; and after Draper's election in 1877 to the National Academy of Sciences, they regularly entertained the members during their New York meetings. During the summer months the Drapers lived in Dobbs Ferry, New York, two miles from the Hastings observatory; and each autumn they returned to their home on Madison Avenue, where Draper maintained an astronomical laboratory that acquired the reputation of being the best-equipped in the world.

Work on a twenty-eight-inch reflecting telescope continued from 1867 to 1872; it was interrupted by the ruling of gratings and by preliminary studies of the spectra of the elements, especially carbon, nitrogen, and hydrogen. As a reference scale for the determination of wavelength, Draper photographed the solar spectrum; and his results far surpassed the best spectra available from 1873 until 1881, attesting to the combined power of photography and his ingenuity.

In May 1872, as soon as the final touches had been added to the twenty-eight-inch reflector, Draper photographed the spectrum of the star Vega, but the initial attempt failed. The low sensitivity of the wet collodion plates and the difficulty of keeping the stellar spectrum motionless on the plate prevented him from obtaining more than a faint continuum without spectrum lines. By August his technique had improved, and he was rewarded with the first photograph of stellar spectrum lines. Later he devised and named a "spectrograph," similar to Huggins' visual spectroscope, employing an entrance slit to purify the resulting spectrum and to permit the impression of reference spectra for the identification of the celestial elements.

When his father-in-law died in 1873, Draper accepted the responsibility of managing the estate; and when he found that this job required several hours a day, he resigned as dean of the medical faculty and accepted the title of professor of analytical chemistry in the academic department. The following year he completely set aside his own research to act as director of the photographic department of the U.S. commission to observe the 1874 transit of Venus. Following the transit the commission asked Congress to order a special gold medal to be struck for Draper, and the following year he was elected to the Astronomische Gesellschaft. In 1876 he attended the Philadelphia Centennial Exposition as a judge of the photographic section.

Draper committed one significant scientific error when, in 1877, he announced the identification of eighteen emission lines of oxygen in the spectrum of the solar disk. His explanation that the emission was due to the "great thickness of ignited oxygen" revealed a failure to appreciate the significance of Kirchhoff's law of radiation. Chemists were delighted by his announcement, but spectroscopists were at once skeptical. Draper repeated the crucial experiment at higher dispersion and carried the new results directly to the Royal Astronomical Society, but he succeeded only in sharpening the debate. After his death his contention that some apparent absorption lines were merely gaps between bright emission lines was definitely refuted by spectroscopy at still higher dispersion.

At the completion of his summer observing, Draper often hunted on horseback in the Rocky Mountains with generals R. B. Marcy and W. D. Whipple, so he was well aware of the clarity of the mountain air. He organized an expedition to observe the summertime solar eclipse of 1878; the party consisted of himself, Mrs. Draper, Thomas Alva Edison (who was able to detect the thermal radiation from the corona), President Henry Morton of the Stevens Institute of Technology, and Professor George F. Barker of the University of Pennsylvania. Their spectroscopic observations during the eclipse revealed the important fact that the corona shines largely by reflected light from the solar disk.

In the spring of 1879 Draper visited Huggins in England and learned that dry photographic plates had become more sensitive than wet collodion. He then called on Lockyer, whose work on the dissociation of the elements had profoundly impressed him. Thus stimulated, he returned to stellar spectroscopy; and in October he wrote to his friend E. S. Holden, "I have had splendid success in stellar spectrum photography this summer, having been able to use a slit only 1/1000 of an inch in width." Draper confirmed Huggins' discovery of hydrogen in Vega, and he noted that the stars so far observed could be placed in Secchi's first two spectrum classes. In his report to the National Academy of Sciences that year he cautioned:

> It is not easy without prolonged study and the assistance of laboratory experiments to interpret the results, and even then it will be necessary to speak with diffidence. . . . It is to be hoped that before long we may be able to investigate photographically the spectra of the gaseous nebulae, for in them the most elementary condition of matter and the simplest spectra are doubtless found.

The convenience of the new dry plates was wonderful; and within the next three years Draper had obtained more than eighty high-quality spectra of bright stars, the moon, Mars and Jupiter, the comet 1881 III, and the Orion nebula. His spectra of the Orion nebula revealed a faint continuous background

that he attributed to the scattering of starlight by meteoritic particles.

Draper also achieved splendid and unique results in the direct photography of the moon and of the Orion nebula. The key to this success was the excellent clockwork he devised after rejecting six earlier attempts, and in October of 1880 he wrote to Holden: "The exposure of the Orion Nebula required was 50 minutes; what do you think of that for a test of my driving clock?" The following March he wrote that he had far surpassed the earlier results with an exposure of 140 minutes, so that "the singular proposition is therefore tenable that we are on the point of photographing stars fainter than we can see with the same telescope." Draper had succeeded in making photography the best means of studying the sky, and in May 1882 he wrote: "I think we are by no means at the end of what can be done. If I can stand 6 hours exposure in midwinter another step forward will result." He died before another winter came.

In 1882 Draper received an honorary LL.D. from his alma mater and from the University of Wisconsin. He was a member of the American Philosophical Society and the American Academy of Arts and Sciences, as well as the National Academy of Sciences and the American Association for the Advancement of Science.

In the fall of 1882 Draper resigned his joint professorship of chemistry and physics, to which he had been elected the previous January upon the death of his father. Having thus ensured himself of the free time to pursue his research, he embarked on a two-month hunting trip in the Rocky Mountains. He was exposed one night to severe cold on a mountain slope without shelter, and he returned to New York with less than his usual vigor. But plans for entertaining the National Academy of Sciences were well advanced; and on 15 November 1882 about forty academicians and a few personal friends dined at the Draper home under the novel light of Edison bulbs. Draper retired early with chills and a fever, and he died five days later of double pleurisy.

Mrs. Draper established the Henry Draper Memorial at the Harvard College Observatory to further its research on the photography of stellar spectra.

BIBLIOGRAPHY

I. Original Works. Draper's published works are "On the Changes of Blood Cells in the Spleen," in *New York Journal of Medicine*, 3rd ser., **5** (1858), 182–189, his M.D. thesis; "On a New Method of Darkening Collodion Negatives," in *American Journal of Photography and the Allied Arts and Sciences*, 2nd ser., **1** (1859), 374–376; "On a Reflecting Telescope for Celestial Photography," in *Report of the British Association for the Advancement of Science,* **2** (1860), 63–64; "On an Improved Photographic Process," in *American Journal of Photography and the Allied Arts and Sciences,* 2nd ser., **5** (1862), 47; "Photography," in *New American Cyclopaedia* (New York, 1863); "On the Construction of a Silvered Glass Telescope 15-1/2 Inches in Aperture, and Its Use in Celestial Photography," in *Smithsonian Contributions to Knowledge,* **14,** pt. 2 (1864); "On the Photographic Use of a Silvered Glass Reflecting Telescope," in *Philosophical Magazine and Journal of Science,* 4th ser., **28** (1864), 249–255; "On a Silvered Glass Telescope and on Celestial Photography in America," in *Quarterly Journal of Science,* **1** (1864), 381–387; "Petroleum: Its Importance, Its History, Boring, Refining," *ibid.,* **2** (1865), 49–59, and in *Dinglers polytechnisches Journal,* **177** (1865), 107–117; "American Contributions to Spectrum Analysis," in *Quarterly Journal of Science,* **2** (1865), 395–401; *A Text Book on Chemistry* (New York, 1866); "Report on the Chemical and Physical Facts Collected From the Deep Sea Researches Made During the Voyage of the School Ship Mercury," in *Report of the Commission on Public Charities* (New York, 1871); "On Diffraction Spectrum Photography," in *American Journal of Science and Arts,* 3rd ser., **6** (1873), 401–409, also in *Philosophical Magazine,* 4th ser., **46** (1873), 417–425; *Annalen der Physik und Chemie,* **151** (1873), 337–350; and *Nature,* **9** (1873), 224–226; "Sur longueurs d'ondes et les caractères de raies violettes et ultraviolettes du soleil," in *Comptes rendus,* **78** (1874), 682–686.

"Photographs of the Spectra of Venus and α Lyrae," in *American Journal of Science and Arts,* 3rd ser., **13** (1877), 95, also in *Philosophical Magazine,* 5th ser., **3** (1877), 238; and *Nature,* **15** (1877), 218; "Astronomical Observations on the Atmosphere of the Rocky Mountains, Made at Elevations of From 4,500 to 11,000 Feet, in Utah and Wyoming Territories and Colorado," in *American Journal of Science and Arts,* 3rd ser., **13** (1877), 89–94; "Discovery of Oxygen in the Sun by Photography and a New Theory of the Solar Spectrum," *ibid.,* **14** (1877), 89–96, also in *Proceedings of the American Philosophical Society* (July 1877), 74–80; *Memorie della Società degli spettroscopisti italiani,* **6** (1877), 69; and *Nature,* **16** (1877), 364–366; "Observations on the Total Eclipse of the Sun of July 29th, 1878," in *American Journal of Science and Arts,* 3rd ser., **16** (1878), 227–230, also in *Philosophical Magazine,* 5th ser., **6** (1878), 318–320; "Speculum," in *New Universal Cyclopedia* (New York, 1878); "On the Coincidence of the Bright Lines of the Oxygen Spectrum with the Bright Lines of the Solar Spectrum," in *American Journal of Science and Arts,* 3rd ser., **18** (1879), 263–277, also in *Monthly Notices of the Royal Astronomical Society,* **39** (1879), 440–447; "On Photographing the Spectra of the Stars and Planets," in *Nature,* **21** (1879), 83–85, also in *American Journal of Science and Arts,* 3rd ser., **18** (1879), 419–425; and *Memorie della Società degli spettroscopisti italiani,* **8** (1879), 81; "Photographs of the Nebula in Orion," in *American Journal of Science and Arts,* 3rd ser., **20** (1880), 433, also in *Philosophical Magazine,* 5th ser., **10** (1880), 388; and *Comptes rendus,* **91** (1880), 688–690; "On a Photograph of Jupiter's Spectrum Showing Evidence of Intrinsic Light From That Planet," in *American Journal of Science and Arts,* 3rd ser., **20** (1880), 118–121, also in *Monthly Notices of the Royal Astronomical Society,* **40** (1880), 433–435; "On Stellar Photography," in *Comptes rendus,* **92** (1881), 964–965; "On Photographs of the Spectrum of Comet b 1881," in *American Journal of Science and Arts,* 3rd ser., **22** (1881), 134–135, also in *Observatory,* **5** (1882), 252–253; "On Photographs of the Nebula in Orion and of Its Spectrum," in *Comptes rendus,* **92** (1881), 173, also in *Monthly Notices of the Royal Astronomical Society,* **42** (1882), 367–368; "On Photographs of the Spectrum of the Nebula in Orion," in *American Journal of Science and Arts,* 3rd ser., **23** (1882), 339–341, also in *Observatory,* **5** (1882), 165–167. An extensive collection of Henry Draper's professional and personal correspondence is on file in the New York Public Library MS collection.

II. SECONDARY LITERATURE. Principal sources are George F. Barker, "Biographical Memoir of Henry Draper 1837–1882," read before the National Academy (Apr. 1888); and "Researches Upon the Photography of Planetary and Stellar Spectra by the Late Henry Draper, M.D., LL.D., with an introduction by Professor C. A. Young, a List of the Photographic Plates in Mrs. Draper's Possession, and the Results of the Measurement of these Plates by Professor E. C. Pickering," in *Proceedings of the American Academy of Arts and Sciences,* **19** (1884), 231–261. Other sources are "'Minute' on Henry Draper," in *Proceedings of the American Philosophical Society* (Dec. 1882); T. W. Webb, "Draper's Telescope," in *Smithsonian Annual Report* (1864), pp. 62–66, repr. from *Intellectual Observer* (London); and George F. Barker, "On the Use of Carbon Disulphide in Prisms; Being an Account of Experiments Made by the Late Dr. Henry Draper of New York," in *American Journal of Science,* 3rd ser., **29** (1885), 1–10.

CHARLES A. WHITNEY

DRAPER, JOHN WILLIAM (*b.* St. Helens, Lancashire, England, 5 May 1811; *d.* Hastings-on-Hudson, New York, 4 January 1882), *chemistry, history.*

Draper was the son of an itinerant Methodist preacher who possessed a Gregorian telescope and who evidently encouraged the boy's scientific interests. The father had purchased two shares in the new London University intended to accommodate scientists, workingmen, and Dissenters, but he died before his son commenced his premedical studies at University College (as it later became) in 1829. There Draper studied chemistry under Edward Turner, an admirer of Berzelius and the author of one of the earliest English textbooks in organic chemistry. Turner interested Draper in the chemical effects of light and thereby gave his career a decisive turn. At a time when Parliament had not yet broken the monopoly of Oxford and Cambridge for granting degrees, Draper had to be contented with a "certificate of honours" in chemistry.

On the urging of maternal relatives, who had gone to America before the Revolution to found a Wesleyan community, Draper immigrated with his mother, his three sisters, and his new wife to Virginia in 1832. He had already collaborated on three minor scientific publications before leaving England and now published eight additional papers between 1834 and 1836 from what he ambitiously described as his "laboratory" in the family farmhouse. The earnings of his sister Dorothy Catharine as a schoolteacher enabled him to take his medical degree at the University of Pennsylvania in 1836. His thesis, "Glandular Action," reflected the interest of his teacher J. K. Mitchell in the researches of Dutrochet on osmosis. His other principal instructor was Robert Hare.

On his return to Virginia, Draper was engaged as chemist and mineralogist to the newly formed Mineralogical Society of Virginia, which had been inspired by the writings of the celebrated pioneer of scientific agriculture in America, the Virginian Edmund Ruffin. A projected school of mineralogy never materialized, but many of the projectors were trustees of Hampden-Sidney College, where Draper served as professor of chemistry and natural philosophy from 1836 to 1839. From 1839 until his death, he was professor of chemistry in the college of New York University. He was also a founding proprietor, in 1841, of the tenuously connected New York University School of Medicine, of which he served as president from 1850. Under his inspiration, the university proper granted the degree of doctor of philosophy five times between 1867 and 1872, to students who had a bachelor's degree in arts or science or a medical degree and had then completed two further years of study in chemistry. This appears to be one of the two earliest attempts in the United States to establish the Ph.D. as a graduate degree. The enterprise petered out with Draper's own advancing years. His other principal institutional exertions were as first president of the American Union Academy of Literature, Science and Art, founded in 1869 as a riposte to the creation of the National Academy of Sciences in 1863. Draper had unaccountably been omitted from the original incorporators of the latter, and the omission was not repaired until 1877. He was, however, elected first president of the American Chemical Society in 1876.

Draper first achieved wide celebrity for his pioneering work in photography. As early as 1837, while still in Virginia, he had followed the example of Wedgwood and Davy in making temporary copies of objects by the action of light on sensitized surfaces. When the details of Daguerre's process for fixing camera images were published in various New York newspapers on 20 September 1839, Draper was ready for the greatest remaining challenge, to take a photographic portrait. A New York mechanic, Alexander S. Wolcott, apparently won the race by 7 October. But if Draper knew of this, he persisted in his own experiments and succeeded in taking a portrait not later than December 1839. His communication to the *Philosophical Magazine,* dated 31 March 1840, was the first report received in Europe of any photographer's success in portraiture. The superb likeness of his sister Dorothy Catharine, taken not later than July 1840, with an exposure of sixty-five seconds, seems to be the oldest surviving photographic portrait.

In the busy winter of 1839–1840, Draper also took the first photograph of the moon and launched, in a very modest way, the age of astronomical photography. He obtained "distinct" representations of the dark spots or lunar maria. He first announced his success to the New York Lyceum of Natural History on 23 March 1840. Fittingly enough, Draper's second son, Henry, became one of the most distinguished astronomical photographers of the nineteenth century. As early as 1850, when Henry was thirteen, Draper enlisted his aid in photographing slides through a microscope to illustrate a projected textbook, *Human Physiology* (1856). In the book they appear as engravings, but the elder Draper was one of the first, if not the very first, to conceive of and execute microphotographs.

Draper's grasp of the uses to which photography could be put and his ingenuity in accomplishing the requisite feats made him a technical innovator of considerable importance; but this was merely incidental to a much deeper concern with the chemical effects of radiant energy in general. By his researches in this field, Draper became easily one of the dozen most important contributors to basic science in the United States before 1870.

He enunciated in 1841 the principle that only absorbed rays produce chemical change—long known as Draper's law but eventually rechristened the Grotthuss or Grotthuss–Draper law from its formulation by the German C. J. D. Grotthuss in 1817. Grotthuss' statement attracted no attention until the close of the nineteenth century, by which time the principle had become well established under Draper's (entirely independent) auspices. In 1843 Draper constructed a "tithonometer," or device for measuring the intensity of light, based on the discovery by Gay-Lussac and Thénard in 1809 that light causes hydrogen and chlorine to combine progressively. The seminal work in this field remained to be done by Bunsen and Roscoe from the mid-1850's onward. Their "actinometer," built after they had rejected Draper's instrument as inaccurate, made use of the identical phenomenon.

With a grating ruled for him by the mechanician of the United States Mint, Joseph Saxton, Draper took, in 1844, what seems to have been the first photograph of the diffraction spectrum. Apparently he was also the first to take with any precision a photograph of the infrared region, and the first to describe three great Fraunhofer lines there (1843). He also photographed lines in the ultraviolet independently of Edmond Becquerel and at about the same time.

In one of his most important memoirs (1847), he proved that all solid substances become incandescent at the same temperature, that thereafter with rising temperature they emit rays of increasing refrangibility, and (a fundamental proposition of astrophysics, later elaborated upon by Kirchhoff) that incandescent solids produce a continuous spectrum. Draper implied in the mid-1840's and stated clearly in 1857 that the maxima of luminosity and of heat in the spectrum coincide. For the sum of his researches on radiant energy, Draper received the Rumford Medal of the American Academy of Arts and Sciences (1875).

By the mid-1850's Draper had become acquainted, directly or indirectly, with the positivism of Auguste Comte and had embraced Comte's law of the three stages of historical development, from the theological through the metaphysical to the "positive," or scientific. Comte had argued for a parallel development of the individual personality from infancy to maturity. Where Draper sharply diverged from Comte was in postulating that the history of mankind had consisted in a succession of dominant nations or cultures, regarded as biological organisms experiencing decrepitude and death as well as birth and development. With this cyclical theory of history, entirely alien to Comte, Draper combined a passionate espousal of environmentalism.

The principal work in which all these notes sounded together was *A History of the Intellectual Development of Europe* (1863). Draper says, however, that the book was sketched by 1856 and completed by 1858. The suspicion that he had been influenced by either Buckle or Darwin is unfounded. Yet he undoubtedly profited from the vogue of both men and blandly assimilated himself to Darwinism whenever he could. Thus he spruced up his totally unamended views on history for the British Association for the Advancement of Science at Oxford in 1860, under the provocative but fraudulent title "On the Intellectual Development of Europe, Considered With Reference to the Views of Mr. Darwin and Others, That the Progression of Organisms Is Determined by Law." This unprofitable paper was the direct occasion for the

famous exchange between Bishop Wilberforce and T. H. Huxley. From this time forward, Draper was regarded as a valiant defender of science against religion. His most popular book, widely read in many translations, was a *History of the Conflict Between Religion and Science* (1874), a vigorous polemic against the persecution of scientists by religionists.

BIBLIOGRAPHY

I. ORIGINAL WORKS. Draper's works include *A Treatise on the Forces Which Produce the Organization of Plants* (New York, 1844); *Human Physiology, Statical and Dynamical; or, The Conditions and Course of the Life of Man* (New York, 1856); *A History of the Intellectual Development of Europe* (New York, 1863); *Thoughts on the Future Civil Policy of America* (New York, 1865); *History of the American Civil War*, 3 vols. (New York, 1867–1870); *History of the Conflict Between Religion and Science* (New York, 1874); and *Scientific Memoirs, Being Experimental Contributions to a Knowledge of Radiant Energy* (New York, 1878).

II. SECONDARY LITERATURE. See Donald Fleming, *John William Draper and the Religion of Science* (Philadelphia, 1950), which has an extensive bibliography.

DONALD FLEMING

DREBBEL, CORNELIUS (*b.* Alkmaar, Netherlands, 1572; *d.* London, England, 1633), *mechanics, optics, technology.*

Drebbel's father, Jacob Jansz, a burgher of Alkmaar, was a landowner or farmer. Nothing is known of his mother. He probably had only an elementary education, learning to read and write Latin in his later years. As a young man Drebbel was apprenticed to the famous engraver Hendrik Goltzius and lived in his home in Haarlem. Drebbel proved to be an apt pupil, as is shown by a number of extant engravings from his hand. In addition, he probably acquired an interest in and some knowledge of alchemy from Goltzius, who was an adept.

After his marriage in 1595 to one of Goltzius' younger sisters, Sophia Jansdocther, he settled at Alkmaar, where he devoted himself to engraving and publishing maps and pictures. He soon turned to mechanical inventions, for in 1598 a patent was granted to him for a pump and a clock with a perpetual motion. He is mentioned as having built a fountain for the city of Middelburg, in the province of Zeeland, in 1601; and in 1602 he was granted a patent for a chimney. About 1605 Drebbel moved to London. Apparently some of his mechanical inventions appealed to James I, and he was soon taken into the special service of Henry, prince of Wales, and was installed in the castle at Elpham.

Drebbel's fame as an inventor became well known on the Continent, and he was visited at Elpham by Emperor Rudolf II and by the duke of Württemberg. He was invited to visit Rudolf, and by October 1610 he was in Prague with his family. Drebbel spent his time at the court of Rudolf showing off his "perpetuum mobile" and probably devoting himself to alchemy. After Matthias, Rudolf's brother, had conquered Prague and deposed Rudolf, Drebbel was imprisoned; through the intervention of Prince Henry, however, he was set free to return to England in 1613.

During the next several years Drebbel lived mostly in London, although there are indications that at various times he was on the Continent and again in Prague. About 1620 he began to devote himself to the manufacture of microscopes and to the construction of a submarine. He became acquainted with Abraham and Jacob Kuffler, who with their two other brothers were to become his disciples. Abraham soon married Drebbel's daughter Anna; and Johannes, another brother, married Katherina Drebbel in 1627. The four Kuffler brothers became agents and promoters for the microscopes and other instruments developed by Drebbel, Johannes being the one who did the most to promote Drebbel's inventions after his death.

For the next several years Drebbel was employed by the British navy and was concerned mainly with the famous expedition to La Rochelle. In spite of the failure of the expedition to raise the siege, Drebbel continued to work for the navy for some time at a fairly high salary. From 1629 until his death Drebbel was extremely poor and earned his living by keeping an alehouse. He was also engaged in various schemes for draining land near London, but apparently none was successful.

According to most of Drebbel's contemporaries, he was a light-haired and handsome man of gentle manners, considered to possess good intelligence, to be sharp-witted, and to have many ideas about various inventions. No absolute information on his religion is available; but his biographers have concluded that he was most likely an Anabaptist, since most of his friends and relatives were.

Drebbel left very few writings of his own, and none of them is concerned with his inventions. His most famous work was *Ein kurzer Tractat von der Natur der Elementum* (Leiden, 1608), an alchemical tract on the transmutation of the elements. Later editions contain a description of his "perpetuum mobile." Another treatise, *De quinta essentia* (Hamburg, 1621), is also alchemical in outlook and was written with the help of a friend. In it Drebbel discusses extracts from metals, minerals, plants, and other materials and their use in medicine.

In the strict sense Drebbel was not a scientist but an inventor or practicing technologist. In certain inventions he made use, however, of well-established scientific principles. Unlike many of his predecessors who had been interested in technological inventions, he actually brought his inventions to the practical state, and his finished models worked.

Among Drebbel's best-known inventions are the following.

(1) "Perpetuum mobile." This elaborate toy operated on the basis of changes in atmospheric temperature and pressure. Many models of it were used, and Drebbel extended the basic idea to the operation of clocks. Probably his initial fame in England and Europe rested on this invention, which delighted the people of the time.

(2) Thermostats. Drebbel apparently learned to apply the principles used in the "perpetuum mobile" to temperature regulators for ovens and furnaces. The principle involved was that as the temperature rose, the air expanded and pushed a column of quicksilver to the point at which it would close a damper. As the temperature fell, the damper would be opened. Drebbel applied the same idea to an incubator for hatching duck and chicken eggs.

(3) Optics. Drebbel was an expert lens grinder; and records indicate that his instruments were bought by several well-known persons, including Constantin Huygens. He made compound microscopes as early as 1619; and some of his biographers insist that he was the actual inventor of the microscope with two sets of convex lenses.

(4) The submarine. While living in London, according to many reliable accounts, Drebbel built a submarine that could carry a number of people. It was based on the principle of a diving bell: the bottom was open, and a rower sitting above the water level controlled the submarine. There was apparently no connection between the submarine and the atmosphere. Such reliable authorities as Robert Boyle have said that Drebbel had some means of purifying the air within the submarine.

(5) Chemical technology. Undoubtedly, Drebbel's most important contribution in this field was his discovery of a tin mordant for dyeing scarlet with cochineal. This process was communicated to his son-in-law, Abraham Kuffler, who had a dyehouse in Bow, London; and for many years the scarlet made with tin was known as "color Kufflerianus." The famous scarlets of the Gobelins made use of Drebbel's invention, and the method soon spread to all parts of the Continent. It is said that the discovery was made by accident when some tin dissolved in aqua regia happened to fall into a solution of cochineal that Drebbel

was planning to use for a thermometer. Although not a dyer, he quickly recognized the importance of his fortunate discovery and his family made good use of it. Among other chemical achievements attributed to Drebbel are the introduction into England of the manufacture of sulfuric acid by burning sulfur with saltpeter and the discovery of mercury and silver fulminates.

BIBLIOGRAPHY

I. ORIGINAL WORKS. Drebbel's most important books are cited in the text.

II. SECONDARY LITERATURE. On Drebbel or his work, see (listed chronologically): F. M. Jaeger, *Cornelis Drebbel en zijne tijdgenooten* (Groningen, 1922); Gerrit Tierie, *Cornelius Drebbel (1572–1633)* (Amsterdam, 1932); L. E. Harris, *The Two Netherlanders* (Cambridge, 1961); and J. R. Partington, *A History of Chemistry,* II (London, 1961), 321–324.

SIDNEY EDELSTEIN

DREYER, JOHANN LOUIS EMIL (*b.* Copenhagen, Denmark, 13 February 1852; *d.* Oxford, England, 14 September 1926), *astronomy.*

Dreyer was the son of Lt. Gen. J. C. F. Dreyer and Ida Nicoline Margarethe Rangrup. He began studying mathematics and astronomy at Copenhagen University in 1869 and won a gold medal in 1874 for an essay entitled "Personal Errors in Observation." He received the M.A. in 1874 and the Ph.D. in 1882. All of Dreyer's astronomical appointments were in Ireland: from 1874 to 1878, assistant at Lord Rosse's observatory, Parsonstown [now Birr], where he observed nebulae through the seventy-two-inch-aperture telescope; from 1878 to 1882, assistant at Dunsink Observatory, Dublin; from 1882 to 1916, director of Armagh Observatory, where he collected and reduced observations made since 1859. This work led to the *Second Armagh Catalogue of 3,300 Stars* (1886). He settled at Oxford after retirement.

Dreyer was a fellow of the Royal Astronomical Society from 1875, gold medalist in 1916, and president from 1923–1926. He married Katherine Hannah Tuthill of Kilmore, Ireland, in 1875; they had three sons and a daughter. Gentle and amiable in disposition, Dreyer was a good astronomical observer and a most erudite scholar, gifted in languages, accurate, painstaking, and devoted to astronomy and astronomical history.

Dreyer enriched astronomy by three monumental works of research, collection, and editing. The first is "New General Catalogue of Nebulae and Clusters of Stars" (1888). The Herschels had discovered and catalogued over 5,000 nebulae and clusters, but by the 1880's numerous discoveries by other astronomers had made Sir John Herschel's catalog out-of-date. Dreyer had tried to remedy this by publishing a supplement listing hundreds of items (1878). Then, at the suggestion of the Royal Astronomical Society, he used the Herschel catalog as a basis for the compilation of the *New General Catalogue,* renumbering all the 7,840 objects discovered up to 1888 and giving their positions and descriptions. During the following twenty years he also published two index catalogs, enumerating all additional discoveries and raising the total to over 13,000. Many galaxies, nebulae, and star clusters are still known by their NGC and IC numbers.

In 1912 Dreyer edited the scientific papers of Sir William Herschel for the Royal Society of London and the Royal Astronomical Society. The two thick volumes contain seventy-one published and some thirty unpublished papers of the elder Herschel. Dreyer prefaced the work with an excellent detailed biography, based mainly on unpublished material.

Interest in a famous figure in his country's history, Tycho Brahe, the last great astronomer of the pretelescope era, had inspired Dreyer from boyhood to become an astronomer. In 1890 his book *Tycho Brahe* provided a scholarly biography rich in information about sixteenth-century astronomy and astronomers. In his last years, Dreyer completed the formidable task of collecting and editing all the works and correspondence of Tycho, including all his observations and those of his assistants. This huge collection (in Latin) was published under the auspices of the Academy of Sciences of Copenhagen between 1913 and 1929.

Among Dreyer's other works are a *History of Planetary Systems* and papers including "Original Form of the Alfonsine Tables" and "A New Determination of the Constant of Precession."

BIBLIOGRAPHY

I. ORIGINAL WORKS. Dreyer's 1874 gold medal essay was expanded and published as "On Personal Errors in Astronomical Transit Measurements," in *Proceedings of the Irish Academy,* 2nd ser., **2** (1876), 484–528. Major works edited by Dreyer are "New General Catalogue of Nebulae and Clusters of Stars," in *Memoirs of the Royal Astronomical Society,* **49** (1888), 1–237; "Index Catalogue of Nebulae Found in the Years 1888–1894 (Nos. 1–1529), With Notes and Corrections to NGC," ibid., **51** (1895), 185–228; and "Second Index Catalogue of Nebulae and Clusters of Stars, Containing Objects Found in the Years 1895–1907 (Nos. 1530–5386), With Notes and Corrections to NGC and to First IC," ibid., **59** (1908), 105–198. These three were republished as *New General Catalogue . . .* in 1 vol. by the

Royal Astronomical Society (1953; repr. 1962). Also of considerable importance are *The Scientific Papers of Sir William Herschel*, 2 vols. (London, 1912); and *Omnia opera Tychonis Brahe Dani*, 15 vols. (Copenhagen, 1913–1929). Vols. I–IV contain the observations made by Brahe and his assistants in the following years: Vol. I, 1563–1585; Vol. II, 1586–1589; Vol. III, 1590–1595; Vol. IV, 1596–1601 and observations of comets. Volumes X–XIII are also entitled *Thesaurus observationum*.

Additional works by Dreyer are "A Supplement to Sir John Herschel's *General Catalogue of Nebulae and Clusters of Stars*," in *Transactions of the Royal Irish Academy*, **26** (1878), 381–426, which was included in the NGC; "A New Determination of the Constant of Precession," in *Proceedings of the Royal Irish Academy*, **3** (1883), 617–623, which includes a historical survey of the subject; *Second Armagh Catalogue of 3,300 Stars for Epoch 1875, Deduced From Observations Made at the Armagh Observatory 1859–1883, and Prepared for Publication by J. L. E. Dreyer* (Dublin, 1886); *Tycho Brahe. A Picture of Scientific Life in the Sixteenth Century* (Edinburgh, 1890); *History of the Planetary Systems From Thales to Kepler* (Cambridge, 1906); and "On the Original Form of the Alfonsine Tables," in *Monthly Notices of the Royal Astronomical Society*, **80,** no. 3 (1920), 243–261, a brilliant research based on medieval manuscripts.

II. SECONDARY LITERATURE. Two works that draw heavily on Dreyer are A. F. O'D. Alexander, *The Planet Saturn* (London, 1962), which draws on Dreyer's works on Brahe and Herschel, and *The Planet Uranus* (London, 1965), which uses the work on Herschel. Obituaries are in *Observatory*, **49** (1926), 293–294; and *Monthly Notices of the Royal Astronomical Society*, **87** (1927), 251–257. There is a biography in *Dictionary of National Biography* for 1922–1930.

A. F. O'D. ALEXANDER

DRIESCH, HANS ADOLF EDUARD (*b.* Bad Kreuznach, Germany, 28 October 1867; *d.* Leipzig, Germany, 16 April 1941), *biology, philosophy.*

Toward the end of the nineteenth century, when Hans Driesch entered upon his unique career, the German universities seemed to be in their prime and members of their scientific faculties were particularly preeminent in the natural sciences, including biology. Yet when Driesch chose his life style, he became an embryologist as an independent rather than as a professional investigator. He was a man of comfortable means, a cosmopolite, and a world traveler. He had no need, and at first no inclination, to join the academic hierarchy; he was not habilitated until twenty years after he had received his doctorate. While working as an amateur, he made numerous contributions of great originality and of far-reaching importance to the new science of experimental embryology. He was always theoretically inclined, and his experimental results turned him eventually toward

philosophical explanations. He had already written, while still an experimental biologist, a number of metaphysical articles and books; and when he finally was habilitated, it was in natural philosophy. He became a professor of philosophy and, as such, the strongest proponent in our times of vitalism.

Driesch was the only child of Paul Driesch, a well-to-do Hamburg merchant who dealt in gold and silver wares, and the former Josefine Raudenkolb. He grew up in Hamburg, where he was first educated at a famous humanistic Gymnasium, Gelehrtenschule des Johanneums, founded by a friend of Martin Luther's. In 1886 he spent two semesters at the University of Freiburg, studying with August Weismann in preparation for becoming a zoologist. He then became a student at the University of Jena, where he received his doctorate under Ernst Heinrich Haeckel in 1889; during the summer of 1888 he interrupted his zoological training to study physics and chemistry at Munich. For ten years after he received his degree he traveled extensively, usually with Curt Herbst, whom he had met at Jena in 1887; many of his scientific ideas were strongly influenced by Herbst's. Driesch performed his most important experiments during these years; they were carried out principally, although not exclusively, at the internationally supported Zoological Station in Naples. He did his last experiments in 1909, the year in which he was habilitated in natural philosophy at the Faculty of Natural Sciences of Heidelberg, where he had settled in 1900. On 23 May 1899 he married Margarete Reifferscheidt; their children were Kurt (*b.* 1904) and Ingeborg (*b.* 1906), both of whom later became musicians.

Driesch became extraordinary professor at Heidelberg in 1912, accepted the ordinary professorship of systematic philosophy at Cologne in 1919, and became professor of philosophy at Leipzig in 1921. He was a visiting professor in China (Nanking and Peking) in 1922–1923, in the United States (University of Wisconsin) in 1926–1927, and in Buenos Aires in 1928. In 1933 he was prematurely placed in emeritus status by the National Socialists because of his lack of sympathy for their regime, but he continued to work until he died in 1941.

Driesch first became attracted to zoology through his mother's collection of exotic birds and animals, maintained in an aviary and in vivaria in her home. He was inspired to specialize in embryology, as were many of his contemporaries, by Haeckel's popular books. Driesch, however, lost interest in phylogeny by 1890. He himself chose the subject for his doctoral dissertation, which played down phylogenetic speculation in favor of an investigation of the laws governing the growth of hydroid colonies (1890, 1891). In the spring of 1891 he performed the experiment for which he is now best remembered, the separation of the blastomeres of the cleaving sea urchin egg.

Shortly before, in 1888, Wilhelm Roux had published the results of experiments showing that when one blastomere of the two-celled frog egg is killed, the remaining cell forms a half-embryo. Roux interpreted this as signifying that each cell is predestined, at the two-cell stage, to form only what it would have formed in the normally developing embryo. Richard and Oskar Hertwig, and later Theodor Boveri, had shaken sea urchin eggs to separate them into nucleated and nonnucleated fragments; Driesch adopted this method to separate the sea urchin blastomeres at the two-cell stage and found that in this egg, in contrast with that of the frog, each blastomere could form a whole, rather than a half, larva. Driesch interpreted these results as signifying that the fate of the cells is not fixed at the two-cell stage and that a cell can form parts that it does not normally form during development. The fate of a cell is a function of its position in the whole; its prospective potency, as Driesch was to put it a few years later (1894), is greater than its prospective significance. Furthermore, the cell not only forms parts that it would not have formed had the experiment not been performed; it also forms an organized, whole individual. It is, as Driesch was to call it, first in 1899, a harmonious equipotential system.

These interpretations were diametrically opposed to those of Roux, who considered that cells self-differentiate independently, forming a sort of mosaic that constitutes the embryo. Driesch's discovery that the development of a cell is not fixed at the two-cell stage and that it can be altered confirmed experimentally that development is epigenetic and opened new paths for exploration by the developing science of experimental embryology. In particular, his emphasis on organic wholeness and his comparison of the prospective potency of a part with its prospective significance provided the conceptual framework for the organizer concept developed by Hans Spemann during the first third of the twentieth century.

Driesch eventually extended his original experiments on the sea urchin eggs by shaking them in calcium-free seawater, according to a method of Herbst's, and separated the cells at later developmental stages. He also performed a corollary experiment, fusing two sea urchin embryos at the blastula stage to produce a single giant larva. He experimented also on eggs of other echinoderms and of ctenophores and ascidians, and he performed a number of experiments on regeneration in adult hydroids and ascidians. The philosophical implications of these experiments were later to influence Driesch's thought profoundly; but in the meantime, during the latter part of the nineteenth century, he performed a number of other strictly embryological experiments of great import and influence in their time, although they are less frequently recalled than the blastomere separation.

Roux and Weismann had postulated that qualitatively unequal nuclear division and subsequent differential distribution of nuclear material to the cells are the prime factors responsible for the formation of particular embryonic parts by particular cells. If this explanation held true, Driesch reasoned, abnormal distribution of the nuclei in the cytoplasm should result in embryonic malformations. He tested this possibility (1892) by compressing sea urchin eggs between glass cover slips at the four-cell stage in order to alter the cleavage pattern. The third cleavage occurred under pressure. The cytoplasm was deformed, with the nuclei displaced and atypically distributed through it. Yet the larvae that developed from the compressed eggs were normal, and Driesch knew that this meant that all the nuclei were equivalent. As Herbst said, "Expressed in terms of modern genetics, this signifies that all the nuclei contain all the genes" ("Hans Driesch als experimenteller und theoretischer Biologe," p. 115).

Driesch had great interest in the mode of nuclear function. He postulated (1894) that factors external to a cell influence its cytoplasm, which in turn influences the nucleus to produce substances that affect the cytoplasm. Furthermore, he postulated that the influence of the nucleus on the cell body is mediated through enzymes (ferments, in the terminology of his times); these concepts were widely disseminated and extremely influential in their day.

Another experiment performed by Driesch on sea urchin eggs, of equal theoretical importance and influence, was one in which he shook sea urchin larvae at the stage when the primary mesenchyme cells were organizing themselves into two clumps, preparatory to developing the larval skeleton. After their displacement by the shaking, the mesenchyme cells returned to their original positions. Driesch believed that they reaggregated there under the influence of the ectoderm and interpreted this in terms of the ability of the mesenchyme cells to react to tactile stimuli from the ectoderm (1896). This is very close to the concept of induction; in 1894 Driesch had written at great length about the possibilities of embryonic induction, including chemical induction and contact induction, in the widely read monograph *Analytische Theorie der organischen Entwicklung.*

Driesch published his first wholly theoretical pamphlet in 1891; in it he expressed his desire to explain development in terms of mechanics and mathematics. In the *Analytische Theorie der organischen Entwicklung* he was still mechanistic in outlook. As early as 1892, however, he had mentioned, in an experimental paper, the possibility that vitalistic interpretation might be compatible with scientific methodology; by 1895, according to his own testimony, he was a convinced vitalist. He despaired of explaining on a mechanistic basis the ability of half of a two-celled egg to form a whole larva, for he could not envisage a machine that could divide itself into two machines, each able to reconstitute itself into a whole. During the first decade of the new century he found himself obliged to invoke an agent-outside-the-machine (for which he borrowed Aristotle's word "entelechy") as a regulator of organic development. Although he believed the entelechy to be a vital agent indefinable in terms of physics and chemistry, he thought its action was somehow brought about by the formation or activation of enzymes (ferments), and he laid strong emphasis on the importance of enzymes as regulatory agents in development.

Driesch was invited to deliver the Gifford lectures in natural theology at the University of Aberdeen in 1907 and 1908. These lectures, first published in 1908 in Driesch's own excellent English under the title *Science and Philosophy of the Organism,* summarized his experiments and the philosophical conclusions to which they led. Driesch later wrote many philosophical articles and books on organic form and organic wholeness, on the mind-body problem, and so forth. As a systematic philosopher he devoted considerable attention to both logic and metaphysics; as a metaphysician, he was strongly influenced by Kant. He also became interested in parapsychology; when he applied for permission to leave Germany to preside at a meeting of the International Society for Psychic Research in Oslo in 1935, he was deprived of his passport by the Nazis.

Driesch received many honors, including honorary degrees from Aberdeen, Hamburg, and Nanking. In honor of his sixtieth birthday, in 1927, eighteen years after he had performed his last experiment, two volumes of *Wilhelm Roux Archiv für Entwicklungsmechanik der Organismen,* including forty-eight articles, were dedicated to him. In his introduction to the *Festschrift,* Spemann wrote: "If Wilhelm Roux's systematic mind discovered and staked out for us a new field of investigation, Driesch's statements of its problems widened its horizons immeasurably" (p. 2). He placed Driesch's work, to which he owed so much, in proper perspective.

Although Driesch's experiments were ingeniously

conceived, he was not particularly deft at carrying them out, a deficiency that he recognized and regretted. The biological interpretations of some of his experimental results, particularly those on later cleavage stages of the sea urchin, were subsequently shown to have been erroneous. Nevertheless, the principal conclusions drawn from his early experiments still hold. They made a positive contribution to the ongoing progress of experimental and analytical embryology that cannot be minimized, even though in his later days Driesch chose what was to him the vitalistic imperative.

BIBLIOGRAPHY

I. ORIGINAL WORKS. The article by Herbst (below) includes a bibliography of 130 items by Driesch, classified into two categories (descriptive and experimental, and biotheoretical). The book edited by Wenzl (below) includes a bibliography of 289 items by Driesch, arranged chronologically. The articles and books listed below deal principally with Driesch's experiments and their interpretations: "Tektonische Studien an Hydroidpolypen," in *Jenaische Zeitschrift für Naturwissenschaft,* **24** (1890), 189–226; "Tektonische Studien an Hydroidpolypen. II. Plumularia und Aglaophenia. Die Tubulariden. Nebst allgemeinen Erörterungen über die Natur tierischer Stöcke," *ibid.,* 657–688; "Entwicklungsmechanische Studien. I. Der Werth der beiden ersten Furchungszellen in der Echinodermenentwicklung. Experimentelle Erzeugung von Theil- und Doppelbildungen. II. Ueber die Beziehungen des Lichtes zur ersten Etappe der thierischen Formbildung," in *Zeitschrift für wissenschaftliche Zoologie,* **53** (1891), 160–184; "Heliotropismus bei Hydroidpolypen," in *Zoologische Jahrbücher,* Abteilung für Systematik . . ., **5** (1891), 147–156; *Die mathematisch-mechanische Betrachtung morphologischer Probleme der Biologie. Eine kritische Studie* (Jena, 1891); "Tektonische Studien an Hydroidpolypen. III (Schluss). Antennularia," in *Jenaische Zeitschrift für Naturwissenschaft,* **25** (1891), 467–479; "Entwicklungsmechanische Studien. III. Die Verminderung des Furchungsmaterials und ihre Folgen (Weiteres über Theilbildungen). IV. Experimentelle Veränderungen des Typus der Furchung und ihre Folgen (Wirkungen von Wärmezufuhr und von Druck). V. Von der Furchung doppeltbefruchteter Eier. VI. Ueber einige allgemeine Fragen der theoretischen Morphologie," in *Zeitschrift für wissenschaftliche Zoologie,* **55** (1892), 1–62; *Die Biologie als selbstständige Wissenschaft* (Leipzig, 1893); "Entwicklungsmechanische Studien. VII. Exogastrula und Anenteria (über die Wirkung von Wärmezufuhr auf die Larvenentwicklung der Echiniden). VIII. Ueber Variation der Mikromerenbildung (Wirkung von Verdünnung des Meereswassers). IX. Ueber die Vertretbarkeit der 'Anlagen' von Ektoderm und Entoderm. X. Ueber einige allgemeine entwicklungsmechanische Ergebnisse," in *Mitteilungen aus der Zoologischen Station zu Neapel,* **11** (1893), 221–254; "Zur Theorie der tierischen

Formbildung," in *Biologisches Zentralblatt,* **13** (1893), 296–312; "Zur Verlagerung der Blastomeren des Echinideies," in *Anatomischer Anzeiger,* **8** (1893), 348–357; *Analytische Theorie der organischen Entwicklung* (Leipzig, 1894); "Von der Entwickelung einzelner Ascidienblastomeren," in *Archiv für Entwicklungsmechanik der Organismen,* **1** (1895), 398–413; "Zur Analyse der ersten Entwickelungsstadien des Ctenophoreies. I. Von der Entwickelung einzelner Ctenophorenblastomeren. II. Von der Entwicklung ungefurchter Eier mit Protoplasmadefekten," *ibid.,* **2** (1896), 204–224, in collaboration with T. H. Morgan; "Die taktische Reizbarkeit von Mesenchymzellen von *Echinus microtuberculatus,*" *ibid.,* **3** (1896), 362–380; "Betrachtungen über die Organisation des Eies und ihre Genese," *ibid.,* **4** (1897), 75–124; "Studien über das Regulationsvermögen der Organismen. 1. Von den regulativen Wachstums- und Differenzirungsfähigkeiten der Tubularia," *ibid.,* **5** (1897), 389–418; "Ueber rein-mütterliche Charaktere an Bastardlarven von Echiniden," *ibid.,* **7** (1898), 65–102; *Die Lokalisation morphogenetischer Vorgänge. Ein Beweis vitalistischen Geschehens* (Leipzig, 1899), also in *Archiv für Entwicklungsmechanik der Organismen,* **8** (1899), 35–111; "Studien über das Regulationsvermögen der Organismen. 2. Quantitative Regulationen bei der Reparation der Tubularia. 3. Notizen über die Auflösung und Wiederbildung des Skelets der Echinidenlarven," *ibid.,* **9** (1899), 103–139; "Studien über das Regulationsvermögen der Organismen. 4. Die Verschmelzung der Individualität bei Echinidenkeimen," *ibid.,* **10** (1900), 411–434; "Studien über das Regulationsvermögen der Organismen. 5. Ergänzende Beobachtungen an Tubularia," *ibid.,* **11** (1901), 185–206; "Studien über das Regulationsvermögen der Organismen. 6. Die Restitutionen der *Clavellina lepadiformis,*" *ibid.,* **14** (1902), 247–287; "Studien über das Regulationsvermögen der Organismen. 7. Zwei neue Regulationen bei Tubularia," *ibid.,* 532–538; "Ueber Aenderungen der Regulationsfähigkeit im Verlauf der Entwicklung bei Ascidien," *ibid.,* **17** (1903), 54–63; "Ueber das Mesenchym von unharmonisch zusammengesetzten Keimen des Echiniden," *ibid.,* **19** (1905), 658–679; *Der Vitalismus als Geschichte und als Lehre* (Leipzig, 1905); "Regenerierende Regenerate," in *Archiv für Entwicklungsmechanik der Organismen,* **21** (1906), 754–755; *The Science and Philosophy of the Organism. The Gifford Lectures Delivered Before the University of Aberdeen in the Year 1907* [*and 1908*], 2 vols. (London, 1908; 2nd ed., 1 vol., 1929); "Zwei Mitteilungen zur Restitution der Tubularia," in *Archiv für Entwicklungsmechanik der Organismen,* **26** (1908), 119–129; "Neue Versuche über die Entwicklung verschmolzener Echinidenkeime," *ibid.,* **30,** pt. 1 (1910), 8–23; and *Lebenserinnerungen. Aufzeichnungen eines Forschers und Denkers in entscheidender Zeit* (Basel, 1951).

Later philosophical and theoretical articles are listed in the bibliographies by Herbst and Wenzl.

II. SECONDARY LITERATURE. Selected writings about Hans Driesch, his work, and his thought are Margarete Driesch, "Das Leben von Hans Driesch," in *Hans Driesch, Persönlichkeit und Bedeutung für Biologie und Philosophie von heute . . . ,* A. Wenzl, ed. (Basel, 1951), pp. 1–20; Curt

Herbst, "Hans Driesch als experimenteller und theoretischer Biologe," in *Wilhelm Roux Archiv für Entwicklungsmechanik der Organismen,* **141** (1941–1942), 111–153; and E. Ungerer, "Hans Driesch. Der Naturforscher und Naturphilosoph (1867–1941)," in *Naturwissenschaften,* 29 Jahrgang (1941), 457–462.

In addition, the work edited by Wenzl, cited above, includes a bibliography of other articles on Driesch and his work, p. 206. The *Festschrift* referred to in the text, dedicated to Driesch and containing 48 articles in his honor, is *Wilhelm Roux Archiv für Entwicklungsmechanik der Organismen,* **111–112** (1927).

JANE OPPENHEIMER

DRUDE, PAUL KARL LUDWIG (*b.* Brunswick, Germany, 12 July 1863; *d.* Berlin, Germany, 5 July 1906), *physics.*

Drude was the son of a medical doctor in Brunswick. He attended the local Gymnasium and then went on to study at the University of Göttingen. His original ambition was to become a mathematician, and he studied mathematics, first at Göttingen and then at Freiburg and Berlin. In his sixth semester he returned to Göttingen, where he came under the influence of W. Voigt and as a result began to study theoretical physics. Drude's dissertation, under Voigt's direction, was a purely theoretical treatment of the equations governing the reflection and refraction of light at the boundaries of absorbing crystals.

Drude worked with Voigt at Göttingen until 1894. He then moved to Leipzig where he pursued both theoretical and practical researches on the propagation of electromagnetic waves and wireless telegraphy, as well as continuing his work on physical optics. His interest in the physical determinants of optical constants led him toward an attempt to correlate and account for the optical, electrical, thermal, and chemical properties of substances. Drude's interest in these problems was stimulated by his own growing conviction, based on studies begun in 1888, that Maxwell's electromagnetic theory was superior to the older mechanical view of light. This conviction led him to publish *Physik des Äthers* (1894), one of the first German books to base explanations of electrical and optical effects on Maxwell's theory. By 1898 Drude had begun to consider these matters within the structure of the theory of electrons; indeed, he thereby laid the foundation for understanding such phenomena as conduction in metals, thermal conductivity, and optical properties of metals as interactions of the electrical charges of substances with their environment.

In 1894 Drude married Emilie Regelsberger, the daughter of a Göttingen jurist. With the death of Wiedemann in 1889, he assumed the editorship of *Annalen der Physik,* the most prestigious of physics journals. In 1901, shortly after the publication of his *Lehrbuch der Optik,* Drude moved to Giessen where he became director of the Institute of Physics.

In Giessen, where he remained until 1905, Drude continued his work in optics and the electron theory. Having declined other appointments, it was only with some reluctance that he answered the call to Berlin to take over directorship of the physics institute. Almost immediately after Drude assumed this position, the size of the institute's staff was enlarged by a third in order to meet the demands of the increase of both the theoretical and the practical work that he brought with him. He died suddenly and unexpectedly within a year of moving to Berlin.

Drude's chief contributions fall into two categories: his early work in physical optics, in which he concentrated on the relationship between the physical properties and the optical characteristics of crystals, and his later work, in which he attempted to explain both physical and optical properties in a unified theory. In both phases theory and experiment were carefully interwoven; the transition in Drude's orientation is closely correlated with his change from a mechanical to an electromagnetic view of optical phenomena.

Drude may be considered the intellectual descendant of Franz Neumann—the first of Germany's great theoretical physicists, who developed a mechanical theory of light propagation based on the work of Fresnel and closely related to Fresnel's own theory. It was a mechanical theory which assumed that light oscillations were of a mechanical-elastic nature, transmitted through an ether conceived of as an elastic solid. Neumann's theory had its counterparts in England and France but was distinguished by the power and rigor of the mathematical analysis and by the assumption that the density of the ether is the same in all bodies. This leads to the conclusion that the displacement of ether particles in a plane polarized ray is in the plane of polarization. (The Fresnel theory assumed that the elasticity of the ether was the same in all bodies, leading to the conclusion that the displacement of ether particles is perpendicular to the plane of polarization.) Neumann was not only a theoretical physicist. At Königsberg he worked both in the physics department and the department of mineralogy. It was quite natural then that he should do extensive work on the optical properties of crystals. His laboratory was well equipped to investigate the structure of crystals and their elastic properties. Voigt, whose work continued that of Neumann, was particularly interested in magneto- and electro-optics. Drude's dissertation was a direct offshoot of Voigt's work. Voigt then set him the problem of checking his work in the laboratory, using crystals of

bournonite. The experimental difficulties were great, and Drude almost immediately realized that the optical constants of such crystals were not independent of the state of the crystal's surface. He discovered that the index of refraction and the coefficient of reflection of a crystal changed steadily from the time it was freshly cleaved. With characteristic care and thoroughness Drude then undertook a reexamination of the optical constants of a wide variety of absorbing substances, making measurements as difficult and exacting as those of the original experiments. When he was finished the optical constants of a wide variety of substances were known to an accuracy hitherto unthinkable.

This work occupied Drude from 1887 to 1891. During this period, too, he first became interested in Maxwell's work in electrodynamics, stimulated by Hertz's detection of electromagnetic radiation. Maxwell's treatise of 1873 was translated into German in 1882; but Maxwell's views were not widely accepted. The mechanical view of light propagation still held sway, and it had been under the influence of that theory that Drude had been working.

Drude did not become an immediate convert to the electromagnetic point of view. In 1888 he began an intensive four-year study, first immersing himself in the electromagnetic point of view, then reexamining the mechanical theory of light. He did not feel obliged to reject the mechanical theory which—although it presented some difficulty, especially in regard to the propagation of transverse waves through an elastic medium—had served so well.

Finally Drude took a phenomenological approach, attempting to remove nonessential elements from the mechanical formulation of optics. He argued that the differential equations and the imposed boundary conditions must be retained while assumptions about the mechanical nature of light waves and the elasticity of the ether were extraneous. He published the fruits of his investigation in a paper entitled "In wie weit genügen die bisherigen Lichttheorien den Anforderungen der praktischen Physik?" (1892). In this paper Drude pointed out that if the investigator restricted himself to differential equations and necessary boundary conditions, which he designated as the "explanation system" (*Erklärungssystem*), the mechanical and electromagnetic theories were equivalent. For example, to transform the mechanical view to the electromagnetic view, instead of such terms as "density," "elasticity," and "velocity of the ether," one needed only to substitute "magnetic permeability," "dielectric constant," and "magnetic field strength." Drude's paper was much in the spirit of Hertz's own assertions about Maxwell's theory—that the Maxwell theory should be considered as Maxwell differential equations.

Drude gradually took up the electromagnetic viewpoint. In another paper of 1892, "Ueber magnetio-optische Erscheinungen," he developed a system of equations directly from Maxwell's equations to account for Kerr's discovery that the reflectivity of magnetic substances (iron, cobalt, and nickel) is influenced by the state of magnetization and for Kundt's observation that the plane of polarization of light is rotated in passing through thin plates of these substances. Although the ease with which Maxwell's theory allowed such work to be done was important to Drude, he did not yet advocate one theory to the exclusion of the other. Rather, for another two years he lectured at Göttingen on the Maxwell theory; these lectures led to the publication of his first book, *Die Physik des Äthers* (1894). As a result of the heuristic effect that Maxwell's theory had on his own work between 1894 and 1898, Drude became an advocate of the electromagnetic view.

With his move to Leipzig, Drude's work on physical constants and his work on electromagnetic radiation began to merge into one set of coherent concerns. Drude had already hinted in some of his published work that by using the electromagnetic theory one might be able to explain electrical and optical properties of matter as the interaction of electromagnetic fields with electrical charges contained within the body. The publication of Lorentz' electron theory between 1892 and 1895 undoubtedly spurred him in that direction.

Shortly after arriving at Leipzig in 1894, Drude undertook further investigations on the relationship between optical and electrical constants and the constitution of substances. Using seventy to eighty centimeters radiation, he measured coefficients of absorption in a wide variety of solutions and compared these to coefficients of conductivity for the same solutions. According to Maxwellian theory, a close correlation should have existed between electrical conductivity and absorption of light—the higher the conductivity, the greater should be the absorption. Drude found, however, that this was not always the case. For example, the absorption coefficients of amyl alcohol and copper salt solutions might be the same, whereas the conductivity of the copper salt solution might be thousands of times greater than the conductivity of the alcohol. By careful and controlled experimentation, Drude found that, in fact, a whole class of substances absorbed seventy-five centimeters electromagnetic radiation—quite independent of their coefficient of conductivity when it was measured by direct current methods. The same substances also exhibited a marked deviation from expected values of their dielectric constants and also exhibited anomalous dispersion. Drude was able to demonstrate that selective absorption of seventy-five centimeters radiation was directly related to the chemical structure of substances and that it was the hydroxyl radical (OH) that was responsible. Thus he developed a new practical analytic tool for chemists.

The problem presented some theoretical difficulties. The obvious explanation for selective absorption would have to be based on the hypothesis that it represented a resonance phenomenon with the natural period of the molecular constituents of the substance; this suggested to Drude that the natural period at the atomic level was not independent of the particular molecular arrangement since a much higher resonance frequency would be expected of independent considerations.

The organization of Drude's *Lehrbuch der Optik* (1900) reflects his own approach to problems in optics. The first half of the book is devoted almost exclusively to the phenomena and to their mathematical characterization. Then, after a brief outline of the mechanical and electromagnetic theories, Drude gives what he considers to be the advantages of the electromagnetic theory: first, transverse waves are a direct consequence of Maxwell's conception of electromagnetic interaction; second, special boundary conditions are not required in the electromagnetic theory for radiation in the optical region of the spectrum; and third, the velocity of light can be determined directly from electromagnetic experiments. "In fact," Drude wrote, "it is an epoch-making advance in natural science when in this way two originally distinct fields of investigation, like optics and electricity, are brought into relations which can be made the subject of quantitative measurements" (*The Theory of Optics*, C. R. Mann and R. A. Millikan, trans., 2nd ed. [New York, 1959], p. 261).

Drude's move to Giessen thus occurred at a time when he was intent on understanding the optical, thermal, and electrical properties of metals by application of the electron theory. Drude was not the only person interested in such a practical application of the electron theory. Both J. J. Thomson and E. Riecke made substantial though different contributions. In the theory developed by Drude every metal contains a large number of free electrons, which he treated as a gas, the electrons having an average kinetic energy equal to the average kinetic energy of the atoms and molecules of the substance. The essential difference between conductors and nonconductors was that nonconductors contained relatively few free electrons. In early versions of his theory, Drude assumed that both positive and negative electrons were part of the "gas" but in a later simplification assumed that only negative electrons were mobile. Using the temperature of the substance as an index of the average kinetic energy of the particles in the electron gas, the velocity of the electrons should be enormous if it were not for the very small mean free path—due, mainly, to collisions with atomic centers.

Consider a neutral conductor, not under the influence of an electric force. Since the motion of the electron gas is perfectly random, there should be no net charge created at any point and no net transfer of electricity from one point to another. Under the influence of an electric field, however, there should be an increase in the average velocity of electrons in one direction and a decrease in their average velocity in the opposite direction. Such a situation would constitute an electric current whose intensity should be theoretically calculable. Drude arrived at the result that the electrical conductivity would be given by

$$\sigma = \frac{e^2 N l}{2mu},$$

where e is the charge on a single electron, N is the number of electrons per unit volume, l is the mean free path, m is the mass of the electron, and u is the average velocity of the electrons. Since the electrons are treated as a gas, the average kinetic energy of the gas should be proportional to the absolute temperature. The coefficient of conductivity may thus be expressed as absolute temperature:

$$\sigma = \frac{e^2 N l u}{4\alpha T},$$

where T is the temperature and α is a universal constant.

The power of Drude's analysis lies in that when one turns to different phenomena, such as thermal conductivity, the analysis is similar. Suppose the ends of a metal bar be maintained at different temperatures. The conduction of heat in the metal is due to collisions between the free electrons. The mean free path, however, is determined as before by collisions with essentially stationary metal atoms. Based on these assumptions, the coefficient of thermal conductivity for a substance is given by

$$k = \frac{\alpha N l u}{3}.$$

Drude used a scheme of this type to account for such things as thermoelectric and magnetoelectric effects. While agreement with experimental results was never perfect, it was usually within the right order of magnitude. For example, the ratio of Drude's values for the thermal and electrical conductivity of a substance is proportional to the absolute temperature:

$$k/\sigma = \frac{4}{3}(\alpha/e)^2 T.$$

Since α and e are both universal constants, Drude would have predicted that the ratio of thermal to electric conductivity at a given temperature was the same for all metals. Although this is not precisely true it is a good approximation to what was known to be the case experimentally.

Drude did not make these researches serially; typically, he had several different research projects in progress at the same time—in addition to lecturing, directing doctoral students, heading the various physical institutes, and editing the *Annalen der Physik*. Drude carried this diverse and taxing load with grace and performed his duties with characteristic thoroughness.

Drude died a week after he had written the foreword to the second edition of his *Lehrbuch der Optik* and six days after he had given his inaugural speech at the Berlin Academy—a speech in which he sketched plans for future research.

BIBLIOGRAPHY

I. ORIGINAL WORKS. Drude's writings include "Ueber die Gesetze der Reflexion und Brechung des Lichtes an der Grenze absorbierende Kristalle," in *Annalen der Physik*, **32** (1887), 584–625; "Beobachtungen über die Reflexion des Lichtes am Antimonglanz," *ibid.*, **34** (1888), 489–531; "Ueber Oberflächenschichten," in *Göttingen Nachrichten* (1888), pp. 275–299; and *Annalen der Physik*, **36** (1889), 532–560, 865–897; "Bestimmung der optischen Konstanten der Metalle," *ibid.*, **39** (1890), 481–554; "Ueber die Reflexion und Brechung ebener Lichtwellen beim Durchgang durch eine mit Oberflächenschichten behaftete planparallele Platte," *ibid.*, **43** (1891), 126–157; "In wie weit genügen die bisherigen Lichttheorien den Anforderungen der praktischen Physik?," in *Göttingen Nachrichten* (1892), pp. 366–412.

"Ueber magnetiooptische Erscheinungen," in *Annalen der Physik*, **46** (1892), 353–422; "Ueber die Phasenänderung des Lichtes bei der Reflexion an Metallen," *ibid.*, **50** (1893), 595–624, and **51** (1894), 77–104; "Zum Studium des elektrischen Resonators," in *Göttingen Nachrichten* (1894), pp. 189–223, and *Annalen der Physik*, **53** (1894), 721–768; *Physik des Äthers auf elektro-magnetischer Grundlage* (Stuttgart, 1894); "Die Natur des Lichtes," "Theorie des Lichtes für durchsichtige Medien," "Theorie der anomalen Dispersion," "Doppelbrechung," "Uebergang des Lichtes über die Grenze zweier Medien," "Rotationspolarisation," "Gesetze der Lichtbewegung für absorbierende Medien," and "Polarisation des gebeugten Lichtes," in *Winkelmanns*

Handbuch der Physik, II, pt. 1, "Optik," (Breslau, 1894), 623–840; "Untersuchungen über die elektrische Dispersion," in *Annalen der Physik,* **54** (1894), 352–370.

"Der elektrische Berchungsexponent von Wasser und wässerigen Lösungen," in *Berichte. Sächsische Akademie der Wissenschaften.* Math.-phys. Kl., **48** (1896), 315–360, and *Annalen der Physik,* **59** (1896), 17–63; "Elektrische Anomalie und chemische Konstitution," in *Berichte. Sächsische Akademie der Wissenschaften.* Math.-phys. Klasse, **48** (1896), 431–435, and *Annalen der Physik,* **60** (1897), 500–509; "Neuer physikalischer Beitrag zur Konstitutionsbestimmung," in *Chemische Berichte,* **30** (1897), 930–965; "Ueber Messung der Dielektrizitätskonstanten kleiner Substanzmengen vermittelst elektrischer Drahtwellen," in *Berichte. Sächsische Akademie der Wissenschaften.* Math.-phys. Klasse, **48** (1896), 583–612; "Theorie der anomalen elektrischen Dispersion," in *Annalen der Physik,* **64** (1898), 131–158; "Zur Elektronentheorie. I," *ibid.,* **1** (1900), 566–613; "Zur Elektronentheorie. II," *ibid.,* **3** (1900), 369–402; *Lehrbuch der Optik* (Leipzig, 1900, 1906), C. R. Mann and R. A. Millikan, trans., as *The Theory of Optics* (Chicago, 1902; repr. New York, 1959).

"Zur Elektronentheorie. III," in *Annalen der Physik,* **7** (1902), 687–692; "Zur Konstruktion von Teslatransformatoren," *ibid.,* **9** (1902), 293–610; "Elektrische Eigenschaften und Eigenschwingungen von Drahtspulen mit angehängten geraden Drähten oder Metallplatten," *ibid.,* **11** (1903), 957–995; "Ueber induktive Erregung zweier elektrischer Schwingungskreise mit Anwendung auf Perioden- und Dämpfungsmessung, Teslatransformatoren und drahtlos Telegraphie," *ibid.,* **13** (1904), 512–561; "Optische Eigenschaften und Elektronen-Theorie. I," *ibid.,* **14** (1904), 677–726; "Optische Eigenschaften und Elektronen-Theorie. II," *ibid.,* 936–961; and "Die Natur des Lichtes," "Theorie des Lichtes für durchsichtige, ruhende Medien," "Doppelbrechung," "Uebergang des Lichtes über die Grenze zweier Medien," "Die Gesetze der Lichtbewegung für absorbierende Medien," "Theorie der Dispersion," "Rotationspolarisation," and "Theorie des Lichtes für bewegte Körper," all in *Winkelmanns Handbuch der Physik,* vol. VI (2nd ed., Breslau, 1906).

II. SECONDARY LITERATURE. On Drude and his work see also M. Plank, "Paul Drude," in *Verhandlungen der Deutschen physikalischen Gesellschaft,* **8** (1906), 599–630; F. Richarz and W. König, *Zur Erinnerung an Paul Drude* (Giessen, 1906); and W. Voigt, "Paul Drude," in *Physikalische Zeitschrift,* **7** (1906), 481–482.

STANLEY GOLDBERG

DRYGALSKI, ERICH VON (*b.* Königsberg, Eastern Prussia [now Kaliningrad, U.S.S.R.], 9 February 1865; *d.* Munich, Germany, 10 January 1949), *geography.*

At the age of seventeen Drygalski began to study mathematics and physics in Königsberg but soon went to Bonn in order to attend the lectures of Ferdinand von Richthofen, whom he followed in 1883 to Leipzig and in 1886 to Berlin. In 1887, while an assistant at the Geodetic Institute in Potsdam, he received his doctorate after completion of a dissertation in geophysics, but Richthofen's strong scientific and personal influence led him to become a geographer. Drygalski qualified as lecturer in geography and geophysics at the University of Berlin in 1898 and became a professor in 1899. In 1906 he accepted a call to the newly established chair of geography at the University of Munich, which he made highly regarded and held until his retirement in 1935.

Ice and oceans figured prominently in Drygalski's lifework. In the summer of 1891 and in 1892–1893 he led the preliminary and main expeditions of the Berlin Geographical Society to western Greenland. This expedition established Drygalski's international reputation. The following years were dedicated to the painstaking preparation of the first German expedition to the South Pole, which was tirelessly advocated and supported by Georg von Neumayer. It was carried out under Drygalski's direction in 1901–1903 on the polar ship *Gauss.* It had little outward publicity in comparison with other South Pole expeditions because of the considerable difficulties of the area allotted to it by international agreement. Of great value, however, were the scientific data, a wealth of scrupulously presented observations of the most varied scientific matters that brought the name "Antarctic University" to the *Gauss* expedition and gave it the highest rank among the South Pole explorations of the "classical" period. Drygalski henceforth was classed among the leading authorities in the fields of polar and oceanic exploration.

Although the expedition's report appeared soon after its return (1904), the scientific conclusions were fully developed only after almost thirty years of indefatigable labor by Drygalski and his co-workers.

Drygalski was a member of many academies, honorary member of numerous geographical societies, and recipient of their medals. In 1944 the Munich Geographical Society, which he had headed for twenty-nine years, established the Erich von Drygalski Medal in his honor.

Drygalski was also an excellent teacher. Thousands of students came to Munich to attend his stimulating classes, which were never confined to his special fields but dealt with many areas of geography, even those in which he had little interest. He emphasized regional geography, especially that of Asia, North America, and Germany. Eighty-four dissertations were written under his guidance; it is characteristic that he did not impose a single one of the subjects, and that none of them was designed to confirm or develop his own views. This absolute scientific freedom was highly appreciated by Drygalski's students and was the reason that the *Festschrift* for his sixtieth birthday was entitled *Freie Wege vergleichender Erdkunde* (1925).

BIBLIOGRAPHY

I. ORIGINAL WORKS. A complete list of Drygalski's writings may be compiled from the following sources: for 1885–1924, his *Festschrift, Freie Wege vergleichender Erdkunde*, pp. 374–386; for 1925–1934, *Zeitschrift für Geopolitik,* **12** (1935), 127–132; and for 1935–1949, *Die Erde. Zeitschrift der Gesellschaft für Erdkunde zu Berlin,* **1** (1949/1950), 69–72.

Among his works are *Grönland-Expedition der Gesellschaft für Erdkunde zu Berlin 1891–1893,* 2 vols. (Berlin, 1897); *Zum Kontinent des eisigen Südens* (Berlin, 1904); *Deutsche Südpolar-Expedition 1901–1903,* 20 vols. text and 2 vols. maps (Berlin–Leipzig, 1905–1931); and "Gletscherkunde," in *Enzyklopädie der Erdkunde,* VIII (Vienna, 1942), written with Fritz Machatschek.

II. SECONDARY LITERATURE. The *Festschrift* issued for Drygalski's sixtieth birthday was L. Distel and E. Fels, eds., *Freie Wege vergleichender Erdkunde* (Munich, 1925). Obituaries are N. Greutzburg, in *Erdkunde,* **3** (1949), 65–68; H. Fehn, in *Berichte zur deutschen Landeskunde,* **8** (1950), 46–48; E. Fels, in *Forschungen und Fortschritte,* **25** (1949), 190–191, and *Die Erde. Zeitschrift der Gesellschaft für Erdkunde zu Berlin,* **1** (1949/1950), 66–72; O. Jessen, in *Geographische Rundschau,* **1** (1949), 116–117, and *Jahrbuch der Bayerischen Akademie der Wissenschaften* (1949/1950), pp. 133–136; W. L. G. Joerg, in *Geographical Review,* **40** (1950), 489–491; W. Meinardus, in *Petermanns geographische Mitteilungen,* **93** (1949), 177–180; and S. Passarge, in *Mitteilungen der Geographischen Gesellschaft in München,* **35** (1949/1950), 105–107.

EDWIN FELS

DUANE, WILLIAM (*b.* Philadelphia, Pennsylvania, 17 February 1872; *d.* Devon, Pennsylvania, 7 March 1935), *physics, radiology.*

William Duane was the younger son, by his second wife, of Charles William Duane, an Episcopalian minister. On his father's side he was a direct descendant of Benjamin Franklin and of several Duanes who had played prominent political roles in the early republic; through his mother he held a good Bostonian pedigree and was distantly related to Charles W. Eliot, president of Harvard. From 1882 to 1890 his father was rector of St. Andrew's Church in West Philadelphia; young William attended private schools in Philadelphia and then the University of Pennsylvania, where he studied mathematics (including quaternions), wrote papers on the Sophists and on the "silver question," and was graduated A.B. in 1892 as valedictorian of his class. Moving on to Harvard—his father was rector of Christ Church (Old North

Church), Boston, from 1893 to 1910—he received an A.B. in 1893; was then two years assistant in physics, aiding John Trowbridge in experiments on the velocity of Hertzian waves; and received an A.M. in 1895.

With a Tyndall fellowship in physics from Harvard, Duane spent the next two or three years in Germany. At the University of Berlin he continued experimental work on electromagnetism under Emil Warburg (discovering an unforeseen effect and then showing it to be a "dirt effect"); heard the philosopher Wilhelm Dilthey; and studied physical chemistry with Landolt, mineralogy with Klein, experimental physics with Neesen, and especially theoretical physics with Planck, who testified in June 1898 that Duane had attended his lectures and exercise sessions for several semesters, displaying genuine aptitude and conscientious application. At Göttingen he heard the organic chemist Wallach but worked especially with Nernst. Duane's experimental and theoretical investigation, *Über elektrolytische Thermoketten,* suggested and guided by Nernst, was accepted by Planck in December 1897 as a University of Berlin doctoral dissertation.

In 1898 Duane was appointed professor of physics at the University of Colorado. He married in 1899 (and eventually had four children) and began to accumulate apparatus for experimental work in physical chemistry (1900–1901). By 1902, however, Duane had lost interest in physical chemistry and turned back to electromagnetism—perhaps because of his teaching in this field. His attention was increasingly to applications, with much effort devoted to a multiplex telegraph based upon synchronous motors at the two stations. It was the sabbatical year 1904–1905 which brought Duane back to fundamental problems; the winter was spent in the Curies' laboratory, where he learned techniques of research in radioactivity, and the spring with J. J. Thomson. In Paris he had determined the total ionization produced by a radioactive source of given intensity; back at the University of Colorado in the winter of 1905–1906 Duane was determining the total charge carried by the α and β rays rather than the ionization they produced.

Duane liked Paris, and the Curies had been impressed by him. Late in 1905 Pierre Curie asked Andrew Carnegie for a fellowship for Duane to continue work in the Laboratoire Curie. At the end of 1906, after Pierre Curie's death, Carnegie provided Mme. Curie with 12,500 francs per year for two or three fellowships. Duane was granted 7,500 francs from that sum for each of three years; in fact, he stayed six, and remained thereafter a member of the Société Française de Physique. His work in this pe-

194

riod, 1907–1913, was very solid but not truly outstanding, either quantitatively or qualitatively. Perhaps the most difficult and most important of these researches was the measurement of the rate of evolution of heat from minute samples of radioactive substances.

In 1913 the physics department at Harvard University had a vacancy due to the retirement of John Trowbridge; and the newly founded Harvard Cancer Commission, at the newly constructed Huntington Hospital, wished the services of a physicist experienced in handling radioactive substances to initiate there the treatment of cancer by implantation of sources of intense radiation. Duane was appointed assistant professor at the Jefferson Physical Laboratory in Cambridge and research fellow in physics at Huntington Hospital in Boston; his time and his salary were thenceforth divided between these two institutions. The techniques of collecting the radium emanation (radon) continually evolving from a dissolved radium salt, purifying it, compressing it, and sealing it into a tube whose volume was a fraction of a cubic millimeter were all familiar to Duane from his Paris period; he now designed a far more efficient apparatus for manufacturing such "radioactive lamps" and himself applied the "lamps" to the patients. In 1917 Duane was promoted to professor of biophysics, a title created for him; he proudly asserted it to be the first such in America.

Besides radioactivity there was a second area of physical research with direct applications to cancer therapy: X rays. Duane had had no experience in this field, but his new position and responsibilities demanded that he make himself thoroughly familiar with it; and so arose his truly important contributions to physics. The time and place were opportune: Laue and the Braggs had just opened the field of X-ray spectroscopy; W. D. Coolidge's high-vacuum, high-voltage, heated cathode X-ray tubes were just becoming available; and Duane had inherited Trowbridge's unique 45,000-volt storage battery—the ideal power supply to exploit the Coolidge tube. Duane's initial concern was with the therapeutically important "Relation Between the Wave-Length and Absorption of X-Rays," the title of a paper read to the American Physical Society at the end of October 1914 but not printed.

Duane's attention soon turned, however, to the relation between the energy of the cathode rays and the frequency of the X rays produced by them, and at the end of December 1914 he described to the American Physical Society experiments showing that the ratio of these two quantities was equal, within a factor of two, to Planck's constant, h. The real advance, reported at the annual meeting of the society in April 1915, was made in collaboration with Franklin L. Hunt,[1] the first of the many graduate students and postdoctoral assistants with whose aid almost all of Duane's subsequent physical researches were carried out. Now for the first time Duane drove his Coolidge tube with the high-tension battery—i.e., with a constant voltage—and was impressed by the fact that "a constant difference of potential . . . does not produce homogeneous X-rays," i.e., X rays whose fractional absorption per unit of path length is independent of the thickness of the (homogeneous) absorber. From this naïve discovery Duane and Hunt jumped to a sophisticated question: "We therefore set ourselves the problem of determining the minimum wave length that can be produced by a given difference of potential."

From David L. Webster, then a young instructor at Harvard, they borrowed his newly constructed X-ray spectrometer. Fixing it at a given angle (i.e., wavelength), they observed the intensity of the X rays as a function of the voltage applied to the tube—possible because, and only because, of the Coolidge-Trowbridge apparatus. With decreasing voltage the intensity plunged to zero, thus showing dramatically that there was indeed a maximum frequency in the radiation produced by electrons of a given energy, and for this frequency the equation $E = h\nu$ held to within a few tenths of a percent. In the next two years Duane developed the "Duane-Hunt law" into a precision method for determining h, and it soon came to be regarded as the most accurate method available.

The war brought only a slight dip in Duane's productivity, and with the aid of Chinese and Japanese students he turned to accurate measurements, on a variety of elements, of the critical potentials and wavelengths for excitation of their characteristic X rays and, again, accurate measurements of the wavelengths of these X-ray spectra. Theoretical atomic physicists, notably Sommerfeld and Bohr, craved data of this sort to fix the number of electron shells and subshells in the various atoms, their energies, their quantum numbers, and the number of electrons in each shell. In the period 1918–1921 Manne Siegbahn's laboratory in Lund—using photographic recording in a closed, evacuated spectrometer—and Duane's laboratory—where the measurement of the intensity of the diffracted X rays at each angle by means of an ionization chamber achieved its highest development—were the two principal reliable sources of this vital data. Moreover, during these and especially the following years Duane gave much effort to the introduction and promotion of the treatment of cancer with high-voltage X rays—designing apparatus, supervising its installation at Huntington Hospital[2] and then at other institutions, developing the technique of measuring X-ray dosage in terms of the ionization of air, and securing the official adoption of this standard in the United States and then internationally in 1928.

In the year 1922–1923 Duane's career reached its zenith—and then fell precipitously. In April 1920 he had been elected to the National Academy of Sciences; in the fall of 1922 he was selected to receive the 1923 Comstock Prize—an award made by the academy at five-year intervals—for having established through his X-ray researches "relations which are of fundamental significance, particularly in their bearings upon modern theories of the structure of matter and of the mechanism of radiation."[3] In 1922–1923 Duane was chairman of the Division of Physical Sciences of the National Research Council and in 1923 president of the Society for Cancer Research. All must have supposed that many more laurels would in the following years be laid upon the brow of this late-blooming, quiet, outwardly modest, unexcitable Episcopalian; this competent pianist and organist; this Beacon Street Bostonian who sought recreation in bridge whist with his friends at the Somerset Club.

At the end of 1921 George L. Clark came into Duane's Cambridge laboratory as a postdoctoral National Research fellow. Three and a half years later it became clear that the several wholly new discoveries to which their fourteen collaborative papers had been devoted were so many pseudo phenomena. Clark was a chemist, then interested in crystal structure. The original goal of their research was a new method of crystal analysis using the Duane-Hunt limit to determine directly the wavelength of the X ray reflected at a given angle, and thus the interatomic distances in the reflecting crystal. With potassium iodide they found, along with other anomalous phenomena, intense reflected X rays not merely with the wavelengths of the characteristic X rays of the anticathode of the X-ray tube but also with the wavelengths of the K series of iodine. They had thus "discovered" the diffraction of the characteristic X radiation emitted by the atoms of the crystal—the very phenomenon which in 1912 Laue, Walter Friedrich, and Paul Knipping had unwarrantably expected to find when they in fact discovered diffraction of the incident X rays.[4] Bohr, among many others, was especially interested in this "discovery," for he felt it had to be explicable from the general viewpoint on the interaction of radiation and matter for which he had been groping and which emerged at the end of 1923 as the Bohr-Kramers-Slater theory.

This "discovery" also led Duane himself to some theoretical considerations of astonishing simplic-ity—and novelty. Reasonably well grounded in classical mathematical physics (as most of the best American experimentalists were) but for want of personal contact with the contemporary European theoretical physicists typically unaware of the extent of his naïveté, Duane had published a number of theoretical papers in the preceding years: on magnetism as the nuclear force (1915); on a new derivation of Planck's law (1916); and on modifications of the electron ring positions, quantum numbers, and populations in the Bohr model (1921). These, quite properly, had been ignored by the theorists.

Now, however, stimulated by the fact that the selective reflection of the characteristic X radiations of the atoms of the diffracting crystal "does not appear to be explicable in a simple manner by the theory of interference of waves," Duane suggested in February 1923 an interpretation of diffraction by a grating or crystal "based on quantum ideas without reference to interference laws."[5] In much the same way that A. H. Compton was simultaneously explaining the increased wavelength of scattered X rays, Duane pictured diffraction as a collision of a light quantum with a grating. He pointed out that if one applies the familiar quantum conditions to the grating, the periodicity of its structure restricts the momentum it can take up from, or impart to, the light quantum, with the result that all the equations expressing the conditions for constructive interference of waves (e.g., the Bragg law, $n\lambda = 2\,d\,\sin\theta$) are retrieved if the energy transferred to the grating can be neglected.

This reinterpretation came as a revelation to many theorists puzzling over the wave versus quantum theory of light (Gregory Breit, Paul Ehrenfest, Paul Epstein, Adolf Smekal, Gregor Wentzel—but not Bohr), although they of course disregarded the *ad hoc* extensions of this mechanism by means of which Duane claimed to have explained the selective reflection. A curious consequence of the theorists' efforts to achieve a more general statement of Duane's reinterpretation of diffraction was to bring forward once again the representation of a grating (or crystal) by a Fourier series or integral. Duane himself then pointed out that since the distribution of intensity in the spectrum is essentially the Fourier transform of the grating producing it, in principle it should be possible to invert the transform and from intensity measurements determine the distribution of electrons in the diffracting crystal.[6] Duane put a National Research fellow to work on this, but the idea, which is the basis of all the subsequent analyses of the structure of biologically important molecules, caught on only through its adoption and advocacy by W. L. Bragg in the following years.

Perhaps even more damaging to Duane's reputation than the "discovery" of selective reflection was his opposition to the Compton effect. The most eminent American X-ray spectroscopist was the last to reproduce Compton's observation and the most vociferous in denying and explaining away his younger compatriot's discovery—even to the point of claiming as his own discovery the tertiary radiation that he had originally advanced as the probable source of Compton's shifted wavelengths.[7] It was not, of course, that Duane was opposed to the notion of light quanta; rather, there was an element of competition between his own and Compton's light quantum theories, which probably disposed Duane, who had in those years so little time for laboratory work, to accept uncritically the various new effects and negative observations with which Clark was plying him.

These disastrous episodes were scarcely behind Duane when, late in 1925, his capacity for work was severely reduced by the onset of acute diabetes, and in 1926 he was obliged to take a year's leave. By 1927 his sight had so deteriorated that he was compelled to do much of his reading and writing through his secretary. In 1931 Duane suffered a paralytic stroke, recovering only slowly and incompletely; in the fall of 1933 he took a leave of absence and retired in the fall of 1934. Six months later he died of a second stroke.

NOTES

1. Duane and Hunt, "On X-Ray Wave-Lengths," in *Physical Review*, **6** (1915), 166–171.
2. "Improved X-Rays for Cancer Work," in *New York Times* (14 Feb. 1921), 7, col. 2.
3. *Report of the National Academy of Sciences* for 1923 (Washington, D.C., 1924), pp. 5, 20.
4. P. Forman, "The Discovery of the Diffraction of X-Rays by Crystals: A Critique of the Myths," in *Archive for History of Exact Sciences*, **6** (1969), 38–71.
5. Duane, "The Transfer in Quanta of Radiation Momentum to Matter," in *Proceedings of the National Academy of Sciences*, **9** (1923), 158–164.
6. Duane, "An Application of Certain Quantum Laws to the Analysis of Crystals," in *Physical Review*, **25** (1925), 881; R. J. Havighurst, "The Application of Fourier's Series to Crystal Analysis," *ibid.;* Duane, "The Calculation of the X-Ray Diffracting Power at Points in a Crystal," in *Proceedings of the National Academy of Sciences*, **11** (1925), 489–493; R. J. Havighurst, "The Distribution of Diffracting Power in Sodium Chloride," *ibid.*, 502–507.
7. Clark and Duane, "On the Theory of the Tertiary Radiation Produced by Impacts of Photoelectrons," in *Proceedings of the National Academy of Sciences*, **10** (1924), 191–196.

BIBLIOGRAPHY

I. ORIGINAL WORKS. The best bibliography of Duane's publications, although still woefully incomplete in both form and content, is in Bridgman (below). A few letters from Duane to Bohr and Sommerfeld in 1924 are in the Archive for History of Quantum Physics, for which see T. S. Kuhn, *et al., Sources for History of Quantum Physics* (Philadelphia, 1967). The Niels Bohr Library, American Institute of Physics, New York, holds some twelve letters to Duane, notably a testimonial by Planck (1898), two letters from J. J. Thomson (1905), and four letters from Marie Curie (1905–1907).

II. SECONDARY LITERATURE. Biographical articles are P. W. Bridgman, "Biographical Memoir of William Duane, 1872–1935," in *Biographical Memoirs. National Academy of Sciences*, **18** (1937), 23–41; and G. W. Pierce, P. W. Bridgman, and F. H. Crawford, "Minute on the Life and Services of William Duane, Professor of Bio-Physics, *Emeritus,*" in *Harvard University Gazette* (11 May 1935). There is also "Charles William Duane," in *National Cyclopaedia of American Biography*, XVIII (New York, 1922), 403–404. Useful information is contained in the *vita* of Duane's dissertation, *Über elektrolytische Thermoketten* (Berlin, 1897). Recollections of the controversy with Compton by one of Duane's postdoctoral students—the one who finally found the effect—may be found in Samuel K. Allison, "Arthur Holly Compton, Research Physicist," in *Science*, **138** (1962), 794–797.

PAUL FORMAN

DUBINI, ANGELO (*b.* Milan, Italy, 8 December 1813; *d.* Milan, 28 March 1902), *medicine, helminthology.*

Dubini took the M.D. at the University of Pavia in 1837. He began his practice at the Ospedale Maggiore in Milan, then returned to Pavia for the academic biennium 1839–1841 as an assistant at the Clinica Medica, where he gave a free course in auscultation. In November 1841 he began a postgraduate trip to France, England, and Germany; in Paris he attended the courses of Gabriel Andral. At the end of 1842 Dubini returned to Milan and resumed his work as a medical assistant at the Ospedale Maggiore. In 1865 he was nominated as both head physician and director of the newly established dermatology department.

At the Ospedale Maggiore Dubini was the most noteworthy exponent of the *médecine d'observation,* which, proceeding along the lines indicated by G. B. Morgagni, had been developed in Parisian hospitals by J. N. Corvisart and R. T. H. Laënnec, among others. This new clinical medicine attempted to formulate in the living being a diagnosis that is substantially anatomical, by means of a continuous dialogue—possible only in the hospital—between clinical medicine and anatomical pathology, with a common purpose and subject.

Indeed, Dubini's most important discovery was precisely the result of his anatomical-pathological work within the hospital and, in particular, of the diligence with which he systematically opened the intestine in accordance with recent studies made by French physicians on typhic and tubercular ulcers. In May 1858 Dubini recorded a "new human intestinal worm" following the dissection of the corpse of a peasant woman who had "died of croupous pneumonia." He confirmed this discovery in November 1842 and published his description of it in April 1843, describing the new worm as *Anchylostoma duodenale*, derived from the hooked mouth of the organism and from its habitat in the human host. Dubini's helminthological description is highly accurate and was further developed in his *Entozoografia* (1850).

As early as his work of 1843 Dubini had stressed the high frequency of occurrence of the worm, "which, although it had not yet been seen by others, nor described, is nevertheless found in *twenty out of one hundred corpses* that are dissected with the aim of finding it." This affirmation—as well as testifying to the high incidence of ancylostomiasis in the countryside around Milan—demonstrates that Dubini (who had also noted that the worm seemed to be hematotrophic) was unwilling to attribute any particular pathogenicity to the duodenal Ancylostoma. (The pathogenicity of Ancylostoma was eventually confirmed in the course of studies on Egyptian chlorosis made by F. Pruner, W. Griesinger, and T. Bilharz and in D. Wucherer's work on tropical chlorosis; it was proven beyond doubt in 1882 in the research of B. Grassi, C. and E. Parona, E. Perroncito, C. Bozzolo, and L. Pagliani on the serious epidemic of miner's cachexia that spread among the miners of the St. Gotthard tunnel.)

Dubini's name is given to the electric chorea that he diagnosed and described, thereby ensuring himself a place in the history of lethargic encephalitis, of which such chorea is a mark.

BIBLIOGRAPHY

I. ORIGINAL WORKS. Dubini's major work is *Entozoografia umana per servire di complemento agli studi d'anatomia patologica* (Milan, 1850). His earlier works are "Nuovo verme intestinale umano (Anchylostoma duodenale), costituente un sesto genere di nematoidei proprii dell'uomo," in *Annali universali di medicina*, **106** (1843), 4-13; and "Primi cenni sulla corea elettrica," *ibid.*, **117** (1846), 5-50.

II. SECONDARY LITERATURE. Works on Dubini are Luigi Belloni, "Per la storia del cuore tigrato," in *L'Ospedale Maggiore*, **44** (1956), 252-258; "La medicina a Milano dal settecento al 1915," in *Storia di Milano*, XVI (Milan, 1962), 991-997; "La scoperta dell'Ankylostoma duodenale," in *Gesnerus*, **19** (1962), 101-118; "Dalla scoperta dell'Anky-

lostoma duodenale alla vittoria sull'anemia dei minatori," in *Folia medica*, **48** (1965), 836-855, and in *Minerva medica*, **57** (1966), 3215-3233; and Ambrogio Bertarelli, "Angelo Dubini (8 dicembre 1813-28 marzo 1902)," in *Bollettino della Associazione Sanitaria Milanese*, **4** (1902), 115-119.

LUIGI BELLONI

DUBOIS, FRANÇOIS. *See* **Sylvius, Franciscus.**

DUBOIS, JACQUES (Latin, **JACOBUS SYLVIUS**) (*b.* Amiens, France, 1478; *d.* Paris, France, 13 January 1555), *medicine*.

Jacques Dubois, hereinafter referred to as Sylvius, came to Paris at the invitation of his brother François, professor at and principal of the Collège de Tournai. Sylvius acquired a good command of Greek and Latin and was particularly attracted to the medical writings of Hippocrates and Galen. He studied medicine informally with members of the Paris Faculty of Medicine and particularly anatomy with Jean Tagault, whom he later described as "mihi in re medica praeceptor." Prevented from having any sort of medical career by lack of a degree, Sylvius went to Montpellier, where he was graduated M.B. in 1529 and M.D. in 1530. Upon returning to Paris, he was incorporated M.B. in 1531, permitted to take the examinations for the degree of licenciate, and thus allowed to teach at the Collège de Tréguier. In 1536 the Faculty of Medicine gave recognition to his course by permitting him to lecture in the Faculty and to receive students' fees.

Sylvius was a very popular teacher of anatomy who, unlike many of his contemporaries, was not unwilling to perform his own dissections. His most distinguished student was Andreas Vesalius; but since Sylvius was the arch-Galenist of Paris, wholly confident of Galen's medical omniscience and determined at all costs to defend him against open, critical attack, he became intensely hostile to his former student upon publication of Vesalius' *Fabrica* (1543). Sylvius' most bitter attack, which appeared under the title of *Vaesani cuiusdam calumniarum in Hippocratis Galenique rem anatomicam depulsio* (1551), was so unrestrainedly abusive that Renatus Henerus, in his later defense of Vesalius, *Adversus Jacobi Sylvii depulsionum anatomicarum calumnias pro Andrea Vesalio apologia* (1555), declared that Sylvius' invective "wearied our ears and aroused the indignation of many of us." Despite such irascibility, Sylvius was genuinely concerned over the welfare of his more orthodox students, for whom he wrote *Victus ratio scholasticis pauperibus partu facilis & salubris* (1540) and *Conseil tresutile contre la famine: & remedes d'icelle* (1546).

Sylvius was a prolific writer of commentaries, of

which the following were the most frequently reprinted and the most influential: *Methodus sex librorum Galeni in differentiis et causis morborum et symptomatum* (1539), *Methodus medicamenta componendi* (1541), *Morborum internorum prope omnium curatio ex Galeno et Marco Gattinaria* (1548), and *De febribus commentarius ex Hippocrate et Galeno* (1555). His major contribution to anatomy is represented by the posthumous *In Hippocratis et Galeni physiologiae partem anatomicam isagoge* (1555). It is a systematic account of anatomy, written at some time after 1536 (possibly in 1542) and based on the writings of Galen, on a certain amount of human anatomical dissection, and, as Sylvius admitted, on the *Anatomiae liber introductorius* (1536) of Niccolo Massa, a Venetian physician and anatomist.

As a self-appointed defender of Galenic anatomy Sylvius could not, like Vesalius, call attention openly to Galen's errors in the course of presenting more nearly correct anatomical descriptions in his *Isagoge*. His procedure was therefore (1) to acknowledge the best of Galenic anatomy; (2) to describe without critical comment such anatomical structures as Galen had overlooked or, where Galen had permitted an alternative, to make a better choice; and (3) if necessary, to criticize not Galen but the human structure, which Sylvius declared to have degenerated and thus to have betrayed Galen's earlier, correct descriptions. In general, Sylvius' systematic presentation is worthy of commendation, as is his relatively modern method of numbering branches of vessels, structures, and relationships. Notably, he provided a clear scheme for the identification of muscles, based, like that of Galen, on their attachments. It has been called the foundation of modern muscle nomenclature. Relative to this contribution, Sylvius introduced and popularized a number of other anatomical terms that have persisted, such as crural, cystic, gastric, popliteal, iliac, and mesentery.

Further examples of his method and contributions are to be found in his description of the heart, where, perhaps influenced by Massa as well as by his own dissections, Sylvius describes the passage of blood by the pulmonary artery from the right ventricle to the lungs and thence to the left ventricle (ed. Venice, 1556, fol. 89*v*). It is true that Galen had described this route, although he considered it of lesser importance than the one that he proposed through "pores" in the cardiac septum. Sylvius, however, does not refer to the latter route or to the implications of his silence—which perhaps he did not realize, for in effect they denied Galenic cardiovascular physiology. Furthermore, he did not accept the standard existence of the *rete mirabile* in the human brain: "This plexus

seen by Galen under the gland still appears today in brutes" (fol. 57*r*). Thus he suggests that through degeneration the *rete mirabile* had disappeared from the human structure. This attitude is clearly expressed in a further statement relative to thoracic structures: "The azygos vein [was] always observed under the heart by Galen in those in whom the sternum formed of seven bones made a longer thorax, but in our bodies, because of the shortness of the sternum and thorax, it arises more or less above the heart and pericardium" (fols. 46*v*–47*r*). In summation, the *Isagoge* may be described as an introduction to human anatomy based on an attempt to reconcile the best of classical teachings with the results of observation, direct or at second hand, of human dissection. Despite such contributions as were mentioned above, and others, the work retains the defects of compromise.

Sylvius died in Paris and was interred in the Cemetery of the Poor Scholars.

BIBLIOGRAPHY

I. ORIGINAL WORKS. Of Sylvius' many publications the following list represents a selection of the most important and representative: *Methodus sex librorum Galeni in differentiis et causis morborum et symptomatum* (Paris, 1539); *Ordo et ordinis ratio in legendis Hippocratis et Galeni libris* (Paris, 1539); *Methodus medicamenta componendi ex simplicibus judicio summo delectis, et arte certa paratis* (Paris, 1541); *Victus ratio scholasticis pauperibus paratu facilis & salubris* (Paris, 1542); *Morborum internorum prope omnium curatio brevi methodo comprehensa ex Galeno praecipue & Marco Gattinario* (Paris, 1545); *Vaesani cuiusdam calumniarum in Hippocratis Galenique rem anatomicam depulsio* (Paris, 1551); *De febribus commentarius ex libris aliquot Hippocratis & Galeni* (Paris, 1554); *Commentarius in Claudii Galeni duos libros de differentiis febrium* (Paris, 1555); *In Hippocratis et Galeni physiologiae partem anatomicam isagoge* (Paris, 1555); *Commentarius in Claudii Galeni de ossibus ad tyrones Libellum* (Paris, 1556); and *Iacobi Sylvii Opera medica,* René Moreau, ed. (Geneva, 1634).

II. SECONDARY LITERATURE. The fullest biography of Sylvius is the "Vita" prefixed to René Moreau's edition of *Iacobi Sylvii Opera medica,* cited above; corrections will be found in Louis Thuasne, "Rabelaesian: Le Sylvius Ocreatus," in *Revue des bibliothèques,* **15** (1905), 268–283. More specialized topics are dealt with in Curt Elze, "Jacobus Sylvius, der Lehrer Vesals, als Begründer der anatomischen Nomenklatur," in *Zeitschrift für Anatomie und Entwicklungsgeschichte,* **114** (1949), 242–250; C. E. Kellett, "Sylvius and the Reform of Anatomy," in *Medical History,* **5** (1961), 101–116; and C. D. O'Malley, "Jacobus Sylvius' Advice for Poor Medical Students," in *Journal of the History of Medicine,* **17** (1962), 141–151.

C. D. O'MALLEY

DU BOIS-REYMOND, EMIL HEINRICH (*b.* Berlin, Germany, 7 November 1818; *d.* Berlin, 26 December 1896), *electrophysiology.*

Emil's father, Felix Henri du Bois-Reymond, moved from Neuchâtel, Switzerland (then part of Prussia), to Berlin in 1804 and became a teacher at the Kadettenhaus. Later he was the representative from Neuchâtel to the Prussian government, and in 1832 he published a fundamental work on linguistics. His orthodox Pietism and authoritarian manner soon aroused his son's spirit of resistance. Emil's mother, the former Minette Henry, was the daughter of the minister who served the French colony in Berlin and the granddaughter of Daniel Chodowiecki, a well-known artist. Emil had two sisters, Julie and Felicie, and two brothers; his brother Paul became a distinguished mathematician. The family's background made them feel that they belonged to the French colony in Berlin. They usually spoke French at home; and Emil attended the French academic high school in Berlin, except for a year in Neuchâtel.

In 1837 du Bois-Reymond began his studies at the University of Berlin, where, at first, somewhat undecided about his future, he attended lectures in theology, philosophy, and psychology. During a short period at the University of Bonn (1838–1839), he studied logic, metaphysics, and anthropology, in addition to botany, geology, geography, and meteorology. In the winter semester of 1839, having returned to Berlin, he was inspired by Eduard Hallmann, assistant to the anatomist Johannes Müller, to study medicine. It was also Hallmann who taught him the basic principles of osteology and botany and worked out a schedule of the lectures he should attend. His letters to Hallmann are splendid proof of du Bois-Reymond's intellectual liveliness, but they also show his initial uncertainty about his course of study and his own talents. He was easily influenced and was able only slowly to eradicate the prejudice for Müller that he had acquired from Hallmann.

Du Bois-Reymond was soon acquainted with such teachers and researchers as Heinrich Dove, Theodor Schwann, and Matthias Schleiden, and became a close friend of Ernst Brücke, Hermann Helmholtz, Carl Reichert, and Carl Ludwig. In 1840 he worked more closely with Müller, concerning himself with anatomical preparations, comparative anatomy, physiology, and microscopy. He was still very interested in morphology. During this period he also studied the philosophical writings of Hegel and Schelling with great interest and attended the clinical lectures of Dieffenbach and Johann Schönlein, among others.

On 10 February 1843 du Bois-Reymond received his degree with a historical-literary paper on electric fishes. This was a subsidiary result of his interest in the history of animal electricity and also a preliminary study for the experimental verification, recommended to him by Müller, of the new papers of Carlo Matteucci, who in 1840 had published his *Essai sur les phénomènes électriques des animaux.* This marked the start of his lifelong, almost monomaniacal experimental analysis of animal electricity. It occupied him constantly from 1840 to 1850; and in the course of his work he developed a strong preference for experimental physics, particularly the application of physical principles and methods of measurement to the problems of physiology. He was encouraged greatly in this by Brücke and later by Helmholtz. On 14 January 1845 he founded the Physikalische Gesellschaft with Brücke, Dove, and others in Berlin. In December 1845 he met Helmholtz and was deeply impressed by him.

Du Bois-Reymond's first experimental and theoretical investigations of animal electricity produced definite conclusions in November 1842. Upon Müller's advice the results were hurriedly submitted for publication in Poggendorff's *Annalen der Physik und Chemie,* appearing as "Abriss einer Untersuchung über den sogenannten Froschstrom und über die electrischen Fische" in January 1843. Through Humboldt he also sent an extract to the Académie des Sciences in Paris.

On 6 July 1846 du Bois-Reymond qualified as a university lecturer with the paper "Über saure Reaktion des Muskels nach dem Tode." He had already completed a great deal of the manuscript of *Untersuchungen über thierische Elektrizität,* mainly the preface of volume I (which became famous), the historical introduction, and the techniques of electrophysiology. From 1848 to 1853 du Bois-Reymond was instructor in anatomy at the Berlin Academy of Art. He did not lecture at the university until 1854, when Müller asked him to lecture on physiology with him. Du Bois-Reymond was now concerned exclusively with physiology, and with his friends Brücke, Ludwig, and Helmholtz he became a pioneer in the new physical orientation of the field, which sought to explain all processes in an organism by means of physical, molecular, and atomic mechanisms, without drawing upon hypothetical vital forces.

Thanks to the great interest which Humboldt had had in galvanism since his youth, du Bois-Reymond was elected to membership in the Prussian Academy of Sciences in 1851, at the age of thirty-three. From 1876 he was one of the permanent secretaries of the academy, and a great part of his work was dedicated to preparing the meetings and the official speeches for the annual celebrations in memory of Leibniz, its founder, and of its great patron, Frederick II.

In 1853 du Bois-Reymond married Jeanette Claude. They had four sons and five daughters. Of the four sons, René became a physician and a physiologist, Claude an ophthalmologist, and Allard and Felix mathematicians and engineers. Of the daughters, Estelle gained fame by editing her father's posthumously published works.

In 1855 du Bois-Reymond was named associate professor. When Müller died suddenly in 1858, the chair was divided. Reichert received the professorship of anatomy and du Bois-Reymond that of physiology. Now he had to carry the entire burden of lecturing as well as a heavy schedule of academy duties. At this time the physiology department was located in the west wing of the university building on Unter den Linden; along with the anatomy department and the museum, there were a few shabby rooms, inadequate for the needs of the physiology department. The conditions for experimentation were so unsuitable that du Bois-Reymond had to conduct the greater part of his experiments in his own apartment. Only after long efforts was a new institute for physiology, located on the Dorotheenstrasse, completed in 1877; after Carl Ludwig's institute in Leipzig it was the largest and most modern in Germany. There were four departments: physiological chemistry (Eugen Baumann, Kossel), physiological histology (Gustav Fritsch), physiological physics (Arthur Christiani), and a special department for experimentation with animals (Karl Hugo Kronecker, J. Gad). Also at this time the *Archiv für Anatomie, Physiologie und wissenschaftliche Medizin,* which had been taken over from Müller and since then edited by Reichert and du Bois-Reymond, was divided into an anatomical section and a physiological section, the latter being edited by du Bois-Reymond. Most of the papers by his colleagues and pupils appeared in this journal, as did most of the publications from Ludwig's institute in Leipzig. Among du Bois-Reymond's pupils were Eduard Pflüger, Ludimar Hermann, Isidor Rosenthal, Hermann Munk, F. Boll, Carl Sachs, and Gad, all of whom became prominent physiologists. A great many Russians worked in the institute also. A list of his colleagues and pupils, along with their publications, is in the dissertation by J. Marseille (1967). Du Bois-Reymond gave his colleagues and pupils great personal freedom and latitude to develop on their own, occupying himself almost exclusively with the problems of electrophysiology. After 1877 his publications are dominated by public speeches at the academy and his investigations of electric fishes.

By heritage du Bois-Reymond was particularly open to things French; he sought contact with French colleagues and visited Paris as early as 1850 in order to present the results of his experiments. He also met Claude Bernard there. However, he obviously felt that he did not receive the recognition he had expected. He reproached French researchers for reading only French publications and later leveled harsh criticism against his French neighbors, particularly during the Franco-Prussian War. He got along better with his English colleagues, traveling to England in 1852, 1855, and 1866 to visit or to attend congresses. H. Bence-Jones, who became a good friend and colleague, published a short version of du Bois-Reymond's papers in 1852.

Du Bois-Reymond was twice rector of the University of Berlin, in 1869–1870 and in 1882–1883. He was of course a member of almost all noteworthy scientific academies. On 11 February 1893 he celebrated the fiftieth anniversary of obtaining his doctorate. The formal address was delivered by Virchow. On 26 December 1896 du Bois-Reymond died of senile heart disease. The eulogy given by his pupil Rosenthal was used as a preface to the second edition of du Bois-Reymond's speeches (1912). The best biography is by his pupil E. Boruttau but it lacks a bibliography. With du Bois-Reymond, the last of that group died which had led German physiology to its position of uncontested leadership at the end of the nineteenth century.

From the beginning du Bois-Reymond directed his research to electrical phenomena that had been thought to be involved in various life processes since the time of Galvani but were long known to exist with certainty only in the discharges of electric fishes. Along with Galvani and Volta, Humboldt (1797) had concerned himself with these phenomena; this was the reason for his great interest in du Bois-Reymond's research. Interest in the phenomenon of animal electricity had generally receded since about 1820; but Aldini, Nobili, and particularly Matteucci continued to concern themselves with its explanation and measurement. In 1828 Nobili, using an improved Schweigger multiplier, was able to demonstrate the presence of an electric current (*courant propre*) on an intact but skinned frog trunk. From 1836 Matteucci concerned himself with the shock of electric fishes and confirmed the existence of the *courant propre.* In 1842 he demonstrated the existence of a *courant musculaire,* the demarcation, or injury, current between the uninjured surface and the cross section of a muscle. Matteucci also observed the "induced contraction" that a nerve-muscle preparation shows when its nerve is laid over the thigh muscle of a second, contracting preparation. In addition, he was the first to observe deflections in the galvanometer when a muscle contracted in strychnine tetanus. His later investigations were published in *Untersuchungen über die thierische Elektrizität* (1848) and in *Gesam-*

melte Abhandlungen zur allgemeinen Muskel- und Nervenphysik (1875–1877).

Du Bois-Reymond's most significant achievement was introducing clear physical methods and concepts into electrophysiology. In 1842–1843 he described (incorrectly at first) an autogenous current from the intact surface of the muscle to the tendon and (correctly) the injury current between the surface and the cross section; he used a multiplier that he had coiled and improved himself. He found this current even in the smallest pieces of muscle and traced it correctly to the individual muscle fibers, the interior of which is negative with respect to the surface of the fibers. The contracting muscle thus reveals a change, the so-called "negative fluctuation" of the injury current (1849). It occurs during every muscle contraction; but during tetanus, which arises from summation of many individual contractions, it becomes much clearer. Du Bois-Reymond confirmed induced contraction and identified it correctly as "secondary contraction" caused by the stimulus that the electric current of a contracting muscle in one nerve-muscle preparation gives to the nerve of a second preparation.

Du Bois-Reymond's interpretation of the basic molecular processes was analogous to Ampère's interpretation of the magnet. He believed that the muscle fiber was made up of numerous peripolar electromotive molecules, each thought to consist of a positive equatorial zone and two negative polar zones. For the tendons he assumed electrically neutral parelectronomic molecules. When Hermann was able to demonstrate the lack of current in intact muscle fibers in 1867–1868, du Bois-Reymond tried in vain to save his theory of preexistence by means of additional assumptions. In any case, he interpreted the currents from intact, injured, and contracting muscles as having a single cause.

Because of the extremely high sensibility of his multiplier, he was able in 1849 to show the injury current also in the nerve. He succeeded further in demonstrating the "negative fluctuation" in tetanized nerves and thus proved the electric nature of the *Nervenprinzip*.

Du Bois-Reymond also discovered that polarization occurs at the points of entry and exit during the flow of direct current through a nerve. It is shown in a change of charge at and near the positive and negative poles of the section through which the current flows. This "electrotonus" was the subject of his work for many years, and his pupil Pflüger continued to investigate the subject intensively. In connection with this du Bois-Reymond proposed the thesis that the effect of the electrical stimulation, apart from the polarization, depends upon the slope of the change

in intensity of the current at the point of stimulation, and not upon the duration or the absolute intensity of the current. After 1869, when Wilhelm Krause developed the theory that the transmission of stimulation from nerves to the muscle fiber is the result of an electrical discharge of the end plate, du Bois-Reymond also pursued these questions. He considered it possible for a chemical mechanism for transmitting stimulation to exist along with the electrical mechanism.

Quite a large part of du Bois-Reymond's research concerned the explanation of the nature and origin of the shock given by electric fishes. Many papers, particularly after 1877, written with Sachs and Fritsch are concerned with the anatomy and the production of electricity in these creatures. From 1857 he studied living examples of the *Malapterurus electricus* (electric catfish), the torpedo, and the *Gymnotus electricus*.

Du Bois-Reymond owed his great scientific success to the development of new electrophysiological methods of deriving and measuring current. He was the first to avoid the many difficulties and sources of error that make it very hard to obtain clear results in electrophysiology, and he created much of the apparatus of electrophysiology. His first multiplier (1842) had almost twice as many wire coils as previous ones, which made it unusually sensitive. In 1849 he once more increased them several times for the measurement of the nerve current. He was also the first to develop a deriving electrode that could not be polarized, by using glass tubes closed with a clay stopper and including a combination of zinc slabs in a solution of zinc sulfate (1859); it remained in use until about 1940. Du Bois-Reymond also was the first to develop the procedure of measuring weak bioelectric currents without loss by means of compensation with a rheochord bus-bar or a handy round compensator (1861). For decades physiologists used the du Bois-Reymond sliding-carriage induction coil for many purposes. The principle of induction had been known since the time of Oerstedt and Faraday. Du Bois-Reymond built an apparatus with a secondary coil that could be moved on a sliding carriage (1849). This made it possible to graduate and calibrate the intensity of the first and last induction shocks. This instrument was the starting point for many devices used in the medical applications of Faradic stimulations in electrotherapy.

Many very useful aids in electrophysiology were developed or adapted to the needs of animal experimentation by du Bois-Reymond. He constructed "simple" switches that guaranteed a definite electrical contact, as well as the mercury switch, the rocker, the electrode holder, stands, and clamps. He was the first to succeed in clarifying, eliminating, or avoiding the many sources of error in electrophysiological procedure, such as losses due to leakage, the polarization phenomena on metal electrodes, the deflection caused by nonparallel muscle fibers, the temporal change in the injury current following death, and the influence of extension on the voltage derived. Du Bois-Reymond also investigated the currents which occur in secretory glands (1851) and believed that he could derive electric currents from the human arm during voluntary contraction.

Most of du Bois-Reymond's experimental findings and technical procedures have remained valid. Some of his theories and several of the conceptions derived from his incorrect molecular hypothesis (such as denying the absence of current in intact muscles) did not last. Students, co-workers, and visitors from all over the world took up electrophysiology; improved the measuring devices; and demonstrated electrical phenomena in glands, the eye, the heart, and the brain. In this way, new areas of physiology originated from his preliminary work.

Du Bois-Reymond's interest in molecular physics led him to lecture during almost every summer semester from 1856, on the "physics of organic metabolism." This involved such processes as diffusion of gases and liquids, diffusion through pores, adsorption, the theory of solutions, capillarity, surface tension, swelling, osmosis, and secretion. The lectures, which were edited by his son René (1900), show du Bois-Reymond's interest in the subject and make one aware that his intellectual effort belonged completely to the period up to the end of the 1860's. His last decades were, for the most part, filled with other work and problems that were much less those of physiology than general problems of scientific knowledge, problems of methods and limitations, and historical questions. After about 1870 du Bois-Reymond became increasingly active in the public discussion of the relation between the natural sciences and the humanities, particularly philosophy, theology, and history. He had uncommonly wide knowledge and judgment in both science and various branches of the humanities. This is shown especially by the two-volume *Reden.*

In France and Germany in the second half of the eighteenth century, the idea had prevailed that the processes of formation, conservation, irritability, sensitivity, and such could not be explained by the laws of inorganic nature. Something like a vital force, a conservative force, or an educative force—analogous to the force of gravity—was supposed to direct the vital processes. Even Müller, du Bois-Reymond's teacher, subscribed to this belief; thus it was significant when Müller's young assistant eloquently demonstrated the inconsistencies in this theory: "Matter is not a wagon to which forces can be arbitrarily hitched

or unhitched like horses." Forces do not exist independently of matter; and where they are expressed, they are the same in the living and the dead. At that time Schwann, Hermann Lotze, Brücke, Ludwig, and Helmholtz thought similarly.

Du Bois-Reymond's detailed, well-documented memorial speech for Müller (1858) is of the greatest historical interest. The same is true of his speech for Helmholtz (1895). His speech at the opening of the new institute for physiology (1877) is also an important document. His speeches on Voltaire (1868), La Mettrie (1875), and Maupertuis (1892) are prime examples of analysis of intellectual history. To him Voltaire was a fighter for intellectual freedom, human dignity, and justice, who had disseminated the significance of Newtonian thought. Du Bois-Reymond also portrayed the astonishing gifts of Diderot (1884), who was equally productive in treatises and novels, in art and science, ethics, metaphysics, philology, and philosophy. He demonstrated in several speeches his excellent knowledge of Leibniz, his philosophy, and his scientific significance. His lively feeling for the history of science was expressed in his address of 1872. He praised the charisma of the master scientists of the past and considered the history of science the most important, but most neglected, part of cultural history.

Du Bois-Reymond's lecture "Kulturgeschichte und Naturwissenschaft" (1876) contains a complete analysis of Western cultural history in relation to the inductive sciences. He saw the absolute organ of culture in the natural sciences and the true history of mankind in the history of the natural sciences. Man had become a "rational animal who travels with steam, writes with lightning, and paints with sunbeams." He portrayed the weaknesses of the contemporary schools, which provide classical languages but are deficient in mathematics and the theory of conic sections. His political speeches "Der deutsche Krieg" (1870), "Das Kaiserreich und der Friede" (1871), and "Über das Nationalgefühl" (1878) are not without exaggerated complaints about the self-praise and chauvinistic feelings of superiority of the French.

In any case, du Bois-Reymond was not afraid to express unpopular thoughts. His inaugural speech as rector, "Goethe und sein Ende" (1882), annoyed a great many intellectuals. He mercilessly portrayed the weaknesses of Goethe's concept of nature, his inclination to deduction, the deficiencies of his theory of color, and even the curious contradictions in his *Faust.* Du Bois-Reymond maintained that natural science had come as far as it had without Goethe's scientific writings: one should leave Goethe alone as a scientist.

Other speeches show how well read du Bois-

Reymond was and his ability to judge questions of art. The greatest excitement and the most bitter opposition were caused by the two speeches "Über die Grenzen des Naturerkennens" (1872) and "Die sieben Welträtsel" (1880). For him there were two insoluble questions for natural science, that of the essence of matter and force and that of the occurrence of consciousness in connection with molecular processes in the brain. Even an intellect like Laplace would not be able to know all of the factors involved in these questions. The seven riddles of the world are, according to du Bois-Reymond, those questions which science can answer only with the words *ignoramus* or *ignorabimus:* (1) the essence of force and matter, (2) the origin of movement, (3) the origin of life, (4) the teleology of nature, (5) the origin of sense perception, (6) the origin of thought, and (7) free will. He considered these questions transcendental.

Du Bois-Reymond's views annoyed both extreme natural scientists, like Ernst Haeckel, and theologians. The controversy he stimulated filled the daily press as well as the scientific literature. Accordingly, du Bois-Reymond significantly affected his own time and posterity on two levels. In electrophysiology he laid the foundations of the methods that were used for a century. In his treatment of problems of scientific boundaries and principles, he developed such brilliant formulations that his arguments still arouse great interest.

Du Bois-Reymond had an unusual gift for language and a finely developed sense of beauty, and he chose his words carefully. He loved figurative comparisons; those he used were sometimes audacious but never dull. His language was clear, his thought structure logical. He loved to introduce quotations from both classical and contemporary poets. French heritage blended with German thoroughness, eloquence with awareness of problems. From his youth du Bois-Reymond was receptive to philosophy and religion; but in protest against his Kantian and pious father, he tended very early toward cognitive-theoretical empiricism and free-thinking atheism. His study of La Mettrie had played not a slight role. He had only little love for nineteenth-century Christianity. Metaphysics, he thought, should not be mixed with natural science: the idea of the vital force was a mistake of this kind because the law of the conservation of energy, the framework for all transformations of energy, forbids such a hypothesis.

The neovitalism of Hans Driesch and Gustav von Bunge drew du Bois-Reymond's sharp condemnation. Thus, as he wrote in 1875, he found in himself a union of "intellectual inclinations which drive me with almost equal intensity in very different directions of perceiving nature." Du Bois-Reymond, for all his modesty, was self-confident and certain. His intellectual vitality and his many talents allowed him to make friends rapidly. He was uncommonly devoted to his friends, such as Hallmann and Ludwig, and did not allow his co-workers, such as Sachs and Fritsch, to go unrecognized. Understandably, he found it difficult in his old age to encounter much hostility and many refutations of his molecular theory of animal electricity. The opposition of his talented student Hermann was a bitter blow, but the scientific world of the nineteenth century never lacked polemics.

BIBLIOGRAPHY

I. ORIGINAL WORKS. Du Bois-Reymond's writings include "Vorläufiger Abriss einer Untersuchung über den sogenannten Froschstrom und über die elektrischen Fische," in Poggendorff's *Annalen der Physik und Chemie,* **58** (1843), 1–30; *Untersuchungen über thierische Elektrizität,* 2 vols. (Berlin, 1849–1884), vol. II in 2 secs., sec. 2 in 2 pts.; and *Abhandlungen zur allgemeinen Muskel- und Nervenphysik,* 2 vols. (Leipzig, 1875–1877). The books contain many papers that had already appeared in the *Monatsberichte . . ., Sitzungsberichten . . .,* and *Abhandlungen der Preussischen Akademie der Wissenschaften* and also those that had been published in Poggendorff's *Annalen* and in *Archiv für Anatomie, Physiologie und wissenschaftliche Medizin.* A complete bibliography of du Bois-Reymond's publications is in the dissertation by J. Marseille (below). The list of academic speeches (incomplete) is in A. von Harnack, *Geschichte der Königlichen Preussischen Akademie der Wissenschaften zu Berlin,* III; and in Otto Köhncke, *Gesamtregister über die in den Schriften der Akademie von 1700–1890 erschienen wiss. Abhandlungen und Festreden* (Berlin, 1900). The 2-vol. 2nd ed. of his *Reden,* Estelle du Bois-Reymond, ed. (Leipzig, 1912), contains almost all of his public speeches. Further sources are *Emil du Bois-Reymond. Jugendbriefe an Eduard Hallmann,* Estelle du Bois-Reymond, ed. (Berlin, 1918); and *Zwei grosse Naturforscher des 19. Jahrhunderts. Ein Briefwechsel zwischen Emil du Bois-Reymond und Karl Ludwig,* Estelle du Bois-Reymond and Paul Diepgen, eds. (Leipzig, 1927).

II. SECONDARY LITERATURE. Accounts based on original sources are H. Bence-Jones, *On Animal Electricity, Being an Abstract of the Discoveries of Emil du Bois-Reymond* (London, 1852); and Ilse Jahn, "Die Anfänge der instrumentellen Elektrobiologie in den Briefen Humboldts an Emil du Bois-Reymond," in *Medizin historisches Journal,* **2** (1967), 135–156. On the history of electrophysiology, see the following by K. E. Rothschuh: "Die neurophysiologischen Beiträge von Galvani und Volta," in L. Belloni, ed., *Per la storia della neurologia italiana* (Milan, 1963), pp. 117–130. In addition see "Alexander von Humboldt und die Physiologie seiner Zeit," in *Archiv für Geschichte der*

Medizin, **43** (1959), 97–113; "Von der Idee bis zum Nachweis der tierischen Elektrizität," *ibid.,* **44** (1960), 25–44; and "Emil du Bois-Reymond und die Elektrophysiologie der Nerven," in K. E. Rothschuh, ed., *Von Boerhaave bis Berger* (Stuttgart, 1964), pp. 85–105. Also of value are Giuseppe Moruzzi, "L'opera elettrofisiologica di Carlo Matteucci," in *Physis,* **4** (1964), 101–140, with a bibliography of works by Matteucci; and J. Marseille, "Das physiologische Lebenswerk von E. du Bois-Reymond mit besonderer Berücksichtigung seiner Schüler," an M.D. dissertation (Münster, 1967), with bibliography.

Biographies, memorials, and obituaries are Heinrich Boruttau, *Emil du Bois-Reymond,* vol. III in the series Meister der Heilkunde (Vienna–Leipzig–Munich, 1922); and I. Munk, "Zur Erinnerung an Emil du Bois-Reymond," in *Deutsche medizinische Wochenschrift,* **23** (1897), 17–19, with portrait. Further references to obituaries are in *Index medicus,* 2nd ser., **2** (1897), 521–522; 3rd ser., **3** (1922), 178.

Further secondary literature and historical evaluations are Erich Metze, *Emil du Bois-Reymond, sein Wirken und seine Weltanschauung,* 3rd ed. (Bielefeld, 1918); Paul Grützner, in *Allgemeine deutsche Biographie,* XLVIII (1903), 118–126; Friedrich Harnack, *Emil du Bois-Reymond und die Grenzen der mechanistischen Naturauffassung* (Festschrift zur 150-Jahr-Feier der Humboldt-Universität Berlin), I (Berlin, 1960), 229–251; F. Dannemann, "Aus Emil du Bois-Reymond's Briefwechsel über die Geschichte der Naturwissenschaften," in *Mitteilungen zur Geschichte der Medizin und der Naturwissenschaften und der Technik,* **18** (1919), 274 ff.; K. E. Rothschuh, *Geschichte der Physiologie* (Berlin–Göttingen–Heidelberg, 1953), pp. 130–139, with portrait; Wolfgang Kloppe, "Du Bois-Reymond's Rhetorik im Urteil einiger seiner Zeitgenossen," in *Deutsches Medizin historisches Journal,* **9** (1958), 80–82; and Rudolf Virchow, "Ansprache zum 50-jährigen Dr.-Jubiläum von Emil du Bois-Reymond," in *Berliner klinische Wochenschrift,* **30** (1893), 198–199.

K. E. Rothschuh

DU BOIS-REYMOND, PAUL DAVID GUSTAV

(*b.* Berlin, Germany, 2 December 1831; *d.* Freiburg, Germany, 7 April 1889), *mathematics.*

Paul du Bois-Reymond was the younger brother of the famous physiologist Emil du Bois-Reymond. He studied first at the French Gymnasium in Berlin, then at the *collège* in Neuchâtel and the Gymnasium in Naumburg. Following the example of his brother, he began to study medicine at the University of Zurich in 1853 and by the next year had published four articles that dealt basically with physiological problems. But soon du Bois-Reymond began to apply his talents to the mathematical and physical sciences. He continued his studies at the University of Königsberg, where, mainly through the influence of Franz Neumann, he turned to the study of mathematical physics, joining his talent for observation with that for making theoretical analyses. He specialized in the study of liquids, especially the areas of liquidity and capillarity. In 1859 he received his doctorate at the University of Berlin on the basis of his dissertation, "De aequilibrio fluidorum." Du Bois-Reymond then became a professor of mathematics and physics at a secondary school in Berlin and continued to devote himself systematically to mathematics until his appointment at the University of Heidelberg in 1865. In 1870 he went from Heidelberg to Freiburg as a professor, and thence to the University of Tübingen, in 1874, as the successor to H. Hankel. From 1884 until the end of his scientific career he occupied a chair of mathematics at a technical college in Berlin.

Du Bois-Reymond worked almost exclusively in the field of infinitesimal calculus, concentrating on two aspects: the theory of differential equations and the theory of the functions of real variables.

Studying the problems of mathematical physics led du Bois-Reymond to the theory of differential equations. He was concerned with these problems at the start of his scientific career and returned to them in the last years of his life. His basic study, *Beiträge zur Interpretation der partiellen Differentialgleichungen mit drei Variablen* (part 1, *Die Theorie der Charakteristiken* [Leipzig 1864]), was one of the first to follow up Monge's idea of the "characteristic" of a partial differential equation. This idea, expressed by Monge for equations of the second order as early as 1784, depended on the geometric expression of the integral of a differential equation as the surface defined by a system of curves. Du Bois-Reymond generalized this for partial differential equations of the nth order. These ideas, such as the simple case of a study of contact transformations, led in generalized form to the studies by Lie and Scheffers.

The chief means of solving partial differential equations at that time was by Fourier series. As early as the 1820's Cauchy, Abel, and Dirichlet had pointed out some of the difficulties of the expansion of "arbitrary" function in a Fourier series and of the convergence of this series. These problems contributed substantially to the rebuilding of the foundations of mathematical analysis. One of the first to deal with them systematically was du Bois-Reymond. He published his main results toward the end of the 1860's and in the 1870's—at first under the influence of Riemann's ideas and at a time when the results of Weierstrass' work had not been published and were little known.

He achieved a number of outstanding results. As early as 1868, when he was studying some properties of integrals, du Bois-Reymond expressed both precisely and generally and demonstrated the mean-value theorem for definite integrals, which was then

205

an important aid in the study of Fourier series. This theorem was later expressed independently by Dini (1878), who ascribed it to Weierstrass. The latter, however, developed a similar but more specialized proposition and made no claim to du Bois-Reymond's discovery.

Like other mathematicians who relied on Dirichlet, du Bois-Reymond also originally tried to show that each continuous function in a given interval is necessarily representable by its Fourier series (or another series analogous to a trigonometric one). A decisive turn came in 1873, when du Bois-Reymond published "Über die Fourier'schen Reihen." This article contains an exposition of the chief idea of a construction of a continuous function with a divergent Fourier series at any point. Later he also attempted to show the properties of this continuous function (which has a very complicated construction) using considerations, difficult to comprehend, that concern the infinitely small and the infinitely large (the so-called *Infinitärcalcul*).

Two of the other results of du Bois-Reymond's work should be mentioned. First and foremost is the solution of the problem of the integrability of Fourier series, which he proposed (but did not publish until 1883) and for which he demonstrated certain conditions that made it possible to distinguish Fourier's from other trigonometric series. The second is the solution to a question that concerned mathematicians of that time: the publication (1873) of an example and the precise demonstration of the properties of the function that is continuous in a given interval but without derivatives. This achievement was inspired by Weierstrass.

Du Bois-Reymond was then led to attempt a general exposition of the fundamental concepts of the theory of functions in his book *Die allgemeine Functionentheorie,* the first part of which was published in 1882. Among other things, this work shows that its author was aware that a precise theory of real numbers was needed for the further progress of the theory of functions, but he did not make any real contributions to that progress. Instead, he wrote of the problems of the philosophy of mathematics, recognizing the advantages of different approaches and expressing grave doubts about the usefulness of formalism.

Du Bois-Reymond's work was directed at the basic questions of the mathematical analysis of the time and is marked by both the personality of the author and the state of the mathematics of the period. It appeared before completion of the revision of the foundations of mathematical analysis for which he was striving. Led by sheer mathematical intuition, he

did not hesitate to publish even vague considerations and assertions that were later shown to be false. Further developments, some while du Bois-Reymond was still alive, disclosed these weaknesses (e.g., Pringsheim's criticism) and also rapidly outdated his results, even on the main questions. Among them is his attempt to give a general theory of convergence tests. This meant that his work, which had been greatly appreciated by his contemporaries, soon sank into oblivion, although it had included very important questions and notions that were later reflected in the work of such mathematicians as W. H. Young, A. Denjoy, and H. Lebesgue.

BIBLIOGRAPHY

Du Bois-Reymond's "Über die Fourier'schen Reihen" appeared in *Nachrichten von der Gesellschaft der Wissenschaften zu Göttingen* (1873), 571–584. *Die allgemeine Functionentheorie* was translated by G. Milhaud and A. Girot as *Théorie générale des fonctions* (Paris, 1887). On du Bois-Reymond and his work, see (in chronological order), L. Kronecker, "Paul du Bois-Reymond," in *Journal für die reine und angewandte Mathematik,* **104** (1889), 352–354; "P. du Bois-Reymond's literarische Publicationen," in *Mathematische Annalen,* **35** (1890), 463–469; H. Weber, "Paul du Bois-Reymond," *ibid.,* **35** (1890), 457–462; *Paul du Bois-Reymond, Zwei Abhandlungen über unendliche (1871) und trigonometrische Reihen (1874),* Ostwalds Klassiker, no. 185 (Leipzig, 1912); *Paul du Bois-Reymond, Abhandlungen über die Darstellung der Funktionen durch trigonometrische Reihen (1876),* Ostwalds Klassiker, no. 186 (Leipzig, 1913); and A. B. Paplauskas, *Trigonometricheskie ryady ot Eylera do Lebega* ("Trigonometrical Series from Euler to Lesbesgue," Moscow, 1966).

LUBOŠ NOVÝ

DUBOSCQ, OCTAVE (*b.* Rouen, France, 1 October 1868; *d.* Nice, France, 18 February 1943), *protistology, cytology.*

The son of a minor railroad employee who was crushed between two cars, Duboscq was orphaned at a very young age; his mother died of grief only a few months later. His aunt took him in and cared for him. He was a brilliant student at the lycée in Coutances. In 1886 he began to study medicine at Caen while preparing for his *licence ès sciences naturelles,* which he obtained in 1889. He went to Paris to complete his medical studies and in 1894 defended his doctoral thesis in medicine.

However, scientific research attracted Duboscq, and he abandoned his medical career. He was named *préparateur* at Caen, then *chef de travaux* at Grenoble. He defended his doctoral thesis in science in 1899 and became lecturer in zoology at Caen (1900), professor of zoology at Montpellier (1904) and then of marine biology at Paris, and director of the Arago Laboratory at Banyuls-sur-Mer (1923), where he remained until his retirement (1 October 1937). He then took up residence in Paris and he spent three months each winter in Nice with his brother, who died of a heart attack in 1942. Grief over this death and malnutrition as a result of the war led to his own death.

Louis Joyeux-Laffuie, professor of zoology at Caen, Georges Pruvot of Grenoble, Louis Léger of Grenoble, and Yves Delage of Paris profoundly influenced Duboscq's work as well as his teaching. His collaboration with Léger lasted nearly a quarter of a century. A brilliant teacher, around 1912 Duboscq created a certificate in cytology and protistology and organized a teaching method that accorded a large place to practical topics.

Duboscq's work, at once original and substantial, began with researches on the microanatomy of the arthropods (venom glands, nervous system of the chilopods, the digestive duct of the insects and crustaceans, spermatogenesis of the *Sacculina*). His essential work, however, represents an effort very important to the knowledge of several classes of the Protista. His investigations concerned the structure and cycle of the schizophytes and the intestinal and sanguicolous spirochetes of saltwater fishes. With Léger he studied the eccrinids, which are filamentous parasitic protophytes of the arthropods, and determined their development cycles; they also studied the sporozoans, establishing their general cycle and that of the gregarines in particular. They also discovered the cycle of the *Porospora*. They studied the coccidiomorphs and made a valuable contribution to the knowledge of the *Pseudoklossia*, of the *Selenococcidium*, and of the *Aggregata*. Moreover, they offered original ideas on the phylogeny and classification of the sporozoans.

Duboscq was also interested in the flagellates, especially in the sexual reproduction of the *Peridinia* and in the sexuality of the flagellate organisms that live in termites. The sporozoans represent the major work of his maturity. In his old age he devoted himself to the sponges. James Brontë Gatenby discovered the indirect fertilization of the sponges, and Duboscq and his student O. Tuzet specified the details and variations of the process.

BIBLIOGRAPHY

Among Duboscq's numerous writings are "Recherches sur les chilopodes," his thesis for the doctorate in science, in *Archives de zoologie expérimentale,* 3rd ser., **7** (1899);

"Les éléments sexuels et la fécondation chez *Pterocephalus,*" in *Comptes rendus hebdomadaires des séances de l'Académie des sciences,* **134** (1902), 1148–1149; "Aggregata vagans, n. sp. grégarine gymnosporée parasite des pagures," in *Archives de zoologie expérimentale,* n. et r., 4th ser., **1** (1903), 147–151; "Notes sur les infusoires endoparasites. II. *Anoplophrya brasili.* III. *Opalina saturnalis,*" ibid., **2** (1904), 337–356; "*Selenococcidium intermedium* et la systématique des sporozoaires," ibid., 5th ser., **5** (1910), 187–238; "Deux nouvelles espèces de grégarines appartenant au genre *Porospora,*" in *Annales de l'Université de Grenoble,* **23** (1911), 399–404; "*Selysina perforans,* description des stades connus de sporozoaire de *Stolonica* avec quelques remarques sur le pseudovitellus des statoblastes et sur les cellules géantes," in *Archives de zoologie expérimentale,* **58** (1918), 1–53; "L'appareil parabasal des flagellés et sa signification," in *Comptes rendus hebdomadaires des séances de l'Académie des sciences,* **180** (1925), 477–480; "Les porosporides et leur évolution," in *Travaux de la Station zoologique de Wimereux,* **9** (1925), 126–139; "L'évolution des *Paramoebidium,* nouveau genre d'eccrinides, parasites des larves aquatiques d'insectes," in *Comptes rendus hebdomadaires des séances de l'Académie des sciences,* **189** (1929), 75–77; "L'appareil parabasal et les constituants cytoplasmiques des zooflagellés," ibid., **193** (1931), 604–605; "L'appareil parabasal des flagellés avec des remarques sur le trochosponge, l'appareil de Golgi, les mitochondries et le vacuome," in *Archives de zoologie expérimentale,* **73** (1933), 381–621; "L'ovogenèse, la fécondation et les premiers stades du développement des éponges calcaires," ibid., **79** (1937), 157–316; and "Recherches complémentaires sur l'ovogenèse, la fécondation et les premiers stades du développement des éponges calcaires," ibid., **81** (1942), 395–466.

A biographical notice with a chronological list of Duboscq's scientific works is P. P. Grassé, in *Archives de zoologie expérimentale,* **84** (1944), 1–46.

ANDRÉE TÉTRY

DU BUAT, PIERRE-LOUIS-GEORGES (*b.* Tortizambert, Normandy, France, 23 April 1734; *d.* Vieux-Condé, Flanders [now part of Nord, France], 17 October 1809), *hydraulics.*

Born in the manor of Buttenval, the second son of a minor nobleman, Du Buat was in all probability educated at Paris, where he became a military engineer at the age of seventeen. By 1787 he had risen to the rank of colonel, which he then resigned to accept appointment as *lieutenant du roi.* His earliest assignments were canal, coastal, harbor, and fortification works in the north of France.

In 1758 Du Buat married a native of Condé (near Valenciennes, on the Belgian border), by whom he eventually had eleven children. On the death of his older brother in 1787, he inherited their late father's title of count; but with the advent of the Revolution he lost titles and properties and was forced in 1793 to flee with his family to Belgium, then Holland, and finally Germany. In 1802 he returned to Vieux-Condé, and a portion of his estate was restored to him.

Du Buat began his hydraulic studies in 1776, and by 1779 he had published the first edition of his major work, *Principes d'hydraulique,* copies of which are now quite rare. This was enlarged in 1786 to two volumes, the first of which was analytical and the second experimental; it is supposed to have been translated into English (no copy can be found) as well as German. A posthumous edition of three volumes appeared in 1816, the third volume (*Pyrodynamique*) having been written during his exile. All three editions carried essentially the same prefatory remarks reviewing the state of the art—in particular those many important topics about which little or nothing was known; portions of the discourse are often quoted in subsequent works because of their continued relevance.

The analytical part of Du Buat's writings was perhaps more effective than that of such contemporaries as Jean Charles Borda and Charles Bossut, for he dealt extensively with matters of boundary resistance, velocity distribution, underflow, overflow, and backwater. It was in experimental work that he excelled. The results of his 200 separate tests on flow in pipes, artificial channels, and natural streams were to be used by engineers for generations. Even more original was his treatment of immersed bodies. He showed that tests in air and in water could be correlated in terms of the relative density of the resisting medium, and calculated, for example, the size of a parachute required to break the fall of a man of a given weight. He was also the first to demonstrate that the shape of the rear of a body is as important in controlling its resistance as is that of the front.

Du Buat also made 100 measurements on the distribution of pressure around bodies and sought through his findings to develop a new form of Henri Pitot's "machine" for the measurement of velocity. The basis for his conclusion that the force exerted upon a stationary body by running water is greater than that required to move the same body at the same relative speed through still water (Du Buat's paradox) is not clear from his writings—i.e., whether the cause is the uneven velocity distribution or the turbulence of the flow. Du Buat is called by some the father of French hydraulics, although at least partial credit should go to several of his contemporaries—not to mention Edmé Mariotte, more than a century his senior.

BIBLIOGRAPHY

Du Buat's major work was *Principes d'hydraulique, ouvrage* . . . (Paris, 1779); 2nd ed. entitled *Principes d'hydraulique vérifiés* . . ., 2 vols. (Paris, 1786); 3rd ed. entitled *Principes d'hydraulique et de pyrodynamique,* 3 vols. (Paris, 1816).

On Du Buat and his work, see H. Rouse and S. Ince, *History of Hydraulics* (New York, 1963), pp. 129–134; and B. de Saint-Venant, "Notice sur la vie et les ouvrages de Pierre-Louis-Georges, comte du Buat," in *Mémoires de la Société impériale des sciences de Lille,* 3rd ser., **2** (1865), 609–692.

HUNTER ROUSE

DUCHESNE, JOSEPH, also known as **Josephus Quercetanus** (*b.* L'Esture, Armagnac, Gascony, France, *ca.* 1544; *d.* Paris, France, 1609), *chemistry, medicine.*

The son of a physician, Duchesne (occasionally referred to as Sieur de la Violette) studied first at Montpellier. He married a granddaughter of the humanist Guillaume Budé and, because of persecution of the French Protestants, spent many years away from his homeland. Duchesne received his medical degree at Basel in 1573 and for some time was settled at Kassel, the capital of the grand duchy of Hesse. At this time and later the grand dukes were noted for their patronage of the new Paracelsian-Hermetic medicine. Later Duchesne moved to Geneva where he was received as a citizen in 1584. After election to the Council of Two Hundred (1587), he was sent on several diplomatic missions. In 1592 he helped determine the peace terms which the Republic of Geneva made with its neighbors. The following year Duchesne returned to Paris, where he was appointed physician in ordinary to King Henry IV.

Duchesne is a figure of some importance in French literature as well as science and medicine. His *La morocosmie* (1583, 1601) and *Poesies chrestiennes* (1594) have been commented on favorably by literary historians while his other poetical work, *Le grand miroir du monde* (1584, 1595), is important for Duchesne's concept of the elements. In addition, he ventured into tragicomedy with *L'ombre de Garnier Stauffacher* (1583), a work which took as its theme the alliance between Zurich, Berne, and Geneva.

Duchesne's medicoscientific works are best seen as part of the late sixteenth- and early seventeenth-century debate on the place of chemistry in medicine and natural philosophy. The flood of Paracelsian texts published in the third quarter of the sixteenth century had gained many adherents to the new medicine, but at the same time it had brought forth strong opposition from the medical establishment. Peter Severinus had attempted to systematize the works of Paracelsus in 1571, and Guinther von Andernach had written in defense of the new chemically prepared medicines in the same year, but Thomas Erastus at Basel had prepared a lengthy and detailed attack on Paracelsus and his views (1572–1573). Alarmed by the increasing internal use of minerals and metals, the Faculty of Medicine at Paris forbade the further prescription of antimony in this fashion (*ca.* 1575).

The strong critique of the views of Paracelsus on chemical medicines and the origin of metals written by Jacques Aubert in 1575 was the occasion for Duchesne's first publication. His *Responsio* to Aubert (1575) was a strong defense of the iatrochemical position, and although it was a short work, it was reprinted often and attracted considerable attention.

In the *Responsio* and many other works Duchesne offered a large number of pharmaceutical preparations. His *Sclopetarius* (1576), which dealt with the cure of gunshot wounds, and his *Pharmacopoea dogmaticorum* (1607) are only two of many works by him that were translated into several languages and went through numerous editions. These works offer a large number of remedies prepared from substances of mineral, vegetable, and animal origin. In all of his practical texts Duchesne placed strong emphasis on chemical procedures and his works contain the first printed directions for the preparation of turpeth mineral (basic mercuric sulfate), antimony sulfide, urea, and—possibly—calomel as medicines. Devaux has pointed to Duchesne's use of sulfur for respiratory problems and iodated substances (calcinated sea sponges) for the goiter.

A series of polemical works debating the value of the new medicine and the extent to which chemistry might be employed by physicians were printed in the last quarter of the century. In France the matter reached a climax when Duchesne published his *De priscorum philosophorum verae medicinae materia . . .* (1603). This work was immediately answered by the elder Jean Riolan who accused him of wishing to sweep away the venerable medicine of the ancients in his *Apologia pro Hippocratis Galeni medicina* (1603). In his reply to Riolan, published the following year, Duchesne denied this charge and answered that he wished only to use the best of the old medicine along with the new chemistry. These works were followed by a series of other works in which both Riolans, Israel Harvet, Theodore Turquet de Mayerne, Andreas Libavius, and many other authors participated.

In the course of this debate it became clear that there was more at stake than the simple acceptance or rejection of chemical remedies. For Duchesne—as for other iatrochemists—chemistry was to serve as a key to all nature. His cosmology was based on the biblical story of the Creation, and in his discussion he pictured the Creator as an alchemist separating the elements from the unformed chaos. In the fifteenth chapter of the *Ad veritatem hermeticae medicinae ex*

Hippocratis veterumque decretis ac therapeusi . . . (1604), Genesis is clearly interpreted in terms of the three Paracelsian principles of salt, sulfur, and mercury. In the earlier *Le grand miroir du monde* (1584) Duchesne had also accepted the Aristotelian water and earth as elementary substances. This five-element principle system has much in common with the five-element descriptions so common in the works of later seventeenth-century chemists.

Duchesne rejected the four humors of the ancients and when discussing the vascular system specifically spoke of the "circulation" of the blood. By this, however, he meant a series of local circulations in different organs, analogous to the heating of liquids in distillation flasks. His was a world view based on a close relation of the macrocosmic and microcosmic worlds. An integral part of this was his sincere belief in the doctrine of signatures, which for him were an important guide to divine gifts existing here on earth. Duchesne wrote of the need of "experientia" and new observations for a proper understanding of nature, and although he objected to being called a Paracelsian, his views were similar to those of Paracelsus in many respects.

Much of Duchesne's influence derives from the debate his work had initiated at Paris. His publications of 1603 and 1604 went through numerous editions in several languages and did much to publicize his version of the chemical philosophy. In these works Duchesne had discussed at length the Creation and the three principles. More than half a century later Robert Boyle still found it necessary to comment on these views in *The Sceptical Chymist* (1661).

In addition, the Parisian debate was influential in bringing about a more general acceptance of chemically prepared medicines. The chemists had been generally agreed that their aim was not to destroy all of the old medicine, but rather to apply what they found valuable in the works of the ancients along with the best of the new chemical medicine. This surely had been the view taken by Duchesne and it was also that of Mayerne, who had been the first of Duchesne's colleagues to support him in 1603. Mayerne was later to become chief physician to King James I of England, and he advocated this compromise position in the publication of the important *Pharmacopoeia* (1618) of the Royal College of Physicians. This work is notable both for its prominent inclusion of chemicals alongside the traditional Galenicals and also for its prefatory defense of the new methods of cure.

BIBLIOGRAPHY

I. ORIGINAL WORKS. There is no complete list of Duchesne's iatrochemical books. Used together, J. Ferguson's

Bibliotheca chemica, 2 vols. (Glasgow, 1906), and J. R. Partington's *A History of Chemistry,* II (London, 1961), will furnish most titles if not all of the editions.

Among his many works, Duchesne's first publication, the *Ad Iacobo Auberti vindonis de ortu et causis metallorum contra chymicos explicationem Iosephi Armeniaci, D. Medici breuis responsio* (Lyons, 1575), was considered a major work in support of the iatrochemical position. It was reprinted often in Latin, French, and German, and an English translation by John Hester was printed in London in 1591. The next year Duchesne published his *Sclopetarius, sive de curandis vulneribus quae sclopetarum ictibus acciderunt* (Lyons, 1576), a work that appeared in French translation in the same year. John Hester made this text available in English in 1590. The *De priscorum philosophorum verae medicinae materia . . .* (St. Gervais, 1603) initiated the debate over the chemical medicine at Paris. Duchesne's reply to Jean Riolan, the *Ad veritatem hermeticae medicinae ex Hippocratis veterumque decretis ac therapeusi . . .* (Paris, 1604), is also a major theoretical statement. The first of these appeared in French translation (Paris, 1626) and selections from both were translated into English by Thomas Timme as *The Practise of Chymicall and Hermeticall Physicke for the Preseruation of Health* (London, 1605). A final—and much less well known—*Ad brevem Riolani excursum brevis incursio* (Marburg, 1605) concluded Duchesne's contributions to this debate.

There is little question that Duchesne's most popular work was the *Pharmacopoea dogmaticorum restituta pretiosis selectisque hermeticorum floribus abunde illustrata* (Paris, 1607). There are twenty-five known editions of this work from the first half of the seventeenth century. The *Opera medica* includes the *Responsio* to Aubert, the *Sclopetarius,* and the *De exquisita mineralium animalium, et vegetabilium medicamentorum spagyrica preparatione et vsu, perspicua tractatio.* This went through at least two Latin editions (Frankfurt am Main, 1602; Leipzig, 1614) and one German edition (Strasbourg, 1631). The most extensive collection was the three-volume *Quercetanus redivivus* prepared by Johann Schröder, a massive text that went through three editions (Frankfurt am Main, 1648, 1667, 1679).

II. SECONDARY SOURCES. Pierre Lordez's *Joseph du Chesne, sieur de La Violette, médecin du roi Henri IV, chimiste, diplomate et poète* (Paris, 1944) contains useful information.

Guy Devaux's "Quelques aspects de la médecine et de la pharmacie au XVIe siècle à travers la 'Pharmacopée des dogmatiques' de Joseph Du Chesne, Sieur de la Violette, conseiller et médecin du roy," in *Revue d'histoire de la pharmacie,* **19** (1969), 271–284, is a study of the pharmaceutical preparations in Duchesne's most popular work, while the discussion of Duchesne in Partington's *History of Chemistry,* II (London, 1961), 167–170, centers on the chemical preparations known to Partington.

W. P. D. Wightman, *Science and the Renaissance,* I (Edinburgh–London–New York, 1962), 256–263, offers a helpful discussion of the complex debate at Paris in the early years of the seventeenth century.

For element theory in Duchesne, see R. Hooykaas, "Die

Elementenlehre der Iatrochemiker," in *Janus,* **41** (1937), 1–18; and Allen G. Debus, *The English Paracelsians* (London, 1965), pp. 87–101. Duchesne's views on the circulation of the blood are discussed in Allen G. Debus, "Robert Fludd and the Circulation of the Blood," in *Journal of the History of Medicine and Allied Sciences,* **16** (1961), 374–393.

Finally, Pagel has pointed to a Paracelsian tract (1635) by Fabius Violet (possibly Duchesne) in which the digestive factor in the stomach is identified with the "hungry acid" of Paracelsus. This is a statement that comes close to van Helmont's position first printed in 1648. The influence of Violet on van Helmont is surely possible although the former did not go on to identify this acid with hydrochloric acid as did the latter. On this see Walter Pagel, *Paracelsus. An Introduction to Philosophical Medicine in the Renaissance* (Basel, 1958), 161–164.

ALLEN G. DEBUS

DUCLAUX, ÉMILE (*b.* Aurillac, Cantal, France, 24 June 1840; *d.* Paris, France, 2 May 1904), *biochemistry.*

Duclaux belonged to that group of physicists and chemists, still limited in the second half of the nineteenth century, who through their work increased our knowledge of living matter. It appears, however, that his lasting fame derives less from his discoveries than from the close ties that bound him to Pasteur and his followers throughout his adult life. He was, in fact, one of the first to believe in microbes, and the books he devoted to them have long remained the "gospel" of the new doctrine.

His father was bailiff of the court at Aurillac, where his mother ran a small grocery. As a child, his long walks through the beautiful Auvergne countryside gave Duclaux a taste for nature and poetry; and his parents' example revealed to him the value of sincerity, simplicity, and perseverance.

In 1857, upon completing his classical education at the local *collège,* Duclaux left Aurillac and went to Paris to attend the special mathematics course at the Lycée St. Louis. Two years later he was accepted at both the École Polytechnique and the École Normale Supérieure; he chose the latter. In 1862 he became *agrégé* in the physical sciences and was then retained by Pasteur as his laboratory assistant (*agrégé-préparateur*) at the school. It was during this period that the discussions of the possibility or impossibility of spontaneous generation were at their liveliest. Pasteur maintained that the microscopic creatures responsible for fermentation came from parents similar to themselves. Nicolas Joly, Pouchet, and Musset asserted that, on the contrary, these creatures were born spontaneously in organic fluids. From time to time Dumas and Balard, members of the commission named by the Académie des Sciences to settle the question, came to the École Normale. Duclaux, who had already participated in the experiments of his mentor, now attended the debates. The impression they made on him showed him his true course in life.

Dissociated from Pasteur's laboratory, an *agrégé-préparateur* faced an uncertain future. After defending his doctoral thesis in physical sciences in 1865, Duclaux decided to leave Paris. He became a teacher first at the *lycée* in Tours, then at the Faculty of Sciences at Clermont-Ferrand, in which city his mother, a widow since 1860, joined him. He was able to renew his collaboration with Pasteur, first at Pont-Gisquet, Gard, where the master was pursuing his work on silkworm diseases, and a little later at Clermont-Ferrand. The experiments—on fermentation—began in a makeshift laboratory set up by Duclaux and were repeated on a much greater scale at the Kuhn brewery in Chamalières, which is between Clermont-Ferrand and Royat. It is well known that these experiments were requested in order to revive the brewing industry.

New professional duties brought Duclaux to Lyons in 1873 and finally to Paris in 1878. In Paris he won a competition for the professorship of meteorology at the Institut Agronomique, and he was also given a lectureship in biological chemistry at the Sorbonne. He immediately used this opportunity to give a course in microbiology, the first of its kind anywhere.

His young wife, the former Mathilde Briot, succumbed suddenly to puerperal fever following the birth of their second son. To forget his grief, Duclaux threw himself into his work with even greater energy. He taught, experimented, and wrote; and he followed, day after day, Pasteur's extraordinary series of accomplishments. These included the development of vaccines against fowl cholera, anthrax, swine fever, and, in 1885, against rabies. In 1888 the Institut Pasteur was founded in Paris on rue Dutot. Duclaux, who meanwhile had become titular professor at the Sorbonne, transferred his teaching activities to the Institut Pasteur. A little earlier, through his efforts a new monthly journal, the *Annales de l'Institut Pasteur,* was created to publish research in microbiology.

Beginning with this period, one may say that Duclaux's life was almost inseparable from that of the Institut Pasteur. At the death of its brilliant founder in 1895, he took over its direction and in a few years made it into a sort of "scientific cooperative," in which each scientist, while preserving the independence of his own ideas, worked toward a common goal. To the original buildings were added, at the beginning of the century, the Institut de Chimie Biologique and a hospital.

Duclaux became a member of the Académie des Sciences in 1888, of the Société Nationale d'Agriculture in 1890, and of the Académie de Médecine in 1894. In 1901 he married Mme. James Darmesteter (the former Mary Robinson), a woman remarkable for both her intelligence and her warmth. He had finally found familial happiness again, but this happiness did not last. In January 1902 he suffered his first stroke. Scarcely recovered, he began to write again for the *Annales* and in the spring of 1903 recommenced his lectures. But this was too much to demand of an overtaxed body. On the evening of 2 May 1904 Duclaux suddenly lost consciousness and died in the night. His place as director of the Institut Pasteur was assumed by one of his pupils from Clermont-Ferrand, Émile Roux. The latter had become well known for his research with Pasteur, his discovery of the diphtheria bacillus, and his development of a specific diphtheria antitoxin.

Duclaux's scientific work is at once that of a physicist and that of a chemist. As a physicist he studied the phenomena of osmosis, of molecular adhesion, and of surface tension. As a chemist he concentrated especially on fermentation processes. In this area he was to some extent following up the work of Pasteur. As the years passed he was led to accord to enzymes (then called *diastases*) an increasingly important role in the phenomena of life. He devoted a long series of investigations to the respective roles played in the intestinal tract of men and animals by enzymes issuing from glands and by those liberated by microbes. He recognized that the microbes had no role in gastric and pancreatic digestion, which involve only juices released from the tissues. Microbial digestion does not begin until the intestine, but then rapidly becomes important. In a related area, Duclaux realized that microbes are indispensable in the formation in the soil of plant nutrients. Without microbes the earth is infertile, because the enzymes in the plant cells cannot leave the cells and thus cannot act outside the plant.

Milk provided Duclaux with a material ideally suited to the study of enzymes. In the first stage, through a great number of analyses, he was able to develop methods permitting the determination of the proportions of its constituents. In the second stage he studied the enzymes capable of modifying the constituents. The great importance of enzymes was shown in the transformation of milk into cheese. In this case, however, the active agents are of external origin. A cheese is in fact the result of microbial cooperation: "Each of the microscopic workers must act in its turn and stop at the right moment. Such a workshop is difficult to direct, and one may say that it has required the experience of centuries to obtain products whose taste and appearance are always the same" (Émile Roux, in *Annales de l'Institut Pasteur,* **18** [1904], 337). Duclaux studied several types of cheese, but undoubtedly with particular relish the cheese from Cantal, one of the riches of his native area.

Duclaux the teacher was no less remarkable than Duclaux the researcher. His pupil Roux, recalling his days as a medical student at Clermont-Ferrand, wrote: "Duclaux presented a subject so clearly that everyone understood. His words were those of a scientist burning with the 'sacred fire.' He set thinking, to the point that when one had finished his course, he seemed to be there still" (*ibid.*).

In addition to his research papers Duclaux wrote a great many didactic works; and the critical reviews he published in the *Annales* remain models. It has been said of them that they display "the logic of the scientist and the style of the poet. . . . He could extract from a memoir . . . possible consequences that the author himself had not always suspected. How many ideas he explored; what new insights he lavishly bestowed. Duclaux sowed the high wind . . ." (Émile Roux, in *Bulletin de l'Institut Pasteur,* **2** [1904], 369).

Duclaux was captivating, full of wit and verve. He was also a just man with a passionate soul. He dreamed of a universal brotherhood under the banner of science—"the common fatherland," as he used to say, "where one could have passions without having hatreds." But he was not oblivious to what was happening outside his laboratory. On several occasions his devotion to the truth led him to enter into political conflicts. In particular he took a very active part in the campaign that finally forced the reinstatement of Captain Dreyfus.

BIBLIOGRAPHY

I. ORIGINAL WORKS. A complete list of Duclaux's scientific publications appears in *Annales de l'Institut Pasteur,* **18** (1904), 354–362.

Among his most important books are *Ferments et maladies* (Paris, 1882); *Le microbe et la maladie* (Paris, 1886); *Cours de physique et de météorologie* (Paris, 1891), a published version of his course at the Institut Agronomique; *Traité de microbiologie,* 4 vols. (Paris, 1891–1901); *Principes de laiterie* (Paris, 1892); *Le lait, études chimiques et microbiologiques* (Paris, 1894); *Pasteur, histoire d'un esprit* (Paris, 1896), which contains the frequently cited phrase, "Chemistry has taken possession of medicine, and will not let go"; and *L'hygiène sociale* (Paris, 1902).

II. SECONDARY LITERATURE. On the life and works of Duclaux, two articles by Émile Roux are classics: "Notice sur la vie et les travaux d'Émile Duclaux," in *Annales de l'Institut Pasteur,* **18** (1904), 337–362; and "Émile Duclaux,"

in *Bulletin de l'Institut Pasteur,* **2** (1904), 369–370. A biography, *La vie d'Émile Duclaux,* was written by his second wife, Mary Darmesteter Duclaux (Paris, 1906).

ALBERT DELAUNAY

DUCROTAY DE BLAINVILLE, HENRI MARIE. *See* **Blainville, Henri Marie Ducrotay de.**

DUDITH (DUDITIUS), ANDREAS (*b.* Buda [now Budapest], Hungary, 16 February 1533; *d.* Breslau, Germany [now Wrocław, Poland], 23 February 1589), *astronomy, astrology, mathematics.*

Andreas Dudith combined political and religious activity with humanist and scientific interests in a manner fairly common in the sixteenth century. Of mixed Hungarian and Italian descent, Dudith was educated in the Hungarian tradition of Erasmian humanism. He traveled widely in Italy, France, and England from 1550 to 1560, serving for a time as secretary to Cardinal Reginald Pole. After attending the Council of Trent in 1562–1563, Dudith received the bishopric of Pécs and performed various diplomatic missions to Poland for the emperors Sigismund II and Maximilian II between 1563 and 1576. Dudith's first marriage in 1567 to Regina Strass, a Polish noblewoman, and his subsequent adherence to Lutheranism brought upon him the condemnation of Rome and weakened his position at the Viennese court. (His second marriage, in 1574, was to Elisabeth Zborowski.) After some political reverses he retired from affairs of state in 1576 and later devoted himself to scientific and theological matters at Breslau, inclining to Calvinist and Socinian doctrines.

Dudith was familiar with the leading intellectual movements of his day; his visits to Italy had acquainted him with humanists and bibliophiles like Paulus Manutius and Giovanni-Vincenzo Pinelli and also with the works of Pietro Pomponazzi and the Paduan Averroists. In the 1570's Dudith took up the study of mathematics and cultivated the friendship of the Englishmen Henry and Thomas Savile and the German Johann Praetorius. Medicine also interested Dudith; he studied Galen and corresponded with many physicians, including the imperial physician Crato. In the breadth of his intellectual interest Dudith was typical of Renaissance humanists, and his library of printed books and manuscripts reflects this encyclopedism. Like many Italians, notably his friend Pinelli, he collected Greek mathematical manuscripts for both their philological and scientific interest. Among his manuscripts were the *Arithmetic* of Diophantus (which he loaned to Xylander to use as the text for the first Latin translation published at Basel in 1575); the *Mathematical Collections* of Pappus; the

Elementa astronomiae of Geminos (used for the *editio princeps* of 1590); and his own transcription of the *Tetrabiblos* of Ptolemy. Several of these manuscripts were lost following the dispersal of his library, but many of his manuscripts and his 5,000 printed books are now in the Vatican, Paris, Leiden, and various Swedish libraries.

Dudith is known mainly for his contribution to the controversy over the comet of 1577. (Hellman lists more than 100 publications on this comet.) He knew several of the personalities involved in the dispute, including Thomas Erastus, Thaddaeus Hagecius (Hayck), and Tycho Brahe; and a collection of tracts on the topic was dedicated to him in 1580. Although originally interested in the astrology of the *Tetrabiblos* of Ptolemy, Dudith became an opponent of the astrologers. His *De cometarum significatione* shows the influence of Erastus in its rejection of astrology as a vain pseudoscience. Both Dudith and Erastus argued that comets could appear without causing or portending natural or political calamities. (In his first letter to Hagecius, Dudith remarked that astrology was condemned by Christian authorities and, despite his own Calvinist leanings, that astrology infringed upon free will.)

Dudith accepted, however, Aristotle's physical explanation of comets as accidental exhalations of hot air from the earth that rise in the sublunar sphere. But an insistence on mathematical astronomy rather than astrology soon led Dudith to the rejection of Aristotelian physical doctrine. In 1581 Dudith learned in a letter from Hagecius, a believer in astrology, of the latter's observation that the parallax of another comet indicated that the comet was beyond the moon. In his letter of 19 January 1581 to Rafanus, Dudith argued that this observation proved the Aristotelian explanation fallacious. If the comets were terrestrial in origin they could not penetrate beyond the sublunar sphere; if, however, they originated in the immanent heavens comets could not be classified as accidental phenomena. Dudith remarked that many recently observed comets seemed to form and dissolve in the region of permanent things. This fact suggested serious flaws in the Aristotelian system. (Tycho arrived at a similar conclusion from his observation that the 1577 comet had no parallax and must therefore be farther from the earth than was the moon. Tycho also attempted to calculate the orbit of that comet.)

Dudith's use of a mathematically precise observation to criticize a general physical theory of Aristotle's betokens the same kind of dissatisfaction with Aristotelian physical doctrines that was most eloquently expounded in the works of Galileo fifty years later.

BIBLIOGRAPHY

I. ORIGINAL WORKS. Dudith's main scientific work is *De cometarum significatione commentariolus . . .* (Basel, 1579), repr. in the 2nd pt. of *De cometis dissertationes novae clariss. Virorum Th. Erasti, Andr. Duditii . . .* (Basel, 1580). Dedicated to Dudith, it includes Dudith's letter to Erastus of 1 Feb. 1579. Subsequent eds. are: Breslau, 1619; Jena, 1665; Utrecht, 1665. The first letter to Hagecius (26 Sept. 1580) is in J. E. Scheibel, *Astronomische Bibliographie,* II (Breslau, 1786), 160–182, with other materials on the comet of 1577. The second letter (1 Feb. 1581), congratulating Hagecius on his observation of a comet's parallax, appears at the beginning of Thaddaeus Hagecius, *Apodixis physica et mathematica de cometis* (Görlitz, 1581). The letter to Rafanus is in Lorenz Scholtz, *Epistolarum philosophicarum medicinalium, ac chymicarum volumen* (Frankfurt, 1598), letter 28. Details of Dudith's voluminous correspondence are given in the Costil biography cited below.

For Dudith's writings on the marriage of priests see Q. Reuter, *Andreae Dudithii orationes in concil. Trident. Habitae . . .* (Offenbach am Main, 1610). See also the references to Dudith in J. L. E. Dreyer, ed., *Tychonis Brahe opera omnia,* 15 vols. (Copenhagen, 1913–1929), IV, 453, 455; VI, 327–328; VII, 63, 123, 182, 214; VIII, 455.

II. SECONDARY LITERATURE. An excellent biography and bibliography is Pierre Costil, *André Dudith: humaniste hongrois 1533–1589, sa vie, son oeuvre et ses manuscrits grecs* (Paris, 1935). For the controversy on the comet of 1577, see Dreyer, *op. cit.,* IV, 509; C. Doris Hellman, *The Comet of 1577: Its Place in the History of Astronomy* (New York, 1944); and Lynn Thorndike, *A History of Magic and Experimental Science,* 8 vols. (New York, 1923–1958), VI, 67–98, 183–186.

PAUL LAWRENCE ROSE

DUDLEY, ROBERT (*b.* Sheen House, Surrey, England, 7 August 1573; *d.* Villa di Castello, Florence, Italy, 6 September 1649), *navigation.*

Dudley was the son of Robert Dudley, earl of Leicester, and Lady Douglas Sheffield. The legitimacy of Dudley's birth was questioned in his lifetime, yet he was given every advantage commensurate with his father's position in Elizabethan England. He was a student at Christ Church, Oxford, and at the age of twenty-one sailed in command of two ships to the West Indies. In 1596 he was in the battle of Cádiz with the earl of Essex and was knighted for his bravery. In 1605 Dudley left his wife and children in England and traveled to Italy, accompanied by one of the beauties of the day, Elizabeth Southwell. He established himself in Florence, became a Catholic, married Miss Southwell, and entered the service of the grand duke of Tuscany. He was put in charge of several major engineering projects, including the building of the port of Leghorn, and the beginnings of land reclamation near Pisa. He never returned to

England; his assumed titles, earl of Warwick and duke of Northumberland, invalid in England, were confirmed by the Holy Roman Emperor Ferdinand II in recognition of his services.

Dudley's first work, an account of his voyage to the West Indies, was printed by Hakluyt in the second edition of his *Voyages* under the title "A Voyage . . . to the Isle of Trinidad and the Coast of Paria." He had become interested in navigation while at Oxford, and the interest had been further stimulated by his close association with the great sea captain Thomas Cavendish, brother of his first wife. He continued to work on the pressing problems of navigation, including the determination of longitude; made a collection of the best and most advanced navigational instruments, now in the Florence Museum of Science; and at the age of seventy-three published his great work, *Dell'arcano del mare* (three volumes, Florence, 1646–1647). It is one of the great sea atlases of all time, magnificently engraved, and may justly be regarded as an encyclopedia of knowledge regarding the sea. It contains a treatise on naval strategy; a manual of shipbuilding; directions on building coastal fortifications; instructions to navigators, including the essential elements of nautical almanacs; and a set of maps of the entire world. It is these maps that give Dudley's work special significance; *Dell'arcano del mare* is the first sea atlas with all maps drawn on Mercator's projections, as modified by Edward Wright. The maps, virtually without ornamentation and restricted to the information essential to the seaman, are, in spite of errors and imperfections, among the milestones of naval cartography.

BIBLIOGRAPHY

See G. F. Warner's biographical sketch and preface to the Hakluyt Society's edition of Dudley's *Voyage* (London, 1899); and Vaughan Thomas, *The Italian Biography of Sir Robert Dudley* (Oxford, 1861?).

GEORGE KISH

DUFAY (DU FAY), CHARLES-FRANÇOIS DE CISTERNAI (*b.* Paris, France, 14 September 1698; *d.* Paris, 16 July 1739), *physics.*

Dufay came from a family that had followed military careers for over a century. He himself joined the Régiment de Picardie as a lieutenant in 1712, at the warlike age of fourteen; apparently he missed the closing battles of the War of the Spanish Succession, but he participated in the successful siege of Fuenterrabia (1718/1719), which helped force Philip V to abandon his adventures in Italy. Shortly after the campaign, Dufay accompanied his father and Cardi-

nal de Rohan, the leading churchman in France, on an extended visit to Rome (1721). This marked the end of his military service. On his return to France in 1722 he became a candidate for the position of "adjunct chemist" in the Académie des Sciences, Paris.

This step did less violence to family tradition than might appear. Dufay's grandfather, an amateur alchemist who appreciated the value of education, had sent his son, Dufay's father, to the Jesuits at the Collège de Clermont. There he met the future cardinal and contracted a bibliomania that dominated his life after the loss of a leg ended his soldiering in 1695. Dufay grew up among his father's books and erudite friends, "raised, like an ancient Roman, equally for arms and for letters" (Fontenelle). It was very likely Cardinal de Rohan who directed the attention of the scientific establishment toward the unknown young officer. The Academy's leading scientist, Réaumur, and its titular head, the Abbé Bignon, managed Dufay's candidacy, which terminated successfully in May 1723. He became associate chemist in 1724, pensionary in 1731, and director in 1733 and 1738.

Dufay very quickly justified the influence exercised in his favor. His first academic paper (1723), on the mercurial phosphorus, already displayed the characteristics which distinguished his later work: full command of earlier writings, clear prescriptions for producing the phenomena under study, general rules or regularities of their action, thorough study of possible complications or exceptions, and cautious mechanical explanations of a Cartesian flavor. This "phosphor"—the light sometimes visible in the Torricelli space when a barometer is jostled—much perplexed the physicists of the era, primarily because it did not always occur under apparently identical conditions. Dufay found that traces of air or water vapor occasioned the failures, which could be entirely eliminated with a technique of purification taught him by a German glassmaker. He explained the light in terms of Cartesian subtle matter squeezed from the agitated mercury; although he knew the work of Francis Hauksbee (the elder), he suggested no connection with electricity.

This maiden effort, however useful for the development of technique, did not provide a continuing line of research. For several years Dufay flitted from one subject to another: he studied the heat of slaked lime (1724), invented a fire pump (1725), touched on optics (1726), plane geometry (1727), the solubility of glass (1727), and the coloring of artificial gems (1728). He eventually published at least one paper in each of the branches of science recognized by the Academy, the only man, perhaps, who has ever done so. In 1728 he took up magnetism, the first subject to enlist his interest for an extended period. In the first of three memoirs he attacked the vexed question of natural magnetism: Under what conditions, and in what positions, do iron tools acquire a magnetic virtue? The apparent answer—oriented vertically—suggested an easy Cartesian model, for the "hairs" which determine the direction in which the magnetic effluvia pass through the pores of iron might be expected to line up under their gravity when the bodies containing them stand upright. The last two memoirs (1730, 1731), which attempt to measure the force of magnetic poles, are most instructive. Although Dufay took the greatest pains over the experiments, varying sizes, shapes, and measuring devices, he failed to find any simple relation between force and distance; the apparently straightforward procedures of Coulomb in fact are far from obvious.

In 1730 Dufay returned to his original subject, phosphorescence, with a memoir of great importance in the development of his method. Chemists had long been acquainted with a few minerals which, like the Bologna stone (BaS) and Balduin's hermetic phosphor (CaS), glowed after exposure to light. Great mystery surrounded these expensive and supposedly rare substances. Dufay detested mysteries and held as a guiding principle that a given physical property, however bizarre, must be assumed characteristic of a large class of bodies, not of isolated species. He set about calcining precious stones, egg and oyster shells, animal bones, etc., most of which became phosphorescent; indeed, he found that almost everything except metals and very hard gems could be made to shine like Bologna stones. He gave clear recipes for producing the phosphors and patiently examined the endless variations in their colors and intensities: "How differently bodies behave which seemed so similar, and how many varieties there are in effects which seemed identical!" This line of work ended in 1735, with a study of the luminescence of gems. Dufay distinguished excitation by friction, by heat, and by light, and tried to find some general rules of their operation; but the phenomena proved altogether too complex, and he established little more than that diamonds usually can be excited in more ways than lesser stones.

In 1732 Dufay at last found a subject ripe for his practiced talents. A year earlier Stephen Gray had published an account of his discovery that "electricity"—the attractive and repulsive "virtue" of rubbed glass, resins, precious stones, etc.—could be communicated to bodies, like metals or human flesh, which could not be electrified by friction. Gray had also succeeded in transmitting the virtue of a glass tube through lengths of stout cord suspended by silk threads. It appeared to Dufay that electricity, far from

being the parochial, effete effect discussed by earlier writers, was one of nature's favorite phenomena. He proceeded as with the phosphors: first a survey of the existing literature, which became his initial memoir on electricity; next, an attempt to electrify every natural object accessible to experiment. As he expected, all substances properly treated—save metals, animals, and liquids—could be electrified by friction; while all bodies whatsoever could be made so by communication. In the process he distinguished insulators from conductors more sharply than Gray had done and ended the desultory search for new electrics which had characterized the study of electricity since the time of Gilbert.

Dufay's most notable discoveries (1733) resulted from an attempt to clarify the connection between electrostatic attraction and repulsion. Ever since Hauksbee had found that light objects drawn to a glass tube are sometimes forcibly driven from it, physicists had tried to understand the relation between motions toward and away from an excited electric. Hauksbee had given incompatible theories; others, like the Dutch Newtonian W. J. 'sGravesande, taught that the tube possessed an electrical "atmosphere" whose pulsations caused alternate "attractions" and "repulsions," an elegant theory which, however, misrepresents the facts; and still others suspected, as Dufay did initially, that repulsion did not exist at all, an object apparently repelled by an excited electric in fact being drawn away by neighboring bodies electrified by communication. Further experiment suggested another possibility to him: Since substances the least excitable by friction, like the metals, respond most vigorously to the pull of the tube, might not "an electric body attract all those that are not so, and repel all those that become electric by its approach, and by the communication of its virtue?" The apparent confirmation of this capital insight—bits of metal electrified by the tube were found to repel one another—may be regarded as the decisive step in the recognition of electrostatic repulsion, the uncovering of the phenomenological connection between motions toward and away from the tube. It also prepared the way for a detection still more surprising.

Experience had taught Dufay not to draw general conclusions without examining a wide range of substances. Accordingly he tried electrifying one of the two metal bits by a rod of gum copal; the resultant attraction, which flabbergasted him, soon forced him to recognize the existence of two distinct "electricities," and to determine their basic rule of operation. This "bizarrie" (as Dufay called the double electricities) proved a great difficulty for the usual theories of electricity, which relied solely on matter in motion. Dufay expected that a representation in terms of vortices might someday be found, but he did not insist; he was concerned first to establish the regularities and only later to add the mechanical pictures. In this point of method Benjamin Franklin—and not Dufay's protégé the Abbé Nollet—was his lineal descendant.

From his classic researches on the two electricities Dufay turned to Gray's quixotic experiment of the charity boy, the electrification of a small insulated orphan. Playing the leading part himself, Dufay received a sharp shock when an assistant tried to touch him, the stroke penetrating even his waistcoat and shirt; and both he and Nollet noticed that a spark passed just before contact when the experiment was repeated at night. These phenomena utterly astounded him, inured though he was to "meeting the marvelous at every turn." He devoted great effort to studying the electric light, to which his earlier research on phosphors naturally inclined him. Here again he was stopped by the vast complexity of the phenomena, which gave no intelligible clue to the advancement of electrical theory.

Dufay's substantial electrical discoveries—the relation between attraction and repulsion, the two electricities, shocks, and sparking—are but one aspect, and perhaps not the most significant, of his achievement. His insistence on the importance of the subject, on the universal character of electricity, on the necessity of organizing, digesting, and regularizing the known facts before grasping for more, all this helped to introduce order and professional standards into the study of electricity at precisely the moment when the accumulation of data began to require them. He found the subject a hodgepodge of often capricious, disconnected phenomena; he reduced the apparent caprice to rule; and he left electricity in a state where, for the first time, it invited prolonged scrutiny from serious physicists.

Electricity by no means exhausted Dufay's energy or talent; between his sixth and seventh memoirs on the subject, he published papers on parhelia (1735), on fluid mechanics (1736), on dew (1736), on sensitive plants (1736), and on dyestuffs (1737). The last two studies were by-products of still another side of Dufay's ceaseless activity. That on dyestuffs related to an onerous charge he had received from the government, namely the revision of standards for the closely regulated dye industry. The botanical paper grew out of an even larger job, the administration of the Jardin Royal des Plantes.

The Jardin, founded in 1635 as a medical garden and a school of pharmacy and medicine, had extended its functions under the inspired direction of the royal physician, Guy Crescent Fagon, who encouraged the study of chemistry and the expansion of the botanical collections. Regrettably Fagon's successor, Pierre Chirac, a much more limited doctor who cared only for his own profession, neglected the garden and alienated the professors. A nonmedical man was needed to repair the damage. Dufay's industry, wide interests, and practical good sense, not to mention his ministerial connections, made him an ideal administrator. With the advice of his friends the brothers Jussieu, who held chairs at the Jardin, Dufay replanted, built new greenhouses for foreign flora, and established close relations, including exchanges of specimens, with the directors of similar institutions elsewhere in Europe. His official visits to Holland and England (1733/1734), accompanied by Bernard de Jussieu and Nollet, advanced not only French botany, but—through connections formed by Nollet—French experimental physics as well. In the seven years of his intendancy Dufay transformed Chirac's collection of weeds into "the most beautiful garden in Europe" (Fontenelle), providing the basis for the great expansion effected by his successor, the comte de Buffon.

Dufay's diverse activities made him a careful economist of his time. Although his position, acquaintance, and good humor opened endless opportunities for social engagements, he preferred to live quietly, finding relaxation in the satires of Swift, in the small circle of his mother's friends, or at the home of a kindred soul like the marquise du Châtelet. He never married. It was a great blow to French science (and a measure of its incompetence) when, at the age of forty, Dufay succumbed to the smallpox.

BIBLIOGRAPHY

Dufay's chief papers were published in the *Mémoires de l'Académie des sciences* (Paris). Among the most important are "Mémoire sur les baromètres lumineux" (1723), 295–306; "Observations sur quelques expériences de l'aimant" (1728), 355–369; "Suite des observations sur l'aimant" (1730), 142–157; "Mémoire sur un grand nombre de phosphores nouveaux" (1730), 524–535; "Troisième mémoire sur l'aimant" (1731), 417–432; "Mémoires sur l'électricité" (1733), 23–35, 73–84, 233–254, 457–476; (1734), 341–361, 503–526; (1737), 86–100, 307–325; and "Recherches sur la lumière des diamants et de plusieurs autres matières" (1735), 347–372. Dufay summarized his first electrical memoirs in "A Letter . . . Concerning Electricity," in *Philosophical Transactions of the Royal Society,* **38** (1733/1734), 258–266.

A full bibliography of the French papers is given in *Nouvelle table des articles contenus dans les volumes de l'Académie royale des sciences de Paris depuis 1666 jusqu'en 1770* (Paris, 1775/1776), and in P. Brunet, "L'oeuvre scientifique de Charles-François Du Fay (1698–1739)," in *Petrus nonius,* **3,** no. 2 (1940), 1–19. Poggendorff omits several items published after 1735. I. B. Cohen, *Franklin and Newton* (Philadelphia, 1956), p. 616, gives complete titles of the memoirs on electricity. Dufay autographs are quite rare. There are a few unimportant letters among the Sloane Manuscripts at the British Museum; a dossier including notes of Hauksbee's work and correspondence with Gray's collaborator, Granville Wheler, at the Institut de France; several letters to Réaumur published in *La correspondance historique et archéologique,* **5** (1898), 306–309; and a few administrative documents noticed in A.-M. Bidal, "Inventaire des archives du Muséum national d'histoire naturelle," in *Archives du Muséum,* **11** (1934), 175–230.

The biographical sources are surprisingly meager. The most important is Fontenelle's "Éloge de M. Du Fay," in *Histoire de l'Académie des sciences* (1739), 73–83; scattered data appear in G. Martin, *Bibliotheca fayana* (Paris, 1725); *Les lettres da la marquise du Châtelet,* T. Besterman, ed. (Geneva, 1958); *Correspondence of Voltaire,* T. Besterman, ed. (Geneva, 1953–1965); and J. Torlais, *Un esprit encyclopédique en dehors de l'Encyclopédie. Réaumur,* 2nd ed. (Paris, 1961).

For assessments of Dufay's scientific work see the publications of Brunet and Cohen cited above; H. Becquerel, "Notice sur Charles François de Cisternai du Fay . . . ," in *Centenaire de la fondation du Muséum d'histoire naturelle* (Paris, 1893), pp. 163–185; J. Daujat, *Origines et formation de la théorie des phénomènes électriques et magnétiques* (Paris, 1945); and E. N. Harvey, *A History of Luminescence* (Philadelphia, 1957). For Dufay's administrative accomplishments see A.-L. de Jussieu, "Quatrième notice historique sur le Muséum d'histoire naturelle," in *Annales du Muséum,* **4** (1804), 1–19; and the bibliography in Y. Laissus, "Le Jardin du Roi," in R. Taton, ed., *Enseignement et diffusion des sciences en France au XVIIIe siècle* (Paris, 1964), pp. 287–341.

JOHN L. HEILBRON

DUFOUR, GUILLAUME-HENRI (*b.* Constance, Switzerland, 15 September 1787; *d.* Les Contamines [near Geneva], Switzerland, 14 July 1875), *technology.*

Dufour's family came from Geneva, where he studied military engineering. He also studied at the École Polytechnique in Paris and the École de Génie at Metz. When Geneva was incorporated into the French territory, he served as a sublieutenant in the army of his new country. In 1813, he was in Napoleon's army defending Corfu and had become a captain by the time of the fall of the Empire. In 1817 he returned to Switzerland and was appointed *ingénieur cantonal.* His work on fortification at Grenoble and his construction works in Geneva—which greatly improved the city—made him well-known. In 1818, he became the chief instructor of the military school that he had helped to establish at Thun.

When Geneva was reintegrated into Switzerland, Dufour joined the Swiss army. He was made a colonel in 1827. In 1831 he became chief of staff, and in 1833 he commanded a division that restored order in Basel. He began his pioneering work in triangulation the same year in order to prepare topographical maps of the Confederation. The maps were later published (1842–1864). He was elected a general of the Swiss army in 1847, during the Sonderbund War, again in 1849 to preserve Swiss neutrality, in 1856 during the conflict with Prussia over Neuchâtel, and finally—for the fourth time—in 1859, when the French threatened to annex Savoy. He was a conservative member of the federal assembly, and in 1864 presided over the Geneva international congress which drew up the rules for treatment of the wounded in wartime and resulted in the creation of the Red Cross.

A bronze equestrian statue of Dufour stands in the Place Neuve in Geneva.

BIBLIOGRAPHY

I. ORIGINAL WORKS. Dufour's works include *Cours de tactique* (Paris, 1840); *De la fortification permanente* (Geneva, 1822); *Mémoire sur l'artillerie des anciens et sur celle du moyen âge* (Paris, 1840); and *Mémorial pour les travaux de guerre* (Geneva, 1820).

II. SECONDARY LITERATURE. See also E. Chapuisat, *Le Général Dufour,* 2nd ed. (Lausanne, 1942); and T. Stark, *La famille du général Dufour et les Polonais* (Geneva, 1955).

ASIT K. BISWAS

DUFRÉNOY, OURS-PIERRE-ARMAND (*b.* Sevran, Seine-et-Oise, France, 5 September 1792; *d.* Paris, France, 20 March 1857), *geology, mineralogy.*

With Élie de Beaumont and under the direction of Brochant de Villiers, Dufrénoy prepared the first modern geological map of France. He published over sixty memoirs on geology and crystallographic and chemical mineralogy and an important mineralogical work entitled *Traité de minéralogie.* As the inspector of courses and later director of the École des Mines, he instituted important changes in the curriculum and teaching methods.

Dufrénoy's father had been Voltaire's literary agent, and his mother, Adélaïde, was a scholar of the classics and an accomplished poet. Thus the boy grew up in an intellectual atmosphere despite the family's extreme poverty, occasioned by the French Revolution and the father's loss of eyesight. Dufrénoy first attended the lycée at Rouen and then the Lycée Louis-le-Grand in Paris. He won the first prize in mathematics at the general examinations in 1810 and entered the École Polytechnique in 1811. In 1813 he was admitted to the École des Mines, at that time located at Peisey in Tarentaise (Savoy), and he returned with it when the school was moved to Paris in 1816. In 1818 he was named engineer of mines and head of the collections at the École des Mines. Stimulated by the publication of Greenough's geological map of England, Brochant de Villiers was successful in gaining authorization for the preparation of a similar map of France. Dufrénoy and Élie de Beaumont were selected to carry out the necessary fieldwork and in 1822 were sent to England for two years to learn Greenough's procedures. As a result of this visit, Dufrénoy and Élie de Beaumont coauthored a work entitled *Voyage métallurgique en Angleterre,* which described in detail the mining and metallurgical industries of England.

For the French geological map Dufrénoy was assigned the area south and west of a line running from Honfleur, Alençon, Avallon, Chalons-sur-Saône, and the Rhone. Each summer from 1825 to 1829 Dufrénoy and Élie de Beaumont made field trips, surveying and taking notes on their respective areas; from 1830 to 1834 they traveled together in order to resolve difficulties and coordinate their work. They published their notes between 1830 and 1838 and the explanation of their map in 1841. The map was on a scale of 1:500,000, and the explanation was essentially a physical description of France, together with the history, composition, and disposition of its terrain. They did not perform any detailed stratigraphic work. The regions of the Pyrenees and Britanny had hardly been explored geologically at that time, and Dufrénoy's work in these areas was excellent. He was admitted to membership in the Académie des Sciences in 1840, and in 1843 the Geological Society of London presented the Wollaston Medal to Dufrénoy and Élie de Beaumont jointly for their work.

While preparing the geological map, Dufrénoy was also engaged in other important studies. In 1830 he determined that the large coal deposits in the department of Aveyron could be used directly in various metallurgical processes, as the English had been doing; his study resulted in the establishment of industries at Decazeville. In 1832 he was sent to Scotland to study the use of high-temperature air in iron blast furnaces, and his detailed report caused the French iron industry to adopt this practice immediately. He also studied the thermal springs at Vichy and drew up plans for their exploitation.

Dufrénoy served as assistant professor of mineralogy at the École des Mines from 1827 to 1835 and as professor from 1835 to 1848. In 1836 he became inspector of courses there and director of the school in 1846, so that, in effect, he governed instruction in

the institution for twenty years, until his death in 1857. During his tenure Dufrénoy introduced to courses the use of specimens from the rich mineralogical collection, and he modernized the curriculum by adding courses in railway construction, law, economics, and paleontology. He entered the Conseil des Mines in 1846 and was promoted to the superior grade in 1851. After Brongniart's death in 1847, Dufrénoy was named professor of mineralogy at the Muséum d'Histoire Naturelle.

BIBLIOGRAPHY

I. ORIGINAL WORKS. With Élie de Beaumont, Dufrénoy published the following works: *Voyage métallurgique en Angleterre,* 2 vols. (Paris, 1827); *Mémoires pour servir à une description géologique de la France,* 4 vols. (Paris, 1830–1838); and *Explication de la carte géologique de la France, rédigée sous la direction de M. Brochant de Villiers,* 3 vols. (Paris, 1841). In addition, Dufrénoy published *Mémoire sur la position géologique des principales mines de fer de la partie orientale des Pyrénées* (Paris, 1834); and *Traité de minéralogie,* 4 vols. (Paris, 1844–1847). His sixty-five memoirs were published principally in the *Journal des mines,* the *Annales des mines,* and the *Annales de chimie et de physique.*

II. SECONDARY WORKS. On Dufrénoy or his work, see A. d'Archiac, *Notice sur la vie et les travaux de P. A. Dufrénoy* (Paris, 1860); A. Daubrée, "Dufrénoy," in *École polytechnique: Livre du centenaire 1794–1894,* I (Paris, 1895), 375–381; and A. Lacroix, "Notice historique sur le troisième fauteuil de la section de minéralogie," in *Académie des sciences—séance publique annuelle du lundi 17 décembre 1928* (Paris, 1928), pp. 24–33.

JOHN G. BURKE

DUGAN, RAYMOND SMITH (*b.* Montague, Massachusetts, 30 May 1878; *d.* Philadelphia, Pennsylvania, 31 August 1940), *astronomy.*

Dugan devoted over half his life to the study of eclipsing variables—those pairs of stars which by chance have orbits almost edge on to us and therefore appear to vary in brightness because of repeated mutual eclipses. His prolonged and careful observations resulted in a wealth of information about many fundamental properties of stars. He also collaborated with Henry Norris Russell in writing one of the best elementary astronomy texts of this century.

His mother, Mary Evelyn Smith Dugan, was of Puritan stock, and his father, Jeremiah Welby Dugan, was but one generation removed from Ireland. After receiving a B.A. degree from Amherst College in 1899, Dugan went to Beirut (then Syria) to serve both as instructor in mathematics and astronomy and as acting director of the observatory in the Syrian Protestant College (now American University). Here he remained until 1902, when Amherst granted him an M.A. degree and he transferred to the University of Heidelberg to work and study for three years under Max Wolf. During this period he discovered eighteen asteroids, found two new variable stars, and earned a Ph.D. degree with a dissertation on the star cluster known as the Pleiades.

Having taken part in the Lick Observatory expedition to Alhama de Aragón, Spain, for the solar eclipse of 30 August 1905, Dugan returned to the United States to become instructor in astronomy at Princeton University. In 1909 he married Annette Rumford Odiorne, and in 1920 he was named professor, which rank he held until death terminated his thirty-five-year association with Princeton.

Endowed with what a contemporary referred to as "the world's most accurate photometric eyes," Dugan used Princeton's twenty-three-inch telescope with a polarizing photometer to make long series of observations on a selected few eclipsing variables; for several of them this involved more than 18,000 individual settings. The resulting light curves, when analyzed according to methods developed in large part by his colleague Russell, revealed the relative sizes of the two stars, how far apart they were, their individual surface brightnesses, mutual tidally induced distortions into ellipsoids, and even how their densities varied from center to periphery. Dugan was the first to detect the so-called reflection effect, a brightening of the fainter member on the side facing its more luminous partner. He also found evidence that even widely separated pairs could be tidally distorted; furthermore he was able to explain some of the gradually lengthening periods of revolution that he observed as resulting from tidal evolution.

Dugan was elected a member of the American Philosophical Society in 1931 and served from 1935 until his death as chairman of the Commission on Variable Stars of the International Astronomical Union. He was also secretary of the American Astronomical Society from 1927 to 1936 and vice-president from 1936 to 1938.

BIBLIOGRAPHY

I. Original Works. The textbook referred to above was by Henry Norris Russell, Raymond Smith Dugan, and John Quincy Stewart, *Astronomy,* I. *The Solar System* (Boston, 1926; rev. ed., 1945), II. *Astrophysics and Stellar Astronomy* (Boston, 1927; repr. with supp. material, 1938).

Dugan's discoveries of asteroids were reported in *Astronomische Nachrichten,* **160** (1902–1903), cols. 183, 216; **161** (1903), col. 143; **162** (1903), cols. 15, 111, 160; **163** (1903), cols. 255, 285, 379; **164** (1903–1904), cols. 15, 191, 224; **165**

(1904), cols. 110, 191; his discovery of two variable stars, *ibid.,* col. 43. A shortened version of his dissertation also appeared in *Astronomische Nachrichten,* **166** (1904), 49–56; the full text, "Helligkeiten und mittlere Örter von 359 Sternen der Plejaden-Gruppe," is in *Publikationen des Astrophysikalischen Observatoriums Königstuhl-Heidelberg,* **2** (1906), 29–55. His work on eclipsing variables, under the general title "Photometric Researches," makes up (if four papers by his students are included) 17 of the 19 *Contributions From the Princeton University Observatory* that appeared between 1911 and 1940: details concerning equipment and observing techniques are in "The Algol System RT Persei," in no. 1 (1911), 1–47, with a shortened version published in *Monthly Notices of the Royal Astronomical Society,* **75** (1915), 692–702; his first detection of the reflection effect is described in "The Algol System Z Draconis," in no. 2 (1912), 1–44, with a shortened version in *Monthly Notices of the Royal Astronomical Society,* **75** (1915), 702–710; confirmation of the reflection effect and observation of ellipsoidal shapes in widely separated pairs appeared in "The Eclipsing Variables RV Ophiuchi and RZ Cassiopeiae," in no. 4 (1916), 1–38, also covered in *Astrophysical Journal,* **43** (1916), 130–144, and **44** (1916), 117–123, and for RZ Cassiopeiae alone in *Monthly Notices of the Royal Astronomical Society,* **76** (1916), 729–739; his first evidence for a lengthening period, indicating tidal evolution, is in "The Eclipsing Variable U Cephei," in no. 5 (1920), 1–34, with a shortened version in *Astrophysical Journal,* **52** (1920), 154–161; the first evidence for radial variation in density appeared in "The Eclipsing Variable Y Cygni," in no. 12 (1931), 1–50; and his critical summary of the first twenty-nine years of his work at Princeton is in the introduction to "A Finding List for Observers of Eclipsing Variables," in no. 15 (1934), 1–33.

For insight into the conditions under which Dugan worked (and a taste of his dry wit), see "The Old Princeton Observatory and the New," in *Popular Astronomy,* **43** (1935), 146–151, repr. from *Princeton Alumni Weekly* (2 Oct. 1934).

The list of Dugan's publications in Poggendorff, VI, 612, and VIIb, 1149–1150, is complete except for some early items (included above).

II. Secondary Literature. Obituary notices on Dugan by Henry Norris Russell appeared in *Popular Astronomy,* **48** (1940), 466–469; *Science,* n.s. **92** (1940), 231; and *Yearbook of the American Philosophical Society* (1940), 419–420. Other brief notices are listed in Poggendorff, VIIb (see above). Dugan's entry in *Who Was Who in America,* I (Chicago, 1943) appears on p. 344.

Sally H. Dieke

DUGGAR, BENJAMIN MINGE (*b.* Gallion, Alabama, 1 September 1872; *d.* New Haven, Connecticut, 10 September 1956), *plant pathology.*

The fourth of six sons of a country practitioner, Duggar entered the University of Alabama shortly before his fifteenth birthday, but a compelling interest in agricultural science led him to transfer after two years to the Mississippi Agricultural and Mechanical College (now Mississippi State College). Shortly after graduation (1891) Duggar found a sympathetic mentor in George F. Atkinson at Alabama Polytechnic Institute, where he served one year as assistant in mycology and plant physiology and received his M.Sc. for the carefully documented thesis "Germination of Teleutospores of Ravenelia Cassiaecola." He spent an additional year as assistant director of the Agricultural Experiment Station at Uniontown, Alabama, before transferring to Harvard. Here, from 1893 to 1895, he worked under W. G. Farlow and Roland Thaxter, taught botany at Radcliffe, and completed required courses in the humanities that finally brought him a highly cherished Harvard M.A. After another year of fieldwork—this one concerned with the wheat-devastating chinch bug in Illinois—Duggar rejoined Atkinson, at Cornell. Here he concentrated on chemistry and fungus spore germination and completed the work required for the Ph.D.

Traveling in Europe for a year (1899–1900) Duggar studied with such eminent authorities as Wilhelm Pfeffer at Leipzig and Georg Klebs and Julius Kühn, both at Halle. Returning to America, he spent one year as plant physiologist with the Bureau of Plant Industry of the U. S. Department of Agriculture. There he developed a lasting interest in cotton diseases and mushroom culture. While continuing to serve as consultant to the bureau, Duggar accepted his first major educational post, as professor of botany and head of the department at the University of Missouri (1902). For an exhibit of mushrooms and other fungi he was awarded a grand prize at the St. Louis Fair (1904). Another foreign tour (1905–1906) took him first to Munich, where he worked with Karl von Goebel at the Botanical Institute, and later to Bonn, Montpellier, and Algiers. Returning to Cornell as professor of plant physiology, Duggar completed two major works: *Fungus Diseases of Plants* (New York, 1909), the first monograph in any language devoted exclusively to the subject of plant pathology, which remained a standard text for many years, and *Plant Physiology With Special Reference to Plant Production* (New York, 1911).

Duggar next returned to Missouri as research professor of plant physiology at Washington University and director of the Missouri Botanical Garden. Studies of this period include those on red pigment formation in the tomato, enzymes in red algae, nitrogen fixation, and methods for determining hydrogen concentration in biological fluids. During World War I, Duggar contributed valuable data on the salt requirements of higher plants. He later (1920) turned his attention to the serious problem of the tobacco mosaic virus, becoming a leading investigator in this field.

After fifteen years at Washington University, Duggar accepted his last university assignment, the professorship of plant physiology and economic botany at the University of Wisconsin, a post he held from 1927 to 1943, when he retired emeritus. But the most rewarding period of his career was yet to come. During World War II he served as adviser to the National Economic Council, and in 1944 he accepted a position as consultant in mycological research with the Lederle Division of the American Cyanamid Company. After a short period devoted to the investigation of antimalarial drugs, Duggar turned his attention to the quest for new antibiotic-producing organisms. A three-year study of *Streptomyces aureofaciens* led to the introduction of chlortetracycline (Aureomycin) (1948), another milestone in the story of man's attempt to conquer pathogenic bacteria.

Duggar, a man of great enthusiasm and physical vitality, played a dynamic role in organizing plant scientists in America. A founder of the American Society of Agronomy (1907) and the American Phytopathological Society (1908), he was also active in the American Association for the Advancement of Science, the American Society of Naturalists, the American Botanical Society (president, 1923), and the American Society of Plant Physiologists (president, 1947). A voluminous writer, he also was editor of several important publications, including *Proceedings of the International Congress of Plant Sciences* (1926); *Biological Effects of Radiation* (1936), for which he wrote a chapter, "Effects of Radiation on Bacteria"; and *Botanical Abstracts for Physiology* (1917–1926). When the latter publication was absorbed by *Biological Abstracts,* he continued as editor of the plant physiology section (1926–1933).

Among the many honors bestowed on Duggar were membership in the American Philosophical Society (1921) and the National Academy of Sciences (1927), as well as honorary degrees from Missouri (LL.D., 1944), Washington (Sc.D., 1953), and Wisconsin (D.Sc., 1956). A modest individual, although always a perfectionist, Duggar enjoyed many aspects of life to the fullest. His marriage in 1901 to Marie L. Robertson (*d.* 1922) produced two sons and three daughters. A second marriage to Elsie Rist (1927) produced one daughter.

As a scientist Duggar helped to advance research in his chosen field from the era of morphology to the modern period, with its emphasis on physiology. Certainly his pioneer work of 1909 has already won a secure place among the classics of American science, and the discovery of Aureomycin assures Duggar an honored position in the history of medicine.

BIBLIOGRAPHY

A biography is J. C. Walker, "Benjamin Minge Duggar," in *Biographical Memoirs. National Academy of Sciences,* **32** (1958), 113–131, with bibliography and photograph.

See also "Benjamin Minge Duggar," in *Current Biography 1952* (1953), pp. 166–169.

MORRIS H. SAFFRON

DU HAMEL, JEAN-BAPTISTE (*b.* Vire, Normandy, France, 11 June 1623; *d.* Paris, France, 6 August 1706), *institutional history.*

Although usually designated an anatomist, this distinguished priest and humanist had in reality no such specialized scientific interests and indeed owes his fame primarily to the high office that he held from 1666 to 1697 in the first great French institution. His successor Fontenelle, who knew him well, suggested that du Hamel inherited from his lawyer father a talent for conciliation. Certainly he inherited from his family a sensitivity to social relations in the legal milieu in general, and the manner in which he exploited his heritage has earned him a place in the history of science.

In Paris, du Hamel completed the studies in rhetoric and philosophy that he had begun in Caen. He immediately applied his talents to mathematics at the scholarly institution called the Académie Royale, which was being enlivened by the Jesuits. His short treatise *Elementa astronomica* (1643), intended as a primer on astronomy, testifies to his ability. Having already taken minor orders, he was admitted to the Institution de l'Oratoire in Paris on Christmas day of 1643. In September 1644 he was sent to the Collège Université of Angers, where he taught philosophy with great success and where he was ordained a priest in 1649. In October 1652 he was recalled to the house in the rue St. Honoré to instruct the young Oratorians in positive theology. But at the request of his lawyer brother, who sought his aid in ecclesiastical matters, he left the Oratory in 1653. He became a curé in Neuilly-sur-Marne until 1663. During these ten years he was both a zealous pastor and an industrious intellectual. The works that he published in 1660 and 1663 assure his reputation and reflect perfectly his scholarly personality.

Directed to a lay audience, these works outlined the then current state of physics and of philosophical disputes. Their originality lies in the effort to emphasize what is valuable in the ancients for the moderns, in an interesting compilation of knowledge in the era following the death of Descartes.

Appointed royal chaplain in 1656, du Hamel relinquished the vicariate of Neuilly in 1663 to assist the bishop of Bayeux in Paris as chancellor. In 1666 the founding of the Académie Royale des Sciences brought him another office. As Fontenelle said, he had given, without intending to, evidence of all the qualities necessary in a secretary of the new organization. The choice proved to be judicious.

From 1668 to 1670 he attended the marquis of Croissy at the negotiations of Aix-la-Chapelle, at which an expert Latinist was required, and then accompanied him to England and the Netherlands on diplomatic missions. Du Hamel resumed his position at the academy, enriched by his contact with foreign scholars, notably Boyle and Oldenburg.

His zeal in the service of secular knowledge was soon tempered, however. He dedicated himself increasingly to important publications for the sacred sciences. Without doubting the sincerity of the scruples that he expressed with regard to his sacerdotal state, one may suppose that with time, and for a variety of reasons, his responsibilities at the Academy became more trying. The Academy had not maintained its original distinction and in the last decade of the seventeenth century was afflicted with various ills that threatened to hasten its demise. Surrounded by the debates of an advancing science and suffering from faults in its administrative organization, the institution was in need of reform as well as protection. By securing his position for as long as possible and by passing it on to Fontenelle in 1697, du Hamel certainly assisted in preserving the Academy, at the same time that he published the first printed summary of its history.

A pensionary anatomist in the revived Academy of 1699, du Hamel once again saw how to make way for a qualified member, Littré Alenis. In the larger interest of science he permitted Varignon, in 1701, to assume the chair of Greek and Latin philosophy, which he had held since 1682, at the Collège de France.

A man of the Church who had a deep inner life, du Hamel put the advantages of his position and background in the service of the broadest scientific progress.

BIBLIOGRAPHY

I. ORIGINAL WORKS. The following list includes only those works concerning science and its history: *Elementa astronomica ubi Theodosii Tripolitae sphaericorum libri tres cum universa triangulorum resolutione nova succincta et facillime arte demonstrantur* (Paris, 1643), some eds. with the commentary on Euclid by P. Georges Fournier, S.J., one of which eds. was repr. (London, 1654); *Astronomia physica, seu de luce, natura et motibus corporum caelestium, libri duo . . . Accessere P.Petiti observationes aliquot eclypsium solis et lunae* (Paris, 1660); *De meteoribus et fossilibus libri duo* (Paris, 1660); *De consensu veteris et novae philosophiae ubi Platonis, Aristotelis, Epicuri, Cartesii aliorumque placita de principiis rerum excutiuntur et de principiis chymicis* (Paris, 1663); *De corporum affectionibus tum manifestis tum occultis libri duo* (Paris, 1670); *De mente humana libri quatuor* (Paris, 1672); *De corpore animato libri quatuor* (Paris, 1673); and *Regiae scientiarum academiae historia* (Paris, 1698), 2nd augmented ed. (Paris, 1701).

II. SECONDARY LITERATURE. On du Hamel and his work, see "Mémoire sur la vie et les écrits de J. B. du Hamel, prieur de St. Lambert," in *Journal des sçavans,* supp. (Feb. 1707), pp. 88–94 (author anon.); Fontenelle, "Éloge de Mr. du Hamel," in *Histoire et mémoires de l'Académie royale des sciences,* pt. 1 (Paris, 1707), pp. 142–153; Louis Batterel, *Mémoires domestiques pour servir à l'histoire de l'Oratoire,* Bonnardet-Ingold, ed., III (Paris, 1904), 142–155; and a medallion in *Museum Mazzuchelianum seu numismata virorum doctrina praestantium,* II (Venice, 1761), 89 and pl. 120, no. 4.

PIERRE COSTABEL

DUHAMEL, JEAN-MARIE-CONSTANT (*b.* St.-Malo, France, 5 February 1797; *d.* Paris, France, 29 April 1872), *mathematics, physics.*

Duhamel's scientific contributions were minor but numerous and pertinent; his teaching and involvement in academic administration were probably the primary sources of his influence. Today his name is best remembered for Duhamel's principle in partial differential equations;[1] Duhamel obtained this theorem in the context of his work on the mathematical theory of heat. Using the techniques of mathematical physics he also studied topics of acoustics. In his interests and approaches Duhamel was clearly in the tradition of the French *géomètres.*

Duhamel entered the École Polytechnique in Paris in 1814, after studying at the lycée of Rennes. The political events of 1816, which caused a reorganization of the school, obliged him to return to Rennes, where he studied law. He then taught in Paris at the Institution Massin and the Collège Louis-le-Grand (probably mathematics and physics) and founded a preparatory school, later known as the École Sainte-Barbe. The subject of his first memoir, presented in 1828,[2] indicates that by this time he was quite involved in current problems of mathematical physics.

Except for one year, Duhamel taught continuously at the École Polytechnique from 1830 to 1869. He was first given provisional charge of the analysis course, replacing Coriolis. He was made assistant lecturer in geodesy in 1831, entrance examiner in 1835, professor of analysis and mechanics in 1836, permanent examiner in 1840, and director of studies in 1844. The commission of 1850 demanded his removal because he resisted a program for change, but he returned as professor of analysis in 1851, replacing Liouville. Duhamel also taught at the École Normale Supérieure and at the Sorbonne. He was known as a good teacher, and students commented especially on his ability to clarify the concept of the infinitesimal, a topic also emphasized in his text.[3] Duhamel's most famous student was his nephew by marriage, J. L. F. Bertrand.

Duhamel's earliest research dealt with the mathematical theory of heat and was based on the work of Fourier and Poisson. It was the subject of the theses, accepted in 1834,[4] that he submitted to the Faculty of Sciences. His first memoir treated heat propagation in solids of nonisotropic conductivity, and the laws that he obtained were later verified experimentally by Henri de Sénarmont.[5] In 1833 Duhamel published a solution for the temperature distribution in a solid with variable boundary temperature. He was considering the situations in which the surface radiates into a medium and in which the temperature of the medium changes according to a known law. His object was to reduce these cases to those of a surface at constant temperature. His method, based on the principle of superposition, generalized a solution by Fourier and substituted, in place of the original temperature function, the sum of a constant temperature term and an integral term (an integral of the rate of change of the temperature function).[6] This method generalizes to Duhamel's principle.

In acoustics Duhamel studied the vibrations of strings, the vibrations of air in cylindrical and conical pipes, and harmonic overtones. For an experimental check on his analysis of a weighted string Duhamel used a novel method whereby a pointer attached to the string leaves a track on a moving plane. His study of the excitation of vibration by the violin bow, based on Poisson's *Mécanique,* used the expression for friction force that had been experimentally determined by Coulomb and Morin. Duhamel was intrigued by harmonic overtones and suggested, independently of Ohm,[7] that one perceives a complex sound as the group of simultaneous sounds into which its vibrations can be decomposed.[8]

NOTES

1. For example, R. Courant and D. Hilbert, *Methods of Mathematical Physics,* II (New York, 1966), 202–204.
2. Published in 1832.
3. Commenting on the disagreement among mathematicians over definitions of the differential, Duhamel pointed out in an introductory note to the second edition of his *Cours d'analyse* (Paris, 1847) that he had changed his own approach. Instead of considering the differential as an infinitely small addition to the

variable, as he had done in the first edition, he was now considering differentials as quantities whose ratios in the limit are the same as the ratios of the variables.

4. *Théorie mathématique de la chaleur* (Paris, 1834) and *De l'influence du double mouvement des planètes sur les températures de leur différents points* (Paris, 1834).

5. "Sur la conductibilité des corps cristallisés pour la chaleur," in *Annales de chimie*, **21** (1847), 457–476; "Second mémoire sur la conductibilité des corps cristallisés pour la chaleur," in *Comptes rendus hebdomadaires des séances de l'Académie des sciences*, **25** (1847), 459–461, 707–710; *Annales de chimie*, **22** (1848), 179–211.

6. For a modern discussion of Duhamel's principle and its use in solving heat problems, see H. S. Carslaw and J. C. Jaeger, *Conduction of Heat in Solids*, 2nd ed. (Oxford, 1959), 30–32.

7. G. S. Ohm, "Ueber die Definition des Tons, nebst daran geknüpfter Theorie der Sirene und ähnlicher tonbildender Vorrichtungen," in *Annalen der Physik*, **59** (1843), 513–566.

8. *Comptes rendus*, **27** (1848), 463.

BIBLIOGRAPHY

I. ORIGINAL WORKS. A partial listing of Duhamel's textbooks includes *Cours d'analyse*, 2 vols. (Paris, 1840–1841; 2nd ed., 1847); *Cours de mécanique*, 2 vols. (Paris, 1845–1846; 2nd ed., 1853–1854); *Éléments de calcul infinitésimal*, 2 vols. (Paris, 1856; 2nd ed., 1860–1861); *Des méthodes dans les sciences de raisonnement*, 3 vols. (Paris, 1865–1873).

His articles include "Sur les équations générales de la propagation de la chaleur dans les corps solides dont la conductibilité n'est pas la même dans tous les sens," in *Journal de l'École polytechnique*, **13** (1832), *cahier* 21, 356–399; "Sur la méthode générale relative au mouvement de la chaleur dans les corps solides plongés dans des milieux dont la température varie avec le temps," in *Journal de l'École polytechnique*, **14** (1833), *cahier* 22, 20–77; "De l'action de l'archet sur les cordes," in *Comptes rendus hebdomadaires des séances de l'Académie des sciences,* **9** (1839), 567–569; **10** (1840), 855–861; *Mémoires présentés par divers savants à l'Académie des sciences*, **8** (1843) 131–162; "Mémoire sur les vibrations des gaz dans les tuyaux de diverses formes," in *Comptes rendus hebdomadaires des séances de l'Académie des sciences*, **8** (1839), 542–543; *Journal de mathématiques pures et appliquées*, **14** (1849), 49–110; "Sur les vibrations d'une corde flexible chargée d'un ou de plusieurs curseurs," in *Journal de l'École polytechnique,* **17** (1843), *cahier* 29, 1–36; "Sur la résonnance multiple des corps," in *Comptes rendus hebdomadaires des séances de l'Académie des sciences,* **27** (1848), 457–463; and "Sur la propagation de la chaleur dans les cristaux," in *Journal de l'École polytechnique,* **19** (1848), *cahier* 32, 155–188.

For an extended list of Duhamel's papers, see the *Royal Society Catalogue of Scientific Papers, 1800–1863,* II (1868), 376–377; and *1864–1873,* VII (1877), 569.

II. SECONDARY LITERATURE. Not much material is available on Duhamel. For short accounts, see Louis Figuier, *L'année scientifique et industrielle* (*1872*), XVI (Paris, 1873), 537–540; M. Maximilien Marie, *Histoire des sciences mathématiques et physiques*, XII (Paris, 1888), 220–224; and E. Sarrau, "Duhamel," in *École polytechnique, livre du centenaire 1794–1894*, I (Paris, 1894–1897), 126–130.

SIGALIA DOSTROVSKY

DUHAMEL DU MONCEAU, HENRI-LOUIS (*b.* Paris, France, 1700; *d.* Paris, 23 August 1782), *agronomy, chemistry, botany, naval technology.*

The son of Alexandre Duhamel (the name can be found variously listed as Hamel, du Hamel, or Monceau), *seigneur* of the estate of Denainvilliers in Gâtinais, Duhamel was a wealthy but minor member of the French landed gentry. Although the stories about Duhamel's problems at the Collège d'Harcourt have been rather exaggerated for effect, there is little doubt that he began to apply himself seriously only after hearing science lectures at the Jardin du Roi in the 1720's. During this time he became acquainted with the younger group of French scientists, such as the chemist Charles-François Dufay and the botanist Bernard de Jussieu, as well as with such established members of the scientific community as Louis Lémery and Étienne-François Geoffroy.

Duhamel first achieved scientific recognition with his explanation of the cause of a blight which attacked the saffron plant with particular ferocity in the 1720's. This study, unusual from its inception because it was given by the Academy to a nonmember, showed that the disease was caused by a plant parasite which spread underground from one saffron bulb to another. The work, read to the Academy in April 1728, was well-conceived, thorough, and conclusive, and led to his election as *adjoint chimiste* in the same year.

The choice of position was partly due to a lack of openings in botany, but it was not unreasonable in absolute terms since Duhamel's breadth of interests was somewhat surprising even for an eighteenth-century polymath. Moreover, although his early researches for the Academy were devoted to botanical subjects, he undertook a series of chemical investigations in the early 1730's in collaboration with the chemist Jean Grosse. These included an attempt to make tartar soluble and the well-known study of Frobenius' ether, which, if one can accept Duhamel's testimony, was carried out largely by Grosse. In the mid-1730's Duhamel investigated contrasting claims for the synthesis of sal ammoniac and examined the nature of the purple dye commonly obtained from shellfish. His most important work in chemistry during this period was "Sur la base du sel marin," read in January 1737, in which he argued that there were different fixed alkaline components of salts and that these were essentially soda and potash. Although challenged by the German chemist J. H. Pott, Duhamel made this important idea credible. He occasionally undertook chemical projects in later years, but other interests, primarily botany and agronomy, occupied most of his remaining working life. One of these interests was in the cultivation and use of timber. With his primary interest in plants, Duhamel was made *associé botaniste* of the Academy in 1730; and in 1732 he was appointed *inspecteur général de la marine,* with the understanding that his duties would include supervising the timber to be used in the French navy. His experiences in this position led to several studies published in the 1740's on the structural properties of wood and on management of tree stands, and to his first book (1747), a treatise on the rigging of ships.

But Duhamel's major interest and contribution to technology and society was in agriculture. The first half of the eighteenth century had witnessed the beginning of a technological renaissance in agriculture, chiefly in England, where it was notably celebrated in the writings of Jethro Tull, whose major work, *Horse-Hoeing Husbandry,* was published in 1733. As the work of the progressive English landed gentry began to bear fruit, traveling French savants were quick to publish critical comparisons of French and English practices. In 1750, stimulated by a trip to England and by wide reading in agronomy, Duhamel published the first volume of his *Traité de la culture des terres.* . . . This was an exposition, rather than a translation, of Tull's writings. Moreover, he adapted Tull's system to France based on his own wide reading in French agronomy and on original experiments. Although a supporter and admirer of Tull's system, he was not a slavish disciple: not only was he critical of Tull's experiments and ideas, but he refused to accept one of Tull's central principles, a doctrinaire rejection of the use of manures. Later volumes of the *Traité* were devoted to clarifications of and additions to the original work and, most important, to case histories—most of which were gleaned from Duhamel's extensive correspondence—of successful applications of the *nouveau système* to support its adherents.

Although the ideas of Tull and Duhamel enjoyed substantial popularity among a progressive group of French landowners, the opposition—either in the form of active criticism or in the passive inertia of an almost medieval agrarian society—was too strong for France to enjoy the rapid agricultural changes which occurred in England and, shortly after, in Scotland. However, enough progress was made for Duhamel to receive recognition for his pioneering work during his lifetime.

Duhamel never married and, according to one biographer, never planned or desired to do so. He divided his time between Paris and Denainvilliers, where his brother carried out many of the agricultural projects which Duhamel designed, and managed the family fortune that allowed Duhamel to pursue various experiments of his own. When his brother died,

Duhamel was looked after by a niece and particularly by his nephew and protégé, Fougeroux de Bondaroy. Straightforward in speech and thought, Duhamel consciously wrote for an audience of technicians rather than scientists. Although his later writings reflect the professed distaste for theory that Condorcet attributed to him, his papers as a whole were not as barren of interpretation as one might suppose from his biographers. Indeed, that his works include ideas as well as simple techniques is amply attested by those who disagreed with his papers and treatises, as well as by the honors he received from more than a dozen learned societies.

BIBLIOGRAPHY

Duhamel had the habit of writing supplements to his books, sometimes years after the original publication. As the supplements were book-length themselves, they were frequently issued as "Vol. II" of the original and sometimes there were minor changes in the titles. The *Traité . . . des terres* thus grew from a one-volume work to a six-volume work and generally bears the dates 1753 (the year of publication of the second supplement as part of a set that included the original and first supplement) and 1761 (the year of the final supplement). I have, however, given original publication dates and not the dates of reissues; that is, all dates in the text and below are those years in which Duhamel's works were first made available to the public.

I. ORIGINAL WORKS. Duhamel is credited with over a hundred entries in the *Histoires de l'Académie royale des sciences, avec des mémoires de mathématique et de physique.* Although he was certainly prolific, this figure is somewhat misleading. More than a third of the *mémoires* under his name are his "Observations botanico-météorologiques," an intellectually routine annual series (1740–1780) of recorded daily weather conditions, including temperature and barometric pressure, with additional data on crops, floods, and plant growth in general. But even subtracting *histoires,* reviews of his books, and the "Observations," Duhamel contributed some fifty-five papers to the French Academy. In addition, he wrote a score of articles for the *Descriptions des arts et métiers* (1760–1775). A few contributions to other journals are also known.

His impressive output of separate works includes *Traité de la fabrique des manoeuvres pour les vaisseaux ou l'art de la corderie perfectionné,* 2 vols. (Paris, 1747–1769); *Traité de la culture des terres suivant les principes de M. Tull,* 6 vols. (Paris, 1750–1761); *Eléments de l'architecture navale* (Paris, 1752); *Avis pour le tránsport par mer des arbres, des plants vivaces, des semences, et de diverses autres curiosités d'histoire naturelle* (Paris, 1753); *Traité de la conservation des grains et en particulier du froment* (Paris, 1753); *Traité des arbres et arbustes qui se cultivent en France en pleine terre,* 2 vols. (Paris, 1755); *Mémoires sur la garance et sa culture* (Paris, 1757); *La physique des arbres,* 2 vols. (Paris, 1758); *Moyens de conserver la santé aux équipages des vaisseaux* (Paris, 1759); *Des semis et plantations des arbres et de leur culture* (Paris, 1760); *Éléments d'agriculture,* 2 vols. (Paris, 1762); *Histoire d'un insecte qui dévore les grains dans l'Angoumois* (Paris, 1762); *De l'exploitation des bois,* 2 vols. (Paris, 1764); *Du transport, de la conservation et de la force des bois* (Paris, 1767); *Traité des arbres fruitiers,* 2 vols. (Paris, 1768); *Traité général des peches, et histoire des poissons qu'elles fournissent,* 3 vols. (Paris, 1769–1777). There are various translations in English, German, Spanish, and Italian.

II. SECONDARY LITERATURE. Most biographies rely heavily on the *éloge* by Condorcet in the *Histoire de l'Académie royale des sciences . . . 1782* (1785), 131–155.

Other material may be found in *Biographie universelle, ancienne et moderne,* XII (Paris, 1814), 185–190; *Dictionnaire de biographie française* (Paris, 1968), p. 22; *Dictionnaire historique de la médecine, ancienne et moderne,* II, pt. 1 (Paris, 1834), 147–149; *Dictionnaire des sciences médicales,* III (Paris, 1821), 538–541; *Nouvelle biographie générale,* XV (Paris, 1868), 106–107.

JON EKLUND

DUHEM, PIERRE-MAURICE-MARIE (*b.* Paris, France, 10 June 1861; *d.* Cabrespine, France, 14 September 1916), *physics, rational mechanics, physical chemistry, history of science, philosophy of science.*

Duhem was that rare, not to say unique, scientist whose contributions to the philosophy of science, the historiography of science, and science itself (in thermodynamics, hydrodynamics, elasticity, and physical chemistry) were of profound importance on a fully professional level in all three disciplines. Much of the purely scientific work was forgotten until recently. His apparent versatility was animated by a single-mindedness about the nature of scientific theories that was compatible with a rigidly ultra-Catholic point of view, an outlook unusual among historians, philosophers, or practitioners of science—Cauchy is the only other example that comes to mind.

Duhem's historical work, the major part of which traces the development of cosmology from antiquity to the Renaissance, was meant partly to redeem the centuries of Scholasticism, the great age for his church, from the reputation of scientific nullity, but mainly to exemplify the central epistemological position of his philosophy. This assigned to scientific theories the role of economizers of experimental laws which approach asymptotically some sort of reality, rather than that of models of reality itself or bearers of truth. Thus would the truth be independent of science and reserved for theology. This position coincided in important, although not all, respects with that of contemporary positivists, who came to it from the other extreme ideologically and without concern for defending theology.

Among the areas of agreement between Duhem,

Ernst Mach, and Wilhelm Ostwald was a common predilection for the energeticist over the mechanistic position in physics itself, involving skepticism about the reality of known physical entities, although he differed from them in allowing the existence of real entities in principle, however unknowable. A similar skeptical view was held by Henri Poincaré.

Duhem's father, Pierre-Joseph, was a commercial traveler from Roubaix in the industrialized north of France. His mother, born Alexandrine Fabre, was of a bourgeois family originally from Cabrespine, a town in Languedoc, near Carcassonne. They settled in Paris and sent Duhem, the eldest of their four children, to the Collège Stanislas from his eleventh year. He was a brilliant student and there acquired the firm grasp of Latin and Greek that he would need in his historical scholarship, while being attracted primarily to scientific studies and especially thermodynamics by a gifted teacher, Jules Moutier. His father hoped that for his higher education he would enter the École Polytechnique, where the training and tradition assured most graduates eminent technical careers in the service of the state. His mother, on the other hand, fearful that science or engineering would diminish his religious faith, urged him to study humanities at the École Normale Supérieure. Having placed first in the entrance examinations, he chose the middle ground of science at the École Normale, indicating his desire for an academic career. He published his first paper, on the application of the thermodynamic potential to electrochemical cells, in 1884, while still a student.

He proceeded with distinction through the *licence* and *agrégation,* after meeting a setback with a thesis for the doctorate that he presented in 1884 (prior to receiving the *licence,* an uncommon event). The subject concerned the concept of thermodynamic potential in chemistry and physics, and the argument included an attack on Marcellin Berthelot's twenty-year-old principle of maximum work, whereby the heat of reaction defines the criterion for the spontaneity of chemical reactions. This principle is false. Duhem, following J. W. Gibbs and Hermann von Helmholtz, properly defined the criterion in terms of free energy. Berthelot was extremely influential, resented the neophyte challenge, and was able to get the thesis refused. At risk to his career, Duhem later published the thesis as a book, *Le potentiel thermodynamique* (1886). Duhem was placed under the necessity of preparing another subject for the doctorate. He received the degree in 1888 for a thesis on the theory of magnetism, this one falling within the area of mathematics.

Unfortunately the enmity between Berthelot and Duhem was not dissipated until after 1900. Moreover, Duhem was of a contentious and acrimonious disposition, with a talent for making personal enemies over scientific matters. He blamed Berthelot, who was minister of education from 1886 to 1887, together with the circle of liberal and free-thinking scientists who advised successive ministers, for preventing him from ever receiving the expected call to a professorship in Paris. Aside from the hearsay evidence of anecdotes from the personalities involved, it must be admitted that there is no other instance in modern French history of a scientist of equivalent productivity, depth, and originality remaining relegated to the provinces throughout his entire postdoctoral career. Duhem taught at Lille (1887–1893), Rennes (1893–1894), and Bordeaux (1894–1916). He spurned an offer of a professorship in the history of science at the Collège de France shortly before his death, on the grounds that he was a physicist and would not enter Paris by the back door of history. In 1900 he was elected to corresponding membership in the Academy of Sciences. In 1913 he was elected one of the first six nonresident members of the Academy, a recognition that, together with various honorary degrees and foreign academic memberships received earlier, mollified his feelings to some degree.

Duhem had few qualified students, but those he did have considered him an extraordinary teacher. His personal friendships were as warm as his professional enmities were bitter. In October 1890 while at Lille he married Adèle Chayet. She died only two years later while giving birth to their second daughter, who also died. Duhem made his home thereafter with the surviving daughter, Hélène. She saw to the publication of the final five volumes (1954–1959) of his historical masterpiece, Le système du monde, left in manuscript after his death. He died at fifty-five of a heart attack brought on by a walking expedition during vacation days at Cabrespine. His health had never been vigorous.

Duhem's interests fell roughly into periods. Thermodynamics and electromagnetism predominated between 1884 and 1900, although he returned to them in 1913–1916. He concentrated on hydrodynamics from 1900 to 1906. His interest in the philosophy of science was mostly in the period 1892–1906, and in the history of science from 1904 to 1916, although his earliest historical papers date from 1895. The extraordinary volume of Duhem's production is impressive—nearly 400 papers and some twenty-two books. Among them, certain wartime writings (La science allemande and La chimie est-elle une science française?) express, as do his philosophical judgments of the style of British science, a certain chauvinism that remains the only unattractive characteristic of his nonscientific writings. It will be best to consider his most important work in the order of philosophy, history, and physics; to do so will reverse its chronology but will respect its intellectual structure.

Philosophy of Science. Duhem published his major philosophical work, La théorie physique, son objet et sa structure, in 1906, after having largely completed his researches in physical science. "A physical theory," he held there, ". . . is a system of mathematical propositions, deduced from a small number of principles, which has the object of representing a set of experimental laws as simply, as completely, and as exactly as possible." In adopting this position, he was explicitly rejecting what he considered to be the two alternatives to which any serious existing or previous account might be reduced.

According to epistemologies of the first sort, proper physical theories have the aim of accounting for observed phenomena by proposing hypotheses about, and preferably by actually revealing, the nature of the ultimate entities underlying the phenomena in question. Duhem rejected this view as illusory because experience showed that acting upon it had had the effect historically of subordinating theoretical physics to metaphysics, thereby encumbering and distracting it with all the difficulties and disputes afflicting that subject. He allowed that physicists may appropriately hope to form theories of which the structure "reflects" reality. It may be thought of such theories that their mode of interrelating empirical laws somehow fits the way in which the real events that give rise to the observations are interrelated. This hope can be based only on faith, however. There is and can be no evidence to support it.

Little in Duhem's philosophical writings clarifies the idea of such a fit, beyond the notion that the evolution of physical theories caused by successive adjustments to conform to experiment should lead asymptotically to a "natural classification" which somehow reflects reality. But his historical writings allude to numerous examples of what he had in mind, and his Notice (1913) indicates that they were in part originally motivated by it. It is no doubt for this reason that, despite his enthusiastic discovery of Scholastic mechanics in the Middle Ages, his favorite philosopher of antiquity was Plato, to whom he attributed the origin of the view (clearly akin to his own) that the healthy role of astronomical or other mathematical theory is to "save the phenomena." At the same time he had great faith in the syllogism as a logical instrument. He believed that mathematical reasoning could in principle be replaced with syllogistic reasoning, and he went so far as to reject Poincaré's argument that mathematical induction involves nonsyllogistic elements.[1]

The second category of philosophies or methodologies of physics that Duhem found unacceptable were those in which theories were expected to provide models in the form of mechanical analogies or constructs that permit visualizing the phenomena and offer handles for thought. He rejected this alternative partly on utilitarian and partly on aesthetic grounds. He felt that physical theories should have practical value, and he preferred the analytic to the geometric mode in mathematical thinking. Theories of the kind he advocated permit deducing many laws from a few principles and thus dispense the physicist from the necessity of trying to remember all the laws. Duhem evidently considered reason a higher faculty than memory. Complex models are distracting to people who can reason but cannot remember a mass of concrete detail. They are not, he believed, likely to lead to discovery of new laws. Merely artificial constructs, they can never attain to the status of natural classifications. Duhem was highly critical of British physics for its reliance upon the use of just such mechanistic models. In his view this national habit resulted from a defect of cultural temperament. He described the British mind in science as wide and shallow, the French as narrow and deep. As will appear in the discussion of his electrodynamics, Maxwell was his bête noire in this respect. It must be acknowledged that a certain rigidity in his opinions accorded ill with the subtle nature of his philosophy.

Duhem's philosophy was certainly empiricist but never naïvely so. He showed very beautifully that there can be no such thing as simply observing and reporting an experiment. The phenomenon observed must be construed—must be seen—in the light of some theory and must be described in the terms of that theory. Laws arrived at experimentally must be expressed by means of abstract concepts that allow them to be formulated mathematically and incorporated in a theory. At their best they can merely approximate experimental observations. It is quite impossible to test or verify the fundamental hypotheses of a theory one by one. Thus there cannot be a crucial experiment, and induction from laws can never determine a unique set of hypotheses. Thus data and logic leave much to the discretion of the theorist. He must supplement their resources with good sense and historical perspective on his problems and his science.

It is an aspect of Duhem's recognition of the role of taste in scientific research that he never insisted that his philosophy require the adoption of an energeticist, to the exclusion of a mechanistic, point of view. That was an empirical, not a philosophical, issue. What his philosophy purported to establish was that an energeticist approach was no less legitimate

than a mechanistic one. The discussion explains how theories are to be judged and looked at merely in point of preference or policy; and in the absence of concrete facts, either type of theory would in principle be acceptable, so long as no metaphysical import be loaded into the choice. The issue was one that Duhem discussed in *L'évolution de la mécanique* (1902) and also in the essay "Physique de croyant," included in later editions of *La théorie physique*.

History of Science. Like Ernst Mach, his contemporary in the positivist school, Duhem relied heavily on historical examples in presenting his philosophy of science. *L'évolution de la mécanique* may be compared to Mach's famous *Die Mechanik in ihrer Entwicklung, historisch-kritisch dargestellt* (1883) as a philosophical critique of a science based upon its history, although Duhem was by far the more faithful to the original texts and the intentions of their authors. A history of the concept of chemical combination appeared in 1902 and a two-volume study of early statics in 1905–1906.

The object of historical examples was to attempt to see the trend toward the "natural classification," which requires the examination of preceding theories. Duhem was primarily led into his historical studies by following such theories backwards. Thus he always claimed that his conception of physical theory was justified by the history of physics, not because it corresponded to views shared by all, or most, or even (as Mach had tended to imply of his own position) by the best physicists, but because it did yield an analysis of the nature of the evolution of physics and of the dialectic responsible for that process.

The most impressive monument to the scholarly fertility of that claim remains his massive contribution to the knowledge of medieval science in his three-volume *Études sur Léonard de Vinci* (1906–1913) and the ten-volume *Système du monde* (1913–1959). These works contain a detailed exposition of two theses: (1) a creative and unbroken tradition of physics, cosmology, and natural philosophy was carried on in the Latin West from about 1200 to the Renaissance, and (2) the results of this medieval activity were known to Leonardo da Vinci and Galileo, and played a seminal role in the latter's transformation of physics. Duhem was led to his theses, and to the almost single-handed discovery of this medieval activity, by recognizing in Leonardo's notebooks statements by earlier writers and references to works fortunately available in manuscript in the Bibliothèque Nationale. Pursuing these citations and references still further he found wholly unsuspected "schools of science." He emphasized the significance of Paris: particularly important was a series of Parisian masters who were relatively unknown before Duhem's researches—Jordanus de Nemore, Jean Buridan, Francis of Méyronnes, Albert of Saxony, and Nicole Oresme. Duhem also brought out of obscurity the contributions of Mersenne and Malebranche. Expressed in dramatic form and supported by extensive quotation from the original texts (particularly in *Le système du monde*), Duhem's discoveries revolutionized, if they did not completely create, the study of medieval physics. While it is true that recent studies have seriously modified and qualified some of his conclusions, Duhem's studies remain the indisputable starting point for the study of medieval natural philosophy.[2]

Scientific Thought and Work. It must be recalled that Duhem's scientific formation took place in the period 1880–1890, well before the discovery of radioactivity and the experiments of Jean Perrin and, later, Henry G. F. Moseley. Discontent with the notion of reducing all physical concepts to classical mechanics or to mechanical models was growing. It was fed by the necessity to modify ad hoc the often contradictory properties of supposedly fundamental atomic or molecular particles in order to maintain the applicability of the model to newly determined phenomena, particularly in chemical dynamics and in the physics of heat and gases. Duhem early became convinced that rather than try to reduce all of physics and chemistry to classical mechanics, the wiser policy would be to see classical mechanics itself as a special case of a more general continuum theory. He believed that such underlying descriptive theory for all of physics and chemistry would emerge from a generalized thermodynamics. The central commitment of his scientific life was the building up of such a science, one that would include electricity and magnetism as well as mechanics. His attempts culminated in the *Traité d'énergétique* (1911), in which valuable work there is not a single word about atoms or molecules. Duhem always considered that it was his most important—and would prove to be his most lasting—contribution to science. He had not succeeded, however, in his goal of including electricity and magnetism in its purview.

His conception of the nature of physical theory had in fact influenced both the direction of his work and the form of his writings. His contemporaries (see Secondary Literature) often remarked that many of his papers opened with the barest of assumptions followed by a series of theorems. In his mode of posing "axioms," he gave little motivation, made hardly any appeal to experiment, and of course made no use whatever of atomic or molecular models. In his concern over extracting the logical consequences of a set of axioms for a portion of physics or chemis-

try, Duhem was a pioneer. Today a flourishing school of continuum mechanics follows a similar path, with a strong interest in foundations and in finding general theorems about more general fluids or elastic bodies with nonlinear constitutive equations or with fading memory. They often cite Duhem and his more famous predecessors such as Euler and Cauchy. However, because of the special hypotheses and restricted constitutive equations built into Duhem's thermodynamics from the beginning, modern workers no longer view his generalized thermodynamics as the best way to approach continuum mechanics.[3,4]

Duhem began his scientific work with the generalization and application of thermodynamics. While still at the Collège Stanislas and under Moutier's guidance, he had read G. Lemoine's description of J. W. Gibbs's work[5] and the first part of Hermann von Helmholtz' "Die Thermodynamik chemischer Vorgänge."[6] These papers emphasized the characteristic functions, closely related to those invented by F. J. D. Massieu,[7] now called the Gibbs and Helmholtz free energies—G and A, respectively. These functions play a role for thermodynamics directly analogous to the one played by the potential of classical mechanics. Duhem was one of the first to see real promise in this, calling Massieu's functions "thermodynamic potentials." Using this idea together with the principle of virtual work, he treated a number of topics in physics and chemistry.

Among the subjects treated systematically were thermoelectricity, pyroelectricity, capillarity and surface tension, mixtures of perfect gases, mixtures of liquids, heats of solution and dilution, saturated vapors, solutions in gravitational and magnetic fields, osmotic pressure, freezing points, dissociation, continuity between liquid and gas states, stability of equilibrium, and the generalization of Le Chatelier's principle. The Duhem-Margules equation was first obtained by Duhem in the course of this work. His success with these problems in the period 1884–1900 rank him with J. H. van't Hoff, Ostwald, Svante Arrhenius, and Henry Le Chatelier as one of the founders of modern physical chemistry.

Duhem's results are of course an extension and elaboration of the pioneer work of Gibbs and Helmholtz. But Duhem's elaboration, explanation, and application of their suggestions in his *Traité de mécanique chimique* (1897–1899) and *Thermodynamique et chimie* (1902) provided a whole generation of French physicists and chemists with their knowledge of chemical thermodynamics.

Duhem made a number of other contributions to thermodynamics. In the first part of his rejected thesis, *Le potentiel thermodynamique* (1886), Duhem presented or rederived by means of the thermodynamic potential a number of known results on vapor pressure of pure liquids and solutions, dissociation of gases and of heterogeneous systems, and the heat effects in voltaic cells. In the second and third parts he obtained new results on solubility and freezing points of complex salt solutions and on electrified systems. There is also the first application of Euler's homogeneous-function theorem to the extensive properties of solutions. This technique, now common, reduces the derivation of relations among the partial molal properties of a solution to the repeated application of this theorem. One of the equations so derived is the Gibbs-Duhem equation. Also included is a discussion of electrified systems which contains an expression equivalent to the electrochemical potential. This book, popular enough to be reprinted in 1896, is historically important for the systematic use of thermodynamic potentials, when others were still using osmotic pressure as a measure of chemical affinity and using artificial cycles to prove theorems.

Duhem was the first (1887) to publish a critical analysis[8] of Gibbs's "Equilibrium of Heterogeneous Substances."[9] In Duhem's paper is the first precise definition of a reversible process; earlier versions by others (unfortunately often preserved in today's textbooks) are too vague. Duhem emphasizes that the reversible process between two thermodynamic states A and B of a system is an unrealizable limiting process. The limit of the set of real processes for getting from A to B is obtained by letting the imbalance of forces between the system and the surroundings at each step tend toward zero. Each member of this set of real processes must pass through nonequilibrium states, or else nothing would happen. However, the limit of this set, where the forces balance at every step, is a set of equilibrium states. Since once the system is in equilibrium nothing can happen, this limit is thus in principle an unrealizable process. This limiting process is now called a "quasi-static" process. If a similar set of realizable processes for getting from B and A has the same (unrealizable) limit, then the common sequence of equilibrium states is defined by Duhem as a reversible process.

Duhem later pointed out in the "Commentaire aux principes de la thermodynamique" (pt. 2, 1893) that there exist situations such as hysteresis where the limiting set of equilibrium states for the direction AB is not the same as that for the direction BA. Therefore, it is possible to go from A to B and back by quasi-static processes, but not reversibly. This distinction was noted fifteen years before the celebrated paper of Carathéodory.[10]

Duhem believed that the "Commentaire" (1892–1894) was one of his more significant contributions.

It contains a very detailed analysis of the steps leading from the statement of the second law of thermodynamics to the definitions of entropy and thermodynamic potential. It also contains an axiomatic treatment of the first law of thermodynamics which is surprisingly good by present-day standards. (A different version is given in the Traité d'énergétique [1911].) The concepts of oeuvre (total energy including kinetic energy) and travail (work) are taken as undefined ideas. Axioms about oeuvre include independence of path, additivity along a path, commutativity, associativity, conservation, plus other matters often left implicit. Important to note is that the concept "quantity of heat" was not assumed but was defined in terms of energy and work. Consequently the definition, although more diffusely stated, was equivalent to and preceded that of C. Carathéodory (1909)[10] and Max Born (1921),[11] and should be called Duhem's definition. Duhem's axiomatic outlook which characterized this discussion of the first law was indeed pioneering for physics and to some extent anticipated the major axiomatic research in mathematics. Thus, although the axiomatization of arithmetic began in the first half of the nineteenth century, the research for axiomatic foundations for other branches of mathematics (Euclidean geometry, fields, groups, Boolean algebra) did not begin in earnest until 1897–1900.

In "Sur les déformations permanentes et l'hystérésis" (1896–1902), Duhem considered in some detail the thermodynamics of nonreversible but quasi-static processes and some irreversible processes, including hysteresis and creep. The results were mostly qualitative, not entirely satisfactory, and of little influence. As of this writing there is no really adequate thermodynamic theory of such systems, although interest in this subject has recently been revived.

Duhem provided the first explicit unrestricted proof of the Gibbs phase rule, based on Gibbs's suggestions, in "On the General Problem of Chemical Statics" (1898). At the same time he extended it beyond the consideration of just the intensive variables, giving the conditions necessary to specify the masses of the phases as well. The conditions are different for the pairs of variables pressure–temperature and volume–temperature, and their statement is called Duhem's theorem.[12] In addition the properties of "indifferent" systems, of which azeotropes are a simple special case, were discussed in some detail.

Duhem attached great importance to his thermodynamics of false equilibrium and friction.[13] According to Duhem, false equilibria can be divided into two classes: apparent, as for example a supersaturated solution, which, as a result of a small perturbation, returns instantly to thermodynamic equilibrium; and *real,* as for example organic compounds, such as diamond or petroleum constituents. Such compounds are unstable thermodynamically with respect to other substances but have remained unchanged for large perturbations throughout geological periods of time. Yet they will transform into the stable products if the perturbations are large enough (diamond to graphite by heating). A similar view was held by Gibbs (his passive resistances). The false equilibrium viewpoint was very useful to E. Jouguet, a major contributor to explosives theory and one of Duhem's disciples.[14] However, real false equilibria can also be considered as instances of extremely slow reaction rates. A violent polemic over this issue took place between 1896 and 1910. Most, but by no means all, of those interested in such questions today prefer the infinitely slow reaction rate view. Since the results are the same from either view, the choice is a personal one.

A major portion of Duhem's interest was focused on hydrodynamics and elasticity. His second book, *Hydrodynamique, élasticité, acoustique* (1891), had an important influence on mathematicians and physicists because it called attention to Hugoniot's work on waves. Jacques Hadamard, a colleague for one year and lifelong friend, remarked that this book and later conversations with Duhem led him into a major portion of his own work in wave propagation, Huygens' principle, calculus of variations, and hyperbolic differential equations. Duhem was both a pioneer and almost alone for years in trying to prove rigorous general theorems for Navier-Stokes fluids and for finite elasticity in Kelvin-Kirchhoff-Neumann bodies. His results are important and of sufficient interest later that his *Recherches sur l'hydrodynamique* (1903–1904) was reprinted in 1961.

In hydrodynamics Duhem was the first to study wave propagation in viscous, compressible, heat-conducting fluids using stability conditions and the full resources of thermodynamics (*Recherches sur l'hydrodynamique*). He showed the then startling result that no true shock waves (i.e., discontinuities of density and velocity) or higher order discontinuities can be propagated through a viscous fluid. This is contrary to the result for rigorously nonviscous fluids. The only discontinuities that can persist are transversal, which always separate the same particles; these Duhem identified with the "cells," observed by Bénard, formed when a liquid is heated from below. Since real fluids are both viscous and heat conducting, how is it possible to have sound waves propagated, as in air? Duhem's answer was that while true waves are not possible, "quasi waves" are. A quasi wave is a thin layer whose properties, including velocity, change smoothly but rapidly. If we consider a series of similar fluids whose values of the heat conductivity k and viscosity η approach zero, then the thickness of the associated quasi wave also approaches zero and the smooth change of properties approaches a discontinuity. When k and η are small, as in air, such quasi waves behave exactly as a true longitudinal shock wave in a perfect fluid with $k = \eta = 0$, i.e, propagating with the Laplace velocity. Duhem's concept and theory of the quasi wave is more general and more precise than the later ideas of Prandtl (1906) about the "shock layer." Some of Duhem's theorems on shock waves have been improved recently. For perspective, it should also be noted that Duhem considered only the then universally accepted Navier-Stokes fluid. There are more general concepts of a fluid with viscosity which do allow wave propagation.[4]

Duhem generalized and completed earlier results on the stability of floating bodies (including those containing a liquid). He showed that while some earlier methods were incorrect, certain results (in particular the famous rule of metacenters) were still correct. Finally, the article "Potentiel thermodynamique et pression hydrostatique" (1893) contains, but does not develop, the idea of an oriented body that consists not only of points but of directions associated with the points. Such an oriented body can represent liquid crystals or materials whose molecules have internal structure. Eugène and François Cosserat adapted this idea to represent the twisting of rods and shells in one and two dimensions (1907–1909). This concept has also been useful for some recent theories of bodies with "dislocations."

In elasticity Duhem was again interested in rigorous general theorems (*Recherches sur l'élasticité* [1906]). He kept a correct finite elasticity alive and inspired other workers. He was the first to study waves in elastic, heat-conducting, viscous, finitely deformed systems. The results are similar to that for fluids; namely, in any finitely deformed viscous elastic system, whether crystalline or vitreous, no true waves can be propagated and the only possible discontinuities always separate the same particles (as in the Bénard problem). Quasi waves are expected in viscous solids, but Duhem did not carry his analysis that far. Duhem was also the first to study the relationships between waves in isothermal (heat-conducting) and adiabatic (nonconducting) finitely deformed systems without viscosity. Duhem was also interested in the general conditions for solids (vitreous or crystalline) to be stable. He had to choose special conditions of stress or strain, but he was able to prove some general theorems. All this was based on the then universally accepted Kelvin-Kirchhoff-

Neumann elastic body. At the present writing, more general concepts of elastic bodies are being considered.

After Gibbs, Duhem was among the few who were concerned about stability of thermodynamic systems. His techniques were a natural consequence of his interest in thermodynamic potentials. He was the first to consider solutions ("Dissolutions et mélanges" [1893]); and he often returned to stability questions ("Commentaire aux principes de la thermodynamique" [1894]; "On the General Problem of Chemical Statics" [1898]; *Recherches sur l'élasticité* [1906]; *Traité d'énergétique* [1911]). Because he tried to be more explicit and more general than Gibbs and because he often took a global point of view, he had to face more difficult problems than did Gibbs. He succeeded fairly well with sufficient conditions but was less successful with necessary ones. In his *Énergétique* he showed familiarity with Liapounoff's work, but his own previous results were based on more special hypotheses. As a result, there is some confusion in Duhem's results over what are the proper necessary and sufficient conditions for thermodynamic stability. Such questions have only recently been rigorously resolved.

Electricity and magnetism and his attempts to bring them into the framework of his *Énergétique* (which was not the same as the philosophical school of "energetics") were important to Duhem. If a system's currents are zero or constant, then its electrodynamic energy is zero or constant. In this case, the total energy divides neatly into internal and kinetic energies, and energetics can be successfully applied. Thus Duhem was able to treat pyroelectricity and piezoelectricity in a general way without needing the special hypotheses of F. Pockels and W. Voigt. However, if currents are not constant, then matters are much more complex, and the electrodynamic energy must be accounted for using some electromagnetic theory.

Although Duhem recognized J. Clerk Maxwell's ingenuity, he could not appreciate Maxwell's theory at its real value because of its contradictions and unrigorous development, its mistakes in sign, and its lack of experimental foundation. Duhem preferred an electromagnetic theory due to Helmholtz, since it could be logically derived from the classical experiments. This theory, which Duhem helped to elaborate—and improve—is more general than Maxwell's because it contains two additional arbitrary parameters. By an appropriate choice of values for these parameters, it can be shown that Maxwell's equations appear as special cases of Helmholtz' theory. In particular, if the Faraday-Mossotti hypothesis is adopted (equivalent to one parameter being infinity), then transverse fluxes propagate with the velocity of light. This results in an electromagnetic theory of light and an explanation of Heinrich Hertz's experiments. If the other parameter (Helmholtz') is chosen to be zero, then no longitudinal fluxes can be propagated, which circumstance is in agreement with Maxwell's equations. Duhem, however, believed that there were experiments showing that such longitudinal fluxes exist and are also propagated at the velocity of light. He suggested (1902) that perhaps the recently discovered X rays might be identified with these longitudinal fluxes.

Duhem was a pitiless critic of Maxwell's theory, claiming that it not only lacked rigorous foundation but was not sufficiently general to explain the existence of permanent magnets (*Les théories électriques de J. Clerk Maxwell* [1902]). Similar reservations about lack of rigor were expressed by many Continental physicists (e.g., Poincaré), and Helmholtz worked out his own electromagnetic theory because of his dissatisfaction with Maxwell's approach. Duhem later admitted that not only had his criticisms not been accepted, they had not even been read or discussed; and of course Maxwell's theory has triumphed. However, both L. Roy[15] and A. O'Rahilly[16] have contended that the logical derivation of Maxwell's equations from a continuum viewpoint comes best through the Helmholtz-Duhem theory with the proper choice of constants.

The foregoing discussion covers an extraordinary output of purely scientific work. It is curious that until recently working scientists were almost completely unaware of these contributions, with the exception of the Gibbs-Duhem and Duhem-Margules equations, which have been well known to physical chemists. The reason for the neglect of Duhem's scientific work, the failure to call him to Paris, and the long delay in his election to the Academy—despite the high quality of his work and the foreign honors accorded him—are interesting and are summarized below. They involve aspects of Duhem's personality as well as differences between competing scientific schools of the period. (A more complete account of the antagonisms and suppression, interwoven with a biography, may be found in Miller, *Physics Today,* **19,** no. 12 [1966], 47–53.)

Duhem's contentious characteristics have already been noted. On the one hand, his extremely conservative religious and political views conflicted sharply with those of the freethinkers and liberals who then dominated French science. On the other hand, the polemical nature of his writings on such controversies as energetics vs. atomism, Maxwell's theory vs. Helmholtz', relativity, false equilibrium, and the maximum work principle made personal enemies of many of his scientific contemporaries. Their combined opposition blocked his career and resulted in partial suppression of his work or in its being taken over without citation.

In part, however, the neglect of his work is to be explained by the triumph of views that he bitterly opposed, such as atomic theories and Maxwell's theory. His objection to relativity derived from its "mutilation" of classical mechanics in order to leave unaltered Maxwell's theory and atomic theories of electrons.

With the crystal clarity of a half century of hindsight, it would seem that Duhem should not have opposed corpuscular models so strongly. Since he had based his whole philosophy on the deliberate avoidance of such aids and given the rigid nature of his personality, he could not change his views as the evidence mounted and the use of such models became more plausible. It is essential to recall, however, that Duhem was not alone in his objection to corpuscular models, Maxwell, and relativity. At the time he was in the company of many eminent scientists.

Pierre Duhem is a fascinating example of a brilliant scientist caught up in historical and personal circumstances that blocked his career and partially suppressed his scientific work. Right-wing, royalist, anti-Semitic, anti-Dreyfus, anti-Republican, and a religious extremist, he was exiled to the provinces and his scientific work was almost systematically ignored in France.

Nevertheless, Duhem's scientific ideas and outlook had a major influence on French physical chemistry and particularly on Hadamard, Jouguet, and the Cosserats. He was a pioneer in attempting to prove rigorous general theorems about thermodynamics, physical chemistry, Navier-Stokes fluids, finite elasticity, and wave propagation. His purely scientific investigations and results in these fields are important, useful, and significant today, although the ascendancy of atomic theories has diminished the relative importance of his contributions to science as a whole.

By midcentury Duhem's scientific work had been almost completely forgotten. Since then, his contributions have been rediscovered, and are being increasingly cited and given the recognition they deserve.[3,4,12] There has never been, of course, any question about the importance of his work in the philosophy and history of science. Since his contributions to any one of the fields of pure science, philosophy, or history would have done credit to one person, the ensemble from the pen of a single man marks Duhem as one of the most powerful intellects of his period.

NOTES

1. "La nature du raisonnement mathématique," in *Revue de philosophie*, **21** (1912), 531–543.
2. M. Clagett, *Science of Mechanics in the Middle Ages* (Madison, Wis., 1959).
3. C. Truesdell and R. Toupin, "The Classical Field Theories," in S. Flügge, ed., *Encyclopedia of Physics,* III, pt. 1 (Berlin, 1960); C. Truesdell and W. Noll, "The Non-Linear Field Theories of Mechanics," *ibid.,* III, pt. 3 (Berlin, 1965).
4. B. D. Coleman, M. E. Gurtin, I. Herrara, and C. Truesdell, *Wave Propagation in Dissipative Materials* (New York, 1965).
5. G. Lemoine, *Études sur les équilibres chimiques* (Paris, 1882).
6. H. von Helmholtz, "Die Thermodynamik chemischer Vorgänge," in *Sitzungsberichte der Deutschen Akademie der Wissenschaften zu Berlin,* **1** (1882), 22–39.
7. F. J. D. Massieu, "Sur les fonctions caractéristiques des divers fluides," in *Comptes rendus hebdomadaires des séances de l'Académie des sciences,* **69** (1869), 858–864, 1057–1061.
8. P. Duhem, "Étude sur les travaux thermodynamiques de J. Willard Gibbs," in *Bulletin des sciences mathématiques,* 2nd ser., **11** (1887), 122–148, 159–176.
9. J. W. Gibbs, "On the Equilibrium of Heterogeneous Substances," in *Transactions of the Connecticut Academy of Arts and Sciences,* **3,** pt. 1 (1876), 108–248; **3,** pt. 2 (1878), 343–520.
10. C. Carathéodory, "Untersuchungen über die Grundlagen der Thermodynamik," in *Mathematische Annalen,* **67** (1909), 355–386.
11. M. Born, "Kritische Betrachtungen zur traditionellen Darstellung der Thermodynamik," in *Physikalische Zeitschrift,* **22** (1921), 218–224, 249–254, 282–286.
12. I. Prigogine and R. Defay, *Chemical Thermodynamics* (New York, 1954), ch. 13.
13. P. Duhem, "Théorie thermodynamique de la viscosité, du frottement, et des faux équilibres chimiques," in *Mémoires de la Société des sciences physiques et naturelles de Bordeaux,* 5th ser., **2** (1896), 1–208; *Thermodynamique et chimie* (Paris, 1902; 2nd ed., 1910).
14. E. Jouguet, *Mécanique des explosifs, étude de dynamique chimique* (Paris, 1917).
15. L. Roy, *L'électrodynamique des milieux isotropes en repos d'après Helmholtz et Duhem* (Paris, 1923).
16. A. O'Rahilly, *Electromagnetics* (London, 1938), ch. 5; repr. as *Electromagnetic Theory,* 2 vols. (New York, 1965).

BIBLIOGRAPHY

I. ORIGINAL WORKS. Duhem published twenty-two books in forty-five volumes, as well as nearly 400 articles and book reviews in scientific and philosophical journals. An extensive bibliography (although lacking some twenty-five articles and more than fifty book reviews) is given by O. Manville, in *Mémoires de la Société des sciences physiques et naturelles de Bordeaux,* 7th ser., **1,** pt. 2 (1927), 437–464.

Duhem's correspondence consists of letters to him from some 500 correspondents and is being copied with the permission of Duhem's daughter, Mlle. Hélène Pierre-Duhem. Copies will ultimately be deposited in the University of California, Berkeley, and University of California, San Diego, libraries. Few letters by Duhem survive. Little of the correspondence seems to have major scientific value, although there are a few interesting historical items.

Duhem's major scientific books are *Le potentiel thermodynamique et ses applications à la mécanique chimique et à la théorie des phénomènes électriques* (Paris, 1886); *Hydrodynamique, élasticité, acoustique,* 2 vols. (Paris, 1891); *Leçons sur l'électricité et le magnétisme,* 3 vols. (Paris, 1891–1892); *Traité élémentaire de la mécanique chimique,* 4 vols. (Paris, 1897–1899); *Les théories électriques de J. Clerk Maxwell: Étude historique et critique* (Paris, 1902); *Thermodynamique et chimie* (Paris, 1902; 2nd ed., 1910), English trans. by G. Burgess (New York, 1903); *Recherches sur l'hydrodynamique,* 2 vols. (Paris, 1903–1904; repr., 1961); *Recherches sur l'élasticité* (Paris, 1906); and *Traité d'énergétique,* 2 vols. (Paris, 1911).

His major historical books are *Le mixte et la combinaison chimique. Essai sur l'évolution d'une idée* (Paris, 1902); *L'évolution de la mécanique* (Paris, 1902); *Les origines de la statique,* 2 vols. (Paris, 1905–1906); *Études sur Léonard de Vinci, ceux qu'il a lus et ceux qui l'ont lu,* 3 vols. (Paris, 1906–1913); and *Le système du monde. Histoire des doctrines cosmologiques de Platon à Copernic,* 10 vols. (Paris, 1913–1959).

His philosophy of science is stated in *La théorie physique, son objet et sa structure* (Paris, 1906; 2nd ed., 1914; 3rd ed., 1933), German trans. by F. Adler, with foreword by E. Mach (Leipzig, 1908); English trans. by Philip P. Wiener as *The Aim and Structure of Physical Theory* (Princeton, 1954; repr. New York, 1963). See also "Notation atomique et hypothèse atomistique," in *Revue des questions scientifiques,* 2nd ser., **31** (1892), 391; *Les théories électriques de J. Clerk Maxwell* (Paris, 1902); "Analyse de l'ouvrage de Ernst Mach," in *Bulletin des sciences mathématiques,* 2nd ser., **27** (1903), 261; and Σωξειν τα φαινομενα (Paris, 1908).

Duhem's most important scientific papers include "Étude sur les travaux thermodynamiques de J. Willard Gibbs," in *Bulletin des sciences mathématiques,* 2nd ser., **11** (1887), 122, 159; "Commentaire aux principes de la thermodynamique," in *Journal de mathématiques pures et appliquées,* **8** (1892), 269; **9** (1893), 293; and **10** (1894), 207; "Le potentiel thermodynamique et la pression hydrostatique," in *Annales scientifiques de l'École normale supérieure,* **10** (1893), 183; "Dissolutions et mélanges," in *Travaux et mémoires des Facultés de Lille,* **3,** no. 11 (1893), no. 12 (1893), and no. 13 (1894); "Sur les déformations permanentes et l'hystérésis," in *Mémoires de l'Académie royale de Belgique. Classe des sciences,* **54,** nos. 4, 5, and 6 (1896); **56,** no. 6 (1898); and **62,** no. 1 (1902); "Théorie thermodynamique de la viscosité, du frottement, et des faux équilibres chimiques," in *Mémoires de la Société des sciences physiques et naturelles de Bordeaux,* 5th ser., **2** (1896), 1; and "On the General Problem of Chemical Statics," in *Journal of Physical Chemistry,* **2** (1898), 91.

Some of Duhem's papers on electrodynamics may be found in *Annales de la Faculté des sciences de l'Université de Toulouse,* **7,** B, G (1893); **10,** B (1896); 3rd ser., **6** (1914), 177; *American Journal of Mathematics,* **17** (1895), 117; *L'éclairage électrique,* **4** (1895), 494; and *Archives néer-*

landaises des sciences exactes et naturelles, 2nd ser., **5** (1901), 227. His principal papers on floating bodies are found in *Journal de mathématiques pures et appliquées,* 5th ser., **1** (1895), 91; **2** (1896), 23; **3** (1897), 389; 6th ser., **7** (1911), 1.

His major historical papers are "Les théories de la chaleur," in *Revue des deux-mondes,* **129** (1895), 869; and **130** (1895), 380, 851.

For Duhem's own assessment of his work to 1913, see *Notice sur les titres et travaux scientifiques de Pierre Duhem* (Bordeaux, 1913), prepared by him for his candidacy at the Académie des Sciences. There remains an unpublished work on capillarity written several years before his death.

II. SECONDARY LITERATURE. *Mémoires de la Société des sciences physiques et naturelles de Bordeaux,* 7th ser., **1,** pt. 2 (1927) is a special issue entitled "L'oeuvre scientifique de Pierre Duhem"; in addition to the bibliography by O. Manville, cited above, it contains Manville's detailed discussion of Duhem's physics, pp. 1–435, and shorter discussions of his mathematical work by J. Hadamard, pp. 465–495, and of his historical work by A. Darbon, pp. 497–548.

See also E. le Roy, "Science et philosophie," in *Revue de métaphysique et de morale,* **7** (1899), 503; and "Un positivisme nouveau," ibid., **9** (1901), 143–144; A. Rey, "La philosophie scientifique de M. Duhem," ibid., **12** (1904), 699–744; a short review of Duhem's scientific work by his best-known disciple, E. Jouguet, in *Revue générale des sciences,* **28** (1917), 40; L. Roy, *L'électrodynamique des milieux isotropes en repos d'après Helmholtz et Duhem* (Paris, 1923); and A. Lowinger, *The Methodology of Pierre Duhem* (New York, 1941).

Biographical sources include P. Humbert, *Pierre Duhem* (Paris, 1932); E. Jordan, in *Annuaire de l'Association des anciens élèves de l'École normale supérieure* (1917), pp. 158–173, and *Mémoires de la Société des sciences physiques et naturelles de Bordeaux,* 7th ser., **1,** pt. 1 (1917); D. Miller, in *Physics Today,* **19,** no. 12 (1966), 47–53, based in part on several interviews with Hélène Pierre-Duhem; E. Picard, *La vie et l'oeuvre de Pierre Duhem* (Paris, 1921), which also includes a summary review of all his work; and Hélène Pierre-Duhem, *Un savant français: Pierre Duhem* (Paris, 1936).

DONALD G. MILLER

DUJARDIN, FÉLIX (*b.* Tours, France, 5 April 1801; *d.* Rennes, France, 8 April 1860), *protozoology.*

Both Dujardin's father and grandfather were skilled watchmakers, originally in Lille, and Félix, who for a time trained in the trade, seems to have acquired some of his interests—as well as his remarkable manual dexterity—from them.

With his two brothers, Dujardin attended the classes of the Collège de Tours as a day pupil. He was originally attracted to art, especially drawing and design. His interest in science was apparently first aroused by a surgeon who was a friend of the family and who lent him some books on anatomy and natural history as well as Fourcroy's *Chimie.* Chemistry became for a time Dujardin's chief interest and, using a textbook by Thénard and some basic chemical reagents, he conducted simple experiments at home. Intending to study chemistry in the laboratories of Thénard and Gay-Lussac at Paris, he began to prepare himself for the entrance examination at the École Polytechnique. He persuaded his older brother to join him in these studies—particularly mathematics—and they both presented themselves for the examination in 1818. His brother succeeded, but Dujardin failed.

Discouraged by this failure, Dujardin went to Paris to study painting in the studio of Gérard, although he did not entirely forsake his scientific studies. In order to make a living, however, he soon accepted a position as a hydraulic engineer in the city of Sedan. He was married to Clémentine Grégoire there in 1823. Still restless, he returned to Tours, where he was placed in charge of a library. He began simultaneously to teach, especially mathematics and literature, and soon achieved sufficient success to give up his duties at the library. In his leisure, he pursued scientific studies of various kinds. His earliest publication, on the Tertiary strata and fossils of the Touraine area, were valuable enough to attract the attention of Charles Lyell.[1]

When in 1826 the city of Tours decided to inaugurate courses in applied science, Dujardin was assigned to teach geometry. In 1829 he was asked to teach chemistry as well and was provided with liberal funds for the establishment of a laboratory. This gave Dujardin the opportunity to return to his initial interest in chemical research. He also pursued studies in optics and crystallography and found time for botanical excursions, which led in 1833 to the publication (with two collaborators) of *Flore complète d'Indre-et-Loire.*

About this time, the diversity of his interests began to trouble Dujardin. On the advice of Henri Dutrochet, he decided to specialize in zoology and left Tours for Paris in pursuit of this goal. For the next several years, he apparently supported himself and his family by writing for scientific journals and encyclopedias.

In 1839, on the strength of his work in geology, Dujardin was appointed to the chair in geology and mineralogy at the Faculty of Sciences at Toulouse. In November 1840 he was called to the newly established Faculty of Sciences at Rennes as professor of zoology and botany and dean of the faculty—a position that for several years embroiled him in disputes with his colleagues. The intensity of these disputes diminished somewhat after he gave up the deanship in 1842. Although he was nominated several times for more important positions in Paris, he seemed always to end up second in the voting. Convinced, with some justice, that he was being persecuted from all sides (his colleagues sought to undermine his authority by such tactics as spreading rumors about his sex life), Dujardin became almost a recluse and spent his final years at Rennes in quiet obscurity. Shortly before his death, he was elected corresponding member of the Académie des Sciences, twelve years after his name was first proposed.

From the beginning of his career in zoology, Dujardin seems to have perceived the importance of observing organisms in the living state. Having already traveled widely during his geological and botanical studies, he expanded his excursions in pursuit of living animal specimens. Some of this spirit is reflected in his rare but charming little book *Promenades d'un naturaliste* (Paris, 1838).

In the autumn of 1834 Dujardin went to the Mediterranean coast to study microscopic marine animals. It was this work that led him to suggest the existence of a new family, the Rhizopods (literally, "rootfeet"). This suggestion was based primarily on his careful examination of several living species belonging to a widely distributed group long known as the Foraminifera. The most obvious feature of these tiny organisms (especially in the fossil state) is a delicate multichambered shell, outwardly similar to the shell of such mollusks as the Nautilus, and they had consequently been classified as "microscopic cephalopods" by Alcide d'Orbigny in 1825. Although d'Orbigny's classification was subsequently supported by the authority of Georges Cuvier, Dujardin rejected it because he was unable to see in the Foraminifera any evidence of the internal structure one ought to find in a mollusk. He perceived that the shell was only a secondary, external structure. By carefully crushing or decalcifying these delicate shells, he exposed a semifluid internal substance having no apparent structure.

As Dujardin observed the Foraminifera in their living state, he was struck by the activity of this contractile internal substance, which exuded spontaneously through pores in the calcareous shells to form pseudopodic rootlets. With equal spontaneity, these rootlets might then retract within the shell again. Dujardin became convinced that he was observing a special sort of amoeboid movement, in effect an amoeba within a porous shell. But pseudopodic rootlets could also be seen in microscopic animals having a less distinct casing than that of the Foraminifera, and Dujardin suggested that all such organisms should be joined in a new family to be called the Rhizopoda. According to this view, the Foraminifera, d'Orbigny's so-called "microscopic cephalopods," were in truth merely rhizopods with shells (*Rhizopodes à coquilles*).

This work in systematics led Dujardin to conclusions of far greater significance. In particular he now denied the famous "polygastric hypothesis" of Christian Ehrenberg, the foremost protozoologist of the era. Ehrenberg had recently revived Leeuwenhoek's view that infusoria were "complete organisms"; more specifically, that they possessed organ systems that imitated in miniature the general features of the organ systems of far more complex organisms, including the vertebrates. Like d'Orbigny, Ehrenberg enjoyed the support of Cuvier, and his theory was generally accepted. In his classificatory scheme, Ehrenberg placed several hundred species of infusoria in a new class, the Polygastrica (literally, "many stomachs"), in conformity with his belief that the globules or vacuoles which appear in most infusoria are tiny stomachs (as many as 200) connected together by an intestine. The strongest evidence for this belief came from experiments in which Ehrenberg had fed infusoria with various dyes (indigo and carmine, for example) and had then observed coloration of the "stomachs."

Dujardin reported that this conception had troubled him for some time. Although he could see neither the intestine nor the anal and oral orifices that Ehrenberg had posited, the "stomachs" were clearly visible. "I would," he wrote, "probably have lost courage and abandoned this research . . . if I had not fortunately found the solution to my problem in the discovery of the properties of *sarcode*."

"Sarcode" (from the Greek word for flesh) was the name Dujardin gave to the structureless substance he had found within the Foraminifera and other rhizopods and that he had found to be in every sense comparable to the substance of the amoeba and other Polygastrica. "The strangest property of *sarcode*," wrote Dujardin, "is the spontaneous production, in its mass, of vacuoles or little spherical cavities, filled with the environing fluid." It was these spontaneously produced vacuoles (*vacuoles adventives*) that Ehrenberg had mistaken for stomachs. Far from being complex organs, they were a natural result of the physical properties of sarcode; vacuoles could be formed at any time, by a spontaneous separating out of a part of the water present in living sarcode.

Ehrenberg's feeding experiments did not prove the existence of true stomachs, since the vacuoles did not become distended upon ingestion as might be expected of walled stomachs and only some of the vacuoles took on color, while others remained colorless. If they were stomachs, how could one explain "this choice of different aliments for different stomachs?" Dujardin thus rejected Ehrenberg's theory "with complete conviction," finding no reason to believe that his microscope and his sight were inferior to Ehrenberg's, especially since in several infusoria he had seen essential details which had escaped the German observer.

Dujardin presented all this work in a memoir of 1835. Ehrenberg did not retract, however. When in 1838 he published his monumental work on the infusoria as complete animals, he took every opportunity to ridicule Dujardin. In 1841 Dujardin gathered his work together in a large but less pretentious treatise on the infusoria. In this work, which became the starting point for later attempts to classify the protozoa, Dujardin reasserted his views but treated Ehrenberg rather more fairly than Ehrenberg had treated him. The polemic between Dujardin and Ehrenberg stimulated great interest in the microscopic animals and focused attention on one of the most important and recurrent issues in the history of biology—the relation between structure and function. By 1870 this issue had been resolved at one level by the general acceptance of the protoplasmic theory of life, according to which the basic attributes of life resided in a semifluid, largely homogeneous ground substance (protoplasm) having no apparent structure.

Dujardin's description of sarcode represents an important step toward this view. In his memoir of 1835, he wrote: "I propose to name *sarcode* that which other observers have called living jelly [*gelée vivante*], this diaphanous, glutinous substance, insoluble in water, contracting into globular masses, attaching itself to dissecting-needles and allowing itself to be drawn out like mucus; lastly, occurring in all the lower animals interposed between the other elements of structure." Dujardin went on to describe the behavior of sarcode when subjected to various chemicals. Potash seemed to hasten its decomposition by water, while nitric acid and alcohol caused it to coagulate suddenly, turning it white and opaque. "Its properties," wrote Dujardin, "are thus quite distinct from those of substances with which it might be confused, for its insolubility in water distinguishes it from albumen (which it resembles in its mode of coagulation), while at the same time its insolubility in potash distinguishes it from mucus, gelatin, etc."

Because this is such a remarkably complete and accurate description of what would later be called protoplasm, some of Dujardin's admirers have insisted that the German-directed (most especially by the histologist Max Schultze) substitution of "protoplasm" for "sarcode" represents "a violation of all good rules of nomenclature and justice."[2] If this attitude is meant to suggest that Dujardin was the rightful discoverer of the substance of life, one major objection can be raised; namely, that it ascribes to Dujardin's work a broader interpretation than he himself seems to have given it. He did suggest, even in 1835, that sarcode was present in a number of animals more complicated than the infusoria (worms and insects, for example), and he did soon after recognize that the white blood corpuscles were also composed of sarcode. The identity between plant protoplasm and animal sarcode seems to have escaped him, however, and was emphasized instead by German workers, most notably Ferdinand Cohn and Max Schultze. Until this identity was recognized, the notion of a substance of life had little meaning. Perhaps Dujardin missed the identity because he never integrated his notion of sarcode with the concept of the cell.

Dujardin published memoirs on a variety of animals other than the infusoria, particularly the coelenterates, intestinal worms, and insects. In 1838 he described a rare species of spiculeless sponge, to which his name was later attached. He also considered the then disputed question whether sponges were animals or plants, and concluded that they were animals. In 1844, he published a major treatise on the intestinal worms, which laid the basis for much of the work done since in helminthology and parasitology.

At the time of his death, Dujardin was engaged in a major study of the echinoderms, although he was by then more interested in questions of broader biological significance. He regretted that this work on the echinoderms kept him from a proper investigation of the "division of germs," of the species problem, and particularly from a new study on sarcode. This last point is especially interesting because by 1852 at least, Dujardin clearly recognized that the properties of sarcode led to an idea of great biological significance—the idea of "life as anterior to organization, as independent of the permanence of forms, as capable of making and defying organization itself."[3] It should be emphasized that Dujardin did not really deny all organization whatever to sarcode. Rather, he argued that its organization could not be compared to the definite structures observable in higher organisms. He seems to have had an almost prophetic vision of the importance of organization at the more subtle molecular level, and with the benefit of hindsight, E. Fauré-Fremiet makes a persuasive case for considering Dujardin a pioneer in the colloidal chemistry of protoplasm.[4]

Apart from this prophetic vision, perhaps the most appealing feature of Dujardin's work is his consistent modesty and rigorous attention to methodology. He always recognized that his work might undergo significant modification through the efforts of later workers and rarely made a claim that was not supported by his own direct observations. In placing the bacteria among the animals rather than the plants, in failing to recognize the significance of the nucleus, and in considering spontaneous generation possible, Dujardin was in the company of most of his contemporaries. His close attention to microscopic method is particularly apparent in his *Manuel de l'observateur au microscope* (1843), but it also informs his major treatise on the infusoria, which contains a brief but suggestive sketch of the historical interrelationship between developments in microscopic technique and developments in knowledge about the microscopic animals.

The breadth of Dujardin's early interests was crucial to his later success in protozoology. His artistic talent and training is evident in the many careful and beautiful plates with which his works are illustrated. His knowledge of optics allowed him to develop an improved method of microscopic illumination which bore his name and which can be considered an ancestor of the present condenser. Finally, his knowledge of physics and chemistry was important in enabling him to describe so completely and so accurately the properties of sarcode. It is easy to agree with Dujardin's admirers that his work was improperly appreciated during his lifetime, and easy to understand why protozoologists still cite his work with admiration today.[5]

NOTES

1. Charles Lyell, "On the Occurrence of Two Species of Shells of the Genus *Conus* in the Lias, or Inferior Oolite, near Caen in Normandy," in *Annals of Natural History,* **6** (1840), 293; and *Principles of Geology* (9th ed., London, 1853), p. 236.
2. Yves Delage, *La structure du protoplasma et les théories sur l'hérédité et les problèmes grands de la biologie générale* (Paris, 1895), p. 19. See also L. Joubin, p. 10.
3. E. Fauré-Fremiet, pp. 261–262.
4. *Ibid.,* 266–268.
5. See, e.g., Reginald D. Manwell, *Introduction to Protozoology* (New York, 1968).

BIBLIOGRAPHY

I. ORIGINAL WORKS. Dujardin's major works are "Recherches sur les organismes inférieurs," in *Annales des sciences naturelles (zoologie),* 2nd ser., **4** (1835), 343–377; *Histoire naturelle des zoophytes. Infusoires, comprenant la physiologie et la classification de ces animaux et la manière de les étudier à l'aide du microscope* (Paris, 1841); and *Histoire naturelle des Helminthes ou vers intestinaux* (Paris, 1845).

A complete bibliography of Dujardin's ninety-six published works can be found in Joubin (see below), pp. 52–57, while sixty-four of his papers are cited in the *Royal Society Catalogue of Scientific Papers,* II, 378–380.

Dujardin's rich collection of manuscripts, including laboratory notes and more than 500 letters, many of which are from the leading scientists of the day, is preserved at the Faculty of Sciences in Rennes. This probably important collection remains largely untapped, although Joubin and E. Fauré-Fremiet have made some use of it.

II. SECONDARY LITERATURE. The basic source is L. Joubin, "Félix Dujardin," in *Archives de parasitologie,* **4** (1901), 5–57. At the time he wrote this paper, Joubin held the chair at Rennes once occupied by Dujardin, and it was his clear intention to bestow on his predecessor all the honor he had been denied in life. The attempt was marred by Joubin's consistent and uncritical tendency to give Dujardin's work an importance that only hindsight can provide.

Also on Dujardin, see Enrique Beltrán, "Felix Dujardin y su *Histoire naturelle des zoophytes. Infusoires,* 1841," in *Revista de la Sociedad mexicana de historia natural,* **2** (1941), 221–232; "Notas de historia protozoologica. I. El descubrimiento de los sarcodarios y los trabajos de F. Dujardin," *ibid.,* **9** (1948), 341–345; and E. Fauré-Fremiet, "L'oeuvre de Félix Dujardin et la notion du protoplasma," in *Protoplasma,* **23** (1935), 250–269.

More generally, see J. R. Baker, "The Cell Theory: A Restatement, History, and Critique. Part II," in *Quarterly Journal of the Microscopical Sciences,* **90** (1949), 87–107; F. J. Cole, *The History of Protozoology* (London, 1926); G. L. Geison, "The Protoplasmic Theory of Life and the Vitalist-Mechanist Debate," in *Isis,* **60** (1969), 273–292; *Toward a Substance of Life: Concepts of Protoplasm, 1835–1870* (unpublished M.A. thesis, Yale University, 1967); and Arthur Hughes, *A History of Cytology* (London, 1959).

GERALD L. GEISON

DULLAERT OF GHENT, JEAN (*b.* Ghent, Belgium, *ca.* 1470; *d.* Paris, France, 19 September 1513), *logic, natural philosophy.*

Dullaert is sometimes confused with John of Jandun, owing to the Latin form of his name, Joannes de Gandavo. At the age of fourteen Dullaert was sent to Paris to study. He was a pupil of, and later taught with, John Major at the Collège de Montaigu; in 1510 he became a master at the Collège de Beauvais. Among his students at Montaigu were the Spaniards Juan de Celaya and Juan Martínez Silíceo, both important for their contributions to the rise of mathematical physics, and the humanist Juan Luis Vives.

At Paris, Dullaert published his questions on the *Physics* and the *De caelo* of Aristotle (1506), which appeared in at least two subsequent editions (1511; Lyons, 1512); a commentary on the *De interpretatione* of Aristotle (1509; Salamanca, 1517, edited by Silíceo); and an exposition of Aristotle's *Meteorology* (1512). The last title was reissued posthumously, "with Dullaert's questions," in 1514 by Vives, who prefaced

a brief biography wherein he states that Dullaert had left unfinished a commentary on the *Prior Analytics;* this apparently was prepared for publication in 1520/1521 by Jean Drabbe, also of Ghent. At the time of his death Dullaert was also working on a general edition of the works of Albertus Magnus that was based on previously unedited manuscripts which he himself had discovered. Earlier he had edited and revised for publication Jean Buridan's questions on Aristotle's *Physics* (1509) and Paul of Venice's *De compositione mundi* (*ca.* 1512) and *Summa philosophiae naturalis* (1513).

Like Paul of Venice, Dullaert was an Augustinian friar, and he showed a predilection for the realist views of this confrere while being strongly attracted also to the nominalist teaching then current at Paris. Perhaps for this reason his questions on the *Physics* are eclectic and, in many passages, inconclusive. At the same time they summarize in great detail (and usually with hopelessly involved logical argument) the teachings of Oxford "calculatores" such as Thomas Bradwardine, William Heytesbury, and Richard Swineshead; of Paris "terminists" such as Jean Buridan, Albert of Saxony, and Nicole Oresme; and of Italian authors such as James of Forlì, Simon of Lendenaria, and Peter of Mantua—while not neglecting the more realist positions of Walter Burley and Paul of Venice. The logical subtlety of Dullaert's endless dialectics provoked considerable adverse criticism from Vives and other humanists, but otherwise his teachings were appreciated and frequently cited during the early sixteenth century.

The structure of Dullaert's treatment of motion, which covers sixty-nine of the 175 folios constituting the questions on the *Physics* and *De caelo,* shows the strong influence of Heytesbury's *Tractatus de tribus praedicamentis,* with some accommodation along lines suggested by Albert of Saxony's *Tractatus proportionum.* Dullaert treats successively the entitative status of local motion, the velocity of local motion (both rectilinear and curvilinear), the velocity of augmentation, and the velocity of alteration, digressing in the latter tract to take up the intension and remission of forms. He is ambiguous in discussing the reality of local motion but holds for the impetus theory of Jean Buridan, regarding impetus as a kind of accidental gravity in the projectile that is corrupted by the projectile's own natural tendencies. He raises the question whether the impetus acquired by a falling body is proportional to the weight of the body but declines an answer. Following John Major, he teaches that God has the power to produce an actual (as opposed to a potential) infinity, and he sees no difficulty in the existence of a void. His views were generally taken over and clarified by Juan de Celaya, Luis Coronel, and others at Paris and in Spanish universities.

BIBLIOGRAPHY

None of Dullaert's works is available in English. A copy of the *Quaestiones super octo libros Aristotelis physicorum necnon super libros de caelo et mundo* (Lyons, 1512) is in Houghton Library of Harvard University. Pierre Duhem, *Études sur Léonard de Vinci*, III (Paris, 1913), gives numerous brief excerpts from this in French translation.

On Dullaert or his work, see Hubert Élie, "Quelques maîtres de l'université de Paris vers 1'an 1500," in *Archives d'histoire doctrinale et littéraire du moyen âge*, **18** (1950–1951), 193–243, esp. 222–223; R. G. Villoslada, *La universidad de Paris durante los estudios de Francisco de Vitoria, O.P., (1507–1522)*, Analecta Gregoriana XIV (Rome, 1938); and William A. Wallace, "The Concept of Motion in the Sixteenth Century," in *Proceedings of the American Catholic Philosophical Association,* **41** (1967), 184–195; and "The Enigma of Domingo de Soto: *Uniformiter difformis* and Falling Bodies in Late Medieval Physics," in *Isis,* **59** (1968), 384–401.

WILLIAM A. WALLACE, O.P.

DULONG, PIERRE LOUIS (*b*. Rouen, France, 12/13 February 1785; *d*. Paris, France, 19 July 1838), *chemistry, physics.*

Dulong's father died shortly after his birth; and when he was four and a half, his mother died. An aunt, Mme. Fauraux, assumed responsibility for the young orphan and took him into her home at Auxerre, where he attended the local *collège*. His teachers encouraged his mathematical ability, and he was able to study some science at the *école centrale* founded in Auxerre in 1796. He succeeded in the competition for the École Polytechnique in Paris, which he entered in 1801 at the minimum age of sixteen. Excessive study ruined Dulong's health, and in his second year he withdrew from the school. He then turned to medicine as a career. He could do this because formal qualifications were not required in post-Revolutionary France. Dulong practiced in one of the poorer districts of Paris. Although the number of patients rapidly increased, his small capital ran out, for the tender-hearted doctor not only treated his patients without charge but offered to pay for their prescriptions.

After leaving medicine, Dulong turned first to botany and then to chemistry, hoping to make a name for himself in this newly famous science. In chemistry he found his métier, although his subsequent work in physics and physical chemistry exhibited the value of his mathematical training at the École Polytechnique. First Dulong obtained a position as an assistant in Louis Jacques Thenard's laboratory, and then Berthollet offered him a place in his private laboratory at Arcueil.

Dulong married Émélie Augustine Rivière on 29 October 1803. They had four children, one of whom died in infancy. Dulong's mature years were dominated by a conflict between his desire to do research and the necessity of accepting numerous teaching, examining, and administrative positions in order to buy apparatus and provide for his family. This conflict often developed into a crisis because of his persistent bad health. His first teaching post (1811) was at the École Normale, and in 1813 he was appointed to teach chemistry and physics at the École Vétérinaire d'Alfort. In 1820 he was appointed professor of chemistry at the Faculté des Sciences in Paris. At the École Polytechnique he was first appointed as examiner (1813–1820) and then professor of physics (1820–1830). Of the latter appointment Dulong wrote:

> Through a weakness of character for which I reproach myself incessantly, I have consented to accept the professorship of physics at the École Polytechnique, which the death of my unfortunate friend [Petit] has left vacant. Even with good health the duties of this post would have left me with little free time, so judge how much of this I have had, sick as I have been for the past eighteen months.[1]

In 1831 Dulong's friend Arago succeeded in relieving him of his teaching duties at the École Polytechnique by securing for him the post of director of studies, an office that was purely administrative. Dulong's health subsequently improved, but he bitterly regretted that he no longer had the laboratory facilities of his teaching post.

Dulong was a member of the Société d'Arcueil (1811) and the Société Philomatique (1812). He was elected to the physics section of the Académie des Sciences on 27 January 1823. In 1828 he became president of the Academy for one year, and later ill-advisedly accepted the position of permanent secretary for a short time (1832–1833).

Dulong's first publication, a report on work that he had carried out at Arcueil, reflects very clearly the influence of his patron, Berthollet. This memoir, read at a meeting of the First Class of the Institute in July 1811, provided a striking confirmation of Berthollet's thesis that chemical affinities were not fixed and that chemical reactions could often be reversed. Dulong showed that when barium sulfate, a notoriously "insoluble" salt, was boiled with a solution containing an equivalent quantity of potassium carbonate, it was partly decomposed. In another experiment, in which "insoluble" barium carbonate was added to a boiling solution of potassium sulfate, a partial exchange took place. From the small amount of barium sulfate formed, Dulong considered that a state of equilibrium had been reached.

It was his work on "insoluble" salts that led Dulong to make a special study of the oxalates of barium, strontium, and calcium. He went on to study the action of heat on oxalates and reached the conclusion that oxalic acid consisted of hydrogen and carbon dioxide;[2] he suggested that it might accordingly be renamed "hydrocarbonic acid." To Dulong, a metal oxalate was a simple compound of the metal and carbonic acid, although this was contrary to current chemical theory, according to which metals could combine with acids only in the form of oxides. Dulong's work therefore contributed to the post-Lavoisier conception of an acid as a compound containing hydrogen that is replaceable by a metal. Dulong compared the carbon dioxide in a metal oxalate to cyanogen in a cyanide or chlorine in hydrochloric acid. He thus deserves mention as a precursor of the radical theory in organic chemistry.

Better known, and certainly more spectacular, was Dulong's discovery of the spontaneously explosive oil nitrogen trichloride. Not realizing the danger involved when he first prepared a small quantity of the substance in October 1811, he lost a finger and the sight of one eye. He began his memoir (1813) by pointing out that only three elements—nitrogen, carbon, and boron—were apparently unable to combine with "oxymuriatic acid" (chlorine). He presented his research as an attempt to make nitrogen and chlorine combine. Although the gases did not combine directly, Dulong was more successful when he passed a current of chlorine through a fairly concentrated solution of ammonium chloride. After the reaction had been going on for two hours at a temperature of between 7° and 8° C., a yellow oil began to form. This was what exploded.

By February 1812 Dulong had sufficiently recovered from his injuries to resume his investigation. He now realized that he could avoid an explosion only if he kept the temperature low. Accordingly, he waited until the following October to carry out further research. He succeeded in determining the qualitative composition of the oil by allowing it to come into contact with copper; the only products were copper chloride and nitrogen. After receiving further injuries, Dulong abandoned this research. His memoir, however, contains the following remarks about the explosive properties of the new compound. They are significant in the light of his later thermochemical studies:

It seems to me that this compound contains a certain amount of combined heat which, when its elements separate from each other, raises their temperature and imparts to them a great elastic force.[3]

In 1816 Dulong carried out two pieces of chemical research prompted by the interest of Berthollet's circle at Arcueil in combining proportions. There was very great divergence between the analyses of phosphoric acid published by various chemists, and there was also some difference of opinion between Gay-Lussac and Thenard on the composition of phosphorous acid. It was in an attempt to clarify this situation that Dulong found that there were at least four acids of phosphorus. In addition to the two mentioned above, the composition of which he determined accurately, Dulong was able to confirm the existence of hypophosphoric acid and discovered a fourth acid that was obtained from the solution remaining after the action of water on barium phosphide. Dulong named this syrupy acid "hypophosphorous acid." His memoir (1817) contained a careful analysis of the new acid and a discussion of its salts.

The various oxides of nitrogen had created some confusion in the early nineteenth century. In 1816 Gay-Lussac had succeeded in distinguishing five oxides of nitrogen and had given their correct chemical composition. Dulong repeated Gay-Lussac's preparation of dinitrogen tetroxide. By heating *dry* crystals of lead nitrate, he excluded water from the product, which was collected as a liquid in a tube surrounded by a freezing mixture. He was the first to make a study of the color changes undergone by this interesting compound over a wide range of temperature, from a colorless solid at −20°C. to a deep red vapor when heated.

In 1819, when Berzelius was in Paris, Dulong collaborated with him in determining the gravimetric composition of water. This was a fundamental datum of chemistry, and it was important that it should be determined with great precision. They passed pure hydrogen over heated copper oxide and absorbed the water formed with anhydrous calcium chloride. The mean of their results gave the ratio $H:O = 11.1:88.9$, or, as Dumas later represented it, $1:8.008$. Dulong and Berzelius had been able to work only to an accuracy of approximately 1/60, and the remarkable accuracy of their result was due largely to the canceling out of errors. Dumas did not carry out his classic redetermination of this ratio until 1842.

In 1815 Dulong's famous collaboration with the mathematical physicist Alexis Thérèse Petit began; it produced three important memoirs on heat. The best-known part of this work is the statement of the law of constant atomic heats that bears their names, which is discussed further below. They began with the fundamental problem of measuring quantities of heat, which involved a critical analysis of thermometric scales. In 1804–1805 Gay-Lussac had carried out a comparison of mercury and air thermometers between 0°C. and 100°C. Dulong and Petit extended the range of comparison up to 300°C. and found an increasing discrepancy between the two scales at higher temperatures.

Dulong and Petit continued their researches in 1817, stimulated by the subjects of the prize to be awarded by the Académie des Sciences in 1818. The first of the three subjects for this prize was to determine the movement of the mercury thermometer as compared with an air thermometer from −20°C. to +200°C. They approached the subject by determining the *absolute* coefficient of expansion of mercury, and to do this they introduced the now classic method of balancing columns. Two vertical columns of mercury, one hot and the other cold, were connected by a thin horizontal tube. Since the columns balanced, the two pressures were equal, or

$$h:d = h':d',$$

where h is the height of the column and d is the density. Since density is inversely proportional to volume, a simple method was now available for direct measurement of the expansion of the mercury without reference to the material of the vessel. A refined version of this apparatus, introduced later by Regnault, became the standard apparatus for determining a liquid's coefficient of absolute expansion.

The second part of the subject for the Academy's prize was to determine the laws of cooling in a vacuum; Dulong and Petit accordingly undertook a complete re-examination of Newton's law of cooling. The most remarkable feature of their work was the way they broke down a complex phenomenon into its constituent parts and dealt with each factor separately. For example, they distinguished losses due to radiation from those due to contact with particles of a gas. They thus arrived at a series of laws relating to different special cases. It was not until 1879 that Stefan was able to reduce the phenomenon of radiation to a simple law. The memoir in which he did this took the work of Dulong and Petit as its starting point, and Stefan was at pains to show that his law agreed with their experimental results.[4] There is no doubt that the young Frenchmen deserved to win the 3,000-franc prize offered by the Academy.

The third and last joint memoir of Dulong and Petit was also on heat. Among its far-reaching implications was a new approach to Dalton's atomic theory, which had been received in France with deep skepticism. In considering some of the implications of the atomic theory, Dulong and Petit therefore began on a defensive note:

> Convinced . . . that certain properties of matter would present themselves under more simple forms, and could be expressed by more regular and less complicated laws, if we could refer them to the elements upon which they immediately depend, we have endeavoured to introduce the most certain results of the atomic theory into the study of some of the properties which appear most intimately connected with the individual action of the material molecules.[5]

They were concerned with the specific heats of elements; but if these elements really existed as atoms, it seemed possible that there might be a connection between the weight of the atom and the amount of heat required to raise the temperature of a given weight of that element by a certain amount.

Dulong and Petit first had to develop a reliable method of determining specific heats, for the published data were quite unreliable. They adopted the method of cooling that used the finely powdered solid packed round the bulb of a thermometer (since the rates of cooling are directly proportional to the thermal capacities and hence to the specific heats). They recorded the specific heats of a dozen metals and sulfur, and then multiplied each by the element's atomic weight. The following table shows the remarkably constant value obtained.

	Specific heat (water = 1)	Atomic weight (oxygen = 1)	Product of specific heat and atomic weight
Bismuth	0.0288	13.30	0.3830
Lead	0.0293	12.95	0.3794
Gold	0.0298	12.43	0.3704
Platinum	0.0314	11.16	0.3740
Tin	0.0514	7.35	0.3779
Silver	0.0557	6.75	0.3759
Zinc	0.0927	4.03	0.3736
Tellurium	0.0912	4.03	0.3675
Copper	0.0949	3.957	0.3755
Nickel	0.1035	3.69	0.3819
Iron	0.1100	3.392	0.3731
Cobalt	0.1498	2.46	0.3685
Sulfur	0.1880	2.011	0.3781

Dulong and Petit said that inspection of this table showed "the existence of a physical law susceptible of being generalized and extended to all elementary substances." Certainly it showed that the specific heats of the elements tested were inversely proportional to their atomic weights. Their interest in the atomic structure of matter is revealed by their conclusion, "The atoms of all simple bodies have exactly the same capacity for heat," and also by their suggestion that the actual distances between the atoms might be calculated from thermal expansion data. Of more immediate concern to chemists, however, was the use of their law of atomic heats in settling disputed values of atomic weights. On the basis of their law, Dulong and Petit changed some of Berzelius' atomic weights—for example, they halved his values for silver and sulfur. Following his success in relating atomic weights to specific heats, Dulong investigated the possibility of a relation between the atomic (or molecular) weights of gases and their refractive indexes, but with little success.

After Petit's death in 1820, Dulong carried out further research on heat by himself and published a memoir on the specific heats of gases (1829). He determined the relation of the specific heats of various gases at constant pressure and constant volume by measuring the effect of change in temperature on the tone produced when the respective gases were passed through a flute. His method was an extension of one used by Chladni in 1807. He concluded that (1) equal volumes of all gases under the same conditions of temperature and pressure, when suddenly compressed or expanded to the same fraction of their original volume, give off or absorb the same quantity of heat; (2) the resulting temperature changes are inversely proportional to the specific heats of the respective gases at constant volume.

Dulong also worked on animal heat, taking up the subject when it was chosen in 1821 for the prize of the Académie des Sciences. He devised a respiration calorimeter in which the heat was absorbed by water rather than by ice, as in the classic apparatus of Lavoisier and Laplace. Because of unsatisfactory agreement between the theoretical and actual quantities of heat obtained (due largely to incorrect data), Dulong was not satisfied with his work and it was not published until after his death. The situation was similar in the case of his work on thermochemistry, where he measured several heats of combustion. In conversations with Hess in 1837, Dulong made such generalizations as "The quantities of heat evolved are approximately the same for the same substances, combining at different temperatures," and "Equal volumes of all gases give out the same quantity of heat." Dulong's concern with generalizing about heats of reaction may have inspired Hess to formulate his law of constant heat summation (1840).

Dulong collaborated with Thenard on a study of catalytic phenomena. They confirmed Döbereiner's discovery that a jet of hydrogen could be kindled by allowing it to impinge in air on spongy platinum. They found that palladium, rhodium, and iridium are active at room temperature and other metals at higher temperatures. They realized that the metal's activity was dependent on its physical state but offered no explanation of the action of these substances, which Berzelius later called *catalysts*.

Dulong collaborated with Arago on a long and perilous study of the pressure of steam at high temperatures. This work was prompted by the French government's concern about the safety of boilers. They first confirmed the validity of Boyle's law at pressures up to twenty-seven atmospheres. They were then able to measure the steam pressure in boilers by means of a manometer, and afterward they calculated the temperatures corresponding to these pressures.

NOTES

1. Letter to Berzelius. 21 Aug. 1821, in Berzelius, *Bref* (Uppsala, 1912-1925), II, pt. 4, 29.
2. Although this was never published by Dulong, Cuvier gave an account of it in *Mémoires de l'Institut* (1813-1815), Histoire, 198-200. See also Gay-Lussac, in *Annales de chimie et de physique,* **1** (1816), 157; and Ampère, *ibid.,* p. 298.
3. *Mémoires de physique et de chimie de la Société d'Arcueil,* **3** (1817), 62.
4. "Über die Bezeihung zwischen der Wärmestrahlung und der Temperatur. I. Über die Versuche von Dulong und Petit," in *Sitzungsberichte der kaiserlichen Akademie der Wissenschaften.* Mathematisch-naturwissenschaftliche Classe, **59,** Abt. 2 (1879), 391-410.
5. *Annales de chimie et de physique,* **10** (1819), 395.

BIBLIOGRAPHY

I. ORIGINAL WORKS. Dulong wrote both alone and in collaboration. Works of which he was the sole author include "Recherches sur la décomposition mutuelle des sels solubles et insolubles," in *Annales de chimie et de physique,* **82** (1812), 273-308; "Mémoire sur une nouvelle substance détonnante," *ibid.,* **86** (1813), 37-43, and in *Mémoires de physique et de chimie de la Société d'Arcueil,* **3** (1817), 48-63; "Observations sur quelques combinaisons de l'azote avec l'oxigène," in *Annales de chimie et de physique,* **2** (1816), 317-328; "Mémoire sur les combinaisons du phosphore avec l'oxigène," in *Mémoires de physique et de chimie de la Société d'Arcueil,* **3** (1817), 405-452; "Recherches sur les pouvoirs réfringents des fluides élastiques," in *Annales de chimie et de physique,* **31** (1826), 154-181; "Recherches sur la chaleur spécifique des fluides élastiques," *ibid.,* **41** (1829), 113-158; "Sur la chaleur dégagée pendant la combustion de diverses substances simples ou composées," in *Comptes rendus de l'Académie des sciences,* **7** (1838), 871-877; and "De la chaleur animale" (1822-1823), in *Annales de chimie et de physique,* 3rd ser., **1** (1841), 440-455.

With Petit, he wrote "Lois de la dilatation des solides, des liquides et des fluides élastiques à de hautes températures," in *Annales de chimie et de physique,* **2** (1816), 240–264; "Recherches sur la mesure des températures, et sur les lois de la communication de la chaleur," *ibid.,* **7** (1817), 113–154, 225–264, 337–367; and "Recherches sur quelques points importants de la théorie de la chaleur," *ibid.,* **10** (1819), 395–413.

Berzelius collaborated with him on "Nouvelles déterminations des proportions de l'eau et de la densité de quelques fluides élastiques," in *Annales de chimie et de physique,* **15** (1820), 386–395.

Dulong and Thenard's researches produced "Note sur la propriété que possèdent quelques métaux de faciliter la combinaison des fluides élastiques," in *Annales de chimie et de physique,* **23** (1823), 440–444; and "Nouvelles observations sur la propriété dont jouissent certains corps de favoriser la combinaison des fluides élastiques," *ibid.,* **24** (1823), 380–387.

Arago and Dulong wrote "Exposé des recherches faites par ordre de l'Académie Royale des Sciences, pour déterminer les forces élastiques de la vapeur d'eau à de hautes températures," in *Annales de chimie et de physique,* **43** (1830), 74–110.

II. SECONDARY LITERATURE. Works on Dulong or his contributions are F. Arago, "Dulong," in *Notices biographiques,* 2nd ed. (Paris, 1865), III, 581–584; M. P. Crosland, *The Society of Arcueil. A View of French Science at the Time of Napoleon I* (Cambridge, Mass., 1967); R. Fox, "The Background to the Discovery of Dulong and Petit's Law," in *British Journal for the History of Science,* **4** (1968–1969), 1–22; J. Girardin and C. Laurens, *Dulong de Rouen. Sa vie et ses ouvrages* (Rouen, 1854); J. Jamin, "Études sur la chaleur statique et la vapeur, travaux de Dulong et Petit," in *Revue des deux mondes,* **11** (1855), 377–397; P. Lemay and R. E. Oesper, "Pierre Louis Dulong, His Life and Work," in *Chymia,* **1** (1948), 171–190; and G. Lemoine, "Dulong," in *Livre centenaire de l'École polytechnique* (Paris, 1895), I, 269–278.

M. P. CROSLAND

DUMAS, JEAN-BAPTISTE-ANDRÉ (*b.* Alès [formerly Alais], Gard, France, 14 July 1800; *d.* Cannes, France, 11 April 1884), *chemistry.*

Dumas, son of the town clerk of Alès, was educated at the classical *collège* in that southern town and then was apprenticed to an apothecary. In 1816 he emigrated to Geneva, where he studied pharmacy and was taught chemistry by Gaspard de La Rive, physics by Marc Pictet, and botany by Augustin de Candolle. He was given permission to conduct experiments in the chemical laboratory of Le Royer, a local pharmaceutical firm.

Dumas's earliest researches were in medicine and physiology. In 1823 he returned to France and was appointed *répétiteur* in chemistry at the École Poly-

technique. Shortly afterward he succeeded to Robiquet's chair of chemistry at the Athenaeum, where evening classes were held for adults.

In 1824, with Adolphe Brongniart and J. V. Audouin, Dumas founded *Annales des sciences naturelles.* Two years later he married Hermine Brongniart, daughter of Alexandre Brongniart, director of the royal porcelain works at Sèvres. In 1828 he published the first volume of his *Traité de chimie appliquée aux arts,* and the following year he was a cofounder of the École Centrale des Arts et Manufactures. Dumas was appointed assistant professor at the Sorbonne and became full professor in 1841, a position he held until his retirement in 1868. Since the contemporary practice was to hold several academic appointments at once, Dumas also occupied a chair at the École Polytechnique (from 1835) and in 1839 became professor of organic chemistry at the École de Médecine. He lectured occasionally at the Collège de France and gave instruction in experimental chemistry at his private laboratory from 1832 to 1848. From 1840 he was an editor of *Annales de chimie et de physique.*

Dumas, a moderate conservative, became actively involved in politics after the February Revolution of 1848 and was elected to the legislative assembly from Valenciennes immediately after the fall of Louis Philippe. He was minister of agriculture from 1850 to 1851, and when Napoleon III became emperor he was made a senator. He was also a member, vice-president (1855), and president (1859) of the Paris Municipal Council. With Haussmann, Dumas undertook the transformation and modernization of the capital, supervising the installation of modern drainage systems, water supply, and electrical systems. He became permanent secretary of the Academy of Sciences in 1868.

Dumas was a brilliant teacher and trained a galaxy of chemists, including Laurent, Stas, Leblanc, and Louis Melsens. The iniquitous system of multiple professorships was responsible for a great deal of bitterness directed against him by some of the younger chemists, a few of them his former pupils. Dumas, however, refrained from indulging in retaliatory measures, even though he was repeatedly subjected to unfounded attacks.

Dumas's work is notable for its wide range rather than for its depth and insight. His most original contributions stemmed from the adaptation of existing ideas and not from the desire to make revolutionary breakthroughs. This was partly the result of his eminently practical personality, always willing to compromise; but it was chiefly the result of his familiarity with the historical tradition of chemistry, which enabled him to situate every problem within a broader perspective. His historically oriented *Leçons sur la philosophie chimique* was very influential upon subsequent studies in the history of chemistry.

Dumas's practical interests resulted in numerous contributions to applied chemistry, including the publication of *Traité de chimie appliquée aux arts*. He investigated problems in metallurgy, such as the preparation of calcium and the treatment of iron ores; he studied the nature and properties of different kinds of commercial glass; and he was interested in questions as diverse as the materials used in thirteenth-century frescoes and the nature of the compounds of phosphorus and of minium. Dumas's researches on dyes were probably his most lasting contributions to industry: he analyzed indigo and established the relationship between the colorless and blue types. He was also the first chemist to show that picric acid, the yellow organic compound commonly used for dyeing during the period, was a derivative of phenol. Dumas made extensive studies in pharmaceutics and established the correct formulas for several alkaloids, chloroform, and other substances. His interest in animal and plant physiology led him to suggest numerous improvements in those fields.

He investigated the mechanism involved in the formation of animal fat and attempted to establish that it was utilized in the maintenance of body heat and combustion while it formed a reserve, stored in the body tissues, which could be released for metabolism whenever required. He also showed that there was a close analogy between vegetable and animal metabolism. Because of the growing exasperation of German scientists with the dominant position of French science, this period saw an increasing number of violent diatribes against any major discoveries made in France. J. Liebig was the undisputed champion of this growing and squalid German nationalism in scientific affairs. Along with the discoveries of most other major French chemists—including Laurent, Gerhardt, and Chevreul—he abusively attacked the physiological discoveries of Dumas in the most violent and unjustified manner.

The most important problem with which Dumas was concerned throughout his career was the classification of chemical substances. He sought to devise comprehensive classificatory schemes for organic compounds and for the elements. Dumas's earliest contribution to organic chemistry was his study of nine alkaloids, published in 1823, jointly with Pierre Pelletier.[1] He analyzed the elemental constituents of these organic "bases" and attempted to prove that their relative proportions of oxygen followed Dalton's law of multiple proportions. He had embraced the ideas of the two reigning theories in contemporary chemistry: dualism, with its division of substances into electronegative (acid) and electropositive (alkaline); and atomism, which Dalton had used to explain his law. Dumas spent the next few years attempting to create an adequate system of classification of organic compounds based upon these two theories.

In 1826 Dumas developed a new method for directly measuring the vapor densities, and indirectly (by calculation) the relative molecular weights of different substances in the gaseous state. His method, which had the merit of being both precise and simple, is still used in chemical analysis. Dumas used the method himself to determine the molecular weights of phosphorus, arsenic, and boron.

Although he explicitly referred to Avogadro and Ampère, Dumas nevertheless failed to make a clear distinction between molecules and atoms. He thought that the atomic weights of gaseous substances could be derived directly by measuring their densities. Dumas circumvented the limitation imposed upon the application of this principle by the small number of elements observed in a gaseous state with the help of Gay-Lussac's law of combining volumes. Since those elements formed gaseous compounds, it was relatively easy to determine the simple volumetric proportions in which they combined. Atomic weights could then be indirectly calculated from the measurement of the density and the application of Boyle's law and Gay-Lussac's law.

However, Dumas's original enthusiasm for this method was soon tempered by his realization of its obvious inadequacies, which could have been removed only by a clearer recognition of Avogadro's distinction between a molecule and an atom. Dumas pointed out several anomalies. For instance, a liter of chlorine and a liter of hydrogen contained the same number of atoms—say 1,000—at a given temperature and pressure. Upon combination, one atom of either element united with an atom of the other to form a single atom of hydrochloric acid gas. If it were true that all gases contained the same number of atoms under the same conditions, hydrogen and chlorine in the example above would have combined to produce one liter of hydrochloric acid gas containing 1,000 atoms. But this was not the case: two liters of the gas resulted. Therefore chlorine and hydrogen atoms could not be indivisible: they must have divided in two before combination in order to produce as many atoms of the compound gas as of the two elemental gases taken together—2,000—assuming that a liter of any gas contained 1,000 atoms. Dumas's initial hypothesis that the vapor density of a gas could give a direct measurement of its relative atomic weight was thus disproved.

Dumas tried to save the situation by postulating a distinction between two types of particles: those corresponding to molecules, which could not be split any further by purely physical means (such as heat), and the true chemical atoms, which were the smallest units entering into any chemical reaction. It was only the former whose relative weights could be determined by comparing vapor densities. In spite of this classification, Dumas's ideas on the subject were not always consistent; he accepted the concept of an atom grudgingly as his career advanced. He cited the particles found in identical numbers in all gases under similar conditions as examples of physical atoms. He found it impossible, however, to ascertain that the smallest particles involved in any chemical reaction were genuine examples of chemical atoms because there was always the chance that reactions were possible only with aggregates of chemical atoms rather than with single atoms.

He was, however, so far from rejecting atomism that from 1840 onward he carried out an important revision of the atomic weights of thirty elements. His most valuable contribution in this field was his very precise determination of the atomic weight of carbon (jointly with his pupil Stas) in 1840.[2] A previously accepted weight, determined by Berzelius as $C = 12.20$ ($O = 16$), was shown to be incorrect. Dumas proved that $C = 12\pm.002$ ($O = 16$) or $C = 75$ ($O = 100$). The analysis was made by burning diamond and artificial and natural graphite in oxygen; the carbon dioxide formed was weighed in potash solution. The results were in close agreement. The "new" weight of carbon had a great effect on the progress of organic chemistry.

Dumas never doubted that organic compounds were to be classified according to their structures, which depended upon their having an atomic (or particulate) constitution. His first important contribution to classificatory organic chemistry came in 1827, when he and his assistant Polydore Boullay published the first part of a study of ether; the final part appeared the following year. This paper assumed that the composition of organic compounds was dualistic, consisting of two parts corresponding to the acidic and basic constituents of an inorganic salt. First, the composition of alcohol and ether was determined by analysis and vapor density measurements. It was concluded that they were both hydrates of ethylene ("hydrogène bicarbone"); alcohol contained twice as much water combined with the hydrocarbon as ether did. Extending the analysis to "compound ethers" (i.e., esters) of nitrous, benzoic, oxalic, acetic,

and other acids with alcohol, it was shown that "compound ethers" could be divided into two kinds: those that were formed by oxyacids, which contained no water and were the salts of ether and anhydrous acids; and those that were formed by hydracids, which contained water and were salts of ether and hydrated acids.

Dumas affirmed that this dualistic interpretation should be related to the nature of ethylene rather than to that of ether. In all these cases it was the hydrocarbon that played the role of a powerful base, having a saturation capacity equal to that of ammonia. If it did not act upon litmus paper and other indicators, this was due to its insolubility in water. (The suggestion that ethylene was a strong base had originally been made by Chevreul.) This view was extended by Dumas to cover a large number of other cases. For instance, he suggested that cane sugar and grape sugar were salts formed by carbonic acid, ethylene, and water.

The dualistic theory was interpreted by Dumas in electrochemical terms in 1828; and he maintained this view for another ten years, although with diminishing enthusiasm as the discrepancies accumulated over the years. Until 1835 he was convinced that the electrochemical theory had been established with almost complete certainty. "All present-day chemistry is based upon the view that there is opposition between substances, which is admirably borne out by the evidence from electrical phenomena."[3] The constitution of oxamide (analogous to ethers), also investigated by Dumas, was explained by postulating the existence of the amide radical (N_2H_4) which remained after ammonia (N_2H_6) had lost hydrogen at the negative pole. Oxamide was a binary compound formed by the combination of carbon [mon]oxide (C_2O) with the amide radical. Even though the latter had not been isolated, its presence was to be assumed because it helped to explain, predict, and classify a large number of phenomena. For example, urea was best understood as being made up of carbon [mon]oxide (C_2O) combined with two amide radicals: $C_2O + 2N_2H_4$ (1830). Similarly, the strongly electropositive alkaline metals, sodium and potassium, formed amides, with the amide radical functioning electronegatively, like chlorine in metallic chlorides.

In 1835, through his investigations into "spirit of wood" (methyl alcohol), Dumas showed how the presence of a radical gave rise to a whole series of compounds. Something new was added to the earlier dualistic theories in this conception: isomerism. He had found that in various hydrocarbons, such as naphthalene and anthracene, or ethylene and isobutylene, carbon and hydrogen were combined in the same relative proportions but were "more closely packed together in one member than in the other." This discovery led Dumas to postulate the existence of a third hydrocarbon analogous to ethylene and isobutylene, where hydrogen and carbon were combined in a 1:1 ratio, although in different states of condensation. He suggested that the three hydrocarbons would constitute a series such that the condensation for each successive term was twice that of its immediate predecessor. In other words, ethylene was C_2H_2 (C = 6) and isobutylene C_4H_4; the new member would be CH, the immediate predecessor of ethylene. By this reasoning, based purely upon analogy, Dumas predicted and succeeded in discovering the whole methyl series. The first member of the series (CH) was called "methyl." In this way Dumas not only established a link between ethyl and methyl alcohols but also discovered the radical of cetyl alcohol, which had been known from Chevreul's earlier investigations.

From the known constitution of ethyl alcohol—interpreted as being composed of a hydrocarbon, ethylene (C_8H_8), and water—Dumas reasoned that there must be similar hydrocarbons to be found in other alcohols if their water could be extracted. Thus he succeeded in discovering, although not necessarily isolating, hydrocarbons combined with water in methyl alcohol, cetyl alcohol, etc.

A second set of analogies, worked out in conjunction with the hydrocarbon contained in methyl alcohol, indicated that this hydrocarbon could be made to combine with a host of substances—nitric acid, ammonia, chlorine, etc.—and give rise to a complete series of compounds in which the hydrocarbon is transferred from one combination to another. At the same time he realized that in certain hydrocarbons, carbon and hydrogen were contained in the same relative proportions, although not in the same relative quantities.

The Theory of Substitutions. The theory of substitutions (or "métalepsie") was stated by Dumas in 1834. Its main assertion was that the hydrogen in any compound could be replaced by an equivalent amount of a halogen, oxygen, or other element. Furthermore, in order to explain the action of chlorine on a substance containing hydrogen linked to oxygen (rather than to carbon), the theory maintained that "if the hydrogenized compound contains water (i.e., hydrogen linked to oxygen), the hydrogen is eliminated without replacement; but if a further quantity of hydrogen in subsequently removed, then it is replaced by an equivalent amount of chlorine, etc."

The importance of this law, which was the first to explain the mechanism of substitution reactions in organic chemistry, cannot be overestimated. Its historical origin has been explained in various fashions. The most likely explanation is the one offered by Dumas himself, which the context renders probable: he was interested in testing the correctness of his dualistic theory of the constitution of alcohols by examining the action of the halogens on these compounds. Both ethyl and methyl alcohol produced chloroform when subjected to the action of chlorine. This led him indirectly to the theory of substitutions.

In January 1834, Dumas had read to the Académie des Sciences the results of significant research[4] in which the correct molecular formulas for chloroform, bromoform, iodoform, and chloral were given for the first time. He had also observed during his investigations of the action of chlorine on alcohol to give chloral that ten volumes of hydrogen (C = 6) were removed from alcohol but were replaced by only six volumes of chlorine. This was contrary to the evidence he had obtained earlier when studying the action of chlorine on essence of turpentine, where each atom of hydrogen had been replaced by one of chlorine. However, the reaction of alcohol and chlorine was explicable if it were assumed that an atom of hydrogen directly combined with oxygen behaved differently from hydrogen atoms combined with carbon in an organic compound. In other words, if Dumas's theory of the constitution of alcohol were correct, it followed that the water molecule would react differently from the ethylene molecule. The action of chlorine on alcohol thus appeared to constitute a direct proof of the correctness of Dumas's dualistic theory: the hydrogen atoms lost by ethylene were replaced by chlorine; those eliminated from water were not, as was shown by the following equation:

$$C_8H_8,H_4O_2 + Cl_{16} = C_8H_2Cl_6O_2 + 5H_2Cl_2$$
$$\text{Alcohol} \quad \text{Chlorine} \quad \text{Chloral} \quad \text{Hydrochloric Acid}$$

Dumas continued his researches on the theory of substitution in order to seek further proof for his view of the constitution of alcohol and the ethers. Paradoxically, the theory was correct only for that part which Dumas had thought was subsidiary to his main proof, a proof based upon erroneous assumptions.

The Theory of Types. From 1837 he became progressively dissatisfied with the electrochemical dualistic theory because of the numerous difficulties that it could not resolve. Encouraged by the example of several young chemists who had developed alternative modes of explanation and classification in organic chemistry while ignoring electrochemical ideas, Dumas was also progressively led to abandon the dualistic theory in favor of a unitary view in which the whole molecule was conceived of as a single structure without polarization into negative and positive parts. Laurent had pointed out (1837) that within a series generated by a hydrocarbon, all the hydrogen molecules could be replaced by their equivalents of the halogens, oxygen, or other substance without the fundamental chemical characteristics of the compound being markedly affected. He therefore assumed that all molecules were unitary structures whose properties were dependent upon the position and arrangement of their component elements and not upon the intrinsic natures of the latter, whether electropositive or electronegative.

In 1839 Dumas discovered that the action of chlorine upon acetic acid formed a new compound (trichloroacetic acid) in which the hydrogen atoms of the acetic acid had been replaced by chlorine. But the new compound had virtually the same physical and chemical characteristics as the acetic acid, even though electronegative chlorine had replaced the strongly electropositive hydrogen. Dumas was converted to the unitary view by this experiment.

The role of his younger contemporaries in his adoption of the unitary theory was admitted by Dumas. He explicitly recognized the contributions of Laurent, Regnault, Faustino Malaguti, Rafaelle Piria, and J. P. Couerbe in his earliest papers, before a rather distasteful set of accusations about priorities were made against him in print by Laurent, Baudrimont, and several others. Dumas's fairness is demonstrated by his reference to Couerbe, who had emphasized the role of arrangement and position of atoms within a molecule in determining its properties: "I attribute the properties of alkaline compounds to the physical form of the molecule, a form produced by the grouping of the elementary atoms of this molecule. This idea, which I have generalized, is the cause, if not primary, at least the secondary cause, of its properties."[5] Dumas affiliated his views on unitary structures with those of his predecessors. In fact, Dumas was so generous that he did not even claim to have discovered the law of substitutions and contented himself with the modest role of having generalized a discovery made by a group of contemporary chemists: "I do not claim to have discovered it (the law of substitutions), for it does no more than reproduce more precisely and in a more generalized form, opinions that could be found in the writings of a large number of chemists. . . ."[6]

It is, however, of interest to see the gradual evolution of Dumas's thought on this subject, even during the period when he was convinced of the quasi certainty of the electrochemical theory. In 1828 he had already declared that the electrochemical theory was powerless to account for the dual behavior of certain elements that were negative in some combinations and positive in others. This implied the contradictory assumption that some molecules were both negatively and positively charged. For example, the halogens—chlorine, bromine, and iodine—were positive toward oxygen and negative toward hydrogen. Even more difficult to explain was the fact that while chlorine was positive toward oxygen and both chlorine and oxygen were negative in their compounds with calcium, chlorine displaced oxygen from calcium oxide.

In order to avoid a complete impasse, Dumas hinted at another mode of explanation: "It must be admitted that electrical relations are not alone in determining chemical reactions; in certain cases, the *number* of molecules, their *relative positions*"[7] were perhaps equally influential in modifying the outcome.

By 1834 these anomalous cases had vastly increased because of Dumas's interpretation that frequently, in binary organic compounds, carbon acted both electronegatively and electropositively. Often it was electropositive in an organic acid and negative in the corresponding base. For example, oxalic ester was composed of an acid (oxalic acid), a base (ethylene), and water; in it carbon functioned positively in the first constituent and negatively in the second. It is strange that the replacement of hydrogen by the electronegative halogens, in alcohols and other compounds, did not appear anomalous to Dumas when he formulated the law of substitution. In fact, he was still persuaded that hydrogen was the only absolutely electropositive element. This is all the more difficult to reconcile with his later (1838) remark to Berzelius that his theory of substitution was a simple empirical rule that described but did not explain phenomena, especially since almost immediately afterward he abandoned electrochemistry because of the anomalous role of hydrogen in substitution reactions. In fact, it is closer to the truth to say that Laurent and Baudrimont's conclusions about the unitary structure of molecules had been associated with the discovery of substitution reactions by Dumas as early as 1836, when a new note of caution crept into the latter's attitude toward electrochemistry. The dogmatic certainty of this theory had been replaced by Dumas's admission that the electrochemical theory was nothing more than a series of hypotheses for which no final proof was forthcoming.

After 1840 Dumas developed the type theory, in which he classified compounds according to two types: chemical and mechanical. The former were substances like acetic and chloroacetic acids, which have similar chemical properties, while the latter had more obscure analogies, basically of a physical kind.

Dumas's mechanical type, whose origin he attributed to Regnault's work on the ethers, was shown to be untenable by Laurent.

Whereas Laurent had adopted a static model for his fundamental types, based upon an analogy with crystalline structures, Dumas had adopted a dynamic planetary model in which the atoms in a molecule were seen as analogous to the planets in the solar system. Laurent's model was ultimately derived from Haüy, while Dumas was influenced by Berthollet.

Dumas and the Classification of Elements. In 1831, after the discovery of isomerism in compounds, Dumas had been led to speculate upon the possibility of isomerism among the elements: different elements might in fact be nothing but multiple structures in which the same fundamental element was duplicated or "condensed." This was supported by the comparison of atomic weights, since several elements had atomic weights which were whole-number multiples of one another, as was shown by the following table[8] drawn up at the time:

	Zinc	403.22
	Yttrium	401.84
1/2	Antimony	403.22
1/2	Tellurium	403.22
1/2	Sulfur	402.33
	Platinum	1233.26
	Indium	1233.26
	Osmium	1244.21
	Gold	1243.01
	Bismuth	1330.37
2	Palladium	1331.68
	Cobalt	369.99
	Nickel	369.67
1/2	Tin	367.64
	Cerium	574.7
	Tantalum	576.8
	Copper	395.7
1/2	Iodine	394.6
	Molybdenum	598.5
1/2	Tungsten	596.5
	Silicium	277.4
2	Boron	271.9

After his revision of atomic weights in the 1840's, Dumas had wanted to revive the speculation about a *materia prima* in conjunction with Prout's hypothesis that all elements were multiples of the hydrogen atom. In 1851 he read a paper to the British Associa-

tion in which he attempted to establish how certain regular patterns might be found in arranging elements, such that the heavier atoms were derived from combinations of lighter ones. He also published two papers[9] in which he tried to develop the view that for the classification of the elements it was possible to discover "generating" relations similar to those defining the series of organic compounds. The elements could be divided into "natural families." The atomic weights of all the members of the same family were linked by a simple arithmetic relationship; they increased by multiples of sixteen:

Li	7
Na	$7 + (1 \times 16) = 23$
K	$7 + (2 \times 16) = 39$
O	16
S	$16 + (1 \times 16) = 32$
Se	$16 + (4 \times 16) = 80$
Te	$16 + (7 \times 16) = 128$
Mg	24
Ca	$24 + (1 \times 16) = 40$
Sr	$24 + (4 \times 16) = 88$
Ba	$24 + (7 \times 16) = 136$

NOTES

1. "Recherches sur la composition eléméntaire et sur quelques propriétés caractéristiques des bases salifiables," in *Annales de chimie et de physique,* **24** (1823), 163–191.
2. "Sur le véritable poids atomique du carbone," *ibid.,* **1** (1841), 5–55, written with J. S. Stas; also in *Comptes rendus hebdomadaires des séances de l'Académie des sciences,* **11** (1840), 991–1008.
3. *Journal de pharmacie,* **20** (1834), 262.
4. "Recherches de chimie organique," in *Annales de chimie et de physique,* **56** (1854), 113–154; repr., with a few adds., as "Recherches de chimie organique, relative à l'action du chlore sur l'alcool," in *Mémoires de l'Académie des sciences,* **15** (1838), 519–556.
5. J. P. Couerbe, "Du cerveau considéré sous le point de vue chimique et physique," in *Annales de chimie et de physique,* **56** (1834), 189 n.
6. "Mémoire sur la loi des substitutions et la théorie des types," in *Comptes rendus hebdomadaires des séances de l'Académie des sciences,* **10** (1840), 178.
7. See the intro. to the *Traité de chimie appliquée aux arts,* I (Paris, 1828), lx; the italics are the author's.
8. "Lettre de M. Dumas à M. Ampère sur l'isomérie," in *Annales de chimie et de physique,* **47** (1831), 335.
9. "Sur les equivalents des corps simples," in *Comptes rendus hebdomadaires des séances de l'Académie des sciences,* **45** (1857), 709–731; **46** (1858), 951–953; and **47** (1858), 1026–1034; also in *Annales de chimie et de physique,* **55** (1859), 129–210.

BIBLIOGRAPHY

I. ORIGINAL WORKS. Dumas published most of his work in the *Annales de chimie et de physique* and in the *Mémoires* and the *Comptes rendus* of the Académie des Sciences. See the indexes for titles.

His books are *Phénomènes qui accompagnent la contraction de la fibre musculaire* (Paris, 1823); *Traité de chimie appliquée aux arts,* 8 vols. (Paris, 1828); *Leçons sur la philosophie chimique* (Paris, 1837); *Thèse sur la question de l'action du calorique sur les corps organiques* (Paris, 1838); *Essai sur la statique chimique des êtres organisés* (Paris, 1841).

II. SECONDARY LITERATURE. On Dumas's life and work see J.-B. Dumas, *La vie de J.-B. Dumas, par le général J.-B. Dumas son fils* (Paris, 1924), 230 mimeographed pp.; S. C. Kapoor, "Dumas and Organic Classification," in *Ambix,* **16** (1969), 1–65; and E. Maindron, *L'oeuvre de J.-B. Dumas* (Paris, 1886).

SATISH C. KAPOOR

DUMBLETON. *See* **John of Dumbleton.**

DU MONCEL, THÉODOSE ACHILLE LOUIS (*b.* Paris, France, 6 March 1821; *d.* Paris, 16 February 1884), *electricity, magnetism.*

Du Moncel studied at the *collège* of Caen and at the age of eighteen published two works on perspective. After graduation he traveled through Turkey and Greece and later published an elaborate account of his travels, for which he drew the lithograph illustrations. His interest in electricity began in 1852, following the publication in Cherbourg the previous year of a work on meteorology. Some sixty-five books and papers on electricity and magnetism followed during thirty years of active writing, his works being translated into English, German, Portuguese, and Italian.

Du Moncel's interest in electricity spanned the most fertile period of its development, from Faraday to Edison, and his publications analyzed each discovery and invention in the framework of the entire science. His early work dealt with the determination of the characteristics of electromagnets and their application to motor design, and the mutual interaction of magnets and energized conductors.

His first popular work, *Exposé des applications de l'électricité,* appeared in Paris in two volumes in 1853–1854 and was expanded to five volumes of 2,870 pages in 1856–1862, making it a valuable reference encyclopedia of electrical development up to that time. In it Du Moncel reviewed Charles Bourseul's proposal for the electric transmission of speech, the earliest approach to practical telephony. Du Moncel wrote of this, "I thought it incredible," yet it was held to have contained the germ of later Bell and Gray inventions. In the contests among telephone inventions, Du Moncel soon differentiated between those devices capable of transmitting only music and those

which could transmit the more complex articulations of the human voice. He gave maximum praise to Bell. Du Moncel also described electromagnetic equipment and its widening use in telegraphy, mechanics, and medicine. His most popular work, *Le téléphone, le microphone et le phonographe,* was first published in Paris in 1878 and was translated into English the following year. He collaborated with Sir William Henry Preece in publishing on electric illumination in 1882 and with Frank Geraldy on electric motors in the following year.

Du Moncel's publications also dealt with the printing telegraph, electromagnetic applications, especially electric motors and railway signals, the Ruhmkorff induction coil, lightning theory and lightning protection, the effect of the sun's passage over telegraph lines, and the forms and operation of electric batteries, clocks, and lamps. He then turned to the Atlantic cable, mathematical analysis of electromagnets, and grounded telegraph circuits. His final work, which concerned the electric motors of P. Elias and the Pacinotti dynamo, was published in 1883.

Although Du Moncel contributed no great discovery or invention of his own, his clear, widely read books and papers spread the advances in electrical science, which was rapidly expanding. His concern was less with electrical theory than with its devices and practical applications. His assiduous experiments and interpretations of the work of his colleagues helped organize the electrical innovations from the 1850's to the 1880's. He accepted tasks on behalf of his nation and profession and was accorded many honors. He became a member of the Technical Committee of the Administration of Telegraphs of France in 1860 and in 1866 was named a *chevalier* of the Legion of Honor. He was made a member of the Institute of France, elected to the Academy of Sciences, and in 1879 became editor of *Lumière électrique.* He was an early member of the Society of Telegraph Engineers and Electricians of London and was awarded the Order of St. Vladimir of Russia.

BIBLIOGRAPHY

Among Du Moncel's many books and monographs on electrical subjects are *Considérations nouvelles sur l'électromagnétisme* (Paris, 1853); *Exposé sommaire des principes et des lois de l'électricité* (Cherbourg, 1853); *Exposé des applications de l'électricité,* 2 vols. (Paris, 1853–1854; 2nd ed., 5 vols., 1856–1862; rev. 3rd. ed., 1872–1878); *Notice sur l'appareil d'inductions électrique de Ruhmkorff* (Paris, 1855; 4th ed., 1859); *Notices historiques et théoriques sur le tonnerre et les éclairs* (Paris, 1857); *Étude du magnétisme et de l'électro-magnétisme* (Paris, 1858); *Revue des applications de l'électricité en 1857 et 1858* (Paris, 1859); *Étude des lois des courants électriques* (Paris, 1860); *Traité théorique et pratique de télégraphie électrique* (Paris, 1864); *Le téléphone, le microphone et le phonographe* (Paris, 1878), Eng. trans. (New York, 1879); *L'éclairage électrique* (Paris, 1880), Eng. trans. (London, 1882), Italian trans. (Turin, 1885–1887); and *L'électricité comme force motrice* (Paris, 1883), Eng. trans. (London, 1883).

BERN DIBNER

DUNCAN, JOHN CHARLES (*b.* Duncan's Mill, near Knightstown, Indiana, 8 February 1882; *d.* Chula Vista, California, 10 September 1967), *astronomy.*

Duncan's chief contribution to astronomy was his photographic demonstration of expansion in the Crab nebula. He is perhaps better known, however, as the author of *Astronomy,* a standard college textbook for over thirty years, which was illustrated with many of his own excellent photographs of nebulae and galaxies.

The son of Daniel Davidson Duncan and his wife, Naomi Jessup, Duncan grew up in Indiana and taught at a country school there from 1901 to 1903 while an undergraduate at Indiana University in Bloomington. Between receiving his B.A. in 1905 and his M.A. in 1906, both from Indiana University, he was a fellow of Lowell Observatory in Flagstaff, Arizona. In 1907, following his marriage to Katharine Armington Bullard the previous year, he enrolled at the University of California, where he received a Ph.D. in 1909; his dissertation, on Cepheid variables, was written under the direction of William Wallace Campbell.

Returning to the East, he served as instructor in astronomy at Harvard University from 1909 to 1916, before becoming professor of astronomy and director of Whitin Observatory at Wellesley College. Upon his retirement from these posts in 1950—at the age of sixty-eight—he spent the next twelve years as visiting professor at the University of Arizona and visiting astronomer at Steward Observatory.

The Crab nebula, located in the constellation of Taurus, is still today a fruitful subject for investigation because of its association with the pulsar NP 0532; it is believed to be the remnant of a supernova observed in Japan and China in A.D. 1054. By comparing a photograph taken with the sixty-inch telescope at Mount Wilson in 1909 by George Willis Ritchey with one he took himself in 1921 with the same instrument, Duncan was able to demonstrate outward motions in the filaments of the Crab. He later confirmed these motions with another photograph taken in 1938, thus showing that it was indeed an expanding envelope such as has been observed around other novae.

Duncan also investigated comets, spectroscopic binary stars, and novae. His long-exposure photographs of nebulae and galaxies were taken during an appointment as astronomer at Mount Wilson in 1920 and during many subsequent summers spent there as a voluntary research assistant.

BIBLIOGRAPHY

I. ORIGINAL WORKS. Duncan's textbook, *Astronomy* (New York, 1926; 5th ed., 1955), also appeared in an abridged version, *Essentials of Astronomy* (New York, 1942).

His dissertation was published as "The Orbits of the Cepheid Variables Y *Sagittarii* and RT *Aurigae;* with a Discussion of the Possible Causes of This Type of Stellar Variation," in *Lick Observatory Bulletin,* **5** (1908–1910), 82–94. His work on the Crab nebula appeared as "Changes Observed in the Crab Nebula in Taurus," in *Proceedings of the National Academy of Sciences,* **7** (1921), 179–180; and as "Second Report on the Expansion of the Crab Nebula," in *Astrophysical Journal,* **89** (1939), 482–485.

Reproductions and descriptions of the best of Duncan's photographs are contained in six papers: "Bright Nebulae and Star Clusters in Sagittarius and Scutum," in *Astrophysical Journal,* **51** (1920), 4–12, with 4 plates; "Bright and Dark Nebulae near ζ Orionis, Photographed with the 100-inch Hooker Telescope," *ibid.,* **53** (1921), 392–396, with 2 plates; "Photographic Studies of Nebulae, Third Paper," *ibid.,* **57** (1923), 137–148, with 11 plates; "Photographic Studies of Nebulae, Fourth Paper," *ibid.,* **63** (1926), 122–126, with 4 plates; "Photographic Studies of Nebulae, Fifth Paper," *ibid.,* **86** (1937), 496–498, with 6 plates; and "Photographic Studies of Nebulae VI. The Great Nebulous Region in Cygnus Photographed in Red Light," *ibid.,* **109** (1949), 479, with 2 plates.

There are 38 articles by Duncan listed in Poggendorff, VI, pt. 1, 615, and VIIb, pt. 2, 1155–1156, which include all those mentioned above except the second.

II. SECONDARY LITERATURE. Joseph Ashbrook's brief, unsigned obituary notice, with photograph, appeared in *Sky and Telescope,* **34** (1967), 283. Other facts about Duncan's life can be found in *Who's Who in America,* XXVII (Chicago, 1952), 690–691, and XXVIII (Chicago, 1954), 746; and in *American Men of Science,* 11th ed., The Physical and Biological Sciences, D–G (New York, 1965), 1313.

SALLY H. DIEKE

DUNDONALD, ARCHIBALD COCHRANE, EARL OF (*b.* Culross Abbey [?], Scotland, 1 January 1749; *d.* Paris, France, 1 July 1831), *chemistry.*

Dundonald was the eldest son of Thomas Cochrane of Culross and Ochiltree, eighth Earl of Dundonald, and his second wife, Jane Stuart. Following family tradition he entered on a military career but subsequently transferred in turn to the navy and back to the army. He inherited his title in 1778 but little else other than saltpans and mineral rights on the Culross

Abbey estate on the north shore of the River Forth. Dundonald spent most of his long life attempting to apply science to the art of manufactures; he achieved considerable technical but little commercial success.

In 1781 he returned to Culross Abbey, where he associated with such Edinburgh intellectuals as Joseph Black, James Hutton, and John Hope. By this time Dundonald had conceived the idea of a substitute for wood tar made from coal, and he built kilns at Culross Abbey. In 1781 he was granted a patent (B.P. 1781 No. 1291) covering not only coal tar but "essential oils, volatile alkali, mineral acids, salts and cinders (coke)." The kilns are described in *The Statistical Account of Scotland,* and there is a drawing, probably by Dundonald, in the Boulton and Watt Collection (Reference Library, Birmingham). In 1782 Dundonald founded the British Tar Company to operate the patent and build kilns associated with various ironworks. He failed, however, to interest the British Admiralty in coal tar. Coal-gas lighting was almost a by-product of the same experiments, but Dundonald missed the possibility.

Failure with coal tar led to interest in other materials: first alum, a mordant used by dyers and by silk and calico printers (B.P. 1794 No. 2015). His chief contribution to late eighteenth-century industrial chemistry was the production of soda from common salt (B.P. 1795 No. 2043), which solved one of the major technical problems of the late eighteenth century: to find a synthetic substitute for the dwindling supplies of barilla, kelp, wood ash, and weed ash that were essential to the soap, glass, and textile industries. In 1790 Dundonald had gone to Newcastle-upon-Tyne, where William Losh and Thomas Doubleday were trying to make alkali from the ash of marine plants by a LeBlanc-like process. Losh was sent to Paris and in 1796, following his return, The Walker Chemical Company, at Walker-on-Tyne, County Durham, was established to operate Dundonald's patent. Similar works were subsequently established near Newcastle and Glasgow. His other patents cover the manufacture of white lead (B.P. 1779 No. 2189); a variety of heavy chemicals (B.P. 1798 No. 2211) including soda, saltpeter, sal ammoniac, alum, Epsom salts, potassium chloride and sulfate, and sodium phosphate, and the production of alkali from vegetable sources (B.P. 1812 No. 3547).

Dundonald's other interests included making bread from potatoes; the substitution of potatoes for grain in alcohol production; finding a substitute for gum senegal; paint, pottery, and textile production; and iron and coal mining. His treatise on the connection between agriculture and chemistry foreshadowed much of Humphry Davy's *Elements of Agricultural Chemistry,* including the recognition of phosphorus as an essential plant nutrient.

So speculative and widespread were his enterprises that he was known in Scotland as "Daft Dundonald." Unhappily none of them helped his family fortunes; he died in poverty in Paris in 1831.

BIBLIOGRAPHY

I. ORIGINAL WORKS. Dundonald's writings include *Account of the Quality and Uses of Coal Tar and Coal Varnish* (London, 1785); *The Present State of Manufacture of Salt Explained* (London, 1785); *Letters of the Earl of Dundonald on Making Bread from Potatoes* (Edinburgh, 1791); *A Treatise Showing the Intimate Connection That Subsists Between Agriculture and Chemistry* (London, 1795); and *Directions by Lord Dundonald for Extracting Gum From Lichen and Tree Moss* (Glasgow, 1801).

See also "Dundonald Papers Concerning The British Tar Company," National Library of Scotland (Edinburgh); "Boulton and Watt Papers," Assay Office Library (Birmingham, England); "Session Papers 241/25," Library of the Writers to H. M. Signet (Edinburgh); *Abridgments of Specifications Relating to Acids, Alkalis . . .,* Patents Office Library (London); and "Newcastle: Chemical Manufacturers in the District," British Association Report (1863), p. 701.

II. SECONDARY LITERATURE. On Dundonald and his work, see W. G. Armstrong, ed., *The Industrial Relations of the Three Northern Rivers, Tyne, Wear, and Tees* (London, 1864); Archibald and Nan L. Clow, "Lord Dundonald," in *Economic History Review,* **12** (1942), 47; "Archibald Cochrane, 9th Earl of Dundonald," in *Chemistry and Industry,* **24** (1944), 217; *The Chemical Revolution* (London, 1952); Thomas Cochrane, 10th Earl of Dundonald, *Autobiography of a Seaman* (London, 1860); and John Sinclair, ed., *The Statistical Account of Scotland,* X (Edinburgh, 1791–1799), 412.

ARCHIBALD CLOW

DUNÉR, NILS CHRISTOFER (*b.* Billeberga, Sweden, 21 May 1839; *d.* Stockholm, Sweden, 10 November 1914), *astronomy.*

Dunér studied astronomy at the University of Lund and obtained his doctor's degree in 1862. From 1864 to 1888 he was senior astronomer at the Lund Observatory. In 1888 he was appointed professor of astronomy at Uppsala University and director of the observatory. He retired in 1909.

Dunér's dissertation of 1862 deals with the determination of the orbit of the planetoid Panopea, which had been discovered the previous year. Swedish astronomy at that time was of necessity strictly nonobservational, as the observatories were obsolete. During the next few years a new observatory was erected at Lund, and Dunér became an observing astronomer, "the strict empiricist," who introduced the "new astronomy" to Sweden. His work covered measurement of visual double stars and discussion of their relative movements; description and measurement of the spectra of red stars (the Vogel spectral type III), of which he discovered more than 100; spectroscopic determination of the rotation of the sun (a spectroscope with the largest grating of the time had been constructed); and observation and reduction of the star positions of the Lund Zone (declination $+35°$ to $+40°$) of the meridian circle survey until the declination $-23°$ of the *Astronomische Gesellschaft.*

Having transferred to Uppsala Observatory, Dunér again had to wait for improved equipment, but he succeeded in developing an efficient observatory. He revived his measurements of solar rotation and obtained further evidence for the decrease in the velocity of rotation from the equator to the latitudes $\pm75°$ (the results of his Lund measurements had also contributed to the waning discussion of the reliability of the Doppler principle). He continued his observations of the red stars; about twenty years later Hale and Ellerman pointed out how Dunér's results, obtained visually and with small and primitive instruments, were confirmed photographically. Also at Uppsala he found the solution to the special problems of the eclipsing binary Y Cygni, pointing out that this system consists of two similar suns moving around their common center of gravity in elliptic orbits, the common line of apsides of which simultaneously rotates in the plane of the orbits. After summing up these results in a few lines Dunér added modestly: "These investigations may well claim some interest."

In 1887 Dunér went to Paris as a Swedish delegate to the meeting concerning the gigantic *Carte photographique du ciel* project, and he was a member of the commission appointed to plan and supervise its effectuation. His foresight is apparent in his suggestion to postpone the project for a quarter of a century, in view of the rapid development of instrumental and photographic facilities that was expected. But his observatory did participate in the photographic campaign of the years 1900–1901 to determine the solar parallax by means of observations of the planetoid Eros.

In 1861 and 1864 Dunér was a member of expeditions to the Spitsbergen Islands as geographer and physicist, and his experiences were later taken into account by a joint Swedish-Russian geodetic survey of these northern islands about 1900.

In characterizing Dunér's qualities as a scientist, Ångström, in his obituary, praised his clear mind for inductive reasoning and his great experimental genius.

BIBLIOGRAPHY

I. ORIGINAL WORKS. A bibliography of Dunér's published papers is in von Zeipel's obituary. Dunér's more important works are "Mesures micrométriques d'étoiles doubles, faites à l'Observatoire de Lund, suivies de notes sur leurs mouvements relatifs," in *Acta Universitatis lundensis,* **12**, no. 2, pt. 1 (1876), 1–266; "Sur les étoiles à spectres de la troisième classe," in *Kungliga Svenska vetenskapsakademiens handlingar,* **21**, pt. 2 (1884), 1–137; "Recherches sur la rotation du soleil," in *Nova acta Regiae Societatis scientiarum upsaliensis,* 3rd ser., **14**, pt. 13 (1891), 1–78; "On the Spectra of Stars of Class III b," in *Astrophysical Journal,* **9** (1899), 119–132; "Calculation of Elliptic Elements of the System of Y Cygni," ibid., **11** (1900), 175–191; "Om den på fotografisk väg framställda stjernkatalogen," in *Öfversigt af Kungliga Vetenskapsakademiens förhandlingar* (1900), 399–407; and "Über die Rotation der Sonne," in *Nova acta Regiae Societatis scientiarum upsaliensis,* 4th ser., **1**, pt. 6 (1907), 1–64.

II. SECONDARY LITERATURE. An article on Dunér by Ö. Bergstrand is in *Svenskt biografiskt lexicon,* XI (1945), 528–535. Obituaries are A. Ångström in *Astrophysical Journal,* **41** (1915), 81–85; Ö. Bergstrand in *Astronomische Nachrichten,* **199** (1914), 391–392; A. Fowler in *Monthly Notices of the Royal Astronomical Society,* **75** (1915), 256–258; B. Hasselberg in *Vierteljahrsschrift der Astronomischen Gesellschaft,* **52** (1917), 2–31; and H. von Zeipel in *Kungliga Svenska vetenskapsakademiens Årsbok för År 1916* (Uppsala), 291–312.

AXEL V. NIELSEN

DUNGLISON, ROBLEY (*b.* Keswick, England, 4 January 1788; *d.* Philadelphia, Pennsylvania, 1 April 1869), *medical education, lexicography, physiology.*

His father, William, and his maternal grandfathers were wool manufacturers; his mother was Elizabeth Jackson, and his maternal grandmother was a Robley, hence his first name. Orphaned as a child, Dunglison received a classical education at Green Row Academy, Abbey Holme, through a legacy from a rich uncle. There he obtained an excellent knowledge of Greek and Latin as well as a fluent pen in English; later he was also to become well-versed in French and German. Having decided upon a medical career, he took a preceptorship with a surgeon at Keswick and went to Edinburgh, Paris, and London for his formal medical education; he obtained his degree by examination from Erlangen. In London he assisted the ailing Dr. Charles Thomas Haden, a prominent practitioner, who greatly influenced the development of Dunglison's professional and social character. Dunglison passed the examinations of the Royal College of Surgeons and of the Society of Apothecaries and commenced practice in 1819 at London, where he was appointed physician-accoucheur to the Eastern

Dispensary. His pen, however, was busier than his lancet, and by 1824 he had published articles on the English Lake Region, belladonna, malaria, and meningitis; a book on the bowel complaints of children; numerous book reviews; translations of Félix-Hippolyte Larrey's *Moxa* and of François Magendie's *Formulary;* and an edition of Robert Hooper's *Vade-Mecum;* and had served on the editorial boards of two medical journals. In 1824 he married Harriet Leadam, daughter of a London apothecary; they had seven children. Shortly after their marriage they went to the University of Virginia where, at the behest of Thomas Jefferson, Dunglison was appointed to the chair of medicine. Responsible only for teaching, Dunglison was able to prepare textbooks on those subjects he taught. (Medical instructors, who had, until then, been actively engaged in practice, relied chiefly upon the European literature for information on current advances.) Dunglison thus became the first full-time professor of medicine in the United States and the first American author of a book on physiology, a medical dictionary, and a history of medicine, as well as a pioneer in the publication of works on public health (or hygiene, as he called it), materia medica and therapeutics, medical jurisprudence and toxicology, medical education, and internal medicine. (He abhorred the knife and completely avoided surgery.) Dunglison also made important contributions to William Beaumont's classic work on the physiology of digestion.

After eight years at the University of Virginia, Dunglison moved to the University of Maryland and then, after three years, to the Jefferson Medical College at Philadelphia, where he taught for the next thirty-two years. When he arrived, faculty dissension and rivalry with another Philadelphia medical school were threatening to destroy the college, but Dunglison's skillful reorganization of the faculty welded it into a coherent, cooperative teaching group, and he succeeded in establishing the school as one of the country's best medical centers. Fluent, lucid, elegant, entertaining, instructive, and stimulating as a lecturer, he attracted many students: more than 5,000 nineteenth-century physicians proudly displayed his signature on their diplomas. Elected to many organizations, he was especially active in the American Philosophical Society and in the Musical Fund Society of Philadelphia. As a member of the Pennsylvania Institution for the Blind he was an early advocate of raised type for the blind. He was also interested in the Elwyn School for the mentally retarded and worked for improved care of the insane poor, preparing several reports that led to reforms in asylums. An Episcopalian, he was a member of the vestry of

St. Stephen's Church, Philadelphia. Two of his sons, Richard James and Thomas Randolph, were physicians. Although medical practice was not to his taste, he attended Thomas Jefferson in his last illness and was consulted by presidents Monroe, Madison, and Jackson and by families connected with the University of Virginia. His importance to American medical history rests in his extraordinary success in sifting from the world literature information of importance to medical students and physicians, and in his ability to present this information effectively. In addition we owe to him the firm establishment of two great medical institutions, the University of Virginia School of Medicine and the Jefferson Medical College.

BIBLIOGRAPHY

I. ORIGINAL WORKS. A fairly complete list of Dunglison's writings appears in "The Autobiographical Ana of Robley Dunglison," ed. with notes and an intro. by Samuel X. Radbill, in *Transactions of the American Philosophical Society,* n.s., **53** (1963), 196–199. His most significant medical publications are *Commentaries on the Diseases of the Stomach and Bowels of Children* (London, 1824); *Syllabus of Lectures on Medical Jurisprudence, and on the Treatment of Poisoning and Suspended Animation* (Charlottesville, Va., 1827); and *Human Physiology,* 2 vols. (Philadelphia, 1832; 8th ed., 1856). *A New Dictionary of Medical Science and Literature,* 2 vols. (Boston, 1833) appeared in 1 vol. in its 2nd and subsequent eds.; the 19th ed. (Philadelphia, 1868) was the last published in Robley Dunglison's lifetime; his son Richard edited several subsequent eds.; in 1911 Thomas Lathrop Stedman continued it as *Stedman's Practical Medical Dictionary,* and it is still appearing, a century after Dunglison's death. Other works are *Elements of Hygiene* (Philadelphia, 1835); *General Therapeutics, or Principles of Medical Practice* (Philadelphia, 1836); *The Medical Student* (Philadelphia, 1837); *New Remedies* (Philadelphia, 1839); and *The Practice of Medicine,* 2 vols. (Philadelphia, 1842). The *Dictionary for the Blind in Tangible Type,* 3 vols. (Philadelphia, 1860) was prepared by W. Chapin under the supervision of Dunglison. Dunglison also edited the following journals: *London Medical Repository* (1823–1824), *Medical Intelligencer* (1823), *Virginia Literary Museum and Journal of Belles Lettres, Arts, Sciences, etc.* (1830), and *American Medical Library and Intelligencer* (1837–1842). Dunglison's interest in the mentally retarded is reflected in *Appeal to the People of Pennsylvania on the Subject of an Asylum for the Poor of the Commonwealth* (Philadelphia, 1838); a *Second Appeal* was pub. in 1840. A posthumous work, *History of Medicine,* was arranged and ed. by his son Richard J. Dunglison, M.D. (Philadelphia, 1872).

II. SECONDARY LITERATURE. On Dunglison and his work, see William B. Bean, "Mr. Jefferson's Influence on American Medical Education," in *Virginia Medical Monthly,* **87** (1960), 669–680; John M. Dorsey, *Jefferson-Dunglison Let-*

ters (Charlottesville, Va., 1960); Chalmers L. Gemmill, "Educational Work of Robley Dunglison, M.D. at the University of Virginia," in *Virginia Medical Monthly,* **87** (1960), 307–309; Chalmers L. Gemmill and Mary Jeanne Jones, *Pharmacology at the University of Virginia School of Medicine* (Charlottesville, Va., 1966), pp. 9–23; Samuel D. Gross, "Memoir of Robley Dunglison," in *Transactions of the College of Physicians of Philadelphia,* n.s., **4** (1874), 294–313, and *Autobiography,* II (Philadelphia, 1887), 334; Mary Jeanne Jones and Chalmers L. Gemmill, "The Notebook of Robley Dunglison, Student of Clinical Medicine in Edinburgh, 1816–1818," in *Journal of the History of Medicine and Allied Sciences,* **22** (1967), 261–273; Henry Lonsdale, *Worthies of Cumberland,* VI (London, 1875), 262–279; Samuel X. Radbill, "Robley Dunglison, M.D., 1788–1869: American Medical Educator," in *Journal of Medical Education,* **34** (1959), 84–94; and "Dr. Robley Dunglison and Jefferson," in *Transactions and Studies of the College of Physicians of Philadelphia,* 4th ser., **27** (1959), 40–44.

SAMUEL X. RADBILL

DUNOYER DE SEGONZAC, LOUIS DOMINIQUE JOSEPH ARMAND (*b.* Versailles, France, 14 November 1880; *d.* Versailles, 27 August 1963), *physics.*

Dunoyer was the son of Anatole Dunoyer, a founder of the École des Sciences Politiques in Paris, and Jeanine Roquet. He married Jeanne Picard, daughter of Émile Picard, on 4 June 1907. They had two sons, whose studies Dunoyer supervised himself.

As a youth, Dunoyer placed first in the general physics competition and was second on the admissions list of the École Polytechnique and first on that of the École Normale Supérieure. He chose to attend the latter (1902–1905), which oriented him toward teaching and research. He placed first in the physics *agrégation* in 1905 and in that year was an assistant to P. Langevin at the Collège de France. His first research concerned the difficulties of compensating compasses in iron and iron-clad ships. This work furnished the subject for his doctoral thesis[1] and took concrete form in the dygograph and the type of electromagnetic compass[2] that was mounted in Lindbergh's *Spirit of St. Louis.* In 1908 he won the Prix Extraordinaire de la Marine[3] for his research in magnetism.

A Carnegie scholar in the laboratory of Marie Curie in 1909, Dunoyer conducted the fundamental experiment on molecular beams in 1912.[4] Originally designed to verify the kinetic theory, the experiment also resulted in the preparation of thin films of alkali metals. "He showed that in a good vacuum one could obtain a linear beam of molecules, but that if the vacuum degenerated, the impacts of the molecules against each other produced a broadening and a

disintegration of the beam."[5] (This work was followed by the studies of the properties of molecules, without perturbation, by Otto Stern and others.) This experimental demonstration of the kinetic theory of gases was the origin of the preparation of thin films by thermal vaporization and of the studies of the properties of atoms and molecules by the so-called molecular ray method.[6] In 1912 Dunoyer was awarded the Subvention Bonaparte[7] for his work on the fluorescence of pure sodium vapor and for the complete investigation of the fluorescence and absorption spectra of the alkaline metals. In 1913 he won the Prix Becquerel for his research on the electrical and optical properties of metallic vapors, notably of sodium vapor.[8] In the same year he was appointed deputy professor at the Conservatoire National des Arts et Métiers. He studied the surface resonance of sodium vapor with R. W. Wood in 1914.

An aviation officer and inspector, Dunoyer was wounded and became *chevalier* of the Legion of Honor, receiving the Croix de Guerre in 1915 as well. He became interested in meteorology and aerial navigation and invented a bombsight.[9] In 1918 he was awarded the Prix Danton for his work on radiant phenomena.[10]

Dunoyer became a lecturer at the Institut d'Optique in 1919. He was physicist at the observatory of Meudon from 1927 to 1929 and professor at the Institut d'Optique from 1921 to 1941. He participated in the founding of the Société de Recherches et de Perfectionnements Industriels, and while secretary-general of the Société Française de Physique he devised a special lens for the illumination of atomic beams. A glassblower and remarkable technician, he improved the procedures of Wolfgang Gaede (1913) and of Langmuir (1916) and developed various diffusion pumps and devices for measuring very low temperatures. These accomplishments brought him the Subvention Loutreuil in 1925.[11]

Simultaneously Dunoyer pursued his research on photoelectricity and the construction of photoelectric cells; the first application (1925) was to talking movies, where a potassium cell was employed. He won the Prix Valz in 1929 for his research on the spirit level and on photoelectric cells.[12] In 1930 he was awarded the Subvention Loutreuil for the continuation of his research on photoelectric cells.[13]

In 1935 Dunoyer's studies on thermal vaporization in a vacuum enabled him to construct the first aluminized mirrors.[14] On 10 February 1937 he was elected artist member of the Bureau des Longitudes, replacing Louis Jolly. From 1941 to 1945 he was titular professor at the Sorbonne and director of the Institut de Chimie Physique, where he taught a remarkable course on the kinetic theory of gases. Dunoyer was named honorary president of the Société des Ingénieurs du Vide, in whose journal, *Le vide,* he published seven articles between 1949 and 1956. The society dubbed him "Grandfather of the Vacuum."

NOTES

1. The thesis was under the direction of E. E. N. Mascart and P. Langevin and was entitled *Étude sur les compas de marine et leurs méthodes de compensation. Un nouveau compas électro-magnétique* (Paris, 1909). It is *thèse* Fac. Sciences Paris, no. 1336.
2. See *Comptes rendus hebdomadaires des séances de l'Académie des sciences,* **145** (1907), 1142–1147, 1323–1325; **147** (1908), 834–837, 1275–1277; *Bulletin de la Société française de physique,* **295** (1909–1910); *Revue maritime,* **315** (1910). The *Comptes rendus* are hereafter cited as *CR.*
3. See *CR,* **147** (1908), 1111, 1113–1117, for his electromagnetic compass tested on the battleship *Patrie* and the dygograph placed on the battleship *Danton.* It replaced the ordinary compass, which was rendered useless by rarefaction of the magnetism, resulting from the ship's armor.
4. See *CR,* **152** (1911), 592–595; **153** (1911), 333–336; **154** (1912), 815–818, 1344–1346; **155** (1912), 144–147, 270–273; **157** (1913), 1068–1070; **158** (1914), 1068–1071, 1265–1267, written with R. W. Wood; *Bulletin de la Société française de physique,* four memoirs between 1912 and 1914; *Journal de physique et radium,* **185** (1913); *Collection de mémoirs relatifs à la physique* (1912); *Radium,* seven memoirs between 1910 and 1914.
5. Robert Champeix, *Le vide* (Paris, 1965).
6. *Le vide,* **106** (July–Aug. 1963).
7. See *CR,* **155** (1912), 93, 1407.
8. See *CR,* **157** (1913), 1287.
9. See *CR,* **165** (1917), 1068–1071, written with G. Reboul; **166** (1918), 293–295; **168** (1919), 47, 138, 457–459 (with Reboul), 785–787 (with Reboul), 726–729, 1102–1105; **169** (1919), 762, 78–79, 191–193 (the last two written with Reboul); **170** (1920), 744–747 (with Reboul); **173** (1921), 1101–1104; *Bulletin de la Société française de physique* (1920); *Technique aéronautique* (1921).
10. See *CR,* **167** (1918), 829.
11. See *CR,* **181** (1925), 1012, 1016. At the same time he was given money from the research fund of the secretary-general of the Société Française de Physique in order to pursue his investigations of certain problems concerning modern methods of measuring high vacuums.
12. See *CR,* **189** (1929), 1123.
13. See *CR,* **191** (1930), 1245. See also *CR,* **174** (1922), 1615–1617 (written with P. Toulon); **176** (1923), 953–955, 1213; **179** (1924), 148–151, 461–464, 522–575 (all written with P. Toulon); **182** (1926), 686–688; **185** (1927), 271–273; **196** (1933), 684–686 (written with Paounoff); **198** (1934), 909–911; **200** (1935), 1835–1838; *Bulletin de la Société française de physique,* 13 memoirs between 1922 and 1930; *Revue d'optique théorique et instrumentale,* 11 memoirs between 1922 and 1948; *Journal de physique et radium,* 2 memoirs.
14. See *CR,* **202** (1936), 474–476; **220** (1945), 520–522, 686–688, 816–817, 907–909; **221** (1945), 97–99; **230** (1950), 57–58; **232** (1951), 1080–1082; **233** (1951), 125, 919–921.

BIBLIOGRAPHY

In addition to the articles cited in the notes, see *La technique du vide* (Paris, 1924); *Les émissions électroniques des couches minces* (Paris, 1932); *Les radiations monochromatiques* (Paris, 1935); "Les cellules photoélectriques," in *Comptes rendus. 2° Congrès international d'électricité* (Paris, 1936); *Allocution pour le vingtième anniversaire de la mécanique ondulatoire* (Paris, 1944); *Le vide et ses applications,* in the series Que Sais-je?, no. 430 (Paris, 1950).

His articles published in *Le vide* are "Étude d'un micromanomètre thermique, précédée de quelques remarques générales sur ce type d'instrument," **4** (1949), 571–581, 603–618, 643–660; "Sur certaines phénomènes de dégagement gazeux observés pendant le pompage de lampes à incandescence à basse tension," **5** (1950), 793–806; "Quelques remarques sur les formules de l'écoulement des gaz raréfiés dans les canalisations," *ibid.,* 881–886; "Bases théoriques de la dessication dans le vide," **6** (1951), 1025–1040, 2077–2090; "Expériences sur l'évaporation de l'eau dans le vide et comparaison avec la théorie," **8** (1953), 1280–1294; "Fonctionnement des condensateurs de vapeur d'eau dans les appareils de dessication dans le vide," **10** (1955), 165–184; and "Quelques appareils pour la production de faisceaux moléculaires et quelques expériences sur ceux de sodium en resonance optique," **11** (1956), 172–189.

P. BERTHON

DUNS SCOTUS, JOHN (*b.* Roxburghshire, Scotland, *ca.* 1266; *d.* Cologne, Germany, November 1308), *philosophy.*

Little is known of the life of John Duns Scotus, who was among the outstanding thinkers of the later Middle Ages. He entered the Franciscan order probably in 1279 or 1280 and was ordained in 1291. He studied first at Oxford University and then at Paris University, returning to Oxford in 1300 to complete the requirement for his doctorate. Before he could take his degree, however, he was once again sent by his superiors to Paris, where he finally became a doctor of theology in 1305, having been temporarily banished from France in 1303, together with about seventy other friars, for supporting Pope Boniface VIII in his quarrel with the French king, Philip the Fair. We last hear of him at Cologne in 1308, teaching in the Franciscan house there.

Duns Scotus' premature death together with the vicissitudes of his career have combined to make his writings more than usually problematical. Only gradually is the correct relation between his lectures at Paris and those at Oxford being established, while the authority of other works ascribed to him has still to be definitively established. His major writings are his two commentaries on the *Sentences* of Peter Lombard, a compendium of theology, which constituted one of the main exercises for a degree in that subject. Because of his studies in the theological faculties of both Oxford and Paris, Duns Scotus wrote two such commentaries, *Opus Oxoniense* and *Reportata Parisiensis.* Each was left in an unfinished state, as were all his other main works; the unraveling of the correct rela-

254

tion of the two commentaries to each other has been one of the preoccupations of the Scotist editorial commission over the past thirty years and is still not complete. Even when it is, Duns Scotus' thought will always be incompletely understood. Within a few years of his death his teaching had been developed by his followers into a definite set of tenets, from which it is sometimes difficult to disentangle his own positions. Scotism became one of the dominant schools of later medieval thought, and much in Duns Scotus' teaching formed the point of departure for William of Ockham's own, more far-reaching radicalism.

Like the majority of medieval thinkers, Duns Scotus was primarily a theologian. He sought to provide a new, metaphysical basis for a natural theology, which would thereby free such discourse from dependence upon natural phenomena. Duns Scotus was writing in the aftermath of the great 1277 condemnations at Paris and at Oxford of over 200 theses that had applied criteria drawn from the sensory world to the articles of Christian faith. The condemnations had crystallized the danger inherent in employing the categories of nature in seeking knowledge of the divine. As a consequence, many theologians in the years immediately before Duns Scotus had sought a return to the older, traditional stress upon inner, nonsensory awareness as the source of higher knowledge. Duns Scotus, however, denied the human mind any but a sensory source for its knowledge. Accordingly, the problem was how to arrive at concepts that could be held independently of sensory experience. Scotus found the answer in metaphysics—the study of being in itself—and more specifically in the notion of being. As a concept, being was the most universal of all categories, under which every other concept fell. In this most generalized form, being was univocal: it applied indifferently to all that is, regardless of different kinds of being. It therefore transcended the physical properties of specific beings known through the senses; thus, if it could be applied to God, it would free any discussion of him from reliance upon physical categories. In that way, God could be the object of metaphysical, as opposed to physical, discourse. Duns Scotus held that the way to this lay in considering being in its two main modes, infinite and finite. Infinite being was by definition necessary and uncaused, while finite being was dependent upon another for its existence and, so, contingent. Accordingly, metaphysics could adduce God's existence as necessary being and that of his creatures as finite. But that was as far as it could go. Beyond saying God was first being, one could know his nature only when one turned from metaphysics to theology; in like manner, what he had

ordained for creation belonged to the articles of faith, not to natural reason.

The effects of Duns Scotus' reorientation of metaphysics were to put a new stress upon infinity and contingency. On the one hand, only God was infinite and, so, beyond the compass of human discourse; once having established God as the first infinite being, metaphysics could offer no analogies between the divine and the created. There was no place for Aquinas' five proofs of God's existence drawn from knowledge of this world, just as Duns Scotus allowed none to the older Augustinian doctrine of divine illumination of the soul, by which the soul was enabled to know eternal truths. On the other hand, creatures, since they were merely contingent, had no other *raison d'être* than God's having willed them. God's will was the only reason for the existence of that which was finite and need not have been. Moreover, God was absolutely free to do anything save contradict himself, which would limit him. Duns Scotus gave a renewed emphasis to God's omnipotence by reviving the distinction between God's ordained power as applied to this world and his absolute power by which he could do anything. Whereas by his ordained power he had decreed the unchanging laws that govern creation, by his absolute power God could supersede those laws and thus, for example, reward a man without first having infused him with grace. Duns Scotus does not appear to have pressed very far the contrast between these two aspects of God's power, but in this, as in stressing God's infinity, he opened the way to a much more radical application by William of Ockham and his followers.

The significance of Duns Scotus in the history of thought is that he broke away from the previous ways of establishing a natural theology. In doing so, he limited the area of meaningful natural discourse about the divine and gave new force to the contingent nature of creation. He thereby took an important step in separating natural experience and reason from revealed theological truth and from the preordained determinism against which the condemnations of 1277 had been especially directed. Those of the next generation, above all William of Ockham, were to make unbridgeable the gulf thus opened between knowledge and faith and to arrive at new and fruitful ways of interpreting natural phenomena.

BIBLIOGRAPHY

Duns Scotus' works were collected as *Opera omnia,* 12 vols. (Lyons, 1639; repr., Paris, 1891-1895). A new critical edition by the Scotist Commission, under C. Balíc, at Rome is in progress.

Modern editions of individual works include *Tractatus de primo principio*, ed. and with English trans. by E. Roche (New York, 1949). Selections from Duns Scotus in English translation are contained in *John Duns Scotus: Philosophical Writings*, A. Wolter, ed. and trans., which also provides a selected bibliography. A fuller bibliography is to be found in E. Gilson, *History of Christian Philosophy* (London, 1955), pp. 763–764.

GORDON LEFF

DUPERREY, LOUIS-ISIDORE (*b.* Paris, France, 21 [22?] October 1786; *d.* Paris, 25 August [10 September?] 1865), *navigation, hydrography, terrestrial magnetism.*

A sailor in the French navy from 1803 onward, Duperrey rose rapidly through the ranks, was assigned to carry out a hydrographic mission off the coast of Tuscany in 1809, and received his first command in 1814. He was in charge of hydrographic activities on Louis de Freycinet's expedition around the world in 1817–1820 and produced valuable observations on the earth's shape and on terrestrial magnetism, together with numerous charts. About one year following his return Duperrey presented to the naval minister a plan for another circumnavigating expedition, and in 1822 he embarked in command of the *Coquille*. Second in command was Jules-Sébastien-César Dumont d'Urville, and the expedition was joined by two naturalists, René-Primevère Lesson and Prosper Garnot.

Before his return to Marseilles in 1825 (accomplished without the loss of a single man), Duperrey and his company discovered a number of unknown islands, prepared charts of previously little-known areas of the South Pacific (especially in the Caroline Archipelago), studied ocean currents, gathered new information on geomagnetic and meteorological phenomena, and collected an impressive array of geological, botanical, and zoological specimens for the Muséum d'Histoire Naturelle. After the return of the expedition Duperrey and his collaborators worked assiduously to prepare the results of the journey for publication. The expedition particularly distinguished itself in producing new knowledge of the behavior of ocean currents in the Atlantic and Pacific oceans (there was a certain fascination with asymmetry in the weather of the Northern and Southern hemispheres) and in its contributions to knowledge of variations in intensity and direction of terrestrial magnetism. Duperrey himself was especially concerned with the determination of the earth's magnetic equator.

Duperrey was elected to membership in the Academy of Sciences (section for geography and navigation) in 1842, became vice-president in 1849, and served as president in 1850.

BIBLIOGRAPHY

I. ORIGINAL WORKS. The results of the voyage of the *Coquille* were published as *Voyage autour du monde, exécuté par ordre du Roi, sur la corvette de Sa Majesté, la Coquille, pendant les années 1822, 1823, 1824 et 1825. . .* (7 vols. plus 4 vols. of plates and maps, Paris, 1825–1830). Duperrey himself prepared the *Histoire du voyage* (1825), *Hydrographie et physique* (1829), *Hydrographie* (1829), and *Physique* (1830); *Botanique* (2 vols., 1828) was prepared by Dumont d'Urville, J. B. Bory de Saint-Vincent, and Adolphe Brongniart; while Lesson, Garnot, and Félix-Édouard Guérin-Méneville collaborated on *Zoologie* (2 vols., 1826–1830). Duperrey also published separately *Mémoire sur les opérations géographiques faites dans la campagne de la corvette de S. M. la Coquille, pendant les années 1822, 1823, 1824 et 1825* (Paris, n.d. [1827]).

Duperrey's publications of the scientific results of his expeditions also appeared in the form of articles, such as "Résumé des observations de l'inclinaison et de la déclinaison de l'aiguille aimantée faites dans la campagne de la corvette de S. M. la *Coquille,* pendant les années 1822, 1823, 1824, et 1825," in *Annales de chimie et de physique,* **34** (1827), 298–320; "Notice sur la configuration de l'équateur magnétique, conclue des observations faites dans la campagne de la corvette la *Coquille,*" ibid., **45** (1830), 371–386; "Notice sur la position des pôles magnétiques de la terre," in *Comptes rendus hebdomadaires des séances de l'Académie des Sciences,* **13** (1841), 1104–1111; and "Réduction des observations de l'intensité du magnétisme terrestre faites par M. de Freycinet et ses collaborateurs durant le cours du voyage de la corvette l'*Uranie,*" ibid., **19** (1844), 445–455. Other articles were published in *Additions à la connaissance des temps* and *Annales maritimes et coloniales.* Information gathered by Duperrey on terrestrial magnetism is set forth extensively in Antoine César Becquerel, *Traité expérimental de l'électricité et du magnétisme, et de leurs rapports avec les phénomènes naturels,* vol. VII (Paris, 1840).

II. SECONDARY LITERATURE. On Duperrey and his work see Dominique F. J. Arago and others, "Rapport fait à l'Académie des Sciences, le lundi 22 août 1825, sur le voyage de découvertes, exécuté dans les années 1822, 1823, 1824 et 1825, sous le commandement de M. Duperrey, lieutenant de vaisseau," in *Additions à la connaissance des temps,* année 1828, pp. 240–272; this appears to be the principal source for a long biographical article by P. Levot in Hoefer's *Nouvelle biographie générale,* vol. XV (Paris, 1856), cols. 278–286. Duperrey published a *Notice sur les travaux de M. L.-I. Duperrey, ancien officier supérieur de la marine* (Paris, 1842). Contemporary biographical notices appear in Figuier's *L'année scientifique et industrielle* (1866), pp. 477–478; and in Edouard Goepp and Henri de Mannoury d'Ectot, *La France biographique illustrée: Les marins,* 2 vols. (Paris, 1877), II, 227–228. A recent sketch by É. Franceschini is in *Dictionnaire de biographie française,* fasc. LXVIII (1968), cols. 338–339. Information on Duperrey's circumnavigating expedition is found in Paul Chack, *Croisières merveilleuses* (Paris, 1937), pp. 131–147;

and in Robert J. Garry, "Geographical Exploration by the French," in *The Pacific Basin: A History of Its Geographical Exploration,* Herman R. Friis, ed. (New York, 1967), pp. 201–220.

KENNETH L. TAYLOR

DUPIN, PIERRE-CHARLES-FRANÇOIS (*b.* Varzy, France, 6 October 1784; *d.* Paris, France, 18 January 1873), *mathematics, economics, education.*

Dupin grew up in his native Nivernais, where his father, Charles-André Dupin, was a lawyer and legislator. His mother was Cathérine Agnès Dupin (her maiden name was also Dupin). The second of three sons, Dupin graduated in 1803 from the École Polytechnique in Paris as a naval engineer. In 1801, under the guidance of his teacher Gaspard Monge, he had made his first discovery, the cyclid (of Dupin). After assignments in Antwerp, Genoa, and Toulon, he was placed in charge of the damaged naval arsenal on Corfu in 1807. He restored the port, did fundamental research on the resistance of materials and the differential geometry of surfaces, and became secretary of the newly founded Ionian Academy. In 1810, on his way back to France, he was detained by illness at Pisa; and during his convalescence he edited a posthumous book by his friend Leopold Vacca Berlinghierri, *Examen des travaux de César au siège d'Alexia* (Paris, 1812). At the Toulon shipyard in 1813, Dupin founded a maritime museum that became a model for others, such as that at the Louvre. That year he published his *Développements de géométrie.*

In 1816, after some difficulty, Dupin was allowed to visit Great Britain to study its arsenals and other technical installations. The results were published in *Voyages dans la Grande Bretagne entrepris relativement aux services publics de la guerre, de la marine . . . depuis 1816* (1820–1824).

Settling down to a life of teaching and public service, Dupin accepted the position of professor of mechanics at the Paris Conservatoire des Arts et Métiers, a position he held until 1854. His free public lectures, dealing with mathematics and mechanics and their industrial applications, became very popular. His *Applications de géométrie et de mécanique* (1822) was a continuation of the *Développements* but placed greater stress on applications. Many of Dupin's lectures on industry and the arts were published in *Géométrie et mécanique des arts et métiers et des beaux arts* (1825); his *Sur les forces productives et commerciales de France* appeared two years later. In 1824 the king made him a baron.

The *Développements* contains many contributions to differential geometry, notably the introduction of conjugate and asymptotic lines on a surface, the so-called indicatrix of Dupin, and "Dupin's theorem," that three families of orthogonal surfaces intersect in the lines of curvature. A particular case Dupin investigated consisted of confocal quadrics. In the *Applications* we find an elaboration of Monge's theory of *déblais et remblais*—and, hence, of congruences of straight lines, with applications to geometrical optics. Here Dupin, improving on a theorem of Malus's (1807), stated that a normal congruence remains normal after reflection and refraction. He also gave a more complete theory of the cyclids as the envelopes of the spheres tangent to three given spheres and discussed floating bodies. In 1840 he introduced what is now called the affine normal of a surface at a point.

In 1828 Dupin was elected deputy for Tarn, and he continued in politics until 1870. In 1834 he was minister of marine affairs, in 1838 he became a peer, and in 1852 he was appointed to the senate. He tirelessly encouraged the establishment of schools and libraries, the founding of savings banks, the construction of roads and canals, and the use of steam power. In 1855 he reported on the progress of the arts and sciences, as represented at the Paris World Exhibition; the part of the report dealing with Massachusetts was published in English (1865).

Dupin married Rosalie Anne Joubert in 1830. He was a correspondent of the Institut de France (1813) and a member of both the Académie des Sciences (1818) and the Académie des Sciences Morales et Politiques (1832). His older brother, André, known as Dupin *aîné,* was a prominent lawyer and politician.

BIBLIOGRAPHY

I. ORIGINAL WORKS. Among Dupin's writings are his ed. of Berlinghierri's *Examen des travaux de César* (Paris, 1812); *Développements de géométrie* (Paris, 1813); *Voyages dans la Grande Bretagne,* 3 vols. (Paris, 1820–1824); *Applications de géométrie et de mécanique des arts et métiers,* 3 vols. (Brussels, 1825); *Sur les forces productives,* 2 vols. (Paris, 1827); "Mémoire sur les éléments du troisième ordre de la courbure des lignes," in *Comptes rendus de l'Académie des sciences,* **26** (1848), 321–325, 393–398; and *Forces productives des nations de 1800 à 1851* (Paris, 1851). For his many economic and technical writings, see A. Legoyt, in *Nouvelle biographie générale,* XIV (1868), 315–326.

II. SECONDARY LITERATURE. On Dupin's life, see J. Bertrand, *Éloges académiques* (Paris, 1890), pp. 221–246; and A. Morin, *Discours funéraires de l'Institut de France* (Paris, 1873). Dupin's mathematical work is discussed in J. G. Darboux, *Leçons sur la théorie générale des surfaces* (Paris, 1887–1896, see index), and *Leçons sur les systèmes orthogonaux et les coordonnées curvilignes* (Paris, 1898; 2nd ed., 1910), ch. 1.

For information on the Dupin family, I am indebted to M. Baron Romain, Corvol d'Embernard (Nièvre).

DIRK J. STRUIK

DUPRÉ, ATHANASE LOUIS VICTOIRE (*b.* Cerisiers, France, 28 December 1808; *d.* Rennes, France, 10 August 1869), *physics, mathematics.*

After early education at the Collège of Auxerre, Dupré entered the École Normale Supérieure in Paris in 1826, gained first place in science in the *agrégation* of 1829, and immediately took a post at the Collège Royal in Rennes. There he taught mathematics and physical science until, in 1847, he was appointed to the chair of mathematics in the Faculty of Science in Rennes. His last post, from 1866, was as dean of the faculty there. He received the Legion of Honor in 1863 but won no other major honor and was never a member of the Académie des Sciences. He was an ardent Catholic throughout his life.

Dupré's scientific career fell into two parts. In the first, which lasted from his years at the École Normale until about 1859, he contributed to several branches of mathematics and physics. The most important of his papers from this period was his entry of 1858 for the competition in mathematics set by the Académie des Sciences. The paper, a study of an outstanding problem in Legendre's theory of numbers, earned Dupré an honorable mention but only half the prize of 3,000 francs.

During the second period, which covered the remaining ten years of his life, Dupré concerned himself exclusively with the mechanical theory of heat, his main interest being the implications of the theory for matter on the molecular scale. He made an important contribution to the dissemination in France of the newly discovered principles of thermodynamics in nearly forty communications to the Academy, in an entry for the Academy's Prix Bordin in 1866 (which again won him only an honorable mention and half the prize money), and in a successful advanced textbook, *Théorie mécanique de la chaleur* (1869).

BIBLIOGRAPHY

I. ORIGINAL WORKS. The most important of Dupré's papers were published in the *Annales de chimie et de physique;* those on the mechanical theory of heat were summarized in the *Théorie mécanique de la chaleur* (Paris, 1869). His entry for the 1858 competition was published as *Examen d'une proposition de Legendre relative à la théorie des nombres* (Paris, 1859).

II. SECONDARY LITERATURE. The only full biographical sketch, by Simon Sirodot, Dupré's successor as dean of the Faculty of Sciences in Rennes, appeared in the annual publi-

cation *Université de France. Académie de Rennes. Rentrée solennelle des facultés des écoles préparatoires de médecine et de pharmacie et des écoles préparatoires à l'enseignement supérieur des sciences et des lettres de l'Académie de Rennes* (Rennes, 1869), pp. 52–57.

ROBERT FOX

DÜRER, ALBRECHT (*b.* Nuremberg, Germany, 21 May 1471; *d.* Nuremberg, 6 April 1528), *mathematics, painting, theory of art.*

Dürer was the son of Albrecht Dürer (or Türer, as he called and signed himself) the Elder. The elder Dürer was the son of a Hungarian goldsmith and practiced that craft himself. He left Hungary, traveled through the Netherlands, and finally settled in Nuremberg, where he perfected his craft with Hieronymus Holper. He married Holper's daughter Barbara. The printer and publisher Anton Koberger stood godfather to the younger Dürer.

Dürer attended the *Lateinschule* in St. Lorenz and learned goldsmithing from his father. From 1486 to 1489 he studied painting with Michael Wolgemut (then the leading church painter of Nuremberg); in Wolgemut's workshop he was able to learn not only all the standard painting techniques but also wood- and copper-engraving. In 1490, in accordance with the custom of the painter's guild, Dürer went on his *Wanderjahre*. Until 1494 he traveled through the Upper Rhine and to Colmar, Basel, and Strasbourg, presumably making his living as a draftsman.

Dürer returned to Nuremberg and on 7 July 1494 married Agnes Frey, the daughter of Hans Frey. Frey, who had been a coppersmith, had become prosperous as a mechanician and instrument maker. He belonged to that school of craftsmen in metals for which Nuremberg was famous. The marriage brought Dürer's family increased social standing and brought Dürer a generous dowry.

As early as his *Wanderjahre* Dürer had come to appreciate the works of Mantegna and other Italian artists. He wished to learn more of the artistic and philosophical rediscoveries of the Italian Renaissance (he knew from books about the Academy of Florence, modeled on Plato's Academy). Moreover, he had become convinced that the new art must be based upon science—in particular, upon mathematics, as the most exact, logical, and graphically constructive of the sciences. It was this realization that led him to the scientific work for which he was, in his lifetime, as celebrated as for his art. He decided to travel to Italy and in 1494 left his wife in Nuremberg and set off on foot to visit Venice.

On his return to Nuremberg in 1495, Dürer began serious study of mathematics and of the theory of art as derived from works handed down from antiquity, especially Euclid's *Elements* and the *De architectura* of Vitruvius. These years were highly productive for Dürer; in 1497 he adopted his famous monogram 𝕬 to protect his work against being counterfeited. At about the same time he formed an important and lasting friendship with Willibald Pirckheimer, subject of one of his most famous portraits. (Dürer was fortunate in his patrons and friends; besides Pirckheimer these included such humanists as Johannes Werner, the mathematician; Johann Tscherte, the imperial architect; and Nicholas Kratzer, court astronomer to the English King Henry VIII.)

Most important, however, this period marked the beginning of Dürer's experiments with scientific perspective and mathematical proportion. The mathematical formulations of Dürer's anatomical proportion are derived both from antiquity and from the Italian rediscoveries; he drew upon both Polyclitus the Elder and Alberti, and to these he added the notion of plastic harmony after the mode of musical harmony taken from Boethius and Augustine. The earliest of Dürer's documented figure studies to be constructed in accordance with one or several strictly codified canons of proportion date from 1500 and include the study of a female nude (now in London). In addition, critics have pointed out that the head of the famous Munich self-portrait may be shown to have been constructed proportionally.

Throughout the years 1501–1504 Dürer continued to work with the problem of proportion, making numerous studies of men and horses. His copper engraving *Adam and Eve* (1504) marks the high point of his theoretical mastery—the figures were methodically constructed, he wrote, with a compass and a ruler. The preliminary studies for the *Adam and Eve* (now in Vienna) reveal Dürer's method. During this time he also mastered the techniques of linear perspective, as may be seen in his series of woodcuts, *The Life of the Virgin.*

In 1505–1507 Dürer returned to Venice. He extended his Italian travels to Bologna on this occasion, "on account," he wrote, "of secret [knowledge of] perspective." He most probably made the journey to meet with Luca Pacioli, a mathematician and theorist of art. Pacioli's book, *Divina proportione* (in which Leonardo da Vinci collaborated), propounded the notion that the *sectio aurea* (the famous "golden mean" of classical sculpture and architecture), being mathematical in nature, related art to that science exclusively. In Venice, at the close of his second Italian trip, Dürer bought Tacinus' 1505 edition of Euclid, which was henceforth to be his model for mathematical formulation. This period of Dürer's life marks

the full maturity of his mathematical, philosophical, and aesthetic theory; in his painting he had begun to realize the full synthesis of late German Gothic and Italian Renaissance painting.

Between 1506 and 1512 Dürer devoted himself to the rigorous study of the problem of form, which presented itself to him in three aspects: true, mathematical form; beautiful, proportional form; and compositional form, used in an actual work of art, ideally the fusion of the preceding. In solving these problems Dürer drew upon the resources of arithmetic and geometry; it was in his achievement as a painter that his formal solutions were meaningful and expressive.

From about 1508 Dürer sketched and wrote down the substance of his theoretical studies (fragments of these notes and drawings are preserved in the notebooks in London, Nuremberg, and Dresden). Some of these fragments may have been intended for inclusion in the encyclopedic *Speis' der Malerknaben* that Dürer had planned to publish; this *Malerbuch* was to have presented his mathematical solutions to all formal problems in the plastic arts. Although the *Malerbuch* was never completed, Dürer extracted a part of it for his major "Treatise on Proportion" (*Proportionslehre*).

In 1520–1521 Dürer traveled to the Netherlands, particularly Bruges and Ghent, where he saw the works of the early Flemish masters. He returned to Nuremberg ill with malaria; henceforth he devoted himself primarily to the composition and printing of his three major theoretical books. (He continued to paint, however; his pictures from this period include several notable portraits of his friends as well as the important diptych of the *Four Apostles,* given to the city council of Nuremberg by Dürer in 1526 and now in Munich.)

Dürer had completed the manuscript of the "Treatise on Proportion" by 1523, but he realized that a more basic mathematical text was necessary to its full comprehension. For that reason, in 1524–1525, he wrote such a text, the *Underweysung der Messung mit Zirckel und Richtscheyt in Linien, Ebnen und gantzen Corporen* ("Treatise on Mensuration With the Compass and Ruler in Lines, Planes, and Whole Bodies"), which was published by his own firm in Nuremberg in 1525.

The *Underweysung der Messung* is in four books. In the first, Dürer treats of the construction of plane curves (including the spiral of Archimedes, the logarithmic spiral, tangential spirals, conchoids, and so forth) and of helices according to the methods of descriptive geometry. In addition he includes a method for the construction of "Dürer's leaf" (the *folium Dureri*), presents the notion of affinity by the example of the ellipse as a related representation of the circle, and, most important, describes the conic sections in top and front views as well as demonstrating their construction.

In book II Dürer develops a morphological theory of regular polygons and their exact or approximate constructions. He shows how to make use of such constructions as architectural ornaments, in parquet floors, tesellated pavements, and even bull's-eye window panes. The book concludes with theoretical investigations (culminating in the Vitruvian approximation for squaring the circle, a process which had already been noted by Dürer in a proportional study made in Nuremberg in 1504 or 1505) and with the computation of π (as 3.141).

The first part of the third book includes bird's-eye and profile elevations of pyramids, cylinders, and columns of various sorts (in 1510, in Nuremberg, Dürer had already sketched a spiral column with spherical processes). The second part of the book deals with sundials and astronomical instruments; Dürer had a small observatory at his disposal in the house that he had acquired from Bernhard Walther, a student of Regiomontanus, and could also make use of Walther's scientific library, part of which he bought. In the third part of the third book Dürer is concerned with the design of letters and illustrates the construction in a printer's quad of capitals of the Roman typeface named after him as well as an upper- and lowercase *fraktur* alphabet.

In book IV Dürer presents the development of the five Platonic solids (polyhedra) and of several semiregular (Archimedean) solids. He additionally shows how to construct the surfaces of several mixed bodies and, of particular importance, presents an approximate development of the sphere (he had begun work on the last for the construction of the first globe in Nuremberg in 1490–1492; his work on other globes, celestial charts, and armillary spheres is well known). He also shows how to duplicate the cube (the Delian problem) and related bodies, demonstrates the construction of the shadows of illuminated bodies, and finally summarizes the theory of perspective.

Except for the *Geometria Deutsch* (*ca.* 1486–1487), a book of arithmetical rules for builders which Dürer knew and used, the *Underweysung der Messung* is the first mathematics book in German. With its publication Dürer could claim a place in the front ranks of Renaissance mathematicians.

Dürer's next technical publication, the *Befestigungslehre* ("Treatise on Fortifications"), was a practical work dictated by the fear of invasion by the Turks, which gripped all of central Europe. This book was published in Nuremberg in 1527; as well as summarizing the science of fortification it contains some of Dürer's chief architectural work (various other architectural drawings and models are extant). Many of his ideas were put to use; the city of Nuremberg was strengthened according to his plan (in particular the watchtowers were fortified), similar work was undertaken at Strasbourg, and the Swiss town of Schaffhausen built what might be considered a model of Dürer's design with small vaults above and below ground, casemates, and ramparts that still survive intact.

Dürer's third book, his "Treatise on Proportion," *Vier Bücher von menschlicher Proportion,* was published posthumously in 1528; Dürer himself saw the first proof sheets (there are no other details of his last illness and death) and his friends saw to the final stages of publication. This book is the synthesis of Dürer's solutions to his self-imposed formal problems; in it, he sets forth his formal aesthetic. In its simplest terms, true form is the primary mathematical figure (the straight line, the circle, conic sections, curves, surfaces, solids, and so forth), constructed geometrically or arithmetically, and made beautiful by the application of some canon of proportion. The resulting beautiful form may be varied within limits of similarity. (In the instance of human form, there should be sufficient variation to differentiate one figure from another, but never so much as that the figure becomes deformed or nonhuman.) Dürer's Platonic idea of form figures in his larger aesthetic; for him beauty was the aggregate of symmetrical, proportionate, and harmonious forms in a more highly symmetrical, proportionate, and harmonious work of art.

Dürer's aesthetic rules are firmly based in the laws of optics—indeed, he even designed special mechanical instruments to aid in the attainment of beautiful form. He used the height of the human body as the basic unit of measurement and subdivided it linearly to reach a common denominator for construction of a unified artistic plan. This canon was not inviolable; Dürer himself modified it continually in an attempt to approximate more closely the canon of Vitruvius (which was also the canon most favored by Leonardo). Thus the artist retains freedom in the act of selecting his canon. In books I and II of the *Vier Bücher* Dürer deals, once again, with the arithmetic and geometrical construction of forms; in books III and IV he considers the problems of variation and movement.

The last of the *Vier Bücher* is perhaps of greatest mathematical interest since in treating of the movement of bodies in space Dürer was forced to present new, difficult, and intricate considerations of descriptive spatial geometry; indeed, he may be considered the first to have done so. At the end of this book he summarizes and illustrates his theories in the construction of his famous "cube man."

Dürer's chief accomplishment as outlined in the *Vier Bücher* is that in rendering figures (and by extension, in the composition of the total work of art) he first solved the problem of establishing a canon, then considered the transformations of forms within that canon, altering them in accordance with a consistent idea of proportion. In so doing he considered the spatial relations of form and the motions of form within space. His triumph as a painter lay in his disposition of carefully proportioned figures in surrounding space; he thereby elevated what had been hit-or-miss solutions of an essential problem of plastic composition to a carefully worked out mathematical theory. No earlier method had been so successful, and Dürer's theoretical work was widely influential in following centuries.

BIBLIOGRAPHY

I. ORIGINAL WORKS. Editions of Dürer's works include *Underweysung der Messung mit Zirckel und Richtscheyt in Linien, Ebnen, und gantzen Corporen* (Nuremberg, 1525; 2nd ed., Nuremberg, 1538; facsimile ed. by Alvin Jaeggli and Christine Papesch, Zurich, 1966); *Etliche Underricht zu Befestigung der Stett, Schloss und Flecken* (Nuremberg, 1927), repr. as W. Waetzoldt, ed., *Dürer's Befestigungslehre* (Berlin, 1917); and *Vier Bücher von menschlicher Proportion* (Nuremberg, 1528), of which there is a facsimile ed. in 2 vols. with text and commentary, Max Steck, ed. (Zurich, 1969).

II. SECONDARY LITERATURE. Max Steck, *Dürer's Gestaltlehre der Mathematik und der bildenden Künste* (Halle-Tübingen, 1948), contains an extensive bibliography of works by and about Dürer as well as a scientific analysis of the sources of the *Underweysung der Messung;* see also Hans Rupprich, *Dürer-Schriftlicher Nachlass*, vols. I and II (Berlin, 1956–1966), vol. III (in preparation); and Max Steck, "Albrecht Dürer als Mathematiker und Kunsttheoretiker," in *Nova Acta Leopoldina*, **16** (1954), 425–434; "Albrecht Dürer als Schrifsteller," in *Forschungen und Fortschritte*, **30** (1956), 344–347; *Dürer: Eine Bildbiographie* (Munich, 1957; 2nd ed. Munich, 1958; other German eds.), trans. into English as *Dürer and His World* (London–New York, 1964); "Ein neuer Fund zum literarischen Bild Albrecht Dürer's im Schrifttum des 16. Jahrhunderts," in *Forschungen und Fortschritte*, **31** (1957), 253–255; "Drei neue Dürer-Urkunden," *ibid.*, **32** (1958), 56–58; "Grundlagen der Kunst Albrechts Dürers," in *Universitas* (1958), pp. 41–48, also trans. for English and Spanish eds.; "Theoretische Beiträge zu Dürers Kupferstich 'Melancolia I' von 1514," in *Forschungen und Fortschritte*, **32** (1958), 246–251; *Albrecht Dürer, Schriften—Tagebücher—Briefe* (Stuttgart, 1961); "Albrecht Dürer as a Mathematician," in *Proceedings of the Tenth International Congress of the History of Science*, II (Paris, 1964), 655–658; "Albrecht Dürer als Mathematiker und Kunsttheoretiker," in *Der Architekt und der Bauingenieur* (Munich, 1965), pp. 1–6; and "Albrecht Dürer: Die exaktwissenschaftlichen Grundlagen seiner Kunst," in *Scientia, Milano*, **1C** (1966), 15–20, with French trans. as "Albert Dürer: Les sciences exactes sont les bases de son art," *ibid.*, pp. 13–17.

MAX STECK

DU TOIT, ALEXANDER LOGIE (*b.* Rondebosch, near Cape Town, South Africa, 14 March 1878; *d.* Cape Town, 25 February 1948), *geology.*

Du Toit was not only the most honored of South African geologists but also, in the words of R. A. Daly, the "world's greatest field geologist." To a remarkable degree he combined two traits not often found together: an extremely careful observer, he noted and drew deductions from details that escaped others, and at the same time he was able to synthesize information in broad fashion. Toward the end of his life he supported the hypothesis of continental drift with arguments drawn from all parts of the world and considerations about the underlying mantle.

Du Toit's versatility of mind is demonstrated by the important contributions he made to such varied subjects as the stratigraphy of both Precambrian and Karroo beds, paleobotany, petrology, hydrogeology, geomorphology, and the economic geology of base metal, nonmetallic, and diamond deposits. He was very active and mapped the geology of more than 100,000 square miles, much of it in detail, using a plane table with a bicycle for transport and a donkey cart as a base.

Those who remember du Toit have a deep respect for his intellect, knowledge, and activity but an even greater regard for his modesty, frugality, and kindness to all. These qualities, coupled with a strong character, made him an outstanding leader of men and a dominant figure in any company.

Du Toit was born on his family's estate near Cape Town. His father's family, one of the largest and most distinguished in South Africa, was of Huguenot descent and had been in the Cape since 1687. His mother was Anna Logie, daughter of a Scottish immigrant. He went to school at the local diocesan college and graduated from South Africa College (now the University of Cape Town) before spending two years qualifying in mining engineering at Royal Technical College, Glasgow, and studying geology at the Royal College of Science, London.

While in Glasgow, du Toit married Adelaide Walker. They had one child, Alexander Robert. Du Toit's wife died in 1923, and two years later he married Evelyn Harvey. At this period of his life he became a proficient musician, his favorite instrument being the oboe, and did some motorcycle racing.

In 1901 du Toit became lecturer at both the Royal Technical College, Glasgow, and the University of Glasgow. In 1903 he returned to South Africa to join the Geological Commission of the Cape of Good Hope. He spent the next seventeen years almost continuously in the field, mapping, at times accompanied by his wife and child. This period laid the foundations for his broad understanding and unrivaled knowledge of the details of South African geology.

His first season, spent with A. W. Rogers in the western Karroo, determined many of what were to become du Toit's abiding interests. Together they established the stratigraphy of the Lower and Middle Karroo system noting the glacial origin of the Dwyka tillite. They recorded systematic phase changes from place to place in the Karroo and Cape systems. They mapped numerous dolerite intrusives, their acid phases, and their metamorphic aureoles.

From 1903 to 1905 du Toit was in the rugged Stormberg area, mapping so well that his accounts of the paleobotany of the coal-bearing Molteno beds and of the volcanicity have remained classics. From 1905 to 1910 he worked in the northern part of the old Cape Colony, mapping nonfossiliferous rocks of early Precambrian to Permian age. He became interested in geomorphology and hydrogeology and collaborated with Rogers in a new edition of the book *Introduction to the Geology of Cape Colony.*

Between 1910 and 1913 du Toit was near the Indian Ocean, mapping Karroo coal deposits, the flexure of the Lebombo Range along the coast, and an immense number of basic intrusions and charnockite rocks that he discovered there. In 1910 he received the D.Sc. degree from the University of Glasgow for his report on the copper-nickel deposits of the Insiza Range. His "Underground Water in South-East Bechuanaland" (1906) and "The Geology of Underground Water Supply" (1913) were important monographs which served to establish him as the leading authority on groundwater in South Africa. In 1914 du Toit visited Australia to study the rocks equivalent to the Karroo System and the groundwater geology of the Great Artesian Basin. From the outbreak of World War I until the campaign in South West Africa was over in 1915, he was hydrogeologist to the South African forces, holding the rank of captain.

Returning to Natal, du Toit became increasingly involved in work for the irrigation department and transferred to it in 1920. The relief from continuous fieldwork that this provided enabled him to produce a series of important papers and books on the Karroo System (1918), Karroo dolerites (1920), Carboniferous glaciation (1921), past land connections with other continents (1921), the South African coastline (1922), and the geology of South Africa (1926).

In 1923 a grant-in-aid from the Carnegie Institution of Washington enabled du Toit to make a trip to South America for the purpose of comparing the geology of that continent with that of Africa. He left Cape Town on 12 June and spent five months in Brazil, Paraguay, and Argentina. He described this visit in *A Geological Comparison of South America with South Africa* (1927), in which he also outlined points of similarity between the two continents.

He found the two continents to be alike in (1) Precambrian crystalline basement with infolded pre-Devonian sediments; (2) in the far north, a gentle syncline of marine Silurian and Devonian strata; (3) farther south, gently dipping Proterozoic and Lower Paleozoic strata cut by granites; (4) an area of flat-lying Devonian strata; (5) in the extreme south, conformable Devonian to Permian strata including Carboniferous tillites crumpled by later mountain building; (6) tillites extending northward transgressing across the Devonian on to the Precambrian basement before dying out; (7) glacial deposits overlain by continental Permian and Triassic strata with *Glossopteris* flora, followed by extensive basalt flows and dolerite intrusives; (8) Gondwana beds extending northward continuously from the southern Karroo to the Kaokoveld in Africa and from Uruguay to Minas Geraes in South America, with further great detached areas in the north, in each instance some distance inland, in the Angola-Congo and Piauhy-Maranhão regions; (9) an intraformational break occurring commonly below the late Triassic; (10) tilted Cretaceous beds occurring only along the coast; (11) widespread horizontal Cretaceous and Tertiary strata; (12) a succession in the Falkland Islands closely resembling that of the Cape, but distinct from that of Patagonia; (13) seven corresponding faunal assemblages in the similar strata; and (14) the geographical outline of the continent.

From 1927 to 1941 du Toit was consulting geologist to De Beers Consolidated Mines but continued to write on many topics; in 1937 he published his well-known book *Our Wandering Continents.* In 1932 he visited North America, in 1937 the Soviet Union, and in 1938 India. From his retirement until his death he lived at Cape Town and maintained his varied interests, extending them to include archaeology and vertebrate zoology.

Du Toit received many honors and awards, including five honorary degrees. He was twice president of the Geological Society of South Africa, a corresponding member of the Geological Society of

America, and a fellow of the Royal Society of London.

More than most scientists, du Toit's reputation, already high, has continued to grow, because in many of his deductions he was ahead of his time. His forte was meticulous and extensive fieldwork which enabled him to grasp virtually all aspects of the geology of South Africa. Many of the ideas that he espoused concerning groundwater, economic deposits of copper and nickel, and geomorphology and stratigraphy of rocks were original but not remarkably different from those held by others. The most significant factor of du Toit's work was his early espousal of the theory of continental drift; he was the first to realize that the southern continents had at one time formed the supercontinent of Gondwanaland, which was distinct from the northern supercontinent of Laurasia. His championship of continental drift, unpopular at the time, is now widely hailed as having been correct.

BIBLIOGRAPHY

I. ORIGINAL WORKS. Du Toit's works include "The Stormberg Formation in Cape Colony," in *Report and Papers, South African Association for the Advancement of Science,* **2** (1905), 47; "Underground Water in South-East Bechuanaland," in *Transactions of the South African Philosophical Society,* **16** (1906), 251–262; "Report on the Copper-Nickel Deposits of the Insizwa, Mount Ayliff, East Griqualand," in *Annual Report of the Geological Commission for the Cape of Good Hope for 1910* (1911), pp. 69–110; "The Geology of Underground Water Supply," in *Mining Proceedings of the South African Society of Civil Engineers for 1913* (1913), pp. 7–31; "The Problem of the Great Australian Artesian Basin," in *Journal and Proceedings of the Royal Society of New South Wales,* **51** (1917), 135–208; "The Zones of the Karroo System and Their Distribution," in *Proceedings of the Geological Society of South Africa,* **21** (1918), 17–36; "The Karroo Dolerites of South Africa: A Study in Hypabyssal Injection," in *Transactions of the Geological Society of South Africa,* **23** (1920), 1–42; "The Carboniferous Glaciation of South Africa," *ibid.,* **24** (1921), 188–227; "Land Connections Between the Other Continents and South Africa in the Past," in *South African Journal of Science,* **18** (1921), 120–140; "The Evolution of the South African Coastline," in *South African Geographical Journal,* **5** (Dec. 1922), 5–12; *The Geology of South Africa* (Edinburgh, 1926); *A Geological Comparison of South America with South Africa,* Carnegie Institution Publication no. 381 (Washington, D. C., 1927); *Our Wandering Continents: An Hypothesis of Continental Drifting* (Edinburgh, 1937); "Tertiary Mammals and Continental Drift," in *American Journal of Science,* **242** (1944), 145–163; and "Palaeolithic Environments in Kenya and the Union—A Contrast," in *South African Archeological Bulletin,* **2** (1947), 28–40.

II. SECONDARY LITERATURE. On du Toit and his work see T. W. Gevers, "The Life and Work of Dr. Alexander L. du Toit," Alexander L. du Toit Memorial Lecture no. 1, in *Proceedings of the Geological Society of South Africa,* **52** (1949), annexure 1–109; S. H. Haughton, "Alexander Logie du Toit, 1878–1948," in *Biographical Memoirs of Fellows of the Royal Society,* **6** (1948), 385–395; and "Memorial to Alexander Logie du Toit," in *Proceedings. Geological Society of America,* Annual Report for 1949 (1950), pp. 141–149.

J. T. WILSON

DUTROCHET, RENÉ-JOACHIM-HENRI (*b.* Néon, France, 14 November 1776; *d.* Paris, France, 4 February 1847), *animal and plant physiology, embryology, physics, phonetics.*

Dutrochet was born at a seignorial mansion near Poitiers; he was the eldest son of wealthy and noble parents. His early childhood was spoiled by clubfoot, which—after unsuccessful medical consultations—was completely healed by a renowned healer, who was also a hangman.

The Revolution brought expropriation of family property after his father emigrated; Dutrochet was therefore forced to rely on his own resources. He volunteered for the navy in 1799, then deserted and joined his brothers in the last Royalist units. Following 18 Brumaire, which with the accession of Bonaparte to the Consulate brought an end to the Royalist resistance and a general amnesty, Dutrochet spent two peaceful years with his family. He was, however, dissatisfied with such an empty and useless life, so in 1802, at the age of twenty-six, he went to Paris to study medicine. Graduating in 1806, he qualified as a military medical officer in 1808 and was sent to Spain. With great devotion and sacrifice and lacking adequate material means, he dealt with a severe outbreak of typhoid in Burgos. He believed that he had found his true vocation until, having contracted the disease himself, he was so weakened that he had to return to France for a long convalescence. He joined his mother in a country house near Château-Renault in Touraine, where he lived in seclusion from society and decided, at the age of thirty-four, to abandon medical practice and devote all his efforts to natural science. In 1819 he was elected corresponding member of the Académie des Sciences; in 1831 he was elected to full membership. After his mother's death he lived in Paris during the winter months and returned in summer to his country residence. In 1845 he suffered a blow on the head which, after a long illness marked by severe headaches, led to his death.

Dutrochet's first scientific interest, which he pursued even before he finished his medical studies, was phonetics. In 1806 he repeated Ferrein's experiments on the larynx and tried to establish the relationship between pitch and tension of the vocal cords under different loads—these experiments, however, have been overshadowed by his subsequent studies and are almost forgotten.

Dutrochet's investigations into the development of birds, reptiles, batrachians, and mammals, published in 1814, are more important. In them he paid special attention to the hitherto neglected early stages of development of the egg within the ovary, to its detachment, and to the fetal membranes. (One of them, the external yolk membrane of the bird's egg, whose fibers are continuous with the chalazae, is called "Dutrochet's membrane.") He also made several original observations on fetal development, but it was his demonstration of the analogy of fetal envelopes in ovipara and vivipara that suggested a unity of the main features in the development of animals and proved extremely valuable for further studies.

The principal field of Dutrochet's studies was plant physiology, although he also studied that of animals. He further explored the areas that were common to both, especially the exchange of gases between the atmosphere and plant or animal tissues—the key to the life processes. He asserted that respiration is of the same nature in both plants and animals. Active breathing in animals had been evident to observers since very early times; in plants, however, the existence of respiration was brought to light much later. In 1832 Dutrochet showed that the minute openings on the surface of leaves (the stomata) communicate with lacunae in deeper tissue. He further demonstrated that only the green parts of the plant can absorb carbon dioxide and thus transform light energy into chemical energy that can then serve to accomplish all kinds of syntheses.

In his studies of excitability and motility Dutrochet tried to demonstrate that these widespread phenomena are essentially the same in both plants and animals, since they utilize the same organs and mechanisms. In contrast to the then current explanation of these phenomena—which was based on *Naturphilosophie* and depended on intervention of the "vital force"—he stressed anatomical and mechanical arguments. For example, he emphasized the importance to plant motility of the turgor of the hinge cells, the passage of water out of the cells on one side into the intercellular spaces, and so forth.

Dutrochet's research on the phenomena of osmosis and diffusion (or endosmosis and exosmosis, as he not very aptly called them) and their applications to the study of previously unexplained vital phenomena attracted general attention. His chief observation was that certain organic membranes allow the passage of water but stop the molecules dissolved in it, so that between two solutions of different concentration, separated by such a membrane, water passes from the less concentrated to the more concentrated, even against gravity. Although the conditions of Dutrochet's experiments were rather simple and did not allow of great accuracy, he made the first important steps toward the study of osmosis and diffusion. He constructed an osmometer for measurements of osmotic pressure and pointed to such pressure as the possible cause of circulation and rise of sap in plants, absorption of nutrients in plants and animals. His experiments were developed by many of his younger colleagues, and his ideas played an important role in their thinking, for example, in Carl Ludwig's hypothesis of the formation of urine in the kidneys (1842).

Among Dutrochet's other discoveries, it may be noted that in 1831 he demonstrated that mushrooms are in fact the fruiting bodies of the mycelium; they had been previously considered to be a particular genus (called *byssus*). He was also the first (1840) to detect, by a thermoelectric technique, the production of heat in an individual plant and in an insect muscle during activity.

Dutrochet is also considered to be the founder of the cell theory; but his ideas are actually more in the nature of shrewd, intuitive anticipations rather than conclusions based on his own microscopic observations. His illustrations are not convincing and it seems that, at least in some cases, Dutrochet's "globules" (cells) were optical artifacts produced by poor lenses and bad illumination. Although he expressed his ideas in language similar to that of the cell theory, these ideas and the observations upon which they were based were not equivalent to it. Dutrochet himself made no claim to priority when Schwann's book was published in 1839.

Dutrochet's observations and experiments were often unsatisfactory; his means were largely inadequate. He was often mistaken in his conclusions or made false parallels between plants and animals. His importance lies more in the systematic endeavor to demonstrate that vital phenomena can be explained on the basis of physics and chemistry, that living organisms use physical and chemical forces, and that there is no reason to suppose the existence of some intervention of a "vital force." He strove to generalize and to show the unity of basic processes in all living things, both plant and animal. His experimental studies and observations led him to the conclusion that there is only one physiology, only one general science of the function of living bodies. His attempt to apply physicochemical forces and phenomena in explanation of physiological processes overcame that mysticism which had been introduced into physiology by teleologically minded physiologists.

A convinced antivitalist, Dutrochet developed a unitary conception of a nature—animate and inanimate, organic and inorganic, all subject to the laws of physics and chemistry. For this reason he had a great influence on his younger colleagues; for example, in 1841 du Bois-Reymond wrote, "I am gradually returning to Dutrochet's view. The more one advances in the knowledge of physiology, the more one will have reason for ceasing to believe that the phenomena of life are essentially different from physical phenomena." Dutrochet's work was also greatly appreciated by the distinguished plant physiologist Julius Sachs.

BIBLIOGRAPHY

I. ORIGINAL WORKS. Dutrochet's writings include *Essai sur une nouvelle théorie de la voix, avec l'exposé des divers systèmes qui ont paru jusqu'à ce jour sur cet objet* (Paris, 1806); *Mémoire sur une nouvelle théorie de la voix* (Paris, 1809); *Mémoire sur une nouvelle théorie de l'harmonie dans lequel on démontre l'existence de trois modes nouveaux, qui faisaient partie du système musical des Grecs* (Paris, 1810); *Recherches anatomiques et physiologiques sur la structure intime des animaux et végétaux* (Paris, 1824); *L'agent immédiat du mouvement vital dévoilé dans sa nature et dans son mode d'action chez les végétaux et animaux* (London-Paris, 1826); and *Nouvelles recherches sur l'endosmose et l'exosmose, suivies de l'application expérimentale de ces actions physiques à la solution du problème de l'irritabilité végétale, et à la détermination de la cause de l'ascension des tiges et de la descente des racines* (Paris, 1828). Further observations on the osmotic phenomena were published as "Nouvelles observations sur l'endosmose et l'exosmose, et sur la cause de ce double phénomène," in *Annales de chimie et de physique*, **35** (1827), 393–400; "Nouvelles recherches sur l'endosmose et l'exosmose," *ibid.*, **37** (1828), 191–201; "Recherches sur l'endosmose et sur la cause physique de ce phénomène," *ibid.*, **49** (1832), 411–437; "Du pouvoir d'endosmose considéré comparativement dans quelques liquides organiques," *ibid.*, **51** (1832), 159–166; and "De l'endosmose des acides," *ibid.*, **60** (1835), 337–368.

II. SECONDARY LITERATURE. On Dutrochet and his work, see *Notice analytique sur les travaux de M. Henri Dutrochet* (Paris, 1832); A. Brongniart, *Notice sur Henri Dutrochet* (Paris, 1852); J. J. Coste, *Éloge historique de Henri Dutrochet* (Paris, 1866); *Gazette médicale de Paris*, no. 11 (1866); and I. Geoffroy Saint-Hilaire, in *Biographie universelle*, XII (Paris, 1855). For Dutrochet's place in the history of the cell theory see A. R. Rich, "The Place of R. J. H. Dutrochet in the Development of the Cell Theory," in *Bulletin of the Johns Hopkins Hospital*, **39** (1926), 330–365; F. K. Studnička, "Aus der Vorgeschichte der Zellentheorie. H. Milne Edwards, H. Dutrochet, F. Raspail, J. E. Pur-

kinje," in *Anatomischer Anzeiger*, **73** (1931), 390–416; and J. W. Wilson, "Dutrochet and the Cell Theory," in *Isis*, **37** (1947), 14–21. His work in plant physiology is discussed by J. Sachs in *Geschichte der Botanik* (Munich, 1875), English trans. by H. E. Garney (Oxford, 1890).

VLADISLAV KRUTA

DUTTON, CLARENCE EDWARD (*b.* Wallingford, Connecticut, 15 May 1841; *d.* Englewood, New Jersey, 4 January 1912), *geology.*

Prepared for college early (he was ready to matriculate at thirteen), Dutton was held back by his parents, Samuel and Emily Curtis Dutton, as too young. Entering Yale at fifteen, he at first showed more literary than scientific aptitude. After graduation in the class of 1860, he entered Yale Theological Seminary. His studies were interrupted by the Civil War; he entered the army, where he quickly discovered a liking for mathematics that led him to make the army his career. Emerging from the war a captain of ordnance, he was stationed first at Watervliet Arsenal, near the Bessemer steelworks in West Troy, New York. His first scientific paper was on the chemistry of the Bessemer process.

Later Dutton was transferred to the Washington Arsenal; here he was led toward geology by the brilliant group of men who were then creating a structure of government-supported science. At Washington Philosophical Society meetings he met S. F. Baird and Joseph Henry of the Smithsonian Institution; E. W. Hilgard of the Coast and Geodetic Survey; Simon Newcomb, Asaph Hall, and William Harkness of the Naval Observatory; and F. V. Hayden and J. W. Powell of the western surveys. By 1875 Powell had enough confidence in Dutton as a geologist to ask that he be assigned to special duty with his geographical and geological survey of the Rocky Mountain region. When the western surveys of Powell, Clarence King, Hayden, and G. M. Wheeler were consolidated in 1879, Dutton continued with the United States Geological Survey until 1890, when he returned to regular army duty.

From the beginning of his geological studies, Dutton was interested in orogenic problems, and during his years of work in the plateau region of Utah, Arizona, and New Mexico he had the opportunity to study not only the faults and monoclines along which uplift and subsidence had taken place but also the extensive volcanism that had accompanied these earth movements. In a number of reports and papers and in two major monographs (*Report on the Geology of the High Plateaus of Utah*, 1880, and *The Tertiary History of the Grand Canyon District*, 1882) he established himself as a brilliant interpreter of physical features. With Powell and Grove Karl Gilbert, his close collaborators, he established some of the basic principles of structural geology—in particular the theory of isostasy, which he developed to explain crustal movements. His geological writings, moreover, are marked by great charm of style; and he virtually formulated a new aesthetic for the startling scenery of the Grand Canyon country.

In 1882 Dutton studied live Hawaiian volcanoes, intending thereafter to examine the extinct volcanoes and lava beds of Oregon. He was diverted by the Charleston earthquake of 1886, on which he prepared a monograph; and from 1888 to 1890 he directed the hydrographic work of the irrigation surveys under Powell. After returning to army duty in 1890, he wrote further papers on volcanism and earthquakes, including several on the possibilities of earthquakes along the route of the proposed Nicaragua Canal. His last major contribution was *Earthquakes in the Light of the New Seismology,* which linked volcanism to radioactivity.

BIBLIOGRAPHY

I. ORIGINAL WORKS. A full listing of Dutton's papers is appended to Wallace Stegner, *Clarence Edward Dutton: An Appraisal* (Salt Lake City, n.d. [1936]). The most important are *Report on the Geology of the High Plateaus of Utah,* vol. XXXII, U.S. Geographical and Geological Survey of the Rocky Mountain Region (Washington, D.C., 1880); *The Tertiary History of the Grand Canyon District,* U.S. Geological Survey Monograph no. 2 (Washington, D.C., 1882); "Hawaiian Volcanoes," in *Report of the United States Geological Survey,* **4** (1884), 75–219; "Mount Taylor and the Zuñi Plateau," *ibid.,* **6** (1885), 105–198; "The Charleston Earthquake of August 31, 1886," *ibid.,* **9** (1889), 203–528; "General Description of the Volcanic Phenomena Found in That Portion of Central America Traversed by the Nicaragua Canal," United States Senate Document no. 357, 57th Congress, 1st Session (1901–1902), XXVI, 55–62; and *Earthquakes in the Light of the New Seismology* (New York, 1904).

II. SECONDARY LITERATURE. In addition to Stegner, above, brief discussions of Dutton's life and work may be found in *Biographical Record, Class of Sixty* (Boston, 1906); and in G. P. Merrill, *The First Hundred Years of American Geology* (New Haven, 1904); as well as in the administrative reports of the Powell Survey and the United States Geological Survey.

WALLACE STEGNER

DUVAL, MATHIAS MARIE (*b.* Grasse, France, 7 February 1844; *d.* Paris, France, 28 February 1907), *histology, physiology, comparative anatomy, embryology.*

The son of Joseph Duval, the botanist and naturalist, and Marie Jouve, he spent his childhood in Grasse, Algiers, and then Strasbourg, where his father had been appointed school inspector. Duval studied medicine there from 1863 to 1869. His doctoral thesis was entitled "Étude sur la valeur relative de la section du maxillaire supérieur." He was a student of Joseph Alexis Stolz, Charles Basile Morel, and Émile Küss; he became an anatomy assistant in 1866 and a prosector in 1869. During the Franco-Prussian War he served under General Charles Bourbaki. The loss of Alsace forced him to pursue his career first in Montpellier and finally in Paris. After defending a thesis entitled "La rétine; structure et usages," he became *agrégé* in anatomy and physiology in 1873.

From 1873 until 1899 he taught—among other subjects—anatomy for artists at the École Nationale Supérieure des Beaux-Arts. His course, greatly influenced by Guillaume Duchenne, dealt mainly with the physiology of the face, the muscles of physiognomy, and the expression of strong emotions. In 1880 Duval succeeded Pierre Paul Broca as professor of zoological anthropology and became director of the anthropology laboratory at the École Pratique des Hautes Études. In December 1885 he was appointed professor of histology at the Faculty of Medicine of the University of Paris. His clear, precise, and efficacious teaching method was highly appreciated by students. In 1882 Duval was elected to the Académie Nationale de Médecine. In 1889 he was president of the Société d'Anthropologie de Paris. Blinded by bilateral cataract, he was forced to reduce and finally to discontinue his teaching activity. He died probably of cancer and was buried in Neuville-les-Dames, near Dieppe.

Duval's work was strongly influenced by that of Charles Darwin and the French histologist Charles Robin. In histology his most important original works involve the microscopic structure of the central nervous system and sensory organs, as well as the true origin of the cranial nerves. Duval declared: "Embryological studies can have no guiding hypotheses other than those expressed in transformist doctrine." He did a great deal to disseminate Darwin's theory of evolution. His research in this area reflects his training as a histologist and physiologist: it concerned the formation of the gastrula, development of the blastoderm, the three primitive germ layers and their derivatives in the various species, segmentation of the egg, and embryonic appendages of birds and mammals. Extremely well-versed in anatomy, he defended the concepts of "animal colonies" and of the invertebrate origin of higher forms of animal life; among other homologies he established relationships between the "primitive lineage" of birds and the "Rusconian orifice" of batrachians. He was also interested in teratology based on fertilization anomalies. His written didactic works exerted tremendous influence both in France and abroad.

BIBLIOGRAPHY

I. ORIGINAL WORKS. Between 1868 and 1900 Duval published more than 250 papers, works, and articles in various dictionaries and journals of anatomy, physiology, anthropology, general biology, and even history and ethnography. A complete list may be found in the two *Notices sur les titres et travaux scientifiques de M. Mathias Duval* (Paris, 1885, 1896) and in E. Retterer, "Mathias Duval; sa vie et son oeuvre," in *Journal de l'anatomie et de la physiologie de l'homme et des animaux,* **43,** no. 3 (1907), 241–331.

His main didactic works are *Cours de physiologie,* which appeared in eight eds. from 1872 to 1897 and was translated into English (Boston, 1875), Spanish (Madrid, 1876, 1884), Greek (Athens, 1887), and Russian (St. Petersburg, 1893); *Manuel du microscope dans ses applications au diagnostic et à la clinique* (with L. Lereboullet, 1873, two eds.); *Précis de technique microscopique et histologique* (1878); *Manuel de l'anatomiste* (with C. Morel, 1882); *Leçons sur la physiologie du système nerveux* (1883); *Précis d'anatomie à l'usage des artistes* (1882, three eds.; English trans., London, 1884 and 1905); *Dictionnaire usuel des sciences médicales* (with Dechambre and Lereboullet, 1885, two eds.); *Le Darwinisme* (1886); *Atlas d'embryologie* (1889); *L'anatomie des maîtres* (with A. Bical, 1890); *Anatomie et physiologie animales* (with P. Constantin, 1892, two eds.); *Le placenta des carnassiers* (1895); *Précis d'histologie* (1897; two eds.; Italian translation by Fusari, Turin, 1899); and *Histoire de l'anatomie plastique* (with E. Cuyer, 1899).

II. SECONDARY LITERATURE. On Duval and his work see A. Gautier, "Notice nécrologique sur M. Duval," in *Bulletin de l'Académie nationale de médecine,* **57** (1907), 343–344; G. Hervé, "Mathias Duval," in *Revue de l'École d'anthropologie,* **17** (1907), 69–74; and H. Roger, "Mathias Duval," in *Presse médicale,* **15,** no. 19 (1907), 145–146.

CHARLES COURY

DUVERNEY, JOSEPH-GUICHARD (*b.* Feurs, France, 5 August 1648; *d.* Paris, France, 10 September 1730), *anatomy.*

Duverney, the son of the village doctor, went to Avignon when he was fourteen years old to study medicine, receiving his medical degree there in 1667. Shortly thereafter he went to Paris, where he soon began to attend the weekly scientific meetings at the house of the Abbé Bourdelot. At these meetings Duverney often spoke on anatomical subjects. Here, too, he probably met Claude Perrault, who asked him to assist in dissections.

Perrault was the leader of a group of anatomists, who came to be known as the "Parisians," who col-

laborated with one another to an uncommon degree, regularly performing dissections as a group and collectively reviewing both the text and plates before publishing their collaborative work. Individually and together they dissected a wide variety of animals, many of which came from the royal menagerie at Versailles. (Duverney performed the dissection of an elephant in the presence of Louis XIV.) These anatomists considered most zoological writings inadequate and wished to assemble a large series of observations to constitute a new *Historia animalium* to replace that of Aristotle—one that would be worthy of their monarch.

The Paris group concentrated on describing unusual species and distinctive anatomical features, barely more than cataloging the commonplace. They used the human body as a standard of reference, not because of its assumed perfection, but for their readers' familiarity with it. When appropriate, domestic animals were used for purposes of comparison, although these were not described in any detail. They published their comparative anatomical studies anonymously at first. Although individual contributions to these earlier papers can only occasionally be determined, there is little question that Duverney contributed to them, probably heavily, presumably beginning with the *Description anatomique . . .* of 1669, which contained descriptions of a chameleon, beaver, dromedary, bear, and gazelle.

Duverney's connection with the Académie des Sciences began in 1674 when he was enlisted to assist in the completion of the two sumptuous elephant-folio volumes of the *Mémoires* that were published anonymously at the king's expense. The work had been begun by Perrault, Louis Gayant, and Jean Pequet but had been interrupted by the deaths of the latter two. The same year, the Academy sent Duverney to Bayonne and lower Brittany to dissect fishes; Phillipe de la Hire accompanied him as his illustrator. Duverney was elected to full membership in 1676.

In 1679 Duverney was appointed to the chair of anatomy at the Jardin du Roi. He was a highly successful lecturer, and his auditors included the curious and the fashionable as well as serious students of anatomy. Jacques-Bénigne Winslow, F. P. du Petit, and J.-B. Senac—who edited two of Duverney's posthumous works—were among his students.

In 1688 Perrault died, and Duverney became responsible for all the comparative-anatomical work sponsored by the Academy. He also inherited Perrault's manuscripts relating to such work, including descriptions of sixteen animals that needed only editing for publication, but these did not appear until after Duverney's death. Duverney had a certain reluctance to publish—for example, he bought the manuscript of Jan Swammerdam's *Biblia natura* with the intention of publishing it, but the book did not appear until Hermann Boerhaave bought it from him. Nor did he ever produce the new edition of the *Mémoires,* despite the urgings of the Academy.

The only major work written by Duverney alone and published during his lifetime was, in fact, his *Traité de l'organe de l'ouie . . .* (1683), the first thorough, scientific treatise on the human ear. In it he describes the structure, functions, and diseases of the ear and includes a further description of the fetal ear, noting its differences from the adult structure. Duverney based his study of the ear on a study of its sensory innervation; to this end he had a new plate engraved to illustrate the base of the brain and the origin of these nerves, since he had found no adequate figure of this region. His interpretation of aural function was mechanical; for example, in the *Traité* he states that sound is transmitted within the ear as vibrations carried by the enclosed air and by the malleus, incus, and stapes. These vibrations reach the end of the nerves and set up a flow of spirits to the brain; the muscles (except for the muscles of the neck that turn the head) are motivated by another flow of spirits from the brain. Duverney believed that there is a direct communication by the nerves from the outer ear to the neck muscles, so that a flow of spirits along this route is responsible for the turning of the head when a noise is heard.

In addition, Duverney read numerous papers to the Academy, of which the most important are a group dealing with the circulatory and respiratory systems in cold-blooded vertebrates. In 1699 he presented a paper on these subjects, especially in the tortoise but also in the carp, frog, and viper. He presented a highly accurate description of the heart of the tortoise, demonstrating the single ventricle and its three cavities, the flow pattern of the blood, and the mixing of the arterial and venous bloods. He noted that the pulmonary artery carries venous blood, and he recognized the respiratory function of the gills. He here displays a knowledge of the piscine circulatory system that surpasses that of any other seventeenth-century work.

In a paper of 1701 Duverney limited himself to fishes with gills, but did not go significantly beyond his earlier work. He did describe the role of the gills in greater detail, however, in particular the diffusion of blood in the gills to provide a greater respiratory surface. He recognized that the change of color in the gills marked the conversion of venous to arterial blood. Knowledge of the cold-blooded vertebrates' circulatory state had been chaotic and disorganized prior to Duverney's work; he systematized it and advanced it considerably.

Three anatomical structures are sometimes given Duverney's name. The first, an incisura in the cartilage of the external auditory meatus, was described in his *Traité;* the second, the *pars lacrimalis musculus orbicularis oculi,* was described in the posthumously published (1749) *L'art de disséquer;* while the third is commonly known as Bartholin's glands, after Caspar Bartholin (1655–1738), who first described them in humans—Duverney had previously observed them in the cow.

BIBLIOGRAPHY

I. ORIGINAL WORKS. The collected works of the Parisians, to which Duverney would have contributed, were the *Mémoires pour servir à l'histoire naturelle des animaux,* 2 vols. (Paris, 1671–1676), trans. into English by Alexander Pitfield (London, 1688; later eds., 1701, 1702). An expanded ed. appeared after Duverney's death but included much of his material, 3 vols. (Paris, 1732–1734). Duverney's principal individual study was the *Traité de l'organe de l'ouie, contenant la structure, les usages & les maladies de toutes les parties de l'oreille* (Paris, 1683). A Latin ed. appeared (Nuremberg, 1684), and there were two English eds., trans. by J. Marshall (London, 1737, 1748).

Individual papers cited in the text are "Observations sur la circulation du sang dans le foetus et description du coeur de la tortue et de quelques autres animaux (du coeur de la grenouille; de la vipère; de la carpe)," in *Mémoires de l'Académie des Sciences de Paris* (1699); and "Mémoire sur la circulation du sang des poissons qui ont des ouyes et sur respiration," *ibid.* (1701).

Duverney's posthumous writings include *L'art de disséquer méthodiquement les muscles du corps humain* (Paris, 1749); *Traité des maladies des os,* J.-B. Senac, ed. (Paris, 1751), English trans., *The Diseases of the Bones,* S. Ingham, trans. (London, 1762); and *Oeuvres anatomiques,* 2 vols., J.-B. Senac, ed. (Paris, 1761), which contains most of his papers published in the *Mémoires de l'Académie des sciences,* including the important ones on the circulatory system of the cold-blooded vertebrates.

II. SECONDARY LITERATURE. Principal biographical sources are the article in *Biographie universelle* (*Michaud*) *ancienne et moderne,* vol. XII (Paris, 1855); and Bernard Le Bovyer de Fontenelle, "Eloge," in *Oeuvres,* new ed., vol. VI (Paris, 1742).

WESLEY C. WILLIAMS

DYCK, WALTHER FRANZ ANTON VON (*b.* Munich, Germany, 6 December 1856; *d.* Munich, 5 November 1934), *mathematics.*

Dyck was the son of Hermann Dyck, a painter and the director of the Munich Kunstgewerbeschule, and

Marie Royko. He married Auguste Müller in 1886; they had two daughters.

Dyck studied mathematics in Munich, Berlin, and Leipzig. He qualified as a university lecturer in Leipzig in 1882 and was an assistant of F. Klein. In 1884 he became a professor at the Munich Polytechnikum. He made noteworthy contributions to function theory, group theory, topology, potential theory, and the formative discussion on integral curves of differential equations. He was also one of the founders of the *Encyclopädie der mathematischen Wissenschaften*. Appointed director of the Polytechnikum in 1900, he brought about its rise to university standing as the Technische Hochschule; and as rector (1903–1906, 1919–1925) he carried out a major building expansion. In 1903 he was enlisted, along with Carl von Linde, by Oskar von Miller to aid in the establishment and early development of the Deutsches Museum; he also served as its second chairman from 1906. As a dedicated member of the Bayerische Akademie der Wissenschaften (and a class secretary in 1924), he prepared the plan and organization of the complete edition of the writings and letters of Kepler, including the posthumous works (for the most part in Pulkovo, near Leningrad). Moreover, as a founder (along with F. Schmitt-Ott) of the Notgemeinschaft der Deutschen Wissenschaften, he concerned himself with assuring financial support for the edition.

Linguistically gifted and a warm, kind-hearted man of wide-ranging and liberal interests, including art and music, Dyck was an outstanding scholar and organizer and an enthusiastic and inspiring teacher.

BIBLIOGRAPHY

I. ORIGINAL WORKS. Dyck's writings include *Uber regulär verzweigte Riemannsche Flächen und die durch sie bestimmten Irrationalitäten* (Munich, 1879), his doctoral dissertation; "Gruppentheoretische Studien," in *Mathematische Annalen,* **20** (1882), 1–44; **22** (1882), 70–108; "Beiträge zur Analysis situs," in *Sitzungsberichte der Sächsischen Akademie der Wissenschaften zu Leipzig* (1885), 314–325; (1886), 53–69; (1888), 40–52; and in *Mathematische Annalen,* **32** (1888), 457–512; **37** (1890), 273–316; *Katalog math.-physik. Modelle . . .* (Munich, 1892; supp., 1893); "Beiträge zur Potentialtheorie," in *Sitzungsberichte der Bayerischen Akademie der Wissenschaften zu München* (1895), 261–277, 447–500; (1898), 203–224; *Spezialkatalog der mathematischen Austellung, Deutsche Unterrichtungsabteilung in Chicago* (Munich, 1897); L. O. Hesse, *Gesammelte Werke,* ed. with S. Gundelfinger, J. Lüroth, and M. Noether (Munich, 1897); "Nova Kepleriana," in *Abhand-*

lungen der Bayerischen Akademie der Wissenschaften, **25** (1910), 1–61; **26** (1912), 1–45; **28** (1915), 1–17; **31** (1927), 1–114, written with M. Caspar; n.s. **17** (1933), 1–58, written with M. Caspar; **18** (1933), 1–58; **23** (1934), 1–88; *G. von Reichenbach* (Munich, 1912), a biography; and *J. Kepler in seinen Briefen,* 2 vols. (Munich, 1930), written with M. Caspar.

II. SECONDARY LITERATURE. Obituary notices by G. Faber are in *Forschungen und Fortschritte,* **34** (1934), 423–424, *Jahresbericht der Deutschen Mathematikervereinigung,* **45** (1935), 89–98, with portrait and bibliography, and *Jahrbuch der Bayerischen Akademie der Wissenschaften* (1934); an anonymous obituary is in *Almanach. Österreichische Akademie der Wissenschaften,* **85** (1935), 269–272; see also J. E. Hofmann, in *Natur und Kultur,* **32** (1935), 61–63, with portrait; J. Zenneck, in *Mitteilungen der Gesellschaft deutscher Naturforscher und Ärzte,* **11** (1935), 2–3. On his seventieth birthday see H. Schmidt, in *Denkschriften der Technische Hochschule München,* **1** (1926), 3–4, with portrait as a youth. On the centenary of his birth see R. Sauer, in *Wissenschaftliche Vorträge, gehalten bei der akademischen Jahresfeier der Technischen Hochschule München* (1957), 10–11. A short biography by G. Faber is in *Neue Deutsche Biographie,* IV (Berlin, 1959), 210. A bronze bust by Hermann Hahn, at the Technische Hochschule in Munich, was unveiled in 1926.

J. E. HOFMANN

DYSON, FRANK WATSON (*b*. Measham, near Ashby-de-la-Zouch, Leicestershire, England, 8 January 1868; *d*. on board ship near Cape Town, South Africa, 25 May 1939), *astronomy.*

On graduating in the mathematical tripos at Cambridge, England, as second wrangler in 1889, Dyson began research on gravitational problems. He was appointed chief assistant at the Royal Observatory at Greenwich in 1894; astronomer royal for Scotland in 1905; and in 1910 he returned to Greenwich to become the eleventh astronomer royal. It was by cooperation in, and direction of, the preparation of fundamental astronomical measurements that he contributed significantly to the progress of astronomy.

From 1894 Dyson improved the methods used at Greenwich for reduction of the measurement of star positions from photographs, and during the opposition of Eros in 1900–1901 he organized the observations and reduction of the data compiled from them to provide new standards of accuracy. With W. G. Thackeray he reobserved the 4,239 stars that had been cataloged by Stephen Groombridge from 1806 to 1816 and compared positions so that proper motions of the stars could be determined over an eighty-year interval. Following this, Dyson extended J. C. Kapteyn's hypothesis of two star streams to fainter stars and rephotographed the stars in the internationally delimited Greenwich astrographic zone to allow more proper motions to be determined.

In observing the total solar eclipses of 1900, 1901, and 1905, Dyson measured the wavelengths of 1,200 lines in the spectrum of the chromosphere and compared the strengths with those for which laboratory evidence was available. His intensity measurements confirmed the work of J. N. Lockyer and A. Fowler, which was then subject to much criticism. It was due to Dyson that two Greenwich expeditions, one to Principe Island off Spanish Guinea and one to Sobral in Brazil, were sent to observe the 1919 solar eclipse. They verified the deflection of starlight by the sun's gravitational field to the degree predicted by relativity theory.

Dyson developed geophysical work at Greenwich by bringing up to date the observatory's equipment and techniques for measurements of terrestrial magnetism and by moving the department to the country when local railroad electrification made this necessary. He also reorganized accurate latitude measurement, developing the methods for using the floating zenith telescope with great success. Dyson took much interest in time determination: he installed the Shortt synchronome free-pendulum clocks in 1924 and arranged for public radio time signals that were soon extended to give worldwide coverage.

Dyson had a genius for collaboration, and the majority of his published work was as joint author. A strong supporter of the International Astronomical Union, he attended every meeting from 1922 to 1935; his charming hospitality at Greenwich was a byword among astronomers from every country. In 1931 W. J. Yapp, a wealthy manufacturer, donated a thirty-six-inch reflector to commemorate Dyson's tenure as astronomer royal; it was first used in April 1934. Dyson retired on 28 February 1933 but continued to offer advice, particularly on the removal of the Radcliffe Observatory from Oxford to Pretoria, South Africa.

Dyson received many honors, including four gold medals from learned societies. He was elected a fellow of the Royal Society in 1901, was president of the Royal Astronomical Society from 1911 to 1913, was created a knight bachelor in 1915, and received the K.C.B. in 1926.

BIBLIOGRAPHY

Dyson's important writings (alone or in collaboration) include "On the Determination of Positions of Stars for the Astrographic Catalogue at the Royal Observatory," *Monthly Notices of the Royal Astronomical Society,* **51** (1896), 114–134; "Determination of the Constant of Precession and the Direction of the Solar Motion From a Comparison of Groombridge's Catalogue (1810) With Modern Greenwich Observations," *ibid.,* **65** (1905), 428–457; "Determinations of Wavelengths From Spectra Obtained at the Total Solar Eclipses of 1900, 1901 and 1905," in *Philosophical Transactions of the Royal Society,* **206A** (1906), 403–452; "A Statistical Discussion of the Proper Motions of the Stars in the Greenwich Catalogue for 1910," in *Monthly Notices of the Royal Astronomical Society,* **77** (1917), 212–219; "A Determination of the Deflection of Light by the Sun's Gravitational Field, From Observations Made at the Total Eclipse of 1919 May 29," in *Philosophical Transactions of the Royal Society,* **220A** (1920), 291–333; "Variability of the Earth's Rotations," in *Monthly Notices of the Royal Astronomical Society,* **89** (1929), 549–557; and *Eclipses of the Sun and Moon* (Oxford, 1937). Manuscript material is in the archives of the Royal Greenwich Observatory, Herstmonceux, Sussex, England.

Obituaries of Dyson are A. S. Eddington, in *Obituary Notices of Fellows of the Royal Society of London,* **3** (1940), 159–172; and J. Jackson, in *Monthly Notices of the Royal Astronomical Society,* **100** (1940), 236–246. A biography is M. Wilson, *Ninth Astronomer Royal* (Cambridge, 1951).

COLIN A. RONAN

EAST, EDWARD MURRAY (*b.* Du Quoin, Illinois, 4 October 1879; *d.* Boston, Massachusetts, 9 November 1938), *genetics.*

East was the only son of William Harvey East, a mechanical engineer, and Sarah Granger Woodruff. The family on both sides had a long history of scholarly pursuits. After graduating from high school at fifteen, he worked for two years in a machine shop before entering the Case School of Applied Science (now Case Western Reserve University) in Cleveland in 1897. He found Case intellectually too narrow and left the next year for the University of Illinois, where he took his bachelor's (1900), master's (1904), and doctorate (1907) degrees. In 1903 he married Mary Lawrence Boggs; they had two daughters. East was ill for much of his life, and this may account for his irascibility with some of his students and colleagues.

East was trained as a chemist at Illinois. While a student there he assisted C. G. Hopkins of the Illinois Agricultural Experiment Station on selection experiments to alter the protein and fat content of corn. His job was to conduct the chemical analysis of the kernels. He soon became dissatisfied with this perfunctory job and wanted to elucidate the genetic mechanisms involved. East was especially intrigued by the decrease in yield which accompanied the success of the selection experiments. He wondered if increased inbreeding in the selected stock caused the decrease in yield, and if so, why. He began experiments on inbreeding in corn before he left the University of Illinois in October 1905 for a position at the Connecticut Agricultural Experiment Station. He remained there four years and conducted numerous experiments on inbreeding and outbreeding in tobacco, potatoes, and corn. These four years of intense experimentation were crucial for East's development as a scientist and determined to a great extent his later scientific interests. In 1909 he received an offer from the Bussey Institution of Harvard University. He accepted, became a full professor in 1914, and remained there until his death.

While conducting experiments on inbreeding and outbreeding between 1905 and 1908, East was struck by the problem of accounting for the inheritance of continuously varying characters. It was widely believed at this time that such blending inheritance could not be accounted for by Mendelian inheritance. East, along with H. Nilsson-Ehle of the Agricultural Research Station at Svalöf, Sweden, showed experimentally that some cases of blending inheritance could indeed be interpreted in terms of Mendelian inheritance. This experimental result was extremely important because Mendelian inheritance could then be seen to cover the entire spectrum of inherited characters, whereas before it was generally known to apply only to phenotypic characters inherited as a unit. East's 1910 paper on this topic, "A Mendelian Interpretation of Variation That Is Apparently Continuous," was particularly influential in America because Nilsson-Ehle's papers were written in German and published in a Swedish journal generally unavailable in the United States. After 1910 East published other papers on the inheritance of quantitatively varying characters. Perhaps the most important of these was his 1916 paper on the inheritance of size in *Nicotiana,* published in the first volume of the new journal *Genetics.* East's work on the problem of quantitative inheritance was widely known and hailed by other geneticists.

Another result of East's experiments in inbreeding and outbreeding was his interpretation of the role of sexual reproduction in the production of heritable variation. An understanding of heritable variation was of course crucial for an understanding of evolution. East popularized the now well-known view that sexual reproduction leads to recombination in the germ plasm and thus to vastly increased numbers of heritable variations. His 1918 article, "The Role of Reproduction in Evolution," came at a time when geneticists were just beginning to understand the importance of sexual reproduction as an immense source of heritable variation upon which selection could act. Thus he contributed significantly to a major tenet in all modern genetic theories of evolution.

By 1912 East had begun planning a book proposing a general theory of the effects of inbreeding and outbreeding. This book, *Inbreeding and Outbreeding: Their Genetic and Sociological Significance,* was finally published in 1919 with the collaboration of Donald F. Jones. The basic theory proposed by East was that inbreeding in a genetically diverse stock caused increased homozygosity. Believing with the *Drosophila* workers (Thomas Hunt Morgan *et al.*) that most mutations were recessive and deleterious, he concluded that the increased homozygosity caused by inbreeding should generally be accompanied by detrimental effects. The theory also explained why inbreeding was not necessarily deleterious in all cases. Unless deleterious recessives were present, inbreeding caused no ill effects. Outbreeding of course had the opposite effect of increasing heterozygosity and was often accompanied by heterosis, or hybrid vigor. In later years East continued to work on the physiological interpretation of heterosis and published a long paper on the subject only two years before his death. The theory of inbreeding and outbreeding was not conceived by East alone, but the 1919 book was well conceived and the theory presented with a wealth of evidence. It was widely read and cited by geneticists.

From the beginning of his work at the Connecticut Agricultural Experiment Station, East was concerned with the problems of the commercial production of agricultural products. With G. H. Shull he pioneered in developing a new method of corn breeding which revolutionized the production of corn in America and elsewhere. He also published papers on the improvement of potato and tobacco yields.

During World War I, East served as a chairman of the Botanical Raw Products Committee of the National Research Council and as acting chief of the Statistical Division of the U.S. Food Administration. While serving in these capacities he became immersed in the problems of world food production, overpopulation, and eugenic improvement of mankind. The gravity of these problems was brought home to him by the effects of World War I and by reading Malthus' *Essay on Population.* He became convinced that biologists had an obligation to speak out on the social implications of their science, and after 1920 his major efforts went in this direction. East believed that there was a genetic aspect to nearly all the problems of society; thus geneticists were qualified to speak on social problems. He himself was outspoken on the major social issues of the time. In 1923 he published *Mankind at the Crossroads,* in 1927 *Heredity and Human Affairs,* and in 1931 *Biology in Human Affairs,* a book which he edited and to which he contributed two chapters.

East was very concerned with the problems of overpopulation because he believed that mankind was reproducing faster than the food supply was increasing. He predicted that the world would soon be faced with mass starvation. Believing in the overwhelming importance of heredity as compared with environment, he proposed a eugenic plan of birth control in which the less desirable elements of society would be prevented from having children. This would solve the overpopulation problem and improve mankind at the same time.

Along with many other geneticists East believed that human races differed in their inherent capacities, both physical and mental, and that crosses between divergent races were biologically detrimental. He was firmly convinced that the racial crossing of whites and blacks in the United States should be prevented at all costs because the Negro was an inferior race: "In reality the negro is inferior to the white. This is not hypothesis or supposition; it is a crude statement of actual fact. The negro has given the world no original contribution of high merit" (*Inbreeding and Outbreeding*, p. 253). East justified his belief in the genetic inferiority of the Negro by pointing to the results of psychological testing of U.S. recruits during World War I. Negroes had scored consistently lower than whites on I.Q. tests. He was unafraid of the prospect that the United States or the world would be inundated by blacks, because he claimed their natural rate of increase was low in comparison with that of whites. He believed the blacks' only chance for extended survival in the United States was amalgamation with the whites, a possibility he clearly wanted to prevent.

One of East's major contributions to biology was his influence as a teacher of geneticists. He and William Castle worked together at the Bussey Institution to produce many of the best-known geneticists in the world, including D. F. Jones, Karl Sax, L. J. Stadler, R. A. Brink, L. C. Dunn, and Sewall Wright. East was known to be harsh and unduly critical of his students at times, but clearly his students were successful.

Another way he helped shape genetic research was by his active participation in professional organizations. He was a member of nearly every group of biologists concerned with genetics and its social import and served as an officer on many occasions. East helped found the journal *Genetics* in 1916 and was on its editorial board for many years. He not only helped direct the progress of genetic research through participation in these activities but also helped direct the interests of other geneticists toward the social implications of their scientific work. Some geneticists were stirred to write about the social im-

plications of genetics because of their opposition to East's ideas.

East contributed significantly to genetic research. His attempts to portray its social implications were less successful, and on some issues, particularly race, he now seems totally misguided. He appears to have examined his evidence much less carefully when analyzing the social implications of genetics than when analyzing a problem within genetics.

BIBLIOGRAPHY

A complete bibliography of East's work may be found in Donald F. Jones, "Edward Murray East," in *Biographical Memoirs. National Academy of Sciences,* **22** (1944), 217–242. This memoir is the only substantial secondary source dealing with the life and work of East.

WILLIAM B. PROVINE

EASTON, CORNELIS (*b.* Dordrecht, Netherlands, 10 September 1864; *d.* The Hague, Netherlands, 3 June 1929), *astronomy, climatology.*

The son of J. J. Easton, a sailor, and M. W. Ridderhof, Easton was principally a journalist. After graduating from high school in 1881, he first attended courses for those wishing to become government employees in Indonesia (then under Dutch rule) and subsequently studied French at the Sorbonne until 1886. After a short period of teaching, he became associated with various newspapers, notably the *Nieuwe Rotterdamsche Courant* (1895–1906), the *Nieuws van den Dag* of Amsterdam (1906–1923), and the *Haagsche Post* (from 1923).

Easton's contributions to astronomy deal mostly with the description and interpretation of the Milky Way. At the age of seventeen, as an amateur astronomer, he made his first drawings of the distribution of its brightness. The subsequent perfection and Easton's interpretation of these drawings gained him international fame and, in 1903, an honorary doctorate in physical sciences from the University of Groningen, at the proposal of the famous astronomer J. C. Kapteyn. The drawings aimed, first of all, at the representation of the northern Milky Way as a whole; detailed descriptions of certain regions of the sky published by such authors as Heis and Otto Boeddicker did not allow the construction of a homogeneous overall picture. The drawings were first published at Paris in 1893, under the title *La Voie Lactée, dans l'hémisphère boréal.*

Subsequent work deals with the comparison of those drawings with the distribution of the stars, and with the problem of the structure of the Milky Way stellar system. Counts of the faint stars in the *Bonner Durchmusterung* (around ninth-magnitude) revealed close correlation between their distribution in the sky and the drawings. In his attempts to interpret these findings, Easton adopted the hypothesis that the Milky Way system resembles other celestial objects showing spiral structure, and he proposed various solutions putting the center of the galaxy in the direction of the constellation Cygnus. The work is synthesized in "A Photographic Chart of the Milky Way and the Spiral Theory of the Galactic System," in *The Astrophysical Journal* (**37** [March 1913]). This concept of the galactic spiral structure has not survived subsequent research, which has led to the establishment of the galactic center in the direction of Sagittarius. But Easton's work inspired, and was highly esteemed by, such contemporary professional astronomers as Kapteyn, Pannekoek, and Seeliger.

Easton was active in many other fields of science besides astronomy. Particular mention should be made of his efforts in climatology. His monumental work *Les hivers dans l'Europe occidentale* (Leiden, 1928) contains a statistical-historical study of the climatological conditions in western Europe that attempts to connect data as far back as the thirteenth century with modern ones and critically studies suggested periodic variations. His accomplishments in this field led to Easton's appointment to the Board of Curators of the Netherlands Meteorological Institute in 1923.

BIBLIOGRAPHY

Easton's principal communications or astronomical studies, apart from those cited in the text, are in the publications of the Royal Netherlands Academy of Sciences (Amsterdam), *The Astrophysical Journal, Astronomische Nachrichten,* and *Monthly Notices of the Royal Astronomical Society.*

For descriptions of Easton's life and works see an article by J. J. Beyermann, in *Nieuwe Rotterdamsche Courant* (10 Sept. 1964); and J. Stein, "C. Easton in Memoriam," in *Hemel en Dampkring* (July, Aug.–Sept. 1929).

A. BLAAUW

EATON, AMOS (*b.* Chatham, New York, 17 May 1776; *d.* Troy, New York, 10 May 1842), *geology, botany, scientific and applied education.*

The son of a farmer, Abel Eaton, of old New England stock, Amos was born in eastern New York, just over the border from Massachusetts. He had a conventional education that culminated in graduation from Williams College in 1799. He taught briefly in a country school, but primarily he read law in New

York City and was admitted to the state bar. Thereafter he established himself in Catskill, New York, as a lawyer and land agent. To these roles he added, as was then usual, practice in surveying. Even in those early years, however, Eaton gave evidence of an interest in popular science and education. In 1802 he published a pamphlet on surveying, *Art Without Science.* In Catskill he offered popular lectures in botany and wrote a manual on the subject that won the approval of David Hosack, an eminent authority in the field.

A tragic turn of events abruptly terminated Eaton's legal career in 1810. He was convicted of an alleged forgery during the Hudson Valley land disputes. Eaton and many others always maintained his innocence, but he spent five years in the Greenwich jail in New York City. There he turned to scientific studies, aided by John Torrey, son of the warden and subsequently a distinguished botanist. On release from jail, almost forty years of age, already married twice and a father, Eaton spent a year at Yale College, studying science under Benjamin Silliman and Eli Ives. Then he returned to Williams College, where he introduced a course of very popular and successful scientific lectures in 1817. In this year too appeared his first ventures in scientific publication, *A Botanical Dictionary* and the first edition of *Manual of Botany for the Northern States.*

Eaton was deeply grateful to the academic communities of Yale and Williams for admitting him to their company after his earlier humiliation. An important effect of his imprisonment was undoubtedly a humble and self-deprecating manner, which expressed itself in an effort at once to suppress and to surmount the resulting handicap. Eaton was gifted with an articulate and even voluble style, which fitted him well for his new career as a popular lecturer. It was an age and an environment lacking a truly professional tradition, and he was able to range widely as an amateur over the whole of science, from botany to chemistry, zoology, and geology. In 1818 he moved westward into the Troy–Albany area, in which he had been born and raised. This was then an active center of growth and internal improvement, as manifested particularly by the Erie Canal. Here he became associated with Governor De Witt Clinton and Stephen Van Rensselaer, both patrons and promoters of science and public improvement, who were convinced that the geological study of western New York could not fail to uncover coal and other mineral resources.

For the next half-dozen years Eaton was busy in several capacities. He was an itinerant lecturer in village and school, from West Point in the lower Hudson Valley to the Castleton Medical Academy in

Vermont. He sponsored the formation of the Troy Lyceum of Natural History, and he compiled textbooks in chemistry, zoology, and geology. Most important, under Stephen Van Rensselaer's patronage he executed geological and agricultural surveys of the local counties and across New York State along the Erie Canal route. He was thus drawn into a kind of specialization in geology, and he described himself as "the only person in North America capable of judging strata." His published reports of these surveys, bridging the earlier surveys of Maclure and the classical stratigraphy of the New York State Survey, earned him recognition in American geology, and the decade of the 1820's has been designated as the "Eatonian era."

His persistent efforts to devise and develop an American nomenclature for New York stratigraphy often led Eaton into opinionated and extravagant theorizing. Basically he was a Wernerian, following Abraham Werner's fivefold classification of Primitive, Transition, Secondary (or *Floetz*), Volcanic, and Alluvial. He thought of his task as primarily one of correlation of American, and particularly New York, strata with their English and Continental equivalents, recognizing at the same time the differences in the lithologic sequence. Although Eaton described fossils, his stratigraphic distinctions were drawn, as were those of Maclure before him, on the basis of lithology and the structural attitude of beds. This led him to repeat Maclure's error in correlating the New York plateau sediments with the English Secondary, although he correctly associated the Catskill brownstones with the Old Red Sandstone.

A characteristic product of the American frontier, Eaton was a kind of "jack-of-all-sciences," opening new vistas and stressing simplicity and practicality. In botany, too, he was very prolific, issuing eight editions of *Manual of Botany for the Northern States.* Asa Gray, like Eaton a product of northern New York, who became America's greatest botanist in the nineteenth century, began his studies with Eaton's *Manual.* In later years, however, he severely criticized Eaton's deficiencies as a botanist.

Eaton's final and most noteworthy contribution was to scientific education. He evolved a pedagogical theory emphasizing "the application of science to the common purposes of life"; students were to learn by doing, in sharp contrast with the conventional method of learning by rote. They were to perform experiments in the laboratory, collect specimens in the field, and even prepare their own lectures, leaving to the instructor and fellow students the role of critic. For the implementation of this then novel theory, Eaton persuaded Stephen Van Rensselaer to establish the Rensselaer School in Troy, New York, in 1824. Here, for the rest of his life, Eaton served as senior professor, struggling to realize his concept of an all-scientific and practical course of education. It was virtually a one-man institution, and Eaton's zeal and dedication were unflagging. In this school he trained a small but significant band of scientists who carried on and diffused his influence widely. Chief among his disciples were James Hall, J. C. Booth, Asa Fitch, Ebenezer Emmons, G. H. Cook, Abram Sager, E. S. Carr, Douglass Houghton, and E. N. Horsford. Although most were concerned primarily with geology, some also acquired an interest in chemistry and botany, as well as mineralogy and zoology.

In 1835 Eaton expanded his program and gave it greater practicality. Renamed the Rensselaer Institute, it was divided into two departments, one for science and one for engineering. Eaton created two degrees new to American education: bachelor of natural science, and civil engineer. In the pragmatic environment of nineteenth-century America, engineering gained headway, and the role of science was eventually subordinated in what became known after the middle of the century as the Rensselaer Polytechnic Institute.

Amos Eaton transmitted his zeal for science to his children. A daughter taught science in a girls' academy. Two of his sons were educated and taught at the Rensselaer School, and a third became a professor of natural science at Transylvania University in Kentucky. All three died young. A grandson, Daniel Cady Eaton, was for many years professor of paleobotany at Yale University. Thus, largely self-taught, Amos Eaton was a zealous and pioneering explorer and teacher of natural science in early America. Above all, he laid the foundations of a novel school and course of scientific and technological education. Perhaps he was also responsible for introducing a basic dichotomy between the traditional and the new technical types of education, a dichotomy that has not been easy to resolve.

BIBLIOGRAPHY

I. ORIGINAL WORKS. For more than a quarter of a century Amos Eaton was a prolific writer of texts, manuals, reports, and articles on many subjects. A full bibliography is in E. McAllister's *Amos Eaton* (see below). Only a few titles need be listed here, chiefly to illustrate the broad scope of his scientific interests: *Art Without Science* (Hudson, 1802; Albany, 1830); *The Young Botanists' Tablet of Memory* (Catskill, 1810); *A Botanical Dictionary* (New Haven, 1817); *Manual of Botany for the Northern States* (Albany, 1817; 8th ed., 1840); *An Index to the Geology of the Northern States* (Albany, 1818); *Chemical Instructor* (Albany, 1822; several eds. to 1836); *A Geological and Agricultural Survey of the District Adjoining the Erie Canal* (Albany, 1824); *Zoological Text-Book* (Albany, 1826); *Geological Nomenclature for North America* (Albany, 1828); *Prodromus of a Practical Treatise on the Mathematical Arts* (Troy, 1838).

II. SECONDARY LITERATURE. Aside from numerous biographical sketches, in the *Dictionary of American Biography* and elsewhere, the sole full-length life of Eaton is Ethel M. McAllister, *Amos Eaton, Scientist and Educator* (Philadelphia, 1941). Other references deal with the various aspects of Eaton's scientific and educational career. To be mentioned are P. C. Ricketts, *History of the Rensselaer Polytechnic Institute* (New York, 1895, 1914, 1934); and Samuel Rezneck, *Education for a Technological Society: A Sesquicentennial History of Rensselaer Polytechnic Institute* (Troy, N.Y., 1968). Other special topics include G. P. Merrill, *The First One Hundred Years of American Geology* (New Haven, 1924); Samuel Rezneck, "Amos Eaton: A Pioneer Teacher of Science in Early America," in *Journal of Geological Education*, **13** (Dec. 1965), 131 ff.; and "Amos Eaton the Old Schoolmaster," in *New York History*, **39** (Apr. 1958), 165 ff.; W. M. Smallwood, "Amos Eaton, Naturalist," *ibid.*, **18** (Apr. 1937), 167 ff.; H. S. Van Klooster, *Amos Eaton as a Chemist*, Rensselaer Science and Engineering Series, no. 56 (Troy, N.Y., 1938); and John W. Wells, *Early Investigations of the Devonian System in New York*, Special Papers, Geological Society of America, no. 74 (New York, 1963), esp. pp. 25–64, "The Eatonian Era." For Eaton's geological bibliography, see J. M. Nickles, *Geological Literature on North America, 1785–1918*, U.S. Geological Survey Bulletin 746 (Washington, D.C., 1923).

SAMUEL REZNECK

EBEL, JOHANN GOTTFRIED (*b.* Züllichau, Germany, 6 October 1764; *d.* Zurich, Switzerland, 8 October 1830), *medicine, geography.*

Ebel's father was a wealthy merchant, and his mother died when he was still young. He went to high school in Neuruppin and in 1780 entered the University of Frankfurt-an-der-Oder to study medicine. After studying there and in Vienna, he received his M.D. degree in 1788 with a thesis on the comparative anatomy of the brain. He continued his scientific work but also entered politics. Ebel lived for some years in Paris, where he came to know several of the leading figures of the French Revolution. During his extensive travels he became fascinated by Switzerland and wrote his famous *Anleitung* (1793), which is essentially a geological and historical guide to the country. During the wars of the French Revolution and the Napoleonic era, Ebel used his influence with the French leaders to improve conditions for the Swiss population and was rewarded with Swiss citizenship (1801). He settled there in 1810.

Like many intellectuals of his time, Ebel worked

in many fields. He translated the political works of Sieyès into German, and he worked extensively in ethnology, statistics, and comparative anatomy. His reputation was such that Goethe suggested him for the chair of surgery and anatomy at the University of Jena (1803). Ebel loved his adopted country and wrote a number of enthusiastic books about it. They contributed to the image of Switzerland, and because of their popular style, especially that of the *Anleitung*, they attracted many visitors to the country. He also participated in establishing new hotels and set up the first lookout point in Switzerland, at Rigi. The purpose of his books was to spread knowledge of Switzerland, and he can thus be considered one of the pioneers of the Swiss tourist industry.

BIBLIOGRAPHY

Ebel's works in medicine are almost forgotten, and his fame rests on his books about Switzerland, the most important of which is *Anleitung auf die nützlichste und genüssvollste Art die Schweiz zu bereisen*, 2 vols. (Zurich, 1793; 2nd ed., 4 vols., 1804–1805; 3rd ed., 4 vols., 1809–1810). The last five eds. (8th ed., 1843) were in 1 vol. This popular work was translated into several languages and also appeared in pirated editions. Ebel's other works include *Schilderungen der Gebirgsvölker der Schwiz*, 2 vols. (Tübingen, 1798–1802; 2nd ed., Leipzig, 1802–1803), an ethnological description of the population in the cantons of Glarus and Appenzell. His most important geological work is *Über den Bau der Erde in Alpengebirge*, 2 vols. (Zurich, 1808). He also wrote a number of popular, descriptive books about Switzerland, such as *Malerische Reise durch Graubünden* (Zurich, 1825).

As a result of his fame and popularity, many (mostly panegyric) biographies of Ebel were written just after his death. Among the later ones is H. Escher, "J. G. Ebel," in *80. Neujahrblatt zum Besten des Waisenhaus in Zürich* (1917).

NILS SPJELDNAES

EBERTH, CARL JOSEPH (*b.* Würzburg, Germany, 21 September 1835; *d.* Berlin, Germany, 2 December 1926), *comparative anatomy, pathology, bacteriology.*

Eberth was the son of an artist, who died when Carl Joseph was still young. The boy helped his mother support the family by cutting out silhouette pictures. Nevertheless, he was able to attend the University of Würzburg, where he was drawn to biology and medicine by some of Germany's foremost teachers: Kölliker, Heinrich Müller, Leydig, and Virchow.

From 1856 to 1859 Eberth worked as an assistant in the Pathological Institute in Würzburg. In the latter year he completed a dissertation on the biology and parasitic characteristics of whipworms and was granted the M.D. degree. He then became a prosector under Heinrich Müller at the Institute of Comparative Anatomy. Here he concentrated on histology, both normal and abnormal. He passed the *Habilitation* in 1863 and two years later moved to Zurich as *extraordinarius* in pathology, becoming *ordinarius* in 1869. From 1874, until his call to Halle in 1881, Eberth also taught histology and embryology in the school of veterinary medicine at the University of Zurich.

In Halle, Eberth was professor of comparative anatomy and histology until 1895, when he assumed directorship of the Pathological Institute. He held the latter position until his retirement at age seventy-five in 1911. As a teacher Eberth was patient and much admired. As a scientist he was thorough, meticulous, and humble, despite wide acclaim for his work.

Eberth married Elisabeth Hohensteiner, a minister's daughter, in Zurich in 1870. They had three daughters. Eberth was an avid naturalist and mountain climber, activities he continued into his seventies. After becoming emeritus, Eberth lived near Berlin with a daughter. He continued to be in excellent health until shortly before his death.

Eberth is best known for his discovery of the typhoid bacillus (*Salmonella typhosa,* earlier known as *Eberthella typhosa*), but this was only one of many important contributions he made in a fifty-year-long career in biological and medical science.

In his earlier scientific papers, many of which were published in *Virchows Archiv für pathologische Anatomie,* Eberth dealt with the histological structure of various parts of human and animal bodies. Particularly noteworthy were his descriptions of the ciliated epithelium and its function and several papers describing the normal and abnormal microscopic anatomy of the liver. As was true of many comparative anatomists and pathologists about 1870, Eberth became interested in the process of inflammation. He clearly differentiated between epithelial degeneration and regeneration in the cornea, and he was drawn to the study of inflammations caused by microorganisms. Along with Edwin Klebs and very few others, Eberth was instrumental in bringing the studies of bacteria and their actions, in which Davaine and Pasteur in France had pioneered, to the attention of German scientists.

In a remarkable small monograph, *Zur Kentniss der bacteritischen Mycose* (1872), Eberth set forth the results of his thorough observational and experimental techniques. Especially noteworthy is that this work was carried out four years before Koch dramatically demonstrated the isolation and cultivation of anthrax bacilli. The first part of Eberth's mono-

graph described his studies of tissues from patients who had died of diphtheria, then a prevalent disease. He saw organisms (not clearly identified as diphtheria bacilli until 1884 by Klebs and Loeffler) that were most plentiful in the exudate covering the tonsils and the necrotic membrane in the pharynx. As a result of his investigations Eberth concluded that the organisms associated with diphtheria appeared first on the mucous membrane or on the edges of wounds. Further growth of the bacteria led to marked tissue destruction. All these conclusions are now known to be essentially correct. He went even further, saying that without these organisms there is no diphtheria ("Ohne diese Pilze keine Diphtherie . . .").

In the case of a newborn baby dying of respiratory failure, Eberth described a gelatinous exudate, rich in bacteria, filling the alveoli of the lungs. He did not clearly identify the organisms, but he stained them with iodine and hematoxylin and showed their existence in the heart and spleen as well as in the lungs. In the final section of the monograph Eberth confirmed experimentally what Davaine in France had shown before: that rod-shaped bodies in the blood of animals sick with anthrax were the cause of the disease. He mixed anthrax-infected blood with large volumes of water and allowed the mixture to settle. When he inoculated experimental animals with the supernatant fluid, no infection resulted. The sediment, however, was capable of producing anthrax. These techniques were to become commonplace in the laboratories of Europe during the next decade, but Eberth's work and his observations made him one of the earliest laboratory bacteriologists. He was thus one of the first of many pathologists seriously to take up bacteriological investigations.

In 1879 Eberth studied twenty-three cases of typhoid fever and reasoned that the characteristic changes found in the spleen and lymph nodes of the abdomen occurred because bacterial activity was most intense in these areas. He found rod-shaped organisms in twelve of his cases and published his results in *Virchows Archiv* in 1880. While he is, therefore, given credit for discovering the typhoid bacillus, he did so by histopathological techniques. The bacillus was not actually isolated and cultivated until 1884, when Gaffky, a student of Koch's, was able to grow it. Eberth, along with Koch and others, demonstrated the pneumonia diplococcus microscopically, but he did not cultivate that organism either.

Eberth contributed many papers describing important techniques and discoveries. He described the process of amyloid deposition in tissues and clearly showed that this substance came from outside the cells and was not a product of the cells in the affected areas. Thus, it was not necessarily a degenerative process of the cells that caused the amyloid to appear; rather, the cells were damaged by the amyloid deposited in the spaces between them.

Perhaps Eberth's major work in pathology was his contribution to the understanding of thrombosis, one of the most common pathological findings. Thrombosis is the process through which clots form in blood vessels during life. Because of its frequency and importance it had received much attention since the earlier part of the century. Virchow, in the 1840's, and others studied the problem, and most thought it was merely a blood coagulum. In the 1870's Zahn carried out systematic studies of thrombosis in the frog's mesentery. By direct observation he noticed that blood cells were deposited on the inner wall of the blood vessels and continued to accumulate in layers until the lumen became completely occluded. Zahn thought the cells were mainly white blood cells. Georges Hayem and Bizzozero in the early 1880's implicated blood platelets. In the mid-1880's Eberth, with his pupil and assistant Curt Schimmelbusch, who later became instrumental in perfecting the aseptic technique for surgery, carried out a thorough study of the role of the platelets.

Eberth and Schimmelbusch, by means of meticulous microscopic studies of experimentally induced thrombi, concluded that slowing of the flow of blood or injury to the inner lining of the vessel caused platelets to adhere to the wall, forming the beginning of a plug. By a process of viscous metamorphosis, now better understood, they believed the platelets adhered to one another and attracted red and white cells as formation of the thrombus continued. Eberth and Schimmelbusch called this process conglutination and were careful to distinguish it from coagulation, which they regarded as a later event in the development of the thrombus.

While some of the details of their explanation were disputed, Eberth and Schimmelbusch's major conclusions—that it was the platelets that were first involved, and that a combination of injury to the vessel and slowing of the blood flow were necessary for thrombosis to occur—have essentially stood the test of time. Their papers and subsequent monograph of 1888 do not give them priority of discovery, yet they deserve major credit for summarizing and elucidating the process in modern terms.

In Zurich and Halle, Eberth had many students. As an aid to them and students everywhere he undertook in 1889 to bring out a new edition of a widely used manual of techniques for pathological studies written by Carl Friedländer. Eberth contributed substantially toward making this popular book even more useful in the fourth and fifth editions. He nearly doubled the text, added many illustrations, and provided an index. Thus, Eberth was able to communicate to others the methods of microscopic investigation of tissues and cells that he had so successfully used himself.

BIBLIOGRAPHY

I. ORIGINAL WORKS. Much of Eberth's work was reported in the major German and Swiss medical journals. He was a frequent contributor to *Virchows Archiv für pathologische Anatomie,* where some of his major discoveries appeared, including "Untersuchungen über die normale und pathologische Leber," **39** (1867), 70–89; **40** (1867), 305–325; "Die amyloide Entartung," **80** (1880), 138–172; "Die Organismen in den Organen bei Typhus abdominalis," **81** (1880), 58–74; and "Neue Untersuchungen über den Bacillus des Abdominaltyphus," **83** (1881), 486–501.

The major monographs were *Zur Kentniss der bacteritischen Mycose* (Leipzig, 1872); *Die Thrombose nach Versuchen und Leichenbefunden* (Stuttgart, 1888), written with C. Schimmelbusch; and new eds. of Carl Friedländer, *Microscopische Technik zum Gebrauch bei medicinischen und pathologisch-anatomischen Untersuchungen* (4th ed., Berlin, 1889; 5th ed., 1894).

II. SECONDARY LITERATURE. See the following, listed chronologically: H. Ribbert, "Karl Joseph Eberth zum 70. Geburtstag," in *Deutsche medizinische Wochenschrift,* **31** (1905), 1511–1512; R. Beneke, "Zu Carl Josef Eberth's 80. Geburtstag," in *Berliner klinische Wochenschrift,* **52** (1915), 1010–1013; and "Carl Josef Eberth," in *Zentralblatt für allgemeine Pathologie und pathologische Anatomie,* **39** (1927), 226–228; W. Wachter, "Carl Joseph Eberth," in *Apothekerzeitung,* **42** (1927), 310–313; R. Beneke, "Zur Erinnerung an Karl Joseph Eberth," in *Münchener medizinische Wochenschrift,* **82** (1935), 1536–1537; Ernst Galgiardi, Hans Nabholz, and Jean Strohl, *Die Universität Zurich 1833–1933 und ihre Vorläufer* (Zurich, 1938), pp. 564–565; Heinrich Buess, "Carl Joseph Eberth," in *Les médecins célèbres,* R. Dumesnil and F. Bonnet-Roy, eds. (Geneva, 1947), pp. 196–197, trans. into German in *Die berühmten Ärzte,* R. Dumesnil and H. Schadewaldt, eds. (Cologne, 1966), pp. 235–236; and H. von Meyenburg, "Geschichte des pathologischen Instituts," in *Zürcher Spitalgeschichte,* 2 vols. (Zurich, 1951), II, 559–580, esp. 565–566.

GERT H. BRIEGER

EDDINGTON, ARTHUR STANLEY (*b.* Kendal, England, 28 December 1882; *d.* Cambridge, England, 22 November 1944), *astronomy, relativity.*

Eddington was the son of a Somerset Quaker, Arthur Henry Eddington, headmaster of Stramongate School in Kendal from 1878 until his death in 1884, and of Sarah Ann Shout, whose forebears for seven generations had been north-country Quakers. Following the death of her husband, Mrs. Eddington took Arthur Stanley, not yet two, and her daughter Winifred, age six, back to Somerset, where they made their home at Weston-super-Mare. In the atmosphere of this quiet Quaker home, the boy grew up. He remained a Quaker throughout his life.

Eddington's schooling was fortunate. Brynmelyn School, to which he went as a day boy, had three exceptionally gifted teachers who imparted to him a keen interest in natural history, a love of good literature, and a splendid foundation in mathematics. Reserved and studious by nature, Eddington was also physically active, playing on the first eleven at both cricket and football and enjoying long bicycle rides through the Mendip Hills. Before he was sixteen, he won an entrance scholarship to Owen's College (now the University of Manchester), where again he was fortunate in his teachers—Arthur Schuster in physics and Horace Lamb in mathematics. In the autumn of 1902, with an entrance scholarship, Eddington went into residence at Trinity College, Cambridge.

After two years of intensive concentration on mathematics under the guidance of the distinguished coach R. A. Herman, who stressed both the logic and the elegance of mathematical reasoning, Eddington sat the fourteen papers of the tripos examinations in 1904. He won the coveted position of first wrangler, the first time that a second-year man had attained this distinction. In 1905 he gained his degree and proceeded to coach pupils in applied mathematics and to lecture in trigonometry during the following term.

In February 1906 Eddington took an appointment as chief assistant at the Royal Observatory, Greenwich, where he remained until 1913. Here he obtained thorough training in practical astronomy and began the pioneer theoretical investigations that placed him in the forefront of astronomical research in a very few years. Besides his participation in the regular observing programs, Eddington had two special assignments: he went to Malta in 1909 to determine the longitude of the geodetic station there, and to Brazil in 1912 as leader of an eclipse expedition. Two further tests of his ability as a practical astronomer came after his return to Cambridge as Plumian professor of astronomy and director of the observatory. During the war years Eddington completed single-handed the transit observations for the zodiacal catalog. In 1919 he organized the two eclipse expeditions that provided the first confirmation of the Einstein relativity formula for the deflection of light in a gravitational field.

During these years Eddington was elected to fellowships in the Royal Astronomical Society (1906) and the Royal Society (1914). He was knighted in 1930, and his greatest honor, the Order of Merit, was conferred on him eight years later.

Eddington was president of the Royal Astronomical Society from 1921 to 1923 and of the Physical Society and the Mathematical Association from 1930 to 1932. In 1938 he became president of the International Astronomical Union. After his death an annual Eddington Memorial Lectureship was established and the Eddington Medal was struck for annual award, the first recipient being a former pupil of Eddington's, Canon Georges Lemaître of Louvain.

Eddington never married. After his appointment in 1913 to the Plumian professorship in Cambridge, he moved into Observatory House as director of the observatory and brought his mother and sister to live with him. Here he remained until the autumn of 1944, when he underwent a major operation from which he did not recover.

Of Eddington's scientific work, particularly in the field of stellar structure, E. A. Milne wrote in 1945 that he "brought it all to life, infusing it with his sense of real physics and endowing it with aspects of splendid beauty. . . . Eddington will always be our incomparable pioneer." His intuitive insight into the profound problems of nature, coupled with his mastery of the mathematical tools, led him to illuminating results in a wide range of problems: the motions and distribution of the stars, the internal constitution of the stars, the role of radiation pressure, the nature of white dwarfs, the dynamics of pulsating stars and of globular clusters, the sources of stellar energy, and the physical state of interstellar matter. In addition, he was the first interpreter of Einstein's relativity theory in English, and made his own contributions to its development; and he formulated relationships between all the principal constants of nature, attempting a vast synthesis in his provocative but uncompleted *Fundamental Theory.*

It is important to remember how rudimentary was much of our knowledge of astrophysics and of stellar movements at the beginning of this century. Proper motion or transverse motion had been known since the time of Halley and radial velocity since Doppler, but the assumption of William Herschel of random motion of the stars relative to the sun had been abandoned of necessity by Kapteyn in 1904. Schwarzschild attempted to show that the radial velocity vectors could be represented as forming an ellipsoid. This problem of the systematic motions of the stars was the subject of Eddington's first theoretical investigations. He chose to work with proper motions and isolated two star streams or drifts. In 1917 he compared the two theories thus:

The apparent antagonism between the two-drift and the ellipsoidal hypotheses disappears if we remember that the purpose of both is descriptive. Whilst the two-drift theory has often been preferred in the ordinary proper motion investigations on account of an additional constant in the formulae which gives it a somewhat greater flexibility, the ellipsoidal theory has been found more suitable for discussions of radial velocities and the dynamical theory of the stellar system [*Monthly Notices of the Royal Astronomical Society,* **77,** 314].

Eddington's remarkable statistical analyses of proper-motion data fully confirmed the existence of the two star streams, and he was able to determine their directions and relative numbers. He went on to other problems, such as the distribution of stars of different spectral classes, planetary nebulae, open clusters, gaseous nebulae, and the dynamics of globular clusters. In his first book, *Stellar Movements and the Structure of the Universe* (1914), Eddington brought together all the material of some fifteen papers, most of which had been published in the *Monthly Notices of the Royal Astronomical Society* between 1906 and 1914. The cosmological knowledge of the period was summarized and the most challenging problems were delineated, and he clearly declared his preference for the speculation that the spiral nebulae were other galaxies beyond our Milky Way, which was itself a spiral galaxy.

Eddington's great pioneer work in astrophysics began in 1916. His first problem was radiation pressure, the importance of which had been pointed out a decade earlier by R. A. Sampson. A theory of the radiative equilibrium of the outer atmosphere of a star was subsequently developed by Schwarzschild in Germany. Eddington delved deeper, in fact to the very center of a star, showing that the equation of equilibrium must take account of three forces—gravitation, gas pressure, and radiation pressure. Replacing the assumption of convective equilibrium of Lane, Ritter, and Emden with radiative equilibrium, he developed the equation that is still in general use. At that time he felt justified in assuming that perfect gas conditions existed in a giant star, and he adopted Emden's equation for a polytropic sphere with index $n = 3$. This is still referred to as Eddington's model of a star. Not until 1924 did he realize that this assumption and, therefore, this model were also applicable to dwarf stars.

That matter under stellar conditions would be highly ionized had been recognized by several astronomers, but it was Eddington who first incorporated this into the theory of stellar equilibrium by showing that high ionization of a gas reduced the average molecular weight almost to 2 for all elements except hydrogen.

Finding that the force of radiation pressure rose with the mass of the star, and with startling rapidity as the mass exceeded that of our sun, Eddington concluded that relatively few stars would exceed ten times the sun's mass and that a star of fifty times the solar mass would be exceedingly rare. To obtain a theoretical relation between mass and luminosity of a star, some assumption was necessary about internal opacity. At first he regarded opacity as mainly a photoelectric phenomenon, a view that drew strong criticism; but when Kramers' theory of the absorption coefficient became available, Eddington adapted it to the stellar problem, introducing his "guillotine" factor, and obtained his important mass-luminosity relation, announced in March 1924. Since the observational data for dwarf stars, as well as for giant stars, closely fitted the theoretical curve, he announced that dwarfs also must be regarded as gaseous throughout, in spite of their densities exceeding unity. He realized that the effective volume of a highly or fully ionized atom is very small, and hence deviations from perfect gas behavior will occur only in stars of relatively high densities. The mass-luminosity relation has been widely used and is still of immense value, although its applicability has been somewhat limited in recent years by the more detailed classification of both giants and dwarfs and by the recognition of the distinctive characteristics, for example, of subdwarfs, which do not conform to the mass-luminosity relation.

Eddington had calculated the diameters of several giant red stars as early as the summer of 1920. In December, G. E. Hale wrote him of the Pease and Anderson interferometer measurement of α Orionis on 13 December "in close agreement with your theoretical value and probably correct within about 10 per cent." Later Eddington applied his calculations to the dwarf companion of Sirius, obtaining a diameter so small that the star's density came out to 50,000 gm./cc., a deduction to which he said most people had mentally added "which is absurd!" However, in the light of his 1924 realization of the effects of high ionization, he claimed these great densities to be possible and probably actually to exist in the white dwarf stars. He therefore wrote W. S. Adams, asking him to measure the red shift in the Mount Wilson spectra of Sirius B, since, if a density of 50,000 or more did exist, then a measurable Einstein relativity shift to the red would result. Adams hastened to comply, and wrote Eddington that the measured shifts closely confirmed the calculated shift and, hence, confirmed both the third test of relativity theory and the immense densities that Eddington had calculated. (This exchange of historic letters in 1924 and 1925 is recorded in *Arthur Stanley Eddington,* pp. 75–77.)

A direct consequence of this work was the challenge it presented to physicists, a challenge taken up in 1926 by R. H. Fowler, who achieved a brilliant investigation of the physics of super-dense gas, afterward called "degenerate" gas, by employing the newly developed wave mechanics of Schrödinger.

A consequence of Eddington's mass-luminosity relation was his realization that a time scale of several trillion (i.e., 10^{12}) years was essential for the age of stars if the then current Russell-Hertzsprung sequence of stellar evolution was to be retained. Except in the rare case of a nova or supernova that hurls out much of its matter, the loss of mass by a star is due to radiation. For a massive O or B class star to radiate itself down to a white dwarf, at least a trillion years would be required. This brought into the limelight the theory of conversion of matter into radiation by annihilation of electrons and protons, a hypothesis that appears to have been first suggested by Eddington in 1917. For seven years, in spite of severe criticism in Great Britain, he defended the general idea that the chief source of stellar energy must be subatomic. After 1924 many astronomers and physicists turned their attention to this. In 1934, after the discovery of the positron, Eddington urged abandonment of the electron-proton annihilation theory, on the ground that electron-positron annihilation was not only a more logical supposition but also an observed fact. In 1938 came the famous carbon-nitrogen-oxygen-carbon cycle of Hans Bethe, elegantly solving some of the problems of stellar energy and invoking the electron-positron annihilation hypothesis.

In 1926 Eddington published his great compendium, *The Internal Constitution of the Stars* (reprinted in 1930). In this book he drew attention to the unsolved problems partially treated in his investigations, among them the problem of opacity and the source or sources of stellar energy, which he called "two clouds obscuring the theory." Another obstinate problem was the phase relation of the light curve and the velocity curve of a Cepheid variable. In 1918 and 1919 he had published papers on the mathematical theory of pulsating stars, explaining many observed features of Cepheid variables but not the phase relation. He returned to this problem in 1941, when more was known about the convective layer and he could apply the physics of ionization equilibrium within this layer with encouraging results.

Other problems dealt with in these years were the central temperatures and densities of stars and the great cosmic abundance of hydrogen (recognized independently by Strömgren). Eddington developed a theory of the absorption lines in stellar atmospheres, extending earlier work of Schuster and Schwarzschild.

This made possible the interpretation of many observed line intensities. When the "nebulium" lines were identified by Bowen in 1927 as the result of so-called forbidden transitions in ionized nitrogen and oxygen atoms, Eddington explained how and why these emission lines can be produced within the highly rarefied gases that constitute a nebula. Another line of adventurous thinking concerned the existence, composition, and absorptive and radiative properties of interstellar matter. He calculated the density and temperature and showed that calcium would be doubly ionized, with only about one atom in 800 being singly ionized. He discussed the rough measurement of the distance of a star by the intensity of its interstellar absorption lines, a relation soon confirmed by O. Struve and by J. S. Plaskett.

In the field of astrophysics Eddington undoubtedly made his greatest—but by no means his only—contributions to knowledge. Here he fashioned powerful mathematical tools and applied them with imagination and consummate skill. But during these same years his mind was active along other lines; thus we have his profound studies on relativity and cosmology, his herculean but unsuccessful efforts to formulate his *Fundamental Theory,* and his brilliant, provocative attempts to portray the meaning and significance of the latest physical and metaphysical thinking in science.

Einstein's famous 1915 paper on the general theory of relativity came to England in 1916, when deSitter, in Holland, sent a copy to Eddington, who was secretary of the Royal Astronomical Society. Immediately recognizing its importance and the revolutionary character of its implications, Eddington threw himself into a study of the new mathematics involved, the absolute differential calculus of Ricci and Levi-Civita. He was soon a master of the use of tensors and began developing his own contributions to relativity theory. At the request of the Physical Society of London, he prepared his *Report on the Relativity Theory of Gravitation* (1918), the first complete account of general relativity in English. He called it a revolution of thought, profoundly affecting astronomy, physics, and philosophy, setting them on a new path from which there could be no turning back. A second edition (1920) contained the results of the eclipse expeditions of 1919, which had appeared to confirm the bending of light in a gravitational field, as predicted by Einstein's theory; it also contained a warning that the theory must meet the test of the reddening of light emitted from a star of sufficient density. This test was met when the measurements on Sirius B made by W. S. Adams at Eddington's request were announced in 1924.

Eddington published a less technical account of relativity theory, *Space, Time and Gravitation,* in 1920. This book brought to many readers at least some idea of what relativity theory was and where it was leading in cosmological speculation. It showed, too, how Eddington's mind had already entered philosophical grooves in which it continued to run—his selective subjectivism, almost universally repudiated, and his logical theory of structure, "a guiding illumination," in the words of Martin Johnson, who added, "As elucidator of the logical status of physics, Eddington led well his generation."

In 1923 came Eddington's great book, *Mathematical Theory of Relativity*. Einstein said in 1954 that he considered this book the finest presentation of the subject in any language, and of its author he said, "He was one of the first to recognize that the displacement field was the most important concept of general relativity theory, for this concept allowed us to do without the inertial system."

In this book Eddington gave the substance of the original papers of Einstein, deSitter, and Weyl but departed from their presentations to give a "continuous chain of deduction," including many contributions of his own, both in interpretation and in derivation of equations. With intuitive brilliance he modified Weyl's affine geometry of world structure by means of a new mathematical procedure, parallel displacement, which in itself was a not unimportant contribution to geometry. This led to his explanation of the law of gravitation ($G_{\mu\nu} = \lambda g_{\mu\nu}$) as implying that our practical unit of length at any point and in any direction is a definite fraction of the radius of curvature for that point and direction, so that the law of gravitation is simply the statement of the fact that the world radius of curvature everywhere supplies the standard with which our measure lengths are compared. This led subsequently to his theoretical determination of the cosmic constant λ. Assuming the principle that the wave equation determining the linear dimensions of an atomic system must give these dimensions in terms of the standard world radius, he obtained a value for λ in terms of the atomic constants that appear in the ordinary form of the wave equation.

This fascination with the fundamental constants of nature—the gravitation constant, the velocity of light, the Planck and Rydberg constants, the mass and charge of the electron, for example—and the basic problem of atomicity had driven Eddington to seek this bridge between quantum theory and relativity. Having found it, he eventually established relationships between all these and many more constants, showing their values to be logically inevitable. From

seven basic constants Eddington derived four pure numbers, including the famous 137 forever associated with his name. This is the fine structure constant. He evolved the equation $10m^2 - 136m + 1 = 0$, the coefficients of which are in accordance with the theory of the degrees of freedom associated with the displacement relation between two charges and the roots of which give the ratio of masses of proton and electron as 1847.60. He showed that the packing factor for helium should be 136/137. Later Eddington identified the total number of protons and electrons in the universe with the number of independent quadruple wave functions at a point; he evaluated this constant as $3/2 \times 136 \times 2^{256}$, which is a number of the order of 10^{79}. In all, he evaluated some twenty-seven physical constants.

As all this work proceeded, Eddington published a succession of books, both technical and nontechnical, dealing with the above problems and also with the new problems that were arising in cosmological theories. The spherical Einstein universe was found to be unstable, and in 1927 Georges Lemaître published in an obscure journal his cosmology of an expanding universe, the result of the catastrophic explosion of a primeval atom containing all the matter of the universe. He sent a reprint to Eddington only in 1930. Immediately his own modification of this became the basis of all of Eddington's further work in this field. In 1928 Dirac published his new interpretation of the Heisenberg symbols q and p, an approach to a recondite subject that sent Eddington's mind racing off in a new direction. He developed a theory of matrices providing "a simple derivation of the first order wave equation, equivalent to Dirac's but expressed in symmetrical form" and also "a wave equation which we can identify as relating to a system containing electrons with opposite spin." He then developed his *E*-number theory, which proved to be a powerful tool in much subsequent work.

The Nature of the Physical World (1928) and *The Expanding Universe* (1933) deal with the above ideas and his epistemological interpretation. *New Pathways in Science* (1935) and *The Philosophy of Physical Science* (1939) carried his ideas further. All these books are rich in literary excellence and in the sparkle of his imagination and humor, as well as being gateways to new ideas and adventures in thinking.

His technical book *The Relativity Theory of Protons and Electrons* (1936), based almost wholly on the spin extension of relativity, spurred Eddington to evolve a statistical extension. Thus, during his last years he worked indomitably toward his dream—"Bottom's dream," he called it—his vision of a harmonization of quantum physics and relativity. The difficulties were immense and, as we now know, the greatest complexities of nuclear physics and subatomic particles were not yet discovered. But he took hurdle after hurdle as he saw them, with daring leaps, always landing, as he believed, surefootedly on the far side, even though he could not demonstrate his trajectories with mathematical rigor.

The obscurities and gaps in logical deduction in *Fundamental Theory* have discouraged most scientists from taking it seriously, but a few able men— Whittaker, Lemaître, Bastin, Kilmister, Slater—have seen Eddington's vision and have felt it worthwhile to explore further. Slater isolated an erroneous numerical factor in Eddington's work, a factor of 9/4 which modified the calculated recessional constant that had agreed reasonably well with the Mount Wilson observed value. Thus, in 1944, although he did not realize it himself, Eddington's theory had really demanded the change in the distance scale of the universe that Baade announced in 1952 from observational studies of the Cepheid variables in the Andromeda galaxy.

Eddington's biographer has referred to *Fundamental Theory* as an "unfinished symphony" standing as a challenge to "the musicians among natural philosophers of the future." His mystical approach to all experience necessarily embraced the sensual, the mental, and the spiritual. He believed that truth in the spiritual realm must be directly apprehended, not deduced from scientific theories. His Swarthmore Lecture to the Society of Friends, published as *Science and the Unseen World* (1929), and his chapter entitled "The Domain of Physical Science" in *Science, Religion and Reality* (1925), as well as passages throughout his books, reveal a deeply sincere, mystical, yet essentially simple, approach to consideration of the things of the spirit. In the search for truth, whether it be measurable or immeasurable, "It is the search that matters," he wrote. "You will understand the true spirit neither of science nor of religion unless seeking is placed in the forefront."

BIBLIOGRAPHY

I. Original Works. Eddington's books are *Stellar Movements and the Structure of the Universe* (London, 1914); *Report on the Relativity Theory of Gravitation* (London, 1918); *Space, Time, and Gravitation* (Cambridge, 1920); *Mathematical Theory of Relativity* (Cambridge, 1923); *The Internal Constitution of the Stars* (Cambridge, 1926); *Stars and Atoms* (Oxford, 1927), Eddington's only popular account of astrophysical researches; *The Nature of the Physical World* (Cambridge, 1928); *Science and the Unseen World* (London, 1929); *The Expanding Universe* (Cambridge, 1933, 1940); *New Pathways in Science* (Cambridge, 1935); *Relativity Theory of Protons and Electrons* (Cambridge, 1936); *The Philosophy of Physical Science* (Cambridge, 1939); and *Fundamental Theory*, Edmund T. Whittaker, ed. (Cambridge, 1946), published posthumously.

II. Secondary Literature. Writings on Eddington or his work include Herbert Dingle, *The Sources of Eddington's Philosophy* (Cambridge, 1954), an Eddington Memorial Lecture; A. Vibert Douglas, *Arthur Stanley Eddington* (Edinburgh and New York, 1956), a biography that includes a comprehensive list of Eddington's books and more than 150 scientific papers on pp. 193–198 and a genealogical table, pp. 200–201; Martin Johnson, *Time and Universe for the Scientific Conscience* (Cambridge, 1952), an Eddington Memorial Lecture; C. W. Kilmister, *Sir Arthur Eddington*, in Selected Readings in Physics series (London, 1966); C. W. Kilmister and B. O. J. Topper, *Eddington's Statistical Theory* (Oxford, 1962); S. R. Milner, *Generalized Electrodynamics and the Structure of Matter* (Sheffield, 1963); J. R. Newman, *Science and Sensibility,* I (London, 1961); A. D. Ritchie, *Reflections on the Philosophy of Sir Arthur Eddington* (Cambridge, 1947), an Eddington Memorial Lecture; Noel B. Slater, *Eddington's Fundamental Theory* (Cambridge, 1957); Edmund Whittaker, *From Euclid to Eddington* (Cambridge, 1949), and *Eddington's Principle in the Philosophy of Science* (Cambridge, 1951), an Eddington Memorial Lecture; and J. W. Yolton, *The Philosophy of Science of A. S. Eddington* (The Hague, 1960).

A. Vibert Douglas

EDER, JOSEF MARIA (*b.* Krems, Austria, 16 March 1855; *d.* Kitzbühel, Austria, 18 October 1944), *chemistry, photography.*

Eder went to Vienna to study chemistry and remained there for his entire professional life. His first independent research was carried out in a competition to explain the reaction between chromic acid or chromates and organic substances, especially gelatin, which in chromate becomes insoluble when exposed to light. He found in 1878 that a labile chromium dioxide is formed and easily decomposes into the lower and higher oxides. This study earned Eder first prize, and he decided to devote his life to photochemistry and photography. He became assistant professor at the Technische Hochschule in 1880 and professor of chemistry at the state vocational high school in 1882. There he founded an institute for education and research in the graphic arts, directing it from its beginning in 1889 until he retired in 1923.

In 1881 Eder extended and improved the use of silver chloride in gelatin emulsion by the method of precipitation, washing, and developing by ferrous citrate or hydroquinone. Such emulsions and techniques became important in the production of transparencies and copying papers. Eder became interested in sensitometry in 1884. He measured the effect of adding the dye eosin to silver chloride or bromide in gelatin or collodion emulsion by determining the depth of "blackening" after exposure for various lengths of time in specific regions of the solar spectrum. He found advantages in using the iodine derivative erythrosin with eosin. With monobromofluorescein and the methyl violet that others had recommended, Eder obtained sensitivities of silver bromide-collodion emulsions that made them suitable for the autotype process of printing in three colors. He recommended mercury oxalate for measurements in the ultraviolet. From spectrophotometry he went to the use of a concave Rowland grating with 13,000 lines per inch for the spectra of many elements, including those of the rare earths.

In 1884 Eder published the first volume of an extensive handbook of photography that grew to four volumes and appeared in a second edition in 1892. Eder was responsible for subsequent editions and enlargements. He also started a yearbook of photography and reproduction techniques in 1887; its thirtieth volume appeared in 1928. His history of photography saw several German editions and was translated into English by Edward Epstein in 1945.

BIBLIOGRAPHY

I. Original Works. Eder's books were published in Halle. In later editions, the four volumes of the *Handbuch* were divided into parts, as follows: I, pt. 1, *Geschichte der Photographie* (4th ed., 1931); pt. 2, *Photochemie* (1906); pt. 3, *Photographie bei künstlichem Licht, Spektrumphotographie, Aktinometrie* (1912); pt. 4, *Photographische Objektive* (1911); II, pt. 1, *Die Grundlagen der Negativ-Verfahren* (1927), written with Lüppo-Cramer; pt. 2, *Photographie mit Kollodium Verfahren* (1927); pt. 3, *Daguerrotypie, Talbotypie, und Niepcotypie* (1927), written with E. Kuchinka; pt. 4, *Autotypie* (1928), written with A. Hay; III, pt. 1, *Fabrikation photographischer Platten, Filme, und Papiere* (1930), written with F. Wentzel; pt. 2, *Verarbeitung der photographischen Platten, Filme, und Papiere* (6th ed., 1930), written with Lüppo-Cramer, M. Andresen, and Tanzen; pt. 3, *Sensibilisierung und Desensibilisierung* (1930), written with Lüppo-Cramer, R. Schuloff, G. Sachs, J. Eggert, W. Ditterle, and M. Biltz; pt. 4, *Sensitometrie und Spektroskopie* (1930); IV, pt. 1, *Die photographischen Kopierverfahren mit Silbersalzen und photographische Rohpapiere* (1928), written with F. Wentzel; pt. 2, *Pigmentverfahren usw.* (4th ed., 1926); pt. 3, *Heliogravüre und Rotationstiefdruck* (1922); pt. 4, *Lichtpausverfahren und Kopierverfahren ohne Silbersalze* (1929), written with A. Trumm. His other works include *Atlas typischer Spektren* (1911); and *Rezepte, Tabellen, und Arbeitsvorschriften für Photographen und Reproduktionstechniker* (13th ed., 1927).

II. Secondary Literature. Obituaries and biographies include W. Greenwood, in *Photographic Journal,* **86A** (1946), 266 ff.; O. Kempel, in *Österreichische Naturforscher und Techniker* (Vienna, 1951), pp. 125–127; and Erich Stenger, in *Zeitschrift für wissenschaftliche Photographie,* **8** (1948), 255–256.

Eduard Farber

EDISON, THOMAS ALVA (*b.* Milan, Ohio, 11 February 1847; *d.* West Orange, New Jersey, 18 October 1931), *technology.*

Edison's parents emigrated from Canada to Milan, Ohio, after his father joined an unsuccessful insurrection in 1837. The elder Edison prospered as a shingle manufacturer until the railroad bypassed the town, and in 1854 the family moved to Port Huron, Michigan, where the father conducted a less profitable grain and lumber business.

Edison's formal schooling was limited to about three months, followed by four years of instruction by his mother. He was an entrepreneur at age twelve, riding the trains to sell newspapers and food and to pick up odd jobs. He had an early and avid interest in chemistry and electricity, performing experiments at home and on the train. He acquired the habit of going for long periods with little sleep—an idiosyncrasy he kept throughout his life. At about age twelve Edison began to grow deaf, to the point where he could hear nothing below a shout. One result of this was to shut him further into himself and to encourage him in a vast self-directed program of reading. A bout with Newton's *Principia* at age fifteen "gave me a distaste for mathematics from which I have never recovered." He was, however, fascinated by various more elementary practical treatises.

In 1863 Edison became a telegraph operator, and this was his main source of income as he moved from city to city, ending up in Boston in 1868. His resolve to become an inventor became dominant, even though some initial attempts proved financially disastrous. He went to New York in 1869 to seek better fortune. In 1870, at age twenty-three, Edison received $40,000 for improving the stock-ticker system and used the money to set up a private fifty-man laboratory. In 1876 this laboratory was moved to Menlo Park, New Jersey, where his most concentrated and productive work was done. Eleven years later he moved to enlarged facilities at West Orange, New Jersey.

Edison was the epitome of the technologist-inventor. He was not unlearned in science—his prodigious reading had carried him through countless semipopular works, and during the year in Boston he obtained the first two volumes of Faraday's *Experimental Researches,* which he later claimed was a source of considerable inspiration to him; certainly the ability of Faraday to get along without mathematics must have been appealing. But his purposes were practical; he invented by design. He would see a gap in the economy, then invent to fill it; and at this he was very good. Examples include his work on stock tickers, multiplex telegraphy, incandescent lighting, magnetic iron-ore separation, and the storage battery. Some items were developed on very short notice to protect a patent position. Edison's chalk-drum telegraph relay and loudspeaking telephone receiver are especially good examples of this. His method in virtually all cases was to try the hundreds or thousands of possibilities that seemed plausible. This was not done in completely haphazard fashion, since he often obtained detailed knowledge of materials before testing them; but his procedure is rightly considered close to the ultimate in "cut-and-try."

The "Edison effect" (emission of electrons from a hot cathode) is often cited as his sole scientific discovery. In 1883 Edison performed a series of experiments to investigate the dark shadow that formed on the inside of a light bulb. He placed a second electrode inside the bulb and found that negatively charged carbon particles were emitted from the filament. He patented the device as a possible meter and then abandoned it. John A. Fleming, a British consultant to Edison, performed some further experiments, and the matter was still in his mind twenty years later when, as a consultant to Marconi, he saw the possibility of using the rectifying properties of a two-element bulb as a radiowave detector.

One product of his practical motivation was that Edison approached certain problems with a point of view different from that of a scientist. Thus some of the latter, contemplating the possibilities of incandescent lighting in the late 1870's, used available information—including indications that the successful lamp (as yet not invented) would have a low resistance—to prove that a system of independently controlled lights was infeasible. Edison changed the parameters by developing a high-resistance lamp and constructed a system that worked. Similarly the experts extolled the value of generators in which the internal and external resistances were equal, hence producing an efficiency of 50 percent. This was the condition for maximum energy transfer. Edison recognized that he did not need maximum energy, and that therefore he could use machines of low internal resistance to obtain much higher efficiencies. Edison may not have been unique in either of these realizations, but he was certainly the first and most successful in putting them together into a practical lighting system.

Edison's laboratories are considered prototypes of the modern industrial research laboratories in terms of the support they gave to manufacturing operations and the training they gave to staff members. The centralization of effort around the ideas of one man, however, was much greater than in later organizations.

In 1915 a consulting board, with Edison as its president, was established to advise the U.S. Navy on the possibilities of using new scientific and technical devices in war. Tangible results were limited, but one of Edison's early suggestions—a permanent scientific laboratory within the Navy—eventually found fruit in the establishment of the Naval Research Laboratory.

Edison was elected to membership in the National Academy of Sciences in 1927.

BIBLIOGRAPHY

I. Original Works. A large body of notebooks, photographs, and other MS materials is preserved at the Edison Laboratory National Monument at West Orange, New Jersey. Other miscellaneous sources can be identified in the Josephson work cited below. Some original apparatus has been saved: in the Menlo Park laboratory building, which has been restored and moved to Greenfield Village in Dearborn, Michigan; in the West Orange laboratory, which has been preserved at its original site; and at the Smithsonian Institution in Washington.

II. Secondary Literature. The best of the Edison biographies is M. Josephson, *Edison* (New York, 1959), although technical details are generally lacking. The Menlo Park years are treated in some depth in F. Jehl, *Menlo Park Reminiscences* (Dearborn, Mich., 1938).

See also H. C. Passer, "Electrical Science and the Early Development of the Electrical Manufacturing Industry in the United States," in *Annals of Science,* **7** (1951), 382–392.

Bernard S. Finn

EDWARDES (or **EDGUARDUS**), **DAVID** (*b.* Northamptonshire, England, 1502; *d.* Cambridge [?], England, *ca.* 1542), *medicine.*

Edwardes was admitted on 9 August 1517 as a scholar to Corpus Christi College, Oxford, where at different times he seems temporarily to have held the readership in Greek, and became B.A. in 1521 and M.A. in 1525. Additionally it appears that he had "seven years study of medicine" at Oxford, and at some undetermined time practiced that profession at Bristol. In 1528–1529 he continued his medical studies at Cambridge, where he became a member of the medical faculty, a position that he retained until his death.

Edwardes produced a small book of two treatises (London, 1532), the first entitled *De indiciis et praecognitionibus,* dealing with uroscopy and medical prognostication; the second, *In anatomicen introductio luculenta et brevis,* dedicated to the earl of Surrey, was the first work published in England to be devoted solely to anatomy. The latter treatise contains reference to Edwardes' dissection of a human body in 1531 at or near Cambridge, the first recorded, although legally unsanctioned, human dissection in England. The work is brief, occupying only fifteen printed pages, and follows the pattern of exposition popularized by Mondino, that is, progressing from the most to the least corruptible parts. It displays a scorn of medieval anatomy and, in contrast, reflects the new, humanistic Greek anatomical nomenclature. In fact, Edwardes' occasional use of words and phrases in Greek letters is one of the first such instances in England. The anatomical content of the treatise is mostly Galenic in character, although the author was sufficiently under Aristotelian and Avicennan influence to describe a three-chambered heart. Astonishingly for the time, he referred to the left kidney as being higher than the right, a statement that ran counter to the accepted Galenic doctrine and clearly demonstrated the use of independent observation and judgment.

Edwardes' treatise on anatomy antedated the development of anatomical studies in England by almost a generation and, perhaps for this reason, appears to have been utterly without influence.

BIBLIOGRAPHY

The combination of Edwardes' two treatises is known today only in the copy in the British Museum Library. There is a second copy of *De indiciis et praecognitionibus* in the library of the Royal Society of Medicine, London. A facsimile of *In anatomicen introductio luculenta et brevis,* with an English translation and such slight biographical information about Edwardes as exists, is to be found in *David Edwardes. Introduction to Anatomy 1532,* C. D. O'Malley and K. F. Russell, eds. (London, 1961).

C. D. O'MALLEY

EDWARDS, WILLIAM FRÉDÉRIC (*b.* Jamaica, West Indies, 6 April 1776; *d.* Versailles, France, 23 July 1842), *physiology, ecology, anthropology, ethnology, linguistics.*

Son of a wealthy planter of English origin, Edwards, like his brother, Henri Milne-Edwards, grew up and was educated in Bruges, where his family had moved. He became keeper of the Bruges Public Library and, interested in natural sciences, began to study medicine. Since Flanders was then a part of France, the family acquired French citizenship. In 1808 Edwards went to Paris to complete his medical studies. He did not graduate until 1814, at the age of thirty-eight, with a dissertation on the inflammation of the iris and black cataract. He worked at that time with the physiologist Magendie, who in his two-volume *Précis élémentaire de physiologie* (1816–1817) acknowledged Edwards' constant assistance in his experiments and in the preparation of the book.

After a short excursion into mineralogy, Edwards devoted much time to the study of the influence of environmental factors on the "animal economy." His early results were honored by the Prix Montyon of the Académie des Sciences (1820), and in 1824 he published his findings in a book. His main idea was that vital processes depend on external physical and chemical forces but are not entirely controlled by them. Life is different from heat, light, or electricity, forces which, however, contribute to the production of vital phenomena. Edwards systematically examined all principal functions, mostly of vertebrate species; and by varying the external conditions, he determined the nature and degree of their modification. Among the phenomena studied were the minimum and maximum temperatures compatible with life; heat production in young and adult animals; resistance of young animals to cold and to lack of oxygen; the importance of humidity, pressure, and movement of air in the loss of heat by transpiration; the role of light in the development of batrachians; and expiration of carbon dioxide by animals deprived of oxygen. Important was his finding that some warm-blooded animals (carnivores, rodents, some birds) are born less developed and have a much smaller capacity for heat production than those not born helpless. The former need external heat and cannot live without it. Body temperature of newborn carnivores and rodents drops by 10–12°C. as soon as they move away from their mother, but in contact with her it differs by only 1–2°C. Similarly, eight-day-old birds (starlings) in the nest maintain a body temperature of 35–37°C., while outside the nest (at 17°) body temperature drops within one hour to 19°C. These findings proved important in the prevention of infant mortality. Adult animals are, according to the conditions of life of their species, adapted to certain external temperature and thus to certain geographical distribution. Edwards' book is a classic pioneer work on animal ecology.

Soon afterward (*ca.* 1826) Edwards turned to some linguistic problems (etymology in Indo-Germanic languages, Celtic idioms) and was impressed during a journey to southern France and northern Italy by the problem of human types (races). In his opinion human races—in spite of their mixing—have fixed features and persist in their original type for centuries, so that descendants of all known great nations of antiquity could still be found among contemporary peoples (he gave several examples). His view, backed by J.-A. Colladon's early mice hybridization experiments, agrees with the more recent views of geneticists.

In 1832 Edwards was elected to the Académie des Sciences. His last studies led him to found the Société Ethnologique de Paris in 1839 (followed soon in England and the United States). Publication of its *Mémoires* drew attention to a field hitherto rather neglected. The word "ethnologie," introduced by Edwards, designates matters later included in the scope of anthropology.

BIBLIOGRAPHY

I. ORIGINAL WORKS. Edwards' writings include *Dissertation sur l'inflammation de l'iris et de la cataracte noire* (Paris, 1814); *De l'influence des agents physiques sur la vie* (Paris, 1824), trans. by Hodgkin and Fisher as *On the Influence of Physical Agents on Life* (London, 1832; Philadelphia, 1838), with observations on electricity and notes to the work of Edwards by Hodgkin; *Des caractères physiologiques des races humaines, considérés dans leurs rapports avec l'histoire* (Paris, 1829); "Animal Heat," in R. B. Todd, ed., *Cyclopaedia of Anatomy and Physiology,* II (London, 1836–1839), 648–684; *Mémoires de la Société ethnologique de Paris,* **1, 2** (1841–1842); and *Recherches sur les langues celtiques,* H. Milne-Edwards, ed. (Paris, 1844).

II. SECONDARY LITERATURE. See *Analyse succincte des principaux travaux de William Edwards, docteur en médecine* (Paris, n.d.); *Funérailles de William Edwards. Discours de Beriat-Saint-Prix* (Paris, 1842); and A. Quatrefages, in Michaud, *Biographie universelle,* XII (Paris, 1855), 280–282.

VLADISLAV KRUTA

EGAS MONIZ, ANTONIO CAETANO DE ABREU FREIRE (*b.* Avança, Portugal, 29 November 1874; *d.* Lisbon, Portugal, 13 December 1955), *neurology.*

Egas Moniz, the son of Fernando de Pina Rezende Abreu and Maria do Rosario de Almeida e Sousa, was educated by his uncle, an *abbé,* before entering the University of Coimbra in 1891. He studied mathematics and considered a career in engineering before deciding to enter medicine; he received his M.D. degree in 1899. Selecting neurology as his specialty, Egas Moniz went to Paris and Bordeaux to study with the leading figures in neurology and psychiatry, such as J. F. F. Babinski, J. J. Dejerine, Pierre Marie, and J. A. Sicard. In 1902 he became professor at

Coimbra and married Elvira de Macedo Dias. Egas Moniz was appointed to the chair of neurology at the new University of Lisbon in 1911, a position he held until his retirement in 1945. His honors included the Nobel Prize in physiology or medicine in 1949, honorary degrees from the universities of Bordeaux and Lyons, and awards from the Portuguese, Spanish, Italian, and French governments. He served as president of the Lisbon Academy of Sciences and was a member or honorary member of many other scientific societies, including the Royal Society of Medicine, the Academy of Medicine in Paris, and the American Neurological Association.

In addition to his scientific achievements, Egas Moniz was an accomplished historian, literary critic, and composer and had a distinguished career in politics. He was a deputy in the Portuguese Parliament from 1900 until his appointment as ambassador to Spain in 1917; he became foreign minister in 1918 and led Portugal's delegation to the 1919 Paris Peace Conference. Egas Moniz retired from politics in 1919 after a political quarrel involved him in a duel.

Egas Moniz' two most outstanding contributions to medicine were the diagnostic technique of cerebral angiography to locate brain tumors, and the first clinical use of psychosurgery. When he entered neurology, the method by which physicians attempted to use the still new technique of X-raying to locate intracranial tumors was the one developed by W. E. Dandy, involving the injection of air into the brain cavities. Seeking a more exact as well as a less hazardous technique, Egas Moniz began a series of cadaver experiments in which he injected various radiopaque solutions into the brain's arteries. After mapping the normal distribution of the intracranial blood vessels, he introduced his method clinically in 1927, outlining with X rays the location and size of a patient's brain tumor by the tumor's displacement of injected arteries. Egas Moniz and his colleagues published over 200 papers and monographs on normal and abnormal cerebral angiography, and the technique has been refined and elaborated for the localization of tumors and vascular disorders throughout the body.

The Nobel Prize went to Egas Moniz "for his discovery of the therapeutic value of leucotomy in certain psychoses." Early in his career he had worked with F. Regis on the problem of toxic psychoses and had become convinced that "only by an organic orientation can psychiatry make real progress." In 1935, at the Second International Neurological Congress in London, he heard J. F. Fulton and G. F. Jacobsen discuss the effects of frontal leucotomy (surgical division of the nerves connecting the frontal lobes to the rest of the brain) on the behavior of two chimpanzees: the animals remained friendly, alert, and intelligent but were no longer subject to temper tantrums or other symptoms of the experimental neuroses that had been successfully induced prior to surgery.

On the basis of this work Egas Moniz and his young surgical colleague, Almeida Lima, worked out a frontal leucotomy technique that they felt might alleviate certain psychiatric conditions, particularly those dominated by emotional tensions. The report of their first clinical trials on mental hospital patients—no operative deaths and fourteen out of twenty patients "cured" or "improved"—created worldwide interest and debate over the possibility that mental illness could be corrected by operating on brains that are not organically diseased. Modifications of their psychosurgical procedure were employed widely for two decades, then declined in use with the advent of psychopharmacology. At the Nobel presentations in 1949, Herbert Olivecrona captured the significance of Egas Moniz' work when he said:

> Frontal leucotomy, despite certain limitations of the operative method, must be considered one of the most important discoveries ever made in psychiatric therapy, because through its use a great number of suffering people and total invalids have recovered and have been socially rehabilitated.

NOTE

The presentation speech by Olivecrona at the Nobel awards, 1949, is in *Nobel Lectures. Physiology or Medicine, 1942–1962* (Amsterdam–New York, 1964), p. 246.

The techniques of frontal leucotomy or lobotomy pioneered by Egas Moniz in treating mental conditions were applied to the alleviation of intractable pain by W. H. Freeman and his colleagues in the mid-1940's. Variations of the surgical procedure have been devised in an effort to minimize some of the undesirable personality changes that were found to follow leucotomy. Use of the procedure to treat conditions such as schizophrenia has declined greatly since the advent of tranquilizers and other psychopharmacological agents.

BIBLIOGRAPHY

I. ORIGINAL WORKS. Egas Moniz' writings include *A vida sexual (fisiologia e patologia)* (Coimbra, 1901); *A neurologia na guerra* (Lisbon, 1917); *Um ano de politico* (Lisbon, 1920); "L'encéphalographie artérielle: Son importance dans la localisation des tumeurs cérébrales," in *Revue neurologique,* 2 (1927), 72–90; *Diagnostic des tumeurs cérébrales et épreuve de l'encéphalographie artérielle* (Paris, 1931); *L'angiographie cérébrale, ses applications et résultats en anatomie, physiologie et clinique* (Paris, 1934); "Essai d'un traitement chirurgical de certaines psychoses," in *Bulletin de l'Académie de médecine,* 115 (1936), 385–392; *Tentatives opératoires dans le traitement de certaines psychoses* (Paris, 1936); *Ao lado da medicina* (Lisbon, 1940); *Como cheguei a realizar a leucotomia pré-frontal* (Lisbon, 1948).

II. SECONDARY LITERATURE. See "Obituary. Antonio Egas Moniz, M.D.," in *Lancet* (1955), 2, 1345; and F. R. Perino, "Egas Moniz, 1874–1955," in *Journal of the International College of Surgeons,* 36 (1961), 261–271.

JUDITH P. SWAZEY

EGOROV, DIMITRY FEDOROVICH (*b.* Moscow, Russia, 22 December 1869; *d.* Kazan, U.S.S.R., 10 September 1931), *mathematics.*

After graduating from the Gymnasium in Moscow, Egorov entered the division of physics and mathematics of Moscow University, from which he received a diploma in 1891. After obtaining his master's degree he remained at the university to prepare for a professorship, and in 1894 he became *Privatdozent* there. In 1901 he received his doctorate with a dissertation entitled "Ob odnom klasse ortogonalnykh sistem," and two years later he was appointed extraordinary professor in the division of physics and mathematics at the University of Moscow. In 1909 Egorov was made ordinary professor and was appointed director of the Mathematical Scientific Research Institute. He was elected corresponding member of the USSR Academy titled "Ob odnom klasse ortogonalnykh sistem," and member. Egorov was a member of the Moscow Mathematical Society; in 1902 he was elected to the French Mathematical Society and the Mathematical Society of Berlin University. From 1922 almost until his death, he was president of the Moscow Mathematical Society, and from 1922 he was editor-in-chief of *Matematicheskii sbornik.*

Egorov's investigations on triply orthogonal systems and potential surfaces, i.e., surfaces *E,* contributed greatly to differential geometry. The results of these investigations were presented by Darboux in his monograph *Leçons sur les systèmes orthogonaux et les coordonnées curvilignes* (2nd ed., Paris, 1910).

Egorov considerably advanced the solution of Peterson's problem on the bending on the principal basis. In the theory of functions of a real variable, wide use is made of Egorov's theorem: Any almost-everywhere converging sequence of measurable functions converges uniformly on a closed set, the complement of which has an infinitely small measure. This theorem, as well as Egorov's scholarship in new trends, led to the creation of the Moscow school dealing with the theory of functions of a real variable. Among the mathematicians belonging to Egorov's school are the well-known Soviet mathematicians N. N. Lusin, V. V. Golubev, and V. V. Stepanov.

Egorov also worked in other areas; for instance,

he initiated an investigation into the theory of integral equations. A brilliant lecturer and scholar, Egorov wrote some college textbooks on the theory of numbers, on the calculus of variations, and on differential geometry.

BIBLIOGRAPHY

Egorov's writings include "Uravnenia s chastnymi proisvodnymi vtorogo poriadka po dvum nezavisimym peremenym," in *Uchenye zapiski Moskovskogo universiteta,* **15** (1899), i–xix, 1–392; "Ob odnom klasse ortogonalnykh sistem," *ibid.,* **18** (1901), i–vi, 1–239, his doctoral diss.; "Ob izgibanii na glavnom osnovanii pri odnom semeystve ploskikh ili konicheskikh linii," in *Matematicheskii sbornik,* **28** (1911), 167–187; "Sur les suites de fonctions mesurables," in *Comptes rendus hebdomadaires des séances de l'Académie des sciences,* **152** (1911), 244–246; and "Sur l'intégration des fonctions mesurables," *ibid.,* **155** (1912), 1474–1475; *Elementy teorii chisel* (Moscow, 1923); *Differentsialnaya geometria* (Moscow–Petrograd, 1924); "Sur les surfaces, engendrées par la distribution des lignes d'une famille donnée," in *Matematicheskii sbornik,* **31** (1924), 153–184; "Sur la théorie des équations intégrales au noyau symétrique," *ibid.,* **35** (1928), 293–310; "Sur quelques points de la théorie des équations intégrales à limites fixes," in *Comptes rendus hebdomadaires des séances de l'Académie des sciences,* **186** (1928), 1703–1705.

A secondary source is V. Steklov, P. Lazarev, and A. Belopolsky, "Zapiska ob uchenykh trudakh D. F. Egorova," in *Izvestiya Rossiiskoi akademii nauk,* **18,** no. 12–18 (1924), 445–446.

A. B. PAPLAUSKAS

EHRENBERG, CHRISTIAN GOTTFRIED (*b.* Delitzsch, near Leipzig, Germany, 19 April 1795; *d.* Berlin, Germany, 27 June 1876), *biology, micropaleontology.*

Ehrenberg's father, Johann Gottfried Ehrenberg, was a municipal magistrate in the small city of Delitzsch; his mother, Christiane Dorothea Becker, was the daughter of an innkeeper. She died when Ehrenberg was thirteen years old. At the age of fourteen he entered school in Schulpforta, near Naumburg, a Protestant boarding school with a high level of instruction and a classical-philological orientation. In 1815, after passing his final examination, Ehrenberg, at his father's request, began to study theology in Leipzig. He then changed to medicine, however, and during his five semesters in Leipzig also attended J. C. Rosenmüller's lectures on anatomy and Schwägrichen's lectures on botany and zoology.

In 1817 Ehrenberg continued his medical studies at the University of Berlin, where in 1818 he passed the state medical examination. He studied under Christoph W. Hufeland, K. A. W. Berends, and K. F. von Graefe and was especially influenced by Karl Rudolphi and Heinrich Link, who encouraged his botanical and zoological studies and stimulated his interest in microscopical technique. With the presentation of a botanical dissertation, "Sylvae mycologicae Berolinensis," he was made a doctor of medicine in November 1818. This work not only depicts some 250 species of fungi found in the vicinity of Berlin (including sixty-two described for the first time) but it also demonstrates the constancy of the fungi species and their origin from seeds, which was still disputed. In a specialized work on the *Syzygites megalocarpus* (1819) he described for the first time the copulatory process among the molds and provided still further proofs of the sexual generation of the mushrooms in the essay *De mycetogenesis epistola* (1821).

These fundamental microscopical investigations led Ehrenberg to reject the then dominant view that spontaneous generation (*generatio aequivoca*) was possible in principle and that "lower" organisms, among which algae and fungi were grouped, could originate directly out of a basic inorganic substance, that is, water and slime. A major portion of Ehrenberg's lifework, above all the later microscopical research, was directed toward the clarification of this question. In the context of this problem, it becomes understandable why throughout his life Ehrenberg placed so much weight on demonstrating the constancy of species even among the lower organisms. Through his research on fungi, Ehrenberg became acquainted with Nees von Esenbeck, the president of the Deutsche Akademie der Naturforscher Leopoldina, of which Ehrenberg had become a member in 1818. His acquaintance with Adelbert von Chamisso was also a result of his botanical studies. While preparing the material from his expeditions, Ehrenberg was able to observe the generation of the lichen.

Ehrenberg's scientific career took a decisive turn in 1820 when he was presented with the opportunity to participate in the archaeological expedition of Count Heinrich von Menu von Minutoli, who planned to travel in Egypt. With a friend from his student days, Wilhelm Hemprich, Ehrenberg joined this expedition, which was advocated by Alexander von Humboldt (then residing in Paris) and by Heinrich Lichtenstein, the director of the university's zoological museum. The expenses of Ehrenberg and Hemprich were financed primarily by the Prussian Academy of Sciences, which also gave the instructions for the expedition. The two men were first to study thoroughly the natural history collections in Vienna and to consult scientists residing in that city. Therefore, in June 1820, Ehrenberg traveled from Berlin to Vienna and then to Trieste, where the party boarded ship for Alexandria on 5 August. The journey led through the Libyan desert to Cyrenaica, to Fayum in 1821, toward the Nile to Dongola, and to the shores of the Red Sea (in 1823) and yielded an unexpectedly large body of scientific results. Of the animal species alone, 3,987 (34,000 individual zoological objects) were sent to the collections of the Berlin Zoological Museum, which in that period were under the supervision of Heinrich Lichtenstein. As for botany, 46,000 plant specimens representing approximately 3,000 species were collected. The poor organization of the journey and its insufficient financing resulted in a considerable loss of time and many privations. Many members of the expedition became seriously ill. Ehrenberg's companion Hemprich fell victim to a fever in Massawa shortly before the end of the trip in 1825. Ehrenberg was forced to halt the journey ahead of schedule, without being able to explore the interior of Abyssinia; however, he had already made the littoral observations that were to make him famous as a zoologist. In his work on the coral polyps of the Red Sea (1834), he presented the first exact investigations on the anatomy, nourishment, and growth of the corals, and in individual works (published mostly in Poggendorf's *Annalen der Physik*) he explained the causes of the coloring of the Red Sea and the composition of the dust of trade winds. He also made drawings, based on microscopical studies, of numerous marine animals (mollusks, echinoderms, medusae, and electric rays) *in situ;* examined vertebrates for endoparasites; and made anatomical and embryological observations on insects, crabs, and spiders. In accordance with the scientific instructions given by the Berlin Academy, the collecting was not confined to plants and animals but also included rocks, fossils, and geographic measurements, as well as historical and ethnographic data and materials, among which were six manuscripts of ancient Arab physicians.

At the beginning of December 1825, Ehrenberg landed again in Trieste, the only survivor of an expedition that had lost nine members, including Hemprich. After his return Ehrenberg, originally humorous and joyful, experienced further disappointments that spoiled his enjoyment of the scientific utilization of this unusual and very productive journey. Even before his return his collections were decimated through the sale of the duplicates, and some of the boxes were damaged during quarantine, resulting in the destruction of their contents; consequently, of the originally immense series of forms of each species, only a fraction was still usable. Moreover, labels and sketches were missing, and Ehrenberg could hardly put the collections in order by himself.

Although in 1826 he published the plan for a comprehensive work (in the journal *Hertha,* pp. 92–94), the first section of which was to contain an account of the expedition, and the second, illustrated descriptions of the individual plants and animals, neither portion was completed, even though draftsmen paid by the state aided in preparing the material. The description of the journey and the first parts of the *Symbolae physicae,* dealing with animal and bird descriptions, appeared in 1828. Moreover, individual results obtained on the expedition had been reported since 1826 in the sessions of the Berlin Academy of Sciences by its members Alexander von Humboldt, Heinrich Lichtenstein, Heinrich Link, Karl Rudolphi, and Christian Weiss.

In July 1827, Ehrenberg was elected a member of the Berlin Academy of Sciences, having already become, on 24 March of that year, an assistant professor at the University of Berlin. In these years Ehrenberg obtained financial aid and scientific support through the influential Alexander von Humboldt, who in May 1827 left Paris to settle permanently in Berlin. He persuaded Ehrenberg to participate in a scientific expedition to Siberia financed by Czar Nicolas I. Ehrenberg used this opportunity not only to collect botanical and zoological specimens but also to undertake geological and paleontological studies, and to make microscopical observations on the Infusoria (or, as they were then called, animalcules). Humboldt's eight-month journey, in which, besides Ehrenberg, the Berlin mineralogist Gustav Rose took part, went from St. Petersburg and Moscow to Nizhni Novgorod (now Gorki), up the Volga to Kazan and to Ekaterinburg (now Sverdlovsk), and from there into the northern Urals. On the return journey, based in Astrakhan, they navigated the Volga and the Caspian Sea, where Ehrenberg, in addition to gathering fish for the St. Petersburg, Paris, and Berlin museums, made observations on living plankton.

Following his return home in 1831, Ehrenberg married Julie Rose, the niece of Gustav Rose and the daughter of Johannes Rose, a businessman and the consul in Wismar. After her early death (1848) he was married again, in 1852, this time to Karoline Friederike Friccius, sister-in-law of the chemist Eilhard Mitscherlich. From his first marriage he had one son, Hermann Alexander, and four daughters. The eldest daughter, Helene, married the botanist Johannes Hanstein, and another married the chemist Karl Friedrich Rammelsberg; the youngest daughter, Clara, aided her father in his scientific research.

When in 1833 Johannes Müller was appointed

successor to the late Karl Rudolphi, Ehrenberg was disappointed in his hope of being named to the chair of comparative anatomy, which would have allowed him to use the zootomical collections (including the material he himself had contributed) unhindered by questions of competence. As a result of Alexander von Humboldt's vigorous intercession, a strengthening of Ehrenberg's academic standing was sought, and in 1839 he was given a full professorship in "Methodologie, Enzyklopädie und Geschichte der Medizin." Ehrenberg did not, however, view this teaching post in terms of an active role. Generally, he hardly functioned as a university teacher, although as a member of the Berlin Academy of Sciences he had the right to lecture at the university even without a teaching appointment.

Ehrenberg's lifework consisted mainly of specific research, which he carried out at the Berlin Academy. It was recognized through his election to the Académie des Sciences of Paris (1841), his appointment as secretary of the Mathematics-Physics Section of the Berlin Academy of Sciences (1842), and by the award of the Order of Merit (1842), in which Alexander von Humboldt's opinion was important.

The scientific work that Ehrenberg undertook in Berlin following his return from the Russo-Siberian expedition was at first still related to the observations he had made on the Middle Eastern journey, especially those from the Red Sea. Included in this category are the publications on Hydrozoa and mollusks, especially the works on the coral polyps of the Red Sea (1831–1834); contributions to the knowledge of the physiology of the coral polyps in general and those of the Red Sea in particular, including an essay on the physiological systematics of these animals (1832); the medusae of the Red Sea (1834, 1835); marine phosphorescence (1835); the development and structure of the gastrotricha and rotatoria (1832); and the first reports on the so-called animalcules (Infusoria), the group that later absorbed Ehrenberg's interest. Already in 1828 and in 1830 he had given lectures at the Berlin Academy on the organization, systematics, and geographical relations of the Infusoria, which were soon followed by a series of papers entitled "Zur Erkenntnis der Organisation in der Richtung des kleinsten Raumes" (from 1832). Ehrenberg first treated this theme in monograph form in 1838, in *Die Infusionsthierchen als vollkommene Organismen,* in which he also presented a detailed historical sketch on the investigation and significance of this heterogeneous class of animals and elucidated the method of study underlying his microscopical researches. Although in all these works Ehrenberg utilized primarily observations and specimens from

his Middle East expedition, he nevertheless almost always completed them with comparative material from the Baltic Sea and North Sea or from the Russo-Siberian expedition.

All Ehrenberg's individual observations were viewed in the light of a fundamental conception held consistently since his student years: this consisted of examining the theory, revived by Leibniz in the eighteenth century, of the existence of a "chain of being" (*scala naturae*) in nature. One of the bases for this theory was the various levels of organization among organisms, combined with the ideas that there exist gradual transitions in structure and performance from the mineral kingdom to man, that transformations from "lower" into more highly organized creatures still take place everywhere in nature, and that the lowest organisms can emerge spontaneously out of inorganic matter. These theories, which were earnestly discussed until the middle of the nineteenth century, were based mainly on that little-investigated group of organisms that Cuvier had united in the fourth class of his "radial animals." The five classes of the "radial animals" were, according to Cuvier, echinoderms, entozoa, medusae, polyps, and Infusoria; and they were considered to be simple organized animals, as opposed to the divisions within the vertebrates, mollusks, and arthropods. From the beginning of his research Ehrenberg strove to investigate the inner organization of the animals of these five classes and particularly to provide a new, systematic grouping for the Infusoria, a task to which he was led in large part by the use of the microscope.

In his opinion, all animals possess with an equal degree of completeness the important organs of life, e.g., nervous and vascular systems, muscles, and digestive and sexual organs. Through comparative anatomical investigations Ehrenberg examined Cuvier's five classes for the presence of these organs. In order to ascertain the nervous capacity of the echinoderms and medusae, he employed, on the advice of Alexander von Humboldt, galvanic currents as stimuli. In exploring the structure of the digestive organs he utilized, beginning in 1833, food colored with indigo or carmine. He carried out an extensive series of studies of this type with the Infusoria in particular. At the time this group still included such heterogeneous organisms as bacteria, all single-celled animals, the many-celled rotatoria, and several worms. Ehrenberg did not yet separate the many-celled animals from the single-celled ones, a concept that became current in systematic zoology only after 1850; rather, he believed that he could demonstrate the presence of complete organ systems in single-celled animals. This was for him an important argument against spontaneous generation and the "chain of being."

In spite of a critical, inductive research method, Ehrenberg succumbed to an optical error, especially when he consciously renounced microscopical magnifications of greater than 300. His error was similar to that of the pioneers of the microscope in the seventeenth century, like Leeuwenhoek and Swammerdam, who considered the indistinct structures in the egg and the sperm to be complete organisms and on these grounds derived the preformation theory. The basis for the correction of Ehrenberg's errors was set out only in 1863, with the union of protozoology and cytology. In his later years Ehrenberg could no longer accept the more correct perceptions of Felix Dujardin (his most vehement opponent), Theodor von Siebold, Max Schultze, and others, since they did not concern an individual error but called into question the entire conception of his system of the animal kingdom.

As a systematist Ehrenberg proceeded from Cuvier, but he had rejected both the latter's graduated hierarchy of the more highly and thoroughly organized animals and his classification of man among the mammals. His own system, which he proposed in 1836 in the sketch of the animal kingdom according to the principle of a single type reaching down to the monad, set man (*Kreis der Völker*) as a systematic category in contrast with the animals (*Kreis der Tiere*). He based this procedure on the "capacity for mental development" (*geistigen Entwicklungsfähigkeit*) of the human race, and even for the classification of the animals he employed social behavior as the most important taxonomic characteristic. This conception remained limited to its time and later hindered Ehrenberg's acceptance of the Darwinian theory of evolution.

So much the greater, then, is the importance of the continuation of the studies on single-celled marine and fossil animals, with which Ehrenberg completed his pioneering achievements. With the microscope he discovered single-celled fossils that built up geological strata; he gave exact descriptions of and discriminated among the shells and skeletons of freshwater and marine animals, thereby becoming the founder of microgeology and micropaleontology in Germany. His collection of samples, containing many types, along with his manuscripts and correspondence, are still available for study in the Museum für Naturkunde in Berlin.

Through his worldwide marine investigations Ehrenberg was invited to participate in oceanographic research projects of international importance. Thus he influenced the instructions, drawn up by Humboldt, for James Ross's Antarctic expedition (1839–

1843) and for the Novara expedition (1857–1859) and worked on the deep-bottom samples of the American researchers Silliman, L. W. Bailey, and M. F. Maury; the latter, beginning in 1853, provided him with material taken from depths of 10,000–12,000 feet. These results made possible L. Brooke's invention of the deep-sea lead, for the employment of which on German ships such as the *Arkona* and the *Thetis* (1860–1862) and the *Nymphe* (1865–1868) Ehrenberg tirelessly campaigned. Finally, the *Gazelle* expedition (1874–1876) was equipped with this device, but Ehrenberg did not live to see the results. Even the investigation of the sea bottom served Ehrenberg in his refutation of the theory of spontaneous generation, which had again come under discussion from the standpoint of the theory of evolution, through the hypothetical prehistoric organism *Bathybius haeckeli*.

In his lifetime and until the present, Ehrenberg has been reproached for not completing the utilization of the collections assembled on his Middle East expedition, for not accepting the findings of cytology and of the theory of evolution, and for not correcting his errors. The first stemmed both from technical problems, extending to a lack of scientific organizational ability, and from his very exact and laborious method of working, which aimed at comprehensive analysis. Moreover, the results were embedded in a philosophical system that presupposed the spiritual origin and constancy of the world order and therefore resisted materialistic and evolutionary interpretations. His method was based on the comparative anatomy and morphology of the first half of the nineteenth century; in these areas, as a pioneer of microscopy, he employed polarized light and pursued a comparative microscopical anatomy—with outmoded optical means. He expressed the program of his life and his research in a youthful letter (1821) to Nees von Esenbeck: "Until now my favorite pursuit has been neither naked systematizing nor unsystematic observation, and whenever time and circumstances, together with my ability, allow it, I prefer getting down to the grass-roots level" (Stresemann, "Hemprich und Ehrenberg. Reisen zweier naturforschender Freunde . . .," p. 42). In later years he considered only purely empirical knowledge to be valid; the lasting merit of his description and classification of the fossil protozoans stems from this position.

BIBLIOGRAPHY

I. ORIGINAL WORKS. Ehrenberg's writings include *Reisen in Aegypten, Libyen, Nubien und Dongola*, I, pt. 1 (Berlin, 1828), not completed; *Symbolae physicae* (Berlin,

1828–1845): *Aves,* pts. 1–2 (1828–1829), *Mammalia,* pts. 1–2 (1828–1832), *Evertebrata excl. Insecta,* pts. 1–2 (1829–1831), *Insecta,* pts. 1–5 (1829–1845), none of the divisions completed; "Ueber die Natur und Bildung der Corallenbänke des rothen Meeres und über einen neuen Fortschritt in der Kenntnis der Organisation im kleinsten Raume durch Verbesserung des Mikroskops von Pistor und Schiek," in *Abhandlungen der Preussischen Akademie der Wissenschaften zu Berlin* (1832), pp. 381–438; "Ueber den Mangel des Nervenmarks im Gehirn der Menschen und Thiere, den gegliederten röhrigen Bau des Gehirns und über normale Krystallbildung im lebenden Tierkörper," in *Annalen der Physik,* **28,** no. 3 (1833); *Ueber die Natur und Bildung der Coralleninseln und Corallenbänke im rothen Meere* (Berlin, 1834); *Das Leuchten des Meeres. Neue Beobachtungen nebst Übersicht der Hauptmomente der geschichtlichen Entwicklung dieses merkwürdigen Phänomens* (Berlin, 1835); *Die Akalephen des rothe Meeres und den Organismus der Medusen der Ostsee erläutert und auf Systematik angewendet* (Berlin, 1836), which contains the first draft and a review of his system; *Beobachtung einer auffallenden bisher unerkannten Structur des Seelenorgans bei Menschen und Tieren* (Berlin, 1836); "Ueber das Massenverhältnis der jetzt lebenden Kiesel-Infusorien...," in *Abhandlungen der Preussischen Akademie der Wissenschaften zu Berlin* (1836), pp. 109–136; *Die Infusionsthierchen als vollkommene Organismen. Ein Blick in das tiefere organische Leben der Natur* (Leipzig, 1838), with an atlas and 64 colored copperplates; "Über noch zahlreich jetzt lebende Tierarten der Kreidebildung," in *Abhandlungen der Preussischen Akademie der Wissenschaften zu Berlin* (1839), pp. 81–174; "Kieselschaligen Süsswasserformen am Wasserfall-Fluss im Oregon" and "Mikroskopisches Leben in Texas," in *Monatsberichte der Akademie der Wissenschaften zu Berlin* (1848–1849), pp. 76–98; "Über das mikroskopische Leben der Galapagos-Inseln," *ibid.* (1853), pp. 178–194; "Über die erfreuliche im Grossen fördernde Teilnahme an mikroskopischen Forschungen in Nord-Amerika," *ibid.,* pp. 203–220; "Über die seit 27 Jahren noch wohl erhaltenen Organisations-Praparate des mikroskopischen Lebens," in *Abhandlungen der Preussischen Akademie der Wissenschaften zu Berlin* (1862), pp. 39–74, with three color plates; "Über die wachsende Kenntnis des unsichtbaren Lebens als felsbildende Bacillarien in Californien," *ibid.* (1870), pp. 1–74, with three plates; "Uebersicht ... über das von der Atmosphäre getragene organische Leben," *ibid.* (1871), pp. 1–150; "Nachtrag zur Übersicht der organischen Atmosphärilien," *ibid.* (1871), pp. 233–275, with three plates; "Mikrogeologische Studien über das kleinste Leben der Meeres-Tiefgründe aller Zonen und dessen geologischen Einfluss," *ibid.* (1873), pp. 131–398, with twelve plates; and "Fortsetzung der mikrogeologischen Studien als Gesammt-Übersicht der mikroskopischen Paläontologie gleichartig analysierter Gebirgsarten der Erde, mit specieller Rücksicht auf den Polycistinen-Mergel von Barbados," *ibid.* (1875), pp. 1–225.

Unpublished travel diaries, MSS, and letters on his journeys to the Middle East and Siberia are in the archives of the Berlin Academy of Sciences, and original drawings are in the library of the zoological museum (Museum für Naturkunde) of Humboldt University, Berlin.

II. SECONDARY LITERATURE. Biographies of Ehrenberg are Clara Ehrenberg, *Unser Elternhaus. Ein Familienbuch* (Berlin, 1905); Johannes von Hanstein, *Christian Gottfried Ehrenberg* (Bonn, 1877); and Max von Laue, *Christian Gottfried Ehrenberg. Ein Vertreter deutscher Naturforschung im neunzehnten Jahrhundert* (Berlin, 1895), with portrait and bibliography.

On specific aspects of Ehrenberg's work, see H. Engel, "Het Levenswerk van Christian Gottfried Ehrenberg," in *Microwereld,* **15** (1960), 19–32; Gerhard Engelmann, "Christian Gottfried Ehrenberg, ein Wegbereiter der deutschen Tiefseeforschung," in *Deutsche hydrographische Zeitschrift,* **22** (1969), 145–157; Siegmund Günther, "Chr. G. Ehrenberg und die wissenschaftliche Erdkunde," in *Deutsche Rundschau für geographische Statistik,* **17** (1895), 529–538; A. von Humboldt, "Bericht über die naturhistorischen Reisen der Herren Ehrenberg und Hemprich," in *Hertha* (1827), 73–92; Otto Koehler, "Christian Gottfried Ehrenberg," in H. Gehrig, ed., *Schulpforta und das deutsche Geistesleben* (Darmstadt, 1943), pp. 58–68; Erwin Stresemann, "Hemprich und Ehrenberg. Reisen zweier naturforschender Freunde im Orient, geschildert in ihren Briefen aus den Jahren 1819–1826," which constitutes *Abhandlungen der Deutschen Akademie der Wissenschaften zu Berlin,* Klasse für Math. und allg. Naturwiss. (1954), no. 1, with a portrait; "Hemprich und Ehrenberg zum Gedenken. Ihre Reise zum Libanon im Sommer 1824 und deren ornithologische Ergebnisse," in *Journal für Ornithologie,* **103** (1962), 380–388; and Sigurd Locker, "Mikrofossilien aus der Sammlung Christian Gottfried Ehrenberg," in *Wissenschaftliche Zeitschrift der Humboldt-Universität zu Berlin,* Math.-Naturwiss. Reihe., **19,** no. 2–3 (1970), 186–189.

There is no comprehensive assessment of Ehrenberg's importance in micropaleontology and geology. Unpublished letters and MSS in these areas are included in the micropaleontological collection of the Museum für Naturkunde, Berlin.

ILSE JAHN

EHRENFEST, PAUL (*b.* Vienna, Austria, 18 January 1880; *d.* Amsterdam, Netherlands, 25 September 1933), *theoretical physics.*

Paul Ehrenfest was the youngest of the five sons of Sigmund and Johanna Jellinek Ehrenfest. His childhood was spent in a working-class district of Vienna, where his father ran a successful grocery business. He grew up surrounded by the crowded and varied life of the many nationality groups in the Austro-Hungarian capital, constantly reminded by the ugly, widespread anti-Semitism that he was a Jew. Ehrenfest's early interest in mathematics and science was stimulated by his oldest brother, Arthur, and this fascination with science helped him through a difficult adolescence. He studied theoretical physics at Vienna, where he received his doctorate in 1904 for a dissertation on the extension of Hertz's mechanics to problems in hydrodynamics. The dissertation was supervised by Ludwig Boltzmann, whose work and style greatly influenced Ehrenfest.

On 21 December 1904 Ehrenfest married Tatyana Alexeyevna Afanassjewa, a Russian student of mathematics whom he had met at Göttingen in 1902, during a year of study there. According to Austro-Hungarian law, the marriage of a Christian to a Jew could occur only if both partners officially renounced their religions, which Ehrenfest and his Russian Orthodox bride therefore did. During the early years of their marriage the Ehrenfests collaborated on several papers that clarified some of the obscurities in the statistical mechanics of Boltzmann and Josiah Willard Gibbs. As a result they were invited by Felix Klein to prepare a monograph on the foundations of statistical mechanics for the *Encyklopädie der mathematischen Wissenschaften.* After their marriage the Ehrenfests lived first in Vienna and Göttingen and in 1907 moved to St. Petersburg, hoping to settle in Russia. Ehrenfest had no regular employment in any of these cities, but they were able to manage on their small inherited incomes. In 1911 he began a difficult and depressing search for an academic position, a search complicated by his anomalous religious status. This search came to an unexpectedly successful conclusion in 1912, when Ehrenfest was appointed to the chair of theoretical physics at Leiden as the successor to H. A. Lorentz, to whom he became deeply attached.

Ehrenfest moved to the Netherlands in October 1912 and immediately brought new vitality to the scientific life of Leiden. He started a weekly colloquium, established a reading room for physics students, revived a student science club, and generally devoted his efforts to maintaining real intellectual and human contact among all members of Leiden's scientific community. As a teacher Ehrenfest was unique. Albert Einstein described him as "peerless" and "the best teacher in our profession whom I have ever known." His lectures always brought out the basic concepts of a physical theory, carefully extracting them from the accompanying mathematical formalism. He worked closely with his students, doing everything in his power to help them develop their own talents. His nickname among the students, "Uncle Socrates," captures his probing questioning, the force of a personality that could sometimes be overwhelming, and the infectious warmth of his humor.

Ehrenfest's special gift as a theoretical physicist was his critical ability, rather than his creative power or his calculational skill. This ability is particularly evident in his writings on statistical mechanics. Boltzmann had developed this subject over a thirty-year period, and his ideas had changed a good deal during this time as he responded to a variety of difficulties pointed out to him by others. As a consequence, there was a certain amount of confusion about what his theory asserted, which assertions had been proved, and how much of the theory had survived the various attacks on it. In 1907 Ehrenfest proposed a simple theoretical model (the Ehrenfest urn model) that showed how the laws of probability could produce an average trend toward equilibrium, even though the behavior of the model was reversible in time and every one of its states would eventually recur. This meant that Boltzmann's *H*-theorem (showing that molecular collisions will produce an approach to equilibrium with the entropy increasing monotonically in time), if interpreted in a suitable statistical way, did not necessarily contradict the reversible laws of mechanics, as Loschmidt had argued, or Poincaré's recurrence theorem, as Zermelo had argued.

In their *Encyklopädie* article, which appeared in 1911, the Ehrenfests brought out both the logical structure and the remaining difficulties of this theory. They made a clear distinction between the older approach (before 1877), which treated the molecules statistically but tried to make universally valid statements about the gas as a whole, and the later work, in which the gas itself was treated by statistical methods. The role of the ergodic hypothesis in relating time averages to averages over an ensemble was brought out clearly; so clearly, in fact, that the attention of mathematicians was drawn to the ergodic problem. The Ehrenfests formulated the sequence of theorems that still needed proving before the statistical foundation of the second law of thermodynamics could be said to be firmly established. Their analysis of Gibbs's approach to the subject was less sympathetic. They found fault with his treatment of irreversibility and underestimated the importance of Gibbs's powerful ensemble methods in dealing with complex systems.

The critical approach also led Ehrenfest to his greatest positive contribution to physics: the adiabatic principle. Ehrenfest was one of the first to try to understand the significance of the strange new concept of energy quanta that Max Planck had introduced into physics in 1900 in his theory of blackbody radiation. In a series of papers culminating in his major study of 1911, "Which Features of the Quantum Hypothesis Play an Essential Role in the Theory of Heat Radiation?," Ehrenfest picked out the essentials of the early quantum theory and showed how they fit together. He proved rigorously that the energy of electromagnetic vibrations cannot take on all values—cannot vary continuously—if the total energy of the blackbody radiation in an enclosure is to be finite: Planck's assumption that energy is a discrete variable was, therefore, logically necessary and not just sufficient. Ehrenfest also showed, by an analysis of Wien's displacement law, that the ratio of energy to frequency was the only variable that could be quantized for a harmonic oscillator, if one wanted to maintain the statistical interpretation of entropy. Planck's quantum condition for the energy E of an oscillator of frequency v,

$$E/v = nh,$$

where n is a nonnegative integer and h is Planck's quantum of action, no longer seemed arbitrary. The quantity E/v was the only one that kept a constant value if one varied the frequency-determining parameters sufficiently slowly, that is, adiabatically.

In a series of papers that appeared from 1913 to 1916, Ehrenfest studied the possibility of generalizing the notion of quantization, previously applied only to oscillators. He showed that every periodic system possesses a property invariant under slow (adiabatic) changes in its parameters: the ratio of the kinetic energy, averaged over one period, to the frequency. Ehrenfest proposed that only such adiabatic invariants could properly be quantized and also that when the parameters of a quantized system are changed adiabatically, the allowed quantum states of the original system continue to be the allowed quantum states. Ehrenfest and his student J. M. Burgers showed that this adiabatic principle encompassed the various quantization methods introduced independently by a variety of physicists. The adiabatic principle was widely used and highly prized as one of the few reliable guides to progress during the difficult years of the "old quantum theory," when even the laws of conservation of energy and momentum were suspect.

During the late 1920's and early 1930's Ehrenfest did his utmost to try to insure the intelligibility of the new quantum mechanics and to stress its relationships with classical physics. He proved the result, still known as Ehrenfest's theorem, that quantum mechanical expectation values of coordinates and momentum obey the classical equations of motion. One of his last papers consisted entirely of a series of fundamental questions on the physical and mathematical aspects of quantum mechanics. These questions were probably troubling many physicists, but only Ehrenfest was willing to risk the odium of asking questions that might be put aside as "meaningless." They were far from that, as Wolfgang Pauli soon demonstrated by writing a paper answering some of Ehrenfest's questions.

Ehrenfest affected the development of physics even more by his personal influence on other physicists than by his writings, particularly in the last decade of his life. He traveled widely, lecturing or attending conferences, and was a welcome visitor at universities from Moscow to Pasadena. When he was at home, there were always visiting physicists—older colleagues like Planck, contemporaries like Abram Fedorovitch Joffe, or young men like Enrico Fermi and Robert Oppenheimer. Ehrenfest's way of living his physics had its effect on all who knew him, and on others through them. Both Albert Einstein and Niels Bohr were his close friends, and Ehrenfest arranged a number of the historic conversations between them on the fundamental ideas of quantum physics.

All his life Paul Ehrenfest suffered from feelings of inadequacy and inferiority. They persisted despite his extraordinary success as physicist and teacher, despite his close and warm ties to many people of many kinds. They were accentuated by the growing difficulty Ehrenfest felt in keeping up with the latest developments in his science. Finally, in September 1933, depressed by the plight of his Jewish colleagues in Nazi Germany (on whose behalf he had been exerting himself to the limit of his powers) and faced with a multitude of personal problems that seemed insuperable, Ehrenfest took his own life.

BIBLIOGRAPHY

I. Original Works. Ehrenfest's scientific papers, including his unpublished dissertation, the *Encyklopädie* article, and several lectures, are reprinted in his *Collected Scientific Papers* (Amsterdam, 1959). An English translation by M. J. Moravcsik of the *Encyklopädie* article appeared under the title *The Conceptual Foundations of the Statistical Approach in Mechanics* (Ithaca, N.Y., 1959).

Ehrenfest's MSS, notebooks, and scientific correspondence are in the National Museum for the History of Science at Leiden. For further information, see T. S. Kuhn, J. L. Heilbron, P. Forman, and L. Allen, *Sources for History of Quantum Physics* (Philadelphia, 1967), pp. 33–35.

II. Secondary Literature. For a full discussion of Ehrenfest's life and work through the period of World War I, see Martin J. Klein, *Paul Ehrenfest, I, The Making of a Theoretical Physicist* (Amsterdam, 1970). The second volume of this biography is in preparation. A biography in Russian by Viktor J. Frenkel has been announced but has not yet appeared.

Valuable information can be found in Albert Einstein's essay, "Paul Ehrenfest in Memoriam," repr. in his *Out of My Later Years* (New York, 1950), pp. 214–217; H. A. Kramers, "Physiker als Stilisten," in *Naturwissenschaften,* **23** (1935), 297–301; Wolfgang Pauli, "Paul Ehrenfest†," *ibid.,* **21** (1933), 841–843; and George E. Uhlenbeck, "Reminiscences of Professor Paul Ehrenfest," in *American Journal of Physics,* **24** (1956), 431–433.

Martin J. Klein

EHRET

EHRET, GEORG DIONYSIUS (*b.* Heidelberg, Germany, 30 January 1708; *d.* London, England, 9 September 1770), *botany.*

Ehret was a gifted artist and teacher whose skillfully executed botanical drawings significantly advanced the knowledge of many new and exotic plants. His work and teaching contributed to the successful introduction of the Linnaean system into England.

Ehret was the son of a poor gardener to the margrave of Baden-Durlach. His father's early death forced him to leave school and begin an apprenticeship as a gardener with his uncle. During the ensuing years he worked as a journeyman gardener in several cities of Germany, executing at the same time a large number of drawings and paintings of the plants under his care. The turning point of his career came about 1732, when Ehret made the acquaintance of the German botanist and physician Christoph Jacob Trew. The financial good fortune resulting from Trew's patronage enabled Ehret to travel across Europe. He visited the most celebrated gardens in France and Holland, collecting and drawing many rare plants. In 1734 he met the French botanist Bernard de Jussieu in Paris, and shortly thereafter the English physician and botanist Hans Sloane in London. His travels culminated with a visit to the great Swedish botanist Linnaeus in 1737, at Haarlem. There he completed all the illustrations for Linnaeus' book *Hortus Cliffortianus,* which was published in the same year. Ehret returned to England in 1740 and began his successful career as an artist and teacher. Among his patrons were the English naturalists Sir Joseph Banks and Griffith Hughes, the physicians Richard Mead and John Fothergill, and the duchess of Portland. He was also temporarily employed at the botanical garden of the University of Oxford in 1750–1751. Ehret was elected fellow of the Royal Society on 19 May 1757 and read several botanical papers before the group. His name was immortalized in the genus *Ehretia,* an honor proposed by his lifelong friend and mentor Trew and confirmed by Linnaeus.

BIBLIOGRAPHY

I. ORIGINAL WORKS. "A Memoir of Georg Dionysius Ehret," translated into English, with notes, by E. S. Barton, is in *Proceedings of the Linnean Society of London* (1894–1895), pp. 41–58; Ehret's original German MS is preserved in the botanical department of the British Museum. With Christoph J. Trew he published *Plantae selectae quarum imagines ad exemplaria naturalia Londini in hortis curiosorum nutrita* (Nuremberg, 1750–1773). Some of his paintings were collected in *Twelve Coloured Reproductions From the Original Paintings on Vellum,* with an introduction and descriptive text by Wilfrid Blunt (Guildford, England, 1953). Among Ehret's articles the following should be mentioned: "An Account of a Species of Ophris," in *Philosophical Transactions of the Royal Society,* **53** (1763), 81–83; "An Account of a New Peruvian Plant Lately Introduced Into the English Gardens," *ibid.,* 130–132; and "A Description of the Andrachne With Its Botanical Characters," *ibid.,* **57** (1767), 114–117.

II. SECONDARY LITERATURE. For a short and almost contemporary account of Ehret's life see Richard Pulteney, *Historical and Biographical Sketches of the Progress of Botany in England* (London, 1790), II, 284–293. Other biographies appeared in *Dictionary of National Biography,* VI, 585; *Proceedings of the Linnean Society of London* (1883–1884), 42–43; and in *Journal of Botany, British and Foreign,* **34** (1896), 316–317. Seven letters written to Ehret by Linnaeus between 1736 and 1769 were published in *Proceedings of the Linnean Society of London* (1883–1884), 44–51.

GUENTER B. RISSE

EHRLICH

EHRLICH, PAUL (*b.* Strehlen, Germany [now Strzelin, Poland], 14 March 1854; *d.* Bad Homburg, Germany, 20 August 1915), *hematology, immunology, chemotherapy.*

Among medical scientists of his generation Ehrlich was probably the most original, stimulating, and successful. The fruitfulness of his concepts initiated advances in all fields of biomedical research to which they were applied. Hematology became a recognized discipline through his pioneering studies of dye reactions on red and white blood cells. In exhaustive experiments on the production of high-potency diphtheria antitoxin and on methods of assaying and standardizing such products, he developed techniques and established fundamental principles of immunity. His crowning achievement was the synthesis of Salvarsan and the demonstration of its therapeutic efficacy in syphilis and allied diseases.

Paul Ehrlich was born into a comfortable, lively household in a country town in Prussian Silesia, about twenty miles south of Breslau (now Wrocław, Poland). He was the only son and fourth child of Ismar Ehrlich, a respected but somewhat eccentric Jewish distiller, innkeeper, and lottery collector, and his wife Rosa Weigert, an industrious woman of notable intelligence, charm, and organizational talent. Her cousin Carl Weigert, the distinguished pathologist, was only nine years older than Paul, and the two became close friends. Besides many of his mother's characteristics the boy had his father's excitability and interjection-ridden manner of speech, and perhaps inherited certain aptitudes from his paternal grandfather, Heimann Ehrlich, a prosperous liqueur merchant, who collected an extensive private library and late in life gave lectures on science to fellow citizens of Strehlen.

In 1860, when he was six years old, Ehrlich entered the local primary school. At age ten he went to the St. Maria Magdalena Humanistic Gymnasium in Breslau and boarded with a professor's family. He accepted Spartan living and classroom conditions; was unobtrusive and conscientious; and though not outstanding, was often near the top of his class. He disliked all examinations, however. His favorite subjects were mathematics and Latin; his weakest was German composition.

After matriculating in 1872, Ehrlich took a disappointing introductory course in natural sciences at Breslau University and then spent three semesters at Strasbourg, which largely determined his life's course. He was impressed by the anatomist Wilhelm von Waldeyer's broad comprehension of medicine, and the professor in turn noted the many extra hours this unusual student devoted to making excellent histological preparations with his own modifications of new aniline dyes. Ehrlich visited the Waldeyer household, and a lasting friendship was established.

Although lacking formal courses in chemistry, Ehrlich became fascinated with the subject while studying for his *Physikum* at Strasbourg. Having passed this examination, he returned in 1874 to Breslau, where he completed studies for his medical degree, except for one semester in 1876 at the Physiology Institute of Freiburg im Breisgau and a final term at Leipzig in 1878. In Breslau he was influenced by the pathologists Julius Cohnheim and Carl Weigert, the physiologist Rudolf Heidenhain, and the botanist Ferdinand Cohn, sponsor of Robert Koch's researches on anthrax bacilli. At the Pathology Institute, Ehrlich became friendly with such outstanding visitors as W. H. Welch, the American pathologist, and C. J. Salomonsen, the Danish bacteriologist. Weigert had introduced aniline dyes into microscopic technique, and in his cousin's laboratory Ehrlich studied their selective action on cells and tissues. His first paper on the properties of these dyes appeared in 1877, in which year he passed the state medical examination. His doctoral dissertation, "Beiträge zur Theorie und Praxis der histologischen Färbung," was approved at Leipzig University in 1878. These two works included descriptions of large, distinctively stained cells containing basophilic granules, for which Ehrlich coined the term "mast cells," differentiating them from the rounded "plasma cells" observed in connective tissue by Waldeyer. In 1879 he defined and named the eosinophil cells of the blood.

Upon graduation Ehrlich was appointed head physician (*Oberarzt*) in Friedrich von Frerichs' renowned medical clinic at the Charité Hospital in Berlin. Frerichs, an imaginative clinician with deep interests in experimental pathology, encouraged Ehrlich's histological and biochemical researches, and the latter thereby gained lasting insights into diagnostic and therapeutic problems. His reports on the morphology, physiology, and pathology of the blood cells advanced hematology into a new era by establishing methods of detecting and differentiating the leukemias and anemias. Further, the observations that basic, acidic, and neutral dyes reacted specifically with such cellular components as leukocyte granules and nuclei implanted in Ehrlich's mind the fundamental concept underlying his future work: that chemical affinities govern all biological processes. He extended comparable staining methods to bacteria and protozoa and rendered Koch's discovery of the tubercle bacillus immediately more important by showing that its failure to stain in aqueous dye solutions could be circumvented by use of basic dyes in an aqueous-aniline oil solution, which penetrated the bacillary coating and then remained acid-fast.

Ehrlich was determined to explore the avidity of living tissues for certain dyes. In 1885 a remarkable monograph, *Das Sauerstoffbedürfnis des Organismus,* reporting his investigations into the distribution of oxygen in animal tissues and organs, gained widespread attention from medical scientists. Using two vital-staining dyes, alizarin blue (reducible to a leuko form with difficulty) and indophenol blue (readily reducible), he demonstrated that while living protoplasm in general has potent reducing properties, bodily organs are classifiable into three categories according to their oxygen avidity. Challenging Pflüger's assertion that tissue oxidation and reduction entail direct entry and exit of oxygen, he contended that these processes involve withdrawal and insertion of hydrogen atoms. Two years later the monograph won the Tiedemann Prize and served as Ehrlich's *Habilitation* thesis before he became *Privatdozent* in internal medicine at Berlin University. In 1886 he described methylene blue as a selective vital stain for ganglionic cells, axis cylinders, and nerve endings. Later, with A. Leppmann, he used this dye therapeutically to kill pain in neuralgias; and in 1891, with P. Guttmann, he pursued to its logical conclusion the finding that malaria parasites stain well with methylene blue, administering the dye to two malarial patients with apparent success.

Further by-products of Ehrlich's ingenuity with dyestuffs were the use of fluorescein to observe the streaming of the optic humors (1882) and his diazo reaction, a color test for the presence of bilirubin in the urine, regarded long afterward as a useful prognostic test in severe acute infections, such as typhoid fever (1883). His other Charité investigations that strengthened the developing conviction that chemical composition, distribution within the body, and pharmacological effect of biologically active substances were interrelated included the treatment of iodine poisoning by detoxification with sulfanilic acid (1885); the lipotropism of thalline and its homologues, and the dependence of thalline's antipyretic action on the ortho-position of the methoxyl group in the molecule (1886); the correlation between lipotropism and neurotropism, as displayed in rabbits inoculated with certain dyes of the basic and the nitrated, but not the sulfonic acid, groups (1887); and the demonstration that liver degeneration in cocaine-poisoned mice was not caused by the benzoyl radical responsible for the drug's anesthetizing properties (1890).

In 1883 Ehrlich had married Hedwig Pinkus, daughter of a prosperous textile industrialist of Neustadt, Upper Silesia, whom he had met during a visit to Strehlen. Ten years his junior, she proved an understanding, faithful companion, and their marriage was happy. They had two daughters—Stephanie, born in 1884, and Marianne, born in 1886—to whom he was greatly attached. One year after his marriage Ehrlich was made a titular professor at Berlin, on Frerichs' recommendation. When Frerichs died suddenly in 1885 and the more conservative Karl Gerhardt succeeded him, Ehrlich found his researches disturbingly impeded. In 1888, discovering tubercle bacilli (presumably of laboratory origin) in his sputum, he ended a decade of fruitful association with the clinic and journeyed with his young wife to Egypt, where he stayed over a year. In 1889 he returned to Berlin apparently cured of pulmonary tuberculosis, received Koch's newly discovered tuberculin treatment, and never had a recurrence.

Now without appointment, Ehrlich set up a small private laboratory in a rented flat and launched a series of fundamental studies in immunity that captured attention for many years. Using as antigens the toxic plant proteins ricin and abrin, he demonstrated that young mice could be protected against these agents if fed or injected with them in initially minute but increasing dosages. Such "actively" immunized mice developed high levels of specific antibodies in their blood. After describing these observations in two papers entitled "Experimentelle Untersuchungen über Immunität" (1891), Ehrlich showed that the progeny of a ricin- or abrin-immunized mother inherited a specific transient immunity, sustainable at higher levels by sucklings through absorption of antitoxin in the maternal milk. A similar state of "pas-

sive" immunity was induced in the progeny of a nonimmune mother that were suckled by an actively immunized mouse. Further, a normal lactating mouse injected with antiserum from an animal highly immunized against abrin, ricin, or tetanus toxin conferred specific passive immunity upon her offspring. These "wet nurse" and related experiments were reported in 1892.

Some of this work was carried out during Ehrlich's brief appointment (arranged by Koch in 1890) as clinical supervisor at the Moabit Municipal Hospital in Berlin. There he and P. Guttmann found that small doses of tuberculin were valuable in pulmonary and laryngeal tuberculosis. Ehrlich reported this finding at the Seventh International Congress for Hygiene and Demography at London in 1891. Thereafter he performed his immunological studies in a small laboratory at the newly founded Institute for Infectious Diseases in Berlin, of which Koch had become director. Ehrlich worked here for more than three years without salary, despite his appointment as extraordinary professor at Berlin University in 1891.

The institute's dedication to problems of infection, his own experiences with tuberculin, and Emil von Behring's discoveries of diphtheria and tetanus antitoxins led Ehrlich to investigate bacterial toxins and antitoxins by methods comparable with those employed in his plant protein studies. With L. Brieger he produced potent antitoxic serums in actively immunized large animals and demonstrated that these substances could be concentrated and partially purified. In 1894 he reported, with H. Kossel and A. von Wassermann, on 220 unselected diphtheritic children treated with antitoxin, stressing the importance of early, liberal dosages. Meanwhile, Behring had overcome serious difficulties in diphtheria antitoxin production by exploiting Ehrlich's assistance, procuring for himself a remunerative contract for supervising commercial manufacture of antitoxin.

Early in 1895, on the initiative of the director of the Prussian Ministry of Educational and Medical Affairs, Friedrich Althoff, an enlightened public servant who admired Ehrlich's ability, an antitoxin control station was established at Koch's institute under the supervision of Ehrlich, assisted by Kossel and Wassermann. This function was transferred in 1896 to a center for serum research and testing at Steglitz, a Berlin suburb. Ehrlich was appointed director, with Wilhelm Dönitz, and later Julius Morgenroth and Max Neisser, as his associates. The Institut für Serumforschung und Serumprüfung consisted of a one-story ramshackle building, variously described as a former almshouse or disused bakery, with an adjacent stable for laboratory animals. Nevertheless,

Ehrlich took pride in his unpretentious establishment, and excellent work was done in it.

After months of arduous work involving "hecatombs" of guinea pigs, he concluded that serum samples should be assayed in terms of a relatively stable international unit of antitoxin, distributable in dried form in vacuum tubes. Moreover, in titration the "test dose" of toxin should be the minimum amount that, added to one standard unit of antitoxin, kills within four days a 250-gram guinea pig injected therewith. These recommendations were widely adopted, and Ehrlich's L†, or *Limes-Tod,* designation for the test dose survives among his striking legacy of biomedical terms. Besides such practical accomplishments he sought theoretical explanations for the instability of diphtheria toxins that involved their lethality for guinea pigs and their ratio of lethality to antitoxin-binding power. He considered the interaction between diphtheria toxin and antitoxin a chemical process in which the reagents combine in constant proportion, as did abrin and ricin with their respective antiserums.

Ehrlich also surmised arbitrarily that one standard unit of antitoxin should fully neutralize exactly 200 minimal doses of pure toxin. When unpredictable rates of toxin degradation and varying avidities among antitoxin samples challenged this oversimplified view, he postulated the formation of toxoids (with combining power intact but toxicity absent) and of epitoxoids or toxones (with lessened combining power and altered toxicity). According to Ehrlich, each preparation of crude toxin had its own "spectrum" (*Giftspektrum*), divided into 200 segments, in which toxin, toxoid, and other designated components showed simple quantitative interrelationships.

Although certain of these proposals, set forth in the papers "Die Wertbemessung des Diphtherieheilserums und deren theoretische Grundlagen" (1897), and "Ueber die Constitution des Diphtheriegiftes" (1898), mystified some readers and aroused opposition from others, in the main they won acceptance and brought their author international recognition. He was appointed *Geheimer Medizinalrat* in 1897. Althoff realized that Ehrlich's genius deserved better facilities, and with the lord mayor of Frankfurt am Main, Franz Adickes, arranged for construction of a suitable building near the city hospital. Opened in 1899, the Royal Prussian Institute for Experimental Therapy was directed by Ehrlich until his death sixteen years later.

The new "Serum Institute" was not only responsible for routine state control of immunotherapeutic agents, such as tuberculin and diphtheria antitoxin, but also for research and training in experimental therapy. To this latter function Ehrlich devoted himself and his disciples, including Dönitz, Neisser, and Morgenroth, who followed him from Steglitz, and such subsequent staff members as Hans Sachs, E. von Dungen, E. Marx, Hugo Apolant, and Alfred Bertheim. In 1906 the adjacent Research Institute for Chemotherapy (designated the Georg-Speyer-Haus) was erected and endowed by Franziska Speyer in memory of her late husband. She did so on the advice of her brother, L. Darmstädter, to whom the promising possibilities of the specific chemotherapy of infectious diseases had been expounded by Ehrlich early in 1905. His spreading fame brought numerous visitors from abroad to work in the combined institutes, including Reid Hunt, Christian Herter, and Preston Keyes from the United States, Carl Browning and H. H. (later Sir Henry) Dale from Britain, and Kiyoshi Shiga and Sahachiro Hata from Japan.

Ehrlich's activities in Frankfurt fall into three periods. The first, 1899–1906, was marked by the emergence and elaboration of his side-chain theory, the conclusion of his work on diphtheria, extensive researches into the mechanisms of hemolytic reactions (with Morgenroth), and his cancer investigations (with Apolant). The second period dates from an address at the ceremonial opening of the Georg-Speyer-Haus in September 1906, in which Ehrlich prophesied the creation of substances "in the chemist's retort" that would "be able to exert their full action exclusively on the parasite harbored within the organism and would represent, so to speak, magic bullets which seek their target of their own accord." It culminated in his announcement before the Congress for Internal Medicine at Wiesbaden, in April 1910, that a synthetic arsenical compound, which he called dioxy-diamidoarsenobenzol (Salvarsan), had shown curative properties in rabbit syphilis and fowl spirillosis, and also in clinical trials on syphilitic patients. The third period, 1910–1915, covered Ehrlich's gallant struggle to handle the multiplex problems that followed the discovery of Salvarsan. The highlights of these periods will be reviewed consecutively.

In the final publications begun at Steglitz, Ehrlich summarized his doctrine of the interrelationship of "composition, distribution, and effect" and outlined his side-chain theory. This theory, presaged in his *Sauerstoffbedürfnis* (1885), was brought into focus mainly to account for diphtheria toxin's two distinct attributes, toxicity and antitoxin-binding power. It postulated two different chemical groups in the toxin molecule, one designated haptophore and the other toxophore. The former "anchors" the toxin molecule to the side chains (later termed "receptors") of a cell for which it has chemical affinity, by a process akin to the "lock and key" simile of the organic chemist

Emil Fischer, thus exposing the cell to damage or destruction by the toxophore group. If the cell survives the attack, the receptors rendered inert by combination with the haptophore group are replicated to excess, following Weigert's theory that tissue injury incites proliferative regeneration. Some of these surplus receptors, adapted to absorbing and neutralizing the toxin molecules, are shed and appear as circulating antitoxin—in Ehrlich's words, "handed over as superfluous ballast to the blood."

The theory was expounded by Ehrlich in his Croonian lecture, "On Immunity With Special Reference to Cell Life," delivered before the Royal Society in 1900. This fertile, heuristic hypothesis was a bold attempt to integrate the newer knowledge of nutrition, immunology, and pharmacology, but the ingenious arguments advanced by Ehrlich to bring fresh data within its purview were sometimes farfetched or obscure. He investigated the hemolytic reactions of animal serums reported by Jules Bordet in 1898 because they showed analogies to bacteriolytic phenomena and could be studied precisely *in vitro*. Bordet's observation—that the heterolysin produced by injecting an animal with red blood cells from an alien species became manifest only in the presence of a heat-labile factor (designated "alexine" by Bordet and "complement" by Ehrlich), found in most fresh normal serums—was confirmed. Whereas Bordet contended that alexine destroyed the red cells after their sensitization by a single immune body (*substance sensibilatrice*), Ehrlich visualized a far more complex situation. In several papers written with Morgenroth (1899–1901) he postulated two haptophore components in the immune body of an active hemolysin, one having strong affinity for the corresponding red blood cell receptor, the other combining with complement. Later he compared the immune body (amboceptor) and complement to the haptophore and toxophore groups of a toxin and presupposed an "extraordinary multiplicity" of hemolysins and a plurality of complements.

From Steglitz, in the midst of illuminating and practically unchallenged toxin-antitoxin titrations, Ehrlich had confided his perplexity and disenchantment to Carl Weigert. The situation now was different. In 1901 Max von Gruber launched a two-year polemic, which became inexcusably insulting, against the side-chain theory. Moreover, Svante Arrhenius and Thorvald Madsen, and Bordet as well, constructively criticized Ehrlich's views on the strictly chemical nature of the union between diphtheria toxin and antitoxin. At Frankfurt pertinacious efforts to clarify the mechanisms of hemolytic and toxin-antitoxin reactions continued. When J. Bang and

J. Forssman criticized the side-chain theory anew in 1909, Ehrlich and Sachs defended it in two final papers. To confound contemporaries who proclaimed the theory without practical value and its creator a "theoretician," Wassermann testified that the complement-fixation test for syphilis could not have been developed without Ehrlich's teaching.

In 1901 Adickes and Althoff persuaded the Theodor Stern Foundation to finance a cancer research station at the Serum Institute. After two rather unproductive years, C. J. Jensen's discovery that mouse mammary tumors are malignant and transplantable incited Ehrlich and Apolant to perform thousands of tumor-grafting experiments. Applying familiar techniques to this new field, they increased the tumor virulence for mice tenfold, until 100 percent of grafts took; and with single injections of slightly virulent cell suspensions they induced high degrees of immunity against virulent transplanted tumors. While closely following over many generations the structural changes that accompanied increased virulence, they observed a strain of mouse carcinoma apparently transforming into sarcoma. To explain the failure of a second graft to grow in an animal already carrying a tumor, whereas after resection of the first tumor a subsequent graft would take, Ehrlich coined the term "athreptic immunity." "Athrepsia," derived from the Greek $\tau\rho\epsilon\phi\omega$, "to nourish," signified exhaustion of the host's supply of nutrients essential for tumor growth. In his second Harben lecture (1907), Ehrlich suggested broader applications of the term—which, however, found little acceptance. This cancer work represented an unsought digression from his main course, and by 1909 chemotherapeutic researches had entirely superseded it.

In his long-standing aim to discover synthetic chemicals that act specifically upon pathogenic microorganisms, Ehrlich was aided by Arthur Weinberg and Ludwig Benda, director and chemist, respectively, of the Farbwerke Cassella & Co. near Frankfurt, who made compounds to his specifications even before the Georg-Speyer-Haus was established. In 1904 he reported with Shiga that one such substance, trypan red, cured mice experimentally infected with *Trypanosoma equinum,* causal parasite of *mal de caderas.* When he and Bechhold investigated the relationship between molecular constitution and disinfectant action of phenolic compounds upon bacterial suspensions, they found these effects inhibited by serum; moreover, the agents proved toxic and failed to produce "internal antisepsis" when injected into artificially infected animals. Hence Ehrlich pursued his earlier chemotherapeutic studies on trypanosome-infected mice and rats.

Recurrent infections in treated animals were ascribed to specific resistance to trypan red and related dyes acquired by the surviving parasites. However, such resistant strains were susceptible to atoxyl, an arsenical compound reported by H. W. Thomas and A. Breinl in 1905 to cure trypanosome-infected rodents. Ehrlich therefore postulated sessile "chemoceptors" (including an "arsenoceptor") in the parasite's protoplasm that were not released into the blood like antitoxin but had anchoring facilities for certain specific radicals. In 1907, having discovered that atoxyl was the sodium salt of *p*-aminophenylarsonic acid, or arsanilic acid, he and Bertheim synthesized and tested several hundred derivative compounds. By tailoring molecular appendages to fit the receptors of broadly resistant trypanosomal strains, they hoped to create drugs of maximum "parasitotropism" and minimum "organotropism."

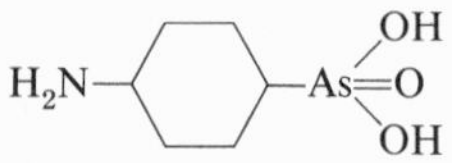

FIGURE 1. *p*-Aminophenylarsonic Acid
(Arsanilic Acid)

Meanwhile, Paul Uhlenhuth and others, stimulated by E. Roux and Elie Metchnikoff's successful transfer of syphilis to apes (1903), Fritz Schaudinn's discovery of the spirochete of syphilis (1905), and certain parallels between spirochetal and trypanosomal infections in animals and man, reported beneficial effects from atoxyl treatment of dourine, fowl spirillosis, and syphilis in rabbits, apes, and man. Since blindness sometimes followed treatment of human sleeping sickness with this agent, Ehrlich sought safer and more effective remedies. For example, arsacetin, prepared by introducing the acetyl radical into the amino group of atoxyl, was less poisonous and cured mice a few hours away from death, but it was still too toxic for clinical use.

Late in 1908, lecturing before the German Chemical Society, Ehrlich described a trivalent arseno-benzene compound of low toxicity for mice that was derived from atoxyl by two-stage reduction. This was arsenophenylglycine, number 418 in the series under test. Its high trypanocidal effectiveness inspired Ehrlich to introduce one of his favorite and best-known Latin tags, "therapia sterilisans magna," denoting "complete sterilization of a highly infected host at one blow." Six weeks later, in his Nobel lecture, "Ueber Partialfunctionen der Zelle," he asserted that through this substance "one can actually, with all kinds of animals and with every kind of trypanosome infection, achieve a complete cure by a single injection." In trials elsewhere, particularly by his friend

from earliest school days, the Breslau dermatologist Albert Neisser, arsenophenylglycine gave excellent results in the treatment of dourine and other treponemal diseases of animals but was less satisfactory in fowl spirillosis and in simian and human syphilis. Moreover, it was unstable, forming toxic oxidation products.

The search for an agent whose therapeutic index (ratio of curative to tolerated dose) was very small halted in 1909. Hata arrived that spring from Tokyo to work with Ehrlich. He was familiar with rabbit syphilis, and the emphasis switched to this and fowl spirillosis for appraisal of the many new compounds now on hand. Hata found number 606, dihydroxy-diamino-arsenobenzene-dihydrochloride (distantly related to arsanilic acid through a three-stage reduction process), had a "dosis curativa" to "dosis tolerata" ratio for fowl spirillosis of only 1:58. Intensive trials on rabbit syphilis confirmed the outstanding spirocheticidal properties of this compound. Ehrlich released limited supplies to selected specialists for clinical trials. Paralytic syphilis cases showed little improvement, but in relapsing fever and early syphilis the results were excellent. After additional favorable trials, Ehrlich, Hata, and several clinicians announced their findings in April 1910, before the Congress for Internal Medicine at Wiesbaden.

The rush for the new remedy was uncontrollable. Ehrlich tried to restrict its distribution to qualified acquaintances in various countries but was importuned by mail and by physicians who flocked to Frankfurt. Five months later, at another congress in Königsberg, he announced that "606" would not be generally available until 10,000–20,000 cases had received treatment, but further enthusiastic reports increased the demand. By the year's end, when the full resources of the Georg-Speyer-Haus had provided about 65,000 doses gratis, large-scale facilities at the nearby Höchst Chemical Works were enlisted and the product patented under the name Salvarsan. In the United States it later became known as arsphenamine.

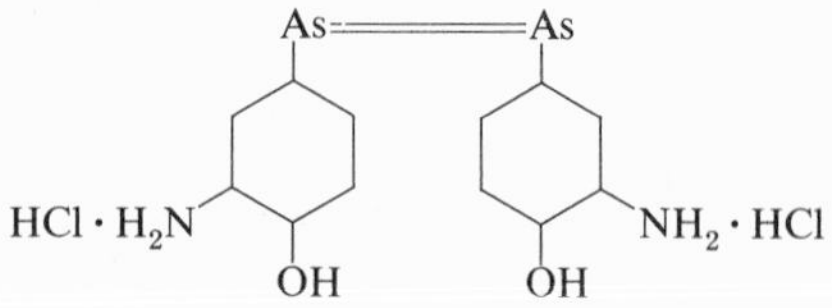

FIGURE 2. Dihydroxydiamino-arsenobenzene-dihydrochloride
(Salvarsan, Arsphenamine)

The invention of Salvarsan brought Ehrlich four years of both tragedy and triumph. He battled problems that stemmed from the drug's imperfections, from the complex pathology of syphilis, and from human carelessness, cupidity, and malice. The tricky manufacturing process and rigid biological tests on every batch came under his scrutiny. The best method of administration for counteracting the product's oxidizability and acidity and for reducing reactions remained uncertain; and although Ehrlich emphasized the therapeutic principle "frapper fort et frapper vite," routes of injection and dosages were still largely empirical. His ideal, "sterilisatio magna," was apparently feasible for relapsing fever, yaws, and certain animal diseases, but it seemed elusive or unattainable in syphilis. Neurological recurrences in undertreated cases and Jarisch-Herxheimer reactions (from hypersensitivity to massively destroyed spirochetes) were alarming, despite Ehrlich's explanations. Again, on every possible patient serological reports on Wassermann's complement-fixation test were correlated with clinical progress. As each complaint or complication was pursued, Ehrlich's correspondence reached staggering proportions and the institute overflowed with visiting physicians and would-be patients. Meanwhile, he published several reviews and edited collections of reports on Salvarsan and chemotherapy. Despite all the turmoil, he devised an arsenical derivative, number 914, which went into neutral solution without loss of effectiveness. It was introduced for clinical use in 1912 as Neosalvarsan. With Paul Karrer, his last collaborator, Ehrlich attempted further improvements by combining Salvarsan with such metals as copper, silver, bismuth, and mercury.

Such burdens would have daunted and overtaxed any man. Ehrlich's frail health began to crumble, and his peace of mind was disturbed by calumnies. Fanatic sensationalists accused him of charlatanism, profiteering, and ruthless experimentalism. The slander continued, led by the Berlin police doctor, until in March 1914 the Reichstag, forced to debate the merits of Salvarsan, endorsed it as "a very valuable enrichment of the remedies against syphilis." Three months later Ehrlich was defense witness for the Frankfurt Hospital when a local newspaper brought suit alleging that prostitutes were being forcibly subjected to dangerous treatment with Salvarsan. The complainant was sentenced to one year in jail. The outbreak of World War I drew public attention elsewhere, and Ehrlich suffered no further indignities.

Ardently although quietly patriotic and on friendly terms at court, Ehrlich was grievously distressed by the war; he brooded over his isolation from scientific friends abroad and was disconcerted by the enforced diversion of the institute's activities. In December 1914 he suffered a slight stroke. The arteriosclerotic and diabetic manifestations were treated by banning the strong cigars that he habitually smoked to excess

and by regimenting his diet, but he regained neither health nor sanguine temperament. Persuaded early in August 1915 to enter a sanatorium for treatment and rest, he shortly had a second, peacefully terminal stroke. He was buried in the Frankfurt Jewish Cemetery.

Many honors came his way. After sharing the 1908 Nobel Prize with Metchnikoff, awarded in recognition of their work on immunity, Ehrlich was renominated in 1912 and 1913 for his contributions to chemotherapy. The value of Salvarsan was considered still too disputed; and before the question was settled, Ehrlich had died. He received the Prussian Great Gold Medal for Science (1903), the Liebig Medal (1911), and the Cameron Prize (1914). Twelve orders (ten from foreign governments) and five honorary doctorates were conferred on him. He was granted the title of *Geheimer Obermedizinalrat* in 1907 and of *Wirklicher Geheimer Rat,* with the predicate *Excellenz,* in 1911. From 1904 he was honorary ordinary professor at Göttingen, and in 1914 he became ordinary professor at the new Frankfurt University. He held honorary or foreign memberships in about eighty scientific and medical societies. In 1912 he received the freedom of the city of Frankfurt, and the street containing his institutes was renamed Paul-Ehrlich-Strasse. His friends and disciples celebrated his sixtieth birthday in 1914 by preparing a remarkable *Festschrift,* each of whose thirty-seven chapters commemorated one aspect of his manifold accomplishments. The Paul Ehrlich Prize for outstanding achievement in one of his fields of research is given biennially by the Paul Ehrlich Institut as a living memorial to him.

Despite the varied nature of his investigations, a unifying principle is discernible throughout. As a student Ehrlich was fascinated by E. H. Heubel's observation (1871) that in chronic lead poisoning the organs showed wide differences in content of the toxic element, differences that were paralleled in organs from normal animals immersed in dilute lead solutions. Thus the fruitful doctrine was initiated that biological activities are determined by specific chemical affinities and are quantitatively measurable. Ehrlich's early work on dyes, on the oxygen need of the tissues, and on methylene blue treatment of malaria strengthened this belief, which also animated his chemotherapeutic strivings. The adapted aphorism "Corpora non agunt nisi fixata," introduced in his address on chemotherapy before the 1913 International Congress of Medicine in London, epitomized a concept that is still valid and fruitful, particularly in cytochemistry.

To the creative momentum of a sound original

principle of broad applicability, Ehrlich harnessed brilliant talents: a darting intelligence linked to untrammeled imagination; compulsive industriousness; the faculty of stereognostically visualizing benzene rings and structural chemical formulas; technical ingenuity and punctiliousness, and unique virtuosity in "test-tube" chemistry; the capacity to direct several lines of research simultaneously, through a system of daily "blocks" carrying written instructions to every co-worker; and the foresight to abandon paths that were unpromising. An autodidact, he was nobody's disciple. His gift for coining words, phrases, and metaphors enriched the common vocabulary of science. Ehrlich conversed and lectured in German only, but he could read English and French and perused relevant scientific publications avidly and rapidly (reading "diagonally"). His tastes in general literature aspired no higher than Conan Doyle and he lacked feeling for art, but he was refreshed by simple music.

By nature Ehrlich was enthusiastic, good-humored, at times even bantering; but meanness, unfair criticism, or false claims to priority aroused fierce indignation. Although genuinely modest, he knew the importance of his work. He never lobbied for his own ends, was devoid of mercenary instinct, and was completely honorable in all his dealings. Lovably loyal to his family and countless friends, he was the very embodiment of minor eccentricity and true genius. As Sir Robert Muir wrote, "Ehrlich must be with the greatest, however small that company may be."

BIBLIOGRAPHY

I. ORIGINAL WORKS. The most complete edition is *The Collected Papers of Paul Ehrlich,* compiled and edited by F. Himmelweit, assisted by Martha Marquardt, under the general direction of Sir Henry Dale (London–New York, 1956–1960). The first 3 vols. contain all his important papers, including a few hitherto unpublished. These are grouped according to topics: vol. I, *Histology, Biochemistry, and Pathology;* vol. II, *Immunology and Cancer Research;* vol. III, *Chemotherapy.* Vol. IV (not yet published) will include his letters and a complete bibliography. Of 158 publications reproduced in this edition, all are in German except 11 articles which originally appeared in English or French. Fresh English translations are appended to 15 of the remaining 147 items.

Ehrlich's pupil and co-worker Hans Sachs compiled a bibliography in 1914 as an appendix to Ehrlich's sixtieth birthday *Festschrift* (see below). This listed 212 separate publications in well-known journals, as well as several monographs, over the period 1877–1913. Ehrlich was sole author of roughly three-quarters of these items, many of which underwent multiple publication. Sachs also appended a bibliography of 400 reports by Ehrlich's disciples.

Apart from the special translations in the *Collected Papers,* Ehrlich's Croonian (1900), Herter (1904), and Harben (1907) lectures were first published in English-language journals (see below). The Harben lectures were republished as *Experimental Researches on Specific Therapy* (London, 1908). *Collected Studies in Immunity* (New York, 1906), C. Bolduan, trans., includes 41 reports by Ehrlich and his co-workers between 1899 and early 1906, of which 38 had appeared previously in *Gesammelte Arbeiten zur Immunitätsforschung* (Berlin, 1904). A later edition of *Collected Studies* (1910) contains Bolduan's translations of Ehrlich's Nobel Prize address and of seven additional papers by his pupils.

Other collections of Ehrlich's papers in book form are *Farbenanalytische Untersuchungen zur Histologie und Klinik des Blutes* (Berlin, 1891); *Constitution, Vertheilung und Wirkung chemischer Körper; ältere und neuere Arbeiten* (Leipzig, 1893); and *Beiträge zur experimentellen Pathologie und Chemotherapie* (Leipzig, 1909). He also published several monographs, including his *Habilitation* thesis, *Das Sauerstoffbedürfnis des Organismus. Eine farbenanalytische Studie* (Berlin, 1885); *Die Anaemie* (Vienna, 1898–1900), written with A. Lazarus; *Leukaemie. Pseudoleukaemie. Haemoglobinaemie* (Vienna, 1901), written with A. Lazarus and F. Pinkus; *Die experimentelle Chemotherapie der Spirillosen* (Berlin, 1910), written with S. Hata; *Aus Theorie und Praxis der Chemotherapie* (Leipzig, 1911); and *Grundlagen und Erfolge der Chemotherapie* (Stuttgart, 1911). Ehrlich was coeditor, with R. Krause, M. Mosse, H. Rosin, and C. Weigert, of *Enzyklopädie der mikroskopischen Technik,* 3 vols. (Vienna, 1902–1903; 2nd ed., 1910; 3rd ed., 1926–1927); he was sole editor of *Abhandlungen über Salvarsan,* 4 vols. (Munich, 1911–1914); contributed chapters and forewords to several monographs; and wrote obituaries of or tributes to E. Albrecht, H. Apolant, A. Bertheim, R. Koch, and C. Weigert.

Among his more important and characteristic reports in scientific and medical journals are "Beiträge zur Kenntnis der Anilinfärbungen und ihrer Verwendung in der mikroskopischen Technik," in *Archiv für mikroskopische Anatomie,* **13** (1877), 263–277, published while he was still a medical student; "Beiträge zur Theorie und Praxis der histologischen Färbung," his inaugural dissertation at Leipzig University (1878); "Beiträge zur Kenntnis der granulirten Bindegewebszellen und der eosinophilen Leukocythen," in *Archiv für Anatomie und Physiologie,* Physiologische Abteilung (1879), 166–169; "Ueber die spezifischen Granulationen des Blutes," *ibid.,* 571–579; "Methodologische Beiträge zur Physiologie und Pathologie der verschiedenen Formen der Leukocyten," in *Zeitschrift für klinische Medizin,* **1** (1880), 553–560; "Ueber paroxysmale Hämoglobinurie," in *Deutsche medizinische Wochenschrift,* **7** (1881), 224–225; "Ueber provocirte Fluorescenzerscheinungen am Auge," *ibid.,* **8** (1882), 21–22, 35–37, 54–55; "Ueber eine neue Methode zur Färbung von Tuberkelbacillen," in *Berliner klinische Wochenschrift,* **20** (1883), 13; "Ueber eine neue Harnprobe," in *Charité-Annalen,* **8** (1883), 140–166; and "Zur biologischen Verwertung des Methylenblaus," in *Zentralblatt für die medizinische Wissenschaft,* **23** (1885), 113–117.

Other papers include "Ueber Wesen und Behandlung des Jodismus," in *Charité-Annalen,* **10** (1885), 129–135; "Zur Physiologie und Pathologie der Blutscheiben," *ibid.,* 136–146; "Ueber die Methylenblaureaction der lebenden Nervensubstanz," in *Deutsche medizinische Wochenschrift,* **12** (1886), 49–52; "Beiträge zur Theorie der Bacillenfärbung," in *Charité-Annalen,* **11** (1886), 123–138; "Experimentelles und Klinisches über Thallin," in *Deutsche medizinische Wochenschrift,* **12** (1886), 849–851, 889–891; "Zur therapeutischen Bedeutung der substitutierenden Schwefelsäuregruppe," in *Therapeutische Monatsheft,* **1** (1887), 88–90; "Ueber die Bedeutung der neutrophilen Körnung," in *Charité-Annalen,* **12** (1887), 288–295; "Ueber schmerzstillende Wirkung des Methylenblau," in *Deutsche medizinische Wochenschrift,* **16** (1890), 493–494, written with A. Leppmann; "Studien in der Cocainreihe," *ibid.,* 717–719; "Die Wirksamkeit kleiner Tuberkulindosen gegen Lungenschwindsucht," *ibid.,* 793–795, written with P. Guttmann; "Recent Experiences in the Treatment of Tuberculosis (With Special Reference to Pulmonary Consumption) by Koch's Method," in *Lancet* (1891), **2,** 917–920, trans. by T. W. Hime from a paper presented by Ehrlich at the Seventh International Congress of Hygiene and Demography, London; "Ueber die Wirkung des Methylenblau bei Malaria," in *Berliner klinische Wochenschrift,* **28** (1891), 953–956, written with P. Guttmann; "Experimentelle Untersuchungen über Immunität. I. Ueber Ricin. II. Ueber Abrin," in *Deutsche medizinische Wochenschrift,* **17** (1891), 976–979, 1218–1219; and "Ueber Immunität durch Vererbung und Säugung," in *Zeitschrift für Hygiene,* **12** (1892), 183–203.

See also "Ueber die Uebertragung von Immunität durch Milch," in *Deutsche medizinische Wochenschrift,* **18** (1892), 393–394, written with L. Brieger; "Ueber Gewinnung und Verwendung des Diphtherieheilserums," *ibid.,* **20** (1894), 353–355, written with H. Kossel and A. Wassermann; "Die staatliche Kontrolle des Diphtherieserums," in *Berliner klinische Wochenschrift,* **33** (1896), 441–443; "Die Wertbemessung des Diphtherieheilserums und deren theoretische Grundlagen," in *Klinische Jahrbuch,* **6** (1897), 299–326; "Zur Kenntnis der Antitoxinwirkung," in *Fortschritte der Medizin,* **15** (1897), 41–43; "Ueber die Constitution des Diphtheriegiftes," in *Deutsche medizinische Wochenschrift,* **24** (1898), 597–600; "Observations Upon the Constitution of the Diphtheria Toxin," in *Transactions of the Jenner Institute of Preventive Medicine,* **2** (1899), 1–16; "Zur Theorie der Lysinwirkung," in *Berliner klinische Wochenschrift,* **36** (1899), 6–9, written with J. Morgenroth, as was "Ueber Haemolysine," *ibid.,* **36** (1899), 481–486; **37** (1900), 453–458; **38** (1901), 251–257, 569–574, 598–604.

Other papers published after 1900 include "On Immunity, With Special Reference to Cell Life," in *Proceedings of the Royal Society,* **66** (1900), 424–448, the Croonian lecture; "Die Schutzstoffe des Blutes," in *Deutsche medizinische Wochenschrift,* **27** (1901), 865–867, 888–891, 913–916; "Ueber die Beziehungen von chemischer Constitution, Vertheilung, und pharmakologischen Wirkung,"

in *Ernst von Leyden-Festschrift,* I (Berlin, 1902), 645–679, address delivered to Verein für innere Medicin, Berlin, 12 December 1898, trans. by C. Bolduan as "The Relations Existing Between Chemical Constitution, Distribution, and Pharmacological Action," in *Studies on Immunity* (1906), pp. 404–442; "Ueber die Vielheit der Complemente des Serums," in *Berliner klinische Wochenschrift,* **39** (1902), 297–299, 335–338, written with H. Sachs, as was "Ueber den Mechanismus der Amboceptorenwirkung," *ibid.,* 492–496; "Ueber die complementophilen Gruppen der Amboceptoren," *ibid.,* 585–587, written with H. T. Marshall; "Ueber die Giftcomponenten des Diphtherie-Toxins," *ibid.,* **40** (1903), 793–797, 825–829, 848–851; "Toxin und Antitoxin. Entgegnung auf den neuesten Angriff Grubers," in *Münchener medizinische Wochenschrift,* **50** (1903), 1428–1432, 1465–1469; "Toxin und Antitoxin. Entgegnung auf Grubers Replik," *ibid.,* 2295–2297; "Vorläufige Bemerkungen zur Mittheilungen von Arrhenius zur Theorie der Absättigung von Toxin und Antitoxin," in *Berliner klinische Wochenschrift,* **41** (1904), 221–223; "The Mutual Relations Between Toxin and Antitoxin," in *Boston Medical and Surgical Journal,* **150** (1904), 443–445; "Physical Chemistry v. Biology in the Doctrine of Immunity," *ibid.,* 445–448; "Cytotoxins and Cytotoxic Immunity," *ibid.,* 448–450, the Herter lectures; "Farbentherapeutische Versuche bei Trypanosomenerkrankungen," in *Berliner klinische Wochenschrift,* **41** (1904), 329–332, 362–365, written with K. Shiga; and "Ueber den Mechanismus der Antiamboceptorenwirkung," *ibid.,* **42** (1905), 557–558, 609–612, written with H. Sachs.

Also of interest are "Beobachtungen über maligne Mäusetumoren," *ibid.,* 871–874, written with H. Apolant; "Beziehungen zwischen chemischer Konstitution und Desinfektionswirkung. Ein Beitrag zum Studium der 'innern Antisepsis,'" in *Hoppe-Seyler's Zeitschrift für physiologische Chemie,* **47** (1906), 173–199, written with H. Bechhold; "On Immunity With Special Reference to the Relationship Between Distribution and Action of Antigens," in *Journal of the Royal Institute of Public Health,* **15** (1907), 321–340; "On Athreptic Functions," *ibid.,* 385–403; "Chemotherapeutic Studies on Trypanosomes," *ibid.,* 449–456, the Harben lectures; "Ueber *p*-Aminophenylarsinsäure. Erste Mitteilung," in *Berichte der Deutschen chemischen Gesellschaft,* **40** (1907), 3292–3297, written with A. Bertheim; "Ueber spontane Mischtumoren der Maus," in *Berliner klinische Wochenschrift,* **44** (1907), 1399–1401, written with H. Apolant; "Ueber den jetzigen Stand der Chemotherapie," in *Berichte der Deutschen chemischen Gesellschaft,* **42** (1909), 17–47; "Ueber Partialfunktionen der Zelle," in *Münchener medizinische Wochenschrift,* **56** (1909), 217–222, Nobel Prize address, 11 December 1908; "Ueber serumfeste Trypanosomenstämme," in *Zeitschrift für Immunitätsforschung,* **3** (1909), 296–299, written with W. Roehl and R. Gulbransen; "Kritiker der Seitenkettentheorie im Lichte ihrer experimentellen und literarischen Forschung. Ein Kommentar zu den Arbeiten von Bang und Forssman," in *Münchener medizinische Wochenschrift,* **56** (1909), 2529–2532, written with H. Sachs, as was "Ist die Ehrlichsche Seitenkettentheorie mit den tatsächlichen

Verhältnissen vereinbar? Bemerkungen zu der II Mittheilung von Bang und Forssman," *ibid.,* **57** (1910), 1287–1289; "Reduktionsprodukte der Arsanilsäure und ihre Derivate. Zweite Mittheilung: Ueber *p, p'*-Diamino-arsenobenzol," in *Berichte der Deutschen chemischen Gesellschaft,* **43** (1910), 917–927, written with A. Bertheim; "Allgemeines über Chemotherapie," in *Verhandlungen des 27. Kongresses für innere Medizin, Wiesbaden,* **27** (1910), 226–234; "Die Behandlung der Syphilis mit dem Ehrlichschen Präparat 606," in *Deutsche medizinische Wochenschrift,* **36** (1910), 1893–1896; "Die Salvarsantherapie. Rückblicke und Ausblicke," in *Münchener medizinische Wochenschrift,* **58** (1911), 1–10; "Ueber Salvarsan," *ibid.,* 2481–2486; "Chemotherapeutics: Scientific Principles, Methods, and Results," in *Lancet* (1913), **2**, 445–451, address in pathology to 17th International Medical Congress, London, 1913; and "Deaths After Salvarsan," in *British Medical Journal* (1914), **1**, 1044–1045.

Ehrlich's former institute at Frankfurt contains a small collection of memorabilia (group photographs and laboratory notebooks). Other relics were donated by his family to the New York Academy of Medicine. His surviving papers, retrieved from the bomb-damaged institute after World War II and from a village hiding place in the Taunus Mountains, were placed by Ehrlich's executor, his grandson, on indefinite loan in the custody of the Wellcome Institute of the History of Medicine, London. These include most of his copybooks of handwritten letters, from late 1898 to early 1903, and of typed ones thereafter to 1915, as well as copies of his "blocks" to collaborators, 1906–1915.

II. Secondary Literature. Obituaries in German include G. Joannovics, "Paul Ehrlich 1854–1915," in *Wiener klinische Wochenschrift,* **28** (1915), 937–942; M. Kirchner, "Paul Ehrlich†," in *Zeitschrift für ärtzliche Fortbildung,* **12** (1915), 513–515; A. Neisser, "Paul Ehrlich, Gestorben den 20 August 1915," in *Archiv für Dermatologie und Syphilis,* **121** (1919), 557–578; F. Pinkus, "Paul Ehrlich geboren 14 März 1854, gestorben 20 August 1915," in *Medizinische Klinik,* **11** (1915), 985, 1116–1117, 1143–1145; H. Sachs, "Paul Ehrlich†," in *Münchener medizinische Wochenschrift,* **62** (1915), 1357–1361; and "Paul Ehrlich, geb. 14.III.1854, †20.VIII.1915," in *Natur und Volk,* **46** (1916), 139–152; A. von Wassermann, "Paul Ehrlich†," in *Deutsche medizinische Wochenschrift,* **41** (1915), 1103–1106, 1135–1136; and A. von Weinberg, "Paul Ehrlich," in *Berichte der deutschen chemischen Gesellschaft,* **49** (1916), 1223–1248.

Obituaries in English include C. H. Browning, "Professor Paul Ehrlich," in *British Medical Journal* (1915), **2**, 349–350; R. Muir, "Paul Ehrlich. 1854–1915," in *Journal of Pathology and Bacteriology,* **20** (1915), 349–360; and the following unsigned tributes: "Wirkl.-Geheimrat Paul Ehrlich," in *Lancet* (1915), **2**, 525–526; "Professor Paul Ehrlich," in *British Medical Journal* (1915), **2**, 349; "Professor Paul Ehrlich," in *Boston Medical and Surgical Journal,* **173** (1915), 637–640; and "Death of Paul Ehrlich," in *Journal of the American Medical Association,* **65** (1915), 814, 1123.

Other references in German to Ehrlich's life and work

are H. Apolant, L. Benda, A. Bertheim, et al., *Paul Ehrlich. Eine Darstellung seines wissenschaftlichen Wirkens* (Jena, 1914), the *Festschrift* for his sixtieth birthday; S. Arrhenius and T. Madsen, "Anwendung der physikalischen Chemie auf des Studium der Toxine und Antitoxine," in *Zeitschrift für physikalische Chemie,* **44** (1903), 7–62; L. Aschoff, *Ehrlich's Seitenkettentheorie und ihre Anwendung auf die künstlichen Immunisierungsprozesse* (Jena, 1902); A. Beyer, *Paul Ehrlich und Emil v. Behring* (Berlin, 1954); W. Dönitz, "Bericht über die Thätigkeit des königlichen Instituts für Serumforschung und Serumprüfung zu Steglitz. Juni 1896–September 1899," in *Klinische Jahrbuch,* **7** (1899), 1–26; A. von Engelhardt, *Hundertjahrfeier der Geburtstage von Paul Ehrlich und Emil von Behring in Frankfurt-Main, Marburg-Lahn und Hoechst,"* (Marburg, 1954); I. Fischer, "Paul Ehrlich," in *Biographisches Lexikon der hervorragender Aerzte,* I (1932), 352–353.

See also W. Greuling, *Paul Ehrlich. Leben und Werk* (Düsseldorf, 1954); M. Gruber, "Zur Theorie der Antikörper. I. Ueber die Antitoxin-Immunität," in *Münchener medizinische Wochenschrift,* **48** (1901), 1827–1830, 1880–1884; "II. Ueber Bakteriolyse und Haemolyse," *ibid.,* 1924–1927, 1965–1968; "Neue Früchte der Ehrlichschen Toxinlehre," in *Wiener klinische Wochenschrift,* **16** (1903), 791–793; "Toxin und Antitoxin. Eine Replik auf Herrn Ehrlichs Entgegnung," in *Münchener medizinische Wochenschrift,* **50** (1903), 1825–1828; and "Bemerkungen zu Ehrlich's 'Entgegnung auf Grubers Replik,'" *ibid.,* 2297; M. Gruber and C. von Pirquet, "Toxin und Antitoxin," *ibid.,* 1193–1196, 1259–1263; B. Heymann, "Zur Geschichte der Seitenkettentheorie Paul Ehrlichs," in *Klinische Wochenschrift,* **7** (1928), 1257–1260, 1305–1309; Janina Hurwitz, "Paul Ehrlich als Krebsforscher," in *Zürcher medizingeschichtliche Abhandlungen,* n.s. no. 7 (1962); G. Joannovics, "Referat: Paul Ehrlich. Eine Darstellung seines wissenschaftlichen Wirkens. Festschrift zum 60. Geburtstage des Forschers," in *Wiener klinische Wochenschrift,* **28** (1915), 93–95; A. Lazarus, "Paul Ehrlich," in M. Neuberger, ed., *Meister der Heilkunde,* I (Vienna, 1921), 9–88; W. Leibbrand, "Paul Ehrlich," in *Neue deutsche Biographie,* IV (1957), 364–365; and "Paul Ehrlich und Emil von Behring zum hundertsten Geburtstag am 14. und 15. März," in *Münchener medizinische Wochenschrift,* **96** (1954), 298–299; H. Loewe, "Paul Ehrlich. Schöpfer der Chemotherapie," in *Grosse Naturforscher,* VIII (Stuttgart, 1950); Leonor Michaelis, "Zur Erinnerung am Paul Ehrlich: Seine wiedergefundene Doktor-Dissertation," in *Die Naturwissenschaften,* **7** (1919), 165–168; A. Neisser, "Ueber das Arsenophenylglyzin und seine Verwendung bei der Syphilisbehandlung," in *Archiv für Dermatologie und Syphilis,* **121** (1916), 579–612; A. Neisser *et al.,* "Die Behandlung der Syphilis mit den Ehrlichschen Präparat 606," in *Deutsche medizinische Wochenschrift,* **36** (1910), 1889–1924; and *Beitrage zur Pathologie und Therapie der Syphilis* (Berlin, 1911); H. Satter, *Paul Ehrlich, Begründer der Chemotherapie* (Munich, 1962); P. Uhlenhuth, *Experimentelle Grundlagen der Chemotherapie der Spirochaetenkrankheiten mit besondere Berücksichtigung der Syphilis* (Berlin–Vienna, 1911); O. H. Warburg, "Paul Ehrlich, 1854–1915," in *Die* *grossen Deutschen,* IV (1957), 186–192; and A. Wasser-mann, "Paul Ehrlich," in *Münchener medizinische Wochen-schrift,* **56** (1909), 245–247.

English and French references to Ehrlich's life and work include J. Almkvist, "Reminiscences of Paul Ehrlich," in *Urologic and Cutaneous Review,* **42** (1938), 214–220; H. Bauer, "Paul Ehrlich's Influence on Chemistry and Biochemistry," in *Annals of the New York Academy of Sciences,* **59** (1954), 150–167; J. Bordet, "Sur le mode d'action des antitoxines sur les toxines," in *Annales de l'Institut Pasteur,* **17** (1903), 161–186; C. H. Browning, "Paul Ehrlich—Memories of 1905–1907," in *British Medical Journal* (1954), **1,** 664–665; and "Emil Behring and Paul Ehrlich. Their Contributions to Science," in *Nature,* **175** (1955), 570–575, 616–619; Henry Dale, "Paul Ehrlich, Born March 14, 1854," in *British Medical Journal* (1954), **1,** 659–663; C. E. Dolman, "A Fiftieth Anniversary Com-memorative Tribute to Paul Ehrlich, With Two Letters to American Friends," in *Clio Medica,* **1** (1966), 223–234; and "Paul Ehrlich and William Bulloch: A Correspondence and Friendship (1896–1914)," *ibid.,* **3** (1968), 65–84; H. Good-man, "Paul Ehrlich. 'A Man of Genius and an Inspiration to Humanitarians,'" in *American Medicine,* **42** (1936), 73–78; L. W. Harrison, "Paul Ehrlich and the Development of 606," in *St. Thomas's Hospital Gazette,* **52** (1954), 37–42; E. Jokl, "Paul Ehrlich—Man and Scientist," in *Bulletin of the New York Academy of Medicine,* **30** (1954), 968–975; Martha Marquardt, *Paul Ehrlich* (London, 1949); and "Paul Ehrlich, Some Reminiscences," in *British Medical Journal* (1954), **1,** 665–667; G. H. F. Nuttall, "Biographical Notes Bearing on Koch, Ehrlich, Behring and Loeffler, With Their Portraits and Letters From Three of Them," in *Parasitology,* **16** (1924), 214–238 ("Paul Ehrlich, 1854–1915", pp. 224–229); H. G. Plimmer, "A Critical Summary of Ehrlich's Recent Work on Toxins and Antitoxins," in *Journal of Pathology and Bacteriology,* **5** (1897), 489–498; C. P. Rhoads, "Paul Ehrlich and the Cancer Problem," in *Annals of the New York Academy of Sciences,* **59** (1954), 190–197; and "Paul Ehrlich in Contemporary Science," in *Bulletin of the New York Academy of Medicine,* **30** (1954), 976–987; L. Vogel, "Paul Ehrlich (1854–1915)," in *Revue d'histoire de la médecine hebraïque,* **22** (1969), 75–85, 107–117; W. Wechselmann, "Beobachtungen an 503 mit Dioxy-diamido-Arsenobenzol behandelten Krankheitsfällen," in *Deutsche medizinische Wochenschrift,* **36** (1910), 1478–1481; and *The Treatment of Syphilis With Salvarsan* (New York–London, 1911), A. L. Wolbarst trans.; and E. Witebsky, "Ehrlich's Side-Chain Theory in the Light of Present Im-munology," in *Annals of the New York Academy of Sciences,* **59** (1954), 168–181.

CLAUDE E. DOLMAN

EICHENWALD, ALEKSANDR ALEKSANDRO-VICH (*b.* St. Petersburg, Russia, 4 January 1864; *d.* Milan[?], Italy, 1944), *physics, engineering.*

Eichenwald's father was a photographer and artist; his mother, a professor of harp at the St. Petersburg Conservatory and, later, a soloist of the Bolshoi Thea-ter orchestra in Moscow. His sisters and brother were also professional musicians, and he himself was a pianist and a connoisseur of music, which stimulated his interest in acoustics.

While in high school, from which he graduated in 1883, he formed his friendship with the future physi-cist P. N. Lebedev. After completing two years of study at the Faculty of Physics and Mathematics of Moscow University, Eichenwald entered the St. Petersburg Railway Institute, from which he gradu-ated in 1888. After working for seven years as an engineer, he went to Strasbourg to continue his edu-cation and devoted himself to physics. K. F. Braun was his instructor in experimental physics, and Emil Cohn in theoretical physics. His Ph.D. dissertation was entitled "Absorption elektrischer Wellen bei Elektrolyten" (1897).

From 1897 to 1921 Eichenwald worked at the Moscow Engineering College (now the Moscow Insti-tute of Railway Engineers). In the excellent scientific laboratory that he organized there, he carried out the fundamental experiments described in his dissertation for a Russian doctorate, *O magnitnom deystvii tel, dvizhushchikhsya v elektrostaticheskom pole* ("On the Magnetic Action of Bodies Moving in an Electrostatic Field," 1904), and undertook investigations of the propagation of electromagnetic and sound waves. In 1905–1908 Eichenwald was director of the Institute of Railway Engineers and from 1901 was also an instructor at the Higher Women's Courses and, in 1906–1911, at Moscow University. After Lebedev's death he headed the Moscow Physics Society, which Lebedev had founded. In 1917–1920 he participated in the reorganization of higher education. After two operations in Moscow and Berlin for cancer, Eichen-wald moved to Milan, where he wrote textbooks that were published in the Soviet Union. His textbook on electricity saw eight editions from 1911 to 1933. In 1926–1932 the first three and the sixth volumes of *Theoretical Physics* were published.

Eichenwald was simultaneously a keen experi-menter, a serious theoretician, a brilliant lecturer and methodologist, and an inventor of demonstration apparatus. He won world fame by his unquestionable proof that the motion of an electrically charged body produces an electric field, by his exact proof of the equivalence of convection and conduction currents, and by the first proof, based on direct measurements, of the existence of a magnetic field when the polariza-tion of a dielectric changes, i.e., a magnetic field of a displacement current (1901–1904).

By his direct and accurate experiments on the detection and measurement of the magnetic field of convection currents, Eichenwald completed the final step in a series of experiments with contradictory results that had been started by H. A. Rowland (1876) and continued by V. Grémieu, Ernst Lecher, and Harold Pender (1902).

Besides the magnetic field created by the motion of charged conductors, Eichenwald measured the currents produced by the motion of a dielectric in a nonuniform electric field (they had been discovered by Roentgen in 1888) and organized a new type of experiment (the Eichenwald experiment), by means of which the existence of the magnetic field of the displacement current in dielectrics was established and its magnitude was measured for the first time.

Half of a disk made from a dielectric and rotating about its axis passed constantly between the plates of one capacitor, and the other half between those of another capacitor. The electric fields in the capacitors were oppositely directed. When each element of the dielectric passed from the zone of one capacitor to that of the other, the polarization of this element became the opposite of what it had been. Eichenwald discovered the magnetic field of the displacement current appearing in the dielectric by observing the change in the oscillations of a small magnetic needle when the disk was stationary and in motion. The needle was arranged so as not to react to convection currents. The experiment was organized in connection with the question of the conduction of ether by moving bodies. The result conformed with the theories of H. A. Lorentz and E. Cohn, in which motionless ether was assumed, but after the appearance of the theory of relativity Eichenwald proved that his experiment could be interpreted in accordance with the new concept.

In "O dvizhenii energii pri polnom vnutrennem otrazhenii sveta" ("On the Motion of Energy With Complete Internal Reflection of Light," 1908), Eichenwald completely explained this phenomenon from the standpoint of J. C. Maxwell's electromagnetic theory of light, indicating the reason for Drude's error. (According to Drude's theory of the motion of light energy along a reflecting surface, the direction of the vector of the electric field coincides with the direction of this motion, instead of being perpendicular to it.)

The equations deduced in this work, reflecting the curvilinear nature of the propagation of light in a reflecting medium, were also applicable in other cases and were published in a generalized form in "Das Feld der Lichtwellen bei Reflexion und Brechung" (1912).

In the investigation "Akusticheskie volny bolshoy amplitudy" ("Sound Waves of Large Amplitude"), a different, simpler, and physically more illustrative

method of calculation than that of Riemann was proposed for strong sounds, when the approximate equations of wave propagation cannot be used.

BIBLIOGRAPHY

I. ORIGINAL WORKS. Some of Eichenwald's works were collected as *Izbrannye trudi* ("Selected Works"), A. B. Mlodzeevsky, ed. (Moscow, 1956), with remarks and a biographical essay. Among his writings are "Absorption elektrischer Wellen bei Elektrolyten," in *Annalen der Physik und Chemie,* **62** (1897), 571–587; "Über die magnetischen Wirkungen elektrischer Konvektion," in *Jahrbuch der Radioaktivität und Elektronik,* **5,** no. 1 (1908), 82–98—see also L. Graetz, *Handbuch der Elektrizität und des Magnetismus,* II (Leipzig, 1914), 337–365; "O dvizhenii energii pri polnom vnutrennem otrazhenii sveta" ("On the Motion of Energy With Complete Internal Reflection of Light"), in *Izvestiya Moskovskago inzhenernogo uchilishcha* (Apr. 1908), 15–41—see also *Annalen der Physik,* **35** (1911), 1037–1040; "Das Feld der Lichtwellen bei Reflexion und Brechung," in *Festschrift Heinrich Weber* (Leipzig, 1912), 37–56; and "Akusticheskie volny bolshoy amplitudy" ("Sound Waves of Large Amplitude"), in *Uspekhi fizicheskikh nauk,* **14,** no. 5 (1934), 552–585—see also *Rendiconti del Seminario matematico e fisico di Milano,* **6,** no. 10 (1932), 1–28.

II. SECONDARY LITERATURE. On Eichenwald and his work, see N. A. Kaptsov, "Aleksandr Aleksandrovich Eichenwald," in *Uchenye zapiski Moskovskogo gosudarstvennogo universiteta,* Jubilee ser., no. 52 (1940), 166–171; G. Mie, *Elektrodynamik* (Leipzig, 1952), pp. 51–54, 60–62; and A. B. Mlodzeevsky, "A. A. Eichenwald," in *Ocherki po istorii fiziki v Rossii* ("Essays on the History of Physics in Russia," Moscow, 1949).

O. LEZHNEVA

EICHLER, AUGUST WILHELM (*b.* Neukirchen, Germany, 22 April 1839; *d.* Berlin, Germany, 2 March 1887), *botany.*

Eichler has been considered one of the most prominent systematic and morphological botanists of his time. He was an enemy of dogmas and philosophical speculations; his main contributions concern the symmetry of flowers and the taxonomy of higher plants. These accomplishments followed in the tradition of another great German botanist, Alexander Braun, and culminated in the introduction of a widely adopted system of plant classification.

The eldest son of a cantor who also taught natural sciences, Eichler demonstrated an early interest in nature, collecting minerals and flowers and becoming skilled in mountain climbing. After his early education in Eschwege and Hersfeld, he studied mathematics and natural science at the University of

Marburg from 1857 to 1861. There Eichler developed a close personal relationship with one of his teachers, the botanist Albert Wigand, an association that proved decisive for his future career. His main interest turned to the study of flowers and their basic structure and, in opposition to Wigand's ideas, he became a vigorous defender of Darwin. Warmly recommended by his teachers, Eichler went to Munich after his graduation, as private assistant to the naturalist Karl Friedrich von Martius. There he assisted Martius in editing the monumental *Flora Brasiliensis*. After becoming a lecturer at the University of Munich, Eichler assumed the sole editorship of this ambitious project upon the death of Martius in 1868. Three years later, in 1871, he accepted an offer to become professor of botany at the Technische Hochschule of Graz and to supervise the local botanical gardens. Eichler occupied this post for only one year, until he heeded a call from the Prussian government to assume the chair of botany at Kiel. There he completed the first part of his most famous work on the comparative structure of flowers, *Blüthendiagramme*. This publication was based on meticulous and repeated observations, and Eichler himself executed some of the woodcuts that illustrated the book.

After the death of Alexander Braun in 1877, Eichler was appointed professor of systematic and morphologic botany at the University of Berlin. In addition he assumed the direction of the university's herbarium and the Royal Botanical Gardens at Schoeneberg. Eichler's contemporaries were impressed with his ability as a teacher as well as with the combination of scholarship, strict objectivity, and personal modesty that he constantly exhibited. What had begun as an eye complaint during the years at Kiel gradually became a disabling systemic disease, diagnosed before his death as leukemia. It greatly hampered his research and teaching during the years in Berlin.

In 1867 Eichler was elected secretary of the International Botanical Congress held in Paris on 16–23 August of that year. After his call to the German capital, he was elected a member of the Berlin Academy of Sciences in 1880. He also became a corresponding or honorary member of several other societies, such as the French Academy of Sciences, the Royal Society of Belgium, the Academy of Sciences of Munich, and in 1881, the Linnean Society of London.

BIBLIOGRAPHY

I. ORIGINAL WORKS. A complete list of Eichler's publications can be found in *Annals of Botany,* **1** (1887–1888), 400–403; and in I. Urban, "A. W. Eichler's botanische Arbeiten," in *Botanisches Centralblatt,* **32** (1887), 123–127.

Among his best-known books are *Zur Entwicklungsgeschichte des Blattes mit besonderer Beruecksichtigung der Nebenblattbildungen* (Marburg, 1861); *Bewegung im Pflanzenreiche* (Munich, 1864); *Blüthendiagramme,* 2 vols. (Leipzig, 1875–1878); *Beitraege zur Morphologie und Systematik der Marantaceen* (Berlin, 1883); and *Syllabus der Vorlesungen ueber specielle und medicinisch-pharmaceutische Botanik,* 4th ed., rev. (Berlin, 1886).

Eichler was also one of the editors of *Flora Brasiliensis,* 15 vols. (Munich–Leipzig, 1840–1906).

Some of his best articles are "On the Formation of the Flower in Gymnosperms." T. Thomson, trans., in *Natural History Review,* **4** (1864), 270–290; "Bemerkungen ueber die Structur des Holzes von Drimys und Trochodendron, sowie ueber die systematische Stellung der letzteren Gattung," in *Flora, oder allgemeine botanische Zeitung,* **47** (1864), 449–458 and **48** (1865), 12–15, partially trans. into English in *Journal of Botany, British and Foreign,* **3** (1865), 150–154; and "Einige Bemerkungen ueber den Bau der Cruciferenbluethe und das Dédoublement," in *Flora, oder allgemeine botanische Zeitung,* **52** (1869), 97–109.

II. SECONDARY LITERATURE. An extensive biography of Eichler is Carl Mueller, "August Wilhelm Eichler, ein Nachruf," in *Botanisches Centralblatt,* **31** (1887), 61–63, 120–128, 155–160, 188–191, 229–232, 261–263, 294–296, 325–327, 357–360; **32** (1887), 27–32, 61–63, 121–123. This biography was also published as a book, together with I. Urban's bibliography, under the same title (Kassel, 1887). Other biographical sketches appeared in *Proceedings of the Linnean Society of London* (1886–1887), 38–39; *Berichte der Deutschen botanischen Gesellschaft,* **5** (1887), xxxiii–xxxvii; and *Flora, oder allgemeine botanische Zeitung,* **70** (1887), 243–249.

GUENTER B. RISSE

EICHWALD, KARL EDUARD IVANOVICH (*b.* Mitau, Latvia [now Jelgava, Latvian S.S.R.], 4 July 1795; *d.* St. Petersburg, Russia, 16 November 1876), *geology, paleontology.*

Eichwald's father, Johann Christian Eichwald, was a private tutor to the family of a baron of Courland and later a lecturer in modern languages and natural history. His mother, Charlotte Elizabeth Louis, was the daughter of the court hairdresser. Eichwald was tutored at home before attending the Gymnasium. He began his studies at Dorpat University in 1814 but soon transferred to Berlin University, where he studied medicine and natural sciences. To expand the range of his knowledge he traveled to Germany, Switzerland, France, and England in 1817, taking specialized courses at the universities of Vienna and Paris. In 1819, upon his return to Russia, Eichwald defended his dissertation at Vilna University and was awarded the M.D. degree; he then worked as a physician for two years.

In 1821 Eichwald became assistant professor at

Dorpat University and lectured on geology and paleontology. Two years later he became ordinary professor of obstetrics and zoology at Kazan University, where he also lectured on botany and mineralogy, directed the botanical garden, founded a laboratory of comparative anatomy, and furthered the development of the department of natural history. While in Kazan he married Sofia Ivanovna Finke, the daughter of a professor at the university.

In 1827 Eichwald moved to Vilna and was given the chair of zoology, comparative anatomy, and obstetrics at the university; from 1831 to 1837 he held the chair of zoology, mineralogy, and anatomy at the Medical-Surgical Academy in Vilna. In 1838 Eichwald moved to St. Petersburg, where he received the same chair in a similar type of academy. Until his retirement in 1855 he simultaneously lectured on paleontology at the Mining Institute and on mineralogy and geognosy at the Engineering Academy. In 1826 the Academy of Sciences in St. Petersburg elected him a corresponding member. In 1846 the Medical-Surgical Academy conferred the doctorate of surgery on him, and the University of Breslau awarded him the Ph.D.

Eichwald was a naturalist of wide interests. At different periods of his life he successfully devoted himself to medicine and zoology, as well as to botany, geology, paleontology, anthropology, ethnography, and archaeology. His major fields of concentration were geology and especially paleontology.

During the first years of his scientific activity Eichwald traveled a great deal, which opportunity enabled him to collect abundant and varied material in natural history. In addition to visiting western Europe, he traveled extensively throughout European Russia, concentrating on the Baltic provinces. He also visited Scandinavia and in 1846 made excursions to Italy, Sicily, and Algeria. The results of his trip in 1825–1826, across the Caspian Sea, the Caucasus, Persia, and western Turkmenistan, were extremely fruitful: he collected extensive material on the existing flora and fauna and on the geology, paleontology, and geography of a region that was virtually unstudied at the time.

In 1829–1831 Eichwald published a three-volume monograph on zoology, in which he gave a classification of animals and supplied comparative anatomical, physiological, and paleontological data. By a natural system of classification Eichwald understood not merely a simple and definite grouping of animals by criteria of similarity in organization, but also an expression of the genetic relations actually existing between them. In his researches on present-day fauna Eichwald described many previously unknown forms of mollusks and fishes of the Caspian, brackish-water animals of the Black Sea area, and reptilians of certain regions of the Caucasus.

In the 1830's Eichwald became increasingly interested in the study of fossil organisms. He soon received general recognition as the leading paleontologist of Russia and retained this reputation for more than thirty years. He demonstrated exceptional erudition in a wide range of areas concerning fossil organisms and studied both the flora and fauna of all orders and classes throughout the entire geologic sequence from Cambrian to Recent deposits.

His researches were not limited to the fossils that he collected but also included numerous collections regularly sent to him by geologists from the most diverse regions of Russia. Amid this vast quantity of material Eichwald discovered and described for the first time a great number of previously unknown forms. Endeavoring to summarize and systematize the accumulated data, he began the compilation of an extensive summary of the paleontology of Russia. As a result, during the period from 1853 to 1868 he published (simultaneously in Russian and French) three volumes, in separate sections, of his fundamental monograph, *Lethaea Rossica*. The total work consists of about 3,500 pages of text and three atlases that contain 133 plates representing more than 2,000 different fossil organisms.

While preparing this exceptionally voluminous work, Eichwald worked alone and tried to do everything without assistants. Having undertaken a task too great for one man, he inevitably produced a number of inaccurate descriptions and made certain errors in determining the systematic position and geologic age of the fossils. Nevertheless, his paleontological summary was a valuable scientific contribution; it was very widely used, and many of the new species that he described have retained his nomenclature.

In paleontology Eichwald sought to study a fossil without separating it from geology, a practice that enabled him to draw conclusions on the age of the strata and on the physicogeographical environment that the extinct organisms had inhabited. His stratigraphic deductions formed the basis for most of the geologic research carried out in Russia during that period. In the early 1830's Eichwald was the first to divide the entire geologic column over the distance from Lithuania to the Black Sea, distinguishing detailed units from Transition beds, i.e., Lower Paleozoic, up to Quaternary deposits, inclusive. He also confirmed the wide development of Silurian deposits in the Baltic provinces and supplied the earliest information on the fauna of Pliocene and Quaternary terraces on the coast of the Caspian Sea. In addition, he correctly resolved the question of the geologic age of deposits found throughout the wide expanses of central Russia.

In studying the lithologic features of the rocks in which the fossils were found, Eichwald, outstripping his mid-nineteenth-century contemporaries, began to draw conclusions on the paleogeographic conditions that had existed in the distant geologic past and on the ecological environments that the organisms had inhabited. On a number of geologic questions he adhered basically to opinions that were progressive for his time. For instance, contrary to the majority of his contemporaries, who in conformity with the views of the catastrophist school considered orogeny to be a rapid process, Eichwald wrote in the 1830's that mountains originate from repeated slow uplifts that do not occur simultaneously in different parts of the mountain range.

Regarding the nature of island arcs of the Aleutian type, Eichwald expressed an opinion congruent with the present concepts of the formation of such arcs in weakened zones of the earth's crust. He also stated that prominent faults exist on the boundaries between the continents and the oceans and that they are marked by volcanoes.

In 1827—before the contraction hypothesis was formulated—Eichwald wrote that folding results from the combined effect of gravity and lateral compression, in other words, that it is caused by a combination of vertical and tangential strains.

Eichwald several times changed his ideas on the development of the organic world. Originally, in the 1820's, his views were transformist: he thought that all types and classes of animals originated from a primal protoplasm. Later, under the influence of proponents of the catastrophist theory, Eichwald wrote of the periodic destruction of every living thing and the subsequent appearance of a completely new fauna and flora as the result of an act of divine creation, this new life being more highly organized than the one that had previously existed. Following the publication of Darwin's *Origin of Species,* however, Eichwald renounced his catastrophist and creativist concepts and became an adherent of evolutionary theory.

Eichwald was interested in the problems of the origin of certain rocks and minerals. He believed, among other things, that dolomite was formed as a result of ordinary sedimentation from water, despite the dominance at that time of Buch's hypothesis, which asserted that this rock was formed from limestones under the influence of "magnesian vapors." Eichwald divided hard coals according to their origin into two types that correspond to the present allochthonous and autochthonous coals. He thought that the process of coal formation takes place at a great depth as a result of the pressure exerted by the rock mass above and the action of heat from below.

Eichwald's textbooks on mineralogy (1844) and on geology (1846) were based on the specific features of the geologic structure of Russia. He was one of the first (1821–1823) to lecture systematically on paleontology, thus laying the foundation for the creation of chairs of paleontology in Russian universities and institutes.

A member of many Russian and foreign scientific societies, Eichwald was especially active in the work of the Free Economic Society of Russia.

BIBLIOGRAPHY

I. ORIGINAL WORKS. Eichwald's major works include *Ideen zu einer systematischen Oryktozoologie oder über verändert und unverändert ausgegrabene Thiere* (Mitau [Jelgava], 1821); *Zoologia specialis quam exposites animalibus, tam fossilibus potissimum Rossiae in universum et Poloniae in specie,* 3 vols. (Vilna, 1829–1831); "Fauna Caspio-Caucasia nonnulis observationibus novis illustravit," in *Nouveaux mémoires de la Société des naturalistes de Moscou,* **7** (1842); *Polny kurs geologicheskikh nauk preimuschestvenno po otnosheniyu k Rossii:* I. *Oriktognozia preimushchestvenno po otnosheniyu k Rossii i s prisovokupleniem upotreblenia mineralov* (St. Petersburg, 1844), and II. *Geognozia, preimushchestvenno po otnosheniyu k Rossii* (St. Petersburg, 1846); and *Lethaea Rossica ou Paléontologie de la Russie,* 3 vols. (Stuttgart, 1853–1868).

II. SECONDARY LITERATURE. On Eichwald and his work, see E. Lindemann, "Das fünfzigjährige Doktorjubiläum Eduard von Eichwald's, Dr. der Philosophie, Medizin und Chirurgie," in *Verhandlungen der Russisch-kaiserlichen mineralogischen Gesellschaft zu St. Petersburg,* 2nd ser., **5** (1870), 278–358.

V. V. TIKHOMIROV

EIGENMANN, CARL H. (*b.* Flehingen, Germany, 9 March 1863; *d.* Chula Vista, California, 24 April 1927), *ichthyology.*

The son of Philip and Margaretha Lieb Eigenmann, Carl intended to study law when he entered Indiana University in 1879, two years after his arrival in the United States with an uncle. A course in biology under David Starr Jordan turned him to an extremely productive career in ichthyology. After receiving his bachelor's degree (1886), he studied the South American fish collections at Harvard University for one year and then became curator at the Natural History Society in San Diego, the home of his wife, Rosa (also an ichthyologist). At Jordan's departure in 1891, Eigenmann replaced him as professor of zoology at Indiana University, having received his Ph.D. there in 1889. In 1892 he was made director of the Biological Survey of Indiana; in 1908 he became the first dean of the graduate school at Indiana; and from 1909 to 1918 he was honorary curator of fishes at the Carnegie Museum in Pittsburgh.

Eigenmann was a member of the National Academy of Sciences, of Sigma Xi and Phi Beta Kappa, a fellow of the American Association for the Advancement of Science, and an honorary member of the California Academy of Sciences and of the Sociedad de Ciencias Naturales of Bogotá, Colombia.

Although he conducted other researches, Eigenmann repeatedly turned to painstaking analyses of the classification, distribution, and evolution of the freshwater fishes of South America, based on studies of many museum collections and the results of his own expeditions. From comparisons of the African and South American Cichlidae and Characidae, he concluded that a pre-Tertiary land connection between the two continents must have existed. In a number of monographs he presented the classification of families of South American fishes, climaxed by the exhaustive five-part "American Characidae" (1917–1925). His brief stay on the West Coast resulted in valuable papers on the taxonomy, variation, and habits of the fishes of San Diego (1892), and at Indiana he published considerably on the fish there. Curiosity about blindness of cave animals led Eigenmann to detailed study of specimens from Indiana, Missouri, Texas, Kentucky, and Cuba. He concluded that the degenerative characteristics of subdued coloration and of blindness become inherited when they have adaptive environmental value.

A significant participant in the "golden age of descriptive ichthyology in the United States," Eigenmann left a legacy of meticulous classification and many grateful students who credited him especially with teaching them self-reliance.

BIBLIOGRAPHY

I. ORIGINAL WORKS. Besides many monographs on fish families and single papers, Eigenmann's major publication was "The American Characidae," in vol. **43** of the *Memoirs of the Museum of Comparative Zoology of Harvard College:* pt. 1 (1917), 1–102; pt. 2 (1918), 103–208; pt. 3 (1921), 209–310; pt. 4 (1927), 311–428; and pt. 5 (1929), 429–558, written with G. S. Myers. The geographic studies of South American fishes appeared in "The Fresh-Water Fishes of Patagonia and an Examination of the Archiplata-Archhelenis Theory," in *Reports of the Princeton University Expedition to Patagonia, 1896 to 1899,* Zoology, III (Prince-

ton, 1909), 225–374. The studies of cave fauna are summarized in *Cave Vertebrates of North America: A Study in Degenerative Evolution,* Publications of the Carnegie Institution, no. 104 (Washington, D.C., 1909), pp. 1–341.

II. SECONDARY LITERATURE. Little is known of Eigenmann's early life, but his professional career is well summarized in Leonard Stejneger, "Carl H. Eigenmann," in *Biographical Memoirs. National Academy of Sciences,* **18** (1937), 305–336, where it is commented that the "middle initial did not stand for a name." A full bibliography accompanies the Stejneger memoir. For a lively account of the "golden age of descriptive ichthyology," see Carl L. Hubbs, "History of Ichthyology in the United States After 1850," in *Copeia,* no. 1 (1964), pp. 42–60.

ELIZABETH NOBLE SHOR

EIJKMAN, CHRISTIAAN (*b.* Nijkerk, Netherlands, 11 August 1858; *d.* Utrecht, Netherlands, 5 November 1930), *medicine, physiology, nutrition.*

Eijkman, who in 1929 shared the Nobel Prize in physiology or medicine with F. G. Hopkins, was the seventh child of a boarding-school proprietor in the small Gelderland town of Nijkerk, situated at the northern border of the Veluwe. His parents, Christiaan Eijkman and Johanna Alida Pool, had several gifted sons: one brother became a chemist and a professor at Tokyo and Groningen; another was a linguist; and a third was one of the first roentgenologists in the Netherlands.

When Eijkman was only three years old the family moved to Zaandam, where he received sufficient instruction to pass the examination that enabled him to enter the university (1875). The costs of his study were defrayed by the government because he enrolled for later service as an army physician. His ability soon became apparent; he passed three examinations cum laude or magna cum laude.

As a student, for two years Eijkman was assistant to the professor of physiology, Thomas Place. In 1883 he qualified as physician and took his medical degree after defending a thesis on polarization in the nerves ("Over Polarisatie in de Zenuwen"). He was immediately sent as medical officer to the Dutch East Indies, where he worked for two years on Java and Sumatra. A severe attack of malaria forced him to repatriate on sick leave in November 1885. Two months later his young wife of three years, Aaltje Wigeri van Edema, died. After his recovery Eijkman decided to train himself in bacteriology, then a new and rising science. After studying under Josef Förster at Amsterdam, he went to work with Robert Koch at Berlin. Here he made some acquaintances that were decisive for his future career.

In the Dutch East Indies and other eastern countries a disease called beriberi was spreading, especially in closed communities—the army, the navy, prisons, and so on. In some cases cardiac insufficiency with massive edema of the legs dominated the clinical picture, in others a progressive paralysis of the legs (hydropic and "dry" forms). In view of its apparent epidemic character, a bacteriological origin seemed obvious. The Dutch government appointed a committee to study the disease on the spot. The committee consisted of C. A. Pekelharing and C. Winkler, then a young reader and later a well-known neurologist. Before undertaking their difficult mission, both men went to Koch at Berlin to learn something of bacteriology. The result of their meeting there with Eijkman was that the latter, at his own request, was added to the committee that departed for the East in October 1886.

After some two years the committee had shown that in beriberi a polyneuritis could be proved by clinical and microscopic examination, and it believed it had isolated from the blood of beriberi patients the causative agent: a micrococcus, the toxins of which caused the polyneuritis. Pekelharing and Winkler returned to Europe in 1887, leaving Eijkman as head of a small laboratory built for the purpose of continuing the research. Eijkman was also director of the Javanese Medical School.

At that time Eijkman also considered beriberi to be an infectious disease, but he did not succeed in producing the disease in animals by inoculation with the micrococci. He then had the good fortune to see a similar disease develop spontaneously in fowls. The animals showed paresis or paralysis of the legs with dyspnea and cyanosis; microscopic examination of the nerves confirmed the presence of a polyneuritis. Eijkman considered this *polyneuritis gallinarum* to be the equivalent of the polyneuritis in beriberi.

In order to extend the observations, the fowls were removed to another place; but then, unexpectedly, the disease inexplicably disappeared. Eijkman noticed that at the same time a slight change had occurred in the food of the fowls: the original food was obtained from the leavings of boiled rice from the officers' table in the military hospital; later they received unpolished rice, or "paddy," because a new cook had refused military rice to "civilian" fowls. Eijkman now supposed that the causative factor must be sought in the food, especially the polished and boiled rice.

On the basis of extensive food experiments, Eijkman proved that unpolished rice had both a preventive and curative effect on polyneuritis in fowls; but he did not perceive the correct explanation and continued to believe that some chemical agent was causing the polyneuritis, for example, a toxic substance originating from the action of intestinal microorganisms on boiled rice. He even adhered to such a hypothesis for some years after Grijns, in 1901, had advanced the idea of a nutritional deficiency. Nevertheless, Eijkman's observations were the starting point for a line of scientific research that led to the discovery of thiamine (vitamin B_1), found in the pericarp of the unpolished rice grains, as the substance protecting against beriberi.

In 1896 Eijkman, who had married Berthe Julie Louise van der Kemp in 1888, returned home again on sick leave. He made statistical studies on beriberi, on osmosis in the blood, and on the influence of summer and winter on metabolism. In comparing the metabolisms of Europeans in the tropics and natives, he had found no disparities in respiratory metabolism, perspiration, and temperature metabolism. In 1898 he was appointed professor of public health and forensic medicine at the University of Utrecht. He took office with a formal address on health and diseases in the tropics, *Gezondheid en Ziekte in Heete Gewesten* (Utrecht, 1898). During the thirty years of his professorship Eijkman guided many research projects in his laboratory. In the academic year 1912–1913 he acted as rector magnificus, leaving this office with a rectorial oration entitled "Simplex non veri sigillum." He was also a member of several governmental committees in the field of public health and of many national and foreign societies, including the Royal Academy of Sciences of the Netherlands, to which he was appointed in 1907. He was a recipient of the John Scott Medal and a foreign associate of the National Academy of Sciences, Washington, D.C.

In 1928, seventy years old, Eijkman retired; the following year the state of his health did not allow him to accept the Nobel Prize personally, but the address he had intended to deliver was published in *Les Prix Nobel.* During his long life he had performed research in various fields, but his discovery of the role of polished rice in causing *polyneuritis gallinarum* remains his claim to fame because it was the foundation of the later doctrine of the role of vitamins in human nutrition.

About the man himself little information is obtainable. By his second marriage he had one son, Pieter Hendrik, who became a physician.

BIBLIOGRAPHY

I. ORIGINAL WORKS. Except for two textbooks on physiology and chemistry and his orations, nearly all of Eijkman's publications appeared in annual reports and periodicals, most of them in Dutch. A full list is given by Jansen.

Of special note are *Specifieke Antistoffen* (Haarlem, 1901); *Onzichtbare Smetstoffen* (Haarlem, 1904); *Een en Ander over Voeding* (Haarlem, 1906); and *Hygiënische Strijdvragen* (Rotterdam, 1907). See also *Nobel Lectures. Physiology or Medicine,* II (Amsterdam–New York, 1965), 199–207.

II. SECONDARY LITERATURE. See J. M. Baart de la Faille, "Christiaan Eijkman," in T. P. Sevensma, ed., *Nederlandsche Helden der Wetenschap* (Amsterdam, 1946), pp. 299–333, with portrait; and B. C. P. Jansen, *Het Levenswerk van Christiaan Eijkman 1858–1930* (Haarlem, 1959).

G. A. LINDEBOOM

EINSTEIN, ALBERT (*b.* Ulm, Germany, 14 March 1879; *d.* Princeton, New Jersey, 18 April 1955), *physics.*

Albert Einstein was the only son of Hermann and Pauline (Koch) Einstein. He grew up in Munich, where his father and his uncle ran a small electrochemical plant. Einstein was a slow child and disliked the regimentation of school. His scientific interests were awakened early and at home—by the mysterious compass his father gave him when he was about four; by the algebra he learned from his uncle; and by the books he read, mostly popular scientific works of the day. A geometry text which he devoured at the age of twelve made a particularly strong impression.

When his family moved to Milan after a business failure, leaving the fifteen-year-old boy behind in Munich to continue his studies, Einstein quit the school he disliked and spent most of a year enjoying life in Italy. Persuaded that he would have to acquire a profession to support himself, he finished the Gymnasium in Aarau, Switzerland, and then studied physics and mathematics at the Eidgenössische Technische Hochschule (the Polytechnic) in Zurich, with a view toward teaching.

After graduation Einstein was unable to obtain a regular position for two years and did occasional tutoring and substitute teaching, until he was appointed an examiner in the Swiss Patent Office at Berne. The seven years Einstein spent at this job, with only evenings and Sundays free for his own scientific work, were years in which he laid the foundations of large parts of twentieth-century physics. They were probably also the happiest years of his life. He liked the fact that his job was quite separate from his thoughts about physics, so that he could pursue these freely and independently, and he often recommended such an arrangement to others later on. In 1903 Einstein married Mileva Marić, a Serbian girl who had been a fellow student in Zurich. Their two sons were born in Switzerland.

Einstein received his doctorate in 1905 from the University of Zurich for a dissertation entitled, "Eine neue Bestimmung der Moleküldimensionen" ("A New Determination of Molecular Dimensions"), a work closely related to his studies of Brownian motion, discussed below. It took only a few years until he received academic recognition for his work, and then he had a wide choice of positions. His first appointment, in 1909, was as associate professor (*extraordinarius*) of physics at the University of Zurich. This was followed quickly by professorships at the German University in Prague, in 1911, and at the Polytechnic in Zurich, in 1912. Then, in the spring of 1914, Einstein moved to Berlin as a member of the Prussian Academy of Sciences and director of the Kaiser Wilhelm Institute for Physics, free to lecture at the university or not as he chose. He had mixed feelings about accepting this appointment, partly because he disliked Prussian rigidity and partly because he was unhappy about the implied obligation to produce one successful theory after another. As it turned out he found the scientific atmosphere in Berlin very stimulating, and he greatly enjoyed having colleagues like Max Planck, Walther Nernst, and, later, Erwin Schrödinger and Max von Laue.

During World War I, Einstein's scientific work reached a culmination in the general theory of relativity, but in most other ways his life did not go well. He would not join in the widespread support given to the German cause by German intellectuals and did what he could to preserve a rational, international spirit and to urge the immediate end of the war. His feeling of isolation was deepened by the end of his marriage. Mileva Einstein and their two sons spent the war years in Switzerland and the Einsteins were divorced soon after the end of the war. Einstein then married his cousin Elsa, a widow with two daughters. Einstein's health suffered, too. One of his few consolations was his continued correspondence and occasional visits with his friends in the Netherlands—Paul Ehrenfest and H. A. Lorentz, especially the latter, whom Einstein described as having "meant more to me personally than anybody else I have met in my lifetime"[1] and as "the greatest and noblest man of our times."[2]

Einstein became suddenly famous to the world at large when the deviation of light passing near the sun, as predicted by his general theory of relativity, was observed during the solar eclipse of 1919. His name and the term *relativity* became household words. The publicity, even notoriety, that ensued changed the pattern of Einstein's life. He was now able to put the weight of his name behind causes that he believed in, and he did this, always bravely but taking care not to misuse the influence his scientific fame had given him. The two movements he backed most forcefully in the 1920's were pacifism and Zionism, particularly the creation of the Hebrew University in Jerusalem. He also took an active part for a few years in the work of the Committee on Intellectual Cooperation of the League of Nations.

Soon after the end of the war, Einstein and relativity became targets of the anti-Semitic extreme right wing. He was viciously attacked in speeches and articles, and his life was threatened. Despite this treatment Einstein stayed in Berlin, declining many offers to go elsewhere. He did accept an appointment as special professor at Leiden and went there regularly for periods of a week or two to lecture and to discuss current problems in physics. In 1933 Einstein was considering an arrangement that would have allowed him to divide his year between Berlin and the new Institute for Advanced Study at Princeton. But when Hitler came to power in Germany, he promptly resigned his position at the Prussian Academy and joined the Institute. Princeton became his home for the remaining twenty-two years of his life. He became an American citizen in 1940.

During the 1930's Einstein renounced his former pacifist stand, since he was now convinced that the menace to civilization embodied in Hitler's regime could be put down only by force. In 1939, at the request of Leo Szilard, Edward Teller, and Eugene Wigner, he wrote a letter to President Franklin D. Roosevelt pointing out the dangerous military potentialities offered by nuclear fission and warning him of the possibility that Germany might be developing these potentialities. This letter helped to initiate the American efforts that eventually produced the nuclear reactor and the fission bomb, but Einstein neither participated in nor knew anything about these efforts. After the bomb was used and the war had ended, Einstein devoted his energies to the attempt to achieve a world government and to abolish war once and for all. He also spoke out against repression, urging that intellectuals must be prepared to risk everything to preserve freedom of expression.

Einstein received a variety of honors in his lifetime—from the 1921 Nobel Prize in physics to an offer (which he did not accept) of the presidency of Israel after Chaim Weizmann's death in 1952.

One of Einstein's last acts was his signing of a plea, initiated by Bertrand Russell, for the renunciation of nuclear weapons and the abolition of war. He was drafting a speech on the current tensions between Israel and Egypt when he suffered an attack due to an aortic aneurysm; he died a few days later. But despite his concern with world problems and his willingness to do whatever he could to alleviate them, his ultimate loyalty was to his science. As he said once

with a sigh to an assistant during a discussion of political activities: "Yes, time has to be divided this way between politics and our equations. But our equations are much more important to me, because politics is for the present, but an equation like that is something for eternity."[3]

Early Scientific Interests. Albert Einstein started his scientific work at the beginning of the twentieth century. It was a time of startling experimental discoveries, but the problems that drew his attention and forced him to produce the boldly original ideas of a new physics had developed gradually and involved the very foundations of the subject. The closing decades of the nineteenth century were the period when the long-established goal of physical theory—the explanation of all natural phenomena in terms of mechanics—came under serious scrutiny and was directly challenged. Mechanical explanation had had great successes, particularly in the theory of heat and in various aspects of optics and electromagnetism; but even the successful mechanical theory of heat had its serious failures and unresolved paradoxes, and physicists had not been able to provide a really satisfactory mechanical foundation for electromagnetic theory. Many were questioning the whole program of mechanism, and alternatives ranging from the energetics of Wilhelm Ostwald to the electromagnetic world view of Wilhelm Wien were widely considered and vigorously debated.

To a young man who looked to science for nothing less than an insight into the "great eternal riddle"[4] of the universe, these basic questions were the most challenging and also the most fascinating. Einstein was impressed by both the successes and the failures of mechanical physics and was attracted to what he later called the "revolutionary" ideas of James Clerk Maxwell's field theory of electromagnetism. His study of the writings of the nineteenth-century masters received a new direction when he read Ernst Mach's *Science of Mechanics.* This concern with general principles required something else to make it fruitful, however, and Einstein himself described what it was. He realized that each of the separate fields of physics "could devour a short working life without having satisfied the hunger for deeper knowledge," but he had an unmatched ability "to scent out the paths that led to the depths, and to disregard everything else, all the many things that clutter up the mind and divert it from the essential."[5] This ability to grasp precisely the particular simple physical situation that could throw light on obscure questions of general principle characterized much of Einstein's thinking.

His earliest papers—"my two worthless beginner's works,"[6] as he referred to them a few years later—

were an attempt to learn something from experimental materials about intermolecular forces with a view toward their possible relationship with long-range gravitational force, a problem going back to Newton's time. This work led nowhere, and Einstein's next series of three articles, published during the years 1902 to 1904, dealt with quite another set of ideas and was clearly the work of a mature scientist. In these articles Einstein rederived by his own methods the basic results of statistical mechanics: the canonical distribution of energy for a system in contact with a heat bath, the equipartition theorem, and the physical interpretations of entropy and temperature. He also emphasized that the probabilities that appear in the theory are to be understood as having a very definite physical meaning. The probability of a macroscopically identifiable state of a system is the fraction of any sufficiently long time interval that the system spends in this state. Equilibrium is dynamic, with the system passing through all its possible states in an irregular sequence. Ludwig Boltzmann had introduced this point of view years before, but Einstein made it very much his own.

It was in the last of this early series of papers, however, that Einstein introduced a new theme. There is one fundamental constant in statistical mechanics, the constant now known as Boltzmann's constant, k. It appears in the typical exponential factor of the distribution law, $\exp(-E/kT)$, where E is the energy of the system and T is its absolute temperature. It appears too in the relation between the entropy S and the probability W of a state

$$S = k \ln W. \tag{1}$$

Einstein asked for the physical significance of this constant k. It was already well-known from the theory of the ideal gas that k was simply related to the gas constant R and to Avogadro's number, N_0, the number of molecules in a gram-molecular weight of any substance,

$$k = \frac{R}{N_0}. \tag{2}$$

Einstein showed that k entered into still another basic equation of the statistical theory, the expression for the mean square fluctuation $\langle \Delta^2 \rangle$ of the energy E about its average value $\langle E \rangle$:

$$\langle \Delta^2 \rangle = \langle (E - \langle E \rangle)^2 \rangle = kT^2 \frac{d\langle E \rangle}{dT}. \tag{3}$$

This meant that k defines the scale of fluctuation phenomena or, as Einstein put it, that it determines the thermal stability of a system. This result shows that fluctuations are normally negligibly small so that

the average or thermodynamic value of the energy is a very good measure of this quantity, but Einstein was more interested in its other implications. If one could actually measure the energy fluctuations of any system, then k could be determined and with it Avogadro's number and the mass of an individual atom. None of these quantities was known with any precision, and previous determinations involved very indirect theoretical arguments. Einstein could not refer to any measurements of fluctuations, but he did give a very plausible analysis of the energy fluctuations in black-body radiation showing how k was related to the constant in Wien's displacement law.

This 1904 paper made little if any impression on Einstein's contemporaries, but it contained the seeds of much of his later work. No one before Einstein had taken seriously the fluctuation phenomena predicted by statistical mechanics, but he saw that the existence of such fluctuations could be used to demonstrate the correctness of the whole molecular theory of heat. The problem was to find a situation in which fluctuations could be observed, and Einstein found a solution to this problem in 1905, in his paper "Die von der molekularkinetischen Theorie der Wärme geforderte Bewegung von in ruhenden Flüssigkeiten suspendierten Teilchen" ("On the Movement of Small Particles Suspended in a Stationary Liquid Demanded by the Molecular-Kinetic Theory of Heat"). This predicted motion of colloidal particles was already widely known as Brownian motion, but at the time Einstein wrote this paper he knew virtually nothing about what had been observed and hesitated to identify the two motions. He was not trying to explain an old and puzzling phenomenon, but rather to deduce a result that could be used to test the atomic hypothesis and to determine the basic scale of atomic dimensions.

One essential assumption Einstein made was that a colloidal particle will come into thermodynamic equilibrium with the molecules of the fluid in which it is suspended, so that the average kinetic energy of the particle associated with its motion in any one direction is just the equipartition value, $kT/2$. The quantity that Einstein calculated for this random motion of colloidal particles was not the velocity, which is unmeasurable even in principle, but rather the mean square displacement $\langle \delta_x^2 \rangle$ in some particular direction x during the time interval τ. For spherical particles of radius a, satisfying the same law of resistance that a macroscopic sphere would obey in this fluid of viscosity η, he obtained the result

$$\langle \delta_x^2 \rangle = \frac{kT}{3\pi\eta a}\tau. \tag{4}$$

The hope Einstein expressed at the end of his paper, that "some enquirer" undertake an experimental test of his predictions, was fulfilled several years later when Jean Perrin's experiments confirmed the correctness of all features of the Brownian motion equation and provided a new determination of Avogadro's number. These results helped to convince the remaining skeptics, such as Wilhelm Ostwald, that molecules were real and not just a convenient hypothesis. The theory of Brownian motion was developed further by both Einstein and Maryan von Smoluchowski. Several years later both men worked on the theory of another fluctuation phenomenon—the opalescence exhibited by a fluid in the immediate neighborhood of its critical point. Einstein's work, published in 1910, was especially notable for its generalization of fluctuation theory in a form independent of the mechanical foundations of the theory, an old idea of his and one that later proved to be of considerable influence.

All the work discussed thus far, significant as it was, does not represent the predominant concern of Albert Einstein throughout his career—the search for a unified foundation for all of physics. Neither the attempts at a mechanical theory of the electromagnetic field nor the recent efforts to base mechanics on electromagnetism had been successful. The disparity between the discrete particles of matter and the continuously distributed electromagnetic field came out most clearly in Lorentz' electron theory, where matter and field were sharply separated for the first time. This theory strongly influenced Einstein, who often referred to the basic electromagnetic equations as the Maxwell-Lorentz equations. The problems generated by the incompatibility between mechanics and electromagnetic theory at several crucial points claimed Einstein's attention. His struggles with these problems led to his most important early work—the special theory of relativity and the theory of quanta.

For the sake of clarity and convenience, Einstein's development of relativity theory is treated in a separate article following the discussion of his contribution to quantum mechanics that occupies the remainder of the present article. It must be pointed out, however, that separating these two main themes in Einstein's work does an injustice to the unity of his fundamental purpose.

Quantum Theory and Statistical Mechanics. Einstein once described his first paper of 1905, "Über einen die Erzeugung und Verwandlung des Lichtes betreffenden heuristischen Gesichtspunkt" ("On a Heuristic Viewpoint Concerning the Production and Transformation of Light"), as "very revolutionary." He was not exaggerating. The heuristic viewpoint of the title was nothing less than the suggestion that light be considered a collection of independent particles of energy, which he called light quanta. Einstein had his reasons for advancing such a bold suggestion, one that seemed to dismiss a century of evidence supporting the wave theory of light. First among these reasons was a negative result: The combination of the electromagnetic theory of light with the (statistical) mechanics of particles was incapable of dealing with the problem of black-body radiation. It predicted that radiation in thermodynamic equilibrium within an enclosure would have a frequency distribution corresponding to an infinite amount of energy at the high-frequency end of the spectrum. This was incompatible with the experimental results, but, worse than that, it meant that the theory did not give an acceptable answer to the problem. Einstein was the first to point to this result, known later on as the "ultraviolet catastrophe," as a fundamental failure of the combined classical theories, although Lord Rayleigh had hinted at this in a paper in 1900.

Although he was convinced that a new unified fundamental theory was needed for an adequate treatment of the radiation problem, Einstein had no such theory to offer. What he did instead was to analyze the implications of the observed radiation spectrum, well-described, except at low frequencies, by Wien's distribution law. To carry out his analysis, Einstein used the methods of thermodynamics ("the only physical theory of universal content concerning which I am convinced that, within the framework of the applicability of its basic concepts, it will never be overthrown") and statistical mechanics. What he found was that the entropy of black-body radiation in a given frequency interval depends on the volume of the enclosure in the same way that the entropy of a gas depends on its volume. And because the latter dependence has its origin in the independence of the gas molecules rather than the details of their dynamics, Einstein leaped to the conclusion that the radiation, too, must consist of independent particles of energy. This identification required the energy E of the particles to be proportional to the frequency ν of the radiation,

$$E = h\nu, \qquad (5)$$

where the universal proportionality constant h was the product of k and one of the constants in Wien's distribution law.

Einstein showed that his strange proposal of light quanta could immediately account for several puzzling properties of fluorescence, photoionization, and especially of the photoelectric effect. His quantitative prediction of the relationship between the maximum energy of the photoelectrons and the frequency of the incident light was not verified experimentally for a decade. The light quantum hypothesis itself attracted only one or two adherents; it represented too great a departure from accepted ideas. It went far beyond the work Max Planck had done in 1900, in which the energy of certain material oscillators was treated as a discrete variable, capable only of values that were integral multiples of a natural unit proportional to the frequency. Planck's quantum hypothesis had been introduced as a way of deriving the complete distribution law for black-body radiation, but in 1905 it was only just starting to receive critical study.

During the years between 1905 and 1913 it was Einstein who took the lead in probing the significance of the new ideas on quanta. He soon decided that Planck's work was complementary to his own and not in conflict with it, as he had first thought. Einstein then realized that if Planck had been right in restricting the energies of his oscillators to integral multiples of $h\nu$, in discussing the interaction of molecular oscillators with black-body radiation, then this same restriction should also apply to all oscillations on the molecular scale. The success of Planck's work had to be looked upon as demonstrating the need for a quantum theory of matter, even as his own 1905 paper demonstrated the need for a quantum theory of radiation.

In 1907 Einstein pointed out how one could use the quantized energy of the oscillations of atoms in solids to account for departures from the rule of Dulong and Petit. This empirical rule, that the specific heat is the same for one mole of any element in solid form, was understood as a consequence of the theorem of equipartition of energy. Many light elements, however, had specific heats at room temperature that were much smaller than the Dulong-Petit value. Einstein showed how one could easily calculate the specific heat of a solid all of whose atoms vibrated with the same frequency (an assumption he made only as a convenient simplification) and obtain a universal curve for the variation of specific heat with temperature. The only parameter in the theory was the frequency of the quantized vibrations. This specific heat curve approached the Dulong-Petit value at high temperatures; accounted qualitatively for all the departures from the equipartition result, including the absence of electronic contributions to the specific heat; and predicted a new and general law: The specific heats of all solids should approach zero as the absolute temperature approaches zero. Einstein indicated how the vibration frequencies could be determined from infrared absorption measurements in

many cases; several years later he suggested another way of determining these frequencies using their relationship to the elastic constants of the solid.

As it turned out, Einstein's quantum theory of specific heats appeared at a time when the behavior of specific heats at low temperatures had just become of interest for very different reasons. Walther Nernst was planning a program of such measurements to establish his own new heat theorem, later known as the third law of thermodynamics. Nernst's results matched the predictions of Einstein's theory in all essential respects and convinced him that there was something really significant in this "odd" and "grotesque" theory,[7] as he called it. The success of Einstein's theory of specific heats in explaining old difficulties, predicting new laws, and establishing unexpected connections among thermal, optical, and elastic properties of crystals was the single most important element in awakening the interest of physicists in the quantum theory.

Wave-Particle Duality. For Einstein, however, the central problem continued to be the nature of radiation. In 1909, speaking in Salzburg at his first major scientific meeting, he argued that the future theory of light which would have to be constructed would be "a kind of fusion of the wave and emission theories."[8] Einstein's prediction was based on the results of his continued probings into the implications of Planck's distribution law for black-body radiation. He had calculated the energy fluctuations of the radiation in a small frequency interval with the help of equation (3) and had found that the fluctuations were the sum of two terms, indicating two apparently independent mechanisms for energy fluctuations. One term was readily intelligible as due to interfering waves, the other as due to variations in the number of light quanta present in the subvolume under study. Neither a wave nor a particle theory could account for the presence of both terms. Einstein confirmed this result by a completely independent calculation of the Brownian motion that a mirror would have to undergo if it were suspended in an enclosure containing a gas and black-body radiation in thermodynamic equilibrium. Once again there were wave and particle contributions to the fluctuations in momentum of the suspended mirror.

Einstein saw this wave-particle duality in radiation as concrete evidence for his conviction that physics needed a new, unified foundation. His view of the role of light quanta in this new fundamental theory had evolved since he put forward the heuristic suggestion of a corpuscular approach to radiation in 1905. Einstein now envisaged a field theory, based on appropriate partial differential equations, probably nonlinear, from which quanta would emerge as singular solutions, along the lines of the electric charges in electrostatics. He found some support for this parallel in the fact that Planck's constant, h, characteristic for light quanta, was dimensionally equivalent to e^2/c, where e is the unit electric charge and c is the velocity of light. To Einstein this suggested that the discreteness of energy and the discreteness of charge might be explained together by the new fundamental theory.

There was unfortunately very little to go on in the search for this new theory. It would have to be consistent with the special theory of relativity, but Einstein saw that theory as only a universal formal principle, analogous to the laws of thermodynamics, which gave no clue to the structure of matter or radiation. The fluctuation properties of radiation, which he had established, "presented small foothold for setting up a theory."[9] We know from Einstein's correspondence as well as from the brief remarks in his papers of this period that he devoted much of his effort to this problem in the years 1908 to 1911, using Lorentz' theory of electrons as one of his points of departure. His efforts along this line seem to have been comparable in their intensity, although not in their fruitfulness, to his efforts during the following years to create the new gravitational theory—the general theory of relativity.

When in 1911 Einstein put aside his intense work on the problem of developing a theory from which he could "construct" quanta—"because I now know that my brain is incapable of accomplishing such a thing"[10]—he did not give up his interest in quanta. He continued to reflect on the questions surrounding the quantum theory. In a paper in 1914, for example, he used familiar thermodynamic arguments to give a new derivation of Planck's expression for the average energy of an oscillator. This work led him to suggest the identity of physical and chemical changes at the molecular level: "A quantum type of change in the physical state of a molecule seems to be no different in principle from a chemical change."[11]

Relation to Bohr's Early Work. When Einstein returned to the radiation problem in 1916, the quantum theory had undergone a major change. Niels Bohr's papers had opened a new and fertile domain for the application of quantum concepts—the explanation of atomic structure and atomic spectra. In addition Bohr's work and its generalizations by Arnold Sommerfeld and others constituted a fresh approach to the foundations of the quantum theory of matter. Einstein's new work showed the influence of these ideas. He had found still another derivation of Planck's black-body radiation law, an "astonishingly

simple and general" one which, he thought, might properly be called "*the* derivation"[12] of this important law. It was based on statistical assumptions about the processes of absorption and emission of radiation and on Bohr's basic quantum hypothesis that atomic systems have a discrete set of possible stationary states. The proof turned on the requirement that absorption and emission of radiation, both spontaneous and stimulated, suffice to keep a gas of atoms in thermodynamic equilibrium. (This paper introduced the concept of stimulated emission into the quantum theory and is therefore often described as the basis of laser physics.) Einstein himself considered the most important contribution of this work to be not the new derivation of the distribution law but rather the arguments he presented for the directional character of energy quanta. Each quantum of frequency v emitted by an atom must carry away momentum hv/c in a definite direction; spherical waves would simply not exist.

Although Einstein put particular emphasis on the directionality of light quanta, there was no direct evidence for it until 1923 when Arthur Compton explained his experiments on the increase in X-ray wavelength after scattering from free electrons. Compton simply treated the process as a collision, obeying the conservation laws, between the electron and a quantum of energy hv and momentum hv/c in the direction of the incident X-ray beam. Even before this, however, Einstein was trying to devise a crucial experiment to settle the question of the nature of radiation. He held fast to his view that light quanta were indispensable since they described the particle properties really manifested by radiation. Light quanta did not have many other supporters until after the Compton effect, and they were particularly unpopular with Bohr and his co-workers. Bohr saw no good way of reconciling them with the correspondence principle and was willing to give up the exact validity of the conservation laws in order to avoid quanta. Experiments to check Bohr's proposals early in 1925 vindicated Einstein's belief in both the conservation laws and the validity of light quanta.

Bose-Einstein Statistics and Wave Mechanics. In 1924 Einstein received a paper from a young Indian physicist, S. N. Bose, setting forth a theory in which radiation was treated as a gas of light quanta. By changing the statistical procedure for counting the states of the gas, Bose had arrived at an equilibrium distribution which was identical with Planck's radiation law. Einstein was much taken with this extension of his old idea. He not only translated Bose's paper into German and saw to its publication, but he also applied Bose's new statistical idea to develop an analogous theory for an ideal gas of material particles. A gas obeying the Bose-Einstein statistics, as the new counting procedure was later called, showed a variety of interesting properties. Even though the particles exerted no forces on each other the gas showed a peculiar "condensation" phenomenon: Below a certain temperature a disproportionately large fraction of the total number of particles are found in the state of lowest energy.

Einstein's interest in the parallel between the gas of particles and the gas of light quanta deepened when he read Louis de Broglie's Paris thesis late in 1924. De Broglie, inspired by Einstein's earlier work on the wave-particle duality, had become convinced that this duality must hold for matter as well as radiation. In his thesis he developed the idea that every material particle has a wave associated with it, the frequency ν and wavelength λ of the wave being related to the energy E and momentum p of the particle by the equations

$$E = h\nu, \quad p = h/\lambda. \tag{6}$$

De Broglie had no experimental evidence to support his idea and deduced no experimentally testable conclusions from it, so it aroused very little interest. Einstein, however, was immediately attracted to the idea of matter waves because he saw its relationship to his new theory of the ideal gas. He found a confirmation of de Broglie's wave-particle duality for matter in the results of his calculation of the density fluctuations of this ideal gas. These fluctuations showed the same structure as had the energy fluctuations of black-body radiation; only now it was the particle term that would have been the only one present in the classical gas theory. Einstein saw the wave term in the fluctuations as a manifestation of the de Broglie waves, and he was sure he was not dealing with a "mere analogy." He proposed several kinds of experiments which might detect the diffraction of de Broglie waves.

Einstein's support for de Broglie's work brought it the attention it deserved, particularly from Erwin Schrödinger. In describing the origins of his wave mechanics a few years later, Schrödinger wrote: "My theory was stimulated by de Broglie's thesis and by short but infinitely far-seeing remarks by Einstein."[13] Those remarks were the ones linking de Broglie's ideas to the properties of the Bose-Einstein gas.

When the new matrix mechanics appeared, in the papers of Werner Heisenberg, Max Born, and Pascual Jordan, Einstein was interested but not convinced. "An inner voice tells me that it is still not the true Jacob,"[14] he wrote to Born in 1926. He looked more favorably on Schrödinger's wave mechanics: "I am convinced that you have made a decisive advance with your formulation of the quantum condition, just as I am equally convinced that the Heisenberg-Born route is off the track."[15]

Discontent With Quantum Mechanics. In 1927 the synthesis that constituted the new quantum mechanics was worked out. One of its key features was Born's statistical interpretation of Schrödinger's wave function. This meant that a full quantum mechanical description of the state of a system would generally specify only probabilities rather than definite values of the dynamical variables of the system. The new theory was intrinsically statistical and renounced as meaningless in principle any attempt to go beyond the probabilities to arrive at a deterministic theory. Bohr expressed what became the generally accepted viewpoint when he described quantum mechanics as a "rational generalization of classical physics," the result of "a singularly fruitful cooperation of a whole generation of physicists."[16]

Einstein dissented from this majority opinion. He never accepted the finality of the quantum mechanical renunciation of causality or its limitation of physical theory to the unambiguous description of the outcome of fully defined experiments. From the Solvay Congress of 1927, when the quantum mechanical synthesis was first discussed, to the end of his life, Einstein never stopped raising questions about the new physics to which he had contributed so much. He tried at first to propose conceptual experiments that would prove the logical inconsistency of quantum mechanics, but these arguments were all successfully refuted by Bohr. In 1935 Einstein began to stress another objection to quantum mechanics, arguing that its description of physical reality was essentially incomplete, that there were elements of physical reality which did not have counterparts in the theory. Bohr answered this argument, saying that Einstein's criterion of physical reality was ambiguous and that from Bohr's own complementarity standpoint the theory satisfied any reasonable standard of completeness.

Einstein never abandoned his opposition to the prevailing mode of thought despite the enormous success of quantum mechanics. He was convinced that a fundamental theory could not be statistical, "that *He* doesn't play dice."[17] Even more serious in Einstein's view was the incompleteness of the theory. He would not give up the idea that there was such a thing as "the real state of a physical system, something that objectively exists independently of observation or measurement, and which can, in principle, be described in physical terms."[18] The search for a theory that could provide such a description of reality was Einstein's program. He never lost his hope that a field theory of the right kind might eventually reach this goal.

That Einstein, without whom twentieth-century physics would be unthinkable, should have chosen to follow a separate path was a source of great regret to his colleagues. In Max Born's words: "Many of us regard this as a tragedy—for him, as he gropes his way in loneliness, and for us who miss our leader and standard-bearer."[19] But to Einstein himself his choice was inevitable; it was the natural outgrowth of all his years of striving to find a unified foundation for physics. This was what he meant when he ended his scientific autobiography by writing that he had tried to show "how the efforts of a lifetime hang together and why they have led to expectations of a definite form."[20]

MARTIN J. KLEIN

EINSTEIN: Theory of Relativity.

Einstein first wrote on radiation in his statistical mechanical discussion of Wien's law in 1904. He had already long thought about the fundamental problems of radiation; at age sixteen he had puzzled deeply over the question of what light would look like to an observer moving with it. As a student, one of the extramechanical applications of mechanics that had most fascinated him was the theory of light as a wave motion in a quasi-rigid elastic ether. In 1901 he was absorbed in unpublished, independent investigations of the critical problem of the motion of matter through the light ether.

At the turn of the century, the focus of discussion of the light ether was the electron theory. The electron theory had not been taught at the Zurich Polytechnic, and Einstein had had to instruct himself in it. Early in 1903 he began an intensive study of the theory, especially H. A. Lorentz' formulation of it. Lorentz' theory was founded on the concept of an absolutely stationary light ether. The ether completely permeated matter, with the consequence that bodies moving through it were not impeded and did not drag the ether with them. The ether was a dynamical substance but clearly not a mechanical one. Its dynamical properties were described precisely by Maxwell's electromagnetic field equations. The sole connection between the ether and matter occurred through the electrons that Lorentz assumed were contained in all ponderable molecules. The two kinds of physical entities in Lorentz' theory were the continuous ether and the discrete electrons; Maxwell's partial differential equations for the continuous field described the

state of ether, and the ordinary differential equations of Newtonian mechanics described the motion of the electrons.

The two entities together with their respective formalisms—continuous field theory and particle mechanics—constituted the characteristic dualism of Lorentz' theory. This dualism, which pervaded late nineteenth-century physics, was most clearly defined and confronted in Lorentz' theory. From 1900 on there was increasing concern to eliminate the dualism by recognizing the mass concept and the laws of Newtonian mechanics as consequences of the more fundamental laws of electron dynamics. This reduction was the program of the electromagnetic view of nature, which was advocated by W. Wien, M. Abraham, and others.

Like the more influential of his contemporaries, Einstein regarded the separateness of the concepts of electromagnetism and particle mechanics as the outstanding fault of physical theory. He did not, however, subscribe to the electromagnetic program but originated new strategies for unifying the parts of physics; his 1905 light-quantum hypothesis and relativity theory were the fruits of such strategies. In his light-quantum study, he attacked the dualism of field and particle concepts by showing reasons to conceive radiation not as a continuous wave phenomenon, but as a finite collection of discrete, independent energy particles, or quanta. Quanta were foreign to the Maxwell-Lorentz theory, and Einstein was convinced that that theory had to be changed—one reason why he could not accept the electromagnetic program, since it posited the existing electromagnetic theory as exact.

Einstein wrote his theory of relativity in full awareness of its relation to his work on light quanta earlier that year; relativity did not depend on the exactness of Maxwell's theory, a fact that was important to Einstein. He recognized that electromagnetism, no less than mechanics, had to be reformed; and he retained certain concepts of both sciences in seeking the synthesis that removed the dualism from physical theory. He introduced the particle concept from mechanics into the theory of light in his light-quantum study, and he introduced the mechanical concept of relativity into field theory in his relativity study. In his light-quantum study he concluded that light is discontinuous; in his relativity study he rejected the concept of the ether outright as being superfluous in a consistent electromagnetic theory. He saw the stationary, continuous ether of the electron theory as the chief impediment to a unified physics, and in 1905 he put forward two distinct arguments against its admissibility.

Special Relativity. The stated purpose of Einstein's first paper on relativity in 1905, "Zur Elektrodynamik bewegter Körper"[21] ("On the Electrodynamics of Moving Bodies"), was to produce a "simple and consistent theory of the electrodynamics of moving bodies based on Maxwell's theory for stationary bodies." Until the publication of his paper, the current theory had been neither simple nor consistent. As an example of what struck Einstein as undesirable complications, there was the sharp theoretical distinction made between the two ways in which the interaction between a magnet and a conductor was supposed to produce a current in the latter. In one case the magnet was assumed to be at rest, with the conductor in motion; in the other case the conductor was assumed to be at rest, with the magnet in motion. Although the resulting current was the same in both cases, the respective explanations differed from one another and invoked different concepts. Given Einstein's strong conviction that the logical simplicity of a scientific theory was an important token of its validity, the foregoing example (a commonplace experiment in elementary physics) suggested the desirability of finding a point of view from which the phenomena could be accounted for more simply. It suggested to him the possibility that, as was already the case in mechanics, a theory of the electrodynamics of moving bodies should specify only relative motions, there being no phenomenological basis for defining absolute motions.

The validity of this point of view was further confirmed for Einstein by the failure of various "ether-drift" experiments designed to detect the "absolute motion" of the earth, through variations in the velocity of light or other optical or electromagnetic effects of such motion. These experiments were undertaken in the expectation that the laws of electrodynamics and optics for a stationary reference system must take different forms in a moving system.

A variety of attempts were made by contemporary physicists to remove the conflicts with accepted theory produced by such experiments. One of the most famous of these expedients was the hypothesis of the Fitzgerald contraction proposed by G. F. Fitzgerald—and, independently, by Lorentz—to account for the failure of the Michelson-Morley experiment. The interferometer employed in this particular attempt to measure the absolute speed, v, of the earth's motion through the ether, was of sufficient sensitivity to detect variations in the speed of light, c, to the second order of the magnitude v/c. The conclusively negative result was explained by Fitzgerald as having been caused by a contraction of the arm of the interferometer in the direction of its motion through the ether, by the

factor $(1 - v^2/c^2)^{1/2}$, this contraction being just sufficient to offset the expected variation in the velocity of light.

This and other similar supplementary hypotheses added further complications to a theory of electrodynamics which in Einstein's opinion was already unnecessarily complex. By his own testimony the failure of the ether-drift experiments did not play a determinative role in his thinking but merely provided additional evidence in favor of his belief that inasmuch as the phenomena of electrodynamics were "relativistic," the theory would have to be reconstructed accordingly.

Another critic of "arbitrary hypotheses" such as the Fitzgerald contraction was the notable mathematician Henri Poincaré, who as early as 1895 had perceived the operation of a general law in the repeated failures of experiments designed to detect the absolute motion of the earth. Poincaré complained about there being certain explanations for the absence of first-order effects and other explanations for the absence of second-order effects,[22] and he was prepared to postulate that no physical experiment, regardless of its degree of accuracy, could detect the earth's absolute motion. He called this postulate the principle of relativity,[23] perhaps borrowing from Maxwell, who had referred to the "doctrine of the relativity of all physical phenomena" in his *Matter and Motion.*

Poincaré anticipated Einstein in asserting that all laws of nature, optical and electrodynamical as well as mechanical, should be brought within the scope of the principle of relativity. But their points of view and their programs were not identical. Poincaré remained in many respects committed to the traditional theory of electrodynamics. He adhered to the concept of the ether; and, while he appealed to the principle of relativity in deducing important results in electrodynamics, he appears to have imagined that the principle of relativity itself might be accounted for by an appropriate modification of the ether theory.

Einstein's approach was both more radical and more consistent. In his "Autobiographical Notes," Einstein recalled that he had long attempted to correct the dualistic fault of Lorentz' electron theory by direct, constructive approaches. But by the middle of 1905 he had come to see that to succeed he must proceed indirectly, by means of some universal principle. The model he had before him was thermodynamics, the science that had already guided his thought in statistical mechanics and radiation theory. He characterized thermodynamics as a theory of principle, one based on statements such as that of the impossibility of perpetual motion. He contrasted thermodynamics with the more common constructive theory built up from hypothetical statements, notably the theory of the continuous ether and the kinetic-molecular theory of gases.

In 1905 Einstein refounded the Maxwell-Lorentz theory on a new kinematics based on two universal postulates. The first postulate, or the "principle of relativity," pointed directly to Einstein's goal of unifying mechanics and electromagnetism; the postulate stipulated that the "same laws of electrodynamics and optics will be valid for all frames of reference for which the equations of mechanics hold good." The second postulate stipulated that light always moves with the same velocity in free space, regardless of the motion of the source. The second postulate was later described by W. Pauli as "the true essence of the old ether point of view."[24]

Both of Einstein's postulates, taken separately, had considerable experimental support, but in the ordinary view they appeared to be irreconcilable. For if the second postulate held true in one inertial system K (as it was assumed to hold true in the ether), then by virtue of the first postulate it would have to hold true in all reference systems in uniform translatory motion relative to K. But if the velocity of light were measured as c in terms of the space and time coordinates x, y, z, t of the reference system K, then it could not in current theory take the same value c in terms of the coordinates x', y', z', t' of another reference system K' in uniform motion v relative to K. For it was taken for granted that the coordinates of the two systems K and K' had to be related by the transformation equations:

$$x' = x - vt,$$
$$y' = y,$$
$$z' = z, \qquad (1)$$
$$t' = t.$$

The correctness of the transformation (1) had been held virtually above suspicion throughout the history of modern science. It was with respect to this transformation that the laws of classical mechanics remained invariant for all inertial systems. The equations of (1) were also obviously true in the common-sense view of space and time.

It was Einstein's fundamental insight into the problems of electrodynamics to perceive that the transformation (1) could not be assumed to be true a priori. Their form was an assumption made plausible by the invariance properties of Newtonian dynamics, but it was by no means necessary. Indeed, the transformation equations relating the space and time measurements between two coordinate systems are part of a physical theory and have to be consistent with experience. Accordingly Einstein was led to undertake a profound analysis of the appropriate procedures by which space and time coordinates are established within a reference system. His object was to provide a physically meaningful and justifiable basis for the derivation of an alternative set of transformation equations consistent with the joint validity of his two postulates.

One step in that direction had been taken ten years earlier by Lorentz. In a treatise on "electrical and optical phenomena in moving bodies," Lorentz introduced a new concept which he called *Ortszeit* ("local time").[25] He used this primarily as a mathematical shortcut to simplify the form of Maxwell's equations in a system K' assumed to be in uniform motion relative to the unique stationary system K in which these equations held true exactly. Local time involved a departure from the transformation equation $t' = t$. Although Lorentz appears to have viewed local time as a mathematical artifice, it represented in embryo a concept of time that Einstein would later justify adopting for the whole of physics.

The "Kinematical Part" of Einstein's paper "On the Electrodynamics of Moving Bodies" begins with an analysis of the meaning of time in physics. This had been a subject relatively exempt from fundamental scrutiny because of the extraordinary strength of traditional intuitive beliefs. Einstein later acknowledged that his familiarity with the writings of David Hume and Ernst Mach had fostered the kind of critical reasoning underlying this part of his work.

The formidable psychological obstacle to revising the transformation equations (1) had been the concept of absolute simultaneity "rooted in the unconscious."[26] But to be physically meaningful, the synchronization of spatially separated clocks must be defined in terms of an actual physical process. Although, as Einstein later emphasized, one is not in principle restricted to light signals as the standard process for coordinating the clock settings, he chose that particular method on the grounds that the propagation of electromagnetic waves was a process about which most was known.[27] Accordingly, he proposed that within an inertial system the clocks at any two points A and B could be synchronized by stipulating that the time interval in which light travels from A to B is the same as from B to A.

Einstein then proceeded to deduce on the basis of his two postulates the transformation equations relating the four coordinates x', y', z', t' in the system K' to the coordinates x, y, z, t in the inertial system K, with respect to which K' was in uniform translatory velocity v along the x-axis. (For simplicity the two x-axes were assumed to coincide, the other pairs of axes remaining parallel.) Fundamental to the derivation and meaning of this transformation was its dependence upon the synchronizing operation he had already defined for establishing the time coordinates in each system.

The following equations were deduced:

$$x' = \frac{x - vt}{(1 - v^2/c^2)^{1/2}}$$
$$y' = y$$
$$z' = z \qquad (2)$$
$$t' = \frac{t - vx/c^2}{(1 - v^2/c^2)^{1/2}}$$

It should be noted here that, unknown to Einstein, the transformation equations (2) had already appeared in a paper published in 1904 by Lorentz, "Electromagnetic Phenomena in a System Moving With Any Velocity Smaller Than That of Light."[28] Therefore, these equations were called the Lorentz transformation by Poincaré. (Einstein did not use this name, either in 1905 or in his 1907 review paper.)

In Einstein's theory the transformation equations (2) express the kinematical content of his two postulates. Solving all four equations (2) for x, y, z, t in terms of x', y', z', t', their symmetry becomes perspicuous, the only change between the two sets being the sign (i.e., the direction) of v. As Einstein perceived, the new transformation presented a revolutionary theory of space and time. Consider any two inertial systems K and K' moving with relative velocities $\pm v$, respectively. By application of the equations (2), it follows that a rigid body of length l as measured in K, in which it is at rest, measures $l(1 - v^2/c^2)^{1/2}$ in K'; and a rigid body of length l as measured in K', in which it is at rest, measures $l(1 - v^2/c^2)^{1/2}$ in K. A clock at rest in K runs slow by $1 - (1 - v^2/c^2)^{1/2}$ seconds per second when timed by the clocks in K'; and reciprocally an identical retardation occurs for the rate of a clock at rest in K' as measured in K. Thus, lengths and time intervals are magnitudes relative to the inertial systems in which they are measured. The reciprocity of length contraction and time dilation between any two inertial systems renders physically meaningless questions as to whether such effects are "apparent" in one system and "real" in the other, or vice versa. For those contemporaries of Einstein who were committed to the ether theory or the concept of absolute simultaneity this conclusion was difficult to accept.

Another important kinematical theorem of "On the Electrodynamics of Moving Bodies" was Einstein's revised law for the addition of velocities. For the simplest case (in which the velocities v and w are in the direction of the x-axis of the inertial system in which they are composed) this law takes the form:

$$V = \frac{v + w}{1 + vw/c^2}. \qquad (3)$$

From this equation the limiting value of the velocity of light, c, can also be deduced. The composition of no two velocities v and w, each of which is less than c, can equal c; and the composition of any velocity less than c with c equals c.

Because of the complete generality of Einstein's first postulate, it follows that the fundamental principle of the special theory of relativity can be expressed by stating that the laws of physics are invariant with respect to the Lorentz transformation. The imposition of this formal restriction on all possible laws immediately facilitated the development of a greatly simplified theory of electrodynamics for both stationary and moving bodies. That, of course, had been Einstein's original objective.

Applications of Special Relativity. In the concluding or "Electrodynamical Part" of Einstein's original paper on relativity, he presented applications of his theory to various phenomena of electrodynamics. He proved that the Maxwell-Hertz equations for the electromagnetic field, both in empty space and when convection currents are taken into account, were invariant under the Lorentz transformation. He also showed how the force acting upon a point charge in motion in an electromagnetic field could be calculated simply by a transformation of the field to a system of coordinates at rest relative to the charge. In the new theory, electric and magnetic forces did not exist independently of the motion of the system of coordinates. From this point of view, the explanation of the currents produced by the relative motion of a magnet and a conductor was not complicated by theoretical distinctions based on their absolute motions.

Einstein derived several other theorems in the optics and electrodynamics of moving bodies on the basis of the theory for stationary bodies. His method was to choose the appropriate coordinate systems in each case and then apply the transformation equations (2). In this way he deduced relativistic (i.e., Lorentz-invariant) laws for Doppler's principle, for aberration, for the energy of light, and for the pressure of radiation on perfect reflectors. In what was a more difficult problem, he derived the three relativistic laws describing the motion of an electron in an electromagnetic field.

The requirement of Lorentz invariance for the laws of physics led Einstein and fellow physicists, including Planck, to the revision of a number of the laws of classical mechanics. This revision had already been initiated by Einstein in his laws of motion for electrons. In their relativistic formulations, masses and, correspondingly, forces could no longer have absolute magnitudes independent of the coordinate systems in which they were measured. Thus the expressions for momentum and energy also took new relativistic forms. Einstein later claimed that one of the foremost achievements of the special theory was its unification of the conservation laws for momentum and energy.[29]

Another demonstration of the heuristic power of the principle of Lorentz invariance was provided by a second paper published by Einstein in 1905, "Ist die Trägheit eines Körpers von seinem Energiegehalt abhängig?" ("Does the Inertia of a Body Depend Upon Its Energy-Content?").[30] In calculating, by means of the Lorentz transformation, the loss of kinetic energy $(K_0 - K_1)$ for a body emitting radiation energy in the amount L, Einstein was able to deduce the equation

$$K_0 - K_1 = Lv^2/2c^2.$$

This expression revealed (in view of the definition of kinetic energy: $mv^2/2$) that as the result of its radiation the mass of the body had been diminished by L/c^2. Arguing that the particular form in which the body lost some of its energy did not affect the calculated diminishment of its mass, Einstein concluded that the mass of a body is a measurement of its energy content. Differences in its energy content equal differences in its mass in accordance with the equation

$$\Delta E = \Delta mc^2.$$

In accordance with his frequent practice of suggesting appropriate experimental research, Einstein proposed that this law might be tested by experiments with radium salts. He observed that the exchange of radiation between bodies should involve an exchange of mass; light quanta have mass exactly as do ordinary molecules, and thus a bridge was established between the concepts of electromagnetism and mechanics. The mechanical concept of mass lost its isolation, becoming a form of energy, as characteristic of radiation as of ordinary matter. The chief value of the mass-energy law for Einstein lay in its contribution to the problem of the dualism in physical theory. In 1907 he carried this viewpoint one step further, assuming that mass and energy are completely equivalent concepts, the rest mass of a body being a measure of its "latent" energy content in accordance with the famous equation[31]

$$E = mc^2.$$

The electromagnetic mass question and other questions central to the work of Lorentz and his contemporaries remained the focus of German electromagnetic research for several years after Einstein's 1905 relativity paper. The universal significance of relativity was not generally recognized at first; Einstein's theory was regarded as merely another statement of Lorentz' electron theory, not as an important statement in its own right.

Geometric Significance of Relativity. The universal implications of Einstein's theory were first clearly revealed by the Göttingen mathematician Hermann Minkowski in 1907 and 1908. Minkowski argued that relativity implied a complete revision of our conception of space and time, and that this revision applied throughout physics and not just to electrodynamics where it originated. His four-dimensional formulation of the theory, his application of it to mechanics, and his advocacy generally had a decisive historical importance in winning physicists to the new theory and in clarifying its revolutionary significance. By 1910 relativity was fairly well understood in its full generality, and it began to be widely accepted, especially in Germany.

Minkowski recast the special theory of relativity in a form which had a decisive influence in the geometrization of physics. (The memoir was published in 1908.) As David Hilbert expressed it in his memorial lecture, Minkowski, in the formalism which he developed, "was able to reveal the inner simplicity and the true essence of the Laws of Nature." Minkowski considered the world as described by the special theory of relativity to be a four-dimensional flat space-time in which the events are points, the histories of particles represented by curves (world lines), and the inertial frames correspond to Cartesian coordinates spanning this space-time. The history of a particle moving in the absence of an external force is the straightest possible, it is a geodesic. This space-time is flat. Given a geodesic it is always possible to find another which does not intersect the first one. (The Euclidean space of elementary geometry is also flat. There the geodesics are straight lines, and parallel straight lines do not intersect.) Going from one inertial frame to another and using the transcription of data as given by the Lorentz transformations (2) corresponds to relabeling the events by changing the coordinate system in space-time. This very strongly geometrical point of view exhibited the fundamental features of the special theory clearly, and ultimately led to Einstein's belief that all laws of nature should be geometrical propositions concerning space-time.

Gravitational Theory. Einstein understood the universal significance of his relativity theory from the start. In the years immediately following 1905, he continued to work and publish on problems in relativistic electron theory; at the same time he tried to frame a relativistic theory of gravitation, a branch of physics that belonged to mechanics, not electromagnetism. In 1905 he had already freed gravitation from its exclusively mechanical context by his law of mass-energy equivalence; radiation too has mass and should gravitate. He tried to revise the Newtonian gravitational law so that it agreed with the demands of relativistic kinematics.

Any theory of gravitation contains three major parts: (a) the field equations relating the gravitational field to its sources (in Newtonian theory, there is just one equation, Poisson's equation for the gravitational potential using the mass density as the source); (b) the equations of motion of material bodies in this gravitational field (the Newtonian equation of motion in the Newtonian theory); and (c) the equations of motion of the electromagnetic field in the presence of gravitational fields (in the classical theory these are Maxwell's equations *uninfluenced* by the gravita-

tional field). (See Table I for an outline of the development of the theory in these terms.)

Einstein, in his first attempt, retained the scalar potential of classical gravitation theory, generalizing the potential equation by adding a second time-derivative term. The field equation of gravitation then transforms correctly, and gravitation becomes, like electromagnetism, a finitely propagated action. He did not get far with this approach and did not publish it. The difficulty was that, according to the mass-energy law, the inertial mass of a body varies with its internal and kinetic energies, so that the acceleration of free fall might depend on these energies; this would contradict the notion, suggested by experience and adopted by Einstein as a premise, that all bodies have the same gravitational acceleration regardless of their velocities and internal states. This persuaded him that his 1905 principle of relativity was an inadequate basis for a gravitational theory and, hence, for a unified, nondualistic physics.

There was another way to approach the gravitational problem, one based on the recognition that the

Date	Equations of Motion in the Presence of Gravitation	Field Equations for Gravitation
1907	Equivalence principle using uniformly accelerated frames; Maxwell's equations in the presence of gravitation	
1911	Equivalence principle rediscussed	Scalar field theory
1912		Nonlinearity of field equations
		Gravitational induction (leading to Mach's principle of 1918)
1913	Equivalence of all frames in which conservation laws hold	
	History of particle as a geodesic in space-time	Introduction of metric in space-time as seat of gravitation and tensorial formulation of laws
1914	Maxwell's equations correctly given in presence of gravitation	
1915	Final formulation of general theory (announced 25 March)	
1916	Equations of motions of particles and of the electromagnetic field	Field equations of gravitation expressed through curvature of space-time

TABLE I.   Evolution of the General Theory

free fall of a body is independent of its energy if its gravitational mass varies with energy in the same way as its inertial mass. Although there was no theoretical reason why the two kinds of mass should behave in the same way, Einstein did not doubt that they did so. He made the strict equivalence of inertial and gravitational mass the key to a proper understanding of gravitation, and he developed this understanding in his first published statement on gravitational theory. In the same survey article on relativity, which contained the energy-mass equation, he elevated the equality of inertial and gravitational mass, or, equivalently, the equality of the acceleration of the free fall of all bodies, to the status of an equivalence principle.

Einstein explained that the principle of relativity must be extended to accelerated coordinate systems; a coordinate system accelerated relative to an inertial frame is equivalent, in a sufficiently small spatial region, to a frame which is not accelerated relative to an inertial one but in which a gravitational field is present. This comes about in the following way: In an inertial frame let bodies be at rest, or move with a uniform motion. From the point of view of an observer at rest in the accelerated frame, these bodies appear to have an acceleration; this acceleration is the same for all bodies independent of their mass (being equal and opposite to the acceleration of the frame accelerated relative to the inertial frame). This acceleration naturally can be transformed away by simply using the original inertial frame as the frame of reference.

Now Einstein observed that a gravitational field locally generates a physical situation which is identical to the one described by the accelerated observer. For all bodies undergo the same acceleration in a gravitational field independent of their mass, and the acceleration of a body can be transformed away using a frame of reference which falls freely with the body whose acceleration we wish to transform away. If this be the case, one can immediately discuss, at least in a heuristic fashion, the influence of gravitational fields on phenomena, by solving another problem, the description of the same phenomena in the absence of a gravitational field but viewed from an accelerated frame. In this way Einstein showed that gravitational fields influence the motion of clocks. Since the frequency of an emitted spectral line can be used as a clock, it follows that there is a frequency shift between an emitted and an observed spectral line, if the gravitational potential at the location of the observer is different from that at the emitter. He also showed that all electromagnetic phenomena are influenced by a gravitational field; for example, the light rays are bent if they pass in the vicinity of gravitating bodies. It had long been suspected that there might be an interaction between electromagnetic and gravitational fields (see, for example, Faraday's experiments); however, this was the first concrete suggestion as to what this interaction should be, how it arises, and what the order of the magnitude of these effects are.

Program for General Relativity. The year 1907 was a turning point in relativity. From then on Einstein (then twenty-eight years old) was interested less in the special theory of relativity and more in its possible generalization. From the point of view of the special theory, space-time was a given framework, within which the natural phenomena took place. These were still described as in classical physics; there were fields of force and material bodies which acted on each other. The next generalization consisted in eliminating the gravitational fields of force by allowing the structure of space-time to change in such a way that the free motion in this altered space-time should in some way correspond to the motion under the influence of gravitational fields in the space-time of the special theory. The final generalization, which was never successfully attained, would have consisted in eliminating the electromagnetic fields of force as well by altering the geometry of space-time in a suitable way. The first generalization, the geometrization of gravitation, led eventually to the general theory of relativity; the additional geometrization of the electromagnetic fields of force led to the invention of the unified field theories.

In 1907 the details of this program were still obscure. The equivalence principle, relating the gravitational field and accelerated frames of reference, was already there. This helped Einstein to discuss some of the effects of a gravitational field on the electromagnetic field. The geometrization of this principle, the mathematical characterization of the gravitational field, its sources, and the relation between the field and its sources, i.e., the gravitational field equations, were still missing. In the next twelve years, Einstein was occupied with building a complete theory of gravitation rising out of his heuristic principle.

Between 1907 and 1911 Einstein published nothing more on gravitation. He was preoccupied with finding a reformed electron theory that incorporated both electric charges and light quanta; his chief heuristic guides in this search were thermodynamics, his fluctuation method in statistical mechanics, and his special theory of relativity. In the context of this largely unpublished work, he came to understand that the solution to the dualism problem was to write physics in terms of continuous field quantities and nonlinear partial differential equations that yield singularity-free particle solutions. The field equations were to account for particles and their interaction; they were to contain the laws of motion of particles, eliminating the dualistic need for particle mechanics in addition to field theory. He was soon to find additional support for this understanding in his general relativity theory, which required that field equations have just those mathematical properties he had decided upon on physical grounds.

For Einstein the connection of the particle and the field was the central problem of physics, and he saw the whole of the problem as contained in the connection of the electron and the electromagnetic field. A cardinal point of his unification objective in physics was to deduce the electron and its motion from the field equations. The whole difficulty was that it proved impossible to find the proper modification of Maxwell's equations that would permit such a deduction; any modification seemed arbitrary without a universal principle to determine its selection. In the years prior to 1911, he believed that the special relativity principle, together with statistical mechanical considerations, was an adequate guide for finding the new electromagnetic equations capable of describing particles. After several years of arduous effort, he recognized that he had been mistaken and shifted his expectations to the more powerful universal principle—the postulate of general relativity—as offering the possibility of avoiding arbitrariness in constructing field theories with particle solutions. The new postulate restricted much more severely the mathematical form the field equations could take.

By 1911 Einstein had become deeply pessimistic over the prospect of soon finding a new electron theory that incorporated quanta in a natural way. That year he returned to his 1907 gravitational theory, and for the next several years he looked to gravitation rather than electromagnetism as the starting point for the reform of physical theory. In 1911 the first Solvay Congress met to discuss the crisis in physics signaled by the quantum theory. Two years later, in 1913, Niels Bohr published his quantum theory of atoms and molecules. Just when the physics community began seriously to reorient itself toward quantum problems, Einstein seemed to move away from them. By 1911 he had come to regard the particle or quantum aspect of nature as secondary to the field aspect. He thought it was futile to attempt a fundamental understanding of the microscopic structure of nature until the macroscopic structure of the field was understood; when it was, quantum phenomena would be deduced from it. He never ceased to struggle with quanta, but his concern was less obvious than it had

once been. His direct contribution to the later development of the quantum theory tended to be in the nature of criticism and suggestion; all the while he struggled to vindicate this way of developing physics by seeking a theory of the total field that would finally clarify the quantum problem.

Following a 1911 paper on the influence of gravitation on the propagation of light,[32] Einstein published two remarkable memoirs in 1912[33] which were efforts to construct a complete theory of gravitation incorporating the equivalence principle. In these memoirs Einstein supposed that the gravitational field can be characterized completely by one function, the local speed of light, analogous to the Newtonian description, where only the gravitational potential appears. The equivalence principle gives no clue to how the field equation describing the gravitational field should be constructed. By an extraordinary argument he extended the potential equation of Newton, which determines in that theory the gravitational potential, and came to the conclusion (a) that the equation must be nonlinear and (b) that this nonlinearity can be interpreted to show that the source of the gravitational field is not only the energy associated with the rest mass of bodies but also depends on the energy residing in the gravitational field itself. This was the first appearance of a nonlinear field equation for gravitation. In the first of his 1912 memoirs, Einstein wrote the differential equation of the static gravitational field as

$$\Delta c = kc\rho,$$

where c is the local velocity of light, k is a universal gravitational constant, and ρ is the density of matter. Next he derived the equations of motion of a body, using the equivalence principle: the force on a material point of mass m at rest in a gravitational field is

$$-m \operatorname{grad} c.$$

In his second memoir in 1912, he used the equivalence principle to show the influence of a static gravitational field on electromagnetic and thermal processes. Also in the same year, Einstein pointed out that from the energy expression which followed from his theory as it then was, one could conclude that if a body is enclosed in an envelope of gravitating matter its mass might be expected to increase. This he considered as a suggestion that perhaps the whole mass of a body could be conceived as arising from the gravitational interaction of this body with all the other bodies in the universe. He further pointed out that a similar point of view, without any theory, had already been advocated by Mach. This suggestion, that the mass of a body is the manifestation of the presence of other bodies in the universe, Einstein later (1918) called Mach's principle; the first appearance of an idea that a theory of gravitation should discuss the problem raised by Mach was in 1912. During this same period, others were more reluctant to take these far-reaching steps and there were several attempts to invent a gravitational theory in which there are preferred frames of reference such that the velocity of light is constant and has the same value as in empty space. Such a theory is, however, in conflict with the equivalence principle. The most comprehensive attempt was G. Nordström's in 1913.

Einstein himself came to the opposite conclusion. Instead of abandoning the investigation of uniformly accelerated frames of reference, he decided that the approach was too narrow and that in the generalization of the special theory not only these special transformations should be permitted, but more general ones. He was as yet unwilling to introduce general coordinate transformations. In his 1913 review article and in his memoir with Grossman, he insisted that only those frames of reference are admissible in which the conservation laws hold true. In fact these conservation laws were used by him to invent the field equations for gravitation. The use of more general frames of reference brought two important aspects into the theory. One was the use of more general mathematical tools which practically forced Einstein toward the final answer; the other was the observation that if more general transformations are permitted the gravitational field must be characterized not by one function but by ten functions. Moreover these ten functions have a simple geometric significance; they characterize the metric properties of space-time at every point.

This step was immense in its implications: (*a*) it forced the abandonment of the Newtonian notion that the gravitational field could be characterized by one scalar function, the gravitational potential; (*b*) it forced on Einstein the notion that gravitation is explicitly related to the geometrical structure of space-time. In his 1913 paper with Grossman,[34] Einstein adopted as the fundamental invariant of this theory the generalization of the four-dimensional line element *ds* originally introduced by Minkowski for a flat space-time. If space-time is not flat, *ds* must be expressed in terms of a general coordinate frame. Then two events, labeled

$$x^1, \ x^2, \ x^3, \ x^4$$

and

$$x^1 + dx^1, \quad x^2 + dx^2, \quad x^3 + dx^3, \quad x^4 + dx^4,$$

have a separation *ds* whose square is given by

$$ds^2 = \sum_{\mu=1}^{4} \sum_{\nu=1}^{4} g_{\mu\nu} \, dx^\mu \, dx^\nu.$$

The sixteen functions $g_{\mu\nu}$ form a symmetric tensor field (thus ten $g_{\mu\nu}$ are independent). Einstein considered these functions as the basic objects of his theory describing the manifestations of gravitation. In particular he assumed that as in the special theory the history of a body will be a geodesic; thus the history will be that curve in space-time for which $\int ds$ is a minimum, $\delta \int ds = 0$. Since the $g_{\mu\nu}$ appear in *ds* this principle will now determine the motion of a body influenced by gravity. Einstein regarded the $g_{\mu\nu}$ as the gravitational potentials, which replaced the single scalar *c* of his 1912 theory. The principal problem of his gravitational theory was, then, to determine the $g_{\mu\nu}$. For this purpose, Einstein sought an extension of Poisson's equation for the gravitational potential ϕ,

$$\Delta\phi = 4\pi\rho,$$

which he wrote

$$\Gamma_{\mu\nu} = X\Theta_{\mu\nu}.$$

$\Gamma_{\mu\nu}$ is constructed from derivatives of the $g_{\mu\nu}$ and is the analogue of $\Delta\phi$; $\Theta_{\mu\nu}$ contains the material sources of the field and is the analogue of ρ; X is a gravitational constant. In any given physical situation, the $\Theta_{\mu\nu}$ may be assumed known. The problem was to determine the $\Gamma_{\mu\nu}$; Einstein believed that the principle of the conservation of energy and momentum is sufficient for this purpose.

Enunciation of General Relativity. Thus in 1913 the situation was as follows: The equation of motion of a particle in a gravitational field had been given; the equations of motion of the electromagnetic field in the presence of a gravitational field were incomplete; the field equations of gravity were incomplete; Newtonian concepts had been retained in order to save the conservation laws together with preferred frames of reference, to wit, precisely those where the conservation laws still held true as laws. This last stage was soon passed. In 1914 the field equations for the electromagnetic field (Maxwell's equations) were given correctly in the presence of a gravitational field. On 25 March 1915 Einstein announced in the Prussian Academy of Sciences that he also had the field equations of gravitation in hand. The results were published in several articles later in the same year,[35] and on 20 November, David Hilbert, in Göttingen, independently found the same field equations. A greatly expanded and detailed memoir appeared in 1916 which, so to speak, became the Authorized Version.[36] Einstein's new understanding in 1915 and 1916 was that the gravitational field can be characterized by Riemann's curvature tensor $G_{\mu\nu}$, a tensor obtained from the $g_{\mu\nu}$ by differentiation. He wrote the gravitational field equations as

$$G_{\mu\nu} = -K(T_{\mu\nu} - \tfrac{1}{2}g_{\mu\nu}\,T),$$

where T is the scalar of the material energy tensor $T_{\mu\nu}$ and K is a gravitational constant. This was his new analogue of Poisson's equation. The $g_{\mu\nu}$ that are determined by the field equations determine, through the separate equations of motion, the history of a body in the gravitational field.

The final theory now presented was of immense sweep and great conceptual simplicity. All frames of reference are equally good; the classical conservation laws fade away—they are no longer laws but mere identities and lose the significance they had before. There are no gravitational forces present in the sense that the theory contains electromagnetic ones, or elastic ones. Gravitation appears in a different way. The fixed, given space-time of the special theory has gone; what before had erroneously been labeled as the influence of a body by gravitation on the motion of another is now given as the influence of one body on the geometry of space-time in which the free motion of the other body occurs. This free motion in the altered space-time is what was mistaken as the forced motion (forced by a gravitational field) in an unaltered space-time. The laws of nature are now geometrical propositions concerning space-time. Space-time is a metric space, which means that we have a rule how to compute the separation of any two points in the space. This can be done if we know ten numbers at any point and thus have ten functions in space-time. Once these ten functions are given, everything that can be known can be computed. As stated before, three questions should be answered by the theory:

(1) *What corresponds to the field equations of gravitation?* The presence of matter alters the metric properties of space-time; in particular, the curvature of space-time at a point is determined by the amount of matter and electromagnetic field and their motion at that point. This alteration of the metric properties has an effect on the history of the motion of a body and on the history of the development of the electromagnetic field. These are embodied in the equations of motion.

(2) *What are the equations of motion of a body?* The equation of motion of a body is given by the statement that the history of a body always be a geodesic. But, of course, a geodesic in a curved space is quite different from a flat one; altering the curvature alters the motion.

(3) *What are the equations of motion of the electromagnetic field?* The equations of motion of the elec-

tromagnetic field are not geometrical propositions. Here we take over Maxwell's equations from the special theory where it was specified for a flat space-time, and simply transcribe them for a curved one. (The fact that these equations do not refer to anything geometrical sent Einstein in search of a more general theory, a unified field theory, where all the laws would have a geometrical significance.)

The equivalence principle is contained in the theory in the following fashion. According to this principle, one can make the effects of a gravitational field, on the motion of a particle or on an electromagnetic field, disappear locally by a transformation to a frame of reference which has the same acceleration as the gravitational field at that point. In this frame one can describe locally all events as in the special theory. Since the effects of the gravitational field are represented in the general theory by the fact that space-time is curved, this must mean that the equations of motion, on the one hand, and space-time, on the other, must be of such nature that the effects of this curvature can be transformed away locally. This arises because (*a*) the equations of motion of a particle, and of the electromagnetic field, are such that the curvature does not appear in them explicitly, and (*b*) space-time can be approximated locally by its flat tangential space, in the same way that a curved surface can be approximated by a flat tangential plane in the immediate vicinity of the point of contact.

Experimental Predictions of General Relativity. What were the experimental predictions? The equivalence principle had already predicted that the gravitational field must influence the electromagnetic field, and this result was also obtained in the developed theory. In addition Einstein in 1915 had already pointed out that according to Newtonian theory a solitary planet moving around the sun describes an elliptic orbit. Because of the presence of the other planets, this motion is perturbed and the axis of the ellipse slowly rotates relative to the fixed stars; i.e., it precesses. If these effects are computed on a Newtonian basis for the planet Mercury, it will be found that the experimentally observed precession is larger than the computed one. Einstein showed that if the motion of the single planet around the sun is calculated from the general theory, there is already a small precession. If this value is added to the Newtonian value of the precession caused by the other planets, the resulting total precisely fits the experimental results. This was the first unexpected success of the theory. The two other predictions concerned the effect of the gravity on light. In testing the first, the sun is treated as the body causing the bending. In order that the effect on the light coming from other stars might be observed, an eclipse was requisite. Although Einstein suggested such an experiment before the 1914 eclipse, the first observations were made in 1919. The values observed scatter around the theoretically predicted value with probable errors large enough to include it. The second prediction concerned the shift of spectral lines in the presence of a gravitating body and, for some time, the astrophysical observations were inaccurate. Not until 1960 was the prediction accurately verified in the laboratory.

Subsequent Investigations. For the rest of his life Einstein's investigations on relativity centered on the following points: (1) mathematical investigations into the structure of the theory; (2) approximate solutions of the general theory and their physical implications; (3) the application of the theory to the universe as a whole, to cosmology, and to Mach's principle; (4) general discussions of relativity and popular expositions; and (5) efforts to incorporate the electromagnetic field into the geometry of space-time. We shall take up the discussion of each point in chronological order.

Mathematical Investigations. As far as the mathematical structure of general relativity was concerned there were three classes of problems which concerned Einstein particularly: the role and meaning of conservation laws; the relation of the equations of motion of bodies to the field equations of gravitation; and the role and nature of singularities in the theory.

During the development of the general theory, Einstein had intended to hold fast to the conservation of energy and momentum in the usual (special relativistic) sense as far as possible. At the same time he was driven by other considerations toward the idea that the laws should be generally covariant, i.e., that the laws should have the same form for all observers in space-time, irrespective of their states of motion. These two desires, the maintenance of these conservation laws and of general covariance, proved mutually incompatible. The final theory is generally covariant; it has conservation identities and not conservation laws in the usual sense, although certain covariant laws do exist for special cases in general relativity.

The problem of the equation of motion of bodies is the following. The 1916 theory had a classical structure in the sense that there were both field equations (the curvature of space-time is determined by the mass and motion of bodies in space-time) and equations of motion of bodies (the world line of small mass is a geodesic). Are these two statements really separate? If the field equations were linear, they indeed would be. They are not linear, however, and Einstein showed that if matter is represented by a

point singularity of the metric field, these singularities are located on world lines that are geodesics of space-time, provided its metric satisfies the equation of general relativity.[37]

The role and nature of singularities in the solutions greatly troubled Einstein both for mathematical and for physical reasons, and the question influenced his thinking on Mach's principle and on the necessity of unified field theories (the latter are discussed below).

Approximate Solutions. Experimentally, we know that there are observers such that the effects of gravitation are quite small in extended portions of space-time. This enables one to solve the equations of the general theory approximately. These approximate solutions show that, contrary to the Newtonian theory, there are gravitational disturbances that travel as waves. Recent experimental observations by Joseph Weber suggest that these waves may occur in nature. If these waves are compared with electromagnetic waves in empty space, significant differences are noted. Their polarization properties are different. They are associated with more complicated modes of motion of the source. They are thus less efficient in carrying away the kinetic energy of the motion of the source. Both types of waves propagate with the same velocity, however—that of light.

Application of the Theory. If we consider the universe as a whole, we cannot consider gravitation as a small effect, a small deformation of an otherwise flat space-time. In particular the following predicament arises. If inertia and gravitation are inseparable, how is it possible to have a situation in which the effects of gravitation are small? After all, that would mean that in the absence of any such small effect, we still would have a flat space-time with an inertial motion possible in it, while gravitation would be entirely absent. Previously (1912),[38] Einstein had considered the possibility that there should be a gravitational induction effect, according to which the presence of other masses alters the value of the mass of a given body. From this consideration he erected the hypothesis that, conceivably, the whole mass of a body is generated by the presence of other masses.[39] If this be true within the general theory, two things should follow:

(*a*) There should be no solution of the field equations applicable to the whole universe which can describe an empty space-time (since then in this empty space-time geodesics would exist, which could be taken as giving the history of the inertial motion of a particle).

(*b*) The value of the mass of a body should be determined by the presence and amount of other masses in the universe. (It is now also believed that

Mach's principle should contain an explanation of why the gravitational interaction is always attractive.)

It was the notion that the existence of inertia and gravitation must be explained along these lines that Einstein called Mach's principle (1918). In 1917 he grappled with the first half of this problem.[40] If matter in the universe is generally distributed uniformly, is it possible to find a time-independent solution of the field equations that describe a spatially finite (closed) space-time, and will this space-time vanish if the total mass of the universe is spatially infinite? He found that no such solution existed unless he modified the field equations, adding to them the so-called cosmological term. This term has no observable effect on any of the local solutions used in the experimental tests but alters the solution as a whole. With this modification, however, a solution does exist. Thereby, the first aspect of Mach's principle would be satisfied. But Einstein was dissatisfied with this answer because an arbitrary modification had had to be introduced into the field equations.

In 1922 A. Friedmann found that even without the cosmological term there are still solutions of the field equations where matter has a finite density everywhere in space, provided this density is not time-independent. In 1929 Hubble announced his discovery that the red shift of spectral lines coming from distant sources increases uniformly with the distance. This phenomenon can be interpreted as evidence for a uniform expansion of the universe as can be described by the Friedmann solutions.

General Discussions and Expositions. During these years Einstein was also concerned to clarify misconceptions about the theory of relativity and to present his views on natural sciences on a less abstract level. Among his efforts in this direction, one particularly beautiful lecture must be mentioned. In 1921, at the Prussian Academy's commemorative session honoring Frederick the Great, Einstein delivered a lecture on geometry and experience in which he summed up his views on the geometrization of physics and relativity and the relation of mathematics to the external world.[41] Here he gave his famous answer to the puzzling question of why mathematics should be so well adapted to describing the external world: "Insofar as the Laws of Mathematics refer to the external world, they are not certain; and insofar as they are certain, they do not refer to reality."

The Electromagnetic Field and the Geometry of Space-Time. There were two main reasons for Einstein's dissatisfaction with the general theory. One was the seemingly still-inadequate geometrization of physics. He felt that not only gravitational but also electromagnetic effects should be manifestations of the geometry of space-time. The other interactions, such as nuclear forces and the forces responsible for beta decay, were not yet known. Einstein never considered the geometrization of the other interactions, although in the 1940's E. Schrödinger made an attempt to invent a unified field theory incorporating gravitational, electromagnetic, and nuclear interactions.

The other problem was the relation of matter to the singularities of the gravitational field. Einstein felt that a complete and correct field theory should be without singularities while in the general theory the field equations are in general singular.[42] This, he believed, is due to the inadequate description of matter as handled in the general theory. Thus the stage was set for a search for a more extended theory. This new theory should have two basic features. It should enlarge the geometry of space-time in such a manner that new geometrical objects could be introduced which can be associated with the electromagnetic field; the physically relevant solutions (whatever that may mean) should be nonsingular. Although the initial steps in this direction were not taken by Einstein himself, he did become more and more preoccupied with this problem and in his later years the construction of such a theory was his main concern. This was Einstein's ultimate response to the mechanical-electromagnetic crisis in physical theory he had first talked about in the opening of his 1905 light-quantum paper. (In 1953 Einstein said to the author that although it is doubtful that a unified field theory of the type he was seeking could exist, even its nonexistence would be of sufficient interest to be worth establishing it. If he did not do it, Einstein said, perhaps nobody ever would.)

How might the geometry of space-time be enriched with new geometrical objects which then could be considered as candidates for the description of electromagnetic phenomena? Since no clear guiding principle stemming from physics existed (or exists even today), we must rely on geometrical intuition, which necessity would also serve as a motivation.

Practically all the work in this direction fell into one of two categories. Either the dimensionality of space-time would be preserved and the geometry altered in a formal fashion, or the dimensionality of space-time would be enlarged in a formal fashion and the metric geometry preserved. Hermann Weyl initiated the first line of thought in 1918; Kaluza the second in 1921.

Weyl's unified field theory considered space-time to be endowed with a more general geometry. This approach enabled him to introduce four extra functions in space-time, in terms of which the electromagnetic field can be expressed. Einstein immediately noticed (1918), however, that if the same physical interpretation for the geometry be maintained as in the general theory, Weyl's theory leads in its original form to results that contradict experience. In 1921 A. S. Eddington observed that Weyl's geometry of space-time is a special case of a much more general class of geometries, usually called affine geometries, which depend on a profound generalization of the notion of parallelism. Einstein's first investigation of these ideas (1923) introduced the notion of distant parallelism. In 1930, however, he found that the new theory admitted solutions that describe gravitating masses represented by singularities at rest relative to each other under the sole influence of their gravitational interaction. Experience clearly contradicts this consequence. Einstein originally rejected these solutions on the grounds that they contain singularities, and later he rejected the theory itself.

In 1931 Einstein and Walter Mayer reformulated Kaluza's five-dimensional theory retaining a four-dimensional space-time. In 1938 and 1941 Einstein again discussed theories of this type, before returning to the notion that space-time may be endowed with an affine geometry. Several different geometries were envisaged in papers written in collaboration with V. Bargmann (1944), E. G. Strauss (1945–1946), and Bruria Kaufmann (1955). The last was his final published memoir.

Summary. If we turn to summarize Einstein's achievements in relativity what we see is a new point of view and innumerable consequences. The basic new point of view was the explicit recognition that the invariance properties of the laws of physics are of fundamental importance and that these invariance properties stem from immediate physical facts and are required by them. The physical notion of invariance arises from the experimental fact that the descriptions change in a specific way if the arrangement of measuring devices is altered in a specific manner. This alteration may be a simple spatial rotation, or a simple transfer of the origin of the coordinate system, or something more complicated that endows the whole laboratory with a uniform motion, or with a motion with a uniform acceleration. That the results so obtained can be linked together implies that these observations, and hence the physical quantities they describe, transform in a given way as the measuring devices are altered.

The special theory concerned itself with that transformation of labeling of space-time points which corresponds physically to uniform translation of the whole laboratory. Einstein's great achievement was the explicit realization that this transformation of

labels cannot be specified without a specific assumption about the operational meaning of simultaneity with respect to events that are spatially separate. From this realization Einstein was led to the only consistent definition of simultaneity, and thus to the correct understanding of the Lorentz transformations and to an appreciation of their great generality.

If invariance properties are of such importance then a strong geometrical interpretation of the laws of nature becomes highly desirable, since a thing that has no definite invariance properties cannot be even thought of geometrically. This consideration led Einstein to accept Minkowski's point of view that space and time should be considered as forming one geometrical object, space-time, a four-dimensional flat space.

The next step was to analyze the relations between the descriptions of phenomena in frames accelerated relative to each other. From these relations Einstein drew the conclusion that this four-dimensional space-time cannot be flat, and that gravitation is the name given to those phenomena that appear because space-time is not flat. The curvature of space-time is due to its energy and mass content. The remarkable success of this theory derived from its automatic explanation of two features of gravitation: Why is the inertial mass equal to the gravitational mass? And why is gravitation a universal property acting on everything in the universe? The answer is that the two masses are equal because they are one and the same, since they appear in the theory uniquely as the cause of the curvature of space-time. Gravitation is a universal manifestation because it is the property of space-time, and hence everything that is in space-time (which is, literally, every thing) must experience it.

The last efforts of Einstein on unified field theories were a logical continuation of his previous efforts. The chain of argument may be said to run as follows. If invariance properties are of utmost importance, physics should be thought of as a geometry, because thought is then occupied only with objects that have invariant properties. This led to a theory according to which the structure of space-time is the seat of gravitation interaction. Is this structure perhaps so rich that not only gravitational interaction but other interactions are also determined by it? That investigation proved to be unsatisfactory, perhaps because only gravitation is a universal interaction. Nevertheless even this effort turned out to be prophetic; in modern physics it is more and more the practice to proceed with a formal guessing at the laws of nature, the guess being based on formal simplicity and on invariance. The interpretation of the theory often emerges only after the structure of the equations guessed at are better understood. In this, Einstein was a forerunner.

When Einstein's total work in physics is considered, it can be said that his achievements are rivaled only by those of Isaac Newton. Both scientists were guided in their work by unique insights into the nature of physical reality and both represent the utmost fulfillment of the creative imagination in science.

NANDOR L. BALAZS

NOTES

1. A. Einstein, "H. A. Lorentz, His Creative Genius and His Personality," in G. L. de Haas-Lorentz, ed., *H. A. Lorentz. Impressions of His Life and Work* (Amsterdam, 1957), p. 5.
2. A. Einstein, *The World As I See It* (New York, 1934), p. 250.
3. Ernst Straus, "Assistant bei Albert Einstein," in C. Seelig, ed., *Helle Zeit–Dunkle Zeit* (Zurich, 1956), p. 71.
4. A. Einstein, "Autobiographical Notes," in P. A. Schilpp, ed., *Albert Einstein: Philosopher-Scientist* (Evanston, Ill., 1949, 1951), p. 5.
5. *Ibid.*, p. 16.
6. A. Einstein to Johannes Stark (7 Dec. 1907); quoted in A. Hermann, "Albert Einstein und Johannes Stark," in *Sudhoffs Archiv*, **50** (1966), 272.
   Einstein's papers can be readily located by consulting the years of publication in the bibliographies listed below.
7. Walther Nernst, "Über neuere Probleme der Wärmetheorie," in *Sitzungsberichte der Preussischen Akademie der Wissenschaften zu Berlin* (1911), p. 86.
8. A. Einstein, "Über die Entwicklung unserer Anschauungen über das Wesen und die Konstitution der Strahlung," in *Physikalische Zeitschrift*, **10** (1909), 817.
9. *Ibid.*, p. 824.
10. A. Einstein to Michele Besso (13 May 1911).
11. A. Einstein, "Beiträge zur Quantentheorie," in *Verhandlungen der Deutschen physikalischen Gesellschaft*, **16** (1914), 823.
12. A. Einstein to M. Besso (11 Aug. 1916).
13. Erwin Schrödinger, "Über das Verhältnis der Heisenberg-Born-Jordanschen Quantenmechanik zu der meinen," in *Annalen der Physik*, **79** (1926), 735.
14. A. Einstein to Max Born (4 Dec. 1926).
15. A. Einstein to E. Schrödinger (26 Apr. 1926).
16. Niels Bohr, *Atomic Physics and Human Knowledge* (New York, 1958), pp. 66, 71.
17. A. Einstein to M. Born (4 Dec. 1926).
18. A. Einstein, "Einleitende Bemerkungen über Grundbegriffe," in *Louis de Broglie, Physicien et penseur* (Paris, 1953), p. 6.
19. M. Born, "Einstein's Statistical Theories," in Schilpp, p. 163.
20. A. Einstein, "Autobiographical Notes," in Schilpp, p. 94.
21. A. Einstein, *Annalen der Physik*, **17** (1905), 891–921.
22. H. Poincaré, *Rapports présentés au Congrès International de Physique de 1900* (Paris, 1900), I, 22–23.
23. H. Poincaré, "L'état actuel et l'avenir de la physique mathématique," in *Bulletin des sciences mathématiques*, **28** (1904), 306; repr. in English as "The Principles of Mathematical Physics," in *Monist*, **15** (1905), 5.
24. W. Pauli, *Theory of Relativity*, G. Field, trans. (New York, 1958), p. 5.
25. H. A. Lorentz, *Versuch einer Theorie der electrischen und optischen Erscheinungen in bewegten Körpen* (Leiden, 1895), pp. 49–50.
26. A. Einstein, "Autobiographical Notes," in Schilpp, p. 52.
27. A. Einstein, *The Meaning of Relativity* (Princeton, N. J., 1922), p. 28.
28. H. A. Lorentz, in *Proceedings of the Royal Academy of Sciences of Amsterdam*, **6** (1904), 809.
29. A. Einstein, "Autobiographical Notes," in Schilpp, p. 60.
30. A. Einstein, in *Annalen der Physik*, **18** (1905), 639–641.
31. A. Einstein, "Über das Relativitätsprinzip und die aus demselben gezogenen Folgerungen," in *Jahrbuch der Radioaktivität*, **4** (1907), 442.
32. A. Einstein, "Einfluss der Schwerkraft auf die Ausbreitung des Lichtes," in *Annalen der Physik*, 4th ser., **35** (1911), 898.
33. A. Einstein, "Lichtgeschwindigkeit und Statik des Gravitationsfeldes," *ibid.*, **38** (1912), 355; "Theorie des statischen Gravitationsfeldes," *ibid.*, p. 443.
34. A. Einstein, "Entwurf einer verallgemeinerten Relativitätstheorie und eine Theorie der Gravitation," in *Zeitschrift für Mathematik und Physik*, **62** (1913), 225, pt. 2 written with M. Grossman.
35. A. Einstein, "Zur allgemeinen Relativitätstheorie," in *Sitzungsberichte der Preussischen Akademie der Wissenschaften zu Berlin*, pt. 2 (1915), pp. 778, 799; "Erklärung der Perihelbewegung des Merkur aus der allgemeinen Relativitätstheorie," *ibid.*, p. 831; "Feldgleichungen der Gravitation," *ibid.*, p. 844.
36. A. Einstein, "Grundlagen der allgemeinen Relativitätstheorie," in *Annalen der Physik*, 4th ser., **49** (1916), 769.
37. A. Einstein, "Allgemeine Relativitätstheorie und Bewegungsgesetz," in *Sitzungsberichte der Preussischen Akademie der Wissenschaften zu Berlin*, Phys.-math. Kl. (1927), pp. 2, 235, pt. 1 written with J. Grommer; "Gravitational Equations and the Problems of Motion," in *Annals of Mathematics*, 2nd ser., **39** (1938), 65, written with L. Infeld and B. Hoffmann; "Gravitational Equations and the Problems of Motion. II," *ibid.*, **41** (1940), 455, written with L. Infeld.
38. A. Einstein, "Gibt es eine Gravitationswirkung die der elektrodynamischen Induktionswirkung analog ist?," in *Vierteljahrschrift für gerichtliche Medizin und öffentliches Sanitätswesen*, 3rd ser., **44** (1912), 37.
39. A. Einstein, "Prinzipielles zur allgemeinen Relativitätstheorie," in *Annalen der Physik*, 4th ser., **55** (1918), 241.
40. A. Einstein, "Kosmologische Betrachtungen zur allgemeinen Relativitätstheorie," in *Sitzungsberichte der Preussischen Akademie der Wissenschaften zu Berlin*, pt. 1 (1917), p. 142.
41. A. Einstein, *Geometrie und Erfahrung* (Berlin, 1921).
42. A. Einstein, "Demonstration of the Non-existence of Gravitational Fields With a Non-vanishing Total Mass Free of Singularities," in *Revista. Instituto de física, Universidad nacional de Tucumán*, **2A** (1941), 11.

BIBLIOGRAPHY

I. There are three principal bibliographies of Einstein's writings. The first, compiled by Margaret C. Shields, covers his writings to May 1951 and includes general works as well as scientific articles and books. It is to be found in P. A. Schilpp, ed., *Albert Einstein: Philosopher–Scientist* (Evanston, Illinois, 1949, 1951), pp. 689–760. This important book also contains Einstein's "Autobiographical Notes," a series of essays on his work by physicists, mathematicians, and philosophers, and Einstein's "Remarks" concerning these essays. The second bibliography, containing only the scientific writings, is E. Weil, *Albert Einstein. A Bibliography of His Scientific Papers 1901–1954* (London, 1960). The third is Nell Boni, Monique Ross, and Dan H. Laurence, *A Bibliographical Checklist and Index to the Published Writings of Albert Einstein* (New York, 1960).

No regular edition of Einstein's scientific papers has

appeared yet. There is a microfilm edition (Readex Microprint, New York).

II. Einstein's books include *Relativity, the Special and the General Theory: A Popular Exposition* (London, 1920); *The Meaning of Relativity* (Princeton, N. J., 1921); *Investigations on the Theory of the Brownian Movement*, R. Fürth, ed. (London, 1926); *The World As I See It* (New York, 1934); *The Evolution of Physics* (New York, 1938), written with Leopold Infeld; *Out of My Later Years* (New York, 1950); and *Ideas and Opinions* (New York, 1954).

III. Portions of Einstein's correspondence have been published: *Albert Einstein, Hedwig und Max Born. Briefwechsel 1916–1955*, M. Born, ed. (Munich, 1969); *Albert Einstein/Arnold Sommerfeld Briefwechsel*, A. Hermann, ed. (Basel, 1968); Albert Einstein, Erwin Schrödinger, Max Planck, H. A. Lorentz, *Letters on Wave Mechanics*, K. Przibram, ed., M. J. Klein, trans. (New York, 1967); Albert Einstein, *Lettres à Maurice Solovine* (Paris, 1956). Also see O. Nathan and H. Norden, eds., *Einstein on Peace* (New York, 1960), and M. J. Klein, *Paul Ehrenfest. Volume 1. The Making of a Theoretical Physicist* (Amsterdam, 1970). Both books quote extensively from Einstein's correspondence.

IV. Many biographies of Einstein have appeared, but nothing like a definitive study of either the man or his work yet exists. Philipp Frank, *Einstein. His Life and Times*, G. Rosen, trans. (New York, 1947), written by a physicist and philosopher of science who knew Einstein for over forty years, is the most thorough work. It does not, however, discuss Einstein's work in any detail. It suffers from having been written during Einstein's lifetime and without the use of manuscript sources. Carl Seelig, *Albert Einstein. A Documentary Biography*, M. Savill, trans. (London, 1956), quotes extensively from Einstein's correspondence and is particularly good on the earlier part of his life.

Another biography of particular interest is that by Rudolf Kayser, Einstein's son-in-law, *Albert Einstein. A Biographical Portrait* (New York, 1930); this was actually written under the pseudonym Anton Reiser.

A recent biography that presents interesting ideas on Einstein's thought is Boris Kuznetsov, *Einstein*, V. Talmy, trans. (Moscow, 1965).

V. Some articles of particular interest are Robert S. Shankland, "Conversations With Albert Einstein," in *American Journal of Physics*, **31** (1963), 37–47; Gerald Holton, "On the Origins of the Special Theory of Relativity," *ibid.*, **28** (1960), 627–636; "Influences on Einstein's Early Work in Relativity Theory," in *American Scholar*, **37** (winter 1968), 59–79; "Mach, Einstein, and the Search for Reality," in *Daedalus*, **97** (1968), 636–673; and "Einstein, Michelson, and the 'Crucial' Experiment," in *Isis*, **60** (1969), 133–197; Tetu Hirosige, "Theory of Relativity and the Ether," in *Japanese Studies in the History of Science* (1968), pp. 37–53; Martin J. Klein, "Einstein's First Paper on Quanta," in *The Natural Philosopher*, **2** (1963), 57–86; "Einstein and the Wave-Particle Duality," *ibid.*, **3** (1964), 1–49; "Einstein, Specific Heats, and the Early Quantum Theory," in *Science*, **148** (1965), 173–180; "Thermodynamics in Einstein's Thought," *ibid.*, **157** (1967), 509–516; and "The First Phase

of the Bohr-Einstein Dialogue," in *Historical Studies in the Physical Sciences*, **2** (1970), 1–39; R. McCormmach, "Einstein, Lorentz, and the Electron Theory," *ibid.*, 41–87.

VI. Einstein's manuscripts, notes, and correspondence have been collected by the estate of Albert Einstein and are kept at present at the Institute for Advanced Study, Princeton, N. J. Information on certain other Einstein manuscripts may be found in T. S. Kuhn, J. L. Heilbron, P. L. Forman, and L. Allen, *Sources for History of Quantum Physics* (Philadelphia, 1967).

EINTHOVEN, WILLEM (*b.* Semarang, Java, 21 May 1860; *d.* Leiden, Netherlands, 28 September 1927), *physiology*.

Einthoven's father was municipal physician of Semarang; he married Louise M. M. C. de Vogel. He died in 1866, and four years later his widow settled in Utrecht with their six children. There Willem Einthoven graduated from high school and registered as a medical student in 1879. In 1886 he married his cousin Frédérique Jeanne Louise de Vogel; they had three daughters and a son.

While a student, Einthoven was active in sports; when he broke his wrist in a fall, he made it the occasion to publish a study on the pronation and supination of the forearm (1882). On 4 July 1885 he received the Ph.D in medicine *cum laude* with a thesis on stereoscopy through color differentiation. The following December he was appointed professor of physiology at Leiden.

In 1895, after the London physiologist A. D. Waller had published the curve for the action current of the heart as deduced from the body surface and had announced that he was unable to calculate its true shape (as recorded with Lippmann's capillary electrometer), Einthoven repeated this experiment. He defined the physical constants of the capillary electrometer and calculated the true curve, which he called the electrocardiogram. Einthoven considered direct registration of the curve's true shape a necessity. Starting from the mirror galvanometer of Deprez-d'Arsonval, he arrived at his brilliant conception of the string galvanometer. In 1896, while working on the construction of this instrument and developing the necessary photographic equipment, he registered electrocardiograms with the capillary electrometer as well as heart sounds of humans and animals.

For making electrocardiograms Einthoven chose the ordinate and abscissa in such a way that all details of the electrocardiogram would appear as clearly as possible. In 1903 he defined the standard measures for general use—one centimeter movement of the ordinate for one millivolt tension difference and a shutter speed of twenty-five millimeters per second, so that one centimeter of the abscissa represented 0.4 second. He indicated the various extremes by the random letters *P, Q, R, S,* and *T* and chose both hands and the left foot as contact points. This gave three possible combinations for contact which he labeled I (both hands); II (right hand–left foot); and III (left hand–left foot).

In 1912 Einthoven's research on the explanation of the respiratory changes in the electrocardiogram led him to the scheme of the equilateral triangle, considering the extremities as elongations of the electrodes. The information received from the contacts thus represents the projection of what takes place in the heart. With simultaneous registration of the three contacts, the size and direction of the resultant of all potential differences in the heart could be calculated minute by minute. Einthoven referred to this as the manifest size and direction of the electrical axis. He indicated the direction by the angle α of this axis with the horizontal and called it positive when it turned clockwise, negative when counterclockwise. Clinical electrocardiograms were studied by connecting patients with heart disease in the academic hospital to the instrument in Einthoven's laboratory by means of a cable 1.5 kilometers long (1906).

These "telecardiograms" acquainted Einthoven with many forms of heart disease. In addition he deepened his insight by registering heart sounds and murmurs simultaneous to the electrocardiogram by means of a second string galvanometer. The construction of a string recorder and a string myograph, both based on the torsion principle, enabled him to prove that the electrocardiogram and muscle contraction are inseparably connected.

While visiting America to give the Dungham lectures (1924) Einthoven was awarded the Nobel Prize for physiology or medicine. Upon his return to Leiden he found two foreign requests to register the action currents of the cervical sympathetic nerve. With the newly constructed vacuum string galvanometer he succeeded, on 28 April 1926, in registering the tonus action current and, after irritation of the organ, the thereupon induced action current of the cervical sympathetic nerve. His last major physical experiment, which he carried out in company with his son, was concerned with the reception of radiotelegrams broadcast by the machine transmitter "Malabar" in Java. In this case the string of 0.1 micron diameter and six millimeters length had to be synchronized with the 40,000 vibrations of the transmitting wave. Einthoven and his son found the resonance point after they achieved a variation in tension of one micromicron, after which telegrams from the machine

transmitter, working at top speed, were perfectly photographed on paper one centimeter wide.

Einthoven's last work was his treatise on the action current of the heart, which appeared posthumously in *Bethe's Handbuch der normalen und pathologischen Physiologie.*

BIBLIOGRAPHY

I. ORIGINAL WORKS. Einthoven's works include "Quelques remarques sur le mécanisme de l'articulation du coude," in *Archives néerlandaises des sciences exactes et naturelles,* **17** (1882), 289–298; "Stéréoscopie dépendant d'une différence de couleur," *ibid.,* **20** (1886), 361–387; "Lippmann's Capillarelektrometer zur Messung schnellwechseln der Potentialunterschiede," in *Pflügers Archiv für die gesamte Physiologie des Menschen und der Tiere,* **56** (1894), 528–540; "Die Registrierung der Herztöne," *ibid.,* **57** (1894), 617–639, written with M. A. J. Geluk; "Über den Einflusz des Leitungswiderstandes auf die Geschwindigkeit der Quecksilberbewegungen in Lippmann's Capillarelektrometer," *ibid.,* **60** (1895), 91–100; "Über die Form des menschlichen Elektrocardiogramms," *ibid.,* 101–123; "Beitrag zur Theorie des Capillarelektrometers," *ibid.,* **79** (1900), 1–25; "Eine Vorrichtung zum Registrieren der Ausschläge des Lippmann'schen Capillarelektrometers," *ibid.,* 25–38; "Über das normale menschliche Elektrokardiogramm und die capillarelektrometrische Untersuchung einiger Herzkranken," *ibid.,* **80** (1900), 139–160, written with K. de Lint; "Un nouveau galvanomètre," in *Archives néerlandaises des sciences exactes et naturelles,* **6** (1901), 625–633; "Die galvanometrische Registrierung des menschlichen Elektrokardiogramms, zugleich eine Beurteilung der Anwendung des Capillarelektrometers in der Physiologie," in *Pflügers Archiv für die gesamte Physiologie des Menschen und der Tiere,* **99** (1903), 472–480.

See also "Über einige Anwendungen des Saitengalvanometers," in *Annalen der Physik,* **14** (1904), 182–191; "Über eine neue Methode zur Dämpfung oszillierender Galvanometerausschläge," *ibid.,* **16** (1904), 20–32; "Weitere Mitteilungen über das Saitengalvanometer. Analyse der saitengalvanometrischen Kurven. Masse und Spannung des Quarzfadens und Widerstand gegen die Fadenbewegung," *ibid.,* **21** (1906), 483–514, 665–701; "Le télécardiogramme," in *Archives internationales de physiologie,* **4** (1906), 132–165; "Die Registrierung der menschlichen Herztöne mittels des Saitengalvanometers," in *Pflügers Archiv für die gesamte Physiologie des Menschen und der Tiere,* **117** (1907), 461–472, written with A. Flohil and P. J. J. A. Battaerd; "Ein dritter Herzton," *ibid.,* **120** (1907), 31–43, written with J. H. Wieringa and E. P. Snijders; "Weiteres über das Elektrokardiogramm," *ibid.,* **122** (1908), 517–585, written with B. Vaandrager; "Die Konstruktion des Saitengalvanometers, *ibid.,* **130** (1909), 287–321; "Über die Deutung des Elektrokardiogramms," *ibid.,* **149** (1913),

65–86; "Eine Vorrichtung zur photographischen Registrierung der Zeit," in *Zeitschrift für biologische Technik und Methodik*, **3** (1912), 1–8; and "Über die Richtung und die manifeste Grösse der Potentialschwankungen im menschlichen Herzen und über den Einfluss der Herzlage auf die Form des Elektrokardiogramms," in *Pflügers Archiv für die gesamte Physiologie des Menschen und der Tiere*, **150** (1913), 275–315, written with G. Fahr and A. de Waart.

Subsequent works are "On the Variability of the Size of the Pulse in Cases of Auricular Fibrillation," in *Heart*, **6** (1915), 107–121, written with A. J. Korteweg; "Die gleichzeitige Registrierung elektrischer Erscheinungen mittels zwei oder mehr Galvanometer und ihre Anwendung auf die Elektrokardiographie," in *Pflügers Archiv für die gesamte Physiologie des Menschen und der Tiere*, **164** (1916), 167–198, written with L. Bergansius and J. Bijtel; and "Über den Zusammenhang zwischen Elektro- und Mechanokardiogramm," in *Berichte über die gesamte Physiologie und experimentelle Pharmakologie*, **2** (1920), 178.

His last works include "L'électrocardiogramme tracé dans le cas où il n'y a pas de contraction visible du coeur," in *Archives néerlandaises de physiologie de l'homme et des animaux*, **5** (1921), 174–183, written with F. W. N. Hugenholtz; "Über die Beobachtung und Abbildung dünner Fäden," in *Pflügers Archiv für die gesamte Physiologie des Menschen und der Tiere*, **191** (1921), 60–98; "Über Stromleitung durch den menschlichen Körper," *ibid.*, **198** (1923), 439–483, written with J. Bijtel; "Functions of the Cervical Sympathetic Manifested by Its Action Currents," in *American Journal of Physiology*, **65** (1923), 350–362, written with Joseph Byrne; "The Relation of Mechanical and Electrical Phenomena of Muscular Contraction, With Special Reference to the Cardiac Muscle," in *The Harvey Society Lectures* (Philadelphia–London, 1924–1925), pp. 111–131; "Das Saitengalvanometer und die Messung der Aktionsströme des Herzens," in *Les Prix Nobel 1924–1925* (Stockholm, 1926), p. 18, his Nobel Prize acceptance speech; "Gehirn und Sympathicus, die Aktionsströme des Hallssympathicus," in *Pflügers Archiv für die gesamte Physiologie des Menschen und der Tiere*, **215** (1927), 443–453, written with S. Hoogerwerf, J. P. Karplus, and A. Kreidl; and "Die Aktionsströme des Herzens," in *Bethe's Handbuch der normalen und pathologischen Physiologie*, **8** (1928), 785–862.

II. SECONDARY LITERATURE. On Einthoven and his work see S. L. Barron, *Willem Einthoven, Biographical Notes*, Cambridge Monograph no. 5 (London, 1952), pp. 1–26; F. L. Bergansius, "Willem Einthoven," in *Wetenschappelijke bladen*, **1** (1925), 257; A. V. Hill, "Obituary. Prof. W. Einthoven," in *Nature*, **120** (1927), 591–592; Leonard Hill, "Willem Einthoven," in *British Medical Journal* (1927), **2**, 665; S. Hoogerwerf, *Leven en Werken van Willem Einthoven* (Hoorn, 1925), 9–93; and "Willem Einthoven," in T. P. Sevensma, ed., *Nederlandsche Helden der Wetenschap* (Amsterdam, 1946), 239–297; J. E. Johansson, "W. Einthoven (1924–1925)," in *Les Prix Nobel 1924–1925* (Stockholm, 1926); C. L. de Jongh, "Het levenswerk van

Einthoven," in *Nederlandsch tijdschrift voor geneeskunde*, **98** (1954), 270–273; T. Lewis, "Willem Einthoven," in *British Medical Journal* (1927), **2**, 664–665; G. van Rijnberk, "Willem Einthoven," in *Nederlandsch tijdschrift voor geneeskunde*, **68** (1924), 2424–2430; "In Memoriam," *ibid.*, **71** (1927), 1502–1503; E. Schott, "Willem Einthoven und die Fortschritte, welche wir der Erfindung des Saitengalvanometers verdanken," in *Münchener medizinische Wochenschrift*, **72** (1925), 391–392; A. Sikkel, "In Memoriam W. Einthoven," in *Geneeskundige gids*, **5** (1927), 925; "Necrologie Einthoven," in University of Leiden, *Jaarboek, 1928;* A. de Waart, *Einthoven* (Haarlem, 1957), with a complete list of his works; K. F. Wenckebach, "W. Einthoven," in *Deutsche medizinische Wochenschrift*, **51** (1927), 2176; F. A. F. C. Went, "Herdenkingsrede," in *Verslagen van de gewone vergadering van de Koninklijke Nederlandsche Academie van Wetenschappen. Afdeling Natuurkunde*, **8** (1927), 936–938; and H. Winterberg, "W. Einthoven," in *Wiener klinische Wochenschrift*, **40** (1927), 1460–1461.

S. HOOGERWERF

EISENHART, LUTHER PFAHLER (*b.* York, Pennsylvania, 13 January 1876; *d.* Princeton, New Jersey, 28 October 1965), *mathematics.*

Eisenhart was the second son of Charles Augustus Eisenhart and the former Emma Pfahler. His father was a dentist, a founder of the Edison Electric Light and York Telephone companies, and secretary of the Sunday school of St. Paul's Lutheran Church. Eisenhart was taught by his mother before he entered school and completed grade school in three years. He then attended York High School until, in his junior year, he was encouraged by the principal to withdraw and devote his time to the independent study of Latin and Greek for early admission to Gettysburg College, which he attended from 1892 to 1896. Being the only upper-division mathematics student, during the last two years of college Eisenhart studied mathematics through independent guided reading.

After teaching for a year at the preparatory school of the college, he began graduate study at Johns Hopkins University in 1897 and obtained the Ph.D. in 1900 with a thesis whose topic, "Infinitesimal Deformations of Surfaces," he had chosen himself. He was introduced to differential geometry through a lecture by Thomas Craig and studied the subject through the treatises of Gaston Darboux. According to his own testimony, the experience of independent study led Eisenhart to propose the four-course plan of study adopted at Princeton in 1923, which provides for independent study and the preparation of a thesis. Eisenhart's scientific career was spent at Princeton; he retired in 1945.

In 1908 Eisenhart married Anna Maria Dandridge Mitchell of Charles Town, West Virginia; she died in 1913. In 1918 he married Katharine Riely Schmidt of York, Pennsylvania. He had one son, Churchill, by his first marriage and two daughters, Anna and Katharine, by his second.

Eisenhart's work in differential geometry covers two distinct periods and fields. The first period, to about 1920, was devoted mainly to the theory of deformations of surfaces and systems of surfaces.

Modern differential geometry was founded by Gaston Darboux as a field of applications of partial differential equations. His methods were taken up by Luigi Bianchi, who created an extensive theory of the deformations of surfaces of constant negative curvature. In another direction, Claude Guichard showed between 1897 and 1899 how the partial differential equations of the deformations of triply orthogonal systems of surfaces can be interpreted in terms of the systems of lines connecting a point and its image point. These discoveries made the theory of deformations of surfaces one of the focal points of geometric research in Europe at the turn of the century. Although there were quite a number of able mathematicians working in America in the field of geometry at that time, Eisenhart was the only one to turn to the topic of deformations. His main contribution to the theory was a unifying principle: The deformation of a surface defines the congruence (two-parameter family) of lines connecting a point and its image (following Guichard). In general, a congruence contains two families of developable surfaces (a developable surface is formed by the tangent to a space curve). Eisenhart recognized that in all known cases, the intersections of these surfaces with the given surface and its image form a net of curves with special properties. This allows not only a unified treatment of many different subjects and a replacement of tricks by methods, but also leads to many new results that round off the theory. Eisenhart gave a coherent account of the theory in *Transformations of Surfaces* (1923). The book also contains most of Eisenhart's previous results either in the text or in the exercises, with references. Some aspects of the theory were taken up later in the projective setting by Eduard Čech and his students. All these investigations deal with small neighborhoods for which existence theorems for solutions of differential equations are available.

Of the few papers not dealing with deformations dating from this period, a noteworthy one is "Surfaces Whose First and Second Forms Are Respectively the Second and First Forms of Another Surface" (1901), one of the first differential geometric characterizations of the sphere, a topic started by Heinrich Liebmann in 1899. Eisenhart proved that the unit sphere is the only surface whose first and second fundamental forms are, respectively, the second and first fundamental forms of another surface.

Einstein's general theory of relativity (1916) made Riemannian geometry the center of geometric research. The analytic tools that turned Riemannian geometry from an idea into an effective instrument were Ricci's covariant differential calculus and the related notion of Levi-Civita's parallelism. These tools had been thoroughly explored in Luigi Bianchi's *Lezioni di geometria differenziale*. As a consequence, the attention of geometers immediately turned to the generalization of Riemannian geometry. Most of Eisenhart's work after 1921 was in this direction. The colloquium lectures *Non-Riemannian Geometry* (1927) contain his account of the main results obtained by him and his students and collaborators. An almost complete coverage of Eisenhart's results, with very good references, is given in Schouten's *Ricci Calculus*. Three directions of generalization of Riemannian geometry were developed in the years after 1920. They are connected with the names of Élie Cartan, Hermann Weyl, and Eisenhart. Cartan considered geometries that induce a geometry of a transitive transformation group in any tangent space. Weyl gave an axiomatic approach to the maps of tangent spaces by parallelism along any smooth curve. Eisenhart's approach, inspired by Oswald Veblen's work on the foundations of projective geometry and started in cooperation with Veblen, is the only one to deal directly with the given space. In Riemannian geometry, the measure of length is prescribed and the geodesic lines are determined as the shortest connections between nearby points. In Eisenhart's approach, the geodesics are given as the solution of a prescribed system of second-order differential equations and the non-Riemannian geometries are obtained by asking that there should exist a Levi-Civita parallelism for which the tangents are covariant constant.

While Cartan's and Weyl's generalizations have become the foundations of the fiber space theory of differentiable manifolds, Eisenhart's theory does not fit the framework of these topological theories. The reason is that the geometric objects intrinsically derived from the "paths" of the geometry, the projective parameters of Tracy Y. Thomas, have a more complicated transformation law than the generalized Christoffel symbols of Cartan and Weyl. However, there are a number of modern developments, such as the theory of Finsler spaces and the general theory of the geometric object, that fit Eisenhart's framework but not that of the algebraic-topological approach.

As far as metric geometry is concerned, the most fruitful approach seems to be to give the geodesics directly as point sets and to throw out all differential equations and analytical apparatus. On the other hand, for nonmetric geometries Eisenhart proved (in "Spaces With Corresponding Paths" [1922]) that for every one of his geometries there exists a unique geometry with the same paths and for which the mapping of tangent spaces induced by the flow of tangent vectors with unit speed along the paths is volume-preserving. For the latter geometry, which would appear to give a natural setting for topological dynamics, the Cartan, Weyl, and Eisenhart approaches are equivalent.

A number of interesting avenues of development of Riemannian geometry were opened by Eisenhart. The papers "Fields of Parallel Vectors in the Geometry of Paths" (1922) and "Fields of Parallel Vectors in a Riemannian Geometry" (1925) started the topic of recurrent fields and harmonic spaces (for a report with later references, see T. J. Willmore, *An Introduction to Differential Geometry*, ch. 7, sec. 13). The so-called Eisenhart's theorem appears in "Symmetric Tensors of the Second Order Whose First Covariant Derivatives Are Zero" (1923): If a Riemannian geometry admits a second-order, symmetric, covariant constant tensor other than the metric, the space behaves locally like the product of two lower-dimensional spaces. Together with a theorem of Georges de Rham to the effect that a simply connected, locally product Riemannian space is in fact a Cartesian product of two spaces, the theorem is an important tool in global differential geometry. An extension of the theorem is given in "Parallel Vectors in Riemannian Space" (1938).

The basic equations for the vectors of a group of motions in a Riemannian space had been given by Killing in 1892. Eisenhart developed a very powerful analytical apparatus for these questions; the results are summarized in *Riemannian Geometry* (1926; ch. 6) and *Continuous Groups of Transformations* (1933). The later developments are summarized in Kentaro Yano's *Groups of Transformations in Generalized Spaces* (1949).

Eisenhart's interest in mathematical instruction found its expression in a number of influential textbooks—such as *Differential Geometry of Curves and Surfaces* (1909), *Riemannian Geometry* (1926), *Continuous Groups of Transformations* (1933), *Coordinate Geometry* (1939), *An Introduction to Differential Geometry With Use of the Tensor Calculus* (1940)—some in fields that until then had been dependent upon European monographs devoid of exercises and other student aids. His interest in history resulted in several papers: "Lives of Princeton Mathematicians" (1931), "Plan for a University of Discoverers" (1947), "Walter Minto and the Earl of Buchan" (1950), and the preface to "Historic Philadelphia" (1953).

BIBLIOGRAPHY

I. ORIGINAL WORKS. Eisenhart's works published between 1901 and 1909 are "A Demonstration of the Impossibility of a Triply Asymptotic System of Surfaces," in *Bulletin of the American Mathematical Society*, **7** (1901), 184–186; "Possible Triply Asymptotic Systems of Surfaces," *ibid.*, 303–305; "Surfaces Whose First and Second Forms Are Respectively the Second and First Forms of Another Surface," *ibid.*, 417–423; "Lines of Length Zero on Surfaces," *ibid.*, **9** (1902), 241–243; "Note on Isotropic Congruences," *ibid.*, 301–303; "Infinitesimal Deformation of Surfaces," in *American Journal of Mathematics*, **24** (1902), 173–204; "Conjugate Rectilinear Congruences," in *Transactions of the American Mathematical Society*, **3** (1902), 354–371; "Infinitesimal Deformation of the Skew Helicoid," in *Bulletin of the American Mathematical Society*, **9** (1903), 148–152; "Surfaces Referred to Their Lines of Length Zero," *ibid.*, 242–245; "Isothermal-Conjugate Systems of Lines on Surfaces," in *American Journal of Mathematics*, **25** (1903), 213–248; "Surfaces Whose Lines of Curvature in One System Are Represented on the Sphere by Great Circles," *ibid.*, 349–364; "Surfaces of Constant Mean Curvature," *ibid.*, 383–396; "Congruences of Curves," in *Transactions of the American Mathematical Society*, **4** (1903), 470–488; "Congruences of Tangents to a Surface and Derived Congruences," in *American Journal of Mathematics*, **26** (1904), 180–208; "Three Particular Systems of Lines on a Surface," in *Transactions of the American Mathematical Society*, **5** (1904), 421–437; "Surfaces With the Same Spherical Representation of Their Lines of Curvature as Pseudospherical Surfaces," in *American Journal of Mathematics*, **27** (1905), 113–172; "On the Deformation of Surfaces of Translation," in *Bulletin of the American Mathematical Society*, **11** (1905), 486–494; "Surfaces of Constant Curvature and Their Transformations," in *Transactions of the American Mathematical Society*, **6** (1905), 473–485; "Surfaces Analogous to the Surfaces of Bianchi," in *Annali di matematica pura ed applicata*, 3rd ser., **12** (1905), 113–143; "Certain Surfaces With Plane or Spherical Lines of Curvature," in *American Journal of Mathematics*, **28** (1906), 47–70; "Associate Surfaces," in *Mathematische Annalen*, **62** (1906), 504–538; "Transformations of Minimal Surfaces," in *Annali di matematica pura ed applicata*, 3rd ser., **13** (1907), 249–262; "Applicable Surfaces With Asymptotic Lines of One Surface Corresponding to a Conjugate System of Another," in *Transactions of the American Mathematical Society*, **8** (1907), 113–134; "Certain Triply Orthogonal Systems of Surfaces," in *American Journal of Mathematics*, **29** (1907), 168–212; "Surfaces With Isothermal Representation of Their Lines of Curvature and Their Transformations (I)," in *Transactions of the American Mathematical Society*, **9** (1908), 149–

177; "Surfaces With the Same Spherical Representation of Their Lines of Curvature as Spherical Surfaces," in *American Journal of Mathematics,* **30** (1908), 19–42; and *A Treatise on the Differential Geometry of Curves and Surfaces* (Boston, 1909; repub. New York, 1960).

Between 1910 and 1919 he published "The Twelve Surfaces of Darboux and the Transformation of Moutard," in *American Journal of Mathematics,* **32** (1910), 17–36; "Congruences of the Elliptic Type," in *Transactions of the American Mathematical Society,* **11** (1910), 351–372; "Surfaces With Isothermal Representation of Their Lines of Curvature and Their Transformations (II)," *ibid.,* 475–486; "A Fundamental Parametric Representation of Space Curves," in *Annals of Mathematics,* 2nd ser., **13** (1911), 17–35; "Sopra le deformazioni continue delle superficie reali applicabili sul paraboloide a parametro puramente immaginario," in *Atti dell'Accademia nazionale dei Lincei. Rendiconti,* Classe di scienze fisiche, matematiche e naturali, 5th ser., **211** (1912), 458–462; "Ruled Surfaces With Isotropic Generators," in *Rendiconti del Circolo matematico di Palermo,* **34** (1912), 29–40; "Minimal Surfaces in Euclidean Four-Space," in *American Journal of Mathematics,* **34** (1912), 215–236; "Certain Continuous Deformations of Surfaces Applicable to the Quadrics," in *Transactions of the American Mathematical Society,* **14** (1913), 365–402; "Transformations of Surfaces of Guichard and Surfaces Applicable to Quadrics," in *Annali di matematica pura ed applicata,* 3rd ser., **22** (1914), 191–248; "Transformations of Surfaces of Voss," in *Transactions of the American Mathematical Society,* **15** (1914), 245–265; "Transformations of Conjugate Systems With Equal Point Invariants," *ibid.,* 397–430; "Conjugate Systems With Equal Tangential Invariants and the Transformation of Moutard," in *Rendiconti del Circolo matematico di Palermo,* **39** (1915), 153–176; "Transformations of Surfaces Ω," in *Proceedings of the National Academy of Sciences,* **1** (1915), 62–65; "One-Parameter Families of Curves," in *American Journal of Mathematics,* **37** (1915), 179–191; "Transformations of Conjugate Systems With Equal Invariants," in *Proceedings of the National Academy of Sciences,* **1** (1915), 290–295; "Surfaces Ω and Their Transformations," in *Transactions of the American Mathematical Society,* **16** (1915), 275–310; "Sulle superficie di rotolamento e le trasformazioni di Ribaucour," in *Atti dell'Accademia nazionale dei Lincei. Rendiconti,* Classe di scienze fisiche, matematiche e naturali, 5th ser., **242** (1915), 349–352; "Surfaces With Isothermal Representation of Their Lines of Curvature as Envelopes of Rolling," in *Annals of Mathematics,* 2nd ser., **17** (1915), 63–71; "Transformations of Surfaces Ω," in *Transactions of the American Mathematical Society,* **17** (1916), 53–99; "Deformations of Transformations of Ribaucour," in *Proceedings of the National Academy of Sciences,* **2** (1916), 173–177; "Conjugate Systems With Equal Point Invariants," in *Annals of Mathematics,* 2nd ser., **18** (1916), 7–17; "Surfaces Generated by the Motion of an Invariable Curve Whose Points Describe Straight Lines," in *Rendiconti del Circolo matematico di Palermo,* **41** (1916), 94–102; "Deformable Transformations of Ribaucour," in *Transactions of the American Mathematical Society,* **17** (1916), 437–458;

"Certain Surfaces of Voss and Surfaces Associated With Them," in *Rendiconti del Circolo matematico de Palermo,* **42** (1917), 145–166; "Transformations *T* of Conjugate Systems of Curves on a Surface," in *Transactions of the American Mathematical Society,* **18** (1917), 97–124; "Triads of Transformations of Conjugate Systems of Curves," in *Proceedings of the National Academy of Sciences,* **3** (1917), 453–457; "Conjugate Planar Nets With Equal Invariants," in *Annals of Mathematics,* 2nd ser., **18** (1917), 221–225; "Transformations of Applicable Conjugate Nets of Curves on Surfaces," in *Proceedings of the National Academy of Sciences,* **3** (1917), 637–640; "Darboux's Contribution to Geometry," in *Bulletin of the American Mathematical Society,* **24** (1918), 227–237; "Surfaces Which Can Be Generated in More Than One Way by the Motion of an Invariable Curve," in *Annals of Mathematics,* 2nd ser., **19** (1918), 217–230; "Transformations of Planar Nets," in *American Journal of Mathematics,* **40** (1918), 127–144; "Transformations of Applicable Conjugate Nets of Curves on Surfaces," in *Transactions of the American Mathematical Society,* **19** (1918), 167–185; "Triply Conjugate Systems With Equal Point Invariants," in *Annals of Mathematics,* 2nd ser., **20** (1919), 262–273; "Transformations of Surfaces Applicable to a Quadric," in *Transactions of the American Mathematical Society,* **20** (1919), 323–338; and "Transformations of Cyclic Systems of Circles," in *Proceedings of the National Academy of Sciences,* **5** (1919), 555–557.

Eisenhart's works published between 1920 and 1929 are "The Permanent Gravitational Field in the Einstein Theory," in *Annals of Mathematics,* 2nd ser., **22** (1920), 86–94; "The Permanent Gravitational Field in the Einstein Theory," in *Proceedings of the National Academy of Sciences,* **6** (1920), 678–682; "Sulle congruenze di sfere di Ribaucour che ammettono una deformazione finita," in *Atti dell'Accademia nazionale dei Lincei. Rendiconti,* Classe di scienze fisiche, matematiche e naturali, 5th ser., **292** (1920), 31–33; "Conjugate Systems of Curves *R* and Their Transformations," in *Comptes rendus du sixième Congrès international des mathématiciens* (Strasbourg, 1920), pp. 407–409; "Darboux's Anteil an der Geometrie," in *Acta mathematica,* **42** (1920), 275–284; "Transformations of Surfaces Applicable to a Quadric," in *Journal de mathématiques pures et appliquées,* 8th ser., **4** (1921), 37–66; "Conjugate Nets *R* and Their Transformations," in *Annals of Mathematics,* 2nd ser., **22** (1921), 161–181; "A Geometric Characterization of the Paths of Particles in the Gravitational Field of a Mass at Rest" (abstract), in *Bulletin of the American Mathematical Society,* **27** (1921), 350; "The Einstein Solar Field," *ibid.,* 432–434; "Sulle trasformazioni *T* dei sistemi tripli coniugati di superficie," in *Atti dell'Accademia nazionale dei Lincei. Rendiconti,* Classe di scienze fisiche, matematiche e naturali, **302** (1921), 399–401; "Einstein Static Fields Admitting a Group G_2 of Continuous Transformations Into Themselves," in *Proceedings of the National Academy of Sciences,* **7** (1921), 328–334, abstract in *Bulletin of the American Mathematical Society,* **28** (1922), 34; "The Riemann Geometry and Its Generalization," in *Proceedings of the National Academy of Sciences,* **8** (1922), 19–23, abstract in *Bulletin of the American Mathematical*

338

Society, **28** (1922), 154, written with Oswald Veblen; "Ricci's Principal Directions for a Riemann Space and the Einstein Theory," in *Proceedings of the National Academy of Sciences,* **8** (1922), 24–26, abstract in *Bulletin of the American Mathematical Society,* **28** (1922), 238; "The Einstein Equations for the Solar Field From the Newtonian Point of View," in *Science,* n.s. **55** (1922), 570–572; "Fields of Parallel Vectors in the Geometry of Paths," in *Proceedings of the National Academy of Sciences,* **8** (1922), 207–212; "Spaces With Corresponding Paths," *ibid.,* 233–238; "Condition That a Tensor Be the Curl of a Vector," in *Bulletin of the American Mathematical Society,* **28** (1922), 425–427; "Affine Geometries of Paths Possessing an Invariant Integral," in *Proceedings of the National Academy of Sciences,* **9** (1923), 4–7; "Another Interpretation of the Fundamental Gauge-Vectors of Weyl's Theory of Relativity," *ibid.,* 175–178; "Orthogonal Systems of Hypersurfaces in a General Riemann Space," in *Transactions of the American Mathematical Society,* **25** (1923), 259–280, abstract in *Bulletin of the American Mathematical Society,* **29** (1923), 212; "Symmetric Tensors of the Second Order Whose First Covariant Derivatives Are Zero," in *Transactions of the American Mathematical Society,* **25** (1923), 297–306, abstract in *Bulletin of the American Mathematical Society,* **29** (1923), 213; "Einstein and Soldner," in *Science,* n.s. **58** (1923), 516–517; "The Geometry of Paths and General Relativity," in *Annals of Mathematics,* 2nd ser., **24** (1923), 367–393; *Transformations of Surfaces* (Princeton, 1923; corr. reiss. New York, 1962); "Space-Time Continua of Perfect Fluids in General Relativity," in *Transactions of the American Mathematical Society,* **26** (1924), 205–220; "Spaces of Continuous Matter in General Relativity," abstract in *Bulletin of the American Mathematical Society,* **30** (1924), 7; "Geometries of Paths for Which the Equations of the Paths Admit a Quadratic First Integral," in *Transactions of the American Mathematical Society,* **26** (1924), 378–384, abstract in *Bulletin of the American Mathematical Society,* **30** (1924), 297; "Linear Connections of a Space Which Are Determined by Simply Transitive Continuous Groups," in *Proceedings of the National Academy of Sciences,* **11** (1925), 243–250; "Fields of Parallel Vectors in a Riemannian Geometry," in *Transactions of the American Mathematical Society,* **27** (1925), 563–573, abstract in *Bulletin of the American Mathematical Society,* **31** (1925), 292; "Einstein's Recent Theory of Gravitation and Electricity," in *Proceedings of the National Academy of Sciences,* **12** (1926), 125–129; *Riemannian Geometry* (Princeton, 1926); "Geometries of Paths for Which the Equations of the Path Admit $n(n+1)/2$ Independent Linear First Integrals," in *Transactions of the American Mathematical Society,* **28** (1926), 330–338, abstract in *Bulletin of the American Mathematical Society,* **32** (1926), 197; "Congruences of Parallelism of a Field of Vectors," in *Proceedings of the National Academy of Sciences,* **12** (1926), 757–760; "Displacements in a Geometry of Paths Which Carry Paths Into Paths," in *Proceedings of the National Academy of Sciences,* **13** (1927), 38–42, written with M. S. Knebelman; *Non-Riemannian Geometry* (New York, 1927; 6th pr., 1968); "Affine Geometry," in *Encyclopaedia Britannica,* 14th ed. (1929), I, 279–

280; "Differential Geometry," *ibid.,* VII, 366–367; "Contact Transformations," in *Annals of Mathematics,* 2nd ser., **30** (1929), 211–249; and "Dynamical Trajectories and Geodesics," *ibid.,* 591–606.

Between 1930 and 1939 Eisenhart published "Projective Normal Coordinates," in *Proceedings of the National Academy of Sciences,* **16** (1930), 731–740; "Lives of Princeton Mathematicians," in *Scientific Monthly,* **33** (1931), 565–568; "Intransitive Groups of Motions," in *Proceedings of the National Academy of Sciences,* **18** (1932), 195–202; "Equivalent Continuous Groups," in *Annals of Mathematics,* 2nd ser., **33** (1932), 665–676; "Spaces Admitting Complete Absolute Parallelism," in *Bulletin of the American Mathematical Society,* **39** (1933), 217–226; *Continuous Groups of Transformations* (Princeton, 1933; repr. New York, 1961); "Separable Systems in Euclidean 3-Space," in *Physical Review,* 2nd ser., **45** (1934), 427–428; "Separable Systems of Stäckel," in *Annals of Mathematics,* 2nd ser., **35** (1934), 284–305; "Stäckel Systems in Conformal Euclidean Space," *ibid.,* **36** (1935), 57–70; "Groups of Motions and Ricci Directions," *ibid.,* 823–832; "Simply Transitive Groups of Motions," in *Monatshefte für Mathematik und Physik,* **43** (1936), 448–452; "Invariant Theory of Homogeneous Contact Transformations," in *Annals of Mathematics,* 2nd ser., **37** (1936), 747–765, written with M. S. Knebelman; "Graduate Study and Research," in *Science,* **83** (1936), 147–150; "Riemannian Spaces of Class Greater Than Unity," in *Annals of Mathematics,* 2nd ser., **38** (1937), 794–808; "Parallel Vectors in Riemannian Space," in *Annals of Mathematics,* 2nd ser., **39** (1938), 316–321; and *Coordinate Geometry* (Boston, 1939; repr. New York, 1960).

In the 1940's Eisenhart published *An Introduction to Differential Geometry With Use of the Tensor Calculus* (Princeton, 1940); *The Educational Process* (Princeton, 1945); "The Far-Seeing Wilson," in William Starr Myers, ed., *Woodrow Wilson, Some Princeton Memories* (Princeton, 1946), pp. 62–68; "Plan for a University of Discoverers," in *The Princeton University Library Chronicle,* **8** (1947), 123–139; "Enumeration of Potentials for Which One-Particle Schrödinger Equations Are Separable," in *Physical Review,* 2nd ser., **74** (1948), 87–89; "Finsler Spaces Derived From Riemann Spaces by Contact Transformations," in *Annals of Mathematics,* 2nd ser., **49** (1948), 227–254; "Separation of the Variables in the One-Particle Schrödinger Equation in 3-Space," in *Proceedings of the National Academy of Sciences,* **35** (1949), 412–418; and "Separation of the Variables of the Two-Particle Wave Equation," *ibid.,* 490–494.

Eisenhart's publications of the 1950's are "Homogeneous Contact Transformations," in *Proceedings of the National Academy of Sciences,* **36** (1950), 25–30; "Walter Minto and the Earl of Buchan," in *Proceedings of the American Philosophical Society,* **94,** no. 3 (1950), 282–294; "Generalized Riemann Spaces," in *Proceedings of the National Academy of Sciences,* **37** (1951), 311–315; *Uvod u diferentsijalnu geometriiu* (Belgrade, 1951), translation of *Introduction to Differential Geometry . . .;* "Generalized Riemann Spaces, II," in *Proceedings of the National Academy of Sciences,* **38** (1952), 506–508; "Generalized Riemann Spaces and

General Relativity," *ibid.,* **39** (1953), 546–550; Preface to "Historic Philadelphia," in *Transactions of the American Philosophical Society,* **43,** no. 1 (1953), 3; "Generalized Riemann Spaces and General Relativity, II," in *Proceedings of the National Academy of Sciences,* **40** (1954), 463–466; "A Unified Theory of General Relativity of Gravitation and Electromagnetism. I," *ibid.,* **42** (1956), 249–251; II, *ibid.,* 646–650; III, *ibid.,* 878–881; IV, *ibid.,* **43** (1957), 333–336; "Spaces for Which the Ricci Scalar *R* Is Equal to Zero," *ibid.,* **44** (1958), 695–698; "Spaces for Which the Ricci Scalar *R* Is Equal to Zero," *ibid.,* **45** (1959), 226–229; and "Generalized Spaces of General Relativity," *ibid.,* 1759–1762.

The early 1960's saw publication of the following: "The Cosmology Problem in General Relativity," in *Annals of Mathematics,* 2nd ser., **71** (1960), 384–391; "The Paths of Rays of Light in General Relativity," in *Proceedings of the National Academy of Sciences,* **46** (1960), 1093–1097; "Fields of Unit Vectors in the Four-Space of General Relativity," *ibid.,* 1589–1601; "Generalized Spaces of General Relativity II," *ibid.,* 1602–1604; "Spaces Which Admit Fields of Normal Null Vectors," *ibid.,* 1605–1608; "The Paths of Rays of Light in General Relativity of the Non-symmetric Field V_4," *ibid.,* **47** (1961), 1822–1823; "Spaces With Minimal Geodesics," in *Calcutta Mathematical Society Golden Jubilee Commemorative Volume* (Calcutta, 1961), pp. 249–254; "Spaces in Which the Geodesics Are Minimal Curves," in *Proceedings of the National Academy of Sciences,* **48** (1962), 22; "The Paths of Rays of Light in Generalized General Relativity of the Nonsymmetric Field V_4," *ibid.,* 773–775; "Generalized Riemannian Geometry II," *ibid.,* **49** (1963), 18–19; and "The Einstein Generalized Riemannian Geometry," **50** (1963), 190–193.

II. SECONDARY LITERATURE. Biographical memoirs are Gilbert Chinard, Harry Levy, and George W. Corner, "Luther Pfahler Eisenhart (1876–1965)," in *Year Book of the American Philosophical Society* for 1966 (Philadelphia, 1967), pp. 127–134; and Solomon Lefschetz, "Luther Pfahler Eisenhart," in *Biographical Memoirs. National Academy of Sciences,* **40** (1969), 69–90.

Eisenhart's work is discussed in Luigi Bianchi, *Lezioni di geometria differenziale,* Nichola Zanichelli, ed., II, pt. 2 (Bologna, 1930); Herbert Busemann, *The Geometry of Geodesics* (New York, 1955); J. A. Schouten, *Ricci Calculus,* 2nd ed. (Berlin–Göttingen–Heidelberg, 1954); T. Y. Thomas, "On the Projective and Equi-projective Geometries of Paths," in *Proceedings of the National Academy of Sciences,* **11** (1925), 198–203; T. J. Willmore, *An Introduction to Differential Geometry* (London, 1959); and Kentaro Yano, *Groups of Transformations in Generalized Spaces* (Tokyo, 1949).

H. GUGGENHEIMER

EISENSTEIN, FERDINAND GOTTHOLD MAX

(*b.* Berlin, Germany, 16 April 1823; *d.* Berlin, 11 October 1852), *mathematics.*

Eisenstein's father, Johann Konstantin Eisenstein, and his mother, the former Helene Pollack, had con-verted from Judaism to Protestantism before Gotthold was born. His father, who had served eight years in the Prussian army, tried his hand at various commercial enterprises, including manufacturing, but without financial success. Not until late in life did he begin to make a decent livelihood. Eisenstein's five brothers and sisters, born after him, died in childhood, nearly all of meningitis, which he also contracted. His interest in mathematics, awakened and encouraged by a family acquaintance, began when he was about six. "As a boy of six I could understand the proof of a mathematical theorem more readily than that meat had to be cut with one's knife, not one's fork" ("Curriculum vitae," p. 150). Early, too, Eisenstein showed musical inclinations that continued throughout his life and that found expression in playing the piano and composing.

Even while he was in elementary school, his persistently poor health prompted his parents to send him for a time to board in the country. From about 1833 to 1837 he was a resident student at the Cauer academy in Charlottenburg (near Berlin), where the quasi-military discipline was little to his taste. The effects upon him of its Spartan pedagogical methods were manifested in frequent, often feverish illnesses and depression. From September 1837 to July 1842 he attended the Friedrich Wilhelm Gymnasium and then, as a senior, the Friedrich Werder Gymnasium in Berlin. In addition, he went to hear Dirichlet and others lecture at the university.

> What attracted me so strongly and exclusively to mathematics, apart from its actual content, was especially the specific nature of the mental operation by which mathematical things are dealt with. This way of deducing and discovering new truths from old ones, and the extraordinary clarity and self-evidence of the theorems, the ingeniousness of the ideas . . . had an irresistible fascination for me. . . . Starting from the individual theorems, I soon grew accustomed to pierce more deeply into their relationships and to grasp whole theories as a single entity. That is how I conceived the idea of mathematical beauty. . . . And there is such a thing as a mathematical sense or instinct that enables one to see immediately whether an investigation will bear fruit, and to direct one's thoughts and efforts accordingly ["Curriculum vitae," pp. 156–157].

Eisenstein had the good fortune to find in the meteorologist Heinrich W. Dove and the mathematician Karl Schellbach teachers who understood and encouraged him. What he learned in class and at lectures led him to deeper, independent study of the works of Euler, Lagrange, and Gauss, although it was the last who influenced him most. In the summer of 1842, before completing school, he accompanied his mother to England to join his father, who had gone there two years earlier in search of a better livelihood. In neither England, Wales, nor Ireland could the family gain a firm footing. Eisenstein used the time to steep himself in Gauss's *Disquisitiones arithmeticae* and started on his own to study forms of the third degree and the theory of elliptic functions. In Dublin in early 1843 he made the acquaintance of W. R. Hamilton, who gave him a copy of his work "On the Argument of Abel, Respecting the Impossibility of Expressing a Root of Any General Equation Above the Fourth Degree," to be presented to the Berlin Academy.

By around mid-June 1843 Eisenstein and his mother were back in Berlin. His parents were now living apart, and from then until his death Eisenstein stayed with his mother only briefly from time to time. In August 1843 he applied to the Friedrich Wilhelm Gymnasium in Berlin for permission, as a nonstudent, to take their final examinations (a prerequisite for admission to regular university study). In the brief autobiography appended to his application he mentioned (at age twenty) the "hypochondria that has been plaguing me for two years." On 22 September 1843 Eisenstein passed his final secondary school examination, and Schellbach wrote of him in his report: "His knowledge of mathematics goes far beyond the scope of the secondary-school curriculum. His talent and zeal lead one to expect that some day he will make an important contribution to the development and expansion of science" (a remarkable opinion, compared with the wrong ones put forth by other teachers, Galois for example).

Immediately after passing his examinations, Eisenstein enrolled at the University of Berlin. In January 1844 he delivered to the Berlin Academy the copy of Hamilton's study that he had received in Dublin, using the occasion to submit a treatise of his own on cubic forms with two variables. A. L. Crelle, whom the Academy had commissioned to evaluate Eisenstein's work and make appropriate reply to him on its behalf, accepted the treatise for publication in his *Journal für die reine und angewandte Mathematik,* thus again demonstrating Crelle's keen eye for mathematical genius, which had earlier spotted Abel, Jacobi, Steiner, and, later, Weierstrass. At the same time, Crelle introduced the young author to Alexander von Humboldt, who immediately took an interest in him. Time and again Humboldt requested financial support for Eisenstein from the Prussian ministry of education, the king, and the Berlin Academy, and often helped him out of his own pocket. Eisenstein had no feeling of economic security, since these official grants were awarded only for short pe-

riods and always had to be reapplied for, with the approved extensions often arriving late and the sums involved being quite modest and certainly not owed to the recipient. His constant dependence on gifts and charity weighed heavily on him, yet he had found in Humboldt a tireless mentor and protector, the like of which few young talents are ever blessed with. And Humboldt made it clear that he valued Eisenstein not only as a promising young scholar but also as a human being, and with tact and sensitivity he tried (albeit in vain) to divert and cheer him.

The twenty-seventh and twenty-eighth volumes of Crelle's *Journal,* published in 1844, contained twenty-five contributions by Eisenstein. These testimonials to his almost unbelievable, explosively dynamic productivity rocketed him to fame throughout the mathematical world. They dealt primarily with quadratic and cubic forms, the reciprocity theorem for cubic residues, fundamental theorems for quadratic and biquadratic residues, cyclotomy and forms of the third degree, plus some notes on elliptic and Abelian transcendentals. Gauss, to whom he had sent some of his writings, praised them very highly and looked forward with pleasure to an announced visit. In June 1844, carrying a glowing letter of recommendation from Humboldt, Eisenstein went off to see Gauss. He stayed in Göttingen fourteen days. In the course of the visit he won the high respect of the "prince of mathematicians," whom he had revered all his life. The sojourn in Göttingen was important to Eisenstein for another reason: he became friends with Moritz A. Stern—the only lasting friendship he ever made. While the two were in continual correspondence on scientific matters, even Stern proved unable to dispel the melancholy that increasingly held Eisenstein in its grip. Even the sensational recognition that came to him while he was still only a third-semester student failed to brighten Eisenstein's spirits more than fleetingly. In February 1845, at the instance of Ernst E. Kummer, who was acting on a suggestion from Jacobi (possibly inspired by Humboldt), Eisenstein was awarded an honorary doctorate in philosophy by the School of Philosophy of the University of Breslau.

The year 1846 found Eisenstein suddenly involved in an unpleasant priority dispute with Jacobi, who accused him of plagiarism and of misrepresenting known results. Writing to Stern on 20 April 1846, Eisenstein explained that "the whole trouble is that, when I learned of his work on cyclotomy, I did not immediately and publicly acknowledge him as the originator, while I frequently have done this in the case of Gauss. That I omitted to do so in this instance is merely the fault of my naïve innocence."

Jacobi charged him with scientific frivolity and appropriating as his own the ideas imparted to him by others, and he maintained that Eisenstein had no original achievements to his credit but had merely cleverly proved certain theorems stated by others and carried out ideas conceived by others. This was in curious contrast with Jacobi's attitude in 1845, when he had recommended Eisenstein for the honorary doctorate.

In 1846–1847 Eisenstein published various writings, mainly on the theory of elliptic functions. Humboldt, who had tried in vain in 1846 to draw the attention of Crown Prince Maximilian of Bavaria to Eisenstein, early in 1847 recommended him for a professorship at Heidelberg—even before he had earned his teaching credentials at the University of Berlin—but again without success. During the summer semester of 1847 Riemann was among those who attended Eisenstein's lecture on elliptic functions. In September 1847 a great honor came to Eisenstein: Gauss wrote the preface to a volume of his collected treatises. No longer extant, unfortunately, is the letter from Gauss to Eisenstein in which, the latter reported to Riemann, Gauss set down the essentials of his proof of the biquadratic reciprocity law with the aid of cyclotomy.

Early in 1848 Eisenstein had attended meetings of certain democratically oriented clubs, although he took no active part in the pre-March political ferment. During the street battles on 19 March, however, he was forcibly removed from a house from which shots had been fired and was taken with other prisoners to the Citadel at Spandau, suffering severe mistreatment en route. Although he was released the next day, the experience gravely affected his health. Moreover, when word spread that he was a "republican," financial support for him dwindled, and it took Humboldt's most strenuous efforts to keep it from drying up altogether. Eisenstein's situation visibly worsened. Alienated from his family and without close friends or any real contact with other Berlin mathematicians, he vegetated. Only occasionally did he feel able to deliver his lectures as *Privatdozent,* from his bed, if he managed to lecture at all. Yet all this time he was publishing one treatise after another in Crelle's *Journal,* especially on the quadratic partition of prime numbers, on reciprocity laws, and on the theory of forms. In August 1851, on Gauss's recommendation, both Eisenstein and Kummer were elected corresponding members of the Göttingen Society, and in March 1852 Dirichlet managed his election to membership in the Berlin Academy. In late July of that year Eisenstein suffered a severe hemorrhage. Funds raised by Humboldt so that Eisenstein could spend a year convalescing in Sicily came too late: on 11 October he died of pulmonary tuberculosis. Despite all the public recognition, he ended his days in forlorn solitude. The eighty-three-year-old Humboldt accompanied the coffin to the graveside.

Eisenstein soon became the subject of legend, and the early literature about him is full of errors. Only latter-day research has illumined the tragic course of his life. For instance, no evidence at all has been found of the dissolute existence that he was frequently rumored to have led. His lectures were usually attended by more than half of Berlin's mathematics students, which was the more remarkable since Dirichlet, Jacobi, and Steiner were then teaching at Berlin. Eisenstein was ever at pains, as he himself emphasized, to bring home to his listeners the most recent research results.

His treatises were written at a time when only Gauss, Cauchy, and Dirichlet had any conception of what a completely rigorous mathematical proof was. Even a man like Jacobi often admitted that his own work sometimes lacked the necessary rigor and self-evidence of methods and proofs. Thus it is not surprising that, as Leo Koenigsberger tells us, Eisenstein's "Study of the Infinite Double Products, of Which Elliptic Functions Are Composed as Quotients" should have been criticized by Weierstrass, who, in representing his own functions in terms of infinite products, was not picking up the torch from his forerunner, Eisenstein, but was drawing directly upon Gauss. Weierstrass correctly rated Riemann over Eisenstein, who was unable to grasp Riemann's general ideas about functions of complex variables. While Klein did concede that the simplest elliptic functions are defined by Eisenstein's everywhere absolutely convergent series, he called Eisenstein a "walking formula who starts out with a calculation and then finds in it the roots of all his knowledge." Unjustly Klein attributed to him a persecution complex and megalomania. Eisenstein's oft-quoted statement to the effect that through his contributions to the theory of forms (including his finding the simplest covariant for the binary cubic form) he hoped "to become a second Newton" (letter to Humboldt, July 1847) is nothing more than a bad joke.

The development that led to the reciprocity law of nth-power residues will be permanently associated with Eisenstein's work on cubic and biquadratic reciprocity laws. The Eisenstein series have become an integral part of the theory of modular forms and modular functions. They and the Eisenstein irreducibility law (along with the Eisenstein polynomial and the Eisenstein equation) continue to bear his name and to assure him a position about halfway between that contemptuous assessment by Klein and the verdict of Gauss (expressed, of course, in a letter intended for display), who held Eisenstein's talents to be such as "nature bestows on only a few in each century" (letter to Humboldt, 14 April 1846).

BIBLIOGRAPHY

I. ORIGINAL WORKS. Nearly all of Eisenstein's scientific writings were published in the *Journal für die reine und angewandte Mathematik,* specifically in vols. **27** (1844) to **44** (1852); see the bibliography by Kurt-R. Biermann in *Journal für die reine und angewandte Mathematik,* **214/215** (1964), 29–30. Selected *Mathematische Abhandlungen besonders aus dem Gebiete der höhern Mathematik und der elliptischen Functionen* (Berlin, 1847) were published with a preface by Gauss; repr., with intro. by Kurt-R. Biermann (Hildesheim, 1967). An autobiography, "Curriculum vitae des Gotth. Ferdinand Eisenstein," ed. and with intro. by F. Rudio, was published in *Zeitschrift für Mathematik und Physik,* **40** (1895), supp., 143–168. The letters from Eisenstein to M. A. Stern were published by A. Hurwitz and F. Rudio in *Zeitschrift für Mathematik und Physik,* **40** (1895), supp., 169–203. A report by Eisenstein on his imprisonment is found in Adalbert Roerdansz, *Ein Freiheits-Martyrium. Gefangene Berliner auf dem Transport nach Spandau am Morgen des 19. März 1848* (Berlin, 1848), pp. 130–135. A bibliography of Eisenstein's writings is given by Kurt-R. Biermann in *Istoriko-matematicheskie issledovaniya,* **12** (1959), 493–502.

Historical records are available primarily at the following institutions: Archiv der Deutschen Akademie der Wissenschaften zu Berlin; Archiv der Humboldt-Universität zu Berlin; Deutsche Staatsbibliothek, Berlin; Niedersächsische Staats- und Universitäts-Bibliothek, Göttingen; Archiv der Akademie der Wissenschaften, Göttingen; and Deutsches Zentralarchiv, Historische Abteilung II, Merseburg. See also the survey by Kurt-R. Biermann in *Journal für die reine und angewandte Mathematik,* **214/215** (1964), 28.

II. SECONDARY LITERATURE. See the bibliography by Kurt-R. Biermann in *Journal für die reine und angewandte Mathematik,* **214/215** (1964), 28–29. Only the literature devoted directly to Eisenstein will be cited here. See Wilhelm Ahrens, "Gotthold Eisenstein," in *Deutsche allgemeine Zeitung,* no. 177 (17 April 1923); Moritz Cantor, "Eisenstein," in *Allgemeine deutsche Biographie,* V (1877), 774, which contains errors; J. Loewenberg, "A. v. Humboldt und G. Eisenstein," in *Allgemeine Zeitung des Judenthums,* **55** (1891), 246–248; and Julius Schuster, "A. v. Humboldt und F. G. Eisenstein," in *Janus,* **26** (1922), 99.

See also the following works by Kurt-R. Biermann: "A. v. Humboldt als Protektor G. Eisensteins und dessen Wahl in die Berliner Akademie," in *Forschungen und Fortschritte,* **32** (1958), 78–81; "Zur Geschichte der Ehrenpromotion G. Eisensteins," *ibid.,* 332–335; "Die Briefe A. v. Humboldts an F. G. M. Eisenstein," in *Alexander von Humboldt, Gedenkschrift* (Berlin, 1959), 117–159; "A. L. Crelles Verhältnis zu G. Eisenstein," in *Monatsbericht der Deutschen Akademie der Wissenschaften zu Berlin,* **1** (1959), 67–72; "Eisenstein," in *Neue deutsche Biographie,* IV (1959), 420–421; "Einige neue Ergebnisse der Eisenstein-Forschung," in *Zeitschrift für Geschichte der Naturwissenschaften, Technik und Medizin,* **1,** no. 2 (1961), 1–12; and "G. Eisenstein, Die wichtigsten Daten seines Lebens und Wirkens," in *Journal für die reine und angewandte Mathematik,* **214/215** (1964), 19–30.

KURT-R. BIERMANN

EKEBERG, ANDERS GUSTAF (*b.* Stockholm, Sweden, 15 January 1767; *d.* Uppsala, Sweden, 11 February 1813), *chemistry, mineralogy.*

Ekeberg studied in Uppsala, Greifswald, and Berlin from 1784 to 1790. He worked at the Council of Mining in 1794 and in the same year became assistant professor of chemistry at the University of Uppsala. In 1799 he became associate professor and a member of the Royal Swedish Academy of Science.

While in Greifswald, Ekeberg had studied under Christian Ehrenfried Weigel, the follower and German translator of Lavoisier. That the New Chemistry was introduced into Germany at such an early date was undoubtedly due to Weigel; as Weigel's enthusiastic pupil, Ekeberg in his turn helped to spread it northward.

Ekeberg's article "Om Chemiska Vetenskapens närvarande skick" ("On the Present State of the Chemical Science"), published in 1795, was the first attempt to present the antiphlogiston theory in Sweden. Ekeberg consolidated his position with a pamphlet, published the same year, entitled *Försök till Svensk nomenklatur för Chemien . . .* ("An Attempt Toward a Swedish Nomenclature for Chemistry"), in which the terminology introduced was Lavoisier's. Both of these outspokenly antiphlogistic works were published anonymously because Ekeberg was anxious to avoid conflicts with Johan Afzelius, his superior in Uppsala, who distrusted the new theories.

Ekeberg was an extraordinarily capable analytic chemist. Shortly after taking up his duties at Uppsala, probably about 1795–1796, he became interested in a remarkable mineral quarried in Ytterby in Sweden; he made a thorough investigation of it and was thus able in 1797 to confirm Gadolin's earlier discovery of yttria. After further prolonged research he announced in 1802 that he had found yttria in a new mineral from Ytterby which also contained a hitherto unknown heavy metal. Ekeberg was the first to define this heavy metal precisely. On the basis of the inability of its oxide to combine with even the smallest particle of acid—even when it was submerged in it—Ekeberg compared the new metal to Tantalus and called it "tantalum."

In addition to his scientific ability Ekeberg possessed a considerable literary talent which he demonstrated in his younger years. He suffered poor health throughout his life, however, and when this was aggravated by an impairment of vision and hearing, his vitality decreased and his promising scientific career came to a premature end.

BIBLIOGRAPHY

I. ORIGINAL WORKS. Ekeberg's publications include "Om Chemiska Vetenskapens närvarande skick," in *Litteratur tidning för år 1795,* **1** (1795), 91–104; *Försök till Svensk Nomenklatur för Chemien, lämpad efter de sednaste uptäckterne* (Uppsala, 1795); "Ytterligare undersökningar af den svarta stenarten från Ytterby och den däri fundne egna jord," in *Kongliga Vetenskaps Academiens nya Handlingar,* **18** (1797), 156–164; "Uplysning om ytterjordens egenskaper, i synnerhet i jämförelse med berylljorden: Om de fossiler hvari förstnämnde jord innehålles, samt om en ny uptäckt kropp af metallisk natur. Tantalum," *ibid.,* **23** (1802), 68–73; "Chemisk undersökning af et hårdt oktaedriskt kristalliseradt fossil ifrån Fahlun," in *Afhandlingar i fysik, kemi och mineralogi,* **1** (1806), 84–90; and "Undersökning af ett natronhaltigt fossil ifrån Hesselkulla," *ibid.* (1807), 144–153.

II. SECONDARY LITERATURE. On Ekeberg's life and work see "Anders Gustaf Ekebergs biographie," in *Kongliga Vetenskaps Academiens Handlingar,* 3rd ser. (1813), 276–279; and Arne Westgren, "Anders Gustaf Ekebergs föreläsningar 1805–1811," in *The Svedberg 1884 $\frac{30}{8}$ 1944* (Uppsala, 1944).

UNO BOKLUND

EKMAN, VAGN WALFRID (*b.* Stockholm, Sweden, 3 May 1874; *d.* Gostad, Stockaryd, Sweden, 9 March 1954), *oceanography.*

Ekman belonged to the group of Scandinavian oceanographers who, at the beginning of this century, started a new and very fruitful line in physical oceanography. He worked with Fridtjof Nansen, Vilhelm Bjerknes, and B. Helland-Hansen and, like them, must be ranked as one of the great oceanographers.

Ekman was the youngest son of Fredrik Laurentz Ekman, a professor who also worked in oceanography. He went to school in Stockholm and then studied at the University of Uppsala. His interest in hydrodynamics and oceanography came through his contact with Bjerknes, who introduced him to the theoretical problem of the "wind spiral," which became the subject of his thesis. The original idea of the spiral came from Nansen, who observed a systematic drift of the ice to the right of the wind direc-

tion during his famous *Fram* expedition. Nansen suggested that Ekman investigate the problem mathematically, reasoning that each layer of the sea must be set in motion by the layer immediately above and be successively more deflected to the right by the Coriolis force (on the northern hemisphere). Ekman's thesis was a short paper in Swedish published in 1902, and it did not immediately attract any attention. Through an enlarged paper, "On the Influence of the Earth's Rotation on Ocean Currents," published in 1905 in *Arkiv för matematik, astronomi och fysik,* his theory became known to the international scientific community. Its importance has since been well established. The "Ekman layer" is one of the cornerstones of modern theories of oceanic circulation, and it plays an important role in practically all theoretical and experimental works on rotating fluids.

Another important theoretical contribution was given in a paper published in 1923 in the same journal. Here Ekman developed, for the first time, a complete mathematical theory for the wind-driven circulation in an oceanic basin. It took almost thirty years before a new generation of theoretical oceanographers was able to catch up with these ideas and build further on Ekman's theory. Both the 1905 and the 1923 papers are masterpieces of clarity and elegance and can certainly be enjoyed by all those interested in the subject, whether professionally or not. The first paper has been reprinted in booklet form by the Royal Swedish Academy of Sciences, Stockholm, and there are plans to print an English edition of the second paper.

Ekman was a very good experimentalist. He made determinations of the equation state for seawater and studied several important hydrodynamic phenomena both in the laboratory and in the sea. Probably the most widely known of his studies is that devoted to dead water, the strong resistance experienced by ships in the Norwegian fjords because of a particular stratification of the water.

Ekman also constructed oceanographic instruments. His current meter, which gives speed and direction by use of a purely mechanical system, is still a standard tool in oceanographic studies. With Helland-Hansen, Ekman made a number of cruises in the Norwegian Sea to test his current meter. Later, in 1930, he cruised to the trade-wind belt in the Atlantic to carry out systematic current measurements. Unfortunately some of the material was lost during World War II, and it was not until 1953, when Ekman was seventy-nine, that the results were finally published. As usual, Ekman had perfected his work in every detail.

While carrying out his oceanographic research,

Ekman was assistant at the International Oceanographic Laboratory in Oslo from 1902 to 1908, then lecturer in mechanics and mathematical physics in Lund, where he received a full professorship in 1910. He became a member of several learned societies and received the Agassiz Medal in 1928 and the Vega Medal in 1939. Ekman published a total of more than 100 scientific articles as well as several articles on philosophical and religious subjects. He was an active member of the Lutheran church and published in its newspaper, *Kyrkobröderna.*

Ekman was extraordinary in his requirements for truth and exactness in every detail, both in his scientific work and in his private life. He believed that no human being has the right to cause injustice or harm to anyone else, and he certainly lived up to his ideals. Governed rigorously by his principles, Ekman may have appeared impersonal to some, but he had a warmth and spontaneity that was revealed to his family and close friends.

BIBLIOGRAPHY

A complete bibliography, with biography by B. Kullenberg, is given in a repr. of "On the Influence of the Earth's Rotation on Ocean Currents" (Uppsala, 1963). Among his works are "On Dead Water," in *The Norwegian North Polar Expedition 1893–1896. Scientific Results,* V (1904), 15; "On the Influence of the Earth's Rotation on Ocean Currents," in *Arkiv för matematik, astronomi och fysik,* 2 (1905), 11; *Tables for Sea Water Under Pressure,* Conseil Permanent International pour l'Exploration de la Mer, Publication de Circonstance no. 49 (1910); "Über Horizontalzirkulation bei winderzeugten Meeresströmungen," in *Arkiv för matematik, astronomi och fysik,* 17 (1923), 26; *On a New Repeating Current Meter,* Conseil Permanent International pour l'Exploration de la Mer, Publication de Circonstance, no. 91 (1926); and "Turbulent, Periodic and Mean Motions. Some Measurements in the Atlantic," in *Procès-verbaux. Association d'océanographie physique,* 4 (1949), written with B. Helland-Hansen.

PIERRE WELANDER

ELHUYAR (or **ELHUYART**), **FAUSTO D'** (*b.* Logroño, Spain, 11 October 1755; *d.* Madrid, Spain, 6 January 1833), *chemistry, mineralogy, assaying.*

The younger brother of Juan José D'Elhuyar, Fausto shared his brother's studies, profession, and travels until 8 October 1781, when they separated in Vienna and Fausto returned to Spain. There he taught mineralogy and structural, or geotectonic, geology at the Real Seminario Patriótico in Vergara and, with François Chabaneau, lecturer in physics and chemistry, founded the Real Escuela Metalúrgica. There too D'Elhuyar collaborated in the experiments conducted by his brother Juan José, the discoverer of metallic tungsten, and in 1784 he distributed the monograph that had been published under both their names and made it well known when Juan José left for South America. Thus Fausto is the better known of the two and often is erroneously credited with having made the larger contribution to the discovery of metallic tungsten.

In 1785 D'Elhuyar abandoned the teaching of mineralogy and worked with Chabaneau on separating platinum and rendering it malleable. On this subject he had his own ideas and methods, which were opposed to those of Carl von Sickingen. He was unable to develop them, however, for the Spanish government commissioned him to visit his friend Ignaz von Born in Hungary, to see at firsthand Born's new method of amalgamation for the treatment of gold and silver ores. Fausto sent this information to his brother, as well as drawings and models of apparatus to assist Juan José in Nueva Granada (now Colombia). The method was regarded as a revolutionary one, but Born conceded that its origins were in Alvaro Alonso Barba's *El arte de los metales.* D'Elhuyar improved it, however, by adding salt and lime and showed that, contrary to the prevailing view, gold and silver ores could be roasted. The French chemist Joseph-Louis Proust extolled his work in his "Extracto de los descubrimientos de Don Fausto D'Elhuyar" (published in Spanish in *Anales del real laboratorio quimico de Segovia,* 1 [1791]). D'Elhuyar was an avid researcher. In the first of his *Disertaciones metalúrgicas* (Madrid, 1933) he asserted that there were no essential differences between chemical substances, and he adopted the phlogiston theory only in order to make himself easily understood. From his experiments he concluded that "there is no other difference between metals than that which distinguishes each in kind"—there are only gradations. D'Elhuyar also discovered chloroargentic acid and obtained new results in combining sulfur and metals.

The Spanish government put him in charge of organizing missions of metallurgists to go to Mexico and Peru. D'Elhuyar selected Friedrich Sonneschmidt to head the first and Baron Nordenflicht to head the second. The development and prosperity of Mexican mining was due largely to D'Elhuyar's efforts, for when he arrived it was on the decline. After Alexander von Humboldt visited Mexico, he wrote in his *Political Essay on the Kingdom of New Spain:* "No city on the New Continent, not even in the United States, offers scientific establishments so vast and so solid as does the capital of Mexico. It is enough to cite here the School of Mines, of which the scholar D'Elhuyar is Director."

With the start of the War of Independence in 1810, the work of the College of Mines was interrupted and it went into decline, as did mining throughout Mexico. During the conflict D'Elhuyar remained loyal to Spain. In 1821 he resigned his post and returned to Madrid, where he became a member of the Directorate General of Public Credit and of the Development Board. His *Memoria para la formación de una ley orgánica para el gobierno de la minería en España* was the basis for the mining law enacted in 1825. Although he was appointed Director General of Mines, he was assigned to other duties, and his learning and research skills were not fully utilized.

BIBLIOGRAPHY

On D'Elhuyar or his work see the following: *Biografía del ilustrísimo Señor Don Fausto D'Elhuyar y de Subice* (sic) (Madrid, 1853); Juan Fages y Virgili, *Los químicos de Vergara y sus obras* (Madrid, 1909); A. de Gálvez-Cañero y Alzola, *Apuntes biográficos de Don Fausto D'Elhuyar* (Madrid, 1933); A. Federico Gredilla, *Biografía de José Celestino Mutis* (Madrid, 1911); J. Guzmán, *Las disertaciones metalúrgicas de Fausto D'Elhuyar* (Madrid, 1933); C. López-Sánchez, *Elhuyar, minero-metalúrgico* (Madrid, 1933); E. Moles, "Elhuyar, químico," in *Anales de la Sociedad española de física y química* (Feb. 1933); Nicolás de Soroluce, *Real sociedad bascongada de amigos del país* (San Sebastián, Spain, 1880); Mary Elvira Weeks, *Discovery of the Elements,* 6th ed. (Detroit, 1956); and Arthur P. Whitaker, "The Elhuyar Mining Missions and the Enlightenment," in *Hispanic American Review* (Nov. 1961); and *Latin America and the Enlightenment* (Ithaca, N.Y., 1961).

Manuscript sources include the author's library, which contains some of D'Elhuyar's correspondence; and the parish records of Logroño, Spain, and Bayonne and Saint Jean-de-Luz, France.

BERNARDO J. CAYCEDO

ELHUYAR (or ELHUYART), JUAN JOSÉ D' (*b.* Logroño, Spain, 15 June 1754; *d.* Bogotá, Nueva Granada [now Colombia], 20 September 1796), *chemistry, mineralogy, metallurgy.*

D'Elhuyar's father, Juan, a well-known surgeon, and his mother, Ursula Lubice, were French Basques who moved to Spain and settled in Logroño. Juan José received his elementary education at Oyón (Navarre) and Logroño. Sent to Paris with his brother Fausto, he studied medicine for five years (1772–1777) and was a pupil of the chemist and mineralogist Hilaire-Marin Rouelle. Upon returning to Spain in 1777 he joined the Sociedad Económica de Amigos del País, founded by the count of Peñaflorida, whose son Antonio had been a schoolmate of D'Elhuyar's. The latter had to give up his medical career, however,

because the minister of the navy, concerned with preparing Spain for war with Great Britain, sent him and his brother Fausto to study geology, mineralogy, and metallurgy at the Mining Academy in Freiberg, Saxony, so that their knowledge could be applied to the treatment of iron and steel in the manufacture of cannon.

In Freiberg, D'Elhuyar attended lectures by Johann W. Charpentier on structural, or geotectonic, geology, by Geller on metallurgical chemistry, and especially those by Werner, on geology and petrography. Both the lectures at the academy and the fieldwork contributed to his earning in later years the cognomen "sabio" (scholar), which was applied to him by his friend José Celestino Mutis, a physician and botanist. After visiting the mercury deposits in Idrija and the mining districts of Rosenau, Hungary, Bohemia, the duchy of Zweibrücken, the Rhenish Palatinate, and Austria with his brother, D'Elhuyar proceeded by himself in 1781 to Sweden, Norway, and Denmark. At the University of Uppsala he attended lectures by Peter Jacob Hjelm and especially those by Bergman. He also met Scheele. Bergman and Scheele were seeking a new element but got no further than obtaining tungstic acid. D'Elhuyar participated in the experiments, and after his return to Spain, he succeeded in isolating the metallic element tungsten.

In 1783 D'Elhuyar and his brother Fausto published *Análisis químico del wolfram y examen de un nuevo metal que entra en su composición,* which attracted great interest in scientific circles and was translated into several languages. In December 1783 he was appointed director of mines of Nueva Granada (now Colombia); his principal occupation consisted of managing the Mariquita silver mines. In 1796 Viceroy Ezpeleta ordered the exploitation of the silver mines stopped, and D'Elhuyar moved to Bogotá, where he died, leaving a widow (the former Josefa Bastida-Lee) and three children. He wrote many reports to and carried on considerable correspondence with three viceroys and other officials of the Spanish Crown. He perfected Born's method for amalgamating silver and mercury and recommended a new process for the isolation of platinum. The colonial authorities interfered with D'Elhuyar's work and did not utilize his abilities as a scientific researcher.

BIBLIOGRAPHY

I. ORIGINAL WORKS. D'Elhuyar's published work is *Análisis químico del wolfram y examen de un nuevo metal que entra en su composición* (Vitoria, Spain, 1783), written with his brother Fausto. Notes taken by D'Elhuyar while attending Bergman's course in special chemistry at the University of Uppsala in 1782, concerning the new discoveries in chemistry, are in *Lychnos* (1959), pp. 162–207, with an introduction by Stig Rydén and Arne Fredga.

II. SECONDARY LITERATURE. On D'Elhuyar or his work, see *Archivo epistolar del sabio naturalista José Celestino Mutis*, I (Bogotá, 1947), 82–163; Juan Fages y Virgili, *Los químicos de Vergara y sus obras* (Madrid, 1909); Federico Gredilla, *Biografía de Don José Celestine Mutis* (Madrid, 1911), 230–246, 301–316; Vicente Restrepo, "Biografía de Juan José D'Elhuyar," in *Estudio sobre las minas de oro y plata de Colombia* (Bogotá, 1888), pp. 230–246; Stig Rydén, *Don Juan José D'Elhuyar en Suecia y el descubrimiento del tungsteno* (Madrid, 1962); Mary Elvira Weeks, *Discovery of the Elements,* 6th ed. (Detroit, 1956), pp. 113–114, 132–147; Arthur P. Whitaker, "The Elhuyar Mining Missions and the Enlightenment," in *Hispanic American Historical Review,* **31,** no. 4 (Nov. 1951), 558–585; and José Zamora Mendoza, *Don Juan D'Elhuyar, prestigioso cirujano del Hospital de Logroño* (Logroño, 1956), and Marcelino Menéndez Pelayo, *La ciencia española,* vol. II.

Manuscript sources are to be found in the following locations: National Archives, Bogotá, Cataloging Room, no. 169, notarial registries; the author's archives, which contain some of D'Elhuyar's correspondence, as well as many documents relating to both his private and his public life; the parish records of Logroño, Spain; Bayonne, France; and Bogotá, Colombia; and the records of the Real Expedición Botánica del Nuevo Reino de Granada, at the Botanical Garden in Madrid, file 24.

                                                                    BERNARDO J. CAYCEDO

ÉLIE DE BEAUMONT, JEAN-BAPTISTE-ARMAND-LOUIS-LÉONCE (*b.* Canon, Calvados, France, 25 September 1798; *d.* Canon, 21 September 1874), *geology.*

Élie de Beaumont was the elder son of Armand-Jean-Baptiste-Anne-Robert Élie de Beaumont and Marie-Charlotte-Eléonore Mercier Dupaty; their marriage united the families of two jurists who had achieved fame under the *ancien régime.*

Following a widespread custom of the bourgeoisie in the eighteenth century, Élie de Beaumont's grandfather, Jean-Baptiste, a Norman lawyer, joined to his patronymic the name of an estate, in order to distinguish himself from his brother Jean-Antoine, *docteur régent* of the Faculté de Médecine of Paris.

Under the Empire, Léonce's parents, who were living at Canon, engaged a Benedictine monk, Dom Raphaël de Hérino, to serve as tutor to him and his brother, Charles-Adolphe-Eugène. At the beginning of the Restoration, when the children had nearly completed their secondary studies, the family moved to the rue de la Muette, in Faubourg Saint-Antoine, a quarter of Paris not far from the Collège Royal Charlemagne. At this *collège,* where he was called

Élie-Debeaumont, Léonce obtained fourth honorable mention in elementary mathematics in the general competition of 1816. In 1817, after a year of higher mathematics at the Collège Henri IV, he won first prize in mathematics and physics in the general competition and was second on the admissions list of the École Polytechnique, which methodically collected the country's most gifted students for intensive training in mathematics. Graduated first in his class from the Polytechnique, he chose the Corps des Mines, which had not received any engineering students from the last three graduating classes. He entered the École Royale des Mines on 15 November 1819.

The École des Mines offered four two-year courses. Baillet du Belloy, in his course on the working of mines, also discussed hydraulic engines, steam engines, and subterranean topography; Berthier taught docimasy (analytic mineral chemistry); Hassenfratz described the primary treatment processes for all kinds of ores (that is, ore dressing, or beneficiation of ore); and Brochant de Villiers alternately taught one year of mineralogy and one of geology. Between the first and second years the engineering students worked in the laboratory, practiced drafting, and made plans of the catacombs. After the second year they undertook study trips of several months' duration in a mining or metallurgical region, following an itinerary outlined in detail by the council of the École des Mines. Their studies were judged complete when they had attained a certain level in each subject area. In general, students had to spend a third year at the École des Mines in order to reach that level and then were required to take a second study trip.

This was the case with Élie de Beaumont, who, beginning in November 1820, also attended the Faculté des Sciences in Paris. During the summer of 1821 he devoted his first study trip to visiting the iron mines and forges in eastern France and began making geological observations in the Vosges, where his guide was Philippe Voltz, a mining engineer in Strasbourg who was particularly interested in paleontology. In 1822 a second study trip took Élie de Beaumont to Switzerland, where his guide was Jean de Charpentier, director of the salt mines of Bex and a former student of Werner's at the Freiberg Bergakademie. Charpentier also acquainted Élie de Beaumont with his observations on glaciers: he was the first to propose that they had transported erratic boulders deposited on the Swiss Jura. Élie de Beaumont returned on foot to Paris, passing through Auvergne. The main portions of his journals of the two trips, which were considered useful in teaching others, were published in the *Annales des mines* in 1822 and 1824.

On 1 January 1823 Élie de Beaumont was named an engineering cadet at the same time as Charles Combes, who had been in the class after his. All the mining engineers, including the older ones like Hassenfratz and Héron de Villefosse, were concerned about France's underdeveloped industry, especially vis-à-vis England. They thought that first priority should be given to putting France on an equal footing with its rival, especially in the use of steam engines, the development of collieries and mines, and in metallurgy. At the Ministry of the Interior their point of view was shared by the director general of bridges, highways, and mines, Louis Becquey.

The absence of outcroppings and the lack of knowledge of the substrata made prospecting for sedimentary deposits, particularly the search for coal beds, extremely uncertain. To all those concerned with the development of a mineral industry in France, the importance of preparing a geological map had become evident. The idea of representing the nature of the terrain on a topographical map was not new in France. In 1664 the monograph of the Abbé Louis Coulon, *Les rivières de France, ou Description géographique et historique du cours et débordement des fleuves, rivières . . . de France, avec un dénombrement des villes, ponts, passages, . . .,* had been reprinted, accompanied by a map indicating the boundaries of the granite and the sedimentary formations.

In the middle of the eighteenth century, when Guettard had surveyed northern France, he had perceived that the different formations that constitute its soil form large concentric bands about Paris. In 1746 he published in the *Mémoires de l'Académie royale des sciences* a map in which he proposed "to show that there is a certain regularity in the distribution of the rocks, the metals, and most of the fossil substances." Subsequently he was commissioned by Bertin to explore the whole of France from the point of view of mineralogy and to publish descriptions and maps of the provinces.

Originally it had been planned to cover all of France by means of 214 mineralogical maps, but a lack of funds permitted only forty-five maps to be made. Monnet published them in 1780 in the *Atlas et description minéralogiques de la France, entrepris par ordre du Roi . . . 1re partie, comprenant le Beauvoisis, la Picardie, le Boulonnais, la Flandre Française, le pays Messin, et une partie de la Champagne.*

On 6 July 1794 the Committee of Public Safety issued a decree (the text of which Hassenfratz had composed) that the engineers of the Corps des Mines were to search for mineral substances in their districts and to map their discoveries. The *Journal des mines* published several geological memoirs written by mining engineers, as well as mineralogical reports on several departments by Coquebert de Montbret. In collaboration with the latter, the geologist Omalius d'Halloy prepared, between 1810 and 1813, "Essai d'une carte géologique de la France, des Pays-Bas et de quelques contrées voisines." It was published in the *Annales des mines,* but not until 1822, when the subject had become of current interest. This map, drawn on a scale of about 1:3,600,000, distinguished six great rock systems: primordial, penean, ammonean, cretaceous, mastozooic, and pyroidic.

Brochant de Villiers, commissioned in 1802 to teach geology at the École des Mines, had seen the importance of preparing a more detailed geological map. In 1811 he had presented to the director-general of mines, Count Laumond, a project for the execution of such a map. But Napoleon and his ministers, who did not understand the revolutionary economic role of the steam engine and were thus unable to grasp the importance of developing the coal industry, considered the establishment of a geological map to be one of those academic exercises that can be postponed indefinitely.

The Corps des Mines had to wait for the fall of the Empire to triumph over Napoleonic obtuseness. The royal order of 5 December 1816 instructed the council of the École des Mines, reestablished in Paris at the Hôtel Vendôme, to assemble all the materials necessary to complete the mineralogical description of France, and subsequently commissioned it to amass mineral collections and to publish geological and mining maps.

In 1820 the English geologist George Bellas Greenough published a geological map of England in six sheets, a copy of which he sent to the director-general of bridges, highways, and mines. On 11 June 1822 the council of the École des Mines, judging the occasion favorable, repeated its intention to produce a geological map of France and invited Brochant de Villiers to present a new report on this subject to Becquey. On 15 June, Brochant proposed that a mission composed of himself and two young mining engineers go the following year to England in order to confer with and study the methods of the English geologists. Dufrénoy, promoted to mining engineer on 1 June 1821, was the first collaborator that Brochant thought of, and Élie de Beaumont's good fortune was to complete his studies at the moment when a second assistant was being sought.

On 25 April 1823 Élie de Beaumont was invited by Becquey to leave immediately for Dover, "in order to improve his knowledge of the English language by speaking with Englishmen," and to wait there for Brochant and Dufrénoy. Their mission lasted six months. They inspected, in particular, tin and copper mines in Cornwall, lead mines in Cumberland and Derbyshire, and coal mines and ironworks in Wales. Upon their return Becquey complimented them for their work and for the smallness of their expenses. Dufrénoy and Élie de Beaumont devoted 1824 to composing memoirs on their mission, which were published in the *Annales des mines.*

Élie de Beaumont, appointed as mining engineer in May 1824, was assigned on 1 September 1824 to the Service des Mines at Rouen and placed in charge of the Seine-Inférieure (now Maritime) and Eure departments. On 29 June 1825 Becquey wrote to Brochant:

> I have reread your report of 15 June 1822 and the opinion of the council of the École des Mines. All these documents have strengthened me in the resolution that I announced to you in 1820: having a geological map of France made. This work is important: its results should be eminently useful and its execution can only bring honor to the Royal Corps of Mining Engineers. Consequently I approve the various measures that you proposed to me in concert with the council of the École des Mines. The mineralogical description of France ought therefore to include all the information relative to the nature of the terrain that could be of interest at once to *geology, the art of mining, and all the other arts practiced on mineral substances,* as well as information on the different kinds of formations, their relationships, their boundaries, exploited and unexploited deposits of useful minerals, and finally, the location of mine mills. In order to present without confusion such manifold and very often closely related data, one should draw up: (1) *a general geological map of France* including all information on the nature of the formations; (2) *departmental geological and mineralogical maps.* The work will commence with the general geological map. . . . Your proposed geological division of the work among the engineers seems to me clear and precise. I easily follow the twisting diagonal line by which you divide France, which goes from the northwest to the southeast, running along the boundary of the great chalk massif from Calvados to the vicinity of Saumur, Châtellerault, and Auxerre, then turning back toward Avallon and Chalon and, beyond that, following the course of the Saône and the Rhone. . . . Each year please inform me in advance of the probable expense, since funds are so limited that I must be sure of being able to meet expenses before authorizing them. According to the information that you have presented, the total expense for 1825 will be approximately 3,000 francs, including everything.

Dufrénoy, in charge of the western division, and Élie de Beaumont, in charge of the eastern division, spent the first five years, from 1825 to 1829, exploring their sectors on foot during the summer months,

noting their observations on Cassini de Thury's map, drawn up on 180 sheets on a scale of 1 line for 100 *toises* (1:86,400). From 1826 to 1828 Dufrénoy was assisted by E. de Billy, and Élie de Beaumont by Fénéon. In 1830 they went to the Alps with Brochant to verify the abnormal contact, observed by Élie de Beaumont, of granite and an underlying calcareous layer; this inaugurated their joint expeditions, which were continued until 1836. On 20 December 1841, they presented to the Académie des Sciences the *Carte géologique générale de la France,* drawn on six sheets on a scale of 1:500,000, and the first volume of the *Explication.* The 100-page introduction to the latter is still the best that can be placed at the beginning of modern treatises on physical geography.

Dufrénoy and Élie de Beaumont, appointed mining engineers first class in May 1832, henceforth received the same promotions at the same time: chief engineer in May 1833 and inspector general in March 1848.

From 1825 Élie de Beaumont devoted himself almost exclusively to geology, on which he started to lecture in 1827 at the École des Mines and in 1832 at the Collège de France, where in 1848 he had as auditors the students of the first École d'Administration.

On 22 June 1829 Élie de Beaumont presented to the Académie des Sciences his first ideas on tectonics, showing that the various mountain chains are of different ages. In this exposition, to which Arago devoted seventeen enthusiastic pages in the *Annuaire pour 1830* of the Bureau des Longitudes, Élie de Beaumont distinguished six systems of uplift, each characterized by one direction. In 1833, in a note inserted in the translation of Henry De la Beche's *Manual of Geology,* he increased the number of systems to twelve. In 1834, at the Sociéte Géologique de France, of which he had been one of the founders in March 1830, his hypotheses were sharply criticized by Ami Boué.

In 1833, in a memoir entitled *Sur les groupes du Cantal, du Mont-Dore et sur les soulèvements auxquels ces montagnes doivent leur relief actuel,* Dufrénoy and Élie de Beaumont unfortunately borrowed from Leopold von Buch the theory of elevation craters. They thought that great lava flows can spread only over surfaces that are almost horizontal. Occasionally a force acting upward from below, which they supposed was the upheaval of a plug of solid lava, would raise the flows thus formed and build what they called an elevation cone. At the point of application of this force, they stated, a crack with divergent fissures was produced; this divided into triangular sectors the fragments of lava that henceforth constituted the sides of the cone. When flows or thrusts produce a gap at the summit, this constitutes an elevation crater. Since there are spaces between the lava sectors thus formed, Dufrénoy and Élie de Beaumont developed formulas for the calculation of their area as a function of the diameter of the base of the cone and the slope of its sides. After stating these formulas, they believed, contrary to the evidence, that they were verified by observation in central France and then at Vesuvius and Etna, which they inspected the following year with Buch.

In 1846–1847 Élie de Beaumont devoted his course at the Collège de France to volcanic and metalliferous emanations; he continued it on 5 July 1847 at the Société Géologique de France in a statement that was the first complete theory of metalliferous veins. It is his most solid scientific work besides his surveys for the geological map.

On 5 May 1838, at the Société Philomathique, Élie de Beaumont appeared like a mathematician lost among the natural sciences, applying to sedimentary folds considerations borrowed from the theory of ruled surfaces; and these considerations, moreover, were not original, since, as Babinet observed, they had already been stated by Monge in another form.

A growing detachment from observation and a love of calculation led Élie de Beaumont, beginning in 1850, to connect the stylized directions of the mountain chains to a system of terrestrial great circles forming regular pentagons in gnomonic projection. This was the point of departure for his delusory theory of the pentagonal grid, which he represented in 1866 on the *Carte géologique générale de la France* and which was taught for some thirty years at the École des Mines.

On 21 December 1835 Élie de Beaumont was elected to the Académie des Sciences, in the mineralogy section; on 19 December 1853 he was named perpetual secretary for the mathematical sciences, replacing Arago. In December 1859 he married Thérèse-Marie-Augusta de Quélen, the widow of the marquis du Bouchet; she died childless in 1866.

Élie de Beaumont was director of the Service de la Carte Géologique from its organization in 1865 until 1868, when, having reached the age of retirement, he had to cede to Combes the chairmanship of the Conseil Général des Mines, an office which he had held since 1861.

A dogmatic, cold, and distant mathematician, Élie de Beaumont appeared to his contemporaries as a misguided pundit—an impression not lessened by his attachment to the theory of elevation craters and to the pentagonal grid, his noncomprehension of the discoveries of Boucher de Perthes, and his unreserved support of the gullible geometer Michel Chasles dur-ing the scandal that developed from the latter's presentation to the Academy of forged manuscripts which he had purchased.

BIBLIOGRAPHY

I. ORIGINAL WORKS. Élie de Beaumont's papers are too numerous to cite individually. A nearly complete list is in the Royal Society of London *Catalogue of Scientific Papers,* I (1868), 476–479; VI (1872), 648; VII (1877), 607; and IX (1891), 787. Poggendorff, I (1863), 657–658, and III (1898), 404, is incomplete.

The major works were written with Dufrénoy: *Voyage métallurgique en Angleterre, ou Recueil de mémoires sur le gisement, l'exploitation et le traitement des minerais d'étain, de cuivre, de plomb, de zinc et de fer dans la Grande-Bretagne,* 2 vols. (Paris, 1827); *Mémoires pour servir à une description géologique de la France,* 4 vols. (Paris, 1830–1838); *Carte géologique de la France (6 feuilles), Tableau d'assemblage des six feuilles de la carte géologique* (Paris, 1841); *Explication de la carte géologique de la France,* 2 vols. (Paris, 1841–1848); *Description du terrain houiller de la France* (Paris, 1842).

II. SECONDARY LITERATURE. Works on Élie de Beaumont are J. Bertrand, *Éloge historique de Élie de Beaumont* (Paris, 1875); P. Fallot, "Élie de Beaumont et l'évolution des sciences géologiques au Collège de France," in *Annales des mines,* 13th ser., *Mémoires,* **15** (1939), 75–107.

Additional materials may be found in the Archives Nationales (Paris), F14.2723[1], and in the library of the École des Mines de Paris (Élie de Beaumont's papers).

ARTHUR BIREMBAUT

ELKIN, WILLIAM LEWIS (*b.* New Orleans, Louisiana, 29 April 1855; *d.* New Haven, Connecticut, 30 May 1933), *positional astronomy, meteoritics.*

At the time of Elkin's birth his father, Lewis, was inspector of public schools for the city of New Orleans, but he later became a manufacturer of carpets and prospered financially. In 1867 he was appointed representative of the state of Louisiana at the forthcoming Paris Exposition but died unexpectedly just before the family's departure for Europe. All arrangements had been made and his widow, Jane Fitch Elkin, was persuaded to go as scheduled, taking with her their twelve-year-old son William, the only survivor of her five children. Mother and son became expatriates, leading an interesting but peripatetic life in various countries, so that Elkin's secondary education was unorthodox. He did, however, attend private schools in Switzerland but at the age of fifteen had a serious illness, which left his health permanently impaired.

Nevertheless, Elkin decided upon a career as an

engineer and enrolled in the Royal Polytechnic School at Stuttgart, from which he graduated in 1876 with a C.E. degree. But by now his interest had changed to astronomy; so he went to Strasbourg to study under Friedrich August Theodor Winnecke, then considered the foremost teacher of astronomy in Europe. He was a third-year graduate student, preparing a dissertation on the star α Centauri, when a chance meeting with David Gill, newly appointed royal astronomer at the Cape of Good Hope, led to an invitation to South Africa for a working (but personally financed) visit. After receiving his Ph.D. in 1880, Elkin joined Gill and his wife at the Cape and lived with them like a son for more than two years. Together Gill and Elkin set up and shared an ambitious observing program with a four-inch heliometer, to determine the parallaxes of nine stars: three observed by each separately and three by both of them. One of the latter was α Centauri, for which they published a value of 0.75″, with a probable error of 0.01″ (compared to today's value of 0.760″ ± 0.005″).

Meanwhile, a six-inch heliometer had been installed in the Yale University Observatory, and Elkin was invited to come there, as "astronomer in charge of the heliometer." He arrived in 1884 and remained in New Haven for the rest of his life, at first actively observing, then serving as director of the Yale observatory from 1896 (the year he married Catharine Adams) until increasing disability forced his retirement in 1910, at the age of fifty-five. The remaining twenty-three years of his life were spent as an invalid, with no further astronomical activities.

During his productive years at Yale, Elkin performed a formidable amount of work with the heliometer. The labor of measuring parallactic angles is great enough with today's photographic techniques but was many times greater with the heliometer, which in addition was an exhausting instrument to use. Elkin, together with his students, used the Yale heliometer to determine the parallaxes of 238 stars; this was, in the words of Frank Schlesinger (Elkin's successor at Yale), "by far the most important single contribution to our knowledge of stellar distances up to that time."

Concurrently Elkin was cooperating with Gill in an attempt to get an improved value for the solar parallax, by making simultaneous observations, from their widely separated locations, of the minor planets Iris, Victoria, and Sappho. Other observatories with heliometers later joined in this program. Their value, published in 1896–1897, was 8.812″ ± 0.009″, close to the 8.790″ obtained in 1930–1931 with photographic techniques; however, both have now been superseded by a value of 8.79415″, derived from 1961 radar observations of the planet Venus.

Elkin also undertook a program for determining the positions of stars near the north celestial pole, at the request of E. C. Pickering (then director of the Harvard College Observatory), who needed good reference points for a projected photographic survey of that part of the sky. Elkin himself never used photography for determining stellar positions, although in papers published in 1889 and 1892 he compared photographic data on stars in the Pleiades cluster with his own heliometer measurements and declared that the new method showed promise. He did, however, apply photographic techniques to the study of meteors: using two "meteorographs," each consisting of a number of cameras mounted on a motor-driven polar axis and placed several miles apart, he was able to determine the heights at which one Leonid meteor appeared and disappeared—many more were observed visually, but apparently his photographic emulsion was not fast enough to record them. Of greater significance was his use of a rotating bicycle wheel with occulting segments placed in front of his cameras to produce the first successful interrupted photographs of meteor trails, thereby providing information on their velocities.

Recognition for his work was international. Elkin was elected a foreign associate of the Royal Astronomical Society in 1892, received an honorary M.A. from Yale in 1893, and became a member of the American Academy of Sciences in 1895. He shared with his student Frederick Lincoln Chase the Prix Lalande of the French Academy of Sciences in 1908 (for work on stellar parallaxes) and was awarded an honorary Ph.D. by the University of Christiania (now Oslo) in 1911.

BIBLIOGRAPHY

I. ORIGINAL WORKS. Elkin's dissertation was published as *Parallaxe von α-Centauri* (Karlsruhe, 1880). His work at the Cape observatory appeared as "I. Heliometer-Determinations of Stellar Parallax in the Southern Hemisphere," in *Memoirs of the Royal Astronomical Society,* **48** (1884), 1–194, written with David Gill. His heliometer work at Yale was published under the general title "Researches With the Heliometer," in *Transactions of the Astronomical Observatory of Yale University,* with those papers mentioned in the text being "Determination of the Relative Positions of the Principal Stars in the Group of the Pleiades," **1,** pt. 1 (1887), 1–105; "Triangulation of Stars in the Vicinity of the North Pole," **1,** pt. 3 (1893), 149–182; and "Catalogue of Yale Parallax Results," **2,** pt. 4 (1912), 385–400, written with Frederick L. Chase and Mason F. Smith.

The solar parallax program is described in *Annals of the Royal Observatory, Cape Town,* **6** (1897) and **7** (1896), "planned and discussed by David Gill . . . with the co-operation of Arthur Auwers and W. L. Elkin"; "Discussion of the Observations of Iris," **6**, pt. 4 (1)–(169), is the only part signed by Elkin.

Elkin's critiques of photographic methods were "Comparison of Dr. Gould's Reductions of Mr. Rutherfurd's *Pleiades* Photographs With the Heliometer-Results," in *Astronomical Journal,* **9** (1889), 33–35; and "The Rutherfurd Photographic Measures of the *Pleiades,*" in *Publications of the Astronomical Society of the Pacific,* **4** (1892), 134–138.

Elkin published only four brief papers on meteors (but see paper by Olivier listed below): "Photography of Meteors," in *Astronomical Journal,* **13** (1893), 132; "Photographic Observations of the Leonids at the Yale Observatory," in *Astrophysical Journal,* **9** (1899), 20–22; "Results of the Photographic Observations of the Leonids, November 14–15, 1898," *ibid.,* **10** (1899), 25–28; and "The Velocity of Meteors as Deduced From Photographs at the Yale Observatory," *ibid.,* **12** (1900), 4–7.

A list of thirty-one publications by Elkin appears in Frank Schlesinger's biographical memoir (see below).

II. SECONDARY LITERATURE. Gill's account of his first encounter with Elkin and their subsequent association at the Cape observatory constitutes the preface to their joint article in *Memoirs of the Royal Astronomical Society* (see above). Further facts about Elkin appear in *Monthly Notices of the Royal Astronomical Society,* **94** (1934), 285–289, with photograph (written by H. Spencer Jones, then astronomer royal); and in Frank Schlesinger, *Biographical Memoirs. National Academy of Sciences,* **18** (1938), 175–188, with portrait and list of publications. Elkin is listed in *Who Was Who in America,* I (Chicago, 1943), 365.

An account of the awarding of the Prix Lalande for 1908 occurs in *Comptes rendus hebdomadaires des séances de l'Académie des sciences,* **147** (1908), 1123. Elkin's unpublished work on meteors was presented and analyzed by Charles P. Olivier as "Results of the Yale Photographic Meteor Work, 1893–1909," in *Astronomical Journal,* **46** (1937–1938), 41–57.

SALLY H. DIEKE

ELLER VON BROCKHAUSEN, JOHANN THEODOR (*b.* Plötzkau, Germany, 29 November 1689; *d.* Berlin, Germany, 13 September 1760), *medicine, chemistry.*

Eller's father, Jobst Hermann Eller, was an eminent military man under the prince of Anhalt; his mother belonged to the Behm family, an ancient family in Livonia. He had an excellent education in law at Quedlinburg College and Jena University, but he changed to the study of medicine while at Jena. In 1711 he left Jena to search for better instruction in anatomy, going to Halle, then Leiden, and finally in 1712 to Amsterdam, where he found the most capable anatomists in Europe, Rau and Ruysch. When Rau moved to Leiden, Eller went with him and performed public dissections for him until 1716. Eller was not prepared at this point to settle down to the practice of medicine, but turned to the study of mineralogy and chemistry, first with Lemery and Homberg in Paris, and then with Hauksbee and Desaguliers in London.

Upon his return to Anhalt-Bernberg in 1721, Eller was made court physician by the prince. He married Catherine Elizabeth Burckhard in October of that year. In 1724 King Frederick William I called Eller to Berlin and made him professor of anatomy and permanent dean of the Medical College, as well as physician to the army. When Frederick the Great became king in 1740, he made Eller his personal physician and appointed him director of the Berlin Academy of Sciences. Eller's wife died in 1751, and in 1753 he married Henrietta Catherine Rosen. In 1755 Frederick made Eller a privy councillor, a position he held until his death.

Eller held the highest medical positions in Prussia during his lifetime. He was a very competent doctor and administrator. In administration, for example, he was responsible, together with Georg Ernst Stahl, for laying the foundation for all subsequent developments in medical services in Prussia. Eller's writings reflect his medical knowledge and consist largely of compilations of case histories, like the one he published in Berlin in 1730, based on his experiences in the Charité Hospital in Berlin. He carried out some studies on human blood, examined human calculi, and warned about the dangers of using copper kitchen utensils, but he is not noted for any significant development in medicine.

Eller's theoretical chemistry is characterized by the central role given to heat (fire). His writings clearly place him in the Continental tradition that considered heat to be material in nature. With Eller, the Stahlian principle of phlogiston became simply another name for the primary element fire in the fixed state. In this state, fire is chemically combined with most substances and generally is released during chemical reactions. In the active state fire is the sole cause of the fluidity of water and fluids in general (air included). This principle is also integrated into his main practical chemical work, which dealt with the solubility of salts in water. Eller argued that since solubility generally increased with temperature, it must be because the fire in the water, whose activity increased with temperature, could more readily break up (dissolve) the salts.

Eller's influence on chemical theory has never been considered of great consequence, yet it is known that

Lavoisier read Eller's papers, especially those dealing with the elements, and his early views have an interesting resemblance to Eller's ideas about heat and fluidity.

BIBLIOGRAPHY

I. ORIGINAL WORKS. Eller's main work in medicine is *Nützliche und auserlesene medicinische und chirurgische Anmerkungen so wohl von innerlichen, als auch äusserlichen Krankheiten, . . .; nebst einer vorangegebenen kurtzen Beschreibung der Stiftung, Anwachs und jetzigen Beschaffenheit dieses Hauses, usw.* (Berlin, 1730). All of Eller's papers, which were originally published in the Berlin Academy *Memoirs* and *Miscellanea Berolinensia,* are found in German translation in his collected papers, *Physikalisch-chymisch-medicinische Abhandlungen, aus den Gedenkschriften der königlichen Akademie der Wissenschaften,* D. Carl Abraham Gerhard, ed. (Berlin, 1764).

II. SECONDARY LITERATURE. There is no biography of Eller. Some information may be obtained from the *éloge* in the Berlin Academy *Memoirs* of 1761 and the *Allgemeine deutsche Biographie,* VI (Leipzig, 1877), 52–53. Only the larger histories of chemistry say anything about his scientific work.

DAVID R. DYCK

ELLIOT SMITH, GRAFTON (*b.* Grafton, Australia, 15 August 1871; *d.* Broadstairs, England, 1 January 1937), *anatomy.*

Elliot Smith was the son of Stephen Sheldrick Smith, a schoolteacher who had emigrated from England to Australia, and of his wife, Mary Jane Evans. At school he was interested in both physics and medicine, and he dated his interest in the brain to the age of ten, when he dissected a shark. He read medicine at the University of Sydney, graduated M.B., Ch.M. in 1892, and took some clinical posts while beginning research on brains. In 1895 Elliot Smith was awarded an M.D. and gold medal for a thesis on the anatomy and histology of the cerebrum of the nonplacental mammal. In 1896 he went to England, where he continued research for a Ph.D. at Cambridge and in 1899 was elected a fellow of St. John's College. He was also asked to help in preparing a catalog of brains of Reptilia and Mammalia in the Museum of the Royal College of Surgeons; this was published in 1902.

Elliot Smith was invited to be professor of anatomy in the new Government School of Medicine in Cairo and went there in 1900 to create an active department and continue his neurological work. In spite of an early determination to resist the lure of Egyptology, he became interested when he was asked to make anatomical investigations of old skeletons and mummies, particularly when there were remains of soft parts, including brains. These investigations led to the *Catalogue of the Royal Mummies in the Cairo Museum,* published in 1912. In 1907 he was elected to fellowship of the Royal Society and was appointed anatomical adviser to the Archaeological Survey of Nubia, which involved examination and description of thousands of skeletons excavated before the Aswan Dam was raised. The report was published in 1910.

Returning to England in 1909 to occupy the chair of anatomy at Manchester, Elliot Smith continued to work on both neurology and the Nubian remains and developed his theory of the diffusion of culture, which has never been generally accepted by anthropologists. He was one of several experts deceived by the Piltdown skull. During World War I, Elliot Smith worked for short periods in hospitals and did research on shell shock, and in 1919 he transferred to the chair of anatomy at University College, London, where he emphasized the importance of studying human biology with its psychological and cultural aspects, and also the history of medicine. He traveled frequently to the United States, China, and Australia, mainly on anthropological work, and trained several assistants who were later prominent anthropologists. He married Kathleen Macredie in 1900, and they had three sons. He was knighted in 1934 and retired in 1936.

The weight of Elliot Smith's work lies in his anatomical studies. His detailed comparative anatomical descriptions of the brains of reptiles and nonplacental and placental mammals contributed to the study of evolution as well as to neurology, and he related the development of the visual area of the brain to arboreal life in primates. His descriptions of Egyptian mummies were the first to be so comprehensive and so detailed; many of them are not yet superseded.

Some of his manuscripts are at the University of Manchester, and a bronze head, done by A. H. Gerrard in 1937, is in the Medical Sciences Library of University College, London.

BIBLIOGRAPHY

The most comprehensive biography, by Warren R. Dawson, forms the longest section of Warren R. Dawson, ed., *Sir Grafton Elliot Smith: A Biographical Record,* by his colleagues (London, 1938); the volume also contains a 434-item bibliography of Elliot Smith's publications and refers to a collection of his letters held by Dawson.

There is an entry by H. A. Harris in the *Dictionary of National Biography, Supplement 1931–1940* (London, 1949), 816–817, with a list of obituaries, including that by J. T. Wilson in *Obituary Notices of Fellows of the Royal Society* of London, **2** (1938), 323–333. Volume **71** of the *Journal of Anatomy* is a memorial volume to Elliot Smith, who had for a time assisted in editing it; included is a bibliography of his anatomical writings. A more recent assessment is A. A. Abbie, "Sir Grafton Elliot Smith," in *Bulletin of the Post Graduate Committee in Medicine, University of Sydney,* **15** (1959), 101–150. Abbie includes a bibliography strong in biographical material and refers to a valuable collection on Elliot Smith in the Sydney University department of anatomy.

DIANA M. SIMPKINS

ELLIS, WILLIAM (*b.* Greenwich, England, 20 February 1828; *d.* Greenwich, 11 December 1916), *geomagnetism, meteorology, astronomy.*

Ellis' father, Thomas, joined the staff of the Royal Observatory at Greenwich in 1825 and obtained employment there for his son when the boy was thirteen.

Twice married but childless, Ellis occupied himself in his spare time with local church affairs and contributed some 100 articles on a wide range of subjects to scientific journals. He was elected fellow of the Royal Astronomical Society in 1864, honorary member of the British Horological Institution in 1865, member of the Institute of Electrical Engineers in 1873, fellow of the Royal Meteorological Society in 1875 (president 1886–1887), and fellow of the Royal Society in 1893.

Ellis joined the Royal Observatory as a temporary computer on 2 August 1841 and was employed on lunar reductions and the comparison of standards of length during the restoration of the British standards. He left the Royal Observatory in March 1852 to become astronomical observer at Durham University but returned to Greenwich on 13 May 1853 to become a second-class assistant on the permanent staff, which then numbered only nine, including the astronomer royal, George Biddell Airy.

Ellis remained a transit circle observer for more than twenty years, took part in the Harton Colliery geodetic experiments in 1854, and assumed charge of the chronometric galvanic department in 1856. His duties included the care and rating of Royal Navy chronometers and supervision of the hourly galvanic time signals (instituted by Airy in 1853) to a central London telegraph office for distribution throughout the country; he was also in charge of arrangements for the telegraphic determination of longitudes.

Promoted to first-class assistant on 1 February 1871, Ellis was at his own request transferred to the magnetic and meteorological department as superintendent in 1875, a position he held until his retirement on 31 December 1893. It was during this later period that he carried out the work for which he is best known in geomagnetism and meteorology. His paper "On the Relation Between the Diurnal Range of Magnetic Declination and Horizontal Force as Observed at Greenwich During the Years 1841–1877 and the Period of Solar Spot Frequency" (1880) was accepted by most people as proof of the relationship between terrestrial magnetism and sunspots suggested in 1852 by Sabine and others. In his eighty-eighth year Ellis contributed his last paper, "Sunspots and Terrestrial Magnetism," to *Observatory* magazine.

BIBLIOGRAPHY

Ellis' own publications include many regular contributions on meteorology to the *Quarterly Journal of the Royal Meteorological Society* from 1877 on. Among his papers on magnetism are "Account of Some Experiments Showing the Change of Rate in a Clock by a Particular Case of Magnetic Action," in *Philosophical Magazine,* **25** (May 1863), 325–331; "On the Relation Between the Diurnal Range of Magnetic Declination and Horizontal Force as Observed at Greenwich During the Years 1841–1877 and the Period of Solar Spot Frequency," in *Philosophical Transactions of the Royal Society,* **171** (1880); "Earth Currents and the Electric Railway," in *Nature,* **44** (June 1891), 127–128; "On the Simultaneity of Magnetic Variations at Different Places on Occasions of Magnetic Disturbance, and on the Relation Between Magnetic and Earth Current Phenomena," in *Proceedings of the Royal Society,* **52** (1892), 191–212; "On the Relation Between the Diurnal Range of Magnetic Declination and Horizontal Force, and the Period of Solar Spot Frequency," *ibid.,* **63** (1898), 64–78; "Magnetic Results at Greenwich and Kew Discussed and Compared, 1889 to 1896," in *Report of the British Association for the Advancement of Science* (1898), 80–108; and "Sunspots and Terrestrial Magnetism," in *Observatory,* **39** (Jan. 1916), 54–59.

P. S. LAURIE

ELSTER, JOHANN PHILIPP LUDWIG JULIUS (*b.* Bad Blankenburg, Germany, 24 December 1854; *d.* Bad Harzburg, Germany, 6 April 1920), *experimental physics.*

Elster's scientific work can be discussed only with that of Hans Geitel; they jointly carried out and published almost all of their investigations from 1884 to 1920. They were teachers of mathematics and physics at the Herzoglich Gymnasium in Wolfenbüttel, near Brunswick.

Elster and Geitel studied together from 1875 to 1877 in Heidelberg, and until 1878 in Berlin. Elster then returned to Heidelberg, to study with Georg Quincke, under whom he received the doctorate in 1879 for his dissertation "Die in freien Wasserstrahlen auftretenden elektromotorischen Kräfte." After taking the examination to become a teacher he went in 1881 to Wolfenbüttel, where Geitel had been teaching since 1880. In 1884 they began collaborating on scientific works, which eventually totaled almost 150. They were especially concerned with the following problems, which were then new: electrical phenomena in the atmosphere, the photoelectric effect and thermal electron emission, photocells and their use in photometry, various aspects of radioactivity, and the development of apparatus and methods for the measurement of electrical phenomena in gases. The vast scope of Elster and Geitel's pioneering work in all these areas can be determined from the contemporary literature and is emphasized in textbooks of both the nineteenth and the twentieth centuries. Many results of their investigations are now part of the accepted foundations of the areas covered. Today, in the age of Geiger and Müller counters, of cloud and bubble chambers, and of electronics, their methods of measurement are no longer employed; but until 1920 they were crucial to research in the respective areas.

Elster and Geitel's first joint work was concerned with the electrification of flames (1884). This was followed by the first investigations of electrical processes in thunderclouds,[1] the development of electricity in rain, and the "dispersion of electricity" in the atmosphere and its dependence on the electric field of the earth and the measurement of that field. The ionization of gas was not yet known; it arose from J. J. Thomson's discovery of the conductivity of air induced by roentgen rays (1896). With the theory of gas ions, a rational treatment of the phenomena of atmospheric electricity was finally possible; a comprehensive presentation of the results obtained up to 1901 is in a report by Geitel[2] (the investigations continued until 1905). Measurements of atmospheric electricity were made in the Austrian Alps in 1891–1893; on Mt. Brocken, Mt. Säntis, and Mt. Gornergrat in 1900; during the total solar eclipses in Algeria in 1900 and on Majorca in 1905; and on Spitsbergen and Capri in 1902.

A series of twenty investigations on the photoelectric effect began in 1889 with the discovery that negatively charged magnesium filaments, freshly ground with emery, are discharged not only by ultraviolet light but even by "dispersed evening daylight."[3] The investigations of the sensitivity of the photocathodes to visible light led to the actinoelectric series—rubidium, potassium, sodium, magnesium, thallium, zinc—and to the discovery (1910) of the sensitivity of the hydrogenized potassium cathode, which was found to extend into the infrared range.[4] By use of a photocathode of a fluid, absolutely smooth potassium-

sodium alloy, the dependence of the photoelectric current on the polarization of the light was discovered,[5] as was the existence of a "normal" and a "selective" photoelectric effect, which later became of decisive importance in the electron theory of metals. The Elster-Geitel photocell was for decades the photometric instrument of physics and astronomy.

In 1887 Elster and Geitel discovered the "electrification of gases by means of incandescent bodies,"[6] a finding that later was very significant in thermionics. Their finding of the emission of negative electricity from incandescent filaments was decisive in the proof that Thomson's "corpuscles" (electrons) are constituents of all matter.

Soon after the discovery (1896) of radioactivity Elster and Geitel began to study Becquerel rays,[7] in order to determine the origin of the energy of these rays. Crookes had proposed the hypothesis that the air molecules with the greatest velocity stimulated the rays; energy was therefore extracted from the surrounding air. Elster and Geitel placed uranium in a glass vessel that was then evacuated: even at the highest vacuum the radiation remained constant. They also placed uranium and a photographic plate in a container: the blackening of the plate was independent of the pressure. Therefore the radiation could not be stimulated by the air.

Mme. Curie suggested another hypothesis: the radioactive emission was a fluorescence of the uranium, which was excited by a very penetrating radiation that fills all of space. She therefore named the new phenomenon *la radioactivité*, i.e., "activated by radiation." Elster and Geitel showed, however, that the intensity of the uranium radiation above the earth is the same as it is in a mine 852 meters below the surface. They also investigated whether uranium emitted stronger Becquerel radiation when under the influence of cathode rays. For this purpose they developed a new Lenard cathode-ray tube, which let pass into the atmosphere an intense electron beam with a cross section of several square centimeters. (They closed off the discharge tube with a copper net covered with a very thin aluminum foil; the cathode rays escaped through the net's interstices.) The result was negative. They also demonstrated that Becquerel radiation is independent of the temperature of the uranium and of the compound in which it occurs. They concluded from these and other experiments that the radioactive emission is not the consequence of an external influence, but can only be a spontaneous release of energy by the atom. They inferred "that the atom of a radioactive element behaves like an unstable compound that becomes stable upon the release of energy. To be sure, this conception would require the acceptance of a gradual transformation of an active substance into an inactive one and also, logically, of the alteration of its elementary properties."[8] With this statement radioactivity was defined for the first time as a natural, spontaneous transformation of an element attendant upon the release of energy.

A magnetic deflection of the Becquerel rays was sought, but it could not be demonstrated unequivocally; nevertheless, the question raised here for the first time was answered definitively by Giessel (1899) and Mme. Curie (1900). Elster and Geitel did not succeed because in their positive tests beta rays were measured, while in their negative tests gamma rays were measured—this distinction, however, was not yet known. Elster and Geitel had already announced in 1898 that they had obtained new, highly radiant substances from the chemical treatment of Joachimstal pitchblende. Polonium, just discovered by the Curies, was immediately prepared by their methods. A short while later Mme. Curie and G. Bémont made known their discovery of radium. At the same time Elster and Geitel communicated their finding that lead extracted from pitchblende is highly radioactive; the radioactivity of ordinary lead and the amount of radium D, E, and F that it contains were repeatedly investigated in later studies. In 1899 the ionization of air by Becquerel rays was examined for the first time: the radiation produced equal numbers of positive and negative ions in the air mass between the electrodes, not at the electrodes themselves, and thus resembled the effect of roentgen rays, which J. J. Thomson and Ernest Rutherford had demonstrated for the first time in 1896. The influence of the Becquerel rays on spark and brush discharge in the air under various pressures was also described.

In 1899 Elster and Geitel had observed and demonstrated that uranium potassium sulfate glows with constant intensity, completely independently of all external influences. They then investigated the visible fluorescence that Becquerel rays excite in many crystals ("radioactive luminous paint"). After the three types of radioactive Becquerel rays (alpha, beta, gamma) were discovered, such experiments could be carried out separately with each of these types. In this process they discovered[9] (at exactly the same time as Crookes) the scintillation of zinc sulfide by alpha rays: the appearance of a flash of light as each alpha particle enters the crystal. The scintillation method was important in radioactivity research until 1920.

With the experience they had gained in radioactivity investigations, Elster and Geitel set themselves the question[10] of whether the ionization of the atmosphere results from radioactive material within it.

Geitel had shown that the ion content of a quantity of air hermetically sealed off from the outside becomes constant after some time; since both positive and negative ions disappear from the air, for example, through recombination to neutral molecules, an ionizing source must be present. Hence a wire one meter long was suspended in the air at a potential of $-2,000$ volts against earth; after several hours it was radioactive. Under definite, accurately determined experimental and measurement conditions, its activity was found to be proportional to the concentration of the radium emanation (radon) of the free atmosphere. (This is known as the Elster-Geitel activation number.)[11] This simple method provided information on the distribution of the emanation in the atmosphere over land and water, its dependence upon the height, upon meteorological data, and upon the earth's local electric field and its high concentration in narrow valleys and caves. Next came extensive measurements of the radioactivity of rocks, lakes, and spring waters and spring sediments, especially at health spas.[12] In 1913 Ernest Rutherford wrote: "The pioneers in this important field of investigation were Elster and Geitel and no researcher has contributed more to our knowledge of the radioactivity of the earth and the atmosphere than they have."[13]

Elster and Geitel, as inseparable in their life as in their work, were called "the Castor and Pollux of physics." They set up their physics laboratory in their residence, which also contained an astronomical telescope, terraria with tropical animals, and all kinds of natural history collections. They took vacation trips together to investigate the electricity in mountain and sea air and to measure the radioactivity of rocks, springs, and spas. When Geitel received a call to the University of Breslau in 1899, it was obvious that he would go there only with Elster. Elster was also considered for a professorship at Breslau, but they both finally rejected the offers: they feared that in Breslau they would not have the independence and quiet for their research that they had in Wolfenbüttel.

Skilled in designing and making equipment, they constructed all of their apparatus but refused to take out patents on their inventions (for example, the electrometer and the photocell). In 1889 they obtained a great deal of financial support from the Elizabeth Thompson Science Fund, of Boston, Massachusetts.

Both were good teachers, beloved by their students; Geitel especially understood how to train students to think independently. Elster's absent-mindedness was almost legendary: When told that he had placed a stamp of too high a value on a letter, he crossed it out and stuck one of the correct value next to it. And the door of his apartment had a large opening and a small one cut out at the bottom because he had a large dog and a small dog.

The general respect in which Elster and Geitel were held is shown by the large (719 pages) *Festschrift* that was dedicated to them in 1914–1915, a gift from older and younger physicists on their sixtieth birthdays. Among the authors who contributed original works were Max Born, Laue, Lenard, Gustav Mie, Planck, R. W. Pohl, Regener, and Sommerfeld.

NOTES

1. "Observations on the Electrical Processes in Thunder-Clouds," in *Philosophical Magazine,* **20** (1885).
2. H. Geitel, *Anwendung der Lehre von den Gasionen auf die Erscheinungen der atmosphärischen Elektrizität* (Brunswick, 1901), 27 pp.
3. "Entladung negativ elektrisierter Körper durch Sonnen- und Tageslicht," in *Annalen der Physik,* **38** (1889), 497.
4. "Über gefärbte Hydride der Alkalimetalle und ihre photoelektrische Empfindlichkeit," in *Physikalische Zeitschrift,* **11** (1910), 257; "Über den lichtelektrischen Effekt im Infrarot und einige Anwendungen hochempfindlicher Kaliumzellen," in *Physikalische Zeitschrift,* **12** (1911), 758.
5. "Abhängigkeit der Intensität des photoelektrischen Stromes von der Lage der Polarisationsebene des erregenden Lichtes zu der Oberfläche der Kathode," in *Sitzungsberichte der Berliner Akademie der Wissenschaften* (1894); *Annalen der Physik,* **55** (1895), 684, and **61** (1897), 445; *Physikalische Zeitschrift,* **10** (1909), 457.
6. "Elektrisierung der Gase durch glühende Körper," in *Annalen der Physik,* **31** (1887), 109, and **37** (1889), 315; *Sitzungsberichte der Akademie der Wissenschaften in Wien,* **97** (1888), IIa, 1175.
7. "Versuche an Becquerel-Strahlen," in *Annalen der Physik,* **66** (1898), 735, and **69** (1889), 83.
8. *Jahresberichte des Vereins für Naturwissenschaft zu Braunschweig,* **10/12** (1902), 39; *Annalen der Physik,* **69** (1899), 83.
9. "Über die durch radioaktive Emanation erregte szintillierende Phosphoreszenz der Sidotblende," in *Physikalische Zeitschrift,* **4** (1903), 439.
10. "Analogie im elektrischen Verhalten der natürlichen Luft und der durch Becquerel-Strahlen leitend gemachten," *ibid.,* **2** (1901), 590; "Radioaktivität der im Erdboden enthaltenen Luft," *ibid.,* **3** (1902), 574.
11. "Radioaktive Emanation in der atmosphärischen Luft," in *Sitzungsberichte der Bayerischen Akademie der Wissenschaften,* **33** (1903), 301–323; and in *Physikalische Zeitschrift,* **4** (1903), 522.
12. "Sédiments radioactives des sources thermales," in *Archives des sciences physiques et naturelles,* 4th ser., **19** (1905), 5.
13. *Handbuch der Radiologie,* II (Leipzig, 1913), 563.

BIBLIOGRAPHY

In addition to the works cited in the text and the notes see the following.

I. ORIGINAL WORKS. Among the writings published by Elster and Geitel are *Ziele und Methoden der luftelektrischen Untersuchungen* (Wolfenbüttel, 1891); and *Ergebnisse neuer Arbeiten über atmosphärische Elektrizität* (Wolfenbüttel, 1897).

II. SECONDARY LITERATURE. Elster's work is discussed in *Handbuch der Radiologie,* Vol. I (Leipzig, 1920), Vol. II (1913); and R. Pohl and P. Pringsheim, *Die lichtelektrischen Erscheinungen* (Brunswick, 1914). An obituary is E. Wiechert, in *Nachrichten der Akademie der Wissenschaften zu Göttingen* (1921), 53–60.

WALTHER GERLACH

ELVEHJEM, CONRAD ARNOLD (*b.* McFarland, Wisconsin, 27 May 1901; *d.* Madison, Wisconsin, 27 July 1962), *biochemistry.*

Elvehjem, the son of Ole and Christine Lewis Elvehjem, grew up on the family farm and was educated in local schools before entering the University of Wisconsin. He received his B.S. in agricultural chemistry in 1923, the M.S. in 1924, and the Ph.D. in 1927. Upon graduation he became an instructor in agricultural chemistry, rising to the rank of full professor in 1936. In 1944 he became chairman of the department (renamed biochemistry), a position he held until he became the university's thirteenth president in 1958. From 1946 to 1958 he served as dean of the graduate school.

Elvehjem married Constance Waltz in 1926. They had two children, Peggy Ann and Robert Stuart. He died unexpectedly of a heart attack suffered while at work in the presidential office. His only extended absence from the university was a year (1929–1930) spent at Cambridge University studying catalytic oxidations in the laboratory of F. G. Hopkins as a National Research Council Fellow. Elvehjem was elected to the National Academy of Sciences in 1942 and to the National Academy of Arts and Sciences in 1953. He received numerous other honors—the Willard Gibbs Medal, the Osborne and Mendel Award, the Nicolas Appert Award, and the Lasker Award—and was a member of numerous national committees.

Elvehjem's entire scientific career dealt with animal nutrition, particularly the role of trace elements and vitamins. He ranged widely in his interests, yet there was an overall interrelationship in the more than 800 research papers published during his career. His first work, undertaken with E. B. Hart and H. Steenbock, dealt with the influence of light on metabolism of calcium and phosphorus in lactating animals. During the next several years, in association with these same investigators, he studied milk-induced anemia and showed that traces of copper are essential for satisfactory iron uptake in hemoglobin formation. Mineral metabolism in animals remained a matter of primary concern and ultimately included work on the roles of zinc, cobalt, manganese, molybdenum, boron, potassium, aluminum, fluorine, and arsenic.

Elvehjem contributed in many ways to the growth of understanding of members of the vitamin B complex. In 1937, after Euler-Chelpin and Otto Warburg showed that Harden's coenzyme I and related coenzymes contained nicotinic acid, Elvehjem and his associates showed that nicotinic acid cured blacktongue in dogs. Goldberger had shown in 1926 that blacktongue is the canine equivalent of human pellagra, and medical investigators soon showed that nicotinic acid cured pellagra in human beings. Elvehjem's group showed the vitamin to be present as the amide in active concentrates of the vitamin prepared from liver.

When it later became evident that most cereal grains are like corn in being low in nicotinic acid yet—unlike corn—are protective or curative against pellagra, the reason for the anomaly was sought. The proteins of corn are lower in tryptophan than are those of other cereals, and corn has traditionally been present in human diets everywhere in the world that pellagra is endemic. Elvehjem and his associates showed that tryptophan can serve as a substitute for nicotinic acid in diets low in that vitamin, and other investigators established the metabolic conversion of tryptophan to nicotinic acid.

Elvehjem and his associates carried out studies on biotin, pantothenic acid, para-aminobenzoic acid, folic acid, and inositol as these substances became available in pure form, and helped to clarify their role in the nutrition of many species, particularly rats, chickens, dogs, and monkeys. All of these vitamins were originally recognized in connection with the growth of bacterial species; Elvehjem's laboratory pioneered in testing their role in the nutrition of higher animals. His laboratory also did extensive work in clarifying the role of intestinal bacteria in the synthesis of various trace nutrients. This work revealed that certain species do not require a dietary source of a particular vitamin, because it is synthesized by their normal intestinal flora. When the normal flora is inhibited by such drugs as sulfaguanidine or succinylsulfathiazole, the animal becomes dependent upon dietary supplements.

Elvehjem's quiet but forceful, perceptive, hardworking example made him a natural leader as a research director. Many of the eighty-eight students who took the Ph.D. under him went on to make significant contributions to the field. This same intensity of effort in the laboratory was evident in his administrative work. As president of the university he encouraged the growth of research in the humanities and social studies while maintaining the strength of the sciences.

BIBLIOGRAPHY

I. ORIGINAL WORKS. The archives at the University of Wisconsin have extensive holdings of Elvehjem's papers: the material associated with his presidency in the presidential papers, that with his deanship in the graduate school papers, that with his research and instruction in the papers of the biochemistry department. More than a third of his research papers were published in the *Journal of Biological Chemistry*. Other journals containing numerous papers are *Journal of Nutrition, American Journal of Physiology*, and *Proceedings of the Society for Experimental Biology and Medicine*. There is no published bibliography of his works other than the incomplete one in Poggendorff and the listings in the author indexes of *Chemical Abstracts*. The University of Wisconsin biochemistry department holds a bound set of his collected works.

The principal paper dealing with copper and its role in anemia is "Iron in Nutrition, VII. Copper as a Supplement to Iron for Hemoglobin Building in the Rat," in *Journal of Biological Chemistry,* **77** (1928), 797–812, written with E. B. Hart, H. Steenbock, and J. Waddell; see also "Mineral Metabolism," in *Annual Review of Biochemistry,* **5** (1936), 271–294, written with E. B. Hart; and "The Biological Significance of Copper and Its Relation to Iron Metabolism," in *Physiological Reviews,* **15** (1935), 471–507. The curative effect of nicotinic acid for blacktongue in dogs was announced in "Relation of Nicotinic Acid and Nicotinic Acid Amide to Canine Black Tongue," in *Journal of the American Chemical Society,* **59** (1937), 1767–1768, and in more detail in "The Isolation and Identification of the Anti-Black Tongue Factor," in *Journal of Biological Chemistry,* **123** (1938), 137–147; both articles were written with R. J. Madden, F. M. Strong, and D. W. Woolley. See also "Relation of Nicotinic Acid to Pellagra," in *Physiological Reviews,* **20** (1940), 249–271; and "The Biological Significance of Nicotinic Acid," in *Bulletin of the New York Academy of Medicine,* **16** (1940), 173–189. On the role of tryptophan see two articles written with W. A. Krehl, L. J. Teply, and P. S. Sarma: "Growth-Retarding Effect of Corn in Nicotinic Acid-Low Rations and Its Counteraction by Tryptophane," in *Science,* **101** (1945), 489–490; and "Factors Affecting the Dietary Niacin and Tryptophane Requirement of the Growing Rat," in *Journal of Nutrition,* **31** (1946), 85–106.

The role of Elvehjem and his associates in nutritional research is brought out in several review articles which place the work of his laboratory into perspective with overall activities in the field. See, in addition to those cited above, the following papers: "The Water Soluble Vitamins," in *Journal of the American Medical Association,* **120** (1942), 1388–1397; "Recent Advances in Our Knowledge of the Vitamins," in *Scientific Monthly,* **56** (1943), 99–104; "Present Status of the Vitamin B Complex," in *American Scientist,* **32** (1944), 25–38; and "Recent Progress in Nutrition and Its Relation to Drug Therapy," in *Journal of the American Medical Association,* **136** (1948), 915–918.

Elvehjem's Willard Gibbs Medal address, "Newer

Members of the Vitamin B Complex. Their Nutritional Significance," in *Chemical and Engineering News,* **21** (1943), 853–857, is somewhat autobiographical, as is "Early Experiences With Niacin—a Retrospect," in *Nutrition Reviews,* **11** (1953), 289–292. His education philosophy is reflected in his inaugural address, "Essentials of Progress," delivered 9 October 1958 (Madison, 1958).

II. SECONDARY LITERATURE. There are no biographies of Elvehjem other than short journalistic pieces. There are lengthy obituary notices in *The Capital Times* (Madison, 27 July 1962) and *The Milwaukee Journal* (27 July 1962); *The Wisconsin State Journal* (28 July 1962); and *Wisconsin Alumnus,* **64,** no. 1 (1962), 9–12.

AARON J. IHDE

EMANUELLI, PIO (*b.* Rome, Italy, 3 November 1888; *d.* Rome, 2 July 1946), *astronomy.*

The son of a clerk at the Vatican, Emanuelli became interested in astronomy when only ten years old. His first astronomical work was the observation of the solar eclipse of 20 May 1900, on which he made a report to the French astronomer Camille Flammarion. Emanuelli studied in Rome, where he served as a volunteer at the Collegio Romano Observatory until, at the age of twenty-two, he became astronomer at the Vatican Observatory.

At that time the great international astronomical enterprise was the *Astrographic Catalogue,* to which the Vatican Observatory contributed, and Emanuelli worked actively in that area. Even during World War I, when he was called into the army, he maintained his scientific contacts and offered advice and suggestions for the continuation of this important work.

Emanuelli computed several orbits of small planets, elements of many solar eclipses, and was particularly interested in the problem of the relativistic deflections of the stars in the neighborhood of the eclipsed sun. For some eclipses, he published celestial maps and tables with data concerning the amount of the expected displacements. Well known to all astronomers are Emanuelli's tables for the conversion of the equatorial in galactic coordinates, which were used until the new position of the galactic poles was established.

Emanuelli had, besides his professional work in astronomy, a deep interest in the history of science and its dissemination. In these two fields he published many writings in different journals. At his death he left a large number of unpublished manuscripts, which are now deposited at the Domus Galileiana in Pisa.

BIBLIOGRAPHY

Emanuelli's writings include "Eclisse Solare del 17 aprile 1912," in *Memorie della Società degli spettroscopisti italiani,* **40** (1912), 123; observations and computations of the elements of planetary orbits, often untitled, in *Astronomische Nachrichten,* **178** (1908), 319; **181** (1919), 209; **215** (1922), 211; **216** (1922), 137, 419; **219** (1923), 161, 219; **223** (1925), 119; **234** (1929), 357; and **237** (1930), 237; "Gli eclissi di Sole totali non centrali," in *Atti dell'Accademia nazionale dei Lincei. Rendiconti della classe di scienze fisiche, matematiche e naturali,* 6th ser., **8** (1928), 214; and "Il polo galattico e la regione circumpolare galattica," *ibid.,* **9** (1929), 1096.

See also "Posizione di Venere nel 25 marzo del 1300, determinazione dell'ora in cui sono sorti Venere ed il Sole il 25 marzo del 1300 nella montagna del Purgatorio," in *Memorie della R. Accademia d'Italia,* **14** (1943), 193. A list of Emanuelli's MSS is P. Maffei, "Gli scritti inediti di Pio Emanuelli," in *Memorie della Società astronomica italiana,* **37** (1966), 803.

G. RIGHINI

EMBDEN, GUSTAV (*b.* Hamburg, Germany, 10 November 1874; *d.* Frankfurt, Germany, 25 July 1933), *physiological chemistry.*

Embden, son of a Hamburg lawyer, studied medicine at the universities of Freiburg im Breisgau, Munich, Berlin, and Strasbourg. His teachers, Johannes von Vries in Freiburg and Franz Hofmeister in Strasbourg, directed his interest toward physiology. In 1903 Embden was appointed assistant at the Physiological Institute, having worked in Hofmeister's laboratory since his graduation in 1899. He also worked for short periods with Gaule in Zurich, Paul Ehrlich in Frankfurt, and Ernst Ewald in Strasbourg. These brief stints increased Embden's skill in experimentation. But it was Hofmeister's influence that was decisive in directing him toward chemicophysiological research and in increasing his ability to think in a biologically oriented way.

In 1904 Carl von Noorden made Embden director of the newly organized chemistry laboratory of the medical clinic at the municipal hospital of Frankfurt-Sachsenhausen. Embden helped to create such a fine reputation for this laboratory that in 1907 it was expanded into the Physiological Institute. In 1909 this institute became autonomous, and in 1914, with the founding of the university, it was renamed the University Institute for Vegetative Physiology, with Embden as director and full professor. In 1907 Embden had qualified as lecturer at the University of Bonn on the basis of his work in Frankfurt. Two years later he was appointed professor. He married Hanni Fellner, granddaughter of Frankfurt's former lord mayor. From 1925 to 1926 he served as rector of the university.

In his lectures, as in his research, Embden preferred

a presentation of the deeper relationships of chemico-physiological processes to a collection of individual facts. At the Physiological Institute he created an atmosphere of dedicated teamwork through his sympathy, helpfulness, and ability to foster close personal contacts and inspire his assistants to cooperate in the solution of common problems. Embden was known as a researcher who made absolutely sure of his results, without impeding his bold conclusions and theories.

At the time Embden began his biochemical research, the physiology of metabolism was still dominated by the energy principle, and pertinent research was concentrated mainly on the initial and final stages of the metabolic processes. Embden focused on the biologically specialized position of the chemical processes in the living organism and particularly investigated the several stages of intermediate metabolism. His works form an important part of the transition from calorimetric investigations to the physiology of the metabolism of the living cell. Embden's scientific works are divided into two large, clearly distinct, and logically related groups. Initially he investigated intermediate metabolic processes in the liver in order to consider the physiological-chemical processes involved in muscular exertion.

Embden recognized that experiments on the undissected animal produced unclear results, while dissected tissue was unsatisfactory because of breakdown of the organic structure and cell damage. Therefore he developed a new method by using the livers of warm-blooded animals, kept in good condition by a special perfusion technique. With the help of this method he recognized oxidative deamination as a way to break down amino acids, the synthesis of sugar from lactic acid, and—in connection with the β-oxidation of fatty acids discovered by Franz Knoop—that acetoacetic acid and acetone are the products of pathological sugar metabolism. This last discovery formed a basis for research into sugar metabolism and diabetes. In their entirety, these investigations showed that the liver is the most important metabolic-physiological organ of the body.

Embden's research work on intermediate carbohydrate metabolism turned his attention to the chemical processes involved in muscular activity. At first he selected the fluid pressed from a muscle—analogous to fluid pressed from yeast—as a cell-free research medium. In 1924 he succeeded in isolating a hexose diphosphate as an intermediate product, naming it lactacidogen. It showed him that—analogous to the processes in the yeast cell—glucose must be esterified with phosphoric acid before it can be broken down further. In 1927 he discovered hexose monophosphate, the so-called "Embden ester," in the muscle cells. During twenty years of tenacious work Embden and his assistants isolated important phosphor-containing intermediate products of carbohydrate metabolism in the muscle. This led to his discovery of adenyl phosphoric acid in the muscle, thus opening a new, large field in biochemistry. Embden was the first to recognize the rapid reversibility of chemical processes in muscle contraction. Finally, in the course of his last experiments, in 1932–1933, he and his assistants succeeded in tracing all stages of the breakdown of glycogen in the muscle to lactic acid. In these biochemical investigations Embden never lost sight of the problem of general cell physiology, always endeavoring to integrate his discoveries of phosphorylation and metabolic processes with the relationships between activity, fatigue, and training on the one hand and the colloidal state of protoplasm on the other.

BIBLIOGRAPHY

I. ORIGINAL WORKS. Embden's inaugural dissertation is *Anatomische Untersuchung eines Falles von Elephantiasis fibromatosa* (Strasbourg, 1899). Posthumously there appeared "Gustav Embdens und seiner Mitarbeiter letzte Arbeiten," in *Hoppe-Seyler's Zeitschrift für physiologische Chemie,* **230** (1934), 1–108, with a biography (not by Embden).

II. SECONDARY LITERATURE. On Embden or his work see H. J. Denticke, "Gustav Embden," in *Ergebnisse der Physiologie (biologischen Chemie und experimentellen Pharmakologie),* **35** (1933), 32–49, with a bibliography; E. Lehnartz, "Gustav Embden," in *Arbeitsphysiologie,* **7,** no. 5 (1934), 475–483; and J. C. Poggendorff, VI, pt. 1, 660; VIIa, pt. 1, 500.

EBERHARD SCHMAUDERER

EMDEN, ROBERT (*b.* St. Gallen, Switzerland, 4 March 1862; *d.* Zurich, Switzerland, 8 October 1940), *astrophysics.*

Emden received his doctorate at Strasbourg in 1887 as a student of the physicist August Kundt. In 1907 he became an assistant professor (*extraordinarius*) of physics and meteorology at the Technische Hochschule in Munich. He held that position until 1928, when he became an assistant professor for astrophysics at the University of Munich. His work *Gaskugeln, Anwendungen der mechanischen Wärmetheorie auf kosmologische und meteorologische Probleme* (Leipzig, 1907) was epoch-making; all subsequent textbooks on astrophysics have been based on it. He was therefore entrusted with writing the article on the thermodynamics of celestial bodies in the *Enzyklopädie der mathematischen Wissenschaften.*

Emden introduced the concept of "polytropic change of state," although he did not need to display the radiation pressure explicit in his calculations. Nevertheless, this pressure appeared mathematically in the exponents of the polytropic lines. Emden was also the first to give a derivation for radiative equilibrium for nondiscernible particles, that is, photon statistics. He thereby became a precursor in the use of the Bose-Einstein statistics. In further works he dealt with astronomical refraction, the thermodynamics of the atmosphere, and propagation of sound in the atmosphere. In addition, he contributed significantly to the development of the theory of balloon flight.

In 1920 he became a member of the Bavarian Academy of Sciences. From 1916 on, formal difficulties kept him from obtaining German citizenship. Consequently, he at least avoided financial losses upon his dismissal when the Nazis came into power in 1933. He died in Zurich, in his native Switzerland, on 8 October 1940.

BIBLIOGRAPHY

Emden's works include, in addition to those cited in the text, "Theoretische Grundlagen der Ballonführung," in *Illustrierte aeronautische Mitteilungen* (1901); *Grundlagen der Ballonführung* (Leipzig, 1910); "Abnorme Hörbarkeit," in *Sitzungsberichte der Bayerischen Akademie der Wissenschaften zu München* (1916), 113–123; "Zur Thermodynamik der Atmosphäre," in *Meteorologische Zeitschrift,* **33** (1916), 351–360; **35** (1918), 13–29, 74–81, 114–123; **40** (1923), 171–177; "Lichtquanten," in *Physikalische Zeitschrift,* **22** (1921), 513–517; "Astronomische Refraktion," in *Astronomische Nachrichten,* **219** (1923), 45–56; "Strahlungsgleichgewicht," in *Zeitschrift für Physik,* **23** (1924), 176–213; and "Freiballon," in *Handbuch der Experimentalphysik,* IV, pt. 3 (1930), 115–131.

J. O. FLECKENSTEIN

EMERSON, BENJAMIN KENDALL (*b.* Nashua, New Hampshire, 20 December 1843; *d.* Amherst, Massachusetts, 7 April 1932), *geology.*

Emerson belonged to a distinguished New England family that was eminent in the educational world. His father, Benjamin F. Emerson, was a lawyer; his mother was Elizabeth Kendall. Emerson received his secondary education at Tilton (Vermont) Academy. Inspired by the work of the famous New England geologist Edward Hitchcock, he went to Amherst College, from which he graduated with distinction. After a period of teaching sciences at the old Groton Academy, he studied geology at Berlin and Göttingen, receiving the Ph.D. at the latter in 1870.

Emerson returned to Amherst as instructor in geology and zoology, became professor of geology in 1872, and of geology and theology in 1881. That he was an inspiring teacher is shown by the number of renowned geologists who had been his students.

Emerson was also distinguished as a field geologist. For thirty years he was on the staff of the U.S. Geological Survey. He was a member of the Harriman expedition to Alaska in 1899 and wrote the geologic section of its report. His outstanding contributions were on the geology of the Connecticut Valley and bordering plateaus of central and southern New England; his *Geology of Old Hampshire County* is a classic and, like his *Geology of Massachusetts and Rhode Island,* still is an important source for field geologists. Many of his interpretations of stratigraphic, petrologic, and metamorphic geology are a marked advance over earlier works and have served as a progressive link between nineteenth-century and early twentieth-century geology. Besides the newer terminology, he brought in modern concepts of petrogenesis and stratigraphy, drastically modifying and adding to the earlier interpretations of Edward and Charles H. Hitchcock and others. He recognized transitional metamorphic facies and the metasomatic effects of granitic solutions, giving some emphasis to their role in promoting regional metamorphism. In *Geology of Old Hampshire County* there is a detailed description of the Bernardston formation (Devonian), basically important in regional correlations; this monograph also provides the first detailed treatment of the igneous and sedimentary rocks of the Triassic basin and of the Pleistocene—chiefly glacial—deposits of the Connecticut Valley. His *Mineralogical Lexicon* . . . provides a remarkable catalog of mineral occurrences in south-central New England.

Emerson was a founder and original fellow of the Geological Society of America and one of its early presidents (1899). He was also a fellow of the American Academy of Arts and Sciences, the Washington Academy of Sciences, the American Philosophical Society, and the American Geographical Society. He was also a member of the Deutsche Geologische Gesellschaft and several other learned societies.

BIBLIOGRAPHY

I. ORIGINAL WORKS. Fifty-one titles are recorded in *Bibliography of Geologic Literature on North America 1785–1918,* U.S. Geological Survey Bulletin no. 746 (Washington, D.C., 1923), pp. 343–344. The following may be considered Emerson's principal contributions: "A Description of the 'Bernardston Series' of Metamorphic Upper Devonian Rocks," in *American Journal of Science,* 3rd ser.,

40 (1890), 263–275, 362–374; *Mineralogical Lexicon of Franklin, Hampshire, and Hampden Counties, Massachusetts,* U.S. Geological Survey Bulletin no. 126 (Washington, D.C., 1895); *Geology of Old Hampshire County, Massachusetts, Comprising Franklin, Hampshire, and Hampden Counties,* U.S. Geological Survey Monograph no. 29 (Washington, D.C., 1898); *Outlines of the Geology of Western Massachusetts: Description of the Holyoke Quadrangle,* U.S. Geological Survey Geologic Atlas, Holyoke Folio, no. 50 (Washington, D.C., 1898); *The Geology of Eastern Berkshire County, Massachusetts,* U.S. Geological Survey Bulletin no. 159 (Washington, D.C., 1899); and *Geology of Massachusetts and Rhode Island,* U.S. Geological Survey Bulletin no. 597 (Washington, D.C., 1917).

Of the remaining forty-five titles in the cited bibliography two major publications were written with J. H. Perry: *The Geology of Worcester, Massachusetts* (Worcester, 1903); and *The Green Schists and Associated Granites and Porphyries of Rhode Island,* U.S. Geological Survey Bulletin no. 311 (Washington, D.C., 1907).

Other titles, short papers, relate mostly to the tetrahedral theory of the earth (discussional); forms, distribution, and mineralogy of Triassic traprocks of Massachusetts; and glacial and postglacial features of the Connecticut Valley. Several short notes on mineralogic and petrologic subjects appeared in various scientific journals.

II. SECONDARY LITERATURE. The principal biographical sketch is by one of Emerson's former students, F. B. Loomis, "Memorial of Benjamin Kendall Emerson," in *Bulletin of the Geological Society of America,* **44,** pt. 2 (1933), 317–325. Briefer sketches are Charles R. Keyes, in *Pan-American Geologist,* **58,** no. 1 (1932), 1–6; and A. C. Lane, in *Proceedings of the American Academy of Arts and Sciences,* **68,** no. 13 (1933), 625–627.

L. W. CURRIER

EMERSON, ROBERT (*b.* New York, N.Y., 4 November 1903; *d.* New York, 4 February 1959), *plant physiology.*

After studying at Harvard, Emerson received his doctorate under Otto Warburg at Berlin in 1927 and joined the California Institute of Technology biology department in 1930. From 1937 to 1940 he worked at the Carnegie Laboratory of Plant Biology at Stanford, California. After returning to Cal Tech, Emerson spent the World War II years working with Japanese deportees from the West Coast, attempting to develop rubber production from guayule, a Mexican desert shrub. In 1947 he became director of the newly founded photosynthesis research laboratory associated with the botany department of the University of Illinois in Urbana, which he built into one of the leading research laboratories in this field. He died, at the height of his research career, in a plane crash in the East River, off New York City. In 1949 Emerson received the Stephen Hales Award of the American Society of Plant Physiologists, and in 1950 he was elected to membership in the National Academy of Sciences.

In appearance and character Emerson was a typical New Englander: tall, lean, long-headed, self-denying, hard-working, expecting (and appreciating) hard work in others. He exerted great influence on his co-workers and students. A pacifist and believer in democratic socialism, he was always defending the underdog—working with deported Japanese, fighting housing discrimination, befriending students from Africa and India. Emerson was a perfectionist in experimental research and skillful in manual work, including cabinetmaking and gardening. He combined pride in the quality of his own work and critical rejection of less careful work with great modesty and deep respect for the achievements of others.

Emerson's lifelong concern was the precise, quantitative study of photosynthesis—the basic process of life on earth by which organic matter is synthesized by plants from water and carbon dioxide with the aid of light absorbed by plant pigments (of which the green pigment chlorophyll is the most important and ubiquitous).

In 1937 Emerson set out to check the conclusions of his teacher Otto Warburg that plants can synthesize sugar (glucose), using only four light quanta (photons) for each molecule of carbon dioxide utilized and of oxygen liberated. This suggested a remarkable efficiency of the process—conversion of up to 30 percent of the absorbed light energy into chemical energy of the products. Steadily improving the measurement techniques and systematically determining the quantum requirement of photosynthesis in green, brown, red, and blue-green algal cells, in monochromatic light of widely different wavelengths, Emerson arrived at a number of important conclusions.

1. The minimum quantum requirement of photosynthesis for all plants is not four but eight. This conclusion led to a drawn-out controversy with Warburg, in which Emerson's conclusions were gradually accepted as correct by most workers in the field, although not by Warburg himself.

2. Quanta absorbed in chlorophyll *a,* chlorophyll *b,* and the red and blue phycobilin pigments of certain algae are about equally effective in producing photosynthesis. Light quanta absorbed by the yellow pigments (the carotenoids) have a much smaller efficiency—with the exception of a special carotenoid, fucoxanthol, present in brown algae and diatoms.

3. At the longwave end of the absorption band of chlorophyll *a* (above 680 nm in green cells and above 650 nm in red algae) the yield of photosynthesis drops sharply ("red drop"); it can be restored to normal

by additional illumination with shortwave light (the "Emerson effect").

This last result has become one of two main foundations of the now widely accepted theory according to which photosynthesis involves two successive photochemical processes brought about by two pigment systems. Light absorption in one system oxidizes water, liberating oxygen and reducing an intermediate product (perhaps a cytochrome); light absorbed in the other system reduces carbon dioxide (sugar is the ultimate product), oxidizing the intermediate product that had been reduced by the first system. Each of the two steps requires four quanta (to move four hydrogen atoms "uphill," that is, with an increase in chemical energy), which explains the total quantum requirement of eight. In the region of the red drop, too many quanta are absorbed in one pigment system and not enough in the other; this can be corrected by supplementary shortwave illumination.

Another important work of Emerson's (together with William Arnold) dealt with photosynthesis in flashing light. Since photosynthesis involves one or two photochemical steps, preceded and followed (and also separated) by nonphotochemical, enzyme-catalyzed "dark" reactions, the study of photosynthesis in flashing light permits the separation of the light stage from the dark stage. By varying the dark interval between flashes, Emerson proved that the dark stage needs about 0.01 second for its completion at room temperature. Another important result was to show that a single, intense flash of light can produce, in normal healthy plants, only one molecule of oxygen (and reduce one molecule of carbon dioxide) per approximately 2,500 chlorophyll molecules present. This finding became the starting point of the theory of the photosynthetic unit, which postulates the association in plant cells of about 300 chlorophyll molecules (2,500 divided by 8) with a single reaction center (an enzyme molecule) to which the light energy absorbed in any one of the 300 associated pigment molecules is conveyed by a special physical mechanism (resonance energy migration). This is one of the basic concepts of the present-day theory of photosynthesis.

Emerson carried out all his experiments himself, alone or with a trusted assistant. Among his students and co-workers were William Arnold, Charleton Lewis, Shimpe Nishimura, Mrs. Marcia Brody, Carl Cederstrand, and Mrs. Ruth Chalmers.

BIBLIOGRAPHY

I. ORIGINAL WORKS. Emerson's principal writings include "A Separation of the Reactions in Photosynthesis

by Means of Intermittent Light," in *Journal of General Physiology,* **15,** no. 4 (1932), 391–420, written with W. Arnold; "The Photochemical Reaction in Photosynthesis," *ibid.,* **16,** no. 2 (1932), 191–205, with W. Arnold; "Photosynthesis," in *Annual Review of Biochemistry,* **6** (1937), 535–556; "Carbon Dioxide Exchange and the Measurement of the Quantum Yield of Photosynthesis," in *American Journal of Botany,* **28,** no. 9 (1941), 789–804, with C. M. Lewis; "The Dependence of the Quantum Yield of Chlorella Photosynthesis on Wave Length of Light," *ibid.,* **30,** no. 3 (1943), 165–178, with C. M. Lewis; "Some Factors Influencing the Long-wave Limit of Photosynthesis," in *Proceedings of the National Academy of Sciences of the United States of America,* **43** (1957), 133–143, with R. Chalmers and C. Cederstrand; "The Quantum Yield of Photosynthesis," in *Annual Review of Plant Physiology,* **9** (1958), 1–24; and "Red Drop and Role of Auxiliary Pigments in Photosynthesis," in *Plant Physiology,* **35** (1960), 377–485, with E. Rabinowitch.

II. SECONDARY LITERATURE. On Emerson and his work, see E. Rabinowitch and Govindjee, *Photosynthesis* (New York, 1969).

EUGENE RABINOWITCH

EMMONS, EBENEZER (*b.* Middlefield, Massachusetts, 16 May 1799; *d.* Brunswick County, North Carolina, 1 October 1863), *geology.*

Ebenezer Emmons was the focus of the great Taconic controversy, the gravest dispute ever to divide American geology. A principal figure in the first geological survey of New York between 1837 and 1843, he played a leading role in the establishment of a geological column for America and a stratigraphy independent of the Anglo-Continental model. Before the New York survey, correlation with the succession of English strata was the principal objective of American geologists from Maclure and Eaton through Edward Hitchcock and David Dale Owen. By 1842 the Transition strata of New York between the Carboniferous of Pennsylvania and the Primary had been separated into the Catskill, Erie, Helderberg, Ontario, and Champlain groups of a New-York system and a separate Taconic system. The Potsdam sandstone, the Chazy limestone, the black marble of Isle La Motte, and the Lorraine shales, as well as the major group names and the two system designations (New-York and Taconic) were bestowed by Emmons. The strata were characterized both paleontologically and lithologically, and type sections were described by Emmons and his colleagues. The system of nomenclature by geographic reference, adopted for the first time in North America, was specifically the work of Emmons. He also named the Adirondack Mountains,[1] and it was at a meeting of the New York Board of Geologists at Emmons' home in Albany in 1838 that the Association of American Geologists, which developed into the American Association for the Advancement of Science, was planned.

Emmons studied at Williams College and later the Berkshire Medical School, in the midst of the Taconic country. At Williams he was protégé and assistant of Chester Dewey, with whom he began his geological surveys. He joined Dewey in 1828 as instructor and later succeeded him as professor of natural history. In 1826 he was studying geology and assisting Amos Eaton at the newly organized Rensselaer School (now Rensselaer Polytechnic Institute) as well as lecturing in chemistry at the Albany Medical College. Emmons achieved a certain financial independence through the practice of medicine, chiefly obstetrics, which he continued throughout his life.

James Hall was a student at Rensselaer from 1830, the year in which Emmons became junior professor, to 1832. Emmons chose Hall as his assistant in the first field season of his survey of the second New York district. W. W. Mather, Lardner Vanuxem, and T. A. Conrad were initially responsible for the first, third, and fourth of the four districts into which the state had been divided. Hall later succeeded Conrad. Lewis C. Beck was attached to the survey as mineralogist.

Emmons began by tracing an orderly succession of scarcely disturbed fossiliferous strata, beginning with the Potsdam sandstone dipping gently away from the crystalline rocks of the Adirondack outlier. Across the Hudson and Champlain valleys to the east, he found the abrupt front of the Taconic Range, consisting of broken slates with intercalated carbonates, generally dipping steeply toward the crystalline rocks of the New England mountains. In spite of the reverse dip, Emmons had always considered these rocks to be older than the less disturbed shales and carbonates of the Hudson and Champlain valleys[2] and now proposed that they constituted a vast new sedimentary series between the Potsdam and the primary, the true primordial system and the base of the sedimentary column. Vanuxem and Conrad, and apparently even Hall at first, agreed. Mather disagreed, as did William and Henry Barton Rogers, whose observations of the merging of the flat rocks of the Allegheny Plateau into the folded strata of the valley and ridge province persuaded Mather that the Taconic strata are an overfolded extension of the Champlain group.

As the original survey was completed, Hall and Emmons were in competition for continuing geological positions with the state, Hall maneuvering to obtain the post of state paleontologist. Although aspiring to the title of state geologist, Emmons was diverted into the position of state agriculturalist.

His Taconic system came under direct attack from the Rogers brothers, who maintained that the entire folded Appalachian chain contained neither faults nor unconformities. In 1844 and again in 1846, in *Agriculture of New York,* Emmons published a vigorous exposition of the Taconic system, by then supported by paleontological evidence.

George T. Foster, a New York schoolteacher, relying on Emmons' expertise, prepared a geological map that he succeeded in selling to the New York Legislature in 1850 for use in the schools of the state. Louis Agassiz and Hall (who hurriedly prepared his own rival map) induced the state to cancel the order—Hall going so far, according to his assistant and, later, successor, J. M. Clarke, as to dump Foster's maps into the Hudson River. Thereupon, Foster sued Agassiz and Hall for libel. The case against Agassiz was heard first, with Emmons the sole witness to the scientific reputability of Foster's chart. Joseph Henry, James Dwight Dana (who later wrote fifteen papers disproving the Taconic system), J. D. Whitney, the Rogers brothers, Eben Horsford, Mather, Hitchcock, and even Sir Charles Lyell volunteered their testimony in Agassiz's behalf. The case, which ended in dismissal, amounted to the excommunication of Emmons from the ranks of American science. The following year he accepted the post of state geologist for North Carolina and moved south, there to be caught by the Civil War. He continued to assemble evidence of the wide extension of his pre-Potsdam system, and before his death in 1863 he had the satisfaction of seeing his claim to be discoverer of the "true primordial fauna" and the base of the sedimentary column supported by the contentious Jules Marcou; Joachim Barrande, by then the acknowledged authority on the Lower Paleozoic; the Canadian geologists William Logan and Elkanah Billings; and T. S. Hunt.

A man of stern appearance and strict religious observance, Emmons was nevertheless a popular teacher and greatly in demand as an obstetrician. His controversial views made him an underground favorite among students and younger faculty in the strongholds of his opponents. Successive editions of his textbooks attest to his extended influence. Perhaps more significantly, the *Manual of Geology* by Dana, his most uncompromising foe,[3] closely follows the organization and basic pedagogy of Emmons' *Manual of Geology* more than any of the available English examples.

The Taconic controversy, continuing in some aspects to the present day, came to overshadow Emmons' major contribution to world geology, which was the extension in New York of the method begun by William Smith, Georges Cuvier, and Alexandre Brongniart. It was the New York survey, but especially the New-York system classification and Emmons' nomenclature, that set the model in America, as Sedgwick and Murchison were setting it in England, for the subsequent development of stratigraphy and the geological time scale in the next century.

NOTES

1. Wherever possible Emmons took his designations from the names for the original Indian inhabitants. The precedent may have been Murchison and Sedgwick's Silurian system, first used in 1835, when the New York survey was beginning.
2. He had convinced Hitchcock of this in 1833, but by 1842 Hitchcock had decided that the Taconic rocks were simply metamorphosed Champlain strata (E. Hitchcock, *Geology of Massachusetts* [Amherst, 1833], p. 300; W. W. Mather, "Geology of the First District," in *Geology,* pt. 4 of the *Natural History of New York* [Albany, 1843]).
3. In 1888, when the evidence of extensive Lower Cambrian fossiliferous strata was incontrovertible, the American Committee of the International Geological Congress recommended the denomination "Taconic system" for the first group of strata above the Archean. The aged and mellowed Hall agreed, but Dana and C. D. Walcott led a successful fight to reject the recommendation.

BIBLIOGRAPHY

I. ORIGINAL WORKS. Emmons' most significant publication was the now almost unobtainable final report, "Geology of the Second District," in *Geology,* pt. 4 of the *Natural History of New York* (Albany, 1842). *Agriculture of New York,* pt. 5 of *Natural History of New York* (Albany, 1846), contains his geology of New York, the only summary publication of the results of the New York survey. It is profusely illustrated with exceptional lithographs by his son, Ebenezer Jr., and engraved sections, some hand-colored. The text speaks of a map but, according to Marcou, although the map was printed, Hall succeeded in suppressing it. Emmons' several textbooks made free and presumably profitable use of the fossil illustrations prepared under the direction of the New York Board of Geologists, thereby infuriating Hall.

Emmons' *Manual of Mineralogy and Geology* (Albany, 1826; 2nd ed., 1832) should be compared with his last textbook, *Manual of Geology* (Philadelphia, 1860), to illustrate his lack of concern with theory and a characteristic pragmatic concentration on historical geology. For a complete bibliography, consult John M. Nickles, "Geologic Literature on North America 1785–1918," *U.S. Geological Survey Bulletin* no. 746 (1922), 345–346.

II. SECONDARY LITERATURE. A major source of information about Emmons is J. M. Clarke, *James Hall of Albany* (Albany, 1923), by Hall's assistant and successor as New York State paleontologist; see pp. 30, 40, 42, 53, 57, 99, 206. The Taconic controversy is extensively treated in G. P. Merrill, *The First One Hundred Years of American*

Geology (New Haven, 1924), pp. 594–614; a biographical essay by Jules Marcou, *American Geologist,* **7** (1891), 1–23, is somewhat overblown; the article by G. P. Merrill in the *Dictionary of American Biography,* III, 149, is unduly deflating. Emmons' own records apparently were lost in the disorders attendant on his wartime death. Any official records of the *Foster* v. *Agassiz* case, beyond the bare fact of its dismissal, were lost in a fire. See C. J. Schneer, "Ebenezer Emmons and the Foundations of American Geology," in *Isis,* **60,** pt. 4 (1970), 439–450.

CECIL J. SCHNEER

EMMONS, SAMUEL FRANKLIN (*b.* Boston, Massachusetts, 29 March 1841; *d.* Washington, D.C., 28 March 1911), *geology, mining.*

Emmons was a descendant of Thomas Emmons, one of the founders of the Rhode Island Colony, who was "admitted to be an inhabitant of Boston" in 1648. His father was Nathaniel Henry Emmons, a highly respected and affluent Boston merchant engaged in the East India and China trade. His mother, Elizabeth Wales, was a descendant of Nathaniel Wales, who emigrated from Yorkshire to Boston in 1635. He was named for a great-grandfather on his father's side, Samuel Franklin, a cousin of Benjamin Franklin.

During his boyhood Emmons attended private schools, including the Dixwell Latin School, where he had rigorous training in English composition and some instruction in physical geography and map-making, all of which stood him in good stead in later years. He entered Harvard College at the age of seventeen and graduated with an A.B. degree in 1861. The next five years were spent in Europe, climbing in the Alps in the summer of 1861 and then studying with private tutors in Paris to gain admission to the École Impériale des Mines, where he was a student during the academic years 1862–1863 and 1863–1864. He then enrolled in the Bergakademie at Freiberg, Saxony, where he remained until midsummer 1865, after which he visited many of the important European mining centers, finally returning to Boston from Rome in June 1866, at which time Harvard awarded him an A.M. degree.

In late 1866 and early 1867 the geological exploration of the fortieth parallel, under the direction of the chief of engineers, U.S. Army, was authorized by Congress and organized by Clarence King, who was chief geologist. Arnold Hague, who had become acquainted with Emmons when they were students at Freiberg, was appointed one of King's assistant geologists. Through Hague's influence King accepted Emmons as a volunteer assistant for the 1867 field season. The following winter Emmons received an official appointment as assistant geologist, a position he held until the completion of his reports in 1877, when he resigned to engage in cattle ranching in Wyoming. The U.S. Geological Survey was created by act of Congress on 3 March 1879. Clarence King was its first director, and one of his first official acts was to appoint Emmons as geologist in charge of the Rocky Mountain Division. Later he was placed in charge of the Division of Economic Geology, where he remained until his death.

Emmons was married three times: on 5 August 1876 to Waltha Anita Steeves of New York, from whom he was subsequently divorced; on 14 February 1889 to Sophie Dallas Markoe of Washington, who died on 19 June 1896; and on 4 August 1903 to Suzanne Earle Ogden-Jones of Dinard, France, who survived him. He left no children.

Emmons was active in many scientific organizations. He was a member of the National Academy of Sciences and its treasurer from 1902 to 1910. He was one of the founders of the Geological Society of America in 1888 and its president in 1903. Earlier he had helped to establish the Colorado Scientific Society and was its first president in 1882. Emmons was a member or fellow of the American Academy of Arts and Sciences, the American Philosophical Society, the American Association for the Advancement of Science, the Washington Academy of Sciences, the Geological Society of Washington (of which he was president for one term), and the American Institute of Mining Engineers, of which he was vice-president in 1882 and again in 1890 and 1891. When the International Geological Congress met in Washington in 1871, he was its general secretary, and at meetings in other countries in 1897, 1903, and 1910 he was one of its vice-presidents. Emmons became a fellow of the Geological Society of London in 1874 and later an honorary member of the Société Helvétique des Sciences Naturelles. Columbia and Harvard conferred honorary Sc.D. degrees upon him in 1909.

Although mining geology, especially the origin of ore deposits, was Emmons' major interest, his contributions to regional and structural geology were notable. His assignment with the fortieth-parallel exploration involved the survey of an area, about 100 miles in width, extending from the Sierra Nevada to the Great Plains. Much of the region was then so little settled that detachments of the U.S. Army accompanied the field parties to protect them from hostile Indians. The report on this pioneer work (1877) promptly became a model for regional studies and was emulated by many geologists.

The directives for Emmons' early work in the U.S. Geological Survey were conflicting. Most desirable from his point of view were the instructions to prepare a monograph on the region of Leadville, Colorado, at that time one of the most productive mining localities in the Rocky Mountains. But this was in 1879, and the Geological Survey had undertaken the collection of statistics on precious metals for the tenth census (1880). That task was also given to Emmons and G. F. Becker. With characteristic energy Emmons fulfilled both duties simultaneously. Volume XIII of the *Tenth Census Reports,* by Emmons and Becker, with its geological descriptions of mining regions, was published in 1885. A preliminary report on the geology and mining industry of the Leadville region was published in 1882 and the definitive monograph in 1886. This immediately attracted widespread attention and stimulated the investigation of the origin of ore deposits in other mining regions.

Emmons' conclusion that the ores had been derived mainly from the intruded igneous rocks and deposited in adjacent sedimentary rocks by hot aqueous solutions led to the classification of many ore bodies all over the world as results of contact metamorphism. His suggestion that the hot aqueous solutions were of meteoric origin, heated at depth by contact with hot igneous rock, provoked long-continuing discussion, and in his later work he modified his original theory to include the idea that they were partly of magmatic origin. This development of Emmons' concepts of ore genesis, as well as of secondary enrichment, appeared in his later publications and profoundly influenced the work of many geologists, including those who studied mining regions under his supervision when he was in charge of the Division of Economic Geology in the U.S. Geological Survey.

BIBLIOGRAPHY

I. ORIGINAL WORKS. Emmons' writings include "Geology of Toyabe Range," in *Geological Exploration of the 40th Parallel,* III (Washington, D.C., 1870), 320–348; "Descriptive Geology of the 40th Parallel," *ibid.,* II (Washington, D.C., 1877), 1–890, written with Arnold Hague; "Abstract of a Report Upon the Geology and Mining Industry of Leadville, Colorado," in *Report of the United States Geological Survey* (Washington, D.C., 1882), pp. 203–290; "Statistics and Technology of the Precious Metals," in *Tenth Census Reports,* XIII (Washington, D.C., 1885), 1–540, written with G. F. Becker; "Geology and Mining Industry of Leadville, Colorado," in *Monographs of the U.S. Geological Survey,* **12** (1886), 1–770; "Structural Relations of Ore Deposits," in *Transactions of the American Institute of Mining Engineers,* **16** (1888), 804–839; "Orographic Movements in the Rocky Mountains," in *Bulletin of the Geological Society of America,* **1** (1890), 245–286; *Geology and Mineral Resources of the Elk Mountains,*

Colorado, U.S. Geological Survey folio no. 9 (Washington, D.C., 1894); "Geology of the Denver Basin in Colorado," in *Monographs of the U.S. Geological Survey,* **27** (1896), 1–556, written with Whitman Cross and G. E. Eldridge; "The Mines of Custer County, Colorado," in U.S. Geological Survey, *Seventeenth Annual Report* (Washington, D.C., 1896), pt. 2, 411–472; *Geology of the Ten-Mile District, Colorado,* U.S. Geological Survey folio no. 48 (Washington, D.C., 1898); "Secondary Enrichment of Ore Deposits," in *Transactions of the American Institute of Mining Engineers,* **30** (1901), 177–217; "Theories of Ore Deposition, Historically Considered," in *Bulletin of the Geological Society of America,* **15** (1904), 1–28; "Development of Modern Theories of Ore Deposition," in *Mining and Scientific Press,* **99** (1909), 400–403; "The Downtown District of Leadville, Colorado," in *Bulletin of the United States Geological Survey,* no. 320 (1907), 1–75, written with J. D. Irving; and "Cananea Mining District of Sonora, Mexico," in *Economic Geology,* **5** (1910), 312–366.

II. Secondary Literature. Biographies of Emmons are George F. Becker, in *Transactions of the American Institute of Mining Engineers,* **42** (1911), 643–661, with a bibliography of 93 titles; Arnold Hague, in *Bulletin of the Geological Society of America,* **23** (1912), 12–28, with a bibliography of 94 titles; and in *Biographical Memoirs. National Academy of Sciences,* **7** (1913), 307–334, with a bibliography of 98 titles.

Kirtley F. Mather

EMPEDOCLES OF ACRAGAS (*b.* Acragas [now Agrigento, Sicily], *ca.* 492 B.C.; *d. ca.* 432 B.C.), *natural philosophy.*

The originator of the four-element theory of matter, Empedocles was the author of two hexameter poems, a physical-cosmological one traditionally entitled "On Nature" (estimated to have been 2,000–3,000 lines in length) and a religious-mystical one, "Purifications," on themes of personal salvation (including lists of taboos), metempsychosis, and eschatology. A total of 450 lines from the two poems, the largest amount of text available to us from any of the pre-Socratics, have been preserved in the form of quotations by later authors (Simplicius, Aristotle, Plutarch, and others). Also attributed to him in antiquity were a treatise on medicine, tragedies, and other works, but the sources tell us nothing about the contents of any of these, and modern scholars are generally of the opinion that the attributions were spurious or confused. It is noteworthy, nevertheless, that Empedocles is often mentioned as a physician by the medical writers (Galen refers to him as founder of the Sicilian school of medicine) and that Aristotle called him the inventor of rhetoric.

The ancient biographical tradition concerning Empedocles is overlaid with legend. Most of the stories told about him can be seen to be fanciful elaborations of personal remarks made in his poems. He is supposed to have stopped an epidemic by diverting and mixing river streams, to have improved climate by erecting a windbreak across a gorge, to have moderated the etesian winds by drawing them into sacks, and to have revived a woman who had had neither breath nor pulse for thirty days. Of his death it was said that, convinced of his immortality, he jumped into one of the craters of Etna. An alternative version (this one not tinted with sarcasm) has him ascending to the sky. An ancient tradition, enthusiastically revived by the Sicilians in the days of Garibaldi, was that Empedocles, although born an aristocrat, became a champion and hero of democratic politics.

The contents and style of his poetry reveal a man of fervid imagination, versatility, and eloquence, with a touch of theatricality. Perhaps some of the traits of the historical Empedocles have indeed been captured in the colorful portrait of the biographical tradition. The legend-making has continued in modern times: Empedocles has been the hero of Romantic tragedy-poems by Hölderlin and Matthew Arnold, and of other literary works (a French play as recently as 1950).

While the religious poem betrays the influence of Pythagoreanism and kindred strands of what has been called Orphism by some scholars and the Greek "puritan psychology" by others, the cosmological poem is unmistakably a development, with crucial modifications, of Parmenidean metaphysics. Parmenides of Elea had deduced that the real must be (a) unborn and imperishable, (b) one and indivisible, (c) immobile, (d) a complete actuality. Since familiar entities of the world of sense fail to conform to these criteria, these entities are a man-made illusion.

Empedocles moderates the extreme transcendent rationalism of the Parmenidean deduction. He postulates four eternal and unchanging elements, earth, water, air, and fire (he actually calls them "roots of all things" and also refers to them by mythological names) and two forces, Love and Hate. Viewed distributively, all six conform, in some sense that Empedocles considers appropriate, to the Parmenidean criteria. The familiar entities of the manifest world (animals, plants, minerals) result from the mixture, in various degrees of combination and according to various proportions of components, of the four elements ("So much does the mixing alter their [the elements'] look," fragment 21.14). Generation and destruction—change in general—are nothing but aggregation and dispersal of the elements by the two cosmic forces acting externally upon them.

Parmenides' requirement for unity and total integration of the real, expressed by him in a comparison with a "sphere well-rounded from all sides," is also fulfilled in a collective sense in Empedocles' system. The latter postulates a cosmic cycle involving four phases: (1) complete mixture of the four elements in a homogeneous sphere; (2) partial and increasing separation owing to the ascendancy of Hate; (3) an interval of total separation; (4) partial and increasing integration owing to the ascendancy of Love. A cosmos like ours can exist, it would seem, only in phases 2 and 4. (What is given here is the traditional interpretation, most recently defended by O'Brien. Bollack and others have argued that the ancient evidence does not support the ascription of a cycle, in the sense of chronological repetition of these phases.)

To explain the origins of animals in phase 4, Empedocles invokes chance and natural selection. From random combinations of stray limbs and organs, monsters emerge at the early stages. Since these are not adapted for survival and reproduction, they perish. Eventually viable organisms come to be assembled; they succeed in producing offspring, and they proliferate. Darwin mentions this Empedoclean theory (indirectly, by citing a passage from Aristotle in which the views of Empedocles are being discussed) in the first note of the historical preface to *The Origin of Species*. But it should be stressed that in Empedocles the mechanism of selection ceases to function precisely where Darwinian evolution starts: when the mechanism of heredity begins to play a role.

Closely related to the cosmic cycle that culminates in the sphere is the Empedoclean picture of our universe as a spherical (or perhaps egg-shaped) plenum, with an encompassing crystalline firmament. Both fixed stars and planets are islands or pockets of fire, the former rigidly attached to the firmament. Empedocles may well have been the first Greek to articulate this influential picture. (Some scholars credit this to Anaxagoras, on the assumption that his date is earlier; others to Parmenides, or to the Pythagoreans, or to even older thinkers, but on evidence that is less firm than what we possess for Empedocles.) That he regarded the earth as spherical is open to doubt, since he explained the inclination of the celestial axis as the result of "tilting" caused by air pressure. Three more doctrines of his astronomy are worth mention. He adopted Parmenides' account of moonlight as a reflection from the sun and gave the correct explanation of solar eclipses. But he was not content to limit the hypothesis of reflection to the moon; he considered the sun itself to be an image of the whole daytime sky as the latter is reflected from the earth's surface.

The macrocosmic cycle reverberates at all levels of the universe. In fragment 100 Empedocles explains respiration and the movement of blood in terms of ebbing and flowing, and gives as illustration the movement of a liquid in the clepsydra, "the water snatcher"—essentially our pipette but wider and with multiple holes at the lower end, suitable for drawing and serving wine from a deep jar. The illustration has often been extravagantly hailed by modern scholars as an experiment. More significantly, the passage represents the earliest statement of the tidal theory of blood movement that remained standard until the time of William Harvey (1628).

The theory of the four elements was adopted by Plato and Aristotle, although both postulated subelemental principles and allowed for transmutation. The Empedoclean theory also inspired or influenced the similar doctrine of four elements and four humors in the Hippocratic school of medicine. Through these three avenues of Platonism, Aristotelianism, and the medical tradition, Empedocles' theory of matter remained the dominant one until the revival of atomism (by Gassendi and Boyle) in the seventeenth century.

While critical of the four-element theory and of Empedocles' conception of the world as a plenum, the ancient atomists nevertheless drew heavily on him. As can be seen very clearly in Lucretius, they adapted Empedoclean ideas not only in the areas of cosmology and zoogony but also in explanations of the phenomena of perception. Empedocles' theory of filmlike "effluences" that are emitted by all things and of corresponding "pores" that serve as selective receptors for these emissions was especially influential.

To trace the various types of Love-Hate metaphysics, speculative physics, and *Naturphilosophie* to Empedocles would be gratuitous, of course, since that particular pair of forces has the universality of a psychological archetype. Freud, who was struck by the resemblance of his later theory of Eros-Destructiveness to the Empedoclean scheme, mused that his own theory might be a case of cryptomnesia of his early readings in pre-Socratic philosophy (*The Standard Edition of the Complete Psychological Works of Sigmund Freud*, James Strachey, trans. [London, 1964], XXIII, 244–246).

Many of Empedocles ideas that did not have historical influence turned out to have been prophetically right. Most often mentioned in this connection is his evolutionary paleontology—a prime example, according to Hans Reichenbach, of how "a good idea stated within an insufficient theoretical frame loses its explanatory power and is forgotten" (*The Rise of Scientific Philosophy* [Berkeley, 1957], p. 197). The same holds for Empedocles' distinction between matter and mechanical force, his ultimate dualism of attractive and repulsive forces, his postulate of the conservation of energy and matter, his doctrine of constant proportions in chemical reactions, and his assumption that light is corporeal and has finite velocity. If one of the two presently competing theories of cosmology (the "big bang" theory) turns out to be right, even his vision of the universe under the influence of Strife will have found a counterpart in modern physics.

The question of the relation between "On Nature" and "Purifications" remains an enigma. The contrast is not only one of mood; the doctrines of personal salvation and metempsychosis cannot easily be reconciled with the essentially materialist metaphysics of the physical poem. Most modern interpreters have despaired of finding more than a psychological or biographical solution. They see the antinomy implicit in the extant fragments as significantly connected with Empedocles' dual reputation as philosopher-scientist and miracle worker. "The last of the Greek shamans," "a Faust," "a Greek Paracelsus" are some of the more suggestive characterizations that have been proposed.

BIBLIOGRAPHY

For the fragments and ancient reports, see Hermann Diels, *Die Fragmente der Vorsokratiker,* Walther Kranz, ed., 6th ed., 3 vols. (Zurich–Berlin, 1951), ch. 31. Selections with English translation and commentary are in G. S. Kirk and J. E. Raven, *The Presocratic Philosophers* (Cambridge, 1957), pp. 320–361. The most recent lengthy accounts are Jean Bollack, *Empédocle:* I, *Introduction à l'ancienne physique* (Paris, 1965); II and III, *Les origines* (Paris, 1969); W. K. C. Guthrie, *A History of Greek Philosophy,* II (Cambridge, 1965), 122–265; and D. O'Brien, *Empedocles' Cosmic Cycle* (Cambridge, 1969), which includes an annotated bibliography of all publications on Empedocles from 1805 to 1965.

ALEXANDER P. D. MOURELATOS

ENCKE, JOHANN FRANZ (*b.* Hamburg, Germany, 23 September 1791; *d.* Spandau [near Berlin], Germany, 28 August 1865), *astronomy.*

The eighth child of a Lutheran preacher, J. Michael Encke, and his wife, M. Elisabeth Misler, Encke displayed an early interest in mathematics but did not enter the University of Göttingen until the autumn of 1811. During his years of study, which were twice interrupted by his military service in the Wars of Liberation, he was greatly impressed and guided by Gauss, who reciprocated his esteem and in May 1816 procured a post for him at the small Seeberg

observatory, near Gotha. After serving as assistant, Encke qualified as professor at and director of this observatory through his theoretical work, of which the computation of the orbit of a comet discovered by Pons is the most essential. This comet was later called Encke's comet. Encke demonstrated that this comet had a period of scarcely four years and that it had been observed repeatedly. Prior to this only a few comets with elliptical orbits and much longer periods had been known. In 1825 Encke—already famous—was offered a professorship at the Academy of Sciences in Berlin and the directorship of the Berlin observatory.

As member of the Academy Encke directed his attention to creating new star charts. This work, only partly based on new observations, was done by many observatories. Those parts finished by the middle of the 1840's led to the discovery of several minor planets and of Neptune in 1846. In 1859 the task was completed, but the charts were soon excelled by those of Argelander.

Encke continued his theoretical work on comets in Berlin, and his investigations into special perturbations are worth attention even today. As a disciple of Gauss, he had already computed the perturbations of the four oldest planetoids, using Gauss's method, which he subsequently improved considerably. As academician Encke was entitled to lecture without passing the *Habilitation* or receiving a doctorate. Upon request by the ministry he lectured until 1862, but without much pleasure.

Encke's lectures were nevertheless influential, since a whole generation of astronomers, including Galle, F. F. E. Brünnow, B. A. Gould, K. N. A. Kruseger, W. J. Förster, Friedrich Tietjen, and K. C. Bruhns were among his disciples. His lectures covered all areas of astrometry and included practical training in the use of measuring instruments, in determining orbits, and in computing perturbations, as well as in fields now considered part of applied mathematics. Encke also lectured on the history of astronomy. He became ordinary professor at the University of Berlin in 1844.

In 1825 the Berlin observatory was obsolete. With the strong support of Alexander von Humboldt, Encke soon succeeded in obtaining funds for a better and more suitably located structure, which began operation in 1835. Besides a meridian circle and a large Fraunhofer refractor, it was equipped with several special-purpose instruments, such as a heliometer. Particular attention was given to observing the positions of stars, particularly of movable stars. Physical observations of planets were of minor interest to Encke. An eager observer himself, he guided his assistants in observing without interfering too much with their work.

After his appointment at Berlin, Encke undertook the editing of the *Berliner astronomisches Jahrbuch.* With the support of his assistants, especially J. P. Wolfers and Bremiker, he issued the yearbooks for 1830–1866. For coverage of minor planets, which was requiring more and more space in the books, several of Encke's disciples were engaged. Apart from 1844–1851, when the yearbook appeared together with the nautical ephemerides as an official publication, its issuance was a private matter, supported by the state but not without economic risk. The opportunity to publish made possible the appearance of Encke's treatises in the yearbooks, dealing particularly with orbit determinations and perturbation computations.

Encke published several of his papers in *Astronomische Nachrichten;* they referred almost exclusively to bodies of our solar system and only to a small extent to fixed stars. In 1823 he married Amalie Becker, who bore him three sons and two daughters. He died peacefully in 1865, after suffering three strokes, and was buried in Berlin.

BIBLIOGRAPHY

Many of Encke's writings were brought together as *Astronomische Abhandlungen,* 3 vols. (Berlin, 1868). Among his papers are "Polhöhe der neuen Berliner Sternwarte," in *Abhandlungen der Preussischen Akademie der Wissenschaften* (1845); "Entwicklung der allgemeinen Störungen der Flora durch Jupiter und Saturn," in *Berichte der Preussischen Akademie der Wissenschaften* (1853); "Berechnung der Pallas-Störungen," *ibid.* (1855); "Telegraphische Bestimmung der Längenunterschiedes Brüssel–Berlin," in *Abhandlungen der Preussischen Akademie der Wissenschaften* (1858); and "Der Comet von Pons," *ibid.* (1859), composed of eight papers. *Vorlesungen über Geschichte der Astronomie im Altertum* was edited by K. C. Bruhns and published after Encke's death (Altona, 1869). Many notices appeared in *Astronomische Nachrichten.*

A biography is K. C. Bruhns, *Johann Franz Encke* (Leipzig, 1869).

H. C. FREIESLEBEN

ENGEL, FRIEDRICH (*b.* Lugau, near Chemnitz [now Karl-Marx-Stadt], Germany, 26 December 1861; *d.* Giessen, Germany, 29 September 1941), *mathematics.*

The son of a Lutheran pastor, Engel attended the Gymnasium at Greiz from 1872 to 1879, studied mathematics in Leipzig and Berlin from 1879 to 1883, and received his doctorate in Leipzig in 1883 under Adolph Mayer. In 1884 and 1885 he studied with Sophus Lie in Christiania (now Oslo). In 1885 Engel qualified as a lecturer in pure mathematics at Leipzig and became an assistant professor there in 1889 and an associate professor in 1899. In 1904 he succeeded his friend Eduard Study as full professor at Greifswald, and in 1913 he went in the same capacity to Giessen, where, after his retirement in 1931, he continued to work until his death.

Although Engel was himself an important and productive mathematician he has found his place in the history of mathematics mainly because he was the closest student and the indispensable assistant of a greater figure: Sophus Lie, after N. H. Abel the greatest Norwegian mathematician. Lie was not capable of giving to the ideas that flowed inexhaustibly from his geometrical intuition the overall coherence and precise analytical form they needed in order to become accessible to the mathematical world. It was no less a mathematician than Felix Klein who recognized that the twenty-two-year-old Engel was the right man to assist Lie and who sent him to Christiania.

Shortly after Engel's return to Leipzig in 1886, Lie succeeded Klein there, and the fruitful collaboration was continued. The result was the *Theorie der Transformationsgruppen,* which appeared from 1888 to 1893 in three volumes "prepared by S. Lie with the cooperation of F. Engel."

Engel performed two further services for the great man long after the latter's death in 1899. In 1932 there appeared Engel's lectures *Die Liesche Theorie der partiellen Differentialgleichungen: Erster Ordnung,* prepared for publication by Karl Faber. For Lie the transformation groups had only been an important aid in handling differential equations; however, he never succeeded in composing a work on his theory of these differential equations. In Faber the seventy-year-old Engel had found the right person to help him in completing this work of his teacher.

Between 1922 and 1937, Engel published six volumes and prepared the seventh of the seven-volume edition of Lie's collected papers, an exceptional service to mathematics in particular and scholarship in general. Lie's peculiar nature made it necessary for his works to be elucidated by one who knew them intimately, and thus Engel's *Anmerkungen* ("Annotations") competed in scope with the text itself. The seventh volume finally appeared in 1960.

Engel's numerous independent works also are concerned primarily with topics in the fields of continuous groups and of partial differential equations: contact transformations (in his dissertation, before his meeting with Lie), Pfaffian equations, Lie's element sets and higher differential quotients, and many others. Lie's ideas were also applied to the *n*-body problem in mechanics (the ten general integrals).

Engel also edited the collected works of Hermann Grassmann, thus bringing posthumous fame to this great mathematician. In addition, with his friend P. Stäckel, Engel investigated the history of non-Euclidean geometry; along with this study he translated the essential works of N. I. Lobachevsky from Russian into German, their first appearance in a Western language.

Engel was a member of the Saxon, Russian, Norwegian, and Prussian academies. He received the Lobachevsky Gold Medal and the Norwegian Order of St. Olaf and was an honorary doctor of the University of Oslo. In 1899 he married Lina Ibbeken, the daughter of a Lutheran pastor. Their only child died very young.

BIBLIOGRAPHY

On Engel's work, see "Friedrich Engel," in *Deutsche Mathematik,* **3** (1938), 701–719, which includes a detailed bibliography with a short summary of each item by Engel himself; G. Kowaleski, "Friedrich Engel zum 70sten Geburtstag," in *Forschungen und Fortschritte* (1931), p. 466; E. Ullrich, "Ein Nachruf auf Friedrich Engel," in *Mitteilungen des Mathematischen Seminars der Universität Giessen,* no. 34 (1945), which contains a supplement to the bibliography in *Deutsche Mathematik* and, with nos. 35 and 36, containing two previously unpublished works of Engel's, is bound to form *Gedenkband für Friedrich Engel;* and "Friedrich Engel, ein Nachruf," in *Nachrichten der Giessener Hochschulgesellschaft,* **20** (1951), 139–154, and in *Mitteilungen des Mathematischen Seminars der Universität Giessen,* no. 40 (1951), which also contains the bibliographical supplement that appeared in his earlier article.

Also see H. Boerner's article in *Neue deutsche Biographie,* IV (1959), 501–502.

H. BOERNER

ENGEL, JOHANN. *See* **Angelus, Johannes.**

ENGELMANN, THEODOR WILHELM (*b.* Leipzig, Germany, 14 November 1843; *d.* Berlin, Germany, 20 May 1909), *physiology.*

Engelmann was the son of the well-known bibliographer and publisher Wilhelm Engelmann and his wife, Christiane Therese Hasse, daughter of the Leipzig historian Friedrich Christian August Hasse. He was very musical and graduated from the Thomas Schule in Leipzig. In the winter semester of 1861–1862 he began his studies in the natural sciences and medicine at Jena, where he was introduced to comparative anatomy by Gegenbaur, to physiology by

his brother-in-law, Adalbert von Bezold, and to botany by Schleiden. He continued his studies at Heidelberg and Göttingen, but it was at Leipzig that he finished his studies and in 1867 took his doctorate under the ophthalmologist Theodor Ruete, with a dissertation on the cornea.

At the beginning of 1867 Engelmann went to Utrecht, at Ruete's recommendation, as assistant to the physiologist and ophthalmologist Franz Cornelis Donders. In 1869 he married Donders' daughter, Marie. Following her early death he married Emma Vick, a well-known pianist whose professional name was Emma Brandes. Engelmann became associate professor of general biology and histology at Utrecht in 1871. In 1888 he was Donders' successor in the chair of physiology, having declined offers of appointment from Freiburg im Breisgau, Zurich, and Jena, primarily because he suffered greatly from migraine headaches. In 1877 he was rector at Utrecht. Oxford conferred an honorary doctorate on him in 1894.

In the winter semester of 1897 Engelmann became professor of physiology at Berlin, succeeding Emil du Bois-Reymond. He not unhesitatingly exchanged his contemplative existence at Utrecht for the activity of the cosmopolitan city of Berlin. Senile diabetes and failing strength forced him to retire on 14 October 1908. He died the following year from progressive arteriosclerosis.

Engelmann became scientifically oriented at an extremely early age. He was a passionate botanist and microscopist while still a schoolboy. Before his dissertation (1867) he had already published eight papers in zoology and biology, especially on Infusoria, the connection between the nerves and the muscle fibers, and the excitability of nerves and muscles under the influence of induction currents. The microscope was also his most important research tool in Utrecht. Engelmann was one of the founders of the cell physiology that was widespread in the second half of the nineteenth century. In Utrecht (1869) he investigated the flagellating movements of protozoa in great detail and described the *Flimmermühle* and the *Flimmeruhr,* physiological devices for measuring oscillatory motion.

At the same time Engelmann began his studies on the transmission of stimuli in the muscles of the ureter and on the physiology of peristalsis. He was an energetic advocate of myogenic formation and conduction of stimuli (1869). He claimed the same thing for the heart and proved his claim with the famous "zig-zag experiment," in which the heart of a frog was dissected spirally. In spite of its nerves being cut, the strip remained capable of forming and conducting stimuli (1875). Engelmann perfected the method of lever suspension with the frog heart and analyzed the laws of extrasystoles, the refractory phase, and the compensatory pause (1892–1895). He was the first to prove the lack of current in the intact and resting heart (1878) in opposition to du Bois-Reymond's theory of the preexistence of the electrical charge in the intact and resting muscle fiber. Earlier he had determined the velocity of the conduction of stimuli in cardiac muscle (1875). He formulated the law of conservation of the physiological stimulus period (1895). Engelmann was the first to distinguish the four types of activity of the heart nerves: inotropic, bathmotropic, chronotropic, and dromotropic (1896). This was the final prerequisite for an improved understanding of cardiac function in general and of the excitatory processes in particular.

Engelmann's second main area of work was the physiology of muscle contraction, in which he made much use of the microscope. He described the diminution of double refraction in the contracted muscle fiber in polarized light (1873) and believed the cause of contraction to be a shifting of fluid from the isotropic to the anisotropic substance, suspecting swelling processes to be the cause. He constructed an artificial model of the muscle fiber (a birefringent violin string) in order to elucidate the contraction process, and believed that he was able to demonstrate that heat was directly transformed into mechanical work in the course of contraction (1893). A lively conflict of scientific opinion arose from this, a battle he finally lost.

A remarkable investigation with Genderen furnished the microscopic proof that the retinal cones of the frog shift in the course of the change from light to darkness (1884) and that such movements are binocular even if only one of the two eyes is illuminated. Finally, Engelmann analyzed the sensitivity of protozoa to light and color and chemotaxis in bacteria. He had a difference of opinion with Ranvier concerning the structure of the axis cylinder of peripheral nerves, since Engelmann (1880) had incorrectly believed that the nodes of Ranvier represented a discontinuity of the axis cylinder.

Engelmann's interests were directed very early to microscopy and cellular physiology. At first, therefore, his subjects were more biological than physiological. Only with cardiac physiology did he enter the central area of experimental animal physiology. Engelmann never expressed himself on questions of theoretical biology or natural philosophy.

He lived a simple, modest, and retiring life. He loved music and musicians. His house in Utrecht and later in Berlin was frequently a meeting place for well-known musicians. He was an avid cellist and a close friend of Johannes Brahms, who dedicated the Quartet in B Major op. 67 to him. His correspondence with Brahms was published in 1918.

BIBLIOGRAPHY

I. ORIGINAL WORKS. His publications usually appeared both in Dutch, in the archives in the Netherlands, and in German, particularly in *Pflügers Archiv für die gesamte Physiologie* and later in *Archiv für Anatomie und Physiologie,* of which he was editor from 1900 to 1909. Of his 245 publications (see the bibliography in Kingreen) only the most important can be listed here.

Engelmann's books and surveys include *Zur Naturgeschichte der Infusionsthiere* (Leipzig, 1862); *Über die Hornhaut des Auges* (Leipzig, 1867), his inaugural dissertation; *Über die Flimmerbewegung* (Leipzig, 1868); "Physiologie des Protoplasma und der Flimmerbewegung," in *Hermanns Handbuch der Physiologie,* I (Leipzig, 1879), 343–408; *Über den Ursprung der Muskelkraft* (Leipzig, 1892); *Tafeln und Tabellen zur Darstellung der Ergebnisse spektroskopischer Beobachtungen* (Leipzig, 1897); and *Das Herz und seine Thätigkeit im Lichte neuerer Forschung* (Leipzig, 1904).

His journal articles include the following, all in *Pflügers Archiv für die gesamte Physiologie:* "Zur Physiologie der Ureter," **2** (1869), 243–293; "Die Hautdrüsen des Frosches," **6** (1872), 97–157; "Mikroskopische Untersuchungen über die quergestreifte Muskelsubstanz," **7** (1872), 33–71, 155–188; "Contractilität und Doppelbrechung," **11** (1875), 432–464; "Über die Leitung der Erregung im Herzmuskel," *ibid.,* 465–480; "Flimmeruhr und Flimmermühle. Zwei Apparate zum Registrieren der Flimmerbewegung," **15** (1877), 493–510; "Über das elektrische Verhalten des thätigen Herzens," **17** (1878), 68–99; "Über die Discontinuität des Axenzylinders und den fibrillären Bau der Nervenfasern," **22** (1880), 1–30; "Zur Anatomie und Physiologie der Flimmerzellen," **23** (1880), 505–535; "Neue Methode zur Untersuchung der Sauerstoffausscheidung pflanzlicher und thierischer Organismen," **25** (1881), 285–292; "Über Licht- und Farbenperception niederster Organismen," **29** (1882), 387–400; "Über Bewegungen der Zapfen und Pigmentzellen der Netzhaut unter dem Einfluss des Lichts und des Nervensystems," **35** (1885), 498–508; "Beobachtungen und Versuche am suspendirten Herzen. I," **52** (1892), 357–393 (Suspensionsmethode); II, **56** (1894), 149–202 (Erregungsleitung); III, **59** (1895), 309–349 (Physiol. Reizperiode); and "Über den Ursprung der Herzbewegung . . .," **65** (1897), 109–214.

Also see "Über die Wirkungen der Nerven auf das Herz," in *Archiv für Anatomie und Physiologie* (1900), pp. 315–361; "Über die bathmotropen Wirkungen der Herznerven," *ibid.* (1902), supp. 1–26; and "Über den causalen Zusammenhang zwischen Kontraktilität und Doppelbrechung (und ein neues Muskelmodell)," in *Sitzungsberichte der Preussischen Akademie der Wissenschaften zu Berlin* (1906).

II. Secondary Literature. Obituaries include *Deutsche medizinische Wochenschrift,* **35** (1909), 1110; R. du Bois-Reymond, in *Berliner klinische Wochenschrift,* **46** (1909), 1097–1099; *Nederlands Tijdschrift voor Geneeskunde,* **22** (1909), 1786–1790; H. Piper, in *Münchener medizinische Wochenschrift,* **56** (1909), 1797–1800; M. Rubner, in *Verhandlungen der Physiologischen Gesellschaft zu Berlin,* **34** (1910), 84–90; and M. Verworn, in *Zeitschrift für allgemeine Physiologie,* **10** (1910), i–vi.

Details of his life and assessments of his work may be found in *Biographisches Lexikon der hervorragendsten Arzte . . .,* I (Vienna–Berlin, 1932), 367; H. Kingreen, "Theodor Wilhelm Engelmann (Biobibliographie)," unpub., inaugural diss. (Münster, 1969); K. E. Rothschuh, *Geschichte der Physiologie* (Berlin–Göttingen–Heidelberg, 1953), pp. 213–214; and M. Stürzbecher, "Beitrag zur Biographie von Th. W. Engelmann," in *Berliner medizinische Wochenschrift,* **27** (1958), 470–474; and the article on Engelmann in *Neue deutsche Biographie,* IV (Berlin, 1959), 517–518.

K. E. Rothschuh

ENGELS, FRIEDRICH (*b.* Barmen, Germany, 28 September 1820; *d.* London, England, 5 August 1895), *philosophy.*

For a detailed study of his life and work, see Supplement.

ENRIQUES, FEDERIGO (*b.* Leghorn, Italy, 5 January 1871; *d.* Rome, Italy, 14 June 1946), *mathematics, philosophy and history of mathematics and science.*

Enriques, the son of S. Giacomo and Matilda Enriques, was educated in Pisa, where the family moved during his childhood. He attended the university and the Scuola Normale with a brilliant record in mathematics and took his degree in 1891. After a year of graduate study in Pisa, a second one in Rome, and some further work in Turin with Corrado Segre, Enriques undertook the teaching of projective and descriptive geometry at the University of Bologna, where in 1896 he was elevated to a professorship in those subjects. He remained there until 1923. He was honored by the University of St. Andrews with an honorary doctorate.

Guido Castelnuovo speaks of the happy years spent at Bologna as being perhaps the most fruitful of Enriques' entire life. His intense interest in all fields of knowledge was nurtured by close contact with professors from all the faculties, and in the period 1907–1913 he served as president of the Italian Philosophical Society. In this capacity he organized the Fourth International Congress of Philosophy, held at Bologna in 1911.

In 1923 Enriques accepted the offer of the chair of higher geometry at the University of Rome. While there he founded the National Institute for the History of Science and a school dedicated to that discipline. Since his way of life and his philosophy made it impossible for him to cooperate with the dictates of a fascist regime, Enriques retired from teaching during the years 1938–1944.

As a young man Enriques studied under Betti, Dini, Bianchi, and Volterra and was influenced in his views on algebraic geometry by Segre. In 1892 he turned to Castelnuovo in Rome for advice on the direction of his work, and their many consultations led to Enriques' specialization in the theory of algebraic surfaces and to their collaboration in the field. The Turin Academy of Sciences published Enriques' first paper on the subject in June 1893.

A short summary of Enriques' contributions to this field—relating them to those of Castelnuovo, Picard, Severi, Humbert, and Baker—may be found in F. Cajori's *A History of Mathematics.*[1] Greater detail is given in each of two other accounts, both by Castelnuovo and Enriques in collaboration. The first, entitled "Sur quelques résultats nouveaux dans la théorie des surfaces algébriques,"[2] summarizes the Italian contribution up to 1906. The second, an earlier paper, carries the title "Sur quelques récents résultats dans la théorie des surfaces algébriques."[3] H. F. Baker's presidential address to the International Congress in Cambridge (12 December 1912), published as "On Some Recent Advances in the Theory of Algebraic Surfaces,"[4] also serves to highlight the contributions in that field and in so doing details Enriques' major contributions.

Enriques also contributed to the differential geometry of hyperspace. In 1907 he and Severi received the Bordin Award of the Paris Academy of Sciences for their work on hyperelliptical surfaces. The French honored him again in 1937 by making him a corresponding member of the Académie des Sciences Morales et Politiques.

As early as 1898 Enriques' interest in foundations of mathematics was reflected in his use of a system of axioms in his textbook writings. Having written, at Felix Klein's request, the article on the foundations of geometry ("Principien der Geometrie") for the *Encyklopädie der mathematischen Wissenschaften* (III, 1–129), he became instrumental in the writing of textbooks for both elementary and high schools that greatly influenced teaching in Italy. He was responsible for the publication, in Italian, of Euclid's *Elements* with historical notes and commentary, and he encouraged the publication of historical and didactic articles in *Periodico di matematiche,* which he headed for twenty years. His interest in teaching and in teachers is well reflected in his service as president of the National Association of University Professors.

By 1895 Enriques had concluded that besides the logical criteria of independence and compatibility, a psychological criterion involving the sensations and experiences that lead to the formulation of the postulates must be considered. In an 1898 paper he set up conditions justifying the introduction of coordinates on surfaces, thus supplementing Riemann's a priori approach in the assumption of such an existence. His interest in physiological psychology led to his writing studies for the *Rivista filosofica* that were later expanded into his *Problemi della scienza* (1906). Castelnuovo describes Enriques' thesis as being that topology and metrical and projective geometry are linked, respectively, to three different orders of sensations: to the general tactile-muscular, to those of the special sense of touch, and to those of vision. In the second part of the *Problemi,* a critical examination is made of the principles of mathematical, physical, and biological sciences. In the treatment of the principles of mechanics Enriques anticipated some of the foundations of Einstein's theory of relativity. His views on structure are given in *Causalité et déterminisme* (1940), and his philosophical thought is found in *Scienza e razionalismo* (1912). A causal explanation involves a "why" as well as a "how" and links effect to cause. Theory should be "plausible in itself" and "satisfy the principle of sufficient reason which is the mental aspect of causality." Determinism thus becomes a premise of scientific research. Enriques' philosophical and historical beliefs pervade *Per la storia della logica* (1922).

In the introductory note to the English translation of *Problemi della scienza* (1914), Josiah Royce writes of the pragmatistic element in Enriques' thought that brings to the thinking process an adjustment to situations; of his stress on the unifying aspect of scientific theory, the association of concepts and of scientific representation. Enriques' philosophical stance differs from that of the Comtean school. He disagrees with Mach and Pearson in their limitation of science to a simple description of physical phenomena, yet writes: "In the formation of concepts, we shall see not only an economy of thought in accordance with the views of Mach, but also a somewhat determinate mental process. . . ." He maintains a positivistic position toward the transcendental and the absolute in his emphasis on the tentative and relative character of scientific theory; yet his theory progresses toward a comprehension of the essential core concealed in every question. Enriques maintained that "It is plainly seen that scientific questions include something essential, apart from the special way in which they are conceived in a particular epoch by the scholars who study such problems."

NOTES

1. (New York, 1961), p. 316.
2. Émile Picard and George Simart, *Théorie des fonctions algébriques de deux variables indépendentes,* II (Paris, 1906), 485–522.
3. *Mathematische Annalen,* **48** (1897), 241–316.
4. *Proceedings of the London Mathematical Society,* **12** (1913), 1–40.

BIBLIOGRAPHY

I. Original Works. *Federigo Enriques: Memorie scelte di geometria,* 3 vols. (Bologna, 1956–1966), is a collection of 74 papers written between 1893 and 1940 and contains a bibliography of his works. Among his writings are *Lezioni di geometria descrittiva,* J. Schimaglia, ed. (Bologna, 1893–1894; 2nd ed., 1894–1895); republished in a new ed., U. Concina, ed. (Bologna, 1902; 2nd ed., 1908); *Lezioni di geometria proiettiva,* C. Pedretti, ed. (Bologna, 1893–1894; 2nd ed., G. Serrazanetti, ed., 1894–1895); republished in a new ed. (Bologna, 1898; 4th ed., 1920); *Conferenze di geometria: Fondamenti di una geometria iperspaziale* (Bologna, 1894–1895); *Elementi di geometria ad uso delle scuole normali* (Bologna, 1903), written with U. Amaldi; *Elementi di geometria ad uso delle scuole secondarie superiori* (Bologna, 1903), written with U. Amaldi; *Problemi della scienza* (Bologna, 1906; 2nd ed., 1908; repr. 1926), trans. into English by K. Royce with introductory note by J. Royce (Chicago, 1914); *Elementi di geometria ad uso delle scuole tecniche* (Bologna, 1909), written with U. Amaldi; *Nozioni di geometria ad uso delle scuole complementari* (Bologna, 1910), written with U. Amaldi; *Nozioni di geometria ad uso dei ginnasi inferiori* (Bologna, 1910), written with U. Amaldi; *Scienza e razionalismo* (Bologna, 1912); *Nozioni di matematica ad uso dei licei moderni,* 2 vols. (Bologna, 1914–1915); *Lezioni sulla teoria geometrica delle equazioni e delle funzioni algebriche,* 4 vols. (Bologna, 1915–1934; new ed. of vol. I, 1929), written with O. Chisini; *Conferenze sulla geometria non-euclidea,* O. Fernandez, ed. (Bologna, 1918); *Per la storia della logica. I principii e l'ordine della scienza nel concetto dei pensatori matematici* (Bologna, 1922), trans. into English by J. Rosenthal (New York, 1929); *Algebra elementare,* 2 vols. (Bologna, 1931–1932), written with U. Amaldi; *Nozioni di geometria ad uso delle scuole di avviamento al lavoro* (Bologna, 1931), written with U. Amaldi; *Nozioni intuitive di geometria ad uso degli istituti magistrali inferiori* (Bologna, 1931), written with U. Amaldi; *Lezioni sulla teoria delle superficie algebriche,* pt. 1 (Padua, 1932), written with L. Campedelli; pt. 2 was published in *Rendiconti del seminario matematico della reale università di Roma* (1934) as "Sulla classificazione delle superficie algebriche particolarmente di genere zero"; both parts were reorganized by G. Castelnuovo and published as *Le superficie algebriche* (Bologna, 1949).

See also *Storia del pensiero scientifico,* I, *Il mondo antico* (Bologna, 1932), written with G. de Santillana; *Nozioni di geometria ad uso delle scuole di avviamento professionale* (Bologna, 1934), written with U. Amaldi; *Il significato della storia del pensiero scientifico* (Bologna, 1936); *Compendio di storia del pensiero scientifico dall'antichità fino ai tempi moderni* (Bologna, 1937), written with G. de Santillana; *Le matematiche nella storia e nella cultura,* A. Frajese, ed. (Bologna, 1938); *La théorie de la connaissance scientifique de Kant à nos jours,* Actualités Scientifiques et Industrielles no. 638 (Paris, 1938); *Le superficie razionali* (Bologna, 1939), written with F. Conforto; *Causalité et déterminisme dans la philosophie et l'histoire des sciences,* Actualités Scientifiques et Industrielles no. 899 (Paris, 1940); *Elementi di trigonometria piana ad uso dei licei* (Bologna, 1947), written with U. Amaldi; *Le dottrine di Democrito d'Abdera, testi e commenti* (Bologna, 1948), written with M. Mazziotti; and *Natura, ragione e storia,* L. Lombardo Radice, ed. (Turin, 1958), a collection of his philosophical writings with a bibliography.

See also *Questioni riguardanti la geometria elementare* (Bologna, 1900), which Enriques collected and arranged; *Questioni riguardanti le matematiche elementari:* I, *Critica dei principii* (Bologna, 1912); II, *Problemi classici della geometria. Numeri primi e analisi indeterminata. Massimi e minimi* (Bologna, 1914); pt. 2, *I problemi classici della geometria e le equazioni algebriche,* 3rd ed. (Bologna, 1926); pt. 3, *Numeri primi e analisi indeterminata. Massimi e minimi,* 3rd ed. (Bologna, 1927), all collected and arranged by Enriques; and *Gli Elementi d'Euclide e la critica antica e moderna,* ed. by Enriques and many others: bks. I–IV (Rome–Bologna, 1925); bks. V–IX (Bologna, 1930); bk. X (Bologna, 1932); bks. XI–XIII (Bologna, 1935).

II. SECONDARY LITERATURE. On Enriques or his work, see H. F. Baker, "On Some Recent Advances in the Theory of Algebraic Surfaces," in *Proceedings of the London Mathematical Society,* 2nd ser., **12** (1913), 1–40; F. Baron, "Enriques, Federigo," in *Enciclopedia filosofica* (Venice–Rome, 1957), cols. 1916–1917; Guido Castelnuovo, "Commemorazione di Federigo Enriques," in *Federigo Enriques: Memorie scelte di geometria,* pp. x–xxii; Poggendorff, IV, 388–389; *Proceedings of the Fifth International Congress of Mathematicians* (Cambridge, 1912), I, 40; II, 22; Ferruccio Rossi-Landi, "Enriques, Federigo," in *Encyclopedia of Philosophy* (New York, 1967), III, 525–526; Ferruccio Rossi-Landi and Vittorio Somenzi, "La filosofia della scienza in Italia," in *La filosofia contemporanea in Italia* (Rome, 1958), pp. 407–432; and Antonio Santucci, *Il pragmatismo in Italia* (Bologna, 1963), pp. 302–322.

CAROLYN EISELE

ENSKOG, DAVID (*b.* Västra Ämtervik, Värmland, Sweden, 22 April 1884; *d.* Stockholm, Sweden, 1 June 1947), *physics.*

Enskog's father, Nils Olsson, was a preacher; his mother was Karolina Jonasdotter. He was educated at the Karlstads Läroverk (high school) and at Uppsala University, where he received the Ph.D. in 1917. After teaching in secondary schools and colleges for several years, he was appointed professor in mathematics and mechanics at the Royal Institute of Technology, Stockholm, in 1930. In 1913 he married Anna Aurora Jönsson.

Enskog is best-known for his development of a method for solving the Maxwell-Boltzmann transport equations in the kinetic theory of gases. These equations, describing the effect of molecular collisions and external variables (such as temperature gradients) on the flow of molecules, momentum, and energy in a gas, had originally been formulated by James Clerk Maxwell in 1867. The solution of the equations, however, depends in general on a determination of the velocity distribution function in a nonequilibrium gas. Maxwell was unable to determine this function. However, he did show that for a special molecular model—point centers of force with repulsive forces varying inversely as the fifth power of the distance between the molecules—the transport coefficients such as viscosity and thermal conductivity can be calculated even if the velocity distribution function is unknown. In 1872 Ludwig Boltzmann reformulated Maxwell's equations as a single integrodifferential equation for the velocity distribution function, but he was not able to find an exact solution except for the same special model that Maxwell had introduced.

Little progress was made toward solving the Maxwell-Boltzmann equations until 1911, when Enskog in Sweden and Sydney Chapman in England began their researches. In that year, Enskog obtained his philosophy licentiate (equivalent to the M.A.), partly for experimental work on gas diffusion, and also published two papers on a generalization of the Maxwell-Boltzmann kinetic theory. In the second of these papers he noted briefly the existence of a term proportional to the temperature gradient in the theoretical formula for the rate of diffusion in a mixture of two gases. Although it was not followed up at the time, this was later recognized as the first theoretical prediction of the important phenomenon known as thermal diffusion, established experimentally by Chapman and F. W. Dootson in 1917.

The calculations of Enskog and of Chapman, published in 1911–1912, while representing an advance over earlier work, were not yet satisfactory, since they depended on arbitrary assumptions about the nonequilibrium velocity distribution function. In 1912, David Hilbert published a short paper on the Maxwell-Boltzmann equation, in which he applied methods developed earlier in his general theory of integral equations. Enskog immediately saw the value of Hilbert's approach and used it with some modifications to work out a systematic series expansion of the velocity distribution function. The results were presented in his 1917 dissertation at Uppsala, shortly after Chapman published his own calculations based on an equivalent method. Chapman was one of the first scientists to recognize the value of Enskog's work, and in the monograph on *The Mathematical Theory of Non-Uniform Gases,* now the standard work on the subject, he used Enskog's procedure for solving the Maxwell-Boltzmann equations in preference to his own. It was also partly on Chapman's recommendation that Enskog obtained his chair at Stockholm in 1930, although according to Chapman, "His transfer to a university chair seemed rather to bring him new duties than increased leisure, and this, with renewed ill-health, reduced his productivity in later years."

With their new methods Chapman and Enskog were able to calculate accurately a number of the transport properties of gases, such as the coefficients of viscosity, thermal conduction, and diffusion, without having to rely on the mean-free-path approximation introduced by Clausius in 1858 and used by Maxwell in his early work. (Although Maxwell himself abandoned the mean-free-path method, it continued to be used by other scientists and is still discussed in most modern textbooks.) Whereas earlier kinetic theories had been limited to the use of very special molecular models, such as elastic spheres or the Maxwellian inverse fifth-power repulsive force, the Chapman-Enskog theory now made it possible to do calculations with a much larger class of models, including both attractive and repulsive forces varying with any power of the distance.

The Chapman-Enskog theory would have been quickly taken up and exploited by many other scientists during the 1920's if that had not been the time when quantum theory was being vigorously developed. It did not become clear until the 1930's that the classical kinetic theory of gases is still valid over a large range of temperatures and densities, even though the nature of the intermolecular force law is determined by quantum-mechanical considerations. Thus the main impact of the work of Enskog and Chapman before 1920 was not apparent until after 1945, when it provided the basis for a revival of activity in kinetic theory, including applications to phenomena such as sound propagation, shock waves, aerodynamics, the behavior of electrons in metals, and the diffusion of neutrons in nuclear reactors.

One other contribution by Enskog played an important role in the postwar development of kinetic theory. In 1922, he proposed a generalization of the Maxwell-Boltzmann equations to higher densities, taking account of the effect of finite diameter of the molecules. He assumed that the frequency of collisions would be changed by an amount that could be related to the equation of state (equilibrium pressure-volume-temperature relation), since that also depends on collision rate. In this way he obtained formulas for the transport coefficients in which the variation with density can be determined empirically if the equation of state is known from experimental measurements, or theoretically for simple models if the equation of state itself can be calculated theoretically. Until 1965 the Enskog theory of dense gases remained the only accepted theory that had been sufficiently worked out to permit experimental verification, although many more elaborate theories had been attempted. It is only in the last few years, as a result of the work of J. Weinstock, J. R. Dorfman, E. G. D. Cohen, R. Goldman, E. A. Frieman, and J. V. Sengers, that the kinetic theory of dense gases has definitely progressed beyond the point reached by Enskog from a fundamental basis; and according to the most recent calculations of Sengers, the numerical results for the transport coefficients computed from Enskog's theory are probably accurate to within 5 percent as compared with the exact theory.

BIBLIOGRAPHY

I. ORIGINAL WORKS. Enskog's major works on kinetic theory include *Kinetische Theorie der Vorgänge in mässig verdünnten Gasen* (Uppsala, 1917) and "Kinetische Theorie der Wärmeleitung, Reibung und Selbstdiffusion in gewissen verdichteten Gasen und Flüssigkeiten," in *Kungliga Svenska vetenskapsakademiens handlingar,* n.s. **63,** no. 4 (1922). Translations of these works and references to others will be found in the book by S. G. Brush cited below.

II. SECONDARY LITERATURE. On Enskog's kinetic theory of gases, see Sydney Chapman and T. G. Cowling, *The Mathematical Theory of Non-Uniform Gases* (Cambridge, 1939; 2nd ed., 1952). On the history of kinetic theory, see S. G. Brush, *Kinetic Theory,* 3 vols. (Oxford, 1965–); vol. III (in press) includes translations of the two major works of Enskog listed above and a discussion of more recent work.

For further biographical details, see Hilding Faxén, *Svenskt biografiskt lexikon,* XIII (Stockholm, 1950), 765–767.

STEPHEN G. BRUSH

ENT, GEORGE (*b.* Sandwich, Kent, England, 6 November 1604; *d.* London, England, 13 October 1689), *medicine.*

Ent was the son of Josias Ent, a merchant from

the Low Countries. His early education was at Rotterdam; he then studied at Sidney Sussex College, Cambridge, from 1624 to 1631, obtaining his M.A. in 1631. Shortly afterward he probably settled in Padua as a student of medicine. He obtained the M.D. there in 1636, the event being celebrated by a volume of poems, *Laureae Apollinari* (Padua, 1636), contributed by his friends—including P. M. Slegel, J. Rhode, and J. Greaves, all of whom became friends and defenders of Harvey.

The rest of Ent's life was spent in London as a successful and moderate medical practitioner. He rapidly reached a position of esteem among his professional and scientific colleagues. Although he probably had royalist sympathies he was not subject to recriminations during the Cromwellian period. During these years he came into prominence at the College of Physicians, in which he was elected to the most important executive positions, serving as president for seven years between 1670 and 1684. He was married to Sarah Meverall, daughter of the treasurer of the college. The Royal Society provided an outlet for his wider scientific interests; he was a founder fellow and member of its council, although playing a relatively small part in its scientific affairs. Ent was one of the last to give the annual anatomy lectures at the College of Physicians. At these lectures in 1665 he was granted a knighthood by Charles II.

Ent owed much of his scientific reputation to his friendship with William Harvey, which dated from their chance meeting in Rome in 1636. In reaction to the mounting published criticism of *De motu cordis*, Ent became one of the first writers to compose a detailed defense of Harvey, *Apologia pro circulatione sanguinis* (1641). This counteracted the criticisms of Emilius Parisianus; Ent quoted primarily from Harvey but also displayed a wide familiarity with ancient and modern authorities. In a series of digressions he showed a distinctive approach, being more receptive to hermetic authors than Harvey. This is particularly obvious in the sections on innate heat and respiration, which point toward the theories of John Mayow and suggest that nitrous particles from the air are absorbed by the lungs or gills, to support the physiological flame burning in the heart—the source of innate heat. Ent further proposed a less fortunate, but popular, theory whereby a highly nutritive fluid is dispensed through the nerves. Accordingly, the nervous role is reduced; Ent emphasized the role of tissue irritability and natural movement. His ideas on irritability are particularly prominent in his unpublished anatomy lecture notes.

Ent's association with Harvey continued. In about 1648 he persuaded the elderly Harvey to release the manuscript of *De generatione,* which Ent edited and published with a commendatory preface in 1651. His transcript of Harvey's correspondence was used in the College of Physicians edition of Harvey's works in 1766. Harvey's gratitude was indicated in the terms of his will, in which Ent was charged with dispersing his library, that is, selling worthless books and buying better ones to be deposited, with the rest of the library, in the College of Physicians. Ent was also given five pounds to purchase a ring in remembrance of Harvey.

Ent's other writings are less important. His proficient studies of the anatomy of *Lophius, Galeus,* and *Rana,* entitled "Mantissa anatomica," were published in one of Charleton's lesser works. This appears to have been the meager outcome of an elaborate mutual comparative anatomy project, conceived in the 1650's. Finally, Ent published a critique of Malachi Thruston's ideas on respiration, which showed little advance on the *Apologia* and lacked the empirical foundation of Mayow's writings on the same theme.

BIBLIOGRAPHY

I. ORIGINAL WORKS. Ent's writings are *Apologia pro circulatione sanguinis: Qua respondetur Aemilio Parisano* (London, 1641; 2nd ed., with some additions, 1685); *ANTIΔIATPIBH. Sive animadversiones in Malachiae Thrustoni, M.D. Diatribam de respirationis usu primario* (London, 1679, 1685); and *Opera omnia medico-physica* (Leiden, 1687), which contains essays on tides. See also "Mantissa anatomica," in Walter Charleton, *Onomasticon zoicum,* 2nd ed. (Oxford, 1677). Ent's anatomy lectures are in Bodleian Library, Ashmolean MS 1476, and Royal College of Physicians, London, MS 110.

II. SECONDARY LITERATURE. On Ent's life and work, see Sir George Clark, *History of the Royal College of Physicians,* vol. I (London, 1964); Sir Geoffrey Keynes, *The Life of William Harvey* (Oxford, 1966); William Munk, *Roll of the Royal College of Physicians,* I (London, 1878), 223–227; J. R. Partington, *History of Chemistry,* II (London, 1962), 564, 573–574; J. and J. A. Venn, *Alumni cantabrigenses,* II (Cambridge, 1924), 104; and C. Webster, "The College of Physicians 'Solomon's House' in Commonwealth England," in *Bulletin of the History of Medicine,* **41** (1967), 393–412.

CHARLES WEBSTER

EÖTVÖS, ROLAND, BARON VON (*b.* Budapest, Hungary, 27 July 1848; *d.* Budapest, 8 April 1919), *physics.*

Most of the world literature lists Eötvös (pronounced ut' vûsh) in the fashion given in the heading, which is the German version of the Hungarian name. The reason for this is that he published most of his major papers in both Hungarian and German. Roland is a translation of the Hungarian name Loránd, and his full name in Hungarian is Vásárosnaményi Báro Eötvös Loránd. The correct full name in English translation is Roland, Baron Eötvös of Vásárosnamény.

Eötvös was the scion of an aristocratic and intellectual family. His father, Joseph, Baron Eötvös of Vásárosnamény, at the time of Roland's birth held the portfolio of public instruction and religious affairs in the first, short-lived, responsible Hungarian cabinet; his mother was the former Agnes Rosty. The family had a long background of public service (the barony was conferred on his great-grandfather in the eighteenth century), but its intellectual tendencies came to full bloom only in his father, who became Hungary's foremost writer and political philosopher of the nineteenth century. Young Roland thus grew up in an environment leading more or less toward a study of law and government (his family, by hereditary right, belonged to the upper house of parliament). He entered the University of Budapest in 1865 as a law student but, already interested in the mathematical and physical sciences, took private lessons in mathematics from Otto Petzval.

At his father's request Joseph Krenner, the future professor of mineralogy at the university, introduced Eötvös to the study of physical sciences; at the same time he worked in the chemistry laboratory of Charles Than.

In 1867 Eötvös definitely abandoned the study of law and entered the University of Heidelberg. His studies included mathematics, physics, and chemistry, taught there by such outstanding teachers as Kirchhoff, Helmholtz, and Bunsen. After three semesters he went to the University of Königsberg but found the lectures of the theoretical physicist Franz Neumann and of the mathematician Friedrich Richelot less to his taste. For a while Eötvös toyed with the idea of joining the arctic expedition headed by August Petermann; but he finally decided, on his father's advice, to return to Heidelberg, where he obtained his doctorate *summa cum laude* in the summer of 1870. Apparently the subject of his doctoral thesis was identical with the subjects of three papers published by him in 1871, 1874, and 1875; they dealt with a problem formulated by Fizeau. The question was raised whether the relative motion of a light source, with respect to an immobile ether, can be detected by measuring the light intensities in both the same and the opposite directions of the motion. Eötvös generalized the calculations for both the emitter and the detector being in motion and extended it to astronomical observations. This purely theoretical

work became, decades later, the object of many important papers, leading ultimately to the theory of relativity.

His professors profoundly influenced Eötvös's working habits. Kirchhoff taught him the importance of accuracy in measurements. Helmholtz liked to spend as much time as possible with his students and showed Eötvös the value of individual discussion. His knowledge of theoretical physics, and in particular of potential theory, came from Franz Neumann.

At the end of his studies in 1870, Eötvös returned to Hungary and in 1871 became *Privatdozent* at the University of Budapest. In 1872 he was promoted to full professor at the same university. At first he taught theoretical physics; in 1874 he added experimental physics to his duties; and in 1878, at the retirement of Ányos Jedlik, professor of experimental physics, he took over that chair.

In 1876 Eötvös married Gizella Horváth, the daughter of the minister of justice, Boldizsár Horváth. They had two daughters, Ilona and Rolanda.

A few years earlier, while he was still a student at the University of Königsberg, Eötvös designed a simple optical method for determining the constant of capillarity (surface tension). He presented the subject at a physics colloquium, and Franz Neumann found the idea quite praiseworthy. Capillarity thus became the first research subject he attacked and led him to his first important discovery. He showed that the temperature coefficient of the molecular surface energy of a liquid—expressible as $\frac{d}{dT}[\gamma(Mv)^{2/3}]$, where M is the molecular weight, v is the specific volume of the liquid, and γ is the capillarity constant or surface tension—is independent of the nature of simple unassociated liquids. The integral form of the law of Eötvös is usually written as $\gamma v^{2/3} = k(T_0 - T)$, where k is a constant for all simple liquids ($k \approx 2.12$) and T_0 is (approximately) the critical temperature.

His investigations on capillarity were published in a few papers between 1876 and 1886. After 1886 there were no further communications by Eötvös on this subject, although the law of Eötvös attracted wide attention and during the next few decades a considerable number of papers appeared, examining and extending the concepts introduced by him.

After 1886 practically all of Eötvös's scientific papers concentrated on his lifework: gravitation. He was interested in this subject on and off before then, and there is some evidence of a gradually awakening interest in earlier papers and speeches. The exact year when his interest swung from phenomena involving van der Waals forces to the weakest known forces in the universe cannot be ascertained. A partial moti-

FIGURE 1

vation may have been a request by the Természet-tudományi Társulat (Hungarian Society for Natural Sciences) in 1881 for the determination of the gravitational acceleration in different parts of Hungary.

Eötvös's first short Hungarian-language publication on gravitational phenomena appeared in 1888. In January 1889 he presented a short paper to the Hungarian Academy of Sciences concerning his search for a difference in gravitational attraction exerted by the earth on different substances. This short paper, published in 1890, reported that within the accuracy achieved with his torsion balance, all substances investigated experienced the same force of attraction per unit of mass.

From the beginning of his gravitational researches Eötvös concentrated on the use of the instrument he called in a later paper the Coulomb balance, in recognition of the invention and use of torsion balance by Charles Coulomb. Actually, the torsion balance had been invented earlier (and independently) by Rev. John Michell, who had applied the principle upon which it is based as early as 1768 and, shortly before his death, completed construction of the particular torsion balance that in the hands of Henry Cavendish became an outstanding instrument for the determination of the attraction between two masses. The original Michell-Cavendish instrument places two masses at the ends of a horizontal bar suspended to allow a horizontal displacement of the masses around the torsion axis (see Figure 1). If the gravitational potential U is a function of the Cartesian coordinates x, y, z, it is possible to determine with that instrument the curvature of the gravitational field in a horizontal plane, i.e.,

$$\left(\frac{\partial^2 U}{\partial x \partial y}\right) \text{ and } \left(\frac{\partial^2 U}{\partial y^2} = \frac{\partial^2 U}{\partial x^2}\right).$$

For this reason Eötvös called this instrument the curvature variometer, to distinguish it from his horizontal variometer. The latter (see Figure 2) still supports two masses on a horizontally suspended bar, but the masses are offset both horizontally and vertically. By using the new geometry, $\left(\frac{\partial^2 U}{\partial x \partial z}\right)$ and $\left(\frac{\partial^2 U}{\partial y \partial z}\right)$ can be measured in addition to the two components measured by the earlier instrument. An added refinement was measurement of the oscillation period of the

torsion pendulum, instead of the static deviation of the suspended bar, thus gaining an added sensitivity for the instrument.

The achievements of Eötvös in the use of his instrument are threefold. By developing the complete theory of the Eötvös balance, he was able to push its sensitivity to such a point that it took decades to devise methods for exceeding his precision. It is only proper to mention that the high degree of precision he achieved was not due solely to the design of the instrument but depended also on the unparalleled skill he displayed in using it.

The other two accomplishments encompassed the clear recognition of the very important applications of the balance: geophysical exploration and the equivalence of gravitational and inertial mass. In both cases the recognition was followed by intense work proving his insight.

Prospecting by gravitational methods is the technique of measuring the gravitational field at the earth's surface and predicting, from the data obtained, the structure beneath the surface. In principle this information can be derived from direct measurements of gravity by means of a gravimeter, or from gradient measurements by means of the Eötvös balance. While the gravimeter can give faster results (the time required for a single observation is a small fraction of that required by the torsion balance) the signal-to-noise ratio was originally more favorable for the gradient measurement. As a consequence the Eötvös balance was, until good gravimeters were developed, the leading instrument for geophysical prospecting.

Between 1888 and 1922 Eötvös, together with his collaborators, published a number of papers on his investigations. These included the theory and design

FIGURE 2

of the instrument and the results of its widespread application in Hungary and abroad.

The second extremely important application of the Eötvös balance involved a redetermination of the rate of gravitational acceleration for different bodies. It had been known from earlier work that all bodies fall with the same acceleration (in a vacuum), but the best previous determinations yielded only a limited accuracy. In response to a prize announcement by the University of Göttingen, Eötvös and his collaborators followed up his early measurements on this subject. The new measurements provided not merely a more accurate proof of a principle believed right until then, but much more: his results, proving that gravitational mass and inertial mass are equivalent, the possible deviation being about five parts in 10^9, became one of the building stones of the theory of general relativity. The experiment proves the "weak" form of the principle of equivalence, which states that the trajectory of a test particle, under the influence of gravitational fields only, depends only on its initial position and velocity, not on its mass and nature. Later confirmation of his results (during the last fifty years) reduced the possible deviation from perfect equivalence by a factor of 1,000.

Late in life Eötvös became interested in the variation of the gravitational acceleration caused by the relative motion of a body with respect to the earth. The experimental proof of this effect was the subject of two posthumous papers.

Parallel to the geophysical application of the torsion balance, he pursued an investigation of the magnetic anomalies accompanying the gravitational effects. His interest in magnetism led him to paleomagnetic work on bricks and other ceramic objects that covered a period of about 2,000 years. Another side issue attracting his interest was the shape of the earth.

Eötvös's intensive research efforts did not prevent him from pursuing other interests. Shortly after his appointment as professor of physics, he became aware of the shortcomings of both high school and university instruction in Hungary, and from then on he devoted considerable effort to improving both. In 1881 the minister of instruction requested him to make a trip to Paris for the purpose of studying the French system of higher education. These efforts led to a short appointment (June 1894–January 1895) as minister of public instruction and religious affairs (the cabinet post held twice by his father). One of the highlights of this period was the founding of the Eötvös Collegium, patterned after the French École Normale Supérieure and named for his father. Its stated purpose was to improve the training of high school teachers. The effort was quite successful; the surprising increase in the number of outstanding Hungarian scientists during the twentieth century may be indirect proof of the effectiveness of the new school.

Eötvös served one year as rector of the University of Budapest. As professor of physics he devoted much care and time to the preparation of his lectures; he also invented many good demonstration experiments and insisted that his students understand the basic principles underlying them. He became a corresponding member of the Hungarian Academy of Sciences in 1873 and a full member ten years later; in 1889 he was elected its president. Although the usual term for the presidency was three years, he was reelected until his resignation in 1905. Many honors were bestowed upon him, including election to a number of foreign academies, as well as prizes and decorations.

In 1885 Eötvös and four friends founded the (Hungarian) Society for Mathematics. A little later physicists were attracted to the new society. In 1891 the Mathematical and Physical Society was founded, and Eötvös was elected its first president, a post he held until his death.

His main relaxation was mountain climbing. For quite a long time he was well-known as one of Europe's foremost climbers: a peak in the Dolomites is named for him, and the mountaineering handbooks record a number of "first climbs" he made either alone or with his daughters, who became his steady climbing companions.

BIBLIOGRAPHY

I. ORIGINAL WORKS. Eötvös's most important papers include "Über den Zusammenhang der Oberflächenspannung der Flüssigkeiten mit ihrem Molekularvolumen," in *Annalen der Physik und Chemie,* **27** (1886), 448–459; "Untersuchungen über Gravitation und Erdmagnetismus," *ibid.,* **59** (1896), 354–400; "Étude sur les surfaces de niveau et la variation de la pesanteur et de la force magnétique," in C.-E. Guillaume and L. Poincaré, eds., *Rapports présentés au Congrès international de physique réuni à Paris en 1900,* III (Paris, 1900), 371–393; "Programme des recherches gravimétriques dans les régions vésuviennes," in *Comptes rendus des séances de la première réunion de la commission permanente de l'Association internationale de sismologie réunie à Rome* (1906), pp. 177–179; "Bericht über Arbeiten mit der Drehwage ausgeführt im Auftrage der königlich ungarischen Regierung in den Jahren 1909–1911," in *Verhandlungen der XVII. allgemeinen Konferenz der internat. Erdmessung in Hamburg,* I (1912), 427–438; and "Beiträge zum Gesetze der Proportionalität von Trägheit und Gravität," in *Annalen der*

Physik, **68** (1922), 11–66, written with D. Pekár and J. Fekete.

Most of these, together with a few other papers, were republished by the Hungarian Academy of Sciences under the title *Roland Eötvös Gesammelte Arbeiten,* P. Selényi, ed. (Budapest, 1953). A complete bibliography, except for posthumous papers, is given (in Hungarian) in the special Eötvös issue of *Matematikai és physikai lapok,* **27** (1918), 284–290. A reproduction of the same bibliography, with the posthumous papers included, is to be found in Elek Környei, *Eötvös Loránd, A tudós és müvelödéspolitikus irásaiból* (Budapest, 1964).

II. Secondary Literature. The book by Környei listed above and the special issue of *Matematikai és physikai lapok* contain discussions (in Hungarian) of his life and theories. His contributions to physics are the subject of an excellent paper by R. H. Dicke, "The Eötvös Experiment," in *Scientific American,* **205** (Dec. 1961), 84–94, as well as R. H. Dicke, "Some Remarks on Equivalence Principles," in *Annales Universitatis scientiarum budapestinensis de Rolando Eötvös Nominatae,* Geological Section, **7** (1964). See also R. H. Dicke, "Remarks on the Observational Basis of General Relativity," in H. Y. Chiu and W. F. Hoffmann, eds., *Gravitation and Relativity* (New York, 1964), pp. 1–16; and P. G. Roll, R. Krotkov, and R. H. Dicke, "The Equivalence of Inertial and Passive Gravitational Mass," in *Annals of Physics,* **26** (1964), 442–517. The latter paper emphasizes also the importance of the Eötvös experiment for the theory of general relativity. An appreciation of the geophysical aspects is given by A. H. Miller, in "The Theory and Operation of the Eötvös Torsion Balance," in *Journal of the Royal Astronomical Society of Canada,* **28** (1934), 1–31, with the most important relevant papers by Eötvös and his collaborators listed in the bibliography (unfortunately with many misprints). Another useful source of information on the geophysical importance of the torsion balance can be found in Donald C. Barton, "Gravity Measurements With the Eötvös Torsion Balance, Physics of the Earth II., The Figure of the Earth," in *Bulletin of the National Research Council. Washington,* **78** (1931), 167–190.

L. Marton

EPICURUS (*b.* Samos, 341 b.c.; *d.* Athens, 270 b.c.), *moral and natural philosophy.*

Epicurus' father, Neocles, a schoolmaster, was an Athenian of the deme Gargettus who emigrated to the Athenian colony in Samos. At eighteen Epicurus was required to go to Athens to do his military service, after which he rejoined his family, who had by then moved to the Ionian mainland town of Colophon. When he was thirty-two he moved to Mytilene, on Lesbos, and then to Lampsacus on the Hellespont; in both places he set up a school. He returned to Athens about 307/306 b.c. and bought a house, with a garden that became the eponymous headquarters of his school of philosophy. His extant writings, apart from fragments of lost works, consist of *Letter to Herodotus,* which is a summary of his philosophy of nature; *Letter to Pythocles,* on celestial phenomena (possibly the work of a pupil); *Letter to Menoeceus,* on morality; and two collections of aphorisms, one called *Kyriai doxai* (*Principal Doctrines*), the other now known as *The Vatican Collection.*

Epicurus' main concern was to teach an attitude toward life that would lead to personal happiness. He rejected the philosophical ideals of the good life propounded by the Platonists and Aristotelians and substituted a moderate hedonism. Pleasure is the good. Pain is the obstacle to be removed or avoided. Unsatisfied desires are painful, so the wise man learns to limit his desires to things that can easily be obtained. The good Epicurean seeks a quiet life with a few like-minded friends and avoids becoming deeply involved in the affairs of the world.

The moral message was reinforced by a cosmology, and it was this that gave Epicurus whatever importance he has for the history of science. Peace of mind, he thought, was threatened by ignorance about the natural world, by certain widespread beliefs in the intervention by supernatural powers in man's environment, and by belief in rewards and punishments in a life after death: "If we were not troubled by doubts about the heavens, and about the possible meaning of death, and by failure to understand the limits of pain and desire, then we should have no need of natural philosophy [$\phi\upsilon\sigma\iota\omicron\lambda\omicron\gamma\iota\alpha$]" (*Kyriai doxai,* 11).

Epicurus found a world view that suited his moral purpose in the atomism of Leucippus and Democritus, which he first learned from his teacher Nausiphanes. The historian is in no position to make an accurate assessment of Epicurus' originality, since information about Democritus is scanty and biased. It is certain that the main framework of the atomist system was completed by Democritus. All phenomena were explained on the assumption that the whole natural world consists of imperceptibly small, indestructible, and changeless atoms, made of a single common substance, differing only in shape and size, moving in the infinite void. Democritus explained how perceptible qualities were generated in compounds according to the shapes and sizes of the component atoms and the quantity of void between them. He gave some account of the origin and destruction of worlds in the infinite universe, brought about by random collisions of atoms moving through the void. He wrote about the natural origin of living forms and the natural development of human society and culture.

All of this was taken over by Epicurus. Several

modifications in the system can be observed, however, and no doubt more would be revealed if the evidence were more complete. Some of the modifications can be seen to be attempts to meet criticisms brought against Democritus by Aristotle. For example, Aristotle's criticism of "indivisible magnitudes" (especially in *Physics,* Z) appears to be the reason for Epicurus' contradicting Democritus about the indivisibility of the atoms; the Epicurean atom has "minimal parts" that can be distinguished theoretically but not split off physically (*Letter to Herodotus,* 56–59). Aristotle's analysis of "the voluntary" (*Nicomachean Ethics,* III, 1–5) was one of the factors that led to the notorious "swerve" of atoms in Epicurean theory. Democritus' theory of motion was thought not to allow human beings to initiate motion, since all the motions of the atoms that constitute a mind could be explained by their own previous motions and their interaction with the environment. Epicurus said that atoms deviated unpredictably from time to time, and thus he provided for breaks in the chains of causation. He also modified Democritus' theory of motion in another way: instead of taking basic atomic motion as an unexplained assumption of the theory, he said that all atoms have a natural motion "downwards," because of weight. The swerve was therefore needed for another purpose, since without it the theory could not explain why atoms do not all drop in parallel straight lines through the infinite void, without colliding.

Some of Epicurus' views about the natural world were extremely naïve and reactionary. His avowed purpose was to pursue the inquiry only as far as was necessary to remove anxiety. His "canonic," or rules of procedure, held that any view not in conflict with the evidence of the senses could be regarded as true. Thus the hypothesis that the cosmos was created by an intelligent deity was ruled out as being in conflict with the observed facts of the world's imperfections and with the true conception of what it is to be a god (*Letter to Herodotus,* 76–77; see also Lucretius, *De rerum natura,* V, 55–234). But the sun's motion in the ecliptic may be due to the tilting of the heavens, or to winds, or to some other cause (*Letter to Pythocles,* 93). *De rerum natura,* book VI, and *Letter to Pythocles* contain many cases in which multiple explanations, ranging from the more or less correct to the ridiculous, are offered for natural phenomena.

The main importance of Epicurus for the history of science is that he reasserted the principles of Democritus' atomic theory in opposition to the teleological natural philosophy of Plato and Aristotle. His own major work, *On Nature,* did not survive long enough to be very influential; but the essentials of his theory were preserved in the letters that Diogenes

Laertius included in book X of his *Lives and Opinions of the Philosophers,* in some of the philosophical works of Cicero, and especially in the poem *De rerum natura* of the devoted Roman Epicurean, Lucretius. These were the main sources from which post-Renaissance philosophers drew their knowledge of ancient atomism, when Aristotelianism began at last to lose its dominant position.

BIBLIOGRAPHY

Text with English translation and commentary is in Cyril Bailey, *Epicurus* (Oxford, 1926; repr. New York, 1970). The most recent critical edition is G. Arrighetti, *Epicuro* (Turin, 1960), with Italian trans. and commentary; this also includes the papyrus fragments of *On Nature.* English translation is in Russel M. Geer, *Epicurus: Letters, Principal Doctrines and Vatican Sayings* (New York, 1964). Text with ancient testimonia is in H. Usener, *Epicurea* (Leipzig, 1887; repr. Stuttgart, 1966).

Studies of Epicureanism include Cyril Bailey, *The Greek Atomists and Epicurus* (Oxford, 1928; repr. New York, 1964); Benjamin Farrington, *The Faith of Epicurus* (New York, 1967); David J. Furley, *Two Studies in the Greek Atomists* (Princeton, 1967); Jürgen Mau, *Zum Problem des Infinitesimalen bei den antiken Atomisten* (Berlin, 1954); W. Schmid, *Epikurs Kritik der platonischen Elementenlehre* (Leipzig, 1936); "Epikur," in *Reallexikon für Antike und Christentum* (Stuttgart, 1961); and Gregory Vlastos, "Minimal Parts in Epicurean Atomism," *Isis,* **56** (1965), 121–147.

A conference on Epicureanism is recorded by Association Guillaume Budé, *Actes du VIIIᵉ congrés, Paris, 5–10 avril 1968* (Paris, 1969).

Later history of Epicureanism is discussed in Marie Boas, "The Establishment of the Mechanical Philosophy," in *Osiris,* **10** (1952), 412–541; Robert H. Kargon, *Atomism in England From Hariot to Newton* (Oxford, 1966); and Kurd Lasswitz, *Geschichte der Atomistik vom Mittelalter bis Newton* (Hamburg, 1890; repr. Hildesheim, 1963).

For fuller bibliography, see Bursian's *Jahresbericht über die Fortschritte der klassischen Altertumswissenschaft,* no. 281 (1943), pp. 1–194; and P. DeLacy, "Some Recent Publications on Epicurus and Epicureanism, 1937–1954," in *Classical Weekly,* **48** (1955), 169 ff.

DAVID J. FURLEY

ERASISTRATUS (*b.* Iulis, Chios, *ca.* 304 B.C.; *d.* Mycale), *anatomy, physiology.*

Erasistratus was born into a medical family. His father, Cleombrotus, was a doctor, and his mother, Cretoxene, was the sister of the doctor Medios. Like his brother Cleophantus, Erasistratus entered the family profession. He studied medicine first in Athens as a pupil of Metrodorus, the third husband of Aristotle's daughter, Pythias; and it was probably, at least in part, through him that he became so strongly influenced by Peripatetic thought.[1] About 280 B.C. he entered the university in Cos, where the medical school of Praxagoras flourished. Cos had strong political and cultural ties with Alexandria, and in that city Erasistratus came under the influence of Chrysippus the Younger (the palace doctor of Ptolemy Philadelphus), especially in the fields of anatomy, physiology, and pathology. In his old age Erasistratus gave up medical practice and entered the Museum at Alexandria, where the unrivaled facilities afforded by the Ptolemies allowed him to devote himself to his researches. According to later tradition, an incurable ulcer on his foot caused him to commit suicide by drinking hemlock.

Erasistratus wrote a large number of works, notably on anatomy, abdominal pathology, hemoptysis, fevers, gout, dropsy, and hygiene. None of these works has survived. He is best-known for his anatomical and physiological researches. In these fields distinguished work had already been done by his immediate predecessors, Diocles and Praxagoras, and by his teachers Chrysippus and Herophilus, and the Museum itself provided highly advantageous conditions for anatomical research. The public dissection of human bodies was an innovation of the Ptolemies and remained almost exclusively the preserve of the Alexandrians. It is possible that familiarity with the Egyptian practice of embalming bodies contributed to the creation of an environment in which the dissection of the human body was not viewed with misgivings. Certain ancient authorities, notably Celsus, followed by Tertullian and St. Augustine, even accused Erasistratus of vivisecting criminals taken out of the royal prisons. Scholarly opinion is divided in its acceptance of this tradition, and Galen's silence in the matter cannot be taken as conclusive evidence against it. It is clear from Galen that Erasistratus vivisected animals, and these dissections enabled him to draw parallels between men and beasts. For example, he made a detailed investigation of the cavities and convolutions in the brains of man, hare, and stag and correctly inferred that the number of convolutions varied with the degree of intellectual development. In addition to his ventures in comparative anatomy, Erasistratus was a pioneer in the field of pathological anatomy, conducting postmortem examinations of the bodies of men who had just died, in order to study structural changes due to morbid conditions.

As the basis for his physiology Erasistratus combined a corpuscular theory with the doctrine of the pneuma. In both these respects it seems likely that he reveals the influence of the Lyceum, where these theories played an important role. A very important factor in persuading Erasistratus to adopt the latter theory must have been the influence of such doctors as Diocles, Praxagoras, and Herophilus, in whose medical theory the pneuma doctrine plays so fundamental a role and who were themselves either directly or at least indirectly influenced by Peripatetic teachings. It is probable, too, that Erasistratus was induced to adopt his corpuscular theory by the direct influence of Strato of Lampsacus, the third head of the Lyceum and the teacher of Ptolemy Philadelphus in Alexandria shortly before Theophrastus' death. It is perhaps worth recording that Strato also seems to have subscribed to the pneuma doctrine.[2] Like Strato, Erasistratus conceived of his particles as very small, imperceptible, corporeal entities surrounded by a vacuum in a finely divided or discontinuous condition.

Upon the basis of these two theories he sought to assign natural causes to all phenomena and rejected the idea that there were hidden forces such as the power of attraction of certain organs, which many medical authors had postulated in order to explain such physiological processes as the assimilation of food and the secretion of humors. For this idea Erasistratus substituted the theory of $\pi\rho\grave{o}s$ $\tau\grave{o}$ $\kappa\epsilon\nu\acute{o}\upsilon\mu\epsilon\nu o\nu$ $\mathring{a}\kappa o\lambda o\upsilon\theta\acute{\iota}a$, the *horror vacui,* derived from Strato, whereby those empty spaces which suddenly form in the living body are continually filled.

Erasistratus may also have derived his experimental method from Strato. The *Anonymus Londinensis* (col. xxxiii) preserves some evidence of his methodology. It describes an experiment of his which anticipates another experiment, generally considered to be the beginning of the modern study of metabolism, performed in the seventeenth century by Santorio. In order to prove that animals give off certain emanations, Erasistratus recommended that a bird or similar creature should be kept in a vessel without food for some time and then weighed together with any excrement that had been passed. A great loss of weight would then be discovered.

To repair the bodily wastage which Erasistratus had so strikingly demonstrated took place not only visibly but in some part invisibly, Galen tells us that he held that Nature had provided mechanism in the form of appetites ($\mathring{o}\rho\acute{\epsilon}\xi\epsilon\iota s$), forces ($\delta\upsilon\nu\acute{a}\mu\epsilon\iota s$), and substances ($\mathring{\upsilon}\lambda a\iota$), i.e., he believed that part of the purposive activity of the pneuma was the absorption of food into the body. He had made the striking discovery that all organic parts of the living creature were a tissue composed of vein, artery, and nerve (the $\tau\rho\upsilon\pi\lambda o\kappa\acute{\iota}a$ $\tau\tilde{\omega}\nu$ $\mathring{a}\gamma\gamma\epsilon\acute{\iota}\omega\nu$), bodies so fine that they were knowable only by reason. The vein carried the food, the artery the pneuma, and the nerve the psychic pneuma. There was no need for Erasistratus to postulate a hidden power of attraction. He held that the supply of nourishment to each particular organ took place by a process of absorption (διάδοσις) through the extremely fine pores (κενώματα) in the walls of the veins contained in it. The particles of nourishment contained in the blood were able to pass through the veins, in accordance with the principle of πρὸς τὸ κενούμενον ἀκολουθία, to fill those spaces left empty by the evacuations and emanations. Growth, then, proceeded on the principle of the accretion of like to like. Galen tells us that Erasistratus likened the growth of an animal to that of a sieve, rope, bag, or basket, since each of these grows by the addition to it of materials similar to those out of which it began to be made. The two materials which serve for the preservation of the creature, then, are blood and pneuma, the former providing the nutriment and the latter helping to transmit the natural activity.

Erasistratus rejected the widely held beliefs that digestion was a process analogous either to cooking (as Aristotle had held) or to fermentation (as Diocles had believed). He was well aware that the epiglottis closes the larynx during swallowing, thereby preventing liquids and solids from entering the trachea. He thus rejected the old and much debated belief held by Plato, Philistion, Diocles, and Dexippus that it was possible for drink to enter the lungs. He held that the food, once in the stomach, was torn to pieces by the peristaltic motion of the gastric muscles under the influence of pneuma. He gave an accurate description of the structure and function of these muscles. Unlike Diocles, he was not of the opinion that the pneuma arrived in the stomach with the food but held that it was introduced there by the gastric arteries. In accordance with this theory he sought to explain why digestion is impaired during a fever. This was due, he thought, to the impediment of the free motion of the pneuma by the blood that had penetrated into the arteries.

A portion of the food broken into pulp in the stomach was subsequently conveyed in the blood vessels to the liver, where, he believed, it was transformed into blood. Galen complains that Erasistratus did not reveal how this transformation takes place. During this process the biliary constituents are separated off and pass to the gallbladder while the pure blood from the liver is conveyed via the vena cava (κοίλη φλέψ) to the heart.

Erasistratus' description of the vascular system and his views on the significance and structure of the heart represent a great advance over his predecessors. Some scholars have claimed that Erasistratus came near to anticipating Harvey's discovery of the circulation of the blood, but such a claim is unwarranted. He did,

however, conceive the function of the heart to be that of a pump and compared it to a blacksmith's bellows actively dilating and contracting by its own innate force. The arteries, on the other hand, which he likened to a skin bag, were passively dilated by the pneuma forced into them by the heart's contraction. In this respect Erasistratus rejected Herophilus' claim, subsequently revived by Galen, that the arteries were subject to dilations and contractions synchronous with those of the heart.

Erasistratus rightly believed that both veins and arteries originated from the heart and that both of these vessels extended throughout the body, dividing into extremely fine capillaries. But, following Praxagoras, he held that only the veins contained blood, the arteries being full of pneuma. His dissections of dead animals would have confirmed this belief. He had not, however, failed to observe that the arteries of a wounded animal spurt blood. To account for this phenomenon he maintained that when an artery was severed, the escaping pneuma caused a vacuum and the pull of this vacuum (the πρὸς τὸ κενούμενον ἀκολουθία) drew blood from the veins through certain fine capillaries which were usually closed (the synanastomoses, συναναστομώσεις). The blood then spurted out of the arteries after the escaping pneuma. This ingenious hypothesis was not disproved until four and a half centuries later, when Galen, who was otherwise greatly influenced by Erasistratus' theory, showed by careful experiments in vivisection that the arteries of living beings carry blood continuously.

Erasistratus rejected the view that the pneuma was innate in the body. He believed that it was ἐπικτητόν, i.e., drawn in from outside through the nose and the mouth in the process of inhalation, that it passed via the bronchi to the lungs and thence through the pulmonary vein to the left ventricle of the heart. From the heart the vital pneuma was carried through the aorta ascendens and aorta descendens to the brain and to the whole body. In the brain the vital pneuma was transformed into psychic pneuma and was carried from the brain to various parts of the body by the nervous system, there to cause muscular movements by its effect upon the muscles. In order to perform this function the inspired pneuma must have a certain density. If it were too fine, it would presumably escape through pores.

The respiratory process Erasistratus held to be due to the muscular activity in the thorax. When the chest is expanded, so are the lungs, which, like the arteries, possess no motion of their own. Into the resulting empty space the outer air streams in accordance with the principle of *horror vacui*. The contraction of the thorax also brings about the contraction of the lungs "like a sponge compressed by the hands," and the air is expired. The purpose of respiration, according to Erasistratus, is not to cool the innate heat, as Philistion and Diocles had believed, but to fill the arteries with pneuma. Galen provides the further information that Erasistratus declared that if the activity of the thorax were to stop, the heart would not be able to draw in any air from the lungs and suffocation would ensue.

As has already been seen, the pneuma passes from the lungs through the so-called ἀρτηρία φλεβώδης, "the artery resembling a vein," i.e., the pulmonary vein, and, with the expansion of the heart, into the left ventricle in accordance with the principle πρὸς τὸ κενούμενον ἀκολουθία. When the heart contracts, the pneuma is then driven, via the aorta, through the arteries all over the body. The return of the pneuma from the heart into the lungs is prevented by the bicuspid valve (mitral valve) and from the aorta into the heart by the semilunar (sigmoid) valves.

Since there is no possibility of any return to the lungs, any superfluous pneuma distributed throughout the arteries is, presumably, ultimately given off from the body by that process of skin respiration which Erasistratus had earlier sought to demonstrate by the experiment with the bird.

Just as the expansion of the heart led to the left ventricle's becoming filled with pneuma, so the right ventricle becomes filled with blood which comes from the liver via the vena cava. With every contraction of the heart the blood is pumped into the lungs through the so-called φλὲψ ἀρτηριώδης, "the vein resembling an artery," i.e., the pulmonary artery, and thence, presumably, distributed by other "veins" to the rest of the organs. The return of the blood from the heart to the vena cava is prevented by the tricuspid valve and from the pulmonary artery to the heart by the semilunar valves. As is the case with the pneuma, no blood is returned to the heart; nor is there any communication between veins and arteries in the heart, the left and right ventricles being quite separate.

Erasistratus, then, wrongly attributed functions of the auricles to the two pulmonary vessels and incorrectly believed, like Galen after him, that the blood was manufactured in the liver and distributed throughout the body by the veins.

The structure of the brain is described by Erasistratus with a greater accuracy than Herophilus had achieved. Galen tells us that in his old age Erasistratus had leisure for research and made his dissections more accurate. The implication of Galen's evidence here is that Erasistratus had not systematically examined the structure of the brain until he was an old man. As a result of these dissections he distinguished the cerebrum (ἐγκέφαλος) from the cerebellum (which

he called the ἐπεγκρανίς, not the παρεγκεφαλίς, as Herophilus had done). He also gave a detailed description of the cerebral ventricles or cavities within the brain and of the meninges or membranes that cover the brain.

Erasistratus rejected the view of those thinkers who, like Empedocles, Aristotle, Diocles, Praxagoras, and the Stoics, had maintained that the heart was the seat of the central intelligence. In agreement with Alcmaeon, the author of the Hippocratic treatise "On the Sacred Disease," and Plato, he placed this central organ in the brain. Herophilus had clearly shown by dissection that the nerves originated in the brain and had specified the "fourth ventricle" of the cerebellum as the seat of *hegemonikon,* or organ of thought. Erasistratus was most probably in agreement with this viewpoint. For, as was seen above, his observations that the cerebellum of the brain of man had more convolutions than that of other animals had led him to the conclusion that the number of convolutions varied with the degree of intellectual development.

He also agreed with Herophilus that the brain was the starting point of all the nerves. Originally he held that they sprang from dura mater (παχεῖα μήνιγξ). He had discovered through vivisection that incisions into this membrane adversely affected the motor ability of living creatures. But later—probably as a result of his more accurate dissections—he succeeded in tracing the nerves into the interior of the brain and discovered the origin of each type of sensory nerve in the cerebrum.

Again in agreement with Herophilus, Erasistratus recognized the difference between sensory and motor nerves, the νεῦρα αἰσθητικά and κινητικά (Herophilus, however, called the latter προαιρητικά). Erasistratus was of the opinion that the nerve fibers were formed "like a sail" out of three different, imperceptible strands of artery, vein, and nerve. He also believed that the nerves were filled with psychic pneuma drawn, most probably, from the ventricles of the cerebrum. The widespread belief that Erasistratus renounced this theory in his old age and maintained that the nerves contained not pneuma but marrow or brain substance[3] is inaccurate and based upon a misunderstanding of the text.[4] Motion, he held, was effected through the agency of the muscles, which were formed from a texture of vein, artery, and nerve. The pneuma, led to the muscles via the arteries, invested them with the capacity of synchronous expansion of length and contraction of breadth and vice versa, which resulted in the movement of the bodily parts containing them.

In pathology Erasistratus rejected the influential humoral theory or, at any rate, the abuses of this theory practiced in the school of Praxagoras. He considered research into the formation of the humors to be superfluous and, according to Galen, did not mention black bile at all in his writings. However, he could not dispense entirely with the assumption of morbid changes in the bodily humors (κακοχυμία); he considered apoplexy, for example, to be a disease of the brain caused by an excessive secretion of cold, viscous, and glutinous humors which prevented the psychic pneuma from passing into the nerves. But the main cause of disease he held to be plethora (πληθώρα or πλῆθος τροφῆς), i.e., the flooding of the veins with a superfluity of blood engendered by an excessive intake of nourishment. As the plethora increases, the limbs begin to swell, then become sore, more sluggish, and harder to move. If the plethora increases still more, the superfluous blood is then discharged through the synanastomoses into the arteries, where it is compressed by the pneuma which is constantly pumped from the heart. This compressed blood collects in the extremities of the arteries and causes local inflammation (φλεγμονή) accompanied by fever. Moreover, since the flow of the pneuma is impeded by the presence of this blood in the arteries, it cannot perform its natural functions. As examples of diseases brought about in this way by plethora he mentions, among others, ailments of the liver, spleen, and stomach, coughing of blood, phrenitis, pleuritis, and peripneumonia.

Erasistratus' treatment for plethora consisted primarily of starvation (ἀσιτία), on the ground that the veins, when emptied, would more easily receive back the blood which had been discharged into the arteries. Unlike many of his contemporaries he did not resort freely to phlebotomy but employed it only upon rare occasions. Erasistratus preferred prevention to therapy and in a separate treatise stressed the importance of hygiene. In general he was opposed to violent remedies, especially purgatives, preferring in their stead carefully regulated exercise and diet and the vapor bath.

Although Erasistratus founded a school of medicine, none of his successors seems to have made any significant mark in the history of medicine. His true importance lies in the fact that he, together with Herophilus, laid the foundations for the scientific study of anatomy and physiology, and their careful dissections provided a basis and stimulus for the anatomical investigations undertaken by Galen over four centuries later.

NOTES

1. There is also a strong tradition that he had heard Theophrastus himself; see Diogenes Laërtius, 5.57, and Galen, 4.729K. For the tradition linking Erasistratus with the Lyceum generally, see Galen, 2.88K; for Strato's influence, see below.
2. See F. Wehrli, *Straton von Lampsakos, die Schule des Aristoteles,* V (Basel, 1950), commentary on fr. 108, p. 71; and F. Solmsen, "Greek Philosophy and the Discovery of the Nerves," in *Museum Helveticum,* **18** (1961), 183.
3. See M. Wellmann, "Erasistratus," in Pauly-Wissowa, VI, 1 (Stuttgart, 1907), 343; and G. Verbeke, *L'évolution de la doctrine du pneuma* (Paris–Louvain, 1945), p. 185.
4. With Solmsen, *op. cit.,* p. 188.

BIBLIOGRAPHY

For a collection of the evidence of Erasistratus' views, see R. Fuchs's dissertation *Erasistratea* (Leipzig, 1892). References in Galen are cited according to C. G. Kuhn, ed., *Claudii Galeni Opera omnia,* 20 vols. (Leipzig, 1821–1833).

See also C. Allbutt, *Greek Medicine in Rome* (London, 1921); H. Diels, "Über das physikalische System des Straton," in *Sitzungsberichte der Preussischen Akademie der Wissenschaften zu Berlin,* **1** (1893), 101 ff.; J. F. Dobson, "Erasistratus," in *Proceedings of the Royal Society of Medicine,* **20** (1926–1927), 825 ff.; R. Fuchs, "De Erasistrato capita selecta," in *Hermes,* **29** (1894), 171–203; W. W. Jaeger, "Das Pneuma im Lykeion," *ibid.,* **48** (1913), 29–72, and *Scripta minora,* I (Rome, 1960), 57–102; *Diokles von Karystos, die griechische Medizin und die Schule des Aristoteles* (Berlin, 1938); "Vergessene Fragmente des Peripatetikers Diokles von Karystos nebst zwei Anhaengen zur Chronologie der dogmatischen Aerzteschule," in *Abhandlungen der Preussischen Akademie der Wissenschaften,* Phil.-hist. Kl. (1938), no. 3, 1–46, and in *Scripta minora,* II (Rome, 1960), 185–241; and "Diocles of Carystus: A New Pupil of Aristotle," in *Philosophical Review,* **49** (1940), 393–414, and in *Scripta minora,* II, 243–265; W. H. S. Jones, *The Medical Writings of Anonymus Londinensis* (Cambridge, 1947); I. M. Lonie, "Erasistratus, the Erasistrateans and Aristotle," in *Bulletin of the History of Medicine,* **38** (1964), 426–443; F. Solmsen, "Greek Philosophy and the Discovery of the Nerves," in *Museum Helveticum,* **18** (1961), 150 ff.; F. Steckerl, *The Fragments of Praxagoras of Cos and His School* (Leiden, 1958); G. Verbeke, *L'évolution de la doctrine du pneuma* (Paris–Louvain, 1945); F. Wehrli, *Straton von Lampsakos, die Schule des Aristoteles,* V (Basel, 1950); M. Wellmann, "Erasistratus," in Pauly-Wissowa, VI, 1 (Stuttgart, 1907), 333–350; and L. G. Wilson, "Erasistratus, Galen, and the Pneuma," in *Bulletin of the History of Medicine,* **33** (1959), 293–314.

I am grateful to the University of Newcastle upon Tyne Research Fund for a grant which enabled me to consult works in London libraries.

JAMES LONGRIGG

ERASTUS (LIEBER), THOMAS (*b.* Baden, Switzerland, 1523; *d.* Basel, Switzerland, 1 January 1583), *medicine, natural philosophy, theology.*

Erastus studied theology and philosophy at Basel

from 1540 to 1544 and medicine at Bologna and Padua from 1544 to 1555, receiving the M.D. in 1552. While in Bologna he married Isotta a Canonici; they had no children. At Meiningen he was physician to Count William of Henneberg in 1557, and the following year he became professor of medicine at Heidelberg. His anti-Calvinist attitude—he believed in granting the state supremacy in all ecclesiastical affairs, a doctrine that came to be called Erastianism—led to his fall from the favor of Frederick III, elector palatine. In 1580, therefore, he left Heidelberg for Basel, where he became professor of theology and moral philosophy.

Erastus is remembered chiefly as an inexorable and abusive critic of astrology, natural magic, and particularly of Paracelsus and iatrochemistry. He condemned such superstitious practices as the curative use of human blood and parts of corpses and of amulets in the cure of epilepsy, but he firmly believed in Satan, demons, and witches—accusing the witches, against the claims of their defenders (Wierus and others) that they were victims of drug-induced hallucinations, of true cohabitation with the devil. A successful physician with great experience in the use of watering places (Bad Kissingen), he strictly adhered to traditional humoralism and ancient medical practice but nevertheless criticized Galen.

Erastus laced his rational arguments heavily with theological dogma and polemics, yet on occasion he made sound observations, such as tracing vitriol and alum in mineral water with oak gall water. Opposing traditional ideas about the brain, he insisted that what mattered was not its substance but its function and its production of impulses ("spirits"). Erastus also demolished the Galenic theory that epilepsy was caused by obstruction of pathways by viscid mucus, since such a theory could not explain why sensation was disturbed but motility was not. He recognized forms of petit mal manifested by dizziness, hiccups, or excessive sneezing.

No two events in nature, Erastus contended, are equal in cause and effect: hence the futility of forecasting. According to him, heaven acts in conformity with a general plan and does not interfere with the course of events that are specific for the individual object. For example, it supplies heat and moisture in spontaneous generation, but the process is due entirely to the specific disposition of certain parts of matter. Attempts at astrological divination work through the invocation of demons and therefore are damnable heresy. Furthermore, Erastus said, comets do not foretell evil events, such as wars, pestilence, and the deaths of kings; they are merely terrestrial exhalations and, as such, produce drought and heat—factors not conducive to the outbreak of epidemics.

Erastus' criticism of Paracelsus was fivefold. First, he criticized Paracelsus' denial of the existence and universal significance of the elements and humors established in ancient science and medicine and their replacement with the three principles, salt, sulfur, and mercury; these had never been isolated from any object by heat or chemical manipulation. Solidity, inflammability, and volatility were not caused by the presence of any of the three Paracelsian principles but by the proportions in which the four elements of the ancients (air, water, fire, earth) were "mixed" in an object. It was the special mixture of water and subtle earth particles that made mercury prone to go up in smoke. Sulfur was inflammable because of the fire and warm air it contained. Without this air, sulfur would become inert and lose its "sulfurousness." The solidity of salt showed its kinship with the earth.

Second, Erastus angrily repudiated the significance attributed by Paracelsus to the power of imagination and the conversion of something spiritual into matter; this he regarded as the main part of the natural magic—the "Neoplatonic fallacy"—practiced by Paracelsus. The concepts of microcosm and quintessence were sheer nonsense: how could the human body contain the virtues and materials of all parts of the outside world? Who could show that bread already and actually contains human blood instead of being converted into it when consumed?

Third, disease, according to Paracelsus, was not the disturbance of humoral balance in an individual man (as the ancients rightly taught); man was merely the passive recipient of an outside agent that, like a parasite, takes possession and inflicts its own schedule of life on the organism, thereby consuming it. (This was the parasitistic or ontological concept.) In this, Erastus said, Paracelsus confused disease with its cause and disregarded the functions of organs, which alone decide the character of a disease.

Fourth, the chemical and notably the metallic (mainly mercury) remedies recommended by Paracelsus were nonassimilable poisons. No therapy could work except through the humors. Therefore, potable gold was a magician's swindle.

Fifth, said Erastus, Paracelsus was an ignorant man, a "grunting swine" who, driven by ambition and vanity, replaced sane teaching with insane delusion, the comprehensible with the incomprehensible, truth with falsehood, and salubrious medicine with pestilential poison. His "cures" were at best temporary and, as a rule, injurious. Although not devoid of some knowledge of chemistry, he was largely a magus informed by the devil and evil spirits.

Many of Erastus' arguments must have seemed unanswerable to his contemporaries, but he fought a losing battle against iatrochemistry, which through Paracelsians (Turquet de Mayerne, inspired by Oswald Croll) appeared in the first British pharmacopoeia (1618). The Paracelsian concept of disease was further developed by J. B. van Helmont and Harvey and finally became the historical root of the modern concept established in the nineteenth century.

BIBLIOGRAPHY

I. ORIGINAL WORKS. Erastus' main writings are *Disputationes de medicine nova Paracelsi,* 4 pts. (Basel, 1572–1573), pt. 2 with supp. against alchemy; *De occultis pharmacorum potestatibus* (Basel, 1574); *Repetitio disputationis de lamiis seu strigibus* (Basel, 1578; repr. Hamburg, 1606); *De astrologia divinatrice epistolae D. Thomae Erasti ad diversos scriptae* (Basel, 1580); and *De auro potabili,* followed by *De cometarum significationibus sententia* (Basel, 1584—*De auro* text at end dated 1576 and preface dated 1578).

II. SECONDARY LITERATURE. Accounts of Erastus' life are Melchior Adam, *Vitae Germanorum medicorum* (Heidelberg, 1620), pp. 242–246; and J. Karcher, "Thomas Erastus (1524–1583), der unversöhnliche Gegner des Theophrastus Paracelsus," in *Gesnerus,* **14** (1957), 1–13. Erastus' criticism of astrology is discussed in Lynn Thorndike, *A History of Magic and Experimental Science,* V (New York, 1941), 652–667; that of Paracelsus and iatrochemistry in Walter Pagel, *Paracelsus. An Introduction to Philosophical Medicine in the Era of the Renaissance* (Basel–New York, 1958), pp. 311–333. On Erastianism, see R. Wiesel-Roth, *Thomas Erastus. Beitrag zur Geschichte der reformierten Kirche und zur Lehre von der Staatssouveränität* (Baden, Switzerland, 1953).

The following, although of no necessity, are a helpful amenity for the student. For Erastiana (correspondence and biographical notes), see Henricus a Leda Smetius, *Miscellanea medica* (Frankfurt, 1611), and H. Pfister, *Bad Kissingen vor Vierhundert Jahren* (Würzburg, 1954), pp. 17–26.

WALTER PAGEL

ERATOSTHENES (*b.* Cyrene [now Shahhat, Libya], *ca.* 276 B.C.; *d.* Alexandria, *ca.* 195 B.C.), *geography, mathematics.*

Eratosthenes, son of Aglaos, was born in Cyrene but spent most of his working life in Alexandria, where he was head of the library attached to the famous Museum from *ca.* 235 until his death. At some period during his early manhood he went to Athens for the ancient equivalent of a university education, and there he associated with the Peripatetic Ariston of Chios, Arcesilaus and Apelles of the Academy, and Bion the Cynic (Strabo, *Geography,* 15). When he was

about thirty, he was invited to Alexandria by King Ptolemy III (Euergetes I), possibly at the instigation of Eratosthenes' fellow countryman Callimachus, who had already been given a post in the library by Ptolemy II (Philadelphus). On the death of the first chief librarian, Zenodotus, *ca.* 235, Eratosthenes was appointed to the post, Callimachus having died *ca.* 240 (*Suda Lexicon, s.v.,* calls Eratosthenes a pupil of Callimachus). At some time during his stay in Alexandria he became tutor to Euergetes' son and remained in favor with the royal court until his death. (See the anecdote related in Athenaeus, *Deipnosophistai,* VII, 276a, concerning Eratosthenes and Queen Arsinoe III.)

The above represents the most probable account of Eratosthenes' life according to the consensus of scholarly opinion, but the exact dates of the stages of his career are disputed and certainty is unattainable. In particular, Knaack puts the date of his birth back to *ca.* 284, and Jacoby (*Fragmente der griechischen Historiker,* IIB [1930], 704) even as far as 296 (suggesting that in the *Suda Lexicon, s.v.,* ρκς' is a copyist's error for ρκα', which then refers to the 121st olympiad, i.e., 296–293, not the 126th, i.e., 276–273), while the date of his death becomes either about 203 (Knaack) or 214 (Jacoby), both scholars accepting the testimony of our sources that Eratosthenes died at eighty (the *Suda Lexicon*) or eighty-one (Censorinus, *De die natali,* p. 15) or eighty-two (Pseudo-Lucian, Μακρόβιοι, p. 27). The reason for supposing that he must have been born earlier than 276 is that Strabo calls him γνώριμος of Zeno of Citium (the founder of Stoicism), a word that often means "pupil" in such a context; but Zeno died in 262, and Eratosthenes could hardly have studied under him at the tender age of fourteen. To this it may be answered that γνώριμος can also mean simply "acquainted with," and that the date of Zeno's death may be as late as 256 (see Diogenes Laertius, VII, 6:28). There is also considerable doubt about the order of succession of the early librarians at Alexandria. A papyrus fragment (*Oxyrhynchus papyri,* X, 1241, col. 2) lists them as Zenodotus (whose name is presumed to have occurred at the damaged end of the previous column), Apollonius Rhodius, Eratosthenes, Aristophanes of Byzantium, Aristarchus of Samothrace, and another Apollonius; but there are several mistakes and chronological difficulties in this list (*cf.* Grenfell and Hunt, *ad loc.*), and it is by no means certain that Apollonius Rhodius succeeded Zenodotus directly—the *Suda Lexicon* (*s.v.* "Apollonius") has him succeeding Eratosthenes, although this may arise from confusion with the later Apollonius (if he is correctly placed).

Eratosthenes was one of the foremost scholars of his time and produced works (of which only fragments remain) on geography, mathematics, philosophy, chronology, literary criticism, and grammar as well as writing poetry. According to the *Suda Lexicon,* he was described as Πένταθλος ("All-Rounder"), "another Plato," and "Beta"—the last possibly because, working in so many fields (and polymathy was greatly admired by the Alexandrians), he just failed to achieve the highest rank in each (see Strabo's remark that Eratosthenes was a mathematician among geographers and a geographer among mathematicians: *Geography,* 94; *cf.* 15), or perhaps simply because he was the second chief librarian. His most enduring work was in geography (particularly notable is his measurement of the circumference of the earth), but he himself seems to have taken most pride, as regards his scientific work, in his solution to the famous problem of doubling the cube, to celebrate which he composed an epigram disparaging previous solutions and dedicated to Euergetes and his son; the authenticity of this poem has been questioned (by Hiller and by Powell), but on inadequate grounds. As a mathematician, Eratosthenes ranked high enough in the estimation of the great Archimedes to have one of the latter's treatises, the *Method,* dedicated to him and to be the recipient of a difficult problem in indeterminate analysis, known as the "Cattle Problem," for communication to the mathematicians of Alexandria. In philosophy, Eratosthenes was an eclectic and, according to Strabo (*Geography,* 15), somewhat of a dilettante. He was the first Greek writer to make a serious study of chronological questions and established the system of dating by olympiads, while as an authority on Old Comedy he is constantly cited in the scholia to Aristophanes' plays.

Eratosthenes' *Geography* (Γεωγραφικά) was in three books, as we learn from Strabo, who quotes from it frequently and is, in fact, the chief source of our knowledge of it. It long remained a prime authority on geographical matters; Julius Caesar evidently consulted it, since in his description of the Germans he mentions that Eratosthenes knew of the Hercynian Forest (*De bello Gallico,* VI, 24), and Strabo (writing around the turn of the Christian era) admits that for the southeastern quarter of the inhabited world (*oikoumene*) he has no better authority than Eratosthenes (*Geography,* 723). The work was the first scientific attempt to put geographical studies on a sound mathematical basis, and its author may be said to have been the founder of mathematical geography. It was concerned with the terrestrial globe as a whole, its division into zones, changes in its surface, the position of the *oikoumene* as then known, and the actual mapping of it, with numerous estimates of distances along a few roughly defined parallels and meridians; but it also contained a certain amount of material descriptive of peoples and places.

Strabo, who disliked the mathematical side of the subject and much preferred purely descriptive geography (see *Geographical Fragments of Hipparchus,* pp. 36, 162, 164, 171, 191), several times complains that Eratosthenes put too much emphasis on mathematical topics such as the above (*Geography,* 48–49, 62, 65). Hipparchus (second century B.C.), on the other hand, criticizes his predecessor for not making sufficient use of astronomical data in fixing the reference lines of his map and not treating the subject in a mathematical enough manner. (Hipparchus wrote a work in three books, *Against the Geography of Eratosthenes,* of which we have substantial fragments quoted by Strabo, often inextricably mingled with citations from Eratosthenes himself—see *Geographical Fragments of Hipparchus.*) One of Eratosthenes' main purposes was to correct the traditional Ionian map, which had a round *oikoumene* with Delphi at the center, wholly surrounded by a circular ocean (as envisaged, e.g., by Anaximander and Hecataeus and already ridiculed by Herodotus, *History,* IV, 36, 2), and to sketch a better one (Strabo, *Geography,* 68), making use of all the data at his command—which, as head of the largest library in antiquity, must have been considerable (*ibid.,* 69).

Eratosthenes used as his base line a parallel running from Gibraltar through the middle of the Mediterranean and Rhodes, to the Taurus Mountains (Toros Dağlari, in Turkey), which were extended due east to include the Elburz range (south of the Caspian), the Hindu Kush, and the Himalayas, which formed the northern boundary of India (such a line, approximately bisecting the known world, had already been suggested in the previous century by Dicaearchus, a pupil of Aristotle—see *Geographical Fragments of Hipparchus,* p. 30). Intersecting this main parallel at right angles was a meridian line taken as passing through Meroë, Syene (modern Aswan, on the Tropic of Cancer), Alexandria, Rhodes, and the mouth of the Borysthenes (modern Dnieper—*ibid.,* pp. 146–147). Wherever Eratosthenes found in his sources data (such as distances in stades, similarities in fauna, flora, climate, or astronomical phenomena, lengths of the longest days, etc., recorded at different places) that he could correlate with one or both of the above base lines, he was enabled to sketch in other parallels. In addition, he divided at least the southeastern quarter of the *oikoumene* (we have no information about his treatment of the remainder) into rough geometrical figures shaped like parallelograms, which he called "seals" (σφραγῖδες), forming the first "seal" out of India and working westward (*ibid.,* pp. 128–129).

Naturally, the data at his disposal, mainly travelers' estimates of days' voyages and marches, which are notoriously unreliable—the only scientific data available were the gnomon measurements of Philo, prefect of Ptolemy, at Meroë (Strabo, *Geography,* 77), of Eratosthenes himself at Alexandria, and of Pytheas at Marseilles (*ibid.,* 63), together with some sun heights recorded by the latter (*Geographical Fragments of Hipparchus,* p. 180)—were of dubious accuracy, and any mapping done on the basis of them was bound to be largely guesswork. Hipparchus has no difficulty in showing that the figures and distances given by Eratosthenes are mathematically inconsistent with each other, and he therefore rejects them, together with some of the sensible alterations proposed by Eratosthenes for the traditional map, thus demonstrating that inspired guesswork sometimes gives better results than scientific caution (*ibid.,* pp. 34–35).

It is uncertain whether the measurement of the earth's circumference was first published in the *Geography* or in a separate treatise; if the latter, it would at any rate have been mentioned in the larger work. The method is described in detail by Cleomedes (*De motu circulari,* I, 10), the only ancient source to give it. Assuming that Syene was on the Tropic of Cancer (because there, at midday on the summer solstice, the gnomon—i.e., a vertical pointer set upright on a horizontal base—cast no shadow and a well, especially dug for this purpose [according to Pliny, *Natural History,* II, 183] was illuminated to its bottom by the sun's rays), and that this town and Alexandria were on the same meridian, Eratosthenes made a measurement of the shadow cast at Alexandria at midday on the solstice by a pointer fixed in the center of a hemispherical bowl, known as a "scaphe" (σκάφη—presumably he used this form of gnomon because the shadow of a thin stylus would be better defined than that of a large pillar or post) and estimated that the shadow amounted to 1/25 of the hemisphere, and thus 1/50 of the whole circle. Since the rays of the sun can be regarded as striking any point on the earth's surface in parallel lines, and the lines produced through the vertical gnomons at each place meet at the center of the earth, the angle of the shadow at Alexandria (*ABC* in Figure 1) is equal to the alternate angle (*BCD*) subtended by the arc *BD,* which is the distance along the meridian between Alexandria and Syene, estimated by Eratosthenes at 5,000 stades; and since it is 1/50 of the whole circle, the total circumference must be 250,000 stades. This

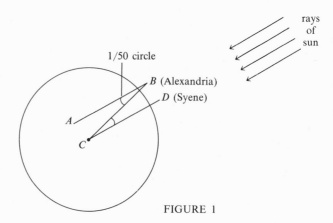

FIGURE 1

is the figure reported by Cleomedes. Hipparchus accepts a figure of 252,000 stades as Eratosthenes' measurement (Strabo, *Geography,* 132, corroborated by Pliny, *Natural History,* II, 247, whose further statement that Hipparchus added 26,000 stades to Eratosthenes' figure is incorrect—see *Geographical Fragments of Hipparchus,* p. 153), and it seems fairly certain that Eratosthenes himself added the extra 2,000 in order to obtain a number readily divisible by 60; he divided the circle into sixtieths only (Strabo, *Geography,* 113–114), the familiar division into 360° being unknown to him and first introduced into Greek science by Hipparchus (*Geographical Fragments of Hipparchus,* pp. 148–149; D. R. Dicks, "Solstices, Equinoxes, and the Pre-Socratics," in *Journal of Hellenic Studies,* **86** [1966], 27–28).

The method is sound in theory, as Hipparchus recognized, but its accuracy depends on the precision with which the basic data could be determined. The figure of 1/50 of the circle (equivalent to 7°12′) for the difference in latitude is very near the truth, but Syene (lat. 24°4′ N.) is not directly on the tropic (which in Eratosthenes' time was at 23°44′ N.), Alexandria is not on the same meridian (lying some 3° to the west), and the direct distance between the two places is about 4,530 stades, not 5,000. Probably Eratosthenes himself was aware that this last figure was doubtful (without trigonometrical methods, which he certainly did not know, it would have been impossible to measure the distance accurately), and so felt at liberty to increase his final result by 2,000. Nonetheless, the whole measurement was a very creditable achievement and one that was not bettered until modern times. On the most probable value of the stade Eratosthenes used (on this vexed question, see *Geographical Fragments of Hipparchus,* pp. 42–46), 252,000 stades are equivalent to about 29,000 English miles, which may be compared with the modern figure for the earth's circumference of a little less than 25,000 miles.

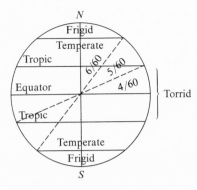

FIGURE 2

Eratosthenes also measured the obliquity of the ecliptic, which he apparently estimated as 11/83 of a circle, equivalent to 23°51′, a figure accepted as accurate by both Hipparchus and Ptolemy; how he obtained this curious ratio (if he did) is not clear (*ibid.,* fr. 41 and comment, pp. 167–168), and whether this measurement was fully described in the *Geography* or elsewhere cannot be determined—Strabo does not mention it, and he was undoubtedly writing with a copy of the *Geography* before him. What certainly would have found a place in this work was Eratosthenes' division of the terrestrial globe into zones. Of these he envisaged five (see Figure 2): a frigid zone around each pole, with a radius of 6/60 each, or 25,200 stades on the meridian circle (in his division of the circle into sixtieths, each sixtieth = 252,000 ÷ 60 = 4,200 stades), a temperate zone between each frigid zone and the tropics, with a radius of 5/60 or 21,000 stades, and a torrid zone comprising the two areas from the equator to each tropic, with a radius of 4/60 or 16,800 stades each (4/60 is equivalent to 24°, an approximate figure for the obliquity of the ecliptic known probably from the time of Eudoxus and used occasionally even by Hipparchus, e.g., *Commentarii in Arati et Eudoxi Phaenomena,* I, 10, 2)—making a total of 126,000 stades from pole to pole, i.e., half the whole circumference (see Geminus, *Isagoge,* XVI, 6 f.; V, 45 f.; Strabo, *Geography,* 113–114; *cf.* 112). The frigid zones were arbitrarily defined by the "arctic" and "antarctic" circles of an observer on the main parallel of latitude (roughly 36° N.), i.e., the circles marking the limits of the circumpolar stars that never rise or set and the stars that are never visible at that latitude (see *Geographical Fragments of Hipparchus,* pp. 165–166). Within this framework the *oikoumene,* according to Eratosthenes, has a "breadth" (north–south, as always in Greek geography) of 38,000 stades from the Cinnamon country (south of Meroë) to Thule, and a "length" (east–west) of 77,800 stades from the further

side of India to beyond the Straits of Gibraltar (Strabo, *Geography,* 62–63, 64).

Although it is clear from the *Geography* that Eratosthenes was familiar with the concept of the celestial sphere, he does not seem to have done any original work in astronomy apart from the above measurements made in a geographical context; his name is not connected with any purely astronomical observation (figures for the distance and size of the sun attributed to him by Eusebius of Caesarea, *Praeparatio evangelica,* XV, 53, and Macrobius, *In somnium Scipionis,* I, 20, 9, are worthless, coming from these sources), he does not appear among the authorities cited by Ptolemy in the *Phaseis* for data relating to the parapegmata or astronomical calendars (see *Geographical Fragments of Hipparchus,* pp. 111–112), and only one astronomical title is attributed to him (and that wrongly): the fragmentary *Catasterismoi* (Robert, ed. [Berlin, 1878]; see Maass, "Analecta Eratosthenica," in *Philologische Untersuchungen,* **6** [1883], 3–55), which tells how various mythical personages were placed among the stars and gave their names to the different constellations, descriptions of which are given. It is possible that an inferior second-century compilation of the same nature, called *Poetica astronomica* (Bunte, ed. [Leipzig, 1875]) and going under the name of the Augustan scholar Hyginus, is based partly on a work of Eratosthenes, who is cited some twenty times (as against, e.g., ten times for Aratus), but this is hardly serious astronomy (see Rose, *Handbook of Latin Literature,* 3rd ed. [1954], p. 447).

In mathematics, Eratosthenes' chief work seems to have been the *Platonicus,* of which we have a few extracts given by Theon of Smyrna, who wrote in the second century (*Expositio rerum mathematicarum ad legendum Platonem utilium,* Hiller, ed. [Leipzig, 1878], pp. 2, 127, 129, 168). In this work, Eratosthenes apparently discussed from a mathematical and philosophical point of view such topics as proportion and progression (essential tools in Greek mathematics) and, arising from this, the theory of musical scales (Ptolemy, *Harmonica,* II, 14, Düring, ed. [Göteborg, 1930], pp. 70 f.; see Düring's ed. of Porphyry's commentary on this [1932], p. 91). Also in this work he gave his solution of the famous Delian problem of doubling the cube and described a piece of apparatus by which a solution could be obtained by mechanical means; the description is preserved for us by Eutocius, a sixth-century commentator on the works of Archimedes, and includes Eratosthenes' epigram (mentioned above) commemorating his achievement (*Eutocii commentarii in libros de sphaera et cylindro,* II, 1, in *Archimedes opera omnia,* Heiberg ed., III,

88 f.; epigram, p. 96); Pappus also describes the apparatus and the method (*Collectio,* III, F. Hultsch, ed. [Berlin, 1876], 22–23, 56–58). Eutocius gives his information in the form of a letter from Eratosthenes to King Ptolemy Euergetes; the "letter" is almost certainly not genuine, but there is no reason to doubt that the contents represent the matter of Eratosthenes' solution (perhaps at least partly in his own words) or that the epigram is his.

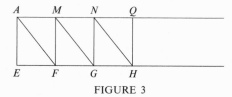

FIGURE 3

The history of the problem of doubling the cube and the various solutions proposed are fully discussed by Heath (*History of Greek Mathematics,* I, 244–270). Briefly, the problem resolves itself into finding two mean proportionals in continued proportion between two given straight lines: if *a* and *b* are the two given straight lines and we find *x* and *y* such that $a:x = x:y = y:b$, then $y = x^2/a = ab/x;$ eliminating *y*, we have $x^3 = a^2b$, and in the case where *b* is twice *a*, $x^3 = 2a^3$, and thus the cube is doubled. Eratosthenes' mechanical solution envisaged a framework of two parallel rulers with longitudinal grooves along which could be slid three rectangular (or, according to Pappus, *loc. cit.,* triangular) plates (marked with their diagonals parallel—see Figure 3) moving independently of each other and able to overlap; if one of the plates remains fixed and the other two are moved so that they overlap as in Figure 4, it can easily be shown that points *A, B, C, D* lie on a straight line in such a way that *AE, BF, CG, DH* are in continued proportion, and *BF* and *CG* are the required mean proportionals between the given straight lines *AE* and *DH.*

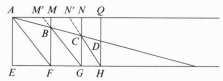

FIGURE 4. Only diagonals and righthand edges of movable plates marked.

In arithmetic Eratosthenes invented a method called the "sieve" (κόσκινον) for finding prime numbers (Nicomachus, *Introductio arithmetica,* I, 13, 2–4). According to this, one writes down consecutively the odd numbers, starting with 3 and continuing as long as desired; then, counting from 3, one passes over

two numbers and strikes out the third (a multiple of 3 and hence not prime) and continues to do this until the end—thus 3 5 7 9̷ 11 13 1̷5̷ 17 19 2̷1̷ 23 25 2̷7̷ 29 31 3̷3̷ 35, etc. The same process is gone through with 5, but this time passing over four numbers and striking out the fifth (a multiple of 5)—3 5 7 9̷ 11 13 1̷5̷ 17 19 2̷1̷ 23 2̷5̷ 2̷7̷ 29 31 3̷3̷ 3̷5̷, etc. The process may be repeated with consecutive odd numbers as many times as one likes, on each occasion, if *n* is the odd number, *n*–1 numbers being passed over and the next struck out; the remaining numbers will all be prime. Pappus (late third century) also attributes to Eratosthenes a work *On Means* (Περὶ μεσοτήτων), the contents of which are a matter of conjecture but which was important enough to form part of what Heath calls the *Treasury of Analysis* (ἀναλυόμενος τόπος), comprising works by Euclid, Apollonius, Aristaeus, and Eratosthenes (Pappus, *Collectio,* Hultsch, ed., VII, 3, p. 636, 24; see Heath, *History of Greek Mathematics,* II, pp. 105, 399 ff.).

In chronology, Eratosthenes apparently wrote two works, *Chronography* (Χρονογραφίαι) and *Olympic Victors* ('Ολυμπιονίκαι); both must have entailed considerable original research (he was the first Greek writer we know to have made a scientific study of the dating of events), and the former seems to have been a popularizing work containing a number of anecdotes, several of which are repeated by Plutarch (e.g., "Demosthenes," Loeb ed., IX, 4; Teubner ed., XXX, 3; "Alexander," Loeb ed., III, 2; Teubner ed., XXXI, 2). Eratosthenes' datings remained authoritative throughout antiquity and in many cases cannot be improved upon today—e.g., the fall of Troy, 1184/1183 B.C.; the Dorian migration, 1104/1103; the first olympiad, beginning 777/776; the invasion of Xerxes, 480/479; the outbreak of the Peloponnesian War, 432/431.

In literary criticism Eratosthenes wrote a work in not less than twelve books entitled *On the Old Comedy,* the contents of which ranged over textual criticism, discussion of the authorship of plays from the dates of performances, and the meanings and usages of words; it was highly thought of by ancient scholars, being frequently cited, and its loss is greatly to be regretted. He also seems to have written a separate work on grammar. Finally, as befitted an Alexandrian polymath, he had a not inconsiderable reputation as a poet; his three main poetical works were *Hermes, Erigone,* and *Anterinys* or *Hesiod* (apparently alternative titles). The first had the same theme at the beginning as the well-known Homeric hymn but went on to draw a picture of the ascent of Hermes to the heavens and to give a vividly imaginative description of the zones of the earth as seen from there (Achilles

Tatius, *Isagoge*, p. 153c in Petavius' *Uranologion* [1630]—the lines are reprinted by Hiller and by Powell); this passage was copied by Vergil (*Georgics*, I, 233–239). The *Erigone* was a star legend dealing with the story of Icarius, his daughter Erigone, and her dog, all of whom in this version were translated to the heavens as Boötes, Virgo, and Sirius, the Dog Star. The subject matter of the third poem is unknown. Only a few fragments of Eratosthenes' poetry are extant (the longest, some sixteen lines, being the passage from the *Hermes* mentioned above), and it is impossible to judge its intrinsic merit from these.

BIBLIOGRAPHY

The only published collection of all Eratosthenes' fragments is G. Bernhardy, *Eratosthenica* (Berlin, 1822), which is now greatly out of date. I have been much indebted in the preparation of this article to R. M. Bentham's unpublished Ph.D. thesis (London) entitled "The Fragments of Eratosthenes of Cyrene." It was made available to me through the kindness of his supervisor, Prof. E. H. Warmington (formerly of Birkbeck College, University of London), following the unfortunate death of the author before he submitted his thesis.

See also G. Knaack, "Eratosthenes," in Pauly-Wissowa, VI (1907), cols. 358–388; E. H. Bunbury, *History of Ancient Geography,* I (London, 1879), ch. 16; E. H. Berger, *Die geographische Fragmente des Eratosthenes* (Leipzig, 1880); A. Thalamas, *La géographie d'Ératosthène* (Versailles, 1921); D. R. Dicks, *The Geographical Fragments of Hipparchus* (London, 1960); E. Hiller, *Eratosthenis carminum reliquiae* (Leipzig, 1872); and J. U. Powell, *Collectanea Alexandrina* (Oxford, 1925).

D. R. DICKS

ERCKER (also **ERCKNER** or **ERCKEL**), **LAZARUS** (*b.* Annaberg, Saxony, *ca.* 1530; *d.* Prague, Bohemia, 1594), *chemistry, metallurgy.*

Ercker was the son of Asmus Erckel. After finishing school at Annaberg, he studied at the University of Wittenberg in 1547–1548. He married Anna Canitz on 7 October 1554, and through the help of one of his wife's relatives, a doctor named Johann Neef, he was appointed assayer at Dresden by Elector Augustus, an enthusiastic admirer of alchemy and metallurgy. A year later he became chief consultant and supervisor in all matters relating to the mineral arts and mint affairs for Freiberg, Annaberg, and Schneeberg but soon was demoted, for unknown reasons, to warden of the mint at Annaberg. In the spring of 1558 he made a trip to the Tyrol to become acquainted with its mines and foundries, and in the autumn of the same year Prince Henry of Brunswick made

him first warden and then master of the mint at Goslar.

After the death of his wife in 1567 Ercker returned to Dresden, where he sought a position with Elector Augustus of Saxony but failed because of intrigue and an unsuccessful attempt to obtain silver from poor ores. He then went to Prague, where his brother-in-law, Casper Richter, was a minter and, through the latter's support, was appointed control tester at Kutna Hora.

In 1574 Ercker published (at Prague) his famous book *Beschreibung allerfürnemisten mineralischen Ertzt.* This brought him to the attention of Emperor Maximilian II, who named him his courier for mining affairs and clerk in the Supreme Office of the Bohemian crown.

During the reign of the next emperor, Rudolf II, a well-known patron of alchemists, Ercker became chief inspector of mines and was knighted on 10 March 1586, receiving the title von Schreckenfels. The motto on his coat of arms was "Erst Prob's dann Lob's." Ercker's second wife, Susanna, for many years managed the mint at Kutna Hora and had the title manager-mistress of the mint. Both of his sons, Joachim and Hans, were assayers.

Through his various posts Ercker acquired extensive experience in chemistry and metallurgy. His first work was *Probierbuchlein* (1556), dedicated to Augustus. In 1563 he wrote *Münzbuch* and in 1569 a book on the testing of ores, *Zkoušeni rud.* In 1574 Ercker published his magnum opus, *Beschreibung allerfürnemisten mineralischen Ertzt.* The only one of Ercker's works to contain many drawings, it presents a systematic review of the methods of testing alloys and minerals of silver, gold, copper, antimony, mercury, bismuth, and lead; of obtaining and refining these metals, as well as of obtaining acids, salts, and other compounds. The last chapter is devoted to saltpeter. Ercker described laboratory procedures and equipment, gave an account of preparing the cupel, of constructing furnaces, and of the assaying balance and the method of operating it. He used as his model Agricola's *De re metallica,* yet he was quite original and included only the procedures he himself had tested. Ercker was so hostile to alchemy that he did not use alchemical symbols, although his *Probierbuchlein* (1556) included a full list of them.

Ercker's *Beschreibung* may be regarded as the first manual of analytical and metallurgical chemistry. Of particular interest to the historian of science is his observation that a cupel containing copper and lead weighs more after roasting in a furnace than before, which, says Ercker, although it is of no importance to the assayer, is surprising (bk. I).

Ercker maintained that precipitating copper from a solution by means of iron does not mean that iron becomes copper and that transmutation takes place; that copper sets silver free from a solution, and if one wants to precipitate copper and silver from solutions of nitrates, one should use iron plates and copper plates; and that iron reduces copper from its solution. This had already been written by Alexander Suchten in *Tractatus secundum de antimonio* (*ca.* 1570, published posthumously in 1604): "Venus so das Eisen aus dem Vitriol reducirt hat." Ercker's account of the fact that zinc precipitates other metals from solutions, cited by J. R. Partington, is to be found only in the 1684 and later editions and therefore was added by an unknown commentator.

Ercker also discovered a new method of refining gold; an exact description was sent to Augustus but is not extant. Ercker's book inspired Löhneyss, Glauber, and others in their own writings on assaying.

BIBLIOGRAPHY

I. ORIGINAL WORKS. Ercker's writings include *Münzbuch, wie es mit den Münzen gehalten sind* (1563); *Beschreibung allerfürnemisten mineralischen Ertzt und Berckwercksarten . . .* (Prague, 1574; Frankfurt, 1580, 1598, 1623, 1629); and *Aula subterranea alias Probierbuch Herrn Lasari Erckers* (Frankfurt, 1672, 1684, 1703, 1736). The *Beschreibung* was translated into English by John Pettus as *Fleta minor, the Laws of Art and Nature* (London, 1683, 1686, 1689) and appeared in a more modern version as *Treatise on Ores and Assaying* (Chicago, 1951); into modern German as *Beschreibung der allevornehmsten mineralischen Erze und Bergwerksarten vom Jahre 1580* (Berlin, 1960), Freiberger Forschungshefte D34; and into Dutch as *Uytvoerige Operinge der onderaarolsche Wereld* (The Hague, 1745).

The MS of the *Probierbuchlein* is in the Sachsisches Landesbibliothek, Dresden, MS J343; that of the *Münzbuch,* in the Herzog Augustus Bibliothek, Wolfenbüttel, MS 2728; and that of *Zkouśeni rud* in the National Archives, Prague, MS 3053.

II. SECONDARY LITERATURE. On Ercker's life and work, see *Allgemeine deutsche Biographie,* VI (1885), 214; E. V. Armstrong and H. S. Lukens, "Lazarus Ercker and His 'Probierbuch.' Sir John Pettus and His 'Fleta Minor,'" in *Journal of Chemical Education,* **16** (1939), 553–562; P. R. Beierlein, *Lazarus Ercker, Bergmann, Hüttenmann und Münzmeister in 16. Jahrhundert* (Berlin, 1955); and in *Beschreibung der allervornehmsten mineralischen Erze und Bergwerksarten vom Jahre 1580* (Berlin, 1960), *passim.* Beierlein's is the best biography (although he consulted only the Landesarchiv in Dresden), but the chemical commentary on Ercker's treatise is incomplete and often in error. See also J. Ferguson, in *Bibliotheca chemica,* I (Glasgow, 1906), 242–245; J. R. Partington, *A History of Chemistry,* II (London, 1961), 104–107; and A. Wrany, in *Geschichte der Chemie* (Prague, 1902), p. 91.

Much material concerning Ercker's activity in Bohemia in 1583–1593, none of which has yet been used, is in the National Archives, Prague, Prazska Mincownia collection, boxes 17–25 (1583–1593). Several letters from Ercker to Wilhelm Rosenberg, burgrave of Prague, are in the Archives of Třeboň, Czechoslovakia. There should also be documents concerning him in the archives of Goslar, Brunswick, and Wolfenbüttel. All the material in the Landesarchiv, Dresden, was used by Beierlein in his study of Ercker.

WŁODZIMIERZ HUBICKI

ERDMANN, OTTO LINNÉ (*b.* Dresden, Germany, 11 April 1804; *d.* Leipzig, Germany, 9 October 1869), *chemistry.*

Erdmann was the son of the physician and botanist Carl Gottfried Erdmann. In 1820, after apprenticeship to a pharmacist, he studied medicine at the Medical-Surgical Academy in Dresden; in 1822 he entered the University of Leipzig, where his interest in chemistry was stimulated by L. W. Gilbert, professor of physics. After graduating in medicine in 1824 and qualifying as a university lecturer in 1825, Erdmann devoted the rest of his life to chemistry. In 1827, after a year directing a nickel mine and foundry at Hasserode, he was appointed extraordinary professor, and in 1830 professor, of technical chemistry at Leipzig, where he established his reputation as a teacher and researcher. Erdmann was Rektor Magnificus of Leipzig from 1848 to 1849, and from 1835 he was a director, and eventually chairman, of the Leipzig-Dresden Railway Company. A prominent Freemason, he devoted much time to the improvement of the cultural facilities and technological prosperity of the city of Leipzig. He married Clara Jungnickel, by whom he had three sons and a daughter.

The Saxon government was persuaded by Erdmann to build chemical laboratories at the university; and after they were opened in 1842[1] Erdmann was able to compete with Liebig at Giessen and attract large numbers of students, many of whom achieved eminence, e.g., C. F. Gerhardt.[2] He toured Germany and France in 1836 in order to meet other chemists, including his future collaborator, R. F. Marchand. Erdmann visited England in 1842, and he was a voluble spokesman for noninterference with the individual chemist's right to freedom of choice between atomic and equivalent weights at the important Karlsruhe Conference in 1860.[3] He greatly enriched chemical communications by the creation in 1834 of the *Journal für praktische Chemie.* His textbooks, and especially his encyclopedia of industrial chemistry, helped to educate the revolutionary generation of Kolbe and Kekulé. To this younger German generation, however, he came to typify the stereotyped, unimaginative chemistry against which they rebelled so passionately and fruitfully.

Erdmann's researches, which spanned mineralogical, industrial, inorganic, and organic chemistry, were primarily descriptive and analytical. In organic chemistry, between 1840 and 1841 (simultaneously with Laurent, who corrected him), he investigated the nature of indigotin and prepared a number of derivatives that were important later, including isatin and tetrachloro-p-benzoquinone.[4] He subsequently investigated and isolated hematoxylin from logwood[5] and euxanthic acid from Indian yellow.[6]

Erdmann's confusion over the empirical formula of isatin led him skeptically to redetermine the atomic weight of carbon in 1841. In collaboration with Marchand he supported Dumas and Stas in lowering its atomic weight from Berzelius' value of 76.43 $(O = 100)$ to 75.08.[7] Subsequently, until the death of Marchand in 1850, they made a number of accurate redeterminations.[8] In most cases they obtained values significantly different from those established by Berzelius and sufficiently close to whole numbers to persuade them that there might be some truth in Prout's hypothesis that atomic weights were multiples of a common unit. There followed a dispute with Berzelius, who abhorred *Multiplenfieber,* in which Erdmann maintained an empirical position that chemists should be guided only by accurate experiments.[9]

NOTES

1. O. L. Erdmann, "Das chemische Laboratorium der Universität Leipzig," in *Journal für praktische Chemie,* **31** (1844), 65–75, with plans.
2. E. Grimaux and C. Gerhardt, *Charles Gerhardt, sa vie, son oeuvre, sa correspondance 1816–1856* (Paris, 1900), pp. 19–21, 85, 218, 264–265, 449, 452.
3. R. Anschütz, *August Kekulé* (Berlin, 1929), I, 671–688.
4. O. L. Erdmann, "Untersuchungen über den Indigo," in *Journal für praktische Chemie,* **19** (1840), 321–362; **22** (1841), 257–299.
5. O. L. Erdmann, "Ueber das Hämatoxylin," *ibid.,* **26** (1842), 193–216, also in *Reports of the British Association for the Advancement of Science,* **11** (1842), 33–34.
6. O. L. Erdmann, "Ueber das Jaune indien und die darin enthaltene organische Säure (Euxanthinsäure)," in *Journal für praktische Chemie,* **33** (1844), 190–209.
7. O. L. Erdmann and R. F. Marchand, "Ueber das Atomgewicht des Kohlenstoffes," *ibid.,* **23** (1841), 159–189.
8. O. L. Erdmann, "Ueber das Atomgewicht des Wasserstoffes und Calciums," *ibid.,* **26** (1842), 461–478; ". . . Calciums, Chlors, Kaliums und Silbers," *ibid.,* **31** (1844), 257–279; ". . . Kupfers, Quecksilbers, und Schwefels," *ibid.,* 385–402; ". . . Eisens," *ibid.,* **33** (1844), 1–6.

9. O. L. Erdmann, "Rechfertigung einiger Atomgewichtsbestimmungen," *ibid.,* **37** (1846), 65–80; "Einige Bemerkungen über die Atomgewichte der einfachen Körper," *ibid.,* **55** (1852), 193–203.

BIBLIOGRAPHY

I. ORIGINAL WORKS. The *Royal Society Catalogue of Scientific Papers* assigns 96 papers to Erdmann, of which 17 were joint researches with Marchand. Unrecorded are several papers on artistic subjects and his many editorial notes to his journals: *Die neuesten Forschungen im Gebiete der technischen und ökonomischen Chemie,* 18 vols. (1828–1833), more familiarly known, through its second title page, as *Journal für technische und ökonomische Chemie.* In 1834 this amalgamated with the well-established *Journal für Chemie und Physik* and was edited jointly by Erdmann and F. W. Schweigger-Seidel as *Journal für praktische Chemie,* 1–9 (1834–1836). Volumes **10–15** (1837–1838) were edited by Erdmann alone, vols. **16–50** (1839–1850) jointly with Marchand, vols. **51–57** (1850–1852) alone, and vols. **58–108** (1853–1869) jointly with G. Werther. The journal was continued after Erdmann's death by Kolbe. Other papers by Erdmann, together with extensive analyses of their contents, may be traced in Berzelius' *Jahres-Bericht über die Fortschritte der physische Wissenschaften,* **7** (1828)–**25** (1846) and its continuation, *Jahresbericht über die Fortschritte der reinen, pharmaceutischen und technischen Chemie* (1849–1870); see annual indexes.

Erdmann published the following books: *Ueber das Nickel* (Leipzig, 1827); *Lehrbuch der Chemie* (Leipzig, 1828; 3rd ed., 1840; 4th ed., 1851), trans. into Dutch (Amsterdam, 1836); *Grundriss der allgemeinen Waarenkunde* (Leipzig, 1833; 2nd ed., 1852; 3rd ed., 1857), with many posthumously revised eds. (after the 7th ed., 1871, edited by C. R. Krönig, it became known as "Erdmann-Krönig" and, with a succession of editors, reached the 17th and final ed. in 1925); and *Ueber das Studium der Chemie* (Leipzig, 1861). He was an editor of *Universel-Lexicon der Handelswissenschaften,* 3 vols. (Leipzig, 1837–1839).

The Karl Marx University, Leipzig, holds 19 of Erdmann's letters, written between 1828 and 1869. There are several letters to Berzelius in the Royal Swedish Academy of Sciences, Stockholm.

II. SECONDARY LITERATURE. The basic sources of information concerning Erdmann's career are the unctuous obituaries by H. Kolbe, in *Journal für praktische Chemie,* **108** (1869), 449–458—an adapted and unacknowledged English version by A. W. Williamson, in *Journal of the Chemical Society,* **23** (1870), 306–310—and in *Berichte der Deutschen chemischen Gesellschaft,* **3** (1870), 374–381. See also *Sitzungsberichte der K. Bayerischen Akademie der Wissenschaften zu München* (1870), pt. 1, 415–417; and J. R. Partington, *A History of Chemistry,* IV, 397. An assessment of Erdmann's atomic weights may be made from G. F. Becker, *Atomic Weight Determinations: A Digest of the Investigations Published Since 1814,* Smithsonian Miscellaneous Collections: Constants of Nature, pt. IV (Washington, D.C., 1880); and F. W. Clarke, *A Recalculation of the Atomic Weights,* Constants of Nature, pt. V (Washington, D.C., 1882; 2nd ed., 1897). For a very important critique of *Grundriss der allgemeinen Waarenkunde,* see R. A. C. E. Erlenmeyer, in *Zeitschrift für Chemie und Pharmacie,* **4** (1861), 217–220, 251–256, 284–287, 320–323, 385–386.

Contemporary opinions of Erdmann may be found in R. Anschütz, *August Kekulé* (Berlin, 1929), I, *passim;* E. Grimaux and C. Gerhardt, *Charles Gerhardt, sa vie, son oeuvre, sa correspondance 1816–1856* (Paris, 1900), pp. 19–21, 85, 218, 264–265, 449, 452; and O. Wallach, ed., *Briefwechsel zwischen J. Berzelius und F. Wöhler,* 2 vols. (Leipzig, 1901), *passim.*

W. H. Brock

ERIUGENA, JOHANNES SCOTTUS (*b.* Ireland, first quarter ninth century; *d.* England [?], last quarter ninth century), *philosophy.*

Nothing is known of Eriugena's life before 847, by which time he had already left Ireland and had been living for some years in France. By 851 the reputation for learning he had acquired was sufficient for his being asked to give his views on the dispute that had arisen over the interpretation of Augustine's teaching on predestined grace (Ebo of Grenoble, *Liber de tribus epistolis,* XXXIX; Migne, *Patrologia,* CXXII, 1052A). In his reply, *De praedestinatione,* he revealed a critical understanding of the relevant texts of Augustine and adopted his precept that the seven liberal arts should be applied to the solution of theological problems. He also gave early evidence of a knowledge of Greek that was to become exceptional, if not unique, in ninth-century Europe.

Eriugena specifically attributed to an inadequate understanding of Greek and the liberal arts the failure of his contemporaries to understand Augustine's teaching (*De praedestinatione,* XVIII; *Patrologia,* CXXII, 403C10–D1) and made these two disciplines the principal subjects in the curriculum of the palace school at Laon, over which he presided with the assistance of his fellow countryman Martin. Here he restored to the arts their ancient classical function of propaedeutic to philosophy and theology. He taught them through the medium of a book that had been forgotten since the end of the ancient world, the *De nuptiis* of Martianus Capella, and used another forgotten work, Boethius' *Consolation of Philosophy,* for more advanced studies. To these texts he and his colleagues appended commentaries that, although not certainly extant in complete form today, established the matter and method of teaching in schools throughout Europe from the ninth to the twelfth centuries. Eriugena and his colleagues at Laon thus founded the educational system of the later Middle Ages and perpetuated the Carolingian renaissance.

The fame of the Greek scholarship at Laon was such that Charles the Bald commissioned Eriugena to translate into Latin the treatises of the pseudo-Dionysius and the *First Ambigua* of Maximus the Confessor. These labors, to which he added for his own purposes translations of the *Quaestiones ad Thalassium* of Maximus and the *De hominis opificio* of Gregory of Nyssa, occupied the years between 860 and 864. They brought Eriugena, already inclined toward Platonism by his reading of Augustine, into direct contact with the fully developed post-Plotinian Neoplatonism which had been absorbed by the Greek Fathers but until then had been a closed book for the Latin West. The immediate consequence of this contact was the composition, between 864 and 866, of Eriugena's greatest work, the *Periphyseon* or *De divisione naturae,* in which the Western and Eastern forms of Neoplatonism are synthesized within a Christian context. In his subsequent writings—the *Expositiones super Ierarchiam caelestem,* his commentary on St. John's Gospel (of which only three fragments survive), and his homily on St. John's Prologue—he enunciates the theories of the *Periphyseon* with greater conviction and expresses them in more precise language, but nowhere does he change or abandon them.

These last works were written between 866 and 870, after which nothing further is known of Eriugena; his end is as obscure as his beginning.

BIBLIOGRAPHY

I. Original Works. Eriugena's principal works, edited by H. J. Floss, are collected in volume CXXII of J. P. Migne's *Patrologiae cursus completus; Series latina,* 2nd ed. (Paris, 1865); but, as will be seen from the following list, the collection is far from complete. It also includes two spurious works, *Expositiones super ecclesiasticam s. Dionysii* and *Expositiones seu Glossae in mysticam Theologiam s. Dionysii.*

De praedestinatione is in *Patrologia . . .,* 355A–440A.

"Iohannis Scotti annotationes in Marcianum," in *Annotationes in Marcianum,* Cora E. Lutz, ed. (Cambridge, Mass., 1939), is an edition of an anonymous commentary on the *De nuptiis* preserved in Paris, Bibliothèque Nationale, MS lat. 12960, one of a group of commentaries that contain Eriugena material and are probably derived from Eriugena's own lost commentary.

H. Silvestre, ed., "Le commentaire inédit de Jean Scot Érigène au mètre ix du livre iii du De consolatione philosophiae de Boèce," in *Revue d'histoire ecclésiastique,* **47** (1952), 44–122, is an edition of an anonymous commentary preserved in Brussels, Bibliothèque Royale, MS 10066–

10067. Silvestre today is less certain that Eriugena is the author, although it is certainly based on his teaching.

Translations of the pseudo-Dionysian works are in *Patrologia . . .*, 1023–1194.

The translation of the *First Ambigua* of Maximus the Confessor is in *Patrologia . . .*, 1193–1222 and 1023A–1024B (introduction and chs. 1–4, sec. 3 only, together with a fragment from a later part printed under the title *Liber de egressu et regressu animae*). The full text is preserved in Paris, MS Mazarine 561, from which one folio has become detached and is now fol. 9 of MS Vat. Reg. lat. 596; Paris, MS Arsenal 237, a contemporary copy of Mazarine MS that lacks the last three folios; and Cambridge, MS Trinity College 0.9, 5, a transcription of the Mazarine MS by Mabillon. Preparatory work for an edition by the late Raymond Flambard based on the two Paris MSS is preserved in Paris, Archives Nationales, AB xxviii[100].

"Scolia Maximi," an unpublished translation of the *Quaestiones ad Thalassium* of Maximus, is preserved in MSS Monte Cassino 333 and Troyes, Bibliothèque Municipale 1234.

De imagine, edited by M. Cappuyns as "Le De imagine de Grégoire de Nysse traduit par Jean Scot Érigène," in *Recherches de théologie ancienne et médiévale*, **32** (1965), 205–262, is an edition of Eriugena's translation of the *De hominis opificio* from the unique MS Bamberg Staatsbibliothek Patr. 78.

Periphyseon (*De divisione naturae*) is in *Patrologia . . .*, 439–1022. Of the new edition in preparation under the auspices of the Dublin Institute for Advanced Studies, the first volume has been published as vol. VII of the series Scriptores latini Hiberniae: I. P. Sheldon-Williams and Ludwig Bieler, eds., *Iohannis Scotti Eriugenae Periphyseon* (*De divisione naturae*) *liber primus* (Dublin, 1968).

Expositiones super Ierarchiam caelestem can be found in *Patrologia . . .*, 125–265 and in H. F. Dondaine, "Les Expositiones super Ierarchiam caelestem de Jean Scot Érigène," in *Archives d'histoire doctrinale et littéraire du moyen âge*, **18** (1951), 245–302—Eriugena's commentary on the *Celestial Hierarchy* of the pseudo-Dionysius, chs. 1, 2, 7–14 in *Patrologia . . .*, the rest in Dondaine.

The *Commentary on St. John's Gospel* is in *Patrologia . . .*, 297A–348B; three fragments are preserved in MS Laon 81.

The homily on the Prologue of St. John's Gospel, was edited by Edouard Jeauneau as *Jean Scot, Homélie sur le Prologue de Jean*, Sources chrétiennes no. 151 (Paris, 1969) and is also in *Patrologia . . .*, 283B–296D.

His poems were edited by L. Traube, in *Monumenta Germaniae historica, Poetae latini aeui Caroli*, III (Berlin 1896), 518–556; an incomplete collection is in *Patrologia . . .*, 1221C–1240C.

II. Secondary Literature. The most important and recent monographs on Eriugena are H. Bett, *Johannes Scotus Erigena: A Study in Mediaeval Philosophy* (Cambridge, 1925; repr. New York, 1964); M. Cappuyns, *Jean Scot Érigène, sa vie, son oeuvre, sa pensée* (Louvain–Paris, 1933; repr. Brussels, 1965), still the best work on Eriugena; and M. Dal Pra, *Scoto Eriugena*, 2nd ed. (Milan, 1951). John J. O'Meara, *Eriugena* (Cork, 1969), is of exceptional importance and resumes the findings of more recent research, to which it makes its own valuable contribution. Extensive bibliographies are given in Cappuyns, *op. cit.*, pp. xi–xvii; I. P. Sheldon-Williams, "A Bibliography of the Works of Johannes Scottus Eriugena," in *Journal of Ecclesiastical History*, **10**, no. 2 (1960), 223–224; and in Jeauneau's translation of the "Homily," pp. 171–198.

I. P. SHELDON-WILLIAMS

ERLANGER, JOSEPH (*b*. San Francisco, California, 5 January 1874; *d*. St. Louis, Missouri, 5 December 1965), *physiology.*

In his late years Erlanger wrote a short but delightful autobiography in which he minimizes his scientific achievements with characteristic modesty but gives interesting details on his early family life. Erlanger's father was born in Württemberg, Germany, and in 1842, at the age of sixteen, landed alone in New York, went to New Orleans, and then became an itinerant peddler along the Mississippi Valley. The gold rush drew him to California, where he became a businessman in San Francisco after having tried his luck at mining. He married the daughter of his business partner. A large family was born to them, Erlanger being their sixth child.

After two years at the San Francisco Boys' High School—during which he acquired a sound knowledge of German and Latin—Erlanger was admitted to the University of California. He enrolled in the college of chemistry to prepare for the medical career that he already had in mind. His native abilities for observation and experimentation were demonstrated in a thesis, written in his senior year, on the development of the eggs of the newt *Amblystoma*.

Erlanger then attended the newly founded Johns Hopkins Medical School in Baltimore. During his medical studies he found time for research, especially during vacations, which he could not spend at home because of the cost of travel. In Lewellys Barker's laboratory Erlanger attacked a fundamental problem of neurophysiology. In 1900 he succeeded in localizing the exact position in the spinal cord of the motor nerve cells that innervate a given muscle, by means of a delicate histological study based on the alterations undergone by the motor nerve cells of the rabbit after the excision of the corresponding muscle. Erlanger's results were the first decisive experimental confirmation of F. Sano's views, according to which each muscle is activated by definite motor nerve cells. Barker's treatise "The Nervous System and Constituent Neurons" describes these findings in detail.

A year later Erlanger published his first paper,

which came to the attention of William H. Howell, professor of physiology at Johns Hopkins, who, shortly after Erlanger took his medical degree, offered him an assistant professorship. In this first paper, "A Study of the Metabolism in Dogs With Shortened Small Intestines," Erlanger sought to ascertain the extent of intestine that could safely be excised in surgical operations. This early research is marked by the dual concern for physiology and medicine with which Erlanger was always to be occupied. This is perhaps the reason why he devoted the major part of his career to the study of circulation and of cardiac physiology.

In 1904 Erlanger imagined and built with his own hands a sphygmomanometer; a form of this instrument bears his name, although others later devised similar apparatuses without mentioning Erlanger's priority. This instrument allowed him to demonstrate that the pulse pressure can also give the precise volume of the pulse wave, a result that was to have an immediate application in the separation of the effects of the pulse pressure from those of the arterial pressure. Erlanger was thus able to demonstrate that in patients affected by albuminuria the discharge of albumin depends much more on the volume of the pulse wave than on the arterial pressure.

From 1904 on Erlanger concerned himself with the conduction of excitation in the heart. He proved that the Stokes-Adams syndrome resulted from an impaired conduction between the auricles and ventricles, similar to the effect obtained through the experimental exercise of pressure on the auriculoventricular junction of the turtle's heart. The fainting spells that characterize the syndrome occur when the partial block of auriculoventricular conduction temporarily becomes complete. The German anatomist Wilhelm His had previously described the only conducting muscular connection between the auricles and ventricles, the narrow auriculoventricular bundle that bears his name. Erlanger devised a clamp with which controlled pressure could be reversibly applied to the His bundle of the beating heart in a dog. He thus produced all degrees of auriculoventricular block, from the normal 1:1 sequence to complete block, through the partial blocks characterized by two or more auricular beats for a simple ventricular contraction. These pioneering experiments are the basis of current knowledge of intracardiac conduction; the finer features of this conduction were to be analyzed many years later by Frank Schmitt.

In 1906 Erlanger was offered the chair of physiology at the University of Wisconsin, an assignment worthy of his abilities. Here he was asked to equip a modern laboratory, and he became responsible for the teaching of the entire field of physiology.

In 1910, when Washington University in St. Louis completely reorganized its medical school (soon to be a research center of worldwide reputation), Erlanger became its professor of physiology. New laboratories devoted to the major fundamental sciences were built close to each other in the vicinity of large hospitals, reinforced by an excellent library.

World War I diverted Erlanger's activity to quite different problems. Among them was the treatment of wound shock, for which he proposed the administration of a solution of glucose and gum acacia, a procedure that was used successfully by the U.S. Army during its campaign in France; this was the first example of treatment by an artificial serum containing a component of large molecular weight—that is, a high polymer.

He also became interested in the problem of blind landing of airplanes. After numerous flights he proposed a new design of the instrument panel so that the major instruments would always remain in the pilot's visual field.

As soon as the war ended, Erlanger resumed his work on circulation. He investigated the mechanism that produces the sounds of Korotkoff (the sounds that are detected by a stethoscope placed on the skin over an arterial region above which a controlled pressure is applied through a pneumatic cuff—the regular procedure for the measurement of arterial pressure). Erlanger showed that these sounds pose a difficult problem of fluid mechanics, which he solved. Working with J. C. Bramwell, he demonstrated, with an elegant and precise technique, that the crest of the pulse wave is unstable. The pulse wave breaks, as does a sea wave on a beach, because its crest dilates the artery and thus proceeds with a higher velocity than the foot of the wave. These two components of the wave can be separated by the observer as corresponding to sharp and dull sounds, respectively. When the dull sound occurs, the pressure applied in the cuff indicates exactly the diastolic pressure.

In 1921 Erlanger and his colleague Herbert Gasser, professor of pharmacology at Washington University, became associated in a new field of research. In about ten years they created, with George Bishop, modern neurophysiology with the use of the cathode-ray oscillograph (then called the Braun tube, after its inventor). Under their able hands this dim and fragile ancestor of the brilliant oscillograph of today immediately proved itself a remarkable instrument. By coupling it with amplifying vacuum tubes they obtained, for the first time, an exact picture of the action potentials that are the electric signs of the nervous impulses. Because of the smallness and brief duration of these action potentials no other instrument could record them; the cathode-ray oscillograph revealed that the nerve action potential is formed by several component waves traveling with unequal velocities. When Gasser showed these records to Louis Lapicque, the professor of physiology at the Sorbonne, Lapicque perceived their significance immediately. Ten years earlier, Lapicque and René Legendre had observed that nerves of slow excitability (that is, of long chronaxies) were constituted of smaller fibers than the nerves of fast excitability (or brief chronaxies). Lapicque had then assumed that the impulse travels more rapidly in large fibers than in small ones. A histological investigation by Lapicque, Gasser, and Henri Desoille immediately showed that multifunctional (motor and sensory) nerves that display a multiwave action potential contain two or three groups of fibers, each of which is characteristically of a different diameter. On the other hand, a unifunctional nerve—the phrenic nerve, for example—that innervates only one muscle and contains no sensory fibers is made up of fibers of uniform diameter. These results led Erlanger and Gasser to formulate their law by which nervous impulse velocity is directly proportional to fiber diameter.

Many further discoveries in neurophysiology arose from Erlanger and Gasser's joint work. They were awarded the Nobel Prize in 1944. The disclosure of the time-course of the excitability cycle of nerve that has had a decisive impact upon all further theoretical attempts toward the formulation of excitatory processes is derived, however, from the work of Erlanger and E. A. Blair.

Although he reached retirement age Erlanger did not cease working. He resumed teaching in the medical school of Washington University during World War II, while his younger colleagues were called to military duties. He remained active after the war and was in close contact with the members of the laboratory, who benefited from his profound knowledge of all the domains of physiology. He also devoted much time to the history of this science, to the profit of the Medical School library. That he was an able and elegant historical writer is testified to by, among other things, his account of William Beaumont's experiments, in which he interpreted Beaumont's observations of the digestive process in the human stomach in the light of modern knowledge and showed how they constitute a most excellent experimental work a century ahead of its time.

Erlanger was a family man. In his last years he sustained with courage the losses of his devoted wife Aimée Hirstel, his only son, Herman, and his son-in-law. His reserve at first approach quickly gave way to his natural kindness and to his generous and smiling inclinations. He was an invaluable source of inspiration for both American and foreign physiologists

and especially for those who had the privilege of working under his guidance in his laboratory.

BIBLIOGRAPHY

Erlanger's works include "A Study of the Metabolism in Dogs With Shortened Small Intestines," in *American Journal of Physiology,* **6** (1901), 1–30, written with W. Hewlett; "An Experimental Study of Blood Pressure and of Pulse Pressure in Man," in *Johns Hopkins Hospital Reports,* **12** (1904), 147–378, written with D. R. Hooker; "On the Physiology of Heart-block in Mammals, With Especial Reference to the Causation of Stokes-Adams Disease," in *Journal of Experimental Medicine,* **7** (1905), 675–724, and **8** (1906), 8–58; "Studies in Blood Pressure Estimations by Indirect Methods. I. The Mechanism of Oscillatory Criteria," in *American Journal of Physiology,* **39** (1916), 401–446; "Studies in Blood Pressure Estimations by Indirect Methods. II. The Mechanism of the Compression Sound of Korotkoff," *ibid.,* **40** (1916), 82–125; "The Compound Nature of the Action Current of Nerve as Disclosed by the Cathode-ray Oscillograph," *ibid.,* **70** (1924), 624–666, written with H. S. Gasser; "'The Action Potential Waves Transmitted Between the Sciatic Nerve and Its Spinal Roots," *ibid.,* **78** (1926), 574–591, written with G. H. Bishop and H. S. Gasser; "The Effects of Polarization Upon the Activity of Vertebrate Nerve," *ibid.,* 630–657, written with G. H. Bishop; "The Role Played by the Sizes of the Constituent Fibres of a Nerve Trunk in Determining the Form of Its Action Potential," *ibid.,* **80** (1927), 1522–1547, written with H. S. Gasser; "Directional Differences in the Conduction of the Impulse Through Heart Muscle and Their Possible Relation to Extra Systolic and Fibrillary Contractions," *ibid.,* **87** (1928), 326–347, written with F. O. Schmitt; "The Irritability Changes in Nerve in Response to Subthreshold Induction Shocks and Constant Currents," *ibid.,* **99** (1931), 108–155, written with E. A. Blair; "William Beaumont's Experiments and Their Present Day Value," in *Bulletin of the St. Louis Medical Society* (8 Dec. 1933); and *Electrical Signs of Nervous Activity* (Philadelphia, 1937).

For further details of Erlanger's life, see his autobiographical "A Physiologist Reminisces," the prefatory chapter to *Annual Review of Physiology,* **26** (1964), 1–14.

A. M. MONNIER

ERLENMEYER, RICHARD AUGUST CARL EMIL (*b.* Wehen, Germany, 28 June 1825; *d.* Aschaffenburg, Germany, 22 January 1909), *chemistry.*

Erlenmeyer was one of the earliest disciples of Kekulé and advocated Kekulé's views on the constitution of organic compounds at a time when many of the leading chemists still adhered to dualistic or to type theories. Erlenmeyer himself was converted from the old chemical types to the newer views on valence and structure. He entered the University of

Giessen in 1845 as a medical student, but on hearing Liebig lecture he decided to study chemistry, first at Giessen and then at Heidelberg, where he became one of Kekulé's first private students. He was professor of chemistry at the Munich Polytechnic School from 1868 until his retirement in 1883. In addition to teaching and publishing many research papers, Erlenmeyer was an editor of the *Zeitschrift für Chemie und Pharmazie* and of Liebig's *Annalen der Chemie.* He was coauthor of the three-volume *Lehrbuch der organischen Chemie* (1867–1894).

Erlenmeyer published important work in both experimental and theoretical organic chemistry. His researches were mostly in the synthesis and constitution of aliphatic compounds. In 1865 he discovered and synthesized isobutyric acid. He synthesized guanidine in 1868 and gave the first correct structural formulas of guanidine, creatine, and creatinine. He prepared several hydroxy acids and explained the formation and structure of the lactones derived from them in 1880. He synthesized tyrosine in 1883. Erlenmeyer invented the conical flask that bears his name (1861).

Erlenmeyer also dealt with many theoretical problems, and his remarks on valence and structure were fundamental to the development of these new ideas. He introduced the term "Strukturchemie" as well as the designations "monovalent," "divalent," and so on, which he employed in place of "monoatomic" and "diatomic."

Alexander Crum Brown in 1864 depicted the structures of organic compounds by drawing chemical bonds with dotted lines and enclosing the atomic symbols in circles. Chemists were hesitant to accept and use these graphic representations until Erlenmeyer in 1866 abandoned the old type formulas and adopted the new structural ones. By modifying Crum Brown's graphic formulas, he introduced the modern structural notation.

Another central problem in the new structural theory concerned the constitution of ethylene and other unsaturated compounds. Crum Brown suggested that their unique feature was the sharing of two valence units by each of two carbon atoms. Erlenmeyer not only adopted the double bond for ethylene but also introduced the triple bond to represent acetylene. His formulas, using lines to represent chemical bonds, proved convincing, and chemists adopted his notation.

Erlenmeyer investigated constitutional problems and proposed structural formulas for many organic substances. He immediately adopted Kekulé's ring structure for benzene and proposed the modern naphthalene formula of two benzene rings with two carbon atoms in common.

In 1880 he formulated what is known as the Erlenmeyer rule: All alcohols in which the hydroxyl group is attached directly to a double-bonded carbon atom become aldehydes or ketones. He had attempted to prepare such alcohols but obtained the isomeric carbonyl compounds in every case. Erlenmeyer concluded that such alcohols were incapable of existence, being converted at the instant of their formation into aldehydes or ketones by an intramolecular rearrangement.

BIBLIOGRAPHY

Erlenmeyer, with others, wrote the *Lehrbuch der organischen Chemie,* 3 vols. (Leipzig–Heidelberg, 1867–1894). He also wrote a small treatise, *Über den Einfluss des Freiherrn J. von Liebig auf die Entwicklung der reinen Chemie* (Munich, 1874), as a tribute to Liebig. His new graphic formulas, the triple bond, and the naphthalene structure are found in his "Studien über die s.g. aromatischen Säuren," in *Annalen der Chemie,* **137** (1866), 327–359; his rule on vinyl alcohols is in "Über Phenylbrommilchsäure," in *Berichte der Deutschen chemischen Gesellschaft,* **13** (1880), 305–310. There is a bibliography of his papers with a detailed account of his life and work by M. Conrad, *ibid.,* **43** (1910), 3645–3664.

William Henry Perkin wrote an interesting brief account of Erlenmeyer's work in *Journal of the Chemical Society,* **99** (1911), 1649–1651.

ALBERT B. COSTA

ERMAN, GEORG ADOLPH (*b.* Berlin, Germany, 12 May 1806; *d.* Berlin, 12 July 1877), *physics, meteorology, geophysics, geography, geology, paleontology.*

Erman was the son of Paul Erman, professor of physics at the University of Berlin. He himself earned the doctorate at that institution in 1826 with a dissertation in physics. In 1832 he became *Privatdozent* there and, in 1834, assistant professor of physics. He married Marie Bessel, daughter of the astronomer; one of their ten children, J. P. A. Erman, became a renowned Egyptologist.

In 1828 Erman accompanied a Norwegian expedition to Russia and Siberia. Leaving the expedition, he began a journey around the world that lasted until 1830 and took him from Kamchatka to San Francisco, Cape Horn, Rio de Janeiro, Portsmouth, and St. Petersburg. The primary purpose of the voyage, which he undertook on a Russian corvette, was geographic and geodesic surveying; Erman made altitude determinations, measurements of terrestrial magnetism, and meteorological observations and correlated these with the corresponding data that he had gathered in Russia and northern Asia. He also made numerous notes on natural history, general geography, ethnology, sociology, and economics; these he combined with an account of his travels in the first five volumes of his *Reise um die Erde* (1833–1848), the second section of which, in two volumes, contains his more purely scientific data.

From 1841 until 1867 Erman edited the *Archiv für wissenschaftliche Kunde von Russland,* a periodical designed to propagate Russian belles lettres, which in addition contained articles on science and the arts, as well as reports on economic and social conditions and events in Russia. Erman himself made many contributions to the journal, some original and some reportorial, on many topics. In particular, he wrote on the earth sciences, and his articles include surveys of the geology of European Russia (1841) and of northern Asia (1842), each illustrated with a geological map. He also wrote on the Tertiary of East Prussia, the Cretaceous of northern Spain, and on the mammalian remains from the Baumann cave in the Harz mountains.

BIBLIOGRAPHY

I. Original Works. Erman's major work is *Reise um die Erde durch Nord-Asien und die beiden Oceane in den Jahren 1828, 1829 und 1830,* 7 vols. (Berlin, 1833–1848). His articles include the series "Beiträge zur Klimatologie des Russischen Reiches," in *Archiv für wissenschaftliche Kunde von Russland,* **1** (1841), 562–579; **3** (1843), 365–438; **4** (1845), 617–640; **6** (1848), 441–488; **9** (1851), 33–130; **12** (1853), 645–665; "Über den dermaligen Zustand und die allmälige Entwickelung der geognostischen Kenntnisse vom Europäischen Russland," *ibid.,* **1** (1841), 59–108, 254–313, with a geological map; "Ueber die geognostischen Verhältnisse von Nord-Asien in Beziehung auf das Gold-Vorkommen in diesem Erdtheile," *ibid.,* **2** (1842), 522–556, 712–789, 808–809, with a geological map, and **3** (1843), 121–177, 185–186; "Bemerkungen über einem am Ural gebräuchlichen Seilbohrapparat," *ibid.,* **12** (1853), 333–357; and "Bemerkungen über ein bei den Jakuten und in Andalusien gebräuchliches Feuerzeug," *ibid.,* **19** (1860), 298–326.

II. Secondary Literature. On Erman and his work, see Poggendorff and *Neue deutsche Biographie,* IV (1959), 598–600; Wilhelm Erman, "Paul Erman. Ein Berliner Gelehrtenleben 1764–1851," in *Schriften des Vereins für die Geschichte Berlins,* **53** (1927), 104–105, 169–172, 187–192, 199–209, 216–222, and 227; a portrait is on p. 184.

Heinz Tobien

ERRERA, LÉO-ABRAM (*b.* Laeken, Belgium, 4 September 1858; *d.* Uccle, Belgium, 1 August 1905), *botany, biology, philosophy.*

The son of a distinguished Venetian banker, Giacomo Errera, and of Marie Oppenheim, who was of German origin, Errera must have spent his early years in an exceptional environment. His father, who was the Italian consul general in Belgium, was an ardent patriot who had fiercely defended Venice against the Austrians in 1849. His maternal grandfather was a revolutionary who fought for new political ideas in 1830 in Frankfurt. Errera was a brilliant student at the Faculty of Letters of the University of Brussels, where he received his baccalaureate. He continued his studies at the Faculty of Sciences of the same university, and was awarded the doctorate in 1879. After spending some time abroad, in 1884 Errera was named university lecturer in anatomy and plant physiology at the University of Brussels. In 1885, he married his first cousin, Rose-Eugénie May. He was elected in 1887 to the Royal Academy of Sciences, Letters, and Fine Arts of Belgium.

In 1894 he succeeded J. E. Bommer in the chair of general botany, a position that he held until his death in 1905 and that he enhanced by such achievements as the creation of the first botany laboratories for students. Among his many students those who were to become outstanding in Belgian biological science were Émile Laurent, Jean Massart, Émile Marchal, and Émile de Wildeman. Errera was, first and foremost, a remarkable teacher and was responsible for countless academic and pedagogical reforms. The first to publish (in 1897) wall charts for the teaching of plant physiology, Errera throughout his life displayed an interest in pedagogy, and his lecture entitled "The Utility of Superfluous Studies" shows clearly the direction of his didactic ideas.

In spite of his early death, Errera left a body of astonishingly varied scientific work. Although not a taxonomist, he undertook, while still very young, studies on the genus *Epilobium* and the phylogeny of the *Salix.* This work led to the publication of a paper entitled "Routines et progrès de la botanique systématique," in which he defined with clarity and foresight what was to become the taxonomy of today. In ethology Errera appears as a precursor because of his research work on the heterostylism of the *Primula*— revived by Jules MacLeod—on the fertilization of *Pentastemon* and *Geranium.* But it is in the domain of plant physiology that Errera's contribution is most striking. He first studied the alkaloids, precisely describing their microchemical characteristics and their localization. He was the first to point out the presence of glycogen, forming protoplasm, in the Ascomycetes. Subsequently he discovered this polysaccharide— which had previously been thought to exist only in animals—in a series of microorganisms. Again, in physiology, Errera was a pioneer in the area of physicochemical analysis. In fact, he was the first, making use of the remarkable work of Henri Devaux, to explain the arrangement of cellular walls by utilizing surface tension. Errera again touched upon biophysics when he investigated the mechanisms of the rising of sap and of the growth of the sporangiferous filaments of the *Phycomycetes*. Errera also took up the study of the transmission of acquired characteristics by the *Aspergillus* in its adaptation to concentrated solutions. Errera seems to have been one of the first biologists to undertake the study of life from a strictly physicochemical perspective, and the title of one of his posthumous works, *Cours de physiologie moléculaire*, is a good illustration.

Errera was a controversialist of the first order and became internationally known for his condemnation of anti-Semitism and for two courageous articles, "L'acte de tolérance" and "Six sermons sur les juifs." A warmhearted man and a poet in his leisure time (he left several collections of verse), Errera may be considered one of the most authentic humanists of the late nineteenth century.

BIBLIOGRAPHY

I. ORIGINAL WORKS. The edition *Recueil des oeuvres de Léo Errera* includes *Botanique générale I* (Brussels, 1908); *Mélanges, vers et prose* (Brussels, 1908); *Botanique générale II* (Brussels, 1909); *Physiologie générale, Philosophie* (Brussels, 1910); and *Pédagogie, Biographies* (Brussels, 1922).

II. SECONDARY LITERATURE. On Errera and his work see L. Frédericq and J. Massart, "Notice sur L. Errera," in *Annales. Académie royale de Belgique* (1908), 131–279; J. Massart, *Léo Errera,* Hayez, ed. (Brussels, 1905); and University of Brussels, Gutenberg, ed., *Commémoration Léo Errera* (Brussels, 1960).

P. E. PILET

ESCHER VON DER LINTH, HANS CONRAD (*b.* Zurich, Switzerland, 24 August 1767; *d.* Zurich, 9 March 1823), *geology, hydraulics.*

Escher came from an old Zurich family. His father was an administrator of the canton of Zurich and ran a prosperous textile factory. Escher, who had eleven brothers and sisters, took over his father's business in 1788, after traveling in France, England, Austria, and Italy, and studying for a year in Göttingen, Germany. In the following years he became involved in politics. His judgment, strength of character, and patriotism gained him responsible administrative positions in his native canton; and in 1798, during the French occupation, he was the head of the Great Council of Switzerland.

Escher began his most important work in hydraulics in 1803 on measures to control the devastation caused by the flooding of the Linth River. The Linth was at that time a rapid mountain river that flowed into the Lake of Zurich and caused heavy high-water damage all year long. According to Escher's plan the Linth River would be conducted into the neighboring Lake of Walen to the east and thereby be rendered harmless. The connection to the Lake of Zurich would be provided by an artificial canal. For this work, largely completed in 1811 and entirely finished in 1823—half a year after his death—Escher and his male descendants obtained the surname "von der Linth." In the last decade of his life Escher was again active in the politics and administration of the canton of Zurich. His only son, Arnold (1807–1872), was an important Alpine geologist.

Soon after he returned from his travels, Escher began the geological investigations of the Alps which occupied him for many years. As early as 1796 he published a geological survey of the Swiss Alps, which was later followed by a series of geological profiles from Zurich to the St. Gotthard Pass. In 1809, in the course of his wanderings in the upper Linth Valley, Escher made an observation that became of great importance for later conceptions of the geological structure of the Alps. He found an older "graywacke formation" (later known as the Permian Verrucano) that lies above the younger "Alpine Limestone Formation" (later known as the Jurassic *Lochseiten* limestone). Escher did not pursue the consequences of this inverse stratification—one reason was undoubtedly the sharp criticism of Leopold von Buch, who rejected his interpretation. Escher's view, that here occurs a tectonic phenomenon connected with the tectonic nappe structure widespread in the Swiss Alps, has long been confirmed, however.

A controversy between Escher and Buch developed on another point. Buch and many other geologists of the time found it difficult to accept water erosion as the fundamental cause of the formation of the great Alpine valleys. They attributed that process instead to ancient tectonic rifts and subsidence. Escher rejected this view, taking for his example the valley of Valais, the widest in the Alps. The direction of this valley does not follow the course and strike of the rocks in the valley walls, but rather intersects them at an angle of thirty to forty degrees. Escher attributed a major influence in the formation of valleys to erosion by rivers (1818).

He further recognized that the distribution of erratic boulders not of local origin in the northern foreland of the Alps corresponds to the watersheds of the great Alpine rivers—the Rhine, the Aare, the Reuss, and the Rhone (1822). Escher thought these boulders were transposed from their watershed in catastrophic floods—today we know that Pleistocene glaciers in the same valleys transported rocks characteristic of the substratum in their moraines into the northern foreland. The occasionally diverse rocks present in the watersheds of the glaciers were thereby distributed separately. Escher's observation, however, was fundamentally sound.

In his geological works Escher showed himself to be a precise, thorough, and critical observer who shied away from hypotheses and the propounding of theories. His modesty led him to publish only a few of his geological studies and investigations.

BIBLIOGRAPHY

I. ORIGINAL WORKS. Escher's works include *Geognostische Übersicht der Alpen in Helvetien* (Zurich, 1796); *Alpina,* 2 vols. (Zurich, 1806–1807); "Geognostische Beschreibung des Linthtales," in *Leonard's Taschenbuch für die gesamte Mineralogie,* **3** (1809), 339–354; "Über die geognostischen Verhältnisse der Gebirge der Linthtäler," *ibid.,* **6** (1812), 369–394; "Die Bildungsart der Täler betreffend," *ibid.,* **12** (1818), 199–221; and "Beiträge zur Naturgeschichte der freiliegenden Felsblöcke in der Nähe des Alpen-Gebirges," *ibid.,* **16** (1822), 631–676.

II. SECONDARY LITERATURE. On Escher and his work see H. Hölder, *Geologie und Paläontologie in Texten und ihrer Geschichte* (Freiburg im Breisgau, 1960), pp. 65–68, 73; J. J. Hottinger, *Hans Konrad Escher von der Linth, Charakterbild eines Republikaners* (Zurich, 1852); R. Lauterborn, "Der Rhein. Naturgeschichte eines deutschen Stromes," in *Berichte der Naturforschenden Gesellschaft zu Freiburg im Breisgau,* **33** (1934), 105–107; G. Meyer von Knonau, in *Allgemeine deutsche Biographie,* VI (Munich, 1877), 365–372; and R. Wolf, "H. C. Escher von der Linth," in *Biographien zur Kulturgeschichte der Schweiz,* IV (Zurich, 1862), 317–348.

HEINZ TOBIEN

ESCHERICH, THEODOR (*b.* Ansbach, Germany, 29 November 1857; *d.* Vienna, Austria, 15 February 1911), *pediatrics.*

Escherich was a pioneer pediatrician whose clinical insights and organizational abilities—linked to profound interests in bacteriology, immunology, and biochemistry—were devoted to improving child care, particularly infant hygiene and nutrition. He was born in a manufacturing town in Franconia, the younger son of *Kreismedizinalrat* Ferdinand Escherich, a medical statistician. His mother was Maria Sophie Frieder, daughter of Baron Carl Stromer von Reichenbach, a Bavarian army colonel. Because of his prankish tendencies in early schooldays, Escherich was sent to the great Jesuit seminary Stella Matutina, in Feldkirch, Austria. It apparently had no repressive effect upon him.

Escherich began his academic and medical education in 1876 at Strasbourg, continued at Kiel, Berlin, and Würzburg, and qualified at Munich in 1881. His doctoral dissertation was entitled "Die marantische Sinusthrombose bei Cholera infantum." In 1882 he joined the medical clinic of the Julius Hospital, Würzburg, becoming first assistant to its director, Karl Gerhardt, a well-known internist with an outstanding knowledge of pediatrics. His interest was thus aroused in this specialty, but since Germany lacked the necessary training facilities, Escherich had to seek them elsewhere, first in Paris and then in Vienna, where he worked for some months under Hermann Widerhofer at the St. Anna Children's Hospital. In 1885 he obtained clinical assistantships in Munich at the Children's Polyclinic of the Reisingerianum and at the Hauner Children's Hospital under Heinrich von Ranke. He habilitated himself at the University of Munich and became *Privatdozent* in pediatrics in 1886.

The increasing impact of Robert Koch's discoveries and his own experiences as scientific assistant in the 1884 cholera epidemic at Naples (to which Gerhardt had sent him) persuaded Escherich that bacteriology could solve or illuminate many pediatric problems. Circumstances at Munich fostered this belief. Koch's pupil, Wilhelm Frobenius, taught him pure culture techniques and methods of bacterial characterization; and he had access to Max von Pettenkofer's hygienic institute, Otto von Bollinger's bacteriological laboratory, Carl von Voit's physiological institute, and Franz von Soxhlet's dairy industry facilities. Escherich's work on cholera had drawn his attention to the bacterial flora of the intestine in infants, and after a further year of intensive laboratory investigations he published a monograph on the relationship of intestinal bacteria to the physiology of digestion in the infant. This work, *Die Darmbakterien des Säuglings und ihre Beziehungen zur Physiologie der Verdauung* (1886), established its author as the leading bacteriologist in the field of pediatrics. During the ensuing years he began studies of artificial nutrition, which led him to formulate a new system of prescribing cow's milk and to become a resolute advocate of breast-feeding for infants.

In 1890, when he was only thirty-three, Escherich was called to Graz to succeed Rudolf von Jaksch as extraordinary professor of pediatrics and director of the provincial children's clinic. Four years later he was promoted to ordinary professor; at that time he also refused a call to Leipzig as Otto Heubner's successor. His happiest years were spent in Graz, where he married Margaretha Pfaundler, daughter of the physicist Leopold Pfaundler. They had two children, a son and a daughter.

In Graz, Escherich instituted a broad program of clinical and laboratory researches and found scope for his organizational talents. He extended the diphtheria investigations that he had already launched in Munich and summarized the findings in two monographs, *Ätiologie und Pathogenese der epidemischen Diphtherie* (1892) and *Diphtherie, Croup, Serumtherapie* (1895). In 1890 he developed an interest in tetany of infants. He became the leading authority on this disease and in his final monograph, *Die Tetanie der Kinder* (1909), correctly ascribed it to parathyroid insufficiency. In 1891, one year after Koch discovered tuberculin, Escherich reported disappointing results in extensive trials of this product on tuberculous children. Thereafter problems of childhood tuberculosis remained among his chief concerns.

Escherich persuaded the Styrian government to build and maintain an infants' division as a branch of the provincial orphanage, attached to the children's clinic. He personally chose the furnishings and laboratory equipment for the expanded institution, designed the auditorium, founded a library, and established a diphtheria division for conducting bacteriological studies on suspected cases. The patient load trebled and a small provincial hospital was transformed into an important scientific and teaching institute.

When Widerhofer died in 1902, Escherich was appointed to his chair at Vienna. Although promised a new clinic, he himself had to draw plans, raise money, and negotiate with the government for this project, which was not completed during his lifetime. Meanwhile he renovated the venerable St. Anna Children's Hospital, making changes whenever he could extract sufficient funds from governmental and charitable sources. In 1903, determined to reduce the capital's infant mortality, Escherich appealed for support to the women of Vienna. The response was such that in the following year he established, with imperial patronage and civic approval, the Infants' Care Association (Verein Säuglingsschutz).

In the St. Anna Hospital, Escherich set up an infants' division and started an exemplary school for infant nursing. Medical students later received clinical instruction in this previously neglected field. The infant care headquarters on the hospital grounds became an educational center for mothers and a distributing point for cow's milk preparations and breast-feeding propaganda. In 1908, the year of the Emperor Franz Joseph's sixtieth jubilee, Escherich again drew attention to the inexcusably high national rate of infant mortality. His efforts resulted in eventual construction of the Imperial Institute for Maternal and Infant Care.

Escherich formed a pediatric section of the Viennese Society for Internal Medicine—serving indefatigably as chairman—and founded the Austrian Society for Child Research. In 1908 he was president of the German Pediatric Association. He coedited several well-known journals, held honorary membership in many foreign medical associations—including the American Pediatric Society—and was the only European pediatrician to address the International Congress of Arts and Sciences at the St. Louis World's Fair in 1904. He received the title *Hofrat* in 1906.

Throughout this decade in Vienna, Escherich worked relentlessly. Consulted professionally by royal families, he attended congresses abroad, published reports on various topics, and encouraged the researches of pupils such as Clemens von Pirquet and Béla Schick, who had accompanied him from Graz. Escherich's health deteriorated when his young son died from appendicitis. About five years later, in February 1911, a succession of cerebral attacks culminated in fatal apoplexy. The Kinderklinik, built to his plans, was officially dedicated soon afterward.

Idealism and progressiveness animated and gave purpose to Escherich's zealous, unbounded industry. Distinguished looking and always meticulously dressed, yet genial and approachable, he disliked intrigue or spiteful gossip. To young patients he showed affection, to older ones respectful candor. His stimulating lectures stressed pathology and reflected a preventive outlook.

More than one quarter of his publications relate to bacteriology. His earliest monograph (1886) included classic descriptions of *Bacterium coli commune* (later eponymously designated *Escherichia coli*) and *Bacterium coli aërogenes*. Although his claims that *B. coli* could cause cystitis and other localized infections were undisputed, his contention that some virulent strains provoked infantile diarrhea and gastroenteritis was verified only after sixty years. He narrowly missed discovering Sonne dysentery bacilli, of which he isolated several cultures, only to discard them because they failed to produce gas in carbohydrate-containing media.

In 1889, Escherich confirmed the causal role of the Klebs-Löffler bacillus in a diphtheria epidemic. He instituted antitoxin therapy in his clinic patients in 1894 and recorded exceptionally favorable results in a subsequent monograph. Through experiments on healthy children he showed the futility of attempting to prevent the disease by oral or rectal administration of antitoxin. In Vienna, he vigorously sponsored Paul Moser's antistreptococcus serum in scarlet fever treatment.

Escherich was intensely interested in the diagnosis,

pathogenesis, and control of tuberculosis. He pioneered in X-ray detection of the disease in children. In his last years he advocated construction of sanatoria, emphasized the tuberculous nature of scrofula, and reinvestigated the *Stichreaktion*—the swelling and redness at the site of subcutaneous injection—observed by him during early therapeutic trials of tuberculin. The diagnostic importance of this test was effectively realized only after von Pirquet modified the technique.

The scope of Escherich's clinical reports ranged from chorea to status lymphaticus, but his biochemical investigations focused on the physiology and pathology of infant nutrition. His breast-feeding edicts stemmed partly from recognition that improper milk formulas induced nutritional disorders, and partly from his observations that whereas healthy mother's milk was bacteriologically sterile, cow's milk might convey scarlet fever as well as intestinal infections. After disproving the prevailing dogma that cow's milk casein was indigestible and showing that bowel fermentation could be influenced by withholding dietary carbohydrates, Escherich evolved new dietary formulas for infants of various ages and weights, based on volumetric intakes by breast-fed counterparts. Characteristically, he devised a sterilizing apparatus to render the mixtures safe and arranged free distribution of the treated material to needy mothers.

Escherich's inspired common sense and technical ingenuity were directed into many channels. Thus his first building in Vienna, which housed separate laboratories for bacteriological, chemical, and X-ray activities, had a flat roof on which infants could lie or children play. The infants' wards were equipped with many novel facilities of his design, such as fully air-conditioned *couveuses* which were used either to protect especially vulnerable infants or to isolate infected ones. His acute social awareness and flair for innovation and coordination, combined with a bent for bacteriological and biochemical research, made Escherich the acknowledged leader of pediatrics in his day. Less versatility and longer life might have won him greater celebrity and more durable renown.

BIBLIOGRAPHY

I. ORIGINAL WORKS. The only bibliography of Escherich's works, listing about 170 items, is the inaccurate and incomplete one provided in an obituary by his former pupil and successor, Clemens von Pirquet (see below). Among his most important published works were four monographs, *Die Darmbakterien des Säuglings und ihre Beziehungen zur Physiologie der Verdauung* (Stuttgart, 1886); *Ätiologie und Pathogenese der epidemischen Diphtherie. I. Der Diphtherie-bacillus* (Vienna, 1892); *Diphtherie, Croup, Serumtherapie nach Beobachtungen an der Universitäts-Kinderklinik in Graz* (Vienna, 1895); and *Die Tetanie der Kinder* (Vienna, 1909). Escherich was also coauthor of a posthumous monograph, *Scharlach* (Vienna, 1912), written with Béla Schick; and of a long chapter on *Bacterium coli commune* in W. Kolle and A. Wassermann's *Handbuch der pathogenen Mikroorganismen*, II (Jena, 1903), 334–474, written with M. Pfaundler.

Many of his shorter contributions appeared in two or more journals. Among the more original and characteristic of these were "Die marantische Sinusthrombose bei Cholera infantum," in *Jahrbuch für Kinderheilkunde*, **19** (1883), 261–274; "Klinisch-therapeutische Beobachtungen aus der Cholera-Epidemie in Neapel," in *Münchener medizinische Wochenschrift*, **31** (1884), 561–564; "Bakteriologische Untersuchungen über Frauenmilch," in *Fortschritte der Medizin*, **3** (1885), 231–236; "Ueber Darmbakterien im allgemeinen und diejenigen der Säuglinge im Besonderen, sowie die Beziehungen der letzteren zur Aetiologie der Darmerkrangungen," in *Centralblatt für Bacteriologie*, **1** (1887), 705–713; "Die normale Milchverdauung des Säuglings," in *Jahrbuch für Kinderheilkunde*, **27** (1888), 100–112; "Zur Reform der künstlichen Säuglingsernährung," in *Wiener klinische Wochenschrift*, **2** (1889), 761–763; "Zur Aetiologie der Diphtherie," in *Centralblatt für Bakteriologie*, **7** (1890), 8–13; "Ueber Milchsterilisirung zum Zwecke der Säuglingsernährung mit Demonstration eines neuen Apparates," in *Berliner klinische Wochenschrift*, **27** (1890), 1029–1033; "Idiopathische Tetanie im Kindesalter," in *Wiener klinische Wochenschrift*, **3** (1890), 769–774; "Die Resultate der Koch'schen Injektionen bei Skrofulose und Tuberculose," in *Jahrbuch für Kinderheilkunde*, **33** (1891–1892), 369–426; "Ueber einen Schutzkörper im Blute der von Diphtherie geheilten Menschen," in *Centralblatt für Bakteriologie*, **13** (1893), 153–161, written with R. Klemensiewicz; "Bemerkungen über den Status lymphaticus der Kinder," in *Berliner klinische Wochenschrift*, **33** (1896), 645–650; "Begriff und Vorkommen der Tetanie im Kindesalter," *ibid.*, **34** (1897), 861–866; "Versuche zur Immunisirung gegen Diphtherie auf dem Wege des Verdauungstractes," in *Wiener klinische Wochenschrift*, **10** (1897), 799–801; "Kritische Stimmen zum gegenwärtigen Stande der Heilserumtherapie," in *Heilkunde* (Vienna), **2** (1897–1898), 593–606; "La valeur diagnostique de la radiographie chez les enfants," in *Revue mensuelle des maladies de l'enfance*, **16** (1898), 233–242; "Pyocyaneusinfectionen bei Säuglingen," in *Centralblatt für Bakteriologie*, **25** (1899), 117–120; "Zur Aetiologie der Dysenterie," *ibid.*, **26** (1899), 385–389; "Zur Kenntniss der Unterschiede zwischen der naturlichen und künstlichen Ernährung des Säuglings," in *Wiener klinische Wochenschrift*, **13** (1900), 1183–1186; "Die Erfolge der Serumbehandlung des Scharlach an der Universitäts-Kinderklinik in Wien," *ibid.*, **16** (1903), 663–668; *Bitte an die Wiener Frauen* [a pamphlet] (Vienna, 1903); "Die Grundlage und Ziele der modernen Kinderheilkunde," in *Wiener klinische Wochenschrift*, **17** (1904), 1025–1027; "Die neue Säuglingsabteilung im St.

Anna-Kinderspital in Wien," *ibid.,* **18** (1905), 977–982; "Antrag auf Einsetzung eines Komitees behufs Ausarbeitung von Vorschlägen zur Förderung der Brusternährung," *ibid.,* **18** (1905), 572–575; "Der Verein 'Säuglingsschutz' auf der hygienischen Ausstellung in der Rotunde 1906," *ibid.,* **19** (1906), 871–875; "Zur Kenntnis der tetanoiden Zustände des Kindesalters," in *Münchener medizinische Wochenschrift,* **54** (1907), 2073–2074; "Hermann Freiherr von Widerhofer 1832–1901," in *Wiener klinische Wochenschrift,* **20** (1907), 1510–1513; "Die Bedeutung des Schularztes in der Prophylaxe der Infectionskrankheiten," in *Monatsschrift für Gesundheitspflege,* **26** (1908), 117–130; "Was nennen wir Skrofulose?," in *Wiener klinische Wochenschrift,* **22** (1909), 224–228; "Die Infektionswege der Tuberkulose, insbesondere im Säuglingsalter," *ibid.,* 515–522; and "Ueber Indikationen und Erfolge der Tuberkulintherapie bei der kindlichen Tuberculose," *ibid.,* **23** (1910), 723–730.

II. Secondary Literature. Obituaries include "Theodor Escherich, M.D.," in *Boston Medical and Surgical Journal,* **164** (1911), 474–475; "Death of Professor Escherich," in *Lancet* (1911), **1,** 626; H. Finkelstein, "Theodor Escherich†," in *Deutsche medizinische Wochenschrift,* **37** (1911), 604–605; I. Fischer, "Escherich, Theodor," in *Biographisches Lexikon der hervorragenden Aerzte der letzten 50 Jarhe,* I (Berlin–Vienna, 1932), 375; F. Hamburger, "Theodor Escherich†" in *Wiener klinische Wochenschrift,* **24** (1911), 263–266; W. Katner, "Theodor Escherich," in *Neue deutsche Biographie,* IV (Berlin, 1959), 649–650; M. von Pfaundler, "Theodor Escherich†," in *Münchner medizinische Wochenschrift,* **58** (1911), 521–523; and C. von Pirquet, "Theodor Escherich," in *Zeitschrift für Kinderkrankheiten,* **1** (1910–1911), 423–441, which includes a bibliography—the same text, without bibliography, may be found in *Mittheilungen der Gesellschaft für innere Medizin und Kinderheilkunde, Beilage VIII,* **9** (1911), 82–93.

Other references to Escherich's life and work are A. Gronowicz, *Béla Schick and the World of Children* (New York, 1954); K. Kundratitz, "Professor Dr. Theodor Escherichs Leben und Wirken," in *Wiener klinische Wochenschrift,* **73** (1961), 722–725; Erna Lesky, *Die Wiener medizinische Schule im 19. Jahrhundert* (Graz, 1965); M. Neuberger, "Zur Geschichte der Wiener Kinderheilkunde," in *Wiener medizinische Wochenschrift,* **85** (1935), 197–203, trans. by R. Rosenthal as "The History of Pediatrics in Vienna," in *Medical Record,* **156** (1943), 746–751; B. Schick, "Pediatrics in Vienna at the Beginning of the Century," in *Journal of Pediatrics,* **50** (1957), 114–124; L. Schönbauer, *Das medizinisches Wien,* 2nd ed. (Vienna, 1947); and R. Wagner, *Clemens von Pirquet. His Life and Work* (Baltimore, 1968).

Claude E. Dolman

ESCHOLT, MIKKEL PEDERSÖN (*b. ca.* 1610; *d.* Christiania [now Oslo], Norway, 1669), *geology.*

The date and place of Escholt's birth are unknown; he first appears in the register of Copenhagen Uni-

versity for 1628 as coming from Malmö. He studied theology in Copenhagen and became chaplain of the castle at Akershus Castle in Christiania in 1646. He seems to have acted as an intelligence officer during the campaigns to reconquer the provinces lost by Denmark-Norway to Sweden by the treaty of Brömsebro (1645). In 1660 he was rewarded with the parish of Vestby in Östfold. When he died his oldest son inherited the parish.

His present scientific reputation stems from his book *Geologia norvegica* (Oslo, 1657). It is the first scientific treatise printed in Norway and also one of the first books printed in Norwegian. The book was written to calm the populace who felt doom approaching because of the slight but distinctly felt earthquake of 24 April 1657. The book gives a clear and surprisingly modern view of geological phenomena, with numerous apt references from both classic and recent literature. Escholt demonstrated the rather unusual regularity of the earthquakes (two each century) in the Oslo region and was aware of the relationship of earthquakes to volcanism. He was the first to use the word "geology" in the modern sense—as the science of the earth. Through an English translation of his book (1662), the word came into use in the scientific literature in the following decade.

His only other known works are brilliantly written but highly polemic theological papers. Escholt does not seem to have influenced or been in contact with contemporary scientists in Copenhagen, and he is barely mentioned in Garboe's exhaustive history of geology in Denmark.

BIBLIOGRAPHY

I. Original Works. Escholt's only scientific work is his *Geologia norvegica* (Oslo, 1657; English trans., 1662). A facsimile ed. was published in 1957.

II. Secondary Literature. See A. Garboe, *Geologiens historie i Danmark,* I (Copenhagen, 1959), 11, 47. A number of short notes, especially concerning Escholt's early use of the word "geology," have appeared in Scandinavian journals and newspapers.

Nils Spjeldnaes

ESCHSCHOLTZ, JOHANN FRIEDRICH (*b.* Dorpat, Russia [now Tartu, Estonian S.S.R.], 1 November 1793; *d.* Dorpat, 7 May 1831), *medicine, zoology.*

Eschscholtz received a medical education at Dorpat University. He took part, as a physician and naturalist, in voyages around the world on the brig *Rurik* from 1815 to 1818, under the command of Captain

O. Kotzebue. His collections, which he made together with A. Chamisso, were given to Dorpat University and the Moscow Society of Naturalists. From 1819 he was extraordinary professor of medicine and dissector at Dorpat University, where from 1822 he was director of the zoological cabinet and, from 1828, ordinary professor of anatomy. He was a member of the Moscow Society of Naturalists, the Deutsche Akademie der Naturforscher Leopoldina and the Swiss Society of Natural Science. A bay in Alaska, an atoll in the Marshall Islands, a genus of plants of the family Papaveraceae, and a genus of ctenophora are named in honor of Eschscholtz.

BIBLIOGRAPHY

I. ORIGINAL WORKS. Eschscholtz' writings include *Ideen zur Aneinanderreihung der rückgratigen Thiere auf vergleichenden Anatomie begründet* (Dorpat, 1819); *Beschreibung des inneren Skelets einiger Insekten* (*Gryllotalpa*) (Dorpat, 1820); *Species insectorum novae descriptae* (*Carabicini*) (Moscow, 1823); *Entomographien* (Berlin, 1824); "Dissertatio de coleopterorum genere Passalus," in *Nouveaux Mémoires de la Société Impériale des Naturalistes de Moscou,* **1** (1829), 13–28; *Zoologisches Atlas enthaltend Abbildungen und Beschreibungen neuer Thierarten, während des Flottenkapitains von Kotzebue zweiter Reise um die Welt in den Jahren 1823–1826 beobachtet* (Berlin, 1829–1833); "Übersicht der zoologischen Ausbeute," in *Reise um die Welt in den Jahren 1823–1826* (Weimar, 1830); and *Beschreibung der Anchinia, einer neuen Gattung der Mollusken* (St. Petersburg, 1835).

II. SECONDARY LITERATURE. On Eschscholtz and his work, see J. F. Recke and C. E. Napiersky, *Allgemeine Schriftsteller- und Gelehrten-Lexicon der Provinzen Livland, Esthland und Kurland* (Mitau, 1827), p. 523; and T. Beise and C. E. Napiersky, *Nachträge und Fortsetzungen* (1859), p. 173.

L. J. BLACHER

ESCLANGON, ERNEST BENJAMIN (*b.* Mison, France, 17 March 1876; *d.* Eyrenville, France, 28 January 1954), *astronomy, mathematics, physics.*

Esclangon came from a family of landed proprietors. The practical attitudes of his class are apparent in his realistic approach to problems in pure mathematics, applied celestial mechanics, relativity, observational astronomy, instrumental astronomy, astronomical chronometry, aerodynamics, interior and exterior ballistics, and aerial and underwater acoustic detection. He contributed to all of these fields to a greater or lesser degree, but always effectively.

Esclangon's first training was as a mathematician. As a student at the École Normale Supérieure (1895–1898) and an *agrégé* in mathematics (1898), he took up the problem of quasi-periodic functions. (Quasi-periodic functions, newly introduced, constitute a remarkable class among the almost periodic functions; their Fourier expansion is formed by a limited number of terms.) Esclangon elaborated a theory for these functions, studied their differentiation and integration, and examined the differential equations which allow them as coefficients. His doctoral thesis established a basis for their employment at a time when their role in mathematical physics was only beginning to be developed.

Esclangon's subsequent career as an astronomer and teacher was the result of chance—in the form of a vacant position—and of his own curiosity that led him to accept it. He was an astronomer at Bordeaux, beginning in 1899, then director of the observatories of Strasbourg (1918) and Paris (1929–1944). In addition, he taught mathematics at the Bordeaux Faculty of Science (from 1902), then became professor of astronomy at Strasbourg (in 1919) and then at Paris (1930–1946).

For fifty years Esclangon explored all the branches of fundamental astronomy. He devoted special attention to perfecting instruments, with a view to increasing the precision of observations. Of particular interest is his solution to a critical problem in positional astronomy, the rigorous definition of the axis of rotation of a transit instrument. Esclangon demonstrated that by fitting an objective in one of the extremities of this axis, which is hollow, and fitting a reticle to the other, the observer is permitted to measure the displacement of the instantaneous axis of rotation continuously throughout the course of the observation.

Esclangon's work in ballistics began in 1914 when, at the beginning of World War I, he proposed to French military authorities that they employ sound-ranging techniques to localize enemy artillery. He was charged with organizing the experimental study of this method; he was thus able to analyze the two components of the wave emitted by the projectile, the conical shock wave and the spherical wave centered on the point of emission. Esclangon then succeeded in 1916 in eliminating the registration of the shock wave and thereby assured a great precision in pinpointing enemy gun locations.

As director of the Bureau International de l'Heure (1929–1944), Esclangon was led to devote himself to problems of time. In addition to making studies on the astronomical determination of time and on its conservation and diffusion, he devised the "talking clock" (employing time signals from an observatory clock) that has made telephonic announcements of the exact time available to the Paris public since 1933.

Esclangon's practical bias and his inclination toward solid demonstrations (whether mathematical or experimental) caused him to be critical of the general theory of relativity. In a memoir of 1937, "La notion de temps. Temps physique et relativité . . .," he discusses the restrictions necessary to certain conclusions that have been stated too absolutely and states how, for example, it is possible to conceive of phenomena faster than light and why the ordinary formulas are not strictly applicable to the motion of masses at great speeds.

Esclangon was a member of the Académie des Sciences (1939) and the Bureau des Longitudes (1932). He served as president of the Union Astronomique Internationale from 1935 to 1938. He assumed his official functions with simplicity and amiability; he was affable and loved to joke, and did not deny himself leisure time. It would almost seem that he accomplished his body of important work without effort.

BIBLIOGRAPHY

I. ORIGINAL WORKS. Esclangon published 247 memoirs, monographs, and articles, of which some of the most important are, in mathematical analysis, "Les fonctions quasi-périodiques," his doctoral thesis, in *Annales de l'Observatoire de Bordeaux,* **11** (1904), 1–276; and "Nouvelles recherches sur les fonctions quasi-périodiques," *ibid.,* **16** (1917), 51–176.

His astronomical works include "Sur les transformations de la comète Daniel . . .," in *Bulletin astronomique,* **25** (1908), 81–91; "Mémoire sur la réfraction astronomique," in *Bulletin de Comité international permanent pour l'exécution photographique de la carte du ciel,* **6** (1913), 319–389; "Sur la précision des observations méridiennes et des mesures de longitudes," in *Annales de l'Observatoire de Strasbourg,* **1** (1926), 373–405; "Mémoire sur l'amélioration des observations méridiennes," in *Bulletin astronomique,* **6** (1930), 229–260; "L'horloge parlante de l'Observatoire de Paris," in *L'astronomie,* **47** (1933), 145–155; "Horloges indiquant simultanément le temps moyen et le temps sidéral," in *Bulletin astronomique,* **11** (1938), 181–189; and "Sur la transformation en satellites permanents de la terre de projectiles auto-propulsés," in *Comptes rendus hebdomadaires des séances de l'Académie des sciences,* **225** (1947), 513–515.

In theoretical physics, Esclangon wrote "Mémoire sur les preuves astronomiques de la relativité," in *Bulletin astronomique,* **1** (1920), 303–329; and "La notion de temps. Temps physique et relativité . . .," *ibid.,* **10** (1937), 1–72.

His work in applied physics includes "Le vol plané sans force motrice," in *Comptes rendus hebdomadaires des séances de l'Académie des sciences,* **147** (1908), 496–498; "Sur un régulateur rotatif de vitesse," *ibid.,* **152** (1911), 32–35; "Sur un régulateur thermique de précision," *ibid.,* **154** (1912), 178–181, 495–497; "Sur un nouveau régulateur de température . . .," *ibid.,* **156** (1913), 1667–1670; "Mémoire sur l'intensité de la pesanteur," in *Annales de l'Observatoire de Bordeaux,* **15** (1915), 99–314; and "Le vol plané sans force motrice," in *Comptes rendus hebdomadaires des séances de l'Académie des sciences,* **177** (1923), 1102–1104.

His publications in military science comprise *Mémoire sur la détection sous-marine . . .* (Paris, 1918), in the Archives de la Marine de Guerre; and *L'acoustique des canons et des projectiles* (Paris, 1925).

II. SECONDARY LITERATURE. On Esclangon and his work, see J. Chazy, "Notice nécrologique sur Ernest Esclangon," in *Comptes rendus hebdomadaires des séances de l'Académie des sciences,* **238** (1954), 629–632; and "Ernest Esclangon (1876–1954)," in *Annuaire du Bureau des longitudes* (1955), C1–C6; A. Danjon, "Obituary Notice: Ernest Esclangon," in *Monthly Notices of the Royal Astronomical Society,* **115** (1955), 124; J. Jackson, "Obituaries: Prof. E. Esclangon," in *Nature,* **173** (1954), 567; and A. Pérard, "Quelques mots de l'oeuvre scientifique d'Ernest Esclangon," in *L'astronomie,* **68** (1954), 201–204.

JACQUES R. LÉVY

ESKOLA, PENTTI ELIAS (*b.* Lellainen, Honkilahti, Finland, 8 January 1883; *d.* Helsinki, Finland, 6 December 1964), *petrology, mineralogy, geology.*

The son of a farmer, Eskola enrolled at the University of Helsinki in 1901 and in 1906 obtained his candidate degree (about equivalent to an M.S.) in chemistry. He obtained his Ph.D. at the same university in 1914 with a dissertation entitled "On the Petrology of the Orijärvi Region in Southwestern Finland." By 1915 he had embarked on his lifework, the study of the mineral facies of rocks. During stays in Norway and the United States in 1920–1921 he worked specifically on eclogites; he spent 1922–1924 as a geologist of the Finnish Survey; and in 1924 he was named extraordinary professor and in 1928 ordinary professor of geology at the University of Helsinki, a position he held until 1953. Eskola was one of the generation of petrologists confronted by the complexities of the Fennoscandian crystalline complex who were inspired by a famous paper of J. J. Sederholm on granites and gneiss to develop a structural-metasomatic school of petrology, influenced also by the application to petrology of physical chemistry by J. H. L. and T. Vogt.

Eskola was a leading petrologist in these and other subjects (mentioned below), within his own field. He held honorary degrees from the universities of Oslo (1938), Padua (1942), Bonn (1943), and Prague (1948). He was honorary president of the Geological Society of Finland and an honorary or corresponding member of many learned societies and academies of science. In 1964 he received the Vetlesen Prize.

Eskola married Mandi Wiiro in 1914. They had two children; a son, Matti, born in 1916 and killed in World War II in 1941; and a daughter, Päivätär, born in 1920, who became a teacher of chemistry. Eskola and his wife were known for their warmth and cooperation in the scientific and personal care of their students, many of whom held important positions in Finland and abroad.

The success of Eskola's scientific work was probably based on the coincidence of three major factors: his thoroughness and steadiness, evident in all his writings and his notable care in rewriting manuscripts; the breadth of his topical experience, including his degree in chemistry, displayed not only in his specific papers but also, especially, in his various textbooks in geology and mineralogy, some of which were written in German; and his constant striving to combine laboratory results with field data, evident in his work in chemistry, his stay at the Geophysical Laboratory in Washington from March 1921 to November 1922, his own fieldwork, and his published work.

Eskola's major contribution to the earth sciences and an idea that he developed throughout his life—indeed, from his first work on solid-state reactions in 1904 to his last years—was the concept of mineral facies, essentially a continuation of Ulrich Gruben-mann's assignment of metamorphic rocks to epi-, meso-, and katazones. In 1914 he wrote on p. 114 of his Ph.D. thesis a definition that is still applicable today: "In any rock of a metamorphic formation which has arrived at a chemical equilibrium through metamorphism at constant temperature and pressure conditions, the mineral composition is controlled only by the chemical composition." Originally he differentiated between five separate facies, stressing their independence of mode of formation. He named them, according to a mineral typical of each, the sanidine, hornfels, greenschist, amphibolite, and eclogite facies. By 1939 in *Die Entstehung der Gesteine* this nomenclature had evolved into a two-dimensional temperature-pressure classification further differentiated into metamorphic and magmatic facies. An early summary of this basic idea was published in 1920 under the title "On Mineral Facies of Rocks" (*Norsk geologisk tidsskrift*, **6**, 143–194).

Through his own work and that of many other colleagues—specifically Paul Niggli, V. M. Gold-schmidt, T. F. W. Barth, F. J. Turner, N. L. Bowen, and H. Yoder—the equilibrium boundaries and stability fields were increasingly specified and modified, until after 1955 an intensive search for new metamorphic facies standards began on a grand scale. As a corollary, Eskola centered repeated efforts on the highest-grade facies, the eclogite problem. An intro-

ductory account is his paper "On the Eclogites of Norway" (*Skrifter utg. af Videnskabsselskabet i Kristiania,* **1**, no. 8 [1921]). The modern concept that deeper layers of the earth do not necessarily differ in composition but rather in the density of their minerals largely originated in Eskola's high-pressure facies idea.

As in his early work on the petrology of Orijärvi, he often interpreted the composition of his mineral facies as the result of metasomatism, specifically of a "replacement of lime, soda, and potash by iron oxides and magnesia." Eskola originally considered the intrusion of granites to be principally responsible for such ionic migrations but was open to a later interpretation by some of his students who derived the same elements from a process of metamorphic differentiations and tectonic energies. A syngenetic interpretation (*in situ* formation) favored more recently by some ore geneticists seems not to have been considered during Eskola's lifetime.

The problem of the origin of metamorphic rocks is indigenous to the geology of Finland. Likewise, the granite problem is a typical Fennoscandian study, and it consequently received almost as much attention from Eskola as the metamorphic rock enigmas. As early as 1932 he summarized his ideas on granites in a paper entitled "On the Origin of Granitic Magmas." He recognized various possible origins, including anatectic processes by which a "pore magma" may form and migrate to produce migmatites. In his later years he agreed that palingenesis or anatexis may have played a more important role than was recognized at first; but he did not share the extreme interpretations of some transformist schools.

Because the problems mentioned so far could be investigated largely through work in Scandinavia, Eskola's contributions to the advancement of Fennoscandian geology were numerous. He was particularly active in the interpretation of pre-Cambrian stratigraphy; for example, the term "Karelian" goes back to his work. In connection with this work, and as a man with a thorough philosophical mind, in 1954 he also presented a book on the possible cosmogenic origin of the earth and of life (*In Quest of a Picture of the World*).

BIBLIOGRAPHY

I. ORIGINAL WORKS. From a list of about 170 original publications (articles, books, and monographs), the following perhaps best represent Eskola's lifework: "The Silicates of Strontium and Barium," in *American Journal of Science,* **4** (1922), 331–375; "On the Origin of Granitic Magmas," in *Mineralogische und petrographische Mit-*

teilungen, n.s. **42** (1932), 455–481; "Wie ist die Anordnung der äusseren Erdsphären nach der Dichte zustande gekommen?," in *Geologische Rundschau,* **27** (1936), 61–73; "Die metamorphen Gesteine," in T. F. W. Barth, Carl W. Correns, and Pentti Eskola, *Die Entstehung der Gesteine; Ein Lehrbuch der Petrogenese* (Berlin, 1939; repr., 1960), pp. 263–407; "Einführung, 'Finnlandheft der geologischen Rundschau,'" in *Geologische Rundschau,* **32** (1941), 401–414; "Kern und Schichten der Erde," in *Sitzungsberichte der Finnischen Akademie der Wissenschaften* (1945), 218–228 (Finnish ed. 1946); *Kristalle und Gesteine. Ein Lehrbuch der Kristallkunde und allgemeinen Mineralogie* (Finnish ed. 1939; repr. Vienna, 1946); "About the Granite Problem and Some Masters of the Study of Granite," in *Comptes rendus de la Société géologique de Finlande,* **28** (1955), 117–130, also in *Bulletin de la Commission géologique de la Finlande,* **168** (1955), 117–130; "On the Mineral Facies of Charnockites," in *Journal of the Madras University,* **27** (1957), 101–119; and "Granitentstehung bei Orogenese und Epirogenese," in *Geologische Rundschau,* **50** (1960), 105–113.

II. Secondary Literature. On Eskola and his work, see T. F. W. Barth, "Memorial to Pentti Eskola (1883–1964)," in *Bulletin of the Geological Society of America,* **76**, no. 9, 117–120; Vladi Marmo, "Pentti Eskola," in *Bulletin de la Commission géologique de la Finlande,* **218** (1965), 20–53; Toini Mikkola, "Memorial of Pentti Eskola," in *American Mineralogist,* **53**, 544–548; and T. G. Sahama, "Pentti Eskola," memorial address given in Helsinki, 10 November 1965.

G. C. Amstutz

ESPY, JAMES POLLARD (*b.* Washington County, Pennsylvania, 9 May 1785; *d.* Cincinnati, Ohio, 24 January 1860), *meteorology.*

Espy was educated at Transylvania University in Lexington, Kentucky, and taught school before embarking upon a full-time career as a meteorologist in the mid-1830's. He did his earliest known work in the field in 1825 while teaching at the Franklin Institute in Philadelphia, his interest stemming from the writings of Dalton and Daniell.

The most common kind of meteorological activity in the antebellum United States was the gathering of observations. From these observations, physical explanations were sometimes deduced (e.g., William Redfield) or the data were analyzed mathematically in some fashion (e.g., Elias Loomis). From such roots arose movements to develop networks of observers and regular systems for processing the resulting data. Espy participated in this tradition in the founding of a system of meteorological observations in Pennsylvania in 1836 and in his labors (*ca.* 1840–1852) to erect a national system of volunteer weather observers which was supplanted by Joseph Henry's telegraph-linked corps of observers.

Espy's principal significance in the history of meteorology arises from a less typical kind of research for his time and place. By direct experimentation, he tried to derive physical concepts supported by quantitative data. Others might talk of the role of atmospheric electricity; Espy flew giant kites.

Espy's most notable experimental work centered on heat effects. He devised an instrument, the "nephelescope," to simulate, as it were, the behavior of clouds and, particularly, to measure the dry and moist adiabatic cooling rates. While the resulting data varied from the correct values, Espy displayed great physical insight in deducing the role of latent heat in cloud formation and rainfall. He was, apparently, the first to point out that the latent heat released by condensation of the vapor in clouds resulted in a considerable expansion of the air, the latent heat, therefore, providing the energy for continued rain and upward movement of the cloud.

As the concept of the saturated adiabatic expansion of rising air currents is basic to meteorology, Espy clearly merits recognition as an important pioneer. Lacking any sophisticated mathematical apparatus or a knowledge of modern thermodynamics and other factors involved in cloud dynamics, Espy's work did not lead directly to the work of Kelvin and others from which the modern theory stems.

It is possible, however, that his enthusiastic proselytizing for his views helped pave the way for the acceptance of the later work. In 1840 Espy addressed the Glasgow meeting of the British Association for the Advancement of Science. An account of his theories sent to the French Academy was favorably reviewed in the *Comptes rendus* in 1841 by a committee whose members were D. F. J. Arago, C. G. M. Pouillet, and J. Babinet. Espy lectured widely in the United States, undoubtedly deserving credit for stirring up popular interest and support for meteorology.

Working against recognition of his theories, however, especially their very real contributions, was this same quality of enthusiastic commitment. Espy was most contentious and not always receptive to criticism. Time would prove W. C. Redfield, with whom Espy was involved in a controversy, correct on the motion of storms; from his results Espy deduced spectacular conclusions, some unconvincing or apparently refutable. (His suggested burning of forests to produce rainfall was disregarded by narrow minds immune to the need for controlled experiments.)

In short, because of his aprofessional behavior the emerging community of professional scientists was inclined to overlook his real contributions, which have been rediscovered periodically by historically inclined meteorologists.

BIBLIOGRAPHY

I. ORIGINAL WORKS. A satisfactory list of Espy's articles is in the *Royal Society Catalogue of Scientific Papers,* II, 522–523. For the full flavor of the man and his ideas, it is necessary to consult his monographic works. The best known is *The Philosophy of Storms* (Boston, 1841). Less known but also quite valuable is *Report on Meteorology,* 4 vols. (Washington, D.C., 1843–1857), submitted by Espy in his anomalous role as the national meteorologist.

Friends of his succeeded in attaching riders to bills authorizing funds for Espy's work. None of the executive establishments requested this work, and as a result these reports were issued separately under rather odd circumstances. The first (1843) is a report to the surgeon general of the army and is fairly rare. The second (1850) and third (1851) are reports to the secretary of the navy. Both are nos. 559 and 560 of the congressional series (Senate executive document no. 30, 31st Congress, 1st session); their being bound together produces problems in determining the dates of the two reports. The fourth and last report was simply submitted by the president to Congress in 1857, but most of the work is of an earlier date. It too is in the congressional series (no. 889) as Senate executive document no. 65, 34th Congress, 3rd session. (For a modern comment on the four *Reports,* see *Meteorological Abstracts* [February 1955], p. 143.)

MS sources for Espy may be found in the archives of the American Philosophical Society and the Franklin Institute, both in Philadelphia. There is much on Espy's activities in the papers of his two leading American contemporaries in meteorology, Elias Loomis and W. C. Redfield, in the Beinecke Library, Yale University, New Haven. The personal papers of Joseph Henry and the archives of the Smithsonian Institution in Washington, D.C., during Henry's secretariat have documents relating to Espy and on the development of American work in meteorology.

II. SECONDARY LITERATURE. The earliest authoritative statement on Espy is the report in the *Comptes rendus hebdomadaires de l'Académie des sciences,* 12 (1841), 454–462, referred to above. After Espy's death, Alexander Dallas Bache, an old friend, wrote a necrology which can stand as a good summary of how Espy was regarded by the professional scientists. It appears in the Smithsonian Institution *Annual Report* for 1859 (Washington, 1860), pp. 108–111. In 1894 William Morris Davis, a fine geographer and geologist, presented a rather superficial view of Espy's period in American meteorological work in "The Redfield and Espy Period," a paper presented at the International Meteorological Congress, Chicago, 21–24 August 1894 (U.S. Weather Bureau, *Bulletin* no. 11, pp. 305–316).

Espy is briefly referred to in W. J. Humphreys, "A Review of Papers on Meteorology and Climatology Published by the American Philosophical Society Prior to the Twentieth Century," in *Proceedings of the American Philosophical Society,* 86 (Sept. 1942), 29–33.

Part of the modest revival of interest in Espy in recent years is undoubtedly the result of his appearance in K. Schneider-Carius, *Wetterkunde Wetterforschung, Ge-schichte ihrere Probleme und Erkenntnisse in Dokumenten aus drei Jahrtausenden* (Munich, 1956), pp. 192–196. Espy is discussed and some of his unpublished documents are printed in Nathan Reingold, *Science in Nineteenth Century America: A Documentary History* (New York, 1964), pp. 92–107, 128–134.

J. E. McDonald, "James Espy and the Beginnings of Cloud Thermodynamics," in *Bulletin of the American Meteorological Society,* 44 (1963), 633–641, is an important recent appraisal. W. E. Knowles Middleton, *A History of the Theories of Rain and Other Forms of Precipitation* (London, 1965), pp. 155–160, is the most recent retrospective appraisal of Espy.

NATHAN REINGOLD

ESSON, WILLIAM (*b.* Carnoustie, Scotland, 17 May 1839 [perhaps 1838]; *d.* Oxford, England, 25 August 1916), *chemistry.*

Esson's father, also William Esson, was a bridge-building engineer, and consequently the family often moved. Esson was an only child. He attended the Royal Academy in Inverness and the grammar school in Cheltenham, then studied mathematics at St. John's College in Oxford. In 1860 he was elected a fellow of Merton College, later becoming a tutor of Merton, where he was a lecturer in mathematics. His teaching was so successful that other colleges sent their students to hear him. In 1872 he married Elisabeth Meek, a pastor's daughter; they had two sons and one daughter. Esson became a deputy professor in 1894 and in 1897 obtained a professorship of geometry. Between 1898 and 1913 he was chairman of the board of the faculty of natural science. He had been a fellow of the Royal Society since 1869. He was a passionate mountain climber and a member of an alpine club.

Although Esson was a mathematician and a professor of geometry, he published almost nothing in his own field; he contributed greatly, however, to the employment of higher mathematics in chemistry (this science had so far been satisfied with the application of arithmetic). Esson worked in his youth as a chemistry demonstrator under Vernon Harcourt, a professor of chemistry at Oxford, and the collaboration between the two researchers continued after Esson himself rose to the rank of professor. Together they considered many problems of chemical kinetics.

In 1864 they investigated the reaction of potassium permanganate with oxalic acid and, in the course of their study, nearly succeeded in formulating the law of mass action ("On the Laws of Connexion Between the Conditions of a Chemical Change and Its Amount," in *Proceedings of the Royal Society,* 14 [1865], 470–475). (The law was formulated at the same time, but in a simpler and more general form, by the

Norwegians C. M. Guldberg and Peter Waage, who are generally credited with it.)

By examining the reaction process, Esson and Harcourt reached the conclusion that "in unit volume of a dilute solution at constant temperature the rate of chemical change varies directly with the mass of each of the interacting substances," or "the velocity of chemical change is directly proportional to the quantity of substance undergoing change." They presented the law of reaction velocity in exponential form: $y = ae^{-\alpha x}$, where x is the time, a the initial concentration and α a constant. Or, in the case of a binary reaction where $u = ae^{-(\alpha+\beta)x}$, it follows that it takes an infinite time for the chemical reaction to go to completion.

In a later article ("On the Observation of the Course of Chemical Change," in *Philosophical Transactions of the Royal Society,* **157** [1867], 117–137), Esson and Harcourt discussed the reaction between hydrogen peroxide and hydroiodic acid. They established that "in the presence of a large excess of iodide, the reaction is of the first order in respect of the hydrogen peroxide." In studying the effect of temperature on the reaction they found that K and K_0 (the velocity coefficient at the two absolute temperatures T and T_0) are related to the temperatures

$$\frac{k}{k_0} = \left(\frac{T}{T_0}\right)^m.$$

To be sure, Esson's formulations were rather too complicated for his contemporaries. Their merits were not recognized until the laws of chemical kinetics were fully stated on the basis of other considerations and the work of many other researchers.

BIBLIOGRAPHY

I. ORIGINAL WORKS. Besides the articles in the text, Esson's writings, all with Harcourt, include "Characters of Plane Curves, a Law of Connexion Between Two Phenomena Which Influence Each Other," in *International Congress of Mathematicians* (1912); and "On the Variation With Temperature of the Rate of a Chemical Change," in *Philosophical Transactions of the Royal Society,* **212** (1913), 187–204, a summary of their work in this field. A more detailed version of the 1865 paper is in *Philosophical Transactions of the Royal Society,* **156** (1866), 193–221. It appears under Harcourt's name only, but Esson's participation is mentioned in the text.

II. SECONDARY LITERATURE. See the article "William Esson," in *Proceedings of the Royal Society,* **93A** (1917), 54; and J. R. Partington, *A History of Chemistry,* IV (London, 1964), 585–587.

F. SZABADVÁRY

ESTIENNE (STEPHANUS), CHARLES (*b.* Paris, France, *ca.* 1505; *d.* Paris, 1564), *anatomy, natural history, scientific publication.*

The son of Henri I Estienne and younger brother of François and Robert I, Charles belonged to the famous dynasty of Parisian printers and publishers. His father died in 1520, and his mother married Simon de Colines, another printer, who was later to publish Estienne's anatomical atlas. After learning Greek under Jean Lascaris, he extended his knowledge of classical philology at the University of Padua. While in Italy (1530–1534) he became interested in botany, horticulture, and medicine. After returning to Paris he followed the extracurricular courses (*cours libres*) in anatomy and medicine given by Jacques Dubois (Sylvius) at the Collège de Tréguier. His literary activity started in 1535 with three abstracts based on the works of the diplomat Lazare de Baïf. Estienne then published several treatises on gardening and the names of plants and birds. *De re hortensi libellus* (1535) and *Seminarium* (1536) were favorably received and republished. In these books Estienne showed himself to be a scholar of importance but a mediocre naturalist in sacrificing observation to history and philology.

In 1536 Charles Estienne had printed by his brother a short treatise entitled *Anatomia.* (This volume is listed in the Estienne firm's catalogues, but no copy seems to have survived.) Around 1538 Estienne married Geneviève de Verley, daughter of Gilles de Verley, surgeon to the king. Estienne was at the time studying medicine but without being formally registered at the Faculté de Médecine. However, the faculty recognized his diligence, and in 1540 he received the degree of bachelor; on 20 June 1542 he was promoted to *docteur régent.* From then on he seems to have devoted himself to the practice of medicine. He taught anatomy from 1544 to 1547 at the Faculté de Médecine in Paris, where he was given the title of *lector ordinarius.* During this period the Latin and French editions of his manual of anatomy were published, although much of this work had been drafted before 1539. In November 1550 Estienne brought out a treatise on diet and a classification of foods, dedicated to the inquisitor Guillaume de Bailly. (This dedication is more easily understood in light of the dangers that threatened the Estienne publishing house; earlier that year Robert, accused of Protestantism, had been obliged to seek refuge in Geneva.) Charles Estienne then gave up his medical practice in order to manage the family business. He printed Belon's zoological treatise, and edited several dictionaries, geographical guides, and works in classical philology, grammar, and history. He translated into

French the treatise of Vegetius on the diseases of horses and also wrote a rural encyclopedia (*Praedium rusticum,* 1554), which when revised by his son-in-law, Jean Liébault, had tremendous success in the book trade. Nevertheless, Estienne was a poor businessman. Accused of having squandered the inheritance of Robert's children and heavily in debt, he was imprisoned in 1561 at the Châtelet, where he spent the last four years of his life.

Estienne's main scientific work, *De dissectione partium corporis humani* (1545), poses a particular problem: although it was published two years after the *Fabrica* of Vesalius, it antedates it in actual composition. Estienne worked it out in collaboration with the surgeon Estienne de la Rivière (Riverius), who had probably done some dissection and also helped in preparing the plates. Estienne first used woodcuts executed by Jollat and stored in his father-in-law's office (four plates are dated from 1530 to 1532); he then used various erotic engravings—among others— and inserted a special section that included internal anatomical details; finally (from 1534 to 1539), he had some original anatomical engravings made. In 1539 Estienne de la Rivière lodged a complaint at the Parlement against Estienne's claiming his rights as author. The lawsuit delayed the publication of the work, two-thirds of which had already been printed and was subsequently submitted in 1541 to the Faculté de Médecine for approval.

In the *De dissectione,* Estienne stated at the outset the principle of the new anatomical method: "One should not believe in books on anatomy but far more in one's own eyes." The book's many original observations include the morphology and physiological significance of the "feeding holes" of bones, the cartilaginous meniscus of the temporomandibular joint, the orbicular ligament of the radius, the three-part composition of the sternum, the path of the trigeminal and phrenic nerves, a sharp distinction between the sympathetic chain (considered as a nerve) and the vagus, the canal of the ependyma and the enlargements of the spinal cord, the cerebrospinal fluid, the valvulae in the hepatic veins, and the scrotal septum. Estienne also described the ideal anatomical theater and expounded the technique of dissecting cadavers and wiring skeletons.

BIBLIOGRAPHY

I. ORIGINAL WORKS. *De dissectione partium corporis humani libri tres, a Carolo Stephano doctore medico editi, una cum figuris et incisionum declarationibus a Stephano Riuerio chirurgo compositis* (Paris, 1545), trans. into French as *La dissection des parties du corps humain* (Paris, 1546;

facsimile ed., Paris, 1965); *De nutrimentis* (Paris, 1550); *Praedium rusticum* (Paris, 1554), trans. into French and revised by Liébault as *L'agriculture et maison rustique* (Paris, 1564).

II. SECONDARY LITERATURE. On Estienne and his work see R. Herrlinger, "Carolus Stephanus and Stephanus Riverius," in *Clio medica,* **2** (1967), 275–287; E. Lau, *Charles Estienne* (Wertheim, 1930); G. Rath, "Charles Estienne, Anatom in Schatten Vesals," in *Sudhoffs Archiv für Geschichte der Naturwissenschaften,* **39** (1955), 35–43; and E. Wickersheimer, *La médecine et les médecins en France à l'époque de la Renaissance* (Paris, 1906). A facsimile edition of *La dissection* with a historical introduction by P. Huard and M. D. Grmek, *L'oeuvre de Charles Estienne et l'école anatomique parisienne* (Paris, 1965), includes a bibliography. A bibliography may also be found in A. A. Renouard, *Annales de l'imprimerie des Estienne* (Paris, 1843). For the anatomical iconography of Estienne, see the manual of L. Choulant and several articles of C. E. Kellett, particularly his brochure *Mannerism and Medical Illustration* (Newcastle, 1961).

M. D. GRMEK

EUCKEN, ARNOLD THOMAS (*b.* Jena, Germany, 3 July 1884; *d.* Chiemsee, Germany, 16 June 1950), *physical chemistry.*

Eucken did experimental and administrative work in physical chemistry. Much of his research was associated with projects of Walther Nernst, and he shared some of Nernst's attitudes toward physical chemistry. His father, Rudolf C. Eucken, was a philosophy professor who received the Nobel Prize for literature in 1908. After graduating from the Gymnasium of Jena in 1902, Eucken entered the University of Kiel, where the inorganic chemistry course, taught by Heinrich Blitz, was oriented to new ideas in physical chemistry. Eucken also studied at the University of Jena. He entered the University of Berlin in 1905 to work in Nernst's laboratory, and he completed his doctorate the following year. From 1908 Eucken was an assistant in Nernst's laboratory. He was *Privatdozent* from 1911 and was in charge of some of the physical chemistry laboratories from 1913. In 1919 he became director of physical chemistry at the Technische Hochschule of Breslau and from 1930 was director of the Institute for Physical Chemistry at the University of Göttingen. Eucken received many academic honors.

After some early work in electrochemistry Eucken became very much involved with heat theory, and conducted experimental research associated with the determination of specific heats. In 1909 he measured specific heats by a method of Nernst's; in the following decades he tested many heat laws experimentally. His work included experiments on the specific heats of hydrogen at low temperatures, Debye's law for specific heats of solids at low temperatures, the range of applicability of Nernst's heat theorem, the difference (predicted by quantum theory) between the specific heats of ortho- and para-hydrogen, and Einstein's theory of specific heats. In the context of his later research on reaction kinetics, Eucken studied contact catalysis and the exchange of vibrational energy between gas molecules.

Eucken was eager to discourage overspecialization in science. For example, he felt that physical chemistry should be studied in terms of physics and mathematics. (He believed, however, that for satisfactory teaching, physical chemistry should remain a separate subject because it is not at all obvious how to apply physics to chemical phenomena.) Similarly, Eucken hoped to increase the interaction between science and technology; some of the research in his laboratory was chosen for the sake of its practical application, and Eucken was chairman of a committee to promote theoretical study of industrial processes.

BIBLIOGRAPHY

I. Original Works. Eucken wrote many physical chemistry texts. An early English version is *Fundamentals of Physical Chemistry,* trans. and adapted by E. R. Jette and V. K. LaMer (New York, 1925). For a listing of Eucken's papers, consult *Chemical Abstracts* for the period 1900–1950.

II. Secondary Literature. See E. Bartholomé, in *Die Naturwissenschaften,* **37** (1950), 481–483; and R. Oesper, "Arnold Eucken," in *Journal of Chemical Education,* **27** (1950), 540–541.

Sigalia Dostrovsky

EUCLID (*fl.* Alexandria [and Athens?], *ca.* 295 B.C.), *mathematics.* The following article is in two parts: Life and Works; Transmission of the Elements.

Life and Works.

Although Euclid (Latinized as Euclides) is the most celebrated mathematician of all time, whose name became a synonym for geometry until the twentieth century,[1] only two facts of his life are known, and even these are not beyond dispute. One is that he was intermediate in date between the pupils of Plato (*d.* 347 B.C.) and Archimedes (*b. ca.* 287 B.C.); the other is that he taught in Alexandria.

Until recently most scholars would have been content to say that Euclid was older than Archimedes on the ground that Euclid, *Elements* I.2, is cited in Archimedes, *On the Sphere and the Cylinder* I.2; but in 1950 Johannes Hjelmslev asserted that this reference was a naïve interpolation. The reasons that he gave are not wholly convincing, but the reference is certainly contrary to ancient practice and is not unfairly characterized as naïve; and although it was already in the text in the time of Proclus, it looks like a marginal gloss which has crept in.[2] Although it is no longer possible to rely on this reference,[3] a general consideration of Euclid's works such as that presented here still shows that he must have written after such pupils of Plato as Eudoxus and before Archimedes.

Euclid's residence in Alexandria is known from Pappus, who records that Apollonius spent a long time with the disciples of Euclid in that city.[4] This passage is also attributed to an interpolator by Pappus' editor, Friedrich Hultsch, but only for stylistic reasons (and these not very convincing); and even if the Alexandrian residence rested only on the authority of an interpolator, it would still be credible in the light of general probabilities. Since Alexander ordered the foundation of the town in 332 B.C. and another ten years elapsed before it began to take shape, we get as a first approximation that Euclid's Alexandrian activities lay somewhere between 320 and 260 B.C. Apollonius was active at Alexandria under Ptolemy III Euergetes (acceded 246) and Ptolemy IV Philopator (acceded 221) and must have received his education about the middle of the century. It is likely, therefore, that Euclid's life overlapped that of Archimedes.

This agrees with what Proclus says about Euclid in his commentary on the first book of the *Elements.* The passage, which is contained in Proclus' summary of the history of geometry,[5] opens:

> Not much younger than these [Hermotimus of Colophon and Philippus of Medma, two disciples of Plato] is Euclid, who put together the elements, arranging in order many of Eudoxus' theorems, perfecting many of Theaetetus', and also bringing to irrefutable demonstration the things which had been only loosely proved by his predecessors. This man lived[6] in the time of the first Ptolemy;[7] for Archimedes, who followed closely upon the first [Ptolemy], makes mention of Euclid,[8] and further they say that Ptolemy once asked him if there were a shorter way to the study of geometry than the *Elements,* to which he replied that there was no royal road to geometry. He is therefore younger than Plato's circle, but older than Eratosthenes and Archimedes; for these were contemporaries, as Eratosthenes somewhere says.[9] In his aim he was a Platonist, being in sympathy with this philosophy, whence he made the end of the whole *Elements* the construction of the so-called Platonic figures.

Since Plato died in 347, Ptolemy I ruled from 323 and reigned from 304 to 285, and Archimedes was born in 287, the chronology of this passage is self-consistent but allows a wide margin according to whether Euclid flourished in Ptolemy's rule or reign. It is clear, however, that Proclus, writing over six centuries later, had no independent knowledge, obviously relying upon Archimedes for his lower date. The story about the royal road is similar to a tale that Stobaeus tells about Menaechmus and Alexander.[10] Euclid may very well have been a Platonist, for mathematics received an immense impetus from Plato's encouragement; what Proclus says about his relationship to Plato's associates, Eudoxus and Theaetetus, is borne out by his own works; and if he were a Platonist, he would have derived pleasure from making the *Elements* end with the construction of the five regular solids. The testimony of so zealous a Neoplatonist as Proclus is not, however, necessarily conclusive on this point.

Confirmation of Proclus' upper date comes from the relationship of Euclid to Aristotle, who died in 322 B.C. Euclid's postulates and axioms or "common notions" undoubtedly show the influence of Aristotle's elaborate discussion of these topics.[11] Aristotle, on the other hand, shows no awareness of Euclid, and he gives a proof of the proposition that the angles at the base of an isosceles triangle are equal which is pre-Euclidean and would hardly have been cited if *Elements* I.5 had been at hand.[12]

If exact dates could be assigned to Autolycus of Pitane, greater precision would be possible, for in his *Phaenomena* Euclid quotes (but without naming his source) propositions from Autolycus' *On the Moving Sphere*. Autolycus was the teacher of Arcesilaus, who was born about 315 B.C. It would be reasonable to suppose that Autolycus was at the height of his activities about 300 B.C., and the date that would best fit the middle point of Euclid's active career is about 295 B.C.; but the uncertainties are so great that no quarrel can be taken with the conventional round date of 300 B.C.[13]

He is therefore a totally different person from Euclid of Megara, the disciple of Plato, who lived about a hundred years earlier.[14] His birthplace is unknown,[15] and the date of his birth can only be guessed. It is highly probable, however, quite apart from what Proclus says about his Platonism, that he attended the Academy, for Athens was the great center of mathematical studies at the time; and there he would have become acquainted with the highly original work of Eudoxus and Theaetetus. He was probably invited to Alexandria when Demetrius of Phalerum, at the direction of Ptolemy Soter, was setting up the great library and museum. This was shortly after 300 B.C., and Demetrius, then an exile from Athens, where he had been the governor, would have known Euclid's reputation. It is possible that this had already been established by one or more books, but the only piece of internal or external evidence about the order in which Euclid wrote his works is that the *Optics* preceded the *Phaenomena* because it is cited in the preface of the latter. Euclid must be regarded as the founder of the great school of mathematics at Alexandria, which was unrivaled in antiquity. Pappus or an interpolator[16] pays tribute to him as "most fair and well disposed toward all who were able in any measure to advance mathematics, careful in no way to give offense, and although an exact scholar not vaunting himself," as Apollonius was alleged to do; and although the object of the passage is to denigrate Apollonius, there is no reason to reject the assessment of Euclid's character. It was presumably at Alexandria, according to a story by Stobaeus,[17] that someone who had begun to learn geometry with Euclid asked him, after the first theorem, what he got out of such things. Summoning a slave, Euclid said, "Give him three obols, since he must needs make gain out of what he learns." The place of his death is not recorded—although the natural assumption is that it was Alexandria—and the date of his death can only be conjectured. A date about 270 B.C. would accord with the fact that about the middle of the century Apollonius studied with his pupils.

Arabic authors profess to know a great deal more about Euclid's parentage and life, but what they write is either free invention or based on the assumption that the so-called book XIV of the *Elements,* written by Hypsicles, is a genuine work of Euclid.

Geometry: Elements (Στοιχεῖα). Euclid's fame rests preeminently upon the *Elements,* which he wrote in thirteen books[18] and which has exercised an influence upon the human mind greater than that of any other work except the Bible. For this reason he became known in antiquity as Ὁ Στοιχειωτής, "the Writer of the Elements," and sometimes simply as Ὁ Γεωμέτρης, "the Geometer." Proclus explains that the "elements" are leading theorems having to those which follow the character of an all-pervading principle; he likens them to the letters of the alphabet in relation to language, and in Greek they have the same name.[19] There had been *Elements* written before Euclid—notably by Hippocrates, Leo, and Theudius of Magnesia—but Euclid's work superseded them so completely that they are now known only from Eudemus' references as preserved by Proclus. Euclid's *Elements* was the subject of commentaries in antiquity by Hero, Pappus, Porphyry, Proclus, and Simplicius; and Geminus had many observations about it in a work now lost. In the fourth century Theon of Alexandria reedited it, altering the language in some places with a view to greater clarity, interpolating intermediate steps, and supplying alternative proofs, separate cases, and corollaries. All the manuscripts of the *Elements* known until the nineteenth century were derived from Theon's recension. Then Peyrard discovered in the Vatican a manuscript, known as *P*, which obviously gives an earlier text and is the basis of Heiberg's definitive edition.

Each book of the *Elements* is divided into propositions, which may be theorems, in which it is sought to prove something, or problems, in which it is sought to do something. A proposition which is complete in all its parts has a general enunciation (πρότασις); a setting-out or particular enunciation (ἔκθεσις), in which the general enunciation is related to a figure designated by the letters of the alphabet; a definition (διορισμός),[20] which is either a closer statement of the object sought, with the purpose of riveting attention, or a statement of the conditions of possibility; a construction (κατασκευή), including any necessary additions to the original figure; a proof or demonstration (ἀπόδειξις); and a conclusion (συμπέρασμα), which reverts to the language of the general enunciation and states that it has been accomplished. In many cases some of these divisions may be missing (particularly the definition or the construction) because they are not needed, but the general enunciation, proof, and conclusion are always found. The conclusion is rounded off by the formulas ὅπερ ἔδει δεῖξαι ("which was to be proved") for a theorem and ὅπερ ἔδει ποιῆσαι ("which was to be done") for a problem, which every schoolboy knows in their abbreviated Latin forms as Q.E.D. and Q.E.F. These formal divisions of a proposition in such detail are special to Euclid, for Autolycus before him—the only pre-Euclidean author to have any work survive entire—had normally given only a general enunciation and proof, although occasionally a conclusion is found; and Archimedes after him frequently omitted the general or particular enunciation.

The Greek mathematicians carefully distinguished between the analytic and the synthetic methods of proving a proposition.[21] Euclid was not unskilled in analysis, and according to Pappus he was one of the three writers—the others being Apollonius and Aristaeus the Elder—who created the special body of doctrine enshrined in the *Treasury of Analysis*. This collection of treatises included three by Euclid: his *Data, Porisms,* and *Surface Loci.* But in the *Elements* the demonstrations proceed entirely by synthesis, that is, from the known to the unknown, and nowhere is appeal made to analysis, that is, the assumption of

the thing to be proved (or done) and the deduction of the consequences until we reach something already accepted or proved true. (Euclid does, however, make frequent use of *reductio ad absurdum* or *demonstratio per impossibile,* showing that if the conclusion is not accepted, absurd or impossible results follow; and this may be regarded as a form of analysis. There are also many pairs of converse propositions, and either one in a pair could be regarded as a piece of analysis for the solution of the other.) No hint is given by Euclid about the way in which he first realized the truth of the propositions that he proves. Majestically he proceeds by rigorous logical steps from one proved proposition to another, using them like stepping-stones, until the final goal is reached.

Each book (or, in the case of XI–XIII, group of books) of the *Elements* is preceded by definitions of the subjects treated, and to book I there are also prefixed five postulates (αἰτήματα) and five common notions (κοίναι ἔννοιαι) or axioms which are the foundation of the entire work. Aristotle had taught that to define an object is not to assert its existence; this must be either proved or assumed.[22] In conformity with this doctrine Euclid defines a point, a straight line, and a circle, then postulates that it is possible

1. To draw a straight line from any point to any point
2. To produce a finite straight line continuously in a straight line
3. To describe a circle with any center and radius.

In other words, he assumes the existence of points, straight lines, and circles as the basic elements of his geometry, and with these assumptions he is able to prove the existence of every other figure that he defines. For example, the existence of a square, defined in I, definition 22, is proved in I.46.

These three postulates do rather more, however, than assume the existence of the things defined. The first postulate implies that between any two points only one straight line can be drawn; and this is equivalent to saying that if two straight lines have the same extremities, they coincide throughout their length, or that two straight lines cannot enclose a space. (The latter statement is interpolated in some of the manuscripts.) The second postulate implies that a straight line can be produced in only one direction at either end, that is, the produced part in either direction is unique, and two straight lines cannot have a common segment. It follows also, since the straight line can be produced indefinitely, or an indefinite number of times, that the space of Euclid's geometry is infinite in all directions. The third postulate also implies the infinitude of space because no limit is placed upon the radius; it further implies that space is continuous, not discrete, because the radius may be indefinitely small.

The fourth and fifth postulates are of a different order because they do not state that something can be done. In the fourth the following is postulated:

4. All right angles are equal to one another.

This implies that a right angle is a determinate magnitude, so that it serves as a norm by which other angles can be measured, but it is also equivalent to an assumption of the homogeneity of space. For if the assertion could be proved, it could be proved only by moving one right angle to another so as to make them coincide, which is an assumption of the invariability of figures or the homogeneity of space. Euclid prefers to assume that all right angles are equal.

The fifth postulate concerns parallel straight lines. These are defined in I, definition 23, as "straight lines which, being in the same plane and being produced indefinitely in both directions, do not meet one another in either direction." The essential characteristic of parallel lines for Euclid is, therefore, that they do not meet. Other Greek writers toyed with the idea, as many moderns have done, that parallel straight lines are equidistant from each other throughout their lengths or have the same direction,[23] and Euclid shows his genius in opting for nonsecancy as the test of parallelism. The fifth postulate runs:

5. If a straight line falling on two straight lines makes the interior angles on the same side less than two right angles, the two straight lines, if produced indefinitely, will meet on that side on which are the angles less than two right angles.

In Figure 1 the postulate asserts that if a straight line (PQ) cuts two other straight lines (AB, CD) in P, Q so that the sum of the angles BPQ, DQP is less than two right angles, AB, CD will meet on the same side of PQ as those two angles, that is, they will meet if produced beyond B and D.

There was a strong feeling in antiquity that this postulate should be capable of proof, and attempts to prove it were made by Ptolemy and Proclus, among others.[24] Many more attempts have been made in modern times. All depend for their apparent success on making, consciously or unconsciously, an assumption which is equivalent to Euclid's postulate. It was Saccheri in his book *Euclides ab omni naevo vindicatus* (1733) who first asked himself what would be the consequences of hypotheses other than that of Euclid, and in so doing he stumbled upon the possibility of non-Euclidean geometries. Being convinced, as all mathematicians and philosophers were until the

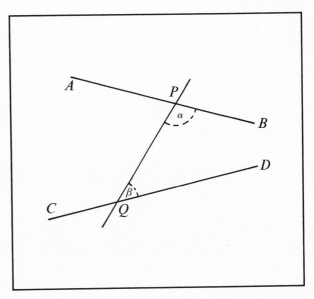

FIGURE 1. Book I, Postulate 5, $\alpha + \beta < 2$ Right Angles

nineteenth century, that there could be no geometry besides that delineated by Euclid, he did not realize what he had done; and although Gauss had the first understanding of modern ideas, it was left to Lobachevski (1826, 1829) and Bolyai (1832), on the one hand, and Riemann (1854), on the other, to develop non-Euclidean geometries. Euclid's fifth postulate has thus been revealed for what it really is—an unprovable assumption defining the character of one type of space.

The five common notions are axioms, which, unlike the postulates, are not confined to geometry but are common to all the demonstrative sciences. The first is "Things which are equal to the same thing are also equal to one another," and the others are similar.

The subject matter of the first six books of the *Elements* is plane geometry. Book I deals with the geometry of points, lines, triangles, squares, and parallelograms. Proposition 5, that in isosceles triangles the angles at the base are equal to one another and that, if the equal straight lines are produced, the angles under the base will be equal to one another, is interesting historically as having been known (except in France) as the *pons asinorum;* this is usually taken to mean that those who are not going to be good at geometry fail to get past it, although others have seen in the figure of the proposition a resemblance to a trestle bridge with a ramp at each end which a donkey can cross but a horse cannot.

Proposition 44 requires the student "to a given straight to apply in a given rectilineal angle a parallelogram equal to a given triangle," that is, on a given straight line to construct a parallelogram equal to a given area and having one of its angles equal to a

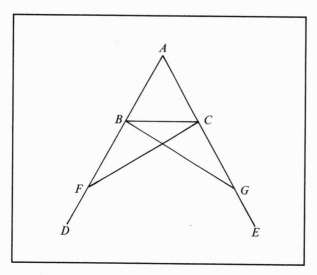

FIGURE 2.   Book I, Proposition 5, Pons Asinorum

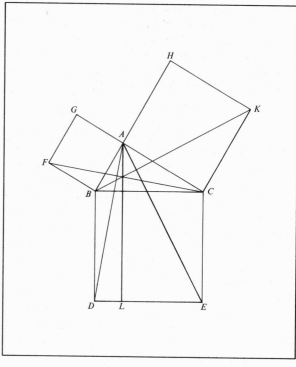

FIGURE 4.   Book I, Proposition 47, "Pythagoras' Theorem,"
$BC^2 = CA^2 + AB^2$

given angle. In Figure 3, *AB* is the given straight line and the parallelogram *BEFG* is constructed equal to the triangle *C* so that $\angle GBE = \angle D$. The figure is completed, and it is proved that the parallelogram *ABML* satisfies the requirements. This is Euclid's first example of the application of areas,[25] one of the most powerful tools of the Greek mathematicians. It is a geometrical equivalent of certain algebraic operations. In this simple case, if $AL = x$, then $x \cdot AB \cos D = C$, and the theorem is equivalent to the solution of a first-degree equation. The method is developed later, as it will be shown, so as to be equivalent to the solution of second-degree equations.

Book I leads up to the celebrated proposition 47,

"Pythagoras' theorem," which asserts: "In right-angled triangles the square on the side subtending the right angle is equal to the [sum of the] squares on the sides containing the right angle." In Figure 4 it is shown solely by the use of preceding propositions that the parallelogram *BL* is equal to the square *BG* and the parallelogram *CL* is equal to the square *AK*, so that the whole square *BE* is equal to the sum of the squares *BG*, *AK*. It is important to notice, for

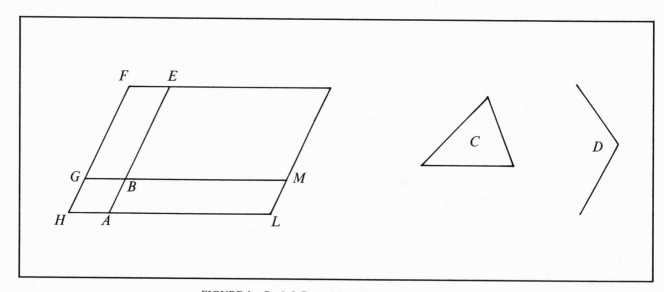

FIGURE 3.   Book I, Proposition 44, Application of Areas

a reason to be given later, that no appeal is made to similarity of figures. This fundamental proposition gives Euclidean space a metric, which would be expressed in modern notation as $ds^2 = dx^2 + dy^2$. It is impossible not to admire the ingenuity with which the result is obtained, and not surprising that when Thomas Hobbes first read it he exclaimed, "By God, this is impossible."

Book II develops the transformation of areas adumbrated in I.44, 45 and is a further exercise in geometrical algebra. Propositions 5, 6, 11, and 14 are the equivalents of solving the quadratic equations $ax - x^2 = b^2, ax + x^2 = b^2, x^2 + ax = a^2, x^2 = ab$. Propositions 9 and 10 are equivalent to finding successive pairs of integers satisfying the equations $2x^2 - y^2 = \pm 1$. Such pairs were called by the Greeks side numbers and diameter numbers. Propositions 12 and 13 are equivalent to a proof that in any triangle with sides a,b,c, and angle A opposite a,

$$a^2 = b^2 + c^2 - 2\,bc \cos A.$$

It is probably not without significance that this penultimate proposition of book II is a generalization of "Pythagoras' theorem," which was the penultimate proposition of book I.

Book III treats circles, including their intersections and touchings. Book IV consists entirely of problems about circles, particularly the inscribing or circumscribing of rectilineal figures. It ends with proposition 16: "In a given circle to inscribe a fifteen-angled figure which shall be both equilateral and equiangular." Proclus asserts that this is one of the propositions that Euclid solved with a view to their use in astronomy, "for when we have inscribed the fifteen-angled figure in the circle through the poles, we have the distance from the poles both of the equator and the zodiac, since they are distant from one another by the side of the fifteen-angled figure"—that is to say, the obliquity of the ecliptic was taken to be 24°, as is known independently to have been the case up to Eratosthenes.[26]

Book V develops the general theory of proportion. The theory of proportion as discovered by the Pythagoreans applied only to commensurable magnitudes because it depends upon the taking of aliquot parts, and this is all that was needed by Euclid for the earlier books of the *Elements*. There are instances, notably I.47, where he clearly avoids a proof that would depend on similitude or the finding of a proportional, because at that stage of his work it would not have applied to incommensurable magnitudes. In book V he addresses himself at length to the general theory. There is no book in the *Elements* that has so won the admiration of mathematicians. Barrow observes: "There is nothing in the whole body of the *Elements* of a more subtile invention, nothing more solidly established and more accurately handled, than the doctrine of proportionals." In like spirit Cayley says, "There is hardly anything in mathematics more beautiful than this wondrous fifth book."[27]

The heart of the book is contained in the definitions with which it opens. The definition of a ratio as "a sort of relation in respect of size between two magnitudes of the same kind" shows that a ratio, like the elephant, is easy to recognize but hard to define. Definition 4 is more to the point: "Magnitudes are said to have a ratio one to the other if capable, when multiplied, of exceeding one another." The definition excludes the infinitely great and the infinitely small and is virtually equivalent to what is now known as the axiom of Archimedes. (See below, section on book X.) But it is definition 5 which has chiefly excited the admiration of subsequent mathematicians: "Magnitudes are said to be in the same ratio, the first to the second and the second to the fourth, when, if any equimultiples whatever be taken of the first and third, and any equimultiples whatever of the second and fourth, the former equimultiples alike exceed, are alike equal to, or alike fall short of, the latter equimultiples respectively taken in corresponding order." It will be noted that the definition avoids mention of parts of a magnitude and is therefore applicable to the incommensurable as well as to the commensurable. De Morgan put its meaning very clearly: "Four magnitudes, A and B of one kind, and C and D of the same or another kind, are proportional when all the multiples of A can be distributed among the multiples of B in the same intervals as the corresponding multiples of C among those of D"; or, in notation, if m, n are two integers, and if mA lies between nB and $(n + 1)B$, mC lies between nD and $(n + 1)D$.[28] It can be shown that the test proposed by Euclid is both a necessary and a sufficient test of proportionality, and in the whole history of mathematics no equally satisfactory test has ever been proposed. The best testimony to its adequacy is that Weierstrass used it in his definition of equal numbers;[29] and Heath has shown how Euclid's definition divides all rational numbers into two coextensive classes and thus defines equal ratios in a manner exactly corresponding to a Dedekind section.[30]

The remaining definitions state the various kinds of transformations of ratios—generally known by their Latin names: *alternando, invertendo, componendo, separando, convertendo, ex aequali,* and *ex aequali in proportione perturbata*—and with remorseless logic the twenty-five propositions apply these various operations to the objects of Euclid's definitions.

It is a sign of the abiding fascination of book V for mathematicians that in 1967 Friedhelm Beckmann applied his own system of axioms, set up in close accordance with Euclid, in such a way as to deduce all definitions and propositions of Euclid's theory of magnitudes, especially those of books V and VI. In his view magnitudes, rather than their relation of "having a ratio," form the base of the theory of proportions. These magnitudes represent a well-defined structure, a so-called Eudoxic semigroup, with the numbers as operators. Proportion is interpreted as a mapping of totally ordered semigroups. This mapping proves to be an isomorphism, thus suggesting the application of the modern theory of homomorphism.

Book VI uses the general theory of proportion established in the previous book to treat similar figures. The first and last propositions of the book illustrate the importance of V, definition 5, for by the method of equimultiples it is proved in proposition 1 that triangles and parallelograms having the same height are to one another as their bases, and in proposition 33 it is proved that in equal circles the angles at the center or circumference are as the arcs on which

they stand. There are many like propositions of equal importance. Proposition 25 sets the problem "To construct a rectilineal figure similar to one, and equal to another, given rectilineal figure."[31] In propositions 27–29 Euclid takes up again the application of areas. It has been explained above that to apply ($\pi\alpha\rho\alpha\beta\acute{\alpha}\lambda\lambda\epsilon\iota\nu$) a parallelogram to a given straight line means to construct on that line a parallelogram equal to a given area and having a given angle. If the straight line is applied to only part of the given line, the resulting figure is said to be deficient ($\acute{\epsilon}\lambda\lambda\epsilon\acute{\iota}\pi\epsilon\iota\nu$); if to the straight line produced, it is said to exceed ($\acute{\upsilon}\pi\epsilon\rho\beta\acute{\alpha}\lambda\lambda\epsilon\iota\nu$). Proposition 28 is the following problem: "To a given straight line to apply a parallelogram equal to a given rectilineal figure and deficient by a parallelogrammatic figure similar to a given one." (It has already been shown in proposition 27 that the given rectilineal figure must not be greater than the parallelogram described on half the straight line and similar to the defect.) In Figure 5 let the parallelogram TR be applied to the straight line AB so as to be equal to a given rectilineal figure having the area S and deficient by the parallelogram PB, which is similar to the given parallelogram D. Let $AB = a$, $RP = x$; let the angle of D be α and the ratio of its sides $b:c$. Let E be the midpoint of AB

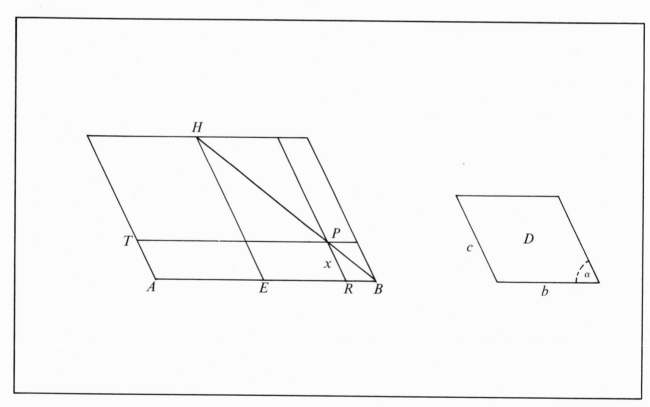

FIGURE 5. Book VI, Proposition 28

and let *EH* be drawn parallel to the sides. Then

(the parallelogram *TR*) = (the parallelogram *TB*)

$$- \text{(the parallelogram } PB)$$

$$= ax \sin \alpha - \frac{b}{c} x \cdot x \sin \alpha.$$

If the area of the given rectilineal figure is *S*, this may be written

$$S = ax \sin \alpha - \frac{b}{c} x^2 \sin \alpha.$$

Constructing the parallelogram *TR* is therefore equivalent to solving geometrically the equation

$$ax - \frac{b}{c} x^2 = \frac{S}{\sin \alpha}.$$

It can easily be shown that Euclid's solution is equivalent to completing the square on the left-hand side. For a real solution it is necessary that

$$\frac{S}{\sin \alpha} \geq \frac{c}{b} \cdot \frac{a^2}{4}$$

i.e., $S \geq \left(\frac{c}{b} \cdot \frac{a}{2}\right)(\sin \alpha)\left(\frac{a}{2}\right)$

i.e., $S \geq HE \sin \alpha \cdot EB$

i.e., $S \geq$ parallelogram *HB*,

which is exactly what was proved in VI.27. Proposition 29 sets the corresponding problem for the excess: "To a given straight line to apply a parallelogram equal to a given rectilineal figure and exceeding by a parallelogrammatic figure similar to a given one." This can be shown in the same way to be equivalent to solving geometrically the equation

$$ax + \frac{b}{c} x^2 = \frac{S}{\sin \alpha}.$$

In this case there is always a real solution. No διορισμός or examination of the conditions of possibility is needed, and Euclid's solution corresponds to the root with the positive sign.

This group of propositions is needed by Euclid for his treatment of irrationals in book X, but their chief importance in the history of mathematics is that they are the basis of the theory of conic sections as developed by Apollonius. Indeed, the very words "parabola," "ellipse," and "hyperbola" come from the Greek words for "to apply," "to be deficient," and "to exceed."

It is significant that the antepenultimate proposition of the book, proposition 31, is a generalization of "Pythagoras' theorem": "In right-angled triangles any [literally "the"] figure [described] on the side subtending the right angle is equal to the [sum of the] similar and similarly described figures on the sides containing the right angle."

Books VII, VIII, and IX are arithmetical; and although the transition from book VI appears sharp, there is a logical structure in that the theory of proportion, developed in all its generality in book V, is applied in book VI to geometrical figures and in book VII to numbers. The theory of numbers is continued in the next two books. The theory of proportion in book VII is not, however, the general theory of book V but the old Pythagorean theory applicable only to commensurable magnitudes.[32] This return to an outmoded theory led both De Morgan and W. W. Rouse Ball to suppose that Euclid died before putting the finishing touches to the *Elements*,[33] but, although the three arithmetical books seem trite in comparison with those that precede and follow, there is nothing unfinished about them. It is more likely that Euclid, displaying the deference toward others that Pappus observed, thought that he ought to include the traditional teaching. This respect for traditional doctrines can be seen in some of the definitions which Euclid repeats even though he improves upon them or never uses them.[34] Although books VII–IX appear at first sight to be a reversion to Pythagoreanism, it is Pythagoreanism with a difference. In particular, the rational straight line takes the place of the Pythagorean monad;[35] but the products of numbers are also treated as straight lines, not as squares or rectangles.

After the numerical theory of proportion is established in VII.4–19, there is an interesting group of propositions on prime numbers (22–32) and a final group (33–39) on least common multiples. Book VIII deals in the main with series of numbers "in continued proportion," that is, in geometrical progression, and with geometric means. Book IX is a miscellany and includes the fundamental theorem in the theory of numbers, proposition 14: "If a number be the least that is measured by prime numbers, it will not be measured by any other prime number except those originally measuring it," that is to say, a number can be resolved into prime factors in only one way.

After the muted notes of the arithmetical books Euclid again takes up his lofty theme in book X, which treats irrational magnitudes. It opens with the following proposition (X.1): "If two unequal magnitudes be set out, and if there be subtracted from the greater a magnitude greater than its half, and from that which is left a magnitude greater than its half, and so on continually, there will be left some magnitude less than the lesser magnitude set out." This is the basis of the "method of exhaustion," as later used by Euclid in book XII. Because of the use made of it by Archimedes, either directly or in an equivalent form, for the purpose of calculating areas and volumes, it has become known, perhaps a little unreasonably, as the axiom of Archimedes. Euclid needs the axiom at this point as a test of incommensurability, and his next proposition (X.2) asserts: "If the lesser of two unequal magnitudes is continually subtracted from the greater, and the remainder never measures that which precedes it, the magnitudes will be incommensurable."

The main achievement of the book is a classification of irrational straight lines, no doubt for the purpose of easy reference. Starting from any assigned straight line which it is agreed to regard as rational—a kind of datum line—Euclid asserts that any straight line which is commensurable with it in length is rational, but he also regards as rational a straight line commensurable with it only in square. That is to say, if m, n are two integers in their lowest terms with respect to each other, and l is a rational straight line, he regards $\sqrt{m/n} \cdot l$ as rational because $(m/n)l^2$ is commensurable with l^2. All straight lines not commensurable either in length or in square with the assigned straight line he calls irrational. His fundamental proposition (X.9) is that the sides of squares are commensurable or incommensurable in length according to whether the squares have or do not have the ratio of a square number to each other, that is to say, if a, b are straight lines and m, n are two numbers, and if $a:b = m:n$, then $a^2:b^2 = m^2:n^2$ and conversely. This is easily seen in modern notation, but was far from an easy step for Euclid. The first irrational line which he isolates is the side of a square equal in area to a rectangle whose sides are commensurable in square only. He calls it a medial. If the sides of the rectangle are l, $\sqrt{k}\,l$, the medial is $k^{1/4}l$. Euclid next proceeds to define six pairs of compound irrationals (the members of each pair differing in sign only) which can be represented in modern notation as the positive roots of six biquadratic equations (reducible to quadratics) of the form

$$x^4 \pm 2alx^2 \pm bl^4 = 0.$$

The first pair are given the names "binomial" (or "biterminal") and "apotome," and Euclid proceeds to define six pairs of their derivatives which are equivalent to the roots of six quadratic equations of the form

$$x^2 + 2alx + bl^2 = 0.$$

In all, Euclid investigates in the 115 propositions of the book (of which the last four may be interpola-

tions) every possible form of the lines which can be represented by the expression $\sqrt{(\sqrt{a} \pm \sqrt{b})}$, some twenty-five in all.[36]

The final three books of the *Elements*, XI–XIII, are devoted to solid geometry. Book XI deals largely with parallelepipeds. Book XII applies the method of exhaustion, that is, the inscription of successive figures in the body to be evaluated, in order to prove that circles are to one another as the squares on their diameters, that pyramids of the same height with triangular bases are in the ratio of their bases, that the volume of a cone is one-third of the cylinder which has the same base and equal height, that cones and cylinders having the same height are in the ratio of their bases, that similar cones and cylinders are to one another in the triplicate ratio of the diameters of their bases, and that spheres are in the triplicate ratio of their diameters. The method can be shown for the circle. Euclid inscribes a square in the circle and shows that it is more than half the circle. He bisects each arc and shows that each triangle so obtained is greater than half the segment of the circle about it. (In Figure 6, for example, triangle *EAB* is greater than half the segment of the circle *EAB* standing on *AB*.) If the process is continued indefinitely, according to X.1, we shall be left with segments of the circle smaller than some assigned magnitude, that is, the circle has been exhausted. (A little later Archimedes was to refine the method by also circum-

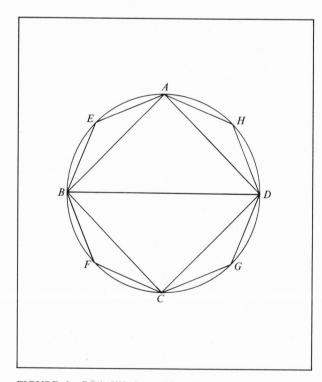

FIGURE 6. Book XII, Proposition 2, Exhaustion of a Circle

scribing a polygon, and so compressing the figure, as it were, between inscribed and circumscribed polygons.) Euclid refrains from saying that as the process is continued indefinitely, the area of the polygon will in the limit approach the area of the circle, and rigorously proves that if his proposition is not granted, impossible conclusions would follow.

After some preliminary propositions book XIII is devoted to the construction in a sphere of the five regular solids: the pyramid (proposition 13), the octahedron (14), the cube (15), the icosahedron (16), and the dodecahedron (17). These five regular solids had been a prime subject of investigation by the Greek mathematicians, and because of the use made of them by Plato in the *Timaeus* were known as the Platonic figures.[37] The mathematical problem is to determine the edge of the figure in relation to the radius of the circumscribing sphere. In the case of the pyramid, octahedron, and cube, Euclid actually evaluates the edge in terms of the radius, and in the case of the icosahedron and dodecahedron he shows that it is one of the irrational lines classified in book X—a minor in the case of the icosahedron and an apotome in the case of the dodecahedron. In a final splendid flourish (proposition 18), Euclid sets out the sides of the five figures in the same sphere and compares them with each other, and in an addendum he shows that there can be no other regular solids. In Figure 7, $AC = CB$, $AD = 2DB$, $AG = AB$, $CL = CM$, and BF is divided in extreme and mean ratio at $N(BF:BN = BN:NF)$. He proves that AF is the side of the pyramid, BF is the side of the cube, BE is the

side of the octahedron, BK is the side of the icosahedron, and BN is the side of the dodecahedron; their values, in terms of the radius r, are respectively $2/3 \sqrt{6} \cdot r$, $\sqrt{2} \cdot r$, $2/3 \sqrt{3} \cdot r$, $r/5 \sqrt{10(5 - \sqrt{5})}$, $r/3(\sqrt{15} - \sqrt{3})$.

Proclus, as already noted, regarded the construction of the five Platonic figures as the end of the *Elements,* in both senses of that ambiguous word. This is usually discounted on the ground that the stereometrical books had to come last, but Euclid need not have ended with the construction of the five regular solids; and since he shows the influence of Plato in other ways, this splendid ending could easily be a grain of incense at the Platonic altar.

Proclus sums up Euclid's achievement in the *Elements* in the following words:[38]

> He deserves admiration preeminently in the compilation of his *Elements of Geometry* on account of the order and selection both of the theorems and of the problems made with a view to the elements. For he included not everything which he could have said, but only such things as were suitable for the building up of the elements. He used all the various forms of deductive arguments,[39] some getting their plausibility from the first principles, some starting from demonstrations, but all irrefutable and accurate and in harmony with science. In addition he used all the dialectical methods, the *divisional* in the discovery of figures, the *definitive* in the existential arguments, the *demonstrative* in the passages from first principles to the things sought, and the *analytic* in the converse process from the things sought to the first principles. And the various species of conversions,[40] both of the simpler (propositions) and of the more complex, are in this treatise accurately set forth and skillfully investigated, what wholes can be converted with wholes, what wholes with parts and conversely, and what as parts with parts. Further, we must make mention of the continuity of the proofs, the disposition and arrangement of the things which precede and those which follow, and the power with which he treats each detail.

This is a fair assessment. The *Elements* is on the whole a compilation of things already known, and its most remarkable feature is the arrangement of the matter so that one proposition follows on another in a strictly logical order, with the minimum of assumption and very little that is superfluous.

If we seek to know how much of it is Euclid's own work, Proclus is again our best guide. He says, as we have seen, that Euclid "put together the elements, arranging in order many of Eudoxus' theorems, perfecting many of Theaetetus', and also bringing to irrefutable demonstration the things which had been only loosely proved by his predecessors."[41] According to a scholiast of book V, "Some say that this book

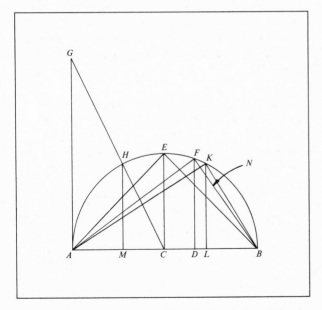

FIGURE 7. Book XIII, Proposition 18, Inscription of Regular Solids in a Sphere

is the discovery of Eudoxus, the disciple of Plato."[42] Another scholiast confirms this, saying, "This book is said to be the work of Eudoxus of Cnidus, the mathematician, who lived about the times of Plato."[43] He adds, however, that the ascription to Euclid is not false, for although there is nothing to prevent the discovery from being the work of another man, "The arrangement of the book with a view to the elements and the orderly sequence of theorems is recognized by all as the work of Euclid." This is a fair division of the credit. Eudoxus also, as we can infer from Archimedes,[44] is responsible for the method of exhaustion used in book XII to evaluate areas and volumes, based upon X.1, and Archimedes attributes to Eudoxus by name the theorems about the volume of the pyramid and the volume of the cone which stand as propositions 7 and 10 of book XII of the *Elements.* Although Greek tradition credited Hippocrates with discovering that circles are to one another as the squares on their diameters,[45] we can be confident that the proof as we have it in XII.2 is also due to Eudoxus.

The interest of Theaetetus in the irrational is known from Plato's dialogue,[46] and a commentary on book X which has survived in Arabic[47] and is attributed by Heiberg[48] to Pappus credits him with discovering the different species of irrational lines known as the medial, binomial, and apotome. A scholium to X.9[49] (that squares which do not have the ratio of a square number to a square number have their sides incommensurable) attributes this theorem to Theaetetus. It would appear in this case also that the fundamental discoveries were made before Euclid but that the orderly arrangement of propositions is his work. This, indeed, is asserted in the commentary attributed to Pappus, which says:

> As for Euclid he set himself to give rigorous rules, which he established, relative to commensurability and incommensurability in general; he made precise the definitions and the distinctions between rational and irrational magnitudes, he set out a great number of orders of irrational magnitudes, and finally he clearly showed their whole extent.[50]

Theaetetus was also the first to "construct" or "write upon" the five regular solids,[51] and according to a scholiast[52] the propositions concerning the octahedron and the icosahedron are due to him. His work therefore underlies book XIII, although the credit for the arrangement must again be given to Euclid.

According to Proclus,[53] the application of areas, which, as we have seen, is employed in I.44 and 45, II.5, 6, and 11, and VI.27, 28, and 29, is "ancient, being discoveries of the muse of the Pythagoreans."

A scholiast to book IV[54] attributes all sixteen theorems (problems) of that book to the Pythagoreans. It would appear, however, that the famous proof of what is universally known as "Pythagoras' theorem," I.47, is due to Euclid himself. It is beyond doubt that this property of right-angled triangles was discovered by Pythagoras, or at least in his school, but the proof was almost certainly based on proportions and therefore not applicable to all magnitudes. Proclus says:

> If we give hearing to those who relate things of old, we shall find some of them referring this discovery to Pythagoras and saying that he sacrificed an ox upon the discovery. But I, while marveling at those who first came to know the truth of this theorem, hold in still greater admiration the writer of the *Elements,* not only because he made it secure by a most clear proof, but because he compelled assent by the irrefutable reasonings of science to the still more general proposition in the sixth book. For in that book he proves generally that in right-angled triangles the figure on the side subtending the right angle is equal to the similar and similarly situated figures described on the sides about the right angle.[55]

On the surface this suggests that Euclid devised a new proof, and this is borne out by what Proclus says about the generalization. It would be an easy matter to prove VI.31 by using I.47 along with VI.22, but Euclid chooses to prove it independently of I.47 by using the general theory of proportions. This suggests that he proved I.47 by means of book I alone, without invoking proportions in order to get it into his first book instead of his sixth. The proof certainly bears the marks of genius.

To Euclid also belongs beyond a shadow of doubt the credit for the parallel postulate which is fundamental to the whole system. Aristotle had censured those "who think they describe parallels" because of a *petitio principii* latent in their theory.[56] There is certainly no *petitio principii* in Euclid's theory of parallels, and we may deduce that it was post-Aristotelian and due to Euclid himself. In nothing did he show his genius more than in deciding to treat postulate 5 as an indemonstrable assumption.

The significance of Euclid's *Elements* in the history of thought is twofold. In the first place, it introduced into mathematical reasoning new standards of rigor which remained throughout the subsequent history of Greek mathematics and, after a period of logical slackness following the revival of mathematics, have been equaled again only in the past two centuries. In the second place, it marked a decisive step in the geometrization of mathematics.[57] The Pythagoreans and Democritus before Euclid, Archimedes in some of his works, and Diophantus afterward showed that

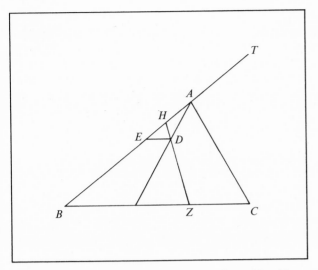

FIGURE 8. *On the Division of Figures,* Proposition 19

Greek mathematics might have developed in other directions. It was Euclid in his *Elements,* possibly under the influence of that philosopher who inscribed over the doors of the Academy "God is for ever doing geometry," who ensured that the geometrical form of proof should dominate mathematics. This decisive influence of Euclid's geometrical conception of mathematics is reflected in two of the supreme works in the history of thought, Newton's *Principia* and Kant's *Kritik der reinen Vernunft.* Newton's work is cast in the form of geometrical proofs that Euclid had made the rule even though Newton had discovered the calculus, which would have served him better and made him more easily understood by subsequent generations; and Kant's belief in the universal validity of Euclidean geometry led him to a transcendental aesthetic which governs all his speculations on knowledge and perception.

It was only toward the end of the nineteenth century that the spell of Euclidean geometry began to weaken and that a desire for the "arithmetization of mathematics" began to manifest itself; and only in the second quarter of the twentieth century, with the development of quantum mechanics, have we seen a return in the physical sciences to a neo-Pythagorean view of number as the secret of all things. Euclid's reign has been a long one; and although he may have been deposed from sole authority, he is still a power in the land.

The Data (Δεδομένα). The *Data,* the only other work by Euclid in pure geometry to have survived in Greek, is closely connected with books I–VI of the *Elements.* It is concerned with the different senses in which things are said to be given. Thus areas, straight lines, angles, and ratios are said to be "given in magnitude" when we can make others equal to them.

Rectilineal figures are "given in species" or "given in form" when their angles and the ratio of their sides are given. Points, lines, and angles are "given in position" when they always occupy the same place, and so on. After the definitions there follow ninety-four propositions, in which the object is to prove that if certain elements of a figure are given, other elements are also given in one of the defined senses.

The most interesting propositions are a group of four which are exercises in geometrical algebra and correspond to *Elements* II.28, 29. Proposition 58 reads: "If a given area be applied to a given straight line so as to be deficient by a figure given in form, the breadths of the deficiency are given." Proposition 84, which depends upon it, runs: "If two straight lines contain a given area in a given angle, and if one of them is greater than the other by a given quantity, then each of them is given." This is equivalent to solving the simultaneous equations

$$y - x = a$$
$$xy = b^2,$$

and these in turn are equivalent to finding the two roots of

$$ax + x^2 = b^2.$$

Propositions 59 and 85 give the corresponding theorems for the excess and are equivalent to the simultaneous equations

$$y + x = a$$
$$xy = b^2$$

and the quadratic equation

$$ax - x^2 = b^2.$$

A clue to the purpose of the *Data* is given by its inclusion in what Pappus calls the *Treasury of Analysis.*[58] The concept behind the *Data* is that if certain things are given, other things are necessarily implied, until we are brought to something that is agreed. The *Data* is a collection of hints on analysis. Pappus describes the contents of the book as known to him;[59] the number and order of the propositions differ in some respects from the text which has come down to us.

Marinus of Naples, the pupil and biographer of Proclus, wrote a commentary on, or rather an introduction to, the *Data.* It is concerned mainly with the different senses in which the term "given" was understood by Greek geometers.

On Divisions of Figures (Περὶ διαιρέσεων βιβλίον). Proclus preserved this title along with the titles of other works of Euclid,[60] and gives an indication of its contents: "For the circle is divisible into parts unlike by definition, and so is each of the rectilineal figures; and this is indeed what the writer of the *Elements* himself discusses in his *Divisions,* dividing given figures now into like figures, now into unlike."[61] The book has not survived in Greek, but all the thirty-six enunciations and four of the propositions (19, 20, 28, 29) have been preserved in an Arabic translation discovered by Woepcke and published in 1851; the remaining proofs can be supplied from the *Practica geometriae* written by Leonardo Fibonacci in 1220, one section of which, it is now evident, was based upon a manuscript or translation of Euclid's work no longer in existence. The work was reconstructed by R. C. Archibald in 1915.

The character of the book can be seen from the first of the four propositions which has survived in Arabic (19). This is "To divide a given triangle into two equal parts by a line which passes through a point situated in the interior of the triangle." Let D be a point inside the triangle ABC and let DE be drawn parallel to CB so as to meet AB in E. Let T be taken on BA produced so that $TB \cdot DE = 1/2\ AB \cdot BC$ (that is, let TB be such that when a rectangle having TB for one of its sides is applied to $DE,$ it is equal to half the rectangle $AB \cdot BC$). Next, let a parallelogram be applied to the line TB equal to the rectangle $TB \cdot BE$ and deficient by a square, that is, let H be taken on TB so that

$$(TB - HT) \cdot HT = TB \cdot BE.$$

HD is drawn and meets BC in Z. It can easily be shown that HZ divides the triangle into two equal parts and is the line required.

The figures which are divided in Euclid's tract are the triangle, the parallelogram, the trapezium, the quadrilateral, a figure bounded by an arc of a circle and two lines, and a circle. It is proposed in the various cases to divide the given figure into two equal parts, into several equal parts, into two parts in a given ratio, or into several parts in a given ratio. The propositions may be further classified according to whether the dividing line (transversal) is required to be drawn from a vertex, from a point within or without the figure, and so on.[62]

In only one proposition (29) is a circle divided, and it is clearly the one to which Proclus refers. The enunciation is "To draw in a given circle two parallel lines cutting off a certain fraction from the circle." In fact, Euclid gives the construction for a fraction of one-third and notes a similar construction for a quarter, one-fifth, "or any other definite fraction."[63]

Porisms (Πορίσματα). It is known both from Pappus[64] and from Proclus[65] that Euclid wrote a three-book work called *Porisms*. Pappus, who includes the work in the *Treasury of Analysis,* adds the information that it contained 171 theorems and thirty-eight lemmas. It has not survived—most unfortunately, for it appears to have been an exercise in advanced mathematics;[66] but the account given by Pappus encouraged such great mathematicians as Robert Simson and Michel Chasles to attempt reconstructions, and Chasles was led thereby to the discovery of anharmonic ratios.

The term "porism" commonly means in Greek mathematics a corollary, but that is not the sense in which it is used in Euclid's title. It is clearly derived from πορίζω, "I procure," and Pappus explains that according to the older writers a porism is something intermediate between a theorem and a problem: "A theorem is something proposed with a view to the proof of what is proposed, and a problem is something thrown out with a view to the construction of what is proposed, [and] a porism is something proposed with a view to the finding [πορισμόν] of the very thing proposed."[67] Proclus reinforces the explanation. The term, he says, is used both for "such theorems as are established in the proofs of other theorems, being windfalls and bonuses of the things sought, and also for such things as are sought, but need discovery, and are neither pure bringing into being nor pure investigation."[68] As examples of a porism in this sense, Proclus gives two: first, the finding of the center of a circle, and, second, the finding of the greatest common measure of two given commensurable magnitudes.

Pappus says that it had become characteristic of porisms for the enunciation to be put in shortened form and for a number of propositions to be comprehended in one enunciation. He sets out twenty-nine different types in Euclid's work (fifteen in book I, six in book II, and eight in book III). His versions suggest that the normal form of Euclid's porisms was to find a point or a line satisfying certain conditions. Pappus says that Euclid did not normally give many examples of each case, but at the beginning of the first book he gave ten propositions belonging to one class; and Pappus found that these could be comprehended in one enunciation, in this manner:

> If in a quadrilateral, whether convex or concave, the sides cut each other two by two, and the three points in which the other three sides intersect the fourth are given, and if the remaining points of intersection save one lie on straight lines given in position, the remaining point will also lie on a straight line given in position.[69]

Pappus proceeds to generalize this theorem for any system of straight lines cutting each other two by two.

In modern notation, let there be n straight lines, of which not more than two pass through one point and no two are parallel. They will intersect in $1/2n(n-1)$ points. Let the $(n-1)$ points in which one of the lines is intersected be fixed. This will leave $1/2n(n-1) - (n-1) = 1/2(n-1)(n-2)$ other points of intersection. If $(n-2)$ of these points lie on straight lines given in position, the other $1/2(n-1)(n-2) - (n-2) = 1/2(n-2)(n-3)$ points of intersection will also lie on straight lines given in position, provided that it is impossible to form with these points of intersection any triangle having for sides the sides of the polygon.[70]

Pappus adds: "It is unlikely that the writer of the *Elements* was unaware of this result, but he would have desired only to set out the first principle. For he appears in all the porisms to have laid down only the first principles and seminal ideas of the many important matters investigated."[71]

Pappus' remarks about the definition of porisms by the "older writers" have been given above. He—or an interpolator—censures more recent writers who defined a porism by an incidental characteristic: "a porism is that which falls short of a locus theorem in respect of its hypotheses."[72] What this means is far from clear, but it led Zeuthen[73] to conjecture that Euclid's porisms were a by-product of his researches into conic sections—which, if true, would be a happy combination of the two meanings of porism. Zeuthen takes the first proposition of Euclid's first book as quoted by Pappus: "If from two points given in position straight lines be drawn so as to meet on a straight line given in position, and if one of them cuts off from a straight line given in position a segment measured toward a given point on it, the other will also cut off from another straight line a segment having to the first a given ratio."[74] He notes that this proposition is true if a conic section, regarded as a "locus with respect to four lines" (see below), is substituted for the first given straight line, with the two given points as points on it.[75] It will be convenient to turn immediately to Euclid's investigations into conic sections and the "three- and four-line locus," noting that, from one point of view, his *Porisms* would appear to have been the earliest known treatise on projective geometry and transversals.

Conics. We know from Pappus that Euclid wrote a four-book work on conic sections, but it has not survived even in quotation. The relevant passage in the *Collection* reads: "Apollonius, having completed Euclid's four books of conics and added four others, handed down eight volumes of conics."[76] The work was probably lost by Pappus' time, for in the next sentence he mentions as still extant the five books

of Aristaeus on "solid loci." Aristaeus preceded Euclid, for Euclid, according to Pappus or an interpolator, thought that Aristaeus deserved the credit for the discoveries in conics he had already made, and neither claimed originality nor wished to overthrow what he had already done. (It is at this point that Pappus contrasts Euclid's character with that of Apollonius, noted above.) In particular, Euclid wrote as much about the three- and four-line locus as was possible on the basis of Aristaeus' conics without claiming completeness for his proofs.[77]

Euclid doubtless shared the early Greek view that conic sections were generated by the section of a cone by a plane at right angles to a generator, and he would have used the names "section of a right-angled cone," "section of an acute-angled cone," and "section of an obtuse-angled cone," which were in use until Apollonius established the terms "parabola," "ellipse," and "hyperbola"; but he was aware that an ellipse can be obtained by any section of a cone or cylinder not parallel to the base, for in his *Phaenomena* he says: "If a cone or cylinder be cut by a plane not parallel to the base, the section is a section of an acute-angled cone which is like a shield [θυρεός]."[78]

Furthermore, Euclid was aware of the focus-directrix property (that a conic section is the locus of a point whose distance from a fixed point bears a constant relation to its distance from a fixed straight line), even though it is nowhere mentioned by Apollonius: Pappus cites the property as a lemma to Euclid's *Surface Loci*,[79] from which it is clear that it was assumed in that book without proof. It is likely, therefore, that it was proved either in Euclid's *Conics* or by Aristaeus.

Euclid was also aware that a conic may be regarded as the locus of a point having a certain relationship to three or four straight lines. He discussed this locus in his *Conics*, and he may be the original author to whom Pappus thinks Apollonius should have deferred.[80] The locus is thus defined by Pappus:

> If three straight lines be given in position, and from one and the same point straight lines be drawn to meet the three straight lines at given angles, and if the ratio of the rectangle contained by two of the straight lines toward the square on the remaining straight line be given, then the point will lie on a solid locus given in position, that is, on one of the three conic sections. And if straight lines be drawn to meet at given angles four straight lines given in position, and the ratio of the rectangle contained by two of the straight lines so drawn toward the rectangle contained by the remaining two be given, then likewise the point will lie on a conic section given in position.[81]

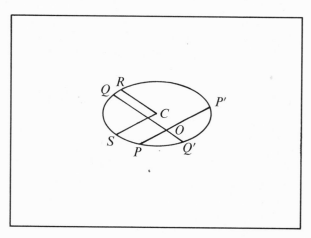

FIGURE 9. $QO \cdot OQ' : PO \cdot OP' = CR^2 : CS^2$

The three-line locus is clearly a special case of the four-line locus in which two of the straight lines coincide. The general case is the locus of a point whose distances x, y, z, u from four straight lines (which may be regarded as the sides of a quadrilateral) have the relationship $xy : zu = k$, where k is a constant.

From the property that the ratio of the rectangles under the segments of any intersecting chords drawn in fixed directions in a conic is constant (being equal to the ratio of the squares on the parallel semidiameters), it is not difficult to show that the distances of a point on a conic from an inscribed trapezium bear the above relationship $xy : zu = k$, and it is only a further step to prove that this is true of any inscribed quadrilateral. It is rather more difficult to prove the converse theorem—that the locus of a point having this relationship to the sides, first of a trapezium, then of any quadrilateral, is a conic section—but it would have been within Euclid's capacity to do so.

Apollonius says of his own *Conics:*

> The third book includes many remarkable theorems useful for the synthesis of solid loci and for determining limits of possibility. Most of these theorems, and the most elegant, are new, and it was their discovery which made me realize that Euclid had not worked out the synthesis of the locus with respect to three and four lines, but only a chance portion of it, and that not successfully; for the synthesis could not be completed without the theorems discovered by me.[82]

In the light of this passage Zeuthen conjectured that Euclid (and the other predecessors of Apollonius) saw that a point on a conic section would have the four-line property with respect first to an inscribed trapezium and then to any inscribed quadrilateral, but failed to prove the converse, even for a trapezium; they failed because they did not realize that the hyperbola is a curve with two branches.[83] It is an attractive suggestion.

Pappus exonerates Euclid from blame on the ground that "he wrote so much about the locus as was possible by means of the *Conics* of Aristaeus but did not claim finality for his proofs" and that "neither Apollonius himself nor anyone else could have added anything to what Euclid wrote, using only those properties of conics which had been proved up to Euclid's time."[84] Since Apollonius implies that he had worked out a complete theory, it is curious that he does not set it out in his treatise; but book III, propositions 53–56 of his *Conics,* when taken together, give what is in effect the converse of the three-line locus: "If from any point of a conic there be drawn three straight lines in fixed directions to meet respectively two fixed tangents to the conic and their chord of contact, the ratio of the rectangles contained by the first two lines so drawn to the square on the third is constant."

Apollonius in his first preface claims originality for his book IV and for parts of book III. He regarded the first four books as an introduction concerned with the elements of the subject. Since Pappus says that Apollonius completed the first four books of Euclid's *Conics,* we may infer from the two passages taken together that Euclid's work covered the same ground as Apollonius' first three books, but not so completely. It would appear that Euclid's work was no advance on that of Aristaeus, which would account for the fact that the latter's *Conics* was still extant, although that of Euclid had been lost, by the time of Pappus.

What Pappus calls "those properties of conics which had been proved up to Euclid's time" can be conjectured from references by Archimedes to propositions not requiring demonstration "because they are proved in the elements of conics" or simply "in the *Conics.*"[85] This would imply that the proofs were given by Aristaeus or Euclid or both. In addition, Archimedes assumes without proof the fundamental properties of the parabola, ellipse, and hyperbola in the form, for the ellipse, of

$$PN^2 : AN \cdot A'N = CB^2 : CA^2,$$

where AA' is the major axis, BB' the minor axis, C the center, P any point on the curve, and N the foot of the perpendicular from P to AA'. More generally he assumes that if QV is an ordinate of the diameter PCP of an ellipse (with corresponding formulas for the parabola and hyperbola), the ratio $QV^2 : PV \cdot P'V$ is constant. It would appear that Euclid must have treated the fundamental characteristics of the curves as proportions, and it was left to Apollonius to develop, by means of the application of areas, the fundamental properties of curves as equations between areas.[86]

Surface Loci (Τόποι πρὸς ἐπιφανείᾳ). *Surface Loci,* a work in two books, is attributed to Euclid by Pappus and included in the *Treasury of Analysis.*[87] It has not survived, and its contents can be conjectured only from remarks made by Proclus and Pappus about loci in general and two lemmas given by Pappus to Euclid's work.

Proclus defines a locus as "the position of a line or surface having one and the same property,"[88] and he says of locus theorems (τοπικά) that "some are constructed on lines and some on surfaces." It would appear that loci on lines are loci which are lines and loci on surfaces are loci which are surfaces. But Pappus says that the equivalent of a quadratrix may be obtained geometrically "by means of loci on surfaces as follows," and he proceeds to use a spiral described on a cylinder (the cylindrical helix).[89] The possibility that loci on surfaces may be curves, of a higher order than conic sections, described on surfaces gets some support from an obscure passage in which Pappus divides loci into fixed, progressive, and reversionary, and adds that linear loci are "demonstrated" (δείκνυνται) from loci on surfaces.[90]

Of the two lemmas to the *Surface Loci* which Pappus gives, the former[91] and the attached figure are unsatisfactory as they stand; but if Tannery's restoration[92] is correct, one of the loci sought by Pappus contained all the points on the elliptical parallel sections of a cylinder and thus was an oblique circular cylinder; other loci may have been cones.

It is in the second lemma that Pappus states and proves the focus-directrix property of a conic, which implies, as already stated, that Euclid must have been familiar with it. Zeuthen, following an insight by Chasles,[93] conjectures that Euclid may have used the property in one of two ways in the *Surface Loci:* (1) to prove that the locus of a point whose distance from a given straight line is in a given ratio to its distance from a given plane is a cone; or (2) to prove that the locus of a point whose distance from a given point is in a given ratio to its distance from a given plane is the surface formed by the revolution of a conic about an axis. It seems probable that Euclid's *Surface Loci* was concerned not merely with cones and cylinders (and perhaps spheres), but to some extent with three other second-degree surfaces of revolution: the paraboloid, the hyperboloid, and the prolate (but not the oblate) spheroid. If so, he anticipated to some extent the work that Archimedes developed fully in his *On Conoids and Spheroids.*

Book of Fallacies (Ψευδάρια). Proclus mentions a book by Euclid with this title which has not survived but is clearly identical with the work referred to as *Pseudographemata* by Michael Ephesius in his com-mentary on the *Sophistici elenchi* of Aristotle.[94] It obviously belonged to elementary geometry and is sufficiently described in Proclus' words:

Do you, adding or subtracting accidentally, fall away unawares from science and get carried into the opposite error and into ignorance? Since many things seem to conform with the truth and to follow from scientific principles, but lead astray from the principles and deceive the more superficial, he has handed down methods for the clear-sighted understanding of these matters also, and with these methods in our possession we can train beginners in the discovery of paralogisms and avoid being misled. The treatise in which he gave this machinery to us he entitled [the *Book of*] *Fallacies,* enumerating in order their various kinds, exercising our intelligence in each case by theorems of all sorts, setting the true side by side with the false, and combining the refutation of the error with practical illustration. This book is therefore purgative and disciplinary, while the *Elements* contains an irrefutable and complete guide to the actual scientific investigation of geometrical matters.[95]

Astronomy: Phaenomena (Φαινόμενα). This textbook of what the Greeks called *sphaeric,* intended for use by students of astronomy, survives in two recensions, of which the older must be the nearer to Euclid's own words.[96] It was included in the collection of astronomical works which Pappus calls Ὁ Ἀστρονομούμενος τόπος, *The Treasury of Astronomy,* alternatively known as *The Little Astronomy,* in contrast with Ptolemy's *Syntaxis,* or *Great Astronomy.* In the older, more authentic recension it consists of a preface and sixteen propositions.

The preface gives reasons for believing that the universe is a sphere and includes some definitions of technical terms. Euclid in this work is the first writer to use "horizon" absolutely—Autolycus had written of the "horizon (i.e., bounding) circle"—and he introduces the term "meridian circle." The propositions set out the geometry of the rotation of the celestial sphere and prove that stars situated in certain positions will rise or set at certain times. Pappus comments in detail on certain of the propositions.[97]

It is manifest that Euclid drew on Autolycus, but both of them cite without proof a number of propositions, which suggests that they had in their hands a still earlier textbook of sphaeric, which Tannery conjectured to have been the composition of Eudoxus. Many of the propositions are proved in the *Sphaerica* of Theodosius, written several centuries later. He naturally uses the theorems of Euclid's *Elements* in his proofs. By examining the propositions assumed by Autolycus, and by further considering what other propositions are needed to establish them, it is thus possible to get some idea of how much of Euclid's

Elements was already known in the fourth century before Christ.[98]

Optics: Optica ('Οπτικά). The *Optica,* which is attributed to Euclid by Proclus, is also attested by Pappus, who includes it, somewhat curiously, in the *Little Astronomy.*[99] It survives in two recensions; there is no reason to doubt that the earlier one is Euclid's own work, but the later appears to be a recension done by Theon of Alexandria in the fourth century, with a preface which seems to be a pupil's reproduction of explanations given by Theon at his lectures.[100]

The *Optica,* an elementary treatise in perspective, was the first Greek work on the subject and remained the only one until Ptolemy wrote in the middle of the second century.[101] It starts with definitions, some of them really postulates, the first of which assumes, in the Platonic tradition, that vision is caused by rays proceeding from the eye to the object. It is implied that the rays are straight. The second states that the figure contained by the rays is a cone which has its vertex in the eye and its base at the extremities of the object seen. Definition 4 makes the fundamental assumption that "Things seen under a greater angle appear greater, and those under a lesser angle less, while things seen under equal angles appear equal." When he comes to the text, Euclid makes a false start in proposition 1—"Of things that are seen, none is seen as a whole"—because of an erroneous assumption that the rays of light are discrete; but this does not vitiate his later work, which is sound enough. From proposition 6 it is easy to deduce that parallel lines appear to meet. In the course of proposition 8 he proves the equivalent of the theorem

$$\frac{\tan \alpha}{\tan \beta} < \frac{\alpha}{\beta},$$

where α and β are two angles and $\alpha < \beta < 1/2\pi$. There are groups of propositions relating to the appearances of spheres, cones, and cylinders. Propositions 37 and 38 prove that if a straight line moves so that it always appears to be the same size, the locus of its extremities is a circle with the eye at the center or on the circumference. The book contains fifty-eight propositions of similar character. It was written before the *Phaenomena,* for it is cited in the preface of that work. Pappus adds twelve propositions of his own based on those of Euclid.

Catoptrica (Κατοπτρικά). Proclus also attributes to Euclid a book entitled *Catoptrica,* that is, on mirrors. The work which bears that name in the editions of Euclid is certainly not by him but is a later compilation, and Proclus is generally regarded as having made a mistake. If the later compilation is the work of Theon, as may well be the case, it would have been quite easy for Proclus to have assigned it to Euclid inadvertently.

Music: Elements of Music (Αἱ κατὰ μουσικὴν στοιχειώσεις). Proclus[102] attributes to Euclid a work with this title and Marinus,[103] in his preface to Euclid's *Data,* refers to it as Μουσικῆς στοιχεῖα. Two musical treatises are included in the editions of Euclid's works, but they can hardly both be by the same author, since the *Sectio canonis,* or *Division of the Scale* (Κατατομὴ κανόνος), expounds the Pythagorean doctrine that the musical intervals are to be distinguished by the mathematical ratio of the notes terminating the interval, while the *Introduction to Harmony* (Εἰσαγωγὴ ἀρμονική) is based on the contrary theory of Aristoxenus, according to which the scale is formed of notes separated by a tone identified by the ear. It is now universally accepted that the *Introduction to Harmony* is the work of Cleonides, the pupil of Aristoxenus, to whom it is attributed in some manuscripts; but there is no agreement about the *Sectio canonis,* except that such a trite exposition of the Pythagorean theory of musical intervals is hardly worthy to be dignified with the name *Elements of Music.* The strongest argument for its authenticity is that Porphyry in his commentary on Ptolemy's *Harmonica* quotes almost the whole of it except the preface and twice, or perhaps three times, refers to Euclid's *Sectio canonis* as though it is the work he is quoting;[104] but the passages cited by Porphyry differ greatly from the text in dispute. Gregory, who was the first to question the attribution to Euclid, would have assigned it to Ptolemy,[105] along with the *Introduction to Harmony;* but his main reason, that it is not mentioned before Ptolemy, is not sufficiently strong to outweigh the primitive character of the work. Tannery thinks that the two last propositions, 19 and 20, which specially justify the title borne by the treatise, may have been added by a later editor who borrowed from Eratosthenes, but that the rest of the work must have been composed before 300 B.C. and would attribute it to the school of Plato.[106] This is not convincing, however, for we have seen how Euclid perpetuated arithmetical theories that had become outmoded, and he could have done likewise for the Pythagorean musical theory. (It is of no significance that there are three arithmetical propositions in the *Sectio canonis* not found in the *Elements.*) As for Platonism, Euclid was himself a Platonist. Jan, who included the book under Euclid's name in his *Musici scriptores Graeci,* takes the view that it was a summary of a longer work by Euclid himself.[107] Menge, who edited it for *Euclidis opera omnia,* considers that it contains some things unworthy of Euclid and is of the opinion that it was extracted by some other writer from the authentic *Elements of Music,* now lost.[108] All that it seems possible to say with certainty is that Euclid wrote a book entitled *Elements of Music* and that the *Sectio canonis* has some connection with it.

Mechanics. No work by Euclid on mechanics is extant in Greek, nor is he credited with any mechanical works by ancient writers. According to Arabic sources, however, he wrote a *Book on the Heavy and the Light,* and when Hervagius was about to publish his 1537 edition there was brought to him a mutilated fragment, *De levi et ponderoso,* which he included as one of Euclid's works. In 1900 Curtze published this side by side with a *Liber Euclidis de gravi et levi et de comparatione corporum ad invicem* which he had found in a Dresden manuscript. It is clearly the same work expressed in rather different language and, as Duhem observed, it is the most precise exposition that we possess of the Aristotelian dynamics of freely moving bodies. Duhem himself found in Paris a manuscript fragment of the same work, and in 1952 Moody and Clagett published a text, with English translation, based chiefly on a manuscript in the Bodleian Library at Oxford. A little earlier Sarton had expressed the view that "It contains the notion of specific gravity in a form too clear to be pre-Archimedean"; but it is not all that clear, and there is no reason to think that Archimedes was the first Greek writer to formulate the notion of specific gravity. It is no objection that the dynamics is Aristotelian, for, as Clagett points out, "The only dynamics that had been formulated at all, in the time in which Euclid lived, was the dynamics of Aristotle." In Clagett's judgment, "No solid evidence has been presented sufficient to determine the question of authenticity one way or the other."[109]

In 1851 Woepcke published under the title *Le livre d'Euclide sur la balance* an Arabic fragment that he had discovered in Paris. The fact that the letters used in the figures follow each other in the Greek order suggests a Greek origin. It contains a definition, two axioms, and four propositions and is an attempt to outline a theory of the lever, not on the basis of general dynamical considerations, as in Aristotle, but on the basis of axioms which may be regarded as self-evident and are confirmed by experience. It is therefore Euclidean in character; and since it falls short of the finished treatment of the subject by Archimedes, it could very well be an authentic work of Euclid, although it owes its present form to some commentator or editor. Woepcke found confirmation of its authenticity in a note in another Paris manuscript, *Liber de canonio.* After citing the proposition that the lengths of the arms of a lever parallel to the

horizon are reciprocally proportional to the weights at their extremities, the author adds: "Sicut demonstratum est ab Euclide et Archimede et aliis." Heiberg and Curtze were unwilling to ascribe to the *Book on the Balance* an earlier origin than the Arabs, but Duhem accepted its authenticity. Clagett, after first allowing as "quite likely that the text was translated from the Greek and that in all probability there existed a Greek text bearing the name of Euclid," has more recently expressed the opinion that it "may be genuine and is of interest because, unlike the statement of the law of the lever in the Aristotelian *Mechanics,* its statement on the subject is proved on entirely geometrical grounds."[110]

Duhem's researches among the Paris manuscripts led him to discover a third mechanical fragment attributed to Euclid under the title *Liber Euclidis de ponderibus secundum terminorum circumferentiam.* It contains four propositions about the circles described by the ends of the lever as it rises and falls. As it stands, it is unlikely to be a direct translation of a Euclidean original, but it could derive from a work by Euclid. Duhem noticed how these three fragmentary works fill gaps in each other and conjectured that they might be the debris of a single treatise. This indeed seems probable, and although Duhem was inclined to identify the treatise with Ptolemy's lost work *On Turnings of the Scale* (Περὶ ῥοπῶν), the ultimate author from whom all three fragments spring could have been Euclid. In view of the Arabic traditions, the high probability that the work on the balance is derived from Euclid, the way in which the fragments supplement each other, and the fact that Euclid wrote on all other branches of mathematics known to him and would hardly have omitted mechanics, this is at least a hypothesis that can be countenanced.

An amusing epigram concerning a mule and an ass carrying burdens that the ass found too heavy is attributed to Euclid. It was first printed by Aldus in 1502 and is now included in the appendix to the *Palatine Anthology,* which Melancthon rendered into Latin verse.[111]

NOTES

1. The identification began in ancient times, for Aelian (second/third century), *On the Characteristics of Animals* VI.57, Scholfield ed., II (London–Cambridge, Mass., 1959), 76.26–78.10, notes that spiders can draw a circle and "lack nothing of Euclid" (Εὐκλείδου δέονται οὐδέν).
2. The reference is Archimedes, *On the Sphere and the Cylinder* I.2, Heiberg ed., I, 12.3: διὰ τὸ β του α τῶν Εὐκλείδου—"by the second [proposition] of the first of the [books] of Euclid." This is the proposition "To place at a given point a straight

line equal to a given straight line." Johannes Hjelmslev, "Über Archimedes' Grössenlehre," in *Kongelige Danske Videnskabernes Selskabs Skrifter,* Matematisk-fysiske Meddelelser, **25,** 15 (1950), 7, considers that the reference should have been to Euclid I.3—"Given two unequal straight lines, to cut off from the greater a straight line equal to the less"—but the reference to Euclid I.2 is what Archimedes needed at that point. Hjelmslev also argues that the reference is inappropriate because Archimedes is dealing with magnitudes, but for Archimedes magnitudes (in this instance, at any rate) can be represented by straight lines to which Euclid's propositions apply. He is on stronger ground, however, in arguing that "Der Hinweis ist aber jedenfalls vollkommen naiv und muss von einem nicht sachkundigen Abschreiber eingesetzt worden sein." Hjelmslev receives some encouragement from E. J. Dijksterhuis, *Archimedes,* p. 150, note, who justly observes: "It might be argued against this that, all the same, Euclidean constructions can be applied to these line segments functioning as symbols. For the rest, the above doubt as to the genuineness of the reference is in itself not unjustified. Archimedes never quotes Euclid anywhere else; why should he do it all at once for this extremely elementary question?" Jean Itard, *Les livres arithmétiques d'Euclide,* pp. 9–10, accepts Hjelmslev's contentions wholeheartedly, and concludes, "Il y a certainement interpolation par quelque scoliaste ou copiste obscur."

The reference was certainly in Proclus' text, for Proclus says that Archimedes mentions Euclid, and nowhere else does he do so. If the reference were authentic, it would be relevant that *On the Sphere and the Cylinder* was probably the fourth of Archimedes' works (T. L. Heath, *The Works of Archimedes,* p. xxxii).

3. It is possible that when Archimedes says in *On the Sphere and the Cylinder* I.6, Heiberg ed., I, 20.15–16, ταῦτα γὰρ ἐν τῇ Στοιχειώσει παραδέδοται, "for these things have been handed down in the *Elements,*" he may be referring to Euclid's *Elements,* particularly XII.2 and perhaps also X.1; but since there were other *Elements,* and the term was also applied to a general body of doctrine not attributable to a particular author, the reference cannot be regarded as certain.

4. Pappus, *Collection* VII.35, Hultsch ed., II, 678.10–12: σχολάσας (Hultsch συσχολάσας) τοῖς ὑπὸ Εὐκλείδου μαθηταῖς ἐν Ἀλεξανδρείᾳ πλεῖστον χρόνον.

5. Proclus, *In primum Euclidis,* Friedlein ed., p. 68.6–23.

6. The word is γέγονε. It literally means "was born"; but E. Rohde in the article "Γέγονε in den Biographica des Suidas," in *Rheinisches Museum für Philologie,* n.s. **33** (1878), 161–220, shows that out of 129 instances in the *Suda* it is certainly equivalent to "flourished" in eighty-eight cases, and probably in another seventeen. This must be the meaning in Proclus, for his anecdote implies that Euclid was not younger than Ptolemy.

7. This was Ptolemy I, commonly called Ptolemy Soter, who was born in 367 or 366 B.C., became ruler of Egypt in 323, declared himself king in 304, effectively abdicated in 285, and died in 283 or 282.

8. The Greek text as printed by Friedlein, p. 68.11–13 from the surviving manuscript M (Monacensis) is γέγονε δὲ οὗτος ὁ ἀνὴρ ἐπὶ τοῦ πρώτου Πτολεμαίου· καὶ γὰρ ὁ Ἀρχιμήδης ἐπιβαλὼν καὶ τῷ πρώτῳ μνημονεύει τοῦ Εὐκλείδου. The second καί is clearly superfluous, or else a miscopying of some other word (to substitute ἐν would ease the problem of interpretation); and ἐπιβαλών is not easy to understand. Grynaeus and August printed the words as Ἀρχιμήδης καὶ ἐν τῷ πρώτῳ in their editions (1533; 1826), and the manuscript Z, which is the basis of Zamberti's Latin translation (1539) did not have ἐπιβαλών. Since Heiberg's discussion in *Litterärgeschichtliche Studien über Euklid,* pp. 18–22, the words ὁ Ἀρχιμήδης ἐπιβαλὼν καὶ τῷ πρώτῳ have generally been understood to mean "Archimedes, following closely on the first [Ptolemy]," but Peter Fraser in *Alexandria,* I, 386–388 and II, note 82, offers a new interpretation. He interprets ἐπιβαλών as meaning "over-

lapping" and thinks it refers not to Ptolemy but to Euclid, with αὐτῷ understood; he sees τῷ πρώτῳ, understood as ἐν τῷ πρώτῳ, as a reference to the first work in the Archimedean corpus, that is, *On the Sphere and the Cylinder.* His translation is therefore "This man flourished under the first Ptolemy; for Archimedes, who overlapped with him, refers to him in his first book [?]." The theory is attractive, but I do not agree with Fraser that there is any awkwardness in τῷ πρώτῳ referring to Ptolemy so soon after ἐπὶ τοῦ πρώτου, nor do I see any difficulty in saying that Archimedes (*b.* 287) followed closely on Ptolemy I (abdicated 285, *d.* 283/282). On the whole, therefore, I prefer Heiberg's intepretation, but Fraser's full discussion merits careful study.

9. Archimedes died in the siege of Syracuse in 212 B.C., according to Tzetzes, at the age of seventy-five; if so, he was born in 287. Eratosthenes, to whom Archimedes dedicated *The Method,* was certainly a contemporary, but the work in which he said so has not survived. The *Suda* records that he was born in the 126th olympiad (276–273 B.C.).

10. Stobaeus, *Eclogues* II, 31.115, *Anthologium,* Wachsmuth and Hense, eds., II (Berlin, 1884); 228.30–33.

11. See T. L. Heath, *The Thirteen Books of Euclid's Elements,* 2nd ed., I, 117–124, 146–151. "On the whole I think it is from Aristotle that we get the best idea of what Euclid understood by a postulate and an axiom or common notion" (*ibid.,* p. 124). See also T. L. Heath, *Mathematics in Aristotle* (Oxford, 1949), pp. 53–57.

12. Aristotle, *Prior Analytics* I, 24, 41b13–22.

13. Hultsch, in Pauly-Wissowa, VI, col. 1004, also gives 295 B.C. as the date of Euclid's ἀκμή. The latest and most thorough discussion is by Peter Fraser, in *Alexandria,* I, 386–388, with notes in II, especially note 82. He concludes that Euclid may have been born about 330–320 B.C. and did not live much, if at all, after about 270 B.C. This would give him a middle date of 300–295. The round figure of 300 B.C. is given by Hankel, Gow, Zeuthen, Cantor, Loria, Hoppe, Heath, and van der Waerden. Michel gives the same date "au plus tard." Thaer puts Euclid's productive period (*Wirksamkeit*) in the last decade of the fourth century B.C. Heinrich Vogt, "Die Entdeckungsgeschichte des Irrationalen nach Plato usw.," in *Biblioteca mathematica,* 3rd ser., **10** (1910), 155, and—in greater detail—in "Die Lebenzeit Euclids," *ibid.,* **13** (1913), 193–202, puts Euclid's birth at about 365 and the composition of the *Elements* at 330–320. Similar dates are given by Max Steck in his edition of P. L. Schönberger, *Proklus Diadochus* (Halle, 1945), and in *Forschungen und Fortschritte,* **31** (1957), 113; but these authors, as Fraser rightly notes, do not pay sufficient attention to the links of Euclid with Ptolemy Soter and of his pupils with Apollonius. The latest date suggested for Euclid's *floruit* is 280 B.C., given in the brief life prefixed by R. N. Adams to the twenty-first and subsequent editions of Robert Simson's *Elements* (London, 1825), but it rests on no reasoned argument.

14. It would hardly be necessary to mention this confusion, of which the first hint is found in Valerius Maximus VIII.12, Externa 1, in the reign of Tiberius (14–37), were it not common in the Middle Ages and repeated in all the printed editions of Euclid from 1482 to 1566. Karl R. Popper, *Conjectures and Refutations,* 3rd ed. (London, 1969), p. 306, has revived it ("Euclid the Geometrician . . . you don't mean the man from Megara, I presume"), but only, it must be assumed, in jest.

Jean Itard has recently advanced the theory that Euclid may not have been an individual but a school. In *Les livres arithmétiques d'Euclide,* p. 11, he advances three hypotheses: (1) that Euclid was a single individual who composed the various works attributed to him; (2) that Euclid was an individual, the head of a school which worked under him and perhaps continued after his death to produce books to which they gave his name; (3) that a group of Alexandrian mathematicians issued their works under the name of Euclid of Megara, just as (he alleges) the chemists of the same period attributed their works to Democritus. Of these speculations he thinks the second "paraît être la plus raisonnable." Itard exaggerates "les difficultés qui surgissent à chaque instant dans la chronologie lorsque l'on admet l'existence d'un seul Euclide"; there is a lack of precise information but no difficulty about Euclid's chronology. No one has hitherto seen any reason for thinking that the author of the *Elements* could not also have been the author of the other books attributed to him. There are differences within the books of the *Elements* themselves, notably the difference between books VII–IX, with which Itard is particularly concerned, and books V and X; but these are explicable by less drastic suggestions, as will be shown later. The reason why the name of Euclid the Geometer ever came to be confused with Euclid of Megara, who lived a century earlier, is clear from the passage of Valerius Maximus cited above. Valerius says that Plato, on being asked for a solution to the problem of making an altar double a cubical altar, sent his inquiries to "Euclid the geometer." One early commentator wished to alter this to "Eudoxus," which is probably right. The first specific identification of Euclid the Geometer with Euclid of Megara does not occur until Theodorus Metochita (d. 1332), who writes of "Euclid of Megara, the Socratic philosopher, contemporary with Plato" as the author of works on plane and solid geometry, data, optics, and so on. Euclid was a common Greek name; Pauly-Wissowa lists no fewer than eight Eukleides and twenty Eukleidas.

15. The idea that he was born at Gela in Sicily springs from the same confusion. Diogenes Laertius II.106 says that he was "of Megara, or according to some, of Gela, as Alexander says in the *Diadochai.*"

16. The passage is bracketed by Hultsch, but he brackets with frequency and not always with convincing reason.

17. Stobaeus, *Eclogues* II, 31.114, Wachsmuth and Hense eds., II, 228.25–29.

18. The so-called books XIV and XV are not by Euclid. Book XIV is by Hypsicles, probably in the second century B.C.; book XV, by a pupil of Isidore of Miletus in the sixth century.

19. Proclus, *In primum Euclidis,* Friedlein ed., p. 72.6–13.

20. This is one of two mathematical uses of the term διορισμός, the other being a determination of the conditions of possibility. In the present sense it is almost part of the particular enunciation. Proclus, Friedlein ed., pp. 203.1–205.12, explains these formal divisions of a proposition.

21. The fullest discussion is in Pappus, *Collection* VII, Pref. 1–3, Hultsch ed., II, 634.3–636.30. It was James Gow, *A Short History of Greek Mathematics,* p. 211, note 1, who first recognized that the correct translation of τόπος ἀναλυόμενος was "storehouse (or treasury) of analysis."

22. Aristotle, *Posterior Analytics* I, 10, 76a31–77a4.

23. The equidistance theory was represented in antiquity by Posidonius, as quoted by Proclus, *In primum Euclidis,* Friedlein ed., p. 176.7–10; Geminus, also as quoted by Proclus, *ibid.,* p. 177.13–16; and Simplicius as quoted by al-Nayrīzī, Curtze ed., pp. 25.8–27.14. (The "philosopher Aganis" also quoted in this passage must be Geminus.) The direction theory is represented by Philoponus in his comment on Aristotle, *Posterior Analytics* II, 16, 65a4 and was probably held by Aristotle himself.

24. For Ptolemy's attempt, see Proclus, *In primum Euclidis,* Friedlein ed., pp. 365.5–367.27; for Proclus' own attempt, *ibid.,* pp. 368.24–373.2.

25. Proclus, *In primum Euclidis,* Friedlein ed., pp. 419.15–420.23, explains at some length what is meant by the application of areas, their exceeding, and their falling short.

26. *Ibid.,* p. 269.8–21.

27. Isaac Barrow, in lecture VIII of 1666, *Lectiones habitae in scholis publicis academiae cantabrigiensis* (Cambridge, 1684), p. 336, states, "Cum hoc elegio praefixum hanc disputationem claudo, nihil extare (me judice) in toto Elementorum opere proportionalitatum doctrinam subtilius inventum, solidius stabilitum, accuratius pertractatum." The English translation

is that of Robert Simson, at the end of his notes to book V of *The Elements of Euclid,* 21st ed. (London, 1825), p. 294. Simson "most readily" agrees with Barrow's judgment.

28. Augustus De Morgan, "Proportion," in *The Penny Cyclopaedia,* XIX, 51. Oskar Becker's theory (see Bibl.) that there was an earlier general theory of proportion hinted at by Aristotle is discussed in the article on Theaetetus.

29. H. G. Zeuthen, *Lehre von den Kegelschnitten im Altertum,* p. 2.

30. Heath, *The Thirteen Books of Euclid's Elements,* I, 124–126.

31. Plutarch, *Quaestiones conviviales* VIII, 2, 4.720a—compare *Non posse suaviter vivi secundum Epicurum,* 11, 1094b—says that the discovery of this proposition, rather than the one about the square on the hypotenuse of a right-angled triangle, was the occasion of a celebrated sacrifice by Pythagoras.

32. According to VII, definition 21 (20), "Numbers are proportional when the first is the same multiple, or the same part, or the same parts, of the second as the third is of the fourth." H. G. Zeuthen, *Histoire des mathématiques,* p. 128, comments: "Sans doute, en ce qui concerne l'égalité des rapports, cette définition ne renferme rien d'autre que ce qu'impliquait déjà la cinquième définition du cinquième Livre." The same author, in his article "Sur la constitution des livres arithmétiques des Éléments d'Euclide," in *Oversigt over det K. Danske Videnskabernes Selskabs Forhandlinger* (1910), 412–413, sees a point of contact between the special and general theories in VII.19, since it shows that the definition of proportion in V, definition 5, has, when applied to numbers, the same significance as in VII, definition 21 (20); and we can henceforth borrow any of the propositions proved in book V.

33. "This book has a completeness which none of the others (not even the fifth) can boast of: and we could almost suspect that Euclid, having arranged his materials in his own mind, and having completely elaborated the tenth Book, wrote the preceding books after it, and did not live to revise them thoroughly" (Augustus De Morgan, "Eucleides," in *Dictionary of Greek and Roman Biography and Mythology,* William Smith, ed., II [London, 1846], 67). See also W. W. Rouse Ball, *A Short Account of the History of Mathematics,* 3rd ed. (London, 1901), pp. 58–59.

34. After defining a point as "that which has no part" (I, definition 1), Euclid says, "The extremities of a line are points" (I, definition 3), which serves to link a line with a point but is also a concession to an older definition censured by Aristotle as unscientific. So for lines and surfaces (I, definition 6). Among unused definitions are "oblong," "rhombus," and "rhomboid," presumably taken over from earlier books.

35. Paul-Henri Michel, *De Pythagore à Euclide,* p. 92.

36. See Augustus De Morgan, "Eucleides," in *Smith's Dictionary of Greek and Roman Biography,* p. 67; and "Irrational Quantity," in *The Penny Cyclopaedia,* XIII, 35–38.

37. See Eva Sachs, *Die fünf Platonischen Körper* (Berlin, 1917).

38. Proclus, *In primum Euclidis,* Friedlein ed., p. 69.4–27.

39. In Greek, συλλογισμοί, but the word can hardly be used here in its technical sense. Two attempts have been made to turn the *Elements* into syllogisms!

40. Geometrical conversion is discussed by Proclus, *In primum Euclidis,* Friedlein ed., pp. 252.5–254.20.

41. *Ibid.,* p. 68.7–10.

42. Scholium 1, book V, *Euclidis opera omnia,* Heiberg and Menge, eds., V, 280.7–9.

43. Scholium 3, book V, *ibid.,* p. 282.13–20.

44. Archimedes, *On the Sphere and the Cylinder* I, preface, *Archimedis opera omnia,* Heiberg ed., I, 2–13; compare *Quadrature of the Parabola,* preface, *ibid.,* 262–266.

45. Simplicius, *Commentary on Aristotle's Physics* A2, 185a14, Diels ed. (Berlin, 1882), 61.8–9.

46. Plato, *Theaetetus,* 147D ff.

47. Franz Woepcke, in *Mémoires présentés à l'Académie des sciences,* **14** (1856), 658–720; W. Thomson, *Commentary of Pappus on Book X of Euclid's Elements,* Arabic text and trans., remarks, notes, glossary by G. Junge and Thomson (Cambridge, Mass., 1930; repr., 1968).

48. J. L. Heiberg, *Litterärgeschichtliche Studien über Euklid*, pp. 169–171.

49. Scholium 62, book X, *Euclidis opera omnia*, Heiberg and Menge, eds., V, 450.16.

50. T. L. Heath, *The Thirteen Books of Euclid's Elements*, III, 3–4; for Thomson's trans., see *op. cit.*, pp. 63–64.

51. *Suda Lexicon, s.v.*, Adler ed., I.2 (Leipzig, 1931), Θ 93, p. 689.6–8.

52. Scholium 1, book XIII, *Euclidis opera omnia*, Heiberg and Menge, eds., V, 654.5–6.

53. Proclus, *In primum Euclidis*, Friedlein ed., p. 419.15–18.

54. Scholium 4, book IV, *Euclidis opera omnia*, Heiberg and Menge, eds., V, 273.13–15.

55. Proclus, *In primum Euclidis*, Friedlein ed., p. 426.6–18.

56. Aristotle, *Prior Analytics* II, 16, 65a4.

57. Compare Karl Popper, *Conjectures and Refutations*, 3rd ed., pp. 88–89: "Ever since Plato and Euclid, but not before, geometry (rather than arithmetic) appears as the fundamental instrument of all physical explanations and descriptions, in the theory of matter as well as in cosmology." Popper has no doubt that Euclid was a Platonist and that the closing of the *Elements* with the construction of the Platonic figures is significant.

58. Pappus, *Collection* VII.3, Hultsch ed., II, 636.19.

59. *Ibid.*, pp. 638.1–640.3.

60. Proclus, *In primum Euclidis*, Friedlein ed., p. 69.4.

61. *Ibid.*, p. 644.22–26.

62. A detailed classification is made in R. C. Archibald, *Euclid's Book on Divisions of Figures*, pp. 15–16.

63. Hero, *Metrica* III.8, Schöne ed., III, *Heronis Alexandrini opera quae supersunt omnia* (Leipzig, 1903), 172.12–174.2, considers the related problem "To divide the area of a circle into three equal parts by two straight lines." "That this problem is not rational," he notes, "is clear"; but because of its utility he proceeds to give an approximate solution.

64. Pappus, *Collection* VII.13, Hultsch ed., II, 648.18–19.

65. Proclus, *In primum Euclidis*, Friedlein ed., p. 302.12–13.

66. If it had survived, it might have led B. L. van der Waerden to modify his judgments in *Science Awakening*, 2nd ed. (Groningen, undated [1956?]), p. 197: "Euclid is by no means a great mathematician . . . Euclid is first of all a pedagogue, not a creative genius. It is very difficult to say which original discoveries Euclid added to the work of his predecessors."

67. Pappus, *Collection* VII.14, Hultsch ed., II, 650.16–20.

68. Proclus, *In primum Euclidis*, Friedlein ed., p. 301.22–26.

69. Pappus, *Collection* VII.16, Hultsch ed., II, 652.18–654. Some words have been added in the translation for the sake of clarity.

70. Robert Simson, *De porismatibus tractatus in Opera quaedam reliqua* (Glasgow, 1776), pp. 392–393, elucidated this passage in elegant Latin, which Gino Loria, in *Le scienze esatte nell'antica Grecia*, 2nd ed. (Milan, 1914), pp. 256–257, first put into modern notation.

71. Pappus, *Collection* VII.17, Hultsch ed., II, 654.16–19.

72. *Ibid.*, VII.14, Hultsch ed., II, 652.2.

73. H. G. Zeuthen, *Die Lehre von den Kegelschnitten im Altertum*, pp. 165–184.

74. Pappus, *Collection* VII.18, Hultsch ed., II, 656.1–4.

75. H. G. Zeuthen, *op. cit.*, p. 152.

76. Pappus, *Collection* VII.30, Hultsch ed., II, 672.18–20.

77. *Ibid.*, pp. 676.25–678.15.

78. Euclid, *Phaenomena*, preface, in *Euclidis opera omnia*, Heiberg and Menge, eds., VIII, 6.5–7.

79. Pappus, *Collection* VII.312, Hultsch ed., II, 1004.23–1006.2.

80. τῷ πρώτῳ γράψαντι, *ibid.*, p. 678.14.

81. *Ibid.*, p. 678.15–24.

82. Apollonius, *Conics* I, preface, *Apollonii Pergaei quae Graece exstant*, Heiberg ed., I (Leipzig, 1891), 4.10–17.

83. H. G. Zeuthen, *Die Lehre von den Kegelschnitten im Altertum*, pp. 136–139.

84. Pappus, *Collection* VII.35, Hultsch ed., II, 678.4–6; *ibid.*, VII.33, p. 676.21–24.

85. Archimedes, *Quadrature of a Parabola*, proposition 3, in *Archimedes opera omnia*, II, 2nd Heiberg ed. (Leipzig, 1910–1915), 268.3; *On Conoids and Spheroids*, proposition 3, Heiberg ed., I, 270.23–24; *ibid.*, p. 274.3. But when the Latin text of *On Floating Bodies*, II.6, Heiberg ed., II, 362.10–11, says of a certain proposition, "Demonstratum est enim hoc per sumpta," it probably refers to a book of lemmas rather than to Euclid's *Conics*.

86. For a full discussion of the propositions assumed by Archimedes, the following works may be consulted: J. L. Heiberg, "Die Kenntnisse des Archimedes über die Kegelschnitte," in *Zeitschrift für Mathematik und Physik*, Jahrgang 25, Hist.-lit. Abt. (1880), 41–67; and T. L. Heath, *Apollonius of Perga*, pp. l–lxvi; *The Works of Archimedes*, pp. lii–liv; *A History of Greek Mathematics*, II (Oxford, 1921), 121–125.

87. Pappus, *Collection* VII.3, Hultsch ed., II, 636.23–24.

88. Proclus, *In primum Euclidis*, Friedlein ed., p. 394.17–19.

89. Pappus, *Collection* IV.51, Hultsch ed., I, 258.20–262.2.

90. *Ibid.*, VII.21, Hultsch ed., II, 660.18–662.22. A large part of the passage is attributed to an interpolator by Hultsch, but without reasons.

91. *Ibid.*, VII.312, p. 1004.17–22.

92. Paul Tannery, review of J. L. Heiberg's *Litterärgeschichtliche Studien über Euklid*, in *Bulletin des sciences mathématiques*, 2nd ser., **6** (1882), 149–150; reprinted in *Mémoires scientifiques*, XI (Toulouse–Paris, 1931), 144–145.

93. Michel Chasles, "Aperçu historique," pp. 273–274; H. G. Zeuthen, *Die Lehre von den Kegelschnitten im Altertum*, pp. 423–431. J. L. Heiberg takes a different view in his *Litterärgeschichtliche Studien über Euklid*, p. 79.

94. Alexander (?), *Commentary on Aristotle's Sophistici elenchi*, Wallies ed., (Berlin, 1898), p. 76.23.

95. Proclus, *In primum Euclidis*, Friedlein ed., pp. 69.27–70.18.

96. The older recension is, however, best illustrated in a Vienna manuscript of the twelfth century; the later recension is found in a Vatican manuscript of the tenth century.

97. Pappus, *Collection* VI.104–130, Hultsch ed., II, 594–632.

98. The task was attempted by Hultsch, *Berichte über die Verhandlungen der Kgl. Sächsischen Gesellschaft der Wissenschaften zu Leipzig*, Phil.-hist. Classe, **38** (1886), 128–155. The method definitely establishes as known before Euclid the following propositions: I.4, 8, 17, 19, 26, 29, 47; III.1–3, 7, 10, 16 (corollary), 26, 28, 29; IV.6; XI.3, 4, 10, 11, 12, 14, 16, 19, and 38 (interpolated). But Hultsch went too far in adding the whole chain of theorems and postulates leading up to these propositions, for in some cases (e.g., I.47) Euclid worked out a novel proof.

99. Proclus, *In primum Euclidis*, Friedlein ed., p. 69.2; Pappus, *Collection* VI.80–103, Hultsch ed., II, 568.12–594.26.

100. Only the later recension was known until the end of the nineteenth century, but Heiberg then discovered the earlier one in Viennese and Florentine manuscripts. Both recensions are included in the Heiberg-Menge *Opera omnia*.

101. See A. Lejeune, *Euclide et Ptolémée: Deux stades de l'optique géométrique grecque*.

102. Proclus, *In primum Euclidis*, Friedlein ed., p. 69.3.

103. Marinus, *Commentary on Euclid's Data*, preface, in *Euclidis opera omnia*, Heiberg and Menge, eds., VIII, 254.19.

104. Καὶ αὐτὸς ὁ Στοιχειωτὴς Εὐκλείδης ἐν τῇ τοῦ Κανόνος κατατομῇ, Porphyry, *Commentary on Ptolemy's Harmonies*, Wallis ed., *Opera mathematica*, III (Oxford, 1699), 267.31–32; ἐν τῇ τοῦ Κανόνος Κατατομῇ Εὐκλείδου, *ibid.*, 272.26–27; Καὶ αὐτῷ τῷ Στοιχειωτῇ καὶ ἄλλοις πολλοῖς κανονικοῖς, *ibid.*, 269.5–6.

105. David Gregory, *Euclidis quae supersunt omnia*, preface.

106. Paul Tannery, "Inauthenticité de la *Division du canon* attribuée à Euclide," in *Comptes rendus des séances de l'Académie des inscriptions et belles-lettres*, **4** (1904), 439–445; also in his *Mémoires*, III, 213–219.

107. *Excerpta potius dicas quam ipsa verba hominis sagacissimi*, in C. Jan, ed., *Musici scriptores Graeci*, p. 118.

108. *Euclidis opera omnia*, Heiberg and Menge, eds., VIII, xxxvii–xlii.

434

109. J. Hervagius, ed., "Euclidis de levi et ponderoso fragmentum," in *Euclidis Megarensis mathematici clarissimi Elementorum geometricorum libri xv* (Basel, 1537), pp. 585–586, and foreword; M. Curtze, "Zwei Beiträge zur Geschichte der Physik im Mittelalter," in *Biblioteca mathematica*, 3rd ser., **1** (1900), 51–54; P. Duhem, *Les origines de la statique*, I, 61–97; and George Sarton, *Introduction to the History of Science*, I, 156.

110. F. Woepcke, "Notice sur des traductions arabes de deux ouvrages perdus d'Euclide," in *Journal asiatique*, 4th ser., **18** (1851), 217–232; M. Curtze, "Das angebliche Werk des Eukleides über die Waage," in *Zeitschrift für Mathematik und Physik*, **19** (1874), 262–263; P. Duhem, *op. cit.*, pp. 61–97; Marshall Clagett, *The Science of Mechanics in the Middle Ages*, p. 28; and *Greek Science in Antiquity* (London, 1957), p. 74.

111. *Anthologia palatina, Appendix nova epigrammatum*, Cougny ed. (Paris, 1890), 7.2; *Euclidis opera omnia*, Heiberg and Menge, eds., VIII.285, with Melancthon's rendering on p. 286.

BIBLIOGRAPHY

I. ORIGINAL WORKS. The definitive edition of Euclid's extant works is *Euclidis opera omnia*, J. L. Heiberg and H. Menge, eds., 8 vols. plus suppl., in the Teubner Classical Library (Leipzig, 1883–1916). It gives a Latin translation of Euclid's works opposite the Greek text and includes the spurious and doubtful works, the scholia, Marinus' commentary on the *Data*, and the commentary on books I-X of the *Elements* by al-Nayrīzī in Gerard of Cremona's Latin translation. The details are: I, *Elementa I–IV*, J. L. Heiberg, ed. (1883); II, *Elementa V–IX*, J. L. Heiberg, ed. (1884); III, *Elementa X*, J. L. Heiberg, ed. (1886); IV, *Elementa XI–XIII*, J. L. Heiberg, ed. (1885); V, *Elementa qui feruntur XIV–XV. Scholia in Elementa*, J. L. Heiberg, ed. (1888); VI, *Data cum commentario Marini et scholiis antiquis*, H. Menge, ed. (1896); VII, *Optica, Opticorum recensio Theonis, Catoptrica cum scholiis antiquis*, J. L. Heiberg, ed. (1895); VIII, *Phaenomena et scripta musica*, H. Menge, ed., *Fragmenta*, collected and arranged by J. L. Heiberg (1916); suppl., *Anaritii in decem libros priores Elementorum Euclidis commentarii*, M. Curtze, ed. (1899).

The *Sectio canonis* and the (Cleonidean) *Introductio harmonica* are also included in *Musici scriptores Graeci*, C. Jan, ed. (Leipzig, 1895; repr. Hildesheim, 1962), pp. 113–166 and 167–208, respectively.

The text of Heiberg's edition of the *Elements* has been reproduced by E. S. Stamatis in four volumes (Athens, 1952–1957), with a trans. into modern Greek, introductions, and epexegeses. Stamatis is also bringing out a new edition of the *Elements* in the Teubner series reproducing Heiberg's text and variant readings. Heiberg's Latin translation is omitted but the notes to it are reproduced and assigned to the corresponding place in the Greek text. The variant readings and notes take account of critical editions later than those available to Heiberg and there are additional notes on the mathematics, ancient testimonies, a bibliography, and relevant papyrus fragments. The first vol. is *Euclidis Elementa I, Libri I–IV, cum appendicibus, post I. L. Heiberg*, E. S. Stamatis, ed. (Leipzig, 1969).

The first printed Latin translation of the *Elements* appeared at Venice in 1482; the first edition of the Greek text, edited by Simon Grynaeus, at Basel in 1533. The first complete edition of the works of Euclid in Greek, edited by David Gregory, was published at Oxford in 1703, and it remained the only complete edition until that of Heiberg and Menge. Most of the early editions and translations are listed in the following works: Thomas L. Heath, *The Thirteen Books of Euclid's Elements*, 3 vols. (Cambridge, 1905, 1925; New York, 1956), I, 91–113—97 titles from 1482 to 1820; Charles Thomas Stanford, *Early Editions of Euclid's Elements* (London, 1926)—84 titles from 1482 to 1600, with bibliographical illustrations; Max Steck, "Die geistige Tradition der frühen Euklid-Ausgaben," in *Forschungen und Fortschritte*, **31** (1957), 113–117—60 titles to 1600; F. J. Duarte, *Bibliografía in Eucleides, Arquimèdes, Newton* (Caracas, 1967)—123 titles of editions of the *Elements*, with bibliographical illustrations.

II. SECONDARY LITERATURE. Two ancient works are of prime importance: the commentary of Proclus on the first book of the *Elements* and the *Collection* of Pappus. Both are available in good editions. Proclus: *Procli Diadochi in primum Euclidis Elementorum librum commentarii*, G. Friedlein, ed. (Leipzig, 1883, repr. 1967); Thomas Taylor, *The Philosophical and Mathematical Commentaries of Proclus on the First Book of Euclid's Elements* (London, 1788–1789, 1791), is superseded by G. R. Morrow, *Proclus. A Commentary on the First Book of Euclid's Elements* (Princeton, N.J., 1970); more useful trans. of the most relevant passages are scattered T. L. Heath, *op cit.*; a German trans. and commentary, *Proklus Diadochus 410–485 Kommentar zum ersten Buch von Euklids Elementen*, P. Leander Schönberger, trans., intro. by Max Steck (Halle, 1945); and a French trans., Paul ver Eecke, *Proclus de Lycie. Les commentaires sur le premier livre des Éléments d'Euclide* (Paris-Bruges, 1948). Pappus: *Pappi Alexandrini Collectionis quae supersunt*, F. Hultsch, ed., 3 vols. (Berlin 1876–1878), with a French trans. by Paul ver Eecke, *Pappus d'Alexandrie: La Collection mathématique*, 2 vols. (Paris–Bruges, 1933).

An extensive modern literature has grown around Euclid. The older works which have not been superseded and the chief recent literature may be classified as follows:

General: J. L. Heiberg, *Litterärgeschichtliche Studien über Euklid* (Leipzig, 1882); F. Hultsch, "Autolykos und Euklid," in *Berichte der Verhandlung der Kgl. Sächsischen Gesellschaft der Wissenschaften zu Leipzig*, Phil.-hist. Classe, **38** (1886), 128–155; Max Simon, "Euclid und die sechs planimetrischen Bücher," in *Abhandlungen zur Geschichte der mathematischen Wissenschaften*, **11** (1901); Thomas L. Heath, *The Thirteen Books of Euclid's Elements* (see above), I, 1–151; F. Hultsch, "Eukleides 8," in Pauly-Wissowa, II (Leipzig, 1907), cols. 1003–1052; Estelle A. DeLacy, *Euclid and Geometry* (London, 1965); E. J. Dijksterhuis, *De Elementen van Euclides*, 2 vols. (Groningen, 1929–1930); Jürgen Mau, "Eukleides 3," in *Die kleine Pauly*, II (Stuttgart, 1967), cols. 416–419.

Elements: General—Max Simon, "Euclid und die sechs planimetrischen Bücher"; T. L. Heath, *The Thirteen Books of Euclid's Elements*; E. J. Dijksterhuis, *De Elementen van Euclides*; Clemens Thaer, *Die Elemente von Euklid*, 5 pts. (Leipzig, 1933–1937); and A. Frajese and L. Maccioni, *Gli Elementi di Euclide* (Turin, 1970).

Postulates and axioms—Girolamo Saccheri, *Euclides ab omni naevo vindicatus* (Milan, 1733), and an English trans. of the part relating to postulate 5, George Bruce Halstead, *Girolamo Saccheri's Euclides Vindicatus Edited and Translated* (Chicago-London, 1920); B. L. van der Waerden, *De logische grondslagen der Euklidische meetkunde* (Groningen, 1937); A. Frenkian, *Le postulat chez Euclide et chez les modernes* (Paris, 1940); Cydwel A. Owen, *The Validity of Euclid's Parallel Postulate* (Caernarvon, 1942); A. Szabó, "Die Grundlagen in der frühgriechischen Mathematik," in *Studi italiani di filologia classica,* n.s. **30** (1958), 1–51; "Anfänge des euklidischen Axiomensystems," in *Archive for History of Exact Sciences,* **1** (1960), 37–106; "Was heisst der mathematische Terminus ἀξίωμα," in *Maia,* **12** (1960), 89–105; and "Der älteste Versuch einer definitorisch-axiomatischen Grundlegung der Mathematik," in *Osiris,* **14** (1962), 308–309; Herbert Meschkowski, *Grundlagen der Euklidischen Geometrie* (Mannheim, 1966); G. J. Pineau, *The Demonstration of Euclid's Fifth Axiom, The Treatment of Parallel Lines Without Euclid's Fifth Axiom, The Self-contradiction of Non-Euclidean Geometry, The Fault of Euclid's Geometry* (Morgan Hill, Calif.); Imre Tóth, "Das Parallelproblem in Corpus Aristotelicum," in *Archive for History of Exact Sciences,* **3** (1967), 1–422; and N. C. Zouris, *Les demonstrations du postulat d'Euclide* (Grenoble, 1968). See also Frankland (below).

Book I—William Barrett Frankland, *The First Book of Euclid's Elements With a Documentary Based Principally Upon That of Proclus Diadochus* (Cambridge, 1905).

Book V—Augustus De Morgan, "Proportion," in *The Penny Cyclopaedia,* XIX (London, 1841), 49–53; O. Becker, "Eudoxus-Studien I. Eine voreudoxische Proportionenlehre und ihre Spuren bei Aristoteles und Euklid," in *Quellen und Studien zur Geschichte der Mathematik,* **2** (1933), 311–333; Friedhelm Beckmann, "Neue Gesichtspunkte zum 5. Buch Euklids," in *Archive for History of Exact Sciences,* **4** (1967), 1–144.

Books VII–IX—Jean Itard, *Les livres arithmétiques d'Euclide* (Paris, 1962).

Book X—[Augustus De Morgan], "Irrational Quantity," in *The Penny Cyclopaedia,* XIII (London, 1839), 35–38; H. G. Zeuthen, "Sur la constitution des livres arithmétiques des Eléments d'Euclide et leur rapport à la question de l'irrationalité," in *Oversigt over det K. Danske Videnskabernes Selskabs Forhandlinger* (1915), pp. 422 ff.; William Tomson (and Gustav Junge), *The Commentary of Pappus on Book X of Euclid's Elements: Arabic Text and Translation,* Harvard Semitic Series, VIII (Cambridge, Mass., 1930; repr. 1968).

Data: M. Michaux, *Le commentaire de Marinus* (Paris, 1947).

On Divisions of Figures: Franz Woepcke, "Notice sur des traductions arabes de deux ouvrages perdus d'Euclide," in *Journal asiatique,* 4th ser., **18** (1851), 233–247; R. C. Archibald, *Euclid's Book on Divisions of Figures With a Restoration Based on Woepcke's Text and the Practica Geometriae of Leonardo Pisano* (Cambridge, 1915).

Porisms: Robert Simson, *De Porismatibus tractatus,* in *Opera quaedam reliqua* (Glasgow, 1776), pp. 315–594; Michel Chasles, *Les trois livres de Porismes d'Euclide* (Paris,

1860); H. G. Zeuthen, *Die Lehre von den Kegelschnitten im Altertum* (Copenhagen, 1886; repr. Hildesheim, 1966), pp. 160–184.

Conics: H. G. Zeuthen, *Die Lehre von den Kegelschnitten im Altertum* (see above), pp. 129–130; T. L. Heath, *Apollonius of Perga* (Cambridge, 1896), pp. xxxi–xl.

Surface Loci: Michel Chasles, "Aperçu historique sur l'origine et le développement des méthodes en géométrie," in *Mémoires couronnés par l'Académie royale des sciences et des belles-lettres de Bruxelles,* II (Brussels, 1837), note 2, "Sur les lieux à la surface d'Euclide," 273–274; H. G. Zeuthen, *op. cit.,* pp. 423–431; T. L. Heath, *The Works of Archimedes* (Cambridge, 1897), pp. lxi–lxvi.

Optics: Giuseppe Ovio, *L'Ottica di Euclide* (Milan, 1918); Paul ver Eecke, *Euclide: L'Optique et la Catoptrique* (Paris–Bruges, 1938); Albert Lejeune, *Euclide et Ptolemée: Deux stades de l'optique géométrique grecque* (Louvain, 1948).

Catoptrica: Paul ver Eecke, *Euclide: L'Optique et la Catoptrique* (see above); Albert Lejeune, "Les 'Postulats' de la Catoptrique dite d'Euclide," in *Archives internationales d'histoires des sciences,* no. 7 (1949), 598–613.

Mechanics: Franz Woepcke, "Notice sur des traductions arabes de deux ouvrages perdus d'Euclide," in *Journal asiatique,* 4th ser., **18** (1851), 217–232; M. Curtze, "Zwei Beiträge zur Geschichte der Physik im Mittelalter," in *Biblioteca mathematica,* 3rd ser. **1** (1900), 51–54; P. Duhem, *Les origines de la statique* (Paris, 1905), pp. 61–97; E. A. Moody and Marshall Clagett, *The Medieval Science of Weights* (Madison, Wis., 1952), which includes *Liber Euclidis de ponderoso et levi et comparatione corporum ad invicem,* Marshall Clagett, ed., with intro., English trans., and notes by Ernest A. Moody; Marshall Clagett, *The Science of Mechanics in the Middle Ages* (Madison, Wis., 1959), which contains "*The Book on the Balance* Attributed to Euclid," trans. from the Arabic by Clagett.

Euclid and his works occupy a prominent place in many histories of mathematics, or Greek mathematics, including Jean Étienne Montucla, *Histoire des mathématiques,* 2nd ed., I (Paris, 1798), 204–217; Hermann Hankel, *Zur Geschichte der Mathematik in Alterthum und Mittelalter* (Leipzig, 1874), pp. 381–404; James Gow, *A Short History of Greek Mathematics* (Cambridge, 1884), pp. 195–221; Paul Tannery, *La géométrie grecque* (Paris, 1887), pp. 142–153, 165–176; H. G. Zeuthen, *Histoire des mathématiques dans l'Antiquité et le Moyen Age* (Paris, 1902)—a translation of a Danish original (Copenhagen, 1893) with additions and corrections—pp. 86–145; Moritz Cantor, *Vorlesungen über Geschichte der Mathematik,* 3rd ed., I (Leipzig, 1907), 258–294; Edmund Hoppe, *Mathematik und Astronomie im klassischen Altertum* (Heidelberg, 1911), pp. 211–239; Gino Loria, *Le scienze esatte nell' antica Grecia,* 2nd ed. (Milan, 1914), pp. 188–268; T. L. Heath, *A History of Greek Mathematics,* I (Oxford, 1921), 354–446; Paul-Henri Michel, *De Pythagore à Euclide* (Paris, 1950), pp. 85–94; and B. L. van der Waerden, *Science Awakening* (Groningen, undated [1956?])—a translation with revisions and additions of a Dutch original, *Ontwakende Wetenschap*—pp. 195–200. Shorter perceptive assessments of his work are in J. L. Heiberg, *Naturwissenschaften*

Mathematik und Medizin im klassischen Altertum, 2nd ed. (Leipzig, 1920), translated by D. C. Macgregor as *Mathematics and Physical Science in Classical Antiquity* (London, 1922), pp. 53–57; J. L. Heiberg, *Geschichte der Mathematik und Naturwissenschaften im Altertum* (Munich, 1925), pp. 13–22, 75–76, 81; George Sarton, *Ancient Science and Modern Civilization* (Lincoln, Nebr., 1954); and Marshall Clagett, *Greek Science in Antiquity* (London, 1957), pp. 58–59. The text of the most important passages, with an English translation opposite and notes, is given in vol. I of the 2-vol. Loeb Classical Library *Selections Illustrating the History of Greek Mathematics* (London–Cambridge, Mass., 1939), especially pp. 436–505.

IVOR BULMER-THOMAS

EUCLID: Transmission of the Elements.

Any attempt to plot the course of Euclid's *Elements* from the third century B.C. through the subsequent history of mathematics and science is an extraordinarily difficult task. No other work—scientific, philosophical, or literary—has, in making its way from antiquity to the present, fallen under an editor's pen with anything like an equal frequency. And with good reason: it served, for almost 2,000 years, as the standard text of the core of basic mathematics. As such, the editorial attention it constantly received was to be expected as a matter of course. The complexity of the history of this attention is, moreover, not simply one of a multiplicity of translations; it includes an amazing variety of redactions, emendations, abbreviations, commentaries, scholia, and special versions for special purposes.

The Elements in Greek Antiquity. The history of the *Elements* properly begins within later Greek mathematics itself. Comments on Euclid's major work were evidently far from uncommon. Indeed, Proclus (410–485), the author of the major extant Greek commentary on the *Elements,* several times refers to similar efforts by his predecessors in a way that makes it clear that the production of works or glosses on or about Euclid was a frequent—even all too frequent and not particularly valuable—activity. It would seem that Proclus had in mind an already considerable body of scholia and remarks (largely, perhaps, in various separate philosophical and scientific works) on the *Elements,* as well as other commentaries specifically devoted to it. We know that at least four such commentaries, or at least partial commentaries, existed. The earliest was written by Hero of Alexandria, but we know of its contents only through the few references in Proclus himself and through fragments preserved in the Arabic commentary of al-Nayrīzī (*d. ca.* 922). Far more important and extensive was the commentary of Pappus of Alexandria, a work whose Greek text is also lost but of which we possess an

Arabic translation of the comments on book X. Proclus also mentions the Neoplatonist Porphyry (*ca.* 232–304), although it is doubtful that his work on Euclid would have been as systematic and penetrating as those of Hero and Pappus. Finally, although he did not compose a commentary specifically on the *Elements* itself, mention should be made of Geminus of Rhodes, whose lost work on the order or doctrine of mathematics (its exact title is uncertain) so often served Proclus with valuable source material. In the period following Proclus, it should be noted that Simplicius, in addition to his well-known commentaries on a number of works of Aristotle, also wrote a *Commentary on the Premises* [or *the Proemium*] *of the Book of Euclid.* Again we are indebted to al-Nayrīzī, who preserved fragments of the work.

To these more formal works on the *Elements,* one should add the substantial number of Greek scholia. Many derive from the commentaries of Proclus and Pappus, the latter being especially significant when they derive from the lost books of his work. Others are of a much later date, to say nothing of an inferior quality, and reach all the way to the fourteenth century (where the arithmetical comments of the monk Barlaam to book II of the *Elements* stand as the most extensive so-called scholium of all).

The event, however, that had the most enduring effect within the Greek phase of the transmission of the *Elements* was the edition and slight emendation it underwent at the hands of Theon of Alexandria (fourth century; not to be confused with the second-century Neoplatonist, Theon of Smyrna). The result of Theon's efforts furnished the text for every Greek edition of Euclid until the nineteenth century. Fortunately, in his commentary to Ptolemy's *Almagest,* Theon indicates that he was responsible for an addendum to the final proposition of book VI in his "edition (ἔκδοσις) of the *Elements*"; for it was this confession that furnished scholars with their first clue in unraveling the problem of the pre-Theonine, "pristine" Euclid. In 1808 François Peyrard noted that a Vatican manuscript (Vat. graec. 190) which Napoleon had appropriated for Paris did not contain the addition Theon had referred to. This, coupled with other notable differences from the usual Theonine editions of the *Elements,* led Peyrard to conclude that he had before him a more ancient version of Euclid's text. Accordingly, he employed the Vatican codex, as well as several others, in correcting the text presented by the *editio princeps* of Simon Grynaeus (Basel, 1533). Others, utilizing occasional additional (but always Theonine) manuscripts or earlier editions, continued to improve Peyrard's text, but it was not until J. L. Heiberg began the reconstruction of the text anew on the basis of the Vatican and almost all other known manuscripts that a critical edition of the *Elements* was finally (1883–1888) established. Heiberg not only in great measure succeeded in getting behind the numerous Theonine alterations and additions, but also was able to sift out a considerable number of pre-Theonine interpolations. In addition to the authority of the non-Theonine Vatican manuscript, he culled papyri fragments, scholia, and every known ancient quotation of, or reference to, the *Elements* for evidence in his construction of the "original" Euclid. The result still stands.

The Medieval Arabic Euclid. A most appropriate introduction to the dissemination of the *Elements* throughout the Islamic world can be had by quoting the entry on Euclid in the *Fihrist* ("Index") of the tenth-century biobibliographer Muḥammad ibn Isḥāq ibn Abī Yaʿqūb al-Nadīm:

> A geometer, he was the son of Naucrates, who was in turn the son of B[a]r[a]nīq[e]s. He taught geometry and is found as an author in this field earlier than Archimedes and others; he belonged among those called mathematical philosophers. On his book *Of the Elements of Geometry:* Its title is στοιχεῖα, which means "elements of geometry." It was twice translated by al-Ḥajjāj ibn Yūsuf ibn Maṭar: one translation, the first, is known under the name of Hārūnian, while the other carries the label Maʾmūnian and is the one to be relied and depended upon. Furthermore, Isḥāq ibn Ḥunayn also translated the work, a translation in turn revised by Thābit ibn Qurra al-Ḥarrānī. Moreover, Abū ʿUthman al-Dimashqī translated several books of this same work; I have seen the tenth in Mosul, in the library of ʿAlī ibn Aḥmad al-ʿImrānī (one of whose pupils was Abuʾl-Ṣaqr al-Qabīsī who in turn in our time lectures on the *Almagest*). Hero commented upon this book [i.e. the *Elements*] and resolved its difficulties. Al-Nayrīzī also commented upon it, as did al-Karābīsī, of whom further mention will be made later. Further, al-Jawharī (who will also be treated below) wrote a commentary on the whole work from beginning to end. Another commentary on book V was done by al-Māhānī. I am also informed by the physician Naẓīf that he saw the Greek of book X of Euclid and that it contained forty more propositions than that which we have (109 propositions) and that he had decided to translate it into Arabic. It is also reported by Yūḥannā al-Qass [i.e., the priest] that he saw the proposition which Thābit claimed to belong to book I, maintaining that it was in the Greek version; and Naẓīf said that he had shown it to him [Yūḥannā?]. Furthermore, Abū Jaʿfar al-Khāzin al-Khurāsānī (who will be mentioned again below) composed a commentary on Euclid's book, as did Abuʾl-Wafāʾ, although the latter did not finish his. Then a man by the name of Ibn Rāhiwayh al-Arrajānī commented on book X, while Abuʾl-Qāsim al-Anṭāqī commented on the whole work and this has come out [been published?]. Further, a commentary was made by Sanad ibn ʿAlī (nine books of which, and a part of the tenth, were seen by Abū ʿAlī) and book X was commented upon by Abū Yūsuf al-Rāzī at the instance of Ibn al-ʿAmīd. In his treatise *On the Aims of Euclid's Book* al-Kindī mentioned that this book had been composed by a man by the name of Apollonius the Carpenter and that he drafted it in fifteen parts. Now, at the time when this composition had already become obsolete and in need of revision, one of the kings of Alexandria became interested in the study of geometry. Euclid was alive at this time and the king commissioned him to rework the book and comment upon it; this Euclid did and thus it came about that it was ascribed to him [as author]. Later, Hypsicles, a pupil of Euclid, discovered two further books, the fourteenth and the fifteenth; he brought them to the king and they were added to the others. And all this took place in Alexandria. Among Euclid's other writings belong: The book *On Appearances* [i.e., the *Phaenomena*]. The book *On the Difference of Images* [i.e., the *Optica*]. The book *On Given Magnitudes* [i.e., the *Data*]. The book *On Tones,* known under the title *On Music* (spurious). The book *On Division,* revised by Thābit. The book *On Practical Applications* [i.e., the *Porisma*] (spurious). The book *On the Canon.* The book *On the Heavy and the Light.* The book *On Composition* (spurious). The book *On Resolution* (spurious).

Al-Nadīm's report immediately reveals the extensive attention Euclid had already received by the end of the tenth century: two complete translations, each in turn revised, perhaps two partial translations, and an amazing variety of commentaries. What is more, this flurry of activity over the *Elements* was to continue for at least 300 years more. But before recounting the more salient aspects of this later history, it will be necessary to expand certain facets of al-Nadīm's account of the earlier efforts to work Euclid into the mainstream of Islamic mathematics. By way of introduction it may be worth indicating that the totally fanciful account reported from al-Kindī of how Euclid came to compose the *Elements* may well have derived, as Thomas Heath has maintained, from a confusing misinterpretation of the Greek preface to book XIV by Hypsicles. More important than Islamic beliefs as to the origin of the *Elements,* however, is the history of how and when this work was introduced to the Arabic-speaking world. Here al-Nadīm is more reliably informed. The first translation by al-Ḥajjāj (*fl. ca.* 786–833) to which he refers was made, as the label he assigns it indicates, under the ʿAbbāsid caliphate of Hārūn al-Rashīd (786–809), at the instance of his vizier Yaḥyā ibn Khālid ibn Barmak. We also know that a manuscript of the *Elements* was obtained from the Byzantine emperor by an earlier caliph, al-Manṣūr (754–775), although apparently without then occasioning its translation into Arabic. And this patronage of science by the ʿAbbāsid caliphs is even more in evidence in Ḥajjāj's realization that a second, shorter recension of his translation would be likely to gain the favor of Maʾmūn (813–833). It is this version alone which appears to be extant (books I–VI, XI–XIII only). The first six books exist in a Leiden manuscript conjoined with al-Nayrīzī's commentary, and from the prefatory remarks of this work we learn that, in preparing his second version of the *Elements*, Ḥajjāj "left out the superfluities, filled up the gaps, corrected or removed the errors, until he had perfected the book and made it more certain, and had summarized it, as it is found in the present version. This was done for specialists, without changing any of its substance, while he left the first version as it was for the vulgar." Although what we have of Ḥajjāj's second version has not yet undergone a thorough analysis, that it was composed with something of the notion of a school text in mind seems evident. For, to cite several instances, the tendency to distinguish separate cases of a proposition and the use of numerical examples to illustrate various proofs point toward a preoccupation with pedagogical concerns that was to become fairly characteristic of the Arabic Euclid and of the medieval Latin versions that derived from it.

The second, largely new translation of Euclid was accomplished, as al-Nadīm tells us, by Isḥāq ibn Ḥunayn, son of Ḥunayn ibn Isḥāq, the most illustrious of all translators of Greek works into Arabic. Again a second recension was prepared, in this instance by a scholar who in his own right holds a major position within the history of Islamic mathematics, Thābit ibn Qurra. Although no copies of Isḥāq's initial version appear to have survived, we do possess a number of manuscripts of the Isḥāq–Thābit recension. Further study of these manuscripts is needed to say much in detail of the character of this translation, but we do know that Thābit utilized Greek manuscripts in whatever reworking he did of the text (as stated in a marginal note to a Hebrew translation of the *Elements* and confirmed by Thābit's own reference to a Greek text). Whether Isḥāq (or even Thābit) relied to any great extent on one of the Ḥajjāj versions for any sort of guidance is problematic. For, in a comparison of a single manuscript of what are presumably books XI–XIII of Ḥajjāj with their corresponding parts in the Isḥāq–Thābit redaction, Martin Klamroth, the first scholar to examine the two translations in depth, confessed that the difference was slight. But perhaps, assuming the ascription of Klamroth's manuscript of XI–XIII to Ḥajjāj correct, this lack of variation occurs only in the later books.

It is at this point perhaps noteworthy that Klamroth was of the opinion that the Arabic tradition as a whole is closer, as we have it, to the original Euclid than the text presented by extant Greek manuscripts. Heiberg, however, marshaled a considerable amount of evidence against Klamroth's contention and clearly confirmed the superior reliability of the Greek tradition. At the same time, he established the filiation of the Isḥāq–Thābit version and a particular divergent Greek manuscript.

To complete al-Nadīm's account of translations, mention should be made that Abū ʿUthman al-Dimashqī (*fl. ca.* 908–932) not only translated parts of the *Elements* but also the commentary of Pappus to book X (the latter alone being extant). Furthermore, al-Nadīm's report of the intention of Naẓīf ibn Yumn (*d. ca.* 990) to translate book X appears to be reflected in various additions and modifications deriving from the Greek that are extant in Arabic under Naẓīf's name. Finally, although it escaped al-Nadīm's notice, the spurious books XIV and XV of the *Elements* were translated by the Baghdad mathematician and astronomer Qusṭā ibn Lūqā.

The full roster of Arabic translations of Euclid's major work only begins to sketch the program of activity concerning the *Elements* within Islamic mathematics and science. The numerous commentaries mentioned by al-Nadīm are adequate testimony to that. But even before one turns to these, attention should be drawn to yet other forms that found expression among Arabic treatments of Euclid. Quite distinct from translations proper (*naql*) there are a number of epitomes or summaries (*ikhtiṣār* or *mukhtaṣar*), recensions (*taḥrīr*), and emendations (*iṣlaḥ*) of the *Elements*.

Undoubtedly the most famous of the epitomes is that included by the Persian philosopher Avicenna (Ibn Sīnā) in the section on geometry in his voluminous philosophical encyclopedia, the *Kitāb al-Shifāʾ*. All fifteen books of the *Elements* are present, but with abbreviated proofs. Nor was Avicenna alone in his attempt to distill Euclid into a more compact dosage; we have already seen that Ḥajjāj considered one of the primary virtues of his second version of the *Elements* to be its shorter length, and other summaries were composed by Muẓaffar al-Asfuzārī (*d.* before 1122), a colleague of Omar Khayyām (al-Khayyāmī), and also, if we can believe a report by the fourteenth-century historian Ibn Khaldūn (*Muqaddima*, VI, 20), by one Ibn al-Ṣalt (presumably the Hispano-Muslim physician, astronomer, and logician Abūʾl-Ṣalt [1067/1068–1134]).

More significant within the history of Islamic mathematics are the various recensions or *taḥrīr* of the *Elements.* The best known is that of the Persian philosopher and scientist Nāṣir al-Dīn al-Ṭūsī, who composed similar editions of many other Greek mathematical, astronomical, and optical works. We know that at least one *Taḥrīr Uṣūl Uqlīdis* ("Recension of Euclid's Elements") was completed by al-Ṭūsī in 1248. It covered all fifteen books and made use of both the Ḥajjāj and Isḥāq-Thābit translations. There is, however, yet another *Taḥrir* of the *Elements* that is traditionally ascribed to al-Ṭūsī. Although it covers only books I–XIII, it is considerably more detailed than the more frequently appearing 1248 version. Printed in Rome in 1594, we know of only two extant manuscripts (both at the Biblioteca Medicea-Laurenziana in Florence) of this thirteen-book *Taḥrīr.* However, one of these codices explicitly asserts that the work was completed on 10 Muḥarram 1298. Since al-Ṭūsī died in 1274, this gives grounds (and there appear to be other reasons as well) for seriously doubting the ascription to him. Yet whatever conclusion may finally be reached concerning its authorship, the preface to this *Taḥrīr* is particularly instructive with respect to the reason for composing such redactions of the *Elements* and with regard to the kind of added material they would be likely to contain. Beginning with a few remarks specifying the place of geometry within the classification of the sciences and several fanciful statements about Euclid's biography, this preface makes special note of the two previously executed translations by Ḥajjāj and (revised by) Thābit and then launches into a more elaborate description of all else Islamic scholars had done with, and to, the *Elements.* This interim "history" of Euclides Arabus tells us that much effort had been spent in removing all difficulties from the text and in clarifying its numerous obscurities. Examples were inserted to make complex things more obvious and, moving in the opposite direction, some things that were too obvious were left out. Some related propositions were combined and treated as one, implicit assumptions were made explicit, and care was taken to specify (at least by number) just which previous theorems were being utilized in a particular proof. And all of this was done, our preface continues, not just in the body of the text of these versions of the *Elements,* but everywhere in the margins and even between lines. The varieties of information produced in such a fashion are now, the author of the present *Taḥrīr* submits, sorely in need of proper arrangement and clarification, and he goes on to reveal his intention of satisfying this need through the presentation as a unified whole of the original text, together with relevant commentary. His resulting *Taḥrīr* needs much closer scrutiny in order to set forth

the complete spectrum of all of the types of added material it contains, but it is clear from the preface we have been summarizing that it presumably includes, in addition to its own original contributions, many features similar to those its author has just recounted among the works of his predecessors.

One other *Taḥrīr* of the *Elements* bears specific mention: that of Muḥyi 'l-Dīn al-Maghribī (*fl.* thirteenth century), a mathematician and astronomer who worked in both Syria and Marāgha and to whom we owe editions (literally "purifications," *tahdhīb*) of Greek works on spherical trigonometry (Theodosius and Menelaus) and of Apollonius' *Conics,* and a similar work entitled *The Essence (Khulāṣa) of the Almagest.* His *Taḥrīr* may have been written shortly after the genuine fifteen-book *Taḥrīr* of al-Ṭūsī, since it is found in a manuscript dated 1260/1261. It contains, on the other hand, a preface that is similar in many ways to that found in the later (1298) *Taḥrīr,* wrongly, it appears, ascribed to al-Ṭūsī. It also complains of the faults in previous attempts to treat Euclid, but it is more specific in assigning at least some of the blame to Avicenna, a certain al-Nīsābūrī, and Abū Ja'far al-Khāzin (cited in al-Nadīm's chronicle). Al-Maghribī's work sets out to remedy these faults and especially to explain all of the puzzles (*shukūk*) occasioned by Euclid and to supply the added lemmas (*muqaddamāt*) necessary for various proofs. In sum, one can say that al-Maghribī's *Taḥrīr,* as well as the others we have mentioned above, began from the existing translations of the *Elements* and, through the incorporation (albeit in revised form) of presumably a good many of the notions contained in earlier commentaries as well as through the creation of much original material, proceeded to the preparation of an improved Euclid that may well have been ultimately intended to serve more adequately than Euclid himself as a school text. Exactly what this improved *Elements* contains as its most salient characteristics will be revealed only after a great deal more analysis of the relevant texts. And the same must be said for the translations of Ḥajjāj and Isḥāq-Thābit.

The third type of redaction of the *Elements* mentioned above, those labeled "Emendations" (*Iṣlāḥ*), is difficult to characterize beyond what is revealed by the title, since no known copies have survived of those to which reference is made by Islamic scholars. We are told, for example, that al-Kindī composed an *Iṣlāḥ* of the *Elements* in addition to his work *On the Aims (Aghrāḍ) of Euclid's Book.* Similarly, *Iṣlāḥ*'s were written by the astronomer al-Jawharī and the Persian philosopher and scientist Athīr al-Dīn al-Abharī (*d.* 1265), but we know of them only through fragmentary quotations in other works. Further, in a way related to the emending of Euclid, it should be mentioned that the contribution of at least a few Islamic mathematicians to the transmission of the *Elements* appeared in the form of specific additions (*ziyādāt*), often merely to particular propositions within the text.

There remain the substantial number of Arabic commentaries, alternatively entitled *tafsīr* or *shurūh*, on Euclid. One can, indeed, extend their sequence considerably beyond that revealed in the *Fihrist*. In another passage of that work al-Nadīm notes what would be, were the reference correct, the very first such commentary on the *Elements:* one ascribed to the central figure of Arabic alchemy, Jābir ibn Hayyān. But this clearly seems to be an error, introduced by a later scribal addition, for the thirteenth-century astronomer Jābir ibn Aflah. When we turn, however, to the list of genuine commentaries in al-Nadīm and supplement it with information drawn from later sources, the number becomes so considerable (nearly fifty, of which more than half are extant in some form or another) that only the most notable can be mentioned here. Among the most significant recorded by al-Nadīm is that by the Persian mathematician and astronomer al-Māhānī, who commented on book X and on book V, and that by the somewhat later al-Nayrīzī. The latter, which is often a source for comments from lost Greek works on Euclid, was translated into Latin in the twelfth century by Gerard of Cremona. When one pushes beyond the Euclid entry of the *Fihrist,* note should be made of the particularly astute commentary on book V written by the Andalusian mathematician Ibn Mu'ādh al-Jayyānī. It contains, apart from Greek mathematics itself, the first known comprehension of the brilliant definition of the equality of ratios formulated by Eudoxus. In fact, apart from several brief glosses in the medieval Latin Euclid, this definition was seldom properly understood in the West before Isaac Barrow in the seventeenth century. Finally, some note should be made of the fact that figures in Islam who derived appreciable eminence from other pursuits also saw fit to expend time in commenting on the *Elements.* Thus, one might cite the philosophers al-Kindī and al-Fārābī, who commented on books I and V. And similar attention should be drawn to the treatises on Euclid written by Alhazen (Ibn al-Haytham), author of the extremely significant textbook on optics, *Kitāb al-Manāzir,* and to the commentary dealing with the problems of parallels, ratios, and proportion by the even more famous Persian mathematician and poet Omar Khayyām.

A somewhat more informative outline of the commentaries can be had if one turns from their authors to the questions and subjects they treat. Although so few have been edited, to say nothing of studied, that only the most tentative attempt can be made to assay the contents of these commentaries, it is nevertheless possible to see at least some of the areas of major concern. To begin with, it should be made clear that the commentaries were more often than not on parts, and not the whole, of the *Elements.* Thus, as one expects within almost any body of Euclidean commentarial literature, considerable effort was spent in mulling over premises, i.e., definitions, postulates, and axioms (for example, in the treatises of al-Karābīsī [see al-Nadīm's report], al-Fārābī, Ibn al-Haytham, and Omar Khayyām referred to above). As a subclass of this genre of concern, emphasis should be placed upon special tracts, or passages in more general commentaries, that carried on the series of attempts already made in Greek mathematics to prove the parallels postulate (thus, to cite but a portion of the literature, we have two separate treatises on this topic written by Thābit ibn Qurra, a separate work dealing with it by al-Nayrīzī, and treatments of it in the *Tahrīr* of both al-Maghrībi and al-Tūsī [both the genuine and the spurious *Tahrīr* of the latter]).

Moving beyond the concern expressed over premises, one is immediately struck by the unusually high proportion of commentaries on books V and X. Although further investigation is needed to establish all of the motives behind the larger share of attention received by these books, a preliminary conjecture can easily be made. On the one hand, the extreme complexity of the treatment of irrational magnitudes in book X undoubtedly required more exposition and explanation to assure comprehension. On the other hand, the central role played by the theory of proportion contained in book V throughout all geometry probably caused Islamic mathematicians, rightly, to view this book as more fundamental than others. This, coupled with the consideration that some trouble was had in appreciating the Eudoxean definition of equal ratios that is included in book V, most likely gave it a position of some priority in the eyes of potential commentators.

One feature of the series of Arabic commentaries on the *Elements* should be recorded: Although the greater number of such commentators were mathematicians, astronomers, or physicians (or some combination thereof), a minority were not that, but rather philosophers. Of course, a philosopher of the mark of al-Kindī was as much concerned with things scientific as he was with things philosophical. But others, such as al-Fārābī and Avicenna, did not have his scientific interests or acumen. Yet they too commented on, or epitomized, the *Elements.* We are also informed that the philosopher and Shāfiʿite theologian Fakhr al-Dīn al-Rāzī (1149–1210) wrote on Euclid's premises and that the Cordovan philosopher, physician, and Aristotelian commentator par excellence Averroës (Ibn Rushd) wrote a treatise on what was needed from Euclid for the study of Ptolemy's *Almagest*. It is likely, to be sure, that such works on the *Elements* written by philosophers (most, unfortunately, are lost) were less penetrating and exacting than the more mathematical product of other commentators; they are, nonetheless, still significant as a measure of the extent to which the importance of Euclid had penetrated Islamic thought. In sum, the Arabic phase of the *Elements'* history may well prove to be not merely the most manifold but, even mathematically, the most creative of all.

Other medieval Near Eastern translations of the *Elements* all seem to have been based on one or another of the Arabic versions already mentioned. This is certainly the case with the Persian translation (completed in 1282–1283) of al-Ṭūsī's fifteen-book *Taḥrīr,* ostensibly made by his pupil Quṭb al-Dīn al-Shīrāzī (1236–1311). Similarly, although there are a fair number of medieval Hebrew compendia and special recensions of the *Elements,* the basic thirteenth-century Hebrew translation (or translations) appears to derive from the revised Isḥāq-Thābit version but contains marginal reference to the Ḥajjāj translation as well. It is still problematic whether we have here two distinct Hebrew translations or the collaborative effort over a number of years (*ca.* 1255–1270) of the two scholars involved: Moses ibn Tibbon and Jacob ben Maḥir ibn Tibbon.

Even more debatable is the issue of the Syriac version of Euclid. It was frequently the case that Arabic translations of Greek works were executed via a Syriac intermediary. It is, however, rather doubtful that this was true with the *Elements.* We do possess fragments of a Syriac redaction in a fifteenth- or sixteenth-century manuscript, and comparison of these fragments with the Arabic tradition clearly indicates a filiation, although without any absolute evidence of the direction in which the parentage must have run. If one asks how early the Syriac edition must be dated, present evidence necessitates moving it back to the eleventh or twelfth century. For instance, we know that the Syriac polymath Abu'l-Faraj (Bar Hebraeus, 1226–1286) lectured on Euclid at Marāgha in 1268. Furthermore, reference to a Syriac version of the *Elements* is made in the 1298 pseudo-al-Ṭūsī *Taḥrīr* and in mathematical opuscula of Ibn al-Sarī (d. 1153). Finally, note should be made of fragments of an Armenian version of the *Elements,* for it too appears to be related to the Arabic (Isḥāq-

Thābit) tradition. It seems most probable that this Armenian Euclid was the work of Gregory Magistros (*d.* 1058), in one of whose letters we find the announcement that he had begun a translation of the *Elements.* If to this we add the fact, as one scholar has urged, that Gregory knew only Greek and Syriac, but no Arabic, it would appear that he based his translation in some way or another on the Syriac version under discussion. This gives us a terminus ante quem of the first half of the eleventh century for this version, but there is no other evidence on the basis of which we can, with any certainty, assign it an earlier date. One can merely indicate that the editor of these Syriac fragments, G. Furlani, judged them to have a very close relation to the Arabic text of Ḥajjāj and that they were, in his view, in some way derived from this text. He dismissed the apparent contrary evidence one might derive from the Syriac transcription of Greek terms, since this often occurs in Syriac works that we know were based on Arabic originals. However, the second scholar to examine the fragments, Mlle. Claire Baudoux, claimed a definite link with the Isḥāq-Thābit translation (not investigated by Furlani) and concluded that the Syriac redaction preceded Isḥāq and served as an intermediary between it and the Greek original. Nevertheless, it would seem that the issue must stand unresolved until a fresh comparison is made with both Arabic translations and all relevant evidence is presented in detail. Until then, it would seem more plausible to hold the tentative conclusion that the Syriac version had an Arabic source, and not vice versa.

As the article we have quoted above from the *Fihrist* already indicates, Euclid's other works also existed in Arabic, although al-Nadīm has omitted the names of their translators. Indeed, we are still not able to identify translators in all instances. Thus, although the original translator of *On the Division of Figures* remains unknown, we do have information that Thābit ibn Qurra revised the translation, and it is, as a matter of fact, on the basis of this revision that, together with other Latin material drawn from the work of the thirteenth-century mathematician Leonardo Fibonacci, we have been able to reconstruct the contents of this Euclidean treatise. Similarly, we know that Thābit also corrected the translation of the work *On the Heavy and the Light.* There is also a treatise extant in Arabic called *The Book of Euclid on the Balance,* but there is no further information concerning its provenance.

Three other minor works, the *Data,* the *Phaenomena,* and the *Optica* (the Arabs were not aware of the pseudo-Euclidean *Catoptrica*), have a similar Islamic history. All three were part of that collection of shorter works known as the "middle books" (*muta-wassiṭāt*), which functioned as appropriate texts for the segment of mathematics falling between the *Elements* and Ptolemy's *Almagest*. Both the *Data* and the *Optica* underwent Isḥāq–Thābit translation-revisions and later *Taḥrīr* at the hands of al-Ṭūsī. Of the *Phaenomena* we are reliably informed only of the recension done by al-Ṭūsī.

The Medieval Latin Euclid: The Greek–Latin Phase. The first known Latin reference to Euclid is found in Cicero (*De oratore,* III, 132)—surely a good number of years before any attempt was made to translate the *Elements.* This latter aspect of the Latin history of Euclid begins, as far as extant sources tell us, with a fragment attributed to the third-century astrologer Censorinus. What we have in this fragment that gives excerpts from the *Elements* might also be reflected in the Euclid passages in the *De nuptiis* of Martianus Capella, although some historians feel that Martianus may have been utilizing a Greek source as well as some Latin adaptation of (or at least of parts of) the *Elements.*

The second piece of evidence in the history of Latin renditions of Euclid is found in a fifth-century palimpsest in the Biblioteca Capitolare at Verona. Treated with chemicals in the nineteenth century, it is now all but impossible to decipher. We can establish, however, that it contains fragments of a translation from books XII–XIII of the *Elements.* Very little else can be said with any surety of the translation, although its most recent editor, M. Geymonat, has urged that the palimpsest be dated slightly later and has suggested that Boethius was the author of the translation of the fragments that it contains.

Whether or not this suggestion is correct, it is to the problem of the Boethian Euclid that we must now turn. We do know that Boethius made such a translation because Cassiodorus refers to it in his *Institutiones* (II, 6, 3: "ex quibus Euclidem translatum Romanae linguae idem vir magnificus Boethius edidit") and also preserved a letter from Theodoric to Boethius himself (*Variae,* I, 45, 4) in which the existence of the translation is again attested. However, we are far less well informed of the extent and nature of this translation, for the "Boethian" geometries—or better, geometrical materials—that have come down to us are in a late fragmentary form. Basically, the excerpts we possess of Boethius' translation derive from four sources, each considerably later than the date of his actual translating efforts: (1) excerpts in the third recension of book II of Cassiodorus' *Institutiones* (eighth or ninth century); (2) excerpts in a number of manuscripts of a later redaction of the *Agrimensores,* a collection (made *ca.* 450) of materials concerned with surveying, land division, mapmaking, the rules of land tenure, etc. (*ca.* ninth century); (3) excerpts within the so-called five-book "Boethian" geometry (eighth century); (4) excerpts within the so-called two-book "Boethian" geometry (eleventh century). Special note might be taken of the full content of the last two sources, inasmuch as they appear in the literature under Boethius' name. The earlier of the two compilations, in five books, consists of gromatic material in book I and in part of book V, of excerpts from Boethius' *Arithmetica* in book II, and of excerpts from his translation of Euclid in books III–IV and in the initial section of book V. The two-book version of the "Boethian" geometry seems to have been compiled by a Lotharingian scholar without especially acute mathematical ability and contains its excerpts from Boethius' translation in book I, as well as a brief preface and a concluding section on the abacus, while book II consists largely of *Agrimensores* material. If one combines the extracts of Boethius' *Elements* from these two works with the extracts found in the Cassiodorus and *Agrimensores* sources listed above, the total schedule, as it were, of translated Euclid amounts to (a) almost all the definitions, postulates, and axioms of books I–V of the *Elements;* (b) the enunciations of almost all the propositions of books I–IV; and (c) the proofs for book I, propositions 1–3. The above four sources containing these extracts often overlap in the items they include, but it is notable that a sequence of the enunciations of propositions from book III (i.e., 7–22) is found only in the five-book "Boethian" geometry, while the definitions of book V appear only in the recension of Cassiodorus. (The relation of the four sources can be seen in the chart below.)

The ninth- through fifteenth-century manuscripts in which these sources (especially the last three) of Euclidean excerpts appear are, for the most part, collections containing other material pertinent to the quadrivium. But even when, with new and more complete translations of the *Elements* in the twelfth century, this kind of collection began to lose the dominant position it once held in medieval Latin mathematics, traces of the Boethian Euclid linger on through occasional conjunction with the newly translated material. Thus, we know of at least two different mélanges of parts of the Boethian excerpts with one of the translations of the *Elements* from the Arabic by Adelard of Bath (that labeled Adelard II below). One of these mélanges dates from about 1200 and seems to have been compiled by a North German scholar with appreciably more mathematical wit than, for example, the author of the two-book "Boethius" discussed above. It is preserved in a single thirteenth-century manuscript: Lüneburg, Ratsbücherei MS miscell. D 4°48. The second mélange occurs in four manuscripts, three of them of the twelfth century, but little has been done to attempt to determine the provenance of its author. Further, cognizance should be taken of the fact that the Boethian "source" of both mélanges seems to have been the two-book *Geometry*. Finally, although we do have these attempts to combine the Greek-Latin Boethian extracts of the *Elements* with the Arabic-Latin tradition deriving from Adelard, it should be made clear that they constituted but a minor part of the medieval Euclid in the West; the Adelardian-based tradition was soon to hold all in sway.

However, before we move to this tradition and to the Arabic-Latin Euclid in general, two other Greek-Latin medieval versions must be mentioned. Of the first we have but a fragment (I, 37–38 and II, 8–9). It exists in a single tenth-century manuscript in Munich. Although extremely literal, its translator, an Italian, knew little of what he was doing, since he translated as numbers the letters designating geometrical figures.

The second Greek-Latin Euclid we must discuss constitutes the most exact translation ever made of the *Elements,* being a *de verbo ad verbum* rendering in which the order of words and occasionally the syntax itself are often more Greek than Latin. Based solely on a Theonine text, the translation is known from two extant manuscripts and covers books I–XIII and XV. Neither manuscript names the translator, but a stylistic analysis of the text has established that he is identical with the anonymous twelfth-century translator of Ptolemy's *Almagest* from the Greek. A preface fortunately attached to the latter translation informs us that our nameless author was a one-time medical student at Salerno who, learning of the existence in Palermo (*ca.* 1160) of a Greek codex of Ptolemy, journeyed to Sicily in order to see this treasure and, after a period of further scientific preparation, set himself to putting it in Latin. Presumably our translator did the same for the *Elements* shortly thereafter (since no mention of such an effort is made in his description of other of his activities in his preface to his version of Ptolemy). When one turns to the translation itself, it is immediately evident that its author was extremely acute, both as an editor and as a mathematician. Not only does he give an extraordinarily exact rendering of the Greek, but on occasion he also employs brackets to indicate several passages in an alternate Greek manuscript he was using. What is more, several times he employs these same brackets to improve the logic of a proof. Unfortunately, the superb Latin Euclid he produced

exerted very little, if any, influence upon his medieval successors. (It might also be indicated that one manuscript of this translation contains a pastiche of books XIV–XV in place of the missing book XIV; it too derives from Greek sources and even castigates translators from the Arabic for being insufficiently careful.)

The Greek-Latin phase of the medieval Euclid is also, perhaps, the most appropriate point at which mention should be made of the minor Euclidean works during this period. For, contrary to what proved to be true for the *Elements,* these shorter works have a medieval Latin history that derives predominantly—in all instances through anonymous translators—from the Greek. Thus, in place of the apparently lost version of the *Data* from the Arabic by Gerard of Cremona (who also translated the *Elements*), we possess several codices of an accurate rendering made in the twelfth century directly from the Greek. Similarly, although there do exist copies of Gerard's Arabic-Latin *Optica,* they are overwhelmingly outnumbered by manuscripts containing Greek-Latin translations. Indeed, there appear to be two distinct versions of the *Optica* from the Greek, some manuscripts of which are so variant as to lead one to expect an even more complicated history. There also seem to be several versions of the pseudo-Euclid *Catoptrica* made from the Greek. What is more, there is a totally separate *De speculis* translated from the Arabic (by Gerard?) and ascribed to Euclid. We know of no Greek or Arabic original from which it may have derived, although it does exist in Hebrew in several manuscripts. The *Sectio canonis* had several propositions from it transmitted through the medium of Boethius' *De institutione musica.* The *Phaenomena,* on the other hand, was not put into Latin before the Renaissance.

The Medieval Latin Euclid: The Arabic-Latin Phase. Once integral translations of the *Elements* from the Arabic were available to the medieval scholar, all Greek-Latin fragments and versions receded into the background. The new, dominant tradition was, however, twofold; one wing derived from the Ḥajjāj Euclid, the other from that of Isḥāq-Thābit, the recensions of al-Ṭūsī and al-Maghribī coming too late, of course, to enter into the competition of translating activity in the twelfth century.

The Latin *Elements* based upon the Isḥāq-Thābit text was the accomplishment of Gerard of Cremona, the most industrious of all translators of scientific, philosophical, and medical works from the Arabic. We know that he translated the *Elements* from its citation in his *Vita,* written by one of his pupils and appended to one of his translations of Galen. Identified among extant manuscripts in 1901, Gerard's Euclid was soon realized to be the closest to the Greek tradition of all Arabic–Latin versions. It alone contains Greek material—for example, the preface to the spurious book XIV—absent from the other versions. Ironically, however, it clearly seems to have been less used, and less influential, than the somewhat more inaccurate (Adelardian-based) editions. It derives its more faithful reflection of the Greek original from the fact that the Arabic of Isḥāq-Thābit, upon which it was based, is itself a more exact reproduction of the Greek. We have no explicit ascription stating that Gerard worked from this particular Arabic translation, but even the most preliminary examination of Gerard's text reveals that this was in all probability the case. For instance, the phrase "Thebit dixit" occurs frequently throughout the body of the translation. At least some of these occurrences—perhaps almost all of them—are not due to Gerard's reflecting on the text he was rendering, but to a direct translation of that text itself, since several citations that have been published by Klamroth from the Arabic and are reproduced in Gerard indicate that Thābit is named therein as well. (Third-person references by an author to himself are, of course, quite common.) While awaiting evidence that will issue from a direct comparison of the Isḥāq-Thābit and Gerard texts, note should be made of the fact that Gerard has the two propositions added after VIII, 25, and the corollaries to VIII, 14–15, which are characteristic of Isḥāq-Thābit. Yet this is not the only Arabic version Gerard had before him, at least not in its pure form. For he includes VIII, 16, which is not, according to Klamroth, in the Isḥāq-Thābit manuscripts examined. Furthermore, after having followed these manuscripts by reproducing VIII, 11–12, as two separate propositions, at the conclusion of book VIII Gerard has an addendum claiming that these two propositions were found as one *in alio libro;* the addendum continues by reproducing this combined version, proof and all. Exactly who found this combined version of VIII, 11–12, in another book is problematic; use of the first person in this passage in Gerard is not conclusive, since it could derive directly from his Arabic text. We do know, however, that the Adelardian tradition ostensibly based on the Ḥajjāj Euclid (of which book VIII is not extant) does conflate the two propositions in question. Therefore, either Gerard utilized texts of both Isḥāq-Thābit and Ḥajjāj in making his translation or, which seems more likely, he based his labors on an Isḥāq-Thābit text that contained material drawn from one or another of the Ḥajjāj versions.

Gerard also contributed to the literature of Euclides Latinus by translating the commentary of al-Nayrīzī on the *Elements,* the commentary of Muḥammad ibn 'Abd al-Bāqī (*fl. ca.* 1100) on book X, and at least part of Dimashqī's translation of Pappus' commentary on book X.

By far the most important share of the medieval Arabic–Latin Euclid belongs to the English translator, mathematician, and philosopher Adelard of Bath. Not only was Adelard himself the author of at least three versions of the *Elements,* but he served as the point of departure for numerous offspring redactions and revisions as well. Taken together as the Adelardian tradition, they soon gained a virtual monopoly when it came to using and quoting Euclid in the Latin Middle Ages.

The first version due to Adelard himself (hereafter specified by the Roman numeral I) is the only one within the whole tradition that is, properly speaking, a translation. As such, there is clear indication that it was based on the Arabic of Ḥajjāj. Thus, the proofs in Adelard I appear to correspond quite well with what we have of Ḥajjāj. Further, Adelard I carries the same three added definitions (at least two, however, going back in some way to the Greek) to book III found in Ḥajjāj and agrees with him in reproducing the maximum of six separate cases in the proof of III, 35. But it also seems clear that Adelard I did not utilize Ḥajjāj as we have him today. The fact that he does not reproduce the arithmetical examples in books II and VI, or the added propositions in book V, that are present in the extant Ḥajjāj is not the point at issue, since these features are most likely from the commentary of al-Nayrīzī to which our Ḥajjāj text is attached. What is significant is the fact that Adelard I does contain the corollaries to II, 4, and VI, 8, which are not present in our Ḥajjāj and, even more suggestive, does not include VI, 12, which is contained in our Ḥajjāj. If one couples the latter fact with the statement in the pseudo-Ṭūsī *Taḥrīr* that Ḥajjāj did not include VI, 12, it then becomes most probable that there existed another Ḥajjāj, slightly variant from the text we possess, and that it was this Arabic version which Adelard I employed. One could argue that it would have been the first version Ḥajjāj prepared under Hārūn al-Rashīd, but we know that this earlier redaction was somewhat longer than the second version—which, presumably, is the one we possess. And Adelard I in other respects (particularly in the length and detail of the proofs) appears to correspond well enough with the second extant version to make derivation from a longer Arabic original unlikely. A variant of Ḥajjāj's second redaction seems a more plausible source.

Adelard II, on the other hand, does not give rise to similar problems, since it is not a translation but an abbreviated edition or, as Adelard himself calls it (in his version III), a *commentum*. Although the briefest of Adelard's efforts in putting Euclid into Latin, it was unquestionably the most popular. This is clear not merely on grounds of the far greater number of extant copies of Adelard II, but also because the translations given here of the "enunciations" (of definitions, postulates, axioms, and propositions) were subsequently appropriated for a good many other versions by editors other than Adelard. Indeed, the diversity thus growing out of Adelard II appears to be present within it as well, since there is considerable variation among the almost fifty manuscript copies thus far identified. The earliest extant codex (Oxford, Trinity College 47) presents, for example, a text that is more concise than any consistently presented by other manuscripts.

The characteristic feature of Adelard II lies in its proofs, which are not truly proofs at all, but *commenta* furnishing relevant directions in the event one should wish to carry out a proof. One is constantly reminded, for instance, of just which proposition or definition or axiom one is building upon, or whether the argument—should it be carried out—is direct or indirect. The *commenta* talk about the proposition and its potential proof; the language is, in our terms, metamathematical. Moreover, this talk about the proof often puts greater emphasis upon the constructions to be utilized than on the proof proper.

Adelard III, referred to by Roger Bacon as an *editio specialis,* continues this fondness for the metamathematical remark, but now embeds them within and throughout full proofs as such. In the bargain, one often finds that such reflections veer from the proposition and the proof at hand to external mathematical matters.

Adelard II and III have much in common besides their author. Both contain Arabisms; both contain Grecisms; and III quotes II. More important, however, both make use of original Latin material: they employ notions drawn from Boethian arithmetic, use classical expressions, and even (Adelard III) allude to Ovid.

A fourth major constituent of the Adelard tradition is the version of the *Elements* prepared by Campanus of Novara. It too takes over the Adelard II enunciations and, through the formulation of proofs that seem largely independent of Adelard, fashions what is, from the mathematical standpoint, the most adequate Arabic–Latin Euclid of all (its earliest dated extant copy being that of 1259). The *additiones* Campanus made to his basic Euclidean text are particularly notable. With an eye to making the *Elements* as self-contained as possible, he devoted considerable

care to the elucidation and discussion of what he felt to be obscure and debatable points. He also attempted to work Euclid more into the current of thirteenth-century mathematics by relating the *Elements* to, and even supplementing it with, material drawn from the *Arithmetica* of Jordanus de Nemore.

Furthermore, Campanus and the three versions of Adelard (especially II and III) served as sources for an amazing multiplication of other versions of the *Elements.* Although the extent to which they diverge from one or another of these sources may not be great or marked with much originality, and although they frequently seem to concentrate on selected books of Euclid, one can still discern among extant manuscripts some fifteen or more additional "editions" belonging to the Adelardian tradition. They range from the thirteenth through the fifteenth centuries and none, as far as a cursory investigation has shown, bears the name of an author or a compiler.

As a whole the Adelardian tradition formed the dominant medieval Euclid. Further, although by far the greatest share of this tradition was not a strict translation from its Arabic source, the divergence from the original Greek thus occasioned caused little difficulty. The few missing propositions were easily remedied, and changes in the order of theorems gave rise to no mathematical qualms at all. Misunderstanding of what Euclid intended also seems to have been quite infrequent, save for the always problematic criterion of Eudoxus for the equality of ratios, which was ensconced in book V, definition 5. Here the most influential medieval interpretation—that of Campanus—curiously seems to have been conditioned by a strange quirk in transmission. For in place of the genuine V, definition 4, Campanus (and all other constituents of the Adelardian tradition) has another, mathematically useless, definition; and in his attempt to make sense of this, Campanus formulated a mechanics of explanation that he in turn extended to his discussion, and consequent misunderstanding, of the "Eudoxean" V, definition 5. Thus, we are witness to a unique instance in which the existence of a spurious fragment within the textual tradition seriously affected interpretation of something genuine.

The most impressive characteristic of the Adelardian-Campanus *Elements* is not, however, to be found in missing or misunderstood fragments of the text, but rather in the frequent additions made to it, additions which often take the form of supplementary propositions or premises but also occur as reflective remarks within the proofs to standard Euclidean theorems. It is not possible to tabulate even a small fraction of these additions, but it is important to realize something of the basis of their concern. To begin with, the motive behind many, indeed most, of them was to render the whole of their Euclid more didactic in tone. The trend toward a "textbook" *Elements,* noted in its Arabic history (and even, in a way, in Theon of Alexandria's new Greek redaction), was being extended. The reflections mentioned above about the structure of proofs are surely part of this increased didacticism. The labeling of the divisions within a proof, express directions as to how to carry out required constructions and how to draw three-dimensional figures, indications of what "sister" propositions can be found elsewhere in the *Elements,* and even clarifying references to notions from astronomy and music are all evidence of the same. We are also witness to the erosion (again pedagogically helpful) of the strict barrier fixed by the Greeks between number and magnitude. For the care not to employ the general propositions of book V in the arithmetical books VII–IX has been pushed out of sight, and one can find admittedly insufficient numerical proofs in propositions (especially in books V and X) dealing with general magnitude.

Of even greater interest is an ever-present preoccupation with premises and with what is fundamental. Axioms are everywhere added (even in the middle of proofs) to cover all possible gaps in the chain of reasoning, and considerable attention is paid to the logic of what is going on. Once again one sees a fit with didactic aims. But this emphasis on basic notions and assumptions was directed not only toward making the geometry of the *Elements* more accessible to those toiling in the medieval faculty of arts; it was also keyed to the bearing of issues within this geometry upon external, largely philosophical problems. Most notable in this regard is the time spent in worrying over the conceptions of incommensurability, of the so-called horn angle (between the circumference of a circle and a tangent to it), and of the divisibility of magnitudes. For these conceptions all relate, at bottom, to the problems of infinity and continuity that so often exercised the wits of medieval philosophers. The Adelardian tradition furnished, as it were, a schoolbook Euclid that admirably fit Scholastic interests both within and beyond the bounds of medieval mathematics.

There is one other medieval Latin version of the *Elements* that is connected, more tenuously to be sure, with the Adelard versions. Its connection derives from its appropriation of most of the Adelard II enunciations, although frequently with substantial change. It exists in anonymous form in a single manuscript (Paris, BN lat. 16646). We know, however, that this codex was willed to the Sorbonne in 1271 by Gérard d'Abbeville and is in all probability identical with a

manuscript described in the *Biblionomia* (*ca.* 1246) of Richard de Fournival. Richard, however, identifies the manuscript as "Euclidis geometria, arismetrica et stereometria ex commentario Hermanni secundi." This version is, therefore, presumably the work of Hermann of Carinthia (*fl. ca.* 1140–1150), well-known translator of astronomical and astrological texts from the Arabic. Its proofs differ from those of the Adelardian tradition, and the occurrence of Arabisms not in this tradition has been viewed as evidence for Hermann's use of another Arabic text in compiling his redaction. The recent suggestion that this text was the Isḥāq–Thābit translation seems doubtful, however, for unlike Gerard of Cremona's version, ostensibly based on that Arabic translation, Hermann not only lacks the references to "Thebit" but also does not have the additions in book VIII (see above) characteristic of Isḥāq–Thābit. On the other hand, it is true that Hermann does show variations from the text of Ḥajjāj as we have it; but all of these, it appears, are also in Adelard I, which clearly derives, as we have seen, from some Ḥajjāj text or another. Hermann repeats the differences noted above in discussing Adelard I and with him alone, among all Latin versions, carries the full six separate cases for III, 35. One other piece of evidence might be noted: In a series of propositions (V, 20–23) dealing with proportion, the Greek Euclid specifies only one (V, 22) for "any number of magnitudes whatever," the others being stated merely for three magnitudes. Now all versions save Adelard I and Hermann, including our Ḥajjāj and, to judge from Gerard's translation, Isḥāq–Thābit, adopt the policy of stating all four propositions in general form. Hermann and Adelard I, on the other hand, retain the "three magnitudes" version of the Greek for V, 20–21, 23 but also substitute *tres* for *quotlibet* in V, 22. The filiation of these two is, therefore, quite close. One can conclude, then, that Hermann used at least both Adelard II (from which he derives many enunciations) and presumably the same version of Ḥajjāj used by Adelard I (and possibly also Adelard I itself). Finally, it has been noticed that Hermann contains the Arabicism *aelman geme* (corresponding to *ʿilm jāmiʿ*) to refer to axioms or common notions, while both Ḥajjāj and, to judge from Klamroth, Isḥāq–Thābit employ *al-ʿulūm al-mutaʿārafa.* Yet here Hermann could still be following some Ḥajjāj text, since *ʿilm jāmiʿ* (also used, incidentally, in Avicenna's epitome of Euclid) occurs as a marginal alternative in our manuscript of Ḥajjāj.

Occasional claims have also been made for two other identifiable medieval Latin versions of the *Elements.* One, purported to be by Alfred the Great, has been shown to derive from erroneous marginal ascriptions (in a single manuscript) of the Adelard II version to "Alfredus." The second, a seventeenth-century manuscript catalogue, refers to a version of the *Elements* as "ex Arab. in Lat. versa per Joan. Ocreatum." We do know of passages at the beginning of book V and in book X (props. 9, 23, 24) in certain manuscripts of Adelard II that do appeal to "Ocrea Johannis," but in such a way that this may be but a reference to separate (marginal?) comments on Euclid or to some other mathematical treatise, rather than to a distinct translation or version of the *Elements.*

If, in conclusion, one compares the very substantial amount of material constituting the Arabic–Latin Euclid with the equally extensive history the *Elements* had in Islam, several rather striking differences are apparent, even at the present, extremely preliminary stage of investigation of these two traditions. In both one finds an overwhelming number of versions, editions, and variants of Euclid proper. Although here one has a common trait, there is, on the other hand, no doubt that the number of commentaries composed in Arabic far exceeds those in Latin. Indeed, there seems to be but one "original" commentary proper in Latin, questionably ascribed to the thirteenth-century Dominican philosopher Albertus Magnus and in any event greatly dependent upon earlier translated material (notably the commentary of al-Nayrīzī). When we do find *Questiones super Euclidem,* they treat more of general problems within geometry, mathematics, or natural philosophy than they do of issues specifically tied to particular Euclidean premises or theorems. In point of fact, this bears upon a second element of contrast between the Arabic and Latin traditions—that the latter seems to have moved more rapidly toward serving the interests of philosophy, while the former remained more strictly mathematical in its concerns. One does not find, for example, anything like the Arabic debate about the parallels postulate in the Latin texts. But then Islamic mathematics itself was more lively and creative than that of the medieval Latin West.

The Renaissance and Modern Euclid. Four events seem to have been the most outstanding in determining the course of the *Elements* in the sixteenth and succeeding centuries: (1) the publication of the medieval version of Campanus of Novara, initially as the first printed Euclid at Venice (1482) by Erhard Ratdolt, and at many other places and dates in the ensuing 100 years; (2) a new Latin translation from the Greek by Bartolomeo Zamberti in 1505; (3) the *editio princeps* of the Greek text by Simon Grynaeus at Basel in 1533; (4) another Greek–Latin translation made in 1572 by Federico Commandino. The publications result-

ing from these four versions show their effect in almost all later translations and versions, be they Latin or vernacular.

Of Campanus we have spoken above. The printed Euclid following his was, ignoring the publication in various forms of the "Boethian" fragments, not the influential one of Zamberti but only portions of the *Elements* included in the gigantic encyclopedia *De expetendis et fugiendis rebus* (Venice, 1501) of Georgius Valla (*d.* 1499). This was not, to be sure, an easily accessible Euclid; for in addition to being an extraordinarily cumbersome book to use, the selections from the *Elements* are scattered among materials translated from other Greek mathematical and scientific texts. The first publication of a Greek-based Latin *Elements* as an integral whole was that at Venice in 1505 prepared by Bartolomeo Zamberti (*b. ca.* 1473). His translation derived from a strictly Theonine Greek text, a factor which has Zamberti attributing the proofs to this Alexandrian redactor (*cum expositione Theonis insignis mathematici*). The work also contains translations of the minor Euclidean works (which were also, in part, in Valla's encyclopedia).

Zamberti was most conscious of the advantages he believed to accrue from his working from a Greek text. This enabled him, he claimed, to add things hitherto missing and properly to arrange and prove again much found in the version of Campanus. Indeed, his animus against his medieval predecessor is far from gentle: his Euclid was, Zamberti complains, replete with "wondrous ghosts, dreams and fantasies" (*miris larvis, somniis et phantasmatibus*). Campanus himself he labels *interpres barbarissimus.*

The attack thus launched by Zamberti was almost immediately answered by new editions of Campanus, the most notable of them being that prepared at Venice in 1509 by the Franciscan Luca Pacioli. Pacioli regarded himself as a corrector (*castigator*) who freed Campanus from the errors of copyists, especially in the matter of incorrectly drawn figures. In direct reply to Zamberti, Campanus was now presented as *interpres fidissimus.*

A kind of détente was subsequently reached between the Campanus and Zamberti camps, for there was soon a series of published *Elements* reproducing the editions of both *in toto,* the first appearing at Paris in 1516. Each theorem and proof first occurs *ex Campano* and is immediately followed by its mate and proof *Theon ex Zamberto.* The *additiones* due to Campanus appear in place but are appropriately set off and indicated as such.

The end of the first third of the sixteenth century brought with it the first publication of the Greek text of the *Elements.* The German theologian Simon

Grynaeus (d. 1541) accomplished this, working from two manuscripts, with an occasional reference to Zamberti's Latin. His edition, which included the text of Proclus' *Commentary* as well, was the only complete one of the Greek before the eighteenth century. The other Greek Euclids of the Renaissance were all partial, most frequently offering only the enunciations of the propositions in Greek (usually with accompanying translation). The most significant of such "piecemeal" *Elements* is unquestionably that of the Swiss mathematician and clockmaker Conrad Dasypodius, or Rauchfuss (1532–1600). Dasypodius makes it abundantly clear that his edition, issued in three parts at Strasbourg in 1564, was intended as a school-text Euclid. For this reason he believed it more convenient to give merely the enunciations of books III–XIII to accompany the full text of books I–II, all in Greek with Latin translation. The pedagogical design of his publication is also seen from the fact that in spite of his exclusion of a great deal of genuine Euclid, he nevertheless saw fit to include the text of the more readily comprehensible arithmetical version of book II that was composed by the Basilian monk Barlaam (d. ca. 1350).

In any event, the printing of the complete Greek text in 1533, plus the earlier appearance of both Campanus and Zamberti, provided the raw material, as it were, for the first, pre-Commandino, phase of the Renaissance Euclid. The irony is that Campanus and Zamberti, and not the Greek *editio princeps,* played the dominant role. Some note of the most significant of the many early Renaissance printed editions of the *Elements* will make this clear. (The substantial, but totally uninvestigated, manuscript material of this period is here excluded from consideration.)

If one focuses, to begin with, upon Latin Euclids, the first important "new" version (Paris, 1536) is that of the French mathematician Oronce Fine (1494–1555). Yet his contribution seems to have been to insert the Greek text of the enunciations for the *libri sex priores* in the appropriate places in Zamberti's Latin translation of the whole of these books. Similarly, his compatriot Jacques Peletier du Mans brought out another six-book Latin version (Lyons, 1557), this time based, as Commandino noted, more on Campanus' Arabic–Latin edition than upon anything Greek. (It should be recorded, however, that Peletier supplemented what he took from Campanus' *additiones* with some interesting ones of his own.) At Paris in 1566 yet a third French scholar, Franciscus Flussatus Candalla (François de Foix, Comte de Candale, 1502–1594) produced a Latin *Elements.* Covering all fifteen books, and appending three more

on the inscription and circumscription of solids, the appeal is once again not to the Greek text as such, but to Zamberti and Campanus. And when there is something not derived from these two, it seems as often as not to have been Candalla's own invention.

A contemporary summary view of the status of Euclid scholarship was revealed when, a few years before Candalla's expanded *Elements,* Johannes Buteo published his *De quadratura circuli* at Lyons in 1559. This work contained as an appendix Buteo's *Annotationum opuscula in errores Campani, Zamberti, Orontii, Peletarii . . . interpretum Euclidis.* Campanus was, he felt, the best of these editors, for his errors derive from his Arabic source and not from an ineptitude in mathematics. Zamberti, on the other hand, although he worked directly from the Greek, showed less acumen in geometry. Even less adequate, in Buteo's judgment, were the works of Fine and Peletier, the latter taking the greatest liberties with the text and ineptly adding or omitting as he saw fit.

We have thus far spoken merely of sixteenth-century Latin translations, but the same pattern reflecting the central impact of Campanus and Zamberti can also be discerned in the most notable vernacular renderings. The earliest of these to be printed was the Italian translation by the mathematician, mechanician, and natural philosopher Niccolò Tartaglia. Its first edition appeared at Venice in 1543. When Tartaglia submits that his redaction was made *secondo le due tradittioni,* there is no question that Campanus—who appears to be heavily favored—and Zamberti are meant. When Campanus has added propositions or premises, Tartaglia has appropriately translated them and noted their absence *nella seconda tradittione,* while things omitted by Campanus but included by Zamberti receive the reverse treatment.

The next languages to receive the privilege of displaying Euclid among their goods were French (by Pierre Forcadel at Paris in 1564) and German (at the hands of Johann Scheubel and Wilhelm Holtzmann in 1558 and 1562). We are better informed, however, of the circumstances surrounding the production of the more elaborate, first complete English edition. Yet before we describe this, it will be well to note an even earlier intrusion of Euclidean materials into English. This is found in *The Pathway to Knowledg* (London, 1551) of the Tudor mathematical practitioner Robert Recorde. Recorde fully recognized the ground he was breaking, for in anticipation of the dismay even Euclid's opening definitions would likely cause in the "simple ignorant" who were to be his readers, he cautioned: "For nother is there anie matter more straunge in the englishe tungue, then this whereof never booke was written before now, in that tungue."

Recorde's purpose was distinctly practical, and he expressly mentioned the significance of geometry for surveying, land measure, and building. The *Pathway* contains the enunciations of books I–IV of Euclid, reworked and reordered to serve his practical aims.

The first proper English translation was the work of Sir Henry Billingsley, later lord mayor of London (*d.* 1606), and appeared at London in 1570 with a preface by John Dee, patron and sometime practitioner of the mathematical arts. A truly monumental folio volume, Billingsley's translation contains "manifolde additions, Scholies, Annotations and Inventions . . . gathered out of the most famous and chiefe Mathematiciens, both of old time and in our age" and even includes pasted flaps of paper that can be folded up to produce three-dimensional models for the propositions of book XI. Each book begins with a summary statement that includes considerable commentary and often an assessment of the views of Billingsley's predecessors, most notably those of Campanus and Zamberti. The role these two scholars played in Billingsley's labors is confirmed in yet another way. There exists in the Princeton University Library a copy of the 1533 *editio princeps* of the Greek text of the *Elements* bound together with a 1558 Basel "combined" edition of Campanus and Zamberti. It is not known how these volumes came into Princeton's possession, but both contain manuscript notes in Billingsley's hand. The fact that these notes are found on only five pages of the Greek text, but on well over 200 of both Campanus and Zamberti, is clearly suggestive of Billingsley's major source. Once again, the two basic Latin versions, one medieval and one Renaissance, have exhibited the considerable extent of their influence.

However, the better part of this influence was interrupted suddenly and decisively by the fourth major version listed above: the publication at Pesaro in 1572 of the Latin translation by Federico Commandino of Urbino. Commandino—who, in addition to the place he holds in the history of physics deriving from his *Liber de centro gravitatis* (Bologna, 1565), prepared exacting Latin versions of many other Greek mathematical works—was clearly the most competent mathematician of all Renaissance editors of Euclid. He was also most astute in his scholarship, for we know that in addition to the 1533 *editio princeps,* he employed at least one other Greek manuscript in establishing the text for his translation. For the first time, save for the anonymous translation in the twelfth century, we now have a version (no matter what language) of the *Elements* that is solidly based on a tolerably critical Greek original. It even includes, also for the first time, a rendering of numerous Greek scholia.

Aware, but critical, of the efforts of his predecessors, Commandino leaves no doubt of the advantage of staying closer to the Greek sources so many of them had minimized, if not ignored. The result of his labors may prove to be of less fascination than other versions, since it so closely follows the Greek we already know, but the importance it held for the subsequent modern history of the *Elements* is immeasurable. It came to serve, in sum, as the base of almost all other proper translations before Peyrard's discovery of the "pristine" Euclid in the early nineteenth century. Thus, to cite only the most notable cases in point, Greek texts of the *Elements* with accompanying Latin translation frequently based the latter on Commandino: for example, Henry Briggs's *Elementorum Euclidis libri VI priores* (London, 1620) and even David Gregory's 1703 Oxford edition of Euclid's *Opera omnia* (which was the standard, pre-nineteenth-century source for the Greek text). Commandino was also followed in later strictly Latin versions: that of Robert Simson, simultaneously issued in English at Glasgow in 1756; and even that of Samuel Horsley, appearing at London in 1802. Vernacular translations often followed a similar course, beginning with the Italian translation, revised by Commandino himself, appearing at Urbino in 1575 and extending to and beyond the English version by John Keill, Savilian professor of astronomy at Oxford, in 1708.

In all translations based heavily on Commandino, one naturally remained close to the (Theonine) Greek tradition; but there were also other efforts after, as well as before, Commandino that did not stay so nearly on course. These were the numerous commentaries on Euclid, the various schoolbook *Elements,* and, in a class by itself, the edition of Christopher Calvius.

The commentaries of the sixteenth through eighteenth centuries were almost always limited to specific books or parts of the *Elements.* We have already noted the 1559 *Annotationum opuscula* of Buteo, but a considerable amount of related commentarial literature began to flourish around the same time. Giovanni Battista Benedetti (1530–1590) brought out his *Resolutio omnium Euclidis problematum . . . una tantummodo circini data apertura* at Venice in 1553 in response to a controversy that had recently arisen out of some reflection by several Italian scholars on Euclid. Petrus Ramus, who had previously produced a Latin version of the *Elements* in 1545, published at Frankfurt in 1559 his *Scholae mathematicae,* in which he scrutinized the structure of Euclid from the standpoint of logic. Along related lines, mention might be made of the curious *Euclideae demonstrationes in syllogismos resolutae* (Strasbourg, 1564) of Conrad Dasypodius and Christianus Herlinus. Such works as these were in a way extensions, perhaps fanciful ones, of the medieval Scholastic concern with the logic of the *Elements*. Yet another development can be seen in the various attempts to reduce the *Elements* to practice. We have already noticed this standpoint in Robert Recorde, and to this one could add the first German translation of books I–VI —published by Wilhelm Holtzmann (Xylander) in 1562—which was written with the likes of painters, goldsmiths, and builders in mind; and the Italian version (1613–1625) of Antonio Cataldi, which expressly declared itself to be an *Elementi ridotti alla practica*.

On a more specific plane, commentaries on book V, and particularly upon the Eudoxean definition of equal ratios that we have already seen to be problematic, continued in the sixteenth and seventeenth centuries. Beginning with the almost totally unknown works of Giambattista Politi, *Super definitiones et propositiones quae supponuntur ab Euclide in quinto Elementorum eius* (Siena, 1529), and of Elia Vineto Santone, *Definitiones elementi quincti et sexti Euclidis* (Bordeaux, 1575), the issue was also broached by Galileo in the added "Fifth Day" of his *Discorsi . . . a due nuove scienze* (an addendum first published at Florence in 1674 in Vincenzo Viviani's *Quinto libro degli Elementi d'Euclide*). Finally, note should be made of two of the most impressive early modern commentaries on selected aspects of Euclid. The first is Henry Savile's lectures *Praelectiones tresdecim in principium Elementorum Euclidis Oxoniae habitae MDCXX* (Oxford, 1621), which cover only the premises and first eight propositions of book I but do so in an extraordinarily penetrating, and still valuable, way. The last work to be mentioned is so famous that one often forgets that it formed part of the commentarial literature on the *Elements*—the *Euclides ab omni naevo vindicatus* (Milan, 1733) of Girolamo Saccheri, in which this Jesuit mathematician and logician fashioned the attempt to prove Euclid's parallels postulate that has won him so prominent a place in the histories of non-Euclidean geometry.

Closely connected with the commentarial literature we have sampled is the magisterial Latin version of the *Elements* composed by another, much earlier Jesuit scholar, Christopher Clavius (1537–1612). The first edition of his *Euclidis Elementorum libri XV* appeared at Rome in 1574. Not, properly speaking, a translation, as Clavius himself admitted, but a personal redaction compiled from such earlier authors as Campanus, Zamberti, and Commandino, the work is chiefly notable, to say nothing of immensely valuable, for the great amount of auxiliary material it

contains. Separate *praxeis* are specified for the constructions involved in the problems, long *excursus* appear on such debatable issues as the horn angle, and virtually self-contained treatises on such topics as composite ratios, mean proportionals, the species of proportionality not treated in Euclid, and the quadratrix are inserted at appropriate places. Indeed, by Clavius' own count, to the 486 propositions he calculated in his Greek-based Euclid, he admits to adding 671 others of his own; "in universum ergo 1234 propositiones in nostro Euclide demonstrantur," he concludes. And the value of what he has compiled matches, especially for the historian, its mass.

The final segment of the modern history of Euclid that requires description is what might most appropriately be called the handbook tradition, both Latin and vernacular, of the *Elements*. Many of the briefer Renaissance versions already mentioned are properly part of this tradition, and if one sets no limit on size, editions like that of Clavius would also qualify. In point of fact, the undercurrent of didacticism we have seen to be present in the medieval Arabic and Latin versions of the *Elements* can justly be regarded as the beginning of this handbook, or school text, tradition.

In the seventeenth century, however, the tradition takes on a more definite form. Numerous examples could be cited from this period, but all of them show the tendency to shorten proofs, to leave out propositions—and even whole books—of little use, and to introduce symbols wherever feasible to facilitate comprehension. This did not mean, to be sure, the disappearance of the sorts of supplementary material characteristic of so many translations and redactions of the *Elements*. On the contrary, such material was often rearranged and retained, and even created anew, when it seemed to be fruitful from the instructional point of view. For instance, one of the most popular (some twenty editions through the first few years of the nineteenth century) handbooks, the *Elementa geometriae planae et solidae* (Antwerp, 1654) of André Tacquet (1612–1660), covers books I–VI and XI–XII, with added material from Archimedes. Its proofs are compendious, but it makes up for its gain in this regard through the addition of a substantial number of pedagogically useful corollaries and scholia. On the other hand, the *Euclidis Elementorum libri XV breviter demonstrati* (Cambridge, 1655) of Isaac Barrow (1630–1677) stubbornly holds to its status as an epitome. Producer of perhaps the shortest handbook of all of books I–XV, Barrow achieved this maximum of condensation by appropriating the symbolism of William Oughtred (1574–1660) that the latter employed in a *declaratio* of book X of Euclid in his *Clavis mathematicae* (Oxford, 1648 ff.). In his preface, Barrow claimed that his goal was "to conjoin the greatest Compendiousness of Demonstration with as much perspicuity as the quality of the subject would admit." Although his success struck some (for example, John Keill) as producing a somewhat obscure compendium, this did not prevent the appearance of numerous (some ten) editions, several of them in English. Vernacular handbooks appeared in other languages as well, perhaps the most notable being *Les Elémens d'Euclide* (Lyons, 1672) of the French Jesuit Claude-François Milliet de Chales (1621–1678). Appearing earlier in Latin (Lyons, 1660), this handbook, covering, like Tacquet's, books I–VI and XI–XII, went through some twenty-four subsequent editions, including translations into English and Italian.

The next stage in the handbook tradition belongs to the nineteenth century, where there occurred a veritable avalanche of Euclid primers, frequently radically divergent from any imaginable text of the *Elements*. Quite separate from these attempts to make Euclid proper for the grammar schools, lycées, and Gymnasia of the 1800's, the rise of classical philology carried with it the efforts to establish a sound and critical text of the *Elements*. These efforts, in turn, gave rise to the annotated translations of the present century, with an audience primarily the historian and the classicist, rather than the mathematician.

Only a paltry few of the almost innumerable versions of the *Elements* dating from the Renaissance to the present have even been mentioned above—most are merely listed in bibliographies and remain totally unexamined. Even the few titles of this period that have been cited have received little more than fleeting attention—often limited to their prefaces—from historians. Further study will, one feels certain, reveal much more of the significance this mass of Euclidean material holds for the history of mathematics and science as a whole.

BIBLIOGRAPHY

Abbreviations of frequently cited works:

Clagett, *Medieval Euclid* = Marshall Clagett, "The Medieval Latin Translations From the Arabic of the *Elements* of Euclid, With Special Emphasis on the Versions of Adelard of Bath," in *Isis*, **44** (1953), 16–42.

Curtze, *Supplementum* = *Anaritii in decem libros priores Elementorum Euclidis ex interpretatione Gherardi Cremonensis*, Maximilian Curtze, ed. (Leipzig, 1899), supplement to *Euclidis Opera omnia*, Heiberg and Menge, eds.

Heath, *Euclid* = Thomas L. Heath, *The Thirteen Books of Euclid's Elements Translated From the Text of Heiberg With Introduction and Commentary*, 3 vols. (2nd ed., Cambridge, 1925; repr. New York, 1956).

Heiberg, *Euclides* = *Euclidis Opera omnia*, J. L. Heiberg and H. Menge, eds., 8 vols. (Leipzig, 1883–1916).

Heiberg, *Litt. Stud.* = J. L. Heiberg, *Litterärgeschichtliche Studien über Euklid* (Leipzig, 1882).

Heiberg, *Paralipomena* = J. L. Heiberg, "Paralipomena zu Euklid," in *Hermes*, **38** (1903), 46–74, 161–201, 321–356.

Klamroth, *Arab. Euklid* = Martin Klamroth, "Ueber den arabischen Euklid," in *Zeitschrift der Deutschen morgenländischen Gesellschaft*, **35** (1881), 270–326, 788.

Sabra, *Simplicius* = A. I. Sabra, "Simplicius's Proof of Euclid's Parallels Postulate," in *Journal of the Warburg and Courtauld Institutes*, **32** (1969), 1–24.

Sabra, *Thābit* = A. I. Sabra, "Thābit ibn Qurra on Euclid's Parallels Postulate," in *Journal of the Warburg and Courtauld Institutes*, **31** (1968), 12–32.

General Euclidean Bibliographies

The most complete bibliography of Euclid is still that of Pietro Riccardi, *Saggio di una bibliografia Euclidea*, in 5 pts., (Bologna, 1887–1893); this work also appeared in the *Memorie della Reale Accademia delle Scienze dell' Istituto di Bologna*, 4th ser., **8** (1887), 401–523; **9** (1888), 321–343; 5th ser., **1** (1890), 27–84; **3** (1892), 639–694. More complete bibliographic information on pre-1600 eds. of the *Elements*, and works dealing with Euclid, can be found in Charles Thomas-Sanford, *Early Editions of Euclid's Elements* (London, 1926). Other bibliographies are listed in the bibliography to pt. I of the present article.

The Elements in Greek Antiquity

1. *Establishment of the "pristine" Greek text.* A history of the text in capsule form was first given in Heiberg, *Litt. Stud.*, pp. 176–186. Heiberg, *Euclides*, V (Leipzig, 1888), xxiii–lxxvi gives a more complete analysis of the Theonine and pre-Theonine texts, together with an outline of the criteria and methods used in establishing the latter. Further material relevant to the textual problem is found in Heiberg, *Paralipomena*, pp. 47–53, 59–74, 161–201. Heath, *Euclid*, I, 46–63, gives a summary of all of the Heiberg material above.

2. *Greek commentaries.* The ed. of the Greek text of Proclus by G. Friedlein is noted in pt. I of the present article, together with several trans. To this one should now add the English trans. of Glenn Morrow (Princeton, 1970). Of the literature on Proclus, the most useful to cite is J. G. van Pesch, *De Procli fontibus* (Leiden, 1900). For the commentary of Pappus, extant only in Arabic, see the following section. Heath, *Euclid*, I, 19–45, gives a convenient summary of Greek commentarial literature. To this one should add Sabra, *Simplicius*, for material on this commentary, extant only in Arabic fragments (and Latin trans. thereof). Finally, Heiberg has treated the commentaries as well as the citations of Euclid in all other later

Greek authors (notably commentators on Aristotle); this material is assembled in Heiberg, *Litt. Stud.,* pp. 154–175, 186–224; and *Paralipomena,* pp. 352–354.

3. *Greek scholia.* Most of these are published in Heiberg, *Euclides,* V (Leipzig, 1888), 71–738, supplemented by Heiberg, *Paralipomena,* pp. 321–352. Scholia to the minor Euclidean works are published in vols. VI–VIII of Heiberg, *Euclides.* The most complete discussion of the scholia is J. L. Heiberg, "Om Scholierne til Euklids Elementer" (with a French résumé), in *Kongelige Danske Videnskabernes Selskabs Skrifter,* Hist.-philosofisk afdeling II, **3** (1888), 227–304. Once again there is a summary of this Danish article in Heath, *Euclid,* I, 64–74.

The Medieval Arabic Euclid

1. *General works.* Serious study of the Arabic Euclid began with J. C. Gartz, *De interpretibus et explanatoribus Euclidis arabicis schediasma historicum* (Halle, 1823) and was continued in J. G. Wenrich, *De auctorum graecorum versionibus et commentariis syriacis, arabicis, armeniacis persicisque commentatio* (Leipzig, 1842), pp. 176–189. The problem of the reports of Euclid in Arabic literature was broached in Heiberg, *Litt. Stud.,* pp. 1–21; but the major step was taken in Klamroth, *Arab. Euklid.* Klamroth's contentions concerning the superiority of the Arabic tradition were answered by Heiberg in "Die arabische Tradition der Elemente Euklid's," in *Zeitschrift für Mathematik und Physik,* Hist.-lit. Abt., **29** (1884), 1–22. This was followed by the summary article, which included material on Arabic commentators, of Moritz Steinschneider, "Euklid bei den Arabern: Eine bibliographische Studie," in *Zeitschrift für Mathematik und Physik,* Hist.-lit. Abt., **31** (1886), 81–110. Cf. Steinschneider's *Die arabischen Uebersetzungen aus dem Griechischen* (Graz, 1960), pp. 156–164 (originally published in *Centralblatt für Bibliothekswesen,* supp. **5,** 1889). See also the article by A. G. Kapp in section 6 below. A summary view of our knowledge (as of the beginning of the present century) of the *Elements* in Islam can be found in Heath, *Euclid,* I, 75–90. M. Klamroth has also published a translation of some of the summaries of Greek works by the ninth-century historian al-Yaʿqūbī which includes a résumé of the *Elements:* "Ueber die Auszüge aus griechischen Schriftstellern bei al-Jaʿqūbī," in *Zeitschrift der Deutschen morgenländischen Gesellschaft,* **42** (1888), 3–9. The standard bibliography of Arabic mathematics and mathematicians is Heinrich Suter, *Die Mathematiker und Astronomen der Araber und ihre Werke, Abhandlungen zur Geschichte der mathematischen Wissenschaften,* X (Leipzig, 1900), with *Nachträge und Berichtigungen, op. cit.,* XIV (Leipzig, 1902), 155–185. The most recent history of Islamic mathematics, with appended bibliography, is contained in A. P. Juschkewitsch [Youschkevitch], *Geschichte der Mathematik im Mittelalter* (Basel, 1964; original Russian ed., Moscow, 1961).

2. *The translation of al-Ḥajjāj.* We know of but a single MS containing (presumably) the second Ḥajjāj version together with Nayrīzī's commentary for books I–VI (and a few lines of VII) alone: Leiden, 399, 1. This has been ed. with a modern Latin trans. by J. L. Heiberg, R. O.

Besthorn, *et al., Codex Leidensis 399, 1: Euclidis Elementa ex interpretatione al-Hadschdschadschii cum commentariis al-Narizii,* in 3 pts. (Copenhagen, 1893–1932). Confirmation is needed of the report of two further MSS containing a Ḥajjāj version of books XI–XII: MSS Copenhagen LXXXI and Istanbul, Fātih 3439. There is no secondary literature specifically devoted to the Ḥajjāj *Elements,* but information is contained in Klamroth, *Arab. Euklid.*

3. *The translation of Isḥāq-Thābit.* The most frequently cited MS of this version is Oxford, Bodleian Libr., MS Thurston 11 (279 in Nicoll's catalogue), dated 1238. This was one of the two basic codices employed in Klamroth, *Arab. Euklid.* The literature also makes continual reference to MS Bodl. Or. 448 (280 in Nicoll) as an Isḥāq-Thābit text; it is not this, but rather a copy of al-Maghribī's *Taḥrīr* (the error derives from a marginal misascription to Thābit that was reported by Nicoll in his catalogue). There are, however, a number of other extant copies of Isḥāq-Thābit. Intention to edit the Isḥāq-Thābit trans. was announced (but apparently abandoned) by Claire Baudoux, "Une édition polyglotte orientale des Eléments d'Euclide: La version arabe d'Isḥāq et ses derivées," in *Archeion,* **19** (1937), 70–71. Of the literature on the reviser of this trans., Thābit ibn Qurra, see Eilhard Wiedemann, "Ueber Thābit, sein Leben und Wirken," in *Sitzungsberichte der physikalisch-medizinischen Sozietät zu Erlangen,* **52** (1922), 189–219; A. Sayili, "Thābit ibn Qurra's Generalization of the Pythagorean Theorem," in *Isis,* **51** (1960), 35–37; and section 7 below. An integral ed. and Russian trans. of Thābit's mathematical works is in preparation.

4. *The epitomes of Avicenna and others.* A. I. Sabra has edited Avicenna's compendium of the *Elements,* and it will appear in the Cairo ed. of Avicenna's *Kitāb al-Shifāʾ.* A brief description of this compendium was published by Karl Lokotsch, *Avicenna als Mathematiker, besonders die planimetrischen Bücher seiner Euklidübersetzung* (Erfurt, 1912). A copy of a poem praising Euclid, ascribed to Avicenna in a MS found in the Topkapi Museum at Istanbul, is the subject of A. S. Unver, "Avicenna's Praise of Euclid," in *Journal of the History of Medicine,* **2** (1947), 198–200 (other occurrences of the poem, however, disagree with this ascription). The only other Euclid compendium treated in the literature is that of al-Asfuzārī, in L. A. Sédillot, "Notice de plusieurs opuscules mathématiques: V. Quatorzième livre de l'épitome de l'Imam Muzhaffar-al-Isferledi sur les Elements d'Euclide," in *Notices et extraits des manuscrits de la Bibliothèque du Roi,* **13** (1838), 146–148.

5. *The Taḥrīr of al-Ṭūsī, pseudo-Ṭūsī, and al-Maghribī.* The genuine, fifteen-book *Taḥrīr* of al-Ṭūsī exists in an overwhelming number of MSS and has also been frequently printed (Istanbul, 1801; Calcutta, 1824; Lucknow, 1873–1874; Delhi, 1873–1874; Tehran, 1881). Indication of the spurious nature of the thirteen-book *Taḥrīr* usually ascribed to al-Ṭūsī is established by Sabra, *Thābit,* n. 11, and *Simplicius,* postscript, p. 18; doubt is also raised in B. A. Rozenfeld, A. K. Kubesov, and G. S. Sobirov, "Kto by avtorom rimskogo izdania 'Izlozhenia Evklida Nasir ad-Dina at-Tusi'" ("Who Was the Author of the Rome

Edition 'Recension of Euclid by Naṣīr al-Dīn al-Ṭūsī'?"),
in *Voprosy istorii estestvoznaniya i tekhniki,* **20** (1966),
51–53. The spurious *Taḥrīr* was printed at Rome in 1594,
and we know of only two extant MSS: Bibl. Laur. Or.
2. and Or. 51; the latter carries the 1298 date, causing,
among other factors, the problems with al-Ṭūsī's authorship. Almost all of the literature dealing with al-Ṭūsī and
Euclid treats of the spurious *Taḥrīr:* H. Suter, "Einiges von
Nasīr el-Dīn's Euklid-Ausgabe," in *Bibliotheca mathematica,* 2nd ser., **6** (1892), 3–6; E. Wiedemann, "Zu der
Redaktion von Euklids Elementen durch *Naṣīr al Din al
Ṭūsī,*" in *Sitzungsberichte der physikalisch-medizinischen
Sozietät zu Erlangen,* **58/59** (1926/1927), 228–236;
C. Thaer, "Die Euklid-Überlieferung durch al-Ṭūsī,"
in *Quellen und Studien zur Geschichte der Mathematik,
Astronomie und Physik,* Abt. B, Studien, **3** (1936), 116–121.
More general works on al-Ṭūsī as a mathematician include
an ed. of the Arabic text of the *Rasā ᶜil al-Ṭūsī,* 2 vols.
(Hyderabad, 1939–1940); E. Wiedemann, "Naṣīr al Din al
Ṭūsī," in *Sitzungsberichte der physikalisch-medizinischen
Sozietät zu Erlangen,* **60** (1928), 289–316; and B. A. Rozenfeld, "O matematicheskikh rabotakh Nasireddina Ṭūsī"
("On the Mathematical Works of Naṣīr al-Dīn al-Ṭūsī"),
in *Istoriko-matematicheskie issledovaniya,* **4** (1951), 489–
512. See also section 7 below. The *Taḥrīr* of al-Maghribī
is found in the thirteenth-century MS Bodl. Or. 448,
as well as two later codices in Istanbul. It is identified and
discussed, together with the ed. and trans. of a fragment
from it in Sabra, *Simplicius,* pp. 13–18, 21–24.

6. *Commentaries. The Arabic translation of the commentary of Pappus on book X.* Extracts of the Arabic text,
together with a French trans., were first published by Franz
Woepcke in "Essai d'une restitution de travaux perdus
d'Apollonius sur les quantités irrationnelles," in *Mémoires
présentés par divers savants à l'Académie des sciences,* **14**
(1856), 658–720 (also published separately). Woepcke also
published the full text of the commentary without date
or place of publication (Paris, 1855[?]). This was in turn
trans. into German with comments by H. Suter, "Der
Kommentar des Pappus zum X Buche des Euklides aus
der arabischen Übersetzung des Abū ᶜOthmān al-Dimashḳī
ins Deutsche übertragen," in *Abhandlungen zur Geschichte
der Naturwissenschaften und der Medizin,* **4** (1922), 9–78.
A new ed. of the Arabic text with notes and English trans.
was published by William Thomson and Gustav Junge,
The Commentary of Pappus on Book X of Euclid's Elements
(Cambridge, Mass., 1930). Critical remarks on this text
were published by G. Bergstrasser, "Pappos Kommentar
zum Zehnten Buch von Euklid's Elementen," in *Der Islam,*
21 (1933), 195–222. A fragment of Gerard of Cremona's
trans. of this Pappus text is printed in G. Junge, "Das
Fragment der lateinischen Übersetzung des Pappus-
Kommentars zum 10. Buche Euklids," in *Quellen und
Studien zur Geschichte der Mathematik, Astronomie und
Physik,* Abt. B, **3,** Studien (1936), 1–17.

Arabic commentaries. Very few of the great number of
these have been published or studied. A list, quite complete
in terms of present knowledge, giving brief indications of
author, subject, and relevant bibliography, can be found

in E. B. Plooij, *Euclid's Conception of Ratio and his Definition of Proportional Magnitudes as Criticized by Arabian
Commentators* (Rotterdam, n.d.), pp. 3–13. More elaborate
is A. G. Kapp, "Arabische Übersetzer und Kommentatoren
Euklids, sowie deren math.-naturwiss. Werke auf Grund
des Ta'rīkh al-Ḥukamā' des Ibn al-Qifṭī," in *Isis,* **22** (1934),
150–172; **23** (1935), 54–99; **24** (1935), 37–79; as the title
indicates, this extensive article contains much material
trans. from the biobibliographical work of Qifṭī (*ca.* 1172–
1248). Arabic commentaries on book X are treated in
G. P. Matvievskaya, *Uchenie o chisle na srednevekovom
blizhnem i srednem vostoke* ("Studies on Number in the
Medieval Near and Middle East"; Tashkent, 1967), pp.
191–229; The following commentaries (listed in approximate chronological order) have been ed. or trans. (if only
partially) and analyzed: (1) al-Nayrīzī: books I–VI in
Arabic in the Heiberg–Besthorn ed. of Ḥajjāj cited in
section 2 above; books I–X (incomplete[?]) in the Latin
trans. of Gerard of Cremona in Curtze, *Supplementum,* pp.
1–252 only (the remainder of this volume containing the
commentary not of al-Nayrīzī, but of ᶜAbd al-Baqi; see
below). Determination through examination of al-Nayrīzī
of various interpolations in the text of the *Elements* was
done in Heiberg, *Paralipomena,* pp. 54–59. (2) Al-Fārābī
on books I and V has been trans. into Russian on the basis
of its two Hebrew copies (MSS Munich 36 and 290, not
edited): M. F. Bokshteyn and B. A. Rozenfeld, "Kom-
mentarii Abu Nasra al-Farabi k trudnostyam vo
vvedeniakh k pervoy i pyatoy knigam Evklida" ("The
Commentary of Abū Naṣr al-Fārābī on the Difficulties in
the Introduction to Books I and V of Euclid"), in *Aka-
demiya nauk SSR, Problemy vostokovedeniya,* no. 4 (1959),
93–104. The Arabic text of this brief work of al-Fārābī
has now also apparently been discovered: Escorial MS
Arab. 612, 109r–111v. A fragment of this, or of another
Euclidean opusculum by al-Fārābī, is Tehran, Faculty of
Theology, MS 123-D, 80v–82r. See also A. Kubesov and
B. A. Rozenfeld, "On the Geometrical Treatise of al-
Fārābī," in *Archives internationales d'histoire des sciences,*
22 (1969), 50. (3) Ibn al-Haytham, *On the Premises of Euclid,*
has also received a (partial) Russian trans. by B. A. Rozenfeld as "Kniga kommentariev k vvedeniam knigi Evklida
'Nachala'" ("Book of Commentaries to Introductions to
Euclid's *Elements*"), in *Istoriko-matematicheskie issledovaniya,* **11** (1958), 743–762. (4) Ibn Muᶜādh al-Jayyānī
on book V has been reproduced in facsimile with accompanying English trans. in the book of E. B. Plooij cited
above. This book also contains a trans. of passages relevant
to book V from the commentaries of al-Māhānī, al-Nayrīzī,
Ibn al-Haytham, and Omar Khayyām. (5) Omar Khayyām's work on Euclid has received the most attention of
all. A. I. Sabra has published a critical Arabic text (without
trans.) as *Explanation of the Difficulties in Euclid's Postulates* (Alexandria, 1961). There is an earlier ed., on the basis
of a single MS, by T. Erani (Tehran, 1936). A Russian trans.,
with commentary, has been published by B. A. Rozenfeld
and A. P. Youschkevitch in *Istoriko-matematicheskie issledovaniya,* **6** (1953), 67–107, 143–168; repr. with a MS facsimile in Omar Khayyām, *Traktaty* (Moscow, 1961). The

English trans. by Amir-Móez in *Scripta mathematica,* **24** (1959), 272–303, must be used with great care. (6) ʿAbd al-Bāqī's commentary on book X in Gerard of Cremona's Latin trans. is printed in Curtze, *Supplementum,* pp. 252–386. H. Suter has given corrections to Curtze's text in "Ueber den Kommentar des Muḥ b. ʿAbdelbāqi zum 10 Buche des Euklides," in *Bibliotheca mathematica,* 3rd ser., **7** (1907), 234–251. See the following section for literature on yet other commentarial material.

7. *On the parallels postulate.* The importance of this postulate in the history of mathematics is reflected not merely in the frequency of its discussion by Islamic authors, but also by the attention it has received from modern historians. As an introduction, see B. A. Rozenfeld and A. P. Youschkevitch, *The Prehistory of Non-Euclidean Geometry in the Middle East, XXV International Congress of Orientalists, Papers Presented by the USSR Delegation* (Moscow, 1960). Compare B. A. Rozenfeld, "The Theory of Parallel Lines in the Medieval East," in *Actes du XIᵉ Congrès International d'Histoire des Sciences, Varsovie-Cracovie 1965,* **3** (Warsaw, etc., 1968), 175–178. More specifically, two treatments of Thābit ibn Qurra are trans. and analyzed in Sabra, *Thābit.* The problem is also the subject of Sabra, *Simplicius.* In fact, these two articles contain a mine of information pertinent to the issue throughout Islamic mathematics. The two Thābit treatises have also been analyzed and trans. into Russian by B. A. Rozenfeld and A. P. Youschkevitch in *Istoriko-matematicheskie issledovaniya,* **14** (1961), 587–597; and **15** (1963), 363–380. Extracts from the treatments of the postulate by al-Jawharī, Qayṣar ibn Abi 'l-Qāsim, and al-Maghribī are found in the two Sabra articles. The greatest amount of attention has been paid to al-Ṭūsī's struggles with the problem, beginning with a trans. into Latin by Edward Pocock of the proof of the postulate in the pseudo-Ṭūsī *Taḥrīr;* this was printed in John Wallis, *Opera mathematica,* II (Oxford, 1693), 669–673. Both this proof and that in the genuine fifteen-book al-Ṭūsī *Taḥrīr* were published and analyzed in Arabic by A. I. Sabra, "Burhān Naṣīr al-Dīn al-Ṭūsī ʿalā muṣādarat Uqlīdis al-khāmisa," in *Bulletin of the Faculty of Arts of the University of Alexandria,* **13** (1959), 133–170. Russian treatment again occurs in G. D. Mamedbeili, *Mukhammad Nasureddin Tusi o teorii parallelnykh liny i teorii otnosheny* ("Muḥammad Naṣīr al-Dīn al-Ṭūsī on the Theory of Parallel Lines and the Theory of Proportion"; Baku, 1959), and in *Istoriko-matematicheskie issledovaniya,* **13** (1960), 475–532. Finally, the article of H. Dilgan, "Demonstration du Vᵉ postulat d'Euclide par Schams-ed-Din Samarkandi, Traduction de l'ouvrage Aschkal-ut-tessis de Samarkandi," in *Revue d'histoire des sciences,* **13** (1960), 191–196, does not contain a proof by Samarqandī, but rather one by Athīr al-Dīn al-Abharī that was reproduced in a commentary to Samarqandī's work.

8. *Translations into other Near Eastern languages.* The most adequate account of Hebrew versions and commentaries is in Moritz Steinschneider, *Die hebräischen Übersetzungen des Mittelalters und die Juden als Dolmetscher* (Berlin, 1893; repr. Graz, 1956), 503–513. The fragments of the Syriac version were published and trans. by G. Furlani,

"Bruchstücke eine syrischen Paraphrase der 'Elemente' des Eukleides," in *Zeitschrift für Semitistik und verwandte Gebiete,* **3** (1924), 27–52, 212–235. Furlani held that the paraphrase was derived from the Arabic of Ḥajjāj. This was questioned, and the opposing view placing it before, and as a source of, the Isḥāq trans., by C. Baudoux, "La version syriaque des 'Eléments' d'Euclide," in *IIᵉ Congrès national des sciences* (Brussels, 1935), pp. 73–75. The fragments of the early Armenian version were published and trans. (into Latin) by Maurice Leroy, "La traduction arménienne d'Euclide," in *Annuaire de l'Institut de philologie et d'histoire orientales et slaves (Mélanges Franz Cumont),* **4** (1936), 785–816. The letter of Gregory Magistros announcing his translating activity with respect to Euclid was published and analyzed by Leroy in the same *Annuaire,* **3** (1935), 263–294. Additional material on Armenian Euclids can be found in the article (not presently examined) by T. G. Tumanyai, " 'Nachala' Evklida po drevnearmyanskim istochnikam" ("Euclid's *Elements* in Ancient Armenian Sources"), in *Istoriko-matematicheskie issledovaniya,* **6** (1953), 659–671, and in G. B. Petrosian and A. G. Abramyan, "A Newly Discovered Armenian Text of Euclid's Geometry," in *Proceedings of the Tenth International Congress of the History of Science, Ithaca, 1962,* II (Paris, 1964), 651–654.

9. *Euclid's minor works.* The Arabic trans. of the Euclidean opuscula, together with a discussion of their role as "middle books" in Islamic mathematics and astronomy, was first examined by M. Steinschneider, "Die 'mittleren' Bücher der Araber und ihre Bearbeiter," in *Zeitschrift für Mathematik und Physik,* **10** (1865), 456–498. There is little material dealing specifically with these shorter works, but in addition to the general literature in section 1 above, see Clemens Thaer, "Euklids Data in arabischer Fassung," in *Hermes,* **77** (1942), 197–205. The prolegomena in vols. VI–VIII of Heiberg, *Euclides,* also contains information on the Arabic phase of these opuscula. For literature dealing with the Islamic role in the work *On the Division of Figures* and the works on mechanics, see pt. I of the present article.

The Medieval Latin Euclid: The Greek–Latin Phase

1. *Euclidean material in Roman authors.* The fragments in Censorinus are appended in F. Hultsch's ed. (Leipzig, 1867) of the *De die natali,* pp. 60–63. For Euclid in Martianus Capella, see the *De nuptiis philologiae et mercurii,* VI, 708 ff.

2. *The Verona palimpsest.* The Euclid fragments have recently been edited, with facsimile and notes, by Mario Geymonat, *Euclidis latine facti fragmenta Veronensia* (Milan, 1964). This work contains references to all other previous literature on the palimpsest, both of paleographers and historians of mathematics.

3. *The Boethian Euclid excerpts.* The best account of all of the variables involved is the absolutely fundamental work of Menso Folkerts, *"Boethius" Geometrie II: Ein mathematisches Lehrbuch des Mittelalters* (Wiesbaden, 1970). This contains a critical ed. of (a) the two-book "Boethian" *Geometry;* (b) the Euclid excerpts preserved in all four earlier medieval sources. The Boethian–Adelard

mélanges in Ratsbücherei Lüneburg MS miscell. D4° 48 have been treated and ed. by Folkerts in *Ein neuer Text des Euclides Latinus: Faksimiledruck der Handschrift Lüneburg D 4° 48, f. 13r-17v* (Hildesheim, 1970), and, together with a consideration of the mélanges in the Paris and Munich MSS (see following section), in "Anonyme lateinische Euklidbearbeitungen aus dem 12. Jahrhundert," in *Denkschriften der Österreichischen Akademie der Wissenschaften,* Math.-naturwiss. Klasse (1970), 5–42. See also Folkerts' earlier article, "Das Problem der pseudo-boethischen Geometrie," in *Sudhoff's Archiv für Geschichte der Medizin und der Naturwissenschaften,* **52** (1968), 152–161. An earlier work that also attempted, as a tangential problem, to sort out the threads of the "Boethian" Euclid is Nicolaus Bubnov, *Gerberti Opera mathematica* (Berlin, 1899; repr. Hildesheim, 1963). Before Folkerts the standard ed. of the two-book geometry was that of Gottfried Friedlein in his text of Boethius' *De institutione arithmetica . . . de institutione musica . . . accedit geometria quae fertur Boetii* (Leipzig, 1867), pp. 372–428. The five-book "Boethian" geometry still does not exist in a critical ed. The first two books have appeared, however, among Boethius' works in J. P. Migne, *Patrologia Latina,* vol. LXIII, cols. 1352–1364 (cols. 1307–1352 contain the two-book geometry now in Folkerts). Books I, III, IV, and part of V are in F. Blume, K. Lachmann, and A. Rudorff, *Die Schriften der römischen Feldmesser,* I (Berlin, 1848), 377–412. The remaining section of book V is unedited. Although the five-book geometry has therefore not received adequate editing, a most exacting analysis of its MS sources and history has been made by C. Thulin, *Zur Überlieferungsgeschichte des Corpus Agrimensorum. Exzerptenhandschriften und Kompendien* (Göteborg, 1911). The Euclid excerpts found in Cassiodorus have been edited by R. A. B. Mynors in his text of the *Institutiones* (Oxford, 1937), pp. 169–172. A recent important article that treats of the role of "Boethian" geometry in the earlier Middle Ages is B. L. Ullman, "Geometry in the Medieval Quadrivium," in *Studi di bibliografia e di storia in onore di Tammaro de Marinis,* IV (Verona, 1964), 263–285. Among the earlier literature on the problems of Boethius and the *Elements* are H. Weissenborn, "Die Boetius-Frage," in *Abhandlungen zur Geschichte der Mathematik,* **2** (1879), 185–240; J. L. Heiberg, "Beiträge zur Geschichte der Mathematik im Mittelalter, II. Euklid's Elemente im Mittelalter," in *Zeitschrift für Mathematik und Physik,* Hist.-lit. Abt., **35** (1890), 48–58, 81–100; Georg Ernst, *De geometricis illis quae sub Boëthii nomine nobis tradita sunt, quaestiones* (Bayreuth, 1903); M. Manitius, "Collationen aus einem geometrischen Tractat," in *Hermes,* **39** (1904), 291–300, and "Collationen aus der *Ars geometrica," ibid.,* **41** (1906), 278–292; and several pieces by Paul Tannery, now included in his *Mémoires scientifiques,* V (Paris, 1922), 79–102, 211–228, 246–250.

4. Boethian–Adelardian mélanges. The Lüneburg MS mélange has been ed. by Folkerts (see above). A second mélange exists in the four MSS Paris, BN lat. 10257; Oxford, Bodl. Digby 98; Munich, CLM 13021, and CLM 23511. The Paris MS has been ed. in the unpublished dissertation of George D. Goldat, "The Early Medieval

Traditions of Euclid's Elements" (Madison, Wisc., 1956).

5. Munich manuscript fragment. This has been ed., from MS Univ. Munich 2° 757, by Curtze, *Supplementum,* pp. xvi–xxvi. Corrections to Curtze's text can be found in Heiberg, *Paralipomena,* pp. 354–356, and *Bibliotheca mathematica,* 3rd ser., **2** (1901), 365–366. A new edition of the text has been prepared by Mario Geymonat in "Nuovi frammenti della geometria 'Boeziana' in un codice del IX secolo?" in *Scriptorium,* **21** (1967), 3–16. Geymonat dates the fragment as of the ninth century rather than the tenth; whether this be correct or not, the question that he poses of Boethius' authorship for this fragment should in all probability be answered negatively.

6. Twelfth-century Greek–Latin translation. This is found in only two extant MSS: Paris, BN lat. 7373, and Florence, Bib. Naz. Centr. Fondo Conventi Soppressi C I 448. The trans. has been analyzed in full in John Murdoch, "Euclides Graeco-Latinus. A Hitherto Unknown Medieval Latin Translation of the *Elements* Made Directly from the Greek," in *Harvard Studies in Classical Philology,* **71** (1966), 249–302. The Greek–Latin version of Ptolemy's *Almagest* made by the same translator is discussed, and its preface edited, in C. H. Haskins, *Studies in the History of Mediaeval Science* (Cambridge, Mass., 1924), ch. 9.

7. Medieval Latin versions of the Euclidean opuscula. General information on the trans. of these minor works can be found in Heiberg, *Euclides,* prolegomena to vols. VI–VIII. In fact, the text of one of the Greek–Latin renderings of the *Optica* has been ed. in Heiberg, *Euclides,* VII (1895), 3–121. The Greek–Latin version of the *Data* was first noted by A. A. Björnbo, "Die mittelalterlichen lateinischen Übersetzungen aus dem Griechischen auf dem Gebiete der mathematischen Wissenschaften," in *Festschrift Moritz Cantor* (Leipzig, 1909), p. 98. It has since been edited in the unpublished dissertation of Shuntaro Ito, "The Medieval Latin Translation of the Data of Euclid" (Madison, Wisc., 1964). The pseudo-Euclidean *De speculis*—to be distinguished from the equally spurious *Catoptrica*—has been edited in A. A. Björnbo and S. Vogl, *Alkindi, Tideus und Pseudo-Euklid. Drei optische Werke, Abhandlungen zur Geschichte der mathematischen Wissenschaften,* vol. XXVI, pt. 3 (Leipzig, 1911); cf. S. Vogl in *Festschrift Moritz Cantor* (Leipzig, 1909), pp. 127–143.

The Medieval Latin Euclid: The Arabic-Latin Phase

1. General. A brief resumé of our earlier knowledge of this wing of the medieval Latin Euclid can be found in Heath, *Euclid,* I, 93–96. The fundamental comprehensive description is now Clagett, *Medieval Euclid,* which includes appendices that present sample texts from all of the basic twelfth-century versions constituting the Arabic-Latin *Elements.*

2. The translation of Gerard of Cremona. The most complete discussion, including a listing of MSS, is Clagett, *Medieval Euclid,* pp. 27–28, 38–41. See also A. A. Björnbo, "Gerhard von Cremonas Uebersetzung von Alkwarizmis Algebra und von Euklids Elementen," in *Bibliotheca mathematica,* 3rd ser., **6** (1905), 239–248. Still useful for Gerard's life and career is B. Boncompagni, "Della vita e delle opere di Gherardo cremonense," in *Atti dell' Accademia pontificia de' Nuovi Lincei,* 1st ser., **4** (1851), 387–493. A more critical text of Gerard's *vita et libri translati* appended in a number of MSS to his trans. of Galen's *Ars parva* has been given, with annotations to the list of works trans., by F. Wüstenfeld, *Die Übersetzungen arabischer Werke in das Lateinische seit dem XI Jahrhundert. Abhandlungen der Königlichen Gesellschaft der Wissenschaften zu Göttingen* (Göttingen, 1877), pp. 57–81. For Gerard's trans. from the Arabic of commentaries on the *Elements,* see section 6 of the Arabic Euclid bibliography above.

3. *The Adelardian tradition.* The first extensive article treating of Adelard's role in the transmission of Euclid was that of Hermann Weissenborn, "Die Übersetzung des Euklid aus dem Arabischen in das Lateinische durch Adelhard von Bath . . .," in *Zeitschrift für Mathematik und Physik,* Hist.-lit. Abt., **25** (1880), 143–166. It was Clagett, *Medieval Euclid,* pp. 18–25, who first distinguished the three separate versions to be ascribed to Adelard. This article also lists a good portion of extant MSS of the three recensions. A more detailed analysis of the nature of these three versions, together with that of Campanus of Novara, is given in J. Murdoch, "The Medieval Euclid: Salient Aspects of the Translations of the *Elements* by Adelard of Bath and Campanus of Novara," in XIIᵉ Congrès International d'Histoire des Sciences, Colloques, in *Revue de synthèse,* **89** (1968), 67–94. For the misinterpretation within the Adelard tradition and within medieval mathematics in general of the Eudoxean definition of equal ratios, see J. Murdoch, "The Medieval Language of Proportions: Elements of the Interaction With Greek Foundations and the Development of New Mathematical Techniques," in A. C. Crombie, ed., *Scientific Change* (London, 1963), pp. 237–271, 334–343. The erroneous ascription of an Adelard version to Alfred the Great was set forth in Edgar Jorg, *Des Boetius und des Alfredus Magnus Kommentar zu den Elementen des Euklid (Nach dem Codex [Z. L. CCCXXXII] B. der Bibliotheca Nazionale di S. Marco zu Venedig), Zweities Buch* (Bottrop, 1935); that this particular MS contains merely both an Adelard II (Boethius) and an Adelard III (Alfred) version was established by M. Clagett, "King Alfred and the *Elements* of Euclid," in *Isis,* **45** (1954), 269–277. Works on Adelard himself are C. H. Haskins, *Studies in the History of Mediaeval Science* (Cambridge, Mass., 1924), ch. 2, and the frequently over-enthusiastic book of Franz Bliemetzrieder, *Adelard von Bath* (Munich, 1935). On the version of Campanus, in addition to the article of Murdoch cited above, see Hermann Weissenborn, *Die Uebersetzungen des Euklid durch Campano und Zamberti* (Halle, 1882). Further biobibliographical information on Campanus is contained in the text and trans. of his *Theorica planetarum,* as edited by Francis S. Benjamin, Jr., and G. J. Toomer (in press).

4. *The translation of Hermann of Carinthia.* See Clagett, *Medieval Euclid,* pp. 26–27, 38–42, and the ed. of books I–VI by H. L. L. Busard, "The Translation of the *Elements* of Euclid From the Arabic Into Latin by Hermann of Carinthia (?)," in *Janus,* **54** (1967), 1–142.

5. *Other translations and commentaries.* The supposed reference to a pre-Adelardian *Elements* in England "Yn tyme of good kyng Adelstones day" (as stated by a fourteenth-century verse) has been shown to apply to masonry, and not geometry, by F. A. Yeldham, "The Alleged Early English Version of Euclid," in *Isis,* **9** (1927), 234–238. For the problem of references to a trans. by Johannes Ocreat, see Clagett, *Medieval Euclid,* pp. 21–22. A commentary on books I–IV of the *Elements* that exists in a single MS (Vienna, Dominik. 80/45) and is there ascribed to Albertus Magnus is discussed by J. E. Hoffmann, "Ueber eine Euklid-Bearbeitung, die dem Albertus Magnus zuschrieben wird," in *Proceedings of the International Congress of Mathematicians, Cambridge, 1958,* pp. 554–566; and by B. Geyer, "Die mathematischen Schriften des Albertus Magnus," in *Angelicum,* **35** (1958), 159–175. An example of later medieval *questiones super Euclidem* are those of Nicole Oresme, recently edited (Leiden, 1961) by H. L. L. Busard; cf. J. E. Murdoch, in *Scripta mathematica,* **27** (1964), 67–91.

The Renaissance and Modern Euclid

1. *General.* There exists very little literature dealing with the transmission of Euclid from 1500 to the present; even bibliographies have not received much attention since the nineteenth century. And there is absolutely no work covering the fairly extensive body of MS materials from the sixteenth and seventeenth centuries. For the printed materials, the most adequate general works are the bibliographies cited above of Riccardi and Sanford, together with the brief survey of the principal eds. of the *Elements* in Heath, *Euclid,* I, 97–113. Dates and places of the versions of the *Elements* that are mentioned above have been given in the body of the text and will not be repeated here.

2. *Latin and Greek editions in the Renaissance and early modern period.* An outline of the major eds. is given in Heiberg, *Euclides,* V (1888), ci–cxiii. Heiberg has also treated of the significance for Euclid and Greek mathematics of Giorgio Valla and his encyclopedic *De expetendis et fugiendis rebus* in "Philologischen Studien zu griechischen Mathematikern: III. Die Handschriften George Vallas von griechischen Mathematikern," in *Jahrbuch für classische Philologie,* **12,** supp. (1881), 337–402; and *Beiträge zur Geschichte Georg Valla's und seiner Bibliothek, Centralblatt für Bibliothekswesen,* Beiheft 16 (Leipzig, 1896). On Zamberti see the monograph of Weissenborn on Campanus and this author that is cited in the section on the Adelardian tradition, above. There is no adequate work on Commandino or Clavius, especially concerning their role in the trans. and dissemination of Greek mathematics. Note has been taken, however, that in the seventeenth century the Jesuit Ricci, a student of Clavius, was instrumental in effecting a Chinese version of the latter's *Elements:* see L. Vanhee, "Euclide en chinois et mandchou," in *Isis,* **30** (1939), 84–88. The possibility of an earlier, thirteenth-century translation of Euclid into Chinese has been briefly discussed by Joseph Needham and Wang Ling, *Science and Civilisation in China,* III (Cambridge, 1959), 105.

Girolamo Saccheri's *Euclidis ab omni naevo vindicatus*

has received a modern ed. and English trans. by G. B. Halsted (Chicago, 1920). But this contains only book I of Saccheri's treatise. For book II (dealing with the theory of proportion) see Linda Allegri, "Book II of Girolamo Saccheri's *Euclides ab omni naevo vindicatus*," in *Proceedings of the Tenth International Congress of the History of Science, Ithaca, 1962*, II (Paris, 1964), 663–665; an English trans. is to be found in the same author's unpublished dissertation, "The Mathematical Works of Girolamo Saccheri, S. J. (1667–1733)" (Columbia University, 1960).

3. *Vernacular translations.* A recent detailed treatment of the appearance of the *Elements* in England up to *ca.* 1700 (in both English and Latin) is Diana M. Simpkins, "Early Editions of Euclid in England," in *Annals of Science,* **22** (1966), 225–249. Robert Recorde and his inclusion of Euclidean material in *The Pathway to Knowledg* is the subject of Joy B. Easton, "A Tudor Euclid," in *Scripta mathematica,* **27** (1964), 339–355. Most extensive attention has been paid to the 1570 English trans. by Sir Henry Billingsley. In addition to the work of Simpkins, above, see G. B. Halsted, "Note on the First English Euclid," in *American Journal of Mathematics,* **2** (1879), 46–48 (which contains the first notice of the volumes at Princeton with marginalia in Billingsley's hand); W. F. Shenton, "The First English Euclid," in *American Mathematical Monthly,* **35** (1928), 505–512; R. C. Archibald, "The First Translation of Euclid's *Elements* Into English and Its Source," in *American Mathematical Monthly,* **57** (1950), 443–452. See also Edward Rosen, "John Dee and Commandino," in *Scripta mathematica,* **28** (1970), 325. An annotated bibliography of French trans. of Euclid is Marie Lacoarret, "Les traductions françaises des oeuvres d'Euclide," in *Revue d'histoire des sciences,* **10** (1957), 38–58. I. J. Depman has written of unnoticed Russian eds. of the *Elements* in *Istoriko-matematicheskie issledovaniya,* **3** (1950), 467–473.

4. *The nineteenth and twentieth centuries.* The most complete survey of the great number of nineteenth-century school-text Euclids is still to be found in the Riccardi bibliography (introductory section above). The most notable twentieth-century trans. that contain considerable historical and analytic annotation are, in English, Heath, *Euclid;* in Italian, Federigo Enriques, *et al.,* eds., *Gli Elementi d'Euclide e la critica antica e moderna,* 4 vols. (Rome–Bologna, 1925–1935); in Dutch, E. J. Dijksterhuis, *De Elementen van Euclides,* 2 vols. (Groningen, 1929–1930); in Russian, D. D. Morduchai-Boltovskogo, *Nachala Evklida,* 3 vols. (Moscow–Leningrad, 1948–1950); in French, of books VII–IX only, Jean Itard, *Les livres arithmétiques d'Euclide* (Paris, 1961).

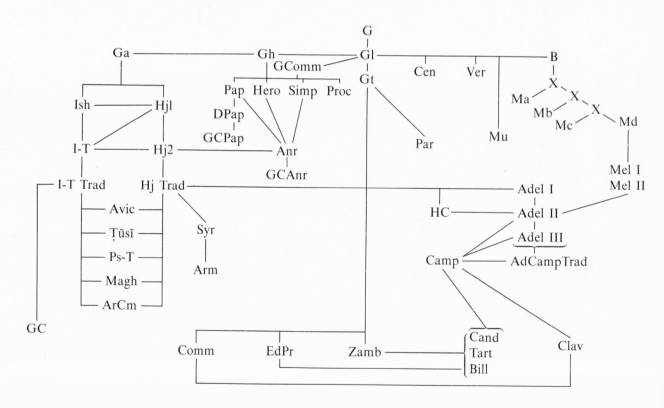

Filiation of the Major Versions of Euclid's *Elements* in the Middle Ages and the Renaissance. Note: Some of the lines of filiation indicated are conjectural. No attempt has been made to differentiate them from those definitely known to be true.

AdCampTrad	= Variant versions deriving from those of Adelard and Campanus
Adel I	= First translation of Adelard of Bath
Adel II	= *Commentum* of Adelard of Bath
Adel III	= *Editio specialis* of Adelard of Bath
Anr	= Commentary of al-Nayrīzī
ArCm	= Arabic commentaries
Arm	= Armenian version presumably made by Gregory Magistros
Avic	= Epitome of Avicenna
B	= Translation of Boethius
Bill	= English translation of Henry Billingsley
Camp	= Version of Campanus of Novara
Cand	= Version of Franciscus Flussatus Candalla
Cen	= Fragments in Censorinus
Clav	= Edition of Christopher Clavius
Comm	= Translation of Federico Commandino
DPap	= Translation by al-Dimashqī of book X of Pappus' commentary
EdPr	= *Editio princeps* of Greek text by Simon Grynaeus
G	= Original Greek text
Gl	= Pre-Theonine Greek text
Ga	= Greek text employed for Arabic translations
GC	= Translation by Gerard of Cremona of Isḥāq-Thābit text
GCAnr	= Gerard of Cremona's translation of al-Nayrīzī's commentary
GComm	= Greek commentaries
GCPap	= Gerard of Cremona's translation of (part of) Dimashqī's translation of Pappus on book X
Gh	= Greek text utilized by Hero of Alexandria
Gt	= Redaction of Greek text by Theon of Alexandria
HC	= Version of Hermann of Carinthia
Hero	= Hero of Alexandria's commentary
Hj1	= First version of Ḥajjāj
Hj2	= Second version of Ḥajjāj
Hj Trad	= Ḥajjāj Arabic tradition
Ish	= Translation of Isḥāq ibn Ḥunayn
I-T	= Translation of Isḥāq as revised by Thābit ibn Qurra
I-T Trad	= Isḥāq-Thābit tradition
Ma	= Boethian excerpts preserved in Cassiodorus
Magh	= *Taḥrīr* of al-Maghribī
Mb	= Boethian excerpts preserved in *Agrimensores* material
Mc	= Boethian excerpts in five-book geometry of "Boethius"
Md	= Boethian excerpts in two-book geometry of "Boethius"
Mel I	= Boethian–Adelardian mélanges in MS Lüneburg D 4° 48
Mel II	= Boethian–Adelardian mélanges in Paris and Munich MSS
Mu	= Fragments of translation in MS Univ. Munich 2° 757
Pap	= Greek commentary of Pappus of Alexandria
Par	= Anonymous Greek–Latin translation of twelfth century
Proc	= Greek commentary of Proclus on book I
Ps-T	= Thirteen-book *Taḥrīr* erroneously ascribed to al-Ṭūsī
Simp	= Commentary of Simplicius on the premises
Syr	= Syriac redaction
Tart	= Italian translation by Niccolò Tartaglia
Ṭūsī	= Genuine fifteen-book *Taḥrīr* by al-Ṭūsī
Ver	= Verona palimpsest of fifth century
X	= Ancestors not further specified here
Zamb	= Translation of Bartolomeo Zamberti of Theonine text

JOHN MURDOCH

EUCTEMON (*fl.* Athens, fifth century B.C.), *astronomy.*

Euctemon is cited (with Meton) by Ptolemy for observations of the summer solstice, including that of 27 June 432 B.C., the reliability of which was doubted by both Ptolemy (*Almagest,* III, 1) and Hipparchus (modern calculations show that the solstice actually occurred about a day and a half later) but which was still used, as the earliest observation available, to confirm the final Hipparchian-Ptolemaic figure of 365.25 less 1/300 of a day for the length of the solar year. Euctemon collaborated with Meton in suggesting a regular intercalation cycle of nineteen years (the Metonic cycle) to correlate the lunar month with the solar year (see B. L. Van der Waerden, in *Journal of Hellenic Studies,* **80** [1960],

170); this cycle contained 235 lunar months (seven of which were intercalary) and 6,940 days, giving a mean lunar month about two minutes too long and a solar year of 365 5/19 days (some thirty minutes too long). According to Geminus (*Isagoge*, VIII, 50), who connects Euctemon but not Meton with this cycle (Meton's name may have dropped out of the text; see Manitius, *ad loc.*), 110 of the months were "hollow" (i.e., twenty-nine days each) and 125 "full" (thirty days).

Euctemon is frequently cited—some forty-five times in the calendar attached to Geminus' *Isagoge* (Manitius, ed., pp. 210 ff.), over fifty times in Ptolemy's *Phaseis,* and often in the other Greek calendars (published in *Sitzungsberichte der Heidelberger Akademie der Wissenschaften,* phil.-hist. Klasse, **1** [1910]; **2** [1911]; **3A** [1913], which contains a conjectural restoration by Rehm of Euctemon's "parapegma"; **4** [1914]; and **5** [1920])—for "weather prognostications" (ἐπισημασίαι) such as formed part of a parapegma, which was a type of almanac, originally engraved on stone or wood, and later transmitted in manuscript form, giving astronomical and meteorological phenomena for the days of each month. His and Meton's parapegma may well have been the first influential text of this kind in Greece (see A. Rehm, "Parapegmastudien," in *Abhandlungen der Bayerischen Akademie der Wissenschaften,* phil.-hist. Abt., n.s. **19** [1941]).

Euctemon is the earliest name mentioned in connection with equinoxes in the extant parapegmata and, according to a second-century B.C. papyrus known as the *Ars Eudoxi* (F. Blass, ed. [Kiel, 1887]—perhaps a student's exercise, containing many errors, partly based on Eudoxus' work with later material added), he gave the lengths of the astronomical seasons, starting from the summer solstice, as ninety, ninety, ninety-two, and ninety-three days, respectively. This shows that he was aware of the nonuniformity of the sun's course round the earth, but it is unlikely that his parapegma was arranged according to zodiacal months, as later ones were. Ptolemy says (*Phaseis,* in *Claudii Ptolemaei opera quae extant omnia,* J. L. Heiberg, ed., II [Leipzig, 1907], 67) that Euctemon made observations at Athens, in the Cyclades, and in Macedonia and Thrace. Rehm thinks that the pseudo-Theophrastian treatise *De signis* (*Theophrasti Eresii opera quae supersunt omnia,* F. Wimmer, ed., III [Leipzig, 1862], fr. 6, pp. 115–130) conceals an original meteorological work by Euctemon, but this is pure conjecture.

Euctemon also did some work in geography and is cited by Avienus (fourth century A.D., but using much older sources) for information concerning the straits of Gibraltar (*Ora maritima,* 337, 350 ff.). Avienus calls him both an Athenian (47–48, 350) and an inhabitant of Amphipolis (337), and he may have been among the Athenian colonists who established a new foundation there in 437 B.C.

BIBLIOGRAPHY

In addition to the works cited in the text, see A. Rehm, "Euktemon 10," in Pauly-Wissowa, XI (1907), cols. 1060–1061.

D. R. Dicks

EUDEMUS OF RHODES (*b.* Rhodes; *fl.* second half of fourth century B.C.), *philosophy, history of science.*

From the title so often given in antiquity to Eudemus the Peripatetic philosopher, it is a fair deduction that he was born at Rhodes; and this is specifically attested by Strabo.[1] The dates of his birth and death are unknown, but his links with Aristotle and Theophrastus show when he flourished.

Nothing is known of his background save that he had a brother Boethus, who had a son, Pasicles.[2] He became a pupil of Aristotle, although whether first at Assos, Mitylene, or Athens must remain uncertain.[3] He won the master's good opinion to such an extent that he and Theophrastus of Lesbos were known as Aristotle's "companions."[4] It is disputed whether it was to him or to Eudemus of Cyprus that Aristotle addressed the moving verses, generally known as the "altar elegy," in which he expressed his veneration for Plato at a time when he had felt compelled to diverge from the Platonic philosophy, but on balance Eudemus of Rhodes would seem to be thus favored. (It is, however, the Cypriot and not the Rhodian Eudemus in whose honor Aristotle's early philosophical dialogue "Eudemus" is named.)

Aulus Gellius recounts that as Aristotle approached death, his disciples gathered round him and asked him to choose his successor; they agreed that Theophrastus and Eudemus were preeminent among them. A little later, when they were again assembled, Aristotle asked for some Rhodian and some Lesbian wine to be brought to him. He pronounced both to be civilized wines—the Rhodian strong and joyful, but the Lesbian sweeter, thus indicating Theophrastus as his successor.[5] Eudemus took the choice of Theophrastus in good part, for Andronicus of Rhodes, in a lost work quoted by Simplicius, records a letter that Eudemus wrote to Theophrastus asking that an accurate copy of passages in the fifth book of Aristotle's *Physics* be sent to him on account of errors in his own manuscript.[6] It is usually deduced from this passage that after Aristotle's death Eudemus set up his own school elsewhere (perhaps in his native Rhodes).

The main importance of Eudemus in the history of thought is that he, Theophrastus, Strato, Phanias, and others brought Aristotle's lectures, lecture notes, their own records, and the recollections of themselves and others to a state fit for publication, thus making the works of Aristotle available to the world. One of the three ethical works in the Aristotelian corpus, the *Eudemian Ethics,* actually bears Eudemus' name,[7] but the significance of the title, which is first attested by Atticus Platonicus[8] in the age of the Antonines, is still an open question, complicated by the fact that books IV–VI are identical with books V–VII of the *Nicomachean Ethics.* At various times it was thought that the treatise was a genuine work of Aristotle dedicated to Eudemus, or that Eudemus was himself its author, or that it was a work of Aristotle edited by Eudemus (opening to discussion whether Eudemus cited the master's words exactly or used them as the basis for what is substantially a work of his own, as he did with the *Physics,* see below).

But in 1841 L. Spengel pronounced the *Eudemian Ethics* to be a restatement of Aristotle's teaching with extensive additions by Eudemus. This view so prevailed that the Greek texts of Fritzsche (1851) and Susemihl (1884) were both entitled *Eudemi Rhodii Ethica,* and the English commentaries on the *Nicomachean Ethics* by Sir Alexander Grant (1857), J. A. Stewart (1892), and J. Burnet (1900) all took it for granted that Eudemus was the author.

Later P. von der Mühl (1909), E. Kapp (1912), and, most notably, W. Jaeger (1923) sought to restore the authenticity of the *Eudemian Ethics.*[9] Jaeger considered it to be intermediate to the ethics *more geometrico demonstrata* in the *Protrepticus,* as recovered from Iamblichus, and the final version of Aristotle's moral teaching in the *Nicomachean Ethics.* This notion of three stages in the development of Aristotle's ethics no longer convinces, and it is generally held nowadays that the differences between the *Eudemian Ethics,* the *Nicomachean Ethics,* and the *Magna moralia* are to be explained by the audiences to which they were addressed; but the belief that the *Eudemian Ethics* is a genuine work of Aristotle has been reinforced by a detailed examination of its language. Its style, in the nature of lecture notes with no literary graces, supports the hypothesis of Aristotelian authorship. It is cited or referred to in other works of Aristotle, notably the *Politics.*[10] If Eudemus were the author of the *Eudemian Ethics,* it is hardly conceivable that he would have allowed such an expression as καθάπερ διαιρούμεθα καὶ ἐν τοῖς ἐξωτερικοῖς

λόγοις, "as we have distinguished in the published writings."[11]

No recent commentators have produced a convincing solution; and it may now be regarded as certain, on grounds of style apart from other considerations, that Eudemus was not the author. In all probability it should be regarded as an authentic work of Aristotle, possibly edited after his death as Gigon believes;[12] why Eudemus' name came to be attached to it remains a puzzle.

Although the moral teaching of the *Eudemian Ethics* is fundamentally the same as that of the other ethical treatises, the final book differs in that it holds up as the ideal τὴν τοῦ θεοῦ θεωρίαν, "the contemplation of God." This has led to a picture of the Rhodian philosopher as the "pious Eudemus" which would lose its force if von Arnim is right in detecting the substitution of θεός ("God") for νοῦς ("mind") by a Christian interpolator.[13]

The sixth-century commentator Asclepius, noting the lack of orderliness and continuity in Aristotle's *Metaphysics,* relates that Aristotle, being himself conscious of these faults, sent the work to Eudemus for his opinion. Eudemus judged it unsuitable to publish such a work to all and sundry—thus implying a belief in an esoteric Aristotelian doctrine—and Asclepius adds that after Aristotle's death, when parts of the work were found to be missing, the school's survivors filled the gaps with extracts from his other works.[14] This is improbable, since the esoteric doctrine did not arise until later and, moreover, such a story would imply that Eudemus left Athens while Aristotle was still head of the school—a contradiction of evidence already given; nor does the *Metaphysics* draw on other works. Another commentator, Alexander of Aphrodisias, implies that Eudemus did some editorial work on the treatise; this is more likely, and accords with a scholium to one of the oldest manuscripts stating that most scholars attributed the second book, α minor, to his nephew Pasicles.[15]

Eudemus wrote a *Physics,* in four books, that covered the same ground as Aristotle's treatise, the first book corresponding to Aristotle's I and II, the second to Aristotle's III and V, the third to Aristotle's IV, and the fourth to Aristotle's VI and VIII, which confirms the belief that VII is not genuine. Simplicius used Eudemus' work extensively in his elucidation of Aristotle; some ninety fragments are gathered together by Wehrli. It is thus possible substantially to reconstruct Eudemus' treatise, but as it so largely overlaps that of Aristotle it is not necessary to discuss the contents here.

Eudemus made contributions of his own to the Aristotelian logic. He wrote a book—or possibly two separate books[16]—on analytics and the categories and another entitled *On Discourse,* which seems to have dealt with the same topics as Aristotle's *De interpretatione.* That Galen wrote a commentary on it is evidence that it had some vogue in antiquity.[17]

According to Boethius, Theophrastus and Eudemus (in one place "or Eudemus") added five moods to the four in the first syllogistic figure,[18] and a Greek fragment of unknown authorship adds that they were later made into a fourth figure.[19] The four moods of the first figure are those known since Peter of Spain as Barbara, Celarent, Darii, and Ferio. Boethius explains that the five new moods are obtained by conversion of the terms of the four original moods. Thus, if *A* is in all *B* and *B* is in all *C,* it follows that *A* is in all *C* (Barbara); and by conversion, if *A* is in all *B* and *B* is in all *C,* we may conclude that *C* is in some *A.* This is the fifth mood, Bramantip, and in the same way the sixth, seventh, eighth, and ninth moods (Carmenes, Dimaris, Fesapo, and Fresison) may be obtained. (It has sometimes been queried why Aristotle himself did not group these last five moods in a fourth figure, for they are implicit in his work; Fesapo and Fresison are specifically mentioned by him, and he explicitly states that a syllogism always results from conversion of the premises.)[20]

The work of Theophrastus and Eudemus on the new moods is bound up with the distinction that they developed between necessary and merely factual premises and conclusions. Aristotle believed that there were combinations of an apodeictic and an assertoric premise which led to an apodeictic conclusion. For the first figure he laid down the rule that an apodeictic major and an assertoric minor may lead to an apodeictic conclusion, while the combination of an assertoric major and an apodeictic minor cannot. According to Alexander of Aphrodisias, the followers of Eudemus and Theophrastus took the opposite view, holding that if either the major or the minor premise is assertoric the conclusion must also be assertoric. Similarly they held that if either premise is negative the conclusion must also be negative, and if either premise is particular the conclusion must be particular. They summarized their doctrine in the saying that the conclusion must be like the "inferior premise,"[21] or as it was later put into Latin, *peiorem semper sequitur conclusio partem.*

Another divergence between Aristotle and his two leading pupils arose over problematic syllogisms. For Aristotle, the proposition "That all *B* should be *A* is contingent" entails "That no *B* should be *A* is contingent"; and "That some *B* should not be *A* is contingent," with related propositions; and the proposition "That no *B* should be *A* is contingent" does not imply "That no *A* should be *B* is contingent." According to

Alexander, Theophrastus and Eudemus rejected this departure from the general principle that universal negative propositions are simply convertible and particular negative propositions not convertible. They have found a supporter in modern times in H. Maier, but W. D. Ross regards Aristotle as completely justified.[22] It depends upon what Aristotle is understood to mean by contingency, and it is unfortunate that Alexander's book, *On the Disagreement Concerning Mixed Moods . . .* has not survived.

It is remarkable that in their development of Aristotle's logic the names of Theophrastus and Eudemus are so often conjoined. Although there are many references to Theophrastus alone, only one to Eudemus alone is recorded; it may thus rightly be inferred that Theophrastus had the major share in the work. Bochenski supposes that the *Organon* represents Aristotle's earlier logical thinking and that in his later lectures he advanced beyond it; and that Theophrastus and Eudemus, who were present at these lectures, separately represent the mature development of Aristotle's logical thought. The coincidence of their views, he thinks, cannot be explained by chance or close and prolonged collaboration.[23]

From a long passage in Damascius[24] it may be inferred that Eudemus wrote a history of theology that appears to have dealt with the origins of the universe and to have ranged over the views of the Babylonians, Egyptians, and Greeks. A single reference in Proclus[25] establishes that Eudemus wrote one purely mathematical work—*On the Angle*—in which he took the view that angularity is a quality rather than a quantity (since angularity arises from an inclination of lines, and since both straightness and inclination are qualities, so also must angularity be).

Eudemus is also important for his studies in the history of science. He wrote three works—a history of arithmetic, a history of geometry, and a history of astronomy—which are of capital value for the transmission of the facts about early Greek science. Although, like all of Eudemus' works, they have been lost, it is mainly through the use made of them by later writers that we possess any knowledge of the rise of Greek geometry and astronomy. Eudemus is not known to have had any predecessors in this field,[26] and he may justly be regarded as the father of the history of science, or at the least as sharing the paternity with his fellow Peripatetics Theophrastus, author of *Views of the Physicists,* and Menon, author of a history of medicine.

The *History of Arithmetic* is known from only one reference, made by Porphyry in his commentary on Ptolemy's *Harmonics,*[27] stating that in the first book Eudemus dealt with the Pythagorean correlation of numbers with musical intervals.

The *History of Geometry,* in at least two books, is known from many ancient references and citations. According to Simplicius, it was written in a summary style like a memorandum.[28] A passage in Proclus' commentary on the first book of Euclid's *Elements*[29] was formerly known as "the Eudemian summary" in the belief that it was an extract from this work. This cannot be so, since it leads up to the work of Euclid, who was later than Eudemus, and there is no stylistic break in the narrative. The earlier part—up to the sentence where Proclus writes, "Those who have compiled histories carry the development of this science up to this point" (*sc.* Philippus of Opus, who lived just before Euclid)—would appear to be a condensation of Eudemus' narrative, written soon after his death, for it is unlikely that a later writer would have stopped at that precise date. The summary tells how Thales introduced the study of geometry from Egypt into Greece and recounts the work of his successors, without, however, ever referring to Democritus. This omission offers further proof that the passage cannot be taken directly from Eudemus, since he would certainly have mentioned this mathematical pioneer who was held in high esteem by Aristotle (although Proclus might not).

One of the most important chapters in the history of Greek mathematics—the work of Hippocrates of Chios on the quadrature of lunes—is known through Eudemus. It is known from the use made of it by Simplicius in his commentary on Aristotle's *Physics.*[30] Simplicius reproduces passages from Eudemus, who may himself be giving the words of Hippocrates along with comments of his own; and many scholars have addressed themselves to the task of separating what Eudemus wrote from what Simplicius added.

From surviving references, Eudemus is also known to have recorded in his *History of Geometry* the theorem that if two triangles have two angles and one side equal, the remaining angle and sides will also be equal (Euclid I.26), discovered by Thales and used by him to find the distances of ships from the shore;[31] the theorem that if two straight lines intersect the vertical and opposite angles are equal (Euclid I.15), discovered but not proved by Thales;[32] the theorem that the interior angles of a triangle are equal to two right angles (Euclid I.32), first proved by the Pythagoreans by means of a line drawn parallel to the base;[33] the "application of areas" (i.e., the erection on a straight line, or on a segment thereof, or on the straight line produced, of a parallelogram with a given angle equal to a given area, which is a species of geometrical algebra), also the discovery of the Pythagoreans;[34] the problem of drawing a straight line perpendicular to a given straight line from a point outside it (Euclid I.12), first investigated by Oeno-

pides,[35] who also first discovered the Euclidean method of constructing a rectilinear angle equal to a given rectilinear angle (Euclid I.23).[36]

Tannery thought that the *History of Geometry* was already lost by the time of Pappus, and that for his knowledge of such matters as the quadrature of the circle and the duplication of the cube Pappus relied on a compilation entitled Ἀριστοτελικὰ κήρια ("Aristotelian apiary"), drawn up, perhaps toward the end of the third century B.C., by his older contemporary Sporus of Nicaea, who in turn would have drawn on Eudemus. This failed to convince Heiberg, who made out a strong case for believing that both Pappus and Eutocius had the text of Eudemus before them.[37]

Eudemus' *History of Astronomy,* also in at least two books, is of further value, through its use by later writers, as a source book. It is, for example, through this work that Oenopides is known to have discovered the obliquity of the ecliptic; and Eudemus recorded its value as being that of the side of a fifteen-sided polygon, that is, twenty-four degrees.[38] Eudemus' history is also the ultimate source, through its use by the Peripatetic philosopher Sosigenes (second century A.D.), of Simplicius' account of Eudoxus' system of concentric spheres on which the poles of the heavenly bodies rotate—the first attempt to account mathematically for the solar, lunar, and planetary motions.[39] Among other topics known to have been dealt with by Eudemus are solar eclipses, particularly Thales' prediction of the eclipse of 28 May 585 B.C.; the cycle of the great year after which all the heavenly bodies are found in the same relative positions; the realization by Anaximander that the earth is a heavenly body moving about the middle of the universe; the discovery by Anaximenes that the moon reflects the light of the sun and his explanation of lunar eclipses; and the inequality of the times between the solstices and the equinoxes.[40]

Aelian, writing in the second or third century A.D., has seven references to a work on animals written by Eudemus,[41] but it has been questioned whether he is to be identified with Eudemus of Rhodes. Apuleius mentions "Aristotle and Theophrastus and Eudemus and Lyco and other lesser Platonists" as having written on the birth and nourishment of animals,[42] and as, in the context, Eudemus of Rhodes must be understood, this would support the identification; but the citations given by Aelian are of fabulous stories about animals which do not fit in well with the serious scientific character of Eudemus of Rhodes.

A history of Lindos was written by a certain Eudemus. Wilamowitz was prepared to believe that this was Eudemus of Rhodes, but Wehrli thinks it highly improbable. There is no evidence on which the question can be settled, as Felix Jacoby sees it;

463

but since Lindos was a port, with a famous temple, in Eudemus' native Rhodes, there is nothing improbable in the suggestion that so prolific an author as Eudemus should have recorded its history, perhaps after his return from Athens.[43]

NOTES

1. Strabo, XIV 2, 13.
2. Asclepius, *In Aristotelis Metaphysica,* I.1, 980ª 22, Hayduck ed., 4.18–22; Scholium to Aristotle's *Metaphysics* α, 993ª 30, *Scholia in Aristotelem (Aristotelis opera IV),* Brandis ed., 589 a 41–43.
3. W. Jaeger, *Aristoteles,* 109 n. 2, takes the view that he (and Theophrastus) became students of Aristotle at Assos; but this seems to be bound up with his view of the date of the *Eudemian Ethics,* and there is no real evidence one way or the other.
4. Ammonius, *In Aristotelis Analytica priora,* I.9, 30ª 15, Wallies ed., 38.38–39, οἱ δ'ἑταῖροι αὐτοῦ, Θεόφραστος καὶ Εὔδημος, is one of many passages in which the expression is used.
5. Aulus Gellius, *Noctes Atticae,* XIII.5, Marshall ed., II. 387, 1–29; Boethius, *De syllogismo hypothetico,* I, in Migne ed., *Patrologia latina,* LXIV, 831D, noted that Theophrastus was a man capable of all learning but tackling only the peaks, whereas Eudemus followed a broader road of learning; but it was as though he scattered seminal ideas without gathering any great harvest. This passage of Boethius, referring to the *Analytica,* is the only evidence of any difference between Theophrastus and Eudemus in the field of logic.
6. Simplicius, *In Aristotelis Physica,* VI, proemium, Diels ed., 923.7–16.
7. It has almost universally been assumed that "Eudemian" refers to Eudemus of Rhodes, but, as Dirlmeier points out, there is no precise evidence whether Eudemus of Rhodes or Eudemus of Cyprus is indicated by the title. He himself makes the suggestion—which has not found favor—that as *Eudemian Ethics* I.5 is a pessimistic reflection on the theme, "It is best not to be born," which plays an impressive part in the dialogue "Eudemus" but not in the other two ethical works, the *Eudemian Ethics* was intended to be a posthumous tribute to his friend the Cypriot (F. Dirlmeier, *Aristoteles magna moralia,* 2nd ed., 1966, p. 97).
8. As preserved by Eusebius, *Praeparatio evangelica XV,* in *Patrologia graeca,* Migne ed., XXI, 1305 A, Dindorf ed., I.344. 24–26: αἱ γοῦν Ἀριστοτέλους περὶ ταῦτα πραγματείαι, Εὐδήμειοί τε καὶ Νικομάχειοι καὶ Μεγάλων Ἠθικῶν ἐπιγραφόμεναι.
9. L. Spengel, "Uber die unter dem Namen des Aristoteles erhaltenen ethischen Schriften," in *Abhandlungen der Bayrischen Akademie der Wissenschaften,* **3** (Munich, 1841), 439–551; P. von der Mühl, *De Aristotelis Ethicorum Eudemiorum auctoritate* (Göttingen, 1909); E. Kapp, *Das Verhaltnis der eudemischen zur nikomanischen Ethik* (Freiburg, 1912); W. Jaeger, *Aristoteles* (Berlin, 1923; 2nd ed., 1955), pp. 237–270, trans. by R. Robinson (Oxford, 1934; 2nd ed., 1948), pp. 228–258.
10. F. Dirlmeier, *Aristoteles Eudemische Ethik,* pp. 112–115; for quotations in the treatise see the same author, "Merkwurdige Zitate in der Eudemischen Ethik des Aristoteles" in *Sitzungsberichte der Heidelberger Akademie der Wissenschaften,* phil.-hist. Klasse (1962), Abh. 2.
11. *Ethica Eudemia,* 1218ᵇ 33–34, Susemihl ed., 16, B. 3–4.
12. O. Gigon, *Aristoteles Die Nikomachische Ethik,* p. 39.
13. H. von Arnim, *Die drei Aristotelischen Ethiken,* p. 68.
14. Asclepius, *In Aristotelis Metaphysica,* I.1, 980ª 22, Hayduck ed., 4.4–15.
15. See note 2. Asclepius in the passage referred to in the same note says that it was book A which Pasicles was alleged to have written, but this, he adds, is untrue.
16. Alexander, *In Aristotelis Analytica priora,* Wallies ed., 31.4–10,

124.8–15, 126.29–127.2, 141.1–5, 173.32–174.3, 220.9–16, 389.31–390.3; Alexander, *In Aristotelis Topica,* Wallies ed., 131.14–19; Philoponus, *In Aristotelis Analytica priora,* Wallies ed., 48.12–18, 123.12–20, 129.15–19; Ammonius, *In Aristotelis Analytica priora,* Wallies ed., 38.38–39.2, 45.42–45, 49.6–12; Olympiodorus, *Prolegomena,* Busse ed., 13.24–25. Eudemus is named by Philoponus, *In Aristotelis Categorias,* proemium, Busse ed., 7.16, along with Phanias and Theophrastus as the author of Κατηγορίαι, Περὶ ἑρμηνείας, and Ἀναλυτικά. He is named by David, *In Porphyrii Isagogen,* Busse ed., 102.4 with Theophrastus alone as the author of Κατηγορίαι; but the individual citations catalogued above make it likely that the Ἀναλυτικά and the Κατηγορίαι are the same work.
17. Alexander, *In Aristotelis Topica,* Wallies ed., 69.13–16, *In Aristotelis Analytica priora,* Wallies ed., 16.12–17, *In Aristotelis Metaphysica,* Hayduck ed., 85.9–11; scholium *In Aristotelis Analytica priora* 1, codex 1917, Brandis ed., 146a 24. As seen in the previous note, Philoponus refers to this work by the same title as that of Aristotle, Περὶ ἑρσηνείας, but this would appear to refer to its subject matter and the title Περὶ λεξέως is better attested.
18. Boethius, *De syllogismo categorico,* II, Migne ed., *Patrologia latina,* LXIV, 813 C ("Theophrastus vel Eudemus"), 814 C ("Theophrastus et Eudemus"), 815 B ("Theophrastus et Eudemus"). Alexander, *In Analytica priora,* I.4, 26ᵇ 30, Wallies ed., 69. 26, attributes the five additional moods to Theophrastus without mention of Eudemus.
19. For references to later publications and discussions of this anonymous Greek fragment see N. Rescher, *Galen and the Syllogism* (Pittsburgh, 1966), p. 2, n. 9.
20. Aristotle, *Analytica priora,* I, 29ª 23.
21. Alexander, *In Aristotelis Analytica priora,* Wallies ed., 124 8–127.16. W. D. Ross, *Aristotle's Prior and Posterior Analytics,* pp. 41–42, suggests that the distinction between Aristotle and his followers is not so sharp as might at first appear.
22. Alexander, *In Aristotelis Analytica Priora,* Wallies ed., 159.8–13, 220.9–221.5; H. Maier, *Die Syllogistik des Aristoteles,* IIa, 37–47; W. D. Ross, *Aristotle's Prior and Posterior Analytics,* p. 45.
23. I. M. Bochenski, *La logique de Théophraste,* p. 125.
24. Damascius, *Dubitationes et solutiones de primis principiis* 124–125, Ruelle ed., I, 319.8–323.17.
25. Proclus, *In primum Euclidis,* definition 8, Friedlein ed., 125.6.
26. It is reading too much into Proclus, *In primum Euclidis,* Friedlein ed., 65.14, to suppose that Hippias wrote a history of mathematics.
27. Porphyry, *In Ptolemaei Harmonica,* Düring ed., in *Göteborgs högskolas Årsskrift,* **38** (1932), 114.23–115.9.
28. Simplicius, *In Aristotelis Physica,* Diels ed., 60.42–44.
29. Proclus, *In primum Euclidis,* Friedlein ed., 64.16–70.18, trans. by Glenn R. Morrow as *Proclus' A Commentary on the First Book of Euclid's Elements* (Princeton, 1970), pp. 51–70.
30. Simplicius, *In Aristotelis Physica,* Diels ed., 60.22–68.32.
31. Proclus, *In primum Euclidis,* Friedlein ed., 352.14–16, the application of the theorem to the distances of ships raises problems, for which see Thomas Heath, *A History of Greek Mathematics,* I, 131–133.
32. Proclus, *In primum Euclidis,* Friedlein ed., 299.1–5.
33. *Ibid.,* 379.2–16.
34. *Ibid.,* 419.15–18.
35. *Ibid.,* 283.7–8. In this case Eudemus is not specifically mentioned as the source, although he must be.
36. *Ibid.,* 333.5–9.
37. Paul Tannery, "Sur les fragments d'Eudème de Rhodes relatifs à l'histoire des mathématiques," in *Annales de la Faculté des Lettres de Bordeaux,* **4** (1882), 70–76, reprinted in *Mémoires scientifiques,* I (Toulouse-Paris, 1912), 156–177; "Sur Sporos de Nicée," in *Annales de la Faculté des Lettres de Bordeaux,* **4** (1882), 257–261, repr. in *Mémoires scientifiques,* I (Toulouse-Paris, 1912), 178–184; *Bulletin des sciences,* **7** (1883), 283–284, repr. in *Mémoires scientifiques,* II (Toulouse-Paris, 1912), 4–5; J. L. Heiberg, in *Philologus,* **43** (1884), 345–346.
38. Theon of Smyrna, *Expositio rerum mathematicarum,* Hiller ed.,

198.14–15, 199.6–8, with Diels's conjecture of Λόξωσιν for διάξωσιν.

39. Simplicius, *In Aristotelis De caelo*, Heiberg ed., 488.18–24, 493.4–506.18. A brief account is given by Aristotle, *Metaphysics*, Λ8, 1073ᵇ17–1074ᵃ 14. For translations and explanations see G. Schiaparelli, *Le sfere omocentriche di Eudosso, di Callippo e di Aristotele*, and T. L. Heath, *Aristarchus of Samos*, 193–211; *A History of Greek Mathematics*, I, 329–334; and *Greek Astronomy*, 65–70.

40. Clement of Alexandria, *Stromata*, I, 14, 65.1, Stählin ed., II (Berlin, 1960), 41.8–15; Diogenes Laertius, I, 23, Long ed., 9.18–21; Theon of Smyrna, Hiller ed., 198.16–199.2; Simplicius, *In Aristotelis De caelo*, Heiberg ed., 471.1–6.

41. Aelian, *On the Characteristics of Animals*, III, 20, 21; IV, 8, 45, 53, 56; V, 7.

42. Apuleius, *Apologia*, 36.

43. *Die Fragmente der griechischen Historiker*, Jacoby, ed., IIIB (Leiden, 1950), nos. 524, 532B-C 10, C32, D1, D2, Εὔδημος ἐν τῷ Λινδιακῷ (*sc. λόγῳ*) pp. 503, 508, 510, 512, 513, *Kommentar*, IIIb (Leiden, 1955), 441–442, and *Noten*, IIIb (Leiden, 1955), 259. Jacoby's conclusion is, "Bei Eudemos denkt man natürlich zuerst an der Schüler des Aristoteles . . . Aber der Name ist gewöhnlich, und es fehlt an entscheidenden Gründen für die Identifikation." For Wilamowitz see "Nachrichten über Versammlungen," reporting a paper by U. von Wilamowitz-Moellendorff to the Archäologische Gesellschaft zu Berlin, 4 March 1913, in *Berliner philologische Wochenschrift* (1913), col. 1372.

BIBLIOGRAPHY

I. ORIGINAL WORKS. From references in ancient writers Eudemus is believed to have written the following works. None has survived except in quotations or paraphrases. There are variants for the Greek titles, but those given are the most probable. A few of the titles are uncertain and are preceded by a question mark: (1) Ἀναλυτικά (?Κατηγορίαι)—possibly a separate work; (2) Περὶ λέξεως; (3) Φυσικά; (4) History of Theology; (5) Περὶ γωνίας; (6) Ἀριθμητικὴ ἱστορία; (7) Γεωμετρικὴ ἱστορία; (8) Ἀστρολογικὴ ἱστορία; (9) (?) Stories of Animals.

In addition, for a reason which cannot now be ascertained, the name of Eudemus is attached to the Ἠθικὰ Εὐδήμεια (or Εὐδημία) of Aristotle. The best text of the Eudemian ethics is still that of F. Susemihl, [*Aristotelis Ethica Eudemia*] *Eudemi Rhodii Ethica* (Leipzig, 1884), but a new critical ed. by R. Walzer for the Oxford Classical Texts series is now in press.

Quotations from Eudemus by ancient writers have been collated in L. Spengel, *Eudemi Rhodii Peripatetici Fragmenta quae supersunt* (Berlin, 1866; 2nd ed., 1870); F. W. A. Mullach, in *Fragmenta philosophorum Graecorum*, III (Paris, 1881), 222–292; and, most recently and most satisfactorily, in Fritz Wehrli, *Eudemos von Rhodos*, in *Die Schule des Aristoteles, Texte und Kommentar*, VIII (Basel, 1955; 2nd ed., 1969).

II. SECONDARY LITERATURE. According to Simplicius, a life of Eudemus was written in antiquity by an otherwise unknown Damas. It has not survived. Modern studies of Eudemus by A. T. H. Fritzsche, *De Eudemi Rhodii philosophi Peripatetici vita et scriptis* (Regensburg, 1851); C. A. Brandis, *Handbuch der Geschichte der Griechisch-Römischen Philosophie*, III, 1 (Berlin, 1860), 215–250; E. Zeller, *Die Philosophie der Griechen in ihrer geschichtlichen*

Entwicklung, II, 2, 3rd ed. (Leipzig, 1879; Obraldruck-Leipzig, 1921), 869–881; and E. Martini in Pauly-Wissowa, VI (Stuttgart, 1907), cols. 895–901, are now superseded by Wehrli (see above), who has also written a new article, "Eudemus von Rhodos," in Pauly-Wissowa, supp. XI (Stuttgart, 1968), cols. 652–658.

For the *Eudemian Ethics* see P. von der Mühl, *De Aristotelis Ethicorum Eudemiorum auctoritate* (dissertation, Göttingen, 1909); E. Kapp, *Der Verhältnis der eudemischen zur nikomachischen Ethik* (dissertation, Freiburg, 1912); W. Jaeger, *Aristoteles, Grundlegung einer Geschichte seiner Entwicklung* (Berlin, 1923; 2nd ed., 1955), 237–270, trans. by R. Robinson as *Aristotle, Fundamentals of the History of His Development* (Oxford, 1934, 2nd ed., 1948), 228–258; H. von Arnim, "Die drei Aristotelischen Ethiken," in *Sitzungsberichte der Akademie der Wissenschaften in Wien, Phil.-hist. Klasse*, **202** (Vienna, 1921); Franz Dirlmeier, *Aristoteles Eudemische Ethik*, in *Aristoteles Werke in Deutscher Übersetzung*, Grumach ed., VII (Berlin, 1962; 2nd ed., 1969) with elaborate intro. and notes (see especially introduction, 110–143), and Franz Dirlmeier, *Aristoteles Magna moralia* in *Aristoteles Werke*, Grumach ed., VIII (Berlin 1958; 2nd ed., 1966), 97–99.

The contribution of Eudemus to the development of Aristotelian logic cannot easily be separated from that of Theophrastus, and may be studied in I. M. Bochenski, *La logique de Théophraste* (Fribourg, 1947) and *Ancient Formal Logic* (Amsterdam, 1951), pp. 72–76; W. D. Ross, *Aristotle's Prior and Posterior Analytics* (Oxford, 1949), pp. 41–42, 45–47; Jan Łukasiewicz, *Aristotle's Syllogistic* (Oxford, 1953; 2nd ed., 1957), pp. 25–28, 38–42; Storrs McCall, *Aristotle's Modal Syllogisms* (Amsterdam, 1963), pp. 2, 15–16.

Eudemus' studies in the history of mathematics are the subject of the following papers by Paul Tannery: "Sur les fragments d'Eudème de Rhodes relatifs à l'histoire des mathématiques," in *Annales de la Faculté des Lettres de Bordeaux*, **4** (1882), 70–76, repr. in *Mémoires scientifiques*, I (Toulouse–Paris, 1912), 168–177; "Le fragment d'Eudème sur la quadrature des lunules," in *Mémoires de la Société des sciences physiques et naturelles de Bordeaux*, 2nd ser. **5** (1883), 217–237, repr. in *Mémoires scientifiques*, I (Toulouse–Paris, 1912), 339–370. His papers on Hippocrates of Chios are also relevant. For the question whether Eudemus' history was directly available to Simplicius and Eutocius, see J. L. Heiberg, *Philologus*, **43** (1884), 345–346. Eudemus' contributions to the history of science are summarized in Thomas Heath, *A History of Greek Mathematics* (Oxford, 1921), I, 118–120; II, 244.

U. Schoebe has written a Latin dissertation on the first book of Eudemus' *Physics* under the title *Quaestiones Eudemeae de primo Physicorum libro* (Halle, 1931).

IVOR BULMER-THOMAS

EUDOXUS OF CNIDUS (*b.* Cnidus, *ca.* 400 B.C.; *d.* Cnidus, *ca.* 347 B.C.), *astronomy, mathematics*.

A scholar and scientist of great eminence, Eudoxus, son of a certain Aischines, contributed to the development of astronomy, mathematics, geography, and philosophy, as well as providing his native city with laws. As a young man he studied geometry with Archytas of Tarentum, from whom he may well have taken his interest in number theory and music; in medicine he was instructed by the physician Philiston; and his philosophical inquiries were stimulated by Plato, whose lectures he attended as an impecunious student during his first visit to Athens. Later his friends in Cnidus paid for a visit to Egypt, where he seems to have had diplomatic dealings with King Nekhtanibef II on behalf of Agesilaus II of Sparta.

Eudoxus spent more than a year in Egypt, some of the time in the company of the priests at Heliopolis. He was said to have composed his *Oktaeteris,* or eight-year calendric cycle, during his sojourn with them. Next he settled at Cyzicus in northwestern Asia Minor and founded a school. He also visited the dynast Mausolus in Caria. A second visit to Athens, to which he was followed by some of his pupils, brought a closer association with Plato, but it is not easy to determine mutual influences in their thinking on ethical and scientific matters. It is unlikely that Plato had any influence upon the development of Eudoxian planetary theory or much upon the Cnidian's philosophical doctrine of forms, which recalls Anaxagoras; but it is possible that Plato's *Philebos* was written with the Eudoxian view of *hedone* (that pleasure, correctly understood, is the highest good) in mind.

Back in Cnidus, Eudoxus lectured on theology, cosmology, and meteorology, wrote textbooks, and enjoyed the respect of his fellow citizens. In mathematics his thinking lies behind much of Euclid's *Elements,* especially books V, VI, and XII. Eudoxus investigated mathematical proportion, the method of exhaustion, and the axiomatic method—the "Euclidean" presentation of axioms and propositions may well have been first systematized by him. The importance of his doctrine of proportion lay in its power to embrace incommensurable quantities.

It is difficult to exaggerate the significance of the theory, for it amounts to a rigorous definition of real number. Number theory was allowed to advance again, after the paralysis imposed on it by the Pythagorean discovery of irrationals, to the inestimable benefit of all subsequent mathematics. Indeed, as T. L. Heath declares (*A History of Greek Mathematics,* I [Oxford, 1921], 326–327), "The greatness of the new theory itself needs no further argument when it is remembered that the definition of equal ratios in Eucl. V, Def. 5 corresponds exactly to the modern theory of irrationals due to Dedekind, and that it is word for word the same as Weierstrass's definition of equal numbers."

Eudoxus also attacked the so-called "Delian problem," the traditional one of duplicating the cube; that is, he tried to find two mean proportions in continued proportion between two given quantities. His strictly geometrical solution is lost, and he may also have constructed an apparatus with which to describe an approximate mechanical solution; an epigram ascribed to Eratosthenes (who studied the works of Eudoxus closely) refers to his use of "lines of a bent form" in his solution to the Delian problem: the "organic" demonstration may be meant here. Plato is said to have objected to the use by Eudoxus (and by Archytas) of such devices, believing that they debased pure or ideal geometry. Proclus mentions "general theorems" of Eudoxus; they are lost but may have embraced all concepts of magnitude, the doctrine of proportion included. Related to the treatment of proportion (as found in *Elements* V) was his method of exhaustion, which was used in the calculation of the volume of solids. The method was an important step toward the development of integral calculus.

Archimedes states that Eudoxus proved that the volume of a pyramid is one-third the volume of the prism having the same base and equal height and that the volume of a cone is one-third the volume of the cylinder having the same base and height (these propositions may already have been known by Democritus, but Eudoxus was, it seems, the first to prove them). Archimedes also implies that Eudoxus showed that the areas of circles are to each other as the squares on their respective diameters and that the volumes of spheres to each other are as the cubes of their diameters. All four propositions are found in *Elements* XII, which closely reflects his work. Eudoxus is also said to have added to the first three classes of mathematical mean (arithmetic, geometric, and harmonic) two more, the subcontraries to harmonic and to geometric, but the attribution to him is not quite certain.

Perhaps the most important, and certainly the most influential, part of Eudoxus' lifework was his application of spherical geometry to astronomy. In his book *On Speeds* he expounded a system of geocentric, homocentric rotating spheres designed to explain the irregularities in the motion of planets as seen from the earth. Eudoxus may have regarded his system simply as an abstract geometrical model, but Aristotle took it to be a description of the physical world and complicated it by the addition of more spheres; still more were added by Callippus later in the fourth century B.C. By suitable combination of spheres the periodic motions of planets could be represented approximately, but the system is also, as geometry, of intrinsic merit because of the hippopede, or "horse fetter," an eight-shaped curve, by which Eudoxus represented a planet's apparent motion in latitude as well as its retrogradation.

Eudoxus' model assumes that the planet remains at a constant distance from the center, but in fact, as critics were quick to point out, the planets vary in brightness and hence, it would seem, in distance from the earth. Another objection is that according to the model, each retrogradation of a planet is identical with the previous retrogradation in the shape of its curve, which also is not in accord with the facts. So, while the Eudoxian system testified to the geometrical skill of its author, it could not be accepted by serious astronomers as definitive, and in time the theory of epicycles was developed. But, partly through the blessing of Aristotle, the influence of Eudoxus on popular astronomical thought lasted through antiquity and the Middle Ages. In explaining the system, Eudoxus gave close estimates of the synodic periods of Saturn, Jupiter, Mars, Mercury, and Venus (hence the title of the book, *On Speeds*). Only the estimate for Mars is seriously faulty, and here the text of Simplicius, who gives the values, is almost certainly in error (Eudoxus, frag. 124 in Lasserre).

Eudoxus was a careful observer of the fixed stars, both during his visit to Egypt and at home in Cnidus, where he had an observatory. His results were published in two books, the *Enoptron* ("Mirror") and the *Phaenomena*. The works were criticized, in the light of superior knowledge, by the great astronomer Hipparchus two centuries later, but they were pioneering compendia and long proved useful. Several verbatim quotations are given by Hipparchus in his commentary on the astronomical poem of Aratus, which drew on Eudoxus and was also entitled *Phaenomena*. A book by Eudoxus called *Disappearances of the Sun* may have been concerned with eclipses, and perhaps with risings and settings as well. The statement in the *Suda Lexicon* that he composed an astronomical poem may result from a confusion with Aratus, but a genuine *Astronomia* in hexameters, in the Hesiodic tradition, is a possibility. A calendar of the seasonal risings and settings of constellations, together with weather signs, may have been included in the *Oktaeteris*. His observational instruments included sundials (Vitruvius, *De architectura* 9.8.1).

Eudoxus' knowledge of spherical astronomy must have been helpful to him in the geographical treatise *Ges periodos* ("Tour [Circuit] of the Earth"). About 100 fragments survive; they give some idea of the plan of the original work. Beginning with remote Asia, Eudoxus dealt systematically with each part of the known world in turn, adding political, historical,

and ethnographic detail and making use of Greek mythology. His method is comparable with that of such early Ionian logographers as Hecataeus of Miletus. Egypt was treated in the second book, and Egyptian religion, about which Eudoxus could write with authority, was discussed in detail. The fourth book dealt with regions to the north of the Aegean, including Thrace. In the sixth book he wrote about mainland Hellas and, it seems, North Africa. The discussion of Italy in the seventh book included an excursus on the customs of the Pythagoreans, about whom Eudoxus may have learned much from his master Archytas of Tarentum (Eudoxus himself is sometimes called a Pythagorean).

It is greatly to be deplored that not a single work of Eudoxus is extant, for he was obviously a dominant figure in the intellectual life of Greece in the age of Plato and Aristotle (the latter also remarked on the upright and controlled character of the Cnidian, which made people believe him when he said that pleasure was the highest good).

BIBLIOGRAPHY

The biography of Eudoxus in Diogenes Laertius 8.86–8.90 is anecdotal but not worthless. The fragments have been collected, with commentary, in F. Lasserre's book *Die Fragmente des Eudoxos von Knidos* (Berlin, 1966). Eudoxian parts of Euclid's *Elements* are discussed by T. L. Heath in his edition of that work, 2nd ed., 3 vols. (Cambridge, 1926). The mathematical properties of the hippopede have been much studied; see especially O. Neugebauer, *The Exact Sciences in Antiquity,* 2nd ed. (Providence, R. I., 1957), 182–183. On the *Ges periodos,* see F. Gisinger, *Die Erdbeschreibung des Eudoxos von Knidos* (Leipzig–Berlin, 1921). A chronology of Eudoxus' life and travels is G. Huxley, "Eudoxian Topics," in *Greek, Roman and Byzantine Studies,* 4 (1963), 83–96.

See also Oskar Becker, "Eudoxos-Studien," in *Quellen und Studien zur Geschichte der Mathematik, Astronomie und Physik,* Abt. B, Studien, 2 (1933), 311–333, 369–387, and 3 (1936), 236–244, 370–410; Hans Künsberg, *Der Astronom, Mathematiker und Geograph Eudoxos von Knidos,* 2 pts. (Dinkelsbühl, 1888–1890); and G. Schiaparelli, *Scritti sulla storia della astronomia antica,* II (Bologna, 1926), 2–112.

G. L. HUXLEY

EULER, LEONHARD (*b.* Basel, Switzerland, 15 April 1707; *d.* St. Petersburg, Russia, 18 September 1783), *mathematics, mechanics, astronomy, physics.*

Life. Euler's forebears settled in Basel at the end of the sixteenth century. His great-great-grandfather, Hans Georg Euler, had moved from Lindau, on the Bodensee (Lake Constance). They were, for the most part, artisans; but the mathematician's father, Paul

Euler, graduated from the theological department of the University of Basel. He became a Protestant minister, and in 1706 he married Margarete Brucker, daughter of another minister. In 1708 the family moved to the village of Riehen, near Basel, where Leonhard Euler spent his childhood.

Euler's father was fond of mathematics and had attended Jakob Bernoulli's lectures at the university; he gave his son his elementary education, including mathematics. In the brief autobiography dictated to his eldest son in 1767, Euler recollected that for several years he diligently and thoroughly studied Christoff Rudolf's *Algebra,* a difficult work (dating, in Stifel's edition, from 1553) which only a very gifted boy could have used. Euler later spent several years with his maternal grandmother in Basel, studying at a rather poor local Gymnasium; mathematics was not taught at all, so Euler studied privately with Johann Burckhardt, an amateur mathematician. In the autumn of 1720, being not yet fourteen, Euler entered the University of Basel in the department of arts to get a general education before specializing. The university was small; it comprised only a few more than a hundred students and nineteen professors. But among the latter was Johann I Bernoulli, who had followed his brother Jakob, late in 1705, in the chair of mathematics. During the academic year, Bernoulli delivered daily public lectures on elementary mathematics; besides that, for additional pay he conducted studies in higher mathematics and physics for those who were interested. Euler laboriously studied all the required subjects, but this did not satisfy him. According to the autobiography:

> . . . I soon found an opportunity to be introduced to a famous professor Johann Bernoulli. . . . True, he was very busy and so refused flatly to give me private lessons; but he gave me much more valuable advice to start reading more difficult mathematical books on my own and to study them as diligently as I could; if I came across some obstacle or difficulty, I was given permission to visit him freely every Saturday afternoon and he kindly explained to me everything I could not understand . . . and this, undoubtedly, is the best method to succeed in mathematical subjects.[1]

In the summer of 1722, Euler delivered a speech in praise of temperance, "De temperantia," and received his *prima laurea,* a degree corresponding to the bachelor of arts. The same year he acted as opponent (*respondens*) at the defense of two theses—one on logic, the other on the history of law. In 1723 Euler received his master's degree in philosophy. This was officially announced at a session on 8 June 1724; Euler made a speech comparing the philosophical ideas of Descartes and Newton. Some time earlier,

in the autumn of 1723, he had joined the department of theology, fulfilling his father's wish. His studies in theology, Greek, and Hebrew were not very successful, however; Euler devoted most of his time to mathematics. He finally gave up the idea of becoming a minister but remained a wholehearted believer throughout his life. He also retained the knowledge of the humanities that he acquired in the university; he had an outstanding memory and knew by heart the entirety of Vergil's *Aeneid.* At seventy he could recall precisely the lines printed at the top and bottom of each page of the edition he had read when he was young.

At the age of eighteen, Euler began his independent investigations. His first work, a small note on the construction of isochronous curves in a resistant medium,[2] appeared in *Acta eruditorum* (1726); this was followed by an article in the same periodical on algebraic reciprocal trajectories (1727).[3] The problem of reciprocal trajectories was studied by Johann I Bernoulli, by his son Nikolaus II, and by other mathematicians of the time. Simultaneously Euler participated in a competition announced by the Paris Académie des Sciences which proposed for 1727 the problem of the most efficient arrangement of masts on a ship. The prize went to Pierre Bouguer, but Euler's work[4] received the *accessit.* Later, from 1738 to 1772, Euler was to receive twelve prizes from the Academy.

For mathematicians beginning their careers in Switzerland, conditions were hard. There were few chairs of mathematics in the country and thus little chance of finding a suitable job. The income and public recognition accorded to a university professor of mathematics were not cause for envy. There were no scientific magazines, and publishers were reluctant to publish books on mathematics, which were considered financially risky. At this time the newly organized St. Petersburg Academy of Sciences (1725) was looking for personnel. In the autumn of that year Johann I Bernoulli's sons, Nikolaus II and Daniel, went to Russia. On behalf of Euler, they persuaded the authorities of the new Academy to send an invitation to their young friend also.

Euler received the invitation to serve as adjunct of physiology in St. Petersburg in the autumn of 1726, and he began to study this discipline, with an effort toward applying the methods of mathematics and mechanics. He also attempted to find a job at the University of Basel. A vacancy occurred in Basel after the death of a professor of physics, and Euler presented as a qualification a small composition on acoustics, *Dissertatio physica de sono* (1727).[5] Vacancies were then filled in the university by drawing lots among the several chosen candidates. In spite of a recommendation from Johann Bernoulli, Euler was not chosen as a candidate, probably because he was too young—he was not yet twenty. But, as O. Spiess has pointed out, this was in Euler's favor;[6] a much broader field of action lay ahead of him.

On 5 April 1727 Euler left Basel for St. Petersburg, arriving there on 24 May. From this time his life and scientific work were closely connected with the St. Petersburg Academy and with Russia. He never returned to Switzerland, although he maintained his Swiss citizenship.

In spite of having been invited to St. Petersburg to study physiology, Euler was at once given the chance to work in his real field and was appointed an adjunct member of the Academy in the mathematics section. He became professor of physics in 1731 and succeeded Daniel Bernoulli, who returned to Basel in 1733 as a professor of mathematics. The young Academy was beset with numerous difficulties, but on the whole the atmosphere was exceptionally beneficial for the flowering of Euler's genius. Nowhere else could he have been surrounded by such a group of eminent scientists, including the analyst, geometer, and specialist in theoretical mechanics Jakob Hermann, a relative; Daniel Bernoulli, with whom Euler was connected not only by personal friendship but also by common interests in the field of applied mathematics; the versatile scholar Christian Goldbach, with whom Euler discussed numerous problems of analysis and the theory of numbers; F. Maier, working in trigonometry; and the astronomer and geographer J.-N. Delisle.

In St. Petersburg, Euler began his scientific activity at once. No later than August 1727 he started making reports on his investigations at sessions of the Academy; he began publishing them in the second volume of the academic proceedings, *Commentarii Academiae scientiarum imperialis Petropolitanae* (*1727*) (St. Petersburg, 1729). The generous publication program of the Academy was especially important for Euler, who was unusually prolific. In a letter written in 1749 Euler cited the importance that the work at the Academy had for many of its members:

> . . . I and all others who had the good fortune to be for some time with the Russian Imperial Academy cannot but acknowledge that we owe everything which we are and possess to the favorable conditions which we had there.[7]

In addition to conducting purely scientific work, the St. Petersburg Academy from the very beginning was also obliged to educate and train Russian scientists, and with this aim a university and a Gymnasium were

organized. The former existed for nearly fifty years and the latter until 1805. The Academy was also charged to carry out for the government a study of Russian territory and to find solutions for various technological problems. Euler was active in these projects. From 1733 on, he successfully worked with Delisle on maps in the department of geography. From the middle of the 1730's he studied problems of shipbuilding and navigation, which were especially important to the rise of Russia as a great sea power. He joined various technological committees and engaged in testing scales, fire pumps, saws, and so forth. He wrote articles for the popular periodical of the Academy and reviewed works submitted to it (including those on the quadrature of the circle), compiled the *Einleitung zur Rechen-Kunst*[8] for Gymnasiums, and also served on the examination board.

Euler's main efforts, however, were in the mathematical sciences. During his fourteen years in St. Petersburg he made brilliant discoveries in such areas as analysis, the theory of numbers, and mechanics. By 1741 he had prepared between eighty and ninety works for publication. He published fifty-five, including the two-volume *Mechanica*.[9]

As is usual with scientists, Euler formulated many of his principal ideas and creative concepts when he was young. Neither the dates of preparation of his works nor those of their actual publication adequately indicate Euler's intellectual progress, since a number of the plans formulated in the early years in St. Petersburg (and even as early as the Basel period) were not realized until much later. For example, the first drafts of the theory of motion of solid bodies, finished in the 1760's, were made during this time. Likewise Euler began studying hydromechanics while still in Basel, but the most important memoirs on the subject did not appear until the middle of the 1750's; he imagined a systematic exposition of differential calculus on the basis of calculus of finite differences in the 1730's but did not realize the intention until two decades later; and his first articles on optics appeared fifteen years after he began studying the subject in St. Petersburg. Only by a complete study of the unpublished Euler manuscripts would it be possible to establish the progression of his ideas more precisely.

Because of his large correspondence with scientists from many countries, Euler's discoveries often became known long before publication and rapidly brought him increasing fame. An index of this is Johann I Bernoulli's letters to his former disciple—in 1728 Bernoulli addressed the "most learned and gifted man of science Leonhard Euler"; in 1737 he wrote, the "most famous and wisest mathematician";

and in 1745 he called him the "incomparable Leonhard Euler" and *mathematicorum princeps."* Euler was then a member of both the St. Petersburg and Berlin academies. (That certain frictions between Euler and Schumacher, the rude and despotic councillor of the St. Petersburg Academy, did Euler's career no lasting harm was due to his tact and diplomacy.) He was later elected a member of the Royal Society of London (1749) and the Académie des Sciences of Paris (1755). He was elected a member of the Society of Physics and Mathematics in Basel in 1753.

At the end of 1733 Euler married Katharina Gsell, a daughter of Georg Gsell, a Swiss who taught painting at the Gymnasium attached to the St. Petersburg Academy. Johann Albrecht, Euler's first son, was born in 1734, and Karl was born in 1740. It seemed that Euler had settled in St. Petersburg for good; his younger brother, Johann Heinrich, a painter, also worked there. His quiet life was interrupted only by a disease that caused the loss of sight in his right eye in 1738.

In November 1740 Anna Leopoldovna, mother of the infant Emperor Ivan VI, became regent, and the atmosphere in the Russian capital grew troubled. According to Euler's autobiography, "things looked rather dubious." [10] At that time Frederick the Great, who had succeeded to the Prussian throne in June 1740, decided to reorganize the Berlin Society of Sciences, which had been founded by Leibniz but allowed to degenerate during Frederick's father's reign. Euler was invited to work in Berlin. He accepted, and after fourteen years in Russia he sailed with his family on 19 June 1741 from St. Petersburg. He arrived in Berlin on 25 July.

Euler lived in Berlin for the next twenty-five years. In 1744 he moved into a house, still preserved, on the Behrenstrasse. The family increased with the birth of a third son, Christoph, and two daughters; eight other children died in infancy. In 1753 Euler bought an estate in Charlottenburg, which was then just outside the city. The estate was managed by his mother, who lived with Euler after 1750. He sold the property in 1763.

Euler's energy in middle age was inexhaustible. He was working simultaneously in two academies— Berlin and St. Petersburg. He was very active in transforming the old Society of Sciences into a large academy—officially founded in 1744 as the Académie Royale des Sciences et des Belles Lettres de Berlin. (The monarch preferred his favorite language, French, to both Latin and German.) Euler was appointed director of the mathematical class of the Academy and member of the board and of the committee directing the library and the publication of

scientific works. He also substituted for the president, Maupertuis, when the latter was absent. When Maupertuis died in 1759, Euler continued to run the Academy, although without the title of president. Euler's friendship with Maupertuis enabled him to exercise great influence on all the activities of the Academy, particularly on the selection of members.

Euler's administrative duties were numerous: he supervised the observatory and the botanical gardens; selected the personnel; oversaw various financial matters; and, in particular, managed the publication of various calendars and geographical maps, the sale of which was a source of income for the Academy. The king also charged Euler with practical problems, such as the project in 1749 of correcting the level of the Finow Canal, which was built in 1744 to join the Havel and the Oder. At that time he also supervised the work on pumps and pipes of the hydraulic system at Sans Souci, the royal summer residence.

In 1749 and again in 1763 he advised on the organization of state lotteries and was a consultant to the government on problems of insurance, annuities, and widows' pensions. Some of Euler's studies on demography grew out of these problems. An inquiry from the king about the best work on artillery moved Euler to translate into German Benjamin Robins' *New Principles of Gunnery.* Euler added his own supplements on ballistics, which were five times longer than the original text (1745).[11] These supplements occupy an important place in the history of ballistics; Euler himself had written a short work on the subject as early as 1727 or 1728 in connection with the testing of guns.[12]

Euler's influence upon scientific life in Germany was not restricted to the Berlin Academy. He maintained a large correspondence with professors at numerous German universities and promoted the teaching of mathematical sciences and the preparation of university texts.

From his very first years in Berlin, Euler kept in regular working contact with the St. Petersburg Academy. This contact was interrupted only during military actions between Prussia and Russia in the course of the Seven Years' War—although even then not completely. Before his departure from the Russian capital, Euler was appointed an honorary member of the Academy and given an annual pension; on his part he pledged to carry out various assignments of the Academy and to correspond with it. During the twenty-five years in Berlin, Euler maintained membership in the St. Petersburg Academy *à tous les titres,* to quote N. Fuss. On its commission he finished the books on differential calculus and navigation begun before his departure for Berlin; edited the mathematical section of the Academy journal; kept the Academy apprised, through his letters, of scientific and technological thought in Western Europe; bought books and scientific apparatus for the Academy; recommended subjects for scientific competitions and candidates to vacancies; and served as a mediator in conflicts between academicians.

Euler's participation in the training of Russian scientific personnel was of great importance, and he was frequently sent for review the works of Russian students and even members of the Academy. For example, in 1747 he praised most highly two articles of M. V. Lomonosov on physics and chemistry; and S. K. Kotelnikov, S. Y. Rumovski, and M. Sofronov studied in Berlin under his supervision for several years. Finally, Euler regularly sent memoirs to St. Petersburg. About half his articles were published there in Latin, and the other half appeared in French in Berlin.

During this period, Euler greatly increased the variety of his investigations. Competing with d'Alembert and Daniel Bernoulli, he laid the foundations of mathematical physics; and he was a rival of both A. Clairaut and d'Alembert in advancing the theory of lunar and planetary motion. At the same time, Euler elaborated the theory of motion of solids, created the mathematical apparatus of hydrodynamics, successfully developed the differential geometry of surfaces, and intensively studied optics, electricity, and magnetism. He also pondered such problems of technology as the construction of achromatic refractors, the perfection of J. A. Segner's hydraulic turbine, and the theory of toothed gearings.

During the Berlin period Euler prepared no fewer than 380 works, of which about 275 were published, including several lengthy books: a monograph on the calculus of variations (1744);[13] a fundamental work on calculation of orbits (1745);[14] the previously mentioned work on artillery and ballistics (1745); *Introductio in analysin infinitorum* (1748);[15] a treatise on shipbuilding and navigation, prepared in an early version in St. Petersburg (1749);[16] his first theory of lunar motion (1753);[17] and *Institutiones calculi differentialis* (1755).[18] The last three books were published at the expense of the St. Petersburg Academy. Finally, there was the treatise on the mechanics of solids, *Theoria motus corporum solidorum seu rigidorum* (1765).[19] The famous *Lettres à une princesse d'Allemagne sur divers sujets de physique et de philosophie,* which originated in lessons given by Euler to a relative of the Prussian king, was not published until Euler's return to St. Petersburg.[20] Written in an absorbing and popular manner, the book was an unusual success and ran to twelve editions in the original

French, nine in English, six in German, four in Russian, and two in both Dutch and Swedish. There were also Italian, Spanish, and Danish editions.

In the 1740's and 1750's Euler took part in several philosophical and scientific arguments. In 1745 and after, there were passionate discussions about the monadology of Leibniz and of Christian Wolff. German intellectuals were divided according to their opinions on monadology. As Euler later wrote, every conversation ended in a discussion of monads. The Berlin Academy announced as the subject of a 1747 prize competition an exposé and critique of the system. Euler, who was close to Cartesian mechanical materialism in natural philosophy, was an ardent enemy of monadology, as was Maupertuis. It should be added that Euler, whose religious views were based on a belief in revelation, could not share the religion of reason which characterized Leibniz and Wolff. Euler stated his objections, which were grounded on arguments of both a physical and theological nature, in the pamphlet *Gedancken von den Elementen der Cörper* . . . (1746).[21] His composition caused violent debates, but the decision of the Academy gave the prize to Justi, author of a rather mediocre work against the theory of monads.

In 1751 a sensational new argument began when S. König published some critical remarks on Maupertuis's principle of least action (1744) and cited a letter of Leibniz in which the principle was, in König's opinion, formulated more precisely. Submitting to Maupertuis, the Berlin Academy rose to defend him and demanded that the original of Leibniz' letter (a copy had been sent to König from Switzerland) be presented. When it became clear that the original could not be found, Euler published, with the approval of the Academy, "Exposé concernant l'examen de la lettre de M. de Leibnitz" (1752),[22] where, among other things, he declared the letter a fake. The conflict grew critical when later in the same year Voltaire published his *Diatribe du docteur Akakia, médecin du pape,* defending König and making laughingstocks of both Maupertuis and Euler. Frederick rushed to the defense of Maupertuis, quarreling with his friend Voltaire and ordering the burning of the offensive pamphlet. His actions, however, did not prevent its dissemination throughout Europe. The argument touched not only on the pride of the principal participants but also on their general views: Maupertuis and, to a lesser degree, Euler interpreted the principle of least action theologically and teleologically; König was a follower of Wolff and Voltaire—the greatest ideologist of free thought.

Three other disputes in which Euler took part (all discussed below) were much more important for the development of mathematical sciences: his argument with d'Alembert on the problem of logarithms of negative numbers, the argument with d'Alembert and Daniel Bernoulli on the solution of the equation of a vibrating string, and Euler's polemics with Dollond on optical problems.

As mentioned earlier, after Maupertuis died in 1759, Euler managed the Berlin Academy, but under the direct supervision of the king. But relations between Frederick and Euler had long since spoiled. They differed sharply, not only in their views but in their tastes, treatment of men, and personal conduct. Euler's bourgeois manners and religious zeal were as unattractive to the king as the king's passion for bons mots and freethinking was to Euler. Euler cared little for poetry, which the king adored; Frederick was quite contemptuous of the higher realms of mathematics, which did not seem to him immediately practical. In spite of having no one to replace Euler as manager of the Academy, the king, nonetheless, did not intend to give him the post of president. In 1763 it became known that Frederick wanted to appoint d'Alembert, and Euler thus began to think of leaving Berlin. He wrote to G. F. Müller, secretary of the St. Petersburg Academy, which had tried earlier to bring him back to Russia. Catherine the Great then ordered the academicians to send Euler another offer.

D'Alembert's refusal to move permanently to Berlin postponed for a time the final decision on the matter. But during 1765 and 1766 grave conflicts over financial matters arose between Euler and Frederick, who interfered actively with Euler's management of the Academy after the Seven Years' War. The king thought Euler inexperienced in such matters and relied too much on the treasurer of the Academy. For half a year Euler pleaded for royal permission to leave, but the king, well-aware that the Academy would thus lose its best worker and principal force, declined to grant his request. Finally he had to consent and vented his annoyance in crude jokes about Euler. On 9 June 1766, Euler left Berlin, spent ten days in Warsaw at the invitation of Stanislas II, and arrived in St. Petersburg on 28 July. Euler's three sons returned to Russia also. Johann Albrecht became academician in the chair of physics in 1766 and permanent secretary of the Academy in 1769. Christoph, who had become an officer in Prussia, successfully resumed his military career, reaching the rank of major-general in artillery. Both his daughters also accompanied him.

Euler settled in a house on the embankment of the Neva, not far from the Academy. Soon after his return he suffered a brief illness, which left him almost completely blind in the left eye; he could not now read and could make out only outlines of large objects. He could write only in large letters with chalk and slate. An operation in 1771 temporarily restored his sight, but Euler seems not to have taken adequate care of himself and in a few days he was completely blind. Shortly before the operation, he had lost his house and almost all of his personal property in a fire, barely managing to rescue himself and his manuscripts. In November 1773 Euler's wife died, and three years later he married her half sister, Salome Abigail Gsell.

Euler's blindness did not lessen his scientific activity. Only in the last years of his life did he cease attending academic meetings, and his literary output even increased—almost half of his works were produced after 1765. His memory remained flawless, he carried on with his unrealized ideas, and he devised new plans. He naturally could not execute this immense work alone and was helped by active collaborators: his sons Johann Albrecht and Christoph; the academicians W. L. Krafft and A. J. Lexell; and two new young disciples, adjuncts N. Fuss, who was invited in 1772 from Switzerland, and M. E. Golovin, a nephew of Lomonosov. Sometimes Euler simply dictated his works; thus, he dictated to a young valet, a tailor by profession, the two-volume *Vollständige Anleitung zur Algebra* (1770),[23] first published in Russian translation.

But the scientists assisting Euler were not mere secretaries; he discussed the general scheme of the works with them, and they developed his ideas, calculated tables, and sometimes compiled examples. The enormous, 775-page *Theoria motuum lunae . . .* (1772)[24] was thus completed with the help of Johann Albrecht, Krafft, and Lexell—all of whom are credited on the title page. Krafft also helped Euler with the three-volume *Dioptrica* (1769–1771).[25] Fuss, by his own account, during a seven-year period prepared 250 memoirs, and Golovin prepared seventy. Articles written by Euler in his later years were generally concise and particular. For example, the fifty-six works prepared during 1776 contain about the same number of pages (1,000) as the nineteen works prepared in 1751.

Besides the works mentioned, during the second St. Petersburg period Euler published three volumes of *Institutiones calculi integralis* (1768–1770),[26] the principal parts of which he had finished in Berlin, and an abridged edition of *Scientia navalis—Théorie complette de la construction et de la manoeuvre des vaisseaux* (1773).[27] The last, a manual for naval cadets, was soon translated into English, Italian, and Russian, and Euler received for it large sums from the Russian and French governments.

The mathematical apparatus of the *Dioptrica* remained beyond the practical opticist's understanding; so Fuss devised, on the basis of this work, the *Instruction détaillée pour porter les lunettes de toutes les différentes espèces au plus haut degré de perfection dont elles sont susceptibles...* (1774).[28] Fuss also aided Euler in preparing the *Éclaircissemens sur les établissemens publics...* (1776),[29] which was very important in the development of insurance; many companies used its methods of solution and its tables.

Euler continued his participation in other functions of the St. Petersburg Academy. Together with Johann Albrecht he was a member of the commission charged in 1766 with the management of the Academy. Both resigned their posts on the commission in 1774 because of a difference of opinion between them and the director of the Academy, Count V. G. Orlov, who actually managed it.

On 18 September 1783 Euler spent the first half of the day as usual. He gave a mathematics lesson to one of his grandchildren, did some calculations with chalk on two boards on the motion of balloons; then discussed with Lexell and Fuss the recently discovered planet Uranus. About five o'clock in the afternoon he suffered a brain hemorrhage and uttered only "I am dying," before he lost consciousness. He died about eleven o'clock in the evening.

Soon after Euler's death eulogies were delivered by Fuss at a meeting of the St. Petersburg Academy[30] and by Condorcet at the Paris Academy of Sciences.[31] Euler was buried at the Lutheran Smolenskoye cemetery in St. Petersburg, where in 1837 a massive monument was erected at his grave, with the inscription, "Leonhardo Eulero Academia Petropolitana." In the autumn of 1956 Euler's remains and the monument were transferred to the necropolis of Leningrad.

Euler was a simple man, well disposed and not given to envy. One can also say of him what Fontenelle said of Leibniz: "He was glad to observe the flowering in other people's gardens of plants whose seeds he provided."

Mathematics. Euler was a geometer in the wide sense in which the word was used during the eighteenth century. He was one of the most important creators of mathematical science after Newton. In his work, mathematics was closely connected with applications to other sciences, to problems of technology, and to public life. In numerous cases he elaborated mathematical methods for the direct solution of problems of mechanics and astronomy, physics and navigation, geography and geodesy, hydraulics and ballistics, insurance and demography. This practical orientation of his work explains his tendency to prolong his investigations until he had derived a convenient formula for calculation or an immediate solution in numbers or a table. He constantly sought algorithms that would be simple to use in calculation and that would also assure sufficient accuracy in the results.

But just as his friend Daniel Bernoulli was first of all a physicist, Euler was first of all a mathematician. Bernoulli's thinking was preeminently physical; he tried to avoid mathematics whenever possible, and once having developed a mathematical device for the solution of some physical problem, he usually left it without further development. Euler, on the other hand, attempted first of all to express a physical problem in mathematical terms; and having found a mathematical idea for solution, he systematically developed and generalized it. Thus, Euler's brilliant achievements in the field are explained by his regular elaboration of mathematics as a single whole. Bernoulli was not especially attracted by more abstract problems of mathematics; Euler, on the contrary, was very much carried away with the theory of numbers. All this is manifest in the distribution of Euler's works on various sciences: twenty-nine volumes of the *Opera omnia* (see Bibliography [1]) pertain to pure mathematics.

In Euler's mathematical work, first place belongs to analysis, which at the time was the most pressing need in mathematical science; seventeen volumes of the *Opera omnia* are in this area. Thus, in principle, Euler was an analyst. He contributed numerous particular discoveries to analysis, systematized its exposition in his classical manuals, and, along with all this, contributed immeasurably to the founding of several large mathematical disciplines: the calculus of variations, the theory of differential equations, the elementary theory of functions of complex variables, and the theory of special functions.

Euler is often characterized as a calculator of genius, and he was, in fact, unsurpassed in formal calculations and transformations and was even an outstanding calculator in the elementary sense of the word. But he also was a creator of new and important notions and methods, the principal value of which was in some cases properly understood only a century or more after his death. Even in areas where he, along with his contemporaries, did not feel at home, his judgment came, as a rule, from profound intuition into the subject under study. His findings were intrinsically capable of being grounded in the rigorous mode of demonstration that became obligatory in the nineteenth and twentieth centuries. Such standards were not, and could not be, demanded in the mathematics of the eighteenth century.

It is frequently said that Euler saw no intrinsic

impossibility in the deduction of mathematical laws from a very limited basis in observation; and naturally he employed methods of induction to make empirical use of the results he had arrived at through analysis of concrete numerical material. But he himself warned many times that an incomplete induction serves only as a heuristic device, and he never passed off as finally proved truths the suppositions arrived at by such methods.

Euler introduced many of the present conventions of mathematical notation: the symbol e to represent the base of the natural system of logarithms (1727, published 1736); the use of letter f and of parentheses for a function $f([x/a] + c)$ (1734, published 1740); the modern signs for trigonometric functions (1748); the notation $\int n$ for the sum of divisors of the number n (1750); notations for finite differences, Δy, $\Delta^2 y$, etc., and for the sum Σ (1755); and the letter i for $\sqrt{-1}$ (1777, published 1794).

Euler had only a few immediate disciples, and none of them was a first-class scientist. On the other hand, according to Laplace, he was a tutor of all the mathematicians of his time. In mathematics the eighteenth century can fairly be labeled the Age of Euler, but his influence upon the development of mathematical sciences was not restricted to that period. The work of many outstanding nineteenth-century mathematicians branched out directly from the works of Euler.

Euler was especially important for the development of science in Russia. His disciples formed the first scientific mathematical school in the country and contributed to the rise of mathematical education. One can trace back to Euler numerous paths from Chebyshev's St. Petersburg mathematical school.

[In the following, titles of articles are not, as a rule, cited; dates in parentheses signify the year of publication.]

Theory of Numbers. Problems of the theory of numbers had attracted mathematicians before Euler. Fermat, for example, established several remarkable arithmetic theorems but left almost no proofs. Euler laid the foundations of number theory as a true science.

A large series of Euler's works is connected with the theory of divisibility. He proved by three methods Fermat's lesser theorem, the principal one in the field (1741, 1761, 1763); he suggested with the third proof an important generalization of the theorem by introducing Euler's function $\varphi(n)$, denoting the number of positive integers less than n which are relatively prime to n: the difference $a^{\varphi(n)} - 1$ is divisible by n if a is relatively prime to n. Elaborating related ideas,

Euler came to the theory of n-ic residues (1760). Here his greatest discovery was the law of quadratic reciprocity (1783), which, however, he could not prove. Euler's discovery went unnoticed by his contemporaries, and the law was rediscovered, but incompletely proved, by A. M. Legendre (1788). Legendre was credited with it until Chebyshev pointed out Euler's priority in 1849. The complete proof of the law was finally achieved by Gauss (1801). Gauss, Kummer, D. Hilbert, E. Artin, and others extended the law of reciprocity to various algebraic number fields; the most general law of reciprocity was established by I. R. Shafarevich (1950).

Another group of Euler's works, in which he extended Fermat's studies on representation of prime numbers by sums of the form $mx^2 + ny^2$, where m, n, x, and y are positive integers, led him to the discovery of a new efficient method of determining whether a given large number N is prime or composite (1751, *et seq.*). These works formed the basis for the general arithmetic theory of binary quadratic forms developed by Lagrange and especially by Gauss.

Euler also contributed to so-called Diophantine analysis, that is, to the solution, in integers or in rational numbers, of indeterminate equations with integer coefficients. Thus, by means of continued fractions, which he had studied earlier (1744, *et seq.*), he gave (1767) a method of calculation of the smallest integer solution of the equation $x^2 - dy^2 = 1$ (d being a positive nonsquare integer). This had been studied by Fermat and Wallis and even earlier by scientists of India and Greece. A complete investigation of the problem was soon undertaken by Lagrange. In 1753 Euler proved the impossibility of solving $x^3 + y^3 = z^3$ in which x, y, and z are integers, $xyz \neq 0$ (a particular case of Fermat's last theorem); his demonstration, based on the method of infinite descent and using complex numbers of the form $a + b\sqrt{-3}$, is thoroughly described in his *Vollständige Anleitung zur Algebra*, the second volume of which (1769) has a large section devoted to Diophantine analysis.

In all these cases Euler used methods of arithmetic and algebra, but he was also the first to use analytical methods in number theory. To solve the partition problem posed in 1740 by P. Naudé, concerning the total number of ways the positive integer n is obtainable as a sum of positive integers $m < n$, Euler used the expansions of certain infinite products into a power series whose coefficients give the solution (1748). In particular, in the expansion

$$\prod_{r=1}^{\infty} (1 - x^r) = \sum_{k=-\infty}^{\infty} (-1)^k x^{(3k^2-k)/2}$$

the right-hand series is one of theta functions, introduced much later by C. Jacobi in his theory of elliptic functions. Earlier, in 1737, Euler had deduced the famous identity

$$\sum_{n=1}^{\infty} \frac{1}{n^s} = \prod_p \left[1 \Big/ \left(1 - \frac{1}{p^s} \right) \right],$$

where the sum extends over all positive integers n and the product over all primes p (1744), the left-hand side is what Riemann later called the zeta-function $\zeta(s)$.

Using summation of divergent series and induction, Euler discovered in 1749 (1768) a functional equation involving $\zeta(s)$, $\zeta(1 - s)$, and $\Gamma(s)$, which was rediscovered and established by Riemann, the first scientist to define the zeta-function also for complex values of the argument. In the nineteenth and twentieth centuries, the zeta-function became one of the principal means of analytic number theory, particularly in the studies of the laws of distribution of prime numbers by Dirichlet, Chebyshev, Riemann, Hadamard, de la Vallée-Poussin, and others.

Finally, Euler studied mathematical constants and formulated important problems relevant to the theory of transcendental numbers. His expression of the number e in the form of a continued fraction (1744) was used by J. H. Lambert (1768) in his demonstration of irrationality of the numbers e and π. F. Lindemann employed Euler's formula $\ln(-1) = \pi i$ (discovered as early as 1728) to prove that π is transcendental (1882). The hypothesis of the transcendence of a^b, where a is any algebraic number $\neq 0,1$ and b is any irrational algebraic number—formulated by D. Hilbert in 1900 and proved by A. Gelfond in 1934—presents a generalization of Euler's corresponding supposition about rational-base logarithms of rational numbers (1748).

Algebra. When mathematicians of the seventeenth century formulated the fundamental theorem that an algebraic equation of degree n with real coefficients has n roots, which could be imaginary, it was yet unknown whether the domain of imaginary roots was restricted to numbers of the form $a + bi$, which, following Gauss, are now called complex numbers. Many mathematicians thought that there existed imaginary quantities of another kind. In his letters to Nikolaus I Bernoulli and to Goldbach (dated 1742), Euler stated for the first time the theorem that every algebraic polynomial of degree n with real coefficients may be resolved into real linear or quadratic factors, that is, possesses n roots of the form $a + bi$ (1743). The theorem was proved by d'Alembert (1748) and

by Euler himself (1751). Both proofs, quite different in ideas, had omissions and were rendered more precise during the nineteenth century.

Euler also aspired—certainly in vain—to find the general form of solution by radicals for equations of degree higher than the fourth (1738, 1764). He elaborated approximating methods of solutions for numerical equations (1748) and studied the elimination problem. Thus, he gave the first proof of the theorem, which was known to Newton, that two algebraic curves of degrees m and n, respectively, intersect in mn points (1748, 1750). It should be added that Euler's *Vollständige Anleitung zur Algebra,* published in many editions in English, Dutch, Italian, French, and Russian, greatly influenced nineteenth- and twentieth-century texts on the subject.

Infinite Series. In Euler's works, infinite series, which previously served mainly as an auxiliary means for solving problems, became a subject of study. One example, his investigation of the zeta-function, has already been mentioned. The point of departure was the problem of summation of the reciprocals of the squares of the integers

$$\sum_{n=1}^{\infty} \frac{1}{n^2} = \zeta(2),$$

which had been vainly approached by the Bernoulli brothers, Stirling, and other outstanding mathematicians. Euler solved in 1735 a much more general problem and demonstrated that for any even integer number $2k > 0$,

$$\zeta(2k) = a_{2k}\pi^{2k},$$

where a_{2k} are rational numbers (1740), expressed through coefficients of the Euler-Maclaurin summation formula (1750) and, consequently, through Bernoulli numbers (1755). The problem of the arithmetic nature of $\zeta(2k + 1)$ remains unsolved.

The summation formula was discovered by Euler no later than 1732 (1738) and demonstrated in 1735 (1741); it was independently discovered by Maclaurin no later than 1738 (1742). The formula, one of the most important in the calculus of finite differences, represents the partial sum of a series, $\sum_{n=1}^{m} u(n)$, by another infinite series involving the integral and the derivatives of the general term $u(n)$. Later Euler expressed the coefficients of the latter series through Bernoulli numbers (1755). Euler knew that although this infinite series generally diverges, its partial sums under certain conditions might serve as a brilliant means of approximating the calculations shown by James Stirling (1730) in a particular case of

$$\sum_{n=2}^{m} \log (n!).$$

By means of the summation formula, Euler in 1735 calculated (1741) to sixteen decimal places the value of Euler's constant,

$$C = 0.57721566\cdots,$$

belonging to an asymptotic formula,

$$\sum_{n=1}^{m} \frac{1}{n} \simeq \ln m + C,$$

which he discovered in 1731 (1738).

The functions studied in the eighteenth century were, with rare exceptions, analytic, and therefore Euler made great use of power series. His special merit was the introduction of a new and extremely important class of trigonometric Fourier series. In a letter to Goldbach (1744), he expressed for the first time an algebraic function by such a series (1755),

$$\frac{\pi}{2} - \frac{x}{2} = \sin x + \frac{\sin 2x}{2} + \frac{\sin 3x}{3} + \cdots.$$

He later found other expansions (1760), deducing in 1777 a formula of Fourier coefficients for expansion of a given function into a series of cosines on the interval $(0,\pi)$, pointing out that coefficients of expansion into a series of sines could be deduced analogously (1798). Fourier, having no knowledge of Euler's work, deduced in 1807 the same formulas. For his part, Euler did not know that coefficients of expansion into a series of cosines had been given by Clairaut in 1759.

Euler also introduced expansion of functions into infinite products and into the sums of elementary fractions, which later acquired great importance in the general theory of analytic functions. Numerous methods of transformation of infinite series, products, and continued fractions into one another are also his.

Eighteenth-century mathematicians distinguished convergent series from divergent series, but the general theory of convergence was still missing. Algebraic and analytic operations on infinite series were similar to those on finite polynomials, without any restrictions. It was supposed that identical laws operate in both cases. Several tests of convergence already known found almost no application. Opinions, however, differed on the problem of admissibility of divergent series. Many mathematicians were radically against their employment. Euler, sure that important correct results might be arrived at by means of divergent series, set about the task of establishing the legitimacy of their application. With this aim, he

suggested a new, wider definition of the concept of the sum of a series, which coincides with the traditional definition if the series converges; he also suggested two methods of summation (1755). Precise grounding and further development of these fruitful ideas were possible only toward the end of the nineteenth century and the beginning of the twentieth century.[32]

The Concept of Function. Discoveries in the field of analysis made in the middle of the eighteenth century (many of them his own) were systematically summarized by Euler in the trilogy *Introductio in analysin infinitorum* (1748),[15] *Institutiones calculi differentialis* (1755),[18] and *Institutiones calculi integralis* (1768–1770). The books are still of interest, especially the first volume of the *Introductio.* Many of the problems considered there, however, are now so far developed that knowledge of them is limited to a few specialists, who can trace in the book the development of many fruitful methods of analysis.

In the *Introductio* Euler presented the first clear statement of the idea that mathematical analysis is a science of functions; and he also presented a more thorough investigation of the very concept of function. Defining function as an analytic expression somehow composed of variables and constants—following in this respect Johann I Bernoulli (1718)—Euler defined precisely the term "analytic expression": functions are produced by means of algebraic operations, and also of elementary and other transcendental operations, carried out by integration. Here the classification of functions generally used today is also given; Euler speaks of functions defined implicitly and by parametric representation. Further on he states his belief, shared by other mathematicians, that all analytic expressions might be given in the form of infinite power series or generalized power series with fractional or negative exponents. Thus, functions studied in mathematical analysis generally are analytic functions with some isolated singular points. Euler's remark that functions are considered not only for real but also for imaginary values of independent variables was very important.

Even at that time, however, the class of analytic functions was insufficient for the requirements of analysis and its applications, particularly for the solution of the problem of the vibrating string. Here Euler encountered "arbitrary" functions, geometrically represented in piecewise smooth plane curves of arbitrary form—functions which are, generally speaking, nonanalytic (1749). The problem of the magnitude of the class of functions applied in mathematical physics and generally in analysis and the closely related problem of the possibility of analytic expression of nonanalytic functions led to a lengthy polemic involving many mathematicians, including Euler, d'Alembert, and Daniel Bernoulli. One of the results of this controversy over the problem of the vibrating string was the general arithmetical definition of a function as a quantity whose values somehow change with the changes of independent variables; the definition was given by Euler in *Institutiones calculi differentialis.*[18] He had, however, already dealt with the interpretation of a function as a correspondence of values in his *Introductio.*

Elementary Functions. The major portion of the first volume of the *Introductio* is devoted to the theory of elementary functions, which is developed by means of algebra and of infinite series and products. Concepts of infinitesimal and infinite quantity are used, but those of differential and integral calculus are lacking. Among other things, Euler here for the first time described the analytic theory of trigonometric functions and gave a remarkably simple, although nonrigorous, deduction of Moivre's formula and also of his own (1743),

$$e^{\pm xi} = \cos x \pm i \sin x.$$

This was given earlier by R. Cotes (1716) in a somewhat different formulation, but it was widely used only by Euler. The logarithmic function was considered by Euler in the *Introductio* only for the positive independent variable. However, he soon published his complete theory of logarithms of complex numbers (1751)—which some time before had ended the arguments over logarithms of negative numbers between Leibniz and Johann Bernoulli and between d'Alembert and Euler himself in their correspondence (1747–1748). Euler had come across the problem (1727–1728) when he discussed in his correspondence with Johann I Bernoulli the problem of the graphics of the function $y = (-1)^x$ and arrived at the equality $\ln(-1) = \pi i$.

Functions of a Complex Variable. The study of elementary functions brought d'Alembert (1747–1748) and Euler (1751) to the conclusion that the domain of complex numbers is closed (in modern terms) with regard to all algebraic and transcendental operations. They both also made early advances in the general theory of analytic functions. In 1752 d'Alembert, investigating problems of hydrodynamics, discovered equations connecting the real and imaginary parts of an analytic function $u(x,y) + iv(x,y)$. In 1777 Euler deduced the same equations,

$$\frac{\partial u}{\partial x} = \frac{\partial v}{\partial y}, \quad \frac{\partial u}{\partial y} = -\frac{\partial v}{\partial x},$$

from general analytical considerations, developing a new method of calculation of definite integrals $\int f(z)\,dz$ by means of an imaginary substitution

$$z = x + iy$$

(1793, 1797). He thus discovered (1794) that

$$\int_0^\infty \frac{\sin x}{x}\,dx = \frac{\pi}{2}.$$

Euler also used analytic functions of a complex variable, both in the study of orthogonal trajectories by means of their conformal mapping (1770) and in his works on cartography (1778). (The term *projectio conformis* was introduced by a St. Petersburg academician, F. T. Schubert [1789].) All of these ideas were developed in depth in the elaboration of the general theory of analytic functions by Cauchy (1825) and Riemann (1854), after whom the above-cited equations of d'Alembert and Euler are named.

Although Euler went from numbers of the form $x + iy$ to the point $u(x,y)$ and back, and used a trigonometric form $r(\cos \varphi + i \sin \varphi)$, he saw in imaginary numbers only convenient notations void of real meaning. A somewhat less than successful attempt at geometric interpretation undertaken by H. Kühn (1753) met with sharp critical remarks from Euler.

Differential and Integral Calculus. Both branches of infinitesimal analysis were enriched by Euler's numerous discoveries. Among other things in the *Institutiones calculi differentialis,* he thoroughly elaborated formulas of differentiation under substitution of variables; revealed his theorem on homogeneous functions, stated for $f(x,y)$ as early as 1736; proved the theorem of Nikolaus I Bernoulli (1721) that for $z = f(x,y)$

$$\frac{\partial^2 z}{\partial x \partial y} = \frac{\partial^2 z}{\partial y \partial x};$$

deduced the necessary condition for the exact differential of $f(x,y)$; applied Taylor's series to finding extrema of $f(x)$; and investigated extrema of $f(x,y)$, inaccurately formulating, however, sufficient conditions.

The first two chapters of the *Institutiones* are devoted to the elements of the calculus of finite differences. Euler approached differential calculus as a particular case, we would say a limiting case, of the method of finite differences used when differences of the function and of the independent variable approach zero. During the eighteenth century it was often said against differential calculus that all its formulas were incorrect because the deductions were based on the principle of neglecting infinitely small summands, e.g., on equalities of the kind $a + \alpha = a$, where α is infinitesimal with respect to a. Euler thought that such criticism could be obviated only by supposing all infinitesimals and differentials equal to zero, and therefore he elaborated an original calculus of zeroes. This concept, although not contradictory in itself, did not endure because it proved insufficient in many problems; a strict grounding of analysis was possible if the infinitesimals were interpreted as variables tending to the limit zero.

The methods of indefinite integration in the *Institutiones calculi integralis* (I, 1768) are described by Euler in quite modern fashion and in a detail that practically exhausts all the cases in which the result of integration is expressible in elementary functions. He invented many of the methods himself; the expression "Euler substitution" (for rationalization of certain irrational differentials) serves as a reminder of the fact. Euler calculated many difficult definite integrals, thus laying the foundations of the theory of special functions. In 1729, already studying interpolation of the sequence $1!, 2!, \cdots, n!, \cdots$, he introduced Eulerian integrals of the first and second kind (Legendre's term), today called the beta- and gamma-functions (1738). He later discovered a number of their properties.

Particular cases of the beta-function were first considered by Wallis in 1656. The functions B and Γ, together with the zeta-function and the so-called Bessel functions (see below), are among the most important transcendental functions. Euler's main contribution to the theory of elliptic integrals was his discovery of the general addition theorem (1768). Finally, the theory of multiple integrals also goes back to Euler; he introduced double integrals and established the rule of substitution (1770).

Differential Equations. The *Institutiones calculi integralis* exhibits Euler's numerous discoveries in the theory of both ordinary and partial differential equations, which were especially useful in mechanics.

Euler elaborated many problems in the theory of ordinary linear equations: a classical method for solving reduced linear equations with constant coefficients, in which he strictly distinguished between the general and the particular integral (1743); works on linear systems, conducted simultaneously with d'Alembert (1750); solution of the general linear equation of order n with constant coefficients by reduction to the equation of the same form of order $n - 1$ (1753). After 1738 he successfully applied to second-order linear equations with variable coefficients a method that was highly developed in the nineteenth century; this consisted of the presentation of particular solutions in the form of generalized power series. Another Eulerian device, that of expressing solutions by definite integrals that depend

on a parameter (1763), was extended by Laplace to partial differential equations (1777).

One can trace back to Euler (1741) and Daniel Bernoulli the method of variation of constants later elaborated by Lagrange (1777). The method of an integrating factor was also greatly developed by Euler, who applied it to numerous classes of first-order differential equations (1768) and extended it to higher-order equations (1770). He devoted a number of articles to the Riccati equation, demonstrating its involvement with continued fractions (1744). In connection with his works on the theory of lunar motion, Euler created the widely used device of approximating the solution of the equation $dy/dx = f(x,y)$, with initial condition $x = x_0$, $y = y_0$ (1768), extending it to second-order equations (1769). This Euler method of open polygons was used by Cauchy in the 1820's to demonstrate the existence theorem for the solution of the above-mentioned equation (1835, 1844). Finally, Euler discovered tests for singular solutions of first-order equations (1768).

Among the large cycle of Euler's works on partial differential equations begun in the middle of the 1730's with the study of separate kinds of first-order equations, which he had encountered in certain problems of geometry (1740), the most important are the studies on second-order linear equations—to which many problems of mathematical physics may be reduced. First was the problem of small plane vibrations of a string, the wave equation originally solved by d'Alembert with the so-called method of characteristics. Given a general solution expressible as a sum of two arbitrary functions, the initial conditions and the boundary conditions of the problem admitted of arriving at solutions in concrete cases (1749). Euler immediately tested this method of d'Alembert's and further elaborated it, eliminating unnecessary restrictions imposed by d'Alembert upon the initial shape and velocity of the string (1749). As previously mentioned, the two mathematicians engaged in an argument which grew more involved when Daniel Bernoulli asserted that any solution of the wave equation might be expressed by a trigonometric series (1755). D'Alembert and Euler agreed that such a solution could not be sufficiently general. The discussion was joined by Lagrange, Laplace, and other mathematicians of great reputation and lasted for over half a century; not until Fourier (1807, 1822) was the way found to the correct formulation and solution of the problem. Euler later developed the method of characteristics more thoroughly (1766, 1767).

Euler encountered equations in other areas of what became mathematical physics: in hydrodynamics; in the problem of vibrations of membranes, which he reduced to the so-called Bessel equation and solved (1766) by means of the Bessel functions $J_n(x)$; and in the problem of the motion of air in pipes (1772). Some classes of equations studied by Euler for velocities close to or surpassing the velocity of sound continue to figure in modern aerodynamics.

Calculus of Variations. Starting with several problems solved by Johann and Jakob Bernoulli, Euler was the first to formulate the principal problems of the calculus of variations and to create general methods for their solution. In *Methodus inveniendi lineas curvas . . .*[13] he systematically developed his discoveries of the 1730's (1739, 1741). The very title of the work shows that Euler widely employed geometric representations of functions as flat curves. Here he introduced, using different terminology, the concepts of function and variation and distinguished between problems of absolute extrema and relative extrema, showing how the latter are reduced to the former. The problem of the absolute extremum of the function of several independent variables,

$$\int_a^b F(x, y, y') \, dx,$$

where F is the given and $y(x)$ the desired minimizing or maximizing function, is treated as the limiting problem for the ordinary extremum of the function

$$W_n(y_0, y_1, \cdots, y_n) = \sum_{k=0}^{n-1} F\left(x_k, y_k, \frac{y_{k+1} - y_k}{\Delta x}\right) \Delta x,$$

where $x_k = a + k\,\Delta x$, $\Delta x = (b - a)/n$, $k = 0, 1, \cdots, n$ (and $n \to \infty$). Thus Euler deduced the differential equation named after him to which the function $y(x)$ should correspond; this necessary condition was generalized for the case where F involves the derivatives $y', y'', \cdots, y^{(n)}$. In this way the solution of a problem in the calculus of variations might always be reduced to integration of a differential equation. A century and a half later the situation had changed. The direct method imagined by Euler, which he had employed only to obtain his differential equation, had (together with similar methods) acquired independent value for rigorous or approximate solution of variational problems and the corresponding differential equations.

In the mid-1750's, after Lagrange had created new algorithms and notations for the calculus of variations, Euler abandoned the former exposition and gave instead a detailed and lucid exposition of Lagrange's method, considering it a new calculus—which he called variational (1766). He applied the calculus of variations to problems of extreme values

of double integrals with constant limits in volume III of the *Institutiones calculi integralis* (1770); soon thereafter he suggested still another method of exposition of the calculus, one which became widely used.

Geometry. Most of Euler's geometrical discoveries were made by application of the methods of algebra and analysis. He gave two different methods for an analytical exposition of the system of spherical trigonometry (1755, 1782). He showed how the trigonometry of spheroidal surfaces might be applied to higher geodesy (1755). In volume II of the *Introductio* he surpassed his contemporaries in giving a consistent algebraic development of the theory of second-order curves, proceeding from their general equation (1748). He constituted the theory of third-order curves by analogy. But Euler's main achievement was that for the first time he studied thoroughly the general equation of second-order surfaces, applying Euler angles in corresponding transformations.

Euler's studies of the geodesic lines on a surface are prominent in differential geometry; the problem was pointed out to him by Johann Bernoulli (1732, 1736, and later). But still more important were his pioneer investigations in the theory of surfaces, from which Monge and other geometers later proceeded. In 1763 Euler made the first substantial advance in the study of the curvature of surfaces; in particular, he expressed the curvature of an arbitrary normal section by principal curvatures (1767). He went on to study developable surfaces, introducing Gaussian coordinates (1772), which became widely used in the nineteenth century. In a note written about 1770 but not published until 1862 Euler discovered the necessary condition for applicability of surfaces that was independently established by Gauss (1828). In 1775 Euler successfully renewed elaboration of the general theory of space curves (1786), beginning where Clairaut had left off in 1731.

Euler was also the author of the first studies on topology. In 1735 he gave a solution to the problem of the seven bridges of Königsberg: the bridges, spanning several arms of a river, must all be crossed without recrossing any (1741). In a letter to Goldbach (1750), he cited (1758) a number of properties of polyhedra, among them the following: the number of vertices, S, edges, A, and sides, H, of a polyhedron are connected by an equality $S - A + H = 2$. A hundred years later it was discovered that the theorem had been known to Descartes. The Euler characteristic $S - A + H$ and its generalization for multidimensional complexes as given by H. Poincaré is one of the principal invariants of modern topology.

Mechanics. In an introduction to the *Mechanica* (1736) Euler outlined a large program of studies embracing every branch of the science. The distinguishing feature of Euler's investigations in mechanics as compared to those of his predecessors is the systematic and successful application of analysis. Previously the methods of mechanics had been mostly synthetic and geometrical; they demanded too individual an approach to separate problems. Euler was the first to appreciate the importance of introducing uniform analytic methods into mechanics, thus enabling its problems to be solved in a clear and direct way. Euler's concept is manifest in both the introduction and the very title of the book, *Mechanica sive motus scientia analytice exposita.*

This first large work on mechanics was devoted to the kinematics and dynamics of a point-mass. The first volume deals with the free motion of a point-mass in a vacuum and in a resisting medium; the section on the motion of a point-mass under a force directed to a fixed center is a brilliant analytical reformulation of the corresponding section of Newton's *Principia;* it was sort of an introduction to Euler's further works on celestial mechanics. In the second volume, Euler studied the constrained motion of a point-mass; he obtained three equations of motion in space by projecting forces on the axes of a moving trihedral of a trajectory described by a moving point, i.e., on the tangent, principal normal, and binormal. Motion in the plane is considered analogously. In the chapter on the motion of a point on a given surface, Euler solved a number of problems of the differential geometry of surfaces and of the theory of geodesics.

The *Theoria motus corporum solidorum,*[19] published almost thirty years later (1765), is related to the *Mechanica.* In the introduction to this work, Euler gave a new exposition of punctual mechanics and followed Maclaurin's example (1742) in projecting the forces onto the axes of a fixed orthogonal rectilinear system. Establishing that the instantaneous motion of a solid body might be regarded as composed of rectilinear translation and instant rotation, Euler devoted special attention to the study of rotatory motion. Thus, he gave formulas for projections of instantaneous angular velocity on the axes of coordinates (with application of Euler angles), and framed dynamical differential equations referred to the principal axes of inertia, which determine this motion. Special mention should be made of the problem of motion of a heavy solid body about a fixed point, which Euler solved for a case in which the center of gravity coincides with the fixed point. The law of motion in such a case is, generally speaking, expressed by means of elliptic integrals. Euler was led to this problem by the study of precession of the equinoxes

and of the nutation of the terrestrial axis (1751).[33] Other cases in which the differential equations of this problem can be integrated were discovered by Lagrange (1788) and S. V. Kovalevskaya (1888). Euler considered problems of the mechanics of solid bodies as early as the first St. Petersburg period.

In one of the two appendixes to the *Methodus...*[13] Euler suggested a formulation of the principle of least action for the case of the motion of a point under a central force: the trajectory described by the point minimizes the integral ∫ *mv ds.* Maupertuis had stated at nearly the same time the principle of least action in a much more particular form. Euler thus laid the mathematical foundation of the numerous studies on variational principles of mechanics and physics which are still being carried out.

In the other appendix to the *Methodus,* Euler, at the insistence of Daniel Bernoulli, applied the calculus of variations to some problems of the theory of elasticity, which he had been intensively elaborating since 1727. In this appendix, which was in fact the first general work on the mathematical theory of elasticity, Euler studied bending and vibrations of elastic bands (either homogeneous or nonhomogeneous) and of a plate under different conditions; considered nine types of elastic curves; and deduced the famous Euler buckling formula, or Euler critical load, used to determine the strength of columns.

Hydromechanics. Euler's first large work on fluid mechanics was *Scientia navalis.* Volume I contains a general theory of equilibrium of floating bodies including an original elaboration of problems of stability and of small oscillations in the neighborhood of an equilibrium position. The second volume applies general theorems to the case of a ship.

From 1753 to 1755 Euler elaborated in detail an analytical theory of fluid mechanics in three classic memoirs—"Principes généraux de l'état d'équilibre des fluides"; "Principes généraux du mouvement des fluides"; and "Continuation des recherches sur la théorie du mouvement des fluides"—all published simultaneously (1757).[34] Somewhat earlier (1752) the "Principia motus fluidorum" was written; it was not published, however, until 1761.[35] Here a system of principal formulas of hydrostatics and hydrodynamics was for the first time created; it comprised the continuity equation for liquids with constant density; the velocity-potential equation (usually called after Laplace); and the general Euler equations for the motion of an incompressible liquid, gas, etc. As has generally been the case in mathematical physics, the main innovations were in the application of partial differential equations to the problems. At the beginning of the "Continuation des recherches" Euler emphasized that he had reduced the whole of the theory of liquids to two analytic equations and added:

> However sublime are the researches on fluids which we owe to the Messrs. Bernoulli, Clairaut and d'Alembert, they flow so naturally from my two general formulae that one cannot sufficiently admire this accord of their profound meditations with the simplicity of the principles from which I have drawn my two equations, and to which I was led immediately by the first axioms of mechanics.[36]

Euler also investigated a number of concrete problems on the motion of liquids and gases in pipes, on vibration of air in pipes, and on propagation of sound. Along with this, he worked on problems of hydrotechnology, discussed, in part, above. Especially remarkable were the improvements he introduced into the design of a hydraulic machine imagined by Segner in 1749 and the theory of hydraulic turbines, which he created in accordance with the principle of action and reaction (1752–1761).[37]

Astronomy. Euler's studies in astronomy embraced a great variety of problems: determination of the orbits of comets and planets by a few observations, methods of calculation of the parallax of the sun, the theory of refraction, considerations on the physical nature of comets, and the problem of retardation of planetary motions under the action of cosmic ether. His most outstanding works, for which he won many prizes from the Paris Académie des Sciences, are concerned with celestial mechanics, which especially attracted scientists at that time.

The observed motions of the planets, particularly of Jupiter and Saturn, as well as the moon, were evidently different from the calculated motions based on Newton's theory of gravitation. Thus, the calculations of Clairaut and d'Alembert (1745) gave the value of eighteen years for the period of revolution of the lunar perigee, whereas observations showed this value to be nine years. This caused doubts about the validity of Newton's system as a whole. For a long time Euler joined these scientists in thinking that the law of gravitation needed some corrections. In 1749 Clairaut established that the difference between theory and observation was due to the fact that he and others solving the corresponding differential equation had restricted themselves to the first approximation. When he calculated the second approximation, it was satisfactorily in accordance with the observed data. Euler did not at once agree. To put his doubts at rest, he advised the St. Petersburg Academy to announce a competition on the subject. Euler soon determined that Clairaut was right, and on Euler's recommendation his composition received

the prize of the Academy (1752). Euler was still not completely satisfied, however. In 1751 he had written his own *Theoria motus lunae exhibens omnes ejus inaequalitates* (published in 1753), in which he elaborated an original method of approximate solution to the three-body problem, the so-called first Euler lunar theory. In the appendix he described another method which was the earliest form of the general method of variation of elements. Euler's numerical results also conformed to Newton's theory of gravitation.

The first Euler lunar theory had an important practical consequence: T. Mayer, an astronomer from Göttingen, compiled, according to its formulas, lunar tables (1755) that enabled the calculation of the position of the moon and thus the longitude of a ship with an exactness previously unknown in navigation. The British Parliament had announced as early as 1714 a large cash prize for the method of determination of longitude at sea with error not to exceed half a degree, and smaller prizes for less exact methods. The prize was not awarded until 1765; £3,000 went to Mayer's widow and £300 to Euler for his preliminary theoretical work. Simultaneously a large prize was awarded to J. Harrison for his construction of a more nearly perfect chronometer. Lunar tables were included in all nautical almanacs after 1767, and the method was used for about a century.

From 1770 to 1772 Euler elaborated his second theory of lunar motion, which he published in the *Theoria motuum lunae, nova methodo pertractata* (1772).[24] For various reasons, the merits of the new method could be correctly appreciated only after G. W. Hill brilliantly developed the ideas of the composition in 1877–1888.

Euler devoted numerous works to the calculation of perturbations of planetary orbits caused by the mutual gravitation of Jupiter and Saturn (1749, 1769) as well as of the earth and the other planets (1771). He continued these studies almost to his death.

Physics. Euler's principal contribution to physics consisted in mathematical elaboration of the problems discussed above. He touched upon various physical problems which would not yield to mathematical analysis at that time. He aspired to create a uniform picture of the physical world. He had been, as pointed out earlier, closer to Cartesian natural philosophy than to Newtonian, although he was not a direct representative of Cartesianism. Rejecting the notion of empty space and the possibility of action at a distance, he thought that the universe is filled up with ether—a thin elastic matter with extremely low density, like super-rarefied air. This ether contains material particles whose main property is impenetrability. Euler thought it possible to explain the diversity of the observed phenomena (including electricity, light, gravitation, and even the principle of least action) by the hypothetical mechanical properties of ether. He also had to introduce magnetic whirls into the doctrine of magnetism; these are even thinner and move more quickly than ether.

In physics Euler built up many artificial models and hypotheses which were short-lived. But his main concept of the unity of the forces of nature acting deterministically in some medium proved to be important for the development of physics, owing especially to *Lettres à une princesse d'Allemagne.* Thus, his views on the nature of electricity were the prototype of the theory of electric and magnetic fields of Faraday and Maxwell. His theory of ether influenced Riemann.

Euler's works on optics were widely known and important in the physics of the eighteenth century. Rejecting the dominant corpuscular theory of light, he constructed his own theory in which he attributed the cause of light to peculiar oscillations of ether. His *Nova theoria lucis et colorum* (1746)[38] explained some, but not all, phenomena. Proceeding from certain analogies that later proved incorrect, Euler concluded that the elimination of chromatic aberration of optic lenses was possible (1747); he conducted experiments with lenses filled with water to confirm the conclusion. This provoked objections by the English optician Dollond, who, following Newton, held that dispersion was inevitable. The result of this polemic, in which both parties were partly right and partly wrong, was the creation by Dollond of achromatic telescopes (1757), a turning point in optical technology. For his part, Euler, in his *Dioptrica,* laid the foundations of the calculation of optical systems.

NOTES

All works cited are listed in the Bibliography. References to Euler's *Opera omnia* (see [1] in Bibliography) include series and volume number.

1. 20, p. 75.
2. "Constructio linearum isochronarum in medio quocunque resistente," in 1, 2nd ser., VI, p. 1.
3. "Methodus inveniendi traiectorias reciprocas algebraicas," in 1, 1st ser., XXVII, p. 1.
4. To be published in 1, 2nd ser., XX.
5. 1, 3rd ser., I, p. 181.
6. 26, p. 51.
7. 13, II, p. 182.
8. *Einleitung zur Rechen-Kunst zum Gebrauch des Gymnasii bey der Kayserlichen Academie der Wissenschafften in St. Petersburg* (St. Petersburg, 1738–1740). See 1, 3rd ser., II, 1–303.
9. *Mechanica sive motus scientia analytice exposita,* 2 vols. (St. Petersburg, 1736). See 1, 2nd ser., I and II.
10. 20, p. 77.

11. *Neue Grundsätze der Artillerie aus dem Englischen des Herrn Benjamin Robins übersetzt und mit vielen Anmerkungen versehen* (Berlin, 1745). See 1, 2nd ser., XIV.
12. See 1, 2nd ser., XIV, 468–477.
13. *Methodus inveniendi lineas curvas maximi minimive proprietate gaudentes* (Lausanne–Geneva, 1744). See 1, 1st ser., XXIV.
14. *Theoria motuum planetarum et cometarum* (Berlin, 1744). See 1, 2nd ser., XXVIII, 105–251.
15. *Introductio in analysin infinitorum,* 2 vols. (Lausanne, 1748). See 1, 1st ser., VIII and IX.
16. *Scientia navalis,* 2 vols. (St. Petersburg, 1749). See 1, 2nd ser., XVIII and XIX.
17. *Theoria motus lunae* (Berlin, 1753). See 1, 2nd ser., XXIII, 64–336.
18. *Institutiones calculi differentialis cum eius usu in analysi finitorum ac doctrina serierum* (Berlin, 1755). See 1, 1st ser., X.
19. *Theoria motus corporum solidorum seu rigidorum ex primis nostrae cognitionis principiis stabilita . . .* (Rostock–Greifswald, 1765). See 1, 2nd ser., III and IV.
20. The work, which comprises 234 letters, was published at St. Petersburg in 3 vols. The first two vols. (letters 1–154) appeared in 1768; vol. III appeared in 1772. See 1, 3rd ser., XI and XII.
21. *Gedancken von den Elementen der Cörper, in welchen das Lehr-Gebäude von den einfachen Dingen und Monaden geprüfet und das wahre Wesen der Cörper entdecket wird* (Berlin, 1746). See 1, 3rd ser., II, 347–366.
22. "Exposé concernant l'examen de la lettre de M. de Leibnitz, alléguée par M. le Professeur Koenig, dans le mois de mars 1751 des Actes de Leipzig, à l'occasion du principe de la moindre action." See 1, 2nd ser., V, 64–73.
23. The work was first published at St. Petersburg in Russian (vol. I, 1768; vol. II, 1769). It then appeared in a two-volume German edition (St. Petersburg, 1770). See 1, 1st ser., I.
24. *Theoria motuum lunae, nova methodo pertractata* (St. Petersburg, 1772). See 1, 2nd ser., XXII.
25. The work was published sequentially, in 3 vols., at St. Petersburg. Vol. I deals with principles of optics (1769); vol. II with construction of telescopes (1770); and vol. III with construction of microscopes (1771). See 1, 3rd ser., III and IV.
26. The work's 3 vols. were published sequentially in St. Petersburg in 1768, 1769, and 1770. See 1, 1st ser., XI, XII, and XIII.
27. To be published in 1, 2nd ser., XXI.
28. See 1, 3rd ser., VII, 200–247.
29. *Éclaircissemens sur les établissemens publics en faveur tant des veuves que des morts, avec la description d'une nouvelle espèce de tontine aussi favorable au public qu'utile à l'état* (St. Petersburg, 1776). See 1, 1st ser., VII, 181–245.
30. See 17.
31. Condorcet's *éloge* was first published in *Histoire de l'Académie royale des sciences pour l'année 1783* (Paris, 1786), pp. 37–68. It is reprinted in 1, 3rd ser., XII, 287–310.
32. See 50, chs. 1–2.
33. "Recherches sur la précession des équinoxes et sur la nutation de l'axe de la terre." See 1, 2nd ser., XXIX, 92–123.
34. See 1, 2nd ser., XII, 2–132.
35. See 1, 2nd ser., XII, 133–168.
36. See 1, 2nd ser., XII, 92, for the original French.
37. See 1, 2nd ser., XV, pt. 1, 1–39, 80–104, 157–218.
38. See 1, 3rd ser., V, 1–45.

BIBLIOGRAPHY

I. ORIGINAL WORKS. Euler wrote and published more than any other mathematician. During his lifetime about 560 books and articles appeared, and he once remarked to Count Orlov that he would leave enough memoirs to fill the pages of publications of the St. Petersburg Academy for twenty years after his death. Actually the publication of his literary legacy lasted until 1862. N. Fuss published about 220 works, and then the work was carried on by V. Y. Buniakovsky, P. L. Chebyshev, and P.-H. Fuss. Other works were found still later. The list compiled by Eneström (25) includes 856 titles and 31 works by J.-A. Euler, all written under the supervision of his father.

Euler's enormous correspondence (approximately 300 addressees), which he conducted from 1726 until his death, has been only partly published. For an almost complete description, with summaries and indexes, see (37) below. For his correspondence with Johann I Bernoulli, see (2) and (3); with Nikolaus I Bernoulli (2) and (4); with Daniel Bernoulli (2) and (3); with C. Goldbach (2) and (5); with J.-N. Delisle (6); with Clairaut (7); with d'Alembert (3) and (8); with T. Mayer (9); with Lagrange (10); with J. H. Lambert (11); with M. V. Lomonosov (12); with G. F. Müller (13); with J. D. Schumacher (13); with King Stanislas II (14); and with various others (15).

1. Euler's complete works are in the course of publication in a collection that has been destined from the outset to become one of the monuments of modern scholarship in the historiography of science: *Leonhardi Euleri Opera omnia* (Berlin-Göttingen-Leipzig-Heidelberg, 1911–   ). The *Opera omnia* is limited for the most part to republishing works that Euler himself prepared for the press. All texts appear in the original language of publication. Each volume is edited by a modern expert in the science it concerns, and many of the introductions constitute full histories of the relevant branch of science in the seventeenth and eighteenth centuries. Several volumes are in course of preparation. The work is organized in three series. The first series (*Opera mathematica*) comprises 29 vols. and is complete. The second series (*Opera mechanica et astronomica*) is to comprise 31 vols. and still lacks vols. XVI, XVII, XIX, XX, XXI, XXIV, XXVI, XXVII, and XXXI. The third series (*Opera physica, Miscellanea, Epistolae*) is to comprise 12 vols. and still lacks vols. IX and X. Euler's correspondence is not included in this edition.

2. P.-H. Fuss, ed., *Correspondance mathématique et physique de quelques célèbres géomètres du XVIIIe siècle*, 2 vols. (St. Petersburg, 1843). See vol. I for correspondence with Goldbach. For correspondence with Johann I Bernoulli, see II, 1–93; with Nikolaus I Bernoulli, II, 679–713; and with Daniel Bernoulli, II, 407–665.

3. G. Eneström, ed., *Bibliotheca mathematica*, 3rd ser., **4** (1903), 344–388; **5** (1904), 248–291; and **6** (1905), 16–87; for correspondence with Johann I Bernoulli. For Euler's correspondence with Daniel Bernoulli, see **7** (1906–1907); 126–156. See **11** (1911), 223–226, for correspondence with d'Alembert.

4. *Opera postuma*, I (St. Petersburg, 1862), 519–549.

5. A. P. Youschkevitch and E. Winter, eds., *Leonhard Euler und Christian Goldbach. Briefwechsel 1729–1764* (Berlin, 1965).

6. A. T. Grigorian, A. P. Youschkevitch, *et. al.*, eds., *Russko-frantsuskie nauchnye svyazi* (Leningrad, 1968), pp. 119–279.

7. G. Bigourdan, ed., "Lettres inédites d'Euler à Clairaut," in *Comptes rendus du Congrès des sociétés savantes, 1928* (Paris, 1930), pp. 26–40.

8. *Bullettino di bibliografia e di storia delle scienze matematiche e fisiche*, **19** (1886), 136–148.

9. Y. K. Kopelevich and E. Forbs, eds., *Istoriko-astronomicheskie issledovania*, V (1959), 271–444; X (1969), 285–308.

10. J. L. Lagrange, *Oeuvres*, J. A. Serret and G. Darboux, eds., XIV (Paris, 1892), 135–245.

11. K. Bopp, "Eulers und J.-H. Lamberts Briefwechsel," in *Abhandlungen der Preussischen Akademie der Wissenschaften* (1924), 7–37.

12. M. V. Lomonosov, *Sochinenia*, VIII (Moscow-Leningrad, 1948); and *Polnoe sobranie sochineny*, X (Moscow-Leningrad, 1957).

13. A. P. Youschkevitch, E. Winter, *et. al.*, eds., *Die Berliner und die Petersburger Akademie der Wissenschaften im Briefwechsel Leonhard Eulers*, 2 vols. See vol. I (Berlin, 1959) for letters to G. F. Müller; vol. II (Berlin, 1961) for letters to Nartov, Schumacher, Teplov, and others.

14. T. Kłado and R. W. Wołoszyński, eds., "Korrespondencja Stanisława Augusta z Leonardem Eulerem . . ." in *Studia i materiały z dziejów nauki polskiej*, ser. C, no. 10 (Warsaw, 1965), pp. 3–41.

15. V. I. Smirnov *et. al.*, eds., *Leonard Euler. Pisma k uchenym* (Moscow-Leningrad, 1963). Contains letters to Bailly, Bülfinger, Bonnet, C. L. Ehler, C. Wolff, and others.

II. SECONDARY LITERATURE.

16. J. W. Herzog, *Adumbratio eruditorum basilensium meritis apud exteros olim hodieque celebrium* (Basel, 1778), pp. 32–60.

17. N. Fuss, *Éloge de Monsieur Léonard Euler* (St. Petersburg, 1783). A German trans. of this is in (1), 1st ser., I, xliii–xcv.

18. Marquis de Condorcet, *Éloge de M. Euler*, in *Histoire de l'Académie royale des sciences pour l'année 1783* (Paris, 1786), pp. 37–68.

19. R. Wolf, *Biographien zur Kulturgeschichte der Schweiz*, IV (Zurich, 1862), 87–134.

20. P. Pekarski, "Ekaterina II i Eyler," in *Zapiski imperatorskoi akademii nauk*, **6** (1865), 59–92.

21. P. Pekarski, *Istoria imperatorskoi akademii nauk v Peterburge*, **1** (1870), 247–308. See also index.

22. M. I. Sukhomlinov, ed., *Materialy dlya istorii imperatorskoi akademii nauk, 1716–1760*, 10 vols. (St. Petersburg, 1885–1900). See indexes.

23. *Protokoly zasedany konferentsii imperatorskoi akademii nauk s 1725 po 1803 god*, 4 vols. (St. Petersburg, 1897–1911). See indexes.

24. A. Harnack, *Geschichte der königlichen preussischen Akademie der Wissenschaften*, I–III (Berlin, 1900).

25. G. Eneström, "Verzeichnis der Schriften Leonhard Eulers," in *Jahresbericht der Deutschen Mathematiker-Vereinigung*, Ergänzungsband **4** (Leipzig, 1910–1913). An important bibliography of Euler's works in three parts, listed in order of date of publication, in order of date of composition, and by subject. The first part is reprinted in (35), I, 352–386.

26. O. Spiess, *Leonhard Euler. Ein Beitrag zur Geistesgeschichte des XVIII. Jahrhunderts* (Frauenfeld–Leipzig, 1929).

27. G. Du Pasquier, *Léonard Euler et ses amis* (Paris, 1927).

28. W. Stieda, *Die Übersiedlung Leonhard Eulers von Berlin nach Petersburg* (Leipzig, 1931).

29. W. Stieda, *J. A. Euler in seinen Briefen, 1766–1790* (Leipzig, 1932).

30. A. Speiser, *Die Basler Mathematiker* (Basel, 1939).

31. E. Fueter, *Geschichte der exakten Wissenschaften in der Schweizerischen Aufklärung, 1680–1780* (Aarau, 1941).

32. Karl Euler, *Das Geschlecht Euler-Schölpi. Geschichte einer alten Familie* (Giessen, 1955).

33. E. and M. Winter, eds., *Die Registres der Berliner Akademie der Wissenschaften, 1746–1766. Dokumente für das Wirken Leonhard Eulers in Berlin* (Berlin, 1957). With an intro. by E. Winter.

34. *Istoria akademii nauk SSSR*, I (Moscow–Leningrad, 1958). See index.

35. Y. K. Kopelevich, M. V. Krutikova, G. M. Mikhailov, and N. M. Raskin, eds., *Rukopisnye materialy Leonarda Eylera v arkhive akademii nauk SSR*, 2 vols. (Moscow–Leningrad, 1962–1965). Vol. I contains an index of Euler's scientific papers, an index of official and personal documents, summaries of proceedings of conferences of the Academy of Sciences of St. Petersburg with respect to Euler's activities, an index of Euler's correspondence, a reedited version of the first part of (24), and many valuable indexes. Vol. II contains 12 of Euler's papers on mechanics published for the first time. See especially I, 120–228.

36. G. K. Mikhailov, "K pereezdu Leonarda Eylera v Peterburg" ("On Leonhard Euler's Removal to St. Petersburg," in *Izvestiya Akademii nauk SSSR. Otdelenie tekhnicheskikh nauk*, no. 3 (1957), 10–38.

37. V. I. Smirnov and A. P. Youschkevitch, eds., *Leonard Eyler. Perepiska. Annotirovannye ukazateli* (Leningrad, 1967).

38. F. Dannemann, *Die Naturwissenschaften in ihrer Entwicklung und in ihrem Zusammenhänge*, II–III (Leipzig, 1921). See indexes.

39. R. Taton, ed., *Histoire générale des sciences*, II (Paris, 1958). See index.

40. I. Y. Timchenko, *Osnovania teorii analiticheskikh funktsy. Chast I. Istoricheskie svedenia* (Odessa, 1899).

41. M. Cantor, *Vorlesungen über Geschichte der Mathematik*, III–IV (Leipzig, 1898–1908). See indexes.

42. H. Wieleitner, *Geschichte der Mathematik*, II (Berlin–Leipzig, 1911–1921). See indexes.

43. D. J. Struik, *A Concise History of Mathematics*, 2 vols. (New York, 1948; 2nd ed., London, 1956).

44. J. E. Hofmann, *Geschichte der Mathematik*, pt. 3 (Berlin, 1957). See index.

45. A. P. Youschkevitch, *Istoria matematika v Rossii do 1917 goda* (Moscow, 1968). See index.

46. Carl B. Boyer, *A History of Mathematics* (New York, 1968).

47. L. E. Dickson, *History of the Theory of Numbers*, 3 vols. (Washington, 1919–1927; 2nd ed., 1934). See indexes.

48. D. J. Struik, "Outline of a History of Differential Geometry," in *Isis*, **19** (1933), 92–120; **20** (1933), 161–191.

49. J. L. Coolidge, *A History of Geometrical Methods* (Oxford, 1940).

50. G. H. Hardy, *Divergent Series* (Oxford, 1949).

51. A. I. Markuschevitsch, *Skizzen zur Geschichte der analytischen Funktionen* (Berlin, 1955).

52. Carl B. Boyer, *History of Analytic Geometry* (New York, 1956). See index.

53. N. I. Simonov, *Prikladnye metody analiza u Eylera* (Moscow, 1957).

54. A. T. Grigorian, *Ocherki istorii mekhaniki v Rossii* (Moscow, 1961).

55. C. Truesdell, "The Rational Mechanics of Flexible or Elastic Bodies," in (1), 2nd ser., XI, pt. 2.

56. S. Timoschenko, *History of the Strength of Materials* (New York–Toronto–London, 1953).

57. A. P. Mandryka, *Istoria ballistiki* (Moscow–Leningrad, 1964).

58. N. N. Bogolyubov, *Istoria mekhaniki mashin* (Kiev, 1964).

59. F. Rosenberger, *Die Geschichte der Physik in Grundzügen*, II (Brunswick, 1884). See index.

60. V. F. Gnucheva, *Geografichesky departament akademii nauk XVIII veka* (Moscow–Leningrad, 1946).

61. E. Hoppe, *Die Philosophie Leonhard Eulers* (Gotha, 1904).

62. A. Speiser, *Leonhard Euler und die deutsche Philosophie* (Zurich, 1934).

63. G. Kröber, *L. Euler. Briefe an eine deutsche Prinzessin. Philosophische Auswahl* (Leipzig, 1965), pp. 5–26. See also intro.

Many important essays on Euler's life, activity, and work are in the following five memorial volumes.

64. *Festschrift zur Feier 200. Geburtstages Leonhard Eulers* (Leipzig–Berlin, 1907), a publication of the Berliner Mathematische Gesellschaft.

65. A. M. Deborin, ed., *Leonard Eyler, 1707–1783* (Moscow–Leningrad, 1935).

66. E. Winter, *et. al.*, eds., *Die deutsch-russische Begegnung und Leonhard Euler* ... (Berlin, 1958).

67. M. A. Lavrentiev, A. P. Youschkevitch, and A. T. Grigorian, eds., *Leonard Eyler. Sbornik statey* (Moscow, 1958). See especially pp. 268–375 and 377–413 for articles on Euler's work in astronomy and his physical concepts.

68. K. Schröder, ed., *Sammelband der zu Ehren des 250. Geburtstages Leonhard Eulers* ... *vorgelegten Abhandlungen* (Berlin, 1959).

69. *Istoriko-matematicheskie issledovania* (Moscow, 1949–1969). For articles on Euler, see II, V–VII, X, XII, XIII, XVI, and XVII.

70. G. K. Mikhailov, "Leonard Eyler," in *Izvestiya akademii nauk SSSR. Otdelenie tekhnicheskikh nauk*, no. 1 (1955), 3–26, with extensive bibliography.

A. P. YOUSCHKEVITCH

EULER-CHELPIN, HANS KARL AUGUST SIMON VON (*b*. Augsburg, Germany, 15 February 1873; *d*. Stockholm, Sweden, 6 November 1964), *biochemistry.*

Hans von Euler-Chelpin was the son of Rigas von Euler-Chelpin, a captain in the Royal Bavarian Regiment, and Gabrielle Furtner and was of the same family lineage as the Swiss mathematician Leonhard Euler. He attended schools in Munich, Würzburg, and Ulm, then from 1891 to 1893 studied art at the Munich Academy of Painting. His concern with the theory of colors caused him to become interested in the spectrum, and he turned his attention to science.

Euler-Chelpin enrolled at the then University of Berlin, where he studied physics under Emil Warburg and Max Planck and organic chemistry under Emil Fischer and A. Rosenheim. During the next two years he worked with W. Nernst in Göttingen. In the summer of 1897 he became an assistant to Svante Arrhenius in Stockholm, where he qualified as *Privatdozent* in physical chemistry at the University of Stockholm in 1898; he spent the summers of 1899 and 1900 with J. H. van't Hoff in Berlin.

Until this time Euler-Chelpin had concentrated on physical chemistry, a subject being developed with much enthusiasm in Germany and Sweden. He now turned toward organic chemistry, visiting the laboratories of Arthur Hantzsch at Würzburg and Leipzig and Johannes Thiele at Strasbourg. He began research in the field at this time, partly in collaboration with his wife, Astrid Cleve. His visits to the laboratories of E. Buchner in Berlin and G. Bertrand in Paris reflected a developing interest in fermentation.

He became professor of general and organic chemistry at the University of Stockholm in 1906. All of his remaining professional work was carried out in Sweden, of which country he became a citizen in 1902. Nevertheless, in World War I he reported for service in the German army, serving in the artillery and, after 1915, in the air force. In the winter of 1916–1917 he was assigned to a military mission in Turkey to stimulate production of munitions and alcohol. He then returned to the air force, where he became commander of a bomber squadron. During this period he had an arrangement with the University of Stockholm that permitted him to compress his teaching activities into a half year. During World War II Euler-Chelpin again made himself available to Germany, but in a diplomatic capacity.

In 1929, the year in which he shared the Nobel Prize in chemistry with Arthur Harden for studies on fermentation, Euler-Chelpin became director of the Vitamin Institute and Institute of Biochemistry founded at the University of Stockholm through the joint support of the Kurt and Alice Wallenburg Foundation and the International Education Board of the Rockefeller Foundation. In 1941 he retired from teaching but continued his research activities almost to the end of his life. He was twice married: to Astrid Cleve (1902–1912), daughter of P. T. Cleve, professor of chemistry at the University of Uppsala, by whom he had five children; and Elisabeth, Baroness Ugglas (1913–1964), by whom he had four children. Both women were associated with him in some of his investigations. His son Ulf Svante von Euler shared the Nobel Prize in medicine or physiology in 1970.

Euler-Chelpin's early interest in inorganic catalysis was soon transferred to biochemical studies and particularly to the enzymes associated with fermentation. His studies on the chemistry of plants led him to concentrate his interest on those fungi that lend themselves to the study of metabolic problems. His studies on vitamins were not really a diversion; most of this work contributed to the understanding of enzyme cofactors. His late work on cancer was also an extension of his work on enzymes.

The work for which Euler-Chelpin received the Nobel Prize in 1929 was closely associated with Buchner's discovery that cell-free yeast juice was still able to ferment sugar, and the observation by Harden and Young that such juice, when passed through an ultrafilter, was separated into two fractions, neither of which alone had the power to ferment sugar but which on mixing again showed normal fermenting activity. Euler-Chelpin studied the low molecular-weight fraction—named cozymase—for more than a decade, starting in 1923. By 1929 he and his associates, particularly K. Myrbäck and R. Nilsson, had clarified the role of cozymase in fermentation.

Harden had shown that phosphoric acid played a role in fermentation by giving rise to certain sugar phosphates. Euler-Chelpin and Nilsson developed the use of inhibitors whereby certain stages in enzyme-catalyzed reactions can be blocked by use of a toxic substance, using fluoride to block that phase of fermentation in which cozymase functions. With Myrbäck, Euler-Chelpin showed that when glucose reacts with phosphoric acid it splits into two three-carbon fragments, one of which remains combined with phosphate. The two other fragments then combine to form glucose diphosphate, while the non-phosphorylated fragment undergoes further degradation. The reaction thereby shows that the sugar molecule undergoing fermentation splits into an energy-rich and an energy-poor fragment.

Euler-Chelpin also investigated the chemical nature of cozymase. Although cozymase is widely distributed in the plant and animal world, Euler-Chelpin and his associates found yeast to be the most practical source for its preparation. Starting with a crude extract having 200 units of activity, they concentrated this into a product having a specific activity of 85,000 units. This product corresponded to a nucleotide, containing sugar, a purine base, and a phosphate; it was clearly related to adenylic acid, which had been isolated by others from muscle. When Warburg showed nicotinamide to be a cofactor in erythrocytes, Euler-Chelpin tested for nicotinamide in cozymase with positive results. Soon thereafter Euler-Chelpin, Fritz Schlenk, and their co-workers showed the chemical structure of cozymase to be that of diphosphopyridine nucleotide (DPN).

In his work on vitamins, Euler-Chelpin assisted in clarifying the role of nicotinamide and thiamine (B_1) in metabolically active compounds. Somewhat earlier, in association with the Swiss chemist Paul Karrer, he had helped clarify the vitamin A activity of the carotenoid pigments. His work on tumors dealt particularly with the role of nucleic acids.

BIBLIOGRAPHY

I. ORIGINAL WORKS. There is no collected bibliography of Euler-Chelpin's more than 1,100 research papers, but see the listings in Poggendorff and in the author indexes of *Chemical Abstracts*. His Nobel Prize lecture, "Fermentation of Sugars and Fermentative Enzymes," is available in *Nobel Lectures, Including Presentation Speeches and Laureates' Biographies, Chemistry, 1922–1941* (Amsterdam, 1966), pp. 144–155. His work is dealt with in detail in his books *Grundlagen und Ergebnisse der Pflanzenchemie*, 3 vols. (Brunswick, 1908–1909); *Chemie der Hefe und der alkoholischen Gärung* (Leipzig, 1915); *Chemie der Enzym*, 2 vols. (Munich-Wiesbaden, 1920–1927); *Biokatalysatoren* (Stuttgart, 1930); *Homogene Katalyse* (Stuttgart, 1931); *Biochemie der Tumoren* (Stuttgart, 1942), written with B. Skarzynski; *Reductone, ihre chemischen Eigenschaften und biochemischen Wirkungen* (Stuttgart, 1950); and *Chemotherapie und Prophylaxe des Krebses* (Stuttgart, 1962).

II. SECONDARY LITERATURE. The best biographical sketch is Feodor Lynen's obituary "Hans von Euler-Chelpin," in *Bayerische Akademie der Wissenschaften, Jahrbuch* (1965), pp. 206–212. Also see R. Lepsius, "Hans Karl August von Euler-Chelpin zum Gedächtnis," in *Chemikerzeitung*, **88** (1964), 933–936. Memoirs on his eightieth birthday are B. Eistert, "Hans von Euler-Chelpin zum 80 Geburtstag," *ibid.*, **77** (1953), 65; and W. Franke,

"Zu Hans von Euler's 80 Geburtstag," in *Naturwissenschaften*, **40** (1953), 177–180. Also see the sketch accompanying his lecture in *Nobel Lectures*, pp. 156–158.

AARON J. IHDE

EUSTACHI, BARTOLOMEO (*b.* San Severino, Ancona, Italy, *ca.* 1500–1510; *d.* on the Via Flaminia en route to Fossombrone, Italy, 27 August 1574), *medicine.*

Bartolomeo was the son of Mariano, a physician, and Francesca (Benvenuti) Eustachi. He had a good humanistic education, in the course of which he acquired such an excellent knowledge of Greek, Hebrew, and Arabic that he was able to edit an edition of the Hippocratic glossary of Erotian (1566) and is said to have made his own translations of Avicenna (Ibn Sīnā) from the Arabic. He appears to have studied medicine at the Archiginnasio della Sapienza in Rome, but it is not known precisely when. He began to practice medicine in his native land about 1540. He was thence invited to be physician first to the duke of Urbino, and then, in 1547, to the duke's brother, Cardinal Giulio della Rovere, whom Eustachi followed to Rome in 1549. There he was invited to join the medical faculty of the Sapienza as the equivalent of professor of anatomy, and to this end he was permitted to obtain cadavers for dissection from the hospitals of Santo Spirito and Consolazione. With advancing years Eustachi was so severely afflicted by gout that he was compelled to resign his chair. He continued, however, to serve Cardinal della Rovere, and it was in response to the cardinal's summons to Fossombrone in 1574 that he set forth, only to die on the way.

Eustachi's first works were *Ossium examen* and *De motu capitis*, both written in 1561 and directed against the anti-Galenism of Vesalius, for whom he had developed a unilateral hostility. Otherwise his researches had a more unbiased scientific purpose and displayed his notable ability as an anatomist.

In 1562 and 1563 Eustachi produced a remarkable series of treatises on the kidney, *De renum structura;* the auditory organ, *De auditus organis;* the venous system, *De vena quae azygos graecis dicitur;* and the teeth, *De dentibus.* These were published, together with the two earlier defenses of Galen, in *Opuscula anatomica* (1564), although the *De dentibus* has a separate title page bearing the date 1563. The treatise on the kidney was the first work specifically dedicated to that organ—it displays a detailed knowledge of the kidney superior to that of any earlier work and contains the first account of the suprarenal gland and a correct determination of the relative levels of the kidneys. It was also in this treatise that Eustachi for the first time emphasized the problem of anatomical variation, which had been previously touched upon briefly by Vesalius.

The second treatise on the auditory organ provides a correct account of the tube (*tuba auditiva*) that is still referred to eponymously by Eustachi's name, and contains a description of the tensor tympani and stapedius muscles. Eustachi's claim to discovery of the stapes is inadmissible, however, since it was mentioned orally by Giovanni Filippo Ingrassia in 1546 and in print by Pedro Jimeno (1549), Luis Collado (1555), and Falloppio (1561).

Eustachi, basing his work on the dissection of fetuses and newborn children, was also the first to make a study of the teeth in any considerable detail. He provided an important description of the first and second dentitions and, in some respects preceded by the account of Falloppio, described the hard outer tissue and soft inner structure of the teeth. He further attempted an explanation of the problem, not yet completely solved, of the sensitivity of the tooth's hard structure. In his work on the azygos vein and its ramifications Eustachi described the thoracic duct and indicated a careful and relatively advanced knowledge of the heart's structure.

In 1552 Eustachi, with the help of Pier Matteo Pini, a relative and an artist, prepared a series of forty-seven anatomical illustrations; these were engraved, two on the obverse and reverse of a single copper plate, by Giulio de' Musi of Rome. The illustrations were prepared for a book entitled *De dissensionibus ac controversiis anatomicis* but were never published. The first eight large octavo plates, labeled Tabula Prima–Octava, were used in the *Opuscula anatomica* to portray aspects of the kidneys, the azygos vein and its ramifications, the veins of the arm, the heart, and the Eustachian valve (*valvula venae cavae* in the right auricle) which is illustrated in Tabula Octava. Somewhat curiously the stapes is illustrated on Tabula Septima with the kidney, perhaps a last-minute addition since this ossicle is also portrayed and more correctly located on one of the plates (XXXXI) discussed below.

Since Eustachi mentioned forty-seven plates (that is, forty-seven copperplate engravings) in the *Opuscula anatomica* but actually made use of only eight of them in that work, the remainder seemed to have been lost after his death and were sought for long and unsuccessfully—by Marcello Malpighi, among others. Ultimately the missing thirty-nine engravings (in folio size and differently labeled Tabula IX–XXXXVII) were discovered in the early eighteenth century in the possession of a descendant of Pier Matteo Pini, to whom Eustachi had, as it was

learned, bequeathed them. They were purchased by Pope Clement XI for 600 scudi and presented to Giovanni Maria Lancisi, his physician and a successor to Eustachi in the chair of anatomy at the Sapienza. Lancisi published the plates, together with the eight smaller ones that had already appeared in 1564, under the title *Tabulae anatomicae Bartholomaei Eustachi quas a tenebris tandem vindicatas* (1714). Although devoid of Eustachi's planned text, the plates alone assure him a distinguished position in the history of anatomy. They are not the first copper-engraved anatomical illustrations to be produced, as has sometimes been declared, however, but rather the third, following those of Giambattista Canano (1541?) and those of Thomas Geminus, *Compendiosa totius anatomie delineatio aere exarata* (1545). Nevertheless, they are strikingly modern in appearance, clearly produced without decorative accompaniment. Sometimes, as in the instance of the "musclemen," they display both sides of the body in juxtaposition, with a numbered rule on three sides of the figures to which numbered references are made in the text for identification of detail.

Despite such modern effects the plates are, oddly enough, arranged in a way that suggests the pattern of dissection that had been followed from medieval times up to that of Vesalius, that is, beginning with the most corruptible parts and continuing thence to the least corruptible. Thus the Eustachian plates begin with the abdominal structures, then those of the thorax, followed by the nervous system, vascular system, muscles, and finally the bones. Despite the apparent detail and precision of representation within the illustrations, their arrangement suggests some sparsity of dissection material—unlike the relative wealth of it available to Vesalius which permitted him to discard the traditional organization of anatomical treatises.

A possible paucity of cadavers is also suggested by a kind of economy of detail in some of the Eustachian figures of the whole body, such as the "musclemen," except in those areas meant expressly for representation of a specific structure. Lack of information on Eustachi's activities prevents more than such surmise of limited dissection material. Whatever the case, examination of the individual plates reveals him to have had remarkable powers of observation. As an example, Tabula XVIII, displaying the base of the brain and in particular the sympathetic nervous system, surpasses in accuracy any similar delineation produced during the sixteenth century. In fact, the illustration of the sympathetic system is generally considered to be one of the best ever produced. The other illustrations of the nervous system are, however, of lesser quality, perhaps inferior to those of Vesalius. Similarly Tabula XXVI, illustrating the vascular system and the relationships of vessels to muscles, is also of notably superior quality, and this may likewise be said of Tabula XXXXII, which represents the dissection of the laryngeal structures. Had the Eustachian anatomical illustrations not been lost to the medical world for over a century, it seems likely that anatomical studies would have reached maturity in the seventeenth rather than the eighteenth century.

BIBLIOGRAPHY

The *Opuscula anatomica* (Venice, 1564) is an exceedingly rare book; it was reprinted in Leiden, 1707, and Delft, 1726. The *Tabulae anatomicae* (Rome, 1714) was republished in Amsterdam, 1722, but with copies of the original plates; in Rome, 1728, with the original plates again used; in Leiden, 1744, with newly engraved copies of the plates accompanied by separate outline plates of equal size on which explanatory letters were engraved. This edition, edited by B. S. Albinus, is the most desirable one for purposes of study. Further editions of the *Tabulae* were published in Venice, 1769; Amsterdam, 1798, in German translation; and Amsterdam, 1800. Finally, there is a commentary as well as an edition of the plates by Gaetano Petrioli, to whom Lancisi bequeathed them, *Riflessioni anatomiche sulle note di Lancisi fatte sopra le tavole del cel. B. Eustachio* (Rome, 1740). It is chiefly of significance for the attached biography of Eustachi by Barnardo Gentili.

There is a biographical study of Eustachi by G. Bilancioni, *Bartolomeo Eustachi* (Florence, 1913), and a collection of documents, *Memorie e documenti riguardanti Bartolomeo Eustachio pubblicati nel quarto centenario dalla nascita* (Fabriano, 1913). The plates as anatomical illustrations are discussed by Ludwig Choulant, Mortimer Frank, trans., *History and Bibliography of Anatomic Illustration* (Chicago, 1920), pp. 200–204, and by Robert Herrlinger, *Geschichte der medizinischen Abbildung* (Munich, 1967), pp. 133–137.

C. D. O'MALLEY

EUTOCIUS OF ASCALON (*b.* Palestine, *ca.* A.D. 480), *mathematics.*

Eutocius was the author of commentaries on three works by Archimedes. He also edited and commented on the first four books of the *Conics* of Apollonius.

His commentary on the first book of Archimedes' *On the Sphere and Cylinder* was dedicated to Ammonius, who was a pupil of Proclus and the teacher of Simplicius and many other sixth-century philosophers, and who could not have lived long after 510. Eutocius' four commentaries on the *Conics* are dedicated to Anthemius of Tralles, the architect of Hagia Sophia in Constantinople, who died about 534. For

these reasons the central point of Eutocius' activities may be put about 510, and it has become conventional to date his birth about 480.

The old belief that Eutocius flourished about fifty years later arose from a note at the end of three of his Archimedean commentaries—on *On the Sphere and Cylinder,* Books I and II, and on the *Measurement of a Circle*—to the effect that each of them was "edited by Isidorus, the mechanical engineer, our teacher." These words, bracketed by Heiberg, cannot refer to Eutocius because they are not compatible with his relationship to Ammonius, for Isidorus of Miletus continued the construction of Hagia Sophia after the death of Anthemius about 534 and could not have been Eutocius' teacher. The words are best understood as an interpolation by a pupil of Isidorus and contain the interesting information that Isidorus revised the commentaries in question. Similarly, a reference in the commentary on *On the Sphere and Cylinder,* Book II (Archimedes, Heiberg ed., III, 84.8–11) to an instrument for drawing parabolas invented by "Isidorus, the mechanical engineer, our teacher" is also best understood as an interpolation. Tannery mentions the possibility that the Isidorus in question may have been a nephew of the successor of Anthemius, who supervised the reconstruction of Hagia Sophia after an earthquake in 557. Ascalon (now Ashkelon), where Eutocius was born, lay between Azotus (now Ashdod) and Gaza on the coast of Palestine; it is the city made famous in the lament of David over Saul and Jonathan: "Tell it not in Gath, publish it not in the streets of Askelon" (II Samuel 1:20). The *Suda Lexicon* relates an unedifying story of a Thracian mercenary named Eutocius who made a lot of money and tried to buy himself into society, first at Eleutheropolis (now Beyt Guvrin, Israel), then at Ascalon, but few have followed Tannery in seeing an ancestor; it seems more probable that Ascalon has been introduced into this story by reason of the mathematician's name and fame.

In his preface to his interpretation of the *Measurement of a Circle* Eutocius refers to his earlier commentaries on *On the Sphere and Cylinder,* and in the commentary on Book I he asks Ammonius to bear with him if he should have erred through youth (Archimedes, Heiberg ed., III, 2.13). He explains that he has found no satisfactory commentaries on Archimedes before his own time and promises further elucidation of the master if his work should meet with the approval of Ammonius. Apart from the *Measurement of a Circle,* he later wrote commentaries on both books of Archimedes' treatise *On Plane Equilibria.* The commentary on Book I was dedicated to an otherwise unknown Peter, whose name reveals him to have been a Christian. It is a fair inference that Eutocius did not know the works of Archimedes entitled *Quadrature of a Parabola* and *On Spirals,* for if he had, he would have referred to them at certain points of his commentary (Archimedes, Heiberg ed., III, 228.25; 278.10; 280.4; 286.13) instead of making less suitable references. Presumably the commentaries on Apollonius' *Conics* were written later than those on Archimedes' works, but there is no direct evidence. All these commentaries have survived. It has been debated whether he also wrote a commentary on Ptolemy's *Syntaxis,* but there is no suggestion of one in a passage of his commentary on the *Measurement of a Circle* (Archimedes, Heiberg ed., III, 232.15–17), where he mentions "Pappus and Theon and many others" as having interpreted that work.

Eutocius is not known to have done any original mathematical work, and his elucidations of Archimedes and Apollonius do not add anything of mathematical significance. Nevertheless, the examples of long multiplication in his commentary on the *Measurement of a Circle* are the best available evidence of the way in which the Greeks handled such operations, and he preserves solutions of mathematical problems by the earlier Greek geometers that are sometimes the sole evidence for their existence and are therefore of major importance for the historian of mathematics.

It is through Eutocius that we have a valuable collection of solutions by Greek geometers of the problem of finding two mean proportionals to two given straight lines, that is, if a and b are two given straight lines, to find two other straight lines x and y such that $a:x = x:y = y:b$. It was to this that a problem which attracted the best Greek mathematicians for several centuries—how to find a cube double another cube—had been reduced by Hippocrates, for if $a:x = x:y = y:b$, then $a^3:x^3 = a:b$, and if $b = 2a$, then x is the side of a cube double a cube of side a. From that time the problem appears to have been attacked exclusively in this form.

The first proposition of Archimedes' *On the Sphere and Cylinder,* Book II, is "Given a cone or cylinder, to find a sphere equal to the cone or cylinder." He shows as analysis that this can be reduced to the problem of finding two mean proportionals and then, in the synthesis, says: "Between the two straight lines, let two mean proportionals be found." It is at this point that Eutocius begins an extended comment (Archimedes, Heiberg ed., III, 54.26–106.24). After noting that the method of finding two mean proportionals is in no way explained by Archimedes, he observes that he had found the subject treated by many famous men, of whom he omits Eudoxus be-

cause in his preface he said he had solved the problem by curved lines but had not used them in the proof and had, moreover, treated a certain discrete proportion as though it were continuous, which a mathematician of his caliber would not have done. In order that the thinking of those men whose solutions have been handed down might be manifest, Eutocius sets out the manner of each discovery. He gives a solution attributed to Plato (but almost certainly wrongly attributed), followed by solutions given by Hero in his *Mechanics* and *Belopoeïca,* by Philo of Byzantium, by Apollonius, by Diocles in his work *On Burning Mirrors,* by Pappus in his *Introduction to Mechanics,* by Sporus of Nicaea, by Menaechmus (two solutions), by Archytas as related by Eudemus, by Eratosthenes, and by Nicomedes in his book *On Conchoidal Lines.* (This is not a chronological order; chronologically the order would probably be Archytas, Eudoxus, Menaechmus, the pseudo-Plato, Eratosthenes, Nicomedes, Apollonius, Philo, Diocles, Hero, Sporus, and Pappus. There is, indeed, no discernible order in Eutocius' list.)

Hero's solution is given in his *Mechanics* I, 11, which has survived only in an Arabic translation, and in his *Belopoeïca,* and is reproduced by Pappus, *Collection* III, 25–26. Pappus' solution is given in *Collection* III, 27 and VIII, 26; it is the latter passage that Eutocius has in mind. The conchoid is described by Pappus, *Collection* IV, 39–40, and he mentions that it was used by Nicomedes for finding two mean proportionals but does not give a proof. The other solutions would not be known but for their preservation by Eutocius. It is a pity that he did not include what purported to be Eudoxus' solution despite the obvious errors in transmission, but for what he has preserved he deserves the gratitude of posterity. The solution ascribed to Eratosthenes is prefaced by a letter, allegedly from Eratosthenes to Ptolemy Euergetes, giving the history of the problem of doubling the cube and its reduction to the problem of finding two mean proportionals; the letter is not authentic, but it closes with a genuine condensed proof and an epigram that Eratosthenes put on a votive monument. The solution attributed to Plato is probably not authentic because, among other reasons, it is mechanical, but the solutions of Eudoxus and Menaechmus show that the problem was studied in the Academy and may be Platonic. According to Eutocius, Nicomedes was exceedingly vain about his solution and derided that of Eratosthenes as impractical and lacking in geometrical sense. The solutions of Diocles, Sporus, and Pappus are substantially identical and so are those of Apollonius, Hero, and Philo.

It is only a little later, in commenting on the fourth

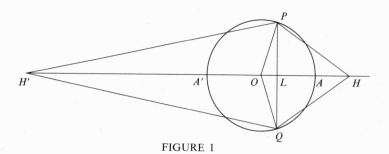

FIGURE 1

proposition of *On the Sphere and Cylinder,* Book II, that Eutocius gives a further precious collection of solutions that would not otherwise be known. Proposition 4 is the problem "To cut a given sphere by a plane so that the volumes of the segments are to one another in a given ratio." In Proposition 2 Archimedes had shown that a segment of a sphere is equal to a cone with the same base as the segment and height $h(3r - h)/(2r - h)$, where r is the radius of the sphere and h is the height of the segment (LA in the figure). In Proposition 4 he proves geometrically that if h, h' are the heights of the two segments, so that $h + h' = 2r$, and they stand in the ratio $m:n$, then

$$h\frac{(3r - h)}{(2r - h)} = \frac{m}{n} h'\frac{(3r - h')}{(2r - h')}.$$

By the elimination of h' this becomes the cubic equation

$$h^3 - 3h^2r + \frac{4m}{m + n} r^3 = 0.$$

The problem is thus reduced (in modern notation) to finding the solution of a cubic equation that can be written

$$h^2 (3r - h) = \frac{4m}{m + n} r^3.$$

Archimedes preferred to treat this as a particular case of a general equation

$$x^2(a - x) = bc^2,$$

where b is a given length and c^2 a given area. For a real solution it is necessary that

$$bc^2 \not> \frac{4}{27}a^3.$$

In the particular case of II, 4, there are always two real solutions.

Before proceeding to the synthesis of the main problem, Archimedes promised to give the analysis and synthesis of this subsidiary problem at the end, but Eutocius could not find this promise kept in any

of the texts of Archimedes. He records that after an extensive search he found in an old book a discussion of some theorems that seemed relevant. They were far from clear because of errors and the figures were faulty, but they seemed to give the substance of what he wanted. The language, moreover, was in the Doric dialect and kept the names for the conic sections that had been used by Archimedes. Eutocius was therefore led to the conclusion, as we also must be, that what he had before him was in substance the missing text of Archimedes, and he proceeded to set it out in the language of his own day. The problem is solved, in modern notation, by the intersection of the parabola and rectangular hyperbola

$$x^2 = \frac{c^2}{a} y, (a - x)y = ab.$$

Others before Eutocius had noticed the apparent failure of Archimedes to carry out his promise, and Eutocius also reproduced solutions by Dionysodorus and Diocles. Dionysodorus solved the particular case of the cubic equation to which II, 4 reduces, that is,

$$(3r - x):\frac{m}{m + n}r = 4r^2:x^2.$$

His solution is the intersection of the parabola and rectangular hyperbola

$$y^2 = \frac{m}{m + n}r (3r - x) \text{ and}$$

$$xy = \frac{m}{m + n}2r^2.$$

Diocles solved not the subsidiary equation but the original problem, II, 4, by means of the intersection of an ellipse

$$(y + a - x)^2 = \frac{n}{m}\{ (a + b)^2 - x^2\}$$

and the rectangular hyperbola

$$(x + a)(y + b) = 2ab.$$

It is clear that the *Measurement of a Circle* was

490

already reduced to three propositions, with the second and third in the wrong order, when Eutocius had it before him. The chief value of his commentary is that he works out in detail the arithmetical steps where Archimedes merely gives the results. Archimedes requires a number of square roots. Eutocius excuses himself from working them out, on the ground that the method is explained by Hero and by Pappus, Theon, and other commentators on Ptolemy's *Syntaxis,* but he multiplies the square root by itself to show how close the approximation is. At the end Eutocius reveals that Apollonius in a work called Ὠκυτόκιον (*Formula for Quick Delivery*) found a closer approximation to the ratio of a circumference of a circle to its diameter than did Archimedes; and he exculpates Archimedes from the censure of Sporus of Nicaea, whose own teacher, Philo of Gadara, also found a more exact value, on the ground that Archimedes was looking for a figure useful in daily life.

Apart from what has been noted above, Eutocius' comments on Archimedes do not add much of value to the text, and occasionally he errs, as in saying that two parabolic segments in Proposition 8 of *On Plane Equilibria* are similar (Archimedes, Heiberg ed., III, 290.23-24). In a commentary on the difficult lemma that is Proposition 9 of the same book and leads to the location of the center of gravity of a portion of a parabola cut off by parallel chords, he admits himself forced to paraphrase.

The commentaries on the *Conics* display more mathematical acumen. In his preface to Book I, Apollonius explains how uncorrected copies came to be in circulation before he had completed his revision. It is therefore probable that there were variant readings and alternative proofs in the manuscripts from earliest days. It is clear that when Eutocius came to comment on Apollonius, he had before him differing versions, and he found it necessary to prepare a recension for his own purposes; in two manuscripts the four books of his comment have the heading "A Commentary of Eutocius of Ascalon on the First (Second, Third, Fourth) of the *Conics* of Apollonius as Edited by Himself." Eutocius' edition suffered at the hands of interpolators, probably in the ninth century, when mathematics had a renaissance at Constantinople under Leo the Mathematician. The best manuscript of the commentary (W, Cod. Vat. gr. 204) was copied in the tenth century, and at a number of points Eutocius' citations from Apollonius are clearly nearer to the original than is the text of the *Conics* as we have it today. In commenting on Apollonius, Eutocius had been preceded by Serenus and Hypatia. The most interesting features of the commentary are in the early pages, where Eutocius emphasizes the generality of Apollonius' method of producing conic sections from any cone.

All the books by Archimedes on which Eutocius commented have survived, and his elucidations may have contributed to their survival. There must also be some significance in the fact that the four books of the *Conics* on which he commented have survived in Greek, whereas Books V–VII have survived only in Arabic and Book VIII is entirely lost. His commentaries on Archimedes were translated into Latin along with the parent works by William of Moerbeke in 1269. The commentaries have usually been printed with the editions of Archimedes and Apollonius and have never been printed separately. The definitive text is to be found in Heiberg's editions of Archimedes and Apollonius with a Latin translation and valuable prolegomena and notes.

BIBLIOGRAPHY

I. ORIGINAL WORKS. Eutocius' commentaries can be found in *Commentarii in libros Archimedis De sphaera et cylindro, in Dimensionem circuli et in libros De planorum aequilibris,* in *Archimedis opera omnia,* J. L. Heiberg, ed., 2nd ed., III (Leipzig, 1915), 1–448; and *Commentaria in Conica,* in *Apollonii Pergaei quae graece exstant,* J. L. Heiberg, ed., II (Leipzig, 1893), 168–361.

II. SECONDARY LITERATURE. See Paul Tannery, "Sur l'histoire des lignes et surfaces courbes dans l'antiquité," in *Bulletin des sciences mathématiques,* 2nd ser., **7** (1883), 278–291; and "Eutocius et ses contemporains," *ibid.,* **8** (1884), 315–329, repr. in *Mémoires scientifiques,* II (Toulouse–Paris, 1912), 1–47, 118–136; and Sir Thomas Heath, *A History of Greek Mathematics* (Oxford, 1921), I, 52, 57–58; II, 25, 45, 126, 518, 540–541.

IVOR BULMER-THOMAS

EVANS, FREDERICK JOHN OWEN (*b.* London [?], England, 9 March 1815; *d.* London, 20 December 1885), *hydrography, geomagnetism.*

Evans came of a naval family, his father, John Evans, being master, R.N. He volunteered for the navy himself at the age of thirteen. Having served on H.M.S. *Rose* and *Winchester* on the American station for five years, he was transferred to the survey ship *Thunder* under Captain Richard Owen. Here he began a long lifetime of work devoted to exact surveying at sea and to geomagnetism.

After three years around the coasts of Central America and the Bahamas, Evans served in a succession of ships in the Mediterranean; in the master's line, he had responsibility for navigation. In 1841 he became master and senior surveying officer of H.M.S. *Fly,* assigned to exploration in the Coral Sea, around the Great Barrier Reef of Australia, and in the Torres Strait; his hydrographic work revealed a safe and easy passage through the strait and was an important contribution to the development of New South Wales. On 12 November 1846 he married Elizabeth Mary Hall of Plymouth, daughter of a naval captain. In 1847 Evans joined the *Acheron* and returned to the antipodes, where for four years he did hydrographic work on the coasts of New Zealand.

After distinguished service in the Baltic during the Crimean War, in 1855 Evans was appointed superintendent of the Compass Department of the Navy; he was promoted to staff commander in 1863, staff captain in 1867, and full captain in 1872. He became chief naval assistant to the hydrographer to the navy in 1865 and himself occupied that important post from 1874 to 1884. He was appointed a companion of the Order of the Bath and knight commander in 1881.

Evans' recognition as an outstanding scientist comes from his solution of the problems associated with compass navigation in iron and armor-plated ships and from his observations leading to the publication of a chart of curves of equal magnetic declination for the navigable world. In his work on compass errors, he had the collaboration of the eminent mathematician Archibald Smith; Evans as experimenter and Smith as theoretician made a formidable team. Together they solved a problem of great importance to the British Navy and to navigation in general at the time when iron ships were coming into wide use. Some of Evans' experiments were carried out on board the pioneer Atlantic steamship *Great Eastern.* The results led to proposals for the proper placing of the needles in the compass in relation to the soft iron magnets and in relation to the ship itself. Both induction effects and the magnetic field created by the metal were fully considered. An important indirect contribution to oceanography was the compilation of the magnetic instructions made by Evans and Smith for the great voyage of the *Challenger* in 1872–1876.

Evans' contribution to science was recognized by his election as fellow of the Royal Society in 1862. He was also a fellow of the Royal Astronomical Society and a fellow and council member of the Royal Geographical Society. In 1884 he represented Britain at the Congress of Washington for the establishment of a prime meridian.

BIBLIOGRAPHY

I. ORIGINAL WORKS. Evans' works include "Reduction and Discussion of the Deviations of the Compass Observed on Board of All the Iron-built Ships, and a Selection of the Wood-built Steamships in Her Majesty's Navy," in *Philosophical Transactions of the Royal Society,* **150** (1860), 337–378; "On the Effect Produced on the Deviations of the Compass by the Length and Arrangement of the Compass-needles; and a New Mode of Correcting the Quadrantal Deviation," *ibid.,* **151** (1861), 161–182, written with A. Smith; "On the Magnetic Character of the Armour-plated Ships of the Royal Navy, and on the Effect on the Compass of Particular Arrangements of Iron in a Ship," *ibid.,* **155** (1865), 263–324, written with A. Smith; "On the Amount and Changes of the Polar Magnetism in Her Majesty's Iron-built and Armour-plated Ship 'Northumberland,'" *ibid.,* **158** (1868), 487–504; *Admiralty Manual for Deviation of the Compass* (London, 1862; 2nd ed., 1863; 3rd ed., 1869); *Elementary Manual for Deviations of the Compass* (London, 1870); and "On the Present Amount of Westerly Magnetic Declination on the Coast of Great Britain, and Its Annual Changes," in *Philosophical Transactions of the Royal Society,* **162** (1872), 319–330.

II. SECONDARY LITERATURE. On Evans and his work see "Sir F. J. O. Evans," in *Nature,* **33** (1886), 246–248; "Captain Sir Frederick J. O. Evans," in *Proceedings of the Royal Geographical Society,* **8** (1886), 112–113; J. B. Jukes, *Narrative of the Surveying Voyage of H.M.S. "Fly." Commanded by Capt. F. P. Backwood, in Torres Strait, New Guinea etc. During the Years 1842–1846,* 2 vols. (London, 1847).

K. C. DUNHAM

EVANS, LEWIS (*b.* Llangwnadl, Carnarvonshire, Wales, 1700; *d.* New York, N.Y., 11 June 1756), *cartography, geography, geomorphology, geology.*

Evans came to Philadelphia sometime before 1736 and became known as surveyor, draftsman, and mapmaker. He also gave lectures on electricity and wrote on climatology. He was a friend and associate of Benjamin Franklin, John Bartram, Governor Thomas Pownall, and Cadwallader Colden, and was very helpful to the visiting Swedish scientist Peter Kalm, who referred to him as "an ingenious engineer."

Based on his own surveys and explorations he made maps of land tracts and boundaries. His two great published maps are "A Map of Pennsylvania, New-Jersey, New-York, And the Three Delaware Counties" (1749; a revision was published in 1752) and "A General Map of the Middle British Colonies in America" (1755). In the booklet that accompanies the latter map Evans not only describes the geography, geomorphology, and some geology and other natural features of the region, but also makes a vigorous attack on the contemporary permissive policy of the British administrators toward the French encroachment in the Ohio Valley, which he vehemently insists must be preserved for English settlement. After a second fiery pamphlet, which even hinted at treasonous collusion with France, Governor

Robert Hunter Morris of Pennsylvania secured Evans' imprisonment in New York, to which he had moved. He was released from jail only three days before he died, leaving his motherless eleven-year-old daughter to the care of friends.

In 1743 Evans traveled with John Bartram and Conrad Weiser to Lake Ontario. In his journal (published in 1776 by Pownall) he recorded observations on raised beaches of the once higher Great Lakes and speculated penetratingly on the drainage of the earlier lakes and the consequent rise of the land because "This part of America was disburthened of such a Load of Waters."

Evans filled in the blank spaces of his maps of 1749 and 1752 with notes on weather, roads, streams, and geology. His notes on the Endless (Appalachian) Mountains were not only descriptive but were also the first analysis of their origin, based on the fossils preserved in their strata and on the erosion of valleys from a former plain (peneplain in modern terms) to form the ridges.

Evans' 1755 "Map of the Middle British Colonies" is partly a geologic map, showing not only the location of economic minerals—"coals," "freestone," pottery clay, and petroleum—but also the trends of the mountains and some indication of rock types. He was keenly aware of the three-dimensional nature of geology and constructed map profiles and sections of strata with their "particular fossils" to accompany the map. Evans said, however, that for "want of room in the plate," these sections would be published on later maps when he had more space. Evans died before these later maps could be published.

The thirty-six-page *Analysis of a General Map of the Middle British Colonies . . . and a Description of the Face of the Country . . .* that accompanied the 1755 map contains (in addition to the discussion of the administration of the Ohio Valley) a long and clear statement of the geomorphic and geologic provinces of the eastern United States. In this prototypical work of American geomorphology, divisions now known as the New England Upland, the Coastal Plain, the Fall Line, the Piedmont, the Blue Ridge, the Folded Appalachians, the Allegheny Front, and the Allegheny Plateau are first delineated. Evans realized that these regions were different because of differing rocks and structures.

Evans' great map was reprinted and copied at least twenty-seven times in the next fifty years. His regional geologic and physiographic classification provided in greater or lesser part the geologic framework for later writers in the sixty years following his death. He was a great cartographer and an early student not only of landscape but also of fossils and the relation of bedrock to surface morphology. He was the first in America to recognize the principles of isostasy.

BIBLIOGRAPHY

I. ORIGINAL WORKS. Evans' maps and publications, now very rare, are reproduced in facsimile, with his extensive unpublished notes, in Laurence H. Gipson, *Lewis Evans* (Philadelphia, 1939). Evans' 1743 journal is published in Thomas Pownall, *A Topographical Description of Such Parts of North America . . .* (London, 1776; Pittsburgh, 1949).

II. SECONDARY LITERATURE. For Evans' life and the history of his maps see Gipson, above; H. N. Stevens, *Lewis Evans, His Map of the Middle British Colonies* (London, 1905, 1924, 1929); and L. C. Wroth, *An American Bookshelf* (Philadelphia, 1934).

For discussion of Evans' geological observations see G. W. White, "Lewis Evans' Early American Notice of Isostasy," in *Science,* **114** (1951), 302–303; "Lewis Evans' Contributions to Early American Geology—1743–1755," in *Transactions of the Illinois Academy of Science,* **44** (1951), 152–158; and "Lewis Evans (1700–56): A Scientist in Colonial America," in *Nature,* **177** (1956), 1055–1056.

GEORGE W. WHITE

EVANS, WILLIAM HARRY (*b.* Shillong, Assam, India, 22 July 1876; *d.* Church Whitfield, Dover, England, 13 November 1956), *entomology.*

Evans' parents were both of military families; his father was General Sir Horace M. Evans (related by marriage to Charles Dickens) and his mother—"the best woman I have known and the greatest influence in my life"—was a keen naturalist, Elizabeth Annie, daughter of Surgeon General T. Tresidder. Conventionally educated at King's School, Canterbury, and the Royal Military Academy, Woolwich, Evans was commissioned an officer in the Royal Engineers at the age of twenty and retired at fifty-five. Apart from the Somaliland Campaign (1903–1904) and World War I (1914–1918), in each of which he was both wounded and decorated, his entire army career was spent in India. He rose to be a distinguished staff officer and was coauthor of several textbooks on administration and military engineering. It is as a naturalist, however, that he will be remembered.

His first tour of army duty (1900–1901) was in Chitral, on the North-West Frontier of India. His hobby there, with a fellow sapper, Major (later Major General) G. A. Leslie, was collecting butterflies. A joint paper, Evans' first publication, listed 139 species, of which, despite the attentions of Lionel de Nicéville, the foremost authority in India, ten could be named only doubtfully and nineteen could not be named at all. Although the relevant literature was voluminous and described a great number of individual genera and species, it contained little analytical or comparative data and did not help in naming fresh material. The concept of linking isolated species as geographically separated races or subspecies of one extensive species had not then been adopted.

Evans resolved to document the butterflies of the Indian region in a way that he himself, with no biological training, could understand. He devoted his spare time to study and collecting; his vacations to touring and visiting museums. He searched the literature for all original descriptions and examined practically every type specimen. From 1910 on he published subregional lists for areas not previously covered, and then in 1923 he began to publish a series of papers on classification in the *Journal of the Bombay Natural History Society.* They were such a success that the Society published them as a volume, *Identification of Indian Butterflies* (Madras, 1927; 2nd ed., rev., 1932).

Here were gathered 695 generic and nearly 4,400 specific names under 320 valid genera and 1,442 species, all readily identifiable through remarkably concise and practical keys. The various subspecies and synonyms were noted, and the whole was well indexed. An informative introduction dealt comprehensively with structure, classification, collecting, and study. This handy volume, in which not a word was wasted, remains the only work dealing fully with the subject of identification, and many popular treatments have stemmed from it. Thus, by the time he retired, Evans had achieved his ambition and published a standard work of the greatest value to oriental entomologists. But now he planned a greater one.

The Hesperiidae (skippers), one of the largest cosmopolitan families of butterflies, had long been neglected owing to their smallness and drab appearance. Evans undertook to reclassify them. He settled near the British Museum (Natural History) in London and worked there as regularly as the staff. In 1937 the Museum published his *Catalogue of the African Hesperiidae . . . in the British Museum,* which, in little more than 200 pages, classified naturally through concise keys 421 species, illustrated 116 species for the first time, and for every species gave diagrams of the male genitalia—features of essential value in distinguishing among this family.

During World War II Evans continued his work in the museum; his deafness was aggravated when a bomb detonated on the road outside the room where he was working on a drawer of specimens, the blast shattering the window and clearing his table, leaving him holding a bare pin. Undeterred, he pub-

lished further catalogues of the Hesperiidae, of which one (1949) covered those of Europe, Asia, and Australia, and a final four volumes (1951–1955) were devoted to those of the Americas. Thus, a year before he died, Evans had established a complete classification of the Hesperiidae of the world, in which he had marshaled 747 published generic names (over a hundred his own) in 525 recognized genera with 3,000 species and nearly 2,000 subspecies, placing a further 3,300 names as synonyms. Not only had he provided comparative keys for the essential features of each natural subfamily, group, and genus, down to subspecies, but he had also given diagrams of the male genitalia of every recognized species and illustrated the majority of the least-known ones in color, for the first time.

BIBLIOGRAPHY

Besides the main works discussed, Evans' many shorter papers are well listed in *The Lepidopterist's News,* **10** (1957), 197–199. Two additions to that list are "Revisional Notes on African Hesperiidae," in *Annals and Magazine of Natural History,* ser. 12, **8,** pt. 4 (1956), 881–885; and "A Revision of the *Arhopala* group of Oriental Lycaenidae," in *Bulletin of the British Museum* (*Natural History*), **5** (1957), 85–141.

C. F. COWAN

EVELYN, JOHN (*b.* Wotton, Surrey, England, 31 October 1620; *d.* London, England, 27 February 1706), *arboriculture, horticulture.*

Evelyn was the grandson of George Evelyn, principal manufacturer of gunpowder under Queen Elizabeth, and the second son of Richard Evelyn, high sheriff of Surrey and Sussex in 1633–1634. He was at Balliol College, Oxford, from 1637 to 1640. On account of the political situation in England he left the country in November 1643 and traveled through France and Italy for the next three years. From June 1645 to April 1646 he was mostly in Padua, studying anatomy and physiology. He brought back anatomical tables which he presented to the Royal Society; these are now in the Royal College of Surgeons.

In July 1646 Evelyn returned to Paris, where he attended courses in chemistry by Nicasius Le Fèvre. In 1649 he went through another course in chemistry at Sayes Court in England. In June 1647 he married Mary, the daughter of Sir Richard Browne, Charles I's diplomatic agent in France. The marriage was a happy one. Of their five sons and three daughters, only one daughter survived her father.

Evelyn spent the last year of the Civil War in England, and his first work, *Of Liberty and Servitude,* a translation of the French treatise against tyranny of F. de la Mothe le Vayer, appeared in January 1649. It was during his last stay in Paris, from 1649 to 1652, that Nanteuil engraved his portrait (1650). Before leaving, he wrote a short treatise on *The State of France, As It Stood in the IXth Yeer of This Present Monarch, Lewis XIIII* (London, 1652). In February 1652 he finally returned to England and settled at Sayes Court, his father-in-law's estate at Deptford in Kent. This was to be his home for the next forty years. After the death of his brother George in 1699, he succeeded to the family estate of Wotton, where he took up residence in 1700.

During his travels Evelyn visited hospitals and was interested in their organization. He showed he had a notion of the importance of isolation during the plague by suggesting the construction of an infirmary. His *Diary* contains a description of touching for the king's evil in 1660 and notices of treatments, medicinal springs, and surgical operations (particularly an amputation of the leg and cutting for the stone). He was present at several dissections and in 1683 attended Walter Charleton's lecture on the heart. He was concerned with hygiene and in *Fumifugium* (1661), a work on the pollution of the air in London, he proposed removing certain trades and planting a green belt of fragrant trees and shrubs around the city. He also possessed some knowledge of zoology.

Horticulture was an enduring interest throughout Evelyn's life and at the beginning of 1653 he started laying out the gardens at Sayes Court, which were to become famous. He began making notes for a vast projected work on horticulture, *Elysium britannicum.* The work, to which Sir Thomas Browne contributed, was never completed and only a synopsis was printed in 1659. But Evelyn continued adding to his notes throughout his life. He also offered valuable practical information to gardeners by publishing translations of important French works, particularly *The Compleat Gard'ner* from Jean de La Quintinie (1693).

Evelyn's principal work, *Sylva,* was the outcome of his association with the Royal Society. Following inquiries made in September 1662 by the commissioners of the navy to the Royal Society concerning timber trees, he drew up a report which he enlarged and presented to the Royal Society on 16 February 1664. *Sylva* was the first book published by order of the Society. It was an immediate success, and more than a thousand copies were sold in less than two years. Evelyn received special thanks from the king and the work appears to have had considerable influence on the propagation of timber trees throughout the kingdom. *Sylva* is not a scientific work but the exhortation of a lover of trees to his countrymen to

repair the damage caused by the Civil War. It contains practical information interspersed haphazardly with classical references. To *Sylva* was annexed *Pomona,* a discourse on the cultivation of fruit trees for the production of cider, and *Kalendarium hortense,* a gardener's almanac, being a chapter of the unfinished *Elysium britannicum. A Philosophical Discourse of Earth* appeared in 1676; it was added to *Sylva* in 1679, as *Terra.* His *Acetaria. A Discourse of Sallets,* also part of *Elysium britannicum,* was published separately in 1699, then added to the 1706 edition of *Sylva. Sylva* was advertised in 1670 and 1671 in the autumn catalogue of books at the Frankfurt fair. Alexander Hunter popularized *Sylva* with an extensively annotated edition, collated from the five original editions, in 1776.

To familiarize his countrymen with the philosophy of Epicurus, Evelyn published his translation of the first book of Lucretius' *De rerum natura* in 1656, followed by a commentary on the works of Gassendi and atomism. Evelyn had taken no part in the affairs of state during the Interregnum, but at the end of 1659 he published an anonymous pamphlet, *An Apologie for the Royal Party,* to induce Colonel Morley, later lieutenant of the Tower, to declare for the king. This proved unsuccessful but may have eased the way for the return of Charles II, to whom Evelyn presented a *Panegyric* on his coronation. In this he suggested that Charles should become the founder of a body for the furthering of experimental knowledge. In 1654, at Oxford, Evelyn had met John Wilkins, the leader of an active group of men interested in science; he thus met Christopher Wren, with whom he collaborated several times during his lifetime. In 1659 he sent Robert Boyle a suggestion for the foundation of a "Mathematical College," or community for scientific study. In December 1660 Evelyn was proposed a member of the society for "the promoting of experimental philosophy," then meeting at Gresham College.

Evelyn was instrumental in obtaining royal patronage and the name of "Royal Society" for the group in 1662. He attended the meetings regularly, served on the council frequently, and was offered the presidency. In January 1661 he drew up a "History of Arts Illiberal and Mechanick" (Royal Society Archives). He was appointed a member of several committees of inquiry, including that for agriculture, and contributed papers on various subjects. In 1665 he sat on the committee for the improvement of the English language.

The fourteen years following the king's return were those of Evelyn's greatest public activity, although the offices he held were only temporary appointments.

He served on several commissions from 1660 to 1674—for the improvement of London streets in 1662, for the Royal Mint in 1663, and for the repair of St. Paul's Cathedral in 1666, during which he worked with Christopher Wren. On 13 September 1666 Evelyn presented his plan for the rebuilding of the city, together with a discourse on the problems involved. But the entire replanning soon appeared impracticable. During the two Dutch wars (1664–1667 and 1672–1674) he was commissioner for the sick and wounded mariners and prisoners of war, his most responsible appointment. From 1671 to 1674 he was a member of the Council for Foreign Plantations, later the Council of Trade and Foreign Plantations. In 1674 *Navigation and Commerce* appeared, being the introduction to a history of the Dutch war that Charles had asked Evelyn to write, which was never finished.

In January 1667 Evelyn obtained for the library of the Royal Society the famous collection of books and manuscripts of the earl of Arundel. The collection of stones bearing Greek and Latin inscriptions was also secured through his good offices for the university of Oxford. *Sculptura: or the History, and Art of Chalcography and Engraving in Copper* (1662) was the outcome of a paper read before the Royal Society. His artistic interests also led him to translate two books from the French of Roland Fréart de Chambray, *A Parallel of the Antient Architecture with the Modern* (1664) and *An Idea of the Perfection of Painting* (1668). To the *Parallel* Evelyn added an *Account of Architects and Architecture,* which he dedicated in the second edition to Christopher Wren. The book appears to have been an indispensable work for later architects. His *Numismata. A Discourse of Medals, Antient and Modern* (1697) closed with a discussion of character as derived from effigies.

Evelyn's translations also include *Instructions Concerning Erecting of a Library* from the French of Gabriel Naudé and Jansenist writings against the Jesuits, for in spite of his tolerance he was hostile to Catholicism. He was a staunch and devout Anglican and found a spiritual advisor in Jeremy Taylor. In 1672 he formed a pious friendship with Margaret Blagge, later Mrs. Godolphin, a maid of honor to the queen, and wrote her *Life* to commemorate her virtues. Among his closest friends was Samuel Pepys, the diarist.

Evelyn lacked detachment and a methodical training to make his contributions scientifically valid. His activity was guided by religious and patriotic motives. His various publications were intended to "give ferment to the curious." His *Diary,* which he kept throughout his life, is his greatest contribution, albeit to letters rather than to science.

BIBLIOGRAPHY

I. ORIGINAL WORKS. Evelyn's works—some of which were published anonymously or pseudonymously—include his trans. of F. de la Mothe le Vayer's *Of Liberty and Servitude* (London, 1649); *The State of France, As It Stood in the IXth Yeer of This Present Monarch, Lewis XIIII* (London, 1652); *An Essay on the First Book of T. Lucretius Carus De rerum natura* (London, 1656); as "Philocepos," *The French Gardiner: Instructing How to Cultivate all Sorts of Fruit-Trees, and Herbs for the Garden,* trans. from N. de Bonnefons (London, 1658); *The Golden Book of St. John Chrysostom, Concerning the Education of Children,* trans. from the Greek (London, 1659); *A Character of England, As It Was Lately Presented in a Letter, to a Noble Man of France* (London, 1659); *An Apologie for the Royal Party: Written in a Letter to a Person of the Late Councel of State* (London, 1659); *Elysium britannicum* (London, ca. 1659), a synopsis of proposed work on gardening, presumably a table of contents, British Museum Add. MS. 15950, f. 143; *The Late News or Message From Bruxels Unmasked, and His Majesty Vindicated, From the Base Calumny and Scandal Therein Fixed on Him* (London, 1660); *The Manner of Ordering Fruit-Trees,* trans. from "Le Sieur Le Gendre" (London, 1660) [attributed to Evelyn by F. E. Budd, in *Review of English Studies,* **14** (1938), 285–297]; *A Panegyric to Charles the Second, Presented to His Majestie the XXIII. of April, Being the Day of His Coronation. MDCLXI* (London, 1661); *Fumifugium: or the Inconveniencie of the Aer and Smoak of London Dissipated* (London, 1661); *Instructions Concerning Erecting of a Library . . .* trans. from Gabriel Naudé (London, 1661); *Tyrannus or the Mode: in a Discourse of Sumptuary Lawes* (London, 1661); *Sculptura: or the History, and Art of Chalcography and Engraving in Copper* (London, 1662); *Sylva, or A Discourse of Forest-Trees, and the Propagation of Timber in His Majesties Dominions . . . To Which Is Annexed Pomona; or, An Appendix Concerning Fruit-Trees in Relation to Cider; The Making and Several Ways of Ordering It . . . Also Kalendarium Hortense; or, Gard'ners Almanac; Directing What He Is to Do Monethly Throughout the Year* (London, 1664); *A Parallel of the Antient Architecture With the Modern,* trans. from the French of R. Fréart de Chambray (London, 1664); Μυστήριον τῆς 'Ανομίας. *That Is, Another Part of the Mystery of Jesuitism,* trans. from the French of A. Arnauld and P. Nicole (London, 1664); *The Pernicious Consequences of the New Heresie of the Jesuites Against the King and the State,* trans. from the French of P. Nicole (London, 1666); *The English Vineyard Vindicated by John Rose Gard'ner to His Majesty* (London, 1666) [Evelyn's authorship identified by G. Keynes]; *Publick Employment and an Active Life Prefer'd to Solitude* (London, 1667); *An Idea of the Perfection of Painting,* trans. from R. Fréart de Chambray (London, 1668); *The History of the Three Late Famous Impostors* (London, 1669); *Navigation and Commerce, Their Original and Progress* (London, 1674); *A Philosophical Discourse of Earth, Relating to the Culture and Improvement of It for Vegetation, and the Propagation of Plants, &c. as It Was Presented to the Royal Society, April 29.1675* (London,

1676) [called *Terra* in later editions]; *The Compleat Gard'ner; or, Directions for Cultivating and Right Ordering of Fruit-Gardens and Kitchen-Gardens; With Divers Reflections on Several Parts of Husbandry,* trans. from J. de La Quintinie (London, 1693); *Numismata. A Discourse of Medals, Antient and Modern* (London, 1697); and *Acetaria. A Discourse of Sallets* (London, 1699).

His occasional contributions include "An Account of Snow-Pits in Italy," in R. Boyle, *New Experiments and Observations Touching Cold* (London, 1665), pp. 407–409; "An Advertisement of a Way of Making More Lively Counterfeits of Nature in Wax, Than Are Extant in Painting: And of a New Kind of Maps in a Low Relievo. Both Practised in France," in *Philosophical Transactions of the Royal Society,* **1** (1665), 99–100; "A Letter . . . Concerning the Spanish Sembrador or New Engin for Ploughing . . . Sowing . . . and Harrowing, at Once," *ibid.,* **5** (1670), 1055–1057; "Panificium, or the Several Manners of Making Bread in France. Where, by Universal Consent, the Best Bread in the World Is Eaten," in J. Houghton, *A Collection of Letters for the Improvement of Husbandry & Trade,* no. 12 (16 Jan. 1683), 127–136; "An Abstract of a Letter From the Worshipful John Evelyn Esq; Sent to One of the Secretaries of the R. Society Concerning the Dammage Done to his Gardens by the Preceding Winter," in *Philosophical Transactions of the Royal Society,* **14** (1684), 559–563; and "Letter to William Cowper Relating to the Anatomical Tables [acquired by Evelyn in Padua]," *ibid.,* **23** (1702), 1177–1179.

Evelyn's shorter works are collected in William Upcott, ed., *The Miscellaneous Writings of John Evelyn, Esq., F. R. S.,* (London, 1825). Posthumous publications are R. M. Evanson, ed., *The History of Religion. A Rational Account of the True Religion* (London, 1850); Geoffrey Keynes, ed., *Memoires for My Grand-son* (Oxford, 1926) and *Directions for the Gardiner at Says-Court But Which May Be of Use for Other Gardens* (Oxford, 1932); Walter Frere, ed., *A Devotionarie Book of John Evelyn* (London, 1936); E. S. de Beer, ed., *London Revived* (Oxford, 1938), the discourse on the replanning of the City of London after the Great Fire; and Harriet Sampson, ed., *The Life of Mrs. Godolphin* (London, 1939).

Evelyn's diary was published first in shortened form by William Bray as *Memoirs* (London, 1818); of many later editions E. S. de Beer, ed., *The Diary of John Evelyn,* 6 vols. (Oxford, 1955), is definitive. Selections from the *Diary* containing important notes may be found in *Voyage de Lister à Paris en MDCXCVIII. . . . On y a joint des Extraits des ouvrages d'Evelyn relatifs à ses voyages en France de 1648 à 1661* (Paris, 1873); H. Maynard Smith, ed., *John Evelyn in Naples 1645* (Oxford, 1914); and *The Early Life and Education of John Evelyn* (Oxford, 1920); and Howard C. Levis, ed., *Extracts from the Diaries and Correspondence of John Evelyn and Samuel Pepys Relating to Engraving* (London, 1915).

Evelyn's correspondence may be found in William Bray, ed., *Diary and Correspondence of John Evelyn . . . To Which Is Subjoined, The Private Correspondence Between King Charles I and Sir Edward Nicholas,* in Bohn's Historical Library (London, 1859 and later issues); F. E. Rowley

Heygate, ed., *Seven Letters of John Evelyn, 1665–1703* (London, 1914); and Clara Marburg, *Mr. Pepys and Mr. Evelyn* (Philadelphia, 1935).

II. SECONDARY LITERATURE. Books on Evelyn include Helen Evelyn, *The History of the Evelyn Family* (London, 1915); Florence Higham, *John Evelyn, Esquire. An Anglican Layman of the Seventeenth Century* (London, 1968); W. G. Hiscock, *John Evelyn and Mrs. Godolphin* (London, 1951) and *John Evelyn and His Family Circle* (London, 1955), which present an adverse view of Evelyn; Geoffrey Keynes, *John Evelyn. A Study in Bibliophily With a Bibliography of His Writings* (Oxford, 1968); and Arthur Ponsonby, *John Evelyn. Fellow of the Royal Society; Author of "Sylva"* (London, 1933).

Lectures and articles that deal with Evelyn and his work are Jackson I. Cope, "Evelyn, Boyle and Dr. Wilkinson's 'Mathematico-Chymico-Mechanical School,'" in *Isis,* **50** (1959), 30–32; Edward Gordon Craig, "John Evelyn and the Theatre in England, France and Italy," in *The Mask,* **10** (1924), repr. in *Books and Theatres* (1925), pp. 3–68; E. S. de Beer, "John Evelyn, F.R.S. (1620–1706)," in *Notes and Records of the Royal Society of London,* Tercentenary Number, **15** (1960), 231–238; Margaret Denny, "The Early Program of the Royal Society and John Evelyn," in *Modern Language Quarterly,* **1** (1940), 481–497; Leonard Guthrie, *The Medical History of John Evelyn, D.C.L., F.R.S., and of His Time 1620–1706* (London, 1905), two lectures delivered before the Harveian Society of London and the King's College Medical Society in October 1902 and October 1903, respectively; George B. Parks, "John Evelyn and the Art of Travel," in *The Huntington Library Quarterly,* **10** (1947), 251–276; W. Barclay Squire, "Evelyn and Music," in *The Times Literary Supplement* (17 Apr. 1924; 16 Oct. 1924; 14 May 1925; 10 Dec. 1925; and 14 Oct. 1926); and F. Sherwood Taylor, "The Chemical Studies of John Evelyn," in *Annals of Science,* **8** (1952), 285–292.

COLETTE AVIGNON

EVERSHED, JOHN (*b.* Gomshall, Surrey, England, 26 February 1864; *d.* Ewhurst, Surrey, England, 17 November 1956), *solar physics.*

The seventh son of John Evershed and Sophia, daughter of David Brent Price of Portsmouth, Evershed came of a family long established in Surrey and was educated at a private Unitarian school in Brighton and later at Croydon. In 1906 he married Mary Acworth Orr, who assisted him in his work until her death in 1949. A year later Evershed married Margaret Randall, who survived him; there were no children from either marriage.

Evershed was introduced into scientific circles by his elder brother Sydney, an inventor of electrical apparatus for the Royal Navy and a researcher in permanent magnetism. As a young man he studied solar spectroscopy and carried out experiments in the production of continuous and absorption spectra of heated gases at his private observatory at Kenley,

Surrey. He was fortunate in inheriting in 1894 the instruments of A. Cowper Ranyard, the distinguished amateur astronomer; these included an eighteen-inch refractor and a spectrograph. A liberal-minded employer (he was engaged in the analysis of oils and other products for a London firm) granted him leave to go on several total solar eclipse expeditions. Professor H. H. Turner provided introductions which led him in 1898 to travel for this purpose to India via the United States (where Evershed spent a month with George E. Hale) and Japan. It was on this expedition that he photographed for the first time the continuous spectrum to the ultraviolet of the Balmer series limit at λ 3646.

Correspondence and meetings with Sir William Huggins, then president of the Royal Society, resulted in Evershed's appointment as assistant to C. Michie Smith, director of the Kodaikanal and Madras observatories in India. Making full use of the high altitude of Kodaikanal (2,343 meters) and of his skill in designing and building instruments, Evershed began a long series of spectroheliograms of the sun's disk. He further began the research which led in 1909 to the discovery in sunspots of the small radial motions of gases parallel to the sun's surface, now known as the Evershed effect. In 1911 he succeeded to the directorship of the Kodaikanal and Madras observatories. During his period of office he carried out a great deal of chromospheric research, made early use of hydrogen α spectroheliograms, and, in 1915, led an expedition to Kashmir, where exceptionally good viewing conditions made it possible for him to measure the small shift to the red of spectrum lines in connection with Einstein's predictions.

Evershed retired in 1923 and returned to England. He settled at Ewhurst, Surrey, where with undiminished enthusiasm he again equipped a private observatory. There he carried out high-dispersion work (employing large liquid prisms) to determine the exact wavelengths of the solar spectrum, sunspots, prominences, and minute line-shifts, and to study the Zeeman effect in assessing the strength of magnetic fields of sunspots. The death of his wife deprived him of her practical assistance, but he continued to make observations until 1953. He then presented some of his instruments to the Royal Greenwich Observatory.

An ingenious designer of optical instruments and an indefatigable and meticulous observer, Evershed contributed much to the knowledge of solar physics during the early decades of this century.

BIBLIOGRAPHY

F. J. M. Stratton, "John Evershed," in *Biographical Memoirs of Fellows of the Royal Society* (1957) contains a full bibliography of Evershed's work. Some representative examples are "Experiments on the Radiation of Heated Gases," in *Philosophical Magazine,* **39** (1895), 460; "Wave-length Determinations and General Results Obtained From a Detailed Examination of Spectra Photographed at the Solar Eclipse of January 22, 1898," in *Philosophical Transactions of the Royal Society,* **197A** (1901), 381; "Solar Eclipse of 1900 May 28—General Discussion of Spectroscopic Results," *ibid.,* **201** (1903), 457; "Radial Motions in Sunspots," in *Monthly Notices of the Royal Astronomical Society,* **70** (1910), 217; "The Spectrum of Nova Aquilae," *ibid.,* **79** (1919), 468; "The Solar Rotation and Shift Towards the Red Derived From the H and K Lines in Prominences," *ibid.,* **95** (1935), 503; "Note on the Zeeman Effect in Sunspot Spectra," *ibid.,* **99** (1939), 217; and "Measures on the Relative Shift of the Line 5250.218 and Neighboring Lines in Mt. Wilson Solar Magnetic Field Spectra," *ibid.,* **99** (1939), 438.

An autobiographical notice is "Recollections of Seventy Years of Scientific Work," in *Vistas in Astronomy,* I (London–New York, 1955), 33.

P. S. LAURIE

EWING, JAMES (*b.* Pittsburgh, Pennsylvania, 25 December 1866; *d.* New York, N.Y., 16 May 1943), *pathology.*

Ewing was the son of Thomas and Julia Hufnagel Ewing, members of a prominent western Pennsylvania family. He completed a classical education at Amherst College, from which he received the A.B. degree in 1888 and the M.A. in 1891. In 1891 he obtained a medical doctorate from the College of Physicians and Surgeons of Columbia University; he subsequently returned there as a tutor in histology (1893–1897), a Clark fellow (1896–1899), and an instructor in clinical pathology (1897–1898). Ewing's mentors at the College of Physicians and Surgeons were Francis Delafield and T. Mitchell Prudden. He also served a brief apprenticeship with another eminent pathologist of the era, Alexander Kolisko, at the Vienna Clinic.

In 1899, following a period of voluntary service as a contract surgeon in the Spanish-American War, Ewing accepted a professorship in clinical pathology at the Medical College of Cornell University in New York. In 1932 he assumed the newly created chair in oncology there, which position he occupied until his retirement in 1939.

A review of Ewing's earlier works reveals the underlying influences of his preceptors at the College of Physicians and Surgeons, and especially the inspiration of Prudden, to whom Ewing dedicated the first and second editions of his *Clinical Pathology of the Blood* (1901; 1903). His contributions of this period include significant reports on the pathogenesis of infectious diseases (see, for example, his Wesley

M. Carpenter Lecture of 1900), immunity and blood serum reactions, and medicolegal questions. Ewing's connection with Cornell University allowed him to do research at the Loomis Laboratory for Research in Experimental Pathology, where an experimental cancer program was begun in 1902 under the auspices of the New York Memorial Hospital (Collis P. Huntington Fund). In 1906 Ewing and his associates published a significant finding on lymphosarcoma in dogs. This investigation showed that the disease was transmitted from one animal to another during coitus by the transfer of viable tumor cells. By virtue of this and other important laboratory discoveries, Ewing soon became one of the foremost American spokesmen in experimental oncology.

By 1910 Ewing recognized the need for a comprehensive organization of anticancer activities. Ewing's scheme for such a center was characterized about 1950 by Leonard Scheele, then surgeon-general of the U.S. Public Health Service, as a plan for "a cancer institute in the modern sense—an institution where scientists of many disciplines combine their efforts and resources in a common mission, cancer research." Ewing was able to implement his idea in 1913, when he was elected president of the Medical Board of the General Memorial Hospital for the Treatment of Cancer and Allied Diseases. In this position and later as first director of research and director of Memorial Hospital (from 1931 to 1939), Ewing supervised the creation of a primary cancer facility—the present Memorial Sloan-Kettering Cancer Center in New York City.

Under Ewing's direction Memorial Hospital entered a new era, one especially fruitful for the clinical management of neoplastic disorders through radiation therapy. As in his studies on the fundamental aspects of cancer research, he brought to the problems of radiology and radiotherapy his own creative and systematic intellect (see his Mutter Lecture of 1922 and the Caldwell Lecture of 1925), and he imparted the wealth of his practical experiences to a younger generation of clinicians. Ewing's stature as the medical administrator of Memorial Hospital is measured precisely in Emerson's dictum that "Every institution is but the lengthened shadow of some man."

The early death of his wife, Catherine Halsted, in 1902 evoked reclusive and eccentric tendencies in Ewing's personality. In later years he suffered the agonizing discomforts of tic doloreux (trigeminal neuralgia), which curtailed his professional activities. He remained an avid sports enthusiast nevertheless, with a marked preference for tennis and baseball, and he possessed a keen artistic temperament.

Ewing's works include several monographs and textbooks. *Clinical Pathology of the Blood* is a rich source on hematologic disorders, while *Neoplastic Diseases* is the cornerstone of modern oncology. In the latter work Ewing recorded a number of significant discoveries in tumor morphology and distinguished that form of malignant osteoma now called "Ewing's sarcoma."

Ewing was a founder and charter member of the American Association for Cancer Research (1907) and the American Cancer Society (1913), and an appointee to the first National Advisory Cancer Council (1937). His services to pathology were acknowledged by numerous international tributes and by his election to the National Academy of Sciences.

BIBLIOGRAPHY

A complete list of Ewing's publications through 1930 (with some biographical detail) appears in a special cancer edition of *The Annals of Surgery,* **93** (1931), xi–xv. See also Frank E. Adair, ed., *Cancer in Four Parts . . . Comprising International Contributions to the Study of Cancer* (Philadelphia, 1931), pp. xi–xv.

Ewing's books and monographs include *Clinical Pathology of the Blood: A Treatise on the General Principles and Special Applications of Hematology* (Philadelphia–New York, 1901; 2nd ed., 1903); *Neoplastic Diseases: A Textbook on Tumors* (Philadelphia–London, 1919; 2nd ed., 1922; 3rd ed., 1928; 4th ed., 1940); and *Causation, Diagnosis and Treatment of Cancer* (Baltimore, 1931).

Ewing's contributions to periodicals include "Conjugation in the Asexual Cycle of the Tertian Malarial Parasite (The Wesley M. Carpenter Lecture)," in *New York Medical Journal,* **74** (1901), 145–151; "A Study of the So-Called Infectious Lymphosarcoma of Dogs," in *Journal of Medical Research,* **15** [n.s. **10**] (1906), 209–228, written with Silas Beebe; "Cancer Problems (The Harvey Society Lecture)," in *Archives of Internal Medicine,* **1** (1908), 175–217; "An Analysis of Radiation Therapy in Cancer (The Mutter Lecture)," in *Transactions of the College of Physicians of Philadelphia,* 3rd ser., **44** (1922), 190–235; and "Tissue Reactions to Radiation (The Caldwell Lecture)," in *American Journal of Roentgenology,* **15** (1926), 93–115.

See also Ewing's articles on "Identity" (pp. 62–103), "The Signs of Death" (pp. 104–137), and "Sudden Death" (pp. 138–160) in Frederick Peterson and Walter S. Haines, eds., *A Textbook of Legal Medicine and Toxicology,* vol. I (Philadelphia–London, 1903); and "Identity" (pp. 132–174), "The Signs of Death" (pp. 175–208), and "Sudden Death" (pp. 209–233) in Frederick Peterson, Walter S. Haines, and Ralph Webster, eds., *Legal Medicine and Toxicology, by Many Specialists,* vol. I (Philadelphia–London, 1923). In addition see Hans Schmaus, trans. by A. E. Thayer, ed. with additions by Ewing, *A Textbook of Pathology and Pathological Anatomy* (Philadelphia–New York, 1902).

Although no formal biography of Ewing exists, a number of Ewing documents are held in the Hayes Martin Collection at the Memorial Sloan-Kettering Cancer Center Library, New York, N. Y. Three peripheral works which in part discuss Ewing's contributions are Victor A. Triolo and Ilse L. Riegel, "The American Association for Cancer Research, 1907–1940: Historical Review," in *Cancer Research,* **21** (1961), 137–167; Victor A. Triolo, "Nineteenth Century Foundations of Cancer Research: Origins of Experimental Research," in *Cancer Research,* **24** (1964), 4–27; and Victor A. Triolo and Michael B. Shimkin, "The American Cancer Society and Cancer Research: Origins and Organization, 1913–1943," in *Cancer Research,* **29** (1969), 1615–1641.

VICTOR A. TRIOLO

EWING, JAMES ALFRED (*b.* Dundee, Scotland, 27 March 1855; *d.* Cambridge, England, 7 January 1935), *physics.*

Ewing's most important research dealt with magnetism. He was one of the first to observe the phenomenon of hysteresis, which he named and studied both experimentally and theoretically. He also did research in seismography and thermodynamics. Although his research was important, Ewing was probably more influential through his continuing efforts to establish engineering education. In three quite different positions—as professor of mechanical engineering in Tokyo, as director of naval education, and as professor at Cambridge—he was involved with the teaching of engineering. In addition, he published many papers and books and participated in numerous committees dealing with engineering problems and the application of science.

Ewing's father was a minister of the Free Church of Scotland; both his brothers became clergymen. Ewing studied at the Dundee high school and then went to the University of Edinburgh on an engineering scholarship. A good student, he came under the influence of Peter Tait and Fleeming Jenkin. Ewing did some early research with Jenkin on the harmonic analysis of vowel sounds (using the traces produced by Edison's phonograph). Through Jenkin, Ewing came in contact with William Thomson and participated in three expeditions for laying transatlantic telegraph cables.

Following Jenkin's recommendation, Ewing went to Japan in 1878 as professor of mechanical engineering at the University of Tokyo. The university provided Ewing with the means to establish a seismological observatory and, beginning in the winter of 1879–1880, he erected instruments and recorded earthquakes. Ewing was especially eager to obtain a continuous record of motion during an earthquake, and he devised a new type of seismograph for this purpose. In the latter part of his stay in Tokyo he was involved in teaching physics and began his experimental study of magnetism. He later received the Japanese Order of the Precious Treasure.

Ewing returned to England in 1883, after five years in Japan. At first he held the chair of engineering at the University of Dundee and continued his research on magnetism. In 1890 Ewing was made professor of mechanism and applied mechanics at Cambridge University. There was at the time disagreement within the university over its involvement with engineering education, and there were some who believed that the subject had no place at Cambridge. (The engineering professorship held by James Stuart, Ewing's predecessor, was not supposed to be renewed.) During Ewing's tenure engineering became accepted, and in 1892 the mechanical sciences tripos was established.

Ewing was director of naval education from 1903 to 1916. Lord Selborne and Admiral John Fisher appointed him to this position as part of their program to reform education in the British navy and to provide training in science and engineering. During World War I he was in charge of "Room 40," a group that intercepted and deciphered German messages.

From 1916 to 1929 Ewing was principal and vice-chancellor of the University of Edinburgh and was active in its expansion—constructing new buildings, founding new chairs, and enlarging the staff. He received honorary degrees from the universities of Oxford, Cambridge, Durham, and St. Andrews. He was made a fellow of the Royal Society in 1887 and received the Royal Medal for his research on magnetism in 1895. He was knighted in 1911 and made honorary member of the Institution of Civil Engineers in 1929 and of the Institution of Mechanical Engineers in 1932.

Ewing began his research on magnetic hysteresis through a project to study the effect of stress on the thermoelectric properties of metals. In 1881 he discovered that the thermoelectric effect lags behind the applied stress. He next suggested that other pairs of variables might also be related in such a cyclic manner, and he studied the transient currents produced by twisting a magnetized wire. He found a lag here also and introduced the term *hysteresis,* from the Greek word meaning "to be late," to describe it. Ewing then turned to the study of hysteresis in magnetization. He observed in 1882 that the area enclosed by the hysteresis loop is proportional to the work done during a complete cycle of magnetization and demagnetization. In 1885 he presented an important paper on this topic to the Royal Society.

The lag, in some processes, between a force and its effect was known in Germany before Ewing's experiments, and Kohlrausch had invented the term *elastische Nachwirkung* for it in 1866. In his 1885 paper Ewing noted that Emil Warburg had independently discovered magnetic hysteresis and had emphasized the physical importance of the area of the hysteresis loop ("Magnetische Untersuchungen," in *Annalen der Physik und Chemie,* **13** [1881], 141–164).

BIBLIOGRAPHY

I. ORIGINAL WORKS. Ewing's writings include "On Friction Between Surfaces Moving at Low Speeds," in *Proceedings of the Royal Society,* **26** (1877), 93–94, written with Fleeming Jenkin; "On the Harmonic Analysis of Certain Vowel Sounds," in *Transactions of the Royal Society of Edinburgh,* **28** (1878), 745–777, written with Fleeming Jenkin; "On a New Seismograph," in *Proceedings of the Royal Society,* **31** (1881), 440–446; "Effects of Stress on the Thermoelectric Quality of Metals," *ibid.,* **32** (1881), 399–402; "On the Production of Transient Electric Currents in Iron and Steel Conductors by Twisting Them When Magnetised or by Magnetising Them When Twisted," *ibid.,* **33** (1881–1882), 21–23; "On Effects of Retentiveness in the Magnetisation of Iron and Steel," *ibid.,* **34** (1882–1883), 39–45; "Earthquake Measurement," in *Memoirs of the Science Department of the University of Tokyo,* **9** (1883), 1–92; "Experimental Researches in Magnetism," in *Philosophical Transactions of the Royal Society,* **176** (1885), 523–640; "Contributions to the Molecular Theory of Induced Magnetism," in *Proceedings of the Royal Society,* **48** (1890), 342–358; *Magnetic Induction in Iron and Other Metals* (London, 1892); *Steam Engine and Other Heat Engines* (Cambridge, 1894); *The Strength of Materials* (Cambridge, 1899); *The Mechanical Production of Cold* (Cambridge, 1908); *Thermodynamics for Engineers* (Cambridge, 1920); and "An Engineer's Outlook," in *Nature,* **130** (1932), 341–350.

For a more extensive listing of Ewing's papers, see the *Catalogue of Scientific Papers of the Royal Society,* IX (London, 1891), and XIV (London, 1915).

II. SECONDARY LITERATURE. On Ewing's life and work, see R. T. Glazebrook, "James Alfred Ewing," in *Obituary Notices of the Royal Society,* I (London, 1932–1935), 475–492; and E. Griffiths, "Sir Alfred Ewing," in *Proceedings of the Physical Society,* **47** (1935), 1135.

SIGALIA DOSTROVSKY

EYTELWEIN, JOHANN ALBERT C. (*b.* Frankfurt am Main, Germany, 31 December 1764; *d.* Berlin, Germany, 18 August 1848), *hydraulic engineering, mechanics.*

Eytelwein, the son of an impoverished tradesman, joined the Prussian artillery at the age of fifteen. Realizing that an army career held little promise, he studied civil engineering privately, passing the state examination for surveyor in 1786. In 1790 he qualified as civil engineer and left the army with the rank of lieutenant to enter the Prussian civil service. His first assignment was to Küstrin [now Kostrzyn] as regional superintendent of dikes of the Oderbruch, the low fertile land on the west bank of the Oder between Lebus and Schwedt.

A concern about the lack of a school or training program for engineers to staff government bureaus led Eytelwein to publish a collection of problems in applied mathematics for surveyors and engineers (*Sammlung . . .*, 1793). Eytelwein, like his French contemporary M. R. de Prony, was one of the first to write on the application of mechanics and mathematics to the design of structures and machines in order to bring rational methods to both the practicing engineer and the student. Called to Berlin in 1794 as director of the Board of Public Works, he became responsible for the regulation of many rivers of eastern Germany, including the Oder, Warthe, and connecting waterways; he also shared in planning the harbors of Memel, Pillau [Baltiysk], and Swinemunde [now Swinoujście]. In 1797 he was a cofounder of a civil engineering journal, the first in Germany, that was later carried on by Crelle as *Journal für die Baukunst.*

Eytelwein's efforts on behalf of an engineering institution were realized with the founding of the Berlin Bauakademie in 1799; this was the first German engineering school of university stature and one of the two nuclei of the later Technische Hochschule-Berlin. He was the first director of the Bauakademie and held that post for seven years; he also lectured on mechanics, hydraulics, hydrostatics, machine design, dike embankments, and stream regulation. In addition to writing books and articles on numerous technical topics, he served on commissions such as that which established a definitive set of weights and measures for Prussia. His *Handbuch der Mechanik . . .* (1801) was the most important book of this era, for it was the first to combine practice and theory. He was elected member of the Academy of Sciences in 1803 and lectured (1810–1815) at the recently founded University of Berlin. A man whose energy matched his ability, he was appointed director of the Prussian Public Works Deputation in 1809, to become in 1816 chief commissioner in charge of all hydraulic works of the kingdom.

Eytelwein's health began to fail in 1825; he retired in 1830 on the fortieth anniversary of his entry into the civil service. Nevertheless, he remained active and published a major work on analytical methods in his seventy-third year. Although he became blind at eighty and deaf before his death, he continued to be concerned in the mathematical instruction of his grandchildren.

Throughout his life Eytelwein was a strong influence in the elevation of the standards of engineering education, bringing to it the analytical methods of the time. His writings were distinguished for their clarity and sweep, practice being viewed and upgraded by developing analysis.

BIBLIOGRAPHY

I. ORIGINAL WORKS. Eytelwein's major works are *Sammlung von Aufgaben aus der angewandten Mathematik für Feldmesser, Ingenieure and Baumeister* (Berlin, 1793); *Grundlehren der Hydraulik* (Berlin, 1796); *Vergleichung der in den Preussischen Staaten eingeführten Maasse und Gewichte* (Berlin, 1798; 2nd ed., 1817); *Anweisung zum Zeichnen* (Berlin, 1799); *Anweisung zur Construction von Faschinenwerken* (Berlin, 1799); *Handbuch der Mechanik fester Körper und Hydraulik* (Berlin, 1801; 3rd ed., Leipzig, 1842); *Handbuch der Statik fester Körper,* 3 vols. (Berlin, 1808; 2nd ed., 1832); *Handbuch der Perspektive,* 2 vols. (Berlin, 1810); *Grundlehren der höheren Analysis,* 2 vols. (Berlin, 1824); *Handbuch der Hydrostatik* (Berlin, 1826); and *Anweisung zur Lösung höherer numerischer Gleichungen* (Berlin, 1837).

II. SECONDARY LITERATURE. Biographical sketches may be found in C. von Hoyer, *Allgemeine deutsche Biographie,* XLVIII (1904), 462; Löbe, *Allgemeine deutsche Biographie,* VI (1877), 464; C. Matschoss, *Männer der Technik* (Düsseldorf, 1925), p. 69; M. Rühlmann, *Vorträge über Geschichte der technischen Mechanik* (Berlin, 1885), pp. 284–286; R. Schröder, *Neue deutsche Biographie,* IV (1959), 714; and S. Timoshenko, *History of Strength of Materials* (New York, 1953), p. 101. For a list of his work see Poggendorff, I, 708.

R. S. HARTENBERG

IBN EZRA, ABRAHAM BEN MEIR, also known as **Abū Isḥāq Ibrāhim al-Mājid ibn Ezra,** or **Avenare** (*b.* Toledo, Spain, *ca.* 1090; *d.* Calahorra, Spain, *ca.* 1164–1167 [?]), *mathematics, astronomy.*

A versatile genius with a charming Hebrew style, Ibn Ezra disseminated rationalistic and scientific Arabic learning in France, England, and Italy. From about 1140 to 1160 he traveled continually, and it was in this last period of his life that his works were written. Ibn Ezra was a Hebrew grammarian, exegete, astrologer, translator from Arabic into Hebrew, and poet, as well as a scientist. His work as a Jewish biblical commentator was much admired by Spinoza. Ibn Ezra considered the physical sciences and astrology fundamental for every branch of Jewish learning.

Three of his treatises were devoted to numbers. *Sefer ha-eḥad* ("Book of the Unit") describes the theory of numbers from one to nine; *Sefer ha-mispar* ("Book of the Number") is on the fundamental operations of arithmetic. The latter describes the decimal system for integers with place value of the numerals from left to right, and the zero is given as *galgal* ("wheel" or "circle") in the preface. In the body of the treatise, however, Ibn Ezra returns to use of the letters of the Hebrew alphabet as numerals. The Indian influence is, nevertheless, unmistakable. The third book, *Yesod mispar* ("The Foundation of Numerals"), is concerned with grammatical peculiarities.

In Ibn Ezra's translation of al-Bīrūnī's *Ta'amē lūḥōt al-Chowārezmī* ("Commentary on the Tables of al-Khwārizmī"; the Arabic original is lost) there is interesting information on the introduction of Indian mathematics and astronomy into Arabic science during the eighth century.

Ibn Ezra was concerned with permutations and combinations, as is shown in his *Sefer ha-'olam* ("Book of the World"). In addition to treatises on the calendar, *Shalosh she'elot* ("Three Chronological Questions") and *Sefer ha-'ibbur* ("Book on Intercalation"), and the astrolabe, *Keli ha-neḥoshet* ("The Astrolabe"), Ibn Ezra wrote a number of astrological works (Steinschneider lists more than fifty) that were very popular and were translated into many languages. Two were printed in Latin in 1482 and 1485, respectively; and all of them appeared in Latin in 1507. Only two of the Hebrew originals have been printed, both in modern times. They are rich in original ideas and in the history of scientific subjects. The astrological works were translated into French in 1213 by Hagin, a Jew in the employ of Henry Bate at Malines (Mechelen), who in turn translated the French into Latin. Both the French and the Catalan translations are of great philological interest.

BIBLIOGRAPHY

Works dealing with Ibn Ezra and his writings are Henry Bate *et al., De luminaribus et diebus criticis* (Padua, 1482–1483); H. Edelmann, *Keli neḥoshet* (Königsberg, 1845); J. L. Fleischer, *Sefer ha-mōrōt* (Bucharest, 1932); Yekuthiel Ginsburg, "Rabbi Ben Ezra on Permutations and Combinations," in *The Mathematics Teacher,* **15** (1922), 347–356, text from *Sefer ha-'olam;* S. J. Halberstam, *Sefer ha-'ibbur* (Lyck [Elk], Poland, 1874); D. Kahana, *Rabi Abraham ibn Ezra,* II (Warsaw, 1894), 107–111; Martin Levey, *Principles of Hindu Reckoning* (Madison, Wis., 1965), pp. 8, 35; Raphael Levy, *The Astrological Works of Abraham ibn Ezra. A Literary and Linguistic Study With Special Reference to the Old French Translation of Hagin* (Baltimore, 1927); Alexander Marx, "The Scientific Work of Some Outstanding Mediaeval Jewish Scholars," in *Essays and Studies in Memory of Linda R. Miller* (New York, 1938), pp. 138–140; Ernst Müller, *Abraham ibn Esra Buch der Einheit aus dem Hebräischen übersetzt nebst Parallelstellen und Erläuterun-*

gen zur Mathematik Ibn Esras (Berlin, 1921); Samuel Ochs, "Ibn Esras Leben und Werke," in *Monatsschrift für Geschichte und Wissenschaft des Judentums,* **60** (1916), 41–58, 118–134, 193–212; M. Olitzki, "Die Zahlensymbolik des Abraham ibn Esra," in *Jubelschrift Hildesheimer* (Berlin, 1890), pp. 99–120; S. Pinsker, *Yesod mispar* (Vienna, 1863), and *Abrahami Ibn Esra, Sepher ha-echad, liber de novem numeris cardinalibus cum Simchae Pinsker interpretatione primorum quatuor numerorum. Reliquorum numerorum interpretationem et proemium addidit M. A. Goldhardt* (Odessa, 1867); George Sarton, *Introduction to the History of Science,* II, pt. 1 (Baltimore, 1931), 187–189; M. Silberberg, ed., *Sefer ha-mispar. Das Buch der Zahl, ein hebräisch-arithmetisches Werk des R. Abraham ibn Esra . . .* (Frankfurt, 1895); D. E. Smith and Yekuthiel Ginsburg, "Rabbi Ben Ezra and the Hindu-Arabic Problem," in *American Mathematical Monthly,* **25** (1918), 99–108; and the following by M. Steinschneider: "Abraham Judaeus-Savasorda und Ibn Esra," in *Zeitschrift für Mathematik,* **12** (1867), 1–44, and **25** (1880), supp. 57–128; *Verzeichniss der hebräische Handschriften der K. Bibliothek zu Berlin* (Berlin, 1897; 1901); *Die hebräischen Übersetzungen . . .* (repr. Graz, 1956), p. 869; *Die arabische Literatur der Juden* (repr. Hildesheim, 1964), p. 156; and *Mathematik bei den Juden* (repr. Hildesheim, 1964), pp. 87–91.

MARTIN LEVEY

FABBRONI (or erroneously **FABRONI**), **GIOVANNI VALENTINO MATTIA** (*b.* Florence, Italy, 13 February 1752; *d.* Florence, 17 December 1822), *economics, physics.*

The son of Orazio Fabbroni, who came from a noble family, and of Rosalind Werner, from Heidelberg, Fabbroni showed his ability so early that in 1768 he was made assistant to Felice Fontana in the Museum of Physics and Natural Sciences in Florence, where he became assistant director in 1780 and director (for a year) in 1805. From 1776 to 1778 he lived in Paris, and then in London. He frequented the enlightened and radical circles of the two capitals, meeting Benjamin Franklin and corresponding with Thomas Jefferson.

Upon his return to Florence in 1782, Fabbroni married the patrician Teresa Ciamignani, from Grosseto, continued his economic studies defending free trade, entered politics, and published many works on agriculture, botany, chemistry, physics, archaeology, and philology. In 1798 he participated in the work of the Commission on Weights and Measures in Paris; in 1802 he was named an honorary professor at the University of Pisa and in 1803, director of the mint. Fabbroni was a member of the Accademia dei Georgofili, of the Società Italiana delle Scienze dell'Accademia dei XL, and of thirty or more other academies, both Italian and foreign.

In a memoir read in 1792 to the Accademia dei Georgofili of Florence (published in 1801) and reworked in a new memoir published in 1799 in the *Journal de physique,* Fabbroni maintained that the phenomena discovered by Galvani (1791) were not due to the action of an electric fluid, but to the reciprocal action of dissimilar metals upon contact, in the presence of moisture. Because of these writings he is often considered the originator of the chemical theory of the battery, even though at the time the two memoirs were written, the battery had not been invented and Fabbroni maintained that the galvanic phenomena were independent of the production of electricity. Nonetheless, his ideas certainly influenced the emergence in the first years of the nineteenth century of the chemical theory of the battery.

BIBLIOGRAPHY

I. ORIGINAL WORKS. A collection of Fabbroni's writings is *Scritti di pubblica economia,* 2 vols. (Florence, 1847–1848). See also "Sur l'action chimique des différens métaux," in *Journal de physique . . .,* **49** (1799), 348–357; and "Dell'azione dei metalli nuovamente avvertita," in *Atti della R. Società economica di Firenze ossia de' Georgofili,* **4** (1801), 349–370. Letters and documents concerning Fabbroni are in the Italian State Archives, the Biblioteca Nazionale in Florence, and the Bibliothèque Nationale in Paris.

II. SECONDARY LITERATURE. On Fabbroni and his work, see Mario Gliozzi, "Giovanni Fabbroni e la teoria chimica della pila," in *Archeion,* **18** (1936), 160–165; Andrea Mustoxidi, "Giovanni Fabbroni," in Emilio de Tipaldo, ed., *Biografia degli italiani illustri,* I (Venice, 1834), 337–345, with list of published and unpublished works; Poggendorff, I, cols. 709–710; Ugo Schiff, "Il museo di storia naturale," in *Archeion,* **9** (1928), 296–297, 318–320; and Franco Venturi, "Giovanni Fabbroni," in *Illuministi italiani,* III (Milan, 1958), 1081–1134, with selections from his works.

MARIO GLIOZZI

FABRE, JEAN HENRI (*b.* Saint-Léons, Aveyron, France, 22 December 1823; *d.* Sérignan, Vaucluse, France, 11 October 1915), *entomology, natural history.*

Fabre was the son of Antoine Fabre, an *homme de chicane* (a sort of law officer), and of Victoire Salgues. He began his studies at the parochial school of his native village, then continued them, beginning in 1833, at the *collège* of Rodez. A scholarship student at the École Normale Primaire in Avignon, he obtained his *brevet supérieur* in 1842 and was appointed a teacher at the lycée of Carpentras in the same year. At Montpellier he prepared for his *baccalauréat,* which he passed, and then earned a double *licence ès sciences* in mathematics and physics. He next went to the lycée of Ajaccio, Corsica, as a physics teacher, remaining there until December 1851. Following this he taught in the lycée of Avignon (1853), then received the *licence* in natural history at Toulouse, and finally defended his thesis for the *doctorat ès sciences naturelles* at Paris in 1854. Henceforth, Fabre devoted himself almost exclusively to the research on the biology and behavior of insects that was to make him one of the great figures of entomology.

In 1855 Fabre published his first work on a hymenopterous vespid (*Cerceris*) that paralyzes its prey (beetles). His second memoir (1857) was concerned with the hypermetamorphosis of the *Meloidae* (coleoptera). In 1856 Fabre was awarded the Prix Montyon (for experimental physiology) of the Institut de France, and in 1859 Charles Darwin cited him in his *Origin of Species,* a valuable encouragement for a poorly paid young teacher.

In an attempt to improve his financial situation, Fabre undertook a research on the coloring principle of madder (alizarin), which he succeeded in isolating in 1866. This discovery resulted in his being awarded the Legion of Honor, and he was received in Paris by Napoleon III. But on his return to Avignon, Fabre learned that alizarin had just been obtained from coal tars and that his process had been superseded. He turned to writing textbooks and gave a free course on the sciences, at the same time forming a friendship with the philosopher John Stuart Mill, who was then living in Avignon. A victim of various jealousies and vexations, Fabre left that city in November 1870 and moved to Orange, and then in 1879 to Sérignan, where he devoted all his time to observations on the life and habits of insects. On 11 July 1887 he was elected a corresponding member of the Académie des Sciences, and his jubilee was celebrated on 3 April 1910.

Fabre's first marriage was to Marie Villard (30 October 1844); they had many children, including three sons and one daughter. Having become a widower shortly after moving to Sérignan, he remarried and had a son and two daughters by his second wife. One of his daughters married the physician G. V. Legros, who was his first biographer.

Fabre's scientific work includes the ten-volume *Souvenirs entomologiques* (1879–1907), which presents a considerable number of original observations on the behavior of insects (and also of arachnids); these had been preceded by various memoirs published as books or periodical articles (1855–1879).

It is the latter group of publications that contains Fabre's principal discoveries: hypermetamorphosis of the *Meloidae;* the relationship between the sex of the egg and the dimensions of the cell among the solitary bees; the habits of the dung beetles; and the paralyzing instinct of the solitary wasps *Cerceris, Sphex, Tachytes, Ammophila,* and *Scolia.*

These last researches, which posed the problem of instinct and its acquisition by insects, were much discussed and were the object of lively criticism by E. Rabaud. Recent works, such as those of A. Steiner (1962) on the wasp *Liris nigra,* which preys on crickets, confirm Fabre's observations and show that the prey is a checkerboard of stimulating zones, each of which provokes a precise and practically unalterable response by the predator.

Although his works were admired by Darwin, Fabre was all his life opposed to evolution, remaining convinced of the fixity of species. For him, each animal species was created as we see it today, with the same instinctual equipment (whereas the modern explanation of instinct draws on the notion of natural selection).

Fabre had the great merit of demonstrating the importance of instinct among the insects, while certain of his predecessors (J. C. W. Illiger, Jean Th. Lacordaire) supposed that insects are endowed "with reasoning or inventing faculties comparable to those of the higher animals, and of man" (J. Rostand, "Jean-Henri Fabre," p. 157).

Responsible for significant discoveries concerning the lives and habits of insects, Fabre remains especially important in the history of science because of the popularity of his *Souvenirs entomologiques;* reading them led more than one person to become a naturalist.

In addition, in order to earn a living, Fabre, between 1862 and 1901, wrote some forty works of scientific popularization, designed chiefly for the young and ranging from mathematics and physics to natural history.

He also composed poems in French and in Provençal; the latter resulted in his being called *felibre di Tavan.*

Fabre remains the very model of the self-taught scientist—solitary, poor, proud, and independent. He was also an attentive and minute observer and a writer of unquestionable talent.

BIBLIOGRAPHY

I. ORIGINAL WORKS. Fabre's major work is *Souvenirs entomologiques,* 10 vols. (Paris, 1879–1907), trans. into English by A. Teixiera de Mattos as *The Works of J. Henri Fabre* (London, 1912 *et seq.*). Among his other writings are two theses presented to the Faculty of Sciences in Paris in 1855, "Recherches sur les tubercules de l'*Himantoglossom hircinum,*" in *Annales des sciences naturelles,* Botanique, ser. 4, **3** (1855), 253–291, with two plates, and "Recherches sur l'anatomie des organes reproducteurs et sur le développment des Myriapodes," *ibid.,* Zoologie, ser. 4, **3** (1855), 257–316, with four plates. See also "Observations sur les moeurs des *Cerceris* et sur la cause de la longue conservation des Coléoptères dont ils approvisionnent leurs larves," *ibid.,* **4** (1855), 129–150; "Recherches sur la cause de la phosphorescence de l'Agaric de l'olivier," *ibid.,* Botanique, ser. 4, **4** (1855), 179–197; "De la germination des Ophrydées et de la nature de leurs tubercules," *ibid.,* **5** (1856), 163–186, with one plate; "Étude sur l'instinct et les métamorphoses des Sphégiens," *ibid.,* Zoologie, **6** (1857), 137–183; "Mémoire sur l'hypermétamorphose et les moeurs des Méloïdes," *ibid.,* **7** (1857), 299–365; "Nouvelles observations sur l'hypermétamorphose et les moeurs des Méloïdes," *ibid.,* **9** (1858), 265–276; *Mémoire sur la recherche des corps étrangers introduits frauduleusement dans la garance en poudre* (Avignon, 1859); *Note sur le mode de reproduction des truffes* (Avignon, 1859); "Rapport sur l'alizarine artificielle de M. Roussin," in *Bulletin de la Société d'agriculture et d'horticulture de Vaucluse,* **10** (Aug. 1861), 235–248; "Étude sur le rôle du tissu adipeux dans la sécrétion urinaire chez les insectes," in *Annales des sciences naturelles,* Zoologie, ser. 4, **19** (1863), 351–389; *Insectes Coléoptères observés aux environs d'Avignon* (Avignon, 1870); and "Étude sur les moeurs et la parthénogenèse des Halictes," in *Annales des sciences naturelles,* Zoologie, ser. 6, **9** (1879), art. 4. His poetry is collected in *Oubreto provençalo dôu Felibre di Tavan* (Avignon, 1909). A list of forty of his textbooks, published between 1862 and 1901, may be found in the biography by Cuny (below), pp. 184–185.

II. SECONDARY LITERATURE. On Fabre and his work see M. Coulon, *Le génie de J. H. Fabre* (Paris, 1924); H. Cuny, *Jean-Henri Fabre et les problèmes de l'instinct* (Paris, 1967); Augustin Fabre, *The Life of Jean Henri Fabre, the Entomologist* (London, 1921), B. Miall, trans.; G. V. Legros, *La vie de J. H. Fabre naturaliste par un disciple* (Paris, 1913); E. Rabaud, *J. H. Fabre et la science* (Paris, 1924); and J. Rostand, "Jean-Henri Fabre," in *Hommes de vérité,* ser. 2 (Paris, 1948), pp. 109–168.

JEAN THÉODORIDÈS

FABRI, HONORÉ, or **HONORATUS FABRIUS** (*b.* Virieu-le-Grand, Dauphiné, France, 5 April 1607; *d.* Rome, Italy, 8 March 1688), *mathematics, natural philosophy.*

Fabri came from a family of judges in Valromey that was probably related to the Vaugelas family.[1] Following his studies at the *institut* in Belley, he entered the Jesuit novitiate in Avignon on 18 October 1626, remaining until 1628. In the fall of that year he went to the Collège de la Trinité[2] in Lyons, where he completed his course in Scholastic philosophy under Claude Boniel. After teaching for two years at the *collège* in Roanne,[3] he returned to Lyons in 1632 in order to begin his course in theology, which

he finished—following his ordination as a priest in 1635—in 1636. In the latter year he was named professor of logic at the *collège* in Arles, where for two years he gave lectures on philosophy that included natural philosophy as well. It was at this time that he discovered—independently of Harvey—the circulation of the blood, which he taught publicly.[4]

Besides being prefect at the *collège* in Aix-en-Provence (1638–1639), Fabri was leader of a sort of circle that, among other things, brought him the acquaintance of—and a long-lasting correspondence with—Gassendi. He was then recalled to Lyons to finish his third year of probation under P. Barnaud and in 1640 was promoted to professor of logic and mathematics, and also to dean, at the Collège de la Trinité.

During the following six years Fabri taught metaphysics, astronomy, mathematics, and natural philosophy. This period was the most brilliant and fruitful of his life; several books that he published later were developed from lectures delivered during this time. Fabri was the first of many famous professors produced by the Collège de la Trinité: his students included Pierre Mousnier, who later edited many of his teacher's lectures; the mathematician François de Raynaud,[5] who became famous through his friendship with Newton; Jean-Dominique Cassini; and Philippe de La Hire. Claude Dechales[6] and the astronomer and mathematician Berthet were also members of this circle. Among these scholars and the two Huygenses (father and son), Leibniz, Descartes, Mersenne, and others an active correspondence developed.

The foci of Fabri's tremendous activity were almost all urgent questions of the science of his day: heliocentrism, Saturn's rings, the theory of the tides, magnetism, optics, and kinematics. In mathematics, infinitesimal methods and the continuum problem were most prominent.

Fabri's favorable reception of certain Cartesian conceptions[7] embroiled him in an intense controversy with his superiors, which finally led to his expulsion from Lyons and his transfer to Rome, where he arrived on 12 September 1646. Although his stay was supposed to be only provisional, he was made a member in the same year of the Penitentiary College (the Inquisition). He served on that body, finally as Grand Inquisitor, for thirty-four years. Despite his important work in Church politics and theology—Fabri was considered the first expert on Jansenism—there was still time for his wide-ranging scientific research.

In mathematics, Fabri showed that despite the influence of Cavalieri and Torricelli, he was an independent and original thinker. This is clear from his principal mathematical work, *Opusculum geometricum.* Through the functional reinterpretation of Cavalieri's concept of indivisibles by means of a dynamically formulated concept of *fluxus,* Fabri approached similar ideas put forth by Newton. Fabri, however, was not able to free himself of a rather cumbersome, purely geometrical representation. In his *Synopsis geometrica* he developed a method of teaching based on his concept of *fluxus* and was not unsuccessful in using his somewhat inadequately formulated principle of homogeneity in his investigations on infinitesimals.

The *Opusculum geometricum* contains, besides an ingenious quadrature of a cycloid which Leibniz found inspiring, various quadratures and cubatures that amount to special cases of $\int x^n \sin x \, dx$, $\int \sin^p x \, dx$, and $\int\int \arcsin x \, dx \, dy$, as well as centroid determinations of sinusoidal and cycloidal segments together with their elements of rotation about both axes. The book doubtless originated in connection with the controversy over cycloids and Pascal's challenge.

In Rome, Fabri became acquainted with Michel Angelo Ricci, who recommended him to the Medici Grand Duke Leopold II. The latter made Fabri a corresponding member of the Accademia del Cimento. In 1660, with an anonymous work,[8] Fabri opened the controversy with Huygens over Saturn's rings which, after five years and a great expenditure of energy, was decided in Huygens' favor. Fabri was a fair opponent: he apologized and openly adopted Huygens' opinion. In the *Brevis annotatio* is a note that reads, more or less, "As long as no strict proof for the motion of the earth has been found, the Church is competent to decide [the issue]. If the proof, however, is found, then there should be no difficulty in explaining that the relevant passages in the Bible must be interpreted in a more symbolic sense." This statement would perhaps have been tolerated later, under Pope Clement IX, on whom Fabri had a strong influence; under Alexander VII, however, it brought Fabri (as a member of the Holy Office) fifty days in prison, and his release was effected only through the intervention of Leopold II. Yet this did not prevent the combative Jesuit from inserting into his *Dialogi physici* (1665) a chapter entitled "De motu terrae." It was also in 1665 that Fabri discovered the Andromeda nebula, which he at first thought was a new comet.

In natural philosophy Fabri was less fortunate than in mathematics. Nevertheless, the following achievements are noteworthy: the constant use of the concept of the static moment; an attempted explanation of tidal phenomena based on the action of the moon,

even though it involved air pressure as the medium; an explanation of the blue color of the sky based on the principle of dispersion; and investigations on capillarity. His attempted explanation of cohesion, however, was completely unsuccessful.

In 1668 Fabri began a year's sick leave in Virieu-le-Grand, where he supervised the publication of various of his works. He continued to work in the Holy Office in Rome until 1680. The last eight years of his life he spent a short distance outside the city, devoting himself to historical studies.[9]

Aside from the individual scientific achievements mentioned, Fabri's efforts to introduce a priori methods in natural philosophy as well as in philosophy are important historically,[10] as is his lasting influence on Leibniz, who richly recompensed Fabri with his friendship. Newton, for his part, mentioned in his second paper on light and colors that he first learned of Grimaldi's experiments through the medium of "some Italian author," whom he identified as Fabri in his dialogue *De lumine.*[11]

NOTES

1. See Gassendi's letter to Mousnier of 1 October 1665, published in Fabri's *Cours de philosophie* (Lyons, 1646).
2. The Collège de la Trinité was transferred by the aldermen of Lyons to the Jesuits in 1565 but was closed in 1594, following the attempt by the Jesuits' pupil Jean Châtel on the life of Henry IV. The Jesuits were expelled from France but returned in 1604 and reestablished the college; it was not completed, however, until 1660.
3. In 1634, at the age of ten, François de La Chaise (later the Jesuit Père Lachaise) entered this *collège;* he was later bound to Fabri by close friendship and an active correspondence.
4. See *Journal des sçavans* (1666), pp. 395–400.
5. Also known as Regnauld and Reynaud.
6. Also known as de Chales.
7. See D.-G. Morhof, *Polyhistori litterarum,* II (Lübeck, 1690), 115; and Adrien Baillet, *La vie de Descartes,* II (Paris, 1691), 299.
8. *Eustachii de divinis septempedani brevis annotatio in systema Saturnium Christiani Hugenii* (Rome, 1660).
9. The manuscripts of the last creative period, most of them unpublished, are in the library of the city of Lyons.
10. See Leibniz's letter to Johann Bernoulli, dated 15 October 1710, in *Leibniz's mathematische Schriften,* C. I. G. Gerhardt, ed., III (Halle, 1856), 856.
11. Newton to Oldenburg, 7 December 1675, in H. W. Turnbull, ed., *The Correspondence of Isaac Newton,* I (Cambridge, 1959), 384.

BIBLIOGRAPHY

I. Original Works. Fabri's mathematical writings include *Opusculum geometricum de linea sinuum et cycloide* (Rome, 1659), written under the pseudonym "Antimus Farbius"; and *Synopsis geometrica* (Lyons, 1669), to which is appended *De maximis et minimis in infinitum proposi-*

tionum centuria, written in 1658/1659. These works, as well as the minor *Brevis synopsis trigonometriae planae* (1658/1659) are discussed in Fellmann, below.

Fabri's works in natural philosophy are *Tractatus physicus . . .* (Lyons, 1646); *Dialogi physici . . .* (Lyons, 1665); *Synopsis optica* (Lyons, 1667); *Dialogi physici . . .* (Lyons, 1669); and *Physica* (Lyons, 1669).

II. SECONDARY LITERATURE. On Fabri's work, see Carlos Sommervogel, *Bibliothèque de la Compagnie de Jésus,* III (Paris-Brussels, 1892), 512–522, which contains an extensive bibliography; and E. A. Fellmann, "Die mathematischen Werke von Honoratus Fabry," in *Physis* (Florence), **1-2** (1959), 6–25, 69–102.

E. A. FELLMANN

FABRI, NICOLAS DE PEIRESC. *See* **Peiresc, Nicolas Fabri de.**

FABRICI, GIROLAMO (or **FABRICIUS AB AQUAPENDENTE, GERONIMO FABRIZIO**) (*b.* Aquapendente, near Orvieto, Italy, *ca.* 1533; *d.* Padua, Italy, 21 May 1619), *anatomy, physiology, embryology, surgery.*

Fabrici was born of a noble and once-wealthy family; that he was the eldest son is indicated by his having been named for his paternal grandfather. Around 1550 his family sent him to Padua where, under the patronage of a patrician Venetian family named Lippomano or Lipamano, he studied Greek and Latin, then logic and philosophy. He went on to medicine and took his degree in medicine and philosophy at Padua in about 1559.

Fabrici studied with Gabriele Falloppio, whom he succeeded as teacher of anatomy upon the latter's death in 1562; from 1563 to 1565 he devoted himself to giving private anatomy lessons. In April 1565 he was nominated by the university to lecture on both anatomy and surgery; the position brought him an annual salary of 100 florins and entailed additional responsibilities in anatomical work. He presented his first lecture on 18 December 1566; he was repeatedly reconfirmed in his academic position (with appropriate raises in pay) and in 1600 was given life tenure, with the title *sopraordinario.* From 1609 on anatomy and surgery were given separately, and Fabrici became *sopraordinario* lecturer in anatomy only, retaining his full salary, however, which by that time amounted to 100 scudi a year. He retired from teaching in 1613, having served the University of Padua for nearly fifty years.

Fabrici's long academic career was not without strife. In 1588 he was publicly accused by his students of neglecting his teaching—a charge that would seem to have some ground in truth, but which may be explained in part by Fabrici's repeated illnesses. Certainly he was of difficult character, as may be seen by his clash with his German students, whom he ridiculed in the course of a public lecture in February 1589 because of their slow and harsh speech—the quarrel was reconciled only in October of that year. He further became embroiled in a protest in 1597 about having been placed after the professors of philosophy on the *Rotula* of the university; had an argument in 1608 with Eustachio Rudio; became involved in a dispute about the schedule of courses with his colleague Annibale Bimbiolo in 1611; and in 1613 attempted to prevent the nomination of a German councillor of the university because he was annoyed with the German students for attending the private anatomy classes given by Giulio Casseri.

It is likely, too, that Fabrici slighted his teaching duties in the interest of scientific research. He did, however, make substantial contributions to the university; among other things, the construction of a permanent anatomical theater, built in 1594 and inaugurated by him in 1595 (still preserved, and now bearing Fabrici's name), was in large part due to his efforts. His merit as a teacher was publicly acknowledged; if some of these acknowledgments are of a formal nature (as for example, those given on the occasions of his academic reconfirmations), others are undoubtedly sincere (the gratitude expressed by the fractious German students for the course in surgery that he conducted in 1606).

Fabrici further took active part in other matters concerning the university: in 1574 he was instrumental in securing the acquittal of a German student from a charge of homicide; in 1591 he intervened on behalf of some German students who had been arrested for carrying arms; in 1592–1593 he concerned himself with the reconstruction of the temporary anatomical theater and in 1595 with free admission to the permanent theater; in 1606 he again acted on behalf of an arrested German student; and in the winter of 1608–1609 he gave a cadaver to the German students (among whom were Olaus Worm and Caspar Bartholin) so that they could prepare the skeleton. It is thus clear that his relations with his students improved with the passage of time.

As a surgeon and physician Fabrici enjoyed high professional acclaim and the patronage of many eminent people. In 1581 he attended a brother of the duke of Mantua; in 1591 he was consulted by the duke of Urbino about the cure for certain fevers that were rampant in Pesaro; and in 1594 he corresponded with Mercuriale and Tagliacozzi about a case of rectogenital fistula. He went to Florence in 1604 to treat Carlo de' Medici, the son of Ferdinand I and Christina di Lorena, while in 1606 he visited Galileo, who subsequently became his patient. He visited Venice with Spigelio on 9 October 1607, and while he was there took care of Paolo Sarpi, who had been wounded a few days before; for these services he was made a knight of St. Mark by the Republic of Venice.

At some unknown time Fabrici married Violante Vidal; they had no children and she died in 1618. He did have an illegitimate son, Francesco, probably born before his marriage. Francesco also took his degree in medicine but was a source of little pleasure or pride to his father—in fact, a quarrel over money brought father and son into legal confrontation; Fabrici had serious disagreements with other close relatives as well. The person to whom he was closest was his great-grandniece, Semidea, whom he adopted on the death of her father and raised as his daughter in Padua. He married her to Daniele Dolfin on 9 May 1619; on 13 May he fell ill and died a few days later, almost certainly at his house in Padua. His funeral took place on 23 May, in the Franciscan church; the oration was given by Giovanni Tuilio, and he was buried, *sine titulo,* in the west cloister.

As a scientist, Fabrici was an indefatigable and scrupulous observer, describing his results with exactitude. His interpretation of observed phenomena was often shaped by tradition, however, and he may not be considered a comparative anatomist in the modern sense because he made no studies of homologous structures and did not attempt to analyze relationships and affinities of the organs that he studied. His primary purpose in his studies of fetal anatomy, for example, was to prepare a tool for the interpretation of the purpose and end of the organs under consideration; he was more concerned with finding philosophically based principles than with morphological detail and tended to modify observations that did not verify such principles. Thus he often failed to pursue his own discoveries to their logical conclusions. His interpretation of nature was, then, a teleological one, and his methods of observation derived largely from Galen.

Fabrici published his results in several volumes, including *De visione, voce, auditu* (Venice, 1600); *De locutione et ejus instrumentis liber* (Venice, 1601); *De brutorum loquela* (1603); *De venarum ostiolis* (1603); *De musculi artificio, ossium de articulationibus* (1614); *De respiratione et eius instrumentis, libri duo . . .* (1615); *De gula, ventriculo, intestinis tractatus* (1618); *De motu locali animalium secundum totum* (1618); and *Hieronymi Senis De totius animalis integumentis opusculum* (1618)—all of which may be considered as parts of the uncompleted but monumental *Totius animalis fabricae theatrum* which he meant to publish

and to which he devoted many years. In addition, there are in the St. Mark's library in Venice 167 *Tabulae anatomicae,* collected in eight volumes, part of the 300 color plates that Fabrici finished in 1600 as his major purely anatomical work.

One of the most famous (and most thoroughly studied) of Fabrici's works is *De venarum ostiolis.* The treatise, published in Padua, consists of twenty-three folio pages, supplemented by eight beautiful plates. In it Fabrici reports that he had first observed the valves of the veins in 1574 (the first demonstration to his students was in 1578 or 1579), as was recognized by his student Salomon Alberti, who published, with Fabrici's permission, a preliminary illustration of the venous valves (Nuremberg, 1585). Although the valves of the veins had been studied previously by G. B. Canano and by Amato Lusitano (indeed, a dispute arising therefrom had involved Vesalius, Eustachi, and Falloppio), Fabrici made no use of their contributions, perhaps intentionally; he describes the venous valves *ex novo,* systematically and accurately.

His interest in reconciling his observations with the traditional Galenic concepts of function misled Fabrici into missing the real significance of the venous valves, however. He accepts the notion of the blood flowing centrifugally, drawn by the viscera, and interprets the function of the venous valves to be the slowing down of the influx of the blood to provide for its even distribution to various parts of the body. He thus gives a teleological account of the number, alternate positioning, and conformation of the valves, pointing out that they are not present in the large veins of the trunk, such as the vena cava, in which the blood flows directly to the viscera and vital organs; they are found instead in the veins of the limbs, where they prevent an excessive inflow of blood, which would both cause swelling and deprive the vital organs of nourishment. He describes the valves as corresponding to the openings of collateral branches of the veins and calls them *ostiola.* In addition to thus regulating the flow of the blood mechanically, the valves also serve to prevent excessive stretching of the blood vessels and to reinforce the walls of the veins.

This is demonstrated by the formation of varicose veins in those who do heavy work; the blood of such persons is more dense and held longer by the valves, which become dilated, then subside as the veins dilate. The valves are further demonstrable by the application of a tourniquet to the upper arm; they then appear as a series of regularly spaced knots on its surface. Fabrici observed that if, after ligating the vein, one pressed upon it with a finger, one could observe the valves in action—acting, he thought, to retard the progress of the blood; his misinterpretation may have been due in part to his confusion of laboratory observation with the clinical symptoms of valvular insufficiency that he had noted, particularly in cases of varicosity.

Perhaps the most notable contribution of *De venarum ostiolis* is that William Harvey drew upon it in beginning his studies of the circulation of blood. Harvey was the pupil of Fabrici—indeed, he even lived for a while in his house—and from Fabrici's work he obtained the illustrations that would, with substantial modifications, serve him for his *De motu cordis.*

Fabrici's embryological studies were written concurrently with his later anatomical works. They include *De formato foetu* (1604) and *De formatione ovi et pulli* (published posthumously in 1621); and these two treatises in themselves would assure Fabrici's place among the most important biologists of his time.

In his introduction to *De formato foetu* (his last embryological treatise, despite its earlier publication), Fabrici divides his studies on generation into three parts. The first of these, dealing with the propagation of the seed and the organs that produce it, is presumably *De instrumentis seminis,* which was never published and is probably lost; the second, his work concerning the nature and properties of the seed and the generation and formation of the fetus, is *De formatione ovi et pulli;* while the third, his treatment of the fetus itself, is the *De formato foetu.* Both of the extant works are of a rather narrative character and are written in a somewhat inelegant Latin; many reputable scholars suggest that these works grew out of Fabrici's classroom lectures.

De formatione ovi et pulli is divided into two parts. The first, in three chapters, deals with the formation of the egg. The first chapter discusses the three bases of animal generation given by Aristotle (the egg, the seed, and spontaneously from decomposing materials); Fabrici differs from Aristotle, however, in asserting that most insects are born from eggs in which there is no differentiation between the formative and the nutritive elements; and in specific opposition to Aristotle he classifies Testacea as oviparous. In some respects, Fabrici's classification approaches the *ex ovo omnia* of Harvey; he excludes from his list of oviparous creatures only mammals and those insects that he believes to have been the products of spontaneous generation. His discussion of the generation of birds involves two aspects, that of the egg (whose *uterus* is the ovaries and oviducts) and that of the chicken (whose *uterus* is the egg itself).

Although Fabrici's embryological studies often surpassed those of Aldrovandi and Coiter, he here makes two mistakes. He interprets the germinal disc of the hen's egg as the scar left on the yolk by the detachment of the peduncle that had attached it to the ovary during its development, and he states that the function of the cloacal bursa in the hen (the bursa of Fabricius, which he discovered) is to store the semen of the rooster.

In the second chapter of *De formatione ovi et pulli* Fabrici states two functions of the "uterus": the formation of the egg and, immediately thereafter, its nutrition. The yolk of the egg is formed in the "upper uterus" (the *ovarium* of the yolk), while the remaining part is formed in the "lower uterus" (the *uterus,* or *ovarium* of the whole egg). The egg thus leaves the ovary as a naked yolk; and the chalazae, the albumen, the two membranes of the shell, and the shell itself develop subsequently in the oviduct. The yolk grows as it is nourished by material brought to it through the blood vessels that run through the ovisac while the egg is still attached to the ovary; after detachment the egg ceases to grow and the albumen, adhering to the yolk, grows by apposition. All parts of the egg are therefore derived from the blood, although from different portions of it. The chapter closes with a discussion of the formation of the shell; the third chapter concerns the usefulness of the uterus.

The second part of the treatise, also in three chapters, is concerned with the generation of the chick within the egg and begins with a description of the eggs of various species. Many of the notions and arguments set forth in the first part of the book are then summarized.

The second chapter of the second part deals with the three basic functions of the egg: the formation, growth, and nutrition of the chick. These considerations draw Fabrici into complex and difficult problems that he is unable to resolve, not because of any inadequacy as an observer but rather because of the science that he has inherited. He concludes his discussion with the trophic functions of both yolk and albumen and goes on to demonstrate that the chalaza attached to the thicker part of the egg is the only possible source of formative material. He considers semen to act as only the effective cause of generation; it never enters the egg, being prevented from doing so by the depth and plication of the uterus, which combine to keep the semen from reaching the upper oviduct—and by the time the egg has reached the lower oviduct it is encased in its protective shell. Fabrici postulates that semen is collected in the cloacal bursa of the hen and thence, through its radiant or spiritual powers, fertilizes the entire egg and uterus.

Thus, in oviparous animals the material and the agent of generation are not only distinct but separated by a notable physical distance; this view in no way contradicts Aristotle's doctrine that all the material for generation is contained in the female. (In dealing with viviparous animals, however, Fabrici adopts the Galenic interpretation by which the male seed is both material and efficient cause of generation.)

Fabrici then speculates further on the various possible causes and conditions of generation, including a discussion of the order in which various parts of the embryo are formed during its development. This question had been debated since Aristotle's time, and Fabrici affirmed that certain structures constituting the "carina" (or "keel") can be seen prior to the development of the heart and viscera; it is probable that his "carina" is in fact the whole one- or two-day-old embryo, in which the head, vertebral column, and ribs are visible to the naked eye. H. B. Adelmann (in *The Embryological Treatises of Hieronymus Fabricius of Aquapendente* [Ithaca, 1942]) maintains, on the basis of Fabrici's rather complicated discussion, that he did not, like Aristotle, consider the heart to be the first organ formed, nor yet, like Galen, the liver; rather, he may be thought to have preceded Harvey in giving priority to the blood.

The last chapter of the treatise returns to teleology to consider the utility of both the egg and the semen of the rooster.

De formatione ovi et pulli is illustrated with seven plates, of which only the first three are labeled. The last five plates are the most significant since they represent the first printed figures of the development of the chick, beginning with the third or fourth day of incubation. Some of these figures—especially those illustrating embryonic appendages—are difficult to interpret, although all are admirable for their subtlety of detail (obtained without magnification). The representation of vascularization at the third and sixth days of incubation is perhaps typical of the series. The time of hatching is, however, somewhat oddly given as twenty-four days, perhaps as the result of retardation induced by the experimental incubation.

Fabrici's other major embryological work, *De formato foetu,* illustrates the way in which nature provides for the necessities of the fetus during its intrauterine life. It treats specifically of the umbilical vessels, the urachus, the fetal membranes, fetal waste products, the "carnea substantia" (placenta), and the uterus. The treatise includes comparative studies of morphological details in dogs, cats, rabbits, mice, guinea pigs, sheep, cattle, goats, roebuck, horses, pigs, birds, sharks, and man. Fabrici's description of the umbilical cord and its vessels is accurate, as is his

differentiation of the action of the umbilical vessels in various animals; he also provides an adequate description of the right and left atria of the heart, the foramen ovale and the ductus arteriosus, the vena cava, and the pulmonary vein in the fetus.

The value of Fabrici's observations is, however, lessened by his need to impose a Galenic interpretation upon them. He posits that no fetal organ exercises any "public" action—that is, any function for the benefit of the whole organism—but only "private" ones; each attracts, utilizes, and voids nutriment for itself alone. The whole fetus needs only nutriment and vital spirit (which helps to digest the nutriment) in order to grow; the nutriment and vital spirit reach the fetus through the umbilical veins and arteries, with the maternal uterus thus doing the work of the fetal heart and liver. (If the umbilical vessels are ligated just above the umbilicus the fetal heart and arteries cease to pulsate, thereby demonstrating that the flow of vital spirit has been interrupted.) Although Fabrici differs from Galen on occasion (as when, for instance, he maintains that the blood which reaches the fetal liver does not need purification), his embryological theories are most often in agreement with him.

Fabrici champions Galen against Aranzio in the question of the relationship between the maternal and fetal blood vessels; he maintains that during pregnancy the uterine vessels terminate in apertures to which the fetal vessels are in some way united (although he does not specify the nature of this union). These connections are always of vein to vein and artery to artery to prevent confusion in the distribution of the vital spirit. Fabrici presents observations of the chorionic villi and the crypts of the placenta and interprets them respectively as the terminals of umbilical and uterine vessels. He considered the chorionic villi as patent, however, whereas Harvey thought them to be blind. Aranzio and Harvey, in their belief in the separateness of maternal and fetal circulation, were closer to the truth than Fabrici. Fabrici's explanation of the atrophy of the umbilical cord following birth is Aristotelian; having served its purpose, it is destined to decay.

Fabrici describes the relationship between the chorion and the allantois in some species in a fuller and more accurate manner than Vesalius, Colombo, or even Harvey. He follows tradition in considering the amnion to be a receptacle for fetal sweat and, in agreement with Falloppio, says that fetal urine is (except in species provided with allantois) stored in the chorion. He next examines the embryonic appendages of some herbivorous animals in light of this theory and states that Aranzio is in error when he says that the human fetus lacks a urachus and discharges urine into the amniotic cavity.

Fabrici then discusses fetal waste products and the Galenic principle whereby there are only six of them: sweat (in the amnion); urine (in the chorion or allantois); bile; phlegm; feces; and the white, caseous residue adhering to the skin, cast off by the fetus in the course of assimilating nutrition.

Although Fabrici's work on the umbilical vessels, the fetal membranes, and fetal waste products are of only limited (if any) originality, he does draw some original, if faulty, conclusions about the significance of the placenta, which he studied more fully than any of his predecessors, including Vesalius and Falloppio. Fabrici is the first to give a reasoned classification of the various forms of placentas and to attempt to correlate these forms with the various types of animals; he limits the term "placenta" (introduced by Colombo) to refer to the discoidal type of placenta found in humans and in some animals (including rabbits, mice, rats, and guinea pigs). He is also the first to study human decidua and the subplacenta of the guinea pig and to print illustrations of the chorionic villi and uterine crypts of horses, pigs, and ruminant animals. In passing he deals with the complex problem of the cotyledons, which had been controversial since the work of Praxagorus and Aristotle.

Fabrici contests Aranzio's view of the function of the placenta—that it acts as a uterine liver to purify the blood of the fetus—although he admits that a small amount of blood is purified by the fleshy placental substance (but only to provide for its own nutrition and hence as a "private" and not a "public" action). The work ends with a chapter containing a highly traditional account of how much nature does to ensure the safe birth of the fetus.

De formato foetu is, like its predecessor, illustrated. It contains thirty-four plates of great interest which illustrate, in some instances for the first time, various aspects of the anatomy of the uterus and of the fetus in humans and in sheep, cows, horses, pigs, dogs, rats, mice, guinea pigs, and sharks. As Fabrici was the first to study he was also the first to illustrate the decidua of the human uterus, the uterine crypts in animals (interpreted as the open ends of uterine vessels), and the subplacenta in guinea pigs. In addition, the work contains interesting plates of the venous and arterial ducts and of the omphalomesenteric vein and artery in the dog; the last plate in the book illustrates the development of serpents, a topic on which Fabrici does not touch in the text. The plates, the work of an unknown artist, are well executed although sometimes lacking clarity (although many fine details are shown), and they are better integrated into the text

than those of De formatione ovi et pulli. Adelmann discusses the embryological color illustrations.

Fabrici's surgical works are gathered in the Pentateuchos cheirurgicum (printed in Frankfurt am Main in 1592, and edited by a pupil of Fabrici, Johann Hartman Beyer, apparently without his consent) and in the Operationes chirurgicae, published in Venice in 1619 as an addendum to the Pentateuchos.

The five books of the Pentateuchos are primarily devoted to the description of tumors, wounds, ulcers and fistulas, fractures, and dislocations; to these the Operationes adds a description of surgical instruments (some of which are illustrated) and classic surgical techniques, including a discussion of particular technical expedients devised by Fabrici himself and emphasizing some differences between Fabrici's technique and that of others. Of particular interest are two plates illustrating an orthopedic device, in the shape of a man, designed to combine in one apparatus the principles for all existing devices for the correction of orthopedic injuries and deformities. A passage by Antonio Vallisneri indicates that this device was actually built and used.

Although Fabrici's surgical works have not yet been studied in any detail it is clear that they rely on both Hippocrates and Galen in diagnostics and therapy. (The medications that Fabrici prescribes are, for example, traditional ones.) Yet the books had great success and went through many editions in many languages; the versification of the first book of the Pentateuchos by Antonio Filippo Ciucci (Rome, 1653) can be taken as an exemplar of Fabrici's fame as a surgeon.

BIBLIOGRAPHY

I. ORIGINAL WORKS. Fabrici's works were collected into Opera omnia anatomica et physiologica (Leipzig, 1687); a later ed. (Leiden, 1738) is more complete. Individual works are cited in the text; unless otherwise specified, all were published in Padua.

Modern eds. are Delle valvole delle vene, with trans. and intro. by Felice Grondona (Milan, 1966); and Dell'orecchio, organo dell'udito and Della laringe, organo della voce, trans. and commentary by Luigi Stroppiana (Rome, 1967).

II. SECONDARY LITERATURE. On Fabrici's life and work see H. B. Adelmann, The Embryological Treatises of Hieronymus Fabricius of Aquapendente (Ithaca, N.Y., 1942); L. Belloni, "Di una avvenuta chiamata di Gaspare Tagliacozzi allo studio di Padova (1594) e di un consulto epistolare tra G. Mercuriali, G. Tagliacozzi e G. Fabrici d'Acquapendente sovra un caso di fistola retto-genitale," in Rivista di storia delle scienze mediche e naturali, 43 (1952); "Die deutsche Aussprache in einer kurzen Abhandlung von Conrad Hofmann an Hieronymus Fabrici ab Aquapendente," in *Sudhoffs Archiv für Geschichte der Medizin und der Naturwissenschaften,* **37** (1953); and "Valvole venose e flusso centrifugo del sangue. Cenni storici," in *Simposi Clinici Ciba,* **5** (1968); A. F. Ciucci, *L'Ospidale di Parnaso,* Bruno Zanobio, ed. (Milan, 1962); G. Favaro, "Contributi alla biografia di Girolamo Fabrici di Acquapendente," in *Memorie e documenti per la storia della Università di Padova* (Padua, 1922); "L'insegnamento anatomico di Girolamo Fabrici d'Acquapendente," in *Monografie storiche sullo studio di Padova. Contributo del R. Istituto Veneto di scienze, lettere ed arti alla celebrazzione del VII centenario della università* (Venice, 1922); K. J. Franklin, *De venarum ostiolis of Hieronymus Fabricius of Aquapendente* (Baltimore, 1933); E. Gurlt, *Geschichte der Chirurgie,* II (Berlin, 1898), 445–481; G. Sterzi, "Le 'Tabulae Anatomicae' ed i Codici marciani con note autografe di Hieronymus Fabricius ab Aquapendente," in *Anatomischer Anzeiger,* **35** (1910); and L. Stroppiana, "Realtà scomparse. Divagando tra G. Fabrizi d'Acquapendente e Antonio Vallisneri," in *Humana studia,* **4** (1952).

BRUNO ZANOBIO

FABRICIUS AB AQUAPENDENTE. *See* **Fabrici, Girolamo.**

FABRICIUS, JOHANN CHRISTIAN (*b.* Tønder, South Jutland, Denmark, 7 January 1745; *d.* Kiel, Germany, 3 March 1808), *entomology.*

Fabricius was undoubtedly one of the most distinguished entomologists and ranks with Carl de Geer, P. A. Latreille, A. G. Oliver, and other prominent specialists of earlier times. In many respects he surpassed them, especially as a theoretical natural scientist. Linnaeus, whose most important contribution hardly lay in the field of entomology, was full of admiration for him—a rather unusual attitude for the Nestor of Swedish science—and his colleagues throughout the world expressed great respect for his work. Quantitatively speaking, the most important part of Fabricius' work was concentrated in the field of descriptive systematics (taxonomy); qualitatively speaking, a very important section of his work fell into the advanced theoretical area of natural history. This is shown clearly in his *Philosophia entomologica* (1778), *Betrachtungen über die allgemeinen Einrichtungen in der Natur* (1781), and *Resultate naturhistorischer Vorlesungen* (1804).

Two basic principles guided Fabricius' approach to entomological systematics: he distinguished, on the one hand, between the artificial and the natural characters; and, on the other hand, he stressed the importance of the various structures of the mouth. The terminology he applied to categories of higher systems differed somewhat from modern terminology: he used the words "classis" for "order" and "ordo" for what

we call "family"; furthermore, he founded his system on the genus and the species, which in his opinion constituted the main bases. It seemed especially important to Fabricius that genera were the natural combinations of related species. He believed that "classes" and "ordines" were artificial concepts. He seems to have understood that even genera can be classified into the natural system—the nearest equivalent to our present "families"—but he probably understood that the time was not yet ripe, that scientific knowledge and general outlook were too narrow for such classification. He thought (not without hesitation) of one large system based on the structure of the mouth organs as being the natural system (see *Philosophia entomologica,* p. 85; *cf.* p. 97).

It was Fabricius' greatest ambition to build a system based on the naturally defined genera, without doubt a definite and new contribution to insect systematics. He considered this more important than a dry description of the various species. In the latter area, however, his contributions are imposing: he named and described some 10,000 insects.

Less known than Fabricius' contributions in the field of insect systematics are his evolutionistic ideas and speculations. He considered systematics to be a means to understanding important scientific functions and phenomena in general. In a frequently quoted sentence he said: "As we would not call a man learned because he can read, so we would not call a man a scientist who knows nothing but the system" (*Resultate natur-historischer Vorlesungen,* p. 138). Many of his ideas concerning evolution sound amazingly modern. For instance, he considered it possible that a species could be formed through mixing existing species (i.e., some form of hybridization) and through morphological adaptation and modification. In his opinion, such phenomena caused an unbelievable wealth of forms and species of living organisms. Fabricius could not believe in haphazard creation and definitely thought that man originated from the great apes (*Resultate,* p. 208). He also discussed the influence of environment on the development of the species, as well as some selective phenomena (females prefer the strongest males, etc.). Henriksen even called Fabricius the "Father of Lamarckism" (1932, p. 80).

Fabricius did not lead the life of a sedentary scientist. He did much traveling, both on the Continent and in Great Britain. He studied for two years under Linnaeus in Uppsala (1762–1764), traveled in Germany on several occasions, in Holland (1766–1767), in Scotland, France, and Italy (1768–1769), and visited London during the summers of 1772–1775 and even later. He also went to Norway, Austria, Switzerland, and Russia. On these trips he came in close contact with the best-known scientists of his time and visited the greatest museums. Fabricius was an extrovert who was liked and appreciated everywhere, and his personality helped to create a fruitful mutual exchange of information and ideas.

Fabricius was professor of natural science and economics, first at the University of Copenhagen, then at Kiel. His extensive collections, as well as the material he described and named, are in the Fabricius collections of the Zoological Museum of Copenhagen, a great part on loan from Kiel. Other collections are in Paris at the Muséum National d'Histoire Naturelle (Bosc Collection), the British Museum (Natural History [Banks Collection]), and in Glasgow (Hunter Collection).

BIBLIOGRAPHY

I. ORIGINAL WORKS. Fabricius' major writings are *Systema entomologiae* (Flensburg–Leipzig, 1775); *Genera insectorum* (Kiel, n.d. [preface dated 26 Dec. 1776]); *Philosophia entomologica* (Hamburg–Kiel, 1778); *Betrachtungen über die allgemeinen Einrichtungen in der Natur* (Hamburg, 1781); *Species insectorum,* 2 vols. (Hamburg–Kiel, 1781); *Mantissa insectorum,* 2 vols. (Copenhagen, 1787); *Entomologia systematica,* 4 vols. and supp. (Copenhagen, 1792–1798); *Systema eleutheratorum,* 2 vols. (Kiel, 1801); *Systema rhyngotorum* (Brunswick, 1803); *Resultate naturhistorischer Vorlesungen* (Kiel, 1804; repr. page for page, Kiel, 1818); *Systema piezatorum* (Brunswick, 1804); *Systema antliatorum* (Brunswick, 1805); *Systema glossatorum* (Brunswick, 1807), only 112 pp. printed, three known copies; facs. ed. by F. Bryk (Neubrandenburg, 1938); and "Autobiographie des Naturforschers Fabricius," in *Kieler Blätter,* **1** (Kiel, 1819), 88–117, trans. from the Danish, with notes and commentary by F. W. Hope, in *Transactions of the Entomological Society of London,* **4** (1845), 1–16.

II. SECONDARY LITERATURE. On Fabricius and his work, see K. L. Henriksen, "Oversigt over Dansk Entomologis Historie," in *Entomologiske Meddelelser* (Copenhagen), **15** (1922–1937); J. Schuster, "Linné und Fabricius. Zu ihrem Leben und Werk," in *Münchener Beiträge zur Geschichte und Literatur der Naturwissenschaften und Medizin,* **4** (1928); R. A. Staig, *The Fabrician Types of Insects in the Hunterian Collection at Glasgow University,* 2 vols. (Cambridge, 1931–1940); S. L. Tuxen, "The Entomologist, J. C. Fabricius," in *Annual Review of Entomology,* **12** (1967), 1–14; and E. Zimsen, *The Type Material of J. C. Fabricius* (Copenhagen, 1964).

BENGT-OLOF LANDIN

FABRY, CHARLES (*b.* Marseilles, France, 11 June 1867; *d.* Paris, France, 11 December 1945), *physics.*

Charles Fabry and his brothers, Eugène, a mathe-

matician, and Louis, an astronomer, all graduated from the École Polytechnique in Paris. Fabry became *agrégé de physique* in 1889 and *docteur ès sciences* in physics in 1892 (University of Paris). After the customary assignment teaching at various lycées in France, Fabry returned to Marseilles to teach and do research at the university; he remained there from 1894 to 1920.

Fabry worked primarily on the precise measurement of optical interference effects, an interest already apparent in his thesis, "Théorie de la visibilité et de l'orientation des franges d'interférence" (Marseilles, 1892). He joined the laboratory of Macé de Lepinay, where this branch of optics was of primary concern. The majority of Fabry's research projects involved an interferometer that he invented with Alfred Pérot.

First devised in 1896, the Fabry-Pérot interferometer is based upon multiple reflection of light between two plane parallel half-silvered mirrors. The distribution of light produced by interference of rays that have undergone different numbers of reflections is characterized by extremely well defined maxima and minima, and monochromatic light produces a set of sharp concentric rings. Different wavelengths in the incident light can be distinguished by the sets of rings produced. This instrument produced sharper fringes than that devised by the American, Albert Michelson. For spectroscopy, their apparatus cheaply duplicates the advantages of the diffraction grating. Fabry and Pérot continued to work together; for about a decade they applied their interferometer to spectroscopy and metrology; an important project, for example, involved determining a series of standard wavelengths.

From 1906 Fabry worked with Henri Buisson on similar experiments and applications of the interference technique. In 1912 they verified for helium, neon, and krypton the Doppler-broadening of emission lines predicted by the kinetic theory of gases—an effect that Michelson had verified for metallic vapors at low pressure. A simple method, devised in 1914, enabled Fabry and Buisson to confirm experimentally in the laboratory the Doppler effect for light (this measurement had previously been made using stellar sources). By their technique a horizontal rotating white disk is illuminated so that points at opposite ends of a diameter constitute equal sources of light moving in opposite directions; the disk is viewed at an oblique angle, and the interferometer then detects the difference in position of the sets of rings produced by light from the two ends of the diameter.

Fabry's interest in astronomy—developed while observing with his brothers when they were students—led him to use the interferometer to study the spectra of the sun and stars, as well as to improve photometric techniques to measure the brightness of the nocturnal sky. As part of this work he showed that the ultraviolet absorption in the upper atmosphere is due to ozone.

As first director of the Institute of Optics and professor of physics both at the Sorbonne and at the École Polytechnique, Fabry spent the latter part of his life mainly in Paris, where he was elected to the Academy of Sciences in 1927. He was also a member of the International Committee on Weights and Measures and the Bureau of Longitudes; he received medals from the Royal Society, the Franklin Institute, and the National Academy of Sciences. Fabry was interested in the popularization of science; he taught a large public course in electrotechnology and wrote some popular works.

BIBLIOGRAPHY

I. ORIGINAL WORKS. Fabry's works include *Les applications des interférences lumineuses* (Paris, 1923); *Optique* (Paris, 1926; 4th ed., 1934), lectures given at the Sorbonne, Jean Mallassez and Maurice Virlogeux, eds.; "Histoire de la physique," in G. Hanotaux, ed., *Histoire de la nation française,* I (Paris, 1924), 165–418; "Mesure de petites épaisseurs en valeur absolue," in *Comptes rendus hebdomadaires des séances de l'Académie des sciences,* **123** (1896), 802–805, written with A. Pérot; "Sur une nouvelle méthode de spectroscopie intérferentielle," *ibid.,* **126** (1898), 34–36, written with A. Pérot; "Sur la largeur des raies spectrales et la production d'interférences à grande différence de marche," *ibid.,* **154** (1912), 1224–1227, written with H. Buisson; and "Vérification expérimentale du principe de Doppler-Fizeau," in *Journal de physique,* 5th ser., **9** (1919), 234–239, written with H. Buisson. Some of Fabry's work is repr. in his *Oeuvres choisies* (Paris, 1938), which includes a list of his publications (pp. 669–689).

II. SECONDARY LITERATURE. On Fabry and his work see Louis de Broglie, "Charles Fabry," in *Obituary Notices of the Royal Society,* V (1945–1948), 445–450; Maurice Caullery, "Notice nécrologique sur Charles Fabry," in *Comptes rendus hebdomadaires des séances de l'Académie des sciences,* **221** (1945), 721–724; and F. A. Jenkins and H. E. White, *Fundamentals of Optics* (New York, 1957), ch. 14.

SIGALIA DOSTROVSKY

FABRY, LOUIS (*b.* Marseilles, France, 20 April 1862; *d.* Les Lecques, near Toulon, France, 26 January 1939), *astronomy, applied celestial mechanics.*

Fabry, the older brother of the physicist Charles Fabry, was admitted to the École Polytechnique in 1880. He obtained his *licence ès sciences* at the Faculté de Marseille in 1883 and the following year was accepted in the school of practical astronomy recently created at the Observatoire de Paris. During his course of study, while practicing on the *équatorial coudé* that had just been placed in use, he had the extraordinary luck of discovering a comet.

The origin of these heavenly bodies was then much discussed—the existence of comets with hyperbolic orbits made it possible to hold the opinion that they originated outside of the solar system. Fabry, in his doctoral thesis in 1893, proved by statistical methods that this hypothesis was not compatible with the distribution presented by the elements of the orbits. He established in particular that the distribution of motions does not yield the dissymmetry that the motion of the sun would introduce if the comets came from infinity.

The subject, however, was not exhausted. Why, in fact, are certain orbits hyperbolic? To solve this problem, the Académie des Sciences posed it as a competition. The prize was shared by Fabry and one of his colleagues, Gaston Fayet; both showed that the orbits known as hyperbolic had become so by the action of planetary perturbations—all of them were originally elliptical.

The observation of the minor planets and the elaboration of rapid methods for identifying them and for calculating and improving their ephemerides constitute, along with his researches on the comets, the essential portion of Fabry's work. He was of that generation of astronomers who strove to cultivate observations for the use of their successors; he lived in a period in which new technology served observation, while the means of calculation were practically nonexistent.

Fabry was named in 1886 to the Observatoire de Nice and then in 1890 to that of Marseilles, where he remained until his retirement in 1925. He was elected a corresponding member of the Académie des Sciences in 1919.

BIBLIOGRAPHY

I. ORIGINAL WORKS. Fabry's principal works on comets are "Découverte d'une comète à l'Observatoire de Paris," in *Comptes rendus hebdomadaires des séances de l'Académie des sciences,* **101** (1885), 1121–1125; "Sur le calcul du grand axe des orbites cométaires," in *Bulletin astronomique,* **11** (1894), 485–488; "Études sur la probabilité des comètes hyperboliques et l'origine des comètes," his doctoral thesis of 1893, in *Annales de la Faculté des Sciences de Marseille,* **4** (1895), 1–214; and "Sur la véritable valeur du grand axe d'une orbite cométaire," in *Comptes rendus hebdomadaires des séances de l'Académie des sciences,* **138** (1904), 335–337.

His writings on the minor planets are "Tables numériques destinées à faciliter le calcul des éphémérides," in

Bulletin astronomique, **2** (1885), 453–463; "Procédé abrégé pour rectifier les éphémérides," *ibid.,* **20** (1903), 243–250; "L'identification des petites planètes," *ibid.,* **30** (1913), 49–64; "Sur la rectification des orbites des planètes," *ibid.,* **31** (1914), 68–79; "Sur l'emploi des latitudes géocentriques pour faciliter l'identification des petites planètes," in *Comptes rendus hebdomadaires des séances de l'Académie des sciences,* **172** (1921), 27–31; and "Nouvelles formules pour le calcul de la ligne de recherche," *ibid.,* **173** (1921), 892–894.

His observations, as well as the numerous orbits of minor planets that he determined, were generally published in *Bulletin astronomique,* beginning in 1885. His seismological writings appeared in *Comptes rendus hebdomadaires des séances de l'Académie des sciences,* **149–152** (1909–1911).

II. SECONDARY LITERATURE. On Fabry's life and work see G. Fayet, "Notice nécrologique sur L. Fabry," in *Comptes rendus hebdomadaires des séances de l'Académie des sciences,* **208** (1939), 545–547.

JACQUES R. LÉVY

AL-FADL IBN HĀTIM AL-NAYRĪZĪ. *See* al-Nayrīzī.

FAGNANO DEI TOSCHI, GIOVANNI FRAN-CESCO (*b.* Sinigaglia, Italy, 31 January 1715; *d.* Sinigaglia, 14 May 1797), *mathematics.*

Giovanni Francesco was the only child of Giulio Carlo Fagnano to show an interest in mathematics. He was ordained a priest and in 1752 was appointed canon of the cathedral of Sinigaglia. Three years later he was made archpriest. He wrote an unpublished treatise on the geometry of the triangle that was inspired by a similar work of his father's. Fagnano made several important contributions to the subject, among them the theorem that the triangle which has as its vertices the bases of the altitudes of any triangle has these altitudes as its bisectors. He also contributed several analytical communications to the *Acta eruditorum* and to other Italian and foreign reviews.

Among his most important results is that, given

$$S_n = \int x^n \sin x \, dx, \quad C_n = \int x^n \cos x \, dx,$$

we obtain

$$S_n = -x^n \cos x + nC_{n-1},$$
$$C_n = x^n \sin x - nS_{n-1}.$$

He also calculated the integrals:

$$\int \tan x \, dx = -\log \cos x, \quad \int \cot x \, dx = \log \sin x.$$

BIBLIOGRAPHY

Among Fagnano's writings is *Nova acta eruditorum* (1774), pp. 385–420. Two further sources of information on

his mathematical work are *Enciclopedia delle matematiche elementari,* I, pt. 2 (1932), 491–492; and Gino Loria, *Storia delle matematiche,* 2nd ed. (Milan, 1950), p. 664.

A. NATUCCI

FAGNANO DEI TOSCHI, GIULIO CARLO (*b.* Sinigaglia, Italy, 6 December 1682; *d.* Sinigaglia, 26 September 1766), *mathematics.*

Fagnano, the son of Francesco Fagnano and Camilla Bartolini, was born into a noble family that had included Pope Honorius II and had been established in his native town for nearly 350 years. In 1723 he was appointed *gonfaloniere* of Sinigaglia; while he held this office he was subjected to calumny by envious fellow citizens. He was the father of many children, among them Giovanni Francesco, a distinguished mathematician.

Fagnano began to study mathematics after reading the first volume of Malebranche's *Recherche de la verité;* and although he was self-educated, he soon made such progress that he became famous both in Italy and abroad. In 1721 Louis XV conferred upon him the title of count; in 1745 Pope Benedict XIV made him a marquis of Sant' Onofrio. He belonged to the Royal Society of London and the Berlin Academy of Sciences, and at his death he had been nominated for membership in the Paris Academy of Sciences. Fagnano maintained correspondence with many contemporary mathematicians, especially Grandi, Riccati, Leseur, and Jacquier; he was praised by Euler and Fontenelle, the permanent secretary of the French Academy. Lagrange, at the age of twenty, turned to him for help in publishing his first work.

Fagnano's works were published at intervals in the *Giornale dei letterati* and in the Raccolta Calogera. These were later collected and with other, unpublished works included in *Produzioni matematiche.*

In algebra Fagnano suggested new methods for the solution of equations of the second, third, and fourth degrees. He also organized in a rational manner the knowledge that scientists had of imaginary numbers, establishing for them a special algorithm that was far better than Bombelli's primitive one. In this field he established the well-known formula

$$\frac{\pi}{4} = \log\left(\frac{1-i}{1+i}\right)^{1/2}.$$

This is reminiscent of Euler's celebrated formula

$$e^{\pi i} = -1,$$

which unites the four most important numbers in mathematics.

In geometry Fagnano formulated a general theory

of geometric proportions that is more noteworthy than the countless writings, published previously, that were intended to illustrate book V of Euclid's *Elements*. Much more important, however, is his work on the triangle, for which he may well be considered the founder of the geometry of the triangle. Some of the problems solved are as follows:

To find in the plane of a triangle, *ABC*, a point, *P*, that will reduce to the minimum the sum *PA* + *PB* + *PC* or the sum $PA^2 + PB^2 + PC^2$.

To find in the plane of a quadrangle, *ABCD*, a point that will render minimum the sum *PA* + *PB* + *PC* + *PD*.

Two of Fagnano's major findings are (1) that the sum of the squares of the distances of the center of gravity of a triangle from the vertices equals one-third the sum of the squares of the sides and (2) that given a triangle, *ABC*, for every point *P* of *BC* we may construct an inscribed triangle, with its vertex at *P*, of minimum perimeter. He also solved the problem proposed by Simon Lhuilier: Draw through a given point the straight line on which two given straight lines cut off the minimum segment. This leads analytically to a third-degree equation.

The most important results achieved by Fagnano, however, were in analytical geometry and in integral calculus. He rectified the ellipse $x^2 + 2y^2 = a^2$, which has as its major axis the mean proportion between the minor axis and its double. The equation

$$(x^2 + y^2)^2 - 2a^2(x^2 - y^2) = 0$$

represents a fourth-degree curve that, owing to its shape, is called "lemniscate," a term derived from the Greek *lemniscata*. This was first studied by Jakob I Bernoulli (1694), but it was made famous by Fagnano's research. He established its rectification and demonstrated that each of its arcs may be divided with ruler and compass into *n* equal parts when *n* is of the form $2 \cdot 2^m$, $3 \cdot 2^m$, $5 \cdot 2^m$.

He gave the name "elliptical integrals" to integrals of the form

$$\int f\left(x_1 \sqrt{P[x]}\right) dx$$

in which *P*(*x*) is a polynomial of the third or fourth degree. Euler found a basic result in their theory, known as the theorem of addition, that includes the results first found by Fagnano in the lemniscate arcs. For this reason some have considered Fagnano's work the forerunner of the theory of elliptic functions—a claim undoubtedly put forward by Legendre.

Disputes, encouraged by Fagnano's uncle Giovanni, arose over who deserved the credit of priority in these studies—Fagnano or Nikolaus I Bernoulli. On the advice of his friend Riccati, Fagnano soon put an end to these arguments.

Fagnano also found the area of the lemniscate, thus demonstrating that Tschirnhausen's opinion was erroneous and that it was impossible to square the area composed of several leaves.

In 1714 Fagnano proposed the following problem: Given a biquadratic parabola of the form $y = x^4$, and given a portion of it, determine another portion of the same curve in such a manner that the difference between the portions is rectifiable. Since no one replied, Fagnano himself published the solution, thus extending the method to infinite species of rectifiable parabolas. Fagnano also studied the problem of squaring hyperbolic spaces.

BIBLIOGRAPHY

I. ORIGINAL WORKS. Among Fagnano's works are *Giornale dei letterati*, **19** (1714), 438; *Produzioni matematiche*, 2 vols. (Pesaro, 1750); and *Opere matematiche del marchese G. C. de' Toschi di Fagnano*, V. Volterra, G. Loria, and D. Gambioli, eds. (Rome, 1911).

II. SECONDARY LITERATURE. On Fagnano or his work, see Luigi Bianchi, *Lezioni sulla teoria delle funzioni di variabile complessa e delle funzioni ellittiche* (Pisa, 1901), p. 250; Gino Loria, *Curve piane speciali algebriche e trascendenti. Teoria e storia* (Milan, 1930), I, 257 ff., and *Storia delle matematiche*, 2nd ed. (Milan, 1950), pp. 664–666; and A. Natucci, "Anton Maria Legendre inventore della teoria delle funzioni ellittiche," in *Archimede*, **4**, no. 6 (1952), 261.

There is an article on Fagnano in *Enciclopedia italiana* (1932), XIV, in which he is called Giulio Cesare. He is mentioned twice by Eugenio G. Togliatti in *Enciclopedia delle matematiche elementari*: II, pt. 1, 184, and in "Massimi e minimi," II, pt. 2. See also *Elogi e biografie d'illustri italiani del conte Giuseppe Mamiani della Rovere* (Florence, 1845), pp. 63–104.

A. NATUCCI

FAHRENHEIT, DANIEL GABRIEL (*b.* Danzig [Gdansk], Poland, 24 May 1686; *d.* The Hague, Netherlands, 16 September 1736), *experimental physics*.

Fahrenheit was the scion of a wealthy merchant family that had come to Danzig from Königsberg in the middle of the seventeenth century. His father, Daniel, married Concordia Schumann, the daughter of a Danzig wholesaler. From this union there were five children, three girls and two boys, of whom Daniel was the eldest.

In 1701 Fahrenheit's parents died suddenly, and his guardian sent him to Amsterdam to learn business. It was there, apparently, that Fahrenheit first became acquainted with, and then fascinated by, the rather specialized and small but rapidly growing business of making scientific instruments. About 1707 he began his years of wandering, during which he acquired the techniques of his trade by observing the practices of other scientists and instrument makers. He traveled throughout Germany, visiting his native city of Danzig as well as Berlin, Halle, Leipzig, and Dresden. He met Olaus Roemer in Copenhagen in 1708, and in 1715 he entered into correspondence with Leibniz about a clock for determining longitude at sea. In 1714 Christian von Wolff published a description of one of Fahrenheit's early thermometers in the *Acta eruditorum.* Fahrenheit returned to Amsterdam in 1717 and established himself as a maker of scientific instruments. There he became acquainted with three of the greatest Dutch scientists of his era: W. J. 'sGravesande, Hermann Boerhaave, and Pieter van Musschenbroek. In 1724 he was admitted to the Royal Society, and in the same year he published in the *Philosophical Transactions* his only scientific writings, five brief articles in Latin. Just before his death in 1736, Fahrenheit took out a patent on a pumping device that he hoped would be useful in draining Dutch polders.

Fahrenheit's most significant achievement was his development of the standard thermometric scale that bears his name. Nearly a century had passed since the construction of the first primitive thermometers, and although many of the basic problems of thermometry had been solved, no standard thermometric scale had been developed that would allow scientists in different locations to compare temperatures. About 1701 Olaus Roemer had constructed a spirit thermometer based upon two universal fiducial points. The upper fixed point, determined by the temperature of boiling water, was labeled 60°; the lower fixed point, determined by the temperature of melting ice, was set at 7-1/2°. This latter, seemingly arbitrary, number was chosen to allow exactly 1/8 of the entire scale to stand below the freezing point. Since 0° on the Roemer scale approximated the temperature of an ice and salt mixture (which was widely considered to be at the coldest possible temperature), all readings on Roemer's thermometer were assumed to be positive.

Roemer did not publish anything about his thermometer, and its existence was unknown to most of his contemporaries except Fahrenheit, who thought mistakenly that his own thermometric scale was patterned after Roemer's. In 1708, while visiting Roemer, Fahrenheit watched the Danish astronomer as he graduated several thermometers. These particular instruments were being graduated to a scale of 22-1/2°, or 3/8 of Roemer's standard scale of 60°.

Since most of the scale would then be in the temperate range, it is probable that Roemer was designing them for meteorological purposes. In a letter addressed to Boerhaave, Fahrenheit gave the following description of Roemer's procedure.

> I found that he had stood several thermometers in water and ice, and later he dipped these in warm water, which was at blood-heat [*welches blutwarm war*], and after he had marked these two limits on all the thermometers, half the distance between them was added below the point in the vessel with ice, and the whole distance divided into 22-1/2 parts, beginning with 0 at the bottom then 7-1/2 for the point in the vessel with ice and 22-1/2 degrees for that at blood-heat.[1]

The problem with Fahrenheit's account is that he took Roemer's "blood-warm" (22-1/2°) to be a primary fiducial point, fixed quite literally at the temperature of the human blood. In fact, 22-1/2° on the Roemer scale is considerably below body temperature (by about 15° on the modern Fahrenheit thermometer). Furthermore, Roemer used boiling water (set at 60°), not blood temperature, as his upper fixed point. The simplest explanation for Fahrenheit's misunderstanding of the Roemer scale seems to lie in the ambiguity of the term "blood-warm." It can mean either a tepid heat or the exact temperature of the human blood.[2] Roemer probably intended to convey the former meaning, and Fahrenheit obviously understood the latter one.

When Fahrenheit began producing thermometers of his own, he graduated them after what he believed were Roemer's methods. The upper fixed point (labeled 22-1/2°) was determined by placing the bulb of the thermometer in the mouth or armpit of a healthy male.[3] The lower fixed point (labeled 7-1/2°) was determined by an ice and water mixture. In addition, Fahrenheit divided each degree into four parts, so that the upper point became 90° and the lower one 30°. Later (in 1717) he moved the upper point to 96° and the lower one to 32° in order to eliminate "inconvenient and awkward fractions."[4]

In an article on the boiling points of various liquids, Fahrenheit reported that the boiling temperature of water was 212° on his thermometric scale. This figure was actually several degrees higher than it should have been. After Fahrenheit's death it became standard practice to graduate Fahrenheit thermometers with the boiling point of water (set at 212°) as the upper fixed point. As a result, normal body temperature became 98.6° instead of Fahrenheit's 96°. This variant of the Fahrenheit scale became standard throughout Holland and Britain. Today it is used for meteorological purposes in most English-speaking countries.

Fahrenheit knew that the boiling temperature of water varied with the atmospheric pressure, and on this principle he constructed a hypsometric thermometer that enabled one to determine the atmospheric pressure directly from a reading of the boiling point of water. He also invented a hydrometer that became a model for subsequent developments.

In the early eighteenth century, it was not at all unusual for a person without formal scientific training to be admitted to the Royal Society. Makers of scientific instruments could be particularly valuable members because they often operated on the farthest frontiers of scientific knowledge, defining universal constants on which to scale their instruments and isolating the variables that affected their operation. In order to make reliable instruments that would be useful to the scientific community as a whole, Fahrenheit was obliged to concern himself with a wide variety of scientific problems: measuring the expansion of glass, assessing the thermometric behavior of mercury and alcohol, describing the effects of atmospheric pressure on the boiling points of liquids and establishing the densities of various substances. His direct contributions, it is true, were small, but in raising appreciably the level of precision that was obtainable in many scientific observations, Fahrenheit affected profoundly the course of experimental physics in the eighteenth century.

NOTES

1. Quoted from W. E. Knowles Middleton, *A History of the Thermometer and Its Use in Meteorology* (Baltimore, 1966), p. 71.
2. J. U. W. Grimm's *Deutsches Wörterbuch* gives "tepid" as the definition of *blutwarm*. Blutwärme ("blood-heat") is defined as the temperature of the blood. Francis Hauksbee, in his *Physico-Mechanical Experiments,* wrote: "I caus'd some water to be heated about Blood-warm" (quoted in the *Oxford English Dictionary*, I, 933). The French translation (Paris, 1754, I, 385) reads ". . . je fis chauffer de l'eau jusqu'à ce qu'elle fût un peu plus que tiède." ("I caused some water to be heated until it was a little more than tepid.")
3. It seems curious that Fahrenheit should have stipulated that the subject be a man. Perhaps this is owing to some remnant of the once widely held notion that women naturally have a lower body temperature than men. (See Jacques Roger, *Les sciences de la vie dans la pensée française du xviiie siècle* [Paris, 1963], pp. 84 ff.)
4. Middleton, *loc. cit.*

BIBLIOGRAPHY

I. ORIGINAL WORKS. All of Fahrenheit's published works appeared in the *Philosophical Transactions of the Royal Society,* **33** (1724): "Experimenta circa gradum caloris liquorum nonnullorum ebullientium instituta," pp. 1–3; "Experimenta & observationes de congelatione aquae

in vacuo factae," pp. 78–84; "Materium quarundum gravitates specificae diversis temporibus ad varios scopos exploratae," pp. 114–115; "Araeometri novi descriptio & usus," pp. 140–141; "Barometri novi descriptio," pp. 179–180. These are translated into German in Ostwalds Klassiker der Exacten Wissenschaften, no. 57 (Leipzig, 1954), pp. 3–18.

II. SECONDARY LITERATURE. There is an enormous quantity of literature on Fahrenheit. The following list is limited to recent articles of importance: Florian Cajori, "Note on the Fahrenheit Scale," in *Isis,* **4** (1921), 17–22; Ernst Cohen and W. A. T. Cohen-De Meester, "Daniel Gabriel Fahrenheit," in *Verhandelingen der Konenklijke akademie van wetenschappen,* sec. 1, **16,** no. 2 (1937), 1–37; N. Ernest Dorsey, "Fahrenheit and Roemer," in *Journal of the Washington Academy of Sciences,* **36,** no. 11 (1946), 361–372; and W. E. Knowles Middleton, *A History of the Thermometer and Its Use in Meterorology* (Baltimore, 1966), pp. 66–79.

J. B. GOUGH

FALCONER, HUGH (*b.* Forres, Scotland, 29 February 1808; *d.* London, England, 31 January 1865), *paleontology, botany.*

After studying successively at the universities of Aberdeen (where he took the M.A.) and Edinburgh (where he obtained the M.D.) Falconer went to India in 1830 as surgeon with the East India Company. In 1832 he was appointed superintendent of the botanic garden at Saharanpur, at the foot of the Siwalik Hills, part of the sub-Himalayan range. He returned to England in 1842 and was appointed in 1844 to superintend the arrangement of Indian fossils for the British Museum. In 1848 he went to Calcutta as superintendent of the botanic garden there and professor of botany at the Calcutta Medical College. He returned again to England in 1855, his health impaired.

Falconer's official posts were thus botanical, and in the course of his duties he explored mountainous country and made immense collections of plants, including new species, the genus *Falconeria* (Scrophulariaceae) being named for him in 1839. He was largely responsible for starting the cultivation of Indian tea (while at Saharanpur) and for the introduction into India of the quinine-bearing plant (while at Calcutta). But his scientific fame rests chiefly on his researches among the vertebrate fossils, particularly the mammals, which he and Captain (later Sir) Proby Cautley brought to light from among the late Tertiary rocks of the Siwalik Hills. He investigated these with extraordinary energy and skill, hunting the living animals around him and preparing their skeletons for comparison with the fossils. This vertebrate fossil fauna was unexampled for extent and richness in any region then known. It included species of mastodon, elephant, rhinoceros, hippopotamus, and giraffe, as well as some reptiles (crocodiles and tortoises) and fishes. This great work accomplished by Falconer and Cautley was recognized in England in 1837 by the bestowal on them jointly of the Geological Society's highest honor, the Wollaston Medal. Unfortunately, their discoveries were never fully described and illustrated.

During the last ten years of his life Falconer made researches into Pleistocene mammals and the evidences of prehistoric man, both in Britain and in various parts of Europe. At the time of his death he was foreign secretary of the Geological Society and a vice-president of the Royal Society.

BIBLIOGRAPHY

I. ORIGINAL WORKS. Falconer's paleontological writings, published and in manuscript, were gathered together and edited, with a biographical sketch, by Charles Murchison in *Palaeontological Memoirs and Notes of the Late Hugh Falconer, A.M., M.D.,* 2 vols. (London, 1868). Of these works the chief was the unfinished *Fauna antiqua Sivalensis,* written with P. T. Cautley, which began publication in 1846 (London). His botanical papers are listed by Murchison, I, lv–lvi.

II. SECONDARY LITERATURE. In addition to Murchison, above, see also W. J. Hamilton, obituary notice in *Proceedings of the Geological Society of London, 21* (1865), xlv–xlix; Charles Lyell, remarks in the course of the president's anniversary address in *Proceedings of the Geological Society of London, 2* (1837), 508–510; obituary notice in *Proceedings of the Royal Society, 15* (1866–1867), 14–20; and H. B. Woodward, *The History of the Geological Society of London* (London, 1908), pp. 128–129.

JOHN CHALLINOR

FALLOPPIO, GABRIELE (*b.* Modena, Italy, 1523 [?]; *d.* Padua, Italy, 3 October 1562), *medicine.*

Gabriele Falloppio, son of Geronimo and Caterina Falloppio, was first educated in the classics, but after the death of his father and ensuing financial difficulties, he was directed toward a career in the church. With improvement in the family's finances he turned to medicine, studying in Modena under Niccolo Machella and, according to the records, dissecting a body for his teacher in December 1544. Although still a student, but perhaps in need of funds, Falloppio began the practice of surgery but displayed so little aptitude for that subject—as demonstrated by the fatal outcome of a number of his cases—that he soon thereafter abandoned it and returned wholly to the study of medicine. There is a possibility that he spent some time at Padua under Giambattista da Monte and Matteo Realdo Colombo, the successor of Vesalius; and it can be stated with certainty that he studied for a period, about 1548, in Ferrara under the direction of "my teacher" Antonio Musa Brasavola and Giambattista Canano.

Falloppio was appointed to the chair of pharmacy in Ferrara and in 1549 accepted the chair of anatomy at the University of Pisa, where he was wrongfully accused of practicing human vivisection. During this period he spent some time in Florence dissecting the bodies of lions in the Medici zoo and thereby disproving Aristotle's statement that the bones of lions are wholly solid and without marrow. Despite the charges against him, he was offered and accepted the famous chair of anatomy at Padua as a successor to Colombo. He took up his duties toward the end of 1551 and lectured and demonstrated with such success as to attract a number of later to be distinguished students, including the comparative anatomist Volcher Coiter. Falloppio was fully appreciated by the university's authorities; he was regularly reappointed to the chair of anatomy until advancing pulmonary tuberculosis first limited his activities and finally killed him.

Of the various works by and attributed to Falloppio only the *Observationes anatomicae* (1561) was published during his lifetime and can be said with certainty to be fully authentic. It is not, however, a general and systematic textbook of anatomy but an unillustrated commentary or series of observations on the *De humani corporis fabrica* of Vesalius, in which Falloppio sought to correct errors committed by his illustrious predecessor and to present new material hitherto overlooked. His criticism, contrary to a characteristic of that age, is temperate and friendly, so that it is not uncommon to find the object of the criticism referred to as the "divine Vesalius," upon whose scientific foundations Falloppio, as a worthy successor, was willing to admit that he had based his own work. Since the *Observationes anatomicae* is not an all-inclusive study of anatomy, it never received the popular acclaim given, for example, to the *De re anatomica* (1559) of Colombo. It is, nevertheless, a work of greater originality.

Falloppio's investigations were the consequence of dissection not only of adult human bodies but also of fetuses, newborn infants, and children "up to the first seven months, and in several beyond" (fol. 17*v*). He was thus able to make a number of observations and contributions to knowledge of primary and secondary centers of ossification. His most notable contributions of this nature were his descriptions of the ossification of the occiput (fols. 21*r* ff.), of the sternum (fols. 51*r*–52*v*), and of the primary centers of the innominate bone (fols. 59*r*–60*r*). In his studies of the teeth Falloppio provided for the first time a clear description of primary dentition, the follicle of the tooth bud, and the manner of growth and replacement of the primary by the secondary tooth, as well as the first denial of the belief that teeth and bones are derived from the same tissues (fols. 39*r*–42*v*). Falloppio's description of the auditory apparatus was superior to that of Vesalius and includes the first clear account of the round and oval windows, the cochlea, the semicircular canals, and the scala vestibuli and tympani (fols. 27*r*–30*v*). He also referred to the third ossicle of the ear, the stapes, actually already mentioned in print (Pedro Jimeno, 1549), but he declared that it had been first described orally in lectures by Giovanni Filippo Ingrassia during a visit to Rome in 1546 (fols. 25*r*–27*r*).

Not the least important of Falloppio's contributions were those dealing with the muscles, among which were his relatively detailed account of the subcutaneous muscles of the scalp and face (fols. 62*r*–*v*, 63*v*–64*r*, 66*v*–68*r*) and his first description of the arrangement of the extrinsic muscles of the ear (fols. 62*v*–63*r*). In his investigation of the muscles of the head and neck he discovered and described the external pterygoid muscle (fol. 72*v*), analyzed the functions of the muscles of mastication (fols. 71*v*–73*r*), described the *tensor* and *levator veli palati* (fols. 76*v*–77*r*), and re-described with greater clarity some of the intrinsic muscles of the larynx (fols. 77*v*–79*r*). His greatest contribution to the study of the muscles of the head, however, was his account of the arrangement and functions of the muscles of the orbit (fols. 64*r*–66*v*, 68*r*–71*v*). For the first time, he described the *levator palpebrae,* even though this honor was later to be claimed by Giulio Cesare Aranzi (1587). He observed the nictitating membrane of mammals, first described by Aristotle and thereafter seemingly disregarded. He recognized the compound action of the oblique muscles, and he was the first to describe and provide the name for the trochlea of the superior oblique muscle. In addition to further, lesser contributions to the study of the muscles of the trunk, he added notably to knowledge of the intrinsic muscles of the hand and of their action (fols. 101*v*–108*v*), separated the adductor mass of the thigh into its three elements, and noted the *quadratus femoris* (fol. 101*v*), which had been previously overlooked.

In considering the vascular system, Falloppio denied the long-held belief that the walls of the vessels were composed of fibers which by their direction controlled the flow of blood (fol. 114*v*). Curiously enough, however, he denied the existence of the venous valves (fol. 118*v*), which were actually known as early as 1546 and described by Vesalius (1555), and he failed to refer to the description of the pulmonary transit of the blood provided in detail by Colombo (1559). He did, on the other hand, give the first relatively adequate account of the distribution of the carotid arteries and of the cerebral circulation (fols. 121*v*–126*r*). He made a major contribution to knowledge of the nervous system through his clear distinction and description of the trochlear nerve (hitherto known only through the briefest mention by Alessandro Achillini [1520]); he traced it to its origin in the brain stem, demonstrated its exclusive termination in the superior oblique muscle of the eye, and satisfied himself beyond any doubt that this nerve was an entity deserving separate classification, and that it was "reflected on a cartilaginous pulley, and it turns the eye inwards" (fols. 155*r*–156*r*). Unwilling to upset the classic number (seven) and arrangement of the cranial nerves, he increased that number only to eight, although in fact he recognized eleven of the twelve cranial nerves.

Falloppio's most important contribution to urology is his account of the kidneys, although it is always difficult to determine whether the priority is properly that of Falloppio or of his contemporary Bartolomeo Eustachi. With this understood, attention may be called to what seems to have been the earliest account of a case of bilateral duplication of the ureter and renal vessels: "Here at Padua I have observed and pointed out to my spectators double urinary passages and double sinuses in the middle of each human kidney, as well as many other things departing from the normal" (fols. 179*v*–180*r*). Falloppio seems, moreover, to have been the first to observe the straight tubules (fol. 180*r*–*v*) that are, however, eponymously named from Bellini's more detailed description of 1662, and he noted the multiple calyxes of the human kidney (fols. 180*v*–181*r*). It was in the course of these remarks on the kidney that Falloppio criticized Vesalius for describing and illustrating in the *Fabrica* (1543) the unipapillary kidney of the dog instead of that of man—although he readily recognized Vesalius' need to use the less fatty kidney of the dog in order to permit a better illustration of that organ's structure. Falloppio further proposed the comparison of the renal papillae to small stills distilling off the urine from the blood (fols. 181*v*–182*r*). He also first described the three muscle coats of the urinary bladder: "It possesses three tunics, as do the stomach and intestines"; and the bladder's internal sphincter "formed by nature to contain the urine and prevent its being strained out" (fol. 182*r*).

Falloppio's name is perhaps most closely associated

with his description of the uterine or fallopian tubes, which in fact he described correctly as resembling small trumpets: "[The extremity] resembles the bell of a brass trumpet, wherefore the seminal passage, with or without its windings, resembles a kind of trumpet" (fol. 197r). Owing, however, to incorrect interpretation of Falloppio's word *tuba,* some of the descriptive meaning has been lost in English. His description of the uterine tubes is sufficiently accurate in detail to justify their bearing his name; he furthermore described the clitoris (fol. 193r–v), asserted the existence of the hymen in virgins, a matter long under dispute (fol. 194r), coined the word "vagina" (192r) for what had previously been called the cervix or neck of the uterus, and disproved the popular notion that the penis entered the uterus during coition (fol. 192v). He described certain vesicle-like structures filled with an aqueous fluid and others with a yellow humor (fol. 195v)—these may represent Graafian follicles or possibly a corpus luteum, and Falloppio's would therefore be the second mention of these structures after a somewhat similar account by Vesalius (1555).

In the preface to the *Observationes anatomicae* there is promise of a much larger, more detailed, illustrated work, mentioned as if it were well on the way toward completion. No trace of it remains today.

Falloppio may be called a student of Vesalius through the latter's books, and both his life and his book indicate a spiritual relationship to the earlier anatomist. In the *Observationes anatomicae* the Vesalian obligation to dissect, observe, and weigh one's findings by independent judgment is everywhere apparent—as well as being consciously expressed by the author, to whose criticisms Vesalius replied in *Anatomicarum Gabrielis Falloppii observationum examen* (1564).

The remainder of Falloppio's writings, originally lecture notes, were edited for publication at various times after his death and may therefore represent more or less than the original content. Of these, *Expositio in librum Galeni de ossibus* (1570), *Observationes de venis* (1570), *De humani corporis anatome compendium* (1571), and *De partibus similaribus humani corporis* (1575) deal with anatomy. Further works are concerned with syphilis, balneology, surgery, and the composition of drugs. The popular *Secreti diversi et miracolosi* (1563), often attributed to Falloppio, is spurious.

BIBLIOGRAPHY

I. ORIGINAL WORKS. Falloppio's works are most accessible in the collected editions *Opera omnia* (Venice, 1584; 2 vols., Frankfurt, 1600; 3 vols., Venice, 1606). The *Observationes anatomicae* has been reproduced in facsimile with Italian translation and notes, *Observationes anatomicae a cura di Gabriella Righi e Pericle Di Pietro,* 2 vols. (Modena, 1964).

II. SECONDARY LITERATURE. The best biographical study remains that of Giuseppe Favaro, *Gabrielle Falloppia Modenese (MDXXIII–MDLXII)* (Modena, 1928). Several studies of particular aspects of Falloppio's work include P. Di Pietro and G. Cavazzuti, "La descrizione falloppiana delle tube uterine," in *Acta medicae historiae patavina,* **11** (1964–1965), 51–60; Pietro Franceschini, "Luci e ombre nella storia delle trombe di Falloppia," in *Physis,* **7** (1965), 215–250; C. D. O'Malley, "Gabriele Falloppia's Account of the Cranial Nerves," in *Medizingeschichte im Spektrum. Festschrift zum fünfundsechzigsten Geburtstag von Johannes Steudel* (Wiesbaden, 1966), pp. 132–137; and "Gabriele Falloppia's Account of the Orbital Muscles," in *Medicine, Science and Culture. Historical Essays in Honor of Owsei Temkin* (Baltimore, 1968), pp. 77–85. On the literary relations of Falloppio and Vesalius, see C. D. O'Malley, *Andreas Vesalius of Brussels* (Berkeley-Los Angeles, 1964), pp. 289 ff.

C. D. O'MALLEY

FANKUCHEN, ISIDOR (*b.* Brooklyn, New York, 19 July 1905; *d.* Brooklyn, 28 June 1964), *crystallography.*

Fankuchen's parents were of modest means; he had two brothers and certainly was not spoiled in his youth. Intelligent and hard-working, he put himself through school by running a radio repair shop. Having obtained the B.S. from Cooper Union in 1926, he entered Cornell University as Hecksher fellow in 1929, married Dina Dardik in 1931, and received the Ph.D. under C. C. Murdock in 1933. In England as a fellow of the Schweinburg Foundation, he worked under Sir Lawrence Bragg in Manchester (1934–1936), then under J. D. Bernal at the Crystallographic Laboratory in Cambridge (1936–1938) and Birkbeck College in London (1938–1939).

On his return to the United States, Fankuchen held a national research fellowship in protein chemistry at the Massachusetts Institute of Technology (1939–1941) and served briefly as associate director of the Anderson Institute for Biological Research in Red Wing, Minnesota (1941–1942). In 1942, the year Cambridge University awarded him his second Ph.D., he joined the faculty of the Polytechnic Institute of Brooklyn, where he soon became head of the division of applied physics (1946) and where he remained until his death.

Fankuchen exerted a great influence on the teaching of crystallography and X-ray diffraction. By 1950 the Polytechnic Institute of Brooklyn had been turned into a teeming center for crystallographic research, as Fankuchen and H. F. Mark were joined by P. P. Ewald, Rudolf Brill, and David Harker. The monthly meetings of the "Point Group," Fankuchen's seminar, regularly attracted a number of crystallographers from outside the New York area. Fankuchen also organized intensive summer courses in X-ray diffraction, intended primarily for scientists in related disciplines, and thereby furthered the dissemination of crystallographic concepts in the scientific community. The Polycrystal Book Service, from which any crystallographic book can be purchased directly, is one of his creations.

From 1948 until his death, Fankuchen was the first American editor of *Acta crystallographica;* he fulfilled his editorial duties with unusual distinction, thanks to his keen critical sense and absolute scientific integrity. He belonged to many scientific societies; he was a charter member of both the American Society for X-Ray and Electron Diffraction and the Crystallographic Society of America; in 1950, when these two organizations merged to form the American Crystallographic Association, he became its first president. At the time of his death, he was chairman of the National Committee for Crystallography.

The mark of Fankuchen's scientific production is its diversity. His interests ranged widely through physics, chemistry, biology, and even mineralogy and metallurgy. He applied X-ray diffraction to new problems and refined or developed the necessary techniques and apparatus, as, for example, his very ingenious condensing monochromator to provide the intense X-ray beam required by his work on tomato mosaic virus. Of the crystal structures that he and his co-workers determined, the most memorable (of which he published a description in 1938, with Bernal and D. P. Riley) is that of the tomato bushy-stunt virus, a living crystalline substance.

For three years Fankuchen was an active member of the Bernal group and contributed to their results in the field of macromolecular compounds. He shared in the determination of the molecular weight of a tobacco-seed globulin (with Dorothy Crowfoot [Hodgkin], 1938) and the taking of the striking 5-degree-oscillation X-ray pattern of a single crystal of wet chymotrypsin (set forth in a paper that also dealt with hemoglobin, with Bernal and M. Perutz, 1938). He collaborated in the 1940 monograph on steroids (with Bernal and Crowfoot), in which crystal data are listed for more than eighty sterol derivatives, and in a famous paper on plant virus preparations (with Bernal, 1941).

In a series of publications, with Mark and others (1943–1949), Fankuchen studied fibers—chrysotile, chain polymers, fibrous proteins, and so forth. For this delicate work he devised a microcamera, in which the bore of a thermometer provided the collimator for the desired microbeam. With M. Bergmann he adapted this microcamera to the study of long spacings (1949), while he simultaneously investigated small-angle scattering from metal films (with B. Carroll, 1948). From 1947 to 1953, with a large number of collaborators, he conducted many studies of bones and teeth, in which investigations the microcamera proved its worth. First with H. S. Kaufman (1949), then with B. Post and R. S. Schwartz (1951), he successfully used diffraction at low temperatures utilizing a clever technique to prevent ice formation.

Fankuchen had a warm and buoyant personality. His kindness and helpfulness were legendary. His boisterous friendliness and deeply human qualities endeared him to all. During his last three years— while he was ill with cancer and knew it—he took great suffering in stride, never permitting it to interfere with his work. The Fankuchen Memorial Lectures perpetuate his name.

BIBLIOGRAPHY

I. Original Works. A complete bibliography of Fankuchen's works may be found in J. D. H. Donnay, "Memorial of Isidor Fankuchen," in *American Mineralogist,* **50** (1965), 539–547.

II. Secondary Literature. On Fankuchen's life and works see also J. D. Bernal, "Prof. Isadore Fankuchen," in *Nature,* **203** (1964), 916–917; J. D. H. Donnay, "Isidor Fankuchen, 1905–1964," in *Bulletin de la Société française de minéralogie (et de cristallographie),* **87** (1964), 299; P. P. Ewald, "I. Fankuchen," in *Acta crystallographica,* **17** (1964), 1091–1093; and E. Ubell, "A Crystal Grows in Brooklyn," in *Norelco Reporter,* **10** (1963), 3, 39.

J. D. H. Donnay

FANO, GINO (*b.* Mantua, Italy, 5 January 1871; *d.* Verona, Italy, 8 November 1952), *geometry.*

Fano was the son of Ugo and Angelica Fano; his father, a Garibaldian, had independent means. Gino studied from 1888 to 1892 at the University of Turin under Corrado Segre; while there, he met Guido Castelnuovo and specialized in geometry. In 1893–1894, while at Göttingen, he met Felix Klein, whose Erlangen program he had translated into Italian (*Annali di matematica,* 2nd ser., **17** [1889–1890], 307–343). From 1894 to 1899 Fano was assistant to Castelnuovo in Rome, was at Messina from 1899 to 1901, and in 1901 became professor at the University of Turin, where he taught until the Fascist laws of 1938 deprived him of his position. During World War

II he taught Italian students at an international camp near Lausanne. After 1946 Fano lectured in the United States and Italy. In 1911 he married Rosetta Cassin; two sons became professors in the United States.

Fano worked mainly in projective and algebraic geometry of n-space S_n. Early studies deal with line geometry and linear differential equations with algebraic coefficients; he also pioneered in finite geometry. Later work is on algebraic and especially cubic surfaces, as well as on manifolds with a continuous group of Cremona transformations. He showed the existence of irrational involutions in three-space S_3, i.e., of "unirational" manifolds not birationally representable on S_3. He also studied birational contact transformations and non-Euclidean and non-Archimedean geometries.

BIBLIOGRAPHY

I. ORIGINAL WORKS. Among Fano's many textbooks are *Lezioni di geometria descrittiva* (Turin, 1914; 3rd ed., 1925) and *Lezioni di geometria analitica e proiettiva* (Turin, 1930; 3rd ed., 1958), written with A. Terracini. Two of his articles appeared in *Encyclopädie der mathematischen Wissenschaften* (Leipzig, 1898–1935): "Gegensatz von synthetischer und analytischer Geometrie in seiner historischen Entwicklung im XIX. Jahrhundert," in III (Leipzig, 1907), 221–288; and "Kontinuierliche geometrische Gruppen," *ibid.*, 289–388.

II. SECONDARY LITERATURE. See A. Terracini, "Gino Fano," in *Bollettino dell'Unione matematica italiana*, 3rd ser., **7** (1952), 485–490; and "Gino Fano, 1871–1952, cenni commemorative," in *Atti dell'Accademia delle scienze* (Turin), classe di scienze fisiche, **87** (1953), 350–360. A bibliography, compiled by the editorial board, is in *Rendiconti del Seminario matematico, Università e politecnico di Torino*, **9** (1950), on pp. 33–45 of this issue dedicated to Fano (with portrait).

DIRK J. STRUIK

AL-FĀRĀBĪ, ABŪ NAṢR MUḤAMMAD IBN MUḤAMMAD IBN ṬARKHĀN IBN AWZALAGH (Latin **Alf[h]arabius, Abunazar,** among other forms) (*b.* Wasīj, district of Fārāb, *ca.* 870; *d.* Damascus, 950), *philosophy, music.*

The district of Fārāb—on both sides of the middle Jaxartes (now the Syr Darya) at the mouth of its tributary, the Aris—was conquered and Islamized by the Samanids in 839–840, and al-Fārābī's grandfather may have been a pagan convert. His father is said to have been an army officer of noble Persian descent, apparently in the service of the Samanid emirs, who claimed descent from the old Sassanid emperors of

Persia and patronized the emerging New Persian literature; but the family almost certainly spoke Sogdian or a Turkic dialect and exhibited Turkish manners and habits of dress. Al-Fārābī probably commenced his study of Islamic sciences (mainly law—the residents of Fārāb followed the legal school of al-Shāfiʿī) and music at Bukhara before going to Marv, where he seems to have begun his study of logic with the Syriac-speaking Nestorian Christian Yūḥannā ibn Ḥaylān, who was to continue teaching him in Baghdad and perhaps in Haran and whom he later acknowledged as his main teacher.

In the caliphate of al-Muʿtaḍid (892–902) both teacher and disciple went to Baghdad. Ibn Ḥaylān devoted himself to his religious duties, either monastic administration or theological instruction in Nestorian monasteries. Al-Fārābī was his only prominent student in logic and philosophy, and his only Muslim student. The complete silence of Arabic sources about Ibn Ḥaylān in any connection except as the teacher of al-Fārābī; Ibn Ḥaylān's isolation from the intellectual life of Baghdad, where Arabic was the main language of instruction in philosophy; and the report that al-Fārābī arrived at Baghdad knowing Turkish and a number of other languages but not Arabic (that is, he did not know Arabic well enough to study philosophy in that language) all indicate that he must have studied with Ibn Ḥaylān in Syriac or Greek or both. It is unlikely that the language of instruction (which included elaborate commentaries on Aristotle's *Organon*) could have been in any of the Turkic dialects, in Sogdian, or even in New Persian. In Baghdad, al-Fārābī set about perfecting his knowledge of Arabic (including the study of advanced Arabic grammar) in about 900 with the well-known philologist Ibn al-Sarrāj, in exchange for lessons in logic and music; he mastered it so well that his writings became a model of simple and clear Arabic philosophic prose. His newly acquired knowledge of Arabic enabled him to participate more fully in the philosophic circles in Baghdad (he is said to have attended the lecture courses of his older contemporary, the Nestorian Christian Mattā ibn Yūnus) and to make fuller use of the extensive body of scientific literature that existed in that language.

In the caliphate of al-Muktafī (902–908) or early in the caliphate of al-Muqtadir (908–932), al-Fārābī left Baghdad to continue his studies in Constantinople. Apparently he traveled first to Haran in the company of Ibn Ḥaylān. "After this [that is, after completing the study of Aristotle's *Posterior Analytics* with Ibn Ḥaylān] he traveled to the land of the Greeks and stayed in their land for eight years until he completed [the study of the] science[s] and learned the entire philosophic syllabus." This report is quoted by al-Khaṭṭābī (931–998) from al-Fārābī's own account of his studies. Al-Fārābī's linguistic interests, his contacts with the Syriac- and Greek-speaking teachers in Baghdad who could have provided him with the incentive and necessary information for the trip, and the relative ease with which a determined Muslim scholar (for example, the historian al-Mas'ūdī) could visit Constantinople during this period make it difficult to doubt the authenticity of the report, which helps to explain a number of facets of al-Fārābī's works and thought, such as his access to certain traditions and texts and the character of his Platonism. Al-Fārābī's works, in turn, can now provide us with a better understanding of the course of philosophic studies at the University of Constantinople in the period between Photius and Michael Psellus.

Sometime between 910 and 920 al-Fārābī returned to Baghdad to spend more than two decades teaching and writing, which established his reputation as the foremost Muslim philosopher and the greatest philosophic authority after Aristotle. His teacher Ibn Ḥaylān died in Baghdad sometime before 932. Although al-Fārābī must have had a number of students who later spread his works and teachings in Persia and Syria, his only students who are known by name are the prominent Jacobite Christian theologian and philosopher Yaḥyā ibn 'Adī, who headed an active but hardly brilliant philosophic school in Baghdad until his death in 975, and his brother Ibrāhīm, who was still with al-Fārābī in Aleppo shortly before the latter's death. Al-Fārābī's true disciples, however, were men like Ibn Sīnā, Ibn Rushd, and Maimonides, and his influence persisted in the learned tradition of the study of and commentary on Aristotle and Plato in Arabic, Hebrew, and Latin.

While defending the claims of philosophy and the philosophic way of life, al-Fārābī carefully avoided the theological, sectarian, and political controversies that raged in Baghdad during this period. He was not a member of the religious or scribal class. He must have had a number of friends among the many officers from his native land who formed the elite corps of the army and occupied high positions as bodyguards of the caliphs. Through them he probably came in contact with the prominent scribes and viziers who patronized the philosophic sciences, such as Ibn al-Furāt, 'Alī ibn 'Isā, and Ibn Muqlah. He wrote his major work on music at the request of Abū Ja'far al-Karkhī, who became vizier in 936. This work was of great importance in the history of music theory and science. It is treated in the next section of the article.

It is unlikely that, at the age of seventy, al-Fārābī would have chosen to leave Baghdad merely in search of additional fame. By 942 the internal political confusion and the threat to the safety and well-being of the city's inhabitants had become extremely grave. The caliph, his viziers, and his bodyguard were so menaced by the rebellion of a former tax collector from the south that the caliph fled and took refuge with the Ḥamdānid prince of Mosul. Al-Fārābī departed to an area which, in 942, seemed more peaceful and was governed by a dynasty more congenial to him than the Hamdānids of Mosul. The Ikhshīdids, who ruled Egypt and Syria, were originally army officers from Farghānah, not far from al-Fārābī's birthplace in central Asia; and the Nubian slave Kāfūr, who held the power as regent, was a liberal patron of the arts. Al-Fārābī stayed in Damascus for about two years (during which he perhaps visited Aleppo) and then went to Egypt, no doubt driven there by the conflict in Syria between the Ikhshīdids and the Ḥamdānids, which was to last until 947. In the meantime, the Ḥamdānid prince Sayf al-Dawlah occupied Aleppo and Damascus and began to surround himself with a circle of learned men, whom he supported liberally. About a year before his death, al-Fārābī left Egypt to join Sayf al-Dawlah's circle. When he died in Damascus in 950, the prince and his courtiers performed the funeral prayers for him. He was buried outside the southern, or minor, gate of the city.

Al-Fārābī believed that science (that is, philosophy) had reached its highest development in the Socratic tradition, as embodied in the writings of Plato and Aristotle, their Greek commentators, and others who developed or made independent contributions to the natural and mathematical sciences. This tradition, which had declined in its original home and the spirit or purpose of which had become extinct or confused, must now find a new home in the civilization of Islam, wherein a new tradition of learning had been developing for more than two centuries; must reassert its claim as the supreme wisdom available to man; must infuse the new learning with critical understanding of its foundations and a sense of harmony, order, and purpose; and must clarify the principles and presuppositions of man's view of himself and the natural whole of which he is a part. Al-Fārābī's effort to recover, explain, defend, and reestablish this view of science as the highest stage of human wisdom took into account the gulf that separated the cultural environment of Greek science from the new Islamic environment in such matters as language, political and legal traditions, and characteristic habits of thought, and especially the pervasive impact of the revealed religions on the character and direction of political life and scientific thought. With persistence and skill, he set about teaching others what must have been the core of his own experience: the reconversion of man and his thought to the natural understanding, as distinguished from the multiplicity of customs, legal and political opinions, and religious beliefs.

Al-Fārābī's teaching activity followed an elaborate philosophic syllabus developed on a number of levels and based on the writings of Aristotle, a number of Platonic dialogues, and the works of Hippocrates and Galen, Euclid and Ptolemy, Plotinus and Porphyry, and the Greek commentators of the schools of Athens and Alexandria.

It began with introductory accounts of the opinions and writings of these authors, comprehensive accounts of the organization of the sciences, and epitomes of individual works. These were followed by a group of paraphrases of individual works, glosses on special difficulties in them, and expositions of particular themes. These led, finally, to a smaller group of lengthy commentaries in which the basic works of Aristotle were explored in great detail, taking into account the contributions, criticisms, and comments of earlier commentators.

Although al-Fārābī wrote commentaries on Euclid's *Elements* and Ptolemy's *Almagest,* the mathematical art to which he devoted particular attention was music. He wrote extensively on its history, theory, and instruments; and it is significant that his chosen art was the practice of music rather than medicine. Unlike the expository and didactic style of his mathematical writings, his specialized writings on natural science are for the most part polemical: against Galen's interpretations of Aristotle's views on the parts of animals; against John Philoponus' criticism of Aristotle's views on the eternity of the world and movement; against the physician al-Rāzī's views on matter, time, place, and atoms; against the theologian Ibn al-Rāwandī's account of dialectic, which was the method used by the theologians in natural science; against the doctrines of the theologians in general concerning atoms and vacuum; and finally against the scientific claims of astrology and alchemy. Judged from two of these writings which have been edited and studied (*On Vacuum* and *Against John Philoponus*), al-Fārābī's intention was not primarily to defend the doctrines of Aristotle against his critics, but rather to clarify the questions at issue, to ascertain the assumptions, coherence, and relevance of the arguments against Aristotle's natural science, and to determine whether they are based on genuine differences between Aristotle and his opponents or merely on a misunderstanding or misinterpretation of Aristotle, overconfidence in the theoretical implications

of certain experiments, or eagerness to support a religious doctrine. Al-Fārābī's openness regarding the foundations of Aristotle's natural science was restrained, however, because of his awareness of the decline of scientific learning since Aristotle's time and the overwhelming odds against free scientific inquiry in the new religious environment.

Al-Fārābī's departure from Aristotle is explicit in his writings on political science, which are inspired by a comprehensive view of Plato's philosophy and modeled after the *Republic* and the *Laws.* The intention of these works is both theoretical and practical. The theoretical intention emerges as al-Fārābī brings together the views of Plato and Aristotle and attempts to harmonize them without removing the underlying polarity between their two philosophies, leaving the reader with the conviction that the residual disagreement between the two leading philosophers may constitute the fundamental unresolved questions of science. The practical intention is expressed through the construction of constitutions proposed for cities whose institutions, doctrines, and practices are meant to promote, support, or at least not inhibit the development of scientific inquiry.

[A full bibliography follows the section below.]

MUHSIN MAHDI

AL-FĀRĀBĪ: Music.

Apart from a brief section in the *Iḥṣāʾ al-ʿulūm* (*Enumeration of the Sciences*), which provided medieval European theorists with one or two definitions but is otherwise of little interest, only one of al-Fārābī's musicological works has been edited, *Kitāb al-mūsīqā al-kabīr.* This is, however, probably the greatest Arabic treatise on music, and in it al-Fārābī not only demonstrates his mastery over the corpus of theory inherited from the Greeks but also justifies his reputation as an executant musician by giving a comprehensive account of some of the main features of contemporary practice.

For his methodology and definitions (set forth in the introduction) al-Fārābī draws upon the techniques of Greek philosophical inquiry. As for subject matter, however, some aspects with which the Greeks were concerned, such as ethical theories, receive scant attention, and the cosmological implications that had been of considerable interest to al-Kindī are ignored. The main theoretical section of the work begins with the physics of sound. Here al-Fārābī follows Aristotle—not uncritically, but nevertheless without any great originality: it was left to the late tenth-century Ikhwān al-Ṣafāʾ (Brethren of Purity) to introduce the concept of the spherical propagation of sound (which had been put forward in Aetius' *De placitis philoso-phorum*). There follow definitions of the basic elements of note, pitch, and interval, and then a detailed exposition of various tetrachord species (diatonic, chromatic, and enharmonic), not all of which are taken from Greek theorists; and of the structure of the Greek two-octave Greater Perfect System. This theoretical section concludes with a highly abstract analysis of rhythm based upon the concept of the *chronos protos*.

Musical practice is examined separately. Particular attention is paid to presenting the differing scales obtainable on the main melody instruments, especially the lutes (ʿud, ṭunbūr khurāsānī, ṭunbūr baghdādī), certain intervals being defined empirically (by halving distances between frets) rather than by ratios, as they are in the theoretical section. A second and less recondite passage on rhythm discusses the various forms taken by the most commonly used rhythmic cycles, and another important aspect of contemporary practice (generally ignored by other theorists) is illuminated by an account of various types of voice production and ornamentation and the way these should be utilized in the course of a composition.

The *Kitāb al-mūsīqā al-kabīr* appears to owe little to the musical treatises of al-Kindī, even when covering the same ground; and although later theorists recognize its importance, they in turn show considerable independence of mind. What influence al-Fārābī had is most apparent on the theoretical side: certain texts reproduce some of the more abstruse passages (especially on scale), but in the main it is his definitions that are cited—and then discussed, enlarged upon, and sometimes modified. Subsequent accounts of musical practice generally employ different descriptive methods and concentrate on other aspects of a complex and constantly evolving musical system.

Al-Fārābī's *Kitāb al-mūsīqā al-kabīr* is translated in R. d'Erlanger, *La musique arabe,* I and II (Paris, 1930–1935).

O. WRIGHT

BIBLIOGRAPHY

I. ORIGINAL WORKS. The following are the main text editions and translations that have appeared since the compilation of Rescher's bibliographies (see below), and many of them give further bibliographical information (especially about MSS) not contained in the bibliographies listed below: *La statistique des sciences,* Osman Amine, ed., 3rd ed. (Cairo, 1968); *Kitāb al-mūsīqā al-kabīr* ("The Great Book on Music"), Ghaṭṭās Khashaba, ed. (Cairo, 1967); "Le Kitāb al-ḥaṭāba," ("Commentary on the Rhetoric"), Jacques Langhade, ed. and trans., in *Mélanges de l'Université Saint-Joseph* (Beirut), **43** (1968), 61–177; Ralph Lerner and Muhsin Mahdi, eds., *Medieval Political Philosophy: A Sourcebook* (New York, 1963), pp. 22–94, which contains selections in English from "Enumeration of the Sciences," "Political Regime," "Attainment of Happiness," and "Plato's Laws"; *Book of Letters: Commentary on Aristotle's "Metaphysics,"* Muhsin Mahdi, ed. (Beirut, 1969); *Book of Religion and Related Texts,* Muhsin Mahdi, ed. (Beirut, 1968); *Utterances Employed in Logic,* Muhsin Mahdi, ed. (Beirut, 1968); *The Political Regime,* Fauzi Najjar, ed. (Beirut, 1964); "Fārābī'nin Peri Hermeneias Muhtasarı," Mübahat Türker-Küyel, ed. and trans., in *Ardṣtirma* (Ankara), **4** (1966), 1–85; and "Un petit traité attribué à al-Fārābī," Mübahat Türker-Küyel, ed. and trans., *ibid.,* **3** (1965), 25–63.

II. SECONDARY LITERATURE. Al-Fārābī's life and works are discussed in Moritz Steinschneider, *Al-Fārābī (Alfarabius)* (St. Petersburg, 1869; repr. Amsterdam, 1966), which gives a comprehensive account of the sources, both printed and MS, available in Europe at that date and which is still indispensable for Hebrew and Latin translations and fragments; and Nicholas Rescher, *Al-Fārābī: An Annotated Bibliography* (Pittsburgh, 1962) and *The Development of Arabic Logic* (Pittsburgh, 1964), pp. 122–128, which list most of the texts and studies that have appeared since Steinschneider, but not the important uncataloged and recently cataloged MSS in the libraries of Turkey, Iran, etc., most of which will be listed in vol. III of Fuat Sezgin, *Geschichte des arabischen Schrifttums* (Leiden, 1967–   ). See also Richard Walzer, "Al-Fārābī," in *Encyclopaedia of Islam,* 2nd ed. (Leiden–London, 1960–   ), II, 778–781; and *Index Islamicus,* J. D. Pearson, ed. (Cambridge, 1958–   ), sec. 4b. Max Meyerhof—"Von Alexandrien nach Baghdad," in *Sitzungsberichte der Preussischen Akademie der Wissenschaft,* Phil.-hist. Kl., **23** (1930), 389–429—studied the few autobiographical fragments that have survived from al-Fārābī's history of philosophy. These should now be supplemented by the fragments reported by al-Khaṭṭābī, in Kabul (Afghanistan) Library of the Ministry of Information, Arabic MS 217, fol. 154r.

The following are the main studies that have appeared since Rescher, many of which provide bibliographical information not found in the works listed above: Muhsin Mahdi, "Alfarabi," in Leo Strauss and Joseph Cropsey, eds., *History of Political Philosophy* (Chicago, 1963), pp. 160–180; "Alfarabi Against Philoponus," in *Journal of Near Eastern Studies,* **26** (1967), 223–260 (the appendix, 253–260, contains a trans. and notes); "The *editio princeps* of Fārābī's *Compendium legum Platonis,*" *ibid.,* **20** (1961), 1–24; Fauzi Najjar, "Fārābī's Political Philosophy and Schīʿism," in *Studia Islamica,* **14** (1961), 57–72; and Richard Walzer, *Greek Into Arabic* (Cambridge, Mass., 1962), *passim;* and "Early Islamic Philosophy," in A. H. Armstrong, ed., *Cambridge History of Later Greek and Early Medieval Philosophy* (Cambridge, 1967), pp. 641–669, 689–691. See also A. Kubesov and B. A. Rosenfeld, "On the Geometrical Treatise of al-Fārābī," in *Archives internationales d'histoire des sciences,* **22** (1969), 50.

MUHSIN MAHDI

FARADAY, MICHAEL (*b.* Newington, Surrey [now part of Southwark, London], England, 22 September 1791; *d.* Hampton Court, Middlesex, England, 25 August 1867), *chemistry, physics.*

Early Life and Education. Michael Faraday was born into a poor family, of which he was the third of four children. His father, James, was a blacksmith who had left his own smithy in Outhgill, near Kirkby Stephen, early in 1791 to seek work in London. His increasing ill health prevented him from providing more than the bare necessities for his family. Faraday later recalled that he was once given a loaf of bread, which was to feed him for a week. James Faraday died in 1809. Michael's mother, the former Margaret Hastwell, was the mainstay of the family. She made do with what she had for material needs, but clearly offered her younger son that emotional security which gave him the strength in later life to reject all social and political distinctions as irrelevant to his own sense of dignity. She died in 1838.

There are no sources for Faraday's early years, so it is impossible to say what effects they had on him; we can only infer them from his adult life. His contemporaries uniformly described him as kind, gentle, proud, and simple in both manner and attitude. He loved children, although he had none of his own, and never lost his enthusiasm for natural beauty, especially such grandiose spectacles as a thunderstorm or an alpine waterfall. Such traits, when taken in conjunction with his solicitude for the success of his older brother, Robert, as a gas fitter and for the education of his younger sister, Margaret, bespeak a close-knit family, enjoying simple pleasures but raised in all propriety by stern but loving parents.

The one early influence of which there can be no doubt was that of religion. Faraday's parents were members of the Sandemanian Church, and Faraday was brought up within its discipline. The Sandemanian religion is a peculiar offshoot of Protestant Christianity. It is fundamentalist in the sense that Sandemanians believe in the literal truth of Scripture, but its emphasis is not on the fire and brimstone of most fundamentalist sects. Rather, it stresses that love and sense of community which marked the primitive Christian Church. It was this love and sense of community which were to sustain Faraday throughout his life. His friend and close associate at the Royal Institution, John Tyndall, a self-styled agnostic, wrote in some puzzlement in his journal for Sunday, 24 October 1852: "I think that a good deal of Faraday's week-day strength and persistency might be referred to his Sunday Exercises. He drinks from a fount on Sunday which refreshes his soul for a week" (Royal Institution, "Tyndall's Journals," MS, V, 163).

Faraday drew more than strength from his religion.

It gave him both a sense of the necessary unity of the universe derived from the unity and benevolence of its Creator and a profound sense of the fallibility of man. Both are worth stressing. The origins of field theory are to be found in Faraday's detailed experimental researches on electricity, but the speculations and imaginings which led him to the experiments and the courage which permitted him to publish physical heresies owe something to his unquestioning belief in the unity and interconnections of all phenomena. This belief, in turn, derived from his faith in God as both creator and sustainer of the universe. The fallibility of man was clearly described in the Book of Job, and this was the book in Faraday's Bible which he had marked the most with marginal emphases. Faraday never engaged in scientific polemics. He presented his results to his peers, having done his best to assure that his experiments were accurate and his reasoning sound. If he were wrong, better experiments and sounder reasoning would prevail and his beloved science would progress. He considered himself to be merely an instrument by which truth was revealed. To insist upon his infallibility would border on blasphemy. He was content to publish his results and let posterity judge how close he had come to being right.

These qualities of Faraday became apparent only when he was in the full tide of fame. In his youth, it seemed unlikely that he would ever have the opportunity to exercise them, at least in the pursuit and presentation of scientific truths. His formal education was almost nil, consisting of the rudiments of reading, writing, and ciphering. When he was thirteen years old, Faraday helped contribute to the family earnings by delivering newspapers for a Mr. G. Riebau of 2 Blandford Street. Riebau was an émigré from France who had fled the political maelstrom of the French Revolution. He not only let out newspapers but also sold and bound books. When Faraday turned fourteen, he was apprenticed to Riebau to learn the art of bookbinding. It was in the seven years of his apprenticeship that Faraday developed the extraordinary manual dexterity that was to distinguish his later experimental researches. The proximity of books stocked for sale and brought in to be rebound stimulated his mind. He became an omnivorous reader, absorbing fact and fancy in equal amounts. The result was a severe case of intellectual indigestion as Faraday became the repository of hosts of unconnected statistics and ideas.

His condition was relieved by the discovery of an elementary treatise, *The Improvement of the Mind,* written by an eighteenth-century clergyman, Isaac Watts. This treatise, as Riebau reported, was "frequent took in his Pocket," and Faraday followed each of Watts's suggestions for self-improvement. He began to keep a commonplace book, in which he could record ideas and interesting observations; he attended lectures and took notes; he began a correspondence with a young man, Benjamin Abbott, with the express hope of improving himself; he later helped found a discussion group devoted to the exchange of ideas. All these things Watts strongly recommended. But Watts went further than providing mechanical aids to learning; he also presented a philosophy which appeared to protect its adherents from false theories and intellectual delusions. Accurate observation of facts and precision in language would prevent a philosopher from premature generalization, which had led many an unwary student astray. This advice, together with his deep sense of human fallibility, reinforced the caution with which Faraday later approached natural philosophy. He never embarked upon an explanation without first testing for himself the facts that needed explanation. Mere reading of the results of others never satisfied him. Some of his most brilliant investigations owed their origin to a casual observation of an anomaly when Faraday checked his facts. And it was not until every fact had been checked and rechecked that Faraday would generalize. Watts had a very attentive pupil.

Faraday's passion for science was first aroused by a chance reading of the article "Electricity" in a copy of the *Encyclopaedia Britannica* which he was rebinding. His curiosity was piqued, and he set out to check what facts he could by means of a small electrostatic generator which he constructed out of some old bottles and waste lumber. The article had been written by one James Tytler, who espoused a somewhat idiosyncratic view of the nature of electricity. For Tytler, all electrical effects could be explained by assuming the existence of a peculiar fluid whose various modes of motion would account for optical and thermal, as well as electrical, phenomena. Electricity was likened by Tytler to a vibration, rather than a flow of material particles through space, and this view permitted him to suggest answers to such thorny questions as why conductors conduct electricity and insulators do not. In the course of his article, Tytler also took the opportunity to demolish the two-fluid theory of electricity then current on the Continent and the Franklinian one-fluid theory popular in Great Britain.

One should be wary of drawing too far-reaching consequences from any single influence, but there are a number of aspects of Tytler's article and its possible effects on Faraday that deserve mention. Tytler was, first of all, a scientific heretic presenting a view that had few supporters. As such, he was both belligerent and challenging, and undoubtedly stirred Faraday to

exercise his own judgment more than if the subject had been presented calmly, without controversy, as Truth. Tytler's defensive posture also forced him to attack the more orthodox theories and underline their very real weaknesses. If nothing else, these criticisms must have made Faraday skeptical of the accepted theories and forced him to keep an open mind on controversial points. When he later challenged both the one-fluid and the two-fluid theories, he was able to do so in precisely those areas where Tytler had first sown doubts. His challenge to orthodox electrical theories in 1838 was couched in Tytlerian terms. Current electricity, for Faraday as for Tytler, was a vibration, not a material flow. How much Faraday owed to Tytler is impossible to assess, but the influence was strong enough to lead Faraday to refer to Tytler's article a number of times in the laboratory diary that he kept from 1820 on.

With the reading of Tytler's article, Faraday began the pursuit of science in earnest. In the London of the early nineteenth century, however, it was difficult for an apprentice bookbinder to find many sources of scientific enlightenment. He could and did attend public lectures, but there were no night schools, no correspondence courses, no public libraries from which he could gain scientific enlightenment. He was, therefore, doubly fortunate to fall in with a group of young men with a common passion for science. They had come together as the City Philosophical Society in 1808 and were led by John Tatum, at whose house they met every Wednesday night. Tatum would deliver a lecture on a scientific subject and then throw open his library to the members of the society.

Faraday was introduced into this company in February 1810, when he attended his first lecture. At the City Philosophical Society, he received a basic education in the sciences, attending and taking careful notes on lectures on electricity, galvanism, hydrostatics, optics, geology, theoretical mechanics, experimental mechanics, chemistry, aerology (pneumatic chemistry), astronomy, and meteorology. These lectures should not be overestimated, for they were often mere catalogs of facts (mineralogy is an example) but, when possible, Tatum illustrated them with experiments and introduced his avid listeners to interesting pieces of scientific apparatus. It was at the City Philosophical Society, for example, that Faraday first saw a voltaic pile in operation.

Faraday's interest was increasingly focused on science. It was this interest that led him to the discovery of a work which he lauded throughout his life, Jane Marcet's *Conversations on Chemistry*. Mrs. Marcet's treatment of chemistry differed considerably from other contemporary, more technical accounts. She had written it for those people, like herself, who had been entranced by the lectures of Humphry Davy at the Royal Institution of Great Britain. Davy approached chemistry as if it were the key to the ultimate mysteries of nature, and Mrs. Marcet did likewise. Here was no dry catalog of chemical facts, or recipes, but a grand scheme which tied together chemical reactions, electrical relations, and thermal and optical phenomena. The impact on Faraday was considerable. The simplicity of his views on electricity was forever destroyed, his thoughts were directed specifically to chemistry, and, most important of all, he was introduced to the thoughts of Humphry Davy, who became, for him, the example of what he would like to be.

Faraday and Humphry Davy. There was, seemingly, little chance that Michael Faraday, bookbinder's apprentice, would ever become anything other than Michael Faraday, bookbinder. But one of Riebau's customers offered him tickets to Davy's lectures at the Royal Institution. He went, took careful notes, and copied them out in a clear hand. Each scientific point made by Davy was grasped eagerly and recounted to his friends at the City Philosophical Society. But this was mere playing at science, and it was with a heavy heart that Faraday, in October 1812, accepted the end of his apprenticeship and prepared to devote himself to bookbinding instead of his beloved chemistry. An accident changed his life and the life of science. In late October, while examining chloride of nitrogen, a very unstable substance, Davy was temporarily blinded by an explosion. Faraday was recommended to Davy as an amanuensis, and Davy was pleased to have him. In December, Faraday sent Davy the carefully bound notes he had taken at Davy's lectures. Davy was flattered but could do nothing at that time to help his young admirer. In February 1813, however, an assistant in the laboratory of the Royal Institution was fired for brawling. Davy immediately sent for Faraday and on 1 March 1813, Faraday took up his new position at the Royal Institution.

Davy exerted the most important influence on Faraday's intellectual development. Davy's mind was both penetrating and wide-ranging. He seems to have been an omnivorous reader interested in metaphysics as well as chemistry, poetry as well as physics. His science was characterized by brilliant flashes of insight soundly supported by experimental evidence. Although he never committed himself to a specific theoretical or metaphysical viewpoint, he was aware of and often used those that offered clues to the nature of matter and its forces. In the early nineteenth century, there were a number of points of view which

could provide the chemist with guidelines worth following. There was, first of all, an English tradition in chemistry which could be traced back to the patron saint of English science, Sir Isaac Newton. It took Newton's work on force and raised it to the level of a universal science. The classic example in the eighteenth century is Gowin Knight's *An Attempt to Demonstrate That All the Phenomena in Nature May Be Explained by Two Simple Active Principles, Attraction and Repulsion* (1748), whose message can be seen from the title. There seems little reason to doubt that both Faraday and Davy had read Knight's work. It was a part of the English scientific tradition and, more important, was easily available in the library of the Royal Institution.

But Knight's work was relatively crude. Although he reduced matter to the forces of attraction and repulsion, he separated the two, hypothesizing one kind of matter with attractive force only and another consisting solely of repulsive force. The association of these two forms of matter gave rise to the phenomena of the sensible world. A more subtle solution to the problem of complexity and of the nature of matter was provided by the Jesuit Rudjer Bošković in his *Philosophiae naturalis theoria redacta ad unicam legem virium in natura existentium,* which first appeared in 1758. Like Knight, Bošković dismissed the reality of matter and substituted forces but, unlike Knight, was able to combine the forces of attraction and repulsion in one "atom." In Figure 1, the pattern of forces of a Boscovichean atom is represented graphically. The point at O is a mathematical point which serves merely as the center of the forces of which the atom consists. Beyond H, the atomic force is attractive, decreasing inversely as the square of the distance, thus satisfying the Newtonian principle of universal attraction. From H to A, the force varies, according to the distance from O, in a continuous fashion from attractive to repulsive and back to attractive. The number of such variations can be multiplied at will to account for phenomena. From A to O, the force becomes increasingly repulsive, reaching infinite repulsion at O and thereby preserving impenetrability as a characteristic of "matter." These point-atoms were likened by Bošković to the points that make up the lines of the letters of the alphabet. A combination of the point-atoms gave the chemical elements, just as a combination of points made up the letters. Combinations of elements yielded the chemical compounds, and so on. Ultimately, then, all "matter" is one; observable complexities were the result of successive levels of complexity of particulate arrangements.

This system was particularly appealing to chemists

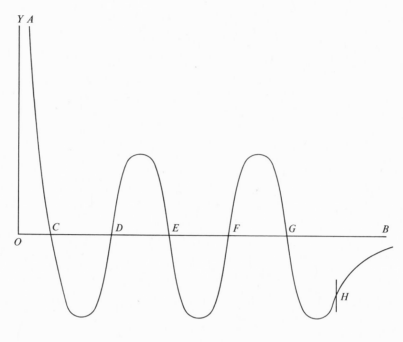

FIGURE 1

of philosophical disposition. It reconciled simplicity and complexity, providing a fundamental order in place of the taxonomic confusion engendered by the myriad chemical compounds and the ever-growing number of chemical elements. It also offered some insight into such specifically chemical problems as elective affinity by referring to the patterns of forces which could interact to create stable compounds. Davy remarked in his last years that he had found Bošković's theory of some importance in the development of his ideas and, in 1844, Faraday publicly declared his preference for Boscovichean atoms over those suggested by Dalton. Just how important Bošković's theory was for Faraday is currently a matter of scholarly dispute. I shall here insist that it was fundamental, but the reader is warned that my discussion of Faraday's use of it is controversial.

Knight and Bošković provided the justification for the unity of matter in which both Faraday and Davy believed. They did not, however, provide the concept of the unity of force. Both Knight and Bošković, after having composed their primary matter(s) from attractive and repulsive forces, gave material explanations for such phenomena as light and electricity. It may, of course, be argued that since all phenomena are ultimately the results of attractive and repulsive forces, then all phenomena are convertible into one another. But no such argument was ever made, to my knowledge, by those within the English tradition or by those who were partial to Bošković. Yet Faraday wrote in 1845: "I have long believed in the unity of

force," and his work from 1831 on was devoted to the conversion of one force into another. Whence came this conviction of the unity and convertibility of forces? Again, what follows is controversial, but it seems to make sense of what otherwise appears inexplicable and is, therefore, worth putting forward, albeit with considerable caution.

The doctrine of the unity and convertibility of forces is the product of German philosophy at the end of the eighteenth century. It was first suggested by Immanuel Kant in his *Metaphysische Anfangsgründe der Naturwissenschaft* (1786) and then developed by F. J. Schelling in his *Naturphilosophie*. The disciples of Schelling—the *Naturphilosophen,* among whom may be counted Hans Christian Oersted, the discoverer of the first force conversion (electromagnetism)—used this idea as the basic guiding thread in their researches. What is extremely difficult is to connect this movement in Germany and Scandinavia to Davy and Faraday. The one possible link, since neither Davy nor Faraday read German and translations were unavailable, is the poet and metaphysician Samuel Taylor Coleridge. He visited Germany in 1798–1799 and came back to England with his head overflowing with *Naturphilosophie.* He and Davy were close friends in the early 1800's and it seems likely, indeed inevitable, given Coleridge's enthusiasm and love of conversation, that he and Davy discussed *Naturphilosophie* in some detail. The unity and convertibility of forces was the kind of idea Davy always liked to keep in the back of his mind without committing himself to it. It might suggest some experiments and was, therefore, a potentially useful way of looking at the world. If he passed it on to Faraday, it fell on eager ears, for there can be no doubt of Faraday's commitment to it. The difference in their reaction may have lain in their different attitudes toward religion rather than toward science. Both men were religious, but Faraday was by far the more intense in his religious feelings and more determined in his devotion. One of the reasons Coleridge had been so enthusiastic in his acceptance of *Naturphilosophie* was that it appeared to contradict materialism and offer a place to spirit in the world. Faraday may have felt the same. Certainly the unity and convertibility of force offered a more appealing view of God's creation than the chaotic interplay of material atoms in which most scientists believed.

If we accept this admittedly hypothetical reconstruction, we can suggest the course of Faraday's development under Davy's tutelage. The unity and convertibility of force would first appeal to the apprentice chemist, for it bound the universe together in an aesthetically and theologically satisfying way. From here, it was a short step to the acceptance of, or at least the willingness to think in terms of, Boscovichean atoms. The English tradition of dynamic atomism made such a step intellectually respectable, for this tradition had based its insistence on the ultimate reality of force on sound empirical arguments which Faraday was to repeat in 1844 and 1846. It is within this intellectual and philosophic framework that his work should be viewed.

There was ample opportunity for Davy and Faraday to discuss these fundamental aspects of the nature and structure of physical reality. Soon after Faraday's employment at the Royal Institution, Davy decided to visit the Continent, and he asked Faraday to accompany him and Lady Davy. The party set out on 13 October 1813 and during 1813 and 1814 visited France and Italy, where Faraday met many of the leading scientists of the day. During this tour, Davy discoursed on every scientific subject under the sun, and Faraday eagerly drank it all in. Faraday became fully conscious, during this period, of the philosophical complexities underlying the apparent simplicity of chemical science and even more aware of the dangers of both methodological and metaphysical complacency.

Journeyman Chemist. Upon his return to London in April 1815, Faraday threw himself into chemistry with the enthusiasm that marked his whole scientific life. He assiduously searched all the scientific journals available to him, keeping a detailed bibliographical record of everything he read and carefully noting everything of interest to him. In 1816 he published his first paper, "Analysis of Caustic Lime of Tuscany," which was followed by a series of short (and inconsequential) articles on subjects suggested to him by the researches of Davy and William T. Brande, Davy's successor as professor of chemistry at the Royal Institution. By 1820 Faraday had established a modest but solid reputation as an analytical chemist, so much so that he was involved in court cases requiring expert testimony. One such case involved the question of the ignition point of heated oil vapor. This, together with his brother's involvement in the new gas lighting of London, led Faraday to investigate the general properties of the various oils used for heating and lighting. From these researches came the discovery of benzene in 1825.

But Faraday's mind ranged far wider than the composition of lime or illuminating gas. One of his earliest chemical enthusiasms had been Davy's work on chlorine, in which Davy had exploded Lavoisier's theory of acids by showing that not all acids contain oxygen, as the name of that element implied. Hydrochloric acid consisted solely of hydrogen and chlorine. Davy's demonstration that chlorine supported combustion also destroyed the unique place among the elements allotted to oxygen as the sole supporter of combustion, and thereby tended to weaken Lavoisier's magistral chemical synthesis. But this demonstration raised an important problem, and it was to this problem that Faraday turned. If chlorine were a supporter of combustion, as the almost explosive nature of the combination of iron with chlorine clearly demonstrated, then why did chlorine not combine with carbon, the combustible substance par excellence? All attempts at "burning" carbon in chlorine were unsuccessful, but Faraday was convinced that compounds of chlorine and carbon must exist. In 1820 he produced the first known compounds of chlorine and carbon, C_2Cl_6 and C_2Cl_4. These compounds had been produced by the substitution of chlorine for hydrogen in "olefiant gas," our modern ethylene. This was the first substitution reaction; such reactions, in the hands of Charles Gerhardt and Augustin Laurent in the 1840's, were to be used as a serious challenge to the dualistic electrochemical theories of J. J. Berzelius.

Beyond his work in analytical and pure chemistry, Faraday showed himself to be a pioneer in the application of chemistry to problems of technology. In 1818, together with James Stodart, a cutler, he began a series of experiments on the alloys of steel. Although he was able to produce alloys of superior quality, they were not capable of commercial production because they required the use of such rare metals as platinum, rhodium, and silver. Nevertheless, Faraday demonstrated that the increasingly urgent problem of producing higher-grade steels could be attacked by science. The later work on steel of Henry Sorby, Henry Bessemer, and Robert A. Hadfield was based directly on Faraday's work in the early part of the century.

In 1824 Faraday was asked by the Royal Society to conduct experiments on optical glass. Again his researches were inconclusive, but he paved the way for later improvements in glass manufacture. It was in these experiments that he produced a glass containing borosilicate of lead and with a very high refractive index. This was the glass he used in 1845 when he discovered the rotation of the plane of polarization of a light ray in an intense magnetic field.

The 1820's were busy years for Faraday beyond his chemical researches. In 1821 he married Sarah Barnard, the sister of one of the friends he had made at the City Philosophical Society. Their marriage was an extremely happy one and sustained Faraday throughout the extraordinary mental exertions of the next forty years. Sarah Barnard was not an intellectual. Once, when she was asked why she did not study chemistry, she replied, "Already it is so absorbing, and exciting to him that it often deprives him of his sleep and I am quite content to be the pillow of his mind." Faraday needed no one to whom to talk about his research. His dialogue was with nature. "I do not think I could work in company, or think aloud, or explain my thoughts . . .," he remarked near the end of his life. He founded no school and left no disciple who had been formed in his laboratory.

In the 1820's the precarious financial position of the Royal Institution also demanded Faraday's attention. He helped support the institution by performing chemical analyses, and he contributed to its fiscal stability by instituting the Friday evening discourses in 1825. He gave more than a hundred of these lectures before his retirement in 1862. They served to educate the English upper class in science, and part of the growing support for science in Victorian England may legitimately be attributed to the efforts of Faraday and his fellow lecturers to popularize science among those with influence in government and the educational establishment.

Early Researches on Electricity. During these busy years, Faraday was forced to push his love for electricity into the background. Yet it was never far from his thoughts, as the events of 1821 and 1831 reveal. In 1821 a series of brilliant researches culminated in the discovery of electromagnetic rotation; in 1831, seemingly out of nowhere, came the discovery of electromagnetic induction and the beginning of the experimental researches in electricity which were to

lead Faraday to the discovery of the laws of electrochemistry, specific inductive capacity, the Faraday effect, and the foundations of classical field theory. These researches, in both 1821 and 1831, are all of a piece; and it would be well here to make explicit what I think is the theoretical thread that holds them together.

By 1821 we know that Faraday was aware of and even toying with the concept of Boscovichean point-atoms. This is not to say that Faraday was a disciple of Bošković, for he certainly did not follow the Boscovichean system in his work. But the notion of atoms as centers of force had a strong appeal for him, and it is this notion that, I should like to suggest, provided the conceptual framework for his work on electricity. In particular, there were two specific consequences of the theory of point-atoms which were to be fundamental to Faraday's discoveries. The first was the emphasis upon complex patterns of force that followed logically from the consideration of the interaction of numbers of Boscovichean particles. It should be remembered that Boscovichean atoms were not the atoms of early nineteenth-century chemistry. Rather, the chemical elements were agglomerates of Boscovichean atoms whose specific chemical properties were the direct result of the patterns of force produced by the intimate association of point-atoms. When Faraday thought of material particles, therefore, he did not envision them as submicroscopic billiard balls with which certain rather simple forces were associated, but rather as centers of a complex web of forces.

Put another way, the orthodox scientist of the 1820's tended to think in terms of central forces emanating from particles, and central forces always act in straight lines between particles. Faraday's vision was far more intricate, and it permitted him to contemplate forces in manifold ways. An example may be useful here. Oersted's discovery of a circular magnetic "force" around a current-carrying wire was explained by André-Marie Ampère as the resultant of central forces emanating from current elements in the wire. To Faraday, the circular "force" was simple and could be used to explain the apparent polarity (or central forces) of magnetic poles. No one but Faraday could or did take a circular "force" seriously, but this was the germ of the idea of the line of force which was to be central to the development of Faraday's theories.

The second consequence involved a subtle shift in point of view away from the orthodox physics of the day. Boscovichean atoms, as force, were infinite in extent because the forces associated with atoms extended to infinity. Thus all material associations on the molecular level were really interpenetrations of fields of force, if I may be excused the anachronism. All particles, then, were associated with one another; the only differences were in the degrees of approximation of molecular or atomic centers of force. A displacement of a particle, anywhere in the universe, ought to affect every other particle. The same conclusion, of course, may be drawn from orthodox action-at-a-distance physics, but it is neither obvious nor obtrusive. In the theory of point-atoms it is both.

Furthermore, it suggests a mode of action which Faraday seized upon in his researches on the nature of electricity. Orthodox theory assumed the existence of one or two "imponderable" electrical fluids with whose particles specific electrical forces were associated. Electrical energy was transferred from place to place by the translation of these particles. The interlocking of force particles permitted energy to be transferred without the permanent displacement of the particles by means of the vibration of the particles. If a line of particles could be put under a strain, this line could then transmit energy either by the rapid breakdown and buildup of the strain or by vibrating transversally to the direction along which the strain was exerted. The first kind of "vibration" was that suggested by Faraday in 1838 to explain spark discharge, electrochemical decomposition, and ordinary electrical conduction. The second sort of vibration was tentatively put forward by Faraday in 1846 in his "Thoughts on Ray Vibrations" to account for the transmission of light through a vacuum without having recourse to a vibrating medium such as the luminiferous ether.

All this was far in the future in 1821, when Faraday was persuaded to take up the subject of electromagnetism by his friend Richard Phillips, an editor of *Philosophical Magazine*. Ever since Hans Christian Oersted's announcement of the discovery of electromagnetism in the summer of 1820, editors of scientific journals had been inundated with articles on the phenomenon. Theories to explain it had multiplied, and the net effect was confusion. Were all the effects reported real? Did the theories fit the facts? It was to answer these questions that Phillips turned to Faraday and asked him to review the experiments and theories of the past months and separate truth from fiction, groundless speculation from legitimate hypothesis. Faraday agreed to undertake a short historical survey but he did so reluctantly, since his attention was focused on problems of chemistry rather remote from electromagnetism.

His enthusiasm was aroused in September 1821, when he turned to the investigation of the peculiar nature of the magnetic force created by an electrical current. Oersted had spoken of the "electrical conflict" surrounding the wire and had noted that "this conflict performs circles," but this imprecise description had had little impact upon Faraday. Yet as he experimented he saw precisely what was happening. Using a small magnetic needle to map the pattern of magnetic force, he noted that one of the poles of the needle turned in a circle as it was carried around the wire. He immediately realized that a single magnetic pole would rotate unceasingly around a current-carrying wire so long as the current flowed. He then set about devising an instrument to illustrate this effect. (See Figure 2.) His paper "On Some New Electro-Magnetical Motions, and on the Theory of Magnetism" appeared in the 21 October 1821 issue of the *Quarterly Journal of Science*. It records the first conversion of electrical into mechanical energy. It also contained the first notion of the line of force. Faraday, it must be remembered, was a mathematical illiterate. His experiments revealed a circular "line" of magnetic force around a current-carrying wire and he found no difficulty in accepting this as a simple fact. To his mathematically trained contemporaries, such a force could not be simple but must be resolved into central forces. This is what Ampère had done so ingeniously in his early papers on electromagnetism. Ampère's sophisticated mathematical reasoning could have no

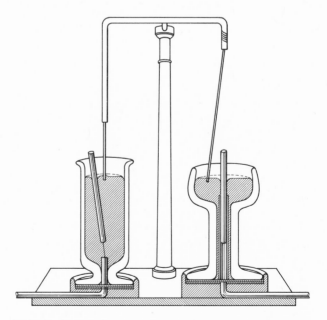

FIGURE 2.   Faraday's apparatus for illustrating electromagnetic rotation. At left, a cylindrical bar magnet, plunged into a beaker of mercury (which was part of the electrical circuit), rotated around the end of a current-carrying wire that made contact with the mercury. At right, the magnet was fixed and the wire was so mounted that it could turn about the point of suspension, and thus rotate around the magnetic pole.

effect on Faraday and he refused to move from what he considered the bedrock of experiment. Stubbornness, however, is no virtue in science and he was forced to face the problem of deriving central forces from his circular force in order to explain the "simple" attractions and repulsions of magnetic poles. His solution was both simple and elegant. If a straight current-carrying wire were bent into a loop, then the circular lines of magnetic force would be arranged in such a way as to concentrate them within the loop and the magnetic "polarity" of the loop would reflect this concentration. That there were no "poles" or termini of the magnetic force, Faraday showed by another simple demonstration. He wound a glass tube with insulated wire and then placed it half-submerged in water. A long magnetic needle was affixed to a cork so that it could float freely on the water. When a current was passed through the wire surrounding the glass tube, "poles" were formed at opposite ends of the tube and the north pole of the needle was attracted to the south pole of the helix. If an ordinary magnet had been used, the needle would have approached the electromagnet and clung to it, giving the illusion that the south pole attracted the north pole.

But in Faraday's setup the result was surprising. The needle moved toward the helix, entered the glass tube and continued through it until the north pole of the needle was situated at the north pole of the helix. The result was as Faraday had expected; it was merely another example of his electromagnetic rotations. A single magnetic "pole" would continue to move around and through the helix and never come to rest. The line of force along which it moved was the resultant of the circular magnetic forces surrounding the wires of the helix and did not emanate in straight lines from the "poles" of the magnet.

Thus Faraday's work on electromagnetic rotations led him to take a view of electromagnetism different from that of most of his contemporaries. Where they focused on the electrical fluids and the peculiar forces engendered by their motion (Ampère's position), he was forced to consider the line of force. He did not know what it was in 1821, but he suspected that it was a state of strain in the molecules of the current-carrying wire and the surrounding medium produced by the passage of an electrical "current" (whatever that was) through the wire. Such a state of strain, he knew, was transmitted some distance from the source of the strain, the current-carrying wire. Might it not be legitimate to speculate that if the strain could be intensified and concentrated, it might induce a similar state in a neighboring wire?

In the years between 1821 and 1831, Faraday re-

turned sporadically to this question. He attempted to detect the strain by passing plane polarized light through an electrolyte through which a current was passing; he queried the best form of magnet to produce the maximum strain, concluding that it might be "a very thick ring"; he attempted to induce an electrical current by means of static electricity; but all to no avail. Yet in these years his ideas gradually developed and clarified. The wave theory of light revealed how strains could transmit energy; the work of his friend Charles Wheatstone on sound, particularly on Chladni figures, which Faraday illustrated to audiences at the Royal Institution, showed how vibrations could produce symmetrical arrangements of particles; the discovery of "magnetism by rotation" by François Arago in 1825 (Arago's wheel) revealed to him the insufficiency of Ampère's electrodynamic theory.

In 1831 Faraday learned of Joseph Henry's experiments in Albany, New York, with powerful electromagnets in which the polarity could be reversed almost instantaneously by a simple reversal of "current" direction. The stage was set. An electromagnet, in the shape of a thick iron ring, wound on one side with insulated wire should set up the powerful strain; the strain should be conducted through the particles of the ring, which would then be thrown into a peculiar arrangement, much as the particles of dust were affected on a neighboring iron plate when one close by was set into vibration by a violin bow; the resultant arrangement would distort the intermolecular forces by which the iron molecules of the ring cohered, and this strain should then be detected by a secondary winding on the other side of the iron ring. On 29 August 1831, Faraday tried the experiment. When the primary circuit was closed, the galvanometer in the secondary circuit moved. An electrical "current" had been induced by another "current" through the medium of an iron ring. This discovery is always called the discovery of electromagnetic induction, but it should be noted that it is no such thing.

It was not until some weeks later that Faraday discovered the conditions under which a permanent magnet could generate a current of electricity (17 October 1831). It was at this date that he could declare that he had demonstrated the reverse of Oersted's effect, namely, the conversion of magnetic force into electrical force. Further investigation led him to the invention of the first dynamo, whereby the reverse of his 1821 discovery of electromagnetic rotations could be accomplished. Mechanical force could be converted into electrical force by a simple machine. A copper disk, rotated between the poles of a magnet, produced a steady electrical current in a circuit run-

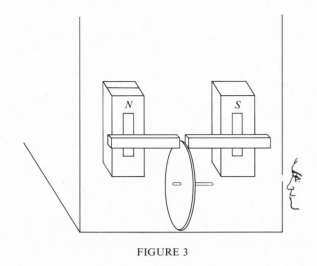

FIGURE 3

ning from the center of the disk through a wire to the edge of the disk. (See Figure 3.)

The concept of the line of force now moved to the very center of Faraday's thought, where it was to remain for the rest of his life. It was the line of force which tied all his researches on electricity and magnetism together. It was therefore with some embarrassment that he confessed, in his second series of *Experimental Researches in Electricity,* that he did not know what the line of force was. In the first series, he had described it as a strain imposed upon the molecules of the conducting wire and the surrounding medium by the passage of the electric "current." This state of strain he christened "the electrotonic state," but it defied every attempt at detection. His abandonment of the electrotonic state in the second series was only temporary, for without it Faraday was deprived of his basic concept. The electrotonic state had to exist, for there could be no doubt of the reality of the line of force. It was his attempts to relate the two which led him onward through the brilliant series of researches which culminated in his general theory of electricity in 1838.

Electrochemistry. The first and second series of *Experimental Researches* had been concerned with the relations between electricity and magnetism. In the summer of 1832 Faraday appeared to go off on a tangent, with an investigation into the identity of the electricities produced by the various means then known. His commitment to the unity of force led him to believe that the electricities produced by electrostatic generators, voltaic cells, thermocouples, dynamos, and electric fishes were identical, but belief was no substitute for proof. Furthermore, this identity had been challenged by Sir Humphry Davy's brother John, who insisted that electrical effects were not produced by a single agent but were the complex

results of a combination of powers. There was little sense in continuing to work on electricity until this question was settled. It seemed like a routine investigation involving mere manipulative skill to demonstrate that electricity, no matter how produced, had the same effects. But in the course of this investigation Faraday was to be led to the laws of electrolysis and, more important, to challenge the concept of action at a distance.

Faraday's attack was straightforward. Searching the literature, he found reports of the similar effects of the various forms of electricity. The only real difficulties arose with static electricity. There were published reports that electrostatic discharges had both magnetic and electrochemical effects but, upon repeating the experiments, Faraday found them equivocal. Electrostatic discharge, for example, could magnetize needles, but Faraday found it impossible to produce a magnet in an electrostatic field. Similarly, William Hyde Wollaston had reported the decomposition of water by an underwater spark in 1801, but it was possible to view this decomposition as the result of the mechanical shock, the heat generated by the discharge, or both. To remove all possible doubts, Faraday turned his experimental skill to the examination of these two effects.

The magnetic effect of an electrostatic discharge was examined by means of a simple galvanometer. The discharge was "slowed down" by passing it through wet string. The galvanometer was deflected, thus settling the question once and for all. Here Faraday might have stopped, but he saw the opportunity to compare static and voltaic electricity quantitatively and was quick to seize it. An electrometer gave him a relative reading of static charge; the deflection of the galvanometer permitted him to correlate the charge with the discharge. Fortunately (and unbeknown to Faraday), his galvanometer here acted like a ballistic galvanometer, and he was able to conclude that "if the same absolute quantity of electricity pass through the galvanometer, whatever may be its intensity, the deflecting force upon the magnetic needle is the same." Faraday immediately proceeded to devise an apparatus by which he could compare, quantitatively, the currents produced by electrostatic and voltaic discharge. Insofar as electricity affected a galvanometer needle, then, Faraday had given conclusive proof of the identity of static and voltaic electricity. He had, furthermore, devised an instrument for the measurement of relative quantities of electricity.

The remaining problem was that of electrochemical decomposition by electrostatic discharge. Once again, the desired effect was produced without the ambiguity of Wollaston's experiment. Faraday might have rested here, since the identity of electricities was what he had set out to prove, but the opportunity for further discoveries was clear and he set out to exploit it. The course was obvious. Both electrostatic and current electricity decomposed water; the "throw" of the galvanometer permitted the accurate measure of electrical quantity. Could not the quantity of electricity be correlated with the products of electrochemical decomposition? In answering this question, Faraday enunciated his two laws of electrochemistry: (1) Chemical action or decomposing power is exactly proportional to the quantity of electricity which passes in solution; (2) The amounts of different substances deposited or dissolved by the same quantity of electricity are proportional to their chemical equivalent weights. Thus, Faraday had not only proved the identity of electricities; he had added another link in the chain of the convertibility of forces. Electricity was not only involved in chemical affinity, as the invention of the voltaic cell had shown, but it was the force of chemical affinity. In 1881 Hermann von Helmholtz was to use Faraday's 1834 papers on electrochemistry as the experimental basis for his suggestion that electricity must be particulate, or Faraday's laws of electrochemistry would make no sense.

In the course of his electrochemical researches, Faraday made a discovery with revolutionary implications. As he varied the conditions under which electrostatic discharge produced electrochemical decomposition, he found to his surprise that no "poles" were required. Ever since the invention of the voltaic cell, electrochemists had assumed that the + and − terminals of the circuit acted as centers of force, which force, acting at a distance upon the molecules in solution, literally tore them apart. Hence the term "poles." But when Faraday passed an electrostatic discharge through some blotting paper soaked with a solution of potassium iodide into the air, the potassium iodide decomposed. Where, now, were the centers of force of orthodox theory? More important, what was "acting at a distance" upon the potassium iodide molecules? The mere passage of the "current" was sufficient to decompose the potassium iodide. The experiment with electrostatic discharge suggested to Faraday that decomposition was not effected by action at a distance.

In a series of ingenious experiments, Faraday went on to show that the molecules were not "torn apart" at all. Instead, the two components of a binary salt seemed to migrate in opposite directions through the solution, without ever becoming free chemical agents, until they reached the terminals upon which they

were deposited. Faraday accounted for this strange behavior by claiming that the electric "current" exalted the affinities of the components of a salt on opposite sides of the compound molecules, thus permitting each component to leave its original partner and join with another close by. The electrical force determined the direction of this recombination, one component moving toward the "positive" terminal, the other toward the "negative." The "exaltation" was passed along from one molecule to the next, beginning from the terminals and moving out into the solution. There was no action at a distance, but only intermolecular forces created by the strain imposed by the electrical force. It is difficult to visualize this process without having recourse to point-atoms and the patterns of force which produced their chemical identity.

Such patterns of force could be distorted by the imposition of other forces, and this appears to be what Faraday meant by his use of the term "exaltation." Under the strain of electrical force, the affinities of the molecular components were both "exalted" and aligned, permitting their transfer through the solution. As in an American square dance "grand right and left," where each partner passes around the square by taking the hands of people passing in the opposite direction, the chemical elements in solution passed through the solution, ever bound to a partner, until they were freed at the termini. The process involved three steps: the creation of the initial strain by the imposition of the electrical force; the exaltation of the affinities along the direction of the electrical force, which exaltation caused the component atoms of the decomposing substances to shift in opposite directions and to be bound by partners moving the other way; and the "shift" in which the strain was momentarily relieved, only to be reimposed immediately by the constant application of the electric force at the termini. The electric force was transmitted by this rapid series of buildups and breakdowns of strain, and electrical energy could be transmitted in this fashion without the transfer of a material agent. It was even possible to deduce the second law of electrochemistry from this scheme. Each shift required the breaking of a chemical bond of specific strength, so it was to be expected that the total force employed (quantity of electricity) should bear some specific and simple relation to the total quantity of matter decomposed by this force.

In his published accounts, Faraday only hinted at what has been presented here as his theory of electrochemical decomposition. The conceptual framework was too conjectural for Faraday to present it to his co-workers in electrochemistry. But what he could and did do was to publish his factual results and also prepare the way for a successful challenge to the prevalent theory by introducing a new nomenclature which was theoretically neutral. Instead of poles, which implied centers of force, Faraday used the term "electrode," which had no such implication. Similarly "cathode," "anode," "electrolysis," "electrolyte," "anion," and "cation" were merely descriptive terms. William Whewell of Trinity College, Cambridge, was the source of most of these neologisms.

Faraday's Theory of Electricity. Faraday's electrochemical researches suggested to him a new perspective on electrostatics. If electrochemical forces did not act at a distance, was it preposterous to think that electrostatic forces also were intermolecular? The researches of Charles Coulomb in the 1780's had appeared to settle that question once and for all in favor of action at a distance, but Faraday drew courage from his electrochemical work and sought to find experimental confirmation for his new point of view. Two consequences flowed logically from the substitution of intermolecular forces for action at a distance. First, the electrostatic force ought to vary if it depended upon the ability of the molecules of a medium to transmit it and, second, this force ought to be transmitted in curved lines, since the transmitting molecules occupied a volume of space, rather than in the straight lines assumed by action-at-a-distance physics. Experimental confirmation of both these conclusions was quick in coming. The inductive force did vary when different substances were used to transmit it. The discovery of specific inductive capacity was an important structural element in the construction of Faraday's novel electrical theory. The inductive force was also shown to be transmitted in curved, not straight, lines, thus confirming once again Faraday's belief in intermolecular forces.

By 1838 Faraday was in a position to put all the pieces together into a coherent theory of electricity. The particles of matter were composed of forces arranged in complex patterns which gave them their individuality. These patterns could be distorted by placing the particles under strain. Electrical force set up such a strain. In electrostatics, the strain was imposed on molecules capable of sustaining large forces; when the line of particulate strain gave way, it did so with the snap of the electric spark. Lightning was the result of the same process on a larger scale. In electrochemistry, the force of the "breaking" strain was that of the chemical affinities of the elements of the chemical compound undergoing electrochemical decomposition. The shift of the particles of the elements toward the two electrodes momentarily relaxed the strain, but it was immediately re-created by the constant application of electric force at the electrodes upon the nearest particles of the electrolyte. This buildup and breakdown of interparticulate strain, passing through the electrolyte, constituted the electrical "current." It was a transfer of energy which did not entail a transfer of matter; Faraday's caution in adopting the term "current" appeared justified. The same situation obtained in ordinary conduction through a wire. The molecules of good conductors could not sustain much of a strain at all, so here the buildup and breakdown of the strain was exceptionally rapid and the "conduction" was therefore correspondingly good.

The theory was elegant, firmly based on experiment, and complete. It was also heretical, challenging almost all the fundamental concepts of orthodox electrical science. Faraday knew this and put it forward with appropriate caution. The experimental results were clearly and firmly reported; the theoretical aspect was hedged with fuzzy and tentative language, hesitantly and sometimes confusedly presented. It is, I think, fair to say that no one in the 1830's took the theory seriously. Even Faraday was unable to advocate it with the necessary vigor. The strain of eight years of unremitting intellectual effort at the farthest frontier of electrical theory ultimately broke his powerful mind. In 1839 he suffered a nervous breakdown, from which he never really recovered. For five years he was unable to concentrate his mental faculties on the problems of electricity and magnetism. He passed this time by devoting himself to the affairs of the Royal Institution and such other researches as did not require his total intellectual commitment. It was in these years, for example, that he extended his earlier work on the condensation of gases. He was able here to use his experimental talents to the full without being forced to focus his mind on the consequences.

Even during these years, Faraday kept returning to his electrical theory. In 1844 he published a small paper entitled "Speculation Touching Electrical Conduction and the Nature of Matter," in which he "proved" to his own satisfaction that only Boscovichean atoms were compatible with the observed conduction and nonconduction of electricity through material bodies. Again, it seems unlikely that Faraday convinced anyone, but this exercise did serve to stimulate him to return to his old preoccupation with the nature of electricity and magnetism. In 1846 he was led, in his "Thoughts on Ray Vibrations," to an embryonic form of the electromagnetic theory of light, later developed by James Clerk Maxwell. In both these essays Faraday was, as it were, conducting a dialogue with himself, attempting to clarify his own ideas and to grasp the full implications of his own speculative hypotheses. These works therefore are of importance more because they reveal Faraday's mind to us than because they are important steps in the progress of electrical and magnetic science.

Last Researches: The Origins of Field Theory. The last, and in many ways the most brilliant, of Faraday's series of researches was stimulated by the quite specific comments of one of the few people who thought his theory of electricity worthy of serious attention. On 6 August 1845, William Thomson, the future Lord Kelvin, addressed a lengthy letter to Faraday, describing his success with the mathematical treatment of the concept of the line of force. At the end of the letter Thomson listed some experiments to test the results of his reasonings on Faraday's theory, and it was this that pushed Faraday once more into active scientific research. One of Thomson's suggestions was that Faraday test the effect of electrical action through a dielectric on plane-polarized light. As Thomson wrote:

> It is known that a very well defined action, analogous to that of a transparent crystal, is produced upon polarized light when transmitted through glass in any ordinary state of violent constraint. If the constraint, which may be elevated to be on the point of breaking the glass, be produced by electricity, it seems probable that a similar action might be observed.

The effect predicted by Thomson was one which Faraday had been seeking to detect since the 1820's, but with no success. Thomson's belief that it should exist reinforced Faraday's, and he returned to the laboratory to find it. As in the 1820's, his search was fruitless, but this time, instead of abandoning his search, he altered the question he put to nature. His own work in the 1830's had illustrated the convertibility of electrical and magnetic force. The failure to detect an effect of electrical force on polarized light might only reflect the fact that electrical force produced a very small effect which he could not detect. The force of an electromagnet was far stronger and might, therefore, be substituted in order to make the expected effect manifest.

On 13 September 1845 his efforts finally bore fruit. The plane of polarization of a ray of plane-polarized light was rotated when the ray was passed through a glass rhomboid of high refractive index in a strong magnetic field. The angle of rotation was directly proportional to the strength of the magnetic force and, for Faraday, this indicated the direct effect of magnetism upon light. "That which is magnetic in the forces of matter," he wrote, "has been affected, and in turn has affected that which is truly magnetic

in the force of light." The fact that the magnetic force acted through the mediation of the glass suggested to Faraday that magnetic force could not be confined to iron, nickel, and cobalt but must be present in all matter. No body should be indifferent to a magnet, and this was confirmed by experiment. Not all bodies reacted in the same way to the magnetic force. Some, like iron, aligned themselves along the lines of magnetic force and were drawn into the more intense parts of the magnetic field. Others, like bismuth, set themselves across the lines of force and moved toward the less intense areas of magnetic force. The first group Faraday christened "paramagnetics"; the second, "diamagnetics."

The discovery of diamagnetism stimulated the production of theories to account for this new phenomenon. Ever since the work of Coulomb in the 1780's, most physicists had assumed (with Coulomb) the existence of polar molecules to account for magnetism. The simple thing to do, when faced with the apparent repulsion of diamagnetic substances by magnetic poles, was simply to assume some kind of "reverse" polarity leading to repulsion rather than attraction. Since such explanations necessarily involved the existence of magnetic or electrical "fluids," Faraday was skeptical. Furthermore, Faraday's attention was increasingly focused on the line of force, rather than on the particles of matter affected by the line of force. In his experiment on the rotation of the plane of polarization of a light ray, Faraday had noted that the "polarity" involved was in the line of magnetic force, not in the interposed glass. Experiments with diamagnetics further convinced him that there were no poles in diamagnetics but only reactions to the line of magnetic force.

He therefore rejected the polar theories of his contemporaries and substituted one of his own. Paramagnetics were substances that conducted the magnetic force well, thereby concentrating lines of force through them; diamagnetic substances were poor conductors of magnetism, thus diverging the lines of magnetic force passing through them. (See Figure 4.) A glance at the patterns of the lines of force was sufficient to disprove the polar theory: the lower figure is *not* the opposite of the top one. There are, in fact, no poles in diamagnetics. The top figure also indicates that there are no "poles" in paramagnetics either, if poles be defined as the termini of the magnetic force. As Faraday went on to show, the lines of magnetic force, unlike their electrostatic cousins, are continuous curves having no termini. They cannot be accounted for in terms of force-atoms under strain, and Faraday ignored his earlier model of interparticulate strain for the transmission of magnetic force.

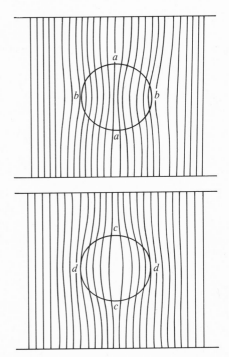

FIGURE 4. Diagrammatic representations of a paramagnetic substance (top) and a diamagnetic substance (bottom) in a uniform magnetic field. The "polarity" of the paramagnetic substance is represented by the compression of the lines of force at *aa*. There is no such compression in the diamagnetic substance; *cc* does not represent polarity opposite to that at *aa*.

was fuzzy and imprecise but capable of clarification and precision if taken up by someone who could share Faraday's vision. Such a man was James Clerk Maxwell, who, in the 1850's and 1860's, built field theory on the foundations Faraday had laid.

Faraday was unable to appreciate what his young disciple was doing. His mind deteriorated rapidly after the mid-1850's, and even if he had been able to understand Maxwell's mathematics, it is doubtful that he would have been able to follow Maxwell's chain of reasoning. As his mental faculties declined, Faraday gracefully retreated from the world. He resigned from all social clubs in the 1850's, concentrating what remained of his energies on his teaching functions at the Royal Institution. His Christmas lectures for a juvenile audience for 1859–1860, on the various forces of matter, and for 1860–1861, on the chemical history of a candle, were edited by William Crookes and have become classics. But even his lecturing abilities began to fade, and he was forced to abandon the lectern in 1861. In 1862 he resigned his position at the Royal Institution, retiring to a house provided for him by Queen Victoria at Hampton Court. On 25 August 1867 he died.

Instead, he spoke of a "flood of power" marked out by the lines of force or compared a magnet to a galvanic circuit in which the magnet was the source of power; but the surrounding medium played the part of the connecting wires to transmit the magnetic "current." A magnet was described as the "habitation of lines of force."

Such explanations were manifestly unsatisfactory, for they provided no mechanism whatsoever for magnetic phenomena. They expressed metaphorically what Faraday felt the phenomena to be, but they gave little insight into their underlying causes. Only one point emerged clearly, and this point was of fundamental importance. Whatever the cause of magnetism, the manifestation of magnetic force took place in the medium surrounding the magnet. This manifestation was the magnetic field and the energy of the magnetic system was in the field, not in the magnet. By extension, the same could be said (and was so said by Faraday) of electrical and gravitational systems. This is the fundamental axiom of classic field theory.

By the mid-1850's Faraday had gone as far as he could go. He had provided a new perspective for those who would look on all manifestations of force in the phenomenal world. His description of this perspective

BIBLIOGRAPHY

I. Original Works. Faraday collected his papers in four vols.: *Experimental Researches in Electricity*, 3 vols. (London, 1839–1855), and *Experimental Researches in Chemistry and Physics* (London, 1859). The course of his thought may be followed in Thomas Martin, ed., *Faraday's Dairy, Being the Various Philosophical Notes of Experimental Investigation Made by Michael Faraday*, 7 vols. and index (London, 1932–1936). For a complete list of Faraday's lectures and writings, see Alan Jeffreys, *Michael Faraday, A List of His Lectures and Published Writings* (London, 1960). Henry Bence Jones was Faraday's close friend and, after his death, collected a large number of letters to and from Faraday, which, together with excerpts from diaries, etc., were published as *Life and Letters of Faraday*, 2 vols. (London, 1870). This volume must be used with great caution, since the editor was not averse to correcting and amending Faraday's language. See also *The Selected Correspondence of Michael Faraday*, L. Pearce Williams, ed., 2 vols. (Cambridge, 1971). There are important MS collections at the Royal Institution of Great Britain, the Royal Society of London, the Institution of Electrical Engineers, London, and the Wellcome Medical Historical Library.

II. Secondary Literature. The most recent and detailed biography is L. Pearce Williams, *Michael Faraday, A Biography* (London–New York, 1965). A complete list of books on Faraday is to be found in the bibliography compiled by M. Lukomskaya as an appendix to the Russian trans. of Faraday's *Experimental Researches in Electricity*

(Moscow, 1951). John Tyndall, *Faraday as a Discoverer* (London, 1869, and many subsequent eds.) reveals what Faraday's orthodox friends thought of his physical heresies. Silvanus P. Thompson, *Michael Faraday. His Life and Work* (London, 1898) depicts Faraday as seen by a famous electrical engineer to whom Faraday's electrical discoveries far outweighed his work on field theory.

There are portraits of Faraday in the Royal Institution of Great Britain and the National Portrait Gallery.

L. Pearce Williams

FAREY, JOHN (*b.* Woburn, Bedfordshire, England, 1766; *d.* London, England, 6 January 1826), *geology.*

Farey was educated in a local school and then sent at the age of sixteen to Halifax, Yorkshire, where he studied mathematics, drawing, and surveying. He married about 1790 and had a large family. In 1792 he was appointed land steward of the Woburn estates belonging to Francis, fifth duke of Bedford; but when the duke died suddenly in 1802, his brother John dismissed Farey, who then went to London, where he resided until his death. There he wrote articles for the new *Cyclopaedia* of Abraham Rees and contributed many papers, mostly on geology but also on the theory of music and decimal coinage, to scientific and other journals. In 1807 he began a survey of Derbyshire for the Board of Agriculture, which occupied him for several years; this was followed by employment as a "mineral surveyor," as he entitled himself. His eldest son, John, Jr., born in 1791, from the age of fourteen assisted his father by making drawings and plans and later became well known as an engineer.

Farey contributed to geology in two ways, one of them indirect. He was taught the principles of geology by William Smith, who was employed by the duke of Bedford in October 1801 to construct water meadows in a boggy part of his estate. Farey was already interested in the distribution of local soils and rocks, and during the next few months he eagerly absorbed Smith's ideas on stratification, which the latter seems to have imparted to him readily. From this time on, Farey took every opportunity to promulgate Smith's claim to be a pioneer in English geology, writing to Sir Joseph Banks on the subject in 1802 and, from 1806, referring to Smith's ideas in the many articles he wrote for the *Philosophical Magazine* and Rees's *Cyclopaedia.* By constantly urging the importance of Smith's discoveries and stressing his priority, Farey undoubtedly helped to make Smith's name better known.

As a geologist, however, Farey is entitled to respect for the work he carried out himself, although it has scarcely been noticed in the standard histories of geology. In 1806 and 1807, while going from London to Brighton to visit his brother, he made a study of the strata visible along the route; and the application of Smith's principles enabled him to construct a geological section from London to Brighton on a scale of an inch to the mile (thus over five feet long), which he presented to Sir Joseph Banks. Farey recognized the anticlinal structure of the district and realized that denudation had removed the overlying Chalk formation between the North Downs and the South Downs, a very advanced concept for his time. He also had a good idea of the succession of the rocks under the Chalk. The section unfortunately was not published but must have been well known, for a few years later he stated that copies were "in the hands of many." Some of the strata shown in the section are described in his article "Clay," in Rees's *Cyclopaedia* (vol. VIII).

Farey's investigation of Derbyshire soils and strata began in 1807, and about this time he drew up a detailed geological section of the succession of strata from Ashover in Derbyshire to the Lincolnshire coast (i.e., from Carboniferous rocks through Triassic and Jurassic to the Cretaceous), quite a remarkable achievement. This section, like the London–Brighton one, was not published, although several manuscript copies exist.

The first volume of Farey's report on Derbyshire appeared in 1811. It contains his detailed account of the soils and rocks, together with a colored geological map of Derbyshire and the adjacent counties, on a scale of six miles to the inch. (The area covered is approximately sixty miles from north to south and forty from east to west.) On this map he depicted with considerable accuracy the geological series now known as Carboniferous Limestone, Millstone Grit, Coal Measures, Magnesian Limestone, and Keuper Marl. His only major error lay in regarding the Bunter Sandstone (Triassic) as alluvial gravel. This, the first geological map of an English county actually published, deserves to be better known. In the same volume are two colored plates illustrating what are now known as block diagrams, perspective drawings showing in two dimensions the effects of different kinds of faulting on bedded strata (a subject that Farey had studied in considerable detail), together with the effects of denudation on the faulted rocks. These alone indicate Farey's capabilities as a geologist. The second and third volumes of the report are devoted mostly to agriculture and transport and have little geological interest.

While the first volume was in press, Farey sent to Sir Joseph Banks "An Account of the Great Derbyshire Denudation," which was published in *Philosophical Transactions of the Royal Society* (1811). A more detailed account of the area, "On the Ashover Denudation in the County of Derby," was read to the Geological Society of London (of which Farey was never a member) in April 1813. It was accompanied by a detailed section and a large map. Unfortunately it was never published, possibly because of its length, and this gave rise to much ill feeling on Farey's part toward the officers of the society.

Farey was an inveterate compiler of lists and indexes, some of which, listing localities of fossils named in Sowerby's *Mineral Conchology* and William Smith's works on fossils, were published in the *Philosophical Magazine.* As a mineral surveyor he visited many parts of the British Isles, and his knowledge was drawn on by G. B. Greenough in the compilation of his *Geological Map of England and Wales* (1819).

BIBLIOGRAPHY

I. ORIGINAL WORKS. *A General View of the Agriculture and Minerals of Derbyshire,* 3 vols. (London, 1811–1817), is Farey's main published work. His signed scientific papers are listed in the Royal Society's *Catalogue of Scientific Papers* (*1800–1863*), II (London, 1868), 561–563, but this list is probably far from complete, since he wrote for the *Monthly Magazine* and agricultural magazines and did not always sign his work. MS geological sections by Farey are in the British Museum (Natural History), the Institute of Geological Sciences (South Kensington), and the Sheffield Central Reference Library. Farey's personal papers were probably destroyed in a fire at his son's house in 1850.

II. SECONDARY LITERATURE. An obituary notice in the *Monthly Magazine,* n.s. **1** (1826), 430, was drawn on by W. S. Mitchell in his "Biographical Notice of John Farey," in *Geological Magazine,* **10** (1873), 25–27. L. R. Cox, in "New Light on William Smith and His Work," in *Proceedings of the Yorkshire Geological Society,* **25** (1942), 1–99, describes Farey's relations with Smith and lists a number of the articles in which he refers to Smith; John Challinor, "From Whitehurst's 'Inquiry' to Farey's Derbyshire," in *Transactions and Annual Report. North Staffordshire Field Club,* **81** (1947), 52–88, provides a valuable commentary on Farey's work in Derbyshire; Trevor D. Ford describes and discusses Farey's MS sections in "The First Detailed Geological Sections Across England, by John Farey (1806–8)," in *Mercian Geologist,* **2** (1967), 41–49, with reproductions (redrawn) of three of Farey's sections.

JOAN M. EYLES

AL-FARGHĀNĪ, ABU'L-ʿABBĀS AHMAD IBN MUHAMMAD IBN KATHĪR (*b.* Farghāna, Transoxania; *d.* Egypt, after 861), *astronomy.*

Al-Farghānī was one of the astronomer-astrologers employed by the Abbasid caliph al-Maʾmūn, who reigned in Baghdad from 813 to 833. His name sometimes occurs in the Arabic sources as Muhammad ibn Kathīr, sometimes as Ahmad ibn Muhammad ibn Kathīr, and it was probably this variation (in addition to variations of the title of his best-known book—see below) that led Ibn al-Qiftī to assume the existence of two Farghānīs, a father and a son. But this assumption has now been generally dismissed as very likely no more than a misunderstanding.[1]

Al-Farghānī's activities extended to engineering, and it is in connection with his efforts as an engineer that we have some biographical information about him. According to Ibn Taghrībirdī, he supervised the construction of the Great Nilometer (*al-miqyās al-kabīr*), also known as the New Nilometer (*al-miqyās al-jadīd*), at al-Fustāt (Old Cairo). It was completed in 861, the year in which the caliph al-Mutawakkil, who ordered the construction, died. (The *Wafayāt al-aʿyān* of Ibn Khallikān reports the event but, in the Cairo edition, gives the name of the engineer as Ahmad ibn Muhammad al-Qarsānī, the last word being no doubt a corruption of "al-Farghānī"—see bibliography.) But engineering was not al-Farghānī's forte, as appears from the following story, which Ibn Abī Usaybiʿa transcribed from the *Kitāb al-Mukāfaʾa* of Ahmad ibn Yūsuf,[2] who heard it from Abū Kāmil.

Al-Mutawakkil had charged the two sons of Mūsā ibn Shākir, Muhammad and Ahmad, with supervising the digging of a canal named al-Jaʿfarī. They delegated the work to "Ahmad ibn Kathīr al-Farghānī who constructed the New Nilometer," thus deliberately ignoring a better engineer, Sanad ibn ʿAlī, whom, out of professional jealousy, they had caused to be sent to Baghdad, away from al-Mutawakkil's court in Sāmarrā. (The caliphal capital had been transferred from Baghdad to Sāmarrā by al-Muʿtasim in 836.) The canal was to run through the new city, al-Jaʿfariyya, which al-Mutawakkil had built near Sāmarrā on the Tigris and named after himself. Al-Farghānī committed a grave error, making the beginning of the canal deeper than the rest, so that not enough water would run through the length of the canal except when the Tigris was high. News of this angered the caliph, and the two brothers were saved from severe punishment only by the gracious willingness of Sanad ibn ʿAlī to vouch for the correctness of al-Farghānī's calculations, thus risking his own welfare and possibly his life. As had been correctly predicted by astrologers, however, al-Mutawakkil was murdered, shortly before the error became apparent.[3] The explanation given for al-Farghānī's mistake is that being a theoretician rather than a practical engineer, he never successfully completed a construction (*wa-kānat maʿrifatuhu awfā min tawfīqihi li-annahu mā tamma lahu ʿamalun qattu*).

Al-Yaʿqūbī (*d.* 897) gives a more charitable reason for al-Farghānī's failure: the stony ground chosen for al-Jaʿfariyya, a place called al-Māḥūza, was simply too hard to dig. He does not mention al-Farghānī by name, but says that work on the canal was entrusted to "Muḥammad ibn Mūsā al-Munajjim and those geometers who associated themselves with him" (*Kitāb al-buldān,* p. 267).

The *Fihrist* of Ibn al-Nadīm, written in 987, ascribes only two works to al-Farghānī: (1) "The Book of [the thirty?] Chapters, a summary of the *Almagest*" (*Kitāb al-Fuṣūl, ikhtiyār*[4] *al-Majisṭī*), and (2) a "Book on the Construction of Sundials" (*Kitāb ʿAmal al-rukhāmāt*). Ibn al-Qifṭī (*d.* 1248) reproduces the same list under Muḥammad ibn Kathīr (the name that occurs in the *Fihrist*) but splits the first title into two: *Kitāb al-Fuṣūl* and *Kitāb Ikhtiṣār* [sic] *al-Majisṭī.* To Aḥmad ibn Muḥammad ibn Kathīr he attributes one work, entitled *Al-Madkhal ilā ʿilm hayʾat al-aflāk wa-ḥarakāt al-nujūm* ("Introduction to the Science of the Structure of the Spheres and of the Movements of the Stars"), which he describes as consisting of thirty chapters (singular, *bāb*) presenting a summary (*jawāmiʿ*) of the book by Ptolemy. This is the only title assigned to al-Farghānī by Ibn Ṣāʿid (*d.* 1244) and Bar-Hebraeus (*d.* 1286). As has been noted, the two Farghānīs are in fact one; and the same work that Ibn al-Qifṭī mistakenly believed to be two has in fact been known by a variety of titles: *Jawāmiʿ ʿilm al-nujūm wa ʾl-ḥarakāt al-samāwiyya, Uṣūl ʿilm al-nujūm, Kitāb al-Fuṣūl al-thalāthīn, ʿIlal al-aflāk,* and so on. This takes us back to the list in Ibn al-Nadīm; but other works must be added to it, notably two(?) treatises on the astrolabe that have come down to us and a commentary on the astronomical tables of al-Khwārizmī.

The *Jawāmiʿ,* or the *Elements,* as we shall call it here, was al-Farghānī's best-known and most influential work. He wrote it after the death of al-Maʾmūn in 833 but before 857. Abuʾl-Ṣaqr al-Qabīsī (*d.* 967) wrote a commentary on it which is preserved in the Istanbul manuscript, Aya Sofya 4832, fols. 97v–114v. Two Latin translations of the *Elements* were made in the twelfth century, one by John of Spain (John of Seville) in 1135[5] and the other by Gerard of Cremona before 1175. Printed editions of the first translation appeared in 1493, 1537, and 1546. (Gerard's translation was not published until 1910.) Jacob Anatoli made a Hebrew translation of the book that served as a basis for a third Latin version, which appeared in 1590, and Jacob Golius published a new Latin text together with the Arabic original in 1669. (For particulars of these editions, see bibliography.) The influence of the *Elements* on medieval Europe

is clearly attested by the existence of numerous Latin manuscripts in European libraries. References to it in medieval writers are many, and there is no doubt that it was greatly responsible for spreading knowledge of Ptolemaic astronomy, at least until this role was taken over by Sacrobosco's *Sphere.* But even then, the *Elements* of al-Farghānī continued to be used, and Sacrobosco's *Sphere* was clearly indebted to it. It was from the *Elements* (in Gerard's translation) that Dante derived the astronomical knowledge displayed in the *Vita nuova* and in the *Convivio.* The following is a summary of the contents of the thirty chapters constituting the *Elements.*

Chapter 1, to which nothing corresponds in the *Almagest,* describes the years of the Arabs, the Syrians, the Romans, the Persians, and the Egyptians, giving the names of their months and days and the differences between their calendars. Chapters 2–5 expound the basic concepts of *Almagest* I.2–8: sphericity of the heaven and of the earth, the central position of the earth, and the two primary movements of the heavens. In chapter 5 al-Farghānī gives the Ptolemaic value for the inclination of the ecliptic as $23°51'$, and reports the value determined at the time of al-Maʾmūn as $23°35'$.[6] (In one of his treatises on the astrolabe he states a different value observed at a later date.) Chapters 6–9 give a description of the inhabited quarter and list the seven climes and the names of well-known lands and cities. In chapter 8 al-Farghānī gives the Maʾmūnic measurements of the circumference and the diameter of the earth: 20,400 miles and approximately 6,500 miles, respectively. Chapters 10–11 discuss ascensions of the signs of the zodiac in the direct spheres, *al-aflāk al-mustaqīma* (i.e., horizons of the equator), and oblique spheres, *al-aflāk al-māʾila* (i.e., horizons of the climes), and equal and unequal (*zamāniyya,* temporal) hours.

There follow descriptions of the spheres of each of the planets and their distances from the earth (chapter 12); movements of the sun, moon, and fixed stars in longitude (chapter 13); movements of the five planets in longitude (chapter 14); retrograde motions of the wandering planets (chapter 15); magnitudes of eccentricities and of the epicycles (chapter 16); and revolutions of the planets in their orbs (chapter 17). The assertion of chapters 13 and 14 is that the slow eastward motion of the sphere of the fixed stars about the poles of the ecliptic through one degree every 100 years (the Ptolemaic value) is shared by the spheres (the apogees) of the sun, as well as of those of the moon and the five planets.

Chapter 18 concerns movements of the moon and of the planets in latitude; chapter 19, the order of the fixed stars in respect of magnitude and the positions of the most remarkable among them (al-Farghānī counts fifteen); chapter 20, lunar mansions; chapter 21, the distances of the planets from the earth (Ptolemy had stated only the distances of the sun and the moon); chapter 22, the magnitudes of the planets compared with the magnitude of the earth ("Ptolemy only showed the magnitude of the sun and of the moon, but not that of the other planets; it is, however, easy to know the latter by analogy with what he did for the sun and the moon"); chapter 23, rising and setting; chapter 24, ascension, descension, and occultation; chapter 25, phases of the moon; chapter 26, emergence of the five planets; chapter 27, parallax; chapters 28–30, solar and lunar eclipses and their intervals.

Al-Farghānī's *Jawāmiʿ* thus gives a comprehensive account of the elements of Ptolemaic astronomy that is entirely descriptive and nonmathematical. These features, together with the admirably clear and well-organized manner of presentation, must have been responsible for the popularity this book enjoyed. It must be noted that, as far as numerical values are concerned, the early printed editions show significant divergences. For example, Mercury's diameter is given no fewer than four different values: 1/28, 1/20, 1/10, and 1/18 the diameter of the earth. Only one edition (Frankfurt, 1590) has the first correct value.[7] And in Golius' 1669 Arabic-Latin edition, which is generally superior to the earlier ones, the value of the same diameter differs in the Latin translation (where it is given as 1/18 the diameter of the earth) from that in the Arabic text (1/28 the diameter of the earth).

Al-Farghānī's writings on the astrolabe survive in a number of manuscripts bearing different titles: *Fī Ṣanʿat al-asṭurlāb, al-Kāmil fī 'l-asṭurlāb, Kitāb ʿAmal al-asṭurlāb.* The thirteenth-century manuscript at the British Museum (Or. 5479)[8] is a substantial work of forty-eight folios (37v–85r) that ought to be counted among the more respectable treatises devoted to this subject in Arabic. Addressed to the scholar who has reached an "intermediate stage in the knowledge of geometry and the computation of the stars" (fol. 38r), it deals at length with the mathematical theory of the astrolabe and purports to correct faulty constructions which were current at the time of its writing. It is no mere rule-of-thumb manual and was in fact intended to resolve doubts and difficulties created by such manuals. In this work al-Farghānī states the inclination of the ecliptic to be 23°33', "as we found by observation in our time" (fol. 46v). On page 49v "our time" is given as the year 225 of Yazdegerd, i.e., A.D. 857–858.

Al-Bīrūnī in his treatise *On the Calculation of Chords in Circles* assigns to al-Farghānī a work entitled *ʿIlal Zīj al-Khwārizmī,* in which, apparently, al-Farghānī gave explanations (*ʿilal,* reasons) for al-Khwārizmī's computational procedures.[9] This work has been lost. But in addition to its having been available to and made use of by al-Bīrūnī in the eleventh century, it had been carefully studied by Aḥmad ibn al-Muthannā ibn ʿAbd al-Karīm in the tenth. Ibn al-Muthannā, whose commentary on al-Khwārizmī's tables survives in Hebrew and Latin translations, tells us that he found al-Farghānī's book lacking in proofs and altogether suffering from omissions and redundancies. But his remarks would suggest that his own book was either based on al-Farghānī's treatise or at least took its starting point from it. The Latin translation, made by Hugo of Santalla in the second quarter of the twelfth century, was reported by C. H. Haskins but, following Suter, was wrongly identified as a commentary on al-Farghānī by al-Bīrūnī.[10] Two Hebrew versions of Ibn al-Muthannā have recently been published with English translation.[11]

NOTES

1. See H. Suter's art. on al-Farghānī in the 1st ed. of the *Encyclopaedia of Islam* and the rev. art. by J. Vernet in the 2nd ed. See also C. Nallino, "Astrologia e astronomia presso i musulmani," in *Raccolta di scritti editi e inediti,* V (Rome, 1944), 135.

2. Ibn Abī Uṣaybiʿa, *Ṭabaqāt al-aṭibbāʾ,* p. 207, refers to *Kitāb Ḥusn al-ʿuqbā,* the title of a ch. in *Kitāb al-Mukāfaʾa.*

3. According to the same story, going back to Abū Kāmil, another victim of the intrigues of the two sons of Mūsā was the philosopher al-Kindī, whom they had caused to be estranged from al-Mutawakkil and whose library they had confiscated. Sanad's condition for getting them out of their difficulty was that the library be restored to al-Kindī.

4. *Ikhtiyār* (selection) is found in G. Flügel's ed. of the *Fihrist* and in the (undated) Cairo ed. But the word should no doubt be read *ikhtiṣār* (summary).

5. See F. Woepcke, "Notice sur quelques manuscrits arabes relatifs aux mathématiques . . .," pp. 116–117.

6. Ibn Yūnus reports that the mission ordered by al-Maʾmūn to prepare the so-called *Mumtaḥan* or *Maʾmūnic zīj* recorded two values of the obliquity at two different places and times: 23°33' at Baghdad in A.H. 214 (A.D. 829–830), and 23°33'52" at Damascus in A.H. 217 (A.D. 832–833). According to the Princeton University Library MS Yahuda 666 (fol. 37v), al-Farghānī reported two values from the *Mumtaḥan:* one equal to the Baghdadian determination of 23°33' and the other the same as that stated in the *Elements:* 23°35'. For Ibn Yūnus, see *Notices et extraits des manuscrits de la Bibliothèque Nationale . . .,* VII (Paris, 1803), 56–57.

7. See P. J. Toynbee, "Dante's Obligations to Alfraganus . . .," p. 424, n. 1.

8. Copies of the same work are in the Berlin MSS nos. 5790, 5791, and 5792. A fourth MS at Berlin, no. 5793, fols. 1r–97v, not seen by the present writer, seems to be a different work. See W. Ahlwardt, *Verzeichnis der arabischen Handschriften der Königlichen Bibliothek zu Berlin,* V (Berlin, 1893), 226–227.

9. See "Risāla fī istikhrāj al-awtār fi 'l-dāʾira," in *Rasāʾil al-Bīrūnī,* I (Hyderabad, 1949), pp. 128, 168.

10. See C. H. Haskins in *Romanic Review,* 2 (1911), esp. 7–9, and

his *Studies in the History of Mediaeval Science,* 2nd ed. (Cambridge, Mass., 1927), p. 74, where the same mistaken identification is repeated. But see Millás Vallicrosa, *Estudios sobre Azarquiel* (Madrid-Granada, 1943-1950), pp. 25-26.

11. See Bernard R. Goldstein, *Ibn al-Muthannā's Commentary on the Astronomical Tables of al-Khwārizmī* (New Haven-London, 1967). Hugo's Latin text is edited by Eduardo Millás Vendrell, S. I., in *El comentario de Ibn al-Muṭannā a las Tablas Astronómicas de al-Jwārizmī* (Madrid-Barcelona, 1963).

BIBLIOGRAPHY

I. ORIGINAL WORKS. The Latin trans. of the *Elements* by John of Spain was first printed at Ferrara in 1493: *Breuis ac perutilis compilatio Alfragani astronomorum pertissimi totum id continens quod ad rudimenta astronomica est opportunum.* This was reprinted at Nuremberg in 1537 as part of *Continentur in hoc libro Rudimenta astronomica Alfragani. Item Albategnius. . . . De motu stellarum, ex observationibus tum proprijs, tum Ptolemaei, omnia cum demonstrationibus geometricis & additionibus Ioannis de Regiomonte. Item Oratio introductoria in omnes scientias mathematicas Ioannis de Regiomonte. . . . Eiusdem introductio in Elementa Euclidis. Item epistola Philippi Melanthonis nuncupatoria, etc.* A second reprint, giving the name of the translator for the first time in print, appeared at Paris in 1546: *Alfragani astronomorum pertissimi compendium, id omne quod ad Astronomica rudimenta spectat complectens, Ioanne Hispalensi interprete, nunc primum peruetusto exemplari consulto, multis locis castigatus redditum.* Francis J. Carmody's ed., *Alfragani Differentie in quibusdam collectis scientie astrorum* (Berkeley, Calif., 1943), gives a critical representation of John's version based on some of the extant MSS.

The Latin trans. by the Heidelberg professor Jacob Christmann, published at Frankfurt in 1590, made use of John's version as well as of a Hebrew trans. by Jacob Anatoli: *Muhamedis Alfragani Arabis Chronologica et astronomica elementa, e Palatinae Bibliothecae verteribus libris versa, expleta, et scholiis expolita. Additus est Commentarius, qui rationem calendarii Romani, Aegyptiaci, Arabici, Persici, Syriaci & Hebraei explicat. . . .* According to Woepcke (see below), p. 120, this version was reprinted in 1618.

Gerard of Cremona's trans., made before 1175, was not printed until 1910: *Alfragano (Al-Fargānī) Il 'Libro dell' aggregazione delle stelle'* (*Dante,* Convivio, *II, vi-134) secondo il Codice Mediceo-Laurenziano, Pl. 29, Cod. 9 contemporaneo a Dante,* introduction and notes by Romeo Campani (Città de Castello, 1910).

An ed. of the Arabic text was prepared by Jacob Golius on the basis of a Leiden MS. It was published (Amsterdam, 1669) after Golius' death with a Latin trans. and copious notes covering only the first nine chs. of al-Farghānī's book: *Muhammedis Fil. Ketiri Fergenensis, qui vulgo Alfraganus dicitur, Elementa Astronomica, Arabice & Latine. Cum notis ad res exoticas sive Orientales, quae in iis occurrunt.*

Ch. 24 of the *Elements, De ortu et occasu Planetarum, et de occultationibus eorum sub radiis solis,* was twice printed together with Sacrobosco's *Sphere: Sphaera*

Ioannis de Sacro Bosco emendata, etc. (Paris, 1556), fols. 53r-54v; (Paris, 1564), fols. 58v-60r.

For the Arabic MSS of al-Farghānī's works, see C. Brockelmann, *Geschichte der arabischen Literatur,* I, 2nd ed. (Leiden, 1943), 249-250; supp. vol. I (Leiden, 1936), 392-393. See also H. Suter, *Die Mathematiker und Astronomen der Araber und ihre Werke* (Leipzig, 1900), pp. 18-19.

MSS of Jacob Anatoli's Hebrew trans. of the *Elements* are listed in M. Steinschneider, *Die hebraeischen übersetzungen des Mittelalters* (repr. Graz, 1956), pp. 554-559 (sec. 343).

For Latin MSS of the *Elements,* see F. Woepcke, "Notice sur quelques manuscrits arabes relatifs aux mathématiques, et récemment acquis par la Bibliothèque impériale," in *Journal asiatique,* 5th ser., **19** (1862), 101-127, esp. 114-120; F. J. Carmody, *Arabic Astronomical and Astrological Sciences in Latin Translation, A Critical Bibliography* (Berkeley-Los Angeles, 1959), pp. 113-116.

A brief but useful description of the early European eds. of the *Elements* is in P. J. Toynbee, "Dante's Obligations to Alfraganus in the *Vita Nuova* and *Convivio,*" in *Romania,* **24** (1895), 413-432, esp. 413-417.

II. SECONDARY LITERATURE. Biographical and bibliographical information is in Ibn al-Nadīm, *al-Fihrist,* G. Flügel, ed., I (Leipzig, 1871), 279; Ibn al-Qifṭī, *Ta'rīkh al-ḥukamā',* J. Lippert, ed. (Leipzig, 1930), pp. 78, 286; Ibn Abī Uṣaybiʿa, *Ṭabaqāt al-aṭibbā',* A. Müller, ed., I (Cairo, 1882), 207-208; Abu 'l-Faraj ibn al-ʿIbrī (Bar-Hebraeus), *Tā'rīkh mukhtaṣar al-duwal,* A. Ṣālḥānī, ed. (Beirut, 1890), pp. 236-237; Ibn Ṣāʿid al-Andalusī, *Ṭabaqāt al-umam,* L. Cheikho, ed. (Beirut, 1912), pp. 54-55; Ibn Khallikān, *Wafayāt al-aʿyān,* I (Cairo, 1882), 483-485—the relevant passage in the ch. on Abu 'l-Raddād is missing from F. Wüstenfeld's ed. of the *Wafayāt,* fasc. 4 (Göttingen, 1837), no. 362, p. 53, and from de Slane's trans., *Ibn Khallikan's Biographical Dictionary,* II (Paris, 1843), 75; Ibn Taghrībirdī, *al-Nujūm al-zāhira,* T. G. J. Juynboll and B. E. Mathes, eds., I (Leiden, 1851), 742-743; Aḥmad ibn Yūsuf, *Kitāb al-Mukāfaʾa,* Aḥmad Amīn and ʿAlī al-Jārim, eds. (Cairo, 1941), pp. 195-198. Gaston Wiet discusses al-Farghānī's construction of the "New Nilometer" in "Une restauration du Nilomètre de l'île de Rawda sous Mutawakkil (247/861)," in *Comptes rendus de l'Académie des inscriptions et belles-lettres* (1924), pp. 202-206. Here Wiet cites a reference in Ibn al-Zayyāt's *al-Kawākib al-sayyāra* to the tomb of al-Farghānī in the *qarāfa* of Cairo, thus giving evidence that al-Farghānī died in Egypt. Material relevant to the episode concerned with the al-Jaʿfarī project is to be found in al-Yaʿqūbī, *Kitāb al-buldān,* in *Bibliotheca geographorum arabicorum,* M. J. De Goeje, ed., **7** (Leiden, 1892), 266-267. See also Yāqūt, *Muʿjam al-buldān,* F. Wüstenfeld, ed., II (Leipzig, 1867), 86-87; III (Leipzig, 1868), 17; and IV (Leipzig, 1869), 413.

A trans. of al-Farghānī's intro. to his treatise on the astrolabe (Berlin MS no. 5790) is included in Eilhard Wiedemann, "Einleitungen zu arabischen astronomischen Werken," in *Weltall,* **20** (1919-1920), 21-26, 131-134; see also Wiedemann's "Zirkel zur Bestimmung der Gebetszeiten," in *Beiträge zur Geschichte der Naturwissenschaften*

62, in *Sitzungsberichte der Physikalish-medizinischen Sozietät in Erlangen,* **52** (1922), 122–125. J. B. J. Delambre, in *Histoire de l'astronomie du moyen-âge* (Paris, 1819), pp. 63–73, gives a detailed account of al-Farghānī's *Elements,* chapter by chapter. See also J. L. E. Dreyer, *History of the Planetary Systems from Thales to Kepler* (Cambridge, 1906), *passim;* P. Duhem, *Le système du monde,* II (Paris, 1914), 206–214; and, concerning the relation of Sacrobosco to al-Farghānī, Lynn Thorndike, *The Sphere of Sacrobosco and Its Commentators* (Chicago, 1949), pp. 15–19. Brief accounts of al-Farghānī are to be found in the *Encyclopaedia of Islam* and in Sarton's *Introduction to the History of Science,* I (Baltimore, 1927), 567.

A. I. SABRA

FARKAS, LASZLO (LADISLAUS) (*b.* Dunaszerdahely, Hungary [now Dunajska Streda, Czechoslovakia], 10 May 1904; *d.* near Rome, Italy, 31 December 1948), *physical chemistry.*

Farkas was the son of a pharmacist and the eldest of several children. After finishing secondary school he studied chemistry from 1922 to 1924 at the Technische Hochschule in Vienna, and then at the Technische Hochschule (now Technische Universität) in Berlin. In 1927 he received his doctorate, and in the same year he entered the Kaiser Wilhelm Institut in Berlin, where he worked under Haber's guidance. When the Nazis came to power, Farkas left Germany and went to England, where he taught colloid chemistry at Cambridge. In 1936 he accepted an offer to serve as professor of physical chemistry at the newly organized Faculty of Sciences of Hebrew University, Jerusalem, and he remained there until his death. He died in a plane crash on his way to the United States to seek support for acquisition of scientific instruments.

Farkas began his scientific activity with work in the field of photochemical sensitizing in the region of the ultraviolet. He then turned to a study of the equilibrium distribution of the two forms of molecular hydrogen—ortho-hydrogen and para-hydrogen.

During this period deuterium was discovered, and Farkas saw in the substance a valuable aid for his investigations into the homogeneous catalysis of ortho- and para-hydrogen conversion. With his brother he developed an electrolytic method which resulted in the simplest known procedure for producing heavy water.

In the following years various investigations involving deuterium constituted the central portion of Farkas' scientific activity. He studied thoroughly the equilibrium of the reaction

$$H_2O + HD \rightleftarrows HOD + H_2$$

and its role in the separation of the hydrogen isotope.

He also investigated the various exchange reactions of heavy hydrogen. Moreover, he established the ratio of heavy to light water in the liquid and vapor phases over an extensive temperature range. Farkas also determined the catalytic activity of heavy hydrogen in various processes. His work was, in many respects, of pioneering importance in the field of deuterium and heavy-water research.

Farkas also left many publications on reaction kinetics and a few on analytical chemistry. During World War II he was secretary of the Scientific Advisory Committee of the Middle East Supply Center. He also contributed to the organization of scientific research in the new state of Israel.

BIBLIOGRAPHY

A list of Farkas' 100 or so publications in German, English, and Israeli journals is in *L. Farkas Memorial Volume* (Jerusalem, 1952), pp. 305–309.

On Farkas, see two articles by E. K. Rideal: "Prof. L. Farkas," in *Nature,* **162** (1949), 313; and "Ladislaus Farkas," in *L. Farkas Memorial Volume* (Jerusalem, 1952), pp. 1–2.

F. SZABADVÁRY

FARMER, JOHN BRETLAND (*b.* Atherstone, Warwickshire, England, 5 April 1865; *d.* Exmouth, Devon, England, 26 January 1944), *botany.*

Farmer was the only son of John Henry and Elizabeth Farmer. After education at grammar school and private tutoring, he went to Oxford in 1883 and took a first-class degree in natural sciences in 1887. He was then appointed demonstrator in botany and was elected to a fellowship in 1889. In 1892 Farmer became assistant professor of botany at the Royal College of Science (which later became the Imperial College of Science and Technology); from 1895 until his retirement in 1929 he was a full professor, playing an active part in the development of the college as one of its governors.

His visit to India and Ceylon in 1892–1893 so impressed Farmer with the need for applied biologists to work in underdeveloped countries that he set about encouraging both instruction and research that would be useful in the tropics: his students worked all over the world, and he was active in advisory work on colonial administration and in setting up research institutes.

Farmer's own research was wide-ranging in pure botany and cytology. His early papers were on morphology and physiology, and it was not until 1893 that he published his first cytological work on nuclear division in the spore mother cells of *Lilium martagon.*

It was followed by several other papers, mostly on spore formation, including a demonstration in 1894 that chromosome reduction was an essential preliminary to fertilization in *Hepaticae,* which provided material for many later studies. With the zoologist J. E. S. Moore, Farmer showed many features in common between reduction division in plant and animal cells, and in 1903 he went on to demonstrate similarities in cell division of malignant and normal growths. Their paper of 1904 introduced the term "maiotic phase" (later changed to "meiotic phase") and illustrated reduction division in species as diverse as a lily, a cockroach, and a fish, discussing its occurrence at different points in the life histories of organisms. Later Farmer worked on the centrosphere and kinoplasm, the dimensions of chromosomes, and water utilization in plants.

He also found time to write a textbook on practical botany and a popular introduction to botany, and to translate, with A. D. Darbishire, de Vries's *Mutationstheorie.* He edited a six-volume work on nature study and, for shorter or longer periods, the journals *Annals of Botany, Science Progress,* and *Gardeners' Chronicle.*

In 1892 he married Edith Mary Pritchard, and they had one daughter. He was elected a fellow of the Royal Society in 1900 and knighted in 1926.

BIBLIOGRAPHY

I. ORIGINAL WORKS. Papers referred to in the text are "On Nuclear Division in the Pollen-Mother-Cells of *Lilium martagon,*" in *Annals of Botany,* **7** (1893), 392–396; "Studies in Hepaticae: On *Pallavicinia decipiens,*" *ibid.,* **8** (1894), 35–52; "On the Resemblance Between the Cells of Malignant Growths in Man and Those of Normal Reproductive Tissues," in *Proceedings of the Royal Society,* **72** (1903), 499–504, written with J. E. S. Moore and C. E. Walker; and "On the Maiotic Phase (Reduction Division) in Animals and Plants," in *Quarterly Journal of Microscopical Science,* **48** (1904), 489–557, written with J. E. S. Moore.

II. SECONDARY LITERATURE. The most important evaluation of Farmer's scientific work is V. H. Blackman's article in *Obituary Notices of Fellows of the Royal Society of London,* **5** (1945–1948), 17–31. The bibliography is comprehensive for papers but omits the 2nd ed. of *A Practical Introduction to the Study of Botany: Flowering Plants* (London, 1902); "The Structure of Animal and Vegetable Cells," in E. Ray Lankester, ed., *A Treatise on Zoology,* I (London, 1903), 1–46; and his popular introduction to botany, *Plant Life* (London, 1913). Blackman also wrote the entry on Farmer in *Dictionary of National Biography, Supplement, 1941–1950,* pp. 245–246.

Other obituaries are an unsigned one in *Gardeners' Chronicle,* 3rd ser., **115** (1944), 64; and R. J. Tabor, in *North Western Naturalist,* **19** (1944), 310–311.

DIANA M. SIMPKINS

FARRAR, JOHN (*b.* Lincoln, Massachusetts, 1 July 1779; *d.* Cambridge, Massachusetts, 8 May 1853), *mathematics, physics, education.*

Farrar was responsible for conceiving and carrying through a sweeping modernization of the science and mathematics curriculum at Harvard College, his alma mater. He brought in the best French and other European writings on introductory mathematics, most of them unknown and unused in the United States. Much of the responsibility for shifting from the Newtonian fluxional notations to Leibniz's algorithm for the calculus was his. In natural philosophy Farrar also relied heavily upon French authors. He introduced current concepts in mechanics, electricity and magnetism, optics, and astronomy.

As the foundation of his curricular reform, Farrar carried through the translation of many French works between 1818 and 1829. Published in separate, topical volumes, they became elements of two series: Cambridge Mathematics and Cambridge Natural Philosophy. He selected and combined the writings most suitable to the needs of his students. The burden of Farrar's presentation in mathematics was carried by Lacroix, Euler, Legendre, and Bézout, but he also drew from John Bonnycastle and Bowditch. In natural philosophy he relied most heavily upon Biot, but used Bézout, Poisson, Louis-Benjamin Francoeur, Gay-Lussac, Ernst Gottfried Fischer, Whewell, and Hare as well.

Farrar's translations provided an excellent introductory program that was used not only at Harvard but also at West Point and other colleges; they went through several editions. Farrar was a fine teacher and, as Hollis professor of mathematics and natural philosophy, played an important role throughout Harvard College. One of his major aspirations, the establishment of an astronomical observatory at Harvard, was not attained until after his death.

In the larger community Farrar made similar contributions. He was active in the American Academy of Arts and Sciences and occasionally translated such topical works as Arago's 1832 *Tract on Comets,* written in preparation for the comet of that year. He published essay reviews in the *North American Review* and occasional observations and a few scientific papers on astronomy, meteorology, and instruments in the *Memoirs of the American Academy of Arts and Sciences* and the *Boston Journal of Philosophy and the Arts.*

BIBLIOGRAPHY

I. ORIGINAL WORKS. Farrar wrote few scientific papers. In the *Memoirs of the American Academy of Arts and Sciences,* he published "An Account of the Violent and Destructive Storm of the 23d of September 1815," **4** (1821), 92–97, and "An Account of a Singular Electrical Phenomenon," *ibid.,* 98–102. His "Account of an Apparatus for Determining the Mean Temperature and the Mean Atmospherical Pressure for Any Period" appeared in *Boston Journal of Philosophy and the Arts,* **1** (1823–1824), 491–494. In the *North American Review* he published several review essays, all of them unsigned: **6** (1817–1818), 205–224; **8** (1818–1819), 157–168; **12** (1821), 150–174; **14** (1822), 190–230; and a few observations: **3** (1816), 36–40, 285–287; **6** (1817–1818), 149, 292.

His primary publishing activity lay in translating and combining French writings with a few others in a manner that effectively produced good college textbooks which were abreast of recent advances. Some appeared without any indication of Farrar's role; others did not name the authors on the title page but always scrupulously noted them at some point. The first editions (often of many) are a translation of S. F. Lacroix, *An Elementary Treatise on Arithmetic* (Boston, 1818); a translation of S. F. Lacroix, *Elements of Algebra* (Cambridge, Mass., 1818); a translation of L. Euler, *An Introduction to the Elements of Algebra* (Cambridge, Mass., 1818); a translation of A. M. Legendre, *Elements of Geometry* (Boston, 1819); translations of S. F. Lacroix and E. Bézout, *An Elementary Treatise on Plane and Spherical Trigonometry* (Cambridge, Mass., 1820); *An Elementary Application of Trigonometry* (Cambridge, Mass., 1822); translations of E. Bézout, *First Principles of the Differential and Integral Calculus* (Cambridge, Mass., 1824); *An Elementary Treatise on Mechanics* (Cambridge, Mass., 1825); *An Experimental Treatise on Optics* (Cambridge, Mass., 1826); *Elements of Electricity, Magnetism, and Electro-Magnetism* (Cambridge, Mass., 1826); *An Elementary Treatise on Astronomy* (Cambridge, Mass., 1827); a translation of E. G. Fischer, *Elements of Natural Philosophy* (Boston, 1827); and a translation of F. Arago, *Tract on Comets* (Boston, 1832).

Letters and other MS records are held by the Harvard University Archives and the Massachusetts Historical Society, and a few by the Boston Public Library.

II. SECONDARY LITERATURE. On Farrar or his work, see Mrs. John Farrar, *Recollections of Seventy Years* (Boston, 1866); Dirk J. Struik, *Yankee Science in the Making* (New York, 1962), pp. 227–229, *passim;* and [John Gorham Palfrey], *Notice of Professor Farrar* (Boston, 1853).

BROOKE HINDLE

IBN AL-FARRUKHĀN. *See* 'Umar ibn al-Farrukhān.

FATOU, PIERRE JOSEPH LOUIS (*b.* Lorient, France, 28 February 1878; *d.* Pornichet, France, 10 August 1929), *mathematics.*

Fatou attended the École Normale Supérieure from 1898 to 1901. The scarcity of mathematical posts in Paris led him to accept a post at the Paris observatory, where he worked until his death. He received his doctorate in 1907 and was appointed titular astronomer in 1928. Fatou worked in practical astronomy: on determining the absolute positions of stars and planets, on instrumental constants, and on measurements of twin stars.

In order to calculate the secular perturbations produced on a planet P' through the movement of another planet, P, Gauss had had the idea of spreading the mass of P' over its orbit, so that the mass of each arc is proportional to the time it takes for the planet to trace it. This proposition is valid only when the distinction between periodic and secular perturbations does not apply, i.e., when n' is very small (n and n' are the mean motions of the planets P and P', respectively). By means of general existence theorems of solutions of differential equations, Fatou studied these motions of material systems subjected to forces whose periods tend to zero. Gauss's intuitive result had often been used in practice but had never been rigorously justified.

Fatou also studied the movement of a planet in a resistant medium. This work was based on the probability that stellar atmospheres had previously been far more extensive than they are now and would thus have given rise to capture phenomena that can be used to explain the origins of twin stars and of certain satellites.

Along with this work Fatou did both related and general mathematical research. He contributed important results on the Taylor series, the theory of the Lebesgue integral, and the iteration of rational functions of a complex variable. When studying the circle of convergence of the Taylor series, several points of view are possible: (1) one can look for criteria of convergence or divergence of the series itself on the circumference; (2) one can consider the limit values of the circle of the analytic function represented by the series and try to determine where these limit values are finite or infinite, as well as the properties of the functions of the argument represented by the real and imaginary parts of the series when these functions are well defined; (3) one can consider what points on the circumference, singular in the Weierstrass sense, also determine the analytic extension of the series. The link between these problems led Fatou to formulate a fundamental theorem in the theory of the Lebesgue integral. He found that the theory of the Lebesgue integral allowed the first two of the above problems to be treated with more precision and more generality, with the following general result: If

$f_n(x) \geqslant 0$ for all values of n, $x \in E$ and $f_n(x) \to f(x)$ as $n \to \infty$, then

$$\int_E f(x)dx \leqslant \lim_{n \to \infty} \int_E f(x)dx.$$

The theorem implies that if the right-hand side is finite, then $f(x)$ is finite almost everywhere and integrable; if $f(x)$ is not integrable or is infinite in a set of positive measure, then

$$\lim_{n \to \infty} \int_E f_n(x)dx = \infty.$$

This work was advanced by Carathéodory, Friedrich and Marcel Riesz, Griffith Evans, Leon Lichtenstein, Gabor Szegö and Nicolas Lusin.

Fatou also showed ways in which the algebraic signs of a_n affect the number and character of singularities in the Taylor series. Given the series $\Sigma a_n x^n$ $0 < R < \infty$, a sequence $\{\lambda_n\}$ exists such that the series obtained by changing the signs of a_{λ_n} has the circle of convergence as a cut. This theorem was proved in general by Hurwitz and George Pólya.

BIBLIOGRAPHY

I. ORIGINAL WORKS. Fatou's writings include "Séries trigonométriques et séries de Taylor," in *Acta mathematica*, **30** (1906), 335–400; "Sur la convergence absolue des séries trigonométriques," in *Bulletin de la Société mathématique de France*, **41** (1913), 47–53; "Sur les lignes singulières des fonctions analytiques," *ibid.*, 113–119; "Sur les fonctions holomorphes et bornées à l'intérieur d'un cercle," *ibid.*, **51** (1923), 191–202; "Sur l'itération analytique et les substitutions permutables," in *Journal de mathématiques pures et appliquées*, 9th ser., **2** (1923), 343–384, and **3** (1924), 1–49; "Substitutions analytiques et équations fonctionnelles à deux variables," in *Annales scientifiques de l'École normale supérieure*, 3rd ser., **41** (1924), 67–142; "Sur l'itération des fonctions transcendantes entières," in *Acta mathematica*, **47** (1926), 337–370; and "Sur le mouvement d'un système soumis à des forces à courte période," in *Bulletin de la Société mathématique de France*, **56** (1928), 98–139. The Société Mathématique de France expects to publish Fatou's papers.

II. SECONDARY LITERATURE. On Fatou or his work, see Jean Chazy, "Pierre Fatou," in *Bulletin astronomique*, **8**, fasc. 7 (1934), 379–384; Griffith Evans, *The Logarithmic Potential* (New York, 1927); P. Fatou, *Notice sur les travaux scientifiques de M. P. Fatou* (Paris, 1929); A. Hurwitz and G. Pólya, "Zwei Beweise eines von Herrn Fatou vermuteten Satzes," in *Acta mathematica*, **40** (1916), 179–183; S. Mandelbrojt, *Modern Researches on the Singularities of Functions Defined by the Taylor Series* (Houston, Tex., 1929), chs. 9, 12; and M. Riesz, "Neuer Beweis des Fatouschen Satzes," in *Göttingensche Nachrichten* (1916); and "Ein Konvergenz satz für Dirichletsche Reihen," in *Acta mathematica*, **40** (1916), 349–361.

HENRY NATHAN

FAUJAS DE SAINT-FOND, BARTHÉLEMY (*b.* Montélimar, Dauphiné, France, 17 May 1741; *d.* Saint-Fond, Dauphiné, 18 July 1819), *geology.*

Faujas (who took his full name from the family estate at Saint-Fond in Dauphiné) was for some years a successful lawyer but, possessed by an overwhelming passion for natural history and coming under the influence of Buffon, he abandoned his legal career and was appointed assistant naturalist at the Muséum d'Histoire Naturelle in Paris in 1778. In 1785 he became royal commissioner of mines and in 1793 was made professor of geology at the museum, a post he held until his death.

Faujas was a wide-ranging naturalist, as was common in his day. His most continuous and concentrated attention was given to rocks, minerals, and fossils (i.e., to geology, a name adopted in the late 1770's), but he was also a physicist and a chemist. He applied his discoveries and investigations to practical affairs: for instance, in 1775 he found, analyzed, and opened up a deposit of a volcanic tuff similar to the Italian pozzolana, which was used industrially in France in the making of cement; he also wrote treatises on the construction and navigation of balloons, a practical scientific activity fashionable at that time.

The existence of a group of old volcanoes in central France had been ascertained by Guettard in 1752 through observations begun at Montélimar itself, but Guettard wrote later that basalt, with its prevalent columnar structure, was a crystallization from water. In the 1760's Desmarest found the true explanation (not published until 1774): this basalt was of volcanic origin. Meanwhile, Faujas had been exploring the hilly districts of Vivarais and Velay in east-central France and found that the basalt there was also volcanic. (It resulted from regional volcanic activity in the Tertiary period which produced as its latest manifestation, particularly in central France, the very new-looking cones of ashes and associated lava flows.) It is not clear to what extent Faujas was familiar with Desmarest's work, but his discoveries were at any rate independent, and he embodied them in 1778 in a great folio work on the ancient volcanoes of Vivarais and Velay (accounts of other researches were included). This work established once and for all that basalt, a rock important scientifically because of its distinctive characteristics, its widespread occurrence, and the manner of its association with other kinds of rock, was the product of volcanic action. The controversy over the origin of basalt was, however, by no means settled; the Wernerian (neptunist) view that it was an aqueous precipitate was vigorously advocated until well into the nineteenth century. In fact, Faujas himself was, except on this question, generally a neptunist.

In 1784 Faujas journeyed through England to Scotland; a full account was published in 1797. He narrated entertaining details of his travels and described arts, industries, and customs, but his most important observations were geological. He realized the volcanic nature of the basalt of the inner Hebrides and paid special attention to the spectacular columnar occurrence on the isle of Staffa, about which his curiosity had been aroused by Banks's account in Thomas Pennant's *Second Tour of Scotland . . .* (1774). (The Staffa basalt was recognized as of volcanic origin by Bishop Uno von Troil in his *Letters From Iceland,* 1780.) He also recognized the volcanic nature of the terraced hills in central Scotland, but he had no idea that these were vastly older (Paleozoic) than those of the western islands (Tertiary). His discrimination between the various kinds of dark, fine-grained rocks was faulty. In particular, Faujas contradicted Whitehurst's correct hypothesis regarding the basaltic nature of the Derbyshire toadstones, and he identified as old lavas some rocks that were unquestionably sedimentary in origin. Unfortunately, his specimens had been lost in a shipwreck on the way back to France; probably a more careful scrutiny of them would have prevented some of his mistakes.

In his monograph on the chalk of Maastricht, Faujas described a huge reptilian skull which he thought was that of a crocodile. Cuvier discussed this at length in his *Ossemens fossiles* (V, pt. 2, [1824]), calling it a "marine serpent-like reptile"; the name mosasaur was proposed by the English geologist W. D. Conybeare in Cuvier's volume. It is now placed as the representative of an extinct group among the lizards. This was perhaps the most notable discovery in the field of vertebrate paleontology up to that time.

BIBLIOGRAPHY

I. ORIGINAL WORKS. Faujas's main geological works are *Recherches sur les volcans éteints du Vivarais et du Velay* (Grenoble, 1778); *Minéralogie des volcans* (Paris, 1784); *Voyage en Angleterre, en Écosse et aux Îles Hébrides,* 2 vols. (Paris, 1797), also trans. into English, 2 vols. (London, 1799) and, later, with notes and a memoir by Archibald Geikie, 2 vols. (Glasgow, 1907); *Histoire naturelle de la montagne de Saint-Pierre de Maestricht* (Paris, 1799); and *Essai de géologie, ou Mémoires pour servir à l'histoire naturelle du globe,* 2 vols. (Paris, 1803–1809).

There is a very full bibliography of Faujas's works,

including his papers in the *Annales du Muséum d'histoire naturelle* (Paris), in *Nouvelle biographie générale,* XVII (Paris, 1856), 167–171; the work was reprinted at Copenhagen in 1963–1969. The list in the *British Museum General Catalogue of Printed Books,* photolith. ed., LXXI (London, 1960), cols. 274–276, is also very full as regards books. The reader should note, though, that in each source there are one or two items that are not in the other.

II. SECONDARY LITERATURE. The chief source in English is A. Geikie, "Memoir of the Author," in his ed. of the *Voyage* (see above). See also *British Museum General Catalogue of Printed Books;* J. Challinor, "The Early Progress of British Geology—III," in *Annals of Science,* **10** (1954), 107–148, esp. 126–129; and T. D. Ford, "Barthélemy Faujas de St. Fond," in *Bulletin of the Peak District Mines Historical Society,* **2** (1965), 236–240.

JOHN CHALLINOR

FAULHABER, JOHANN (*b.* Ulm, Germany, 5 May 1580; *d.* Ulm, 1635), *mathematics.*

The Faulhaber family lived in Ulm from the middle of the fifteenth century and had been vassals of the abbot of Fulda from 1354 to 1461. Like his father, who died in 1593, Faulhaber first learned weaving. Ursula Esslinger of Ravensburg, whom Faulhaber married in 1600, bore him nine children, several of whom distinguished themselves as mathematicians. His son Johann Matthäus, born in 1604, learned weaving from his father before he turned to mathematics. In 1622 he accompanied his father to Basel to survey the fortifications and became director of the assignment following his father's death. A second son, also named Johann, born in 1609, was captain in the Corps of Engineers at Ulm.

His natural abilities led Faulhaber from weaving to mathematics. His first teacher in Ulm was the writing and arithmetic teacher David Saelzlin. The mathematicians of the sixteenth century concerned with algebra called themselves Cossists (from the Italian *cosa,* or "thing," which was used to designate the quantity being sought). Max Jaehns calls Faulhaber one of the most significant of the Cossists and the first to take algebra into equations higher than the third degree.[1]

His education did not make Faulhaber proficient in Latin, but with laborious effort he translated the Latin texts that he needed, lent by Michael Maestlin in Tübingen, as we learn from his letter of 16 April 1617 to Matthäus Beger, in Reutlingen:

> . . . since then I have taken the trouble to get the most distinguished books in German . . . as a person who never studied Latin and only now have attained some understanding of the language . . . to translate from Latin into simple German so that I now have at hand in German the books of Euclid, Archimedes,

Apollonius, Serenus, Theodosius, Regiomontanus, Cardano. . . .

After Faulhaber had helped Johann Kraft, arithmetic master in Ulm, to publish an arithmetic text, he founded his own school in Ulm in 1600.[2]

From 1604 on, Faulhaber received a salary of 30 guldens for running this school, but it was withdrawn in 1610 for a few months because he was concerning himself more and more with physical and technical inventions and developing an extensive literary activity that took him away from his pedagogic duties. Above and beyond this, he incurred the displeasure of the municipal council because he published *Neu erfundener Gebrauch eines Niederländischen Instruments zum Abmessen und Grundlegen, mit sehr geschwindem Vortheil zu practiciren* without the permission of the office responsible for supervision of the schools. About this time Faulhaber set up the formulas for the sum of the powers for natural numbers up to the thirteenth power, a problem with which Leonhard Euler was later concerned in a general way. He knew of the expression for the final difference of the arithmetic series obtained by raising the terms of an arithmetic series of the first order to a higher power.[3] More and more his school became an educational institute for higher mathematical sciences, and an artillery and engineering school was later added. In the pedagogic field Faulhaber's particular merit was in the dissemination of mathematical knowledge for general use. His arithmetic text, *Arithmetischer Wegweiser zu der hochnutzlichen freyen Rechenkunst* (1614), is a very clear textbook for the period. In the early editions he got as far as the "rule of three"; in later editions he treated all of the computations for ordinary use and even the fundamentals of equations. His writings on algebra are difficult to interpret because he used symbols that are no longer common. His particular concerns in these works are the theory of progressions, theory of magic squares, and the nature of numbers.

Like Michael Stifel, the Augustinian monk and promotor of calculation with logarithms, Faulhaber was noted for his mystical consideration of pseudomathematical problems. He attempted to interpret future events from numbers in the Bible: from Genesis, Jeremiah, Daniel, and Revelation. Together with the master baker from Ulm, Noah Kolb, he predicted the end of the world by 1605 and was put in jail for this in 1606. On the basis of his confession that he had not acted with evil intent, but from an irresistible impulse of conscience, he was released. As early as seven years later he again believed that he could see "numeri figurati"—figured numbers—in certain numbers from the Bible, and his view that God had used pyramidal numbers in the prophecies of the Bible was expressed in *Neuer mathematischer Kunstspiegel* (1612). Faulhaber meditated on the numbers 2,300 (Daniel VIII: 14), 1,335 (Daniel XII: 12), 1,290 (Daniel XII: 11), 1,260 (Revelation XI: 3), and 666 (Revelation XX: 2). These are the same numbers with which Stifel concerned himself.[4]

The extent to which this mystic arithmetic had affected Faulhaber can be seen in his books *Andeutung einer unerhörten neuen Wunderkunst . . .* (1613) and *Himmlische geheime Magia . . .* (1613). In the latter book he attempted to solve the hidden riddles of his sealed numbers by a peculiar transposition of the German, Latin, Greek, and Hebrew alphabets, a puzzle in which he refers to the tribes Gog and Magog mentioned in Revelation XX: 8. This biblical interpretation being contrary to Christian teachings, he drew the enmity of the clergy upon himself, and at their instance he was warned by the magistrate in Ulm that he should no longer print such interpretations without the knowledge and permission of the censor, upon pain of losing his civil rights. Since other theologians, such as Hasenreffer, the chancellor of Tübingen University, also sent warning letters to the Ulm city council, the prohibition of *Himmlische geheime Magia* was intensified.

Faulhaber also devoted himself to alchemy, which he practiced as a believer in Johann Valentin Andreae's *Chymische Hochzeit des Christiani Rosencreutz,* first published anonymously about 1604. On 21 January 1618 he wrote to Rudolph von Bünau: ". . . I am not sparing any efforts in inquiring about the commendable Rosicrucian Society . . ."; and on 21 March 1621, to Bünau: ". . . with the help of God, I have come to the point where I can make 2 grains of gold out of 1 grain of gold in a few days, which is why I give praise and thanks to the Almighty, and although one-tenth is supposed to become 10, up to now, I have not been able to get it any further and have worked it with my own hands."

These mysterious arts brought Faulhaber into contact with Duke Johann Friedrich von Württemberg. In 1619 he obtained permission to teach his arts and sciences freely in the duchy, and he continued to have that permission until after he again distributed his forbidden writings about Gog and Magog.

The reputation of Faulhaber's mathematics school extended so far that Descartes studied with him in 1620.[5] According to Veesenmayer, Descartes had already corresponded with Faulhaber concerning questions of plane analytic geometry[6] and had been stimulated to write *Discours sur la méthode . . .* (1637).[7] Descartes called him a "mathematicum insignem et imprimis in numerorum doctrina versatum et praeceptorem."[8]

Faulhaber's lasting accomplishment was the dissemination and explanation of the logarithmic method of calculation. The dissemination of the logarithms associated with Stifel, Bürgi, and Napier occurred through his chief work, *Ingenieurs-Schul,* the *Appendix oder Anhang . . . Ingenieurs-Schul,* and the *Zehntausend Logarithmi. . . .* He gives the logarithms of the numbers 1–10,000 to seven places and the values of the six natural goniometric functions to ten places. Along with the solution of plane and spherical triangles, with the applications to fortification and astronomical geography, we find the reason in the *Appendix:* ". . . that the entire foundation and correct basis of the logarithms from which they originate and are made, briefly indicated and explained. . . ." In addition, it was the first publication of the Briggs logarithms in German.[9] Faulhaber devoted himself to the stereometric analogue to the Pythagorean theorem, which he found and to which he was led by an apocalyptic number, 666. He first published this theorem as a numerical example in his "Miracola arithmetica," which is part of the *Continuatio des neuen mathematischen Kunstspiegel* (1620). Descartes, who probably learned it from Faulhaber, reproduced it in 1620: "In tedraedro rectangula basis potentia aequalis est potentistrium facierum simul." If one imagines a rectangular system of coordinates intersected by an inclined plane; if A, B, and C are the areas of the right triangles that occur on the planes of the coordinates; and if D is the area of the triangle determined by the intersections of the axes on this intersecting plane, then $D^2 = A^2 + B^2 + C^2$.

Faulhaber usually gives the solutions of his mathematical problems only in hints. Among the problems treated in the first part of his *Ingenieurs-Schul,* the question concerning an irregular circle-heptagon (p. 168) attained some measure of fame because the well-known nineteenth-century mathematicians Moebius and Siebeck concerned themselves with it. Faulhaber inscribed within a circle a heptagon with sides of lengths 2,300, 1,600, 1,290, 1,000, 666, 1,260, and 1,335, then asked how the radius of this circle could be found and how many degrees and minutes each angle contained. The numbers again are those of Michael Stifel. Faulhaber does not say how he solved this problem, but in the *Ingenieurs-Schul* (ch. 13, p. 157), he gives the result according to which the radius of the circle is "found to be $1582\frac{6223}{10,000}$."[10]

Faulhaber's prestige as a fortifications engineer is based on his many assignments in this field. Besides Duke August von Brunswick-Lüneburg, his services were sought by Duke Johann Friedrich von Württemberg, Cardinal Dietrichstein of Nicholsburg (near Vienna), King Gustavus Adolphus of Sweden, and the cities of Randegg, Schaffhausen, and Fürstenberg. Unfortunately, in this area too his full development was hindered by his religious fanaticism. On 5 December 1618 he entered the service of Landgrave Philipp von Butzbach, who sought him as an adviser, but he continued to live in Ulm. He wanted to make "all his inventions" known to the landgrave except his work in "munitions," i.e., in fortifications, which he was forbidden to divulge by the municipal council of Ulm.[11] Soon thereafter Faulhaber concerned himself anew with his interpretations of biblical numbers, and in April 1619 his mathematical and astronomical writings to the landgrave suddenly ended. Perhaps it was because the prince, who was firmly grounded in Christian teachings, believed that he had deceived himself about Faulhaber, or perhaps it was, as Faulhaber claims, that he was supposed to give the prince secrets which he had to consider in total confidence. In spite of this, the landgrave remained interested in his former adviser. In 1622 he received news about Faulhaber through Konrad Dietrich, superintendent in Ulm; and we learn from his letter of 23 March 1625 that Faulhaber "has been reconciled with an honorable councilman in Ulm and has promised in the name of the Almighty to let his whims fall."[12]

The full picture of Faulhaber's character is revealed from the controversies into which he was drawn. To be sure, we do not find his scientific importance reduced, but he nevertheless appears shady in view of the interplay of serious perception and speculative fantasy. Having been ordered by the municipal council of Ulm to publish an almanac for the year 1618, he used the ephemerides of Johannes Kepler. In it Kepler listed two rare constellations that were supposed to appear before and after 1 September, which means that the appearance of a comet cannot be regarded as excluded. In his almanac Faulhaber predicted a comet for 1 September 1618, on the basis of a consideration of the longitude and latitude of Mars and the moon. When one of the greatest comets of that era appeared in November 1618, Faulhaber no longer doubted the efficacy of his secret numbers and had this opinion published through his friend J. G. Goldtberg.[13] Attacked as vehemently by Hebenstreit and Zimpertus Wehe in Ulm as he was defended by Matthäus Beger in Reutlingen, Faulhaber appealed to the municipal council in Ulm and the ecclesiastical authorities, who decided in his favor.

He had a lively contact with Johannes Kepler. Upon the order of the magistrate, in 1622 he and Kepler designed a gauging kettle for the measurement of length, volume, and weight, which was cast by Hans Braun in 1627.[14]

NOTES

1. *Geschichte der Kriegswissenschaften,* vol. XXI of *Geschichte der Wissenschaften in Deutschland* (Munich–Leipzig, 1890), sec. 2, ch. 4, p. 1115, par. 118.
2. Although he was the author, it did not appear under his name. Georg Veesenmayer, *De Ulmensium in arithmeticam meritis* (Ulm, 1794), p. 6.
3. L. E. Ofterdinger, "Beiträge zur Geschichte der Mathematik in Ulm," in *Programmschrift des Königlichen Gymnasiums zu Ulm* (Ulm, 1866–1867).
4. Joseph E. Hofmann, "Michael Stifel," in *Sudhoffs Archiv für Geschichte der Medizin und Naturwissenschaften,* supp. 9 (1968), 2–5.
5. J. G. Doppelmayer, *Historische Nachricht von den Nürnbergischen Mathematicis und Künstlern* (Nuremberg, 1730), p. 209.
6. Veesenmayer, *op. cit.,* p. 7.
7. Christian Thomasius, *Historia sapientiae et stultitiae* (Halle, 1693), II, 113.
8. Ofterdinger, *op. cit.,* p. 5.
9. MS notes for and drafts of this work are in the Ulm municipal archives.
10. A. Germann, "Das irreguläre Siebeneck des Ulmer Mathematikers Joh. Faulhaber," in *Programmschrift des Königlichen Gymnasiums zu Ulm* (Ulm, 1875–1876), pp. 3–13.
11. *Ulmer Ratsprotokolle,* no. 61 (1611), fol. 674b.
12. Wilhelm Diehl, *Landgraf Philipp von Butzbach,* no. 4 of the series *Aus Butzbachs Vergangheit* (Giessen, 1922), pp. 37 ff.
13. Conrad Holzhalbius, *Herrn Faulhabers . . . Continuatio seiner neuen Wunderkunsten oder arithmetischen Wunderwerken* (Zurich, 1617).
14. K. E. Haeberle, *10,000 Jahre Waage* (Balingen, 1966), pp. 109–111.

BIBLIOGRAPHY

I. ORIGINAL WORKS. Faulhaber's writings are *Arithmetischer cubicossischer Lustgarten mit neuen Inventionibus gepflanzet* (Tübingen, 1604, 1708); *Neu erfundener Gebrauch eines Niederländischen Instruments zum Abmessen und Grundlegen . . .* (Augsburg, 1610); *Neue geometrische und perspectivische Inventiones etlicher sonderbarer Instrument . . .* (Frankfurt, 1610); *Neue geometrische und perspectivische Inventiones zu Grundrissen der Pasteyen und Vestungen* (Frankfurt, 1610); *Neuer mathematischer Kunstspiegel . . .* (Ulm, 1612); *Andeutung einer unerhörten neuen Wunderkunst . . .* (Nuremberg, 1613), Latin ed., *Ansa inauditae et novae artis . . .* (Ulm, 1613); *Himmlische geheime Magia oder neue cabalistische Kunst und Wunderrechnung vom Gog und Magog* (Nuremberg, 1613), trans. by Johannes Remmelin as *Magia arcana coelestis, sive Cabalisticus novus, artificiosus et admirandus computus de Gog et Magog . . .* (Nuremberg, 1613); *Arithmetischer Wegweiser zu der hochnutzlichen freyen Rechenkunst . . .* (Ulm, 1614, 1615, 1675, 1691, 1708, 1736, 1762, 1765), the last two eds. entitled *Arithmetischer Tausendkünstler . . .; Neue Invention einer Haus- und Handmühle* (Ulm, 1617); *Solution, wie man die Fristen, welche ohne Interesse auf gewisse Ziel zu bezahlen verfallen . . .* (Ulm, 1618); *Continuatio des neuen mathematischen Kunstspiegel . . .* (Tübingen, 1620), which contains thirty-two inventions; *Zweiundvierzig Secreta . . .* (Augsburg, 1621), which contains the inventions in the *Continuatio* plus ten new ones; *Appendix oder Anhang der Continuation des neuen mathematischen Kunstspiegel . . .* (Augsburg, 1621); *Erste deutsche Lection . . . das Prognosticon vom Gog und Magog . . .* (Augsburg, 1621); *Tarif über das kurze und lange Brennholz . . .* (Ulm, 1625); *Ingenieurs-Schul . . .,* 4pts. (Frankfurt, 1630–1633), which is partly extracted from the works of Adrian Vlacq, John Napier, and Matthias Bernegg; *Appendix oder Anhang des ersten Theils der Ingenieurs-Schul . . .* (Augsburg, 1631); and *Zehntausend Logarithmi der absoluten oder ledigen Zahlen . . .* (Augsburg, 1631). A holograph MS of Faulhaber's, entitled "Beobachtungen von Mund- und Sonnenringen" (1619), is in the Darmstadt Landesbibliothek, 4° 3044. Ten letters from Faulhaber to Philipp von Butzbach are in the Darmstadt Staatsarchiv, 55, 1618–1619.

II. SECONDARY LITERATURE. On Faulhaber's work, see Matthias Bernegger, *Sinum, tangentium et secantium canon . . .* (Strasbourg, 1619[?]), which refers to *Neue geometrische und perspectivische Inventiones etlicher sonderbarer Instrument . . .;* and *Phantasma qua Joh. Faulhaber de ansa inauditae et admirabilis artis . . .* (Strasbourg, 1614), a refutation of *Andeutung einer unerhörten neuen Wunderkunst;* Benjamin Bramer, *Beschreibung eines sehr leichten Perspectiv und grundreissenden Instruments auf einem Stande . . .* (Kassel, 1630), which refers to *Appendix oder Anhang der Continuation des neuen mathematischen Kunstspiegel . . .;* Georg Galgemair, *Centiloquium circini proportionum. Ein neuer Proportionalzirkel von 4, 5, 6 oder mehr Spitzen* (Nuremberg, 1626), which refers to *Neue geometrische und perspectivische Inventiones etlicher sonderbarer Instrument . . .;* J. G. Goldtberg, *Fama syderea nova. Gemein offentliches Ausschreiben . . .* (Nuremberg, 1618, 1619); *Expolitio famae sidereae novae Faulhabereanae . . .* (Prague, 1619); *Postulatum aequitatis plenissimum, Das ist: Ein billiges und rechtmässiges Begehren, die Expolitionem famae Faulhaberianae betreffend . . .* (Prague, 1619); *Fama syderea nova, das ist weitere Continuatio der Göttlichen neuen Wunderzeichen und grossen Miraculn . . .* (Nuremberg, 1620); and *Vindiciarium Faulhaberianum continuatio . . .* (Ulm, 1620); Conrad Holzhalbius, *Herrn Faulhabers . . . Continuatio seiner neuen Wunderkünsten oder arithmetischen Wunderwerken* (Zurich, 1617); Petrus Roth, *Arithmetica philosophica . . .,* II (Nuremberg, 1608), which refers to *Arithmetischer cubicossischer Lustgarten mit neuen Inventionibus gepflanzet;* and David Verbez, *Miracula arithmetica zu der Continuation des arithmetischen Wegweisers* (Augsburg, 1622).

Biographical literature includes C. G. Jöcher, in *Allgemeinen Gelehrten-Lexikon,* II (Leipzig, 1750), col. 527; Hermann Keefer, "Johannes Faulhaber, der bedeutendste Ulmer Mathematiker und Festungsbaumeister," in *Württembergische Schulwarte,* 4 (1928), 1–12; Emil von Loeffler, "Ein Ingenieur und Artillerie-Offizier der Festung Ulm in 30-jährigen Kriege," in *Ulmer Tagblatt* (1886), Sonntagsbeilage no. 52 and (1887), Sonntagsbeilage nos. 1–6, also in *Allgemeine Militarzeitung,* 60 (1885), which refers to Faulhaber and Joseph Furtenbach; Max Schefold, "Ein Zyklus von Faulhaberbildnissen," in *Ulmer Tagblatt* (30 Apr. and 7 May 1926); Albrecht Weyermann, *Nachrichten von Gelehrten, Künstlern und andere merkwürdigen Per-*

sonen aus Ulm (Ulm, 1798), pp. 206–215; and J. H. Zedler, in *Universal-Lexikon,* IX (Halle–Leipzig, 1735), col. 317.

Documents concerning Faulhaber are in the Darmstadt Staatsarchiv, 55 XVII. The Faulhaber family's coat of arms is reproduced in J. F. Schannat, *Fuldischer Lehnhof, sive de clientela Fuldensi beneficiaria nobili et equestri tractatus historico-iuridicus . . .* (Frankfurt, 1736), pp. 83, 91.

PAUL A. KIRCHVOGEL

FAVORSKY, ALEXEI YEVGRAFOVICH (*b.* Pavlovo, Russia, 6 March 1860; *d.* Leningrad, U.S.S.R., 8 August 1945), *chemistry.*

One of A. M. Butlerov's outstanding students, Favorsky graduated from St. Petersburg University in 1882. A professor from 1896, in 1921 he became an associate member, and in 1929 a full member, of the Soviet Academy of Sciences. His entire career was devoted to the study of the reactions of organic unsaturates, primarily the acetylenic hydrocarbons. The results of his work form the basis of many general methods of synthesis, including a number that are of industrial significance.

In 1884 Favorsky discovered the isomerization phenomena of acetylenic hydrocarbons (e.g., $C-C-C{\equiv}C \to C-C{\equiv}C-C$) and explained their mechanism, advancing a hypothesis concerning the intermediary formation of derivatives of allene ($CH_2{=}C{=}CH_2$) and vinyl ethers ($C{=}C-OR$). In 1891 he confirmed the latter experimentally with the reaction

$$CH_3-C{\equiv}CH + ROH \xrightarrow{KOH} CH_3-\underset{\underset{OR}{|}}{C}{=}CH_2.$$

Subsequently, Favorsky and his students broadly applied the "vinylization of alcohols" as a quantitative method for obtaining vinyl ethers. From these ethers they prepared aldehydes, acids, and polymers related to the balsams. Verification of the hypothesis concerning the formation of allenes led to the development of methods for the synthesis of dienes:

$$\underset{\underset{C}{|}}{C}-C-C{\equiv}C \longrightarrow \underset{\underset{C}{|}}{C}-C{=}C{=}C \longrightarrow \underset{\underset{C}{|}}{C}{=}C-C{=}C.$$

As a result, Favorsky's school was the first to synthesize isoprene ($CH_2{=}\underset{\underset{CH_3}{|}}{C}-CH{=}CH_2$; V. N. Ipatiev, 1897) and butadiene 1,3 ($CH_2{=}CHCH{=}CH_2$; S. V. Lebedev, 1928). These were recognized as intermediates in the synthesis of rubber.

Between 1905 and 1907 Favorsky studied the condensation of ketones with acetylenic hydrocarbons:

$$CH_3-\underset{\underset{CH_3}{|}}{CO} + HC{\equiv}C-R \longrightarrow CH_3-\underset{\underset{CH_3}{|}}{COH}-C{\equiv}C-R.$$

He used this reaction in the development of a simple method for synthesizing isoprene (1932):

$$CH_3-\underset{\underset{CH_3}{|}}{COH}-C{\equiv}CH \longrightarrow$$

$$CH_3-\underset{\underset{CH_3}{|}}{COH}-CH{=}CH_2 \longrightarrow CH_2{=}\underset{\underset{CH_3}{|}}{C}-CH{=}CH_2.$$

More recently, Walter Reppe has used an analogous technique to synthesize acrylic acid ($CH_2{=}CHCOOH$) and its derivatives by condensing ketones with hydrogen cyanide.

In 1900–1910 Favorsky established the reversibility of the isomeric conversions (or transformations) for a series of acetylene, allene, and diene compounds and explained the phenomena of tautomerism and reversible isomerization in one set of reactions. He discovered the simultaneous isomerization of bromine derivatives into six isomeric forms, given an equilibrium system. Developing one of the most effective theories of affinity capacity, Favorsky pointed out the stability of free radicals among metal ketyls of the fatty series and substantiated this experimentally. Between 1933 and 1936 he studied the limits of dehydrogenation of carbocyclic hydrocarbons and stated the maximum possible nonsaturation of $C-C$ bonds for each isomer from C_3- to C_8-. This work led Favorsky's school to the synthesis of a great many thermodynamically unstable compounds, such as cyclopropene (by I. A. Dyakonov). In 1891 Favorsky predicted the existence of polyene compounds (cumulenes), the stability of which, according to his theory, must increase with an increase in methylation of the end group; these substances were discovered in the middle of the twentieth century by F. Bohlmen:

$$(CH_3)_3C-C{\equiv}C-C{\equiv}C-C(CH_3)_3.$$

As a result of the systematic investigation of compounds found in an unstable state, Favorsky concluded that isomerization, polymerization, and cracking could all be reduced to a common cause. This conclusion allowed him to determine the path taken by the original reagent activated by means of heat or a catalyst and to explain the action of catalysts applied to acetylene and diene compounds. Favorsky concluded that prototropic transfer, or the "migration of hydrogen," is elicited by alkaline catalysts in the initial act of isomerization, polymerization, and cracking. In addition, he developed general methods for the synthesis of various unsaturated alcohols, α-keto alcohols, dichloro ketones, displaced derivatives of the acrylic acids, and dioxane—a solvent for many organic compounds and completely miscible with water.

Favorsky was responsible for a large school of chemists, including V. N. Ipatiev, S. V. Lebedev, I. N. Nazarov, A. E. Poray-Koshits, Z. Jotsich, Y. S. Zalkind, and M. F. Shostakovsky. From 1900 to 1930 he was editor-in-chief of the *Zhurnal Russkago fiziko-khimicheskago obshchestva.*

BIBLIOGRAPHY

I. ORIGINAL WORKS. Favorsky's selected writings are in *Izbrannye Trudy* ("Selected Works," Moscow-Leningrad, 1940; 2nd ed., 1960).

II. SECONDARY LITERATURE. On Favorsky or his work, see V. I. Kuznetsov, *Razvitie issledovany polimerizatsii nepredelnykh soedineny v SSSR* (Moscow, 1959), issued on the centennial of Favorsky's birth; *Voprosy teorii stroenia organicheskikh soedineny* (Leningrad, 1960), a collection honoring the centennial of Favorsky's birth; and M. F. Shostakovsky, *Akademik Alexei Yevgrafovich Favorsky* (Moscow-Leningrad, 1953).

V. I. KUZNETSOV

FAVRE, PIERRE ANTOINE (*b.* Lyons, France, 20 February 1813; *d.* Marseilles, France, 17 February 1880), *chemistry.*

Favre received a medical degree from the Faculty of Medicine in Paris in 1835. Inspired by Jean Dumas's lectures in chemistry at the School of Medicine in 1840, he turned to chemistry. He was admitted to Eugène Peligot's private laboratory and helped in the latter's classic work on uranium compounds; he became Peligot's *préparateur* at the Conservatory of Arts and Manufactures. He was named fellow of the Faculty of Medicine of Paris in 1843 and worked in G. Andral's laboratory on physiological problems. In 1851 he became head of the analytical chemistry laboratory of the Central School of Arts and Manufactures, while continuing as a fellow of the Faculty of Medicine. In 1853 he received the degree of Doctor of Physical Science. He was named professor of chemistry of the Faculty of Science of Besançon in 1854 and was called to the newly created Faculty of Science at Marseilles in 1856.

Twice laureate of the French Academy of Sciences, Favre was elected a correspondent of the chemistry section in 1864 and a correspondent of the physics section in 1868. Favre became dean of the Faculty of Science in Marseilles in 1872, retiring in 1878 because of ill health.

Favre's earliest independent researches were determinations of the equivalent weight of zinc and studies of cupric carbonate and the ammonium carbonates of zinc and magnesium. He wrote several papers on such physiologically important compounds as lactic acid, mannitol, and the constituents of human perspiration.

His interests turned to thermochemistry about 1848—indeed, Favre is perhaps best-known for using the term "calorie" (1853) to denote the unit of heat. Between 1845 and 1853, he and Johann T. Silbermann, a French physicist, collaborated in a series of important thermochemical researches. They demonstrated the falsity of Dulong's rule, which states that the heat of combustion of a compound composed of carbon and hydrogen is the sum of the heats of combustion of the elements it contains. Particularly valuable was their study of the heats of combustion and formation of a large number of substances using a newly devised "mercury calorimeter." The instrument was somewhat inaccurate, and their results were superseded after some years but were nevertheless widely used. They also showed that the heat of combustion of carbon in oxygen is less than that of carbon in nitrous oxide, evidence that helped to strengthen the case for the diatomicity of the oxygen molecule. The collaboration between Favre and Silbermann was influential in replacing the vague notion of chemical affinity with more precise thermodynamic expressions.

In 1857 Favre elegantly substantiated Joule's ideas about the conservation of energy by means of a voltaic battery operating an electric motor which raised a weight. He showed that the total heat evolved in the battery and the circuit, when added to the equivalent in heat required to raise the weight, was equal to that evolved by the battery alone when it was short-circuited.

Shortly before retirement Favre and the mathematician Claude Valson determined both the heats and the volume changes of solution of many salts. This study was cited by Arrhenius in defense of the theory of electrolytic dissociation. Favre was often called upon by the state and by commercial interests; he served as a consultant in the preparation of canned foods, salt, and petroleum distillates for house and street illumination.

Favre was a careful and skillful experimenter. Highly regarded by his contemporaries for his diligence and chemical ability, his mission was to gather data, not to devise the bold new hypotheses which alter the scientific paradigm.

BIBLIOGRAPHY

I. ORIGINAL WORKS. Favre's works include more than seventy papers (alone or with collaborators), which are listed by Poggendorff and in the first series of the *Catalogue of Scientific Papers* of the Royal Society of London.

II. SECONDARY LITERATURE. J. S. Partington gives a brief analysis of Favre's work in *A History of Chemistry*, IV (London, 1964), 691 and *passim*. A short biography by F. LeBlanc, "Notice nécrologique sur P. A. Favre . . .," is in *Bulletin de la Société chimique de Paris*, **33** (1880), 390–400; see also *Comptes rendus hebdomadaires des séances de l'Académie des sciences*, **90** (1880), 329. There is no detailed study of his life and achievement.

LOUIS KUSLAN

FAYE, HERVÉ (*b.* St. Benoît-du-Sault, France, 1 October 1814; *d.* Paris, France, 4 July 1902), *astronomy, geodesy.*

Son of a civil engineer, Faye entered the École Polytechnique in 1832. His vocation for astronomy emerged after a few years of work in France under the supervision of his father. He entered the Paris Observatory in 1836. While working there, under Arago's direction, Faye discovered the periodic comet of 1843 (since known by his name) and computed its orbit. His career thereafter was manifold. He taught geodesy at the École Polytechnique as lecturer from 1848 to 1854 and became full professor in 1873; meanwhile he was professor of astronomy at Nancy. As academic administrator he was rector of the Academy at Nancy and general inspector of secondary schools. He was honored for his achievements throughout his life, beginning with his election to the Académie des Sciences at the age of thirty-three. A member of the Bureau des Longitudes, he served as president for more than twenty years.

Most of Faye's research is contained in the more than 200 notes that he published in the *Comptes rendus hebdomadaires des séances de l'Académie des sciences*. These researches were essentially theoretical in character, including, among other things, an explanation of the tails of comets as well as a discussion of the discrepancies produced in normal Newtonian orbits by radiation pressure from the sun (*Comptes rendus*, **47** [1858], 836). He understood that meteorites follow cometary orbits and are therefore related objects (*ibid.*, **64** [1867], 549). He improved observational techniques in astronomy, advocating the use of photography, designing a zenith telescope (*ibid.*, **23** [1846], 872), and studying carefully refraction as the major cause of errors (*ibid.*, **39** [1854], 381).

Faye's theory of the sun was widely adopted. He considered the sun to be a gaseous sphere with large convective motions (*ibid.*, **60** [1865], 89 and 138), the sunspots being holes (*ibid.*, **61** [1865], 1082) with internal cyclonic motions (*ibid.*, **76** [1873], 509). He also studied earth cyclones. In a book on the origin of

worlds (1884) he developed and improved Laplace's cosmological theory.

Faye also spent much effort in developing geodetic projects in France and all over the world. He first introduced an idea close to isostasy, that the figure of the earth is almost an equilibrium figure, continents being lighter than the crust under the oceans (*ibid.*, **90** [1880], 1185).

Faye's ideas were widely publicized during his lifetime. Some of them remain valid to this day, while others contributed significantly to the development of science in his time.

BIBLIOGRAPHY

I. ORIGINAL WORKS. Faye's most important works are listed in the text. His theory of the sun is described in *Annuaire du Bureau des longitudes* (1873), p. 443, and (1874) p. 407; his theory of comets is in the same publication, (1883), p. 717. See also *Cours d'astronomie*, 2 vols. (Paris, 1882), which includes his most important ideas, and *Sur l'origine des mondes* (Paris, 1884) for his cosmological theory.

II. SECONDARY LITERATURE. Several notices on Faye may be found in *Annuaire du Bureau des longitudes* for 1903.

J. KOVALEVSKY

AL-FAZĀRĪ, MUḤAMMAD IBN IBRĀHĪM (*fl.* second half of the eighth century), *astronomy.*

Al-Fazārī came from an old Arab family (his genealogy is traced back twenty-seven generations by Yāqūt) which had settled in Kūfa. He is first heard of in connection with the building of Baghdad in the latter half of 762, when he was associated with the other astrologers—Nawbakht, Māshā'allāh and 'Umar ibn al-Farrukhān al-Ṭabarī—who were involved in that work. He apparently remained at the Abbasid court; for, when an embassy arrived from Sind which included an Indian astronomer (whose identity is unknown, although it was certainly not Kanaka), the Caliph al-Manṣūr asked al-Fazārī to work with this Indian on an Arabic translation of a Sanskrit astronomical text. The date of this embassy is variously given as 771 or 773. Another Arab astronomer who worked with this Indian was Ya'qūb ibn Ṭāriq.

The Sanskrit astronomical text that was translated with the assistance of al-Fazārī was apparently entitled *Mahāsiddhānta* and belonged to what later became known as the *Brahmapakṣa* (see essay IV on Indian astronomy in supplement); its most immediate cognates were the *Paitāmahasiddhānta* of the *Viṣnudharmottarapurāṇa* and the *Brāhmasphuṭasiddh-*

ānta of Brahmagupta; but the Indian astronomer evidently also conveyed to his Arab collaborators information about the *Āryabhaṭīya* of Āryabhata I. The Arabic translation of this Sanskrit text was entitled *Zīj al-Sindhind;* from it descends a long tradition within Islamic astronomy, which survived in the East until the early tenth century and in Spain until the twelfth. The first derivative work was evidently the *Zīj al-Sindhind al-kabīr* of al-Fazārī himself.

Already in this work the elements of the *Brahmapakṣa* begin to be contaminated with those of other schools. Although the system of the *kalpa* and the mean motions of the planets, their apogees, and their nodes remain within the tradition of the *Zīj al-Sindhind,* the maximum equations are derived primarily from the *Zīj al-Shāh,* which represents the *ardharātrika* school in Indian astronomy (see essay VI), and also from the *Āryabhaṭīya;* the geographical section of the work also reveals the influence of the *Āryabhaṭīya* and of a Sassanian tradition ascribed to Hermes. Moreover, al-Fazārī allows great inconsistencies in this *zīj,* as he extracted convenient rules from one source or another without trying to make them coincide. Thus, he displays three values of *R*—3,438 (from the *Āryabhaṭīya*), 3,270 (from the *Zīj al-Sindhind*), and 150 (from the *Zīj al-Shāh*)—and two values of the maximum equation of the sun—2;11,15° and 2;14° (from the *Zīj al-Shāh*).

After writing this *zīj* al-Fazārī composed another, probably about 790, called the *Zīj ʿalā sinī al-ʿArab* ("Astronomical Tables According to the Years of the Arabs"). In this *zīj* he apparently tabulated the mean motions of the planets for one to sixty *saura* days, 1,0 to 6,0 *saura* days (6,0 *saura* days being equal to one sidereal year), one to sixty sidereal years, and an unknown number of sixty-year periods; and he evidently added tables for converting *kalpa aharganas* into Hegira dates. Of this latter set of tables we still have copies of the *Mujarrad* table for finding the day of the week with which each Arab year and month begins. Moreover, we have al-Fazārī's list of the countries of the world and their dimensions from this *zīj;* the dimensions presuppose a much larger earth than that allowed by the circumference of the earth which he introduced into his *Zīj al-Sindhind al-kabīr* from the *Āryabhaṭīya.*

Very little else is known of al-Fazārī's works. A few lines of his *Qaṣīda fī ʿilm al-nujūm* ("Poem on the Science of the Stars") are preserved by Yāqūt and al-Ṣafadī, and the bibliographers record books on the use of the plane astrolabe (al-Fazārī is said to have been the first in Islam to construct one) and the armillary sphere, and on the measurement of noon. But we do have enough of his *zījes* to know that his

work was almost entirely derivative and that he could not even combine his disparate sources into a unified system. His significance lies entirely in that he helped to introduce a large body of Indian astronomical parameters and computational techniques to Islamic scientists.

BIBLIOGRAPHY

The numerous references to al-Fazārī are collected and discussed in D. Pingree, "The Fragments of the Works of al-Fazārī," in *Journal of Near Eastern Studies,* **29** (1970), 103–123.

David Pingree

FECHNER, GUSTAV THEODOR (*b.* Gross-Särchen, near Halle, Germany, 19 April 1801; *d.* Leipzig, Germany, 18 November 1887), *psychology.*

Fechner was the second of five children of Samuel Traugott Fechner, a rural, innovative Lutheran preacher, and Johanna Dorothea Fischer Fechner. The precocious child had learned Latin from his father by the time of the latter's death, when Fechner was five. After attending the Gymnasium at Soran (near Dresden, where the family moved in 1815), in 1817 Fechner matriculated at the University of Leipzig, where he spent the rest of his life. He took the M.D. there in 1822 but never practiced medicine. In 1833 he married Clara Volkmann, the sister of his colleague and friend A. W. Volkmann, a physiologist in vision.

Fechner's first writings were satirical pieces that he published under the pseudonym "Dr. Mises." The first of these was written in 1821; they appeared sporadically over the next twenty-five years. Fantastical and by turns strained or brilliant, these pieces usually attack the materialism popular in Germany early in the nineteenth century—or *Nachtansicht,* as Fechner called it—in contrast with his own *Tagesansicht,* in which life and consciousness are coequal with matter.

Fechner's first scientific work was in physics, lecturing on it in 1824 (as *ordinarius,* without pay), translating physics and chemistry texts from the French (by which he earned his living), and conducting investigations in electricity, particularly on Ohm's law. In 1831 he published *Massbestimmungen über die galvanische Kette,* a paper of great importance on quantitative measurements of the galvanic battery. This made his reputation as a physicist, and he was appointed professor of physics in 1834. During this period, the only indications of his future interest in psychological problems were his satires, two papers on complementary colors and subjective colors (1838), and his famous paper on subjective afterimages, published in 1840.

Fechner then plunged into a long, serious neurotic illness which necessitated his resignation from his chair of physics in 1839. This began somatically with a partial blindness brought on by gazing at the sun through colored glasses in the experiments on colors and afterimages; it then deepened psychologically into an inability to take food, various psychotic symptoms, and a year of severe autistic thinking. Then on 5 October 1843, having lived for three years in the dark and despairing of ever seeing again, Fechner ventured into his garden, unwound the bandages he wore around his eyes, and found his vision not only regained but abnormally powerful, since he had semihallucinatory experiences of seeing the souls of flowers. His recovery was then slow and progressive.

This peak experience in the garden is reflected in his next work, *Nanna oder über das Seelenleben der Pflanzen* ("Nanna, or the Soul Life of Plants," 1848). In this philosophically diffuse book as well as in his 1851 book, *Zend-Avesta oder über die Dinge des Himmels und des Jenseits* ("Zend-Avesta, or Concerning Matters of Heaven and the World to Come"), Fechner developed what has been called his panpsychism, a development of his *Tagesansicht:* since mind and matter were two aspects of the same thing, the entire universe could be looked at from the point of view of its mind.

But how could this be made scientific? On the morning of 22 October 1850 (called commemoratively by psychophysicists Fechner Day), while Fechner was awaking in bed, the solution came. It was to make the relative increase of stimulation the measure of the increase of the corresponding sensation; and this suggested that the arithmetical series of perceived intensities might correspond to a geometrical series of external energies.

In part, this solution to Fechner's problem was based upon Helmholtz's famous "On the Conservation of Force," published three years earlier. Since energy could neither be created nor be destroyed, all energy impinging on sense organs traversed the nervous system and ended in effectors. Sensation was the mental aspect of this, which had to be just as orderly and related to these physical events in an orderly manner. The relation between sensation and these neurological events he called "inner psychophysics." This was impossible to study. It was, therefore, the relationship of sensation to the external stimulus energy, or outer psychophysics, that could alone be studied.

These ideas, after a decade of thought and experiment, resulted in 1860 in Fechner's classic work, the *Elemente der Psychophysik,* a text of the "exact science of the functional relations or relations of dependency between body and mind." Through its sometimes redundant details are developed three of the basic methods of a new science to be called psychophysics:

1. The method of just noticeable differences, later called the method of limits. The difference between two discriminable stimuli is gradually decreased until discrimination is just lost; and conversely, the difference between two stimuli that are not discriminable is gradually increased until discrimination is barely possible: the average of these two determinations is a measure of the just noticeable difference.

2. The method of right and wrong cases, later called the method of constant stimuli, or simply the constant method, which has become, since the work of G. E. Müller and F. M. Urban, the most important. A range of stimuli are used, none of which is adjustable; a standard stimulus is compared in some given respect with each of a series of similar stimuli, presented in chance order: from the percentage of correct judgments with each comparison stimulus, a threshold is mathematically determined.

3. The method of average error. Whereas the two foregoing methods are partly systematizations of work by others, this method was original with Fechner in collaboration with his brother-in-law, Volkmann. A variable stimulus is adjusted sundry times to apparent equality with a standard, the average adjustment being the "constant error" and its standard deviation the sensitivity. These methods were used by Fechner in classical experiments in lifted weights, visual brightnesses, tactual and visual distances, temperature sensitivity, and even a classification of stars by magnitude following Steinheil.

But this methodology is mere apparatus to carry the central and pervading conception of the *Elemente,* Fechner's fascinating development of the Weber fraction into what has come to be known as the Weber-Fechner law. E. H. Weber, a senior colleague of Fechner at Leipzig, concluded after a series of elegant studies on lifted weights, judged line lengths, and various tactual sensations, that the just noticeable difference in stimulus intensity is a constant fraction of the total intensity at which it is measured. These experiments were first described in Latin in 1834 but achieved attention only when brought together with other facts in Weber's famous chapter on touch in Rudolph Wagner's *Handwörterbuch der Physiologie* (Brunswick, 1846). This may be expressed as

$$\frac{\Delta R}{R} = \text{constant},$$

where R is *Reiz,* or stimulus, and ΔR is the amount of increase in R necessary for a subject to see any difference. This is approximately true for the middle range of sensory stimulation in any modality in men, or in animals where a behavioral response takes the place of an introspected difference in sensation.

Fechner assumed that on the mental side there is a corresponding increase in sensation, ΔS, and that all such ΔS's are equal and can be treated as units, whence

$$\Delta S = C \frac{\Delta R}{R},$$

where C is the constant of proportionality. Integrating, and solving for the constant of integration at threshold where $S = 0$,

$$S = C \log R,$$

where R is measured in units of its threshold value. This is the fundamental relation between mind on the left-hand side of the equation, and matter on the right. It is now known as the Weber-Fechner law, although Fechner with confusing generosity called it Weber's law.

While the methodology of the *Elemente* is sound and permanent, its theoretical purpose and its working out into Fechner's law kindled immediate controversy, which is still far from being resolved. Even before 1860, Fechner's ideas resulted in papers by Helmholtz and Mach on the new psychophysics. And Wilhelm Wundt, in his first psychological publications from 1862 on, made Fechner's work centrally important. His detractors, on the other hand, claimed that Fechner had not measured sensation at all. Their fundamental objections were (1) that it is meaningless to say that one ΔS equals another unless S is independently measurable, and (2) what has been called the quantity objection: in experience, pink is not part of scarlet, nor a thunderclap a summation of murmurs.

As Fechner founded psychophysics with this decade of work, so in the next decade (1865–1876) he founded experimental aesthetics, publishing his *Vorschule der Ästhetik* in 1876. This work treats of its methods, principles, and problems, particularly that of the "golden section," or most aesthetically pleasing relation of length to breadth of an object, a kind of Weber's fraction for aesthetics. He endlessly measured the dimensions of pictures, cards, books, snuffboxes, writing paper, and windows, among other things, in an attempt to develop experimental aesthetics "from below," in rebellion against the Romantic attempt "from above down" first to formulate abstract principles of beauty.

In the final decade of his life, the turbulent wake of his *Elemente* drew Fechner back into psychophysics. In 1882 he answered his critics with his last important book, *Revision der Hauptpunkte der Psychophysik.* This helped to place Fechner's psychophysics even more securely as a cornerstone of the new so-called experimental psychology as it was to be developed in the latter part of the century by Wundt and others.

BIBLIOGRAPHY

I. ORIGINAL WORKS. Fechner's chief works are *Massbestimmungen über die galvanische Kette* (Leipzig, 1831), which is available on microfilm in the "Landmarks of Science" series, I. Bernard Cohen, Charles C. Gillispie, *et al.,* eds. (New York, 1967); *Das Büchlein vom Leben nach dem Tode* (Dresden, 1836; Leipzig, 1841, 1915, 1922; Hamburg, 1887, 1906), English trans. by H. Wernekke as *On Life After Death* (London, 1882; Chicago, 1906, 1914), another English trans. by M. C. Wadsworth, intro. by W. James, as *The Little Book of Life After Death* (Boston, 1904; New York, 1943); *Nanna oder über das Seelenleben der Pflanzen* (Leipzig, 1848, 1920; Hamburg, 1903); *Zend-Avesta oder über die Dinge des Himmels und des Jenseits,* 3 vols. (Leipzig, 1851; Hamburg, 1906); *Elemente der Psychophysik,* 2 vols. (Leipzig, 1860, 1889)—of which vol. I of the 1889 ed. includes a bibliography, originally compiled by R. Müller, of 175 of Fechner's publications—English trans. of vol. I only by H. E. Adler, as *Elements of Psychophysics,* E. G. Boring and D. Howes, eds. (New York, 1966); *Vorschule der Ästhetik* (Leipzig, 1876); *Die Tagesansicht gegenüber der Nachtansicht* (Leipzig, 1879, 1904); and *Revision der Hauptpunkte der Psychophysik* (Leipzig, 1882).

II. SECONDARY LITERATURE. On Fechner's life, see the sympathetic biography by his nephew, J. E. Kuntze, *Gustav Theodor Fechner (Dr. Mises), Ein deutsches Gelehrtenleben* (Leipzig, 1892), which reprints the bibliography of Fechner's works cited above. See also K. Lasswitz, *Gustav Theodor Fechner* (Stuttgart, 1896, 1910); and G. S. Hall, *Founders of Modern Psychology,* (New York, 1912), pp. 123–177.

On Fechner's scientific contributions, see, in addition to the foregoing, T. Ribot, *German Psychology of Today* (New York, 1886), pp. 134–187; W. Wundt, *Gustav Theodor Fechner* (Leipzig, 1901); and M. Wentscher, *Fechner und Lotze* (Munich, 1925). Other bibliographical items on Fechner's scientific work, as well as a good short introduction to him, are given in E. G. Boring, *A History of Experimental Psychology* (New York, 1929), pp. 265–287. William James's scornful evaluation of Fechner and his work may be found in his *Principles of Psychology,* I (New York, 1890), 533–549. See also R. I. Watson, *The Great Psychologists* (Philadelphia, 1968), pp. 229–241.

Of recent revisions of the Weber-Fechner law, the most important are H. Helson and W. C. Michels, "A Reformulation of the Fechner Law in Terms of Adaptation Level Applied to Rating Scale Data," in *American Journal of Psychology,* **62** (1949), 355–368; S. S. Stevens, "On the Psychophysical Law," in *Psychological Review,* **64** (1957), 153–181; R. D. Luce and W. Edwards, "The Derivation of Subjective Scales From Just Noticeable Differences," *ibid.,* **65** (1958), 222–237; and R. D. Luce and E. Galanter, "Discrimination," in R. D. Luce, R. R. Bush, and E. Galanter, eds., *Handbook of Mathematical Psychology,* I (New York, 1963), 191–243, esp. 206–213.

See also H. Eisler, "A General Differential Equation in Psychophysics: Derivation and Empirical Test," in *Scandinavian Journal of Psychology,* **4** (1963), 1–8; M. Mashhour, "On Eisler's General Psychophysical Differential Equation and His Fechnerian Integration," *ibid.,* **5** (1964), 225–233, a highly critical paper on Eisler; and J. C. Falmagne, "The Generalized Fechner Problem and Discrimination," in *Journal of Mathematical Psychology,* in press.

On the quantity objection specifically, see E. B. Titchener, *Experimental Psychology,* II, pt. 2 (London, 1905), xlvii–lxviii. E. G. Boring, "The Stimulus Error," in *American Journal of Psychology,* **32** (1921), 449–471, particularly pp. 451–460, contains other references on the problem.

On Fechner's more philosophical thought, see W. James, *A Pluralistic Universe* (New York, 1909), pp. 133–177; R. B. Perry, *Philosophy of the Recent Past* (New York, 1926), pp. 81–86; and G. S. Brett, *History of Psychology,* ed. and abridged by R. S. Peters (Cambridge, Mass., 1965), pp. 580–590.

JULIAN JAYNES

FEDDERSEN, BEREND WILHELM (*b.* Schleswig, Germany, 26 March 1832; *d.* Leipzig, Germany, 1 July 1918), *physics.*

Not much is known of Feddersen's early life or parentage, except that he was an only child. He studied in Göttingen, Berlin, Leipzig, and Kiel, where he received the doctorate in 1858 with a dissertation on the nature of electric-spark discharges, which he studied by improving a rotating-mirror technique of Wheatstone's. In the same year he moved to Leipzig, where he spent the rest of his life.

By his early and subsequent investigations, Feddersen showed that the discharge of a Leiden flask produces a train of damped oscillations, which he contrived to record in a series of splendid photographs. The finding that a circuit made up of a capacitance, a resistance, and an inductance produces oscillations whose frequency and amplitude depend on these components also proved to be of considerable technological importance. Feddersen's photographs served to confirm the 1853 theory of William Thomson (the future Lord Kelvin), who had been occupied—as had Faraday—with the analysis of long-distance signaling in connection with the first

attempt to lay a transatlantic cable and had developed the formula for the frequency of a damped resonant circuit; Thomson's public acknowledgment of his debt to Feddersen brought the latter worldwide renown. The beginnings of radiotelegraphy likewise depended on spark-discharge techniques, which dominated radio transmission well on into the twentieth century.

Feddersen is also remembered for his contributions to scientific bibliography, because of his personal participation in (and financial support of) Poggendorff's *Biographisch-literarisches Handwörterbuch* (now in its seventh edition). He undertook the editorship of the third volume after the death of the first editor, Johann Christian Poggendorff, in 1877; but its appearance was delayed because of a quarrel with the publisher, and the work was finally taken over by a third physicist, Arthur Joachim von Oettingen. (All three died octogenarians, a useful trait for bibliographers.) Feddersen supported the publication of volumes III and IV by donating the substantial sum of 30,000 marks and a few weeks before his death sought to assure the appearance of further volumes by setting up, jointly with his wife, a 100,000-mark endowment that was unfortunately wiped out by the runaway German inflation of 1919–1923.

In 1866 Feddersen married a distant cousin, Dora Feddersen, who was sickly and on whose account he practically withdrew from scientific activity. She died in 1889, and in 1890 he married Helga Kjär, who survived him until 1936. There were no children from either marriage.

BIBLIOGRAPHY

I. ORIGINAL WORKS. A list of Feddersen's publications appears in Poggendorff's *Biographisch-literarisches Handwörterbuch,* vols. I–V. His diss., *Beiträge zur Kenntniss des elektrischen Funkens,* was published by the University of Kiel (a copy is in the British Museum). The article based on the diss. and his subsequent papers in *Annalen der Physik,* 2nd ser., **103, 108, 112, 113, 115, 116,** form vol. CLXVI of Ostwald's Klassiker der exakten Wissenschaften, T. Des Coudres, ed. (Leipzig, 1908), which also contains a portrait.

II. SECONDARY LITERATURE. Obituaries are A. von Oettingen, in *Berichte der königlichen sächsischen Gesellschaft der Wissenschaften,* **70** (1918), 353; T. Des Coudres, in *Physikalische Zeitschrift,* **19** (1918), 393; and G. von Eichhorn, in *Jahrbuch der drahtlosen Telegraphie,* **13** (1918/1919), 345. An appreciation on the centenary of his birth by W. Dudensing is in *Hochfrequenztechnik und Elektroakustik,* **39** (1932), 77. For the subsequent history of Poggendorff's bibliography, see *Isis,* **57** (1966), 389.

CHARLES SÜSSKIND

FÉE, ANTOINE-LAURENT-APOLLINAIRE (*b.* Ardentes, France, 7 November 1789; *d.* Paris, France, 21 May 1874), *botany.*

From 1809 to 1815 Fée was a pharmacist with the French army, mostly in Spain. For about nine years he operated his own pharmacy in Paris, but in 1825 he resumed his military career and in succeeding years received appointments to the teaching staffs of military hospitals in Lille, Paris, and Strasbourg. While in Strasbourg, he earned an M.D. degree from the Faculty of Medicine in 1833 and shortly thereafter obtained a professorship of botany at that institution. Fée had many interests—literature and the humanities, natural history, pharmacy—but botany remained his chief preoccupation throughout his life. In 1824 he was elected to membership in the Paris Academy of Medicine, and in 1874 he became president of the Société Botanique de France.

Fée's major contribution was to cryptogamic botany and, to a lesser extent, plant physiology. His most ambitious work was an extensive descriptive study of ferns published in eleven memoirs between 1844 and 1866. This investigation won praise from Adolphe Brongniart (1868), who characterized it as "un travail considérable," although he felt that Fée had relied too heavily on veins in differentiating genera. In plant physiology Fée conducted research on movement in plants, especially as such movements were affected by light. Also noteworthy was his work on lichens and cryptogams occurring on medicinal barks imported into France, such as cinchona, angostura, and cascarilla. His early enthusiasm for classical literature prompted him to write about the plants mentioned by Vergil, Theocritus, Pliny, and other literary figures of antiquity.

Among Fée's publications were a number of biographies of prominent botanists. During the last few years of his life, Fée's botanical investigations were concerned mainly with the cryptogams of Brazil.

BIBLIOGRAPHY

I. Original Works. Fée's writings include *Flore de Virgile* . . . (Paris, 1822); *Essai sur les cryptogames des écorces exotiques officinales* (Paris, 1824; supp. and rev., 1837); *Méthode lichénographique et genera* . . . (Paris, 1824); *Cours d'histoire naturelle pharmaceutique* . . ., 2 vols. (Paris, 1828); *Mémoires sur la famille des fougères,* 11 pts. (Strasbourg-Paris, 1844–1866), repr. as no. 52 of Historia Naturalis Classica (Codicote, England–New York, 1966); *Cryptogames vasculaires du Brésil* (Strasbourg, 1869; supp. and revs., Paris-Nancy, 1872–1873). For a comprehensive listing of Fée's publications in botany and other fields, see *Bulletin. Société botanique de France,* **21** (1874), 173–178.

II. Secondary Literature. For an evaluation of Fée's work on ferns, see A. T. Brongniart, *Rapport sur les progrès de la botanique phytographique* . . . (Paris, 1868), pp. 39–41; Fée's research in plant physiology is described by P. E. S. Duchartre, *Rapport sur les progrès de la botanique physiologique* . . . (Paris, 1868), pp. 343 ff. Biographical material about Fée is in J. F. C. Hoefer, ed., *Nouvelle biographie générale* . . ., XVII (Paris, 1858), 255–259. See also A. Balland, *Les pharmaciens militaires français* (Paris, 1913), pp. 169–171, 302–304, and "Quelques pensées et quelques opinions littéraires de Fée," in *Bulletin de la Société d'histoire de la pharmacie,* **4** (1926), 314–315; *Bulletin. Société botanique de France,* **21** (1874), 168–178; and P. Durrieu, "Les goûts archéologiques d'un pharmacien militaire de l'armée française en Espagne sous le Premier Empire," in *Journal des savants,* n.s. **13** (1915), 364–373.

Alex Berman

FEIGL, GEORG (*b.* Hamburg, Germany, 13 October 1890; *d.* Wechselburg, Germany, 25 April 1945), *mathematics.*

Feigl was the son of Georg Feigl, an importer, and Maria Pinl, from Bohemia. He attended the Johanneum in Hamburg and began to study mathematics and physics at the University of Jena in 1909. A severe chronic stomach disorder forced him to interrupt his studies several times, and he did not finish them until 1918, when he received the doctorate with a dissertation on conformal mapping that was supervised by Paul Koebe. In 1919 Feigl became a teaching assistant to Erhard Schmidt, a well-known mathematician at the University of Berlin. Schmidt was the scientist who most influenced Feigl and also developed his gift for teaching. Generations of students in mathematics at the University of Berlin took the introductory course "Einführung in die höhere Mathematik," which Feigl created and which after his death was published, in enlarged form, as a textbook (1953) by Hans Rohrbach.

In 1925 Feigl married Maria Fleischer, daughter of Paul Fleischer, an economist and member of the Reichstag. In 1927 he became assistant professor and in 1933 associate professor at the University of Berlin. From 1928 to 1935 he was, by appointment of the Prussian Academy of Sciences in Berlin, the managing editor of the *Jahrbuch über die Fortschritte der Mathematik,* at that time the only periodical that reviewed papers on mathematics.

Feigl's field of research was geometry, especially the foundations of geometry and topology. But his scientific activity was rather limited because of his illness, and he soon had to choose between research and teaching. His talents led Feigl to devote himself to a reform of the teaching of mathematics. He became a leading member of the National Council of

German Mathematical Societies, and it was essentially through him that the new fundamental concepts of Felix Klein and David Hilbert and the modern mode of mathematical thinking based on axioms and structures were introduced into universities and even high schools.

In 1935 Feigl was called as full professor to the University of Breslau. There during World War II he formed a computing team that worked for the German Aeronautic Research Institute. In January 1945, when the Russians marched into Breslau, he moved with his team to the castle of Graf Schönburg at Wechselburg, Saxony, near Chemnitz (now Karl-Marx-Stadt). There it proved impossible to maintain his necessary medical supervision, a circumstance that led to Feigl's death a few months later.

BIBLIOGRAPHY

Feigl's writings include "Elementare Anordnungssätze der Geometrie," in *Jahresbericht der Deutschen Mathematikervereinigung,* **33** (1924), 2–24; "Zum Archimedesschen Axiom," in *Mathematische Zeitschrift,* **25** (1926), 590–601; "Eigenschaften der einfachen stetigen Kurven," *ibid.,* **27** (1927), 162–168; "Fixpunktsätze für spezielle n-dimensionale Mannigfaltigkeiten," in *Mathematische Annalen,* **98** (1927–1928), 355–398; "Erfahrungen über die mathematische Vorbildung der Mathematik-Studierenden des 1. Semesters," in *Jahresbericht der Deutschen Mathematikervereinigung,* **37** (1928), 187–199; "Geschichtliche Entwicklung der Topologie," *ibid.,* 273–286, repr. in the series Wege der Forschung, vol. CLXXVII (Darmstadt, in press); "Das Unendliche im Schulunterricht," in *Zeitschrift für mathematischen und naturwissenschaftlichen Unterricht,* **60** (1929), 385–393; "Der Übergang von der Schule zur Hochschule," in *Jahresbericht der Deutschen Mathematikervereinigung,* **47** (1937), 80–88; "Ausbildungsplan für Lehramtsanwärter in der Fächern reine Mathematik, angewandte Mathematik und Physik," in *Deutsche Mathematik,* **4** (1939), 98–108, 135–136, written with Georg Hamel; "Erfahrungen über das Mathematikstudium der Lehramtsanwärter nach der neuen Ausbildungsordnung," *ibid.,* **6** (1942), 467–471. His textbook is *Einführung in die höhere Mathematik,* Hans Rohrbach, ed. (Berlin-Göttingen-Heidelberg, 1953).

Some biographical information may be found in *Neue deutsche Biographie,* V (1961), 57.

HANS ROHRBACH

FEJÉR, LIPÓT (*b.* Pécs, Hungary, 9 February 1880; *d.* Budapest, Hungary, 15 October 1959), *mathematics.*

Fejér became interested in mathematics while in the higher grades of the Gymnasium, and in 1897 he won a prize in one of the first mathematical competitions held in Hungary. From 1897 to 1902 he studied mathematics and physics at the universities of Budapest and Berlin. During the academic year 1899–1900 H. A. Schwarz directed his attention, through a suggestion made by C. Neumann concerning Dirichlet's problem, to the theory of Fourier series. Later in 1900 Fejér published, in the *Comptes rendus* of the Paris Academy, the fundamental summation theorem that bears his name and was also the basis of his doctoral dissertation at Budapest (1902). After participating in mathematical seminars in Göttingen and Paris, he taught at the University of Budapest from 1902 to 1905 and at that of Kolozsvár (now Cluj, Rumania) from 1905 to 1911. He was professor of higher analysis at the University of Budapest from 1911 until his death. Collaborating with F. and M. Riesz, A. Haar, G. Pólya, G. Szegö, O. Szász, and other mathematicians of international rank, Fejér became the head of the most successful Hungarian school of analysis.

Fejér was a vice-chairman of the International Congress of Mathematicians held at Cambridge in 1912. In 1933 he and Niels Bohr, two of the four European scientists invited to the Chicago World's Fair, were awarded honorary doctorates by Brown University. Fejér was elected to the Hungarian Academy of Sciences in 1908 and was also a member of several foreign academies and scientific societies. Besides receiving a number of state and academic prizes for his work, he was honorary chairman of the Bolyai Mathematical Society from its founding and the holder of an honorary doctorate from Eötvös University, Budapest (1950).

Fejér's main works deal with harmonic analysis. His classic theorem on (C, 1) summability of trigonometric Fourier series (1900) not only gave a new direction to the theory of orthogonal expansions but also, through significant applications, became a starting point for the modern general theory of divergent series and singular integrals. Through a Tauberian theorem of G. H. Hardy's the convergence theory of Fourier series was considerably affected by Fejér's theorem as well; it is closely connected with Weierstrass' approximation theorems and with the more advanced theory of power series and harmonics (potential theory), and makes possible a number of analogues for related series, such as Laplace series. In 1910 Fejér found a new method of investigating the singularities of Fourier series that was suitable for a unified discussion of various types of divergence phenomena. These results were continued and generalized in several directions by Fejér himself, by Lebesgue (1905), by M. Riesz and S. Chapman (1909–1911), by Hardy and Littlewood (1913), by T. Carleman (1921), and others.

Fejér's contributions to approximation theory and the constructive theory of functions are of great importance. In 1918 he solved Runge's problem on complex Lagrange interpolation relating to an arbitrary Jordan curve, and in the following decades he enriched the field of real Lagrange and Hermite interpolation and mechanical quadrature by introducing new procedures. His work in mechanical quadrature produced wide response in the literature (Akhiezer, Erdös, Grünwald, Natanson, Pólya, J. A. Shohat, Szegö, and Turán, among others). As for Fejér's results in complex analysis, particular stress may still be laid on a joint paper with Carathéodory (1907), of which the basic ideas influenced considerably the literature on entire functions, and a new standard proof of the fundamental theorem of conformal mappings, found in 1922 with F. Riesz.

BIBLIOGRAPHY

I. ORIGINAL WORKS. Fejér's collected works, with bilingual comments in Hungarian and German, are *Fejér Lipót Összegyüjtött Munkái / Leopold Fejér, Gesammelte Arbeiten,* 2 vols. (Budapest, 1970). The summation theorem was first printed as "Sur les fonctions bornées et intégrables," in *Comptes rendus hebdomadaires des séances de l'Académie des sciences,* **131** (1900), 984–987; the author's name is here printed incorrectly as "Tejér."

II. SECONDARY LITERATURE. The proof found with F. Riesz was published (with the permission of the authors) in T. Rado, "Über die Fundamentalabbildung schlichter Gebiete," in *Acta litterarum ac scientiarum R. Univertatis hungarica Francisco-Josephina,* **1** (1922), 240–251. See also C. Carathéodory, "Bemerkungen zu dem Existenztheorem der konformen Abbildung," in *Bulletin of the Calcutta Mathematical Society,* **20** (1930), 125–134.

Other works on Fejér are Émile Borel, *Leçons sur les séries divergentes* (Paris, 1901), p. 88, n.; the article in *Encyclopaedia Brittanica,* 12th ed. (1922), XXXI, 877; and P. Turán, "Fejér Lipót matematikai munkássága" ("The Mathematical Work of Lipót Fejér"), in *Matematikai lapok,* **1** (1950), 160–170.

An obituary by P. Szász, G. Szegö, and P. Turán is in *Magyar tudományos akadémia III osztályának közleményei,* **10** (1960), 103–148; and in *Matematikai lapok,* **11** (1960), 8–18, 225–228.

MIKLÓS MIKOLÁS

FENNEMAN, NEVIN MELANCTHON (*b.* Lima, Ohio, 26 December 1865; *d.* Cincinnati, Ohio, 4 July 1945), *geology.*

Fenneman was the son of William Henry Fenneman, a Reformed Church clergyman, and Rebecca Oldfather. He attended Heidelberg College in Tiffin, Ohio, and then taught high school. He joined the faculty of the Colorado State Normal School in 1892, and in 1893 he married Sarah Alice Glisan, also a faculty member. In 1900 Fenneman undertook graduate work under T. C. Chamberlin, whom he had met with C. R. Van Hise while doing fieldwork in Wisconsin ten years before. Meanwhile, a Harvard summer course in 1895 had brought him under the influence of William Morris Davis. At the University of Chicago he was also a protégé of R. D. Salisbury, receiving the Ph.D. in the near-record time of three semesters.

Returning to Colorado in 1902, Fenneman served as professor of geology at the University of Colorado, where he studied the Boulder oil fields, which were opening at this time. After three semesters at Colorado, Fenneman was called to the geology faculty of the University of Wisconsin, where he taught for four years. Here he began pioneering work in applying regionally the scientific principles of landform study.

In 1907 Fenneman went to the University of Cincinnati, where he started a department of geology and geography. His tenure at Cincinnati may be said to have ended only with his death. Even during his eight years as professor emeritus (he retired as professor of geology and head of the department in 1937, at the age of seventy-three) he continued his studies and publications and taught advanced courses. He spent every summer with geological parties in the field.

From 1900 to 1902 Fenneman was geologist with the Wisconsin Geological and Natural History Survey; from 1906 to 1908, with the Illinois State Geological Survey; and from 1914 to 1916, with the Ohio Geological Survey. He served with the U.S. Geological Survey as assistant geologist (1901–1919), associate geologist (1919–1924), and geologist (for a period from 1924 on), publishing a steady flow of papers and reports. These included the most famous work of his career, the map "Physiographic Divisions of the United States" (1916), which was the original for all such maps and was adopted by the U.S. Geological Survey and all other government agencies, as well as serving as the basis of regional work in the United States and university courses on the subject.

Primarily a geographer who approached his subject from the point of view of the college teacher of introductory courses, Fenneman had long been concerned with the search for classificatory principles in what was largely a descriptive field. By 1915 the proposal for a physiographic and topographic classification of the United States based on natural subdivisions led to the formation of a committee consisting of Eliot Blackwelder, Marius R. Campbell, Douglas Johnson, and F. E. Matthes. It was headed by Fenneman, who went on leave to work in Washington for the year. Fenneman published the *Physiography of Western United States* (New York, 1931) and *Physiography of Eastern United States* (New York, 1938). The two works were the definitive genetic description and analysis of the physiography of the United States, subdivision by subdivision.

His fields of research also included the action of waves and currents on shores and surveys of the Wisconsin lakes and the oil fields of Colorado, Missouri, and Ohio.

Fenneman's scientific work brought him many honors, among them the presidency of the American Association of Geographers in 1918 and of the Geological Society of America in 1935. In 1938 he was awarded the gold medal of the Geographical Society of Chicago "for eminent achievements in physiography."

His colleagues regarded him as "the last of the great trio of American physiographers—Davis, Fenneman, and Johnson—. . . who . . . developed a rigid application of logic to the study of land forms and their evolution" (Raymond Walters, "Memorial," p. 142).

BIBLIOGRAPHY

See Walter Bucher, "Memorial to Nevin M. Fenneman," in *Proceedings. Geological Society of America.* Annual Report for 1945, pp. 215–228, which has a complete bibliography; and Raymond Walters, "Obituary. Nevin M. Fenneman," in *Science,* **102** (10 Aug. 1945), 142–143.

GEORGE B. BARBOUR

FENNER, CLARENCE NORMAN (*b.* near Clifton, New Jersey, 19 July 1870; *d.* near Clifton, 24 December 1949), *petrology, volcanology.*

Fenner was the son of William Griff Fenner and Elmina Jane Carpenter Fenner. He received the degree of Engineer of Mines from the School of Mines of Columbia University in 1892. After fifteen years of experience in the field he returned to Columbia to earn the M.A. in 1909 and the Ph.D. in 1910. On graduation he joined the staff of the Geophysical Laboratory, Carnegie Institution of Washington, remaining there until his retirement in 1938. Fenner then returned to his childhood home, where he lived with his brother Herbert and continued his petrological studies until his death.

Fenner's principal contributions to petrology are his experimental determination of the thermal stability of the various polymorphs of silica; field description, chemical analysis, and structural and theoretical study of the great eruption of Mt. Katmai, in Alaska

(1912); recognition of a type of basalt crystallization leading to iron enrichment; and a physicochemical theory of rock solution and of ore deposition by gaseous emanations. In addition he investigated uranium and thorium minerals bearing on the age of the earth and devised chemical methods for their separation and analysis. During World War I, Fenner was in charge of the optical glass plant of the Spencer Lens Company at Hamburg, New York. He succeeded in putting optical glass on a production basis, thereby helping to establish in the United States that industry which had formerly been reliant on Germany.

In the laboratory Fenner investigated silica, the principal constituent of silicates and of the earth's crust. He showed that the lowest-temperature form of SiO_2—quartz—inverts to tridymite at $870° \pm 10°$ C. and that tridymite inverts to cristobalite at $1470° \pm 10°$ C. He found that the velocity of transformation of one form of silica into another was very sluggish and that one stable form did not always pass directly into the next most stable form, but progressed through successive steps. Fenner attributed the appearance of tridymite and cristobalite in some natural occurrences to this process. The transformations in the laboratory were speeded up by the use of a sodium tungstate flux. Although it has been suggested that this technique may have led to contamination of the material and hence to incorrect values for pure SiO_2, the values of transformation ascertained by Fenner have been confirmed and accepted. His concern with equilibrium, high precision, and detailed definition of products—as well as the application of laboratory data to natural occurrences—set a sound foundation for subsequent study of all silicate systems.

Fenner was a member of the 1919 National Geographic Society expedition to Mt. Katmai, Alaska, to study the violent eruption of 1912, believed to be the second largest energy release by a volcano in historic time. In 1923 he returned to the Katmai region as the leader of an expedition sponsored by the Geophysical Laboratory, Carnegie Institution of Washington.

The principal deduction that Fenner drew from these field studies and subsequent laboratory work was that assimilation of andesitic wall rock by rhyolitic magma had proceeded by means of escaping volatile substances whose exothermic reactions underwent continually increasing acceleration which finally led to explosion (1950, p. 604). The large volume of ejecta was laid down mainly in the Valley of Ten Thousand Smokes as dust and gas mixtures—incandescent tuff flows—issuing through fissures in the valley from a sill or very similar body of magma in the underlying sedimentary strata. The many fumaroles, after which the valley was named, were presumed by Fenner to be due to the continued evolution of gases from that body of magma.

Chemical analyses of the various rocks carried out by Fenner demonstrated that the quantitative variation of each chemical oxide is essentially linear for the series of intermediate rocks. He regarded the nearly linear relationship as evidence of the primary role of assimilation in the formation of rocks intermediate in composition between the end members andesite and rhyolite. On a much later occasion he agreed in part with Norman L. Bowen that the deviations from linearity for some of the rocks suggest that crystal differentiation had played some part in the production of the Katmai rocks.

Fenner's emphasis on assimilative processes was also apparent in his study (1938) of a rhyolite flow that he described as following a valley in an eroded basalt surface on Gardiner River, Yellowstone Park, Wyoming. The older basalts were impregnated and mobilized, according to Fenner, by the rhyolite magma, and the compositions of the resulting soaked rocks were represented by straight lines between the basalt and rhyolite. It was his belief that in their origin in the depths of the earth, the two magmas would have formed a conjugate pair of immiscible liquids (1948, p. 500). (It is interesting to note that at an early stage of his field studies, in 1914, he had been impressed by the apparent chemical attack of magma injected into country rock in New Jersey.)

Fenner assigned volatiles a major role in the assimilation process, a view no doubt acquired from his experimental work with George W. Morey in water-containing systems (1917). He also assigned a primary role to gaseous emanations in transporting metals from a magma into surrounding rocks, thereby producing some types of ore deposits (1933). Further concern with volatiles led to studies (1934, 1936) in the geyser basins of Yellowstone Park, Wyoming, where he deduced the manner in which emanations modified the composition of the rocks through which they had passed and were in turn modified. He made a major contribution to the understanding of ash flow mechanics through his emphasis of their high mobility because of entrapped gases.

Fenner was a leading antagonist of Norman L. Bowen's prevailing theory that magmatic fractionation and differentiation lead to silica and alkali enrichment. His own arguments led Fenner to believe that differentiation of magma proceeded in the direction of iron enrichment, producing ferrogabbro, not granite. Later work showed that both Bowen and Fenner were correct in their views, if the partial pres-

sure of oxygen under which the magma crystallizes is taken into consideration. The "Fenner trend" obtains where the partial pressure of oxygen is relatively low in a magma, whereas the "Bowen trend" obtains if the same magma crystallizes under a relatively high partial pressure of oxygen. The "Fenner trend" was particularly well illustrated in the layered intrusion of Skaergaard, Greenland. Fortunately, both men remained friends; their discussion of the subject in debate was carried out only in print after thoughtful review.

Although Fenner was most experienced as a field petrologist, he had a deep understanding of the limitations of experimental studies and theory that purported to elucidate natural phenomena. He applied the data on simplified systems bearing on rocks and related theoretical deductions with great caution, relying mainly on geological field relations and petrographic observations. Even his own strong support of the roles played by gaseous emanations and by assimilation was tempered by the belief that other processes may be of quantitative importance.

Fenner was elected, with Norman L. Bowen and Joseph P. Iddings, to the Petrologists' Club of Washington in the year of its founding, 1910. Although he was a quiet and unassuming man, the records of the club indicate that he was not reluctant to debate the issues with other petrological leaders such as Whitman Cross, Esper S. Larsen, Jr., Frederick E. Wright, Adolf Knopf, and Henry S. Washington.

BIBLIOGRAPHY

Fenner published widely, on a variety of subjects. On silica polymorphs, see "The Stability Relations of the Silica Minerals," in *American Journal of Science,* 4 (1913), 331–384; and "The Relations Between Tridymite and Cristobalite," in *Transactions of the Society of Glass Technology,* 3 (1919), 116–125.

The Katmai area of Alaska is discussed in "The Katmai Region, Alaska, and the Great Eruption of 1912," in *Journal of Geology,* 28 (1920), 569–606; "The Origin and Mode of Emplacement of the Great Tuff Deposit in the Valley of Ten Thousand Smokes," in *National Geographic Society, Contributed Technical Papers,* 1 (1923), 1–74; "Earth Movements Accompanying the Katmai Eruption," in *Journal of Geology,* 34 (1926), 673–772; and "The Chemical Kinetics of the Katmai Explosion," in *American Journal of Science,* 248 (1950), 593–627, 697–725.

Two articles on the Gardiner River area of Wyoming are "Contact Relations Between Rhyolite and Basalt on Gardiner River, Yellowstone Park," in *Bulletin of the Geological Society of America,* 49 (1938), 1441–1484; and "Rhyolite Basalt Complex on Gardiner River, Yellowstone

Park, Wyoming: A Discussion," *ibid.,* **55** (1944), 1081–1096.

Additional field studies are "The Watchung Basalt and the Paragenesis of Its Zeolites and Other Secondary Minerals," in *Annals of the New York Academy of Sciences,* **20** (1910), 93–187; "The Mode of Formation of Certain Gneisses in the Highlands of New Jersey," in *Journal of Geology,* **22** (1914), 594–612, 694–702; and "Pleistocene Climate and Topography of the Arequipa Region, Peru," in *Bulletin of the Geological Society of America,* **59** (1948), 895–917.

The basalt fractionation trend is discussed in "The Crystallization of Basalts," in *American Journal of Science,* **18** (1929), 225–253; "The Residual Liquids of Crystallizing Magmas," in *Mining Magazine,* **22** (1931), 539–560; and "A View of Magmatic Differentiation," in *Journal of Geology,* **45** (1937), 158–168.

On immiscibility in magmas, see "Immiscibility in Igneous Magmas," in *American Journal of Science,* **246** (1948), 465–502.

Articles on the role of volatiles include "The Ternary System $H_2O—K_2SiO_3—SiO_2$," in *Journal of the American Chemical Society,* **39** (1917), 1173–1229, chemical study by George W. Morey, microscopic study by Fenner; "Hydrothermal Metamorphism in Geyser-Basins of Yellowstone Park, as Shown by Deep Drilling," in *Transactions of the American Geophysical Union,* **15** (1934), 240–243; and "Bore-Hole Investigations in Yellowstone Park," in *Journal of Geology,* **44** (1936), 225–315.

Ore deposits are discussed in "Study of a Contact Metamorphic Ore-Deposit. The Dolores Mine at Matehuala, S. L. P., Mexico," in *Economic Geology,* **7** (1912), 444–484, written with J. E. Spurr and G. H. Garrey; "Pneumatolytic Processes in the Formation of Minerals and Ores," in American Institute of Mining and Metallurgical Engineers, *Ore Deposits of the Western States* (New York, 1933), pp. 58–106; and "The Nature of the Ore-Forming Fluid: A Discussion," in *Economic Geology,* **35** (1940), 883–904.

On the optical glass industry, see "The Technique of Optical Glass Smelting," in *Journal of the American Ceramic Society,* **2** (1919), 102–145; and "The Use of Optical Pyrometers for Control of Optical Glass Furnaces," in *Bulletin of the American Institute of Mining and Metallurgical Engineers,* no. 151 (1919), 1001–1011, and in *Pyrometry* (New York, 1920), pp. 495–505.

HATTEN S. YODER, JR.

FERCHAULT, RENÉ ANTOINE. *See* **Réaumur, René Antoine Ferchault de.**

FERGUSON, JAMES (*b.* near Rothiemay, Banffshire, Scotland, 25 April 1710; *d.* London, England, 16 November 1776), *astronomy, instrument making.*

Son of tenant farmer John Ferguson and his wife, Elspet Lobban, James was the second of six children. His formal education consisted of three months at Keith Grammar School in 1717. While working at a variety of domestic jobs from 1720 until 1735, he mastered the elements of surveying, horology, astronomy, and portraiture. In 1739 he married Isabella Wilson, and they lived in Edinburgh until sailing for London in 1743.

Colin Maclaurin discovered Ferguson's mechanical abilities and introduced him to Martin Folkes, who encouraged Ferguson to lecture to the Royal Society about his astronomical contrivances. A skilled designer of clocks and planispheres (as well as a "solar eclipsareon"), he became an accomplished public lecturer and expounder of Newtonian ideas, especially after the publication of his *Astronomy Explained Upon Sir Isaac Newton's Principles* (1756), which went through seventeen editions. He lectured extensively in London and the provinces (including Bath, Bristol, Derby, Leeds, Liverpool, and Newcastle) and was unofficial "popularizer in residence" to the court of George III. Elected fellow of the Royal Society in 1763, Ferguson spent his last years in London, pained by an unhappy marriage and the disgrace of the prostitution of his only daughter. He wrote a short, partial autobiography, which served as the preface to his *Select Mechanical Exercises* (1773).

Ferguson's scientific work, while both careful and extensive, was neither original nor distinguished. His forte was popularization, and his confessedly weak mathematical background stood him in good stead in writing books for the lay public, particularly his classic *Young Gentleman's and Lady's Astronomy* (1768). He published several technical papers in the *Philosophical Transactions* on eclipses, celestial globes, hygrometers, and horological instruments. His models of the planetary system were classics of engineering design whose accuracy far surpassed anything previously available. Several of his books were used in British grammar schools as late as the 1840's.

BIBLIOGRAPHY

I. ORIGINAL WORKS. Ferguson's major works include *The Use of a New Orrery* (London, 1746); *A Brief Description of the Solar System* (Norwich, 1753); *An Idea of the Material Universe* (London, 1754); *Astronomy Explained Upon Sir Isaac Newton's Principles* (London, 1756); *Lectures on Select Subjects in Mechanics, Hydrostatics, Pneumatics, and Optics* (London, 1760); *Analysis of a Course of Lectures* (London, 1761); *Syllabus of a Course of Lectures* (Edinburgh, 1768); *The Young Gentleman's and Lady's Astronomy* (London, 1768); *An Introduction to Electricity* (London, 1770); and *Select Mechanical Exercises* (London, 1773).

II. SECONDARY LITERATURE. F. Henderson, *Life of James Ferguson* (Edinburgh, 1867) contains Ferguson's short autobiographical notice as well as a very useful discussion of Ferguson's many tracts and shorter works. Some useful information is also found in H. Mayhew, *The Story of the Peasant-Boy Philosopher* (London, 1857).

Laurens Laudan

FERMAT, PIERRE DE (*b.* Beaumont-de-Lomagne, France, 20 August 1601; *d.* Castres, France, 12 January 1665), *mathematics.*

Factual details concerning Fermat's private life are quite sparse.[1] He apparently spent his childhood and early school years in his birthplace, where his father, Dominique Fermat, had a prosperous leather business and served as second consul of the town. His uncle and godfather, Pierre Fermat, was also a merchant. To the family's firm financial position Fermat's mother, Claire de Long, brought the social status of the parliamentary *noblesse de robe.* Hence, his choice of law as his profession followed naturally from the social milieu into which he was born. Having received a solid classical secondary education locally, Fermat may have attended the University of Toulouse, although one can say with certainty only that he spent some time in Bordeaux toward the end of the 1620's before finally receiving the degree of Bachelor of Civil Laws from the University of Orleans on 1 May 1631.

Returning to Toulouse, where some months earlier he had purchased the offices of *conseiller* and *commissaire aux requêtes* in the local *parlement,* Fermat married his mother's cousin, Louise de Long, on 1 June 1631. Like his in-laws, Fermat enjoyed as *parlementaire* the rank and privileges of the *noblesse de robe;* in particular he was entitled to add the "de" to his name, which he occasionally did. Fermat's marriage contract, the price he paid for his offices, and several other documents attest to the financial security he enjoyed throughout his life.

Five children issued from Fermat's marriage. The oldest, Clément-Samuel, apparently was closest to his father. As a lawyer he inherited his father's offices in 1665 and later undertook the publication of his father's mathematical papers.[2] Fermat's other son, Jean, served as archdeacon of Fimarens. The oldest daughter, Claire, married; her two younger sisters, Catherine and Louise, took holy orders. These outward details of Fermat's family life suggest that it followed the standard pattern for men of his social status. The direct male line ended with the death of Clément-Samuel's son, Jean-François, from whom Claire's grandson inherited the offices originally bought by Fermat.

As a lawyer and *parlementaire* in Toulouse, Fermat seems to have benefited more from the high rate of mortality among his colleagues than from any outstanding talents of his own. On 16 January 1638 he rose to the position of *conseiller aux enquêtes* and in 1642 entered the highest councils of the *parlement:* the criminal court and then the Grand Chamber. In 1648 he acted as chief spokesman for the *parlement* in negotiations with the chancellor of France, Pierre Séguier. However, Fermat's letters to Séguier and to his physician and confidant, Marin Cureau de La Chambre,[3] suggest that Fermat's performance in office was often less than satisfactory; and a confidential report by the *intendant* of Languedoc to Colbert in 1664 refers to Fermat in quite deprecatory terms. A staunch Catholic, Fermat served also—again probably by reason of seniority—as member and then president of the Chambre de l'Édit, which had jurisdiction over suits between Huguenots and Catholics and which convened in the Huguenot stronghold of Castres.

In addition to his fame as a mathematician, Fermat enjoyed a modest reputation as a classical scholar. Apparently equally fluent in French, Italian, Spanish, Latin, and Greek, he dabbled in philological problems and the composition of Latin poetry (see appendixes to his *Oeuvres,* I).

Except for an almost fatal attack of the plague in 1652, Fermat seems to have enjoyed good health until the years immediately preceding his death. He died in Castres, two days after having signed his last *arrêt* for the Chambre de l'Édit there. At first buried in Castres, his remains were brought back to the family vault in the Church of the Augustines in Toulouse in 1675.

The Development of Fermat's Mathematics. Fermat's letters and papers, most of them written after 1636 for friends in Paris, provide the few available hints regarding his development as a mathematician. From them one can infer that his stay in Bordeaux in the late 1620's most decisively shaped his approach to mathematics; almost all of his later achievements derived from research begun there. It was apparently in Bordeaux that Fermat studied in depth the works of François Viète. From Viète he took the new symbolic algebra and theory of equations that served as his basic research tools. More important, however, Viète's concept of algebra as the "analytic art" and the program of research implicit in that concept largely guided Fermat's choice of problems and the manner in which he treated them. Fermat himself viewed his work as a continuation of the Viètan tradition.

From Viète, Fermat inherited the idea of symbolic algebra as a formal language or tool uniting the realms of geometry and arithmetic (number theory). An algebraic equation had meaning in both realms, depending only on whether the unknowns denoted line segments or numbers. Moreover, Viète's theory of equations had shifted attention away from solutions of specific equations to questions of the relationships between solutions and the structures of their parent equations or between the solutions of one equation and those of another. In his own study of the application of determinate equations to geometric constructions, Viète laid the groundwork for the algebraic study of solvability and constructibility. Fermat sought to build further on this foundation. An overall characteristic of his mathematics is the use of algebraic analysis to explore the relationships between problems and their solutions. Most of Fermat's research strove toward a "reduction analysis" by which a given problem could be reduced to another or identified with a class of problems for which the general solution was known. This "reduction analysis," constituted from the theory of equations, could be reversed in most cases to operate as a generator of families of solutions to problems.

At first Fermat, like Viète, looked to the Greek mathematicians for hints concerning the nature of mathematical analysis. Believing that the so-called "analytical" works cited by Pappus in book VII of the *Mathematical Collection,* most of which were no longer extant,[4] contained the desired clues, Fermat followed Viète and others in seeking to restore those lost texts, such as Apollonius' *Plane Loci* (*Oeuvres,* I, 3–51) and Euclid's *Porisms* (*Oeuvres,* I, 76–84). Another supposed source of insight was Diophantus' *Arithmetica,* to which Fermat devoted a lifetime of study. These ancient sources, together with the works of Archimedes, formed the initial elements in a clear pattern of development that Fermat's research followed. Taking his original problem from the classical sources, Fermat attacked it with the new algebraic techniques at his disposal. His solution, however, usually proved more general than the problem that had inspired it. By skillful application of the theory of equations in the form of a "reduction analysis," Fermat would reformulate the problem in its most general terms, often defining thereby a class of problems; in many cases the new problem structure lost all contact with its Greek forebear.

In Fermat's papers algebra as the "analytic art" achieved equal status with the traditional geometrical mode of ancient mathematics. With few exceptions he presented only the algebraic derivation of his results, dispensing with their classical synthetic proofs. Convinced that the latter could always be provided, Fermat seldom attempted to carry them out, with the result in several cases that he failed to see how the use of algebra had led to the introduction of concepts quite foreign to the classical tradition.

In large part Fermat's style of exposition characterized the unfinished nature of his papers, most of them brief essays or letters to friends. He never wrote for publication. Indeed, adamantly refusing to edit his work or to publish it under his own name, Fermat thwarted several efforts by others to make his results available in print. Showing little interest in completed work, he freely sent papers to friends without keeping copies for himself. Many results he merely entered in the margins of his books; e.g., his "Observations on Diophantus," a major part of his work on number theory, was published by his son on the basis of the marginalia in Fermat's copy of the Bachet edition of the *Arithmetica.* Some other work slipped into print during Fermat's lifetime, although only by virtue of honoring his demand for anonymity. This demand allows no clear or obvious explanation. Fermat knew of his reputation and he valued it. He seemed to enjoy the intellectual combat of the several controversies to which he was a party. Whatever the reason, anonymity and refusal to publish robbed him of recognition for many striking achievements and toward the end of his life led to a growing isolation from the main currents of research.

Fermat's name slipped into relative obscurity during the eighteenth century. In the mid-nineteenth century, however, renewed interest in number theory recalled him and his work to the attention of mathematicians and historians of mathematics. Various projects to publish his extant papers culminated in the four-volume edition by Charles Henry and Paul Tannery, from which the extent and importance of Fermat's achievements in fields other than number theory became clear.

Analytic Geometry. By the time Fermat began corresponding with Mersenne and Roberval in the spring of 1636, he had already composed his "Ad locos planos et solidos isagoge" (*Ouevres,* I, 91–103), in which he set forth a system of analytic geometry almost identical with that developed by Descartes in the *Géométrie* of 1637. Despite their simultaneous appearance (Descartes's in print, Fermat's in circulated manuscript), the two systems stemmed from entirely independent research and the question of priority is both complex and unenlightening. Fermat received the first impetus toward his system from an attempt to reconstruct Apollonius' lost treatise *Plane Loci* (loci that are either straight lines or circles). His completed restoration, although composed in the traditional style of Greek geometry, nevertheless gives clear evidence that Fermat employed algebraic analysis in seeking demonstrations of the theorems listed by Pappus. This application of algebra, combined with the peculiar nature of a geometrical locus and the slightly different proof procedures required by locus demonstrations, appears to have revealed to Fermat that all of the loci discussed by Apollonius could be expressed in the form of indeterminate algebraic equations in two unknowns, and that the analysis of these equations by means of Viète's theory of equations led to crucial insights into the nature and construction of the loci. With this inspiration from the *Plane Loci,* Fermat then found in Apollonius' *Conics* that the *symptomata,* or defining properties, of the conic sections likewise could be expressed as indeterminate equations in two unknowns. Moreover, the standard form in which Apollonius referred the *symptomata* to the cone on which the conic sections were generated suggested to Fermat a standard geometrical framework in which to establish the correspondence between an equation and a curve. Taking a fixed line as axis and a fixed point on that line as origin, he measured the variable length of the first unknown, *A,* from the origin along the axis. The corresponding value of the second unknown, *E,* he constructed as a line length measured from the end point of the first unknown and erected at a fixed angle to the axis. The end points of the various lengths of the second unknown then generated a curve in the *A,E* plane.

Like Descartes, then, Fermat did not employ a coordinate system but, rather, a single axis with a moving ordinate; curves were not plotted, they were generated. Within the standard framework

> Whenever two unknown quantities are found in final equality, there results a locus [fixed] in place, and the end point of one of these unknown quantities describes a straight line or a curve ["Isagoge," *Oeuvres,* I, 91].

The crucial phrase in this keystone of analytic geometry is "fixed in place";[5] it sets the task of the remainder of Fermat's treatise. Dividing the general second-degree equation $Ax^2 + By^2 + Cxy + Dx + Ey + F = 0$ into seven canonical (irreducible) forms according to the possible values of the coefficients, Fermat shows how each canonical equation defines a curve: $Dx = Ey$ (straight line), $Cxy = F$ (equilat-

eral hyperbola), $Ax^2 \pm Cxy = By^2$ (straight lines), $Ax^2 = Ey$ (parabola), $F - Ax^2 = Ay^2$ (circle), $F - Ax^2 = By^2$ (ellipse), and $F + Ax^2 = By^2$ (axial hyperbola). In each case he demonstrates that the constants of the equation uniquely fix the curve defined by it, i.e., that they contain all the data necessary to construct the curve. The proof relies on the construction theorems set forth in Euclid's *Data* (for the straight line and circle, or "plane loci") or Apollonius' *Conics* (for the conic sections, or "solid loci"). In a corollary to each case Fermat employs Viète's theory of equations to establish the family of equations reducible to the canonical form and then shows how the reduction itself corresponds to a translation (or expansion) of the axis or the origin or to a change of angle between axis and ordinate. In the last theorem of the "Isagoge," for example, he reduces the equation $b^2 - 2x^2 = 2xy + y^2$ to the canonical form $2b^2 - u^2 = 2v^2$, where $u = \sqrt{2}x$ and $v = x + y$. Geometrically, the reduction shifts the orthogonal x,y system to a skew u,v system in which the u-axis forms a 45° angle with the x-axis and the v-ordinate is erected at a 45° angle on the u-axis. The curve, as Fermat shows, is a uniquely defined ellipse.

Although the analytic geometries of Descartes and Fermat are essentially the same, their presentations differed significantly. Fermat concentrated on the geometrical construction of the curves on the basis of their equations, relying heavily on the reader's knowledge of Viète's algebra to supply the necessary theory of equations. By contrast, Descartes slighted the matter of construction and devoted a major portion of his *Géométrie* to a new and more advanced theory of equations.

In the years following 1636, Fermat made some effort to pursue the implications of his system. In an appendix to the "Isagoge," he applied the system to the graphic solution of determinate algebraic equations, showing, for example, that any cubic or quartic equation could be solved graphically by means of a parabola and a circle. In his "De solutione problematum geometricorum per curvas simplicissimas et unicuique problematum generi proprie convenientes dissertatio tripartita" (*Oeuvres,* I, 118–131), he took issue with Descartes's classification of curves in the *Géométrie* and undertook to show that any determinate algebraic equation of degree $2n$ or $2n - 1$ could be solved graphically by means of curves determined by indeterminate equations of degree n.

In 1643, in a memoir entitled "Isagoge ad locos ad superficiem" (*Oeuvres,* I, 111–117), Fermat attempted to extend his plane analytic geometry to solids of revolution in space and perhaps thereby to restore the content of Euclid's *Surface Loci,* another

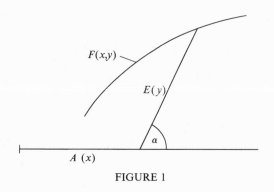

FIGURE 1

text cited by Pappus. The effort did not meet with success because he tried to reduce the three-dimensional problem to two dimensions by determining all possible traces resulting from the intersection of a given solid by an arbitrary plane. The system required, first of all, an elaborate catalog of the possible traces for various solids. Second, the manipulation of the equation of any trace for the purpose of deriving the parameters that uniquely determine the solid requires methods that lay beyond Fermat's reach; his technique could at best define the solid qualitatively. Third, the basic system of the 1636 "Isagoge," lacking the concept of coordinates referred to two fixed orthogonal axes, presented substantial hurdles to visualizing a three-dimensional correlate.

Although Fermat never found the geometrical framework for a solid analytic geometry, he nonetheless correctly established the algebraic foundation of such a system. In 1650, in his "Novus secundarum et ulterioris ordinis radicum in analyticis usus" (*Oeuvres*, I, 181–188), he noted that equations in one unknown determine point constructions; equations in two unknowns, locus constructions of plane curves; and equations in three unknowns, locus constructions of surfaces in space. The change in the criterion of the dimension of an equation—from its degree, where the Greeks had placed it, to the number of unknowns in it—was one of the most important conceptual developments of seventeenth-century mathematics.

The Method of Maxima and Minima. The method of maxima and minima, in which Fermat first established what later became the algorithm for obtaining the first derivative of an algebraic polynomial, also stemmed from the application of Viète's algebra to a problem in Pappus' *Mathematical Collection*. In a lemma to Apollonius' *Determinate Section*, Pappus sought to divide a given line in such a way that certain rectangles constructed on the segments bore a minimum ratio to one another,[6] noting that the ratio would be "singular." In carrying out the algebraic analysis of the problem, Fermat recognized that the division of the line for rectangles in a ratio greater than the minimum corresponded to a quadratic equation that would normally yield two equally satisfactory section points. A "singular" section point for the minimum ratio, he argued, must mean that the particular values of the constant quantities of the equation allow only a single repeated root as a solution.

Turning to a simpler example, Fermat considered the problem of dividing a given line in such a way that the product of the segments was maximized. The algebraic form of the problem is $bx - x^2 = c$, where b is the length of the given line and c is the product of the segments. If c is the maximum value of all possible products, then the equation can have only one (repeated) root. Fermat then sought the value for c in terms of b for which the equation yielded that (repeated) root. To this end he applied a method of Viète's theory of equations called "syncrisis," a method originally devised to determine the relationships between the roots of equations and their constant parameters. On the assumption that his equation had two distinct roots, x and y, Fermat set $bx - x^2 = c$ and $by - y^2 = c$, whence he obtained $b = x + y$ and $c = xy$. Taking these relationships to hold generally for any quadratic equation of the above form, he next considered what happened in the case of a repeated root, i.e., when $x = y$. Then, he found, $x = b/2$ and $c = b^2/4$. Hence, the maximum rectangle results from dividing the given line in half, and that maximum rectangle has an area equal to one-quarter of the square erected on the given line b.

Amending his method in the famous "Methodus ad disquirendam maximam et minimam" (*Oeuvres*, I, 133–136), written sometime before 1636, Fermat expressed the supposedly distinct roots as A and $A + E$ (that is, x and $x + y$), where E now represented the difference between the roots. In seeking, for example, the maximum value of the expression $bx^2 - x^3$, he proceeded as follows:

$$bx^2 - x^3 = M^3$$
$$b(x + y)^2 - (x + y)^3 = M^3,$$

whence $\quad 2bxy + by^2 - 3x^2y - 3xy^2 - y^3 = 0.$

Division by y yields the equation

$$2bx + by - 3x^2 - 3xy - y^2 = 0,$$

which relates the parameter b to two roots of the equation via one of the roots and their difference. The relation holds for any equation of the form $bx^2 - x^3 = M^3$, but when M^3 is a maximum the equation has a repeated root, i.e., $x = x + y$, or $y = 0$. Hence, for that maximum, $2bx - 3x^2 = 0$, or $x = 2b/3$ and $M^3 = 4b^3/27$.

Fermat's method of maxima and minima, which is clearly applicable to any polynomial $P(x)$, originally rested on purely finitistic algebraic foundations.[7] It assumed, counterfactually, the inequality of two equal roots in order to determine, by Viète's theory of equations, a relation between those roots and one of the coefficients of the polynomial, a relation that was fully general. This relation then led to an extreme-value solution when Fermat removed his counterfactual assumption and set the roots equal. Borrowing a term from Diophantus, Fermat called this counterfactual equality "adequality."

Although Pappus' remark concerning the "singularity" of extreme values provided the original inspiration for Fermat's method, it may also have prevented him from seeing all its implications. Oriented toward unique extreme values and dealing with specific problems that, taken from geometrical sources and never exceeding cubic expressions, failed to yield more than one geometrically meaningful solution, Fermat never recognized the distinction between global and local extreme values or the possibility of more than one such value. This block to an overall view of the problem of maxima and minima vitiates an otherwise brilliant demonstration of Fermat's method, which he wrote for Pierre Brûlard de St.-Martin in 1643 (*Oeuvres,* supp., 120–125) and which employs the sophisticated theory of equations of Descartes's *Géométrie.* There Fermat established what today is termed the "second derivative criterion" for the nature of an extreme value ($f''(x) < 0$ for a maximum, $f''(x) > 0$ for a minimum), although his lack of a general overview forestalled investigation of points of inflection ($f''(x) = 0$).

The original method of maxima and minima had two important corollaries. The first was the method of tangents[8] by which, given the equation of a curve, Fermat could construct the tangent at any given point on that curve by determining the length of the subtangent. Given some curve $y = f(x)$ and a point (a,b) on it, Fermat assumed the tangent to be drawn and

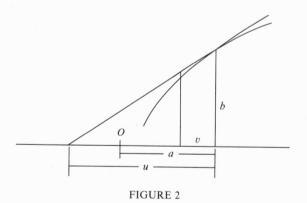

FIGURE 2

to cut off a subtangent of length u on the x-axis. Taking an arbitrary point on the tangent and denoting the difference between the abscissa of that point and the abscissa a by v, he counterfactually assumed that the ordinate to the point on the tangent was equal to the ordinate $f(a - v)$ to the curve, i.e., that the two ordinates were "adequal." It followed, then, from similar triangles that

$$\frac{b}{u} \approx \frac{f(a - v)}{u - v}.$$

Fermat removed the adequality, here denoted by $\approx$, by treating the difference v in the same manner as in the method of maxima and minima, i.e., by considering it as ultimately equal to zero. His method yields, in modern symbols, the correct result, $u = f(a)/f'(a)$, and, like the parent method of maxima and minima, it can be applied generally.

From the method of maxima and minima Fermat drew as a second corollary a method for determining centers of gravity of geometrical figures (*Oeuvres,* I, 136–139). His single example—although again the method itself is fully general—concerns the center of gravity of a paraboloidal segment. Let CAV be the generating parabola with axis AI and base CV. By symmetry the center of gravity O of the paraboloidal segment lies on axis $AI = b$ at some distance $AO = x$

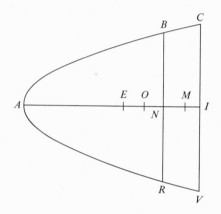

FIGURE 3

from the vertex A. Let the segment be cut by a plane parallel to the base and intersecting the axis at an arbitrary distance y from point I. Let E and M denote the centers of gravity of the two resulting subsegments. Since similar figures have similarly placed centers of gravity (Archimedes), $b/x = (b - y)/AE$, whence $EO = x - AE = xy/b$. By the definition of the center of gravity and by the law of the lever, segment $CBRV$ is to segment BAR as EO is to OM. But, by Archimedes' *Conoids and Spheroids,* proposition 26, paraboloid CAV is to paraboloid BAR as AI^2 is to AN^2, or as b^2 is to $(b - y)^2$, whence

$$\frac{EO}{OM} = \frac{CBRV}{BAR} = \frac{b^2 - (b - y)^2}{(b - y)^2}.$$

Here Fermat again employed the notion of adequality to set OM counterfactually equal to OI, whence

$$OI = b - x \approx OM = \left(\frac{xy}{b}\right)\left(\frac{b^2 - 2by + y^2}{2by - y^2}\right).$$

He removed the adequality by an application of the method of maxima and minima, i.e., by dividing through by y and then setting $y (= OI - OM)$ equal to zero, and obtained the result $x = 2b/3$. In applying his method to figures generated by curves of the forms $y^q = kx^p$ and $x^p y^q = k$ (p,q positive integers), Fermat employed the additional lemma that the similar segments of the figures "have the same proportion to corresponding triangles of the same base and height, even if we do not know what that proportion is,"[9] and argued from that lemma that his method of centers of gravity eliminated the problem of quadrature as a prerequisite to the determination of centers of gravity. Such an elimination was, of course, illusory, but the method did not depend on the lemma. It can be applied to any figure for which the general quadrature is known.

Fermat's method of maxima and minima and its corollary method of tangents formed the central issue in an acrid debate between Fermat and Descartes in the spring of 1638. Viewing Fermat's methods as rivals to his own in the *Géométrie*, Descartes tried to show that the former were at once paralogistic in their reasoning and limited in their application. It quickly became clear, however, that, as in the case of their analytic geometries, Fermat's and Descartes's methods rested on the same foundations. The only substantial issue was Descartes's disapproval of mathematical reasoning based on counterfactual assumptions, i.e., the notion of adequality. Although the two men made formal peace in the summer of 1638, when Descartes admitted his error in criticizing Fermat's methods, the bitterness of the dispute, exacerbated by the deep personal hatred Descartes felt for Fermat's friend and spokesman, Roberval, poisoned any chance for cooperation between the two greatest mathematicians of the time. Descartes's sharp tongue cast a pall over Fermat's reputation as a mathematician, a situation which Fermat's refusal to publish only made worse.[10] Through the efforts of Mersenne and Pierre Hérigone, Fermat's methods did appear in print in 1642, but only as bare algorithms that, by setting the difference y of the roots equal to zero from the start, belied the careful thinking that originally underlay them. Moreover, other mathematicians soon were publishing their own, more general algorithms; by 1659, Huygens felt it necessary to defend Fermat's priority against the claims of Johann Hudde. In time, Fermat's work on maxima and minima was all but forgotten, having been replaced by the differential calculus of Newton and Leibniz.

Methods of Quadrature. Fermat's research into the quadrature of curves and the cubature of solids also had its beginnings in the research that preceded his introduction to the outside mathematical world in 1636. By that time, he had taken the model of Archi-

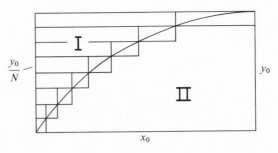

FIGURE 4

medes' quadrature of the spiral[11] and successfully extended its application to all spirals of the forms $\rho = (a\vartheta)^m$ and $R/R - \rho = (\alpha/\vartheta)^m$. Moreover, he had translated Archimedes' method of circumscription and inscription of sectors around and within the spiral into a rectangular framework. Dividing a given ordinate y_0 (or the corresponding abscissa x_0) of a curve $y = f(x)$ into N equal intervals and drawing lines parallel to the axis, Fermat determined that Area I in Figure 4 lay between limits $\dfrac{y_0}{N} \sum\limits_{i=1}^{N} x_i$ and $\dfrac{y_0}{N} \sum\limits_{i=1}^{N-1} x_i$, where x_i is the abscissa that corresponds to ordinate $(i/N)y_0$. Since he possessed a recursive formula for determining $\sum\limits_{=1}^{N} i^m$ for any positive integer m, Fermat could prove that

$$\frac{1}{N^{m+1}} \sum_{i=1}^{N} i^m > \frac{1}{m+1} > \frac{1}{N^{m+1}} \sum_{i=1}^{N-1} i^m$$

for all values of N. In each case the difference between the bounds is $1/N$, which can be made as small as one wishes. Hence, for any curve of the form $y^m = kx$, Fermat could show that the curvilinear Area I $= [1/(m + 1)]x_0 y_0$ and the curvilinear Area II $= [m/(m + 1)]x_0 y_0$. As an immediate corollary, he found that he could apply the same technique to determine the volume of the solid generated by the rotation of the curve about the ordinate or axis, with the restriction in this case that m be an even integer.

Sometime before 1646 Fermat devised a substantially new method of quadrature, which permitted the treatment of all curves of the forms $y^q = kx^p$ and $x^p y^q = k$ (p,q positive integers; in the second equation $p + q > 2$). The most striking departure from the earlier method is the introduction of the concept of adequality, now used in the sense of "approximate equality" or "equality in the limiting case." In the first example given in his major treatise on quadrature[12] Fermat derives the shaded area under the curve $x^2 y = k$ in Figure 5 as follows (we use modern

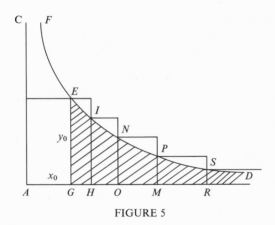

FIGURE 5

notation to abbreviate Fermat's lengthy verbal description while preserving its sense): the infinite x-axis is divided into intervals by the end points of a divergent geometric sequence of lengths AG, AH, AO, $\cdots$, or x_0, $(m/n)x_0$, $(m/n)^2x_0$, $\cdots$, where $m > n$ are arbitrary integers. Since $(m/n)^i - (m/n)^{i-1} = (m/n)^{i-1}(m/n - 1)$, each interval can, by suitable choice of m and n, be made as closely equal to another as desired and at the same time can be made as small as desired. Fermat has, then, $GH \approx HO \approx OM \approx \cdots$ and $GH \to 0$. From the curve and the construction of the intervals, it follows directly that the approximating rectangles erected on the intervals form the convergent geometric series

$$(m/n - 1)x_0y_0, \ (n/m)(m/n - 1)x_0y_0,$$
$$(n/m)^2(m/n - 1)x_0y_0, \ \cdots.$$

Its sum is $(m/n - 1)x_0y_0 + x_0y_0$, which is "adequal" to the shaded area. It approaches the curved area ever more closely as the size of the intervals approaches zero, i.e., as $m/n \to 1$. In the limiting case, the sum will be x_0y_0, which in turn will be the exact area of the shaded segment. Generalizing the procedure for any curve $x^py^q = k$ and a given ordinate y_0, Fermat determined that the area under the curve from y_0 on out is $[q/(p - q)]x_0y_0$. Adapting the procedure to curves $y^q = kx^p$ (by dividing the finite axis from 0 to x_0 by a convergent geometric sequence of intervals), he was also able to show that the area under the curve is $[q/(p + q)]x_0y_0$.

In the remainder of his treatise on quadrature, Fermat shifted from the geometrical style of exposition to the algebraic and, on the model of Viète's theory of equations, set up a "reduction analysis" by which a given quadrature either generates an infinite class of quadratures or can be shown to be dependent on the quadrature of the circle. To carry out the project he introduced a new concept of "application of all y^n to a given segment," by which he meant the limit-sum of the products $y^n \triangle x$ over a given

segment b of the x-axis as $\triangle x \to 0$ (in the absence of any notation by Fermat, we shall borrow from Leibniz and write $Omn_b \, y^n$ to symbolize Fermat's concept). Fermat then showed by several concrete examples that for any curve of the form $y^n = \Sigma a_i x^i / b_j x^j$ the determination of $Omn_b y^n$ follows directly from setting $y^n = \Sigma u_i$, where $u_i = a_i x^i / b_j x^j$. For each i the resulting expression $u_i = f(x)$ will denote a curve of the form $u_i^q = kx^p$ or the form $x^p u_i^q = k$. For each curve, the determination of $Omn_b u_i$ corresponds to the direct quadrature set forth in the first part of the treatise, and hence it is determinable. Therefore $Omn_b y^n = \Sigma Omn_b u_i$ is directly determinable.

Fermat next introduced the main lemma of his treatise, an entirely novel result for which he characteristically offered no proof. For any curve $y = f(x)$ decreasing monotonically over the interval $0,b$, where $f(0) = d$ and $f(b) = 0$, $Omn_b y^n = Omn_d nxy^{n-1}$. This result is equivalent to the modern statement

$$\int_0^b y^n \, dx = n \int_0^d xy^{n-1} \, dy.$$

One example from Fermat's treatise on quadrature suffices to display the subtlety and power of his reduction analysis. Can the area beneath the curve $b^3 = x^2y + b^2y$ (i.e., the "witch of Agnesi") be squared algebraically? Two transformations of variable and an application of the main lemma supply the answer. From $by = u^2$ and $bv = xu$, it follows first that $Omn_x y = 1/b \, Omn_x u^2 = 2/b \, Omn_u xu = 2 \, Omn_u v$. Hence, the quadrature of the original area depends on that of the transformed curve $F(u,v)$. But substitution of variables yields $b^2 = u^2 + v^2$, the equation of a circle. Therefore, the quadrature of the original area depends on the quadrature of the circle and cannot be carried out algebraically.

Fermat's treatise first circulated when it was printed in his *Varia opera* of 1679. By then much of its contents had become obsolescent in terms of the work of Newton and Leibniz. Even so, it is doubtful what effect the treatise could have had earlier. As sympathetic a reader as Huygens could make little sense of it.[13] In addition, Fermat's method of quadrature, like his method of tangents, lacks even the germ of several concepts crucial to the development of the calculus. Not only did Fermat not recognize the inverse relationship between the two methods, but both methods, conceptually and to some extent operationally, steered away from rather than toward the notion of the tangent or the area as a function of the curve.

Fermat's one work published in his lifetime, a treatise on rectification appended to a work on the cycloid by Antoine de La Loubère,[14] was a direct corollary of the method of quadrature. Cast, however, in the strictly geometrical style of classical Greek mathematics, it hid all traces of the underlying algebraic analysis. In the treatise Fermat treated the length of a curve as the limit-sum of tangential segments $\triangle S$ cut off by abscissas drawn through the end points of intervals $\triangle y$ on a given y ordinate. In essence, he showed that for any curve $y = y(x)$,

$$\frac{\triangle S^2}{\triangle y^2} = [x'(y)]^2 + 1.$$

Taking $u^2 = [x'(y)]^2 + 1$ as an auxiliary curve, Fermat used the relation $S = Omn_y u$ to reduce the problem of rectification to one of quadrature. He used the same basic procedure to determine the area of the surface generated by the rotation of the curve about an axis or an ordinate, as the results in a 1660 letter to Huygens indicate.

Number Theory. As a result of limited circulation in unpublished manuscripts, Fermat's work on analytic geometry, maxima and minima and tangents, and quadrature had only moderate influence on contemporary developments in mathematics. His work in the realm of number theory had almost none at all. It was neither understood nor appreciated until Euler revived it and initiated the line of continuous research that culminated in the work of Gauss and Kummer in the early nineteenth century. Indeed, many of Fermat's results are basic elements of number theory today. Although the results retain fundamental importance, his methods remain largely a secret known only to him. Theorems, conjectures, and specific examples abound in his letters and marginalia. But, except for a vague outline of a method he called "infinite descent," Fermat left no obvious trace of the means he had employed to find them. He repeatedly claimed to work from a method, and the systematic nature of much of his work would seem to support his claim.

In an important sense Fermat invented number theory as an independent branch of mathematics. He was the first to restrict his study in principle to the domain of integers. His refusal to accept fractional solutions to problems he set in 1657 as challenges to the European mathematics community (*Oeuvres,* II, 332–335) initiated his dispute with Wallis, Frénicle, and others,[15] for it represented a break with the classical tradition of Diophantus' *Arithmetica,* which served as his opponents' model. The restriction to integers explains one dominant theme of Fermat's work in number theory, his concern with prime numbers and divisibility. A second guiding theme of his

research, the determination of patterns for generating families of solutions from a single basic solution, carried over from his work in analysis.

Fermat's earliest research, begun in Bordeaux, displays both characteristics. Investigating the sums of the aliquot parts (proper divisors) of numbers, Fermat worked from Euclid's solution to the problem of "perfect numbers"—$\sigma(a) = 2a$, where $\sigma(a)$ denotes the sum of all divisors of the integer a, including 1 and a—to derive a complete solution to the problem of "friendly" numbers—$\sigma(a) = \sigma(b) = a + b$—and to the problem $\sigma(a) = 3a$. Later research in this area aimed at the general problem $\sigma(a) = (p/q)a$, as well as $\sigma(x^3) = y^2$ and $\sigma(x^2) = y^3$ (the "First Challenge" of 1657). Although Fermat offered specific solutions to the problem $\sigma(a) = na$ for $n = 3, 4, 5, 6$, he recorded the algorithm only for $n = 3$. The central role of primeness and divisibility in such research led to several corollaries, among them the theorem (announced in 1640) that $2^k - 1$ is always a composite number if k is composite and may be composite for prime k; in the latter case, all divisors are of the form $2mk + 1$.

Fermat's interest in primeness and divisibility culminated in a theorem now basic to the theory of congruences; as set down by Fermat it read: If p is prime and a^t is the smallest number such that $a^t = kp + 1$ for some k, then t divides $p - 1$. In the modern version, if p is prime and p does not divide a, then $a^{p-1} \equiv 1 \pmod{p}$. As a corollary to this theorem, Fermat investigated in depth the divisibility of $a^k \pm 1$ and made his famous conjecture that all numbers of the form $2^{2^n} + 1$ are prime (disproved for $n = 5$ by Euler). In carrying out his research, Fermat apparently relied on an extensive factual command of the powers of prime numbers and on the traditional "sieve of Eratosthenes" as a test of primeness. He several times expressed his dissatisfaction with the latter but seems to have been unable to find a more efficient test, even though in retrospect his work contained all the necessary elements for one.

A large group of results of fundamental importance to later number theory (quadratic residues, quadratic forms) apparently stemmed from Fermat's study of the indeterminate equation $x^2 - q = my^2$ for nonsquare m. In his "Second Challenge" of 1657, Fermat claimed to have the complete solution for the case $q = 1$. Operating on the principle that any divisor of a number of the form $a^2 + mb^2$ (m not a square) must itself be of that form, Fermat established that all primes of the form $4k + 1$ (but not those of the form $4k + 3$) can be expressed as the sum of two squares, all primes of the form $8k + 1$ or $8k + 3$ as the sum of a square and the double of a square, all primes of the form $3k + 1$ as $a^2 + 3b^2$, and that the product of any two primes of the form $20k + 3$ or $20k + 7$ is expressible in the form $a^2 + 5b^2$.

Another by-product of this research was Fermat's claim to be able to prove Diophantus' conjecture that any number can be expressed as the sum of at most four squares. Extending his research on the decomposition of numbers to higher powers, Fermat further claimed proofs of the theorems that no cube could be expressed as the sum of two cubes, no quartic as the sum of two quartics, and indeed no number a^n as the sum of two powers b^n and c^n (the famous "last theorem," mentioned only once in the margin of his copy of Diophantus' *Arithmetica*). In addition, he claimed the complete solution of the so-called "four-cube problem" (to express the sum of two given cubes as the sum of two other cubes), allowing here, of course, fractional solutions of the problem.

To prove his decomposition theorems and to solve the equation $x^2 - 1 = my^2$, Fermat employed a method he had devised and called "infinite descent." The method, an inverse form of the modern method of induction, rests on the principle (peculiar to the domain of integers) that there cannot exist an infinitely decreasing sequence of integers. Fermat set down two rather vague outlines of his method, one in his "Observations sur Diophante" (*Oeuvres,* I, 340–341) and one in a letter to Carcavi (*Oeuvres,* II, 431–433). In the latter Fermat argued that no right triangle of numbers (triple of numbers a, b, c such that $a^2 + b^2 = c^2$) can have an area equal to a square ($ab/2 = m^2$ for some m), since

If there were some right triangle of integers that had an area equal to a square, there would be another triangle less than it which had the same property. If there were a second, less than the first, which had the same property, there would be by similar reasoning a third less than the second which had the same property, and then a fourth, a fifth, etc., ad infinitum in decreasing order. But, given a number, there cannot be infinitely many others in decreasing order less than it (I mean to speak always of integers). From which one concludes that it is therefore impossible that any right triangle of numbers have an area that is a square [letter to Carcavi, *Oeuvres,* II, 431–432].

Fermat's method of infinite descent did not apply only to negative propositions. He discovered that he could also show that every prime of the form $4k + 1$ could be expressed as the sum of two squares by denying the proposition for some such prime, deriving another such prime less than the first, for which the proposition would again not hold, and so on. Ultimately, he argued, this decreasing sequence of primes would arrive at the least prime of the form $4k + 1$—

namely, 5—for which, by assumption, the proposition would not hold. But $5 = 2^2 + 1^2$, which contradicts the initial assumption. Hence, the proposition must hold. Although infinite descent is unassailable in its overall reasoning, its use requires the genius of a Fermat, since nothing in that reasoning dictates how one derives the next member of the decreasing sequence for a given problem.

Fermat's letters to Jacques de Billy, published by the latter as *Doctrinae analyticae inventum novum,*[16] form the only other source of direct information about Fermat's methods in number theory. In these letters Fermat undertook a complete treatment of the so-called double equations first studied by Diophantus. In their simplest form they required the complete solution of the system $ax + b = \square$, $cx + d = \square$. By skillful use of factorization to determine the base solution and the theorem that, if a is a solution, then successive substitution of $x + a$ for x generates an infinite family of solutions, Fermat not only solved all the problems posed by Diophantus but also extended them as far as polynomials of the fourth degree.

The importance of Fermat's work in the theory of numbers lay less in any contribution to contemporary developments in mathematics than in their stimulative influence on later generations. Much of the number theory of the nineteenth century took its impetus from Fermat's results and, forced to devise its own methods, contributed to the formulation of concepts basic to modern algebra.

Other Work. *Probability.* Fermat shares credit with Blaise Pascal for laying the first foundations of the theory of probability. In a brief exchange of correspondence during the summer of 1654, the two men discussed their different approaches to the same solution of a problem originally posed to Pascal by a gambler: How should the stakes in a game of chance be divided among the players if the game is prematurely ended? In arriving at specific, detailed solutions for several simple games, Fermat and Pascal operated from the basic principle of evaluating the expectation of each player as the ratio of outcomes favorable to him to the total number of possible outcomes. Fermat relied on direct computations rather than general mathematical formulas in his solutions, and his results and methods quickly became obsolete with the appearance in 1657 of Christiaan Huygens' mathematically more sophisticated *De ludo aleae.*

Optics (Fermat's Principle). In 1637, when Fermat was engaged with traditional and rather pedestrian problems in geostatics, he read Descartes's *Dioptrique.* In a letter to Mersenne, which opened the controversy between Descartes and Fermat mentioned above,

Fermat severely criticized the work. Methodologically, he could not accept Descartes's use of mathematics to make a priori deductions about the physical world. Philosophically, he could not agree with Descartes that "tendency to motion" (Descartes's basic definition of light) could be understood and analyzed in terms of actual motion. Physically, he doubted both the assertion that light traveled more quickly in a denser medium (he especially questioned the meaning of such a statement together with the assertion of the instantaneous transmission of light) and Descartes's law of refraction itself. Mathematically, he tried to show that Descartes's demonstrations of the laws of reflection and refraction proved nothing that Descartes had not already assumed in his analysis, i.e., that Descartes had begged the question. The ensuing debate in the fall of 1637 soon moved to mathematics as Descartes launched a counterattack aimed at Fermat's method of tangents, and Fermat returned to the original subject of optics only in the late 1650's, when Claude Clerselier reopened the old argument while preparing his edition of Descartes's *Lettres*.

Fermat, who in his earlier years had fervently insisted that experiment alone held the key to knowledge of the physical world, nonetheless in 1662 undertook a mathematical derivation of the law of refraction on the basis of two postulates: first, that the finite speed of light varied as the rarity of the medium through which it passed and, second, that "nature operates by the simplest and most expeditious ways and means." In his "Analysis ad refractiones" (*Oeuvres*, I, 170–172), Fermat applied the second postulate (Fermat's principle) in the following manner: In Figure 6 let the upper half of the circle represent the rarer of two media and let the lower half represent the denser; further, let *CD* represent a given incident ray. If the "ratio of the resistance of the denser medium to the resistance of the rarer medium" is expressed as the ratio of the given line *DF* to some line *M*, then "the motions which occur along lines *CD* and *DI* [the refracted ray to be determined] can be

measured with the aid of the lines *DF* and *M;* that is, the motion that occurs along the two lines is represented comparatively by the sum of two rectangles, of which one is the product of *CD* and *M* and the other the product of *DI* and *DF*" ("Analysis ad refractiones," pp. 170–171). Fermat thus reduces the problem to one of determining point *H* such that that sum is minimized. Taking length *DH* as the unknown *x*, he applies his method of maxima and minima and, somewhat to his surprise (expressed in a letter to Clerselier), arrives at Descartes's law of refraction.

Although Fermat took the trouble to confirm his derived result by a formal, synthetic proof, his interest in the problem itself ended with his derivation. Physical problems had never really engaged him, and he had returned to the matter only to settle an issue that gave rise to continued ill feeling between him and the followers of Descartes.

In fact, by 1662 Fermat had effectively ended his career as a mathematician. His almost exclusive interest in number theory during the last fifteen years of his life found no echo among his junior contemporaries, among them Huygens, who were engaged in the application of analysis to physics. As a result Fermat increasingly returned to the isolation from which he had so suddenly emerged in 1636, and his death in 1665 was viewed more as the passing of a grand old man than as a loss to the active scientific community.

NOTES

1. All published modern accounts of Fermat's life ultimately derive from Paul Tannery's article in the *Grande encyclopédie*, repr. in *Oeuvres*, IV, 237–240. Some important new details emerged from the research of H. Blanquière and M. Caillet in connection with an exhibition at the Lycée Pierre de Fermat in Toulouse in 1957: *Un mathématicien de génie, Pierre de Fermat 1601–1665* (Toulouse, 1957).

2. *Diophanti Alexandrini Arithmeticorum libri sex et de numeris multangulis liber unus. Cum commentariis C. G. Bacheti V. C. et observationibus D. P. de Fermat Senatoris Tolosani* (Toulouse, 1670); *Varia opera mathematica D. Petri de Fermat Senatoris Tolosani* (Toulouse, 1679; repr. Berlin, 1861; Brussels, 1969).

3. Cureau shared Fermat's scientific interests and hence provided a special link to the chancellor. There is much to suggest that the *parlement* of Toulouse took advantage of Fermat's ties to Cureau.

4. Regarding book VII and its importance for Greek geometrical analysis, see M. S. Mahoney, "Another Look at Greek Geometrical Analysis," in *Archive for History of Exact Sciences*, **5** (1968), 318–348. On its influence in the early seventeenth century, see Mahoney, "The Royal Road" (diss., Princeton, 1967), ch. 3.

5. Fermat's original Latin reads: *fit locus loco.* The last word is not redundant, as several authors have thought; rather, the phrase is elliptic, lacking the word *datus.* Fermat's terminology here comes directly from Euclid's *Data* (*linea positione data:* a line given, or fixed, in position).

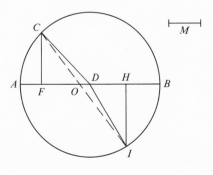

FIGURE 6

Regarding the algebraic symbolism that follows here and throughout the article, note that throughout his life Fermat employed the notation of Viète, which used the capital vowels for unknowns and the capital consonants for knowns or parameters. To avoid the confusion of an unfamiliar notation, this article employs Cartesian notation, translating Fermat's A uniformly as x, E as y, etc.

6. Pappus, *Mathematical Collection* VII, prop. 61. The geometrical formulation is too complex to state here without a figure and in addition requires some interpretation. In Fermat's algebraic formulation, the problem calls for the determination of the minimum value of the expression

$$\frac{bc - bx + cx - x^2}{ax - x^2},$$

where a, b, c are given line segments.

7. The modern foundation of Fermat's method is the theorem that if $P(x)$ has a local extreme value at $x = a$, then $P(x) = (x - a)^2 R(x)$, where $R(a) \neq 0$.
8. Fermat's original version of the method is contained in the "Methodus ad disquirendam maximam et minimam" (*Oeuvres*, I, 133–136); in its most finished form it is described in a memoir sent to Descartes in June 1638 (*Oeuvres*, II, 154–162).
9. Fermat to Mersenne, 15 June 1638 (*Oeuvres*, supp., pp. 84–86).
10. Descartes's most famous remark, made to Frans van Schooten, who related it to Huygens (*Oeuvres*, IV, 122), was the following: "Monsieur Fermat est Gascon, moi non. Il est vrai, qu'il a inventé plusieurs belles choses particulières, et qu'il est homme de grand esprit. Mais quant à moi j'ai toujours étudié à considerer les choses fort généralement, afin d'en pouvoir conclure des règles, qui aient aussi ailleurs de l'usage." The connotation of "troublemaker" implicit in the term "Gascon" is secondary to Descartes's charge, believed by some of his followers, that Fermat owed his reputation to a few unsystematic lucky guesses.
11. In his treatise *On Spirals*.
12. "De aequationum localium transmutatione et emendatione ad multimodam curvilineorum inter se vel cum rectilineis comparationem, cui annectitur proportionis geometricae in quadrandis infinitis parabolis et hyperbolis usus" (*Oeuvres*, I, 255–285). The treatise was written sometime between 1657 and 1659, but at least part of it dates back to the early 1640's.
13. Huygens to Leibniz, 1 September 1691 (*Oeuvres*, IV, 137).
14. "De linearum curvarum cum lineis rectis comparatione dissertatio geometrica. Autore M.P.E.A.S." The treatise was published with La Loubère's *Veterum geometria promota in septem de cycloide libris, et in duabus adjectis appendicibus* (Toulouse, 1660).
15. The dispute is recorded in Wallis' *Commercium epistolicum de quaestionibus quibusdam mathematicis nuper habitum* (Oxford, 1658). The participants were William Brouncker, Kenelm Digby, Fermat, Bernard Frénicle, Wallis, and Frans van Schooten.
16. Published as part of Samuel Fermat's edition of Diophantus in 1670 (see note 2).

BIBLIOGRAPHY

I. ORIGINAL WORKS. The modern edition of the *Oeuvres de Fermat*, Charles Henry and Paul Tannery, eds., 4 vols. (Paris, 1891–1912), with supp. by Cornelis de Waard (Paris, 1922), contains all of Fermat's extant papers and letters in addition to correspondence between other men concerning Fermat. The edition includes in vol. III French translations of those papers and letters that Fermat wrote in Latin and also a French translation of Billy's *Inventum novum*. English translations of Fermat's "Isagoge" and "Methodus ad disquirendam maximam et minimam" have been published in D. J. Struik's *A Source Book in Mathematics, 1200–1800* (Cambridge, Mass., 1969).

II. SECONDARY LITERATURE. The two most important summaries of Fermat's career are Jean Itard, *Pierre Fermat*, Kurze Mathematiker Biographien, no. 10 (Basel, 1950); and J. E. Hofmann, "Pierre Fermat—ein Pionier der neuen Mathematik," in *Praxis der Mathematik*, **7** (1965), 113–119, 171–180, 197–203. Fermat's contributions to analytic geometry form part of Carl Boyer, *History of Analytic Geometry* (New York, 1956), ch. 5; and the place of Fermat in the history of the calculus is discussed in Boyer's *Concepts of the Calculus* (New York, 1949), pp. 154–165. The most detailed and enlightening study of Fermat's work in number theory has been carried out by J. E. Hofmann; see, in particular, "Über zahlentheoretische Methoden Fermats und Eulers, ihre Zusammenhänge und ihre Bedeutung," in *Archive for History of Exact Sciences,* **1** (1961), 122–159; and "Studien zur Zahlentheorie Fermats," in *Abhandlungen der Preussischen Akademie der Wissenschaften,* Mathematisch–Naturwissenschaftliche Klasse, no. 7 (1944). Fermat's dispute with Descartes on the law of refraction and his own derivation of the law are treated in detail in A. I. Sabra, *Theories of Light From Descartes to Newton* (London, 1967), chs. 3–5.

MICHAEL S. MAHONEY

FERMI, ENRICO (*b.* Rome, Italy, 29 September 1901; *d.* Chicago, Illinois, 28 November 1954), *physics.*

His father, Alberto Fermi, was an administrative employee of the Italian railroads; his mother, Ida de Gattis, was a schoolteacher. Fermi received a traditional education in the public schools of Rome, but his scientific formation was due more to the books he read than to personal contacts. It is possible to gather exact information on his readings from an extant notebook, and later in life he mentioned having studied such works as Poisson's *Traité de mécanique*, Richardson's *Electron Theory of Matter*, Planck's *Vorlesungen über Thermodynamik*, and several by Poincaré.

Fermi was fundamentally an agnostic, although he had been baptized a Catholic. In 1928 he married Laura Capon, the daughter of an admiral in the Italian navy. His wife's family was Jewish and was severely persecuted during the Nazi-Fascist period. Fermi, who enjoyed excellent health until his fatal illness, led a very simple, frugal life with outdoor activities as his main recreations. His unusual physical strength and endurance enabled him to hike, play tennis, ski, and swim; although in none of these sports was he outstanding.

Fermi was a member of a great many academies and scientific societies, including the Accademia dei Lincei, the U.S. National Academy of Sciences, and the Royal Society of London. He received the Nobel Prize in 1938 and the Fermi Prize, named for him, a few days before his death. His prominent part in the development of atomic energy involved him in numerous extrascientific activities that were not particularly attractive to him. He undertook administrative duties conscientiously and ably but without great enthusiasm.

Fermi's scientific accomplishments were in both theoretical and experimental physics, an unusual feat in the twentieth century, when increasing specialization tends to narrow the field of study. Fermi's statistics (independently found also by Paul Dirac) and his theory of beta decay were his greatest theoretical contributions. Artificial radioactivity produced by neutron bombardment, slow neutrons, and the realization of a nuclear chain reaction were his greatest experimental achievements. These highlights and his many other results have left their imprint on the most diverse parts of physics.

When Fermi attended school, humanistic literary studies were emphasized: Italian, Latin, and Greek. He was a model student and obtained consistently top marks. But he was primarily self-taught, from a very early age, and he said later that by age ten he had succeeded by concentrated effort in understanding practically unaided why the equation $x^2 + y^2 = r^2$ represents a circle. His older sister, Maria, and his older brother, Giulio, contributed to this early schooling. In grade school he also exhibited a prodigious memory for poems. In 1915 Giulio died unexpectedly, and the sad event left a deep mark on Enrico. Fortunately he then struck up a friendship with a schoolmate, Enrico Persico, and the two boys' common scientific interests led to a lifelong friendship. They became the first two professors of theoretical physics in Italy.

A colleague of Fermi's father, Adolfo Amidei, was perhaps the first adult to recognize Fermi's unusual talent. He lent him books on mathematics and physics in a pedagogically graduated progression. Fermi himself acquired some secondhand books on mechanics and mathematical physics, mainly Poisson's *Mécanique* and A. Caraffa's *Elementa physicae mathematicae* (Rome, 1840). By his seventeenth year, while still in high school, he had acquired a thorough knowledge of classical physics, comparable to that of an advanced graduate student in a university. Furthermore, Fermi and Persico had performed many experiments with apparatus they had built themselves, and thus had acquired an excellent grasp of contemporary experimental physics. For example, they determined precisely the value of the acceleration of gravity at Rome, the density of Rome tap water, and the earth's magnetic field. Fermi was also proficient at building small electric motors.

At Amidei's suggestion, Fermi competed for a

fellowship at the Scuola Normale Superiore in Pisa, where he could acquire an education at no expense to his family. He had to write an assigned essay for the competition, "Distinctive Characters of Sound." (Fortunately the essay was preserved and after his death was found in the archives of the school.) On the first page is the partial differential equation for vibrating reeds, followed by about twenty pages for its solution through eigenfunctions, the determination of the characteristic frequencies, etc. One can easily imagine the surprise of the examiner who received this essay from a seventeen-year-old boy just out of high school. He was convinced of the candidate's genius and assured Fermi of that fact when he met him.

From the Scuola Normale Superiore, Fermi wrote regularly to Persico, and the letters give a vivid insight into his life there. He was by no means bashful, and after about a year in Pisa he said that he was the authority on quantum theory and that everybody, including the professors, depended on him to teach them the new physics. At Pisa he became a close friend of Franco Rasetti, another physics student of great ability.

Fermi received his doctorate from the University of Pisa in 1922 and then returned to Rome. At that time he met Orso Mario Corbino, director of the physics laboratory at the University of Rome. Corbino immediately recognized Fermi's talent and became his lifelong friend and patron. Above all, he saw Fermi as the instrument for one of his fondest aspirations—the rebirth of Italian physics.

To acquire a direct knowledge of modern physics beyond the provincial state of Italian physics, Fermi had to see the world, and to be in touch with foreign scientists. He therefore competed for a foreign fellowship and spent some time at Max Born's institute at Göttingen and then with Paul Ehrenfest at Leiden. With the latter he struck up a warm friendship, and Ehrenfest greatly encouraged him. He and Arnold Sommerfeld helped to introduce Fermi to other physicists. When the fellowship expired in 1924, Fermi returned to Florence with the post of lecturer. He then competed for a chair of mathematical physics; he did not win although he was supported by Tullio Levi-Civita and Vito Volterra.

Up to this time Fermi's work had been primarily in general relativity (tensor analysis), where he had developed a theorem of permanent value: that in the vicinity of a world line, space can always be approximated by a pseudo-Euclidean metric (FP no. 3 in *Collected Papers*). In statistical mechanics he had written subtle papers on the ergodic hypothesis (FP no. 11) and on quantum theory. Here he had developed an original form of analyzing collisions of charged particles. He developed the field produced by the charged particle by the Fourier integral and used the information from optical processes to determine the result of the collision (FP no. 23). This method was later refined and better justified on the basis of quantum mechanics and is generally known as the Weizsäcker-Williams method. Other studies on the entropy constant of a perfect gas are historically important as preparation for things to come. An experiment done with Rasetti, who was also in Florence, on the depolarization of resonance light in an alternating magnetic field was the subject of Fermi's first important experimental paper (FP no. 28). This experiment was the first of a series that, in subsequent years, was to become extremely important in the hands of other physicists.

In 1925 Wolfgang Pauli discovered the exclusion principle, which in the language of the old quantum theory prevents more than one electron from occupying an orbit completely defined by its quantum numbers. This principle had far-reaching consequences in statistical mechanics for a particulate gas when its temperature and density are such that the cube of the de Broglie wavelength is large compared with the total volume divided by the number of particles in the formula $N/V \gg (2\pi kmT)^{3/2} h^{-3}$. Peculiar phenomena, comprised under the technical name of "degeneracy," then appear: for instance, the specific heat of the gas vanishes. The problems of gas degeneracy had been known for many years. Bose and Einstein had shown in 1924 that they could be solved by a modification of classical statistical mechanics (Bose-Einstein statistics). Bose-Einstein statistics are applicable to light quanta and account for Planck's radiation formula. But Bose-Einstein statistics are not applicable to particles obeying Pauli's principle, for which one needs the new type of statistics discovered by Fermi early in 1926 (FP no. 30). Dirac independently found the same result a few months later and connected it to the new quantum mechanics. Fermi statistics, which are applicable to electrons, protons, neutrons, and all particles of half integral spin, have a pervading importance in atomic and nuclear physics and in solid-state theory. The importance of Fermi statistics was immediately appreciated by physicists and established Fermi as a leader in the international community of theoreticians, as was obvious at the International Conference in Physics held at Como in 1927.

In 1927, mainly through the efforts of Corbino, a chair in theoretical physics, the first such in Italy, was established at the University of Rome. In the competition for the position Fermi placed first and Persico second. Fermi then came to Rome, to the Physics Institute in Via Panisperna, to join Corbino. He had

friends there among the mathematicians also, and he was soon joined by Rasetti.

They strove to establish a modern school of physics in Rome. The first task was to recruit students suitable for advanced training and capable of later becoming independent scientists. The first was Emilio Segrè, who was then an engineering student but who had always had a strong interest in physics. When he became acquainted with Rasetti and Fermi through mutual friends, he enthusiastically joined the group as an advanced student. Segrè informed his schoolmate and friend Ettore Majorana of the new opportunity and introduced him to Fermi and Rasetti. Majorana soon (1928) transferred from engineering to physics. Edoardo Amaldi was recruited directly from undergraduate work in physics. Later they were joined by many others. Some came as temporary visitors: Giulio Racah, later rector of the University of Jerusalem and known mainly for his studies on the Racah coefficients and atomic spectra; Giovanni Gentile, Jr., later professor of theoretical physics at Milan; Gilberto Bernardini, later an experimental physicist and director of the Scuola Normale Superiore; and Bruno Rossi, who was a pioneer in the study of cosmic rays. Others joined them as students or fellows: Bruno Pontecorvo; Ugo Fano, later professor of theoretical physics at the University of Chicago; Eugenio Fubini; Renato Einaudi, later professor of mechanics at the University of Turin; and Leo Pincherle, later professor of physics at London University. Gian Carlo Wick came at a later date as an assistant professor. The activity in Rome helped to reanimate several other centers, including Florence (Rossi, Bernardini, Giuseppe Occhialini, Racah) and Turin (Gleb, Wataghin, Wick), and brought about a notable rebirth of physics in Italy.

Fermi's next important study was the application of his statistics to an atomic model. This had been anticipated, however, by L. H. Thomas, who was working independently. The Thomas-Fermi atom gives very good approximations in a great number of problems. The fundamental idea was to compute the density of the electronic cloud around the nucleus as an atmosphere of a totally degenerate gas of electrons attracted by the nucleus. Fermi made numerous applications of his method to X-ray spectroscopy, to the periodic system of the elements, to optical spectroscopy, and later to ions. This work required a considerable amount of numerical calculation, which he performed with a primitive desk calculator. Many of these results were summarized in a paper he read at the University of Leipzig in 1928 (FP no. 49). Other studies in atomic and molecular physics followed.

Another important group of papers which were

devoted to the reformulation of quantum electro-dynamics made this important subject accessible to many physicists (FP no. 67). Dirac had written a fundamental but difficult paper on the subject. Fermi, after reading the paper, decided to obtain the same results by more familiar methods. He developed by Fourier analysis the electromagnetic field which obeys Maxwell's equations, and he quantized the single harmonic components as oscillators. He thus wrote the Hamiltonian of the free field, giving a Hamiltonian form to Maxwell's theory. To this Hamiltonian, he added the Hamiltonian of an atom and a term representing the interaction between atom and radiation. The complete system was then treated by perturbation theory.

Corbino did not miss any occasion to extol Fermi's work, and early official recognition followed. Mussolini named Fermi to the newly created Accademia d'Italia. He was the only physicist so honored, and this singular recognition was also accompanied by a substantial stipend. He was subsequently elected to the Accademia dei Lincei, at an unusually young age. In spite of some grumbling by older professors, it became clear to the academic world and to the cultivated public that Fermi was indeed the leading Italian physicist. His economic position became comfortable although not affluent.

At this time quantum mechanics had reached its full development; nonrelativistic problems, at least in principle, were soluble except for mathematical difficulties. In this sense atomic physics was showing signs of exhaustion, and one could expect the next really important advances to be in the study of the nucleus. Realizing this, Fermi decided to switch to nuclear physics. He initially investigated the theory of the hyperfine structure of the spectral lines and the nuclear magnetic momenta (FP no. 57), a suitable subject for making the transition from atomic to nuclear physics.

The development of experimental physics at Rome presented greater problems than had theoretical physics. In the latter Fermi was a leader of worldwide reputation at the peak of his powers; no substantial amount of money was needed; and it was relatively easy to attract young people from Italy and from abroad. Indeed, very early promising physicists destined to leave their mark in science came to Rome. Besides the Italians mentioned earlier, several foreign physicists studied there, among them Hans Bethe, Edward Teller, Rudolf Peierls, Fritz London, Felix Bloch, George Placzek, and Homi Bhabha. The state of experimental physics was different. Rasetti was the senior man, and although he had outstanding ability he was no Fermi. The only techniques known locally were spectroscopic, and therefore the equipment available was predominantly spectroscopic. Shops were poor and money was scarce. In this situation, with the object of widening the techniques available and ultimately turning to nuclear physics, Rasetti, Amaldi, and Segrè spent periods of about a year in the laboratories of Lise Meitner, Peter Debye, and Otto Stern, respectively, learning various experimental techniques.

In Rome, about 1929, Rasetti and Fermi began experiments on nuclear subjects. In the meantime the great discoveries of the early 1930's, the portents of the impending revolution in nuclear physics, were being made: positron, neutron, deuterium, and artificial acceleration. The Solvay Conference of 1933 was devoted to the nucleus, and shortly thereafter Fermi developed the theory of beta decay, based on the hypothesis of the neutrino formulated for the first time in 1930 by Wolfgang Pauli. Beta decay—the spontaneous emission of electrons by nuclei—presented major theoretical difficulties. Apparently, energy and momentum were not conserved. There were also other difficulties with angular momentum and the statistics of the nuclei. Pauli sought a way out of the apparent paradoxes by postulating the simultaneous emission of the electron and of a practically undetectable particle, later named "neutrino" by Fermi. There remained the task of giving substance to this hypothesis and of showing that it could account quantitatively for the observed facts.

An entirely new type of force had to be postulated, the so-called weak interaction. This new force, together with gravity, electromagnetism, and the strong interaction which binds the particles of the nucleus, constitutes the family of forces presently known in physics. They should account for the whole universe. Weak interactions occur between all particles and are thus unlike electromagnetic or strong interactions, which are restricted to certain particles. The first manifestation of the weak interaction to be treated in detail was the beta decay. The treatment was accomplished by applying second quantization and destruction and creation operators for fermions and by adopting (or better, guessing) a Hamiltonian for weak interactions on the basis of formal criteria, such as relativistic invariance, linearity, and absence of derivatives. Of the five possible choices which satisfied the formal requirements, Fermi treated the vector interaction in detail, mainly because of its analogy with electromagnetism.

In his paper on beta decay, Fermi also introduced a new fundamental constant of nature, the Fermi constant, G, which plays a role analogous to that of the charge of the electron in electromagnetism. This constant has been experimentally determined from the energy available in beta decay and the mean life of the decaying substance. Its value is 1.415×10^{-49} erg cm^3. To clarify its significance we point out that the electromagnetic interaction is of the order of 10^{12} times stronger than the weak interaction. More precisely, the dimensionless number $e^2/\hbar c = 1/137$ is to be compared with $G^2(\hbar c)^{-2}(\hbar/mc)^{-4} \sim 5.10^{-14}$, where m is the mass of the pion. The famous paper in which Fermi developed this theory had far-reaching consequences for the future development of nuclear and particle physics (FP no. 80). For instance, it served as an inspiration to Hideki Yukawa in his theory of the nuclear forces. It is probably the most important theoretical paper written by Fermi.

Soon thereafter Frédéric Joliot and Irène Joliot-Curie discovered artificial radioactivity—the creation of radioactive isotopes of stable nuclei by alpha particle bombardment. The Joliots' discovery provided the occasion for experimental activity which Fermi continued for the rest of his life. Fermi reasoned that neutrons should be more effective than alpha particles in producing radioactive elements because they are not repelled by the nuclear charge and thus have a much greater probability of entering the target nuclei.

Acting on this idea, Fermi bombarded several elements of increasing atomic numbers with neutrons. He hoped to find an artificial radioactivity produced by the neutrons. His first success was with fluorine. The neutron source was a small ampul containing beryllium metal and radon gas. The detecting apparatus consisted of rather primitive Geiger-Müller counters. Immediately thereafter Fermi, with the help of Amaldi, D'Agostino, Rasetti, and Segrè, carried out a systematic investigation of the behavior of elements throughout the periodic table. In most cases they performed chemical analysis to identify the chemical element that was the carrier of the activity. In the first survey, out of sixty-three elements investigated, thirty-seven showed an easily detectable activity. The nuclear reactions of (n, α), (n, p), and (n, γ) were then identified, and all available elements, including uranium and thorium, were irradiated. In uranium and thorium the investigators found several forms of activity after bombardment but did not recognize fission. Fermi and his collaborators, having proved that no radioactive isotopes were formed between lead and uranium, put forward the natural hypothesis that the activity was due to transuranic elements. These studies, which were continued by Otto Hahn, Lise Meitner, Irène Joliot-Curie, Frédéric Joliot, and Savitch, culminated in 1938 in the discovery of fission by Hahn and Fritz Strassmann.

In October 1935 Fermi and his collaborators, now including Pontecorvo, observed that neutrons passed through substances containing hydrogen have in-creased efficiency for producing artificial radioactivity. Fermi interpreted this effect as due to the slowing down of the neutrons by elastic collisions with hydrogen atoms. Thus slow neutrons were discovered. The study of slow neutrons was to form the main object of Fermi's work for several years thereafter. Among other things, Fermi and his collaborators showed that the neutrons reached thermal energy and that neutrons of a few electron volts of energy could show sharp peaks (resonances) in the curve of the collision and absorption cross section, versus neutron energy. Fermi then developed a mathematical theory of the slowing down of neutrons, and he tested it experimentally in considerable detail. This work lasted until about 1936. All the neutron work, which cost approximately a thousand American dollars, was supported by the Consiglio Nazionale delle Ricerche of Italy. The tremendous experimental activity of the years 1934–1938 brought a considerable change in the working habits at the Rome Institute. Because of the lack of time, it became impossible for Fermi to follow all the developments in physics as he had done before. He was forced to curtail the extracurricular teaching of promising young men, nor could he spare time for foreign visitors, who practically stopped coming.

The Ethiopian War marked the beginning of the decline of the work at the Institute, and the death of Corbino on 23 January 1937 brought further serious complications. The deteriorating political situation also materially hampered the work, and finally the Fascist racial laws of 1938 directly affected Fermi's wife. The foregoing problems and his deep, although mute, resentment against injustice were the final arguments that convinced Fermi to leave Fascist Italy. He passed the word to Columbia University, where he had been previously, that he was willing to accept a position there. In December 1938 he received the Nobel Prize in Stockholm. He then proceeded directly from there to New York. He was not to return to Italy until 1949.

Fermi had barely settled himself at Columbia when Bohr brought to the United States the news of the discovery of fission. This discovery made a tremendous impression on all physicists. Fermi and others immediately saw the possibility of the emission of secondary neutrons and perhaps of a chain reaction; he started at once to experiment in this direction.

In the early period at Columbia, Fermi was helped by H. L. Anderson, a graduate student who later took his Ph.D. under Fermi and remained a close collaborator and friend to the end of Fermi's life. The young physicist Walter Zinn was also associated with Fermi for an extended period. Leo Szilard was independently pursuing similar studies, and there were active interchanges of ideas and even some collaboration with other Columbia and Princeton University groups during early research on the chain reaction.

The first problem was to investigate whether on the fission of uranium secondary neutrons were in fact emitted—as was expected because the fragments have excess neutrons for their stability. If such did occur, it might be possible to use these neutrons to produce further fission, and under favorable circumstances one could obtain a chain reaction. To make this possible it is necessary to use the fission neutrons economically, i.e., to employ the neutrons to produce other fissions and not to lose them in parasitic captures by uranium, by other materials used as a moderator to slow down the neutrons, or by escape from the body of the reactor. If one uses natural uranium and a graphite moderator with unseparated isotopes, the margin by which one can obtain a chain reaction is very small and utmost care is needed in husbanding the neutrons. It soon became apparent that more than two neutrons were emitted per fission. This is a necessary but not sufficient condition for a chain reaction. But the number, now known to be about 2.5, is small enough to create an extremely difficult technical problem.

Of the two isotopes contained in natural uranium, only the isotope of mass 235, present in one part out of 140, is fissionable by slow neutrons and the cross section is large at low energy. On the other hand, most of the fission neutrons are unable to produce fission in the abundant isotope uranium 238, but if they are slowed down they are easily captured by U^{235} and produce fission. Neutrons must therefore be slowed down, but in the collisions that reduce the energy of the neutrons there is always a fraction of neutrons which are captured without producing fission. The moderator must thus be carefully chosen. Hydrogen, the first obvious choice, captures too many neutrons, and deuterium was unavailable in sufficient quantities. So for practical purposes the only suitable, and available, substance in 1939 was graphite, and several physicists independently suggested its use. In a long series of measurements of great ingenuity, Fermi and his collaborators studied the purity of the materials (impurities were often important neutron capturers) and the best configuration in which to assemble them. In order to analyze the problems facing him, Fermi needed a great amount of quantitative information on cross sections, delayed neutrons, branching ratios of the fission reactions, and nuclear properties of several nuclei to be used in a future reactor. This information was not available. He then proceeded to collect it with the help of many collaborators. Other independent groups were of course working on the same problems, but exchange of information was limited by self-imposed secrecy.

The potential overwhelming practical importance of this work was clear to physicists, and Fermi, together with George B. Pegram, chairman of the physics department at Columbia and a close personal friend, tried to alert the U.S. government to the implications of the recent discoveries. A small subsidy for further research was obtained from the U.S. Navy, and the studies that were to culminate in the atomic bomb were initiated. At the beginning the staff and equipment were completely inadequate. Perhaps Fermi thought he might be able to repeat, on a somewhat larger scale, work similar to the neutron research in Rome. He certainly did not realize, as very few scientists did, the project's colossal requirements of manpower and means for its successful completion. Fermi was always reluctant to take administrative responsibilities and he concentrated his efforts on the scientific side, leaving to others the staggering problems of organization and procurement. As an expert of exceptional ability and great authority, he naturally helped; but his activity was directed primarily to the scientific aspects of the problems. It must also be remembered that his position—first as an alien, and later, after the United States entered World War II, as an enemy alien—rendered his situation difficult.

Fermi concentrated his efforts on obtaining a chain reaction using ordinary uranium of normal isotopic composition. As soon as it was established that of the two isotopes present in natural uranium, only U^{235} is fissionable by slow neutrons, it became apparent that if one could obtain pure U^{235} or even enrich the mixture in U^{235}, the making of a reactor or possibly even of an atom bomb would be comparatively easy. Still, the isotope separation was such a staggering task that it discouraged most physicists. By the end of the war even this task had been mastered, and isotope separation was soon a normal industrial operation.

In 1939 and 1940, however, isotope separation was very uncertain and other avenues had to be explored. In December 1940, Fermi and Segrè discussed another possibility: the use of the still undiscovered element 94 (plutonium) of mass 239 (Pu^{239}). This substance promised to undergo slow neutron fission and thus to be a replacement for U^{235}. If it could be produced by neutron capture of U^{238} in a natural-uranium reactor, followed by two beta emissions, one could separate it chemically and obtain a pure isotope with, it was hoped, a large slow-neutron cross section. Similar ideas had independently occurred in England and Germany. J. W. Kennedy, Glenn Seaborg, Segrè, and Arthur Wahl undertook the preparation and measurement of the nuclear properties of Pu^{239}, using the Berkeley cyclotron. The favorable results of these experiments (January–April 1941) added impetus to the chain-reaction project because it opened another avenue for the realization of a nuclear bomb. By December 1941, the whole world was engulfed in war, and military applications were paramount. The United States developed, under government supervision, an immense organization, which evolved according to the technical necessities and led to the establishment of the Manhattan Engineer District (MED). The purpose of the MED was to make an atomic bomb in time to influence the course of the war. The history of this development is admirably recounted in the Smyth report. Fermi had a technically prominent part in the whole project. His work at Columbia was still on a small scale, but in 1942 he transferred to Chicago, where it was expanded. It culminated on 2 December 1942 with the first controlled nuclear chain reaction at Stagg Field at the University of Chicago.

The industrial and military developments of the release of nuclear energy, which are of immense importance, will not be treated here. The nuclear reactor, however, is also a scientific instrument of great capabilities, and these were immediately manifest to Fermi. Even during the war, under the extreme pressure of the times, he took advantage of these capabilities to begin research on neutron diffraction, neutron reflection and polarization, measurements of scattering lengths, etc. These investigations, developed later by other physicists, opened up whole new areas of a science sometimes called neutronology, i.e., application of neutronic methods to solid state and various other branches of physics.

When his work at Chicago was finished, Fermi went to Los Alamos, New Mexico, where the Los Alamos Laboratory of the Manhattan Engineer District, under the direction of J. R. Oppenheimer, had the assignment of assembling an atomic bomb. Fermi spent most of the period from September 1944 to early 1946 at Los Alamos, where he served as a general consultant. He also collaborated in the building of a small chain reactor using enriched uranium in U^{235} and heavy water. Fermi actively participated in the first test of the atomic bomb in the desert near Alamogordo, New Mexico, on 16 July 1945.

Following the successful test of the bomb, he was appointed by President Truman to the interim committee charged with advising the president on the use of the bomb and on many fundamental policies concerning atomic energy.

In 1946 the University of Chicago created the Institute for Nuclear Studies and offered a professorship to Fermi. The Institute was promising in its financing and organization; and Fermi, although very influential in its direction, would be spared administrative duties. The offer proved attractive to Fermi, and early in 1946 he and his family left Los Alamos for Chicago. He remained at the University of Chicago for the rest of his life.

The new institute had Samuel K. Allison as director and a faculty in which the new generation of physicists who had been active in the Manhattan Project was strongly represented: Herbert Anderson, Maria Goeppert Mayer, Edward Teller, and Harold C. Urey were among the first members. At Chicago, Fermi rapidly formed a school of graduate students whom he instructed personally, in a fashion reminiscent of his earlier days in Rome. Among those who later distinguished themselves as physicists were Richard L. Garwin, Murray Gell-Mann, Geoffrey Chew, Owen Chamberlain, Marvin L. Goldberger, Leona Marshall, Darragh E. Nagle, T. D. Lee, and C. N. Yang. Chicago thus became an extremely active center in many different areas of physics.

Fermi himself had concluded, at the end of the war, that nuclear physics was reaching a stage of maturity and that the future fundamental developments would be in the study of elementary particles. He thus prepared himself for this new field by learning as much as possible of the theory and by fostering the building of suitable accelerators with which to perform experiments. We have a hint of his effort to assimilate the theory in his Silliman lectures at Yale in the spring of 1950, which were published as *Elementary Particles* (New Haven, 1951). He systematically organized a great number of calculations on all subjects, numerical data, important reprints, etc., which he called the "artificial memory." This material was a daily working tool for him and substituted for books, which he scarcely used any more. It also helped his memory, which, although still excellent, was not as amazing as in his early youth and could not cope with the avalanche of new results.

During the postwar Chicago years, Fermi traveled a good deal, particularly to research centers, where he could meet young, active physicists. He repeatedly visited the Brookhaven National Laboratory, the Radiation Laboratory in Berkeley, the Los Alamos Laboratory, and many universities. He was welcomed everywhere, especially by the younger men who profited from these contacts with him and, in turn, helped Fermi to preserve his youthful spirit. He attended all the Rochester conferences on high-energy physics and taught in several summer schools. In 1949 he revisited Italy, where he was very well received by his former colleagues and by the new generation of physicists who had heard of him as an almost legendary figure.

As soon as the Chicago cyclotron was ready for operation, Fermi again started experimental work on pion-nucleon scattering. (He had coined the word "pion" to indicate pi-mesons.) He found experimentally the resonance in the isotopic spin 3/2, ordinary spin 3/2 state, which had been predicted by Keith Bruckner. The investigation became a major one. With H. L. Anderson and others, Fermi worked out the details up to an energy of about 400 MeV lab of the nucleon-pion interaction. The methods and techniques employed, including the extensive use of computers, were for many years models for the subsequent host of investigators of particle resonances.

In addition to this experimental activity, Fermi did theoretical work on the origin of cosmic rays, devising a mechanism of acceleration by which each proton tends to equipartition of energy with a whole galaxy. These ideas had an important influence on the subsequent studies on cosmic rays. He also developed a statistical method for treating high-energy collision phenomena and multiple production of particles. This method has also received wide and useful applications.

In 1954 Fermi's health began to deteriorate, but with great will power he carried on almost as usual. He spent the summer in Europe, where he taught at summer schools in Italy and France, but on his return to Chicago in September he was hospitalized. An exploratory operation revealed an incurable stomach cancer. Fully aware of the seriousness of his illness and his impending death, he nevertheless maintained his remarkable equanimity and self-control. He died in November and was buried in Chicago.

It is too early to give a historically valid assessment of Fermi's place in the history of physics. He was the only physicist in the twentieth century who excelled in both theory and experiment, and he was one of the most versatile. His greatest accomplishments are (chronologically) the statistics of particles obeying the exclusion principle, the application of these statistics to the Thomas-Fermi atom, the recasting of quantum electrodynamics, the theory of beta decay, the experimental study of artificial radioactivity produced by neutron bombardment and the connected discovery of slow neutrons and their phenomenology, the experimental realization of a nuclear chain reaction, and the experimental study of pion-nucleon collision. In addition there are Fermi's innumerable, apparently isolated contributions to atomic, molecular, nuclear, and particle physics, cosmic rays, relativity, etc., many of which initiated whole new chapters of physics.

BIBLIOGRAPHY

Fermi's *Collected Papers,* E. Segrè, E. Amaldi, H. L. Anderson, E. Persico, F. Rasetti, C. S. Smith, and A. Wattenberg, eds., 2 vols. (Chicago, 1962–1965), contains most of Fermi's papers and a complete bibliography, a biographical introduction by E. Segrè, introductions to the various papers by members of the editorial committee, a chronology of Fermi's life, and subsidiary material.

Secondary literature includes Laura Fermi, *Atoms in the Family* (Chicago, 1954), a biography by Fermi's wife emphasizing the human aspects of their life; Emilio Segrè, *Enrico Fermi, Physicist* (Chicago, 1970), a scientific biography; and H. D. Smyth, *Atomic Energy for Military Purposes* (Princeton, 1945), which gives an excellent account of the history of the development of atomic energy up to 1945.

See also R. G. Hewlett and O. E. Anderson, Jr., *The New World* (University Park, Pa., 1962); R. G. Hewlett and F. Duncan, *Atomic Shield* (University Park, Pa., 1969); and *Review of Modern Physics,* **27** (1955), 249–275, which contains the memorial symposium in honor of Fermi held at Washington, D.C. (Apr. 1955).

EMILIO SEGRÈ

FERNALD, MERRITT LYNDON (*b.* Orono, Maine, 5 October 1873; *d.* Cambridge, Massachusetts, 22 September 1950), *botany.*

Fernald achieved a complete revision in 1950 of Asa Gray's *Manual of the Botany of the Northern United States* (1908), the most critical comprehensive floristic work ever published for any part of North America, and propounded the theory of persistence of plants on nunataks—"the largest single contribution to the science of phytogeography since the time of Darwin" (Merrill, p. 53). The son of Merritt Caldwell Fernald, president of Maine State College of Agriculture and Mechanic Arts (later the University of Maine), and Mary Lovejoy Heyward Fernald, he published his first botanical paper at seventeen. About 830 titles were to follow, chiefly concerning the identities, accurate definitions, and verified distributions of plants of the northeastern United States. Fernald's taxonomic papers were carefully prepared and provocative, although sometimes they were more commentary than conclusion. His approach was to trace types back, often to pre-Linnaean botanists, then to search for clarifying evidence in the field. His masterly acquaintance with botanical literature led him along old paths to fresh decisions.

A short, stout man, Fernald was tireless in the field, boyishly joyous, given to punning, and optimistic throughout his life. His tremendous industry and total absorption with systematic botany were the mainsprings of his success. A "mere grind" was his own appraisal, but his friend Ludlow Griscom called him a "one-pointed, one-sided botanical machine." On the invitation of Sereno Watson, Fernald had become an assistant in the Gray Herbarium early in 1891 and enrolled that fall in Harvard's Lawrence Scientific School. He graduated in 1897 with the B.S. degree, *magna cum laude,* his only earned degree.

Fernald wrote monographs on such genera as *Potamogeton* and *Draba,* which in turn led to his classic paper "Persistence of Plants in Unglaciated Areas of Boreal America" (1925), a documented rebuttal to the generally held view that a moving ice sheet had annihilated all the plants and animals before it. His "nunatak theory" excited debate among geologists and biologists. It stands, somewhat sculptured, like Botanist's Dome of the Gaspé Peninsula, a landmark of plant geography.

"His trenchant criticism . . . [assisted] in maintaining the standards of American botanical scholarship" (Merrill, p. 54). His humor enhances the descriptions and recipes of *Edible Wild Plants of Eastern North America* (1943), which he wrote with A. C. Kinsey.

Fernald married Margaret Howard Grant of Providence, Rhode Island, on 5 April 1907, and a son and two daughters were born to them. His association with Harvard spanned nearly sixty years. He was unforgettable to his students, and his work was avidly followed by readers of *Rhodora,* which he edited for thirty-two years. Fernald was acknowledged doyen in the study of the flora of the eastern United States. "When he was formed," wrote Merrill (p. 61), "the mold was destroyed; there never can be another Fernald."

BIBLIOGRAPHY

I. ORIGINAL WORKS. A bibliography of Fernald's publications, by Katherine Fernald Lohnes and Lazella Schwarten, forms an appendix to Merrill's sketch (see below). Among his writings are "Persistence of Plants in Unglaciated Areas of Boreal America," in *Memoirs of the American Academy of Arts and Sciences,* **15** (1925), 239–342; and *Edible Wild Plants of Eastern North America* (Cornwall, N.Y., 1943), written with A. C. Kinsey, revised ed. by Reed C. Rollins (New York, 1958).

II. SECONDARY LITERATURE. The fullest, and an eminently fair, appraisal of Fernald is by Elmer D. Merrill, in *Biographical Memoirs. National Academy of Sciences,* **28** (1954), 45–98. Other sketches are Arthur Stanley Pease, in *Rhodora,* **53** (1951), 33–39; John M. Fogg, Jr., *ibid.,* 39–43; Harley Harris Bartlett, *ibid.,* 44–55; Reed C. Rollins, *ibid.,* 55–61; and Ludlow Griscom, *ibid.,* 61–65. Rollins published a shortened version of his appraisal in *Bulletin of the Torrey Botanical Club,* **78** (1951), 270–272. A few salient comments appear in Una F. Weatherby, *Charles Alfred Weatherby* (Cambridge, Mass., 1951), pp. 128, 144, 178.

JOSEPH EWAN

FERNEL, JEAN FRANÇOIS (*b.* Montdidier, France, 1497 [?]; *d.* Fontainebleau, France, 26 April 1558), *medicine.*

Fernel's year of birth was probably 1497, according to Sherrington's scrutiny of the various reports available. The son of a well-to-do innkeeper at Montdidier, he was twelve years old when the family moved to Clermont, twenty miles from Paris. In his writings Fernel calls himself "Ambianus," apparently because Montdidier was within the diocese of Amiens.

After schooling at Clermont, Fernel went to the Collège de Ste. Barbe in Paris (1519) and, at the age of twenty-two, took his M.A. degree. For the next five years he was virtually a recluse, feeling that it was necessary to improve his mind and extend his knowledge, particularly in philosophy, astronomy, and mathematics. These studies were interrupted in 1524 by a serious illness ("quartan fever") that forced him to go to the country for a period of convalescence. After that time Fernel's father ceased to support his studies because of his duties to his other children. Obliged to support himself in Paris, Fernel lectured on philosophy and began studying medicine, apparently halfheartedly at first. In 1527 he published his first book, *Monalosphaerium,* which was followed in 1528 by *Cosmotheoria,* both of them mathematical and astronomical. At the time, astrology occupied an important position in mathematics and astronomy; the *Cosmotheoria,* however, contained measurements made by Fernel—his estimate of a degree of meridian was good enough to be in close agreement with that of Jean Picard 140 years later and thus was an important contribution to geophysics.

In the meantime Fernel had married, and he was now severely criticized by his father-in-law, a senator of Paris, for neglecting his medical studies and his duties as head of a family in favor of these unprofitable interests. The young man had done well as a teacher of philosophy at his college and in astronomy. He had also acquired a collection of instruments, among them an astrolabe of his own design for finding the hour and for measuring time, but he was now compelled to sell these instruments and to take his medical studies seriously. These were completed in 1530, when he obtained his *venia practicandi.*

Within six years Fernel became one of the most famous physicians in France. Students flocked to his lectures, and "from his School there went forth skilled physicians more numerous than soldiers from the Trojan horse, and spread over all regions and quarters of Europe" (Plancy, in C. S. Sherrington, *Endeavour of Jean Fernel*). His reputation at the court of the dauphin (later Henry II) became firmly established when he saved the life of Henry's mistress, Diane de

Poitiers. The prince wanted to keep him at Fontaine-bleau as court physician, but Fernel begged "in all charity" to be allowed to return to Paris, to his books, his students, and his patients. Fernel was less successful with Francis I, Henry's father, who died in 1547. He had treated the king for syphilis with a decoction of his own, although the established cure at that time was treatment with mercury. Fernel had criticized this method and later wrote a book on his cure of syphilis. Popular though he was at the court and in the city, he had many enemies at the university; he was, however, too powerful to be suppressed. In 1534 he was appointed professor of medicine.

In 1536, while teaching medicine at the Collège de Cornouailles, Fernel began writing his *De naturali parte medicinae* (1542), addressed to medical subjects that he later named "physiology," thus introducing this term for the science of the functions of the body. The new title was destined to remain, and the book was read for a century, until Harvey's discovery of the circulation of the blood (1628) gave physiology its present experimental direction. Fernel's physiology was still the humoral medicine of his time. It did not discuss respiration, circulation, digestion, and such; the six chapters following that on anatomy concern the elements, the temperaments, the spirits, the innate heat, the faculties, the humors, and the procreation of man. The spirit is said to enter the fetus on the fortieth day of pregnancy; the substance of the soul and its faculties are hidden from us, and therefore we must treat its instruments as "immediate causes" in studying the body.

In spite of his orthodox Galenic physiology Fernel had something new to offer his contemporaries. The medicine of that time acknowledged the influence of magic and sorcery on the origin and development of disease, and people of sufficient means employed private astrologers. Fernel, who had believed in astrology, of which there was still a trace in his *De abditis rerum causis* (1548, but begun before his "Physiologiae"), gradually came to the view that the "whole book of healing was nothing other than a copy of inviolable laws observable in Nature," as formulated in his unfinished last work. His first biographer, Guillaume Plancy (1514–1568), explained Fernel's change of attitude toward contemporary medicine by his respect for facts. Fernel was an observer who emphasized the value of practice and experience; and the astrological predictions did not agree with the lessons of these masters. In the end he utterly condemned astrology. To the young he must have seemed a reformer; to his Scholastically trained colleagues at the University of Paris, a nonsensical if not a dangerous heretic.

With his observant mind, breadth of knowledge, and new attitude toward his profession, Fernel was a man of the Renaissance, which was well under way both at the court of Francis I and among educated citizens, scholars, architects, and painters of Paris. The university, which had remained the stronghold of the old type of scholarship, conservative and against innovation, did not honor its great son until long after his death.

Fernel's *De abditis rerum causis* is written as a dialogue among three characters: Brutus, a cultured man of the sixteenth century; Philiatros, whose name denotes a senior candidate for the doctor's degree; and Eudoxus, a physician older than his two friends and speaking with the voice of Fernel himself. It is an exposition of the beliefs of the educated citizen of that period, what he thinks about God, nature, the soul, matter, medicine, the preternatural, etc., as well as a plea for observation and common sense in the experienced world of nature, but it also admits the existence of a world of incorporeal beings between earth and heaven. "God" may have meant the Supreme Being, but the other words had different meanings. Matter, for instance, was substance composed of the traditional four elements; the soul was the principle of life and mind and had come from the stars. There were three kinds of soul, as Aristotle had taught: the soul of plants, which was nutritive and reproductive; the soul of animals, which was sentient and vegetative; and the soul of man, which partaking of these qualities incorporates reason also with them in a unified way. This book had great appeal for the educated citizens in European cultural centers and went through at least thirty editions. Yet today it seems of less importance than Fernel's contributions to medicine and astronomy (geophysics).

Fernel worked tirelessly to complete his textbook *Medicina*, first published in 1554. His future biographer, Plancy, who lived in his household from 1548 until Fernel's death, tells of the struggle of his last years, torn as he was between a great practice, the writing of his books, and, from 1556, the service of Henry II as physician to the court after the death of his substitute, Maître de Bourges. Fernel was then about sixty and counted on a measure of peace at Fontainebleau. Wars with Spain and England interfered with this expectation. He was compelled to follow the king to the battlefield, all the while trying to write his *Febrium curandarum methodus generalis* ("Treatment of Fevers"). He witnessed the capture of Calais, which the English had held for some two hundred years, then finally settled at the court in Fontainebleau, bringing his wife with him. She died a few months later. This was a severe shock, and he was soon taken ill and died, in spite of the ministrations of all the other physicians at the court.

On his deathbed Fernel was greatly worried that he had found no time to put the finishing touches to his *Medicina.* It fell upon Plancy to edit the full text of the *Universa medicina* (1567), which contained chapters on physiology, pathology, therapeutics, and such. Fernel's latest biographer, Sir Charles Sherrington, has raised the question of whether there were any original observations of value in Fernel's *Medicina.* The important contribution was undoubtedly the "Physiologiae," in which he had noted peristalsis and the systole and diastole of the heart; he did not, however, realize that the veins and arteries were connected by capillaries. Also of interest is his notion that the veins hinder clotting. Fernel's anatomical observations, among them the earliest description of the spinal canal, were good and clearly presented, before or simultaneous with Vesalius' *De humani corporis fabrica* (1543), the shadow of which may well have lain too heavily over significant contributions from contemporaries and predecessors. In medicine Fernel gave early descriptions of appendicitis and endocarditis. His ranking in the history of medicine, however, rests mainly upon his role as a reformer fighting to replace magic, sorcery, and astrology with observations at the sickbed.

BIBLIOGRAPHY

I. ORIGINAL WORKS. Some of Fernel's books are *Monalosphaerium* (Paris, 1527); *Cosmotheoria* (Paris, dated 1527 but apparently not issued until March 1528); *De abditis rerum causis* (Paris, 1548); *Medicina* (Paris, 1554), of which the first seven chapters, called collectively "Physiologiae," represent a reedited version of *De naturali parte medicinae,* also trans. into French as *Les VII livres de la physiologie* (Paris, 1655); *Universa medicina,* Guillaume Plancy, ed. (Paris, 1567), which also includes Plancy's *Vita Fernelii; Febrium curandarum methodus generalis* (Frankfurt am Main, 1577); and *De luis venerae perfectissima cura liber* (Antwerp, 1579).

II. SECONDARY LITERATURE. A scholarly appraisal of Fernel's work, together with an English trans. of Plancy's *Vita Fernelii,* is in C. S. Sherrington, *Endeavour of Jean Fernel* (Cambridge, 1946).

RAGNAR GRANIT

FERRARI, LUDOVICO (*b.* Bologna, Italy, 2 February 1522; *d.* Bologna, October 1565), *algebra.*

Little is known of Ferrari's life. His father, Alessandro, was the son of a Milanese refugee who had settled in Bologna. Following his father's death Ferrari went to live with his uncle Vincenzo. In November 1536 he was sent to Milan by his uncle to join the household of Girolamo Cardano, replacing his uncle's son Luca, who was already in Cardano's service. Although he had not received a formal education, Ferrari was exceptionally intelligent. Cardano therefore instructed him in Latin, Greek, and mathematics and employed him as amanuensis. In Cardano's autobiography, written many years later, Ferrari is described as having "excelled as a youth all my pupils by the high degree of his learning" (*De vita propria liber* [1643], p. 156).

In 1540 Ferrari was appointed public lecturer in mathematics in Milan, and shortly afterward he defeated Zuanne da Coi, a mathematician of Brescia, at a public disputation. He also collaborated with Cardano in researches on the cubic and quartic equations, the results of which were published in the *Ars magna* (1545). The publication of this book was the cause of the celebrated feud between Ferrari and Niccolò Tartaglia of Brescia, author of *Quesiti et inventioni diverse* (1546). In the wake of the resulting public disputation, Ferrari received offers of employment from many persons of importance, including Emperor Charles V, who wanted a tutor for his son, and Ercole Gonzaga, cardinal of Mantua. He accepted Gonzaga's offer and, at the request of the cardinal's brother, Ferrante, then governor of Milan, he carried out a survey of that province. After this he was in the cardinal's service for some eight years. On his retirement because of ill health Ferrari went to Bologna to live with his sister. From September 1564 until his death in October 1565, he held the post of *lector ad mathematicam* at the University of Bologna.

When Ferrari went to live with Cardano, the latter was earning his livelihood by teaching mathematics. Although Cardano was a qualified physician, he had not yet been accepted by the College of Physicians and was then preparing his first works on medicine and mathematics for publication. It is likely that Ferrari was introduced to mathematics through Cardano's *Practica arithmetice* (1539). While this work was in preparation, news reached Cardano that a method of solving the cubic equation of the form $x^3 + ax = b$, where a and b are positive, was known to Niccolò Tartaglia of Brescia. Until then Cardano had accepted Luca Pacioli's statement in the *Summa de arithmetica, geometria, proportioni et proportionalita* (1494) that the cubic equation could not be solved algebraically. On learning that Tartaglia had solved the equation in the course of a disputation with Antonio Maria Fiore in 1535, Cardano probably tried to find the solution himself, but without success. In 1539, before his book was published, he asked Tartaglia for the solution, offering to include it in his forthcoming book under Tartaglia's name. Tartaglia refused, on the ground that he wished to publish his discovery himself. But when he visited Cardano in Milan in March 1539, he gave him the solution on the solemn promise that it would be kept secret. In 1542, however, Cardano learned that the cubic equation had been solved several years before Tartaglia by Scipione Ferro, *lector ad mathematicam* at the University of Bologna from 1496 to 1526. During a visit to Bologna, Cardano and Ferrari were shown Ferro's work, in manuscript, by his pupil and successor Annibale dalla Nave. After this Cardano did not feel obliged to keep his promise.

Having learned the method of solving one type of cubic equation, Cardano and Ferrari were encouraged to extend their researches to other types of cubics and to the quartic. Ferrari found geometrical demonstrations for Cardano's formulas for solving $x^3 + ax = bx^2 + c$ and $x^3 + ax^2 = b$; he also solved the quartic of the form $x^4 + ax^2 + b = cx$ where a, b, c, are positive. The results were embodied in Cardano's *Ars magna* (1545). In it he attributed the discovery of the method of solving the equation $x^3 + ax = b$ to Scipione Ferro and its rediscovery to Tartaglia. That this apparent breach of secrecy angered Tartaglia is evident from book IX of his *Quesiti et inventioni diverse* (1546), where he recounted the circumstances in which he had made his discovery and Cardano's attempts to obtain the solution from him. He also gave a verbatim account of the conversation at their meeting in Milan, along with his comments.

Ferrari, loyal to his master and impetuous by nature, reacted quickly. In February 1547 he wrote to Tartaglia, protesting that the latter had unjustly and falsely made statements prejudicial to Cardano. Having criticized the mathematical content of Tartaglia's work and accused him of repetition and plagiarism, Ferrari challenged him to a public disputation in geometry, arithmetic, and related disciplines. Scholarly disputations, common in those days, were often the means of testing the professional ability of the participants. Since both Ferrari and Tartaglia were engaged in the public teaching of mathematics, a disputation was a serious matter. In his reply Tartaglia, while insisting that Cardano had not kept his promise, said that he had used injurious words in order to provoke Cardano to write to him. He asked Ferrari to leave Cardano to fight his own battles; otherwise, Ferrari should admit that he was writing at Cardano's instigation. Saying that he would accept the challenge if Cardano at least countersigned Ferrari's letter, Tartaglia went on to raise objections to the conditions of the proposed disputation—the subjects, the location, the amount of caution money to be deposited, and the judges.

Twelve letters were exchanged, full of charges and insults, each party trying to justify his position. Tartaglia maintained that Cardano had broken his promise and that Ferrari was writing at Cardano's instance. Ferrari asserted that the solution of the cubic equation was known to both Scipione Ferro and Antonio Maria Fiore long before Tartaglia had discovered it and that it was magnanimous of Cardano to mention Tartaglia in the *Ars magna*. He also denied that he was writing on Cardano's behalf. In the course of this correspondence each party issued a series of thirty-one problems for the other to solve. Tartaglia sent his problems in a letter dated 21 April 1547. The problems were no more difficult than those found in Pacioli's *Summa*. On 24 May 1547 Ferrari replied with thirty-one problems of his own but did not send the solutions to those set by Tartaglia. In his reply (July 1547) Tartaglia sent the solutions to twenty-six of Ferrari's problems, leaving out those which led to cubic equations; a month later he gave his reasons for not solving these five problems. In a letter dated October 1547 Ferrari replied, criticizing Tartaglia's solutions and giving his solutions to the problems set by the latter. Tartaglia, replying in June 1548, said he had not received Ferrari's letter until January and that he was willing to go to Milan to take part in the disputation. In July 1548 both parties confirmed their acceptance.

There is no record of what happened at the meeting except for scattered references in Tartaglia's *General trattato di numeri, et misure* (1556–1560). The parties met on 10 August 1548 in the church of Santa Maria del Giardino dei Minori Osservanti in the presence of a distinguished gathering that included Ferrante Gonzaga, governor of Milan, who had been named judge. Tartaglia says that he was not given a chance to state his case properly. Arguments over a problem of Ferrari's that Tartaglia had been unable to resolve lasted until suppertime, and everyone was obliged to leave. Tartaglia departed the next day for Brescia, and Ferrari was probably declared the winner.

Ferrari's method of solving the quartic equation $x^4 + ax^2 + b = cx$ was set out by Cardano in the *Ars magna*. It consists of reducing the equation to a cubic. The discovery was made in the course of solving a problem given to Cardano by Zuanne da Coi: "Divide 10 into three proportional parts so that the product of the first and second is 6." If the mean is x, it follows that $x^4 + 6x^2 + 36 = 60x$, or $(x^2 + 6)^2 = 60x + 6x^2$. This last equation can be put in the form

$$(x^2 + 6 + y)^2 = 6x^2 + 60x + y^2 + 12y + 2yx^2$$

or

$$(x^2 + 6 + y)^2 = (2y + 6)x^2 + 60x + (y^2 + 12y),$$

where y is a new unknown. If y is chosen so that the

right-hand side of the equation is a perfect square, then y satisfies the condition

$$60^2 = 4(2y + 6)(y^2 + 12y),$$

which can be reduced to the cubic equation

$$y^3 + 15y^2 + 36y = 450.$$

That Ferrari's method of solution is applicable to all cases of the quartic equation was shown by Rafael Bombelli in his *Algebra* (1572).

BIBLIOGRAPHY

I. ORIGINAL WORKS. The letters exchanged by Ferrari and Tartaglia were printed, and copies were sent to several persons of influence in Italy. (A complete set of these letters is in the Department of Printed Books of the British Museum.) They have been published by Enrico Giordani in *I sei cartelli di matematica disfida, primamente intorno alla generale risoluzione delle equazioni cubiche, di Lodovico Ferrari, coi sei contro-cartelli in risposta di Nicolò Tartaglia, comprendenti le soluzioni de' quesiti dall'una e dall'altra parte proposti* (Milan, 1876). Ferrari's work on the cubic and quartic equations is described in Cardano's *Artis magnae, sive de regulis algebraicis* (Nuremberg, 1545).

II. SECONDARY LITERATURE. Cardano wrote a short biography of Ferrari, "Vita Ludovici Ferrarii Bononiensis," in his *Opera omnia* (Lyons, 1663), IX, 568–569. References to Ferrari in Cardano's other works are cited in J. H. Morley, *Life of Girolamo Cardano of Milan, Physician* (London, 1854), I, 148–149, 187. The history of mathematics in sixteenth-century Italy is outlined in Ettore Bortolotti, *Storia della matematica nella Università di Bologna* (Bologna, 1947), pp. 35–80. Arnaldo Masotti, "Sui cartelli di matematica disfida scambiati fra Lodovico Ferrari e Niccolò Tartaglia," in *Rendiconti dell'Istituto lombardo di scienze e lettere,* **94** (1960), 31–41, cites the important secondary literature on Ferrari.

S. A. JAYAWARDENE

FERRARIS, GALILEO (*b.* Livorno Vercellese, Italy, 31 October 1847; *d.* Turin, Italy, 7 February 1897), *electrical engineering, physics.*

One of four children of a pharmacist, Ferraris became one of the prime electrical innovators of the 1880's. At age ten he went to live in Turin with a physician uncle, who guided the boy's education in the sciences and classics. He subsequently spent three years at the University of Turin and two years at the Scuola d'Applicazione di Torino, graduating in 1869 with the title engineer. His doctoral thesis at the university in 1872 was *Teoria matematica della propagazione dell'elettricità nei solidi omogenei.*

Ferraris then taught technical physics at the Regio Museo Industriale in Turin and also investigated light waves and the optical characteristics of telescopes, especially the phase difference of two waves in sinusoidal motion. This led to the concept of phase-displaced electrical waves and a rotating electromagnetic field. Further studies in polyphonic acoustics and interference in telephone circuits sharpened Ferraris' grasp of coacting forces in and out of phase. His continued interest in optics resulted in the publication, in 1876, of the *Proprietà degli strumenti diottrici.* . . .

Ferraris represented the Italian government on the awards jury at the 1881 International Electricity Exposition at Paris, where he learned of the Deprez system of high-voltage alternating current transmission and low-voltage distribution. He was also a delegate to the Paris conference of 1882 to determine standard electrical units, and in 1883 he was his country's delegate to the electrical exposition in Vienna. These duties prepared Ferraris for his service in 1883 as president of the international section of the Electricity Exposition at Turin, where he saw the Gaulard-Gibbs transformer. A paper on the transformer, presented before the Academy of Science at Turin in 1885, led to an intensive study of the interlocking relationships of electrical and magnetic forces in the primary and secondary circuits of the transformer system, and he drew heavily on the optical analogy of light polarized elliptically and circularly.

Carrying the notion further, Ferraris visualized the placing of two electromagnets, each fed by a current displaced 90° out of phase, at right angles to each other, thereby producing the equivalent of a revolving magnetic field. This could induce currents in an included copper drum (or rotor), and the resulting torque would be equivalent to the power of an alternating current electric motor—then still the missing unit in the production of an alternating current system. Ferraris constructed such a device and tested it in August–September 1885 by feeding one coil with current from a small Siemens alternator and the second coil with current from a Gaulard transformer. Switching the currents reversed the direction of rotation. Ferraris freely discussed his principle and openly showed his models in classroom and laboratory. He did not apply for patents because he felt a professional pride in discovery and the extension of all knowledge. This was indicated when he wrote: "Above industrial importance I perceive scientific importance, above material use, intellectual use."

The Ferraris principle led to the design and construction of an alternating-current motor without commutator or brushes, which had a squirrel-cage copper rotor revolving by induction from its surrounding "rotating" stator field; it was asynchronous and self-starting. This type of motor today is responsible for the bulk of conversion of electrical power to mechanical power. Ferraris announced his discovery before the Royal Academy of Sciences at Turin on 18 March 1888. Others later claimed priority for the concept of the rotating field—especially Deprez, Walter Baily, and Nikola Tesla. In litigation in German and U.S. courts between 1895 and 1900, it was established that Ferraris had anticipated the principle but that Tesla had applied it, independently, to motor design. The original Ferraris devices are still preserved at the Istituto Elettrotecnico Nazionale Galileo Ferraris in Turin, an institute inaugurated in 1935 as a center for all forms of electrical research and study.

Ferraris participated in the AEG-Oerlikon effort to extend alternating current systems, as demonstrated in the 175-kilometer Lauffen–Frankfurt transmission line that inaugurated the Frankfurt Electrical Exposition of 1891 (at which he was awarded highest honors). He represented his government and was elected vice-president of the electrical exposition in Chicago in 1893, where the standards for the henry, the joule, and the watt were adopted.

BIBLIOGRAPHY

Ferraris' *Opere* were published in 3 vols. by the Associazione Elettrotecnica Italiana (Milan, 1902–1904); see also *Sulla illuminazione elettrica* (Turin, 1879); "Rotazioni elettrodinamiche prodotte per mezzo di correnti alternate," in *Atti dell'Accademia della scienze*, **23** (1888), 360–363; and *Lezioni di elettrotecnica dettate nel R. Museo industriale italiano in Torino* (Turin–Rome, 1897; 2nd ed., 1904).

BERN DIBNER

FERREIN, ANTOINE (*b.* Frespech, near Agen, Lot-et-Garonne, France, 25 October 1693; *d.* Paris, France, 28 February 1769), *anatomy.*

Ferrein was the son of Antoine Ferrein and Françoise d'Elprat, both members of old Agenois families. At his father's wish he began legal studies and did so at Cahors, although he was much more interested in mathematics and the natural sciences. After reading a work by Borelli, in which physiological propositions were purportedly derived from anatomical information by means of mathematical procedures, Ferrein decided to devote himself entirely to medical and anatomical research. Certain ideas of iatromechanics deeply influenced his thinking throughout his life. He followed the idea of an *anatomie subtile* which would seek out in the *petites machines* of the body the explanation of most physiological and pathological phenomena.

In 1714 Ferrein left Cahors to go to Montpellier, where he studied medicine under Raymond Vieussens and Antoine Deidier. In 1716 he received his bachelor's degree, but family obligations forced him to interrupt his studies and move to Marseilles, where he gave private classes in anatomy, physiology, and surgery. He later returned to Montpellier, and on 27 September 1728 he received the title of Doctor of Medicine. He then taught in the Montpellier Faculty of Medicine as *suppléant* to Astruc. After his applications for the chairs of medicine and chemistry were refused (1731–1732), however, he left Montpellier for Paris.

Since he had no right to practice medicine in Paris, Ferrein gave public instruction in anatomy there. Later he became the chief medical officer of the French army in Italy (1733–1735). During this period he sought to combat several epidemics of miliary fever. He finally met the requirements of the Paris Faculty of Medicine, and although he was fully accredited by Montpellier, he requested and obtained another bachelor's degree in 1736 and that of Doctor of Medicine in 1738. From then on, Ferrein, an ambitious, tireless worker and brilliant speaker, made an extraordinary career for himself. On 22 February 1741 he was elected to the Academy of Sciences as assistant anatomist; in 1742 he became associate; and on 21 May 1750, pensioner.

The decade 1740–1750 was the most fruitful of Ferrein's life. He published a series of memoirs on the structure and function of several organs. In 1742 he was named professor of medicine at the Collège Royal and also became professor of surgery at the Faculty of Medicine. He was awarded the chair of pharmacy in 1745. Ferrein's courses became famous, but more for the clarity and order of his exposition than for the originality of his ideas. In 1751, in addition to all his teaching duties and an exhausting medical practice, Ferrein replaced Winslow as professor of anatomy at the Jardin du Roi. He died following a stroke.

In 1731, while he was competing for the chair of medicine at Montpellier, Ferrein propounded a theory on the shape of the heart during systole that was the origin of a long dispute within several learned societies. Against his rival Antoine Fizès and an opinion then generally prevalent, Ferrein maintained that the heart shrank during systole and that its tip curled over and forward. This was a new and accurate explanation of the heart's beating against the thoracic wall. In 1733 Ferrein published the results of his microscopic research on the parenchymatous and vascular structure of the liver. He was the first to glimpse certain anatomical peculiarities of the hepatobiliary system, but unfortunately he drew erroneous physiological conclusions. Ferrein's researches on lymph ducts, hepatic inflammation, and the movements of the jaw were little valued by subsequent generations.

In 1741 Ferrein reviewed and modified Dodart's theory of phonation. According to Ferrein, the lips of the glottis form two true "vocal cords"; sounds arise solely from the vibration of these cords, which is produced by the stream of exhaled air. Thus the air performs the same function as a violin bow. In this hypothesis the larynx is considered to be a combination of wind and string instrument. Apart from Leonardo da Vinci's experiments, Ferrein was the first to study phonation experimentally by forcing air through the detached larynxes of various animals.

According to his histological researches (1749), the kidney is not composed of glomerules, as Malpighi believed, nor are the blood vessels coiled, as was taught by Ruysch; rather, it is made up of a collection of "white tubes." Ferrein described the "pyramids" and the tubular structure of the kidneys, but he misconstrued their function.

It was also Ferrein who formulated the rules for examination of the abdominal organs by palpation. He also denied the existence of true hermaphroditism.

BIBLIOGRAPHY

I. ORIGINAL WORKS. Almost all Ferrein's scientific studies were published in the *Mémoires de l'Académie royale des sciences;* of particular interest are "De la formation de la voix de l'homme" (1741), p. 50; and "Sur la structure des viscères nommés glanduleux, et particulièrement sur celle des reins et du foie" (1749), pp. 489–530. The most famous of his competition theses is *Quaestiones medicae duodecim* (Montpellier, 1732). The great success of his courses led some of his students to publish them directly from the original MSS or their class notes—these publications include *Cours de médecine pratique rédigé d'après les principes de M. Ferrein par M. Arnault de Nobleville* (Paris, 1769); *Matière médicale,* published by Andry (Paris, 1770); and *Éléments de chirurgie pratique,* published from Ferrein's MSS by H. Gauthier (Paris, 1771). Some of the original MSS are in the library of the Paris Faculty of Medicine.

II. SECONDARY LITERATURE. The biography by Grandjean de Fouchy, "Éloge de M. Ferrein," in *Histoire de l'Académie royale des sciences pour l'année 1768* (1772), pp. 151–162, is the basic secondary source. Biographical information is also in N. F. J. Eloy, "Ferrein," in *Dictionnaire historique de la médecine,* II (Mons, 1778), 223–224; J. R. Marboutin, "Antoine Ferrein," in *Revue de l'Agenais,* **61** (1934), 309–311; and A. Portal, *Histoire de l'anatomie et de la chirurgie,* V (Paris, 1770). A concise appraisal of Ferrein's publications is in J.-E. Dezeimeris, *Dictionnaire historique de la médecine,* II (Paris, 1834), 297–300. His researches on the kidney are analyzed in F. Grondona, "La struttura dei reni da F. Ruysch à W. Bowman," in *Physis,* **7** (1965), 281–316.

M. D. GRMEK

FERREL, WILLIAM (*b.* Bedford [now Fulton] County, Pennsylvania, 29 January 1817; *d.* Maywood, Kansas, 18 September 1891), *mathematical geophysics.*

After Laplace, Ferrel was the chief founder of the subject now known as geophysical fluid dynamics. He gave the first general formulation of the equations of motion for a body moving with respect to the rotating earth and drew from them the consequences for atmospheric and oceanic circulation. He contributed to meteorological and tidal theory and to the problem of "earth wobble" (changes in the axis and speed of the earth's rotation).

Born in remote south-central Pennsylvania, Ferrel was the eldest of six boys and two girls born to Benjamin Ferrel and his wife, whose maiden name was Miller. In 1829 the family moved across Maryland into what is now West Virginia, where Ferrel received the usual rudimentary education during a couple of winters in a one-room schoolhouse. A shy and solitary boy, he avidly devoured the few scientific books he acquired by arduous trips to Martinsburg, West Virginia, or Hagerstown, Maryland. Stimulated in 1832 by a partial solar eclipse, by 1835 he had taught himself, with only a crude almanac and a geography book as guides, to predict eclipses. Not until 1837, when he was twenty, did he learn "the law of gravitation, and that the moon and planets move in elliptic orbits."[1] With money saved from schoolteaching, in 1839 Ferrel entered Marshall College, Mercersburg, Pennsylvania (later merged with Franklin College in Lancaster), where he "saw [for] the first time a treatise on algebra."[2] Lack of money forced him to leave after two years of study, and he returned home to teach school for two years. He completed his degree in 1844 at the newly founded Bethany College in Bethany, West Virginia.

Ferrel then went west to teach school, first in Missouri and then in Kentucky. In Liberty, Missouri, he found a copy of Newton's *Principia* (presumably the Glasgow edition, with the 1740 tidal papers added), and later he sent to Philadelphia for a copy of Laplace's *Mécanique céleste* (in Bowditch's translation). In 1853, aged thirty-six, Ferrel wrote his first scientific paper. He moved to Nashville, Tennessee, the first city in which he had ever lived, in 1854, and there, while teaching school, he became an important contributor to the *Nashville Journal of Medicine and Surgery.* Through Benjamin Apthorp Gould, in whose *Astronomical Journal* he had published his first and some subsequent papers, Ferrel was offered his first scientific post, on the *American Nautical Almanac* staff. He remained with the *Almanac* in Cambridge, Massachusetts, from 1858 to 1867, when Benjamin

Peirce of Harvard persuaded Ferrel to go to Washington to join the U.S. Coast Survey, of which Peirce was the new superintendent. In 1882 Ferrel joined the U.S. Army's Signal Service (predecessor of the Weather Bureau), where he remained until 1886. On his retirement at age seventy he moved to Kansas City, Kansas, to be with his brother Jacob and other relatives, but the lack of "scientific associations and access to scientific libraries"[3] in the West led him to return to Martinsburg, West Virginia, in 1889 and 1890. He died in Maywood, Kansas, at the age of seventy-four.

A painfully shy man, Ferrel never married, nor did he found a school in his subject. He did not apply for any of his scientific positions, yet he became a member of the National Academy of Sciences (1868), an associate fellow of the American Academy of Arts and Sciences, an honorary member of the meteorological societies of Austria, Britain, and Germany, and a recipient of the honorary degrees of A.M. and Ph.D.

Ferrel's career as a scientist began about 1850 with his study of Newton's *Principia.* Concentrating on tidal theory—in which Newton's work had been extended in papers presented to the French Academy in 1740 by Daniel Bernoulli, Euler, and Maclaurin and published in editions of the *Principia* after Newton's death—Ferrel conjectured "that the action of the moon and sun upon the tides must have a tendency to retard the earth's rotation on its axis."[4] In his *Mécanique céleste* Laplace had discounted any effect of the tides on the earth's rate of axial rotation. In his first published paper (1853) Ferrel showed that Laplace had neglected the second-order terms that should cause tidal retardation. Since Laplace had claimed to account for all the observed acceleration in the moon's orbit without tidal friction, Ferrel suggested that the latter might be counteracted by the earth's shrinking as it cooled. When about 1860 it became clear that Laplace's theory could not account for the observed value of the moon's acceleration, Ferrel returned to the problem in a paper read to the American Academy of Arts and Sciences in 1864. Although others reached the same general conclusion independently, Ferrel's was the first quantitative treatment of tidal friction, a problem that continues to be of scientific interest.

After three more papers published locally, Ferrel returned to tidal theory in 1856 with his second paper in Gould's *Astronomical Journal.* In it he suggested that Laplace was in error when he claimed that the diurnal tide would vanish in an ocean of uniform depth. Ferrel's criticisms were parallel to Airy's, and both were strongly opposed by Kelvin. The problem

of "oscillations of the second kind" to which they relate remains of current scientific interest.

In both these early papers Ferrel established the basis of his contributions to the theory of tides. Laplace had ignored fluid friction, which was not successfully treated mathematically until Navier and Poisson in the 1820's and Saint-Venant and Stokes in the 1840's inaugurated the modern theory. In tidal studies Airy (1845) assumed friction to be proportional to the first power of the velocity, in which case (as in Laplace's) the equations are linear. Thomas Young (1823), although he assumed friction to be proportional to the square of the velocity, failed to introduce the required equation of continuity. Ferrel's major contribution to tidal theory was thus to begin the full nonlinear treatment necessitated by realistic assumptions concerning friction.

After joining the Coast Survey, Ferrel made important contributions to the techniques of tidal prediction. He extended the nonharmonic developments of the tide-producing potential beyond the points reached by Laplace and Lubbock, and he gave the first reasonably complete harmonic development. Here his endeavors were parallel to those of Kelvin, who was responsible for the first tide-predicting machine (probably the earliest piece of large-scale computing machinery). In 1880 Ferrel, too, designed a tide predictor, which went into service in 1883. Although it was an analogue machine like Kelvin's, Ferrel's gave maxima and minima rather than a continuous curve as its output. Ferrel also made considerable progress in dealing with the shallow-water tidal components and in using tidal data to calculate the mass of the moon.

His studies of astronomical and geophysical tides established Ferrel's claim to a modest place in the history of science. His claim to a major place in this history lies elsewhere: He was the first to understand in mathematical detail the significance of the earth's rotation for the motion of bodies at its surface, and his application of this understanding to the motions of ocean and atmosphere opened a new epoch in meteorology. From Maury's *Physical Geography of the Sea* (1855) Ferrel learned of the belts of high pressure at 30° latitude and of low pressure at the equator and the poles. Looking for the cause of this distribution of pressure, Ferrel realized that since Laplace's tidal equations were of general application, both winds and currents must be deflected by the earth's rotation.

Pressed to write a critical review of Maury's book, Ferrel instead put his own ideas into "An Essay on the Winds and Currents of the Ocean" (*Nashville Journal,* October 1856), a precise but nonmathematical account of the general circulation, and on joining the *Nautical Almanac* staff he began to develop his ideas in mathematical form. In Gould's *Astronomical Journal* early in 1858 Ferrel made explicit the notion of an inertial circle of motion on the earth and used it to explain the gyratory nature of storms (although purely inertial motions are now known to be common in the ocean but almost absent from the atmosphere). In a series of papers published in his colleague J. D. Runkle's *Mathematical Monthly* in 1858 and 1859, then collected to form a separate pamphlet published in New York and London in 1860, Ferrel developed a general quantitative theory of relative motion on the earth's surface and applied it to winds and currents. His result, now known as Ferrel's law, was "that if a body is moving in any direction, there is a force, arising from the earth's rotation, which always deflects it to the right in the northern hemisphere, and to the left in the southern" (1858).[5] This theory and its derivation were carried to a wider audience by a summary article in the *American Journal of Science* for 1861.

Like others who treated relative motion and its geophysical consequences at about the same time, Ferrel appears to have been indebted to Foucault's pendulum (1851) and gyroscope (1852). Ferrel's treatment was remarkable for its clarity and generality, and by continuing to develop his ideas in a series of publications extending over thirty years, he pioneered in the development of meteorology from a descriptive science to a branch of mathematical physics.

When he began, meteorological thought was dominated by the unphysical ideas of Dove, who, drawing on Hadley's explanation of the trade winds (1735), insisted that the earth's rotation acted only on meridional atmospheric motions to deflect them only zonally. Although Ferrel agreed that temperature differences between equatorial and polar regions drove both atmosphere and ocean, he supported by mathematical deduction his insistence that all atmospheric motions, whatever their direction, were deflected by the earth's rotation. His application of this principle to explain both the general circulation and the rotary action of cyclonic storms began to be generally accepted in the 1870's, as weather forecasting services spread over Europe and North America. In his theory of the general circulation Ferrel developed the basic principle that on the rotating earth, convection between equator and pole must be chiefly by westerly winds. He gave the traditional three-cell diagram of the circulation, abandoned only since about 1950, as it has become clear that this scheme of an average circulation pattern along any meridian, although

heuristically useful, is not supported by the data. Ferrel modified Espy's convection-condensation theory of cyclonic storms, and he gave a plausible account of the great force of tornadoes.

By 1880 meteorology seems to have caught up with Ferrel's ideas, and he was not always able to accept the advances of the following decade that built upon his innovations. The Ferrel-Espy convection-condensation theory explains tropical hurricanes but not midlatitude storms, yet about 1890 Ferrel argued vigorously against Hann's ideas on the latter type of storm. He was also unwilling to admit the role of wind stress in the generation of ocean currents. Yet Ferrel had led in bringing sound physical principles, expressed with the tools of mathematical analysis, to bear on the largest problems of oceanic and atmospheric motion: thus at his death he was called "the most eminent meteorologist and one of the most eminent scientific men that America has produced."[6] This eminence came to Ferrel for "having given to the science of meteorology a foundation in mechanics as solid as that which Newton laid for astronomy."[7]

NOTES

1. MS autobiography, printed with minor changes in *Biographical Memoirs. National Academy of Sciences,* **3** (1895), 291.
2. *Ibid.,* 292.
3. Quoted from a letter of Ferrel by Frank Waldo in *American Meteorological Journal,* **8** (1891), 360.
4. Autobiography, 294.
5. "The Influence of the Earth's Rotation Upon the Relative Motion of Bodies Near Its Surface," in *Astronomical Journal,* **5** (1858), 99.
6. W. M. Davis, *American Meteorological Journal,* **8** (1891), 359.
7. Cleveland Abbe, *Biographical Memoirs. National Academy of Sciences,* **3** (1895), 281.

BIBLIOGRAPHY

I. ORIGINAL WORKS. Ferrel's most significant paper, "The Motions of Fluids and Solids Relative to the Earth's Surface," appeared originally in *Mathematical Monthly,* **1** and **2** (Jan. 1859–Aug. 1860) and was republished with notes by Waldo as Professional Papers of the U.S. Signal Service, no. 8 (Washington, D.C., 1882). Other papers on meteorology, including his 1856 "Essay on the Winds and Currents of the Ocean," were reprinted as no. 12 of the same series (Washington, D.C., 1882). Ferrel also wrote three treatises: "Meteorological Researches for the Use of the Coast Pilot," published in three pts. as appendixes to *Report of the Superintendent of the U.S. Coast Survey for 1875* (Washington, D.C., 1878), *1878* (Washington, D.C., 1881), and *1881* (Washington, D.C., 1883); "Recent Advances in Meteorology," published as app. 71 to *Report of the Chief Signal Officer to the Secretary of War for 1885* (Washington, D.C., 1886), as Professional Papers of the

Signal Service, no. 17, and as House Executive Document no. 1, pt. 2, 49th Congress, 1st session; *A Popular Treatise on the Winds* (New York, 1889). Ferrel's major work on tides is his *Tidal Researches,* appended to the *Coast Survey Report for 1874* (Washington, D.C., 1874); and he described his tide predictor in app. 10 to the *Coast Survey Report for 1883* (Washington, D.C., 1884). Ferrel's bibliography, in *Biographical Memoirs. National Academy of Sciences,* **3** (1895), 300–309, lists more than 100 items; it is preceded (287–299) by an edited version of his autobiography, the holograph MS of which is in the Harvard College Library.

II. SECONDARY LITERATURE. Cleveland Abbe's memoir, in *Biographical Memoirs. National Academy of Sciences,* **3** (1895), 267–286, is the fullest; more concise is William M. Davis' in *Proceedings of the American Academy of Arts and Sciences,* **28** (1893), 388–393. Alexander McAdie wrote a biographical article, accompanied by a portrait, in *American Meteorological Journal,* **4** (1888), 441–449; memorial articles by Simon Newcomb, Abbe, Davis, Waldo, and others are *ibid.,* **8** (1891), 337–369. K. Schneider-Carius, *Wetterkunde. Wetterforschung* (Freiburg, 1955), a source-book in the Orbis Academicus series, is useful on the history of meteorology. Among the older works, Frank Waldo, *Modern Meteorology* (London, 1893), in the Contemporary Science Series, gives—if anything—too much attention to Ferrel. Ferrel's place in the history of tidal theory is easier to assess, thanks to Rollin A. Harris, *Manual of Tides—Part I,* app. 8 to *Coast Survey Report for 1897* (Washington, D.C., 1898); pp. 455–462 of this excellent history are devoted to Ferrel.

HAROLD L. BURSTYN

FERRIER, DAVID (*b.* Aberdeen, Scotland, 13 January 1843; *d.* London, England, 19 March 1928), *neurophysiology, neurology.*

Ferrier was the second son of David Ferrier and Hannah Bell. His early education was at the Aberdeen Grammar School and later at Aberdeen University, where he was graduated M.A. in 1863. He won first-class honors in classics and philosophy and thus the Ferguson scholarship, which was open to all Scottish students of philosophy and was considered their premier award. It was at this time that he came under the influence of Alexander Bain, the famous logician and psychologist, and at his suggestion went to Heidelberg in 1864 to study psychology for a year.

In the following year Ferrier entered the medical school of the University of Edinburgh, and after receiving the M.B. degree in 1868 with all possible distinction, he served for a brief period as assistant to Thomas Laycock, professor of practical medicine at the university and the man who had influenced the young Hughlings Jackson. Ferrier supplemented his income by teaching but, finding this distasteful, he spent two years as assistant to a general practitioner, a Dr. Image of Bury St. Edmunds, and used

his spare time to study comparative anatomy. The latter provided his M.D. thesis, "The Comparative Anatomy and Intimate Structure of the Corpora Quadrigemina," for which he was awarded a gold medal in 1870.

Since he disliked general practice, in 1870 Ferrier obtained an appointment as lecturer on physiology at the medical school of the Middlesex Hospital; one year later he moved to King's College Hospital and Medical School, where he remained for the rest of his professional life. At first he was demonstrator in physiology, but in 1872 he succeeded to the chair of forensic medicine vacated by William Augustus Guy and held it until 1889; Ferrier helped Guy to compile a popular textbook of medical jurisprudence that bore both their names. In 1874 he was elected assistant physician to the hospital and became physician in charge of outpatients and full physician in 1890. His last academic appointment was as professor of neuropathology, the chair having been specially instituted for him in 1889. Ferrier also held appointments at the West London Hospital and, from 1880 to 1907, at the National Hospital, Queen Square, where it is said that he was one of the last physicians to conduct his ward rounds wearing the traditional top hat and black tailcoat. He retired from King's College in 1908, when he was elected emeritus professor of neuropathology and consulting physician to the hospital.

Ferrier was one of the original members of the Physiological Society, founded in 1876, and he was made an honorary member in 1927. He was also a founding editor of *Brain,* along with J. C. Bucknill, J. Crichton-Browne, and Hughlings Jackson; the first number appeared in April 1878. In 1876 he was elected a fellow of the Royal Society and in the following year a fellow of the Royal College of Physicians of London. Ferrier received a number of medals from these societies, and he gave several of their important lectures. Many other honors were bestowed upon him, including *lauréat* of the Institut de France, honorary degrees from the universities of Cambridge and Birmingham, and in 1911 a knighthood.

Ferrier was quiet and reserved and disliked controversy. He possessed an outstandingly active and agile mind, and his philosophical training stood him in good stead in his scientific work. He had an unquenchable thirst for knowledge but lacked the patience and powers of observation of some of his contemporaries in clinical neurology. It was ironic that although Ferrier was exceedingly fond of animals, he was accused, along with Gerald Yeo, of cruelty to experimental subjects. At the trial in 1882 he successfully upheld animal experimentation and won his case by proving that his colleague Yeo, who had carried out the operations on living animals, possessed a license to do so. Ferrier was a lover of classical literature, art, and the sea, and it is recorded that he "remained alert and dapper to the end." In 1874 he married Constance Waterlow; they had a son, Claude, who became a well-known architect, and a daughter.

Ferrier's work as a clinical neurologist was not outstanding, although he always had a large private practice. In this field he was dwarfed by such famous contemporaries as Jackson, W. R. Gowers, H. C. Bastian, and E. F. Buzzard, who were busy creating the British school of neurology at the National Hospital, Queen Square. On the other hand, Ferrier excelled all of these in experimental physiology, which he pursued together with medical practice. In this field he will always be remembered for his contributions to the problem of the localization of function in the cerebral cortex.

In the 1860's Jackson had suggested that the cerebral cortex must represent bodily function in an orderly fashion, but he based his contentions on clinical observation and hypothesis alone. The French clinicians J. B. Bouillaud, Aubertin, and P. P. Broca had already put forward this idea, but again without experimental proof. The first experimental support came from G. T. Fritsch and E. Hitzig in 1870, and early in 1873 Ferrier discussed it with his friend and fellow student at Edinburgh, Sir James Crichton-Browne, director of the West Riding Lunatic Asylum at Wakefield. As a result, during the spring and summer of that year Ferrier carried out investigations in the laboratory recently installed at the asylum. So began his detailed, systematic exploration of the cerebral cortex in different vertebrates, ranging from the lowest to the highest and including the ape, which was conducted over the next decade and more. He set about this work with the express purpose of confirming or refuting the theoretical suggestions made by Jackson with respect to the localized cortical areas of function. But whereas Fritsch and Hitzig had used only the dog and galvanic electric current, Ferrier employed faradic stimulation to the cortex, an important technical advance that remained universally popular until the introduction of improved methods in the 1920's. Ferrier, moreover, studied mainly primates and his researches were more fully and methodically planned.

He mapped much of the cerebral cortex and carefully delineated the "motor-region," as he termed it; the scheme of localized function that he put forward was based on the concept of "motor" and "sensory" regions. Like Fritsch and Hitzig, Ferrier carried out ablations of local areas of cerebral cortex as well as

stimulation and observed the resulting functional deficit. Jackson's concept of "discharging" and "destroying" lesions was therefore reproduced experimentally and his theories put to the test. As far as primates were concerned, they were shown to be correct.

Ferrier's fame as an experimental neurologist was made by these studies, which he first published in the *West Riding Lunatic Asylum Reports* of 1873 and later in book form as *The Function of the Brain* (1876). The latter, which contains the substance of his Croonian lecture of the Royal Society given in February 1874, is one of the most significant publications in the field of cortical localization. It was supplemented by a later and detailed review of his results and those of others, which he delivered as *The Croonian Lectures* [of the Royal College of Physicians of London] *on Cerebral Localisation* in the same year. Wide publicity was given to Ferrier's findings at the International Medical Congress of 1880, in London.

Ferrier was one of the contributors to the spectacular advances made in the neurological sciences toward the end of the nineteenth century, although he was occasionally in error. For instance, he considered that the cortical visual area was in the angular gyrus rather than in the calcarine cortex; no doubt his cortical lesions had involved the nearby optic radiation. He was also guilty of unwarranted extrapolation from his findings in animals to the human brain, although he was by no means alone in the procedure. Thus, he transferred the results from his monkey experiments to a diagram of the human brain, and this was widely accepted. In the first case the interchange of data among the different species is now known to be impossible, and in the second, the belief in well-defined "centers," to which Ferrier's work contributed, is no longer acceptable.

The influence of Ferrier's work was widespread, and he and Fritsch and Hitzig inspired many attempts to chart the cortex. In addition he had an important influence on the embryonic field of brain surgery, for he urged his surgical colleagues to attack cerebral lesions operatively. Throughout his life he was passionately fond of laboratory work, and in addition to his classic studies of the cerebral cortex, he also carried out investigations of the cerebellum, the limb plexuses, and further studies on the quadrigeminal bodies, thereby extending his earlier work.

BIBLIOGRAPHY

I. ORIGINAL WORKS. Ferrier published many articles on the physiology of the nervous system and on clinical neurological topics. The most important are "Experimental

Researches in Cerebral Physiology and Pathology," in *West Riding Lunatic Asylum Medical Reports,* **3** (1873), 30–96; *The Function of the Brain* (London, 1876; 1886); *The Localisation of Cerebral Disease* (London, 1878), the Gulstonian lectures for 1878; *The Croonian Lectures on Cerebral Localisation* (London, 1890); and "The Regional Diagnosis of Cerebral Disease," in *A System of Medicine,* C. Allbutt and H. D. Rolleston, eds., VIII (London, 1911), 37–162.

II. SECONDARY LITERATURE. Obituaries are C. S. S[herrington], "Sir David Ferrier, 1843–1928," in *Proceedings of the Royal Society,* **103B** (1928), viii–xvi; *British Medical Journal* (1928), **1,** 525–526, 574–575; and *Lancet* (1928), **1,** 627–629. Each includes a portrait. See also H. W. Lyle, *King's and Some King's Men* (London, 1935), pp. 279–281; H. R. Viets, "West Riding, 1871–1876," in *Bulletin of the History of Medicine,* **6** (1938), 477–487; and David McK. Rioch, in *The Founders of Neurology,* W. Haymaker, ed. (Springfield, Ill., 1953), pp. 122–125, with portrait. For Ferrier's contribution to knowledge of the visual pathway, see S. Polyak, *The Vertebrate Visual System* (Chicago, 1957), pp. 147–149.

EDWIN CLARKE

FERRO (or **FERREO, DAL FERRO, DEL FERRO), SCIPIONE** (*b.* Bologna, Italy, 6 February 1465; *d.* Bologna, between 29 October and 16 November 1526), *mathematics.*

Scipione was the son of Floriano Ferro (a papermaker by trade) and his wife, Filippa. He was a lecturer in arithmetic and geometry at the University of Bologna from 1496 to 1526, except for a brief stay in Venice during the last year. In 1513 he is recorded as an "arithmetician" by Giovanni Filoteo Achillini, in the poem *Viridario.* After Scipione's death, the same subjects were taught by his disciple, Annibale dalla Nave (or della Nave). Nave married Scipione's daughter, Filippa, and inherited his father-in-law's surname, thereby calling himself dalla Nave, alias dal Ferro. Scipione's activity as a businessman is demonstrated by various notarial documents from the years 1517–1523.

No work of Scipione's, either printed or in manuscript, is known. It is known from several sources, however, that he was a great algebraist. We are indebted to him for the solution of third-degree, or cubic, equations, which had been sought since antiquity. As late as the end of the fifteenth century, Luca Pacioli judged it "impossible" by the methods known at that time (*Summa,* I, dist. VIII, tractate 5). Scipione achieved his solution in the first or second decade of the sixteenth century, as is known from the texts of Tartaglia and Cardano. He did not print any account of his discovery, but divulged it to various people and expounded it in a manuscript that came into the possession of Nave, but which today is unknown.

In 1535 a disciple of Scipione, named Antonio Maria Fiore, in a mathematical dispute with Tartaglia proposed some problems leading to cubic equations lacking the second-degree term, of which he claimed to know the method of solution, having learned "such a secret," thirty years before, from a certain "great mathematician" (Tartaglia, *Quesiti,* bk. ix, question 25). Tartaglia (who had concerned himself with cubic equations as early as 1530) was now (1535) induced to seek and find the solution to them. Some years later, yielding to entreaties, he communicated his solution to Cardano (1539).

Still later (1542), in Bologna, Nave made known to Cardano the existence of the aforementioned manuscript by Scipione: this is attested by Ludovico Ferrari, Cardano's famous disciple, who was with the master (Ferrari to Tartaglia, *Secondo cartello,* p. 3; see also Tartaglia to Ferrari, *Seconda risposta,* p. 6). Cardano, who published the *Ars magna* (1545) somewhat later, represented the solution of cubic equations as the distinguished discovery of Scipione and Tartaglia. The following is taken from the *Ars magna* (chs. 1, 11):

> Scipione Ferro of Bologna, almost thirty years ago, discovered the solution of the cube and of things equal in number [that is, the equation $x^3 + px = q$, where p and q are positive numbers], a really beautiful and admirable accomplishment. In distinction this discovery surpasses all mortal ingenuity and all human subtlety. It is truly a gift from heaven, although at the same time a proof of the power of reason, and so illustrious that whoever attains it may believe himself capable of solving any problem. In emulation of him Niccolò Tartaglia of Brescia, a friend of ours, in order not to be conquered when he entered into competition with a disciple of Ferro, Antonio Maria Fiore, came upon the same solution, and revealed it to me because of my many entreaties to him.

The coincidence of Scipione's and Tartaglia's rules was confirmed by Ettore Bortolotti by means of an ancient manuscript (MS 595N of the Library of the University of Bologna), which reproduces Scipione's rule, which had been obtained from him by Pompeo Bolognetti, lecturer *ad praxim mathematicae* at Bologna in the years 1554–1568. Basing his conclusion on another text by Cardano and on a manuscript of the *Algebra* of Rafael Bombelli (MS B.1569 of the Library of the Archiginnasio of Bologna, assignable to about 1550), Bortolotti concludes, with plausibility, that Scipione did indeed solve both the equations $x^3 + px = q$, and $x^3 = px + q$.

How Scipione arrived at the solution of cubic equations is not known. But there is no lack of attempts at reconstructing his method. For example, in his examination of the *Liber abbaci* of Leonardo Fibonacci and of the *Algebra* of Bombelli, Giovanni Vacca seemed to be able to reproduce, in the following simple procedure, the one used by Scipione: If the sum of square roots is expressed as

$$x = \sqrt{a + \sqrt{b}} + \sqrt{a - \sqrt{b}}, \qquad (1)$$

it can be seen, by raising to the square, that this satisfies the second-degree equation (lacking the term in x)

$$x^2 = (2\sqrt{a^2 - b}) + 2a. \qquad (2)$$

Analogously, if the sum of cube roots is expressed as

$$X = \sqrt[3]{a + \sqrt{b}} + \sqrt[3]{a - \sqrt{b}}, \qquad (3)$$

then it can be seen, raising to the cube, that this satisfies the third-degree equation (lacking the term in X^2)

$$X^3 = (3\sqrt[3]{a^2 - b})X + 2a. \qquad (4)$$

Therefore, equation (4) is solved by means of (3). If one writes

$$p = 3\sqrt[3]{a^2 - b}, \quad q = 2a \qquad (a)$$

or

$$a = \frac{q}{2}, \quad b = \frac{q^2}{4} - \frac{p^3}{27}, \qquad (b)$$

the cubic equation (4) and the formula which solves it (3) assume the accustomed form:

$$X^3 = pX + q, \qquad (5)$$

$$X = \sqrt[3]{\frac{p}{2} + \sqrt{\frac{q^2}{4} - \frac{p^3}{27}}} + \sqrt[3]{\frac{p}{2} - \sqrt{\frac{q^2}{4} - \frac{p^3}{27}}}. \qquad (6)$$

This latter is called Cardano's formula, but incorrectly because Cardano does not deserve credit for having discovered it but only for having published it for the first time.

Another of Scipione's contributions to algebra concerns fractions having irrational denominators. The problem of rationalizing the denominator of such a fraction, when there are square roots intervening, goes back to Euclid. In the sixteenth century, the same problem appears with roots of greater index. And here one can single out the case of fractions of the type

$$\frac{1}{\sqrt[3]{a} + \sqrt[3]{b} + \sqrt[3]{c}},$$

which Scipione was the first to deal with, as can be seen by the manuscript of Bombelli, cited above. In that manuscript, Bombelli calls Scipione "a man uniquely gifted in this art."

Finally, it should be noted that Scipione also applied himself to the geometry of the compass with a fixed opening, although this theory was ancient, the first examples going back to Abu'l-Wafa' (tenth century). In the first half of the sixteenth century, this question arose again, particularly because of Tartaglia, Cardano, and Ferrari. And it is because of the testimony of the last-named (Ferrari to Tartaglia, *Quinto cartello,* p. 25) that we can state that Scipione also took up this problem, but we know nothing about his researches and his contributions.

BIBLIOGRAPHY

I. ORIGINAL WORKS. We possess no original works by Scipione Ferro, and the sources from which knowledge of his activity is derived are indicated in the text. Of the printed sources, the following later eds. are more accessible than the originals: Cardano, *Ars magna,* in *Opera omnia,* C. Spon, ed., vol. IV (Lyons, 1663); facs. repr. of the *Opera omnia,* with intro. by A. Buck (Stuttgart–Bad Cannstatt, 1966); Tartaglia, *Quesiti et inventioni diverse,* facsimile of the edition of 1554, sponsored by the Atheneum of Brescia, A. Masotti, ed. (Brescia, 1959); and Ferrari, *Cartelli,* and Tartaglia, *Risposte,* in the autograph ed. by E. Giordani (Milano, 1876), or in the facs. ed. of the original, sponsored by the Atheneum of Brescia, A. Masotti, ed. (in press). Concerning the two Bolognese manuscripts which have been cited, see E. Bortolotti, "L'algebra nella scuola matematica bolognese del secolo XVI," in *Periodico di matematiche,* 4th ser., **5** (1925), 147–184, as well as the collection of extracts entitled *Studi e ricerche sulla storia della matematica in Italia nei secoli XVI e XVII* (Bologna, 1928).

II. SECONDARY LITERATURE. See C. Malagola, *Della vita e delle opere di Antonio Urceo detto Codro* (Bologna, 1878), pp. 352–355, and app. XXVII, pp. 574–577, which contains "Documenti intorno a Scipione dal Ferro"; L. Frati, "Scipione dal Ferro," in *Bollettino di bibliografia e storia delle scienze matematiche,* **12** (1910), 1–5; and in *Studi e memorie per la storia dell'Università di Bologna,* **2** (1911), 193–205; E. Bortolotti, "I contributi del Tartaglia, del Cardano, del Ferrari, e della scuola matematica bolognese alla teoria algebrica delle equazioni cubiche," in *Studi e memorie per la storia dell'Università di Bologna,* **10** (1926), 55–108, thence in the aforementioned volume of *Studi e ricerche;* and G. Vacca, "Sul commento di Leonardo Pisano al Libro X degli Elementi di Euclide e sulla risoluzione delle equazioni cubiche," in *Bollettino dell'Unione matematica italiana,* **9** (1930), 59–63.

On Annibale dalla Nave, see A. Favaro, note in Eneström, *Bibliotheca mathematica,* 3rd ser., **2** (1901), 354.

On A. M. Fiore, see A. Masotti, note in *Atti* of the

meeting in honor of Tartaglia, held at the Atheneum of Brescia in 1959, p. 42.

Ferro's role in the solution of cubic equations, is discussed in all histories of mathematics. See, for example, M. Cantor, *Vorlesungen über Geschichte der Mathematik;* J. Tropfke, *Geschichte der Elementar-Mathematik;* and D. E. Smith, *History of Mathematics, passim.*

Also of interest are D. E. Smith, *A Source Book in Mathematics* (New York, 1929; repr. New York, 1959), pp. 203–206, where one can read the solution of the cubic equation given in Cardano, *Ars magna,* ch. 11, English trans. by R. B. McClenon; O. Ore, *Cardano, the Gambling Scholar* (Princeton, 1953), pp. 62–107, where can be found the history of the solution of cubic equations, with English translations of various texts by Tartaglia, Cardano, and Ferrari, and various mentions of Ferro; and, finally, G. Sarton, *Six Wings: Men of Science in the Renaissance* (Bloomington, Ind., 1957), pp. 28–36, 246–249.

ARNALDO MASOTTI

FERSMAN, ALEKSANDR EVGENIEVICH (*b.* St. Petersburg, Russia, 8 November 1883; *d.* Sochi, U.S.S.R., 20 May 1945), *mineralogy, geochemistry.*

Fersman's father, Evgeny Aleksandrovich Fersman, was an architect and later a soldier. The atmosphere of his home, which encouraged both art and thought, was unusual in the military environment of that day. Fersman's mother, Maria Eduardovna Kessler, was a talented pianist and painter; her brother, A. E. Kessler, who studied under the well-known chemist A. M. Butlerov, was also an important influence on the boy's education.

The Fersman family usually spent the summer holidays on Kessler's estate near Simferopol, and there, in the Crimean mountains, young Fersman was attracted to mineralogy and began his first mineral collection. The development of his interests was furthered by a trip to Czechoslovakia, to which the family was obliged to go because of the mother's illness. There, in Karlovy Vary (Carlsbad), an old mining area that was no longer prosperous, he could purchase crystals and druses to fill out his mineral collection. Thus, by the time he graduated from the Odessa Classical Gymnasium in 1901, with a gold medal, Fersman's interests had already been formed; he was very much interested in mineralogy, he had a good mineralogical collection, and he had accumulated a substantial store of personal observations.

In Novorossisk University, which Fersman entered, the lecture course in descriptive mineralogy was extremely boring, and Fersman at first wished to give up mineralogy and study the history of art instead. Friends of his family, Professor P. G. Melikashvili and the chemist A. I. Gorbov, advised him to give up this idea and to study the structure of matter and

questions of molecular chemistry. To B. P. Veynberg, a student of D. I. Mendeleev and a specialist in physical chemistry, Fersman owed his acquaintance with ideas on the nature of crystalline substances, such as ice and frost patterns.

In 1903 Fersman's father was given command of the First Moscow Cadet Corps, and the son transferred to Moscow University. Here he approached the head of the department of mineralogy, V. I. Vernadsky, who found him a place in his laboratory. There Fersman mastered the goniometric method of measuring crystals. He worked persistently, and while still a student (1904–1907) he published his first seven scientific works, devoted to crystallography and the mineralogy of stolpenite, gmelinite, and other substances.

When Fersman graduated from the university in 1907, Vernadsky retained him in his department to prepare to become a professor. In 1908 Fersman worked in Victor Goldschmidt's laboratory at Heidelberg University, where he perfected his crystallographic and optical methods. He was commissioned by Goldschmidt to make a tour of the most important jewelers of western Europe and select the most interesting crystals of natural diamonds for study. In Frankfurt, Hanau, and Berlin tens of thousands of carats of diamonds were displayed before him on special tables. As a result of these observations Goldschmidt and Fersman wrote a joint monograph on the crystallography of the diamond (1911) that is still significant.

At Heidelberg, Fersman attended Rosenbusch's lectures on petrography. In France he visited Lacroix's laboratory in Paris and made a trip to study the pegmatites of the islands in the Elbe. This trip played a large role in determining his scientific interests, for Fersman later dedicated many years to research on pegmatites.

In 1912 Fersman became senior curator in the mineralogical section of the Geological Museum of the Russian Academy of Sciences. In the same year, for the first time he gave a course in geochemistry at Shanyavsky University in Moscow. He also took part in the organization of a popular scientific journal, *Priroda,* to which he gave considerable attention throughout his life. In it he published major articles and notes on geochemistry and mineralogy, diamonds, alloys of radium, emeralds, zeolites, platinum, gases, and other useful minerals found in Russia and other countries.

In 1914 the first period of Fersman's scientific activity came to a close, when his great gift for and inclination toward scientific synthesis and theoretical generalization became apparent.

At the beginning of 1915 a commission was organized in the Academy of Sciences for the study of the natural resources of Russia, and Fersman was elected scientific secretary. In connection with the work of the commission he studied the deposits of various useful minerals in the Crimea, Mongolia, Trans-Baykal, the Urals, the Altai, and various regions of European Russia.

During World War I, Fersman traveled to the front and compiled geological maps showing the location of construction materials and water-bearing and waterproof horizons, knowledge of which was important for successful military operations. During this period Fersman faced, in the broadest form, the problems of use of mineral raw materials. He was interested in economics and technology, as well as in mineralogy and geology.

Soon after the Russian Revolution, Lenin turned to the Academy of Sciences for definitions of the new problems facing science. He talked with Fersman, who was impressed with his concern for efficient placement of industry nearer to mineral raw materials and for guaranteeing the Soviet Republic a domestic supply of raw materials. All this awakened Fersman's interest and influenced the direction and planning of his scientific research.

In 1919 Fersman was elected to the Academy of Sciences and was chosen director of its mineralogical museum. Besides imparting his own enthusiasm for science to his students and colleagues, he was modest and encouraged the progress of other researchers. In the winter of 1919–1920 Fersman gave a course of lectures at Petrograd (now Leningrad) University on the geochemistry of Russia, and in the following year repeated it at the Geographical Institute of Petrograd.

Fersman made sizable contributions to the solution of an important theoretical problem of geochemistry: the frequency of distribution of the chemical elements in the rocks of the earth's crust (clarkes). The term "clarke" (the concentration of an element in the earth's crust) was proposed by Fersman in honor of the American scientist F. W. Clarke, one of the first to consider this problem in his fundamental work, *The Relative Abundance of the Chemical Elements* (1889). Fersman calculated the clarkes for most of the elements. Before Fersman, clarkes were expressed in weight percentages. He showed that for geochemical purposes the atomic percentages were more important, thus introducing into science the concept of "atomic clarkes." As a result he discovered the independence of geochemical abundances from the positions of the elements in the periodic system and the concentration and depletion of the various elements. He showed that abundances within the earth's crust

were determined by the effects of the migration of the elements, while abundances in space were related to the stability of the atomic nucleus. He was the first to consider the problem of regional geochemistry and the division of European Russia into geochemical districts, and he provided a classification of hypogene processes. An expanded course of these lectures was published in 1922.

Fersman published the monograph *Dragotsennye i tsvetnye kamni Rossii* ("Precious and Colored Stones of Russia," 1920), as well as works on feldspar, fuller's earth, and saline mud.

Noteworthy among his numerous investigations and expeditions in the 1920's and 1930's is his work in the Khibiny Mountains (Kola Peninsula). He first traveled to the Khibiny Mountains in May 1920, as a member of the commission of the Murmansk railroad, which was headed by the president of the Academy of Sciences, A. P. Karpinsky, and the geologist A. P. Gerasimov. Fersman later expended much of his creative energy in the study of the Khibiny Mountains. He led many expeditions, and his research enabled him to combine separate facts and observations into a coherent system providing an integrated view of the formation processes of the geological structures of the Fenno-Scandinavian shield.

The mineralogical and geochemical research in the Khibiny was crowned by the discovery of great deposits of apatite. Fersman was not only a scientist but also the developer of this inhospitable region. At his initiative the Khibiny mining station was opened in 1937, and Fersman was its first director. This station later grew into an important scientific institution: the Kola branch of the Soviet Academy of Sciences.

Fersman's study of central Asia began in 1924 and continued until the 1940's. At the beginning of his work it was believed that central Asia had few deposits of useful minerals. He carried out considerable scientific research to show the mineral riches there and thus refuted that erroneous belief. Fersman discovered in the Karakum Desert deposits of virgin sulfur; with his help a sulfur refinery was built on the site of the discovery and has supplied the Soviet Union with sulfur ever since.

In the Urals, Fersman investigated pegmatite, rare elements, and deposits of copper, chromium, and other useful minerals. In Siberia he began research showing the value of further study and the great richness of the deposits there. Fersman wrote the important works *Geokhimicheskie problemy Sibiri* ("Geochemical Problems of Siberia") and *Geokhimicheskie problemy Soyuza* ("Geochemical Problems of the [Soviet] Union," 1931).

During World War II, Fersman was concerned with military geology and problems of securing strategic materials. He headed the Commission for the Geological-Geographical Services of the Red Army, to which he attracted many important specialists. He traveled to the front many times with reports and lectures on strategic materials and military geology. In this period he wrote several books and articles on strategic materials of the Soviet Union and Germany, and by comparing them showed that the Soviet Union's military potential guaranteed its victory.

Fersman gave much attention to the history of science. He tried to show the origins of scientific ideas and the achievements of researchers, in particular his predecessors D. I. Mendeleev and V. I. Vernadsky. With particular warmth he wrote of those who, with him, created the new science of geochemistry and of his teachers Vernadsky, Goldschmidt, and G. Hevesy, among others. Fersman had the ability to write sketches that give clear pictures of scientists. Reading his *Zanimatelnaya geokhimia* ("Entertaining Geochemistry," 1948), one can learn of the remarkable work of Marie Curie, A. P. Karpinsky, N. S. Kurnakov, P. I. Preobrazhensky, V. G. Khlopin, and many other distinguished scientists. Through his popular articles, sketches, and books, such as *Zanimatelnaya mineralogia* ("Entertaining Mineralogy," 1928), *Puteshestvia za kamnem* ("Traveling for Rocks," 1956), *Vospominania o kamne* ("Recollections About Rocks," 1940), *Rasskazy o samotsvetakh* ("Tales of Semiprecious Stones," 1957), Fersman helped explain the practical significance of theoretical research in geology.

Fersman gave much attention to his students, many of whom became outstanding scientists: D. I. Shcherbakov, A. A. Saukov, V. V. Shcherbina, and O. A. Vorobeva, among others.

For his achievements and services in geochemistry, mineralogy, geology, and geography Fersman was elected member or corresponding member of sixteen scientific organizations and societies in his native country and abroad. He was awarded the Lenin Prize (1929), the State Prize of the U.S.S.R. of the First Degree (1941), medals from the University of Belgium (1936) and the Wollaston Medal (1942), and the order of the Red Banner of Labor.

Fersman was an active leader of the Academy of Sciences of the U.S.S.R., occupying at various times the posts of vice-president, member of the Presidium, academician-secretary of the Section of Mathematics and Natural Sciences, president of the Council for the Study of Natural Resources, and director of publications.

His scientific creativity was characterized by an exceptionally broad scope and an integral view of nature. With a good understanding of the underlying relationships between various phenomena, he was a master of theoretical generalization and scientific synthesis.

Of major significance were Fersman's works in geochemistry, which he, like his teacher Vernadsky, understood more deeply and more broadly than his contemporaries. According to his definition, geochemistry should concern the history of atoms of chemical elements in the earth's crust and their behavior under various thermodynamic, physical, and chemical conditions of nature. Fersman showed with great clarity the significance of Mendeleev's periodic law for geochemistry.

All his life Fersman did research in mineralogy and geochemistry; he showed graphically, vividly, and in a fascinating way that these sciences do not consist of dry ideas, of inanimate, dead objects of nature; rather, they are sciences of the origins and history of natural phenomena, the complex chemical processes that form the face of the earth and that slowly but inexorably transform what appears to be lifeless stone into new chemical compounds. The idea of geochemical character lay at the basis of all his further work, which was closely connected with the study of the useful minerals of the U.S.S.R. It appeared to him that at the foundation of all surrounding life, all surrounding transformations, and even of the very life processes themselves lay the laws of the dispersion and combination of ninety chemical elements, from which the earth and all of space are constructed, and that one cannot, by studying it only in the laboratory, tear lifeless stone away from the great laboratory of nature in which its transformations take place.

In *Khimicheskie elementy zemli i kosmosa* ("The Chemical Elements of the Earth and Space," 1923), Fersman extended the problem of the history of the elements to the universe; in *Geokhimia Rossii* ("Geochemistry of Russia," 1922) he had tried to apply these ideas to the understanding of those different phenomena which take place in widely distant regions of the U.S.S.R. Most important in Fersman's work is his constant recurrence to the basic problems posed in the past, introducing the study of chemical processes into the chemistry of space while still taking each element back from space to earth and giving attention to its use by man.

In 1932 Vernadsky, following the publication of the monograph *Pegmatity* ("Pegmatites"), expressed pleasure with this new and important work, through which scientists have come to a deeper understanding of the world's structure and of the role of atoms in that structure, about which C. F. Shönbein and Faraday had theorized in the late 1830's. The periodicity of properties in space pointed to a spiral pattern of phenomena, the more so since for the periodic system the spiral was very important.

Fersman asserted that the whole course of chemical processes in space is simply a great Mendeleevian system, in which the laws of energetics and the level of energy govern separate cells, moving elements and combinations of elements about in time and space. The places of the elements in the periodic system reflected a definite step in the chemical history of earth and the universe, between which there is an inner connection.

Fersman's ideas frequently were ahead of his time, and in many of his works he foresaw the future, describing future science and technology. In a special sketch in *Zanimatelnaya geokhimia* attention is drawn to future achievements: the use of atmospheric gases, the ozone screen, the warmth of the earth's depths, atomic energy, the energy of ocean waves and winds, and of new synthetic carbon compounds, and of man's penetration into space.

In calling the geochemical activity of mankind "technogenesis," Fersman meant the economic and industrial activity of man, according to his own scale and significance, compared with the processes of nature herself. Technogenesis basically leads to the extraction of chemical elements from the earth, the redistribution of elements from the depths on the earth's surface, and the agricultural and engineering regrouping of elements. Analyzing the pattern of use of separate elements, its connection with clarkes, and the role of clarkes of concentration, Fersman showed that man concentrates certain elements (gold, platinum, silver, and so forth) and disperses others (carbon, tin, magnesium, silicon, and so forth). As a result he defined the basic geochemical relations between man and nature and noted that the laws of geochemistry force man to seek technical solutions in the use of poor lodes with scattered and rare elements. Technogenesis represents a distinguished theoretical and practical achievement of science, especially in the light of contemporary achievements (atomic experiments and space research). Fersman's work in this area will long light the way for new research, inventions, and the conservation of natural resources.

BIBLIOGRAPHY

I. ORIGINAL WORKS. Fersman's writings include *Der Diamant* (Heidelberg, 1911), written with V. Goldschmidt; *Dragotsennye i tsvetnye kamni Rossii* ("Precious and Colored Stones of Russia," Petrograd, 1920); *Geokhimia Rossii* ("Geochemistry of Russia," Petrograd, 1922); *Puti k nauke budushchego* ("Paths Toward the Science of the Future," Petrograd, 1922); *Khimicheskie elementy zemli i kosmosa* ("The Chemical Elements of the Earth and Space," Petrograd, 1923); *Khimia mirozdania* ("The Chemistry of the Universe," Petrograd, 1923); *Istoria almaznogo fonda* ("History of Diamond Stocks," Moscow, 1924); *Zanimatelnaya mineralogia* ("Entertaining Mineralogy," Leningrad, 1928); *Pegmatity* ("Pegmatites," Leningrad, 1931); *Geokhimicheskie problemy Sibiri* ("Geochemical Problems of Siberia," Moscow-Leningrad, 1931); *Geokhimicheskie problemy Soyuza* ("Geochemical Problems of the [Soviet] Union," Moscow-Leningrad, 1931); *Geokhimia* ("Geochemistry"), 4 vols. (Leningrad, 1933–1939); *Vospominania o kamne* ("Recollections about Rocks," Moscow, 1940); *Voyna i strategicheskoe syre* ("The War and Strategic Raw Material," Krasnoufimsk, 1940); *Geologia i voyna* ("Geology and War," Moscow-Leningrad, 1943); *Khimia zemli na novykh putyakh* ("The Chemistry of the Earth on New Paths," Moscow, 1944); *Mineralnoe syre zarubezhnykh stran* ("The Mineral Raw Materials of Foreign Countries," Moscow-Leningrad, 1947); *Zanimatelnaya geokhimia* ("Entertaining Geochemistry," Moscow-Leningrad, 1948); *Ocherki po istorii kamnya* ("Essays on the History of Rocks"), 2 vols. (Moscow, 1954–1961). Many of his works were brought together as *Izbrannye trudy* ("Selected Works"), 7 vols. (Moscow, 1952–1962).

II. SECONDARY LITERATURE. On Fersman or his works, see G. P. Barsanov, "Kharakternye cherty tvorchestva akademika A. E. Fersmana i ego raboty po mineralogii" ("Characteristic Features of the Creative Work of Academician A. E. Fersman and His Work in Mineralogy"), in *Trudy mineralogicheskogo muzeya Akademii nauk, USSR* no. 5 (1953), 7–18; R. F. Gekker, "Akademik A. E. Fersman i ego rabota vo Vserossyskom obshchestve okhrany prirody" ("Academician A. E. Fersman and His Work in the All-Russian Society for the Conservation of Nature"), in *Okhrana prirody,* no. 3 (1948), 113–119; D. P. Grigoriev and I. I. Shafranovsky, *Vydayushchiesya russkie mineralogi* ("Distinguished Russian Mineralogists," Moscow-Leningrad, 1949), pp. 196–233; O. V. Isakova, ed., *Aleksandr Evgenievich Fersman* (Moscow, 1940), a bibliographical collection; O. Pisarzhevsky, *Fersman* (Moscow, 1959); and A. A. Saukov, "Raboty A. E. Fersmana po geokhimii" ("The Work of A. E. Fersman in Geochemistry"), in *Yubileyny sbornik, posvyashchenny tridtsatiletiyu Velikoy Oktyabrskoy sotsialisticheskoy revolyutsii* ("Jubilee Collection, Dedicated to the Thirtieth Anniversary of the Great October Socialist Revolution"), I (Moscow-Leningrad, 1947), 57–60.

See also I. I. Shafranovsky, "Trudy A. E. Fersman po kristallografii" ("The Work of A. E. Fersman in Crystallography"), in *A. E. Fersman. Kristallografia almaza* ("A. E. Fersman. Crystallography of the Diamond," Moscow, 1955), pp. 532–546; D. I. Shcherbakov, "Aleksandr Evgenievich Fersman i ego tvorchestvo" ("Aleksandr Evgenievich Fersman and His Work"), *ibid.,* pp. 490–531; "A. E. Fersman i ego puteshestvia" ("A. E. Fersman and His Travels," Moscow, 1953); "Osnovnye cherty tvorchestva A. E. Fersmana i drugikh" ("Basic Features of the Creative Work of A. E. Fersman and Others," in *Voprosy geokhimii i mineralogii* ("Questions of Geochemistry and Mineralogy," Moscow, 1956), pp. 1–175; and *Aleksandr Evgenievich Fersman. Zhizn i deyatelnost* ("Aleksandr Evgenievich Fersman. Life and Work"), of which Shcherbakov was editor (Moscow, 1965).

Other sources include V. V. Shcherbina *et al.,* in *Byulleten Moskovskogo obshchestva ispytateley prirody,* n.s. **51,** no. 1 (1946), 90–97; O. M. Shubnikova, "Ocherk zhizni i deyatelnosti A. E. Fersman i drugikh" ("Essay on the Life of A. E. Fersman and Others"), in *Zapiski Vserossyskogo mineralogicheskogo obshchestva,* 2nd ser., **75,** no. 1 (1946), 55–64; A. V. Sidorenko, "Issledovania A. E. Fersmana v Turkmenii i ikh znachenie" ("The Research of A. E. Fersman in Turkmen and Its Significance"), in *Izvestiya Turkmenistanskogo filiala Akademii nauk USSR,* no. 1 (1950), 28–39; and N. D. Zelinsky, "Pamyati akademika A. E. Fersmana" ("Memories of Academician A. E. Fersman"), in *Uspekhi khimii,* **14,** no. 6 (1945), 463–467.

A. MENIAILOV

FESSENDEN, REGINALD AUBREY (*b.* Milton, Quebec, 6 October 1866; *d.* Hamilton, Bermuda, 22 July 1932), *radio engineering.*

Fessenden was the son of Rev. E. J. Fessenden and Clementina Trenholme Fessenden; his father had charge of a small parish in East Bolton, Quebec. When the boy was nine, the family moved to Niagara Falls, Ontario, where he entered De Veaux Military College; he later attended Trinity College School at Port Hope, Ontario, and Bishop's College at Lennoxville, Quebec. Fessenden's first position was as principal of Whitney Institute in Bermuda, but he gave it up after two years and took up a relatively lowly job as tester in the New York factory of Thomas Edison, who was his idol. He soon graduated to Edison's New Jersey laboratory, where he was encouraged to specialize in solving chemical problems. In 1890 Fessenden went to work for the Westinghouse Electric and Manufacturing Co.

In 1892 Fessenden was named professor of electrical engineering at Purdue University; after a year he moved to a similar position at the Western University of Pennsylvania (now the University of Pittsburgh), where he remained for seven years. He next served as a special agent for the U.S. Weather Bureau from 1900 to 1902; his assignment was to adapt radiotelegraphy to weather forecasting and storm warning.

Fessenden's first contribution was the development of the electrolytic detector in 1900 (patent granted in 1903), a device sufficiently more sensitive than the primitive radiotelegraphy detectors of the day to make radiotelephony feasible for the first time. This invention led to other ideas, such as the use of a specially designed alternator as the source of high-frequency oscillations (one machine produced 50,000 cycles per second) and the invention of the heterodyne receiver, forerunner of the superhet. Many of his ideas were in advance of the times and were not elaborated until many years later, by others.

In 1902 two Pittsburgh financiers, Thomas H. Given and Hay Walker, Jr., formed the National Electric Signalling Company to exploit Fessenden's ideas and made him general manager. The firm made many contributions during the eight years of its existence; its station at Brant Rock, Massachusetts, transmitted the first voice signals over long distances in 1906, and the company manufactured radio equipment. But its dreams of competing with the American Marconi Company in establishing an international communications network came to naught when Fessenden demanded that a Canadian subsidiary controlled by himself should run a link with Britain, an arrangement opposed by his backers. Fessenden sued and won a judgment of $406,000, sending the company into bankruptcy.

During his career Fessenden obtained some 300 patents. Not a few became the subject of litigation; in one case, he sued the Radio Corporation of America for $60 million, asserting that he was being prevented from selling devices based on his own patents. The suit was settled out of court. He remained a controversial figure. Among his admirers was Elihu Thomson, himself a prominent inventor and engineer, who is said to have described Fessenden as "the greatest wireless inventor of the age—greater than Marconi." It is difficult to escape the conclusion that many of the fights in which Fessenden became involved were traceable to a choleric temperament and a persistent fear that men of business were getting the best of him—a fear not entirely without justification in the early days of radio.

BIBLIOGRAPHY

There is a biography by his widow, Helen M. Fessenden, *Fessenden, Builder of Tomorrows* (New York, 1940). For an account of Fessenden's role in the development of radio, see G. L. Archer, *History of Radio to 1926* (New York, 1938), pp. 67 ff. An obituary is in the *New York Times* (24 July 1932), p. 22.

CHARLES SÜSSKIND

FEUERBACH, KARL WILHELM (*b.* Jena, Germany, 30 May 1800; *d.* Erlangen, Germany, 12 March 1834), *mathematics.*

Karl Wilhelm was the third of the eleven children of Eva Wilhelmine Maria Troster and the famed

German jurist Paul Johann Anselm Feuerbach. By the age of twenty-two, the gifted young mathematician had been awarded the Ph.D., had made a significant contribution to a pleasant and active branch of mathematical research, and had been named professor of mathematics at the Gymnasium at Erlangen.

Feuerbach's scientific output was small, and his fame as a mathematician rests entirely upon three publications, which constitute the total output of his scientific career. His most important contribution was a theorem in Euclidean geometry, the theorem of Feuerbach:

> The circle which passes through the feet of the altitudes of a triangle touches all four of the circles which are tangent to the three sides of the triangle; it is internally tangent to the inscribed circle and externally tangent to each of the circles which touch the sides of the triangle externally [*Eigenschaften*].

In this statement one recognizes the nine-point circle of a triangle, which had been fully described though not named by Brianchon and Poncelet in 1821. The proof of this theorem was presented with a number of other conclusions on the geometry of the triangle in his small book *Eigenschaften einiger merkwürdigen Punkte . . .*, published in 1822. In this work Feuerbach developed a number of algebraic identities involving the lengths of the sides and other parts of a triangle and then proved that the two circles in question were tangent by showing that the distance between their centers was equal to the sum of their radii. He used as a model for this investigation Euler's "Solutio facilis problematum," a paper that had been published in 1765. Recognition came slowly, but many years after his death a number of papers appeared devoted to a discussion of the nine-point circle of a triangle and the theorem of Feuerbach.

In 1827 Feuerbach brought out the results of his second investigation. After an exhaustive analysis of this work, Moritz Cantor concluded that Feuerbach had proved to be an independent co-discoverer with Moebius of the theory of the homogeneous coordinates of a point in space. In the meantime, however, Feuerbach's teaching career was beset by difficulties and his health had become seriously impaired. At the age of twenty-eight he retired permanently and spent the rest of his life in Erlangen as a recluse.

BIBLIOGRAPHY

I. ORIGINAL WORKS. Feuerbach's works are *Eigenschaften einiger merkwürdigen Punkte des geradlinigen Dreiecks und mehrerer durch sie bestimmten Linien und Figuren. Eine analytisch-trigonometrische Abhandlung* (Nuremberg, 1822), a portion of which was ed. and trans. by R. A. Johnson as "Feuerbach on the Theorem Which Bears His Name," in D. E. Smith, ed., *A Source Book in Mathematics* (New York–London, 1929), paperback repr. (New York, 1959); "Einleitung zu dem Werke Analysis der dreyeckigen Pyramide durch die Methode der Coordinaten und Projectionen. Ein Beytrag zu der analytischen Geometrie," in L. Oken, *Isis*, VI (Jena, 1826), 565; and *Grundriss zu analytischen Untersuchungen der dreyeckigen Pyramide* (Nuremberg, 1827). An unpublished MS on the theory of the triangular pyramid, dated 7 July 1826, is in the Feuerbach family archives.

II. SECONDARY LITERATURE. On the man and his work, see C. J. Brianchon and J. V. Poncelet, "Géométrie des courbes: Recherches sur la détermination d'une hyperbole équilatère, au moyen de quatre conditions données," in *Annales de mathematiques,* **11** (1 Jan. 1821); M. Cantor, "Karl Wilhelm Feuerbach," in *Sitzungsberichte der Heidelberger Akademie der Wissenschaften,* Math.-naturwissen. Klasse, Abh. 25 (1910); L. Euler, "Solutio facilis problematum quorumdam geometricorum difficillimorum," in *Novi commentarii academiae scientiarum imperialis Petropolitanae,* **11** (1765), 103; H. Eulenberg, *Die Familie Feuerbach* (Stuttgart, 1924); L. Feuerbach, *Anselm Ritter von Feuerbachs biographischer Nachlass* (Leipzig, 1853); L. Guggenbuhl, "Karl Wilhelm Feuerbach, Mathematician," in *Scientific Monthly,* **81** (1955), 71; R. A. Johnson, *Modern Geometry: An Elementary Treatise on the Geometry of the Triangle and the Circle* (Boston–New York, 1929), repr. in paperback as *Advanced Euclidean Geometry* (New York, 1960); J. Lange, "Geschichte des Feuerbachschen Kreises," in *Wissenschaftliche Beilage zum Jahresbericht der Friedrichs Wederschen Ober-Realschule zu Berlin Programme No. 114* (1894); J. S. Mackay, "History of the Nine Point Circle," in *Proceedings of the Edinburgh Mathematical Society,* **11** (1892), 19; G. Radbruch, *Paul Johann Anselm Feuerbach* (Vienna, 1934) and *Gestalten und Gedanken. Die Feuerbachs, Eine geistige Dynastie* (Leipzig, 1948); T. Spoerri, *Genie und Krankheit* (Basel–New York, 1952); J. Steiner, *Die geometrischen Constructionen ausgefuhrt mittelst der geraden Linie und eines festen Kreises* (Berlin, 1833); and Olry Terquem, "Considération sur le triangle rectiligne," in *Nouvelles annales de mathématiques,* **1** (1842), 196.

LAURA GUGGENBUHL

FEUILLÉE, LOUIS (*b.* Mane, Basses-Alpes, France, 1660; *d.* Marseilles, France, 18 April 1732), *astronomy, botany.*

Feuillée made astronomical observations when he was only ten years old. He was then in the service of the Minims, having entered that order in Avignon on 2 March 1680. In 1699 he accompanied Jacques Cassini on his exploration of the Greek coast and in 1703 went to the Antilles and the South American coast, returning to Brest in 1706. As a result of this mission he was appointed royal mathematician and corresponding member of the Académie des Sciences in Paris.

In 1707 Feuillée sailed for the west coast of South America, via Cape Horn, landing in Chile, where he remained until 1709. He explored the Chilean and Peruvian coasts, returning to Brest by 27 August 1711. Louis XIV placed in his care an observatory built at Marseilles. In 1724 he was again commissioned by the Academy to establish the longitude of the meridian of Hierro Island in the Canaries.

The work of Feuillée is interesting and reliable, although it was marred by his controversy with A. F. Frézier, who explored the west coast of South America between 1711 and 1714. His description of the flora of the coasts of Peru and Chile is still much appreciated.

BIBLIOGRAPHY

Feuillée's astronomical observations were published in the *Mémoires de l'Académie des sciences* (1699–1710). His best-known work is the *Journal des observations physiques, mathématiques, et botaniques, faites sur les côtes orientales de l'Amérique Méridionale et dans les Indes Occidentales de 1707 à 1712* (Paris, 1714), which was followed by the *Suite du journal . . .* (Paris, 1725). In the *Histoire des plantes médicinales qui son les plus d'usage aux royaumes du Pérou et du Chili* (Paris, 1714–1725) he incorporated the description, illustration, and uses of 100 medicinal plants.

Francisco Guerra

FEULGEN, ROBERT JOACHIM (*b.* Werden, Germany, 2 September 1884; *d.* Giessen, Germany, 24 October 1955), *biochemistry, histochemistry.*

The son of a textile worker, Feulgen was educated in Werden, Essen, and Soest; in 1905 he entered the medical faculty of the University of Freiburg im Breisgau. For the completion of his training he went to Kiel, and while working in the city hospital he prepared his dissertation on the purine metabolism of patients afflicted with chronic gout. The years 1912–1918 were spent in Berlin at the Physiological Institute, the chemistry section of which was headed by the nucleic acid chemist Hermann Steudel. Feulgen's extension and criticism of Steudel's work formed the subject of his *Habilitationsschrift* in 1919. The following year he was appointed to the Physiological Institute at Giessen, where he spent the rest of his life, rising from assistant professor in 1923 to associate professor in 1927 and director of the Physiological-Chemical Institute in 1931.

In Berlin, Feulgen improved on Steudel's extraction technique for thymonucleic acid (DNA), so that the

product gave no biuret reaction and dissolved readily in water to give a colorless solution. By combining nucleic acid with Congo red and malachite green, extracting the salts formed, and subjecting these to an elementary analysis, he believed he had obtained more reliable percentage compositions. His matching of the resulting nitrogen:phosphorus ratios with the ratios predicted from various molecular structures strengthened rather than shook his confidence in the tetranucleotide hypothesis.

Feulgen's major discovery came in 1914, when he took up Steudel's observation (1908) of the reducing action of apurinic acid (then called thymic acid) on Fehling's solution. Feulgen found that phenylhydrazine reacted with this acid, indicating the presence of aldehyde groups, and that Schiff's reagent gave the magenta color indicative of furan. By the use of aldehyde blocking controls Feulgen was led to the correct conclusion that in the mild hydrolysis of thymonucleic acid to apurinic acid, loss of purines exposes aldehyde groups, which easily give rise to the furan structure. By treating thymonucleic acid with NHCl for ten minutes (optimum is pH 7) before application of Schiff's reagent, he obtained the magenta color. Untreated thymonucleic acid failed to produce it, as did the RNA of yeast nucleic acid. It was already known that the carbohydrates in thymonucleic and yeast nucleic acid differ, the latter being a pentose sugar and the former probably a hexose sugar, in Feulgen's opinion glucal—a compound discovered that year by Fischer—because it contains the furan structure, and he called his discovery the nucleal reaction.

In 1923, nine years after his discovery of the nucleal reaction, Feulgen applied it as a histochemical stain. In this way he was able to show that thymonucleic acid is found only in the nucleus and that both plant and animal cells give a positive nucleal reaction. Although he failed to detect the nuclei in yeast cells, he rightly concluded that the pentose nucleic acid of yeast is localized in the cytoplasm. At Feulgen's first demonstration of these results, at the Congress of Physiology held at Tübingen in 1923, Albrecht Kossel was impressed, but otherwise there was skepticism. By a thorough examination of the technique and by the use of aldehyde blocking, Feulgen established his test. In 1937 he succeeded in isolating rye germ nuclei that gave the nucleal reaction. This work effectively banished the old division of nucleic acids into the thymonucleic acids of animals and the yeast (pentose) nucleic acids of plants and established in its place the occurrence of both in the same cell. Although modern research has shown the presence of RNA in the nucleus and of DNA in the cytoplasm, the major part of these acids is still distributed in the way shown by Feulgen's test.

In 1924 Feulgen and Voit discovered a positive nucleal reaction in the cytoplasm without previous mild hydrolysis. This "plasmal" reaction they showed to be due to aldehyde groups; and finding that lipide solvents negative the test, they concluded that a lipide precursor is responsible. In 1928 they isolated "plasmalogen," and eleven years later they identified it as an acetal phosphatide.

Feulgen was orthodox in his acceptance of the tetranucleotide hypothesis, according to which thymonucleic acid is an oligonucleotide formed from a nucleotide of each of the bases thymine, cytosine, adenine, and guanine. Later he expressed reservations, and in 1936 it was clear to him that the undegraded material is a polymer and that the usual extractive procedures yield a mixture of depolymerized fragments. Studies of viscosity and optical activity gave him evidence of this change from what he termed the *a* form to the *b* form. He also discovered that conversion of *a* to *b* can be achieved by the action of a commercial preparation of the pancreatic juice. The depolymerizing enzyme that he believed to be present he called nucleogelase. From the same material M. McCarthy later obtained DNA depolymerase. These findings received little attention, and today Feulgen is remembered not for them but for his introduction of the nucleal reaction, which transformed nucleic acid cytochemistry. He was a skillful experimentalist whose certainty of the specific character of his nucleal reaction has been justified despite nearly thirty years of disputation over its nature and specificity.

BIBLIOGRAPHY

I. ORIGINAL WORKS. Feulgen and his co-workers published seventy original papers, four contributions to biochemical textbooks, and a scholarly review of nucleic acid chemistry: "Chemie und Physiologie der Nucleinstoffe," in A. Kanitz, ed., *Die Biochemie in Einzeldarstellungen* (Berlin, 1923). A complete list of his publications will be found in F. H. Kasten and in K. Felix (see below). The majority of his papers appeared in *Hoppe-Seyler's Zeitschrift für physiologische Chemie;* the most important are "Über die 'Kohlenhydratgruppe' in der echten Nucleinsäure. Vorläufige Mitteilungen," **92** (1914), 154–158, announcing the nucleal reaction; "Mikroskopisch-chemischer Nachweis einer Nucleinsäure vom Typus der Thymonucleinsäure und die darauf beruhende elektive Färbung von Zellkernen in mikroscopischen Präparaten," **135** (1924), 203–248, on the Feulgen stain, written with H. Rossenbeck; and "Die Darstellung der b-Thymonucleinsäure mittels der Nucleogelase," **238** (1936), 105–110. The plas-

mal reaction was described in "Über einen weitverbreiteten Stoff (Plasmal, Plasmalogen), seinen histologischen Nachweis und seiner Beziehungen zum Geruch des gekochten Fleisches," in *Klinische Wochenschrift,* **4** (1925), 1330, written with K. Voit.

II. SECONDARY LITERATURE. The best scientific biography of Feulgen is K. Felix, "Robert Feulgen zum Gedächtnis," in *Hoppe-Seyler's Zeitschrift für physiologische Chemie,* **307** (1957), 1–13, with portrait and full bibliography. An English summary of this essay plus additional biographical data is in F. H. Kasten, "Robert Feulgen," in W. Sandritter, ed., *Hundred Years of Histochemistry in Germany* (Stuttgart, 1964), pp. 97–101, also with portrait and bibliography. For brief details of Feulgen's life see *Leopoldina,* **1** (1955), 52–53; and Poggendorff, VIIa, pt. 2 (Berlin, 1958), 31. The most authoritative account of the debate over the mechanism and specificity of the Feulgen reaction is A. G. E. Pearse, *Histochemistry Theoretical and Applied,* 2nd ed. (London, 1960), pp. 193–201.

ROBERT OLBY

FIBONACCI, LEONARDO, or **LEONARDO OF PISA** (*b.* Pisa, Italy, *ca.* 1170; *d.* Pisa, after 1240), *mathematics.*

Leonardo Fibonacci, the first great mathematician of the Christian West, was a member of a family named Bonacci, whose presence in Pisa since the eleventh century is documented. His father's name is known to have been Guilielmo. It is thus that Fibonacci is to be understood as a member of the Bonacci family and not as "son of a father of the name of Bonacci," as one might suppose from the words "filio Bonacij" or "de filiis Bonacij," which appear in the titles of many manuscripts of his works. The sobriquet "Bigollo" (from *bighellone,* loafer or ne'er-do-well), used by Leonardo himself, remains unexplained. Did his countrymen wish to express by this epithet their disdain for a man who concerned himself with questions of no practical value, or does the word in the Tuscan dialect mean a much-traveled man, which he was?

Life. Leonardo himself provides exact details on the course of his life in the preface to the most extensive and famous of his works, the book on calculations entitled *Liber abbaci* (1202). His father, as a secretary of the Republic of Pisa,[1] was entrusted around 1192 with the direction of the Pisan trading colony in Bugia (now Bougie), Algeria. He soon brought his son there to have him learn the art of calculating, since he expected Leonardo to become a merchant. It was there that he learned methods "with the new Indian numerals," and he received excellent instruction (*ex mirabili magisterio*). On the business trips on which his father evidently soon sent him and which took him to Egypt, Syria, Greece (Byzantium), Sicily, and

Provence, he acquainted himself with the methods in use there through zealous study and in disputations with native scholars. All these methods, however—so he reports—as well as "algorismus" and the "arcs of Pythagoras" (apparently the abacus of Gerbert) appeared to him as in "error" in comparison with the Indian methods.[2] It is quite unclear what Leonardo means here by the "algorismus" he rejects; for those writings through which the Indian methods became known, especially after Sacrobosco, a younger contemporary of Leonardo, bear that very name. Could he mean the later *algorismus linealis*, reckoning with lines, the origin of which is, to be sure, likewise obscure?

Around the turn of the century Leonardo returned to Pisa. Here for the next twenty-five years he composed works in which he presented not only calculations with Indian numerals and methods and their application in all areas of commercial activity, but also much of what he had learned of algebraic and geometrical problems. His inclusion of the latter in his own writings shows that while the instruction of his countrymen in the solution of the problems posed by everyday life was indeed his chief concern, he nevertheless also wished to provide material on theoretical arithmetic and geometry for those who were interested in more advanced questions. He even speaks once of wanting to add the "subtleties of Euclid's geometry";[3] these are the propositions from books II and X of the *Elements*, which he offers to the reader not only in proofs, in Euclid's manner, but in numerical form as well. His most important original accomplishments were in indeterminate analysis and number theory, in which he went far beyond his predecessors.

Leonardo's importance was recognized at the court of the Hohenstaufen emperor Frederick II. Leonardo's writings mention the names of many of the scholars of the circle around the emperor, including Michael Scotus, a court astrologer whom Dante (*Inferno*, XX, 115 ff.) banished to hell; the imperial philosopher, Master Theodorus; and Master Johannes of Palermo. Through a Master Dominicus, probably the Dominicus Hispanus mentioned by Guido Bonatti (see Boncompagni, *Intorno ad alcune opere di Leonardo Pisano*, p. 98, n.), Leonardo was presented to the emperor, who evidently desired to meet him, when Frederick held court in Pisa about 1225.[4] After 1228 we know almost nothing more concerning Leonardo's activity in Pisa. Only one document has survived, from 1240, in which the Republic of Pisa awards the "serious and learned Master Leonardo Bigollo" (*discretus et sapiens*) a yearly *salarium* of "libre XX denariorem" in addition to the usual al-

lowances, in recognition of his usefulness to the city and its citizens through his teaching and devoted services. He evidently had advised the city and its officials, without payment, on matters of accounting, a service the city expected him to continue. This decree of the city, which was inscribed on a marble tablet in the Pisa city archives in the nineteenth century,[5] is the last information we have on Leonardo's life.

Writings. Five works by Leonardo are preserved:
1. The *Liber abbaci* (1202, 1228);
2. The *Practica geometriae* (1220/1221);
3. A writing entitled *Flos* (1225);
4. An undated letter to Theodorus, the imperial philosopher;
5. The *Liber quadratorum* (1225). We know of further works, such as a book on commercial arithmetic, *Di minor guisa*;[6] especially unfortunate is the loss of a tract on book X of the *Elements*, for which Leonardo promised a numerical treatment of irrationals instead of Euclid's geometrical presentation.[7]

Leonardo's works have been collected in the edition by Boncompagni; in 1838 Libri edited only one chapter of the *Liber abbaci*. Boncompagni, however, provides only the Latin text without any commentary. Hence, despite much specialized research on the *Flos* and on the *Liber quadratorum*, which Ver Eecke has translated into French, there is still no exhaustive presentation of Leonardo's problems and methods. The most detailed studies of the substance of the works are those by Cantor, Loria, and Youschkevitch.

Liber abbaci. The word *abacus* in the title does not refer to the old abacus, the sand board; rather, it means computation in general, as was true later with the Italian masters of computation, the *maestri d'abbaco*. Of the second treatment of 1228, to which "new material has been added and from which superfluous removed," there exist twelve manuscript copies from the thirteenth through the fifteenth centuries; but only three of these from the thirteenth and the beginning of the fourteenth centuries are complete. Leonardo divided this extensive work, which is dedicated to Michael Scotus, into fifteen chapters; it will be analyzed here in four sections.

Section 1 (chapters 1–7; *Scritti*, I, 1–82). Leonardo refers to Roman numerals and finger computation, which the student still needs for marking intermediate results.[8] Then the Indian numerals are introduced; following the Arabic manner, the units stand "in front" (on the right), and the fractions are on the left of the whole numbers. In addition, he introduces the fraction bar. All the computational operations are taught methodically through numerous examples and the results are checked, mostly by the method of casting out nines (seven and eleven are also used in this way). Rules are developed for the factoring of fractions into sums of unit factors. Various symbols are introduced for the representation of fractions. Thus, for example, $\dfrac{6\ \ 2}{7\ \ 5}$ is to be read as $\dfrac{2}{5} + \dfrac{6}{7 \cdot 5}$; $0\,\dfrac{6\ \ 2}{7\ \ 5}$ means $\dfrac{2}{5} \cdot \dfrac{6}{7}$; and $\dfrac{6\ \ 2}{7\ \ 5}\,0$ is to be understood as $\dfrac{2}{5} + \dfrac{6}{7}$. Finally, $\dfrac{1\ \ 1\ \ 1\ \ 5}{5\ \ 4\ \ 3\ \ 9}$ signifies $\dfrac{5}{9} + \left(\dfrac{1}{3} + \dfrac{1}{4} + \dfrac{1}{5}\right) \cdot \dfrac{5}{9}$. The first—and the most frequently employed—of these representational methods corresponds to the ascending continued fraction $\dfrac{2 + \dfrac{6}{7}}{5}$. Numerous tables (for multiplication, prime numbers, factoring numbers, etc.) complete the text.

Section 2 (chapters 8–11; *Scritti*, I, 83–165). This section contains problems of concern to merchants, such as the price of goods, calculation of profits, barter, computation of interest, wages, calculations for associations and partnerships, metal alloys, and mixture calculations; the computations of measurements and of currency conversions in particular reflect the widespread trade of the medieval city with the lands bordering the Mediterranean. One of the mixture problems included is known from Chinese mathematics, the "problem of the 100 birds"; a problem in indeterminate analysis, it requires that one purchase for 100 units of money 100 birds of different sorts, the price of each sort being different.

Section 3 (chapters 12 and 13; *Scritti*, I, 176–351). This is the most extensive section and contains problems of many types, which are called *erraticae questiones*. They are mostly puzzles, such as are found in the mathematical recreations of all times. Among them are the "cistern problems" (A spider climbing the wall of a cistern advances so many feet each day and slips back so many feet each night. How long will it take it to climb out?) and, from Egyptian mathematics, the famous so-called "hau calculations," which can be expressed in the form $ax \pm b/c \cdot x = s$. Leonardo calls them *questiones arborum* after the first example, in which a tree is supposed to stand twenty-one ells above the ground with 7/12 of its length in the earth; therefore, $x - 7/12\,x = 21$. Another group are "motion problems," involving either pursuit (as in the famous "hare and hound" problem, in which one must determine how long it will take a hound chasing a hare at a proportional speed to catch the hare) or opposite movements. In both cases the motions can be delayed through backward movements. Since in many problems the speed is not con-

stant, but increases arithmetically, rules for the summation of series are given at the beginning of chapter 12. A group of problems that had already appeared in the epigrams of *The Greek Anthology* (a recent edition is W. R. Paton, ed. [Cambridge, Mass., 1953], V, 25 ff.) and can be designated as "giving and taking," is called by Leonardo *de personis habentibus denarios;* in these there are two or more people, each of whom demands a certain sum from one or several of the others and then states what the proportion now is between his money and that of the others. A simple example is (1) $x + 7 = 5 \cdot (y - 7)$; (2) $y + 5 = 7 \cdot (x - 5)$. In the problem of "the found purse" (*de inventione bursarum*) two or more people find a purse, and we are told for each individual what ratio the sum of his money and the total money in the purse has to the sum of the remaining individuals' monies; for example, with three people the modern arrangement would be (1) $x + b = 2 \cdot (y + z)$; (2) $y + b = 3 \cdot (x + z)$; (3) $z + b = 4(x + y)$. They are, therefore, problems in indeterminate analysis.

Another very extensive group, "one alone cannot buy," takes the form of "horse buying" (*de hominibus equum emere volentibus*). In this case it is given that one of those concerned can buy an object only if he receives from the other (or others) a portion of his (or their) cash.[9] Variations are also given that involve up to seven people and five horses; in these cases, if the price of the horse is not known, the problem is indeterminate. A problem of this type involving three people, where the equation would be

$$x + \frac{y + z}{3} = y + \frac{z + x}{4} = z + \frac{x + y}{5} = s,$$

corresponds to Diophantus II, 24. A further group treats the business trips of a merchant, which are introduced as *de viagiis*. These are the famous problems of the "gate-keeper in the apple garden." It is here that the problems involving mathematical nesting of the form $\langle [(a_1 x - b_1) \cdot a_2 - b_2] \cdot a_3 - \cdots \rangle \cdot a_n - b_n = s$ are to be solved.[10] Of the multitude of other problems treated in the *Liber abbaci*, the following should be mentioned: numerous remainder problems, in which, for example, a number n is sought with the property $n \equiv 1$ (mod. 2, 3, 4, 5, and 6) $\equiv 0$ (mod. 7); the Chinese remainder problem *Ta yen*,[11] the finding of perfect numbers; the summation of a geometric series; the ancient Egyptian problem of the "seven old women" (to find $\sum\limits_{i=1}^{n} 7^i$, the seven wives of St. Ives); the Bachet weight problem; the chess problem (to find $\sum\limits_{i=0}^{64} 2^i$); and the rabbit problem. This last problem assumes that a pair of rabbits requires one month to mature and thereafter reproduces itself once each month. If one starts with a single pair, how many pairs will one have after n months? The answer leads to the famous Fibonacci series, the first recurrent series. Its general form for any term k_n is $k_n = k_{n-1} + k_{n-2}$; and, in this case, it can be expressed as

$$k_n = \frac{1}{\sqrt{5}} \cdot \left[\left(\frac{1 + \sqrt{5}}{2} \right)^n - \left(\frac{1 - \sqrt{5}}{2} \right)^n \right].$$

Leonardo demonstrates an astonishing versatility in the choice of methods of solution to be used in particular instances; he frequently employs a special procedure, for which he usually has no specific name and which has been tailored with great skill to fit the individual problem. He also shows great dexterity in the introduction of an auxiliary unknown; in this he is like Iamblichus, who demonstrated the same talent in his explanation of the *Epanthema* of Thymaridas of Paros. At other times Leonardo makes use of definitely general methods. These include the simple false position, as in the "hau calculations" and the *regula versa,* in which the calculation is made in reverse order in the nesting problems in *de viagiis;* there is also the double false position, to which the whole of chapter 13 is devoted and which is called—as in Leonardo's Arabic models—*regula elchatayn.* With this rule, linear and pure quadratic problems can be solved with the aid of two arbitrarily chosen quantities, a_1 and a_2, of unknown magnitude and the resulting errors, f_1 and f_2. Leonardo knew this procedure, but he generally used a variation. The latter consists in ascertaining from the two errors how much closer one has come to the true answer (*veritati appropinquinare*)[12] in the second attempt and then determining the number that one must now choose in order to obtain the correct solution. A special solution for an indeterminate problem is provided by the *regula proportionis.* If, for example, in the final equation of a problem $63/600\, x = 21/200\, b,$ then, according to this rule, $x = 21/200$ and $b = 63/600$ or, in whole numbers, $x = 63$ and $b = 63$.

Leonardo also employed, as easy mechanical solutions, formulas (especially in the "horse buying," "found purse," and "journey" problems) that can have been obtained only by means of algebra. He knew the algebraic methods very well; he called them *regulae rectae* and stated that they were used by the Arabs and could be useful in many ways. He called the unknown term *res* (Arabic *shai',* "thing"); and since he used no operational symbols and no notations for further unknowns here (see, however, under *Practica geometriae*), he had to designate them as

denarii secundi or, as the case might be, *denarii tercii hominis* and take the trouble to carry them through the entire problem. For most of the problems Leonardo provided two or more methods of solution.

An example of the "giving and taking" type is the following, in which the system named above—(1) $x + 7 = 5 \cdot (y - 7)$; (2) $7 \cdot (x - 5) = y + 5$—is involved. First, $x + y$ is presented as a line segment; at the point of contact $y = 7$ and $x = 5$ is marked off along both sides. Then the segment $y - 7$ (or $x - 5$) is equal to $1/6$ (or $1/8$) of the whole segment $x + y$, and together, therefore, the two segments equal $7/24 \cdot (x + y)$. The further solution is achieved by means of the simple false position $x + y = 24$. There follows still another algebraic solution, this one using the *regulae rectae.* First, $y - 7$ is designated as *res;* then (1) $x = 5\ res - 7$ and (2) $res + 12 = 7 \cdot (5\ res - 12)$.[13]

In some cases the problem is not solvable because of mutually contradictory initial conditions. In other cases the problem is called *insolubilis, incongruum,* or *inconveniens,*[14] unless one accepts a "debit" as a solution. Leonardo is here thinking of a negative number, with which he also makes further calculations. Our operations $22 + (-9) = 22 - 9$ and $-1 + 11 = +10$ he represents with *adde denarios,* as 22 *cum debito secundi* ($=9$) *scilicet extrahe* 9 *de* 22 and *debitum primi* ($= -1$) *cum bursa* ($=11$) *erunt* 10.[15]

Section 4 (chapters 14 and 15; *Scritti,* I, 352–387). Leonardo here shows himself to be a master in the application of algebraic methods and an outstanding student of Euclid. Chapter 14, which is devoted to calculations with radicals, begins with a few formulas of general arithmetic. Called "keys" (*claves*), they are taken from book II of Euclid's *Elements.* Leonardo explicitly says that he is forgoing any demonstrations of his own since they are all proved there. The fifth and sixth propositions of book II are especially important; from them, he said, one could derive all the problems of the *Aliebra* and the *Almuchabala.* Square and cube roots are taught numerically according to the Indian-Arabic algorithm, which in fact corresponds to the modern one.

Leonardo also knew the procedure of adding zeros to the radicands in order to obtain greater exactness; actually, this had already been done by Johannes Hispalensis (*fl.* 1135–1153) and al-Nasawī (*fl. ca.* 1025). Next, examples are given that are illustrative of the ancient methods of approximation. For $\sqrt{A} = \sqrt{a^2 + r}$ the first approximation is $a_1 = a + r/2a$. With $r_1 = a_1^2 - A$, the second approximation is then $a_2 = a_1 - r_1/2a_1$. With the cube root $\sqrt[3]{A} = \sqrt[3]{a^3 + r}$, the first approximation is

$$a_1 = a + \frac{r}{(a+1)^3 - a^3} = a + \frac{r}{3a^2 + 3a + 1}.$$

For a second approximation Leonardo now set $r_1 = A - a_1^3$ and

$$a_2 = a_1 + \frac{r_1}{3a_1 \cdot (a+1)}.$$

He was no doubt thinking of this further approximation when he spoke of his own achievement,[16] for the first approximation was already known to al-Nasawī. The chapter then goes on systematically to carry out complete operations with Euclidean irrationals. There are expressions such as

$$a \pm \sqrt{b}, \quad \sqrt{a} \pm \sqrt{b}, \quad \sqrt{a} \cdot \sqrt{b}, \quad \sqrt{a} \cdot \sqrt[4]{b},$$

$$\sqrt[4]{a} \cdot \sqrt[4]{b}, \quad \sqrt[4]{a} \pm \sqrt[4]{b}, \quad (a + \sqrt{b}) \cdot (c \pm \sqrt{d}),$$

$$(a + \sqrt[4]{b}) \cdot (\sqrt{c} \pm \sqrt[4]{d}), \quad \frac{a - \sqrt{b}}{\sqrt{c} + \sqrt{d}}, \quad \sqrt{a + \sqrt{b}},$$

$$\frac{a}{b + \sqrt{c} + \sqrt[4]{d}}, \quad \sqrt[3]{a} + \sqrt[3]{b}.$$

The proof, which is never lacking, of the correctness of the calculations is presented geometrically. On one occasion the numbers are represented as line segments, for example, in the computation of

$$4 + \sqrt[4]{10} = \sqrt{16 + \sqrt{10} + 8 \cdot \sqrt[4]{10}},$$

where proposition 4 of book II of the *Elements* is used as a "key." On the other hand, the proof is made by means of rectangular surfaces. An example is $\sqrt{4 + \sqrt{7}} + \sqrt{4 - \sqrt{7}} = \sqrt{14}$. Here $(4 + \sqrt{7})$ is conceived as the area of a square, to which at one corner, through the elongation of the two intersecting sides, a square of area $(4 - \sqrt{7})$ is joined. Thus $\sqrt{4 + \sqrt{7}} + \sqrt{4 - \sqrt{7}}$ is the side of a larger square, which consists of the squares $4 + \sqrt{7}$ and $4 - \sqrt{7}$ and the two rectangles each equal to $\sqrt{4 + \sqrt{7}} \cdot \sqrt{4 - \sqrt{7}}$.

With respect to mathematical content Leonardo does not surpass his Arab predecessors. Nevertheless, the richness of the examples and of their methodical arrangement, as well as the exact proofs, are to be emphasized. At the end of chapter 15, which is divided into three sections, one sees particularly clearly what complete control Leonardo had over the geometrical as well as the algebraic methods for solving quadratic equations and with what skill he could use them in applied problems. The first section is concerned with proportions and their multifarious transformations. In one problem, for example, it is given

that (1) $6 : x = y : 9$ and (2) $x + y = 21$. From (1) it is determined that $xy = 54$; then, using Euclid II, 5,

$$\left(\frac{x-y}{2}\right)^2 = \left(\frac{21}{2}\right)^2 - 54$$

and

$$x - y = 15.$$

From this follow the solutions 3 and 18.[17] The end points of the segments are denoted by letters of the alphabet ($abgd \cdots$ or $abcd \cdots$); for example, $.a.b$ signifies a segment. Leonardo, however, also speaks about the numbers $a.b.c.d.,$ by which he means $(ab) \cdot (cd)$. Sometimes, though, only a single letter is given for the entire segment.

The second section first presents applications of the Pythagorean theorem, such as the ancient Babylonian problem of a pole leaning against a wall and the Indian problem of two towers of different heights. On the given line joining them (i.e., their bases) there is a spring which shall be equally distant from the tops of the towers. The same problem was solved in chapter 13 by the method of false position. Many different types of problems follow, such as the solution of an indeterminate equation $x^2 + y^2 = 25$, given that $3^2 + 4^2 = 25$; or problems of the type *de viagiis*, in which the merchant makes the same profit on each of his journeys. Geometric and stereometric problems are also presented; thus, for example, the determination of the amount of water running out of a receptacle when various bodies, including a sphere (with $\pi = 3\frac{1}{7}$), are sunk in.

The third section contains algebraic quadratic problems (*questiones secundum modum algebre*). First, with reference made to "Maumeht," i.e., to al-Khwārizmī, the six normal forms $ax^2 = bx$, $ax^2 = c$, $bx = c$, $ax^2 + bx = c$, $ax^2 + c = bx$ (here Leonardo is acquainted with both solutions), and $ax^2 = bx + c$ are introduced; they are then exactly computed in numerous, sometimes complicated, examples. Frequently what is sought is the factorization of a number, usually 10, for example,

$$\frac{x}{10-x} + \frac{10-x}{x} = \sqrt{5}.$$

Another problem is $\sqrt{8x} \cdot \sqrt{3x} + 20 = x^2$, and still another is $x^2 - 2x - 4 = \sqrt{8x^2}$. Here Leonardo represents x^2 as a square divided into three rectangular parts: $\sqrt{8x^2}$, $2x$, and 4. With the aid of Euclid II, 6 he then obtains $x = \sqrt{7 + \sqrt{8}} + (1 + \sqrt{2})$. Since in the problem a "fortune" (x^2 = avere) was sought, the final solution is $x^2 = 10 + 2 \cdot \sqrt{8} + \sqrt{116 + 40 \cdot \sqrt{8}}$. Leonardo also includes equations of higher degrees that can be reduced to quadratics. For example, it is given that (1) $y = 10/x$; (2) $z = y^2/x$; and (3) $z^2 = x^2 + y^2$. This leads to $x^8 + 100x^4 = 10,000$. The numerical examples are taken largely from the algebra of al-Khwārizmī and al-Karajī,[18] frequently even with the same numerical values. In this fourth section of the *Liber abbaci* there also appear further names for the powers of the unknowns.

When several unknowns are involved, then (along with *radix* and *res* for x) a third unknown is introduced as *pars* ("part," Arabic, *qasm*); and sometimes the sum of two unknowns is designated as *res*. For x^2, the names *quadratus, census,* and *avere* ("wealth," Arabic, *māl*)[19] are employed; for x^3, *cubus;* for x^4, *census de censu* and *censuum census;* and for x^6, *cubus cubi.* The constant term is called *numerus, denarius,* or *dragma.*

Practica geometriae (*Scritti,* II, 1–224). This second work by Leonardo, which he composed in 1220 or 1221, between the two editions of the *Liber abbaci,* is dedicated to the Magister Dominicus mentioned above. Of the nine extant manuscripts one is in Rome, which Boncompagni used, and two are in Paris.[20] In this work Leonardo does not wish to present only measurement problems for the layman; in addition, for those with scientific interests, he considers geometry according to the method of proof. Therefore, the models are, on the one hand, Hero and the *Agrimensores,* and Euclid and Archimedes on the other. Leonardo had studied the *Liber embadorum* of Plato of Tivoli (1145) especially closely and took from it large sections and individual problems with the same numerical values. This work by Plato was a translation of the geometry of Savasorda (Abraham bar Hiyya), written in Hebrew, which in turn reproduced Arabic knowledge of the subject.

The *Practica* is divided into eight chapters (*distinctiones*), which are preceded by an introduction. In the latter the basic concepts are explained, as are the postulates and axioms of Euclid (including the spurious axioms 4, 5, 6, and 9) and the linear and surface measures current in Pisa.[21] The first chapter presents, in connection with the surfaces of rectangles, examples of the multiplication of segments, each of which is given in a sum of various units (rod, foot, ounce, etc.). The propositions of book II of the *Elements* are also recalled. The second chapter and the fifth chapter treat, as a preparation for the following problems, square and cube roots and calculation with them in a manner similar to that of the *Liber abbaci.* Next, the duplications of the cube by Archytas, Philo of Byzantium, and Plato, which are reported by Eutocius, are demonstrated, without reference to their source. The solutions of Plato and Archytas, Leonardo

took from the *Verba filiorum* of the Banū Mūsā, a work translated by Gerard of Cremona. That of Philo appears also in Jordanus de Nemore's *De triangulis,* and probably both Leonardo and Jordanus took it from a common source. (See M. Clagett, *Archimedes in the Middle Ages,* I, 224, 658–660.) The third chapter provides a treatment with exact demonstrations of the calculation of segments and surfaces of plane figures: the triangle, the square, the rectangle, rhomboids (*rumboides*), trapezoids (*figurae quae habent capita abscisa*), polygons, and the circle; for the circle, applying the Archimedean polygon of ninety-six sides, π is determined as $864:275 \sim 3.141818 \cdots$. In addition, Leonardo was acquainted with quadrilaterals possessing a reentrant angle (*figura barbata*) in which a diagonal falls outside the figure.

Many of the problems lead to quadratic equations, for which the formulas of the normal forms are used. They are given verbally. Hence, for example, in the problem $4x - x^2 = 3$, we are told: If from the sum of the four sides the square surface is subtracted, then three rods remain. Attention is also drawn here to the double solution. Along with this, Leonardo gives practical directions for the surveyor and describes instrumental methods, such as can be used in finding the foot of the altitude of a triangular field or in the computation of the projection of a field lying on a hillside. Among the geodetic instruments was an archipendulum. With the help of it and a surveyor's rod, the horizontal projections of straight lines lying inclined on a hillside could be measured. For the surveyor who does not understand the Ptolemaic procedure of determining half-chords from given arcs, appropriate instructions and a table of chords are provided. This is the only place where the term *sinus versus arcus,* certainly borrowed from Arabic trigonometry, appears. The fourth chapter is devoted to the division of surfaces; it is a reworking of the *Liber embadorum,* which ultimately derives from Euclid's lost *Book on Divisions of Figures;* the latter can be reconstructed (see Archibald) from the texts of Plato of Tivoli and of Leonardo and from that of an Arabic version. In the sixth chapter Leonardo discusses volumes, including those of the regular polyhedrons, in connection with which he refers to the propositions of book XIV of Euclid. The seventh chapter contains the calculation of the heights of tall objects, for example, of a tree, and gives the rules of surveying based on the similarity of triangles; in these cases the angles are obtained by means of a quadrant.

The eighth chapter presents what Leonardo had termed "geometrical subtleties" (*subtilitates*) in the preface to the *Liber abbaci.* Among those included is the calculation of the sides of the pentagon and the decagon from the diameter of circumscribed and inscribed circles; the inverse calculation is also given, as well as that of the sides from the surfaces. There follow two indeterminate problems: $a^2 + 5 = b^2$ and $c^2 - 10 = d^2$. The *Liber quadratorum* treats a similar problem: $a^2 + 5 = b^2$, together with $a^2 - 5 = c^2$. Finally, to complete the section on equilateral triangles, a rectangle and a square are inscribed in such a triangle and their sides are algebraically calculated, with the solution given in the sexagesimal system.

Flos (*Scritti*, II, 227–247). The title of this work, which—like two following ones—is preserved in a Milanese manuscript of 1225, is *INCIPIT flos Leonardi bigoli pisani super solutionibus quarumdam questionum ad numerum et ad geometriam vel ad utrumque pertinentium.* Sent to Frederick II, it contains the elaboration of questions that Master Johannes of Palermo posed in the emperor's presence in Pisa. The work had been requested by Cardinal Raniero Capocci da Viterbo; Leonardo, moreover, provided him with additional problems of the same type. For the first problem (involving the equations $x^2 + 5 = y^2$ and $x^2 - 5 = z^2$) only the solution is presented; it is treated in the *Liber quadratorum.* The second question that Master Johannes had posed concerns the solution of the cubic equation $x^3 + 2x^2 + 10x = 20$. Leonardo, who knew book X of the *Elements* thoroughly, demonstrates that the solution can be neither a whole number, nor a fraction, nor one of the Euclidean irrational magnitudes. Consequently, he seeks an approximate solution. He gives it in sexagesimal form as $1° 22' 7'' 42''' 33^{IV} 4^V 40^{VI}$, the 40 being too great by about 1 1/2. We are not told how the result was found. We know only that the same problem appears in the algebra of al-Khayyāmī,[22] where it is solved by means of the intersection of a circle and a hyperbola. One may suppose that the solution follows from the Horner method, which was known to the Chinese and the Arabs.

Next Leonardo presents a series of indeterminate linear problems. If the first of these (*tres homines pecuniam communem habentes*),[23] which had already been solved by various methods in the *Liber abbaci*, was really posed by Master Johannes, then he must have taken it from the algebra of al-Karajī.[24] The following examples are well-known from the *Liber abbaci* as "the found purse" and "one alone cannot buy" problems. Here, too, negative solutions are given. In one problem with six unknowns, one of them is chosen arbitrarily, while *causa* and *res* are taken for two of the others.

Letter to Master Theodorus (undated; *Scritti*, II, 247–252). The principal subject of the letter is the "problem of the 100 birds," which Leonardo had

already discussed in the *Liber abbaci.* This time, however, Leonardo develops a general method for the solution of indeterminate problems. A geometrical problem follows that is reminiscent of the conclusion of the *Practica geometriae.* A regular pentagon is to be inscribed in an equilateral triangle. Leonardo's treatment is a model for the early application of algebra in geometry. The solution is carried through to the point where a quadratic equation is reached, and then an approximate value is determined—again sexagesimally. The letter concludes with a linear problem with five unknowns; instead of a logically constructed calculation, however, only a mechanical formula is given.

Liber quadratorum (*Scritti*, II, 253–279). This work, composed in 1225, is a first-rate scientific achievement and shows Leonardo as a major number theorist. Its subject, which had already appeared among the Arabs[25] and was touched upon at the end of the *Practica geometriae* and in the introduction to the *Flos,* is the question, proposed by Master Johannes, of finding the solution of two simultaneous equations $x^2 + 5 = y^2$ and $x^2 - 5 = z^2$, or $y^2 - x^2 = x^2 - z^2 = 5$. The problem itself does not appear until late in the text; before that Leonardo develops propositions for the determination of Pythagorean triples. He knows that the sum of the odd numbers yields a square. He first considers the odd numbers from 1 to $(a^2 - 2)$ for odd a; the sum is $\left(\frac{a^2-1}{2}\right)^2$. If a^2 is added to this expression, then another square results, $\left(\frac{a^2+1}{2}\right)^2$. For even a the corresponding relation is

$$\left[1 + 3 + \cdots \left(\frac{a^2}{2}\right) - 3\right] + \left[\frac{a^2}{2} - 1 + \frac{a^2}{2} + 1\right]$$
$$= \left[\left(\frac{a}{2}\right)^2 + 1\right]^2.$$

Leonardo was acquainted with still further number triples, such as the Euclidean: $2pq$, $p^2 - q^2$, $p^2 + q^2$; and he had already given another one in the *Liber abbaci.*[26]

He obtains still more triples in the following manner: if $(a^2 + b^2)$ and $(x^2 + y^2)$ are squares and if, further, $a:b \neq x:y$ and $a:b \neq y:x$, then it is true that $(a^2 + b^2) \cdot (x^2 + y^2) = (ax + by)^2 + (bx - ay)^2 = (ay + bx)^2 + (by - ax)^2$. The problem was known to Diophantus, and a special case exists in a cuneiform text from Susa. Next Leonardo introduces a special class of numbers: $n = ab \cdot (a + b) \cdot (a - b)$ for even $(a + b)$, and $n = 4ab \cdot (a + b) \cdot (a - b)$ for odd $(a + b)$. He names such a number *congruum* and demonstrates that it must be divisible by 24. He finds that $x^2 + h$ and $x^2 - h$ can be squares simultaneously only if h is a *congruum*. For $a = 5$ and $b = 4$, $h = 720 = 5 \cdot 12^2$. The problem now, therefore, is to obtain two differences of squares $y^2 - x^2 = x^2 - z^2 = 720$. He determines that $2401 - 1681 = 1681 - 961$, or $49^2 - 41^2 = 41^2 - 31^2$. Following division by 12^2 he gets

$$\left(3\frac{5}{12}\right)^2 + 5 = \left(4\frac{4}{12}\right)^2$$

and

$$\left(3\frac{5}{12}\right)^2 - 5 = \left(2\frac{7}{12}\right)^2.$$

One does not learn how Leonardo obtains the squares 961, 1681, and 2401; however, one can ascertain it from a procedure in Diophantus.[27] Leonardo then proves a further series of propositions in number theory, such as that a square cannot be a *congruum*, that $x^2 + y^2$ and $x^2 - y^2$ cannot simultaneously be squares, that $x^4 - y^4$ cannot be a square, etc. Next Leonardo considers expressions such as the following: $x + y + z + x^2$, $x + y + z + x^2 + y^2$, and $x + y + z + x^2 + y^2 + z^2$. They are all to be squares and they are to hold simultaneously. This was another of Master Theodorus' questions. In the questions treated in the *Liber quadratorum,* Leonardo was long without a successor.

In surveying Leonardo's activity, one sees him decisively take the role of a pioneer in the revival of mathematics in the Christian West. Like no one before him he gave fresh consideration to the ancient knowledge and independently furthered it. In arithmetic he showed superior ability in computations. Moreover, he offered material to his readers in a systematic way and ordered his examples from the easier to the more difficult. His use of the chain rule in the "Rule of Three" is a new development; and in the casting out of nines he no longer finds the remainder solely by division, but also employs the sum of digits. His rules for factoring numbers and the formation of perfect numbers are especially noteworthy, as is the recurrent series in the "rabbit problem." He treated indeterminate equations of the first and second degrees in a manner unlike that of anyone before him; ordinarily he confines himself to whole-number solutions—in contrast with Diophantus—where such are required. In geometry he demonstrates, unlike the *Agrimensores,* a thorough mastery of Euclid, whose mathematical rigor he is able to recapture, and he understands how to apply the new methods of algebra to the solution of geometric problems. Moreover, in his work a new concept of number

seems to be emerging, one that recognizes negative quantities and even zero as numbers. Thus, on one occasion[28] he computes $360 - 360 = 0$ and $0:2 = 0$. Especially to be emphasized is his arithmetization of the Euclidean propositions and the employment of letters as representatives for the general number.

Leonardo's Sources. Early in his youth Leonardo already possessed the usual knowledge of a merchant of his time, as well as that preserved from the Roman tradition (abacus, surveying, formulas, etc.). Then came his journeys. What he absorbed on them cannot in most cases be determined in detail. The knowledge of the Greeks could have reached him either from the already existing Latin translations of the Arabic treatments or in Constantinople, where he had been. One can, to be sure, establish where individual problems and methods first appear, but one cannot decide whether what is involved is the recounting of another's work or an original creation of Leonardo's. The only clear cases are those in which a problem is presented with the same numerical values or when the source itself is named.

Leonardo is fully versed in the mathematics of the Arabs; for example, he writes mixed numbers with the whole numbers on the right. Algebra was available to him in the translations of the works of al-Khwārizmī by Adelard of Bath, Robert of Chester, and Gerard of Cremona or in the treatment by Johannes Hispalensis. The numerical examples are frequently taken directly from the algebra of al-Khwārizmī or from the *Liber embadorum* of Plato of Tivoli, e.g., the paradigm $x^2 + 10x = 39$. The calculation with irrationals and the relevant examples correspond to those in the commentary on Euclid by al-Nayrīzī (Anaritius), which Gerard of Cremona had translated. Countless problems are taken, in part verbatim, from the writings of Abu-Kāmil and of al-Karajī. The cubic equation in the *Flos* stems from al-Khayyāmī. Leonardo readily refers to the Arabs and to their technical words, such as *regula elchatayn* (double false position), *numerus asam* (the prime number), and *figura cata* (which he uses in connection with the chain rule); this is the "figure of transversals" in the theorem of Menelaus of Alexandria.

The geometry of the Greeks had become known through the translations from the Arabic of Euclid's *Elements* by Adelard of Bath, Hermann of Carinthia, and Gerard of Cremona, through al-Nayrīzī's commentary, and perhaps to some extent through the anonymous twelfth-century translation of the *Elements* from the Greek (see *Harvard Studies in Classical Philology,* **71** [1966], 249–302); for the measurement of circles there existed the translations of Archimedes' work by Plato of Tivoli and Gerard of

Cremona.[29] For the geometric treatment of the cone and sphere, of the measurement of the circle and triangle (with Hero's formula), and of the insertion of two proportional means, the *Verba filiorum* of the Banū Mūsā was available in Gerard of Cremona's translation and was used extensively by Leonardo. On the other hand, problems from the arithmetic of Diophantus could have come only from Arabic mathematics or from Byzantium. On this subject Leonardo had obtained from the "most learned Master Muscus" a complicated problem of the type "one alone cannot buy," which is also represented in Diophantus. (That Leonardo actually had access to the Greek is shown by his rendering of ῥητοί as "riti.") Other problems that point to Byzantium are those of the type "giving and taking" and the "well problems," which had already appeared in the arithmetical epigrams of *The Greek Anthology*.

Leonardo also includes problems whose origin lies in China and India, such as the *Ta yen* rules, remainder problems, the problem of the "100 birds," and others. Concerning the course of their transmission, nothing definitive can be said. Nevertheless, they were most likely (like the "100 birds" problem found in Abū Kāmil) transmitted through the Arabs. Problems that appeared in ancient Babylonia (quadratic equations, Pythagorean number triples) or in Egypt (unit fraction calculations, "the seven old women") had been borrowed from the Greeks.

Influence. With Leonardo a new epoch in Western mathematics began; however, not all of his ideas were immediately taken up. Direct influence was exerted only by those portions of the *Liber abbaci* and of the *Practica* that served to introduce Indian-Arabic numerals and methods and contributed to the mastering of the problems of daily life. Here Leonardo became the teacher of the masters of computation (the *maestri d'abbaco*) and of the surveyors, as one learns from the *Summa* of Luca Pacioli, who often refers to Leonardo. These two chief works were copied from the fourteenth to the sixteenth centuries. There are also extracts of the *Practica,* but they are confined to the chapters on plane figures and surveying problems; they dispense with exact proofs and with the *subtilitates* of the eighth chapter.

Leonardo was also the teacher of the "Cossists," who took their name from the word *causa,* which was used for the first time in the West by Leonardo in place of *res* or *radix.* His alphabetical designation for the general number or coefficient was first improved by Viète (1591), who used consonants for the known quantities and vowels for the unknowns.

Many of the problems treated in the *Liber abbaci,* especially some of the puzzle problems of recreational arithmetic, reappeared in manuscripts and then in printed arithmetics of later times: e.g., the problem types known as "giving and taking," "hare and hound," "horse buying," "the found purse," "number guessing," "the twins' inheritance," and the indeterminate problem of the "100 birds," which reappeared as the "rule of the drinkers" (*regula coecis, regula potatorum*) and whose solution Euler established in detail in his algebra (1767). Cardano, in his *Artis arithmeticae tractatus de integris,* mentions appreciatively Leonardo's achievements when he speaks of Pacioli's *Summa.* One may suppose, he states, that all our knowledge of non-Greek mathematics owes its existence to Leonardo, who, long before Pacioli, took it from the Indians and Arabs.[30]

In his more advanced problems of number theory, especially in the *Liber quadratorum,* Leonardo at first had no successor. This situation lasted until the work of Diophantus became available in the original text and was studied and edited by Bachet de Méziriac (1621); he, and then Fermat, laid the foundation for modern number theory. Leonardo, however, remained forgotten. Commandino's plan to edit the *Practica* was not carried out. While the historians Heilbronner (1742) and Montucla (1758) showed their ignorance of Leonardo's accomplishments, Cossali (1797) placed him once more in the proper light; however, since the texts themselves could not be found, Cossali had to rely on what was available in Pacioli. It is thanks to Libri and Boncompagni that all five of Leonardo's works are again available.

NOTES

1. In Italian his title is *deputato della patria pubblico* (Biblioteca Magliabechiana, Florence, Palchetto III, no. 25) and *pubblico cancelliere* (Biblioteca Comunale, Siena, L.IV.21).
2. *Scritti,* I, 1: "quasi errorem computavi respectu modi indorum."
3. *Ibid.:* "quedam etiam ex subtilitatibus euclidis geometrice artis apponens."
4. On the dating, see Cantor, *Vorlesungen über Geschichte der Mathematik,* II, 41.
5. Illustration in Arrighi, *Leonardo Fibonacci,* p. 15.
6. Boncompagni, *Intorno ad alcune opere di Leonardo Pisano,* p. 248.
7. *Ibid.,* p. 246: "ideo ipsum Xᵐ librum glosare incepi, reducens intellectum ipsius ad numerum qui in eo per lineas et superficies demonstratur."
8. He should "hold the numbers in his hand" ("retinere in manu," *Scritti,* I, 7). Thus the student "should bring memory and understanding into harmony with the hands and the numerals" (*Scritti,* I, 1).
9. Youschkevitch, *Geschichte der Mathematik im Mittelalter,* p. 377; Vogel, "Zur Geschichte der linearen Gleichungen mit mehreren Unbekannten."
10. See Vogel, *Ein byzantinisches Rechenbuch des frühen 14. Jahrhunderts,* p. 157.
11. See Cantor, *op. cit.,* p. 26.

12. *Scritti,* I, 318: "adpropinquacio veritati."
13. *Ibid.,* 191: "una res et denarii 12 sunt septuplum quinque rerum et de denariis 12."
14. *Ibid.,* 228, 351.
15. *Ibid.,* 228, 352.
16. *Ibid.,* 378: "inveni hunc modum reperiendi radices."
17. *Ibid.,* 396.
18. A list of the common examples is in Woepke, *Extrait du Fakhrī, Traité d'algèbre par Aboū Bekr Mohammed ben Alhaçan Alkarkhī,* p. 29.
19. *Scritti,* I, 442 ff.
20. See Libri, *Histoire des sciences mathématiques en Italie,* II, 305.
21. See Arrighi, *op. cit.,* p. 18.
22. See Woepke, *L'algèbre d'Omar Alkayyāmī,* p. 78.
23. See Cantor, *op. cit.,* pp. 48 f.
24. See Woepke, *Extrait du Fakhrī . . .,* pp. 141 ff.
25. See Youschkevitch, *op. cit.,* p. 235.
26. *Scritti,* I, 402. The example there involves $x^2 + y^2 = 41$.
27. See Ver Eecke, *Léonard de Pise,* p. 44.
28. *Scritti,* I, 296.
29. See Clagett, *Archimedes in the Middle Ages,* I, *The Arabo-Latin Tradition,* chs. 1, 2.
30. G. Cardano, *Opera,* X (Lyons, 1663), 118, col. 2.
31. See Loria, *Storia delle matematiche,* I, 383.

BIBLIOGRAPHY

I. ORIGINAL WORKS. The only complete edition of Leonardo's works is *Scritti di Leonardo Pisano,* B. Boncompagni, ed., 2 vols. (Rome, 1857–1862). Earlier, G. Libri, in his *Histoire des sciences mathématiques en Italie,* 4 vols. (Paris, 1838–1841), published the introduction and ch. 15 of *Liber abbaci* (II, note 1, 287 ff.; note 3, 307 ff.) and the introduction of *Practica geometriae* (II, note 2, 305 f.). Also, B. Boncompagni published three short works in *Opuscoli di Leonardo Pisano* (Florence, 1852). The *Liber quadratorum* was translated into French by P. Ver Eecke as *Léonard de Pise. Le livre des nombres carrés* (Bruges, 1952). An Italian adaptation of the *Practica geometriae* of 1442 is G. Arrighi, *Leonardo Fibonacci. La pratica di geometria, volgarizzata da Cristofano di Gherardo di Dino cittadino pisano. Dal codice 2186 della Biblioteca Riccardiana di Firenze* (Pisa, 1966). There are also two Italian translations of the introduction to the *Liber abbaci* in the MSS cited in note 1.

II. SECONDARY LITERATURE. General criticism includes B. Boncompagni, "Della vita e delle opere di Leonardo Pisano matematico del secolo decimoterzo," in *Atti dell'Accademia pontificia dei Nuovi Lincei,* 5 (1851–1852), 5–91, 208–246; and *Intorno ad alcune opere di Leonardo Pisano matematico del secolo decimoterzo, notizie raccolte* (Rome, 1854); M. Cantor, *Vorlesungen über Geschichte der Mathematik,* II (Leipzig, 1913), 3–53; G. Loria, "Leonardo Fibonacci," in *Gli scienziati italiani,* Aldo Mieli, ed. (Rome, 1923), pp. 4–12; and *Storia delle matematiche,* I (Turin, 1929), 379–410; G. Sarton, *Introduction to the History of Science,* II (Baltimore, 1931), 611–613; D. E. Smith, *History of Mathematics,* 2 vols. (New York, 1958), *passim.;* J. Tropfke, *Geschichte der Elementarmathematik* (Berlin–Leipzig: I, 3rd ed., 1930; II, 3rd ed., 1933; III, 3rd ed., 1937; IV, 3rd ed., 1939; V, 2nd ed., 1923; VI, 2nd ed., 1924; VII, 2nd ed., 1924), *passim ;* and A. P. Youschkevitch, *Geschichte der Mathematik im Mittelalter* (Leipzig, 1964), 371–387, trans. from the Russian (1961).

Special criticism includes the following on the *Liber abbaci:* A. Agostini, "L'uso delle lettere nel *Liber abaci* di Leonardo Fibonacci," in *Bollettino dell'Unione matematica italiana,* 3rd ser., 4 (1949), 282–287; and K. Vogel, "Zur Geschichte der linearen Gleichungen mit mehreren Unbekannten," in *Deutsche Mathematik,* 5 (1940), 217–240.

On *Practica geometriae:* R. C. Archibald, *Euclid's Book on Divisions of Figures* (Cambridge, 1915); M. Curtze, "Der *Liber embadorum* des Abraham bar Chijja Savasorda in der Übersetzung des Plato von Tivoli," in *Abhandlungen zur Geschichte der mathematischen Wissenschaften mit Einschluss ihrer Anwendungen,* 12 (1902), 3–183; and J. Millás-Vallicrosa, *Abraam bar Hiia. Llibre de Geometriá* (Barcelona, 1931).

On *Flos:* F. Woepke, "Sur un essai de déterminer la nature de la racine d'une équation du troisième degré, contenue dans un ouvrage de Léonard de Pise," in *Journal de mathématiques pures et appliquées,* 19 (1854), 401–406.

On the *Liber quadratorum* and number theory: L. E. Dickson, *History of the Theory of Numbers,* vols. I and II (1919–1920), *passim.;* F. Lucas, "Recherches sur plusieurs ouvrages de Léonard de Pise et sur diverses questions d'arithmétique supérieure," in *Bullettino di bibliografia e storia delle scienze matematiche e fisiche,* 10 (1877), 129–193, 239–293; and R. B. McClenon, "Leonardo of Pisa and His 'Liber Quadratorum,'" in *American Mathematical Monthly,* 26 (1919), 1–8.

On the history of the problems: E. Bortolotti, "Le fonti arabe di Leonardo Pisano," in *Memorie. R. Accademia delle scienze dell'Istituto di Bologna,* fis.-mat. cl., 7th ser., 8 (1929–1930), 1–30; Marshall Clagett, *Archimedes in the Middle Ages,* I, *The Arabo-Latin Tradition* (Madison, Wis., 1964), see index under "Leonardo Fibonacci"; P. Cossali, *Origine, trasporto in Italia, primi progressi in essa dell'algebra,* I (Parma, 1797), ch. 5, 96–172; II (Parma, 1799), 41, l. 16; M. Dunton and R. E. Grimm, "Fibonacci on Egyptian Fractions," in *The Fibonacci Quarterly,* 4 (1966), 339–354; V. Sanford, *The History and Significance of Certain Standard Problems in Algebra* (New York, 1927); K. Vogel, *Die Practica des Algorismus Ratisbonensis* (Munich, 1954), index, p. 267; and *Ein byzantinisches Rechenbuch des frühen 14. Jahrhunderts* (Vienna, 1968), pp. 153 ff.; J. Weinberg, *Die Algebra des Abū Kāmil Sogā᾽ben Aslam* (Munich, 1935); and F. Woepke, *L'algèbre d'Omar Alkayyāmī* (Paris, 1851; *Extrait du Fakhrī, Traité d'algèbre par Aboū Bekr Mohammed ben Alhaçan Alkarkhī* (Paris, 1853); and "Recherches sur plusieurs ouvrages de Léonard de Pise et sur les rapports qui existent entre ces ouvrages et les travaux mathématiques des Arabes," in *Atti dell'Accademia pontificia dei Nuovi Lincei,* 10 (1856–1857), 236–248; 14 (1860–1861), 211–356.

See also Archibald; Boncompagni, *Opuscoli;* Ver Eecke; and G. Loria, "Leonardo Fibonacci." Sarton, II, 613, cites B. Boncompagni, *Glossarium ex libro abbaci* (Rome, 1855), not known to be in German or Italian libraries.

KURT VOGEL

FICHOT, LAZARE-EUGÈNE (*b*. Le Creusot, Saône-et-Loire, France, 18 January 1867; *d*. Tabanac, Gironde, France, 17 July 1939), *marine hydrography*.

Fichot entered the École Polytechnique in 1884, and upon graduation in 1886 he joined the Marine Corps of Hydrographic Engineers. In November 1926 he was made chief of the Marine Hydrographic Service, and at the time of his death he was its director. In 1912 Fichot received the Binoux Award of the Académie des Sciences for his contributions to geography and navigation, and in 1925 he was elected a member of the academy. He was made an officer of the Legion of Honor in 1911 and a member of the Bureau des Longitudes in 1923. He was elected president of the Geodesy Section of the National Committee on Geodesy and Geophysics in 1923.

Fichot's main interests were in hydrography, geodesy, geography, terrestrial physics, and the theory of the tides. His major contributions, however, were in hydrography and tidal theories. During his work in the hydrographic service he made numerous hydrographic, geologic, and meteorologic observations along the coasts of France and the French colonies in Asia and Africa and prepared maps of the coastal regions. In 1908 he discovered a new navigational route along the coast of Indochina by accurately mapping obstructions between Cam Ranh Bay and Nha Hang. In 1912 he prepared hydrographic maps of the Gironde estuary, which became an important navigational route during World War I.

One of Fichot's major works, *Les marées et leur utilisation industrielle* (1923), contained a comprehensive synthesis of existing knowledge on tides as well as results of some of his own research on the subject. Later, in collaboration with Henri Poincaré, he tried to expand his work on tides. Parts of their research were published as *Exposé critique de la théorie des marées* (1938–1941). Nevertheless, the study remained unfinished at the time of Fichot's death.

BIBLIOGRAPHY

Fichot's writings include "Rapport sur la reconnaissance hydrographique de l'embouchure de la Gironde en 1912," in *Recherches hydrographiques sur le régime des côtes*, XIX (Paris, 1911–1914), 12–82; "Rapport sur les travaux de la Mission hydrographique de l'Indo-Chine en 1909–1910," in *Annales hydrographiques*, **33**, no. 2 (1913), 357–393; "Marées océaniques et marées internes," in *Encyclopédie des sciences mathématiques pures et appliquées*, VI, pt. 8 (Leipzig–Paris, 1916), 1–96; *Les marées et leur utilisation industrielle* (Paris, 1923); and "L'influence de la rotation terrestre sur la physionomie des marées," in *Annuaire publié par le Bureau des longitudes* (Paris, 1925), pp. A.1–A.71.

Asit K. Biswas
Margaret R. Peitsch

FICK, ADOLF EUGEN (*b*. Kassel, Germany, 3 September 1829; *d*. Blankenberge, Belgium, 21 August 1901), *physiology, physical medicine*.

Fick's father, Friedrich Fick, a senior municipal architect in Kassel, was instrumental in reorganizing street construction in that city. His mother, Nanni Sponsel, had nine children, of whom Adolf was the youngest. Two of his brothers were professors (one of anatomy and the other of law) at Marburg when Fick began to study there. In the winter semester of 1847–1848, he began his work in mathematics and physics, fields for which he possessed great aptitude, although he soon switched to medicine.

The descendant of Protestant émigrés from Salzburg, Fick was raised in that faith. He was a man of high moral sense, pious but without any formal church affiliation. He married Emilie von Coelln on 24 October 1862. They had five children, two of whom died in early childhood. One son became a jurist; another became an anatomist in Berlin.

As a medical student at Marburg, Fick was guided in anatomy not only by his brother Ludwig but also by his early friendship with Carl Ludwig, then lecturing at Marburg on anatomy and physiology. Fick became one of the main proponents (with Carl Ludwig) of the new orientation of physiology toward physics, to which Hermann von Helmholtz, Ernst Brücke, and Emil du Bois-Reymond also subscribed. It was their objective to determine quantitatively, whenever possible, the fundamental capabilities of the organism's components and to explain them on the basis of general physicochemical laws of nature. Fick wrote his first scientific paper, an investigation on the torque exerted by the motor muscles of the femur in the hip joint (1849), when he was still a student. In this he demonstrated his gift for planning, executing, and mathematically evaluating mathematical-physical research of physiological processes. In the fall of 1849 he continued his studies at Berlin, where he became friends with Helmholtz and du Bois-Reymond. In Berlin the anatomist Johannes Müller, because of his entirely different approach in theory and practice, was unable to exert any great influence on Fick, who was said, moreover, to have been then a genius in the art of enjoying a carefree student life.

Upon his return to Marburg, Fick obtained his doctorate on 27 August 1851, with a thesis on visual errors due to astigmatism. He then accepted the position of a prosector in anatomy with his brother but followed Carl Ludwig to Zurich six months later. This was the beginning of a scientific career characterized by an unusually diversified scientific output. Fick remained in Zurich from 1852 until 1868, first as prosector in anatomy with Ludwig until 1855, subsequently as associate professor of the anatomical and physiological auxiliary sciences until 1861, and later as full professor of physiology. In the winter semester of 1868 he assumed the same position in the Faculty of Medicine at Würzburg, which he held for more than thirty years. In 1883 he moved into a new physiological institute.

During 1878–1879 Fick was rector of the University of Würzburg. He retired at the age of seventy, in 1899. On 21 August 1901 he died from the aftereffects of a cerebral hemorrhage. In 1929 his sons founded the Adolf Fick Fund, which every five years awards a prize for an outstanding contribution to physiology.

Fick's lifework is concerned primarily with problems on the borderline between medicine, physiology, and physics. Accordingly, his monograph *Medizinische Physik,* published in 1856, when he was twenty-six years old, is most characteristic of the problems he preferred, particularly (1) molecular physics: diffusion of gases and water, filtration, endosmosis, and porous diffusion; (2) mechanics of solids, including the geometry of articulations, and the statics and dynamics of muscles; (3) hydrodynamics, as applied to the motion of fluids in rigid and/or elastic vessels (blood vessels), and pulse variations and their accurate recording; (4) sound; (5) the theory of heat in physics and physiology, the origin of heat, and the law of the conservation of energy in the body; (6) optics: the path of rays in the eye and ophthalmoscopy, the microscope, the horopter, and color perception and the theory of color sense; and (7) the theory of electricity: the origin, derivation, and measurement of bioelectric phenomena.

All of these fields were treated with great success by Fick. He showed himself to be an analyst who reflected in strict conformity with physical laws and arrived at the precise mathematical expression of physiological processes. In similar form he analyzed the mechanics of the saddle joint of the thumb (1854) and, in the same year, the torsional movement of the several muscles that move the bulbus oculi. In addition, he studied molecular biophysics, e.g., the expansion of bodies by heat (1854). He then examined, on the basis of the investigations of Brücke, Jolly, Ludwig, and Max Cloëtta, the process of diffusion and developed a differential equation for the flow between a saturated sodium chloride solution and distilled water (1855). In experimental analysis, he introduced the collodion membrane into the study of porous diffusion in endosmosis (1857).

The physics of the vision process had occupied Fick since his doctoral thesis, "De errore optico," which was concerned with perceptual illusions due to astigmatism (1851). He also analyzed the blind spot in the eye and the phenomenon of monocular polyopia through unequal ratios of curvature in the refractive media (1854). Beginning in 1853, Fick became interested in the sequence of excitation in the retina, in adaptation, in the phenomenon of the latent stage, and then in the slow initiation of retinal stimulation (1864). He reflected on the phenomena of color vision and arrived at a confirmation of Helmholtz' three-component theory (1880) but raised essential reservations in regard to Ewald Hering's theory. Later, he was successful in building the first practical instrument for measurement of intraocular pressure, the ophthalmotonometer (1888). Fick had a particular gift for and ingenuity in constructing physiological measuring devices and developed, among other apparatus, an improved aneroid manometer for measurement of the pressure gradient in the vascular system and a pneumograph for recording peripheral variations of the thorax in breathing (1869–1897).

Fick also made outstanding contributions to hemodynamics. He developed a principle, which came to be called Fick's law (1870), that permits calculation of the cardiac output from the measurement of the minute volume of oxygen consumption and arteriovenous oxygen difference in the living organism. The arteriovenous differences of oxygen level indicate the amount of oxygen per 100 cc. carried off by the blood flowing through the lung, and the oxygen consumption per minute indicates how many times per minute 100 cc. of blood have circulated through heart and lung; this result is called the minute volume, and its division by the heart rate yields the stroke volume.

Fick considered mathematical expression to be the most exact and, indeed, the only adequate language of science. In this spirit he theorized on the speed of the flow of blood in the vascular system, on its conditions, and on its measurability. He also introduced the principle of plethysmography. In this procedure the arm, for example, is placed in a rigid, water-filled vessel to which a narrow upright tube is attached. If the supply of blood to the arm exceeds the outflow of blood within the same interval, water is displaced and the meniscus in the tube will rise (1869). Fick also constructed a model of the blood-vessel ramifications from rigid and elastic tubes in order to simulate and analyze the pressure drop in the circulation, especially in the capillaries (1888).

Fick's gift for mathematical-physical thinking is most clearly exhibited in his numerous studies on the nature of heat, on the causes of thermal expansion of bodies (1854–1855), and on the nature, magnitude, and origin of body heat. These problems occupied him again and again, and he maintained that questions of thermal production and consumption should be kept separate from temperature topography. He ascribed all processes of heat generation to the expenditure of chemical energy, which takes place, for instance, to provide the mechanical energy for muscular effort. This raises the question of the substances supplying the energy through their decomposition. Liebig declared them to be the proteins. In 1865 Fick decided the question during a climb of the Faulhorn, in Switzerland, by determining the energy consumed (in m. kg. of climbing effort) and through calculation of protein catabolism from the nitrogen passed in the urine. He found that protein is insufficient to provide the energy requirements.

Fick further investigated the generation of heat in the muscle with sensitive thermometers and related its magnitude to the effort of contraction produced. In order to increase accuracy in such investigations, he introduced the concept and the methodology of isotonic and isometric determination of the process of muscular contraction (1867, 1882, 1889). He constructed an apparatus for measuring the output of m. kg. with the aid of a rotating wheel, the dynamometer (1891). He was always concerned with testing the validity of the law of the conservation of energy in the body. In this connection, Fick also encountered the need for adequate and graduated stimulation of muscles and nerves.

His physiology of stimulation attempted in this connection to find new quantifiable parameters. In contrast with generally held views, Fick found that contraction is a function not only of the intensity of nerve stimulation but also the duration of the stimulus. He demonstrated this specifically for the smooth muscle, in this case the shell adductor of mussels (1863). Fick further investigated electrotonus under optimum exact conditions (1866–1869) and the effect of transversal nerve stimulation. Notable was his successful attempt to demonstrate, against the opinion held by French scientists, that electrical stimulation of the anterior marginal bundles of the spinal cord was possible. He made this an occasion (1869) for an interesting discussion of his research principle of clarifying the fundamental properties of the elemental components of the animal organism, as opposed to a method of research preferring observations and tests of the entire animal.

The similarity of the physiological objectives of Helmholtz and Fick is astonishing. Both were particularly interested in the clarification of the physicochemical and quantitatively determinable processes. Both performed outstandingly in this field. The prerequisites here were always to work under the simplest possible arrangements, under constant or known conditions, or both, and to test the consequences produced by a measurable variation of one of the conditions. Causal analysis within the context of the exact natural sciences, quantification, construction of measuring devices and apparatus—these were the objectives and paths of the generation of German physiologists in the second half of the nineteenth century which included, besides Adolf Fick and Helmholtz, Carl Ludwig and many others.

Fick's acumen was not concentrated in scientific analysis alone. He was also greatly interested in the methodology of scientific investigation, as his philosophical articles demonstrate. He dismissed the romantic physiology of Schelling and Hegel as "superior nonsense" (1870). Like Helmholtz, he followed Kant and believed the empiricism of John Stuart Mill to be inadequate. His epistemological attempt at refutation of Kirchhoff (1882) and his *Philosophischer Versuch über die Wahrscheinlichkeiten* (Würzburg, 1883) reflect these views.

Fick possessed a crystal-clear manner of thinking and writing. He was modest, without intellectual arrogance, and stood by his convictions fearlessly. When he realized the consequences of alcohol abuse, he ceaselessly called public attention to this problem. Among Fick's disciples and collaborators were Friedrich Schenck, Magnus Blix, Johannes Gad, A. Gürber, and Jacques Loeb.

BIBLIOGRAPHY

I. ORIGINAL WORKS. All of Fick's publications were collected and published posthumously in *Adolf Fick. Gesammelte Abhandlungen,* 4 vols. (Würzburg, 1903–1905), with portraits, bibliographic data, and a biography by F. Schenck. Among his writings are *Medizinische Physik* (Brunswick, 1856); *Compendium der Physiologie des Menschen mit Einschluss der Entwicklungsgeschichte* (Vienna, 1860); *Beiträge zur vergleichenden Physiologie der irritablen Substanzen* (Brunswick, 1863); *Lehrbuch der Anatomie und Physiologie der Sinnesorgane* (Lahr, 1864); *Untersuchungen über elektrische Nervenreizung* (Brunswick, 1864); "Über die Entstehung der Muskelkraft," in *Vierteljahrsschrift der Naturforschenden Gesellschaft in Zürich,* **10** (1865), 317 ff.; "Spezielle Bewegungslehre," in L. Hermann, *Handbuch der Physiologie,* I, pt. 2 (Leipzig, 1879); "Dioptrik und Lichtempfindung," *ibid.,* III, pt. 1 (Leipzig, 1879); *Mechanische Arbeit und Wärmeentwicklung bei der Muskeltätigkeit* (Leipzig, 1882); and *Myothermische Untersuchungen aus* *dem physiologischen Laboratorium zu Zürich und Würzburg* (Wiesbaden, 1889).

The journal publications are easily accessible in *Gesammelte Abhandlungen* and need not be listed here in detail.

II. SECONDARY LITERATURE. Notices and obituaries are René du Bois-Reymond, "Nachruf," in *Naturwissenschaftliche Rundschau* (Stuttgart), **16** (1901), 576–577; Friedrich Fick, "Adolf Fick, Professor der Physiologie (1829–1901)," in *Lebensläufe aus Franken,* I (1919), 94 ff., a biography; Max von Frey, "Gedächtnisrede," in *Sitzungsberichte der Physikalische-medizinischen Gesellschaft zu Würzburg* (1901), 65 ff., with references to the literature; Adam Kunkel, "Nachruf," in *Münchener medizinische Wochenschrift,* **48** (1901), 1705–1708; Kurt Quecke, "Adolf Fick (1829–1901). Physiologe," in *Lebensbilder aus Kurhessen und Waldeck,* **4** (1950), 82–90; K. E. Rothschuh. *Geschichte der Physiologie* (Berlin-Göttingen-Heidelberg, 1953), pp. 150–153; F. Schenck, "Zum Andenken an A. Fick," in *Pflügers Archiv für die gesamte Physiologie des Menschen und der Tiere,* **90** (1902), 313–361, with portraits and biography, a good analysis of his work; Dietrich Trincker, "Adolf Fick," in *Neue deutsche Biographie,* V (Berlin, 1961), 127–128; and Edgar Wöhlisch, "A. Fick und die heutige Physiologie," in *Die Naturwissenschaften,* **29** (1938), 585–591; and *Biographisches Lexikon der hervorragenden Ärzte . . . ,* II (Berlin–Vienna, 1930), 515–516.

K. E. ROTHSCHUH

FIELDS, JOHN CHARLES (*b.* Hamilton, Ontario, Canada, 14 May 1863; *d.* Toronto, Ontario, Canada, 9 August 1932), *mathematics, education.*

Fields was the son of John Charles Fields and Harriet Bowes. His father died when the boy was eleven, and his mother, when he was eighteen. Fields matriculated at the University of Toronto in 1880 and received the B.A. in 1884, with a gold medal in mathematics. Johns Hopkins University awarded him a Ph.D. in 1887. He was appointed professor of mathematics at Allegheny College in 1889 and resigned in 1892 in order to continue his studies in Europe. The next decade found Fields primarily in Paris and Berlin, where associations with Fuchs, Frobenius, Hensel, Schwarz, and Max Planck contributed to his intellectual growth. In 1902 he was appointed special lecturer at the University of Toronto, where he remained until his death. He was appointed research professor in 1923.

Fields's lifelong interest in algebraic functions is first evident in his papers of 1901–1904. His treatment is completely algebraic, without recourse to geometric intuition. The structure has both elegance and generality; its machinery is simple, its parts coordinated.

His involvement in mathematical societies was of an international nature. Fields was elected a fellow of the Royal Society of Canada (1907) and of London (1913). He held various offices in the British and American Associations for the Advancement of Science and the Royal Canadian Institute (of which he was president from 1919 to 1925). He was also a corresponding member of the Russian Academy of Sciences and the Instituto de Coimbra (Portugal). The success of the International Congress of Mathematicians at Toronto in 1924 was due to his untiring efforts as president.

Fields conceived the idea of establishing an international medal for mathematical distinction and provided funds for this purpose in his will. The International Congress of Mathematicians at Zurich in 1932 adopted his proposal, and the Fields Medal was first awarded at the next congress, held at Oslo in 1936.

BIBLIOGRAPHY

I. ORIGINAL WORKS. Fields's writings include "Symbolic Finite Solutions by Definite Integrals of the Equation $d^n y/dx^n = x^m y$," in *American Journal of Mathematics,* **8** (1886), 178–179, his Ph.D. thesis; and *Theory of the Algebraic Functions of a Complex Variable* (Berlin, 1906), which establishes a general plan for proving the Riemann-Roch theorem. With the assistance of J. Chapelon, Fields edited the *Proceedings* of the 1924 International Congress of Mathematicians (Toronto, 1928).

Fields's papers are held by the Rare Books and Special Collections Department of the University of Toronto. They include reprints of some of his published speeches and papers, as well as notebooks of lectures and seminars that he attended in Berlin. In addition, the collection contains two bound volumes of notes made by students of the lectures of Weierstrass, *Theorie der elliptischen Functionen* (recorded by A. Darendorff) and *Theorie der hyperelliptischen Functionen* (taken down by an anonymous auditor in the summer semester of 1887).

II. SECONDARY LITERATURE. J. L. Synge, "Obituary Notice of John Charles Fields," in *Obituary Notices of Fellows of the Royal Society of London,* **2** (1933), 129–135 (with portrait), is quite extensive. It contains a full bibliography of Fields's publications (39 titles) and an analysis of the works by his former pupil and colleague, S. Beatty. It also includes the final form of his theorems leading up to and including the proof of the Riemann-Roch theorem. See also Synge, "John Charles Fields," in *Journal of the London Mathematical Society,* **8,** pt. 2 (1933), 153–160. A short statement in *The Royal Canadian Institute Centennial Volume 1849–1949* (Toronto, 1949), William Stewart Wallace, ed., p. 163, gives evidence of Fields's personal dedication to the Royal Canadian Institute.

HENRY S. TROPP

FIESSINGER, NOËL (*b.* Thaon-les-Vosges, France, 24 December 1881; *d.* Paris, France, 15 January 1946), *medicine, biology.*

Fiessinger was descended from a family of Alsatian physicians. His great-grandfather served as field surgeon at Waterloo, and his father, Charles Fiessinger, was a celebrated cardiologist and author. Fiessinger was recognized early as a brilliant physician and a renowned biologist and biochemist. The highest responsibilities in the Paris hospitals were entrusted to him, particularly the great laboratory of the Hôpital Beaujon and the chair of experimental medicine and the renowned chair of clinical medicine at the Hôtel-Dieu. He was prominent among those who brought about a major revolution in clinical thinking—that is, the idea that clinical medicine must be closely associated with biological research.

He elucidated the histogenesis of cirrhosis. This degenerative process of the liver cells is the same whatever the conditions, pathological or otherwise, which determine it (1908). Fiessinger demonstrated the existence of enzymes in the white cells of the blood. He showed that these cells, according to their type, contain either protease or lipase. The presence of protease accounts for the dissolution of internal blood clots or purulent collections, while lipase weakens the lipidic membrane of the Koch bacilli, thus permitting their attack by the protease-carrying white cells.

World War I turned Fiessinger's efforts away from this pioneer work in biochemistry. He made major observations in the biology of war wounds, observations gathered under the precarious conditions in field hospitals, often under severe artillery fire.

After the war Fiessinger revealed himself to be an eminent physiologist. He was among the first to define the principles of functional exploration of an organ, which he applied most successfully to the liver, through such new tests as galactose and Bengal pink dye. Fiessinger's achievements as a biologist are matched by his many contributions to clinical medicine, especially by his discovery of the Fiessinger-Leroy-Retter disease, which up to that time was undefined. His influence as a renowned teacher was considerable, and numerous prominent physicians in many countries are his former students.

BIBLIOGRAPHY

Fiessinger's papers appeared in various medical journals, but all his essential contributions are included in the last editions of his books, which were standard texts for the medical profession.

See *Nouveaux procédés d'exploration fonctionnelle du foie* (Paris, 1934), written with H. Walter; *Syndromes et maladies* (Paris, 1942); *Diagnostics difficiles* (Paris, 1943); and *Diag-*

nostics biologiques (Paris, 1944), written with H. R. Oliver and M. Herbain.

A. M. MONNIER

FINE, HENRY BURCHARD (*b.* Chambersburg, Pennsylvania, 14 September 1858; *d.* Princeton, New Jersey, 22 December 1928), *mathematics.*

Fine was the son of Lambert Suydam Fine, a Presbyterian minister. After the death of his father, his mother settled in Princeton, where Fine attended the university. During Fine's undergraduate years, his interest in mathematics was awakened by the young instructor George Halstead, who promoted the study of non-Euclidean geometry in the United States. After a year as an assistant in physics and three years as a mathematics tutor at Princeton (1880–1884), Fine, like many of his colleagues, went to Germany to study. At Leipzig he attended Felix Klein's lectures and in 1885 wrote a dissertation on an algebraic geometric problem suggested by Eduard Study, with whom he became friendly. After a summer in Berlin attending Leopold Kronecker's lectures, Fine returned to Princeton, where he taught mathematics until his death. In 1888 Fine married Philena Forbes.

In 1903, Woodrow Wilson's first year in the presidency of Princeton, Fine was appointed dean of the faculty; and when Wilson resigned to run for governor of New Jersey, Fine acted as president of the university until a successor was named in 1912. He then became dean of the departments of science, a post he held until his death. Fine was a founding member of the American Mathematical Society in 1891 and its president in 1911–1912.

Fine's impact on science lies mainly in his support of science and mathematics at Princeton. As dean of the faculty he promoted the mathematician Luther Eisenhart and brought in Oswald Veblen, G. A. Bliss, George Birkhoff, and J. H. M. Wedderburn. A professorship of mathematics and a mathematics building at Princeton were named for Fine.

Among his few contributions to mathematics were an expansion of his dissertation; several papers on differential equations; and, most important, a paper on Newton's method of approximation (1916) and an exposition of a theorem of Kronecker's on numerical equations (1914). Fine was the author of several undergraduate textbooks and an exposition of the number system of algebra.

BIBLIOGRAPHY

For a complete bibliography of Fine's publications and related secondary sources, see "Henry Burchard Fine," in

American Mathematical Society Semicentennial Publication, I (New York, 1938), 167–169. Also consult Oswald Veblen, "Henry Burchard Fine," in *Bulletin of the American Mathematical Society,* **35** (1929), 726–730.

C. S. FISHER

FINK (FINCKE), THOMAS (*b.* Flensburg, Denmark [now Germany], 6 January 1561; *d.* Copenhagen, Denmark, 24 April 1656), *mathematics, astronomy, medicine.*

The son of Raadmand Jacob Fincke and Anna Thorsmede (who died six days after his birth), Fink studied from 1577 to 1582 in Strasbourg. Afterward he attended many universities: Jena, Wittenberg, Heidelberg (matriculated 6 February 1582), Leipzig (matriculated summer of 1582), Basel (studied medicine in 1583), and Padua (from 6 November 1583 to 1587). This varied education led to his receipt of the M.D. at Basel on 24 August 1587. After three years of traveling through Germany and Austria, Fink became physician-in-ordinary to Duke Philip of Holstein-Gottorp. When Philip died in 1591, Fink was appointed professor of mathematics at Copenhagen, his field of instruction being changed to rhetoric in 1602 and to medicine in 1603. He held high university posts and carried out his duties until only a few years before his death at the age of ninety-five.

Fink's most famous book is the *Geometriae rotundi* (1583), published when he was twenty-two. This important work is divided into fourteen books. The elementary theses on the circle are collected in the four opening books and the remaining books treat trigonometry, the last three being devoted to spherical trigonometry. A central place is occupied by Rheticus' goniometric tables, but here Fink took a step backward, giving the tables for each function separately and always from 0° to 90°, rather than using the complementary character of the functions, as Rheticus had done. In Strasbourg, Fink had been a pupil of the mathematician Dasypodius but seems to have learned mainly astrology from him. He makes it clear that he was an autodidact in mathematics. His inspiration and guide was not Euclid's *Elements*—this work disturbed him—but Ramus' *Geometria* (1569). Therefore the *Geometriae rotundi* is based mainly on Ramus, many proofs being comprehensible only after consulting the *Geometria*. Even the word "rotundum" in Fink's title, meaning both circle and sphere, was introduced by Ramus. Fink also adopted the term "radius" from him and himself introduced such terms as "tangent" and "secans." He devised new formulas, such as the law of tangents, and proved in this work that he was abreast of the mathematics of his time.

The *Geometriae rotundi* was meant as a textbook, since it treats basic formulas and refers the reader to Regiomontanus for more detail. As a textbook it was very influential. Such mathematicians as Lansbergen, Clavius, Napier, and Pitiscus recommended the work and adopted much from it. Fink's other works show his interest in astrology and astronomy. He was in contact with Tycho Brahe and Magini. But never again in a long series of publications did he reach the level of the *Geometriae rotundi.*

BIBLIOGRAPHY

I. ORIGINAL WORKS. For a bibliography see H. Ehrencron-Müller, *Forfatterlexikon omfattende Danmark . . .,* III (Copenhagen, 1926), 46–49; this work does not mention *Methodica tractatio doctrinae sphaericae* (Coburg, 1626); *Theses logicae* (Copenhagen, 1594); C. Ostenfeld, *Oratio in orbitum T. Finckii* (Copenhagen, 1656). Fink's most important works are *Geometriae rotundi libri XIIII* (Basel, 1583); and *Horoscopographia sive de inveniendo stellarum situ astrologia* (Schleswig, 1591), which includes a horoscope of Heinrich Graf von Rantzau.

II. SECONDARY LITERATURE. On Fink or his work, see Niels Nielsen, *Matematikken i Danmark 1528–1800* (Copenhagen, 1912), pp. 69–70; and H. F. Rördam, *Kjöbenhavns Universitets historie fra 1537 til 1621* (Copenhagen, 1873–1877), III, 550–562. On *Geometriae rotundi,* see A. von Braunmühl, *Vorlesungen über Geschichte der Trigonometrie,* I (Leipzig, 1900), 186–193; and J. Tropfke, *Geschichte der Elementar-Mathematik,* vols. IV (Berlin, 1922; new ed., 1940) and V (Berlin, 1923), see index in vol. VII (Berlin, 1927).

J. J. VERDONK

FINLAY, CARLOS JUAN (*b.* Puerto Príncipe [now Camagüey], Cuba, 3 December 1833; *d.* Havana, Cuba, 20 August 1915), *medicine.*

Finlay was the son of a Scotch father and a French mother whose family lived in Trinidad. An aunt who had had a school in Edinburgh taught him at home until he was eleven; he then went to France for further, more formal schooling. There he developed severe chorea which left him with a speech impediment—a lisp—that he never lost. In 1851, having returned home to Cuba, he nearly died of typhoid fever. Undaunted, Finlay became and remained all his life an avid sportsman, swimmer, and horseback rider. Besides Spanish, he became fluent in English, French, and German.

Finlay attended Jefferson Medical College in Philadelphia, where he studied under Robley Dunglison and John K. Mitchell and his son, Weir. He graduated in 1855, rejecting lucrative offers to practice in the Spanish colony of New York City. After

619

a brief trip to Peru, he settled in Havana, where he practiced general medicine and ophthalmology.

In Philadelphia, John Mitchell taught that malaria and other epidemic fevers were caused by living organisms. In 1879 the U.S. Yellow Fever Commission in Havana concluded that yellow fever was transmissible and that its vector was probably airborne, would attack a person once only, and produced a specific, self-limiting disease. Finlay had written much about yellow fever as arising from telluric influences, miasmata, and meteorological conditions. He had theorized that filth was converted into some hypothetical vegetable-animal germ and had suggested that alkalinity of air caused yellow fever. Working closely with the Commission, he shortly suggested that the disease was transmitted by the household mosquito, *Culex fasciatus,* now called *Aedes aegypti.*

Finlay thought that the mosquito's bill acted in transferring virus in the same way as a dirty needle acts in transferring hepatitis. He considered that the morbific cause of the disease was carried from the blood of an infected patient to a healthy person, but did not mention any change in the material thus transferred. From 1881 until 1898 he conducted 103 experiments wherein he induced mosquitoes to bite yellow fever patients and then bite healthy recent immigrants (who volunteered for the experiment, knowing that they would eventually get yellow fever anyway, since everyone did). The experiments lacked control, because none of Finlay's subjects was kept within screens or away from patients who had yellow fever. From the protocols we know that yellow fever probably was not transmitted; nor were the experiments accepted by physicians and students of the disease in Cuba or elsewhere. Finlay became the laughingstock of the orthodox physicians of Havana.

Finlay thought that a mosquito which drew only a little blood and was only slightly infected would produce mild disease which would confer immunity. Although a shrewd observer and a splendid and kindly physician, he was not trained as an investigator and that he experimented at all was remarkable. When the Yellow Fever Board—Reed, Lazear, Agramonte, and Carroll—came to Havana in 1900 Finlay provided them with mosquitoes, eggs, and instructions for raising mosquitoes. He was also one of a team of physicians who verified the diagnosis of epidemic and experimental yellow fever, an essential function, since there was no laboratory test.

In 1900 Walter Reed and the Board excluded filth as the route for infection, found that Sanarelli's yellow fever bacillus was the familiar hog cholera organism, and showed that the virus was transmittable to the female mosquito from an affected patient only during the first two to three days of the course of the illness. The mosquito then must incubate the virus for about two weeks before her bite could infect a susceptible person.

Finlay was exactly right in naming the mosquito as the vector of the disease and in identifying the variety of mosquito. The precision of his hypothesis is admirable, but his ideas were neglected—as were the similar proposals made by Josiah Nott in Alabama in 1854. Perhaps in atonement for their rejection of his ideas, Cubans have made Finlay a national hero, an honor well deserved for the brilliant hypothesis that he staunchly stuck to against universal disbelief. Happily he lived to see it proved correct.

BIBLIOGRAPHY

I. Original Works. Finlay's works have been collected as *Obras completas,* 4 vols. (Havana, 1965–1970).

II. Secondary Literature. The best biographical source is his son, Carlos E. Finlay, *Carlos Finlay and Yellow Fever* (New York, 1940). See also William B. Bean, "Carlos Finlay," in *Current Medical Digest,* **37** (1970), 366–367; S. Bloom, *Dr. Carlos J. Finlay* (Havana, 1959); J. A. Del Regato, "Carlos Finlay and the Carrier of Death," in *Américas* (May 1968); "Editorial. Carlos J. Finlay (1833–1915). Student of Yellow Fever," in *Journal of the American Medical Association,* **198** (1966), 188–189. A further source of information on Finlay's life and work is Cesar Rodriguez Exposito, *Centenary of the Graduation of Dr. Carlos J. Finlay in Jefferson Medical College* (Havana, 1956).

William B. Bean

FINSEN, NIELS RYBERG (*b.* Thorshavn, Faeroe Islands, 15 December 1860; *d.* Copenhagen, Denmark, 24 September 1904), *therapeutic medicine.*

Finsen, a descendant of the Viking Icelanders and son of a governor of the Faeroe Islands, was educated at Reykjavik and obtained a medical degree at the University of Copenhagen in 1891. He was subsequently appointed a demonstrator in anatomy at the surgical academy of the same university; but his interest in the therapeutic uses of light became his exclusive professional preoccupation by 1892 and led him shortly thereafter to abandon a career in academic medicine. This decision appears to have been prompted by his affinity for a sunlit environment, which he valued especially because of his attachment to outdoor life.

Yet Finsen's earliest studies were not centered on the salubrious effects of sunlight. His first investigations were devoted to an antithetical question: the nature of light-induced inflammations. Such inflammations were exhibited in patients with smallpox after prolonged exposures to solar radiations, which gave rise to severe blistering of the irritated skin. As a consequence, the patients became more susceptible to infection, secondary fever, and excessive scar formation. Finsen found that the injurious influences of light were produced by the so-called chemical rays placed in the blue, violet, and especially the ultraviolet (actinic) parts of the spectrum. The other extremity of the spectrum presented the opposite phenomenon: the red and ultrared rays, which gave a minimum chemical effect, were found to promote rapid healing of the smallpox lesions and to obviate the unfortunate complications of the disease under the conditions of ordinary light. These initial results in photobiology, including the "red room" (red light) treatment of variola, were issued by Finsen in 1893 and 1894.

Finsen's investigations were sufficiently advanced by 1894 to permit the conclusion that light harbored a direct therapeutic quality. Evidence for this argument was gathered from the contemporary researches of Émile Duclaux and others on the lethal effects of light upon bacteria. In 1895 Finsen applied this finding to the treatment of lupus vulgaris, an intractable and highly disfiguring form of tuberculosis of the skin. He employed for this purpose a powerful source of light from a carbon arc, filtered through a quartz prism, whereby the diseased tissues were exposed to high concentrations of the "incitant," or ultraviolet, rays. A series of publications reporting successful cures of lupus vulgaris by means of the concentrated-light treatment brought Finsen an international reputation and inaugurated the modern era of phototherapy.

This discovery was especially acclaimed in Copenhagen, where an institute for the study of phototherapy was founded in 1896 through philanthropic efforts and was placed under Finsen's direction. He and his associates in subsequent years reported from this Lysinstitut numerous clinical experiences with the "light-bath" method.

Finsen's health had begun to fail in his twenty-third year. By the age of thirty he was almost totally incapacitated from a constrictive pericarditis, which he attributed to a hydatid infection contracted during his student days in Iceland. This led him to perform a self-study on the problem of water and salt metabolism, the results of which laid the scientific foundations for the low-fluid and low-salt-intake therapy. Despite his rapid decline, Finsen labored with formidable vigor. He lived to witness a final tribute in the form of the Nobel Prize for Medicine or Physiology, awarded to him in 1903.

BIBLIOGRAPHY

I. ORIGINAL WORKS. Finsen's writings on photobiology include "Om lysets indvirkninger paa huden," in *Hospitalstidende,* **1** (1893), 721–728; "Om de kemiske straalers skadelige virkning paa den dryiske organisme," *ibid.,* 1069–1083; "Endnu et par ord om koppebehandling," *ibid.,* 1269–1273; "Les rayons chimiques et la variole," in *La semaine médicale,* **14** (1894), 483–488; and "The Red Light Treatment of Smallpox," in *British Medical Journal* (1895), **2**, 1412–1414.

His reports on the treatment of lupus vulgaris are *Om anvendelse i medicinen af koncentrerede kemiske lystraaler* (Copenhagen, 1896); *Über die Anwendung von concentrirten chemischen Lichtstrahlen in der Medicin* (Leipzig, 1899); *La photothérapie* (in three parts: "Les rayons chimiques et la variole;" "La lumière comme agent d'excitabilité;" and "Traitement du *Lupus vulgaire* par les rayons chimiques concentrés") (Paris, 1899), trans. from the German ed. with an app. on the light treatment of *Lupus* by James H. Sequeira, as *Phototherapy* (London, 1901); *Om bekaempelse af Lupus vulgaris med en rede gørelse for de i Denmark opennaaede resultaten* (Copenhagen, 1902); *Die Bekampfung des Lupus vulgaris* (Jena, 1903); and *La lutte contre le Lupus vulgaire* (Paris, 1903).

II. SECONDARY LITERATURE. A good popular account of Finsen's work appears in Paul De Kruif, *Men Against Death* (New York, 1932), ch. 10, pp. 283–299. For Finsen's treatment of his own pericarditis, see Hugo Roesler, "Niels Ryberg Finsen's Disease and His Self-Instituted Treatment," in *Annals of Medical History,* n.s. **8** (1936), 353–356, esp. 356 for a list of Finsen's publications on this subject.

VICTOR A. TRIOLO

FIRMICUS MATERNUS (*b.* Sicily, *fl.* A.D. 330–354), *astrology.*

Our only information about Firmicus' life comes from his two extant works, the *Mathesis,* a popular handbook on astrology, and the *De errore profanarum religionum,* an attack upon pagan cults. Nearly all scholars accept his authorship of both works, but doubts still remain about the date of composition of the *Mathesis.* The author of the *De errore* was a Christian, and the seeming pagan character of the *Mathesis* suggests that Firmicus was converted to Christianity before he composed the *De errore* (*ca.* 346). It is, however, quite possible to reconcile the two works from a religious standpoint, particularly since they were written at a time when pagan and Christian doctrines were being freely intermingled in philosophical and religious literature. Firmicus dedicated the *Mathesis* to Lollianus Mavortius as ordinary consul elect, an office that we know Lollianus held in 355. Book I was composed in Constantine's lifetime (*d.* 337); and since Firmicus informs us that he was engaged for a long time in writing the work, it is reasonable to suppose that it was composed intermittently over a period of nearly twenty years before 354.

The *Mathesis* has been called "the most comprehensive handbook of astrology to come down to us from antiquity" (Franz Boll). Compiled as a handy guide for practitioners of the art, it best represents popular traditions of the previous four centuries and bears little resemblance to Ptolemy's quasi-scientific manual of astrology, the *Quadripartitum.* Sources for such compilations cannot be assigned with any assurance; citations are traditional and wholly unreliable. Firmicus' citations include the legendary Hermes, Orpheus, Abraham, Petosiris, Nechepso, and Aesculapius.

Book I presents a defense of astrology and book II a preliminary conspectus of the elements. Book III deals with the *thema mundi* (the aspect of the heavens at the beginning of the present cosmos) and with the effects of each of the seven planets in the twelve *loci;* book IV, with the relations of the moon with the other planets; book V, with the effects of the planets in the signs, together with houses and decans; and book VI, with planets in trine and quartile aspect and in opposition and conjunction, with the horoscopes of such notables as Paris, Oedipus, Homer, and Archimedes, and with more precise definitions of *loci.* Book VII takes up the horoscopes of individual types and occupations and is marked by undue attention to sexual and moral deviates. Book VIII presents a composite of the traditional Mesopotamian and Egyptian "barbaric" spheres. Prepared by an admitted amateur, the *Mathesis* contains many gross errors in astronomical knowledge, such as a

nocturnal culmination of Mercury and an elongation of 90° for Venus.

Firmicus' injunctions to astrologers to pronounce their responses in public in a loud voice indicate the effectiveness of the measures of Christian emperors to curb divinatory activities. Firmicus is mentioned only once, by Sidonius Apollinaris, before the eleventh century, at which time his book appears to have begun to enjoy a vogue.

BIBLIOGRAPHY

I. ORIGINAL WORKS. The standard editions of Firmicus are *Matheseos libri VIII,* W. Kroll and F. Skutsch, eds., 2 vols. (Leipzig, 1897–1913); and *De errore profanarum religionum: Traduction nouvelle avec texte et commentaire,* G. Heuten, ed. (Brussels, 1938).

II. SECONDARY LITERATURE. For the best general introduction, see Franz Boll, "Firmicus Maternus," in Pauly-Wissowa, *Real-Encyclopädie,* VI (Stuttgart, 1909), cols. 2365–2379. For a detailed account of Latin astrological literature, including the "barbaric" spheres, and for comparisons between the *Mathesis* and Manilius' *Astronomica,* see Boll's *Sphaera* (Leipzig, 1903). The most complete account in English of Latin astrology and its Hellenistic backgrounds is in F. H. Cramer, *Astrology in Roman Law and Politics* (Philadelphia, 1954). The article on Firmicus in Schanz-Hosius, *Geschichte der römischen Literatur,* IV, pt. 1 (Munich, 1914), 129–137, is valuable for bibliography and documentation. L. Thorndike, *A History of Magic and Experimental Science,* I (New York, 1923), 525–538, argues cogently for a single authorship of both works and a long period of composition for the *Mathesis.*

WILLIAM H. STAHL

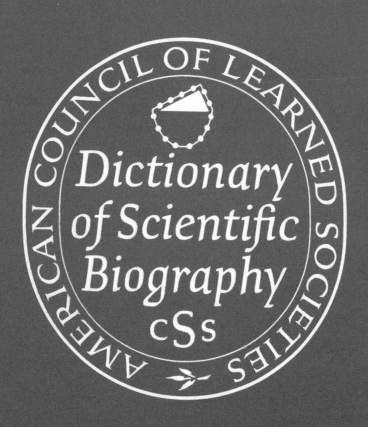

AMERICAN COUNCIL OF LEARNED SOCIETIES

Dictionary
of Scientific
Biography
cSs